PSYCHOLOGY

FIFTH
EDITION

JOHN W. SANTROCK

University of Texas at Dallas

Madison, WI Dubuque Guilford, CT Chicago Toronto London
Mexico City Caracas Buenos Aires Madrid Bogotá Sydney

Book Team

Executive Publisher *Edgar J. Laube*
Acquisitions Editor *Steven Yetter*
Developmental Editor *Linda Falkenstein*
Production Editor *Jayne Klein*
Proofreading Coordinator *Carrie Barker*
Designer *Christopher E. Reese*
Art Editor *Miriam Hoffman*
Photo Editor *Carol Judge*
Permissions Coordinator *Karen L. Storlie*
Production Manager *Beth Kundert*
Production/Costing Manager *Sherry Padden*
Production/Imaging and Media Development Manager *Linda Meehan Avenarius*
Marketing Manager *Carla Aspelmeier*
Copywriter *Jennifer Smith*
Proofreader *Mary Svetlik Anderson*

Basal Text *10/12 Minion*
Display Type *Minion*
Typesetting System *Macintosh® QuarkXpress®*
Paper Stock *45# Bulkton*

Executive Vice President and General Manager *Bob McLaughlin*
Vice President, Business Manager *Russ Domeyer*
Vice President of Production and New Media Development *Victoria Putman*
National Sales Manager *Phil Rudder*
National Telesales Director *John Finn*

A Times Mirror Company

The credits section for this book begins on page 689 and is considered an extension of the copyright page.

All new art for this edition was rendered by Wilderness Graphics

Cover image: © Libyan Sibyl/Sistine Chapel/Nippon Television Network Corporation, Tokyo 1994

Copyedited by *Wendy Nelson;* proofread by *Francine Buda Banwarth*

Library of Congress Catalog Card Number: 95—80643

ISBN 0—697—29678—4

Printed in the United States of America by Times Mirror Higher Education Group, Inc., 2460 Kerper Boulevard, Dubuque, IA 52001

10 9 8 7 6 5 4 3 2 1

With special appreciation to my wife Mary Jo

About the Author

John W. Santrock

John Santrock received his PH.D. from the University of Minnesota in 1973. He taught at the University of Charleston and the University of Georgia before joining the psychology department at the University of Texas at Dallas. He is a member of the editorial board of Developmental Psychology. *His research on father custody is widely cited and used in expert witness testimony to promote flexibility and alternative considerations in custody disputes. John has also authored these exceptional Brown & Benchmark texts:* Child Development, *Sixth Edition,* Life-Span Development, *Sixth Edition,* Children, *Third Edition, and* Adolescence, *Fifth Edition. He is co-author, with Jane Halonen, of* Psychology, The Contexts of Behavior, *Second Edition.*

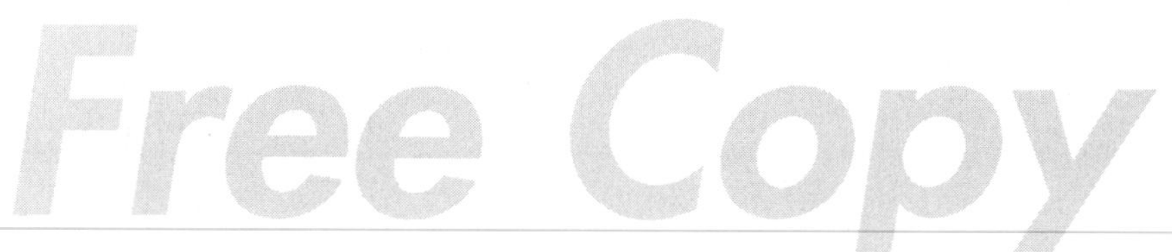

Brief Contents

Free Copy

Contents

CHAPTER
HMD
Human Development 301

CHAPTER
M&E
Motivation and Emotion 357
with Laura King

Chapter PER

Personality 399

Chapter ABN

Abnormal Psychology 441

Chapter THR

Therapies 475

Chapter SCH

Stress, Coping, and Health 513

Chapter STI

Social Thinking and Influence 553

Chapter SOR

Social Relations, Group Behavior, and Sociocultural Diversity 579

APPENDIX
DAT

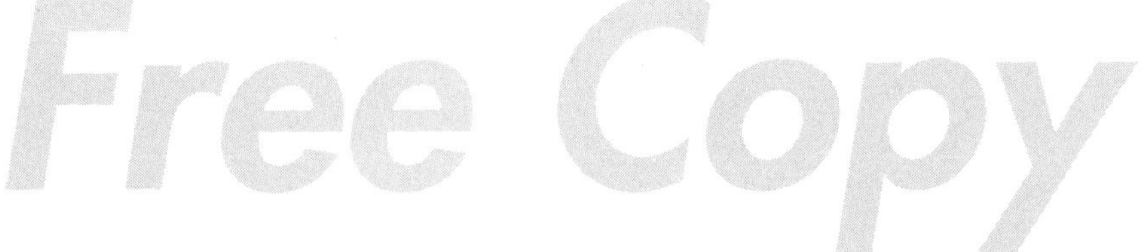

Concept Tables

Explorations in Psychology

Preface

The first three editions of *Psychology* were conventional textbooks of 17 chapters. The fourth edition of *Psychology* was a completely customized book with no standard version, a unique departure from the standard 15–19 chapter text. Instructors could construct their own book from any of the 30 chapters and have them bound in any order they wished. This, the fifth edition of *Psychology,* is available in **both** a standard version of 17 chapters ***and*** as a completely customizable, 4-color text, with 40 different chapters from which to choose.

Throughout all 40 chapters, the fifth edition of *Psychology* has:

- Solid, outstanding research content that expert consultants, among the leading psychologists in the world, praised as being among the best of all introductory psychology texts
- Contributions to individual chapters by leading psychologists in their fields
- Full color throughout (the fourth edition was not in color)
- Excellent pedagogy, clear writing, and a student-friendly character
- New chapter end pieces: overview/cognitive tree, critical thinking about behavior, and resources and readings in psychology
- Flexibility by allowing instructors to package their notes, readings, and virtually any other material with the text

New Chapters for the Fifth Edition, Standard Version, of *Psychology*

Psychology, Fifth Edition, Standard Version, has 3 new chapters:

What Is Psychology?
Methods
Human Development

The introductory chapter from the third edition has been split into two chapters: What Is Psychology? and Methods. Moving the methods material to the second chapter makes the first chapter less overwhelming to students. The methods chapter has been significantly expanded so that students will have a more comprehensive understanding of psychology's scientific underpinnings. The third edition of *Psychology* had two developmental chapters. In response to instructors who indicated they prefer a more concise presentation of development, we discuss human development in a single chapter in the fifth edition of the book.

New Chapters Available for Custom Versions of *Psychology*, Fifth Edition

There are nine completely new chapters available for instructors choosing to customize their texts:

Chapter BRN: The Brain (without Evolution/Heredity)
Chapter EHR: Evolution and Heredity
Chapter ANB: Animal Behavior
Chapter GEN: Gender
Chapter SEX: Human Sexuality
Chapter CLP: Introduction to Clinical Psychology
Chapter ENP: Environmental Psychology
Chapter APP: Applied Psychology
Chapter REL: The Psychology of Religion

Summary of Main Changes in *Psychology*, Fifth Edition

Besides the addition of nine completely new chapters available for customized versions of the text, all of the chapters previously available have been thoroughly updated and revised. What are some of the significant new changes in content?

- New discussion of the sociocultural approach as a major approach in psychology (What Is Psychology?)
- New sections on internal and external validity, cross-cultural research, research with ethnic minority individuals, and reducing sexism in research (Methods)
- New sections on the contemporary perspective of evolutionary psychology, nature and nurture, and brain damage, plasticity, and repair (Biological Foundations and the Brain)
- New sections on signal detection, information processing and ecological theories (Sensation and Perception)
- New section on cultural factors in learning (Learning)
- Revised and updated discussions of types of memory, automatic, and effortful processing, and new sections on priming and repressed memories (Memory)
- New sections on characteristics of problem solving, improving problem-solving skills, hypothesis testing and inductive reasoning, and how problems differ (Thinking and Language)
- Revised and updated sections on homosexuality, achievement, and happiness; new section on anger (Motivation and Emotion)
- New section on individualism and collectivism (Personality)
- Expanded and updated discussions of culture, ethnicity and gender, DSM-IV, and personality disorders (Abnormal Psychology)
- New sections on managed health care, culture and ethnicity in therapy, and feminist therapies (Therapies)
- New sections on poverty, social class, and stress and stress management techniques (Stress, Coping, and Health)
- New research on social comparison and revised section on impression management (Social Thinking and Influence)
- New section on sociocultural diversity and issues; updated discussion of prejudice, stereotyping, and ethnocentrism (Social Relations, Group Behavior and Sociocultural Diversity)

All of the remaining chapters have equally significant new, revised, and updated material. *Psychology,* Fifth Edition, has more than 600 1995, 1996, 1997, and in press references (approximately 300 in the Standard Version alone).

Solid, Outstanding Research Content Praised by Expert Consultants

Thirteen expert consultants went over the content of *Psychology,* Fifth Edition, in their area of expertise and made detailed recommendations. The photographs and brief biographies of the expert consultants, many of them among the world's leading psychologists in their fields, appear in this preface. In many instances, the expert consultants offered glowing praise of *Psychology,* Fifth Edition's, content.

Co-Authors of Individual Chapters by Leading Psychologists in Their Fields

The task of creating a 40-chapter introductory psychology text was a formidable one. To include outstanding content across psychology's many areas, I not only obtained the input of expert consultants as reviewers, but I also asked a number of psychologists to co-author individual chapters. They wrote material for the following chapters:

James Bartlett
Ph.D. Yale; University of Texas at Dallas
Memory; Thinking and Language

Robert Gifford
Ph.D. Simon Fraser; University of Victoria
Environmental Psychology; Applied Psychology

Morton Harmatz
Ph.D U. of Washington; University of Massachusetts
Introduction to Clinical Psychology

William Katz
Ph.D. Brown; University of Texas at Dallas
Thinking and Language

Laura King
Ph.D. U. of California at Davis; Southern Methodist University
Motivation; Motivation and Emotion

David Neufeldt
Ph.D. U. of Arkansas; Hutchinson Community College
Industrial/Organizational Psychology and Career Development; Applied Psychology

Alice O'Toole
Ph.D. Brown; University of Texas at Dallas
Methods; Sensation; Perception; Sensation and Perception

Raymond Paloutzian
Ph.D. Claremont Graduate School; Westmont College
The Psychology of Religion

Barry Stein
Ph.D. Vanderbilt; Tennessee Technological University
Thinking and Language

After each of these experts completed their writing, I rewrote the material in my style and added the appropriate pedagogy.

Writing and Pedagogy

I continue to strive to make *Psychology* a book that has excellent pedagogy, is well-written, and is student-friendly. The fifth edition of the book has a comprehensive, effective pedagogical system that will help students learn the material. The highlights of this learning system are presented in a **visual preface** that follows this preface.

In addition to the pedagogy and clear writing, high-interest chapter introductions (called Images of Psychology), special feature boxes, beautiful photographs and art, and personalized, applied examples of concepts are among the other features that make the fifth edition of *Psychology* a student-friendly book.

Three new chapter-ending features in *Psychology,* Fifth Edition, are:

1. **Overview/Cognitive Tree Section.** This section briefly summarizes the main chapter topics and provides a visual cognitive tree of those topics.

2. **Critical Thinking About Behavior.** This section presents high-interest topics and encourages students to think critically about the topics. The critical thinking pieces were written by leading expert Jane Halonen of Alverno College. These appear in the 17 standard chapters.
3. **Resources and Readings in Psychology.** This innovative feature includes research-oriented books; popular, easy-to-read trade books of high quality; and telephone numbers and addresses of resources related to the chapter's contents.

How to Customize *Psychology,* Fifth Edition

In addition to the standard, 17-chapter version of *Psychology,* it is possible to customize this text to meet your individual needs, with a menu of 40 chapters to choose from—all in full color!

Perhaps you prefer to cover motivation and emotion in depth, with separate chapters devoted to each. Perhaps you prefer combined coverage of learning and memory together in one chapter instead of separate chapters dedicated to each. Perhaps you always skip the development chapters in your course. Perhaps you like to start your semester with social psychology—an order found in virtually no standard introductory textbook. Customizing from the full menu of *Psychology,* Fifth Edition, will allow you to tailor your textbook exactly to the way you teach your course.

If you have been eager to enhance your introductory course by teaching important and high-interest topics that are not usually found in standard introductory psychology texts—subjects such as animal behavior, evolution and heredity, environmental psychology, clinical psychology, or the psychology of religion—*Psychology,* Fifth Edition, allows you to include them. Customizing from the full menu of *Psychology* will allow you to include chapters on gender, sexuality, industrial/organizational psychology, and interpersonal communication, among others. If these topics are important in your class, at your institution, and for your students, take a closer look at the options available through customizing your version of *Psychology,* Fifth Edition.

All of the chapters found in this standard text are available for customization. The full menu of 40 chapters is outlined on the following page. Another helpful way to choose chapters is to think of *Psychology,* Fifth Edition, as having 12 areas from which instructors can select one or more chapters in constructing the text that meets their needs. A visual depiction of the content areas can be found on page xxv.

If you think customization is right for your classroom, or if you just want to learn more, contact your Brown & Benchmark Sales Representative, or call our Educational Resources Department at 1–800–338–5371 to order your examination copy of the Alternative and Enhancement chapters of *Psychology,* Fifth Edition.

Your Brown & Benchmark Sales Representative can help answer all your questions about custom publishing, including how long it takes to produce custom versions of *Psychology,* pricing, packaging options, bookstore orders, and returns. Further information regarding custom publishing can be obtained through our CourseWorks custom publishing unit at 1–800–446–8979, or e-mail <bbcw@tmhe.com>.

Ancillary Materials for the Instructor

We've tried to combine a student-oriented textbook with an integrated ancillary package designed to meet the unique needs of instructors and students. Our goal has been to create a teaching package that is as enjoyable to teach with as it is to study from.

The ***Instructor's Course Planner*** was prepared by Steven A. Schneider of Pima Community College. This flexible planner provides many useful tools to enhance your teaching. For each chapter, learning objectives, an extended chapter outline, suggestions for teaching, lecture/discussion suggestions, video and film suggestions, classroom activities and handout forms are provided. The *Instructor's Course Planner* is also available on disk for IBM and Macintosh computers.

The Brown & Benchmark ***Introductory Psychology Activities Handbook*** offers additional activities, in-class and out-of-class projects, and discussion questions. The activities handbook will help you get your students actively engaged and thinking critically.

A ***Test Item File*** will be available to instructors who adopt *Psychology,* Fifth Edition. Dr. Al Cohen, director of the Office of Testing and Evaluation Services at the University of Wisconsin–Madison, provides valuable feedback in the construction of all Brown & Benchmark test item files.

The questions in the test item file are also available on ***MicroTest III,*** a powerful but easy-to-use test-generating program by Chariot Software Group. MicroTest is available for your use in DOS (3.5 size disks), Windows, and Macintosh versions. With MicroTest, instructors can easily select questions from the Test Item File and print tests and answer keys. Instructors can also customize questions, headings, and instructions; add or import their own questions; and print tests in a choice of printer-supported fonts.

Or take advantage of Brown & Benchmark's free call-in **Testing Service.** With 48-hours notice, our Educational Resources Department will prepare your test and fax you the questions and the answer key. Simply select your questions in advance and call 1–800–338–5371 and our Educational Resources Representatives will be glad to help you.

The ***Student Study Guide*** was also created by Instructor's Manual author, Steven A. Schneider. For each chapter of the text, the student is provided with learning objectives, a detailed outline of the chapter, a guided review of terms and concepts, and two multiple-choice practice tests. For all custom versions of the text, the Student Study Guide will be available on disk only, in DOS and Macintosh versions.

Introductory Psychology Transparency Set. Over 100 additional transparencies illustrating key concepts in general psychology in the *Introductory Psychology Transparency Set*

STANDARD TEXT CHAPTERS		ALTERNATIVE CHAPTERS		ENHANCEMENT CHAPTERS	
Choose from these chapters for coverage similar to a standard introductory psychology text.		*Choose from these chapters for more in-depth coverage of the standard subject areas or in some areas, more concise coverage.*		*Choose from these chapters for in-depth coverage of areas not usually found in standard introductory psychology texts.*	
WIP	What Is Psychology? (w/o Methods)	WPM	What Is Psychology? (w/ Methods)		
MET	Methods				
BFB	Biological Foundations and the Brain	BRN EHR	The Brain (w/o Heredity and Evolution) Evolution and Heredity	ANB	Animal Behavior
S&P	Sensation and Perception	SEN PCP	Sensation Perception		
SOC	States of Consciousness				
LRN	Learning	L&M	Learning and Memory		
MEM	Memory				
T&L	Thinking and Language	TLI	Thinking, Language, and Intelligence		
INT	Intelligence				
HMD	Human Development	CHD AAA	Child Development Adolescence, Adult Development, and Aging	GEN G&S	Gender Gender and Sexuality
M&E	Motivation and Emotion	MOT EMO	Motivation Emotion	SEX	Human Sexuality
PER	Personality				
ABN	Abnormal Psychology			CLP	Introduction to Clinical Psychology
THR	Therapies				
SCH	Stress, Coping, and Health			ENP	Environmental Psychology
STI	Social Thinking and Influence	SOP	Social Psychology (Inclusive)	APP I/O	Applied Psychology Ind./Org. Psychology and Career Development
SOR	Social Relations, Group Behavior, and Sociocultural Diversity			INC REL	Interpersonal Communication The Psychology of Religion
DAT	Analyzing the Data				

(ISBN 0–697–17354–2) or slides (ISBN 0–697–17355–0) and accompanying handbook with specific suggestions for classroom use by Susan J. Shapiro of Indiana University East.

New! ***The Brown & Benchmark Electronic Image Bank*** (ISBN 0–697–29647–4) provides you with the same outstanding graphics on a CD-ROM for presentation from your PC or Macintosh. We provide our own generic viewer, but the contents are .pic files, so they can be downloaded into your own favorite presentation program, for instance, PowerPoint.

The Critical Thinker, Second Edition, by Richard Mayer and Fiona Goodchild, both of the University of California–Santa Barbara, explicitly teaches strategies for understanding and evaluating material in any introductory psychology textbook. This 70-page booklet is available free to adopters.

The AIDS Booklet, Third Edition, by Frank D. Cox of Santa Barbara City College, is a brief but comprehensive introduction to the Acquired Immune Deficiency Syndrome, HIV, and related viruses.

MENU OF CHAPTERS

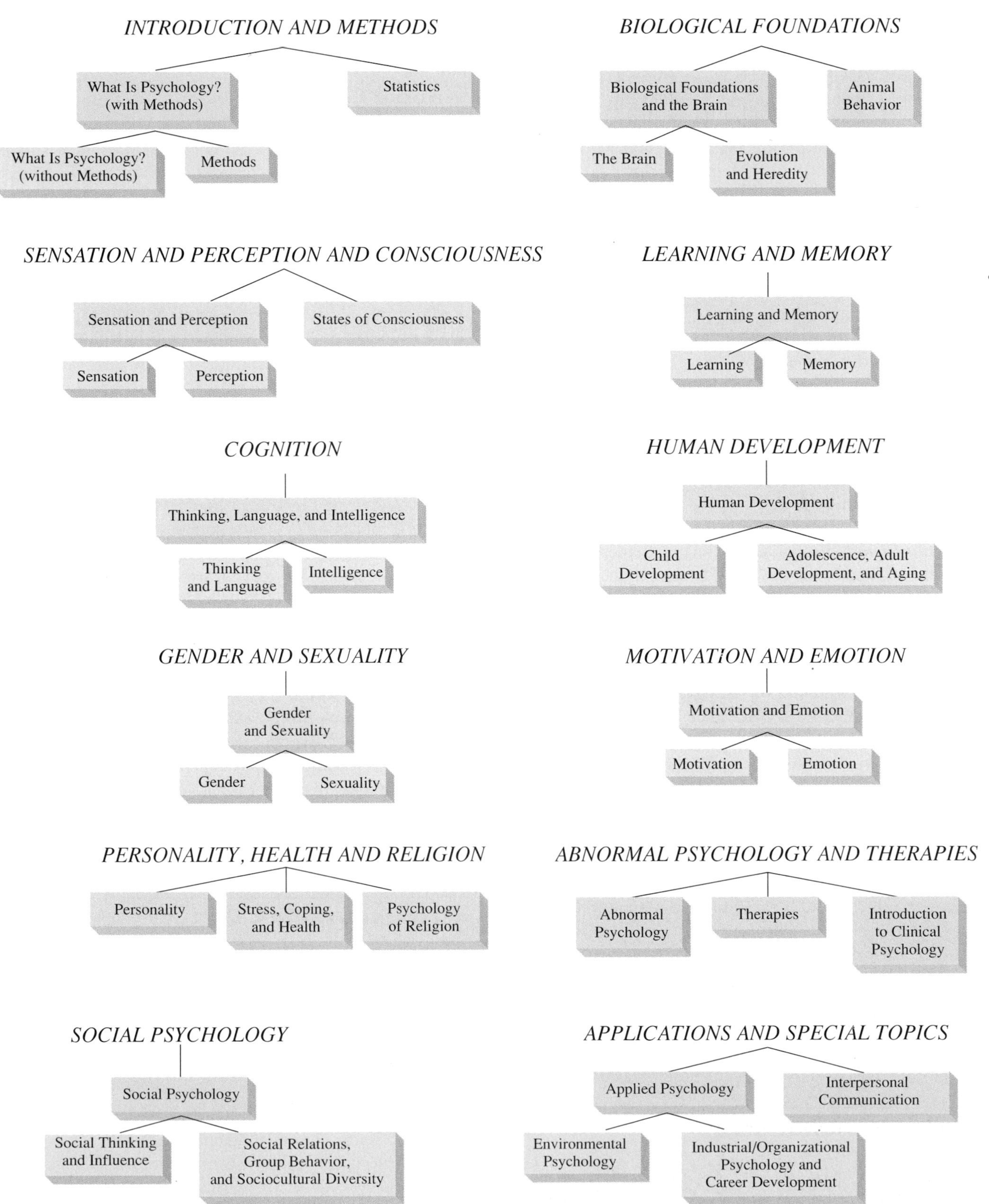

INTRODUCTION AND METHODS
What Is Psychology? (with Methods)
Statistics
What Is Psychology? (without Methods)
Methods
BIOLOGICAL FOUNDATIONS
Biological Foundations and the Brain
Animal Behavior
The Brain
Evolution and Heredity
SENSATION AND PERCEPTION AND CONSCIOUSNESS
Sensation and Perception
States of Consciousness
Sensation
Perception
LEARNING AND MEMORY
Learning and Memory
Learning
Memory
COGNITION
Thinking, Language, and Intelligence
Thinking and Language
Intelligence
HUMAN DEVELOPMENT
Human Development
Child Development
Adolescence, Adult Development, and Aging
GENDER AND SEXUALITY
Gender and Sexuality
Gender
Sexuality
MOTIVATION AND EMOTION
Motivation and Emotion
Motivation
Emotion
PERSONALITY, HEALTH AND RELIGION
Personality
Stress, Coping, and Health
Psychology of Religion
ABNORMAL PSYCHOLOGY AND THERAPIES
Abnormal Psychology
Therapies
Introduction to Clinical Psychology
SOCIAL PSYCHOLOGY
Social Psychology
Social Thinking and Influence
Social Relations, Group Behavior, and Sociocultural Diversity
APPLICATIONS AND SPECIAL TOPICS
Applied Psychology
Interpersonal Communication
Environmental Psychology
Industrial/Organizational Psychology and Career Development

The Encyclopedic Dictionary of Psychology (ISBN 0–87967–885–2) provides easy reference access to the key figures, concepts, movements, and practices of the field of psychology.

Psychology: The Active Learner CD-ROM by Jane Halonen, Marilyn Reedy, and Paul Smith is an innovative interactive product that will help students learn key concepts taught in introductory psychology in a fun and dynamic way. Focusing on concepts that tend to be most difficult for the beginning psychology student, this program contains 15 modules containing tutorial review and critical thinking exercises for biological foundations, sensation and perception, states of consciousness, learning, memory, development, social psychology, and more.

The CD-ROM ***Explorations in Health and Psychology*** by George B. Johnson of Washington University in St. Louis will help students actively investigate processes vital to their understanding of psychology as they should be explored—with movement, color, sound, and interaction. This set of 10 interactive animations on CD-ROM allows students to set and re-set variables in each (including modules on Life-Span and Lifestyle, Drug Addiction, Nerve Conduction, AIDS, Immune Response, and more) and then evaluate those results. In addition to the colorful and precisely labeled graphics and animated illustrations, the CD-ROM also offers **narration in English and Spanish,** a glossary with written and oral pronunciations, and lists of additional recommended readings. Contact your local Brown & Benchmark Representative for more information or call the Times Mirror Higher Education Group Customer Service at 1–800–338–5578.

A large selection of ***videotapes*** is also available to adopters based on the number of textbooks ordered. Consult your Brown & Benchmark Representative for ordering policies.

The Brain Modules on Videodisc created by WNET in New York, Antenne 2 TV/France, the Annenberg/CPB Foundation and Professor Frank J. Vattano of Colorado State University, is based on the Peabody award-winning series "The Brain." Thirty segments, averaging 6 minutes each, illustrate an array of topics in psychology. Consult your Brown & Benchmark Representative for details.

The Brown & Benchmark ***Human Development Interactive Videodisc Set,*** produced by Roger Ray of Rollins College, vividly introduces life-span development with instant access to over 30 brief video segments from the highly acclaimed *Seasons of Life* series. Consult your Brown & Benchmark Representative for details.

The ***Brown & Benchmark Reference Disks*** are available free to adopters. The disks include over 15,000 journal and book references arranged in files by topic. The complete set of five disks is available on IBM (3.5″) or Macintosh disks.

B&B CourseKits™

B&B CourseKits™ are course-specific collections of for-sale educational materials, custom packaged for maximum convenience and value. CourseKits offer you the flexibility of customizing and combining Brown & Benchmark course materials (B&B CourseKits™, Annual Editions®, Taking Sides®, etc.) with your own or other materials. Each CourseKit contains two or more instructor-selected items conveniently packaged and priced for your students. For more information on B&B CourseKits™, please contact your local Brown & Benchmark Sales Representative.

Annual Editions®

Magazines, newspapers, and journals can provide current, first-rate, relevant educational information. *Annual Editions* provides convenient, inexpensive access to a wide range of current, carefully selected articles from magazines, newspapers, and journals. Written by psychologists, researchers, and educators, *Annual Editions: Psychology* provides useful perspectives on important and timely topics. *Annual Editions* is updated yearly, and includes a number of features designed to make it particularly useful including a topic guide, annotated table of contents, and unit overviews. For the professor using Annual Editions in the classroom, an Instructor's Resource Guide with test questions is available. Consult your Brown & Benchmark Sales Representative for more details.

Taking Sides®

Are you interested in generating classroom discussion? In finding a tool to fully involve your students in their experience of your course? Would you like to encourage your students to become more active learners and critical thinkers? *Taking Sides: Clashing Views on Psychological Issues* is a debate-style reader designed to introduce students to controversies in psychology. By requiring students to analyze opposing viewpoints and reach considered judgments, *Taking Sides* actively develops students' critical thinking skills.

Sources: Notable Selections in Psychology (ISBN 1–56134–263–7) brings together 46 selections including classic articles, book excerpts, and research studies that have shaped the study of psychology. If you want your students to gain greater background knowledge in reading and interpreting firsthand from source material, *Sources* collects a diverse array of accessible but significant readings in one place.

CourseWorks

CourseWorks (formerly Kinko's CourseWorks in the U.S.) is the Brown & Benchmark custom publishing service. With its own printing and distribution facility, CourseWorks gives you the flexibility to add current material to your course at any time. CourseWorks provides you with a unique set of options:

- Customizing Brown & Benchmark CourseBooks
- Publishing your own material
- Including any previously published material for which we can secure permissions
- Adding photos
- Performing copyediting
- Creating custom covers

ACKNOWLEDGMENTS

I owe special debts to the following expert consultants who provided detailed reviews of content.

Jackson Beatty is a Professor of Behavioral Neuroscience in the UCLA Department of Psychology. He received both his B.A. and Ph.D. degrees from the University of Michigan. He is a member of the UCLA Brain Research Institute and a Fellow of the American Association for the Advancement of Science in psychology.

He has earned an international reputation for his research on neurobiological issues in the study of higher cognitive processes of the human brain.

Professor Beatty is currently principal investigator on a National Science Foundation grant to expand undergraduate neuroscience laboratory instruction at UCLA.

Charles L. Brewer received his Ph.D. in general experimental psychology from the University of Arkansas in 1965 and did postdoctoral work at Harvard University and the University of Michigan. He has taught at the College of Wooster and Elmira College and is now a professor of psychology at Furman University. Author of numerous book chapters and journal articles, he is coeditor of handbooks for teachers of introductory psychology and of statistics and research methods and is editor of the journal *Teaching of Psychology.* In the American Psychological Association (APA), he is a fellow of Divisions 1, 2, and 26 and is a charter fellow of the American Psychological Society. He is a past President of APA's Divisions 1 and 2 and of the Southeastern Psychological Association. He received the American Psychological Foundation's Distinguished Teaching Award in 1989 and APA's Distinguished Career Contributions to Education and Training Award for 1995.

Richard Brislin is the Senior Fellow and Director of Intercultural Programs at the East-West Center in Honolulu, Hawaii. He has taught courses in cross-cultural psychology, intercultural communication, cross-cultural counseling, and cross-cultural research methods. He is the author of several books which have been used as texts in college courses, including *Cross-Cultural Research Methods* (1973), *Cross-Cultural Encounters: Face to Face Interaction* 1981), *Intercultural Interactions: A Practical Guide* (1986), *Understanding Culture's Influence on Behavior* (1993), and *Intercultural Communication Training: An Introduction* (1994). He was a G. Stanley Hall Lecturer for the American Psychological Association and is coeditor of *Improving Intercultural Interactions: Modules for Cross-Cultural Training Programs* (1994).

Lillian Comas-Díaz received her Ph.D. in Clinical Psychology from the University of Massachusetts. She is the Executive Director of the Transcultural *Mental Health Institute,* and maintains a private practice of clinical psychology in Washington, D.C.

Dr. Comas-Díaz is the former director of the APA's Office of Ethnic Minority Affairs, and the former director of the Hispanic Clinic, at Yale University School of Medicine.

She has also published extensively on the topics of ethnocultural mental health, gender and ethnic factors in psychotherapy, treatment of torture victims, international psychology, and Latino mental health. Her book, *Ethnocultural Psychotherapy,* is in preparation and will be published by Basic Books.

Florence L. Denmark is an internationally recognized scholar, administrator, leader, researcher, and policy maker. She received her Ph.D. in Social Psychology from the University of Pennsylvania and has since made many contributions in that area, particularly to the psychology of women. Denmark has authored more than 75 articles and 15 books, presented over 100 talks and invited addresses, and appeared on numerous radio and television shows. Denmark has been the Thomas Hunter Professor of Psychology at Hunter College of the City University of New York and at present is the Robert Scott Pace Distinguished Professor of Psychology at Pace University, where she is chair of the Department of Psychology.

Jane Halonen (Critical Thinking) earned her Ph.D. in Clinical Psychology from the University of Wisconsin–Milwaukee and is a professor in the Behavioral Science Division at Alverno College. Jane has served as a consultant to numerous psychology departments and has authored two texts for teachers, *Teaching Critical Thinking in Psychology* and *Teaching Social Interaction.* She is past President of the Council of Teachers of Undergraduate Psychology and is a fellow and program chair for Division 2 of the American Psychological Association.

John H. Harvey is a professor of psychology at the University of Iowa. He obtained his Ph.D. in social psychology at the University of Missouri–Columbia, working with Judson Mills, was an NIMH Postdoctoral Fellow at UCLA, working with Harold Kelley, and assumed his first faculty position at Vanderbilt University.

Harvey currently works on topics in the areas of attribution and accounts in close relationships, and how people deal with personal and interpersonal loss. He is the editor of *Contemporary Psychology* and of a journal started in 1996 entitled the *Journal of Personal and Interpersonal Loss.* He is the author of 18 books including most recently *Odyssey of the Heart* (Freeman, 1995) and *Embracing Their Memory: Loss and the Social-Psychology of Story-Telling* (Allyn & Bacon, 1996).

James Jones has written extensively in the area of race relations over the past twenty years. After earning a B.A. degree from Oberlin College in 1963, and an M.A. from Temple University in 1967, Dr. Jones undertook his doctoral training in experimental social psychology at Yale University, earning his Ph.D. in 1970. In 1972 Dr. Jones' book *Prejudice and Racism* was published and continues to be one of the most comprehensive treatments of the relationships among prejudice, group conflict, and racism. Dr. Jones is currently professor of psychology at the University of Delaware and at APA, Director of the Minority Fellowship Program and Affirmative Action Officer.

Seth C. Kalichman is an Assistant Professor in the Department of Psychology at Georgia State University. His research focuses on three main areas: factors related to AIDS risk behavior and using this information to develop better programs for AIDS prevention; sexually aggressive behavior, including rape, date rape, and child sexual abuse; and finally, how psychologists and other mental health professionals can help prevent child abuse.

Dr. Kalichman received his Ph.D. in Clinical-Community Psychology from the University of South Carolina and did his undergraduate work at the University of South Florida. Dr. Kalichman is the author of *Understanding AIDS: A Guide for Mental Health Professionals* and *Mandated Reporting of Suspected Child Abuse: Ethics, Law, and Policy,* both published by the American Psychological Association.

James W. Pennebaker is Professor and Chair of Psychology at Southern Methodist University. Since receiving his Ph.D. in 1977 from the University of Texas at Austin, he has been on the faculty at the University of Virginia and, in 1989, was the Hilgard Visiting Professor at Stanford University. In 1993, he was awarded an honorary doctorate degree from the University of Louvain in Belgium.

Since joining the faculty of Southern Methodist University in 1983, Pennebaker and his students have explored the links between traumatic experiences and physical and mental health. He has published almost 100 scientific articles and 5 books. His most recent studies are focusing on the nature of language and emotion.

Daniel Schacter is a Professor of Psychology at Harvard University. He received a B.A. degree from the University of North Carolina in 1974 and a Ph.D. from the University of Toronto in 1981. He remained at Toronto for the next six years as director of the Unit for Memory Disorders and Assistant Professor of Psychology. In 1987, he moved to the University of Arizona as an Associate Professor, and was promoted to Professor in 1989. He became Professor of Psychology at Harvard in 1991. Schacter received the Arthur Benton Award from the International Neuropsychological Society in 1989, the Distinguished Award for an Early Career Contribution to Psychology from the American Psychological Association in 1990, and the Troland Research Award from the National Academy of Sciences in 1991.

Charles T. Snowdon is John T. Emlen Professor of Psychology and Zoology at the University of Wisconsin–Madison. He and his students study primate behavior with special interests in vocal and chemical communication and the breeding behavior and biology of endangered primates.

Professor Snowdon has served as editor of *Animal Behaviour* and is currently editor of the *Journal of Comparative Psychology.* He has been President of the Animal Behavior Society and has served on grant review committees for animal behavior research for the National Science Foundation and the National Institute of Mental Health. He teaches courses in Animal Behavior and Animal Communication.

Helen Tager-Flusberg is a Professor of Psychology at the University of Massachusetts–Boston. She received her B.Sc. with first class honors from the University of London in 1973 and her Ph.D. from Harvard University in 1978. Her writings include *Constraints on Language Acquisition* (1994) and *Language and Communication in Autism* (1995), and she is coeditor of the book *Understanding Other Minds* from Oxford University Press.

In addition, I also benefitted enormously from the comments of the following reviewers who provided detailed recommendations about individual chapters for *Psychology,* Fifth Edition.

Richard D. Barnes, *Randolph-Macon Women's College*
Belinda Blevins-Knabe, *University of Arkansas–Little Rock*
Galen V. Bodenhausen, *Michigan State University*
Ross Buck, *University of Connecticut*
David M. Buss, *University of Michigan*
Gerald S. Clack, *Loyola University of the South*
Charles M. Cortwright, *Northwestern College*
Mark Costanzo, *Claremont McKenna College and the Claremont Graduate School*
Robert T. Croyle, *University of Utah*
Robert P. Delprino, *SUNY College at Buffalo*
Gregory J. Feist, *College of William and Mary*
Laura Freberg, *California Polytechnic State University–San Luis Obispo*
Stanley O. Gaines, *Pomona College and Claremont College*
Judith L. Gibbons, *St. Louis University*
Martin Heesacker, *University of Florida–Gainesville*
N. Chris Higgins, *University of Northern British Columbia*
William Ickes, *University of Texas–Arlington*
Linda A. Jackson, *Michigan State University*
Robin Kowalski, *Western Carolina University*
Roger J. Kreuz, *University of Memphis*
Randy J. Larsen, *University of Michigan–Ann Arbor*
Fred Levitt, *California State University–Hayward*
Susan D. Lima, *University of Wisconsin–Milwaukee*
Mark E. Mattson, *Fordham University*
David I. Mostofsky, *Boston University*
David C. Munz, *St. Louis University*
Illene C. Noppe, *University of Wisconsin–Green Bay*
Cynthia D. O'Dell, *Indiana University Northwest*
Michelle Perry, *University of Illinois at Urbana–Champaign*
Lawrence A. Pervin, *Rutgers University*
David A. Saarnio, *Arkansas State University*
Ken Sheldon, *University of Rochester*
James Shepperd, *University of Florida–Gainesville*
Sara Shettleworth, *University of Toronto*
Steven M. Smith, *Texas A&M University*
Steve Tolson, *Northeast Louisiana University*
Benjamin Wallace, *Cleveland State University*
Criss Wilhite, *California State University–Fresno*
Todd Zakrajsek, *Southern Oregon State College*

I also want to thank the following individuals for their reviews of previous editions of *Psychology:*

Christopher Aanstoos, *West Georgia College*
Robert Adams, *Eastern Kentucky University*
Karen Ahlm, *Indiana University*
Bernard A. Albaniak, *University of South Carolina*
Ira B. Albert, *Dundalk Community College*
Alva Desoit Allen, *Southern Arizona University*
J. Whorton Allen, *Utah State University*
Paul Amhrein, *University of New Mexico*
Barbara Anderson, *Ohio State University*
Robin Anderson, *St. Ambrose University*
Emir Andrews, *Memorial University of Newfoundland*
Jennifer Appersen, *Longwood College*
JoAnn Armstrong, *Patrick Henry Community College*
Paul Ansfield, *University of Wisconsin–Oshkosh*
William Atkinson, *Shippensburg University of Pennsylvania*
Norma Baker, *Belmont College*
Bill Balance, *University of Windsor*
Barbara Ann Banas, *Rochester Community College*
Lewis M. Barker, *Baylor University*
Jerrold E. Barnett, *Northwest Missouri State University*
James Bartlett, *University of Texas at Dallas*
John D. Batson, *Furman University*
Don Baucum, *Birmingham–Southern College*
Richard Bauer, *Middle Tennessee State University*
Gordon Bear, *Ramapo College of New Jersey*
Robert J. Bell, *Texarkana Community College*
James O. Benedict, *James Madison University*
John B. Benson, *Texarkana Community College*
David Berger, *SUNY–Cortland*
Ann Berland, *University of South Dakota*
John B. Best, *Eastern Illinois University*
Michael Beyerlein, *Fort Hays State University*
James Biglin, *Northern Arizona University*
Tom Billimek, *San Antonio College*
Percy Black, *Pace University of Pleasantville*
Ann Blake, *St. Martins College*
Evelyn Blanch, *Wilberforce University*
Belinda Blevins, *University of Arkansas*
Maria L. Bocchia, *Oklahoma Baptist University*
George Boeree, *Shippensburg University of Pennsylvania*
Ken Bordens, *Indiana University–Purdue*
Marolyn Boswell, *Elon College*
Betty N. Bowers, *North Central Technical Institute*
Peter Brady, *Clark Technical College*
Jay Braun, *Arizona State University*
Charles L. Brewer, *Furman University*
John P. Broida, *University of Southern Maine*
Susan Bromley, *University of Northern Colorado*
Davina Brown, *The Defiance College*
Larry T. Brown, *Oklahoma State University*
James Calhoun, *University of Georgia*
William H. Calhoun, *University of Tennessee–Knoxville*
N. D. Carlsley, *Vancouver Community College*
Ralph L. Casebolt, *University of New Mexico*

Parnell W. Cephus, *Jefferson State Junior College*
Davis Chambliss, *Tulane University*
George A. Cicala, *University of Delaware*
John Clark, *Macomb Community College*
J. B. Clement, *Daytona Beach City College*
James T. Closson, *Graceland College*
Randall Clouser, *Montgomery Community College*
C. Dwaine Cochran, *Stetson University*
David Cohen, *University of Texas*
William Colson, *Norfolk State University*
A. L. Cone, *Pikeville Community College*
Roy Connally, *University of Central Florida*
James V. Couch, *James Madison University*
Norm Culbertson, *Yakima Valley Community College*
Paul Cunningham, *Rivier College*
Ira Dasgupta, *St. Gregory's College*
Stephen Davis, *Emporia State University*
Joan Digby, *Long Island University*
Joan Fimbel DiGiovanni, *Western New England College*
Kim Dolgin, *Ohio Wesleyan University*
W. Jay Dowling, *University of Texas at Dallas*
Mary Dudley, *Howard College*
Rolf Dyke, *Grant MacEwan Community College*
Katherine Ellison, *Montclair State College*
Laurel End, *Salve Regina College*
Robert O. Engbretson, *Southern Illinois University–Edwardsville*
Robert Enright, *University of Wisconsin–Madison*
Martha Ewing, *Collin County Community College*
Thomas Fitzpatrick, *Rockland Community College*
Roy Fontaine, *Williamsport Area Community College*
Paul Foos, *Florida International University*
Cynthia A. Ford, *Jackson State University*
Donelson Forsyth, *Virginia Commonwealth University*
Christopher Frederickson, *University of Texas at Dallas*
Gilbert M. French, *University of South Dakota*
William Frey, *Middlebury College*
Gabriel P. Frommer, *Indiana University*
Gloria Galanes, *Southwest Missouri State University*
Angel Garcia, *Northeastern Illinois State University*
Bill E. Gardner, *Walters State Community College*
Robert L. Gassette, *Hofstra University*
Al Geno, *St. Clair County Community College*
Ed Gilbert, *Albright College*
W. Glassman, *Ryerson Polytechnical Institute*
Richard H. Glessner, *Mount Ida College*
William Gnagey, *Illinois State University*
Sanford Golin, *University of Pittsburgh*
John N. Goodwin, *School of the Ozarks*
Norman Gordon, *SUNY–Oswego*
John R. Goss, *Pennsylvania State University*
Peter Gram, *Pensacola Junior College*
Richard A. Griggs, *University of Florida–Gainesville*
Ralph Grippin, *Metropolitan Community College*
Michael Guile, *Northeastern Oklahoma State University*
Katherine Haffner, *St. Francis College*
Charles G. Halcomb, *Texas Tech. University*
Gordon Hammerle, *Adrian College*
Reed Hardy, *Saint Norbert College*
Renee L. Harrangue, *Loyola Marymount University*
Anne E. Harris, *Arizona State University*
Robert C. Harris, *Mount Royal College*
Nancy S. Harrison, *California State University*
John Harvey, *University of Iowa*
Linda Hatzenbuehler, *Idaho State University*
Glen Hawks, *Virginia Commonwealth University*
W. Heater, *Lansing Community College*
Susan Heidenreich, *Loyola University*
William J. Hepler, *Butler University*
Romayne Hertweck, *Mira Costa College*
J. Hess, *Black Hills State College*
A. George Hetzel, *College of Santa Fe*
Thomas Hewett, *Drexel University*
Annette R. Hiedemann, *West Virginia Wesleyan University*
Garth Hines, *University of Arkansas–Little Rock*
Don Hockenbury, *Tulsa Junior College*
Gordon Hodge, *University of New Mexico*
Steven L. Hopp, *Emory and Henry College*
Marilynn B. Jackson, *Howard Payne University*
James E. Jans, *Concordia University*
Charles W. Johnson, *University of Evansville*
Fern Johnson, *Oklahoma State Technical*
J. Walter Johnson, *St. Thomas Aquinas College*
James J. Johnson, *Illinois State University*
Per Johnson, *University of Wisconsin*
Eric Jolly, *Eastern New Mexico University*
Judi Jones, *Georgia Southern College*
Seth Kalichman, *University of Mississippi*
Katrina Kay, *University of California–Irvine*
Bruce Kenna, *SUNY College of Agriculture & Technology at Cobleskill*
Melvyn King, *SUNY–Cortland*
William B. King, Jr., *University of Wisconsin–Platteville*
Al Knudson, *Concordia College–Moorhead*
Ralph H. Kolstoe, *University of North Dakota*
John Krato, *Schoolcraft College*
R. Eric Landrum, *Boise State University*
Ronald A. Latorre, *Douglas MacArthur State Technical College*
David E. Leas, *New Mexico State University*
Jane Leonard, *Ohio University*
T. C. Lewandowski, *Delaware County Community College*
Gloria Lewis, *Tennessee State University*
David Linden, *West Liberty State College*
Peter R. McCormack, *St. Thomas University*
Mark McCourt, *North Dakota State University*
Lynne McCutcheon, *Northern Virginia Community College*
Thomas A. McGrath, *Fairfield University*
Kathleen McNamara, *Colorado State University*
Sharon McNeely, *Northeastern Illinois University*
K. Katherine Maffner, *St. Francis College*
Jacob Mandel, *Kutztown University of Pennsylvania*
Hal Mansfield, *Fort Lewis College*
Renee L. Marrangue, *Loyola Marymount University*
Francis A. Martin, *Belmont College*
Leonard J. Mather, *Northern Virginia Community College*
Charles Matter, *University of Wisconsin–Green Bay*
Dorothy Mattson, *Lakewood Community College*
Richard Mayer, *University of California*
Sara Medley, *Indiana University*
Joe Meir, *Shepherd College*
Janet L. Merrill, *Dallas Baptist College*
Joe Merz, *Shepherd College*
Frederick Metcalfe, *West LA, California, Suicide Prevention Center*
R. R. Miller, *SUNY–Binghamton*
David Mitchell, *Southern Methodist University*
Kevin Moore, *DePauw University*
John Mortisugu, *Pacific Lutheran University*
David Mostofsky, *Boston University*
Karen Murphy, *Seward County Community College*
Linda Musun-Miller, *University of Arkansas–Little Rock*

Ruth Ann Myers, *Silver Lake College*
Shinken Naitoh, *Honolulu Community College*
John M. Nash, *Worcester State College*
Paul Nay, *Porterville College*
David Neufeldt, *Hutchinson Community College*
John Nichols, *Tulsa Junior College*
Steve Nida, *Franklin University*
David Novak, *Lansing Community College*
Michael O'Boyle, *Iowa State University*
Dennis H. Ofstein, *South Dakota Schools of Mines and Technology*
Judy Ogden, *St. Clair County Community College*
Daniel Ozer, *Boston University*
Wendy Palmquist, *Plymouth State College*
Patricia Parmelee, *California State University–Fullerton*
Hal Pashler, *University of California–San Diego*
James Pate, *Georgia State University*
C. Patrick, *San Diego Mesa College*
L. L. Pearce, *Southern West Virginia Community College*
Ron Peters, *Iowa State University*
Sharyl Peterson, *Colorado College*
Mark W. Phillips, *York College*
Walter Pieper, *Georgia State University*
Ralph Pifer, *Sauk Valley College*
Jack Powell, *Missouri Baptist College*
Dean Powers, *Volunteer State Community College*
Jay B. Pozner, *Jackson Community College*
JoAnn Preston, *University of Richmond*
Janet Procter, *Auburn University*
Tom Prutsman, *Mansfield University*
Bob Rainey, *Florida Community College*
Donald Ratcliff, *Tococa Falls College*
Celia C. Reaves, *Monroe Community College*
Phillip L. Rice, *Moorhead State University*
Matt L. Riggs, *California State University–San Bernardino*
Harold Robbins, *Ohio Wesleyan University*
Eloise Roberts, *Elizabeth City State University*
Ernest E. Roberts, *University of South Alabama*
Dick Rose, *Indiana University*
Milt Rosenbaum, *University of Iowa*
John A. Ross, *St. Lawrence University*
Sherman Ross, *Howard University*
William S. Royce, *University of Portland*
Craig Rush, *Mater Dei College*
Dan Sapin, *Los Angeles Southwest College*
Mary Jo Scheible, *Gateway Technical Institute*
Steve Schneider, *Pima Community College*
David Schroeder, *University of Arkansas*
Dean Schroeder, *Laramie County Community College*
Martin Schroth, *Santa Clara University*
Richard Seefeldt, *University of Wisconsin–River Falls*
David G. Sequin, *Jamestown Community College*
Owen Sharkey, *University of Prince Edward's Island*
Joe B. Shelton, *Southwest Baptist University*
Jack P. Shilkret, *Anne Arundel Community College*
Barbara K. Sholley, *University of Richmond*
David Shwalb, *Westminster College*
Ed Smith, *Longwood College*
Gene Smith, *Western Illinois University*
Robert F. Smith, *George Mason University*
Theresa Socha, *Frostburg State College*
David Solly, *Pittsburgh State University*
Ralph H. Song, *University of Wisconsin–Whitewater*
James R. Speer, *Stephen F. Austin State University*
Martha S. Spiker, *University of Charleston*
Don Stanley, *North Harris County College*
Cathy Stevenson, *University of Kansas*
Michael R. Stevenson, *Ball State University*
John Stoudenwire, *University of Southern Mississippi*
Robert J. Stout, *St. Petersburg Junior College*
Mark Strauss, *University of Pittsburgh*
Barbara Streitfeld, *University of Hartford*
Mary Beth Susman, *Community College of Denver*
Gilles Talbot, *Champlain College*
Robert Tallmon, *American River College*
Christopher Taylor, *Western Washington University*
George Taylor, *University of Missouri*
Freddie Thomason, *Wallace Community College*
Burt Thompson, *Niagara University*
Carol Parker Thompson, *Muskegon Community College*
Glenn W. Thompson, *Allegheny College*
Frank Tikalsky, *Western Montana College*
Irving Tucker, *Shepherd College*
Dennis A. Vanderweele, *Occidental College*
Sylvia Von Kluge, *Eastern Michigan University*
William Walker, *University of Richmond*
William J. Walsh, *Diablo Valley College*
Y. George Wang, *Cooke County College*
Everett Washington, *Virginia Commonwealth University*
Cynthia Whissell, *Laurentian University*
M. L. Whitehill, *Montgomery Community College*
Paul Whitney, *Washington State University*
William M. Wickham, *St. Petersburg Junior College*
Anvy Wicks, *Northeast Iowa Technical Institute*
William Williams, *Eastern Washington University*
Michael Wolff, *Florida State University*
H. D. Woodyard, *University of Windsor*
Lonnie R. Yandell, *Belmont College*
Lugenia D. Young, *Gordon College*
Margaret Zimmerman, *Virginia Wesleyan University*
Roger Zimmerman, *University of Southern Maine*

The editorial and production group at Brown & Benchmark Publishers did an excellent job on this project. Special thanks go to Steven Yetter and Linda Falkenstein of the editorial group, and to Victoria Putman and Jayne Klein of the production group.

Finally, I want to thank my wife, Mary Jo, for her continued support, affection, and wisdom.

TO THE STUDENT

How the Learning System Works

This book contains a number of learning devices, each of which presents the field of psychology in a meaningful way. The learning devices in *Psychology* will help you learn the material more effectively.

Chapter Outlines

Each chapter begins with an outline, showing the organization of topics by heading levels. The outline functions as an overview to the arrangement and structure of the chapter.

CHAPTER WIP

What Is Psychology?

CHAPTER OUTLINE

IMAGES OF PSYCHOLOGY
Portrait of a Psychologist WIP—3
PREVIEW WIP—3
DEFINING PSYCHOLOGY WIP—3
THE BEGINNINGS OF PSYCHOLOGY AS A SCIENCE WIP—4
From Myth to Philosophy to Psychology WIP—4
Early Contributors WIP—4
EARLY AND CONTEMPORARY APPROACHES TO PSYCHOLOGY WIP—5
The Behavioral Approach WIP—5
The Psychoanalytic Approach WIP—7
The Humanistic Approach WIP—7
The Cognitive Approach WIP—8
The Neurobiological Approach WIP—9
The Sociocultural Approach WIP—9
Which Approach Is Best? WIP—10
Women and Ethnic Minorities in Psychology's History WIP—10
PSYCHOLOGY AND PSEUDOPSYCHOLOGY WIP—12
PSYCHOLOGY'S CAREERS AND AREAS OF SPECIALIZATION WIP—15
Careers in Psychology WIP—15
Areas of Specialization in Psychology WIP—15

CRITICAL THINKING ABOUT BEHAVIOR
The Importance of Asking Questions WIP—18

OVERVIEW WIP—19
KEY TERMS WIP—20
RESOURCES AND READINGS IN PSYCHOLOGY WIP—21

CHAPTER BOXES

EXPLORATIONS IN PSYCHOLOGY
Astrology and Psychology's Skepticism WIP—14

The thirst to know and understand . . . these are the goods in life's rich hand.
—Sir William Watson

WIP—5

(a) (b)

FIGURE 1
The Beginning of Psychology as a Science
(*a*) Wilhelm Wundt established the first research laboratory in psychology at Germany's University of Leipzig in 1879. (*b*) To help you place Wundt's achievement in history, consider that Alexander Graham Bell invented the telephone in 1876.

Wundt was the master of introspection training. Before his students were permitted to describe their images and perceptions, they had to participate in a minimum of 10,000 practice observations. Philosophers had used introspection for several thousand years, but they had never varied conditions so systematically. The technique of introspection, however, came under heavy fire. The introspectionists thought they were studying immediate experience, but, in reality, it takes time to introspect. Introspection was actually retrospection; thus, the act of introspection changed the observer's experience, thereby modifying or contaminating the observation.

But psychology's initial emphasis on conscious experience, because it lacked objectivity and investigated mental processes that were too vague, went the way of the dinosaur. Other approaches to mental processes and behavior soon emerged (Hothersall, 1996).

their world. Wundt's and Titchener's attempts to classify the structures of the mind were not unlike a chemist's breaking down chemicals into their component parts—water into hydrogen and oxygen, for example. This approach became quite logically known as **structuralism,** *the early theory of psychology developed by Wundt and Titchener that emphasized the importance of conscious thought and classification of the mind's structures.*

James and Functionalism

The first of the new psychologists in the United States was not Titchener, but William James. James (1890/1950) did not believe that the elementary, rigid structures for which Titchener searched existed. James argued that our minds are characterized by a continuous flow of information about our experiences rather than by discrete components. Following in the steps of Darwin, James emphasized the mind's ability to continuously evolve as it adapts to information about the environment. This approach became known as **functionalism,** *William James' theory that psychology's role is to study the functions of the mind and behavior in adapting to the environment.*

Many of the early psychologists, such as Wundt, Titchener, and James, used introspection to discover information about conscious experiences. **Introspection** *is a technique whereby specially trained people carefully observe and analyze their own mental experiences.* It is a process of turning inward in search of mind's nature.

EARLY AND CONTEMPORARY APPROACHES TO PSYCHOLOGY

Whether psychologists study behavior and the external factors that influence behavior, or mental processes and the internal factors that influence behavior, depends on their approach. There are six important approaches to psychology: behavioral, psychoanalytic, humanistic, cognitive, neurobiological, and sociocultural. We will briefly study each of these approaches in turn, but we will return to them in much greater detail in later chapters. Because the abstract principles of psychological approaches can be difficult to remember—almost like swimming upstream against an onrushing current—we'll apply each approach to something each of us has done in our lives: dating.

The Behavioral Approach

The year is 1898. You are ushered into a room, where you see a dog hooked up to a harness. The dog is salivating profusely, and you wonder what is going on. A gentleman in a white laboratory coat walks over and quietly informs you that an experiment on learning is taking place. He explains that it is a very simple form of learning, in this case documented by the dog's salivation in anticipation of being fed. The man is Ivan Pavlov, who shows you that if he puts the dog's tray down or allows the dog to catch a glimpse of the attendant who fed him the previous day, the dog will begin to salivate.

What Is Psychology? 5

Page Numbering

You may have noticed that your book has two sets of page numbers, one at the top of the page that begins with an abbreviation and one at the bottom. Although you are using the standard 17-chapter version of *Psychology,* the fifth edition is also a 40-chapter book! We have created a customizable "menu" of 40 chapters to choose from, designed to be used in any order. Customizable versions of this book can be designed by an instructor to match exactly the topics that will be covered in that class.

Because the chapters in a customized version of *Psychology* can be used in any order, there could be no standard, consecutive pagination. Instead, in customized versions of this book, each chapter is numbered separately. The page number consists of the three-letter chapter abbreviation and is numbered starting with page 1. However, since your instructor has ordered the standard version of *Psychology,* we have also provided the standard, consecutive paging at the bottom of the page.

My friend . . . care for your psyche, and . . . make it as good as possible. . . . Know thyself, for once we know ourselves, we may learn how to care for ourselves, but otherwise we never shall.

—Socrates

Images of Psychology

Portrait of a Psychologist

Imagine you are seated at dinner next to someone you have never met and learn that she is a psychologist. What comes to mind when you find out that she is a psychologist? To many people, it would mean that she likely has a special insight into human nature and treats people who have problems. But might that expectation be wrong?

You will learn in this book that the word *psychologist* refers to a broad spectrum of occupations, some of which have nothing to do with insight into human nature. Also, many psychologists are research scientists, not healers. No single image encompasses the varied activities of psychologists.

For example, consider the following descriptions of some contemporary psychologists at work:

- A research psychologist trained in cognitive psychology painstakingly constructs the thousands of steps of a computer program that, presented with hundreds of sentences, will learn language as an infant does.
- Another research psychologist trained in physiological psychology and neuroscience injects epinephrine into a rat that has learned a maze, to determine how the hormone affects its memory.
- A clinical psychologist probes a depressed client's thoughts for clues about the cause of the depression and thinks about ways to help the client cope more effectively.
- An educational psychologist gives children a number of psychological tests and recommends the most effective learning environment for each child.
- A psychologist interested in gender and women's issues teaches at a small college and works with her college and the community to eliminate sexual harassment.
- An organizational psychologist has a consulting firm that advises corporations on ways to improve communication and work productivity.

These are but a few of the many different portraits of psychologists. As you read this book, you will discover that psychology is a diverse field and psychologists have heterogeneous interests.

Preview

What is psychology? To provide you with a reasonable answer to this complex question, in this chapter we will take a general look at the field of psychology and psychologists. We will define psychology, explore the beginnings of psychology as a science, examine early and contemporary approaches to psychology, compare psychology with pseudopsychology, and describe psychology's careers and areas of specialization.

Defining Psychology

To some extent, psychology's findings may strike you as being simple common sense, but studies often turn up the unexpected in human behavior. For example, it may seem obvious that couples who live together before marriage have a better chance of making the marriage last. After all, practice makes perfect, doesn't it? But researchers have found a higher success rate for couples who marry before living together (Teachman & Polonko, 1990). It might also seem obvious that we would experience more stress and be less happy if we have to function in many different roles than if we only functioned in a single role. However, women who engage in multiple roles (such as wife, mother,

What Is Psychology? 3

Images of Psychology

This easy-to-read, high-interest piece introduces you to some aspect of the chapter's contents.

Preview

This section tells you what the chapter's contents are.

34—S&P

Explorations in Psychology 2

The Perceptual Worlds of Art

Look at figure A. If you stood very close to this painting and looked at one area, you would see only daubs of colored pigments on a canvas. If you stood back and considered the whole painting, however, you would see the brilliantly colored landscape with a tree, a village, a church, and a turbulent sky. The painting is nineteenth-century Dutch artist Vincent van Gogh's masterpiece *Starry Night.* This is not likely the scene most of us would paint if we were trying to recreate the real world. Stars do not race about in frenzied whirlpools. What caused van Gogh to paint *Starry Night* the way he did? For one thing, he was a tormented, intense, mystical man. Some of the torment, and a kind of ecstasy, are built into the painting. Another artist, not experiencing van Gogh's mental anguish, would likely have painted the same starry night very differently.

Was van Gogh painting what he actually saw? We don't know the answer to that question, but we do know that, at some points in history, artists have strived to mirror the world just as it appears to their eyes; at others they have deliberately distorted reality. The Renaissance masters tried to paint the world as accurately as possible, as if their canvas were a photograph (see figure B). They relied on many of the cues for depth perception to portray three-dimensional reality on a flat surface.

Whereas the Renaissance artists tried to paint the world as their eyes saw it, other schools of art strove for something different. For example, the nineteenth-century French Impressionists focused on the *impression* a scene makes on the observer instead of trying to paint the scene as accurately as possible. They strove to capture the viewer's perception of nature's fleeting sensations of light. Their technique involved the creation of a patchwork of varying daubs of brightly colored paint

Figure A

Vincent van Gogh's *Starry Night*

Figure B

Raphael's *Fire in the Borgo*

The Renaissance masters used depth cues to give their paintings three-dimensional appearance. Notice the detailed attention to perspective, such as how the roofs above the columns extend backward. Notice also the smaller size of the people in the distance and the overlapping of people and buildings.

120 *John W. Santrock*

Explorations in Psychology

You'll find one or more of these boxed features in every chapter, giving you an in-depth look at issues of interest to psychologists today.

S&P—27

Concept Table 3

The Auditory, Skin, Chemical, Kinesthetic, and Vestibular Senses

Concept	Processes/Related Ideas	Characteristics/Description
The Auditory System	The nature of sound and how we experience it	Sounds or sound waves are vibrations in the air that are processed by the auditory (or hearing) system. Sound waves vary in wavelength, which determines the frequency of the sound wave or the number of cycles (or full wavelengths) that pass through a point in a given time. Pitch is the perceptual interpretation of the frequency of sound. Amplitude is measured in decibels (dB), the amount of pressure produced by a sound wave relative to a standard. Loudness is the perception of a sound wave's amplitude. Complex sounds are those in which numerous frequencies of sound blend together. We experience the particular combination of frequencies in a sound as the quality or timbre of a sound.
	Structures and functions of the ear	The ear serves the function of transmitting a high-fidelity version of sounds in the world to the brain for analysis and interpretation. The ear is divided into the outer ear, middle ear, and inner ear. The outer ear consists of the pinna and the external auditory canal. The middle ear consists of the eardrum, hammer, anvil, and stirrup. The main parts of the inner ear are the oval window, cochlea, and the organ of Corti. The basilar membrane, located inside the cochlea, is where vibrations are changed into nerve impulses.
	Theories of hearing	Place theory states that each frequency produces vibrations at a particular spot on the basilar membrane. Frequency theory states that the perception of a sound's frequency is due to how often the auditory nerve fires. Volley theory is a modification of place theory, stating that high frequencies can be signaled by teams of neurons that fire at different offset times to create an overall firing rate that could signal a very high frequency. Frequency theory is better at explaining lower-frequency sounds, volley and place theories higher-frequency sounds.
	Neural-auditory processing	Information about sound is carried from the cochlea to the brain by the auditory nerve. Information is integrated in the temporal lobe.
The Skin Senses	Touch	In touch, we detect mechanical energy, or pressure against the skin.
	Temperature	Thermoreceptors, which are receptors located under the skin, respond to increases and decreases in temperature.
	Pain	Pain is the sensation that warns us that damage to our bodies is occurring. Gate-control theory states that the spinal column contains a neural gate that can be opened (allowing the perception of pain) or closed (blocking the perception of pain). Gate-control theory has been proposed as one explanation of acupuncture, a technique in which thin needles are inserted at specific points in the body to produce various effects, including local anesthesia. Gate-control theory does not completely explain how we experience pain.
The Chemical Senses	Taste	We use our sense of taste to select food and to regulate food intake. Papillae are rounded bumps above the surface of the tongue that contain taste buds, the receptors for taste. The taste qualities we can respond to are classified as sweet, sour, bitter, and salty.
	Smell	The functions of smell include deciding what to eat, tracking, and communication. The olfactory epithelium, located at the top of the nasal cavity, contains a sheet of receptor cells for smell.
The Kinesthetic and Vestibular Senses	Their nature	The kinesthetic senses provide information about movement, posture, and orientation, while the vestibular sense provides information about balance and movement. The semicircular canals, located in the inner ear, contain the sensory receptors that detect head motion that is caused when we tilt or move our heads and/or bodies.

113

Concept Tables

Two or three times in each chapter, you can review what has been discussed so far in that chapter by scanning the information in concept tables. This learning device helps you get a handle on material several times a chapter so you don't wait until the end of the chapter and have too much information to digest.

MET—23

Critical Thinking About Behavior

Personal Versus Psychological Evidence

> *What is needed is not the will to believe, but the wish to find out.*
>
> **Bertrand Russell**

You have read about the history and scope of psychology and the current methods psychologists use in observing, describing, explaining, and predicting behavior. Just how different are psychology-based ways of thinking from the processes you go through when you are making judgments about behavior? There are some critical differences.

1. **Precise descriptions of behaviors.** Psychologists are exacting in how they define and describe behaviors, being especially careful to distinguish descriptions of behavior from other inferences or interpretations that can be made *about* behavior. We are constantly confronted with behaviors that we must examine and interpret, prompting us to come to conclusions, infer meanings, or make predictions about behavior; however, psychologists are inclined to be precise in their observations and cautious about their inferences. When confronted with a challenging behavior, critical thinkers trained in psychology are likely to ask, "*What exactly do you mean by . . . ?*"
2. **Reliance on systematic observation.** Nonscientific explanations of behavior correspond reasonably well to the first stage of the scientific method: identifying and analyzing a problem. It is in the second stage of the scientific method that scientific and nonscientific ways of interpreting behavior diverge. Scientists collect data systematically, interpret the data, and revise their conclusions or beliefs, based on these interpretations.

   This procedure reflects a strong preference for conclusions that are based on objective data derived from carefully planned behavioral research rather than subjective conclusions that might not be carefully considered or are more likely to reflect unknown biases of the observer. When confronted with a conclusion about behavior, the critical thinker trained in psychology is likely to ask, "*What's your evidence for this conclusion?*"
3. **Pursuit of alternative explanations.** Many questions that we ponder about behavior might not lend themselves easily to objective research. In the absence of systematic observation and scientific interpretation, psychologists are likely to question whether there could be other explanations for the behavior being examined. They actively speculate about other variables that could influence the behavior, demonstrating a thinking characteristic that could be described as being *variable-minded.* Psychologists are likely to ask, "*Are there other plausible ways to explain the behavior?*"

You might already have formed some conclusions about the following examples of behaviors. What happens to your conclusions when you adopt psychological ways of examining behavior, when you ask for clarity, inquire about evidence, and look for alternative explanations?

- Magicians are well known for making objects disappear. *Do they really make objects vanish, or can you think of an alternative explanation for this compelling illusion?*
- Seeing a loved one ushering you through a tunnel toward a bright white light is an example of an experience commonly reported by people having a near-death experience. *Is this a confirmation of an afterlife, or could this phenomenon be explained in another way?*
- In psychotherapy, some individuals are startled by their recovery of memories that suggest they have been physically or emotionally abused in childhood. How could it be that something so horrifying isn't remembered until some point quite distant from the event? *How many variables or influences might be involved in understanding this phenomenon?*
- Some people are convinced that they have extrasensory powers. They claim to know in advance or from a distance when bad things happen to their relatives, to be able to predict songs that are about to come on the radio, and so on. *Is this phenomenon real? What evidence is there for extrasensory abilities? Are there other explanations that account for the behavior?*
- Two twins, separated at birth and raised apart, are reunited to discover that they have an uncanny number of similarities. Their reunion prompts strong speculation regarding the power of genetic influence in shaping behavior. *Is this research definitive "proof" of the power of inheritance, or are there other plausible ways to explain the remarkable number of similarities?*
- Many individuals believe that the growing problem of violence in our culture is a direct influence of violence portrayed in movies and television. *What evidence supports this position? Is violence really growing? What other factors might contribute to this important problem?*

You may have thought about some research strategies that could help you to evaluate the quality of conclusions about behavior. You will find out how these questions and others will be evaluated in the chapters that follow.

Critical Thinking About Behavior

This section appears at the end of each standard chapter and involves an elaborate exploration of critical thinking about psychology and behavior.

Overview

The overview section consists of two parts. (1) a cognitive map that provides you with a visual organization of the chapter's main topics and (2) a brief summary of the chapter's main contents.

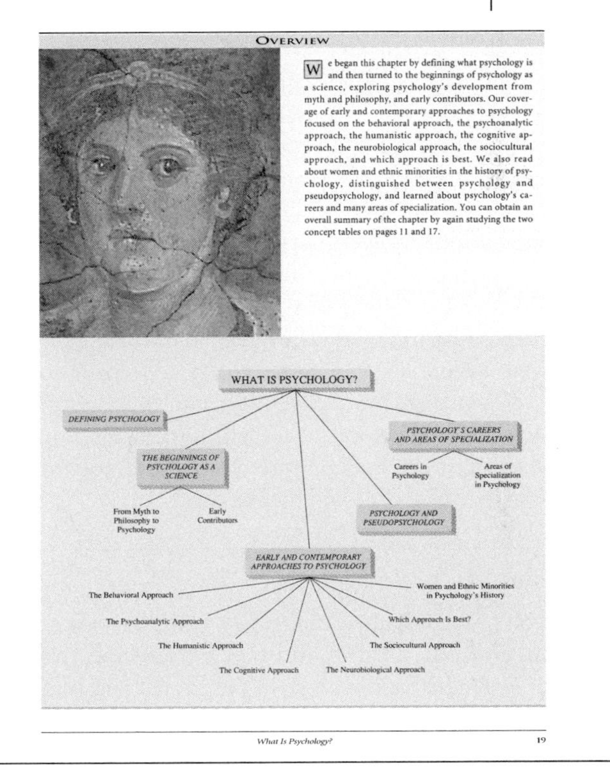

OVERVIEW

We began this chapter by defining what psychology is and then turned to the beginnings of psychology as a science, exploring psychology's development from myth and philosophy, and early contributors. Our coverage of early and contemporary approaches to psychology focused on the behavioral approach, the psychoanalytic approach, the humanistic approach, the cognitive approach, the neurobiological approach, the sociocultural approach, and which approach is best. We also read about women and ethnic minorities in the history of psychology, distinguished between psychology and pseudopsychology, and learned about psychology's careers and many areas of specialization. You can obtain an overall summary of the chapter by again studying the two concept tables on pages 11 and 17.

What Is Psychology? 19

EMO—27

Key Terms

emotion Feeling, or affect, that involves a mixture of arousal (a fast heartbeat, for example), conscious experience (such as thinking about being in love with someone), and overt behavior (such as smiling or grimacing). p. EMO—4

positive affectivity (PA) The range of positive emotion, from high energy, enthusiasm, and excitement, to calm, quiet, and withdrawn. Joy and happiness involve positive affectivity. p. EMO—6

negative affectivity (NA) Emotions that are negatively toned, such as anxiety, anger, guilt, and sadness. p. EMO—6

Yerkes-Dodson law The law that performance is best under conditions of moderate rather than low or high arousal. p. EMO—6

flow Optimal experiences in life that are most likely to occur when people develop a sense of mastery. Flow involves a state of concentration in which an individual becomes absorbed while engaging in an activity. p. EMO—7

James-Lange theory The theory that emotion results from physiological states triggered by stimuli in the environment. p. EMO—10

Cannon-Bard theory The theory that emotion and physiological states occur simultaneously. p. EMO—10

autonomic nervous system The system that takes messages to and from the body's internal organs, monitoring such processes as breathing, heart rate, and digestion. p. EMO—11

sympathetic nervous system The part of the autonomic nervous system that is involved in the arousal of the body, being responsible for quick reactions to a stressor—sometimes referred to as the fight-or-flight response. p. EMO—12

parasympathetic nervous system The part of the autonomic nervous system that calms the body and promotes relaxation and healing. p. EMO—12

polygraph A machine that is used to try to determine if someone is lying by monitoring changes in the body—heart rate, breathing, and electrodermal response (an index that detects skin resistance to passage of a weak electric current)—thought to be influenced by emotional states. p. EMO—14

Maximally Discriminative Facial Movement Coding System (MAX) Izard's system of coding infants' facial expressions that are related to emotion. p. EMO—18

display rules Sociocultural standards that determine when, where, and how emotions should be expressed. p. EMO—22

Resources and Readings in Psychology

Anger: The Misunderstood Emotion (1989)
by Carol Tavris
New York: Touchstone Books

Anger: The Misunderstood Emotion covers a wide terrain of anger. Indeed, it is hard to think of any facet of anger—from wrecked friendships to wars—that Tavris does not tackle. In addition to extensive coverage of anger between marital partners, she addresses highway anger, violence in sports, and young women's anger. Tavris debunks myths about anger, attacks the catharsis, ventilationist approach to anger, describes the toll of anger on the body, and tells readers how to rethink anger and make more adaptive choices.

The Dance of Anger (1985)
by Harriet Lerner
New York: HarperPerennial

The Dance of Anger is written mainly for women about the anger in their lives, both their own anger and the anger of people they live with, especially men. Lerner believes that women have more difficulty coping with anger than men do. Rooted in both family systems and psychoanalytic theory, *The Dance of Anger* discusses styles of managing anger that don't work for women in the long run—silent submission, ineffective fighting and blaming, and emotional distancing. She also paints the cultural context of an American society that has created these ineffective styles in women, and she motivates women to develop the courage to change these old, protective ways.

Emotions and Culture (1994)
edited by Shinobu Kitayama and Hazel Markus
Washington, DC: American Psychological Association

This volume contains chapters by leading authorities in the field of emotion who believe that emotions are influenced and shaped by social and cultural experiences. Major sections of the book focus on emotion as a social product; emotion, language, and cognition; and emotion as moral category and phenomenon.

Flow (1990)
by Mihaly Csikszentmihalyi
New York: Harper & Row

Flow is about the optimal experiencing of life. Csikszentmihalyi (pronounced "chik-*sent*-me-high-yee") has been investigating the concept of flow for more than two decades. Earlier in this chapter we discussed the author's view of what flow is, namely, a deep happiness people feel when they have a sense of mastering something. Flow is a state of concentration in which a person becomes absorbed while engaging in an activity. We can develop flow by setting challenges for ourselves, by stretching ourselves to the limits to achieve something worthwhile, by developing competent coping skills, and by combining life's many experiences into a meaningful pattern.

Telling Lies: Clues to Deceit in the Marketplace, Politics, and Marriage (1985)
by Paul Ekman
New York: W. W. Norton

Ekman explains how to read facial expressions and gestures to determine whether people are lying.

Key Terms

Listed at the end of each chapter are key terms that are defined throughout the chapter. They are listed with page references and are defined again in a glossary at the end of the book.

Resources and Readings in Psychology

This section lists books, brochures, agencies, phone numbers, research journals, and psychological organizations. The extensive description of resources is designed to provide you with more information about psychology's many domains and practical information for improving people's lives.

Your Study Skills

You have taken courses in history, math, English, and science, but have you taken a course in study skills? Have you ever seriously sat down and mapped out a time management program for yourself? Have you ever studied how to improve your memory, then tried the techniques to see if they work? Have you ever had an organized plan to "attack" a textbook? Before you begin reading the specific content of this book, take time to read this section on how to improve your study skills. You will be motivated to think about ways to manage your time, to improve your concentration, to memorize more effectively, and to function more efficiently in the classroom. You will learn skills to understand this and other books more clearly, and you will discover how to prepare for and take exams.

Managing Your Time

A student named Tom came to the author's office about 2 weeks before the final exam in an introductory psychology course. He had a *D* average in the course and wanted to know what was causing him to get such a low grade. It turned out that he wasn't doing well in any of his classes, so we talked about his background. Eventually the conversation turned to his study techniques and what he could do to get better grades on his final exams. I asked Tom to put together a study schedule for the four final exams he was getting ready to take in 2 weeks. He planned to study a total of 4 hours for his psychology exam; only 1 of those hours was scheduled for the night before the exam, and no study time was allotted to the morning before the exam (the exam was in the late afternoon).

I told Tom that, although the psychology exam probably was not the most difficult one he would ever take in college, I thought the material would require more than 4 hours of study time if he wanted to improve his grade for the course. As we talked further, it became evident that Tom was a terrible manager of time. True, he had a part-time job in addition to the 12 credit hours he was taking, but, as we mapped out how he used his time during the day, Tom quickly became aware that he was wasting big chunks of it.

A week is made up of 168 hours. A typical college student sleeps 50 hours, attends classes 19 hours, eats 11 hours, and studies 20 hours per week. For Tom, we allotted 15 hours a week for his part-time job and 6 hours a week for transportation to and from school, work, and home. Subtracting the 20 hours of study time, Tom found that his main activities accounted for 101 of the week's 168 hours, suggesting that, even though he works, he still has 68 hours in which to find time for studying.

You may find it helpful to fill out a weekly schedule of your activities to see where your time goes. Figure 1 provides an example of one student's daily time schedule, along with comments about how and where time could have been used more effectively. Some students are afraid that a schedule will make them too rigid; however, successful students usually follow organized schedules and manage their time efficiently. If you waste less time, you actually will have much more free time for personal activities, and, in managing your time effectively, you will feel a sense of control over your life. Try taking 5 minutes every morning to chart your plan for the day. Before you go to bed at night, review your day to see how well you met your schedule. After you have done this for several weeks, it should become routine.

Study Skills

Given that you manage your time efficiently, how can you effectively use the study time you have? First, you need to concentrate on *really* studying in the time set aside for that purpose. Second, you can use a number of memory techniques to help you recall information. Third, you can discover strategies for learning more effectively from textbooks, such as this one. Fourth, you can reduce your

Time Start	Time End	Time Used	ACTIVITY-DESCRIPTION	
7:45	8:15	:30	Dress	Paste on mirror 3 × 5 cards: Laws of economics; psychological terms; statistical formulas—study while brushing teeth, etc.
8:15	8:40	:25	Breakfast	
8:40	9:00	:20	Nothing	Look over textbook assignment and previous lecture notes to establish continuity for today's psychology lecture.
9:00	10:00	1:00	Psychology-Lecture	
10:00	10:40	:40	Coffee-Talking	Break too long and too soon after breakfast. Should work on psychology notes just taken; also should look over economics assignment.
10:40	11:00	:20	Nothing	
11:00	12:00	1:00	Economics-Lecture	
12:00	12:45	:45	Lunch	
12:45	2:00	1:15	Reading-Magazine	Should re-work the lecture notes on economics while still fresh in mind. Also, look over biology assignment to recall the objective of the coming lab.
2:00	4:00	2:00	Biology-Lab	
4:00	5:30	1:30	Recreation-Volleyball	
5:30	6:00	:30	Nothing	Use this time for reading a magazine or newspaper.
6:00	7:00	1:00	Dinner	
7:00	8:00	1:00	Nap	Not a good idea. Better finish work, then get a good night's sleep.
8:00	8:50	:50	Study-Statistics	
8:50	9:20	:30	Break	Break too long.
9:20	10:00	:40	Study-Statistics	
10:00	10:50	:50	Rap Session	Good as a reward if basic work is done.
10:50	11:30	:40	Study-Accounting	Insufficient time allotted, but better than no time.
11:30	11:45	:15	Ready for Bed	While brushing teeth, study the 3 × 5 cards. Replace cards that have been mastered with new ones.
11:45	7:45	8:00	Sleep	

FIGURE 1

Record of One Day's Activities and Suggestions for Better Time Management

study time by functioning more effectively during class. Fifth, you can learn some important tips in preparing for and taking exams. Let's consider each of these.

Concentration

There are many distractions that keep you from studying or remembering what you have studied. Select your place of study carefully. Most individuals need a desk—a place where pens, paper, and a book can be placed. Use your desk *only* for studying. If you nap or daydream while you are at your desk, the desk can act as a cue for napping or daydreaming. Use your desk as a cue for studying. When you want to nap or daydream, go somewhere else. Be sure the area where you study is well lighted and does not have glare. Do your utmost to find a place that is quiet when you study. If the library is the right place for you, then go there, especially if there are people in the dorm or at home who distract you. Noise is one of the main distractions to effective studying. For the most part, it is a good idea to turn off the stereo, radio, or television while you are studying.

So far we have talked about the physical aspects of the environment that may help or hinder your ability to concentrate on what you are studying. Psychological and personal situations may also interfere with your ability to concentrate. Daydreaming is one way to avoid hard work. Even though daydreaming may seem pleasant at the time we are doing it, we pay the consequences later, possibly with a poor grade on a test or in a course. Everyone has personal relationships that may intrude on study time. Force yourself to put personal relationships and problems out of your mind during the time you have set aside for studying. Tell yourself you will deal with them after you have finished studying.

If the problems seem overwhelming and you cannot avoid thinking about them, you may want to contact the student counseling service at your college or university. Most college and university counseling centers not only have counselors who help students with personal problems, but they often have study skills counselors who help students with such matters as time management and concentration.

Memory Techniques

At a certain point in this course and in the other courses you are taking this semester, you will have to remember what you have heard in class and read in books. How can you remember more effectively?

First, make up your mind to remember. If you really want to improve your memory, you can, but you have to motivate yourself to improve it. Second, keep refreshing your memory. Almost everything tends to fade unless you periodically think about what it is you need to remember. Periodically rehearsing what you have heard in class or read in this book will help you store the information and retrieve it when you have a test. Third, organize, outline, or otherwise structure what you want to remember. Pick out the main points in the material you are studying and arrange them in a meaningful pattern or outline. Then recite and repeat them until you can recall them when needed. Select, organize, and repeat—these are time-tested steps for helping you remember.

A number of memory tricks also can be helpful. One memory trick is to relate what you have read to your own life. You will be encouraged to do so throughout this book. You can also use a number of organized systems to improve your memory. One such system involves using the first letter of each word in an ordered series to form a new name or sentence. For example, the colors in the light spectrum are *r*ed, *o*range, *y*ellow, *g*reen, *b*lue, *i*ndigo, and *v*iolet. You can learn this order quickly by thinking of the name Roy G. Biv.

Learning from This and Other Textbooks

This textbook has a number of built-in devices to improve your learning. You can read about many of these in the preface. One extraordinary technique that can make your reading more efficient is called the SQ3R method, and it was developed by Dr. Frances P. Robinson more than 40 years ago. *S* stands for *S*urvey, *Q* for *Q*uestion, and *3R* signifies *R*ead, *R*ecite, and *R*eview.

To *survey,* glance over the headings in each chapter to find the main points that will be developed. The outline at the beginning of each chapter will help in this regard. This orientation will help you organize the ideas as you read them later.

To *question,* you may want to begin by turning each heading into a question. This will arouse your curiosity and should increase your comprehension. The question may help make important points stand out. Ask yourself questions as you read through the chapter. As you find information that answers your questions, underline or mark the material with a felt pen.

To accomplish the third step in the SQ3R method, you begin *reading* the book as you normally would. In the SQ3R method, though, your reading should be more efficient because you have already built a foundation for understanding the material by surveying and questioning.

The fourth step in the SQ3R method involves *reciting* information periodically as you go through a chapter. To help you use this strategy, reviews appear several times per chapter; they encourage you to recite what you have read in particular parts of the chapter. In many chapters, you will want to do this more than two or three times. Every several pages, you should stop, think about what you have just read, and briefly recite the main points.

After you have used the techniques suggested so far, you need to *review* the material you have read several times before you take a test. Do not think that just because you have read a chapter you will be able to recall all of its information. By reciting the information over and over and continuing to review the material, you will improve your test performance. At the end of each chapter in this book, you will find a summary outline that will help you in the review process.

The Classroom Lecture

What goes on in your classroom is just as important as what is in this textbook. You would not skip a chapter in this book if you knew it was assigned for a test, so it is not a good idea to skip a class just to reach the allowable number of cuts or to cram for an exam. Some students feel that, because they go to class and listen passively to the lecture, they do not need to devote further time to it; however, by preparing for a lecture, using your learning skills during the lecture, and doing some follow-up work, you should be able to improve your performance on tests.

In preparing for a lecture, motivate yourself by telling yourself that it is important for you to stay alert, listen carefully to what is said, and take organized notes throughout the class period. During the lecture, record your notes in simple paragraph form. Strive to capture general ideas rather than minute details. Skip lines to show the end of one idea and the beginning of another. Use abbreviations to save time to listen more. Write legibly so that, when you review, you will know what you have written. It also is a wise idea to consolidate your notes during your first free time after the class. At that time, you may want to underline key ideas with a felt-tip pen, just as you would in the book, and, just before the next class period, go over the notes to further improve your ability to recall the information and to prepare yourself for what will be said.

How to Prepare for and Take Exams

In most cases, your grade in this course will depend on how well you do in 4 to 5 hours of exams spaced periodically throughout the semester or quarter. It is important to devote some time to thinking about how to prepare for and take exams.

All of your textbook reading should be completed several days before an exam. All of your classroom notes should be in order so you can review them easily. All term papers should be written and handed in. In the last few days before an exam, your mind should be free to concentrate on organizing and consolidating the information.

How can you arrive at this ideal state of affairs several days before an exam? Go back to the first day of class. If you have been following a routine of managing your time effectively, taking notes during every lecture, keeping up with textbook assignments, following the SQ3R method, and continuing to recite and review the material you have read and heard, you should be ready to summarize and consolidate what you have learned to prepare for the exam. You may want to develop a summary system, which would follow closely what you did for each chapter or lecture. Several days before the exam, you probably will have to review several chapters and a number of lectures. Try putting them together in an overall system the last day or so before the exam.

Should you cram for an exam? If you have not studied much until several days before the exam, you will probably have to do some cramming. However, be aware that cramming can never replace methodical, consistent study throughout the course.

To ensure success on an exam, you need to be physically and psychologically ready in addition to having the facts, ideas, and principles in your mind. First, you need to have enough rest; second, you need to feel confident. If you keep creating mountains of work for yourself, especially by not studying until the last minute, you will rob yourself of sleep, food, and exercise, probably leaving both your mind and your body in no shape to perform well on an exam. By following the advice given earlier about time management, concentration, memory techniques, the SQ3R method, the classroom lecture, and how to prepare for exams, you will feel confident going into the exam. You are less likely to panic and will have a positive attitude about taking the test.

Further Reading About Study Skills

We have briefly focused on some important ideas that will help you perform better in the courses you are taking. Several books go into much greater detail. If you want to read more about improving your study skills, check your library for the following books:

Shaw, H. (1976). *30 ways to improve your grades.* New York: McGraw-Hill. This is a fun book with interesting chapters, such as "Taking Care of Your Body and Your Brain," "Learn to Listen While Listening to Learn," and "Put into Your Own Words What You Read and Hear." Twenty-seven other chapters provide valuable information about note taking, time management, thinking clearly, and many other aspects of study skills.

Walter, T., & Siebert, A. (1987). *Student success: How to succeed in college and still have time for your friends.* New York: Holt, Rinehart & Winston. This book covers the academic, social, and emotional aspects of meeting college's challenges; an extensive number of tips are provided that will help you study more effectively and still find enough time to enjoy yourself.

Your Critical Thinking Skills

Much of the knowledge you are exposed to in the course of your education passes through your mind like grains of sand washed through a sieve. In other words, it goes in one ear and out the other. You need to do more than just memorize or passively absorb new information; you need to learn how to *think critically.* It is the ability to *think* that you should carry beyond this course, an ability that will enable you to acquire new knowledge about mind and behavior, to replace old knowledge about mind and behavior, and to recognize what types of knowledge about mind and behavior are worth acquiring in the first place. How can you cultivate the ability to think critically and clearly?

According to a leading cognitive psychologist, Robert J. Sternberg (1987), you need to use the right thinking processes, to develop problem-solving strategies, to improve your mental representation, to expand your knowledge base, and to become motivated to use your newly learned thinking skills. Let's consider each of these ideas.

The Right Thinking Processes

What are the right thinking processes? To think critically—or to solve any problem or learn any new information—you need to take an active role. This means that you must call on a variety of active thinking processes, such as the following:

Listening carefully
Identifying or formulating questions
Identifying or formulating criteria for judging possible answers
Organizing your thoughts
Noting similarities and differences
Deducing
Distinguishing between logically valid and invalid inferences
Making value judgments

Finally, you need to be able to ask and answer questions of clarification, such as "What is the main point?" "What did the author mean by that?" and "Why?"

This textbook asks you many questions, often at the beginning of a topic, encouraging you to think about the topic. As you go through the book, you should not simply accept all of the information that is presented. Psychology is a changing discipline—in the 1990s, new information is being acquired about mind and behavior. Have an inquiring mind. Remember to ask, "If the researcher had conducted her experiment this way instead of that way, what would she have discovered?" Do not be afraid to think, "That research study does not make sense to me. I think the conclusion fails to take into account the changing role of females in today's society," for example. It is through such critical thinking that psychology has advanced as a science.

Strategies

Good thinkers do more than just use the right thinking processes—they also know how to combine them into workable strategies for solving problems. It is the rare problem that can be solved by a single type of thought process used in isolation. We need to learn to *combine* thinking processes in order to master a new task.

For example, Robert Ennis (1987), who has developed a well-known taxonomy of critical thinking skills, describes the importance of multiple thinking processes in his experience as a juror serving on a murder trial. Ennis did not study "juries" or "murder" in college, but he and his fellow jurors were called on to judge the credibility of the witnesses; interpret a complicated set of legal criteria for murder and voluntary manslaughter; draw conclusions about the intentions, beliefs, and truthfulness of the defendant; and determine how the victim might have been stabbed. Critical thinking involves combining such complex thought processes in a way that makes sense, not just by jumbling them together.

Mental Representation of Both Sides of Issues and the Multiple Determination of Behavior

We need to be able to see things from multiple points of view. Unless we can mentally represent information from more than one viewpoint, we may well rely on an inadequate set of information. If we do not seek alternative explanations and interpretations of problems and issues, our conclusions may be based on our own expectations, prejudices, stereotypes, and experience.

Throughout this book, you will be encouraged to think about both sides of issues and the multiple determination of behavior, and you will be challenged to think critically. It is easy to fall into the trap of thinking that there is only one side to an issue. For example, you might be inclined to think that behavior is determined only by environmental experiences, to the exclusion of hereditary influences. In many places in the book, you will be encouraged to think critically about the manner in which heredity and environment interact to produce behavior. When we think about what causes behavior, we sometimes lean toward explaining the behavior in terms of a single cause. For example, a friend might tell you, "My marriage didn't work because he couldn't let go of his mother." The husband's inability to relinquish his strong attachment to his mother may have been one cause of the divorce, but undoubtedly there were others—perhaps economic problems, sexual difficulties, personality conflicts, and so on. One of psychology's great lessons is that behavior is multiply determined. Understanding and applying this principle will be encouraged throughout the book and can help you think critically about mind and behavior.

Knowledge Base

It is important for you to keep in mind that thinking does not occur in the absence of knowledge: we need to have something to think about. It is a mistake, however, to concentrate only on information to the exclusion of thinking skills, because you simply would become a student who has a lot of knowledge but who is unable to evaluate and apply it. It is equally a mistake to concentrate only on thinking skills, because you would become a student who knows how to think but has nothing to think about. The material on Study Skills that begins on p. xxxvi will help you acquire this knowledge base about psychology.

Motivation to Use Thinking Skills

All of the thinking skills you possibly could master would be irrelevant if they were not put to use. As you read this book, you will be encouraged to use your critical-thinking skills as you study and go about your everyday activities. Critical thinking is both a matter for academic study and a part of living. Considering both sides of issues, contemplating the multiple determinants of behavior, using the right thought processes, combining the right thought processes into workable strategies, and having access to psychology's knowledge base can help you think critically about issues and problems as you go through the course of your daily life.

Suggested Reading

Baron, J. B., & Sternberg, R. J. (Eds.). (1987). *Teaching thinking skills: Theory and practice.* New York: W. H. Freeman. This book presents essays by 10 eminent psychologists, educators, and philosophers that portray the current state of knowledge about critical thinking skills. It offers various exercises and strategies that can be performed both inside and outside the classroom to enhance your critical thinking skills.

CHAPTER

WIP

What Is Psychology?

ARTIST UNKNOWN
Lady Playing the Kithara, detail

C H A P T E R

What Is Psychology?

Chapter Outline

Chapter Boxes

The thirst to know and understand . . . these are the goods in life's rich hand.

—**Sir William Watson**

> *My friend . . . care for your psyche, and . . . make it as good as possible. . . . Know thyself, for once we know ourselves, we may learn how to care for ourselves, but otherwise we never shall.*
>
> **—Socrates**

Images of Psychology

Portrait of a Psychologist

Imagine you are seated at dinner next to someone you have never met and learn that she is a psychologist. What comes to mind when you find out that she is a psychologist? To many people, it would mean that she likely has a special insight into human nature and treats people who have problems. But might that expectation be wrong?

You will learn in this book that the word *psychologist* refers to a broad spectrum of occupations, some of which have nothing to do with insight into human nature. Also, many psychologists are research scientists, not healers. No single image encompasses the varied activities of psychologists. For example, consider the following descriptions of some contemporary psychologists at work:

- A research psychologist trained in cognitive psychology painstakingly constructs the thousands of steps of a computer program that, presented with hundreds of sentences, will learn language as an infant does.
- Another research psychologist trained in physiological psychology and neuroscience injects epinephrine into a rat that has learned a maze, to determine how the hormone affects its memory.
- A clinical psychologist probes a depressed client's thoughts for clues about the cause of the depression and thinks about ways to help the client cope more effectively.
- An educational psychologist gives children a number of psychological tests and recommends the most effective learning environment for each child.
- A psychologist interested in gender and women's issues teaches at a small college and works with her college and the community to eliminate sexual harassment.
- An organizational psychologist has a consulting firm that advises corporations on ways to improve communication and work productivity.

These are but a few of the many different portraits of psychologists. As you read this book, you will discover that psychology is a diverse field and psychologists have heterogeneous interests.

Preview

What is psychology? To provide you with a reasonable answer to this complex question, in this chapter we will take a general look at the field of psychology and psychologists. We will define psychology, explore the beginnings of psychology as a science, examine early and contemporary approaches to psychology, compare psychology with pseudopsychology, and describe psychology's careers and areas of specialization.

Defining Psychology

To some extent, psychology's findings may strike you as being simple common sense, but studies often turn up the unexpected in human behavior. For example, it may seem obvious that couples who live together before marriage have a better chance of making the marriage last. After all, practice makes perfect, doesn't it? But researchers have found a higher success rate for couples who marry before living together (Teachman & Polonko, 1990). It might also seem obvious that we would experience more stress and be less happy if we have to function in many different roles than if we only functioned in a single role. However, women who engage in multiple roles (such as wife, mother, and career) report more satisfaction with their lives than do women who engage in a single or fewer roles (such as wife or wife and mother) (Cozby, 1991). As you can see, psychology doesn't accept assumptions about human nature at face value, however reasonable they may sound. It is a rigorous discipline that tests assumptions.

Psychology *is the scientific study of behavior and mental processes.* There are three aspects to this definition: science, behavior, and mental processes. Let's examine behavior first. **Behavior** *is everything we do that can be directly observed*—two people kissing, a baby crying, a college student riding a motorcycle.

Mental processes *are trickier to define than behavior; they are the thoughts, feelings, and motives that each of us experiences privately, but which cannot be observed directly.* While we cannot directly see thoughts and feelings, they are no less real. They include *thinking* about kissing someone, a baby's *feelings* when its mother leaves the room, and a college student's *memory* of the motorcycle episode.

As a **science,** *psychology uses systematic methods to observe, describe, predict, and explain behavior.* Psychology's methods are not casual. They are carefully and precisely planned and conducted. They are often verified by checking to see if they *describe* the behavior of many different people. For example, researchers might construct a questionnaire on sexual attitudes and give it to 500 individuals. They might spend considerable time devising the questions and determining the background of the people who are chosen to participate in the survey. The researchers may try to *predict* the sexual activity of college students based on their liberal or conservative religious attitudes, or on their sexual knowledge, for example. After the psychologists analyze their data, they will also want to *explain* what they *observe.* If the researchers discover from their survey that college students are less sexually active than they were a decade ago, they seek to explain why this change has occurred. They might ask, Is it because of increased fear of sexually transmitted diseases? As can be seen, psychology is recognized as a scientific discipline.

Psychology is not a cure-all for every knotty problem, and it doesn't tell us the meaning of life. It does, however, contribute enormously to our knowledge about why people are the way they are, why they think and act the way they do, and how they can cope more effectively with their lives. Psychologists are enthusiastic about psychology's potential to improve our lives as we approach the twenty-first century. *It is an exciting time of discovery in the field of psychology.*

The Beginnings of Psychology as a Science

How did the field of psychology emerge? Who were its earliest contributors?

From Myth to Philosophy to Psychology

Ever since our ancestors first gathered around a fire to create and embellish myths, we've been trying to explain why things are the way they are. Myths attributed most events to the pleasure or displeasure of the gods: When a volcano erupted, the gods were angry; if two people fell in love, they were the target of Cupid's arrows. As we became more sophisticated, myths gave way to *philosophy,* the rational investigation of the underlying principles of being and knowledge.

The early Greek philosophers Socrates (469–399 B.C.) and Aristotle (384–322 B.C.) urged us to know ourselves, to use logic to make inferences about mind, and to systematically observe behavior. It was Aristotle who argued that an empirical approach, rather than dialogue, was the best route to knowledge. Direct observation remains an important dimension of psychology today.

For centuries, philosophers enjoyed arguing and debating questions like these: How do we acquire knowledge? Does information come to us through our senses and our experiences with the environment, or is it inborn? Although such speculation fueled a great deal of intellectual passion, it didn't yield much in the way of concrete answers. It wasn't until the late nineteenth century, in Germany, that psychology emerged as a science.

Early Contributors

What was the first psychology lab like? What conceptual orientation did psychology's earliest contributors have?

Wundt's Laboratory

Imagine a room in Leipzig, Germany, in the year 1879, where a bearded man with a wrinkled forehead and pensive expression is sitting on a chair. He turns his head toward a soft sound coming from the far side of the room. After several minutes he turns his head again, this time toward a loud sound. The scenario is repeated with sounds of varying intensity. The man is Wilhelm Wundt, who is credited with developing the first scientific psychology laboratory (figure 1). By exposing himself to environmental conditions that he systematically varied, and then recording his reactions to different stimuli, Wundt investigated the elements, or "structures," of the mind.

Wundt, Titchener, and Structuralism

The year is now 1892. You are a student sitting in a class at Cornell University in Ithaca, New York. You and the other students wait with anticipation as a man strides into the lecture hall wearing a flowing black gown. Three assistants follow him. Instruments that demonstrate the nature of psychological experimentation are laid out on the stage. This was the protocol of E. B. Titchener, who popularized Wundt's ideas in America. Like Wundt, Titchener was intrigued by how people consciously experience and perceive

(a)

(b)

FIGURE 1

The Beginning of Psychology as a Science
(*a*) Wilhelm Wundt established the first research laboratory in psychology at Germany's University of Leipzig in 1879. (*b*) To help you place Wundt's achievement in history, consider that Alexander Graham Bell invented the telephone in 1876.

their world. Wundt's and Titchener's attempts to classify the structures of the mind were not unlike a chemist's breaking down chemicals into their component parts—water into hydrogen and oxygen, for example. This approach became quite logically known as **structuralism,** *the early theory of psychology developed by Wundt and Titchener that emphasized the importance of conscious thought and classification of the mind's structures.*

James and Functionalism

The first of the new psychologists in the United States was not Titchener, but William James. James (1890/1950) did not believe that the elementary, rigid structures for which Titchener searched existed. James argued that our minds are characterized by a continuous flow of information about our experiences rather than by discrete components. Following in the steps of Darwin, James emphasized the mind's ability to continuously evolve as it adapts to information about the environment. This approach became known as **functionalism,** *William James' theory that psychology's role is to study the functions of the mind and behavior in adapting to the environment.*

Many of the early psychologists, such as Wundt, Titchener, and James, used introspection to discover information about conscious experiences. **Introspection** *is a technique whereby specially trained people carefully observe and analyze their own mental experiences.* It is a process of turning inward in search of mind's nature. Wundt was the master of introspection training. Before his students were permitted to describe their images and perceptions, they had to participate in a minimum of 10,000 practice observations. Philosophers had used introspection for several thousand years, but they had never varied conditions so systematically. The technique of introspection, however, came under heavy fire. The introspectionists thought they were studying immediate experience, but, in reality, it takes time to introspect. Introspection was actually retrospection; thus, the act of introspection changed the observer's experience, thereby modifying or contaminating the observation.

But psychology's initial emphasis on conscious experience, because it lacked objectivity and investigated mental processes that were too vague, went the way of the dinosaur. Other approaches to mental processes and behavior soon emerged (Hothersall, 1996).

Early and Contemporary Approaches to Psychology

Whether psychologists study behavior and the external factors that influence behavior, or mental processes and the internal factors that influence behavior, depends on their approach. There are six important approaches to psychology: behavioral, psychoanalytic, humanistic, cognitive, neurobiological, and sociocultural. We will briefly study each of these approaches in turn, but we will return to them in much greater detail in later chapters. Because the abstract principles of psychological approaches can be difficult to remember—almost like swimming upstream against an onrushing current—we'll apply each approach to something each of us has done in our lives: dating.

The Behavioral Approach

The year is 1898. You are ushered into a room, where you see a dog hooked up to a harness. The dog is salivating profusely, and you wonder what is going on. A gentleman in a white laboratory coat walks over and quietly informs you that an experiment on learning is taking place. He explains that it is a very simple form of learning, in this case documented by the dog's salivation in anticipation of being fed. The man is Ivan Pavlov, who shows you that if he puts the dog's tray down or allows the dog to catch a glimpse of the attendant who fed him the previous day, the dog will begin to salivate.

B. F. Skinner was a tinkerer who liked to make new gadgets. The younger of his two daughters, Deborah, was raised in Skinner's enclosed Air-Crib, which he invented because he wanted to control her environment completely. The Air-Crib was soundproofed and temperature controlled. Some critics accused Skinner of monstrous experimentation with his children; however, the early controlled environment has not had any noticeable harmful effects. Debbie, shown here as a child with her parents, is currently a successful artist, is married, and lives in London.

Pavlov's experiments emphasized careful observation of overt behavior following precise manipulation of the environment. The observations were very different from the information collected through Wundt's introspection, which emphasized inferences about the conscious mind. Pavlov's interest in the overt behavior of organisms and the precise manner in which he observed behavior impressed a young American psychologist by the name of John B. Watson. Watson believed that conscious thought and mental processes had no place in psychology—they lacked objectivity and could not be measured, he said. The view of Pavlov and Watson is called the **behavioral approach,** *which emphasizes the scientific study of behavior and its environmental determinants.* According to behaviorists, we do well in school because of the rewards we experience; we behave in a well-mannered fashion for our parents because of the controls they place on us; and we work hard at our jobs because of the money we receive for our effort. We don't do these things, according to behaviorists, because of an inborn motivation to be a competent person or because a reward makes us feel better about ourselves. We do them because of the environmental conditions we have experienced and are continuing to experience.

Contemporary behaviorism also emphasizes the importance of observing behavior to understand an individual, and the rigorous methods for obtaining information about behavior advocated by Pavlov and Watson remain a cornerstone of the behavioral approach. Contemporary behaviorists continue to stress the importance of environmental determinants of behavior as well.

Although an emphasis on observable behavior and environmental determinants is characteristic of all behavioral views today, different forms of behaviorism have developed. One form is close to the beliefs of Watson and is best represented by the well-known behaviorist B. F. Skinner (1938, 1989). Like Watson, Skinner argued that looking into the mind for the determinants of behavior detracts the investigator from the true cause of behavior—the external environment. Behaviorists who follow Skinner's approach modify and rearrange environmental experiences to determine their effects on an organism, whether rat, pigeon, or human. A father complains that his son misbehaves at home. Careful observation reveals that the father rarely rewards his son, even though his son gets good grades in school, is well liked by his peers, and does a number of chores around the house. The behaviorist calls the father's attention to this pattern of behavior and instructs him to tell the child how pleased he is whenever the child behaves positively, such as when the child does a chore. In this example, the behaviorist is not interested in what the father or the son is thinking or feeling. The behaviorist is only interested in their behavior, which can be directly observed.

Not every behaviorist accepts Skinner's rejection of thought processes. **Social learning theorists,** such as Albert Bandura (1986, 1994), *believe that behavior is determined not only by its controlling environmental conditions, but also by how thought processes modify the impact of environment on behavior.* Perhaps the son in our example has observed other children misbehaving and remembers that event. The son may imitate their behavior, especially if the children are popular with peers. Bandura believes that imitation is one of the main ways we learn about our world. To reproduce a model's behavior, we must code and store the information in memory, which is a mental, or cognitive, process. Thus, social learning theorists broadened the scope of behaviorism to include not only observed behavior but also the ways in which information about the environment is cognitively processed.

What can the behavioral approach tell us about dating? The behavioral approach tells us not to look inside an individual for clues about dating behavior. Inner motives and feelings about another person cannot be directly observed, so they will be of no help in understanding dating. The behaviorists say we should be sensitive to what goes on before and after a date and search for the rewarding aspects that attracted us to the other person in the first place (perhaps a flirtatious smile or a particular appearance). A certain date may be rewarding because it gets us attention from others, possibly increasing our status in a group. Social learning theory tells us that dating behavior may come from watching what others do and listening to what they say—for example, observing an older brother's strategies of what to do (or what not to do) to get a date.

The Psychoanalytic Approach

The year is 1904. You are lying on an incredibly comfortable couch in an office in Vienna, Austria. A gentleman with a stern look on his face walks in and sits down near you. He asks you to close your eyes. After several minutes of silence, he inquires about your childhood experiences. The man asking the questions is Sigmund Freud.

Unlike many pioneer psychologists, Freud was intrigued by the abnormal aspects of people's lives. Others were interested in either the conscious aspects of mind or in directly observable (overt) behavior. For Freud, the key to understanding mind and behavior rested in the unconscious aspects of mind—the aspects of which we are unaware. Freud compared the human mind to an iceberg. The conscious mind is only the tip of the iceberg, the portion above water; the unconscious mind is the huge bulk of the iceberg, the portion under water.

Freud (1917) believed that unlearned biological instincts influence the way individuals think, feel, and behave. These instincts, especially sexual and aggressive impulses, often conflict with the demands of society. For example, in Freud's view, a child inherits the tendency to act aggressively. The aggressive instinct is located in the child's unconscious mind; it is responsible, for example, for the aggressive energy a boy shows in destroying a friend's sand castle, in punching his brother in the nose, or in running wildly through a neighbor's flower garden. The aggressive instinct conflicts with acceptable social behavior, so the child must learn to adapt.

Although Freud saw much of psychological development as instinctually based, he argued that our early relationships with parents were the chief environmental contribution to our personality. That is why he asked you about your childhood as you relaxed on the couch. By getting you to talk about your early family life, Freud hoped you would unconsciously reveal clues about the conflicts causing your problems. The **psychoanalytic approach,** then, *emphasizes the unconscious aspects of the mind, conflict between biological instincts and society's demands, and early family experiences.*

The psychoanalytic approach has survived, although its form has changed somewhat from Freud's original theory. Many contemporary psychoanalytic theorists place less emphasis on sexual instincts and more emphasis on cultural experiences as determinants of personality. Unconscious thought remains a central theme, but contemporary psychoanalytic theorists believe conscious thought makes up more of the iceberg than Freud did.

Erik Erikson (1968) is an important revisionist of Freud's views. Erikson believes we progress through a series of personality stages over the human life span, unlike Freud, who thought personality virtually was etched in stone by 5 years of age. Erikson believes Freud shortchanged the role of culture in personality. Consider, for example, the adolescent years. In Erikson's approach, the key developmental task to be achieved during adolescence is identity, a search for who one is, what one is all about, and where one is going in life. For Freud, adolescents were primarily sexual beings, not wrapped, as Erikson believes, in an exploration of many different roles, some sexual but also some vocational, ideological, religious, lifestyle, and gender. Erikson believes that, by exploring alternatives in many different roles, an adolescent moves toward an identity. Erikson's view fits with our achievement-oriented culture, where exploration of alternative career options is a salient part of finding out who one is and where one is headed in life.

What can psychoanalytic theory tell us about dating? Above all, psychoanalytic theory tells us we will have a difficult time understanding our own dating behavior. The reasons for our dating behavior are pushed deep within our unconscious mind and are primarily sexual in nature. Sex is an unlearned human instinct that dominates our dating behavior. Society's job is to keep this instinct in check, which conflicts with our inner sexual motivation. Our dating behavior can be traced to experiences with our parents during our childhood years as well. Possibly we are dating someone whose appearance and behavior unconsciously remind us of our early relationship with our mother or father. Erikson would instruct us to give more attention to the cultural standards involved in dating and to the ways in which dating fits into our identity as a person.

The Humanistic Approach

Some psychologists are not satisfied with either the behavioral approach, with its emphasis on environmental determinants of behavior, or the psychoanalytic approach, with its focus on instincts, abnormality, and unconscious thoughts. The **humanistic approach** *stresses a person's capacity for personal growth, freedom to choose their destiny, and positive qualities.* Humanistic psychologists take particular opposition to behaviorists, saying that individuals have the ability to control their lives rather than be manipulated by the environment. Humanists stress that our subjective, personal perception of ourselves and the world is more important than behavior itself. Humanists believe we have a tremendous potential for self-understanding. They also think we can help others achieve this self-understanding by providing a nurturant, warm social climate—in other words, by being supportive.

The humanists believe that we have a natural tendency to be loving toward each other and that each of us has the capacity to be a loving person if we would recognize it.

Carl Rogers (1961) and Abraham Maslow (1971) were the main architects of the humanistic approach. Rogers placed special emphasis on improving an individual's self-conception by providing a warm, supportive therapeutic environment. Maslow stressed the importance of achieving our potential, which he thinks is virtually limitless. Maslow called humanistic psychology the "third force" in psychology, believing it deserved the attention accorded the first two forces, behaviorism and psychoanalytic theory. The humanistic approach is a more recent view than behaviorism and psychoanalytic theory, so its staying power in psychology is yet to be determined. Critics call the humanistic approach unscientific, but it has been applauded for helping us reach our human potential and cope more effectively with our problems.

What can the humanistic approach tell us about dating? Humanistic psychologists do not believe dating is based on sexual instinct. Rather, it is a natural tendency of human beings to be loving toward each other. Humanistic psychologists believe each of us has the potential to be a loving person if only we would recognize it. This approach underscores that dating can be better understood if we focus on subjective perceptions of each other instead of on actual dating behaviors. For example, your perception that you are in love with someone you are dating is more important than the number of kisses exchanged on a date. Your perception that you are in love gives meaning to your kisses. Without knowing how you perceive the kisses, they cannot be adequately understood.

The Cognitive Approach

For many contemporary psychologists, the cognitive approach is an extremely important force in psychology. The **cognitive approach** *emphasizes the mental processes involved in knowing: How we direct our attention, how we perceive, how we remember, and how we think and solve problems.* For example, cognitive psychologists want to know how we solve algebraic equations, why we remember some things only for a short time but remember others for a lifetime, and how we can use imagery to plan for the future.

A cognitive psychologist views the mind as an active and aware problem-solving system (Mandler, 1996; Simon, 1996). This positive view contrasts with the pessimism of the psychoanalytic approach, which sees the individual as controlled by instincts, and the behavioral view, which portrays behavior as controlled by external environmental forces. In the cognitive view, an individual's mental processes are in control of behavior. The use of memories, perceptions, images, and thinking allows greater cognitive control over behavior than is possible in either the psychoanalytic or the behavioral approach. In the humanistic approach, emotions play a much stronger role than in the cognitive approach, and the humanistic approach does not emphasize the scientific study of mental processes, as does the cognitive approach.

Information processing *is the most widely adopted cognitive approach. Information-processing psychologists study how individuals process information—how they attend to information, how they perceive it, how they store it, how they think about it, and how they retrieve it for further use.* Computers played an important role in the development of the information-processing perspective. Essentially, computers are high-speed information-processing systems. In the 1950s, it was discovered that if computers were programmed appropriately, they could perform tasks that previously only humans could perform, such as playing chess or computing the answers to complex math problems. Computers provide a logical and concrete, though perhaps oversimplified, model of how information is processed in the mind.

Herbert Simon (1969) was among the pioneers of the information-processing approach. He reasoned that the human mind is best understood by comparing it to a computer processing information. In this model, the sensory and perceptual systems provide an "input channel," similar to data being entered into a computer. As information (input) comes into the mind, mental processes, or operations, act on it, just as the computer's software program acts on data. The transformed input generates information that remains in memory much in the way a computer stores what it has worked on. Finally, the information is retrieved from memory and put to use in the form of an overt response that can be observed, not unlike a computer searching for, finding, and printing out information.

What can the cognitive approach tell us about dating? According to the cognitive approach, our conscious thoughts are the key to understanding dating. Memories and images of people we want to date, or have dated, influence our behavior. As you read these words, you can stop and think about your most memorable dates, including some you probably want to forget. You can think about your current dating or marital situation or project what it will be like in the future: Is she loyal to me? What will the future of our relationship be like? Is he getting tired of me? You can imagine what it would be like to go out with someone for the first time, or a second time.

The cognitive approach says that beliefs and values are important in understanding dating. What are your thoughts about the most important qualities of a date? Is personality more important than looks? Should sex be postponed, or should you engage in premarital sex? According to the cognitive approach, these kinds of conscious thoughts and many more aspects of our rich mental life help us understand dating.

The Neurobiological Approach

According to the **neurobiological approach,** *an understanding of the brain and nervous system is central to understanding behavior, thought, and emotion.* Our remarkable capabilities as human beings would not be possible without our brains. The human brain and nervous system constitute the most complex, intricate, and elegant system imaginable. Rather than study only thoughts, as cognitive psychologists do, neurobiologists believe that thoughts have a physical basis in the brain. The human brain is only a 3-pound lump of matter, but in this lump are more than 100 billion interconnected nerve cells. Electrical impulses zoom throughout our brain cells, and chemical substances are released as we think, feel, and act.

Neurobiologists do study human brains, but much of their work is with simpler brains having far fewer nerve cells (Changeux & Chavillion, 1995). Consider the elegant memory of the inelegant sea slug, a tiny snail with only about 10,000 nerve cells. The sea slug is a slow creature, but if given an electric shock to its tail, the sea slug withdraws its tail quickly. It withdraws the tail even faster if it was previously shocked. In a primitive way, the sea slug remembers. The memory is written in chemicals. Shocking the sea slug's tail releases a chemical that basically provides a reminder that the tail was shocked. This memory informs the nerve cells to send out chemical commands to retract the tail the next time it is touched (Kandel & Schwartz, 1982). If nature builds complexity out of simplicity, the mechanism used by the sea slug may work in the human brain as well. In humans, the memory may come from the sight of a close friend, a dog's bark, or the sound of a car horn. Chemicals, then, may be the ink with which memories are written.

The human brain is divided into left and right sides. Roger Sperry (1964) made one of the most exciting discoveries in neuroscience when he revealed that some aspects of our behavior are controlled more by one side of the brain than by the other. Our own human gift of speech, for example, primarily involves the left side of our brain.

What can the neurobiological approach tell us about dating? The neurobiological approach reminds us that underlying our thoughts, emotions, and behaviors in a dating situation is a physical brain and nervous system. Have you ever thought about how your brain changes when you are attracted to someone? We sometimes say that when your heart pitter-patters, "the chemistry is right." Attraction might literally involve the chemistry of the brain. When your feelings for someone increase, the chemistry of the brain changes. Your feelings for someone may involve the right side of your brain more than the left side. In these ways, dating behavior is wired into the circuitry of the brain.

Neuroscientists have studied the elegant memory of the sea slug, a tiny snail with only about 10,000 nerve cells. How did they investigate this elegant memory?

The Sociocultural Approach

The **sociocultural approach** *emphasizes that culture, ethnicity, and gender are essential to understanding behavior, thought, and emotion.* **Culture** *is the behavior patterns, beliefs, and other products of a particular group of people, such as values, work patterns, music, dress, diet, and ceremonies, that are passed on from generation to generation.* A cultural group can be as large and complex as the United States, or it can be as small as an African hunter-gatherer tribe, but whatever its size, the group's culture influences the identity, learning, and social behavior of its members (Katicibasi, 1995, 1996; Matsumoto, 1996; Triandis, 1994).

Ethnicity (*the word* ethnic *comes from the Greek word for "nation") is based on cultural heritage, nationality characteristics, race, religion, and language.* Ethnicity involves descent from common ancestors, usually in a specifiable part of the world. Given the descent of individuals from common ancestors, people often make inferences about someone's ethnicity based on physical features believed to be typical of an ethnic group. For example, one of the downed American flyers in the Gulf war had features that would be considered "Arab." He was treated worse than the other prisoners of war, who had non-Arab features. This reminds us that ethnicity is a category that is often applied to people even if they don't want to be categorized that way and feel the inferences are wrong and unfair (Brislin, 1990).

In Xinjiang, China, a woman prepares for horseback courtship. Her suitor must chase her, kiss her, and evade her riding crop—all on the gallop. A new marriage law took effect in China in 1981. The law sets a minimum age for marriage—22 years for males, 20 years for females. Late marriage and late childbirth are critical efforts in China's attempt to control population growth.

What can the sociocultural approach tell us about dating? The sociocultural approach tells us that dating behavior may vary according to the person's cultural, ethnic, and gender background. For example, some cultural and ethnic groups have extremely conservative beliefs about dating, especially for females. The age at which young people first date varies from culture to culture. Cultures also differ in the value they place on dating as precursor to marriage, and the importance of sexuality in dating.

Our American culture is becoming increasingly diverse. Ethnic minority groups—African Americans, Latinos, Native Americans (American Indians), and Asian Americans, for example—made up 20 percent of all the individuals under the age of 17 in the United States in 1980. By the year 2000, the percentage will rise to about 33 percent. This changing demographic tapestry promises not only the richness that diversity produces but also difficult challenges in extending the American dream to all ethnic minority individuals (Cauce, 1996; McLoyd & Ceballos, 1995).

So far we have discussed two aspects of sociocultural influences—culture and ethnicity. A third important aspect is **gender,** *the sociocultural dimension of being female or male.* **Sex** *is the biological dimension of being female or male.* Few aspects of our existence are more central to our identity and to our social relationships than our sex or gender. Our gender attitudes and behavior are changing, but how much? Is there a limit to how much society can determine what is appropriate behavior for females and males? A special concern on the part of many feminist writers is that in much of its history psychology has portrayed human behavior with a "male-dominant theme" (Paludi, 1995; Rollins, 1996).

The sociocultural approach is psychology's newest lens for examining behavior and mental processes. As the future brings increasing contact between people from quite different backgrounds, the sociocultural approach will help to expand psychology's role as a relevant discipline in the twenty-first century.

Which Approach Is Best?

All of these approaches to psychology are in a sense correct. They are all valid ways of looking at human behavior, just as blueprints, floor plans, and photographs are all valid ways of looking at a house. Some approaches are better for some purposes. A floor plan, for instance, is more useful than a photograph for deciding how much lumber to buy, just as the neurobiological approach is more useful than the sociocultural approach for explaining how cells in the brain communicate with each other. And, in turn, the sociocultural approach is more useful than the neurobiological approach for understanding how to reduce prejudice and discrimination. But no single approach is "right" or "wrong."

At this point we have discussed a number of ideas about what psychology is, the beginnings of psychology as a science, and early and contemporary approaches. A summary of these ideas is presented in concept table 1.

Women and Ethnic Minorities in Psychology's History

Until recently, psychology, like so many professions, kept women out. During its first 75 years, few women broke through to psychology's inner sanctum (DeAngelis, 1996). In fact, the first woman to complete requirements for a doctorate in psychology, Christine Ladd-Franklin, was denied the degree in 1892 simply because she was a woman. Mary Calkins' history is another example of the barriers women faced. In 1891 she introduced psychology into Wellesley College's curriculum and established its first psychology laboratory. In 1892 she returned to Harvard for additional training. By 1894, Calkins had developed a technique for investigating memory and had completed the requirements for a doctorate degree. Her Harvard psychology professors enthusiastically recommended that she be awarded the degree, but the administration refused because Calkins was a woman (Furumoto, 1989).

Concept Table 1

Psychology: Its Nature, Approaches, and History

Concept	Processes/Related Ideas	Characteristics/Description
Defining Psychology	Its nature	Psychology is the scientific study of behavior and mental processes. Behavior is everything people do that can be directly observed. Mental processes are thoughts, feelings, and motives that each individual experiences. As a science, psychology uses systematic methods to observe, describe, predict, and explain behavior.
The Beginnings of Psychology as a Science	From myth to philosophy to psychology	Myths gave way to the rational logic of philosophy, but the intellectual debate of philosophers did not yield much in the way of concrete, empirical answers.
	Early contributors	Wundt developed the first scientific psychology laboratory in 1879. E. B. Titchener popularized Wundt's ideas in the United States; his psychology was known as structuralism because of its emphasis on structures of the mind. James emphasized the functions of the mind in adapting to the environment; his view was called functionalism. Many early approaches used introspection, which later came under fire.
Early and Contemporary Approaches	Behavioral	This approach emphasizes the scientific study of behavior and its environmental determinants. Pavlov and Skinner developed important behavioral approaches. Social learning theorists take a behavioral approach, but also emphasize that thought processes modify environment-behavior connections.
	Psychoanalytic	This approach stresses the unconscious aspects of mind, conflict between biological instincts and society's demands, and early childhood experiences. Freud was the main architect of psychoanalytic theory. Erikson presented an important revision of psychoanalytic theory.
	Humanistic	This approach emphasizes a person's capacity for personal growth, freedom to choose one's destiny, and positive qualities. Rogers and Maslow were the main developers of the humanistic approach.
	Cognitive	This approach places a premium on cognitive, or thought, processes. A person's mind is viewed as an active, aware problem-solving system. Information processing is the most widely adopted cognitive approach.
	Neurobiological	This approach stresses that the brain and nervous system play important roles in understanding behavior and mental processes. Sperry conducted important research on the brain's two hemispheres.
	Sociocultural	This approach, psychology's newest lens, emphasizes that culture, ethnicity, and gender are essential to understanding behavior, thought, and emotion.
	Which approach is best?	No single theory offers all the answers; each contributes to the science of psychology.

The first woman actually to be awarded a doctorate in psychology was Margaret Washburn in 1908. By 1906, about 1 in every 10 psychologists was a woman. Today, the number of men and women receiving a doctorate in psychology is approximately equal (Furumoto & Scarborough, 1986).

The tapestry of American culture has changed dramatically in recent years. Nowhere is the change more noticeable than in the increasing ethnic diversity of America's citizens. Ethnic minority groups—African American, Latino, Native American, and Asian, for example—will make up approximately one-third of all individuals under the age of 17 in the United States by the year 2000. Two of psychology's challenges are to become more sensitive to race and ethnic origin and to provide improved services to ethnic minority individuals.

Similarly, discrimination has barred African Americans, Latinos, Asian Americans, and Native Americans from entering the field of psychology. The first African American to become a professor of psychology was Gilbert Jones. He obtained his doctorate at the University of Jena in Germany in 1909. Ethnic minority women, especially, faced overwhelming odds. It wasn't until 1934 that an African American woman, Ruth Howard, at the University of Minnesota, finally received a doctorate in psychology. Over a period of about 50 years the ten universities with the most prestigious programs in psychology granted several thousand doctoral degrees. Yet by 1969, these universities had awarded only eight doctoral degrees to African American students. Few Latinos have been awarded doctoral degrees—surveys indicate that less than 2 percent of all psychologists are Latino (Cervantes, 1987). George Sanchez is one of the few. His pioneering research demonstrated that intelligence tests are culturally biased against ethnic minority children. There are also very few Native American psychologists.

Over the last three decades the women's movement and the civil rights movement helped put the rights and needs of women and ethnic minorities on politicians' agendas and led to social change (Bronstein & Quina, 1988). Similarly, psychologists, especially those belonging to these groups, were spurred to reexamine psychology's basic premises and to question the relevance to their own experiences and concerns. This reexamination sparked new inquiry that focuses on populations that previously had been omitted from psychological research and the mainstream theories of psychology. Journals such as *Psychology of Women Quarterly, Sex Roles,* the *Hispanic Journal of Behavioral Science,* and the *Journal of Black Psychology* address the growing interest in gender and ethnic minority issues.

Recognizing the dearth of ethnic minority psychologists, the American Psychological Association formed the Board of Ethnic Minority Affairs to ensure that the concerns of its ethnic group members are heard. The Association of Black Psychologists directly involves its members in issues that are important to the African American community (Jones, 1987). The Asian American Psychological Association identifies resources, develops ideas for education and training, and fosters scientific research on issues of importance in the Asian American community (Suinn, 1987).

At this point we have discussed a number of important approaches to psychology and a number of individuals who were pioneers in various areas of psychology. For a glimpse at some of the most important people in psychology's history, turn to figure 2. Most of these people and their views will be discussed in greater detail at appropriate places in this book.

Psychology and Pseudopsychology

In May of 1988 astrology was on the front page of every newspaper and on every national newscast. *Time* magazine made it a cover story. It was big news that Nancy Reagan used astrologers to advise President Reagan when to schedule political appointments. Suddenly, astrology was both the focus of serious scientific examination and the butt of endless jokes.

At the beginning of this chapter we defined psychology as the *scientific* study of behavior and mental processes. We said that as a science, psychology uses systematic observations to describe, explain, and predict behavior. These observations are carefully and precisely planned and conducted. And we also said that these observations are often *verified* to check their accuracy. Astrology is not psychology. Astrology is a **pseudopsychology**—*a nonscientific system that resembles psychology. Pseudopsychologies, like astrology, lack a scientific base. Their descriptions, explanations, and predictions either cannot be directly tested, or when tested, turn out to be unfounded.*

Among the most popular pseudopsychologies today are astrology, graphology, and the New Age movement. **Astrology** *is the pseudopsychology that uses the position of*

Wilhelm Wundt (1832–1920)

William James (1842–1910)

Alfred Binet (1857–1911)

Ivan Pavlov (1849–1936)

Ruth Howard (1900–)

B. F. Skinner (1904–1990)

Erik Erikson (1902–1994)

Abraham Maslow (1908–1970)

Carl Rogers (1902–1987)

Albert Bandura (1925–)

Sandra Bem (1944–)

Eleanor Maccoby (1917–)

1879: Wilhelm Wundt develops the first psychology laboratory at the University of Leipzig.

1890: William James publishes *Principles of Psychology*, which promotes functionalism.

1891: Mary Calkins establishes a laboratory for psychology at Wellesley.

1892: E. B. Titchener popularizes structuralism in the United States. G. Stanley Hall founds the American Psychological Association at Clark University.

1900: Sigmund Freud publishes *The Interpretation of Dreams*, reflecting his psychoanalytic view.

1905: Alfred Binet (with Theodore Simon) develops the first intelligence test to assess French schoolchildren.

1906: The Russian Ivan Pavlov publishes the results of his learning experiments with dogs.

1908: Margaret Washburn becomes the first woman to receive a Ph.D. in psychology.

1913: John Watson publishes his volume on behaviorism, promoting the importance of environmental influences.

1934: Ruth Howard becomes the first African American woman to receive a Ph.D. in psychology.

1938: B. F. Skinner publishes *The Behavior of Organisms*, expanding the view of behaviorism.

1939: Mamie Phipps Clark and Kenneth Clark conduct research on African American children's self-conceptions and identity. Later, in 1971, Kenneth Clark becomes the first African American president of the American Psychological Association.

1945: Karen Horney criticizes Freud's psychoanalytic theory as male-biased and presents her sociocultural approach.

1950: Erik Erikson publishes *Childhood and Society*, a psychoanalytic revision of Freud's views.

1954: Abraham Maslow presents the humanistic view, emphasizing the positive potential of the individual.

1954: Gordon Allport writes his now classic book, *The Nature of Prejudice*.

1958: Herbert Simon presents his information-processing view.

1961: Carl Rogers publishes *On Becoming a Person*, highlighting the humanistic approach.

1961: Albert Bandura presents ideas about social learning theory, emphasizing the importance of imitation.

1964: Roger Sperry publishes his split-brain research, showing the importance of the brain in behavior.

1969: John Berry, a Canadian psychologist, presents his ideas on the importance of cross-cultural research in psychology.

1974: Sandra Bem and Janet Spence develop tests to assess androgyny and promote the competence of females; Eleanor Maccoby (with Carol Jacklin) calls attention to the importance of sex and gender in understanding behavior and analyzing gender similarities and differences.

1977: Judith Rodin (with Ellen Langer) conducts research showing the powerful influence of perceived control over one's environment on behavior.

Mary Calkins (1863–1930)

G. Stanley Hall (1844–1924)

Margaret Washburn (1871–1939)

John B. Watson (1878–1958)

Mamie Clark (1917–)

Karen Horney (1885–1952)

Gordon Allport (1897–1967)

Sigmund Freud (1856–1939)

Roger Sperry (1913–1994)

John Berry (1939–)

Judith Rodin (1944–)

Herbert Simon (1916–)

FIGURE 2

Important Pioneers and Theorists in Psychology's History

the stars and planets at the time of a person's birth to describe, explain, and predict their behavior. Scientific researchers have repeatedly demonstrated that astrology has no scientific merit. When astrologers' predictions are successful, it is because they usually are so vague that they are virtually guaranteed to happen (for example, "Money is

Explorations in Psychology 1

Astrology and Psychology's Skepticism

Let's examine some astrologers' comments:

> Astrology is a major influence in your life. It's not your only one. We do have environment, and we do have heredity. It's not the only influence. However, it's a major influence.
>
> —Henry Weingarten,
> New York Astrology Center
> "Nightline," May 3, 1988

> I advise them (the Reagans) when to be careful. I don't make decisions for them. An astrologer just picks the best possible time to do something that someone else has already planned to do. It's like being in the ocean; you should go with the waves, not against them. I know his (President Reagan's) horoscope upside down, but I don't know him. I deal with Nancy.
>
> —Joan Quigley, San Francisco astrologer
> *Time,* May 16, 1988

Could your belief in astrology be influenced by the way it is presented in the media? Consider the possibility that you were tuned in to a recent "Oprah" television show. Popular showhost Oprah Winfrey included Roger Culver, an astronomer at Colorado State University, and a skeptic on her panel of experts, but the other three experts on the panel were astrologers, supported by an audience packed with believers. On a "Geraldo" show, the panel of experts consisted of five astrologers and no scientists. On a "Donahue" show, host Phil Donahue's panel of experts included an astrologer, a spiritual counselor, and two psychics; no scientists were present. Regrettably, following the lead of the *National Enquirer,* the media are often more interested in high audience ratings than in the truth of astrologers' claims.

On some responsible television shows, such as "Nightline," scientists were given adequate time to explain their view of astrology:

> It sounds a lot like science, it sounds like astronomy. It's got technical terms. It's got jargon. It confuses the public. The fact is that astrological beliefs go back at least 2500 years. Now that should be a sufficiently long time for astrologers to prove their case. They have not proved their case. It's just simply gibberish. The fact is, there's no theory for it, there are no observational data for it. It's been tested and tested over the centuries. Nobody's ever found any validity to it at all. It is not even close to a science. A science has to be repeatable, it has to have a logical foundation . . . astrology is really quite something else.
>
> —Astronomer Richard Berendzen,
> President American University
> "Nightline," May 3, 1988

Science's battle against astrology is uphill. Despite the assertions of scientists that astrology is a false system of beliefs, the public's belief in astrology has increased. In 1976, 29 percent of the population said they believed in astrology, but in 1986 this figure increased to 36 percent. One reason for the increased interest in astrology is that astrology sells. It is a profitable business. Some kinds of horoscopes are sold in much the same manner as are cornflakes, candy, and beer. Another reason is that many television directors and producers either lack critical judgment about astrology or cater to public taste rather than exercising their responsibility to provide the public with facts.

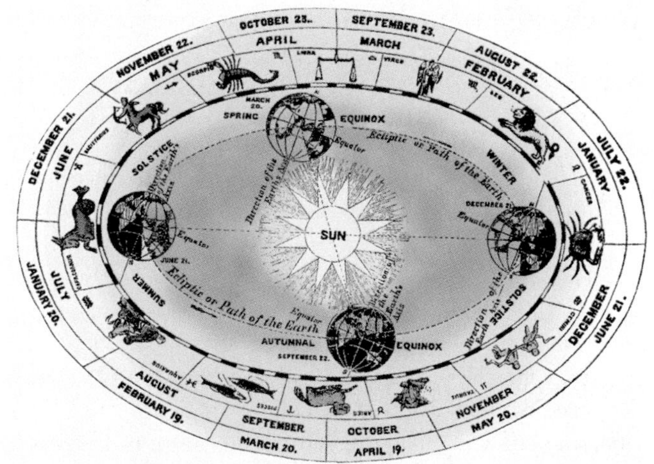

Why does the science of psychology urge you to be skeptical of astrology?

likely to be a source of concern for you this month," or "A tragic plane crash will occur in the southern United States this winter"). Astrologers' more specific predictions ("An unidentified flying object will land on the field during the halftime of the ABC Monday Night Football game on October 4, 1998") never hold up. To read further about astrology and psychology's skepticism about it, see Explorations in Psychology 1.

The **New Age movement** *is a broad-based pseudopsychology that expresses a distrust of science and seeks to develop new levels of spiritual awareness. New Age proponents maintain that there are hidden "spiritual dimensions" to reality that cannot be discovered by science's experimental strategies.* Astrology, crystal power (the use of quartz crystals for healing), channeling (the ability to enter a trance state and communicate with someone in another place and time, even centuries ago), and a belief in reincarnation (past lives) are just some of New Age doctrines. Actress Shirley MacLaine, a leading popularizer of the New Age movement, claims she lived one of her lives as a prostitute during the French Revolution and was beheaded. While many of the New Age movement's tenets are fanciful and intriguing, there is no scientific evidence to support them.

Science urges you to be skeptical about astrology, the New Age movement, and anything that claims access to wondrous powers and supernatural forces (Ward & Grashial, 1995). There is a clear danger in following the advice of astrologers and New Age advocates: People become diverted from coping with their lives in a rational and realistic way. For most people who dabble in the pseudopsychologies, all that will be lost is some time and money for whatever comfort was gained. But for people with serious problems or who are in real distress, following the advice of astrologers or other "mystics" can prevent them from solving their problems and living productive lives.

Psychology's Careers and Areas of Specialization

Psychologists don't spend all of their time in a laboratory, white-smocked with clipboard in hand, observing rats and crunching numbers. Some psychologists spend their days seeing people with problems, others teach at universities and conduct research. Still others work in business and industry, designing more efficient criteria for hiring. In short, psychology is a field with many areas of specialization.

Careers in Psychology

You may already be wondering whether or not to major in psychology. Studying psychology as an undergraduate can give you a sound preparation for what lies ahead by helping you understand, predict, and control the events in your own life. You'll also gain a solid academic background that will enable you to enter various careers and go on to graduate programs, not just in psychology but in other areas as well, such as business and law (Woods & Wilkinson, 1987). A bachelor's degree in psychology will not automatically lead to fame and fortune, but it is a highly marketable degree for a wide range of jobs, including parent educator, drug-abuse counselor, mental health aide, teacher for mentally retarded children, and staff member at a crisis hot-line center. An undergraduate degree in psychology also provides excellent training for many jobs in business, especially in the areas of sales, personnel, or training. If you choose a career in psychology, you can greatly expand your opportunities (and income) by obtaining a graduate degree, although a master's or doctoral degree is not absolutely necessary. Also, because there are so few ethnic minority psychologists, job opportunities are increasingly available to qualified ethnic minority applicants. Where do psychologists work? Slightly more than one-third are teachers, researchers, or counselors at colleges or universities. Most psychologists—almost half—work in clinical and private practice settings (see figure 3).

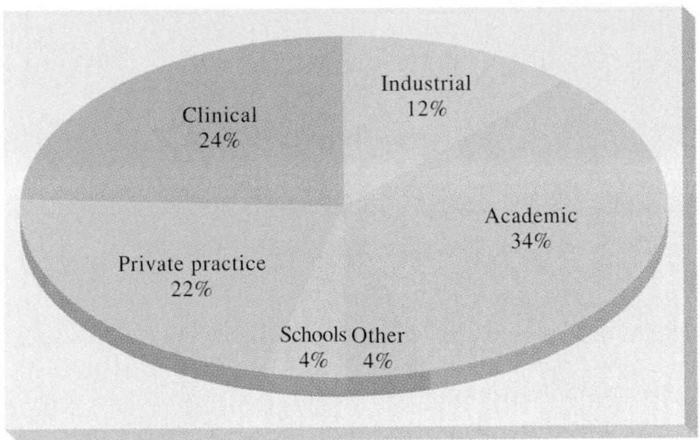

FIGURE 3

Settings in Which Psychologists Work

Areas of Specialization in Psychology

If you go to graduate school, you will be required to specialize in a particular area of psychology. Following is a list of some of the specializations: clinical and counseling; community; experimental and physiological; developmental, social, and personality; school and educational; industrial and organizational; cross-cultural; and the psychology of women. Sometimes the categories are not mutually exclusive. For example, some social psychologists are also experimental psychologists.

Clinical and counseling psychology *is the most widely practiced specialization in psychology: clinical and counseling psychologists diagnose and treat people with psychological problems* (see table 1). The work of clinical psychologists often does not differ from that of counseling psychologists, although a counseling psychologist sometimes deals with people who have less serious problems. In many instances, counseling psychologists work with students, advising them about personal problems and career planning.

Clinical psychologists are different from psychiatrists. Typically a clinical psychologist has a doctoral degree in psychology, which requires 3 to 4 years of graduate work, plus 1 year of internship in a mental health facility. **Psychiatry** *is a branch of medicine practiced by physicians with a doctor of medicine (M.D.) degree who subsequently specialize in abnormal behavior and psychotherapy.* Clinical psychologists and psychiatrists both are interested in improving the lives of people with mental health problems. One important distinction is that psychiatrists can prescribe drugs, whereas clinical psychologists cannot.

Community psychology *focuses on providing accessible care for people with psychological problems. Community-based mental health centers are one means of providing such services as outreach programs to people in need, especially those who traditionally have been underserved by mental health professionals.* Community psychologists view human behavior in terms of adaptation to resources and to one's situation. They work to create communities that are more supportive of residents by pinpointing needs, by providing needed services, and by teaching people how to gain access

ABLE 1

Specialties in the Fields of Clinical and Counseling Psychology, and in Industrial and Organizational Psychology

Clinical and Counseling Psychology*
Psychotherapy With many subspecialties such as family therapy, group therapy, drug therapy, individual therapy, biofeedback, and sex therapy
Clinical Child Psychology Assessment (giving tests), severely disordered children, learning disabilities, reading problems, mental retardation, and parent education
Behavior and Mental Disorders Alcoholism, delinquency, crime, suicide, eating disorders, and depression
Medical Psychology Often working in hospitals in concert with physicians and other medical personnel, hospital care
Gerontology Specializing in the growing area of older adults' mental disturbances
Community Mental Health Working in community mental health clinics
Physically Handicapped Working with the disabled, blind, and hearing impaired
Industrial and Organizational Psychology*
Management and Organization Behavior in organizations, labor-management relations, human relations, and compensation
Personnel Career development and training, job satisfaction and attitudes toward work, selection and placement of employees, retirement
Vocational Counseling Personal or adjustment counseling, test construction, diagnosis and assessment, rehabilitation counseling, employee counseling, employment counseling, and counseling disabled and handicapped employees
Advertising Evaluation of how people perceive and think about advertisements, examination of motivational and emotional factors involved in advertising effectiveness
Marketing Consumer surveys, market analysis

*These lists are meant to be exemplary, not exhaustive.

to resources already available. Finally, community psychologists are also concerned about *prevention.* They try to prevent mental health problems by identifying high-risk groups and then intervening to provide appropriate services and by stimulating new opportunities in the community.

Experimental and physiological psychology *are areas that often involve pure research. Although psychologists in other areas conduct experiments, virtually all experimental and physiological psychologists follow precise, careful experimental strategies.* These psychologists are more likely to work with animals, although many do not. Experimental psychologists explore the mental terrain of memory, sensation and perception, motivation, and emotion. Physiological psychologists investigate a range of topics—from the role of the brain in behavior to the influence of drugs on hormones. The neurobiological approach to psychology is closely aligned with physiological psychology.

Developmental psychology *is concerned with how we become who we are, from conception to death.* In particular, developmental psychologists focus on the biological and environmental factors that contribute to human development. For many years the major emphasis was on child development. However, an increasing number of today's developmental psychologists show a strong interest in adult development and aging. Their inquiries range across the biological, cognitive, and social domains of life.

Social psychology *deals with people's social interactions, relationships, perceptions, and attitudes.* Social psychologists

Concept Table 2

Women and Ethnic Minorities in Psychology's History, Psychology and Pseudopsychology, and Psychology's Careers and Areas of Specialization

Concept	Processes/Related Ideas	Characteristics/Description
Women and Ethnic Minorities in Psychology	Their history in psychology	Until recently, psychology, like so many professions, kept women and ethnic minorities out. Over the last three decades, in concert with the women's and civil rights movements, women and ethnic minorities have gained a stronger voice in psychology. Psychology especially needs more ethnic minority researchers in all of its areas.
Psychology and Pseudopsychology	Nature of the distinction	Pseudopsychology is a nonscientific system that resembles psychology. Pseudopsychologies, like astrology and the New Age movement, lack a scientific base. Their descriptions, explanations, and predictions either cannot be directly verified or, when tested, turn out to be unfounded. There is a clear danger in following the advice of the pseudopsychologies—people can become diverted from coping with their lives in a rational and realistic way.
Psychology's Careers and Areas of Specialization	Their variety	There are many ways to be a psychologist. Careers range from improving the lives of people with mental problems to teaching at a university and conducting research. The areas of specialization in psychology include clinical and counseling; community; experimental and physiological; developmental; social; personality; school and educational; industrial and organizational; cross-cultural; and women's psychology.

believe we can better understand mind and behavior if we know something about how people function in groups.

Personality psychology *focuses on the relatively enduring traits and characteristics of individuals.* Personality psychologists study such topics as self-concept, aggression, moral development, gender roles, and inner or outer directedness.

School and educational psychology *is concerned with children's learning and adjustment in school.* School psychologists counsel children and parents when children have problems in school. They often give children psychological tests to assess personality and intelligence. Most educational psychologists, like other academic psychologists, also teach and conduct research.

Industrial/organizational psychology *deals with the workplace, focusing on both the workers and the organizations that employ them.* Industrial/organizational psychologists are concerned with training employees, improving working conditions, and developing criteria for selecting employees. For example, an organizational psychologist might recommend that a company adopt a new management structure that would increase communication between managers and staff. The background of industrial and organizational psychologists often includes training in social psychology.

Cross-cultural psychology *examines the role of culture in understanding behavior, thought, and emotion. Cross-cultural psychologists compare the nature of psychological processes in different cultures, with a special interest in whether or not psychological phenomena are universal or culture specific.* The International Association for Cross-Cultural Psychology promotes research on cross-cultural comparisons and awareness of culture's role in psychology.

The **psychology of women** *emphasizes the importance of promoting the research and study of women, integrating this information about women with current psychological knowledge and beliefs, and applying the information to society and its institutions.* The Division of the Psychology of Women in the American Psychological Association was formed in 1973.

In sum, the avenues an individual can follow as a psychologist are richly varied. We have only touched on this enormous variety in our description of psychology's main areas. For example, within each area numerous specializations are possible. Table 1 presents some specializations that are available in clinical and counseling psychology and in industrial and organizational psychology. Salaries are especially good in the area of industrial and organizational psychology, recently averaging in the $50,000 range for master's-level positions and $70,000 for doctoral-level jobs.

At this point we have discussed many ideas about women and ethnic minorities in the history of psychology, psychology and pseudopsychology, as well as psychology's many areas of specialization. A summary of these ideas is presented in concept table 2.

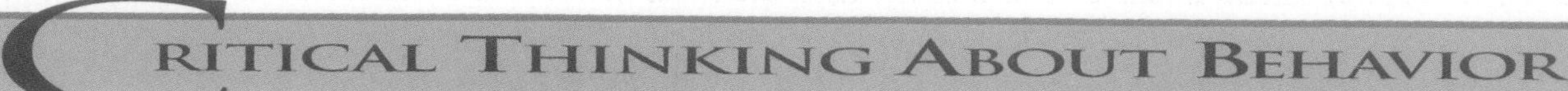

Critical Thinking About Behavior

The Importance of Asking Questions

Not to know is bad; not to wish to know is worse.

Nigerian proverb

Why do we do what we do? This is the fundamental question that drives the study of psychology and fuels our curiosity about what we experience. This question is at the heart of day-to-day interactions with others. It also drives psychological research that establishes new knowledge about human behavior.

Curiosity about behavior is one of our most valuable human characteristics. We are natural question askers. Sometimes human behavior is especially compelling: We might never before have seen anything like the behavior in question, so we don't have a ready explanation to account for what we see. The discrepancy from "business as usual" stimulates us to make sense of the behavior.

Once our curiosity is aroused, we typically go through reliable thinking processes that might seem rather scientific. We observe behavior carefully, make inferences about what we observe, and—if it still does not make sense—we go after more "data" to get to a point of understanding the behavior. We can get more information through research, through purposefully relating the behavior to general ideas we have acquired from observing more familiar behavior, and through asking questions.

Asking questions is evidence of an active curiosity. Children are remarkable for their ability to ask questions, sometimes even embarrassing ones. As strong as this behavior is early in our lives, most of us experience a decline in this ability as we get older. Sometimes we wish not to be rude. Sometimes our experiences in school favor "content loading" over exploring questions. Sometimes we may feel overwhelmed by the complexity or the mystery being proposed.

Psychological perspectives offer us tools for exploring behaviors that we don't understand. Each perspective encourages certain kinds of questions (and ignores others). The following are a few of the questions that are typical of the perspectives presented throughout this text.

The Behavioral Perspective
What role does learning play in the behavior?
Is the behavior performed because it is rewarded?
Is the behavior modeled after someone else's?

The Psychoanalytic Perspective
Does the behavior have unconscious underpinnings?
Does sexuality influence the behavior?
What early childhood experiences contributed to the behavior?

The Humanistic Perspective
How does the behavior fulfill needs?
How does the behavior enhance self-esteem?
How well does the behavior fit with character?

The Cognitive Perspective
How does judgment affect the behavior?
Does cognitive developmental change influence the behavior?
What is the role of emotion in the behavior?

The Neurobiological Perspective
How does genetic endowment influence the behavior?
What role does the brain play in the behavior?
How do hormonal changes contribute to the behavior?

The Sociocultural Perspective
Does socioeconomic status affect the behavior?
What role does ethnicity play in the behavior?
Is the behavior influenced by gender?

Try out these perspectives on a behavior that intrigues you. Is there some event in the news that seems especially perplexing? Could you clarify a friend's behavior by looking at it through the lens of different psychological perspectives? Systematic analysis of behavior can lead to some questions you had not considered and to a more complete picture of what accounts for behavior.

I hope that your study of psychology will enrich the way you look at behavior. As you complete each chapter, you will have more material to draw upon in understanding and explaining behavior. I hope that this increased awareness and knowledge will motivate you to pursue alternative explanations that help to explain behavior more comprehensively.

OVERVIEW

We began this chapter by defining what psychology is and then turned to the beginnings of psychology as a science, exploring psychology's development from myth and philosophy, and early contributors. Our coverage of early and contemporary approaches to psychology focused on the behavioral approach, the psychoanalytic approach, the humanistic approach, the cognitive approach, the neurobiological approach, the sociocultural approach, and which approach is best. We also read about women and ethnic minorities in the history of psychology, distinguished between psychology and pseudopsychology, and learned about psychology's careers and many areas of specialization. You can obtain an overall summary of the chapter by again studying the two concept tables on pages 11 and 17.

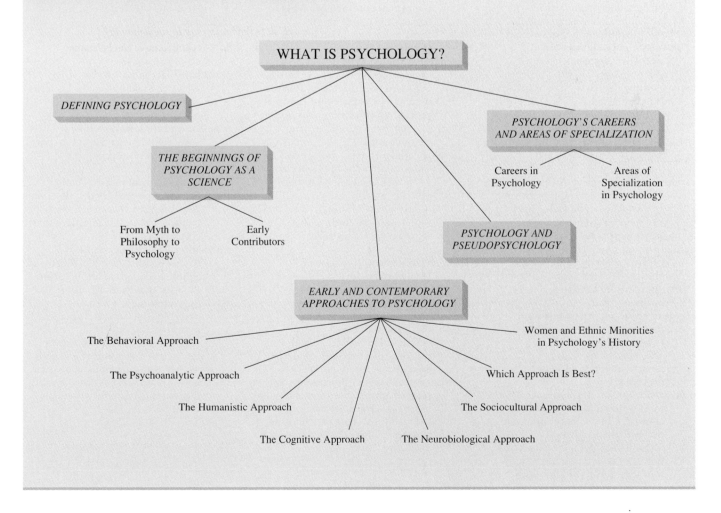

WHAT IS PSYCHOLOGY?

- *DEFINING PSYCHOLOGY*
- *THE BEGINNINGS OF PSYCHOLOGY AS A SCIENCE*
  - From Myth to Philosophy to Psychology
  - Early Contributors
- *EARLY AND CONTEMPORARY APPROACHES TO PSYCHOLOGY*
  - The Behavioral Approach
  - The Psychoanalytic Approach
  - The Humanistic Approach
  - The Cognitive Approach
  - The Neurobiological Approach
  - The Sociocultural Approach
  - Which Approach Is Best?
  - Women and Ethnic Minorities in Psychology's History
- *PSYCHOLOGY AND PSEUDOPSYCHOLOGY*
- *PSYCHOLOGY'S CAREERS AND AREAS OF SPECIALIZATION*
  - Careers in Psychology
  - Areas of Specialization in Psychology

KEY TERMS

psychology The scientific study of behavior and mental processes. p. 4

behavior Everything we do that can be directly observed. p. 4

mental processes The thoughts, feelings, and motives that each of us experiences privately but that cannot be observed directly. p. 4

science In psychology, the use of systematic methods to observe, describe, explain, and predict behavior. p. 4

structuralism The early theory of psychology developed by Wundt and Titchener that emphasized the importance of conscious thought and classification of the mind's structures. p. 5

functionalism William James' theory that psychology's role is to study the functions of the mind and behavior in adapting to the environment. p. 5

introspection A technique whereby specially trained people carefully observe and analyze their own mental experiences. p. 5

behavioral approach An emphasis on the scientific study of observable behavioral responses and their environmental determinants. p. 6

social learning theorists Theorists who believe that behavior is determined by its controlling environmental conditions but also by how thought processes modify the impact of the environment on behavior. p. 6

psychoanalytic approach An emphasis on the unconscious aspects of the mind, conflict between biological instincts and society's demands, and early family experiences. p. 7

humanistic approach An emphasis on a person's capacity for personal growth, freedom to choose their own destiny, and positive qualities. p. 7

cognitive approach An emphasis on the mental processes involved in knowing: How we direct our attention, perceive, remember, think, and solve problems. p. 8

information-processing approach The most widely adopted cognitive approach. Information-processing psychologists study how individuals process information—how they attend to information, how they perceive it, how they store it, how they think about it, and how they retrieve it for further use. p. 8

neurobiological approach An approach that emphasizes the importance of understanding the brain and nervous system if we are to understand behavior, thought, and emotion. p. 9

sociocultural approach An approach that emphasizes the influences of culture, ethnicity, and gender, among other sociocultural factors, on behavior, thought, and emotion. p. 9

culture The behavior patterns, beliefs, and other products of a particular group of people, such as the values, work patterns, music, dress, diet, and ceremonies that are passed on from generation to generation. p. 9

ethnicity A person's heritage based on cultural heritage, nationality characteristics, race, religion, and language. p. 9

gender The sociocultural dimension of being female or male, especially how we learn to think and behave as females and males. p. 10

sex The biological dimension of being female or male. p. 10

pseudopsychology Systems, like astrology, that resemble psychology but lack a scientific basis. Their descriptions, explanations, and predictions either cannot be directly tested or, when tested, turn out to be unfounded. p. 12

astrology The pseudopsychology that uses the position of the stars and planets at the time of a person's birth to describe, explain, and predict their behavior. Scientific researchers have repeatedly demonstrated that astrology has no scientific merit. p. 12

New Age movement A broad-based pseudopsychology that expresses a distrust of science and seeks to develop new levels of spiritual awareness. New Age proponents maintain that there are hidden "spiritual dimensions" to reality that cannot be discovered by science's experimental strategies. p. 14

clinical and counseling psychology The most widely practiced specialization in psychology; clinical and counseling psychologists diagnose and treat people with psychological problems. p. 15

psychiatry A branch of medicine practiced by physicians with a doctor of medicine (M.D.) degree who subsequently specialize in abnormal behavior and psychotherapy. p. 15

community psychology A branch of psychology that focuses on providing accessible care for people with psychological problems. Community-based mental health centers are one means of providing such services as outreach programs to people in need, especially those who traditionally have been underserved by mental health professionals. p. 15

experimental and physiological psychology Areas that involve pure research. Although psychologists in other areas conduct experiments, virtually all experimental and physiological psychologists follow precise, careful experimental strategies. p. 16

developmental psychology A branch of psychology concerned with how we become who we are, from conception to death. p. 16

social psychology An area that deals with people's social interactions, relationships, perceptions, and attitudes. p. 16

personality psychology An area that focuses on relatively enduring traits and characteristics of individuals. p. 17

school and educational psychology An area of psychology that is concerned with children's learning and adjustment in school. p. 17

industrial/organizational psychology A branch of psychology that deals with the workplace, focusing on both the workers and the organizations that employ them. p. 17

cross-cultural psychology An area of psychology that examines the role of culture in understanding behavior, thought, and emotion. p. 17

psychology of women An area of psychology that emphasizes the importance of promoting the research and study of women, integrating this information about women with current psychological knowledge and beliefs, and applying the information to society and its institutions. p. 17

Resources and Readings in Psychology

American Psychological Association

750 First Street, NE
Washington, DC 20002–4242
202–336–5500

The American Psychological Association is the largest organization of psychologists in the United States. It publishes a number of journals on different psychological topics and has a number of books and brochures available, including the free booklet *Careers in Psychology,* which describes a wide range of career opportunities in psychology. Undergraduate students are welcome to join the APA.

American Psychological Society

1010 Vermont Avenue, NW, Suite 1100
Washington, DC 20005
202–783–2077

The American Psychological Society promotes and advances research and applications in psychology. Student affiliate memberships are available.

Canadian Psychological Association/Société canadienne de psychologie

151 Slater Street, Suite 205
Ottawa ON K1P 5H3 Canada
613–237–2144

The Canadian Psychological Association (CPA) is a national voluntary organization with over 4,000 members. It represents the interests of psychologists, advocates the development of national standards and ethical principles, and sponsors national conferences, scientific journals, and mainstream publications to disseminate information. The CPA collaborates with other provincial and national associations and with government departments to advance its objectives.

Guidelines for Ethical Conduct in the Care and Use of Animals (1993)

Science Directorate
American Psychological Association
750 First Street, NE
Washington, DC 20002–4242

This pamphlet was developed by the American Psychological Association's Committee on Animal Research and Ethics (CARE). It profiles guidelines for the appropriate care and use of animals in research.

How to Think Like a Psychologist (1996)

by Donal McBurney
Upper Saddle River, NJ: Prentice-Hall

This book focuses on misconceptions and impediments to understanding psychology. Using a question-answer format, it evaluates such questions as why do psychologists have so many theories, why do I have to learn about so many methods, Why do I have to learn about the brain, can you prove there is no ESP, how can psychology be a science when everybody is unique, and why can't psychologists predict who will commit a violent act?

Is Psychology the Major for You? (1987)

by P. J. Woods and C. S. Wilkinson
Washington, DC: American Psychological Association

This book is must reading for any student interested in a career in psychology. It explains how a psychology degree can be valuable preparation for many diverse careers, including careers in human services, management, and marketing. It also includes chapters on women, Native Americans, Alaska natives, Asian Americans, African Americans, and Latinos in psychology, and on reentry in the field of psychology.

Library Use: A Handbook for Psychology (1992, 2nd ed.)

by Jeffrey Reed and Pam Baxter
Washington, DC: American Psychological Association

This book will show you how to select, define, and locate topics for a library search in psychology. The topics chosen appeal to the interests of many psychology students, and you don't need to have highly technical knowledge to use this book.

Portraits of Pioneers in Psychology, Volume II (1996)

by Gregory Kimbal, C. Alan Boneau, and Michael Wertheimer
Washington, DC: American Psychology Association

Portraits of 21 important figures in the history of psychology are illuminated, including Dorothea Dix, John Dewey, and Robert Yerkes. The authors argue that many of these important contributors have been neglected when the history of psychology has been chronicled.

Psychology and Public Policy (1996)

by Raymond Lorion, Ira Iscoe, Patrick DeLeon, and Gary VanDeBos (eds.)
Washington, DC: American Psychological Association

As a science and health service profession, psychology is relevant to public policy debates and decisions. A number of psychology's leading researchers, clinicians, and policymakers offer their views on ways to improve psychology's impact on public policy.

The Story of Psychology (1993)

by Morton Hunt
New York: Doubleday

This engaging, well-written book journeys through psychology's history and portrays its founders, pioneers, and contemporary figures.

Understanding Culture's Influence on Behavior (1993)

by Richard Brislin
San Diego: Harcourt Brace Jovanovich

This very up-to-date book by a leading authority in cross-cultural psychology introduces you to cultural influences on behavior and ways we can communicate more effectively with people from cultural backgrounds that are different from our own.

CHAPTER

MET

Methods

WASSILY KANDINSKY
Ribbon with Square, detail

CHAPTER

MET

Methods

with Alice O'Toole

Chapter Outline

Chapter Boxes

Truth is arrived at by the painstaking process of eliminating the untrue.

—**Arthur Conan Doyle, Sherlock Holmes**

Science is always profound. It is only the half-truths that are dangerous.

—**George Bernard Shaw, The Doctor's Dilemma, 1913**

Images of Psychology

Scientific Research and You

When you turn on the six o'clock news in the evening or open a newspaper or magazine, you are bombarded with reports about recent research results in medicine, nutrition, and psychology. You are told that a particular vitamin minimizes the risk of cancer; that a particular educational program is effective in helping the mentally handicapped cope in social situations; that certain nutritional factors, such as eating a healthy, balanced breakfast, help young children to concentrate in school; and that certain styles of parenting produce mentally healthy or mentally unhealthy children. How do you respond to this barrage of information? Many of us immediately double our intake of the vitamin in question, vote for candidates who support the educational programs that agree with the latest research on the issue, and make a mental note of (or if you are already a parent, apply) the parenting strategies that you hear produce "healthy" children.

What we know, *or think we know,* about scientific research affects nearly every aspect of daily life, from deciding what foods to eat, to deciding how to vote, and even to deciding what to say to a frightened child in our care. We live in the information age. Research results are no longer the domain of the experts who carry out the studies or the paid professionals who carefully examine and apply the results on a case-by-case basis. For better or for worse, the mass media in our society make research results in psychology the property and concern of every aware citizen. As an active member of society, by voting and paying taxes, you affect the course of scientific research in helping to determine not only which studies scientists carry out, but how they will affect your life in terms of the funding that you will make available for implementing the results of the studies. You will see in this chapter that properly conducted scientific research is a powerful tool for uncovering the laws of physical and mental nature. You will see also that this tool has limits. While scientific inquiry in psychology is the most sophisticated and accurate way of acquiring information about the laws of human behavior, it is also a slow and painstaking process. The results we come to believe from scientific inquiry are rarely the results of a single study; rather, they derive from mountains of data, collected over many years, that converge on a single conclusion, such as "Smoking tobacco causes cancer." The purpose of this chapter is to make you skeptical and to make you aware, not of the truth or falsehoods of the "scientific" claims that you encounter daily, but of the factors you need to understand in order to evaluate the basis of such claims.

Preview

Nothing captures the essence of psychology more than the methods used by psychologists when they conduct scientific research. Psychologists use these methods to describe, predict, and explain behavior. The main topics of this chapter are theory and the scientific method, methods, and challenges in psychological research.

Theory and the Scientific Method

Some people have difficulty thinking of psychology as being a science in the same way that physics, chemistry, and biology are sciences. Can a discipline that studies why people are attracted to each other, how they reason about moral values, and the way ethnicity affects identity be equated with disciplines that examine gravity, the molecular structure of a compound, and the flow of blood in the circulatory system? Science is not defined by *what* it investigates but by *how* it investigates. Whether you investigate photosynthesis, butterflies, Saturn's moons, or why some people bite their fingernails, it is the way you investigate that makes the approach scientific or not.

To be a scientist is to be skeptical. When we think about ourselves and our world, we speculate about mind and behavior: people don't change; love is blind; happiness is the key to success; people are mentally disabled because society makes them that way; communication with spirits is possible. Such claims spark a psychologist's curiosity and skepticism. Psychology seeks to sort fact from fancy by critically questioning the nature of mind and behavior (Martin, 1996).

Theory

A **theory** *is a coherent set of ideas that helps to explain data and to make predictions. A theory has* **hypotheses,** *assumptions that can be tested to determine their accuracy.* For example, a theory about depression explains our observations of depressed people and predicts why they get depressed. We might predict that people get depressed because they fail to focus on their strengths and dwell on their weaknesses. This prediction directs our observations by telling us to look for exaggerations of weaknesses and underestimations for strengths and skills.

The Scientific Method

The **scientific method** *is an approach used to discover accurate information about mind and behavior. It includes the following steps: identifying and analyzing the problem, collecting data, drawing conclusions, and revising theories.* We often generate hypotheses as we identify and analyze problems, and then again as we draw conclusions and revise theories (Rosnow & Rosenthal, 1996). Let's apply the scientific method to the investigation of depression. For example, you decide that you want to help people overcome depression. You have *identified a problem,* which does not seem to be a difficult task. As part of this first step, however, you need to go beyond a general description of the problem by isolating, analyzing, narrowing, and focusing on what you hope to investigate. What specific strategies do you want to use to reduce depression? Do you want to look at only one strategy, or several strategies? What aspect of depression do you want to study—its biological characteristics, cognitive characteristics, or behavioral characteristics?

Peter Lewinsohn and his colleagues (1984), for example, chose to study the behavioral and cognitive characteristics of depression. They analyzed depression's many components and chose to focus on whether people's lives could be improved by taking a course on coping with depression. One of the course's components involved teaching depressed people to control their negative thoughts. In this first step of the scientific method, the researchers identified and analyzed a problem.

The next step in the scientific method involves *collecting information (data).* Psychologists observe behavior and draw inferences about thoughts and emotions. In their investigation of depression, Lewinsohn and his colleagues observed how effectively people who completed the course on coping with depression monitored their moods and engaged in productive work.

Once psychologists collect data, they *use statistical (mathematical) procedures* to understand the meaning of the quantitative data. Psychologists then draw conclusions. In the investigation of depression, statistics helped the researchers determine whether or not their observations reflected real differences in how people cope with depression, or whether they were due to chance or random fluctuations in the data. After psychologists analyze data, they compare their findings with what others have discovered about the same issue or problem.

The final step in the scientific method is *revising theory.* Psychologists have developed a number of theories about why we become depressed and how we can cope with depression. Data, such as that collected by Lewinsohn and his associates, force us to reexamine existing theories of depression to see if they still hold up. (Theories of depression are discussed in the chapter on abnormal psychology.) Over the years some psychological theories have been discarded, others revised. Wundt's theory of introspection was discarded, while behaviorism and psychoanalytic theory were substantially revised. The cognitive, neurobiological, and sociocultural approaches are undergoing revision as the scientific method is applied to the questions they raise. Figure 1 summarizes the main steps in the scientific method and provides an example of each.

Methods

When psycholologists conduct research, two of the most important questions they must answer are these: (1) What kind of measure(s) am I going to use to collect data? and (2) What strategy will I use to carry out the research study?

Measures

Systematic information is collected in a variety of ways. For example, we can watch behavior in the laboratory or in a more natural setting such as on a street corner. We can question people using interviews and surveys, develop and administer standardized tests, conduct case studies, or carry out physiological research or research with animals. To help you understand how psychologists use these methods, we will apply each method to the study of aggression.

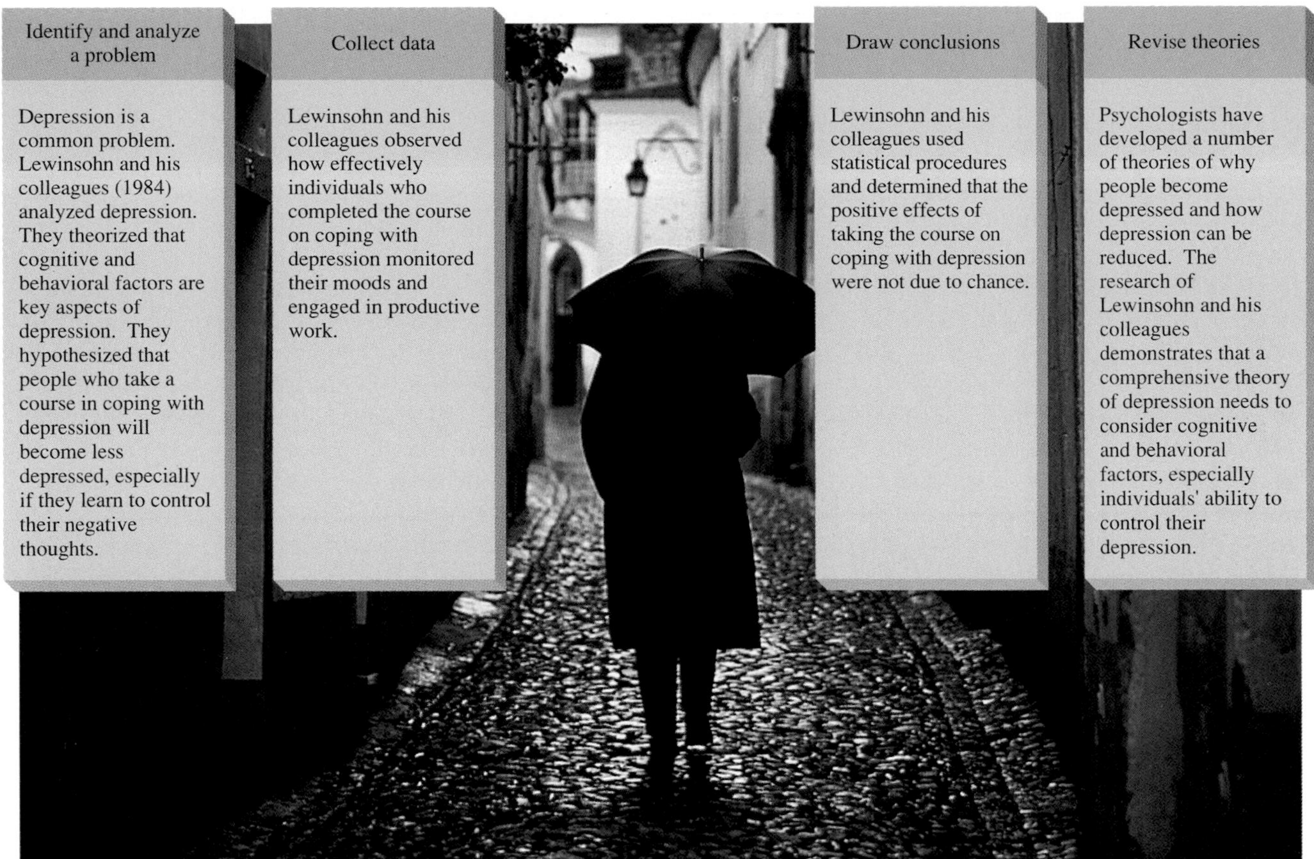

Identify and analyze a problem
Depression is a common problem. Lewinsohn and his colleagues (1984) analyzed depression. They theorized that cognitive and behavioral factors are key aspects of depression. They hypothesized that people who take a course in coping with depression will become less depressed, especially if they learn to control their negative thoughts.
Collect data
Lewinsohn and his colleagues observed how effectively individuals who completed the course on coping with depression monitored their moods and engaged in productive work.
Draw conclusions
Lewinsohn and his colleagues used statistical procedures and determined that the positive effects of taking the course on coping with depression were not due to chance.
Revise theories
Psychologists have developed a number of theories of why people become depressed and how depression can be reduced. The research of Lewinsohn and his colleagues demonstrates that a comprehensive theory of depression needs to consider cognitive and behavioral factors, especially individuals' ability to control their depression.

FIGURE 1

The Main Steps in the Scientific Method Applied to a Study of Depression

Observation

Sherlock Holmes chided Watson, "You see but you do not observe." We look at things all the time, but casually watching a friend cross the campus is not scientific observation. Unless you are a trained observer and practice your skills regularly, you might not know what to look for, you might not remember what you saw, what you are looking for may change from one moment to the next, and you might not communicate your observations effectively.

For observations to be effective, we have to know what we are looking for, whom we are observing, when and where we will observe, how the observations will be made, and in what form they will be recorded. That is, we need to observe in some *systematic* way (Zeren & Makosky, 1995). Consider aggression. Do we want to study verbal or physical aggression, or both? How will we know it when we see it? If one man punches another in the arm, will we mark that down as aggression? If both men are laughing and one punches the other in the arm, will we still count the punch as aggression? Do we want to study men, or women, or children, or all of these? Do we want to evaluate them in a university laboratory, at work, at play, in their homes, or at all of these locations? Do we want to audiotape or videotape their behavior, or both? A common way to record observations

"For crying out loud, gentlemen! That's us! Someone's installed the one-way mirror in backward!"

Explorations in Psychology 1

Hans, the Clever Horse

To understand the importance of controlled observation in psychology, we will consider a horse by the name of Hans. According to experts, Hans could reason and "talk." Hans had been trained by a retired math teacher, Mr. von Osten, to communicate by tapping his forefoot and moving his head. A head nod meant yes, while a shake suggested no. Mr. von Osten developed a code for verbal information in which each letter was represented by a pair of numbers. The letter *A* was coded as one tap, pause, one tap, and the letter *I* was three taps, pause, two taps. Once Hans learned to tap his foot or move his head when questioned, he was given simple problems and then fed a piece of bread or carrot for correct responses. By the end of his training, Hans could spell words spoken to him, and he excelled in math. He became a hero in Germany—his picture was on liquor bottles and toys. Experts were so impressed that an official commission of thirteen scientists, educators, and public officials examined the horse, testing him to see if he really could do all of the things claimed. They came away even more impressed and issued a statement saying that there was no evidence of any intentional influence or aid on the part of Han's questioners.

But there was one scientist who was not so sure that Hans was as intelligent as he had been portrayed. Oskar von Pfungst, a very sharp observer, had detected that Hans always faced his questioner. Von Pfungst hypothesized (developed the hunch or belief) that this might have something to do with his math ability. The scientist set up a very simple experiment. He wrote numbers on a card and held them up one at a time, asking Hans to tap out the numbers written on each card. Half of the cards von Pfungst held so that only Hans, not von Pfungst, could see what was on them. With the cards von Pfungst could see, Hans was his usual brilliant self, getting 92 percent of them correct. But for the numbers von Pfungst could not see, Hans was no longer a brilliant horse, getting only 8 percent correct.

Von Pfungst repeated the experiment over and over again with nearly the same results. He then carefully observed Hans with his other questioners, including von Osten. As soon as they stated the problem to Hans, most questioners would turn their head and upper body slightly. When the correct number of foot taps had been made by Hans, the questioner would move his head upward. Despite his years of work with the horse, Mr. von Osten had never dreamed that Hans had learned to "read" him. Von Osten commented that he actually was angry at the horse and felt betrayed by him.

Thus we can see that experts sometimes can be wrong and that what sometimes seems to be the truth may be a false impression. Even experts can be fooled if they don't make appropriate use of research procedures to check their observations.

This researcher is using observation as part of a research study on infant development. Videotaped observation has allowed researchers to become increasingly precise in coding various behaviors because they can play the tape over and over to discover micro aspects of behavior.

is to write them down, using shorthand or symbols; however, psychologists increasingly use tape recorders, video cameras, special coding sheets, and one-way mirrors to make observations more efficient. To read further about the importance of systematic observation in accurately obtaining information about behavior, see Explorations in Psychology 1.

When we observe, we often need to *control* certain factors that determine behavior but are not the focus of our inquiry. For this reason much psychological research is conducted in a **laboratory,** *a controlled setting with many of the complex factors of the "real world" removed.* For example, in one experiment Albert Bandura (1965) had an adult repeatedly hit a Bobo doll—a plastic, inflated doll about three feet tall.

Jane Goodall was a young woman when she made her first trip to the Gombe Research Center in Tanzania, Africa. Fascinated by chimpanzees, she dreamed about a career that would allow her to explore her hunches about the nature of chimpanzees. She embarked on a career in the bush that involved long and solitary hours of careful, patient observation. A specialist in animal behavior, her observations spanned 30 years, years that included her marriage, the birth of her son, untold hardship, and inestimable pleasure. Due to her efforts, our understanding of chimpanzees in natural settings dramatically improved.

Bandura wondered to what extent the children would copy the adult's behavior. After the children saw the adult attack the Bobo doll, they too aggressively hit the inflated toy. By conducting his experiment in a laboratory with adults the children did not know, Bandura controlled when the child witnessed aggression, how much aggression the child saw, and what form the aggression took. Bandura could not have conducted his experiment as effectively if other factors, such as parents, siblings, friends, television, and a familiar room, had been present.

Laboratory research, however, does have some drawbacks. First, it is almost impossible to conduct research without the participants' knowing they are being studied. Second, the laboratory setting is unnatural and therefore can cause the participants to behave unnaturally. Research participants usually show less aggressive behavior in a laboratory than in a more familiar or natural setting, such as a park or at home. They also show less aggression when they are aware they are being observed than when they are unaware they are being observed. Third, people who are willing to come to a university laboratory are unlikely to represent groups from diverse cultural backgrounds. Those who are unfamiliar with university settings, and with the idea of "helping science," may be intimidated by the setting. Fourth, some aspects of mind and behavior are difficult if not impossible to examine in the laboratory. Certain types of stress are difficult (and unethical) to study in the laboratory. Alcohol, for instance, consistently increases aggression in an individual who is provoked. In 1985 at a soccer game in Brussels, Belgium, a riot broke out. The English fans, intoxicated by alcohol, aroused by the competition, and taunted by the Italian fans, attacked the Italians. As the Italians retreated, they were crushed against a wall—the death toll was 38. Recreating circumstances in a laboratory that even remotely resemble the Brussels soccer game is impossible and unethical.

Although laboratory research is a valuable tool for psychologists, naturalistic observation provides insight that we sometimes cannot achieve in the laboratory (Pellegrini, 1996). In **naturalistic observation,** *psychologists observe behavior in real-world settings and make no effort to manipulate or control the situation.* Psychologists conduct naturalistic observations at soccer games, day-care centers, college dormitories, rest rooms, corporations, shopping malls, restaurants, dances, and other places people live in and frequent. In contrast to Bandura's observations of aggression in a laboratory, some psychologists use naturalistic methods to observe the aggression of children in nursery schools, the aggression of marital partners at home, and the arguments and violence of people at sporting events and political protests (Mahoney, 1995).

Interviews and Questionnaires

Sometimes the best and quickest way to get information from people is to ask them for it. Psychologists use interviews and questionnaires to find out about a person's experiences and attitudes. Most interviews occur face-to-face, although they can take place over the telephone.

Interviews range from highly unstructured to highly structured. Examples of unstructured interview questions are *How aggressive do you see yourself as being?* and *How aggressive is your child?* Examples of structured interview questions are *In the last week how often did you yell at your spouse?* and *How often in the last year was your child involved in fights at school?* Structure is imposed by the questions themselves, or the interviewer can categorize answers by asking the respondent to choose from several options. For example, in the question about your level of aggressiveness, you might be asked to choose from these options: highly aggressive, moderately aggressive, moderately unaggressive, and highly unaggressive. In the question about how often you yelled at your spouse in the last week, you might be asked to choose from these options: 0, 1–2, 3–5, 6–10, or more than 10 times.

An experienced interviewer knows how to put respondents at ease and encourage them to open up. A competent interviewer is sensitive to the way the person responds to questions and often probes for more information (Yoder, 1995). A person may respond to questions about the nature of marital conflict with fuzzy statements, such as "Well, I don't know whether we have a lot of conflict or not." The skilled interviewer pushes for more specific, concrete answers, possibly asking, "If you had it to do over again, would you get married?" or "Tell me the worst things you and your wife said to each other in the last week." Using these strategies forces researchers to be involved with, rather than detached from, the people they interview and yields a better understanding of mind and behavior (Schutte & Malouff, 1995). Interviews also have shortcomings. Perhaps the most critical is known as the factor of "social desirability," in which participants might give responses that they consider to be socially desirable rather than tell interviewers what they really think and feel. When asked about his marital conflict, Sam may not want to disclose that arguments have been painfully tense in the last month. Jane, his wife, may not want to divulge her extramarital affair when asked about her sexual relationships. Skilled interviewing techniques and questions to help eliminate such defenses are critical in obtaining accurate information.

Psychologists also question people using questionnaires or surveys. A **questionnaire** *is similar to a highly structured interview except that respondents read the questions and mark their answers on paper rather than responding verbally to the interviewer.* One major advantage of surveys and questionnaires is that they can be given to a large number of people easily. Good surveys have concrete, specific, and unambiguous questions, and assess the authenticity of the replies (Jackson, 1995).

Sometimes we want information about a small set of people, such as all African American graduates of a particular high school in the last 5 years or all college students from your campus who participated in a nuclear arms protest. At other times, we want to know something about a large population of people, such as all people in the United States. In each instance, it is important that the people surveyed represent the group we wish to describe. We accomplish this important task by surveying a random sample of subjects. In a **random sample** *every member of a population or group has an equal chance of being selected.*

Random samples are important because, in most instances, we cannot survey everyone we are trying to describe—for example, all people in the United States. The National Crime Survey is an example of a random sample survey (U.S. Department of Justice, 1983). If we asked people from a high-crime area of Miami, Florida, if they had been a victim of crime and used this information to project the frequency of crime in the United States, projections would be inflated. While certain pockets of Miami do have extremely high crime rates, the recent National Crime Survey, giving each household in the United States an equal chance of being surveyed, indicated that crime is high across the country—close to one-third of the households surveyed were victimized by violence or theft.

How do researchers obtain a random sample of subjects? In cases like the National Crime Survey, methods increase the likelihood that those sampled are representative of the proportion of White American, African American, Latino, Asian American, Native American, low-income, middle-income, high-income, rural, and urban individuals in the United States. A national random sample of 5,000 subjects, for example, has fewer African Americans than Whites, fewer high-income than low-income persons, and fewer rural than urban subjects.

Unfortunately, appropriate sampling methods are not always followed (Heiman, 1995). Newspapers and magazines often conduct surveys of their readership. Those who participate by mailing or calling in their opinions probably feel more strongly about the issue in question than those who do not respond. Issues such as whether or not drunk driving laws should be tougher or whether or not premarital sex is morally wrong are likely to galvanize those with strong feelings into action. Surveys encounter problems similar to interviews—people don't necessarily tell the truth, and the willingness to answer questions varies between groups.

Case Studies

A **case study** *is an in-depth look at a single individual; this method is used mainly by clinical psychologists when, for either practical or ethical reasons, the unique aspects of an individual's life cannot be duplicated.* A case study provides information about one person's fears, hopes, fantasies, traumatic experiences, upbringing, family relationships, health, or anything that helps the psychologist understand the person's mind and behavior (Stake, 1995).

Traumatic experiences have produced some truly fascinating case studies in psychology. Consider the following. A 26-year-old schoolteacher met a woman with whom he fell intensely in love. But several months after their love affair began, the schoolteacher became depressed, drank heavily, and talked about suicide. The suicidal ideas progressed to images of murder and suicide. His actions became bizarre. On one occasion he punctured the tires of his beloved's car. On another he stood on the side of the road where she passed frequently in her car, extending his hand in his pocket so she would think he was holding a gun. Only eight months after meeting her, the teacher shot her while he was a passenger in the car she was driving. Soon after the act, he ran to a telephone booth to call his priest. The girlfriend had died (Revitch & Schlesinger, 1978).

This case reveals how depressive moods and bizarre thinking can precede violent acts, such as murder. Other vivid case studies appear throughout this text, among them a woman with three personalities, each of which is unaware of the others, and a modern-day wild child named Genie, who lived in near total isolation during her childhood.

While case histories provide dramatic, in-depth portrayals of people's lives, we need to exercise caution when generalizing from this information. The subject of a case study is unique, with a genetic makeup and experiences no one else shares. In addition, case studies involve judgments of unknown reliability. Psychologists who conduct case studies rarely check to see if other psychologists agree with their observations.

Standardized Tests

Standardized tests *require people to answer a series of written and oral questions, and they have two distinct features: (1) An individual's score is totaled to yield a single score, or set of scores, that reflects something about that individual; and (2) the individual's score is compared with the scores of a large group of similar people to determine how the individual responded relative to others.* Scores are often stated in terms of percentiles. For example, suppose you scored in the 92nd percentile on the SAT. This measure tells you that 92 percent of a large group of individuals who previously took the test received scores lower than yours. Among the most widely used standardized tests in psychology are the Stanford-Binet intelligence test and the Minnesota Multiphasic Personality Inventory (MMPI).

To continue our look at how psychologists use different methods to evaluate aggression, consider the MMPI, which includes a scale to assess an individual's delinquency and antisocial tendencies. The items on this scale ask you to respond whether or not you are rebellious, impulsive, and have trouble with authority figures. The 26-year-old teacher who murdered his girlfriend would have scored high on a number of the MMPI scales, including one designed to measure how strange and bizarre our thoughts and ideas are.

The main advantage of standardized tests is that they provide information about *individual differences* among people. But information obtained from standardized tests does not always predict behavior in nontest situations. Standardized tests are based on the belief that a person's behavior is consistent and stable. Although personality and intelligence, two of the primary targets of standardized tests, have some stability, they can vary, depending on the situation. For example, a person may perform poorly on a standardized intelligence test in an office setting but display a much higher level of intelligence at home where he or she is less anxious. This criticism is especially relevant for members of minority groups, some of whom have been inappropriately classified as mentally retarded on the basis of their scores on intelligence tests. And cross-cultural psychologists caution that while many psychological tests developed in Western cultures might work reasonably well in Western cultures, they might not always be appropriate in other cultures (Cushner & Brislin, 1995). For example, people in other cultures simply might not have had as much exposure to the information on the test. Next we will examine cross-cultural research and research with ethnic minority groups.

Standardized tests require individuals to answer a series of written or oral questions. The individual on the right is being given a standardized test of intelligence.

Cross-Cultural Research and Research with Ethnic Minority Groups

Researchers who are unfamiliar with the cultural and ethnic groups they are studying must take extra precautions to shed any biases they bring with them from their own culture. For example, they must make sure they construct measures that are meaningful for each of the cultural or ethnic minority groups being studied (Padilla, 1995).

In conducting research on cultural and ethnic minority issues, investigators distinguish between the emic approach and the etic approach. In the **emic approach,** *the goal is to describe behavior in one culture or ethnic group in terms that are meaningful and important to the people in that culture or ethnic group, without regard to other cultures or ethnic groups.* In the **etic approach,** *the goal is to describe behavior so that generalizations can be made across cultures.* That is, the emic approach is culture-specific; the etic approach

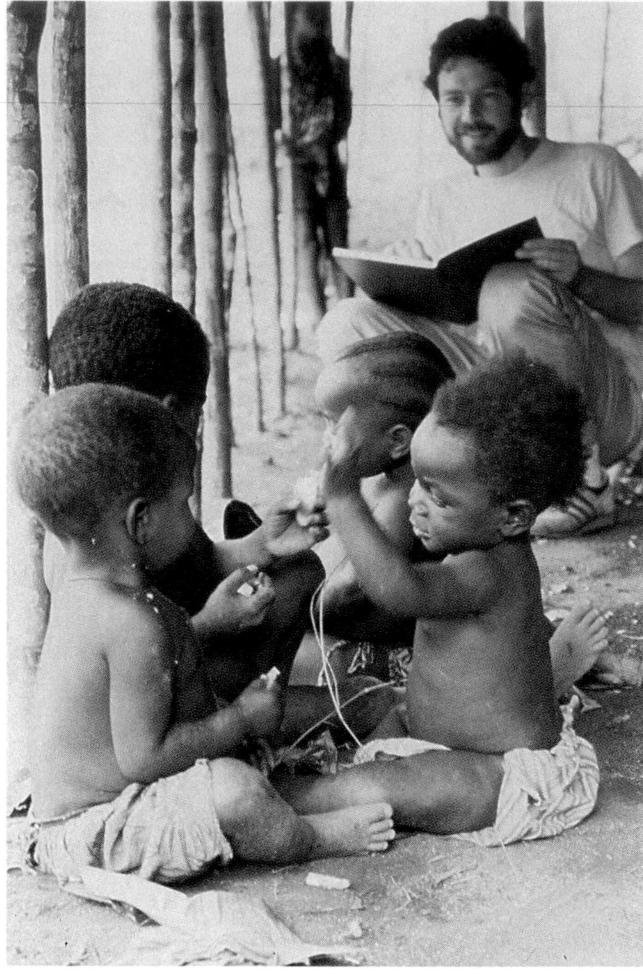

Systematic observations in natural settings provide valuable information about behavior across cultures. For example, in one investigation, observations in different cultures revealed that American children often engage in less work and more play than children in many other cultures (Whiting & Whiting, 1975). However, conducting cross-cultural research using such methods as systematic observation in natural settings is difficult and requires attention to a number of methodological issues.

is culture-universal. If researchers construct a questionnaire in an emic fashion, their concern is only that the questions be meaningful to the particular culture or ethnic group being studied. If, however, the researchers construct a questionnaire in an etic fashion, they want to include questions that reflect concepts familiar to all cultures involved (Berry, 1969).

How might the emic and etic approaches be reflected in the study of family processes? In the emic approach, the researchers might choose to focus only on middle-class White families, without regard for whether the information obtained in the study can be generalized or is appropriate for ethnic minority groups. In a subsequent study, the researchers may decide to adopt an etic approach by studying not only middle-class White families, but also lower-income White families, African American families, Latino families, and Asian American families. In studying ethnic minority families, the researchers would likely discover that the extended family is more frequently a support system in these families than in White American families. If so, the emic approach would reveal a different pattern of family interaction than would the etic approach, documenting that research with middle-class White families cannot always be generalized to all ethnic groups.

Cross-cultural psychologist Joseph Trimble (1989) is especially concerned about researchers' tendencies to use ethnic gloss when they select and describe ethnic groups. By **ethnic gloss,** Trimble means *using an ethnic label, such as* Black, Latino, Asian, *or* Native American, *in a superficial way that makes an ethnic group seem more homogeneous than it actually is.* For example, the following is an unsuitable description of a research sample, according to Trimble: "The subjects included 28 African Americans, 22 Latinos, and 24 Whites." Acceptable descriptions of the groups require much more detail about the participants' countries of origin, socioeconomic status, language, and ethnic self-identification, such as this: "The 22 subjects were Mexican Americans from low-income neighborhoods in the southwestern area of Los Angeles. Twelve spoke Spanish in the home, while 10 spoke English; 11 were born in the United States, 11 were born in Mexico; 16 described themselves as Mexican, 3 as Chicano, 2 as American, and 1 as Latino." Trimble believes that ethnic gloss can cause researchers to obtain samples of ethnic groups and cultures that are not representative of their ethnic and cultural diversity, leading to overgeneralizations and stereotypes.

Let's go back to the study of aggression. Cross-cultural psychologists have found that aggression is universal, appearing in every culture. In this sense, it is an etic behavior; however, the expression of aggression may be culture-specific, so aggression is also an emic behavior. For example, the !Kung of southern Africa actively dissuade one another from behaving aggressively, whereas the Yanomamo Indians of South America promote aggression. Yanomamo youth are told that adult status cannot be achieved unless they are capable of killing, fighting, and pummeling others.

Physiological Research and Research with Animals

Two additional methods that psychologists use to gather data are physiological research and research with animals. Research on the biological basis of behavior and technological advances continue to produce remarkable insights about mind and behavior. For example, researchers have found that electrical stimulation of certain areas of the brain turns docile, mild-mannered people into hostile, vicious attackers; and higher concentrations of some hormones have been associated with anger in adolescents (Tremblay and Schaal, 1995).

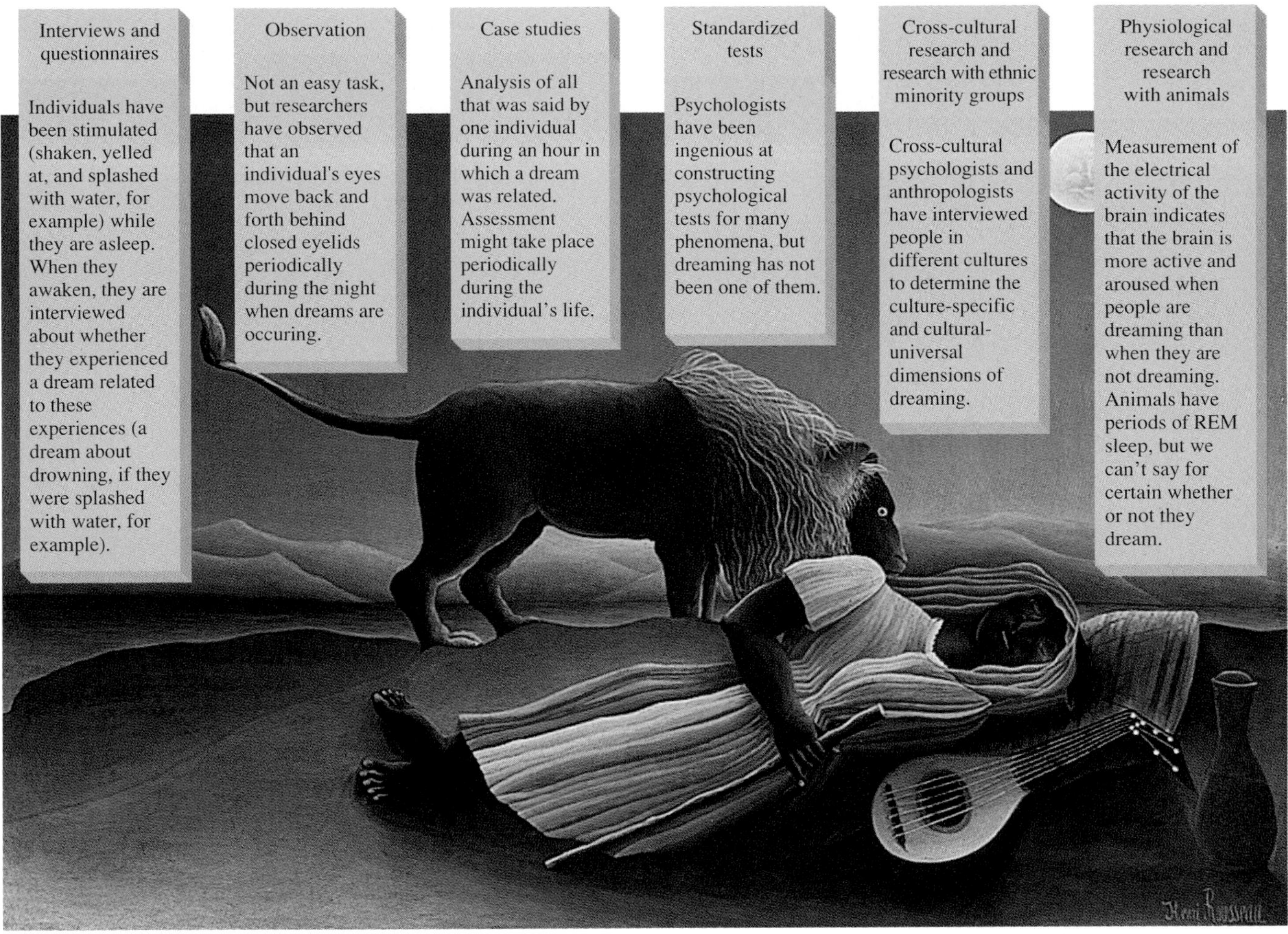

FIGURE 2

Psychology's Measures and an Application to the Study of Dreaming

Henri Rousseau, *The Sleeping Gypsy*, from The Museum of Modern Art, New York, gift of Mrs. Simon Guggenheim.

Since much physiological research cannot be carried out with humans, psychologists sometimes use animals. Animal studies permit researchers to control genetic background, diet, experiences during infancy, and countless other factors. In studying humans, psychologists treat these factors as random variation, or "noise," that may interfere with accurate results. In addition, animal researchers can investigate the effects of some treatments (brain implants, for example) that would be unethical with humans. Moreover, it is possible to track the entire life span of some animals over a relatively short period of time. Laboratory mice, for instance, have a life span of approximately 1 year.

With regard to aggression, we know that castration turns ferocious bulls into docile oxen by acting on the male hormone system. After a number of breedings of aggressive mice, researchers have created mice who are absolutely ferocious (Manning, 1989). Do these findings with animals apply to humans? Hormones and genes do influence human aggression, but the influence is less powerful than in animals. Because humans differ from animals in many ways, one disadvantage of research with animals is that the results may not apply to humans.

In sum, psychologists call on diverse measures to discover new information about mind and behavior. A brief overview of the main categories of measures appears in figure 2, along with examples of the measures psychologists use to investigate dreams. Notice in figure 2 that no standardized test to assess dreaming exists, but that many interviews to discover information about dreaming do exist. It is not unusual in psychology for some measures to be better at obtaining information about an aspect of mind and behavior than others, although the absence of a standardized test of dreaming does not rule out the possibility that someone will develop such a test in the future.

At this point we have discussed a number of ideas about theory, the scientific method, and measures. A summary of these ideas is presented in concept table 1. Next, we turn our attention to strategies for setting up research studies.

Concept Table 1

Theory, the Scientific Method, and Measures

Concept	Processes/Related Ideas	Characteristics/Description
Theory	Its nature	Theories are coherent sets of ideas that help us to explain data and make predictions. A theory has hypotheses, which are assumptions that can be tested to determine their accuracy.
The Scientific Method	Definition	The scientific method is an approach used to discover accurate information about mind and behavior. It includes the following steps: identifying and analyzing the problem, collecting data, drawing conclusions, and revising theory.
Measures	Observation	It is a key ingredient in research that includes both laboratory and naturalistic observation. A laboratory is a controlled setting with many of the complex factors of the "real world" removed. Laboratory research has its pluses and minuses. In naturalistic observation, psychologists observe behavior in real-world settings and make no effort to manipulate or control the situation.
	Interviews and questionnaires	They are used to assess perceptions and attitudes. A questionnaire is similar to a highly structured interview except that respondents read the questions and mark their answers on paper rather than responding verbally to the interviewer. An important concern is whether the survey has been given to a random sample of subjects with every member of the population group having an equal chance of being selected. Social desirability and lying are problems that are sometimes associated with the use of interviews and questionnaires.
	Case studies	They provide an in-depth look at an individual; caution in their generalization is warranted.
	Standardized tests	They require people to answer a series of written and oral questions. They have two distinct features. First, psychologists usually total an individual's score to yield a single score, or set of scores, that reflects something about the individual. Second, psychologists compare the individual's score to the scores of a large group of similar people to determine how the individual responded relative to others. The main advantage of standardized tests is that they provide information about individual differences among people. Sometimes, though, standardized test scores do not predict behavior in nontest situations.
	Cross-cultural research and research with ethnic minority groups	This research focuses on the culture-universal (etic approach) and culture-specific (emic approach) nature of mind and behavior. A special concern in research with ethnic minority groups is ethnic gloss.
	Physiological research and research with animals	Physiological research provides information about the biological basis of behavior. Since much physiological research cannot be carried out with humans, psychologists sometimes use animals. Animal studies permit researchers to control genetic background, diet, experiences in infancy, and countless other factors. One issue is the extent research with animals can be generalized to humans.

Strategies for Setting Up Research Studies

How can we learn if listening to rock music deadens a person's hearing? How can we discover if overeating is influenced by one's state of mind? How can we figure out if high blood pressure is due to stress? To answer such questions, psychologists not only choose a measure or measures, they also decide whether to use a correlational or an experimental research strategy.

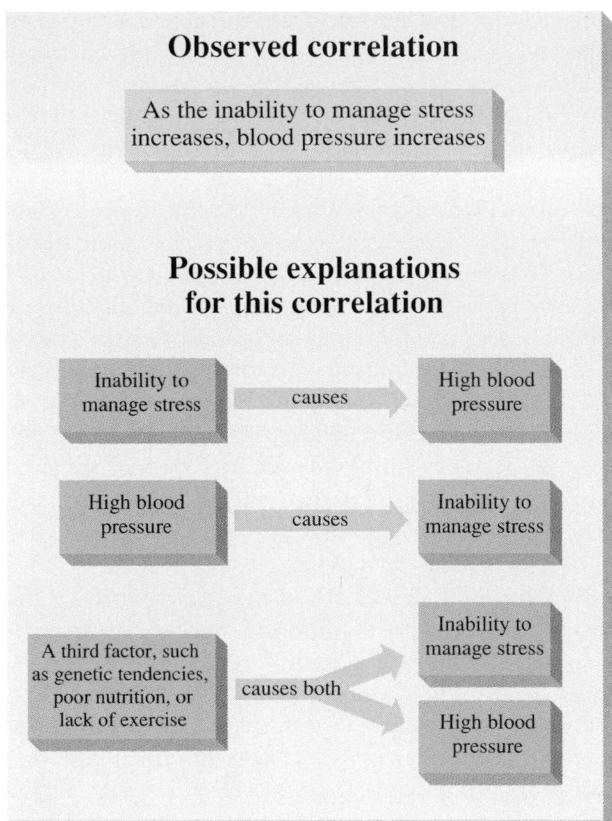

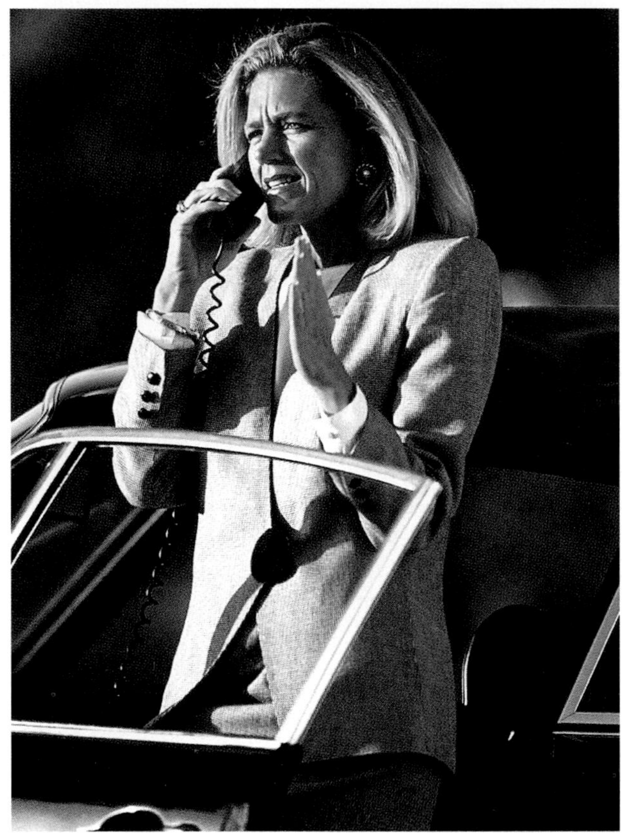

FIGURE 3

Possible Explanations of Correlational Data
An observed correlation between two events cannot be used to conclude that one event causes a second event. Other possibilities are that the second event causes the first event or that a third, unknown event causes the correlation between the first two events.

Correlational Strategy

In the **correlational strategy,** *the goal is to describe the strength of the relation between two or more events or characteristics.* This is a useful strategy because the more strongly events are correlated (related or associated), the more effectively we can predict one from the other. For example, consider one of our major national health problems, high blood pressure. If we find that high blood pressure is strongly associated with high stress levels on the job, then we can use the high levels or work-related stress to predict high blood pressure.

The next step, taken all too often, is to conclude from such evidence that one event causes the other. Following this line of reasoning, we would erroneously conclude that the high job-related stress causes high blood pressure. Why is this reasoning faulty? Why doesn't a strong correlation between two events mean that one event causes the other? A strong correlation could mean that the job-related stress causes high blood pressure, but it also could mean that high blood pressure causes the perception of high levels of stress at work. And a third possibility exists: although strongly correlated, the job-related stress and high blood pressure do not cause each other at all. It is possible that a third factor, such as a genetic tendency, poor nutrition, or lack of exercise, underlies their association (see figure 3). We will see shortly that being able to predict one event from another event is a necessary, but not sufficient, condition for showing that one event causes another. We will see how each of the alternative explanations for a causal link between stress and high blood pressure can be controlled for using an experimental procedure.

To ensure that your understanding of correlation is clear, let's look at another example. People who make a lot of money have higher self-esteem than those who make less money. We could mistakenly interpret this to mean that making a lot of money causes us to have high self-esteem. What are the two other interpretations we need to consider? It could be that developing high self-esteem causes us to make a lot of money, or that a third factor, such as education, social upbringing, or genetic tendencies, causes the correlation between making a lot of money and high self-esteem. Throughout this text, you will read about numerous studies that were based on a correlational strategy. Keep in mind how easy it is to assume causality when two events or characteristics are merely correlated.

Experimental Strategy

While the correlational strategy allows us to say only that two events are related, the **experimental strategy** *allows us to precisely determine behavior's causes.* The psychologist accomplishes this task by performing an **experiment,** *which is a carefully regulated procedure in which one or more of the factors believed to influence the behavior being studied is manipulated and all others are held constant. If the behavior under study changes when a factor is manipulated, we say that the manipulated factor causes the behavior to change.* Experiments are used to establish cause and effect between events, something correlational studies cannot do. Cause is the event being manipulated and effect is the behavior that changes because of the manipulation. Remember that in testing correlation, nothing is manipulated; in an experiment, the researcher actively changes an event to see the effect on behavior (Bordens & Abbott, 1996).

How can we establish that one thing causes something else? The first prerequisite in establishing a causal relationship between two factors is to show that the two factors **covary,** *or that the value of one factor varies with the other factor.* We have just seen that establishing a correlation between two factors is one way of showing that two factors covary. If high levels of stress at work cause high blood pressure, it must be true that people who experience high stress levels at work tend to have high blood pressure. In addition, **time precedence,** *or the appearance of the causal factor before the caused factor,* must be established. If high levels of stress cause high blood pressure, then it must be true that changes in stress precede changes in blood pressure. This eliminates the possibility that having high blood pressure causes people to believe that they are experiencing high levels of stress.

The third and perhaps trickiest part of establishing a causal relation between two factors is to eliminate **confounding factors,** *which are other uncontrolled factors that covary coincidentally with the causal factor.* This usually takes the form of a third factor that causes changes in both of the factors of interest. Let's consider the example of high stress and blood pressure again. Perhaps people who seek out and take on high-stress situations (jobs, conflicted relationships, and so on) have a particular kind of personality, or come from a particular kind of family background. In this case, it might be personality type or family history that is the cause of high blood pressure. Other possibilities might also explain a relationship between the two factors. For example, people with high stress may not have good eating habits, or they may get less sleep than those with low stress. In this case, sleeplessness or vitamin deficiencies, rather than stress per se, might actually lie at the cause of the high blood pressure problems observed in people with high stress.

Finally, it is important to remember that even with the establishment of covariation, time precedence, and the elimination of any known or suspected confounding factors, the establishment of cause is still tentative. Cause cannot be observed, but only inferred from the observed covariation, time precedence, and elimination of any other factors that potentially affect the results of the experiment. Psychologists must always be conscious of these limits and what they suggest about the tentative nature of scientific inquiry.

Most researchers define a good experiment as one that meets three criteria: internal validity, external validity, and reliability. First, good experiments have **internal validity,** *which means that causal inferences can be generated from the experiment.* Confounding variables such as those just mentioned in our hypothetical blood pressure study can threaten internal validity. In this case, the inference that job stress causes high blood pressure might not be valid since variations in nutrition or sleep patterns may actually be causing differences in blood pressure. We will see another example of a threat to internal validity caused by introducing a confounding variable in the procedure used to assign subjects to experimental groups.

A second characteristic of a good experiment is that it has **external validity,** *which means that the experiment provides information that will generalize to the population of interest.* Researchers occasionally joke that experimental psychology is the study of the college freshman or sophomore. While in many cases college freshmen and sophomores are wonderful, cooperative, and easily available subjects, they are not always the best group from which to select subjects. For example, when a researcher studies problem solving in order to learn how to help poor problem solvers to become better problem solvers, the use of college freshmen and sophomores as subjects may threaten the external validity of the study. It is likely that even relatively poor problem solvers in college are not typical of poor problem solvers in the population as a whole, and so the applicability of the results gained from such a study may be limited.

Finally, good experiments have high reliability. **Reliability** *is the extent to which an experiment can be repeated and yield the same results.* Experimental reliability can be affected by many factors, ranging from simple instrumentation problems to much more complex issues concerning the quality and thoroughness of a particular measurement scheme. For example, a reliable measure of hyperactivity or depression in children will consistently identify the same children as hyperactive or depressive and will not yield different results depending on what the children ate for breakfast or on whether the measure was taken during their favorite activity or during a less pleasurable task.

Random Assignment

The following example illustrates the nature of an experiment. Let's say we want to find out if marijuana impairs alertness and increases confidence. Since marijuana is not legally available, we obtain permission from the appropriate authorities to use the drug in an experiment. We decide that to conduct our experiment we need one group of participants who will smoke marijuana and one group who will not. We randomly assign the participants to these groups. **Random assignment** *occurs when psychologists assign subjects to experimental and control conditions by chance, thus reducing the likelihood that the results of the experiment will be due to some preexisting differences in the two groups.* For example, random assignment controls for the probability that the two groups will differ on such factors as prior use of marijuana, health problems, intelligence, alertness, social class, age, and so forth.

Assigning participants to groups without random assignment can threaten the validity of research in subtle and surprising ways. This mistake is easily made if a researcher takes shortcuts in carrying out an experiment for reasons of convenience.

Let's take an example. A researcher wants to find out whether a moralistic film will produce more negative attitudes on the part of adolescents toward drug abuse. The researcher randomly selects a large high school in the area and obtains permission to show different films, an experimental "moralistic" film and a control "informative" film, to two randomly chosen homerooms from the high school. After viewing the film, the students fill out a questionnaire about their attitudes on drug use. The researcher finds that the students who viewed the moralistic film have more negative views about drug use than do those who viewed the informative film. Perhaps the researcher was not aware, however, that for reasons of bureaucratic convenience, many large high schools assign students to homerooms alphabetically. By chance, the researcher may have shown the moralistic film to a homeroom full of students whose names began with "O," like O'Flynn, O'Hara, O'Malley, and O'Shea, and the second control film to a homeroom full of students whose names began with a "P," like Pagano, Paccliacci, Palantino, and Puccini. It is easy to see that the differences obtained by the researcher on the questionnaire might be due entirely to differences in the student's ethnic background rather than due to the experimental manipulation.

Experimental and Control Groups

Now let's return to the marijuana experiment. The participants who smoke the marijuana are called the **experimental group**—*that is, the group whose experience is manipulated.* Those who do not smoke marijuana are the **control group**—*that is, a comparison group treated like the experimental group in every way except for the manipulated factor. The control group serves as a baseline against which the effects found in the manipulated condition can be compared.* The importance of an appropriate control group cannot be underestimated.

In designing the experiment on the effects of marijuana on alertness, we have been careful to see that the participants in our study are randomly assigned to the experimental and control groups, and so are likely to be similar to each other in all important ways (for example, their history of marijuana use), *before* the experiment begins. But what about other aspects of the experimental procedure that may affect the alertness of participants *after* they have been assigned to the experimental or control group? Control groups must be cleverly designed to equalize *all* of these factors, and not only the "evident" ones.

Let's look at some of these factors. Because of the nature of the experiment, all participants must sign a consent form to smoke a controlled substance. Most people know about the typical effects of marijuana and most people have preconceptions (or pre-misconceptions) about how the drug is likely to affect their perceptual and motor abilities. A person assigned to the experimental group may become anxious as they begin to smoke the marijuana. A person in the control group, however, may realize that their role as a participant in the experiment will be to provide a baseline of alertness. Depending upon the way the experiment is carried out, a participant in the control group may become bored waiting to take the alertness test, while the experimental group members are kept continually occupied smoking marijuana.

If a difference in alertness is found between the two groups, how can the experimenter be sure that it is not due to the different expectations of the participants in the two groups? For example, the participants who smoked marijuana might expect that they will be unable to do the task and may try less than those in the control group. The participants in the control group may be bored or annoyed at having to wait for the other group. To eliminate this, and other related possibilities, the experimenter must design a control group experience that equalizes these factors. The experimenter must make all of the participants in this experiment believe that they are being treated in the same way (that is, that they are all smoking marijuana prior to the alertness test) and must keep them occupied to the same degree. To do this, the experimenter might create an inert substance that smells like marijuana. The participants in the control group would smoke this inert substance and would be told that they are smoking marijuana. They would, therefore, be subject to all of the same anticipatory effects as those in the experimental group and would also be similarly occupied throughout the experimental session. The experimenter can then be more certain that the differences in alertness found between the experimental and control groups can be attributed to the experimental manipulation, or in this case, the potency of the marijuana.

After the participants in the experimental group have smoked the marijuana, the behaviors of the two groups are compared. We choose to study how fast the subjects will react when asked to make a simple hand movement in response to a flash of light. We also decide to ask them how well they thought they performed this task. When we analyze the results, we find that the subjects who smoked the marijuana were slower in reacting to the flash of light but actually thought they did better than those who did not smoke marijuana. We then conclude that smoking marijuana decreases alertness but increases confidence.

Independent and Dependent Variables

The **independent variable** *is the manipulated, influential, experimental factor in an experiment.* The label *independent* is used because this variable can be changed independently of other factors. In the marijuana experiment, the amount of marijuana smoked was the independent variable. The experimenter manipulated how much marijuana the subjects used *independently* of all other factors. The **dependent variable** *is the factor that is measured in an experiment;* it may change as the independent variable is manipulated. The label *dependent* is used because this variable depends on what happens to the subjects in the experiment. In the marijuana experiment, the dependent variable was represented by two measures: a task that measures reaction time to determine alertness and a question to evaluate confidence. The subjects' responses on these measures depended on the influence of the independent variable (whether or not marijuana was smoked). An illustration of the nature of the experimental strategy, applied to the marijuana study, is shown in figure 4.

Remember that the correlational study of the relation between stress and blood pressure gave us little indication of whether stress influences blood pressure, or vice versa. This is because we had not established time precedence, or in other words, showed that the job stress preceded the high blood pressure condition. This leaves open the possibility that a third confounding factor may have caused the correlation. The following example of stress management and high blood pressure allows us to make conclusions about *causality* (Irvine & others, 1986). Thirty-two men and women with high blood pressure were randomly assigned to either a group who were trained in relaxation and stress management (experimental group) or a group who received no training (control group). This random assignment minimizes the possibility of confounding factors due to the groups' differing in any important ways before the experiment. This strategy is highly preferable to one in which participants are chosen and assigned to groups based on whether they have high- or low-stress jobs, or based on their own complaints of an inability to manage stress.

The independent variable consisted of ten weekly 1-hour sessions that included educational information about the nature of stress and how to manage it, as well as extensive training in learning to relax and control stress in everyday life. The blood pressure of both groups was assessed before the training program and 3 months after it was completed. The measurement of stress management both before and after the treatment allows the researcher to assess the time precedence of the blood pressure reduction with respect to the treatment. At the 3-month follow-up, the subjects' blood pressure was measured by nurses who did not know which groups the subjects had been in. The results indicated that the relaxation and stress management program (the independent variable) was effective in reducing high blood pressure.

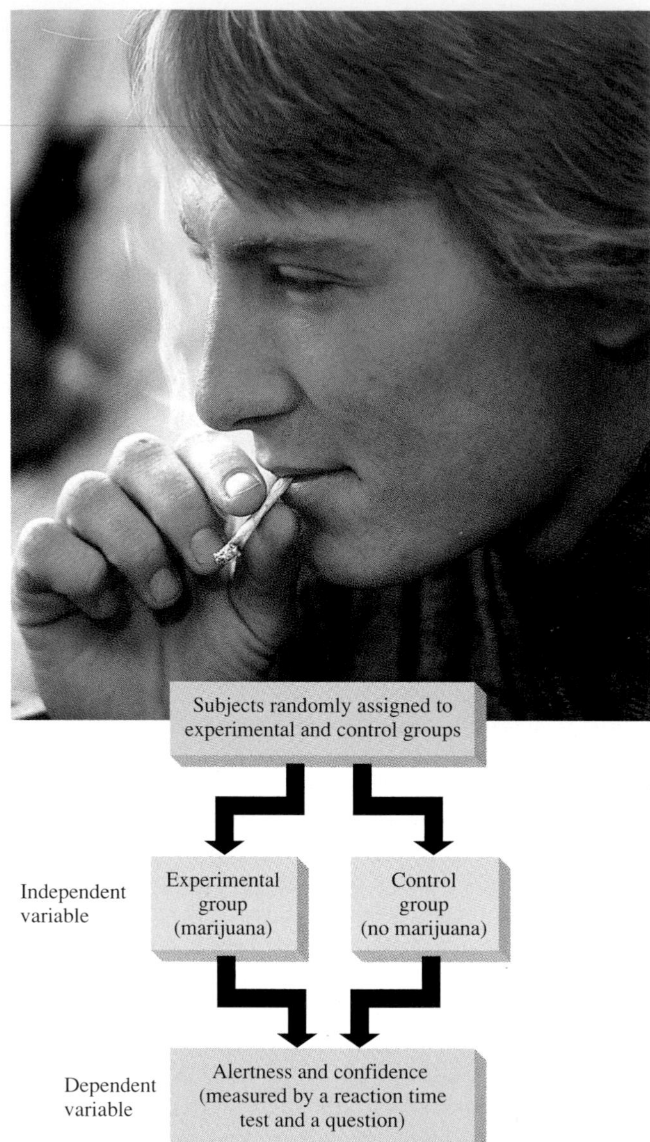

FIGURE 4

The Experimental Strategy in Psychology
This example of the experimental strategy regards the effects of marijuana on alertness and confidence.

It might seem that we should always choose an experimental strategy over a correlational strategy, since the experimental strategy gives us a better sense of the influence of one variable on another. But there are three instances when a correlational strategy might be preferred: (1) when the focus of the investigation is so new (as when AIDS first appeared) that we have little knowledge of which variables to manipulate; (2) when it is impossible to manipulate the variables (such as factors involved in suicide); and (3) when it is unethical to manipulate the variables (for example, determining the association between illness and exposure to dangerous chemicals).

Challenges in Psychological Research

Now that we have considered the basic ways that psychologists conduct research, let's explore some of the challenges in psychological research, such as ethical considerations and whether psychology is value free, sexist bias, and how to become a wise consumer of psychological information.

Ethics and Values

There are three reasons why you need to know about ethics and values in psychology (and in other related disciplines). The first, and most important, is that we are active members of society in the age of information and technology. At the beginning of this chapter, we read about some of the ways that the results of scientific research in psychology and other domains affect our daily lives. As technology advances, the tools and methods available to scientists are becoming more and more sophisticated. Research in the United States and in many other countries is often supported by government grants. Since the allocation of grant money is highly competitive—not only within the scientific community, but also between science and other government-sponsored projects—we must continually set an agenda prioritizing the lines of research we believe are the most beneficial to society. In recent years, for example, the crisis of AIDS has necessitated a shifting of priorities in ways that could not have been anticipated only a decade ago. In addition to questions about what lines of research are important and beneficial, with the explosion in technology society must grapple with looming ethics questions concerning research applications that were unimaginable only a few decades ago (Kimmel, 1996). Should parents be able to determine the sex of their children? Should embryos left over from procedures for increasing fertility in sterile couples be frozen and potentially be used in other research; or should they be discarded?

Science must walk a fine line between the pursuit of knowledge and the application of such knowledge (Hoagwood, Jensen, & Fisher 1996). What science learns through research, society must continually evaluate and apply in ways that it deems ethical. The same line of research that may some day enable previously sterile couples to have children may also enable perspective parents "to call up order" the characteristics they prefer in their children. Similarly, the knowledge that may someday noticeably tip the balance of males and females in the world may also prevent suffering and unnecessary death. The line of research that enables previously sterile couples to have children is the line of research capable of creating excess frozen embryos to be passed about in the courts as a part of a divorce settlement: the house, the car, and the frozen embryos.

The second reason that you need to understand ethics and values in psychology is that some, if not all, of you will undoubtedly serve as participants in psychological research at some point in your life. As such, you need to know about your rights as a participant and about the responsibilities researchers have in assuring that these rights are carefully safeguarded. For the time being, questions concerning ethics in research in psychology are somewhat less dramatic than the analogous questions discussed in the biological sciences. Nonetheless, the issues concerning ethics in research are just as real in psychology as in these other domains. When Anne and Pete, two 19-year-old college students, agreed to participate in an investigation of dating couples, they did not consider the possibility that the questionnaire they completed would stimulate them to think about issues that might lead to conflict in their relationship, and possibly even end it. One year after the study was conducted, 9 of 10 participants said they had discussed their answers with their dating partner (Rubin & Mitchell, 1976). In most instances the discussions helped to strengthen the relationships. But in some cases the participants used the questionnaire as a springboard to discuss problems or concerns previously hidden. One participant said, "The study definitely played a role in ending my relationship with Larry." In this case, the couple had different views about how long they expected to be together. She was thinking of a short-term dating relationship only, while he was thinking in terms of a lifetime. Their answers to the questions brought the disparity in their views to the surface and led to the end of their relationship.

The last, but by no means the least, of the reasons you need to know about ethics and values in conducting psychological research is that many of you may some day be experimenters. This may take the form of carrying out an experimental project in a psychology course, in graduate school, or ultimately in a career in experimental psychology. Students, even very smart and concerned students, frequently do not consider the rights of the participants who serve in their experiments. One student might think, "I volunteer in a home for the mentally retarded several hours per week. I can use the residents of the home in my study to see if a particular treatment helps improve the resident's memory for everyday tasks." We will see below that well-meaning, kindly, and considerately conceived studies like this one, without proper permissions and consents from the people responsible for the welfare of these individuals, constitute flagrant violations of the rights of the participants. We next turn to the exact nature of these rights and the concomitant responsibilities of experimenters.

Ethics Guidelines of the American Psychological Association

At first glance, you would not imagine that a questionnaire on dating relationships would have any substantial impact on those who participate in the research. But psychologists increasingly recognize that considerable caution must be taken to ensure the well-being of the participants in a psychological study. Today colleges and universities have review boards that evaluate the ethical nature of research conducted at their institutions. Proposed research plans must pass the scrutiny of a research ethics committee before the research can be initiated. In addition, the American Psychological Association (APA) has developed ethics guidelines for its members.

The code of ethics adopted by the APA instructs psychologists to protect their participants, often called research subjects, from mental and physical harm. The best interest of the subjects needs to be kept foremost in the researcher's mind (Rosnow, 1995). All subjects must give their informed consent to participate in the research study, which requires that subjects know what their participation will involve and any risks that might develop. For example, research subjects who are dating should be told beforehand that a questionnaire may stimulate thoughts about issues in their relationship that they haven't considered. Subjects also should be informed that in some instances a discussion of the issues raised can improve their dating relationship, while in other cases it can worsen the relationship and even end it. Even after informed consent is given, subjects retain the right to withdraw from the study at any time and for any reason. Experimenters are responsible for keeping all of the data that they gather on individuals completely confidential and when possible completely anonymous. Experimenters have a responsibility to debrief subjects. **Debriefing** *consists of informing subjects of the purpose and methods used in a psychological study when the study is completed.* In most cases it is possible to inform subjects generally about the purpose of the experiment beforehand without "giving away" information about the predicted results that might enable subjects to anticipate how the experimenter wants them to behave or respond.

Deception is an ethical issue that has been debated extensively by psychologists (Whitley, 1996). In some circumstances, telling the subject beforehand what the research study is about substantially alters the subject's behavior and invalidates an investigator's data. For example, a psychologist wants to know whether a bystander will report a theft. A mock theft is staged, and the psychologist observes which bystanders report it. Had the psychologist informed the bystanders beforehand that the study intended to discover the percentage of bystanders who will report a theft, the whole study would have been undermined. In all cases of deception, the psychologist must ensure that the deception will not harm the subject and that the subject will be told the complete nature of the study (debriefed) as soon as possible after the study is completed.

Values

Questions are asked not only about the ethics of psychology, but also about the values of psychology. Values involve standards about what is worthwhile and desirable. Some psychologists argue that psychology should be value free and morally neutral. From their perspective, the psychologist's role as a scientist is to present facts in as value-free a fashion as possible (Kimble, 1989). Others believe that, since psychologists are human, they are not value free, even if they try to be. On the other hand, some people argue that psychologists should take stands on value-laden issues. For example, if research shows that day care in the first year of life is harmful to children's development, shouldn't psychologists support reforms to improve day care or mandates to have businesses give one parent up to a year of paid leave after the child is born? More information about psychology and values appears in Explorations in Psychology 2.

How Ethical Is Research with Animals?

The annual meetings of the American Psychological Association (APA) over the past decades have frequently been the target of animal welfare and animal rights activists, who often chant slogans like "Psychologists are killing our animals!" and "Stop the pain and abuse!"

For generations, some psychologists have used animals in their research, which has provided a better understanding of, and solutions for, many human problems. Neal Miller, a leading figure in contemporary psychology who has made important discoveries about the effects of biofeedback on health, listed the following areas where animal research has benefited humans (Miller, 1985):

- Psychotherapy and behavioral medicine
- Rehabilitation of neuromuscular disorders
- Understanding and alleviating effects of stress and pain
- Discovery and testing of drugs to treat anxiety and severe mental illness
- Knowledge about drug addiction and relapse
- Treatments to help premature infants gain weight so they can leave the hospital sooner
- Knowledge about memory used to alleviate deficits of memory in old age

How widespread is animal research in psychology? Only about 5 percent of APA members use animals in their research. Rats and mice are by far the most widely used, accounting for 90 percent of all psychological research with animals. How widespread is abuse to animals in psychological research? According to animal welfare and rights activists, it is extensive. It is true that researchers sometimes use procedures that would be unethical with humans, but they are guided by a stringent set of standards that address such matters as housing, feeding, and the psychological well-being of animals. Researchers are required to weigh the potential benefit of the research against the possible harm to the animal and to avoid inflicting unnecessary pain. Animal abuse simply is not as common as animal activist groups charge. However, stringent ethical guidelines must be followed when animals or humans are the subjects in psychological research (Herzog, 1995).

Reducing Sexist Research

Traditional science is presented as being value free and, thus, a valid way of studying mental processes and behavior. However, there is a growing consensus that science in

Explorations in Psychology 2

Psychology and Values

Controversy swirls about the issue of whether psychology is value free. As a science, psychology is dedicated to discovering facts about behavior and creating theories to explain those facts. In this abstract description, values do not crop up. The scientific system requires only that psychology discover the most dependable facts and generate the best theories possible (Kimble, 1989). Is this reality, though? No, reality is more complex (Reed, Turiel, & Brown, 1995; Seligman, Olson, & Zanna, 1996).

Reality is more complex because psychology deals with living organisms. Researchers' values influence their choice of research questions. A divorced single parent may decide to study the inadequate involvement of male noncustodial parents in their children's development rather than the increased role of males in caring for children, for example. Each of us also has preconceived ideas about behavior. Consider the values involved in such questions as the right to own guns versus handgun control, bans on sexually explicit books versus freedom of literary expression, the public's right to know versus an individual's right to privacy, retribution versus rehabilitation as the goal of criminal codes, a verdict of "not guilty by reason of insanity" versus "guilty but insane," and "freedom of choice" versus "right to life." Our personal values related to these questions may influence the way we perceive and label behavior. One individual may call a sexual act "a sexual variation"; another individual may label the same act "sick." One individual may label a female's assertive behavior as "too aggressive"; another individual may label the same behavior as "competent." One individual may observe a male's long hours of work and label the behavior "overachieving" or "workaholic," whereas another individual may call the same behavior "maximizing potential."

When psychologists are called on as experts, they often make statements and recommendations that also are laden with values. The therapist you consult about your problems may have certain personal values about sexual conduct that influence the advice he gives; the professor in your class may have certain personal values about moral behavior, child rearing, and how to get ahead in life that she communicates to you; and a psychologist interviewed by Ted Koppel on "Nightline" may have certain values about government's responsibility in caring for the homeless, an adolescent's level of responsibility in dealing cocaine, and a mentally disordered individual's responsibility in committing mass murder. In sum, although psychology often strives to reduce the role of values as it seeks the truths of human behavior, in the court of life, which is psychology's setting, values and psychology are difficult to disentangle.

Florence Denmark (shown here talking with a group of students) has developed a number of guidelines for nonsexist research. Denmark and others believe that psychology needs to be challenged to examine the world in a new way, one that incorporates girls' and women's perspectives.

general and psychology in particular are not value free (Paludi, 1995). A special concern is that the vast majority of psychological research has been male oriented and male dominated. Some researchers believe that male-dominated sciences, such as psychology, need to be challenged to examine the world in a new way, one that incorporates girls' and women's perspectives and respects their ethnicity, sexual orientation, age, and socioeconomic status. For example, Florence Denmark and her colleagues (1988) provided the following three recommendations as guidelines for nonsexist research:

1. **Research methods**

   Problem: The selection of research participants is based on stereotypic assumptions and does not allow for generalizations to other groups.
   Example: On the basis of stereotypes about who should be responsible for contraception, only females are studied.
   Correction: Both sexes should be studied before conclusions are drawn about the factors that determine contraception use.

2. **Data analysis**

   Problem: Gender differences are inaccurately magnified.
   Example: "Whereas only 24 percent of the girls were found to . . . fully 28 percent of the boys were . . ."
   Correction: The results should include extensive descriptions of the data so that differences are not exaggerated.

3. **Conclusions**

   Problem: The title or abstract (summary) of an article makes no reference to the limitations of the study participants and implies a broader scope of the study than is warranted.
   Example: A study purporting to be about "perceptions of the disabled" examines only blind White boys.
   Correction: Use more precise titles and clearly describe the sample and its selection criteria in the abstract or summary.

Being a Wise Consumer of Psychological Information

Psychological research is increasingly talked about in the media. Television, radio, newspapers, and magazines all frequently report on research that is likely to be of interest to the general public. Many professional and mental health and psychological organizations regularly supply the media with information about research. In many cases, this information has been published in professional journals or presented at national meetings, and most major colleges and universities have a media relations department that contacts the press about current research by their faculty.

Not all psychological information that is presented for public consumption comes from professionals with excellent credentials and reputations at colleges or universities or in applied mental health settings. Because journalists, television reporters, and other media personnel are not trained in psychology, it is not an easy task for them to sort through the widely varying material they see and make a sound decision about the best psychological information to present to the public.

Unfortunately, the media often focus on sensationalistic and dramatic psychological findings. They want you to read what they have written or stay tuned to their channel. They hope to capture your attention and keep it by presenting dramatic, sensationalistic, and surprising information. As a consequence, media presentations of psychological information tend to go beyond what actual research articles and clinical findings really say.

Even when excellent research is presented to the public, it is difficult for media personnel to adequately inform people about what has been found and the implications for their lives. For example, throughout this text you will be introduced to an entirely new vocabulary. Each time we present a new concept we precisely define it and give examples of it as well. We have an entire book to carry out our task of carefully introducing, defining, and elaborating on key concepts and issues, research, and clinical findings. The media, however, do not have the luxury of time and space to detail and specify the limitations and qualifications of research. They often have only a few minutes or a few lines to summarize as best they can the complex findings of a study or a psychological concept.

Nomothetic Research and Idiographic Needs

In being a wise consumer of psychological information it is important to understand the difference between nomothetic research and idiographic needs. **Nomothetic research** *is conducted at the level of the group.* Most psychological research is nomothetic research. Individual variations in how subjects respond is often not a major focus of the research. For example, if researchers are interested in the effects of divorce on an adult's ability to cope with stress, they might conduct a study of 50 divorced women and 50 married women. They might find that divorced women, as a group, cope more poorly with stress than married women do. This is a nomothetic finding that applies to divorced women as a group. Nomothetic findings are commonly reported in the media. In this particular study, some of the divorced women were probably coping better with stress than some of the married women—not as many, but some. Indeed, it is entirely possible that of the 100 women in the study, the two or three women who were coping the very best with stress were divorced women; it would still be accurate, though, to report the findings as showing that divorced women (as a group) cope more poorly with stress than married women (as a group) do.

As a consumer of psychological information, you want to know what the information means for you *individually,* not necessarily what it means for a group of people. **Idiographic needs** *are needs that are important for the individual, not for the group.* The failure of the media to adequately distinguish between nomothetic research and idiographic needs is not entirely their fault—researchers have not adequately done this either. Researchers too often fail to examine overlap between groups and present only the differences that are found. When those differences are reported, too often they are stated as if there is no overlap between the groups being compared (in our example, divorced and married women), when in reality there is substantial overlap. If you read a study in a research journal or a media report which states that divorced women coped more poorly with stress than married women did, it does not mean that all divorced women coped more poorly than all married women. It simply means that as a group divorced women coped better—it does not mean that you, if you are a divorced woman, cope poorly.

Overgeneralization Based on a Small Sample

There often isn't space or time in media presentations of psychological information to go into details about the nature of the sample. Sometimes you will get basic information about the sample's size—whether it is based on 10 subjects, 50 subjects, or 200 subjects, for example. In many cases, small or very small samples require that care be exercised in generalizing to a larger population of individuals. For example, if a study of divorced women is based on only 10 or 20 divorced women, study findings may not generalize to all divorced women because the sample investigated may have some unique characteristics. The sample might have a high income, be White American, be childless, live in a small southern town, and be undergoing psychotherapy. In this study, then, we clearly would be making unwarranted generalizations if we thought the findings might automatically characterize divorced women who have moderate to low incomes, are from other ethnic backgrounds, have children, are living in different contexts, and are not undergoing psychotherapy.

A Single Study Is Usually Not the Defining Word About an Issue or Problem

The media might identify an interesting piece of research or a clinical finding and claim that it is something phenomenal with far-reaching implications. While such studies and findings do occur, it is rare for a single study to provide earth-shattering and conclusive answers, especially answers that apply to all people. In fact, in most psychological domains where there are many investigations, finding conflicting results about a particular topic or issue is not unusual. Answers to questions in research usually emerge after many scientists have conducted similar investigations that yield similar conclusions. Thus, a report of one research study should not be taken as the absolute, final answer on a problem.

In our example of divorce, if one study reports that a particular therapy conducted by a therapist has been especially effective with divorced adults, we should not conclude that the therapy will work as effectively with all divorced adults and with other therapists until more studies are conducted.

Causal Conclusions Cannot Be Made from Correlational Studies

Drawing causal conclusions from correlational studies is one of the most common mistakes made by the media. In studies in which a true experiment has not been conducted (in an experiment, subjects are randomly assigned to treatments or experiences), two variables or factors might have only a *noncausal* relation to each other. Remember from our discussion of correlation earlier in the chapter that causal interpretations cannot be made when two or more factors are simply correlated. We cannot say that one causes the other. In the case of divorce, a headline might read "Low income causes divorced women to have a high degree of stress." We read the article and find out the headline was derived from the results of a research study. Since we obviously cannot, for ethical or practical purposes, randomly assign women to become divorced or stay married, and for the same reasons we cannot randomly assign divorced women to be poor or rich, this headline is based on a correlational study, on which such causal statements cannot be accurately based. The low income might have caused the divorced women to have low self-esteem, but for some of the women low self-esteem might have hurt their chances for having a higher income. Their low self-esteem likely is related to other factors as well—factors such as inadequate societal supports, a history of criticism from an ex-husband, and so on.

Always Consider the Source of the Psychological Information and Evaluate Its Credibility

Studies conducted by psychologists are not automatically accepted by the research community. The researchers usually must submit their findings to a research or clinical journal where it is reviewed by their colleagues, who make a decision about whether to publish the paper or not. While quality of research and clinical findings in journals is not uniform, in most cases they have undergone far greater scrutiny and careful consideration of the quality of the work than for what is reported in the media. Within the media, though, a distinction can usually be drawn between what is presented in respected newspapers, such as the *New York Times* and *Washington Post,* as well as credible magazines, such as *Time* and *Newsweek,* and much less respected and less credible tabloids, such as the *National Inquirer* and *Star.*

At this point we have discussed a number of ideas about strategies for conducting research and challenges in psychological research. A summary of these ideas is presented in concept table 2.

Concept Table 2

Strategies for Setting Up Research Studies and Challenges in Psychological Research

Concept	Processes/Related Ideas	Characteristics/Description
Strategies for Setting Up Research Studies	Correlational strategy	This strategy describes how strongly two or more events or characteristics are related. The correlational strategy does not allow causal statements to be made.
	Experimental strategy	The experimental strategy allows us to precisely determine behavior's causes. The psychologist accomplishes this task by performing an experiment, which is a carefully regulated procedure in which one or more of the factors believed to influence the behavior being studied is manipulated and all others are held constant. If the behavior under study changes when a factor is manipulated, we say that the manipulated factor causes the behavior to change. To establish cause, we have to show that the two factors covary, that time precedence occurs, and that confounding factors have been eliminated. Good experiments meet three criteria: internal validity, external validity, and reliability.
	Random assignment	This occurs when psychologists assign subjects to experimental and control groups by chance, thus reducing the likelihood that the results of the experiment will be due to some preexisting differences in the two groups.
	Experimental and control groups	The experimental group is the group whose experience is manipulated. The control group is a comparison group treated like the experimental group in every way except for the manipulated factor.
	Independent and dependent variables	The independent variable is the manipulated, influential, experimental factor in an experiment. The label *independent* is used because this variable can be changed independently of other factors. The dependent variable is the factor that is measured in an experiment; it may change as the independent variable is manipulated.
Challenges in Psychological Research	Ethics and values	Researchers must ensure the well-being of subjects. The risk of physical and mental harm must be reduced, informed consent should occur, and deception should be used with caution. Whether psychology should be value free is currently debated. Controversy also currently surrounds the use of animals in psychological research, although abuse is not nearly as widespread as some activists charge.
	Reducing sexist research	A special concern is that the vast majority of psychological research has been male oriented and male dominated. Some researchers believe that psychologists need to be challenged to examine behavior in a new way, one that incorporates the female's perspective. Recommendations have been made for conducting nonsexist research.
	Being a wise consumer of psychological information	This requires being skeptical about what is presented in the media, understanding the distinction between nomothetic research and idiographic needs, evaluating overgeneralization based on a small sample, knowing that a single study is usually not the defining word about an issue or problem, recognizing that causal conclusions cannot be drawn from correlational studies, and always considering the source of the psychological information and evaluating its credibility.

Critical Thinking About Behavior

Personal Versus Psychological Evidence

What is needed is not the will to believe, but the wish to find out.

Bertrand Russell

You have read about the history and scope of psychology and the current methods psychologists use in observing, describing, explaining, and predicting behavior. Just how different are psychology-based ways of thinking from the processes you go through when you are making judgments about behavior? There are some critical differences.

1. **Precise descriptions of behaviors.** Psychologists are exacting in how they define and describe behaviors, being especially careful to distinguish descriptions of behavior from other inferences or interpretations that can be made *about* behavior. We are constantly confronted with behaviors that we must examine and interpret, prompting us to come to conclusions, infer meanings, or make predictions about behavior; however, psychologists are inclined to be precise in their observations and cautious about their inferences. When confronted with a challenging behavior, critical thinkers trained in psychology are likely to ask, *"What exactly do you mean by . . . ?"*
2. **Reliance on systematic observation.** Nonscientific explanations of behavior correspond reasonably well to the first stage of the scientific method: identifying and analyzing a problem. It is in the second stage of the scientific method that scientific and nonscientific ways of interpreting behavior diverge. Scientists collect data systematically, interpret the data, and revise their conclusions or beliefs, based on these interpretations.

   This procedure reflects a strong preference for conclusions that are based on objective data derived from carefully planned behavioral research rather than subjective conclusions that might not be carefully considered or are more likely to reflect unknown biases of the observer. When confronted with a conclusion about behavior, the critical thinker trained in psychology is likely to ask, *"What's your evidence for this conclusion?"*
3. **Pursuit of alternative explanations.** Many questions that we ponder about behavior might not lend themselves easily to objective research. In the absence of systematic observation and scientific interpretation, psychologists are likely to question whether there could be other explanations for the behavior being examined. They actively speculate about other variables that could influence the behavior, demonstrating a thinking characteristic that could be described as being *variable-minded.* Psychologists are likely to ask, *"Are there other plausible ways to explain the behavior?"*

You might already have formed some conclusions about the following examples of behaviors. What happens to your conclusions when you adopt psychological ways of examining behavior, when you ask for clarity, inquire about evidence, and look for alternative explanations?

- Magicians are well known for making objects disappear. *Do they really make objects vanish, or can you think of an alternative explanation for this compelling illusion?*
- Seeing a loved one ushering you through a tunnel toward a bright white light is an example of an experience commonly reported by people having a near-death experience. *Is this a confirmation of an afterlife, or could this phenomenon be explained in another way?*
- In psychotherapy, some individuals are startled by their recovery of memories that suggest they have been physically or emotionally abused in childhood. How could it be that something so horrifying isn't remembered until some point quite distant from the event? *How many variables or influences might be involved in understanding this phenomenon?*
- Some people are convinced that they have extrasensory powers. They claim to know in advance or from a distance when bad things happen to their relatives, to be able to predict songs that are about to come on the radio, and so on. *Is this phenomenon real? What evidence is there for extrasensory abilities? Are there other explanations that account for the behavior?*
- Two twins, separated at birth and raised apart, are reunited to discover that they have an uncanny number of similarities. Their reunion prompts strong speculation regarding the power of genetic influence in shaping behavior. *Is this research definitive "proof" of the power of inheritance, or are there other plausible ways to explain the remarkable number of similarities?*
- Many individuals believe that the growing problem of violence in our culture is a direct influence of violence portrayed in movies and television. *What evidence supports this position? Is violence really growing? What other factors might contribute to this important problem?*

You may have thought about some research strategies that could help you to evaluate the quality of conclusions about behavior. You will find out how these questions and others will be evaluated in the chapters that follow.

We began this chapter by exploring the nature of theory and the scientific method. Then we turned our attention to methods, including measures and strategies for setting up psychological research. Our coverage of measures focused on observation, interviews and questionnaires, case studies, standardized tests, cross-cultural research and research with ethnic minority groups, and physiological research and research with animals. The discussion of strategies for setting up research studies emphasized the correlational strategy and the experimental strategy. To conclude the chapter, we studied some challenges in psychological research—ethics and values, sexism, and being a wise consumer of psychological information. Don't forget that you can obtain an overall summary of the chapter by again studying the two concept tables on pages 34 and 44.

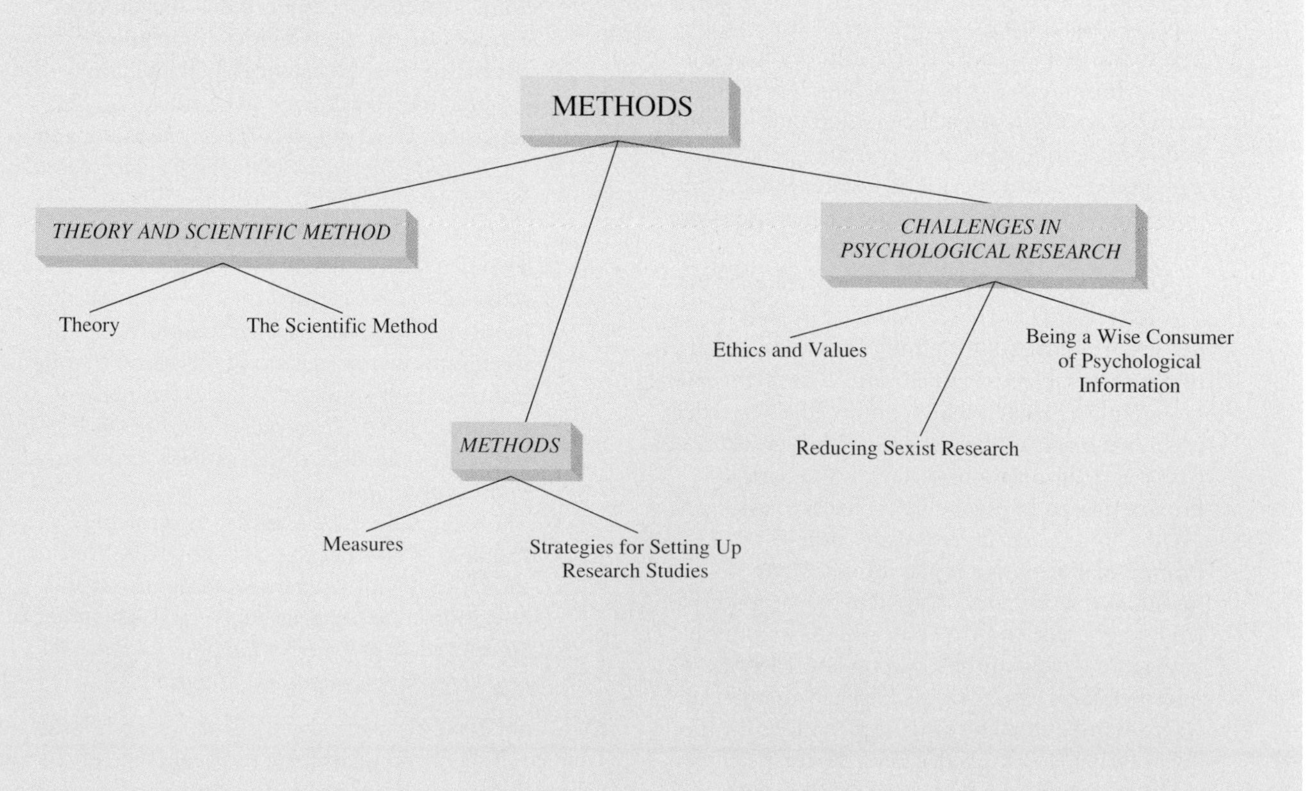

Key Terms

theory A coherent set of ideas that helps to explain data and make predictions. A theory has hypotheses. p. 26

hypotheses Assumptions that can be tested to determine their accuracy. p. 26

scientific method An approach used to discover accurate information. It includes the following steps: identify and analyze the problem, collect data, draw conclusions, and revise theories. p. 26

laboratory A controlled setting with many of the complex factors of the "real world" removed. p. 28

naturalistic observation The observation of behavior in real-world settings, with no effort made to manipulate or control the situation. p. 29

questionnaire A measure that is similar to a highly structured interview except that respondents read the questions and mark their answers on a sheet of paper rather than respond directly to the interviewer. p. 30

random sample A sample for which every member of a population or group had an equal chance of being selected. p. 30

case study An in-depth look at one individual. Clinical psychologists use case studies when, for either practical or ethical reasons, they cannot duplicate the unique aspects of an individual's life for study. p. 30

standardized tests Test that requires people to answer a series of written or oral questions and that has two distinct features: (1) The individual's score is totaled to yield a single score, or set of scores, that reflects something about that individual; and (2) the individual's score is compared with the scores of a large group of similar people to determine how the individual responded relative to others. p. 31

emic approach An approach to research in which the goal is to describe behavior in one culture or ethnic group in terms that are meaningful and important to the people in that culture or ethnic group, without regard to other cultures or ethnic groups. p. 31

etic approach An approach to research in which the goal is to describe behavior in terms that allow cross-cultural generalizations to be made. p. 31

ethnic gloss The use of an ethnic label, such as *African American, Latino, Asian,* or *Native American,* in a superficial way that makes an ethnic group seem more homogeneous than it actually is. p. 32

correlational strategy A strategy in which the goal is to describe the strength of the relation between two or more events or characteristics. p. 35

experimental strategy A strategy that allows us to precisely determine behavior's causes. p. 36

experiment A carefully regulated procedure where one or more of the factors believed to influence the behavior being studied is manipulated and all the others are held constant. If the behavior under study changes when a factor is manipulated, we say that the manipulated factor causes the behavior to change. p. 36

covary The value of one factor varies with the other factor. p. 36

time precedence The appearance of the causal factor before the caused factor. p. 36

confounding factors Other uncontrolled factors that covary coincidentally with the causal factor. p. 36

internal validity In experimental psychology, an experiment's capacity to generate causal inferences; a good experiment has internal validity. p. 36

external validity The capacity of an experiment's results to be generalized to the population of interest; a good experiment has external validity. p. 36

reliability The extent to which an experiment can be repeated with the same results; a good experiment has high reliability. p. 36

random assignment The assignment of subjects to experimental and control conditions by chance. This practice reduces the probability that the results of the experiment will be due to preexisting differences in the two groups. p. 37

experimental group The group whose experience is manipulated. p. 37

control group A comparison group treated in every way like the experimental group except for the manipulated factor. The control group serves as a baseline against which the effects found in the manipulated condition can be compared. p. 37

independent variable The manipulated, influential, experimental factor in an experiment. p. 38

dependent variable The factor that is measured in an experiment; it might change when the independent variable is manipulated. p. 38

debriefing Informing subjects of the purpose and methods used in a psychological study when the study is completed. p. 40

nomothetic research Research that takes place at the level of the group. p. 42

idiographic needs Needs that are important for the individual, not for the group. p. 43

Resources and Readings in Psychology

Ethics for Psychology (1994)
by Mathilda Center, Bruce Bennett, Stanley Jones, and Thomas Nagey
Washington, DC: American Psychological Association

This book provides an overview of the process of ethical decision making and describes the nature of the American Psychological Association. The ethical standards that guide psychological research are clearly spelled out.

Guidelines for Ethical Conduct in the Care and Use of Animals (1993)
Science Directorate
American Psychological Association
750 First Street, NE
Washington, DC 20002–4242

This pamphlet was developed by the American Psychological Association's Committee on Animal Research and Ethics (CARE). It profiles guidelines for the appropriate care and use of animals in research.

How to Think Straight About Psychology (1996, 4th ed.)
by David Stanovich
New York: HarperCollins

This charming text explores how psychologists think about behavior, with a special emphasis on creating and defending arguments about the validity of cause-and-effect relations. The author offers many examples of classic research in psychology and also explores why psychologists struggle to gain respect from other sciences. The author refers to psychology as the "Rodney Dangerfield of the sciences" because of its image problem. Among the important psychological concepts examined by Stanovich are operationism, converging evidence, experimental control, the role of statistics, correlation, and causation.

Publication Manual of the American Psychological Association (4th ed., 1994)
Washington, DC: American Psychological Association

This is the style manual used by researchers and students in psychology and other behavioral and social sciences. The manual provides publication information that includes the topics of organization, writing, submitting manuscripts, reducing bias in the language, referencing, and general policies and ethics in scientific publication.

The Science Game (1993)
by Sandra Pyke and Neil Agnew
Englewood Cliffs, NJ: Prentice Hall

This popular book covers, in an entertaining and informative way, a number of important ideas about conducting research in psychology.

CHAPTER

BFB

Biological Foundations and the Brain

JEAN DUBUFFET
Table de Barbe, detail

CHAPTER

BFB

Biological Foundations and the Brain

Chapter Outline

Chapter Boxes

Swiftly the brain becomes an enchanted loom, where millions of flashing shuttles weave a dissolving pattern—always a meaningful pattern—though never an abiding one.

—Sir Charles Sherrington

There is a grandeur in this view of life. . . whilst this planet has gone cycling on according to the fixed law of gravity, from so simple a beginning endless forms most beautiful and wonderful have been, and are being evolved.

—Charles Darwin

Images of Psychology

The Jim and Jim Twins

Jim Springer and Jim Lewis are identical twins. They were separated at the age of 4 weeks and didn't see one another again until they were 39 years old. Even so, they share uncanny similarities that read more like fiction than fact. For example, they have both worked as a part-time deputy sheriff, have vacationed in Florida, have driven Chevrolets, have had dogs named Toy, and have married and divorced women named Betty. In addition, one twin named his son James Allan, and the other named his son James Alan. Both like math but not spelling, and both enjoy carpentry and mechanical drawing. They have chewed their fingernails down to the nubs and have almost identical drinking and smoking habits. Both have had hemorrhoids, put on ten pounds at about the same time, and first suffered headaches at the age of 18. They also have similar sleep patterns.

The Jim twins: how coincidental? Springer, right, and Lewis were unaware of each other for 40 years.

Jim and Jim have some differences as well. One wears his hair over his forehead, whereas the other wears it slicked back with sideburns. One expresses himself better verbally; the other is more proficient in writing. For the most part, however, they are more alike than different.

The Jim and Jim twins were part of the Minnesota Study of Twins Reared Apart, directed by Thomas Bouchard and his colleagues (1996). The researchers brought identical (genetically identical because they come from the same fertilized egg) and fraternal (genetically dissimilar because they come from different fertilized eggs) twins from all over the world to Minneapolis to investigate the psychological aspects of the twins' lives. For example, the twins were interviewed and asked more than 15,000 questions about their family and childhood environment, personal interests, vocational orientation, values, and aesthetic judgments. Detailed medical histories were obtained, including information about their smoking, diet, and exercise habits. The researchers also took chest X rays, and gave heart stress tests, as well as EEGs (brain-wave tests). The twins were also given a number of personality, ability, and intelligence tests (Bouchard & others, 1981).

Separated at birth, the Mallifert twins meet accidentally.

Drawing by Chas. Addams; © 1981 The New Yorker Magazine, Inc.

Critics of conclusions drawn about the genetic basis of behavior in the Minnesota twins study point out that some of the separated twins had been together several months prior to their adoption, that some twins had been reunited prior to their testing (in some cases a number of years earlier), that adoption agencies often place twins in similar homes, and that even strangers who spend several hours together and start comparing their lives are likely to come up with coincidental similarities (Adler, 1991). Still, even in the face of such criticism, the Minnesota study demonstrates the interest scientists have shown in the genetic basis of behavior.

Preview

The bizarre similarities of the Jim and Jim twins raise questions about the role that genes play in human behavior. For example, how are characteristics transmitted from one generation to the next? How did the human species come to be? What gives us our extraordinary ability to adapt to our world? These questions focus on heredity, evolution, nature/nurture, and the brain, this chapter's main topics. We will spend considerable time exploring the brain, one of the most remarkable structures in the universe.

Heredity, the Evolutionary Perspective, and Nature/Nurture

In the words of twentieth-century French essayist Antoine de Saint-Éxupéry, "The seed of the cedar will become cedar, the seed of the bramble can only become bramble." An English proverb says, "That which comes of a cat will catch mice." Why does the bramble become only bramble? Why does the cat catch mice? No matter what the species, there must be a mechanism used to pass the message of inheritance from one generation to the next. That mechanism is heredity.

Heredity

You began life as a single cell, a fertilized human egg, weighing about one-twenty-millionth of an ounce. From this single cell, you developed into a human being made of trillions of cells. The nucleus of each human cell contains 46 **chromosomes,** *which are threadlike structures that come in 23 pairs, one member of each pair coming from each parent.* Chromosomes contain the remarkable genetic substance **deoxyribonucleic acid,** or **DNA,** *a complex molecule that contains genetic information* (see figure 1). **Genes,** *the units of hereditary information, are short segments of chromosomes, composed of DNA. Genes act like blueprints for cells to reproduce themselves and manufacture the proteins that maintain life.* Chromosomes, DNA, and genes can be mysterious. To help you turn your mystification into understanding, see figure 2.

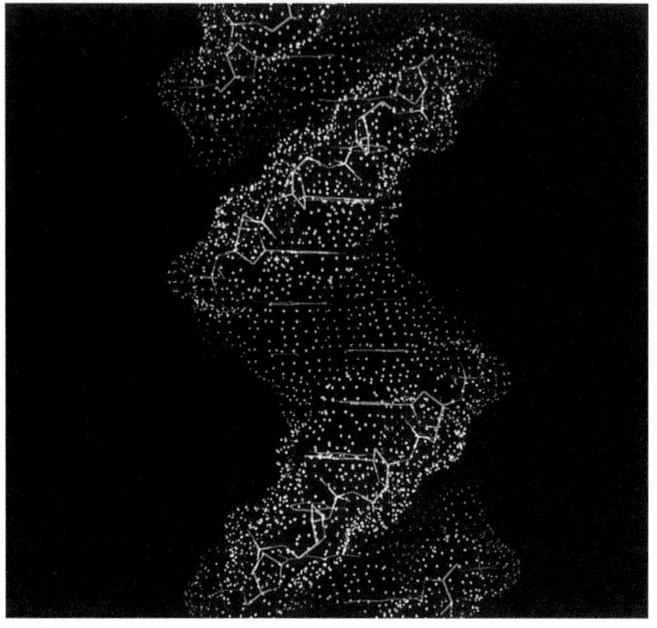

FIGURE 1

The Remarkable Substance Known as DNA

Although we have a long way to go before we unravel all the mysteries about the way genes work, some aspects of heritability are well understood. Every person has two genes for each characteristic governed by heredity. When genes combine to determine our characteristics, some genes are dominant over others. According to the **dominant-recessive genes principle,** *if one gene of a pair is dominant and one is recessive, the dominant gene exerts its effect, overriding the potential influence of the recessive gene. A recessive gene exerts its influence only if both genes of a pair are recessive.* If you inherit a recessive gene from only one parent, you may never know you carry the gene. In the world of dominant-recessive genes, brown eyes, farsightedness, and dimples rule over blue eyes, near-sightedness, and freckles. If you inherit a recessive gene for a trait from both of your parents, you will show the trait. That's why two brown-eyed parents can have a blue-eyed child: Each parent would have a dominant gene for brown eyes and a recessive gene for blue eyes. Since dominant genes override recessive genes, the parents have brown eyes. However, the child can inherit a recessive gene for blue eyes from each parent. With no dominant gene to override them, the recessive genes make the child's eyes blue.

Long before people wondered how brown-eyed parents could possibly bear a blue-eyed child, they wondered what determined a child's sex. Aristotle believed that as the father's sexual excitement increased, so did the odds of producing a son. He was wrong, of course, but it was not until the 1920s that researchers confirmed the existence of human sex chromosomes, the genetic material that determines sex. As already mentioned, humans normally have 46 chromosomes arranged in pairs. The 23rd pair may have two X-shaped chromosomes to produce a female, or it may

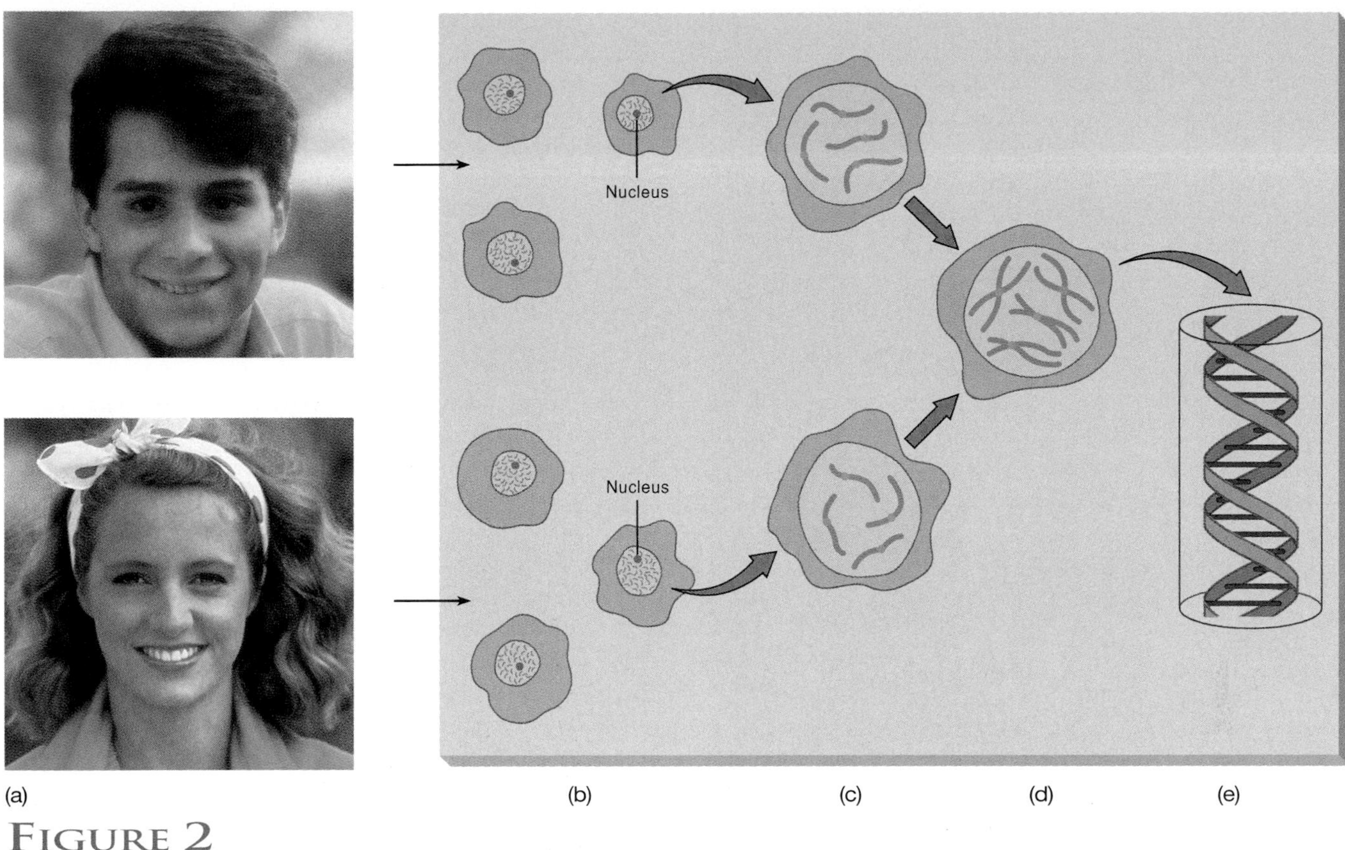

FIGURE 2

Facts About Chromosomes
(*a*) The body contains billions of cells that are organized into tissue and organs. (*b*) Each cell contains a central structure, the nucleus, which controls reproduction. (*c*) Chromosomes reside in the nucleus of each cell. The male's sperm and the female's eggs are specialized reproductive cells that contain chromosomes. (*d*) At conception the offspring receives paired chromosomes from the mother's egg and the father's sperm. (*e*) The chromosomes contain DNA, a chemical substance. Genes are short segments of the DNA molecule. They are the units of hereditary information that act as a blueprint for cells to reproduce themselves and manufacture the proteins that sustain life.

have both an X-shaped and a Y-shaped chromosome to produce a male. The 23rd pair of chromosomes also carries some sex-linked characteristics, such as color blindness or hairy ear rims, both of which are more common in men.

Most genetic transmission is more complex than these rather simple examples. Few psychological characteristics are the result of a single gene pair. Most are determined by the combination of different genes (Tamarin, 1996). Each of us has at least 50,000 genes in our chromosomes. When the 50,000 genes from one parent combine at conception with the 50,000 genes of the other parent, the number of possible combinations—in the trillions—is staggering. No wonder scientists are struck by the complexity of genetic transmission.

The Evolutionary Perspective

Humans are relative newcomers to Earth. If we consider evolution in terms of a calendar year, humans arrived on the planet late in December (Sagan, 1980). Despite our brief existence, we have established ourselves as the most successful and dominant species. As our earliest ancestors left the forests to form hunting societies on the grassy savannas, their thinking and behavior changed. How did these changes in thinking and behavior come about?

Natural Selection

Over time entire species can change through **natural selection,** *the evolutionary process that favors genes that code for design features that are most likely to lead to reproduction and survival.* Also known as "the survival of the fittest," natural selection lies at the heart of Charles Darwin's theory of evolution. Darwin, a nineteenth-century naturalist, sailed to South America to study a multitude of plant and animal species in their natural surroundings. He observed that most organisms reproduce at rates that should result in overpopulation, yet somehow populations remain nearly constant.

Darwin reasoned that each new generation must engage in an intense, constant struggle for food, water, and other resources. In the course of this struggle, many of the young would die. Those who survive would be those who had better adapted to their environment. The survivors would reproduce and, in turn, pass on some of their characteristics to the next generation. Over the course of many generations, the organisms with the characteristics needed for survival (speed and sharp claws in predators or thick fur in Arctic animals, for instance) would make up an increasingly larger percentage of the population. Over many, many

FIGURE 3

The Better an Animal Is Adapted, the More Successful It Becomes Humans, more than any other mammal, adapt to and control most types of environments. Because of longer parental care, humans learn more complex behavior patterns, which contribute to adaptation.

generations, this process could modify the entire population. If environmental conditions were to change, however, other characteristics might be needed and would move the process in a different direction. Darwin published his observations and thoughts in *On the Origin of Species* (1859).

Over a million species have been classified, from bacteria to blue whales, with many varieties of beetles in between. The work of natural selection produced the disappearing acts of moths and the quills of porcupines. The effects of evolution also produced the technological advances, intelligence, and longer parental care of human beings (see figure 3).

Generally, evolution proceeds at a very slow pace. The lines that led to the emergence of human beings and the great apes diverged about 14 million years ago. Modern humans, *Homo sapiens,* came into existence only about 50,000 years ago, and civilization as we know it began about 10,000 years ago. No sweeping evolutionary changes in humans have occurred since then—for example, our brains haven't become 10 times bigger, we haven't developed a third eye in the back of our heads, and we haven't learned to fly.

Sociobiology

Sociobiology *relies on evolutionary biology to explain social behavior.* Sociobiologists believe that psychologists have a restricted understanding of social behavior because they have studied only one mammalian species—*Homo sapiens.* Sociobiology derives its information from the comparison of any of the tens of thousands of animal species that have evolved some form of social life.

According to E. O. Wilson (1975, 1995), the purpose of sociobiology is not to make crude comparisons between animal species or between animals and humans, such as simply comparing wolf and human aggression. Its purpose is to develop general laws of the evolution and biology of social behavior. The hope also is to be able to extend the principles of sociobiology to help explain human behavior.

Let's consider a sociobiology inquiry. In some species of birds, the young born in one year might not breed the next year, but instead help their parents rear the next year's brood. In other instances, adult birds that have lost their mates might help close relatives rear their young. These social systems that involve helping at the nest occur in Florida scrub jays (Woolfenden, 1975), African white-fronted bee-eaters (Emlen, 1984), and acorn woodpeckers in the western United States (Koenig, Mumme, & Pitelka, 1984). Nests with helpers are more successful—the number of young fledged is higher. But in engaging in such helping behavior, helpers expend energy that does not benefit their own progeny. Sociobiologists are interested in how such helping behavior evolved and what the advantages are for helping or not helping.

Sociobiology has stimulated interest in the relation between animal and human behavior, focused attention on the costs and benefits of behavior, directed inquiry toward individual and group differences, highlighted the role of ecology in behavior, and broadened our understanding of behavior's causes (Crawford, 1987).

Nonetheless, sociobiology is not without its critics, especially when sociobiology is applied to human behavior. The critics argue that sociobiologists do not adequately consider human adaptability and experience, and that sociobiology reduces human beings to mere automatons in thrall to their genes. They also say that sociobiologists explain behavior after the fact: that sociobiology lacks the predictive ability that characterizes any good theory. Critics also point out that sociobiology promotes discrimination against women and ethnic minorities under the guise of being scientific (Paludi, 1995). As you can see, when sociobiology is applied to human behavior it is controversial.

How do sociobiologists respond to such criticisms? They argue that most psychologists have not given adequate attention to the evolutionary basis of behavior, that sociobiologists do consider both the biological and the experiential sides of behavior, that much of their work does have predictive validity, and that the use of sociobiology to discriminate against women and ethnic minorities has been inappropriate. Such misuses of sociobiology have included the work of "eugenicists," who focus on genetics as a basis for producing superior human beings or a superior race of humans. In addition, sociobiologists believe that political and ideological issues need to be clearly separated from the scientific issues; they hold that the fact that someone finds a scientific theory to be politically objectionable is irrelevant to whether the theory is true or false.

Evolutionary Psychology

Many sociobiologists have skipped or neglected the psychological level of analysis. They go directly from principles of evolution to patterns of social organization—such as the mating system (polygamy versus monogamy)—without describing or investigating the psychological mechanisms involved. **Evolutionary psychology** *is a contemporary approach that emphasizes that behavior is a function of mechanisms, requires input for activation, and is ultimately related to successful survival and reproduction.*

David Buss (1995) recently described the basic principles of evolutionary psychology. In evolutionary psychology, mechanisms (both psychological and physiological) are the product of evolution by selection. These mechanisms owe their existence to the successful solution to an adaptive problem that humans faced in ancestral environments. The adaptive problems are numerous, and they are all related to successful survival and reproduction, with reproduction being the engine that drives evolution, and survival being important because it aids reproduction. Evolutionary psychology is not about genetic determinism but rather is an interactionistic framework—no behavior can be produced without input into the evolved psychological mechanisms of humans.

The central issue for evolutionary psychologists is the nature of psychological mechanisms created by selection and the adaptive functions they were designed to serve. According to evolutionary psychologists, human psychological mechanisms are domain-specific, or modular. Once developed, all mechanisms require particular forms of input to be activated and to function properly.

The domain-specific, or modular, psychological mechanisms that have been revealed include these:

- A highly patterned distribution of fears and phobias that correspond to hazards faced by humans in ancestral environments—for example, the fear of strangers that emerges between 8 to 24 months of age, as well as fear of snakes, spiders, heights, open spaces, and darkness (Marks, 1987).
- Specialized mechanisms for color vision (Shepard, 1992).
- Perceptual adaptations for tracking and predicting animal motion (Freyd, 1993).
- Children's imitation of high-status rather than low-status models (Bandura, 1977).
- The worldwide preference of men and women for mates who are kind, intelligent, and dependable (Buss & others, 1990).

Thus, evolutionary psychologists believe that research increasingly supports the concept that numerous mechanisms have evolved because of the large number of diverse adaptive problems humans needed to solve in their evolutionary environments (Charlesworth, 1995).

Nature and Nurture

Although genes play a role in human behavior, they alone do not determine who we are. Genes exist within the context of a complex environment and are necessary for an organism to exist. Biologists who study even the simplest animals agree it is virtually impossible to separate the effects of an animal's genes from the effects of its environment (Mader, 1996). **Environment** *refers to all of the surrounding conditions and influences that affect the development of living things.* Environment includes the food we eat, the air we breathe, and the many different physical and social contexts we experience—the cities and towns we live in; our relationships with our parents, peers, and teachers; and our continuing interactions at work, at home, and at play. The term **nurture** *is often used to describe an organism's environmental experiences.* The term **nature** *is often used to describe an organism's biological inheritance.* The interaction of nature *and* nurture, genes *and* environment, influences every aspect of mind and behavior to a degree. Neither factor operates alone (Brown, 1995; Loehlin, 1995; Miller 1995).

To illustrate how both genes and the environment mold human behavior, let's consider shyness. Imagine we could identify the precise genetic combination that predisposes a person to become either outgoing or shy. Even with that information, we couldn't predict how shy a person might become, because shyness is also shaped by life's experiences. Parents, for example, may support and nurture a shy child in a way that encourages the child to feel comfortable

Concept Table 1

Heredity, the Evolutionary Perspective, and Nature/Nurture

Concept	Processes/Related Ideas	Characteristics/Description
Heredity	Chromosomes, DNA, and genes	The nucleus of each human cell contains 46 chromosomes which are composed of DNA. Genes are short segments of DNA and act as blueprints for cells to reproduce and manufacture proteins that maintain life. Most genetic transmission involves combinations of genes.
The Evolutionary Perspective	Natural selection	Over time, entire species can change through natural selection, the evolutionary process that favors genes that code for design features that are most likely to lead to reproduction and survival.
	Sociobiology	This approach relies on the principles of evolutionary biology to explain the social behavior of animals. Sociobiology's purpose is to develop general laws of the evolution and biology of social behavior. The hope also is that sociobiology can assist in the explanation of human behavior. Sociobiology has made important contributions to the understanding of social behavior.
	Evolutionary psychology	This contemporary approach emphasizes that behavior is a function of mechanisms, requires input for activation, and is ultimately related to successful survival and reproduction. Psychological mechanisms are the product of evolution. The central issue for evolutionary psychologists is the nature of the psychological mechanisms created by selection and the adaptive functions they were designed to serve. Evolutionary psychologists believe that human psychological mechanisms are domain-specific, or modular.
Nature/Nurture	Gene-environment interaction	The term *nature* is often used to refer to an organism's biological inheritance. The term *nurture* is often used to refer to an organism's environmental experiences. Every behavior is, to some degree, the product of both genetic heritage and environment, or what is called gene-environment interaction.

in social situations. On the other hand, an initially outgoing child may experience a traumatic event and become shy and withdrawn in response.

At this point, we have discussed some important ideas about heredity, evolution, and nature and nurture. A summary of these ideas is presented in concept table 1. Of all the aspects of human behavior that have evolved, none helps us adapt to our world more than the brain does. To its knowns and unknowns we now turn.

The Brain and Nervous System

Your nervous system's central command center, your brain, controls all of your thoughts and movements. It weighs about 3 pounds and is slightly larger than a grapefruit. With its "crinkled" outer layer, it looks like a large, shelled walnut. Inside, the brain has the consistency of undercooked custard or a ripe avocado. **Neurons,** *or nerve cells, are the basic units of the nervous system.* Highly organized, your nervous system is continuously at work processing information about everything you do—whether you are taking out the garbage, spotting a loved one across a crowded room, or preparing a speech. Let's explore what the brain and nervous system are really like.

Early Approaches

Since the ancient Greeks, people have struggled to explain the work of the brain. For Aristotle, thinking took place in the heart; the brain cooled the blood. For seventeenth-century philosopher René Descartes, the mind functioned like a machine, in which nerves were compared to the plumbing of fountains. In the twentieth century, the brain has been compared to the latest complex machines; however, as we will discover in this chapter, even a supercomputer—the most recent comparison—falls short of the real thing (see figure 4). After all, nature has had a 7-million-year head start, and researchers have never encountered anything as complex and ingeniously designed as the 3-pound lump of tissue inside your skull.

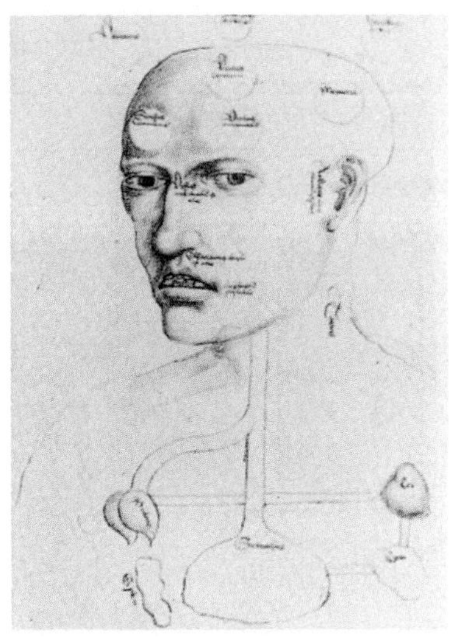
(a)

(b)

(c)

FIGURE 4

Analogies to Explain the Brain
Since the ancient Greeks, individuals have struggled to discover analogies to explain the machinery of the brain, invoking everything from plumbing to computing: (*a*) an artist's rendition of Aristotle's radiator analogy; (*b*) an artist's rendition of Descartes' plumbing analogy; (*c*) supercomputer analogy.

The 3-pound lump of tissue belonging to Phineas T. Gage, a 25-year-old foreman who worked for the Rutland and Burlington Railroad in Vermont, met with an interesting experience on September 13, 1848. Phineas and several co-workers were using blasting powder to construct a roadbed. The crew drilled holes in the rock and gravel, poured in the blasting powder, and then tamped down the powder with an iron rod. While Phineas was still tamping it down, the powder blew up, driving the iron rod up through the left side of his face and out through the top of his head (see figure 5). Phineas was thrown to the ground, but, amazingly, he was still conscious and able to talk. His co-workers placed him on an oxcart and drove him almost a mile to his hotel. Phineas got out of the cart himself and walked up the flight of stairs to his room. A physician was called, and he discovered he could put the entire length of his index finger through the cylindrical hole in Phineas' skull.

Though the wound in his skull healed in a matter of weeks, Phineas became a different person. He had been a mild-mannered, hardworking, emotionally calm individual prior to the accident, well liked by all who knew him. Afterward, he became obstinate, moody, irresponsible, selfish, and incapable of participating in any planned activities. Phineas' misfortune illustrates the brain's importance in determining the nature of personality.

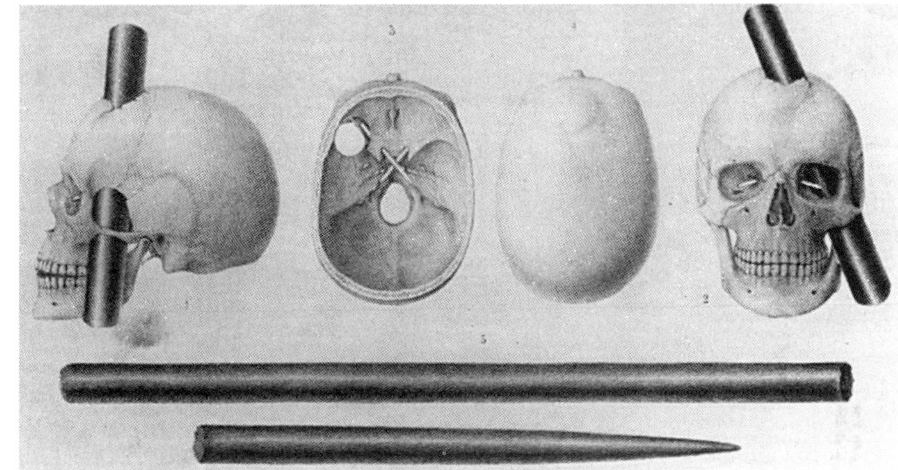

FIGURE 5

The Injury to Phineas T. Gage
Remarkably, Gage's wounds healed in a matter of weeks, but his personality changed dramatically, suggesting the brain's role in personality.

Early in the nineteenth century, the realization that certain parts of the brain are responsible for certain types of behavior began to emerge. **Phrenology** *was an approach developed by a German physician named Franz Joseph Gall, who argued that the bumps on the skull were associated with personality and intelligence.* Gall mapped out a large number of psychological functions: benevolence, destructiveness, mirthfulness, and individuality, for example.

Gall's basic idea was right; different brain regions do have different functions. Where Gall went wrong (besides thinking that skull bumps accurately reflect brain shape) was in the types of psychological functions he assigned to different

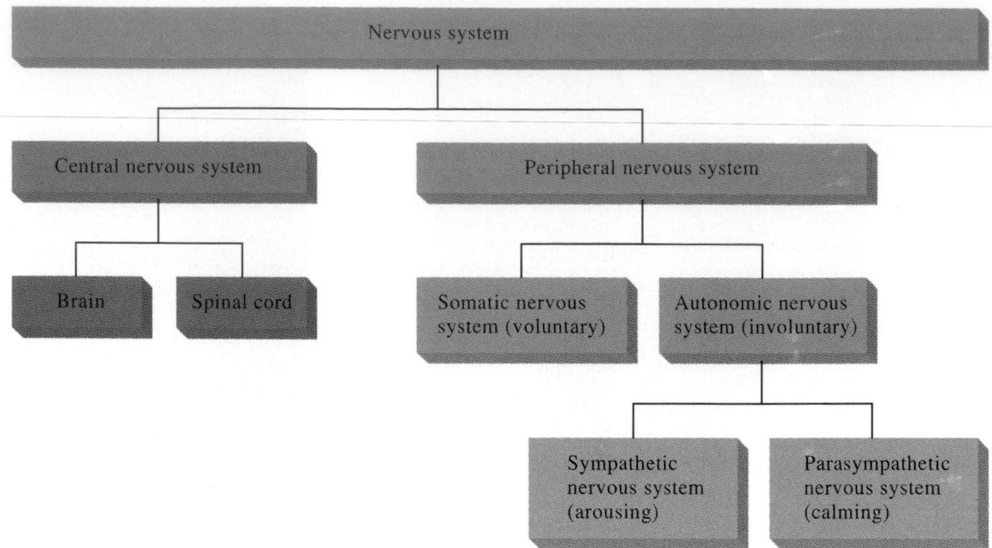

FIGURE 6

Major Divisions of the Human Nervous System

brain regions. His phrenology maps were quickly rejected by scientists of his time, but the notion that functions are localized has prevailed.

More scientific support of the localization concept came from a study by Paul Broca in 1861. One of Broca's patients had received an injury to the dominant side of his brain about 31 years earlier. The injury was to a precise part of the dominant side of the brain called the third frontal convolution. The patient became known as Tan, because *tan* was the only word he could speak. Tan suffered from aphasia, a language disorder associated with brain damage. Tan died several days after Broca evaluated him, and an autopsy revealed the location of the injury. Today we refer to this region of the brain as Broca's area, and we know that it plays an important role in language.

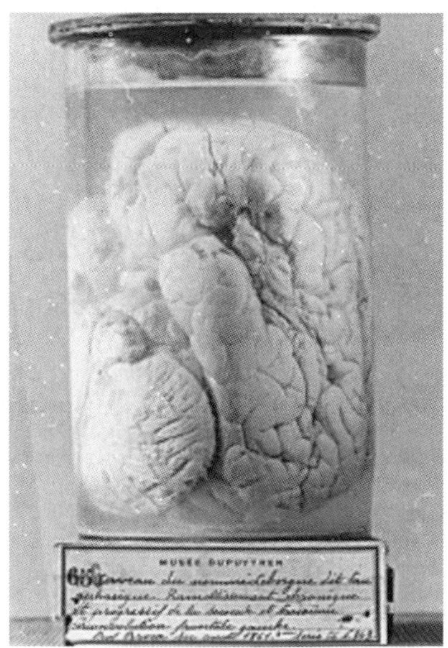

Tan's brain is shown here in the cellars of the Musée Dupuytren in Paris, where it was found by the curator. The brain was so well preserved it could be examined to reveal the damage first observed by Paul Broca.

The degree to which functions are localized in the brain is an important issue. Today psychologists believe that although a particular structure of the brain might be involved with one psychological function more than another, for the most part psychological function is based not on a specific structure, but rather on the interaction of *various* areas of the brain.

The Elegant Organization of the Nervous System

When Emerson said, "The world was built in order and the atoms march in tune," he must have had the human nervous system in mind. This truly elegant system is highly ordered and organized. It is at work processing information in everything we do, whether stumbling across a tiger in the jungle or stretching out for a lazy nap on a hammock. The human nervous system is made up of bundles of nerve cells.

The nervous system is divided into two parts: the central nervous system and the peripheral nervous system. The **central nervous system (CNS)** *is made up of the brain and spinal cord.* More than 99 percent of all neurons (nerve cells) in our body are located in the CNS. The **peripheral nervous system** *is the network of nerves that connects the brain and spinal cord to other parts of the body. The peripheral nervous system brings information to and from the brain and spinal cord and carries out the commands of the CNS to execute various muscular and glandular activities.* Figure 6 displays the hierarchical organization of the nervous system's major divisions.

The two major divisions of the peripheral nervous system are the somatic nervous system and the autonomic nervous system. The **somatic nervous system** *consists of sensory* *nerves, which convey information from the skin and muscles to the CNS about such matters as pain and temperature, and motor nerves, which inform muscles when to act.* The **autonomic nervous system** *takes messages to and from the body's internal organs, monitoring such processes as breathing, heart rate, and digestion.* It too is divided into two parts, the **sympathetic nervous system,** *the division of the autonomic nervous system that arouses the body,* and the **parasympathetic nervous system,** *the division of the autonomic nervous system that calms the body* (see figure 7).

To get a better feel for how the human nervous system works, imagine that you are preparing to give a speech in a class. As you go over your notes one last time, your peripheral nervous system carries information about the notes to your central nervous system. Your central nervous system processes the marks on the paper, interpreting the words as you memorize key points and plan ways to keep the audience interested. After studying the notes several minutes longer, you scribble a joke midway through them. Your peripheral nervous system is at work again, conveying to the muscles in your arm and hand the information from your brain that enables you to make the marks on the paper. The information transmitted from your eyes to your brain and from your brain to your hand is being handled by the somatic nervous system. This is your first speech in a while, so you are a little uptight. As you think about getting up in front of the class, your stomach feels queasy and your heart begins to thump. This is the sympathetic division of the autonomic nervous system functioning as you become aroused. You regain your confidence after reminding yourself that you know the speech cold. As you relax, the parasympathetic division of the autonomic nervous system is working.

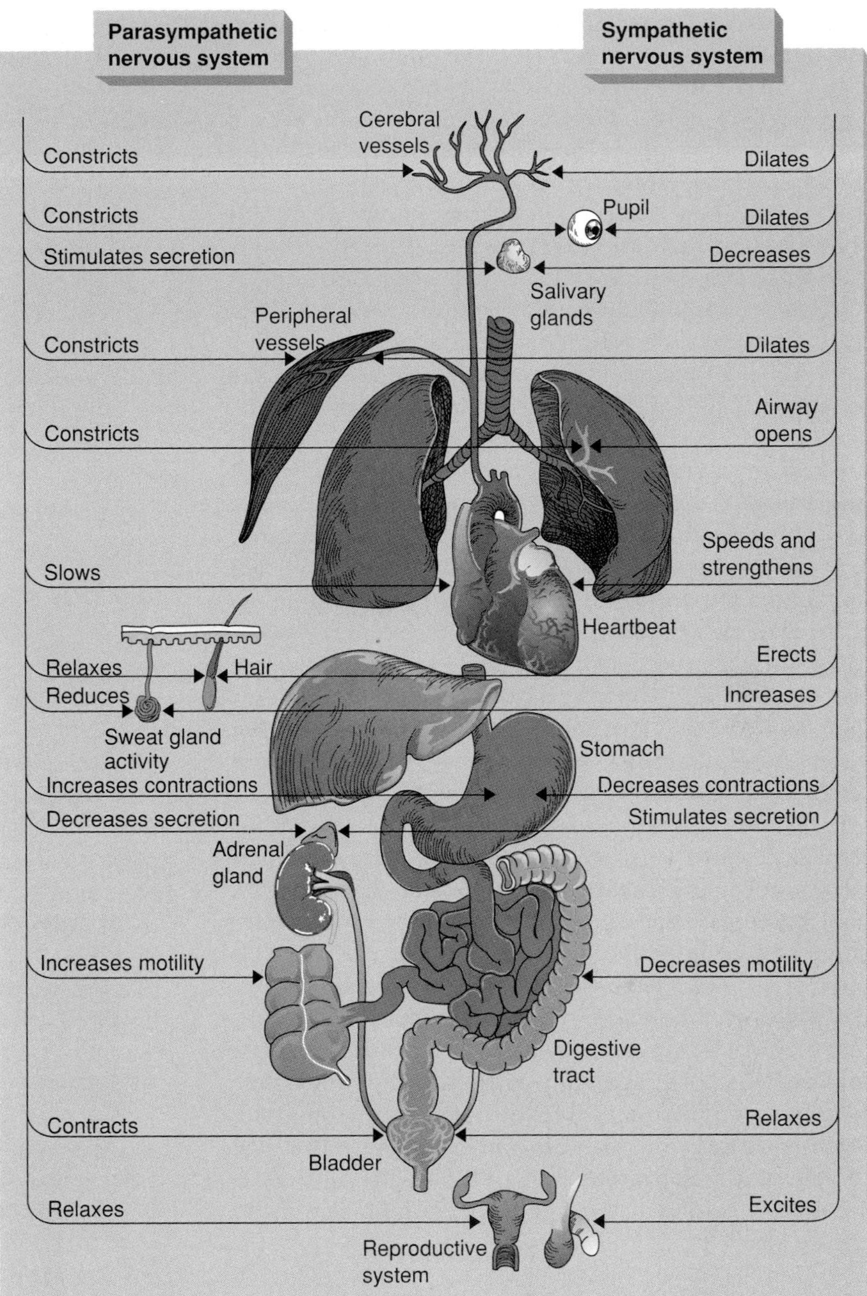

FIGURE 7

Autonomic Nervous System
Parasympathetic and sympathetic divisions. The sympathetic system is at work when we are aroused; the parasympathetic system is at work when we are calm. Both systems influence most organs. For example, the sympathetic system speeds and strengthens heartbeat; the parasympathetic system slows heartbeat.

Neurons

So far we have described the nervous system's major divisions. But there is much more to the intriguing story of how the nervous system processes information. Let's go inside the huge nervous system and find out more about the cells, chemicals, and electrical impulses that are the nuts and bolts of this operation.

Neuron Pathways

Information flows to the brain, within the brain, and out of the brain along specialized nerve cells known as afferent nerves, interneurons, and efferent nerves. **Afferent nerves,** *or sensory nerves, carry information to the brain.* The word *afferent* comes from the Latin word meaning "bring to." **Efferent nerves,** *or motor nerves, carry the brain's output.* The word *efferent* is derived from the Latin word meaning "bring forth."

To see how afferent and efferent nerves work, let's consider a well-known reflex, the knee jerk. When your knee jerks in response to a tap just below your kneecap, afferent cells transmit information directly to efferent cells, so the information processing is quick and simple.

The information involving the knee jerk is processed at the spinal cord and does not require the brain's participation. More complex information processing is accomplished by passing the information through systems of **interneurons,** *central nervous system neurons that mediate sensory input and motor output. Interneurons make up most of the brain.* For example, as you read the notes for your speech, the afferent input from your eye is transmitted to your brain, then passed through many interneuron systems, which translate (process) the patterns of black and white into neural codes for letters, words, associations, and meanings. Some of the information is stored in the interneuron systems for future associations and, if you read aloud, some is output as efferent messages to your lips and tongue.

Your gift of speech is possible because human interneuron systems are organized in ways that permit language processing. Although the neurons in a canary's brain are exactly the same as those in a frog's brain, frogs croak and canaries sing because the neurons are organized differently in the two brains. The interneurons in the frog's vocalization system are connected in such a way that they produce croaking, whereas the canary's produce singing. This is why the study of brain organization—the anatomy and fine structure of the brain—is so important. Brain organization is the key to understanding all of the complex and wondrous things that brains do. We'll tackle the brain's anatomy later; first, let's examine neurons in greater detail.

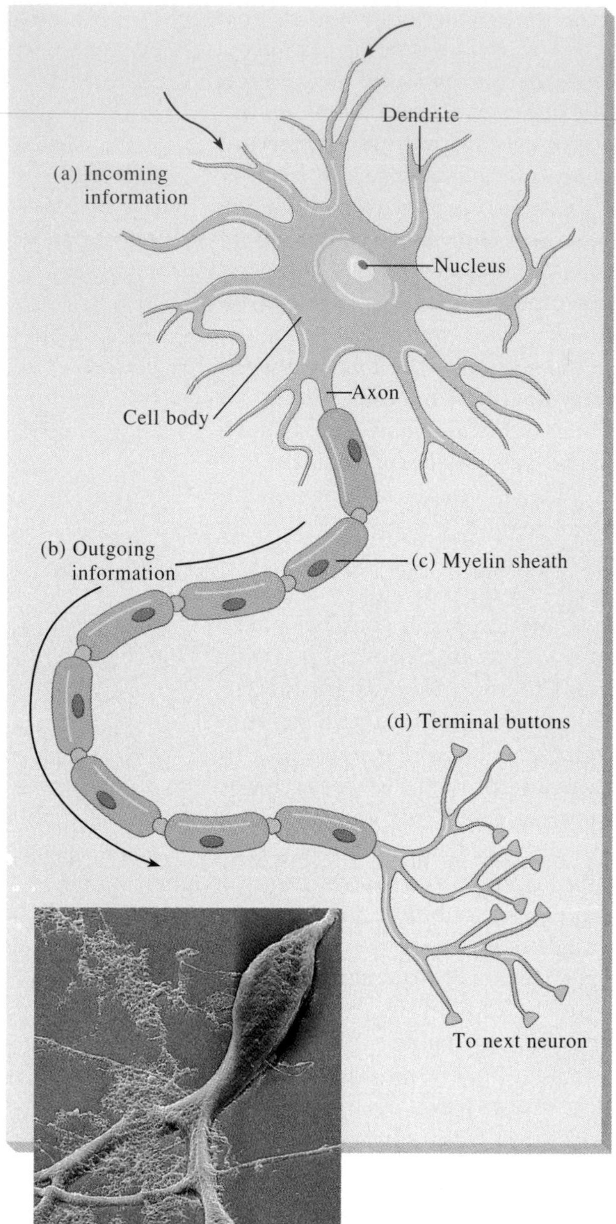

FIGURE 8

The Neuron
(*a*) The dendrites of the cell body receive information from other neurons, muscles, or glands through the axon. (*b*) Axons transmit information away from the cell body. (*c*) A myelin sheath covers most axons and speeds information transmission. (*d*) As it ends, the axon branches out into terminal buttons. Shown in the insert is a photograph of an actual neuron. Notice the branching dendrites at the bottom and the cell body at the top right.

Structure of the Neuron

As indicated earlier, *neuron* is the neuroscientist's label for nerve cells. The neuron handles information processing in the nervous system at the cellular level. There are about 100 billion neurons in the human brain. The average neuron is as complex as a small computer, with as many as 15,000 physical connections with other cells. At times the brain may be "lit up" with as many as a quadrillion connections.

The three basic parts of the neuron are the cell body, the dendrites, and the axon (see figure 8). The neuron's **cell body** *contains the nucleus, which directs the manufacture of the substances the neuron uses for its growth and maintenance.* Most neurons are created very early in life and will not be replaced if they are destroyed. However, most neurons also are capable of changing their shape, size, and connections throughout the life span.

The **dendrite** *is the receiving part of the neuron, serving the important function of collecting information and orienting it toward the cell body.* Most nerve cells have a number of dendrites. Although there are many dendrites radiating from the cell body of the neuron, there is only one axon. The **axon** *is the part of the neuron that carries information away from the cell body to other cells.* The axon is much thinner and longer than a dendrite and looks like an ultrathin cylindrical tube. The axon of a single neuron may extend all the way from the top of the brain to the base of the spinal cord, a distance of over three feet. A **myelin sheath,** *a layer of fat cells that insulates the axon, encases most axons. Not only does the myelin sheath serve as insulation for the nerve cell, it also helps the nerve impulse to travel faster.* The myelin sheath developed as brains evolved and became larger, which made it necessary for information to travel over long distances in the nervous system. This is similar to the appearance of freeways and turnpikes as cities grew. The newly developed roadways keep the fast-moving long-distance traffic from getting tangled up with slow-moving traffic.

The Nerve Impulse

Neurons send information down the axon as brief impulses, or waves, of electricity. Perhaps in a movie you have seen a telegraph operator sending a series of single clicks down a telegraph wire to the next station. That is what neurons do. To send information to other neurons, they send a series of single, electrical clicks down their axons. By changing the rate and timing of the clicks, the neuron can vary the nature of the message it sends. As you reach to turn this page, hundreds of such clicks will stream down the axons in your arm to tell your muscles just when to flex and how vigorously.

The wave of electrical charge that sweeps down the axon abides by the **all-or-none principle,** *which means that once the electrical impulse reaches a certain level of intensity, it fires and moves all the way down the axon, remaining at the same strength throughout its travel.* The electrical impulse traveling down an axon is much like a fuse to a firecracker. It doesn't matter whether a match or blowtorch is used to light the fuse; as long as a certain minimal intensity has been reached, the spark travels quickly and at the same level of strength down the fuse until it reaches the firecracker.

To understand how a neuron, which is a living cell, creates and sends electrical signals, we need to examine this cell and the fluids in which it floats. A neuron is a balloonlike bag filled with one kind of fluid and surrounded by a slightly different kind of fluid. A piece of this balloonlike bag is stretched and pulled to form a long, hollow tube, which is the axon. The axon tube is very thin; a few dozen in a bundle would be about the thickness of human hair.

To see how this fluid-filled "balloon" called a neuron creates electrical signals, we must look at two things: the particles that float in the fluids and the actual wall of the cell, the membrane. The important particles in the fluids are the elements sodium and chloride (which we get from common table salt—sodium chloride) and potassium. **Ions** *are electrically charged particles. The neuron creates electrical signals by moving these charged ions back and forth through its membrane; the waves of electricity that are created sweep along the membrane.*

How does the neuron move these ions? It's really fairly simple; the membrane, the wall of our balloon, is covered with hundreds of thousands of small doors or gates,

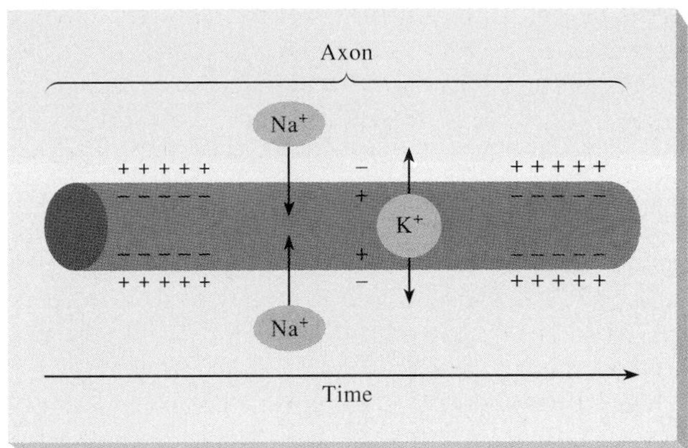

FIGURE 9

Movement of Sodium and Potassium Ions Down the Axon and the Action Potential
Electrical/chemical changes in the neuron produce an action potential. The sodium and potassium ions are shown moving down the axon. As the nerve impulse moves down the axon, electrical stimulation of the membrane makes it more permeable to sodium ions (Na^+). Sodium rushes into the axon, carrying an electrical charge, and that charge causes the next group of gates on the axon to flip open briefly. So it goes, all the way down the axon. After the sodium gates close, potassium ions (K^+) flow out of the cell.

that open and close to let the ions pass in or out to the cell. Normally, when resting or not sending information, the membrane gates for sodium are closed, and those for potassium and chloride are partly open. Therefore, the membrane is in what is called a semipermeable state, and the ions separate; sodium is kept outside, lots of potassium ends up inside, and most of the chloride goes outside. Because the ions are separated, a charge is present along the membrane of the cell (see figure 9). **Resting potential** *is the stable, negative charge of an inactive neuron.* That potential, by the way, is about one-fourteenth of a volt, so fourteen neurons could make a one-volt battery. The electric eel's 8,400 cells could generate 600 volts.

When the neuron gets enough excitatory input to cause it to send a message, the sodium gates at the base of the axon open briefly, then shut again. While those gates are open, sodium rushes into the axon, carrying an electrical charge, and that charge causes the next group of gates on the axon to flip open briefly. And so it goes all the way down the axon, just like a long row of cabinet doors opening and closing in sequence. After the sodium gates close, potassium ions flow out of the cell and bring the membrane charge back to the resting condition. **Action potential** *is the brief wave of electrical charge that sweeps down the axon* (see figure 10).

Synapses and Neurotransmitters

What happens once the neural impulse reaches the end of the axon? Neurons themselves do not touch each other directly, but they manage to communicate. The story of the connection between one neuron and another is one of the most intriguing and highly researched areas of contemporary

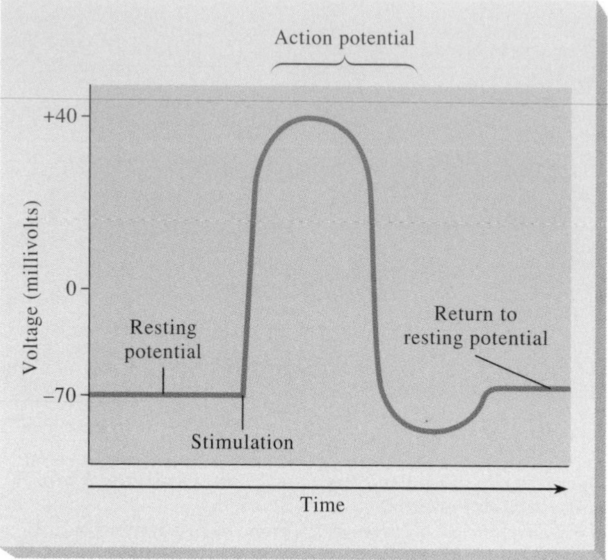

FIGURE 10

Action Potential
The action potential is shown on this graph in terms of its electrical voltage. The action potential is the positive charge in the cell generated by the influx of sodium (Na^+) ions. In the example shown here, the wave of electrical charge reaches about 40 millivolts. After the sodium gates close, potassium ions (K^+) flow out of the cell and bring the voltage back to its resting potential.

neuroscience. **Synapses** *are tiny gaps between neurons.* Most synapses are between the axon of one neuron and the dendrites or cell body of another neuron.

How does information get across this gap to the next neuron? The end of an axon branches out into a number of fibers that end in structures called terminal buttons. Neurotransmitters are found in the tiny synaptic vesicles (chambers) located in the terminal buttons. **Neurotransmitters** *are chemical substances that carry information across the synaptic gap to the next neuron.* The molecules of these chemical substances wait for a nerve impulse to come down through the axon. Once the nerve impulse reaches the terminal buttons, the electrical signal causes these miniature springlike molecules to contract, pulling the vesicles out to the edge of the terminal buttons. At the edge, the vesicles burst open, and the neurotransmitter molecules spew forth into the gap between the two neurons. In the synaptic gap, the neurotransmitter molecules bump about in random motion, and some land on receptor sites in the next neuron, where they fit like small keys in equally small locks. The key in the lock, in turn, opens a "door" and electrical signals begin to sweep through the next neuron. Think of the synapse as a river that cuts two sections of a railroad track in two. When the train gets to the river via the tracks on one side of the river, it crosses the water by ferry and rolls right onto the second section of track to continue its journey. Similarly, a message in the brain is "ferried" across the synapse by a neurotransmitter, which pours out of the end of the cell just as the message approaches the synapse. Synapses and neurotransmitters might sound mysterious; to help turn your mystification into understanding, turn to figure 11.

More than fifty neurotransmitters, each with a unique chemical makeup, have been discovered, and the list will probably grow to a hundred or more in the near future. Most creatures that have been studied, from snails to whales, use the same neurotransmitter molecules that our own brains use. And many animal venoms, such as that of the black widow, actually are neurotransmitter-like substances that disturb neurotransmission.

What are some of these neurotransmitters, and how are they related to our behavior? **GABA,** *gamma aminobutyric acid, is a neurotransmitter that inhibits the firing of neurons.* It is found throughout the brain and spinal cord and is believed to be the neurotransmitter in as many as one-third of the brain's synaptic connections. GABA is so important in the brain because it keeps many neurons from firing. This inhibition helps to control the preciseness of the signal being carried from one neuron to the next. The degeneration of GABA may be responsible for Huntington's chorea, a deadly disease that includes a loss of muscle control. Without GABA's inhibiting influence, the nerve impulse becomes imprecise and muscles lose their coordination. GABA may also be involved in modifying anxiety.

Acetylcholine (ACh) *is a neurotransmitter that produces contractions of skeletal muscles by acting on motor neurons* (see figure 12). While GABA inhibits neurons from firing, in most instances ACh excites neurons and stimulates them to fire. Black widow venom causes ACh to gush through the synapses between the spinal cord and skeletal muscles, producing violent spasms. The drug curare, found on the tips of some South American Indians' poison darts, blocks some receptors for ACh. This paralyzes skeletal muscles.

Norepinephrine *is a neurotransmitter that usually inhibits the firing of neurons in the brain and spinal cord, but excites the heart muscles, the intestines, and the urogenital tract.* Too little norepinephrine is associated with depression, and too much of it is linked to highly agitated, manic states. **Dopamine** *is a neurotransmitter that is related to mental health—too much dopamine in the brain's synapses is associated with the severe mental disorder called schizophrenia, in which an individual loses contact with reality.* More about the role of neurotransmitters in mental health and how drugs can be used to control their action appears in the chapters on abnormal psychology. **Serotonin** *is a neurotransmitter involved in the regulation of sleep, and, like norepinephrine, seems to play a role in depression as well.*

As early as the fourth century B.C. the Greeks used the wild poppy to induce euphoria. But it was not until more than 2,000 years later that the magical formula behind opium's addictive action was discovered. In the early 1970s, scientists found that opium plugs into a sophisticated system of natural opiates lying deep within the brain's pathways

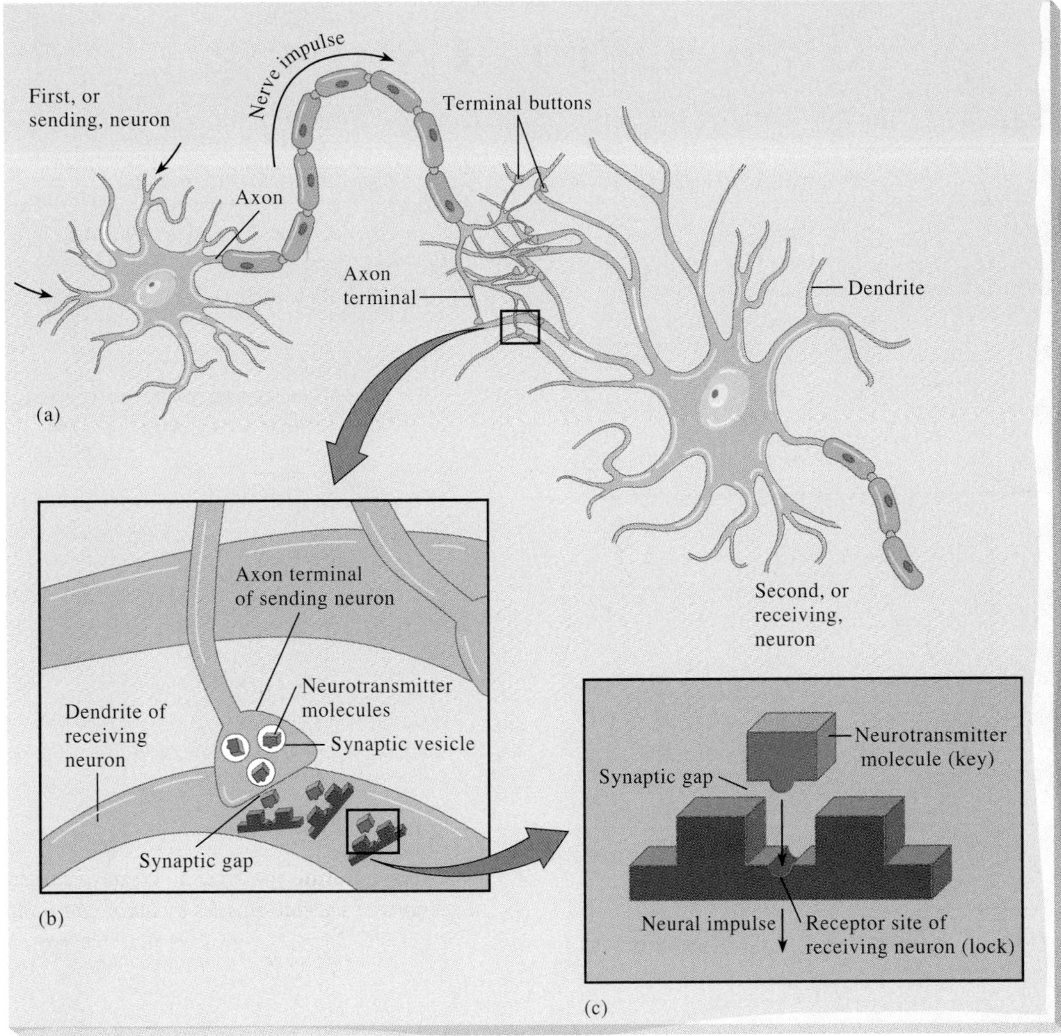

FIGURE 11

How Synapses and Neurotransmitters Work
(*a*) When an axon reaches its destination, it branches out into a number of fibers that end in terminal buttons. There is a tiny gap between these terminal buttons at the tip of the axon terminal and the next neuron. (*b*) When it reaches the terminal buttons, the neural impulse releases tiny chemical molecules that are stored in synaptic vesicles in the knobs. These chemical substances are called neurotransmitters. They bump around in the synaptic gap between the sending and receiving neurons. Some of them land on receptor sites in the next neuron, where the neural impulse continues its travel. (*c*) Neurotransmitter molecules fit like small keys in equally small locks, once they reach the receptor site in the receiving neuron. The key in the lock opens the "door," and the neural impulse begins its travel through the second neuron.

(Pert & Snyder, 1973). The system is involved in shielding the body from pain and elevating feelings of pleasure. A long-distance runner, a woman giving birth, and a person in shock after a car wreck all have elevated levels of **endorphins,** *natural opiates that are neurotransmitters. Endorphins are involved in pleasure and the control of pain.*

The influence of some neurotransmitters is excitatory, whereas the effect of others is inhibitory, and some can function in both excitatory and inhibitory ways, depending on what information-processing job is to be done. As the neurotransmitter moves across the synaptic gap to the receiving neuron, its molecules may spread across a large spatial area or be confined to a small space. The molecules may come in rapid sequence or be spaced out. The receiving neuron must integrate all of this information and decide whether or not to fire.

Glial Cells

The Spanish neuroanatomist Santiago Ramón y Cajal discovered that the brain is made up of two types of cells—neurons, or nerve cells, and **glial cells,** *non-neuron cells that provide supportive and nutritive functions.* Somewhat amazingly, there are many more glial cells in the nervous system than there are neurons. Ramón y Cajal used advances in

Concept Table 2

Early Approaches, the Elegant Organization of the Nervous System, Neurons, and Glial Cells

Concept	Processes/Related Ideas	Characteristics/Description
Early Approaches	Their nature	They suggested that distinct parts of the brain were responsible for different aspects of behavior.
The Elegant Organization of the Nervous System	Central nervous system	The central nervous system consists of the brain and spinal cord; it contains more than 99 percent of all neurons.
	Peripheral nervous system	The peripheral nervous system is a network of nerves that connect the brain and spinal cord to other parts of the body. Two major divisions are the somatic nervous system and the autonomic nervous system. The autonomic nervous system is divided into the sympathetic and parasympathetic systems.
Neurons	Pathways of neurons	Afferent nerves (sensory nerves) carry input to the brain; efferent nerves (motor nerves) carry output away from the brain; interneurons do most of the information processing within the brain.
	Structure of the neuron	The three basic parts of the neuron are the cell body, dendrite, and axon. The myelin sheath speeds information transmission.
	The nerve impulse	Neurons send information in the form of brief impulses, or "waves," of electricity. These waves are called the action potential and operate according to the all-or-none principle.
	Synapses and neurotransmitters	Synapses are gaps between neurons. The neural impulse reaches the axon terminal and stimulates the release of neurotransmitters from tiny vesicles. These carry information to the next neuron, fitting like keys in locks. Important neurotransmitters include GABA, acetylcholine, norepinephrine, serotonin, and endorphins. Some neurotransmitters are excitatory, others are inhibitory.
	Glial cells	They provide support for neurons and are thought to be involved in the regulation and nutrition of neurons.

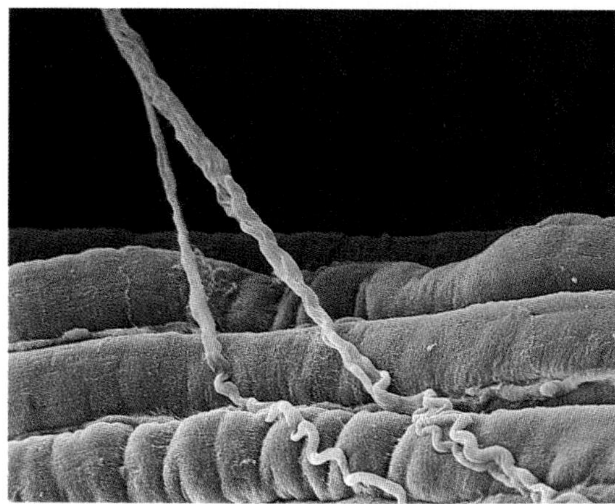

Figure 12

Nerves, Acetylcholine, and Muscles
The nerve impulse, conducted down a nerve fiber that ends in skeletal muscle, releases a small amount of the chemical acetylcholine. The action of acetylcholine at the motor endplate initiates the chemical changes that cause the muscle to contract. The photo shows a number of nerve fibers leading to and crossing several striated muscle cells.

microscope techniques to discover the glial cells early in the twentieth century. He described the cells as looking like glue between the nerve cells.

Unfortunately, we do not know as much about glial cells as we do about neurons. We do know that glial cells do not have axons or dendrites, and they are not specialized to send or receive information. They probably function as physical supports for neurons. They seem to regulate the internal environment of the brain, especially the fluid surrounding neurons, and provide nutrition for neurons. For example, neurons placed in a solution containing glial cells grow more rapidly and prolifically than neurons floating in the same solution without glial cells (Kennedy & Folk-Seang, 1986). The myelin sheath that covers most axons is made up of glial cells.

It has been some time since you read about Phineas Gage, Franz Joseph Gall, and Broca's patient Tan. Since then you have read about the elegant organization of the entire nervous system and how information processing works at the cellular level in the brain. A summary of these aspects of the nervous system is presented in concept table 2.

Brain Structure and Function

Most of the information we have covered about the brain has been about one or two cells. Earlier we indicated that about 99 percent of all neurons in the nervous system are located in the brain and the spinal cord. Neurons do not simply float in the brain. Connected in precise ways, they compose the various structures of the brain.

Embryological Development

As a human embryo develops inside the womb, the nervous system begins as a long, hollow tube on the embryo's back. At three weeks or so after conception, the brain forms into a large mass of neurons and loses its tubular appearance.

The elongated tube changes shape and develops into three major divisions: the hindbrain, which is the portion of the brain adjacent to the spinal cord; the midbrain, which is above the hindbrain; and the forebrain, which is the highest region of the brain (see figure 13).

Hindbrain

The **hindbrain,** *located at the skull's rear, is the lowest portion of the brain. The three main parts of the hindbrain are the medulla, cerebellum, and pons.* Figure 14 shows the location of these brain structures as well as some of the forebrain's main structures. The **medulla** *begins where the spinal cord enters the skull. It helps to control our breathing and regulates a portion of reflexes that allow us to maintain an upright posture.* The **cerebellum** *extends from the rear of the hindbrain and is located just above the medulla. It consists of two rounded structures thought to play important roles in motor behavior.* Leg and arm movements are coordinated at the cerebellum, for example. When we play golf, practice the piano, or perfect our moves on the dance floor, the cerebellum is hard at work. If a higher portion of the brain commands us to write the number 7, it is the cerebellum that integrates the muscular activities required to do so. If the cerebellum becomes damaged, our movement becomes uncoordinated and jerky. The **pons** *is a bridge in the hindbrain that contains several clusters of fibers involved in sleep and arousal.*

Midbrain

The **midbrain,** *located between the hindbrain and forebrain, is an area where many nerve-fiber systems ascend and descend to connect the higher and lower portions of the brain. In particular, the midbrain relays information between the brain and the eyes and ears.* The ability to attend to an object visually, for example, is linked to one bundle of neurons in the midbrain. Parkinson's disease, a deterioration of movement that produces rigidity and tremors in the elderly, damages a section near the bottom of the midbrain.

Two systems in the midbrain are of special interest. One is the **reticular formation** (see figure 15), *a diffuse collection of neurons involved in stereotyped patterns of behavior such as walking, sleeping, or turning to attend to a sudden noise.* The other system consists of small groups of neurons that use the special neurotransmitters serotonin, dopamine, and norepinephrine. These three groups contain relatively few cells, but they send their axons to a remarkable variety of brain regions, perhaps explaining their involvement in high-level, integrative functions (Shier, Butler, & Lewis 1996).

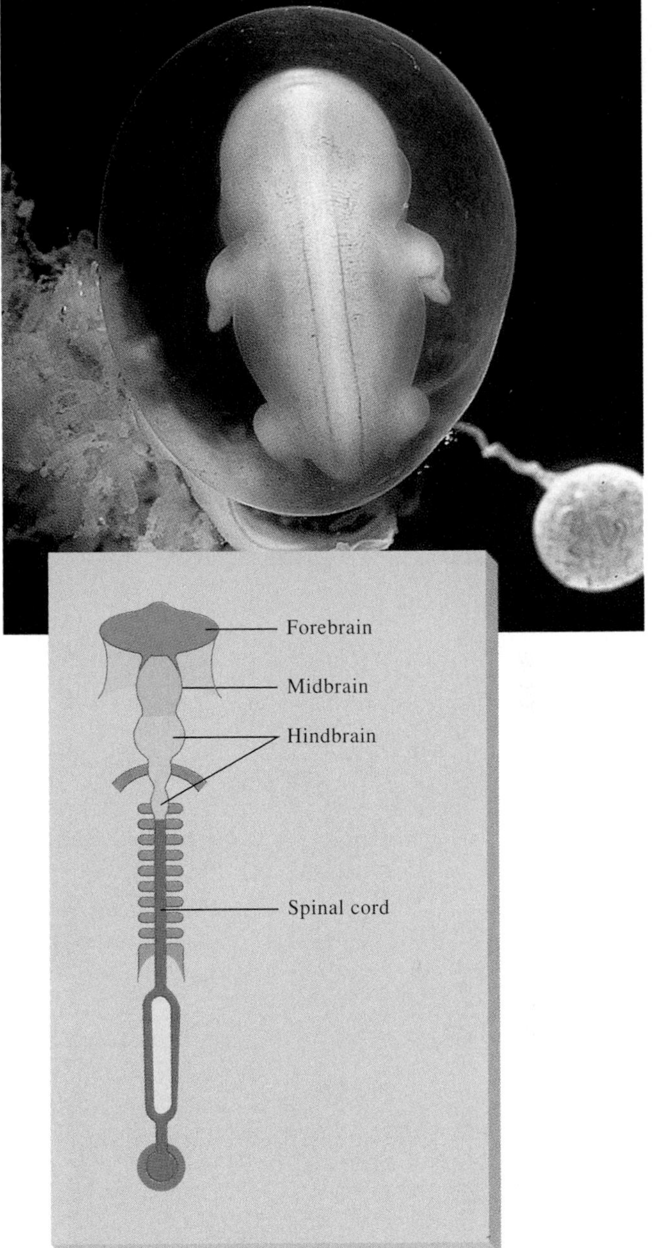

FIGURE 13

Embryological Development of the Nervous System
In this photograph you can see the primitive, tubular appearance of the nervous system at 6 weeks in the human embryo. The drawing shows the major brain regions and spinal cord as they appear early in the development of a human embryo.

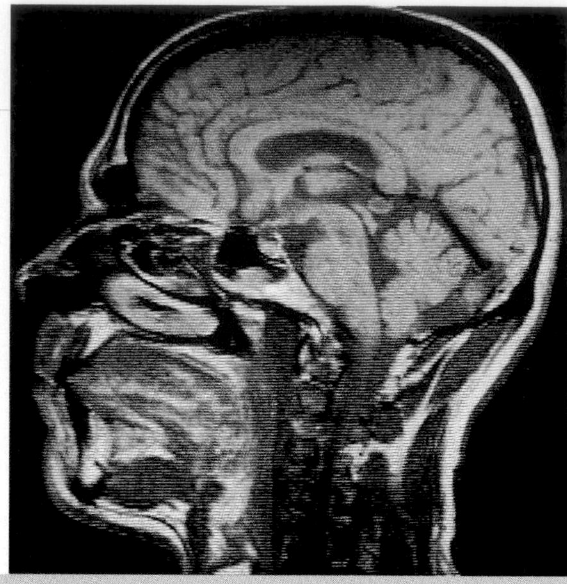

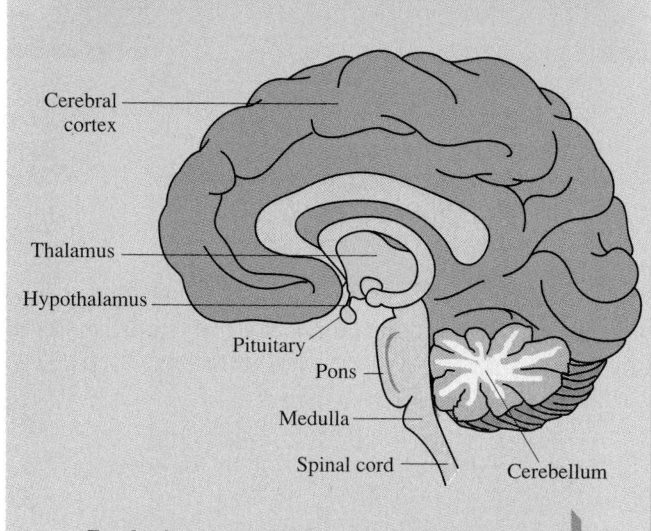

Forebrain structures

Cerebral cortex	Extensive, wrinkled outer layer of the forebrain governs higher brain functions, such as thinking, learning, and consciousness
Thalamus	Relays information between lower and higher brain centers
Hypothalamus	Governs eating, drinking, and sex; plays a role in emotion and stress
Pituitary	Governs endocrine system

Hindbrain structures

Pons	Governs sleep and arousal
Medulla	Governs breathing and reflexes
Cerebellum	Rounded structure involved in motor behavior
Spinal cord	Connects the brain with the rest of the body; governs simple reflexes

FIGURE 14

Structure and Regions in an Actual Image of the Human Brain

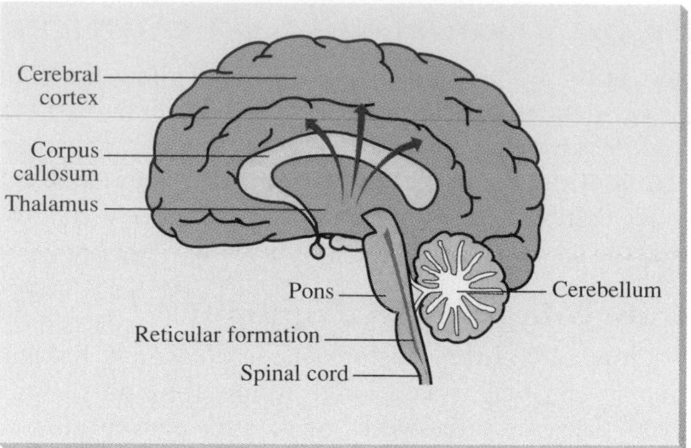

FIGURE 15

Reticular Formation
The reticular formation is a network of nerve fibers that runs through the brain stem. The arrows shown radiating from the brain stem are drawn to show the connections of the reticular formation to the higher portions of the brain in the neocortex. The reticular formation is involved in arousal and attention.

It is not the hindbrain or midbrain that separates humans from animals, however. In humans, it is the forebrain that becomes enlarged and specialized.

Forebrain

You try to understand what all of these terms and parts of the brain mean. You talk with friends and plan a party for this weekend. You remember it has been 6 months since you went to the dentist. You are confident you will do well on the next exam in this course. All of these experiences and millions more would not be possible without the **forebrain,** *the highest region of the human brain. Among its most important structures are the limbic system, amygdala, hippocampus, thalamus, basal ganglia, hypothalamus, and neocortex,* each of which we will discuss in turn.

Limbic System

The **limbic system,** *a loosely connected network of structures under the cerebral cortex, plays important roles in both memory and emotion.* Its two principal structures are the amygdala and hippocampus (see figure 16).

The **amygdala** (named in Latin for its "almond" shape) *is a limbic system structure located within the base of the temporal lobe and is involved in the discrimination of objects that are important in the organism's survival, such as appropriate food, mates, and social rivals.* Neurons in the amygdala often fire selectively at the sight of such stimuli, and lesions in the amygdala can cause animals to attempt to eat, fight, or mate with inappropriate objects such as chairs.

The **hippocampus** *is a limbic system structure that has a special role in the storage of memories.* Individuals suffering

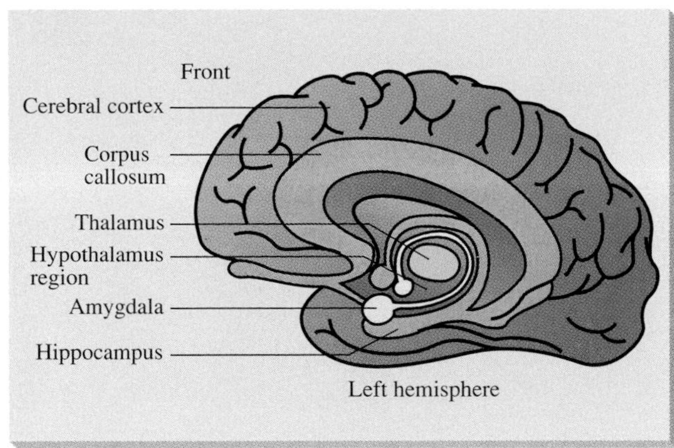

FIGURE 16

Limbic System
The limbic system includes the amygdala, which is involved in fear and anxiety; the hippocampus, which is involved in memory and learning; part of the hypothalamus, which is involved in controlling motivational states; and part of the thalamus, which relays information from the senses to the higher levels of the cerebrum.

extensive hippocampal damage simply cannot retain any new conscious memories after the damage. It is fairly certain, though, that memories are not stored "in" the limbic system. Instead, the limbic system seems to control what parts of all the information passing through the cortex should be "printed" into durable, lasting neural traces in the cortex (Gluck, 1996).

Thalamus

The **thalamus** *is a forebrain structure that sits at the top of the brain stem in the central core of the brain. It serves as a very important relay station, functioning much like a telephone switchboard.* While one area of the thalamus works to orient information from the sense receptors (hearing, seeing, and so on), another region seems to be involved in sleep and wakefulness, having ties with the reticular formation (see figure 14 for the location of the thalamus).

Basal Ganglia

The **basal ganglia** *are forebrain structures essential to starting and stopping voluntary movements.* Individuals with damage to basal ganglia suffer from either unwanted movement (such as constant writhing or jerking of limbs) or too little movement (as in the slow and deliberate movements of those with Parkinson's disease).

Hypothalamus

The **hypothalamus,** *much smaller than the thalamus and about the size of a kidney bean, is a forebrain structure located just below the thalamus. The hypothalamus monitors three enjoyable activities—eating, drinking, and sex; it helps direct the endocrine system through the pituitary gland; and it is involved in emotion, stress, and reward.* Perhaps the best way to describe the function of the hypothalamus is in terms of a regulator. It is sensitive to changes in the blood and neural input, and it responds by influencing the secretion of hormones and neural outputs. For example, if the temperature of circulating blood near the hypothalamus is increased by just 1 or 2 degrees, certain cells in the hypothalamus start increasing their rate of firing. As a result, a chain of events is set in motion. Increased circulation through the skin and sweat glands occurs immediately to release this heat from the body. The cooled blood circulating to the hypothalamus slows down the activity of some of the neurons there, stopping the process when the temperature is just right—37.1 degrees Centigrade. These temperature-sensitive neurons function like a finely tuned thermostat in returning the body to a balanced state.

The hypothalamus also is involved in emotional states and stress, playing an important role as an integrative location for handling stress. Much of this integration is accomplished through the hypothalamus' action on the pituitary gland, located just below it. If certain areas of the hypothalamus are electrically stimulated, a feeling of pleasure results. In a classic experiment, James Olds and Peter Milner (1954) implanted an electrode in the hypothalamus of a rat's brain. When the rat ran to a corner of an enclosed area, a mild electric current was delivered to its hypothalamus. The researchers thought the electric current was punishment for the rat and would cause it to avoid the corner. Much to their surprise, the rat kept returning to the corner. Olds and Milner believed they had discovered a pleasure center in the hypothalamus.

Olds (1958) conducted further experiments and found that rats would press bars until they dropped over from exhaustion just to continue to receive a mild electric shock to their hypothalamus. One rat pressed a bar more than 2,000 times an hour for a period of 24 hours to receive the stimulus to its hypothalamus (figure 17). Today researchers agree that the hypothalamus is involved in pleasurable feelings, but that other areas of the brain, such as the limbic system and a bundle of fibers in the forebrain, are important in the link between brain and pleasure as well.

Neocortex

The **neocortex** *is a region of the forebrain that is the most recently developed part of the brain in the evolutionary scheme. The neural tissue that comprises the neocortex is the largest part of the brain in volume (about 80 percent) and covers the lower portions of the brain almost like a large cap.* Let's look at the neocortex in more detail.

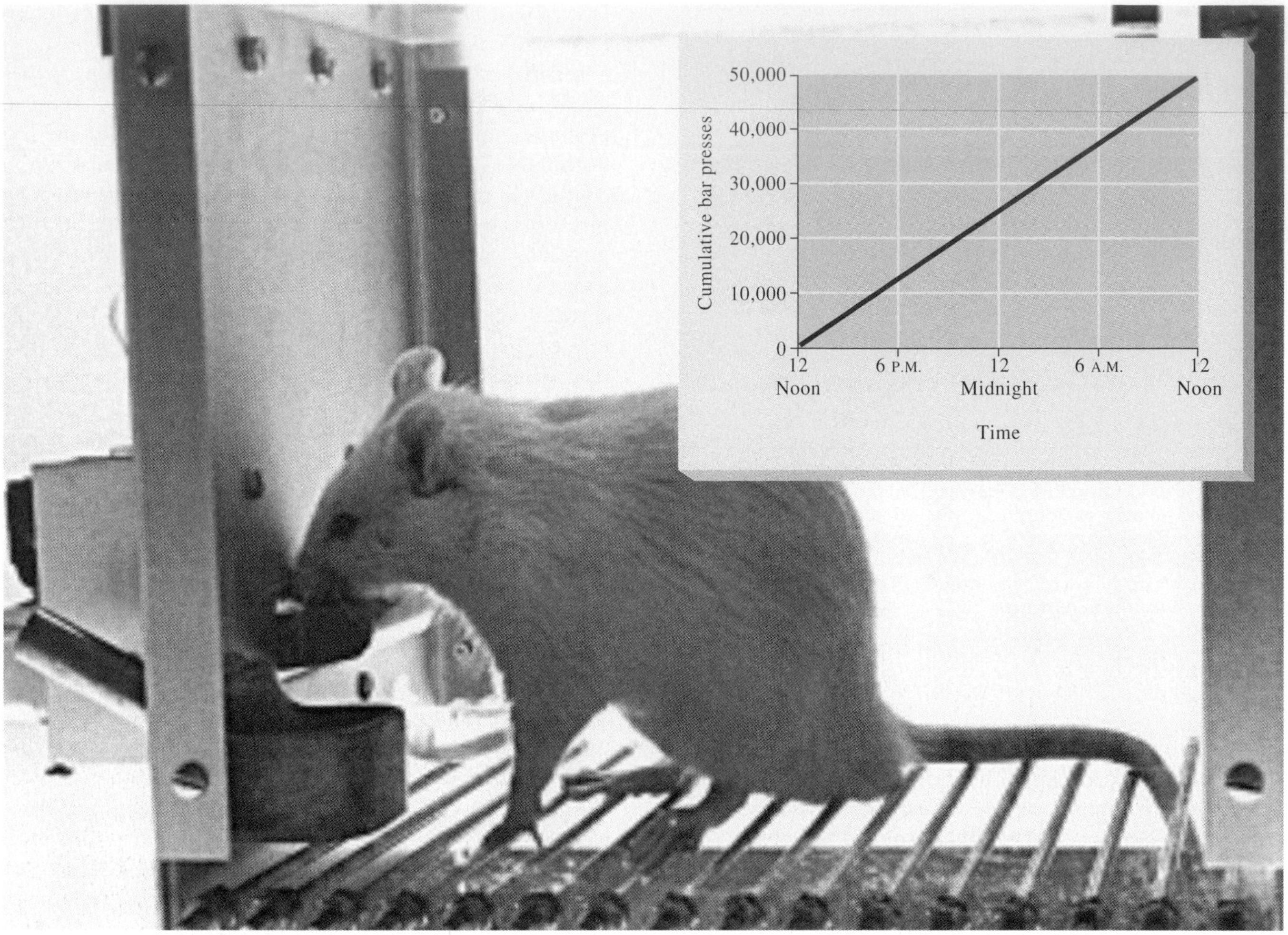

FIGURE 17

Results of the Experiment by Olds (1958) on the Role of the Hypothalamus in Pleasure
The graphed results for one rat show that it pressed the bar more than 2,000 times an hour for a period of 24 hours to receive the stimulus to its hypothalamus. One of the rats in Olds and Milner's experiments is shown pressing the bar to receive stimulation to its hypothalamus.

The wrinkled surface of the neocortex is divided into two halves (see figure 18). These two halves are called hemispheres, and each is divided into four lobes—frontal, parietal, temporal, and occipital (see figure 19). It is important to know that these lobes are not strictly functional regions but, rather, conveniently labeled anatomical regions. Nonetheless, there are functional differences among the lobes, and they are often associated somewhat loosely with functions. For example, the **occipital lobe,** *the portion of the neocortex at the back of the head, is involved in visual functioning;* the **temporal lobe,** *the portion of the neocortex just above the ears, is involved in hearing;* the **frontal lobe,** *the portion of the neocortex behind the forehead, is involved in the control of voluntary muscles and in intelligence;* and the **parietal lobe,** *the portion of the neocortex at the top of the head and toward the rear, is involved in bodily sensation.*

In the same way that the different lobes of the neocortex are associated with different processes, different regions of the lobes have different jobs. Scientists have determined this primarily through topographic mapping.

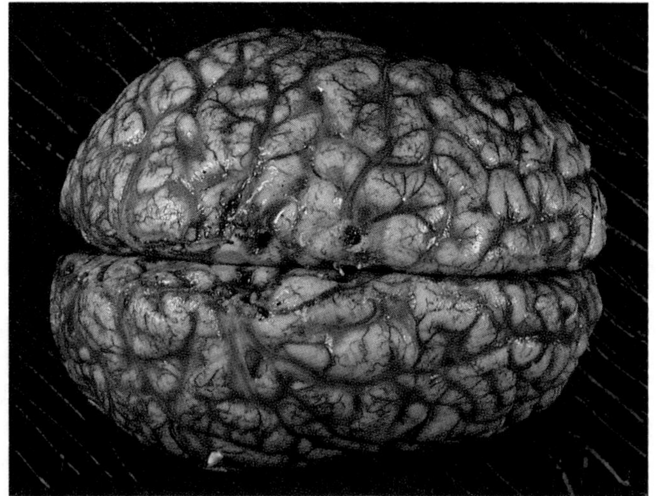

FIGURE 18

The Human Brain's Two Hemispheres
The two halves (hemispheres) of the human brain are clearly seen in this photograph.

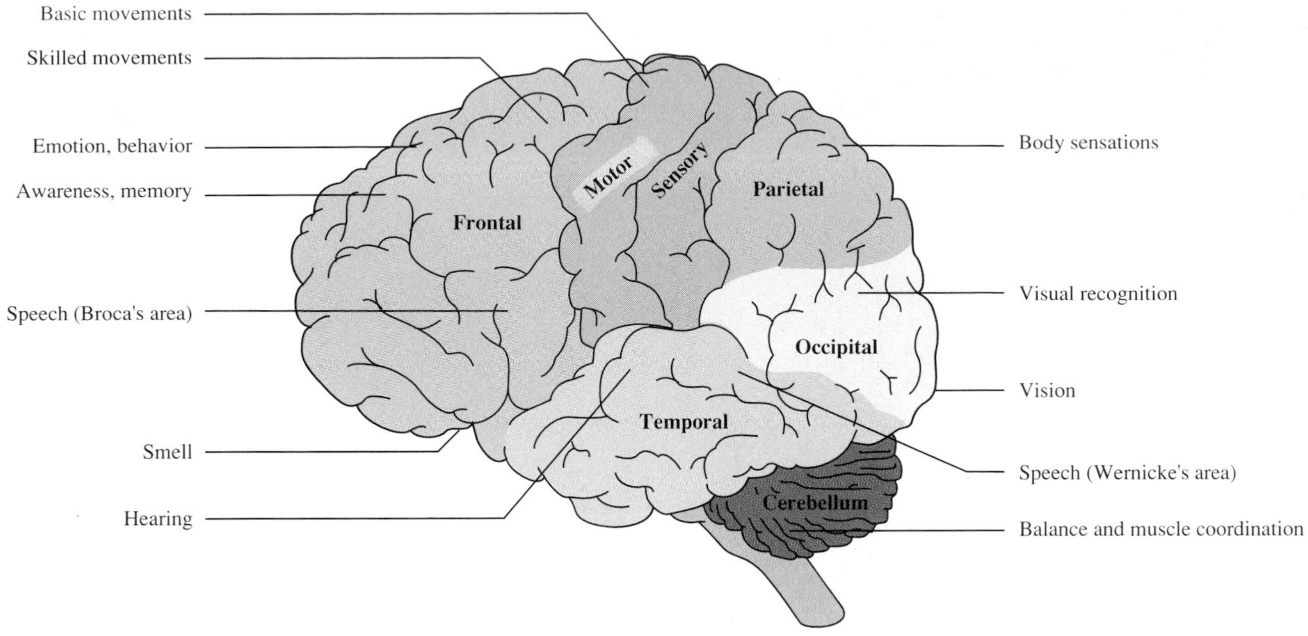

FIGURE 19

The Brain's Four Lobes
Shown here are the locations of the brain's four lobes: occipital, temporal, frontal, and parietal.

Two of the most widely used types of topographic maps are projection maps and functional maps. Projection maps are made by electrically stimulating areas of the brain and detecting the resulting behavior or by recording the electrical activity of the neocortex during certain behaviors.

Wilder Penfield (1947), a neurosurgeon at the Montreal Neurological Institute, worked with a number of patients who had very serious forms of epilepsy. Penfield often performed surgery to remove portions of the epileptic patients' brains, but he was concerned that removing a portion of the brain might impair some of the individuals' functions. Penfield's solution was to map the cortex during surgery by stimulating different cortical areas and observing the responses of the patients, who were given a local anesthetic so they would remain awake during the operation. He found that, when he stimulated certain sensory and motor areas of the brain, different parts of a patient's body moved (see figure 20). For both sensory and motor areas, there is a point-to-point relation between a part of the body and a location on the neocortex (see figure 21). The face and hands are given proportionally more space than other body parts. Because the face and hands are capable of finer perceptions and movements than are other body areas, they need more neocortex representation.

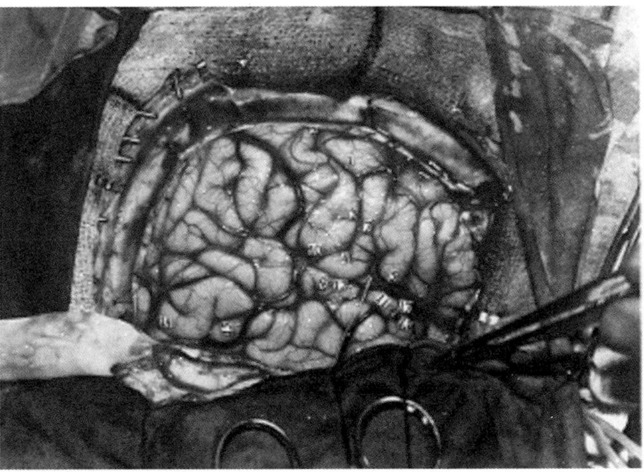

FIGURE 20

Penfield's Research
Penfield stimulated specific locations with a very thin electric probe. When he stimulated a specific area, the patient opened his mouth, sneezed, and began chewing.

The point-to-point mapping of sensory fields onto the cortex's surface is the basis of our orderly and accurate perception of the world (Fox, 1996). When something touches your lip, for example, your brain knows what body part has been touched (your lip) because the nerve pathways from your lip are the only pathways that project to the lip region of the sensory cortex. This arrangement is analogous to the private hot line that connects Washington and Moscow. If the red phone rings in the president's office in Washington, the call must be from Moscow, because Moscow is the only city that is connected to the other end of the hot line. In the sensory cortex, every small region has its own neural hot line bringing in information directly from the corresponding part of the sensory field. In our telephone analogy, it would be as if the president (the cortex) had hundreds of telephones, each one connected to the capital city of a different

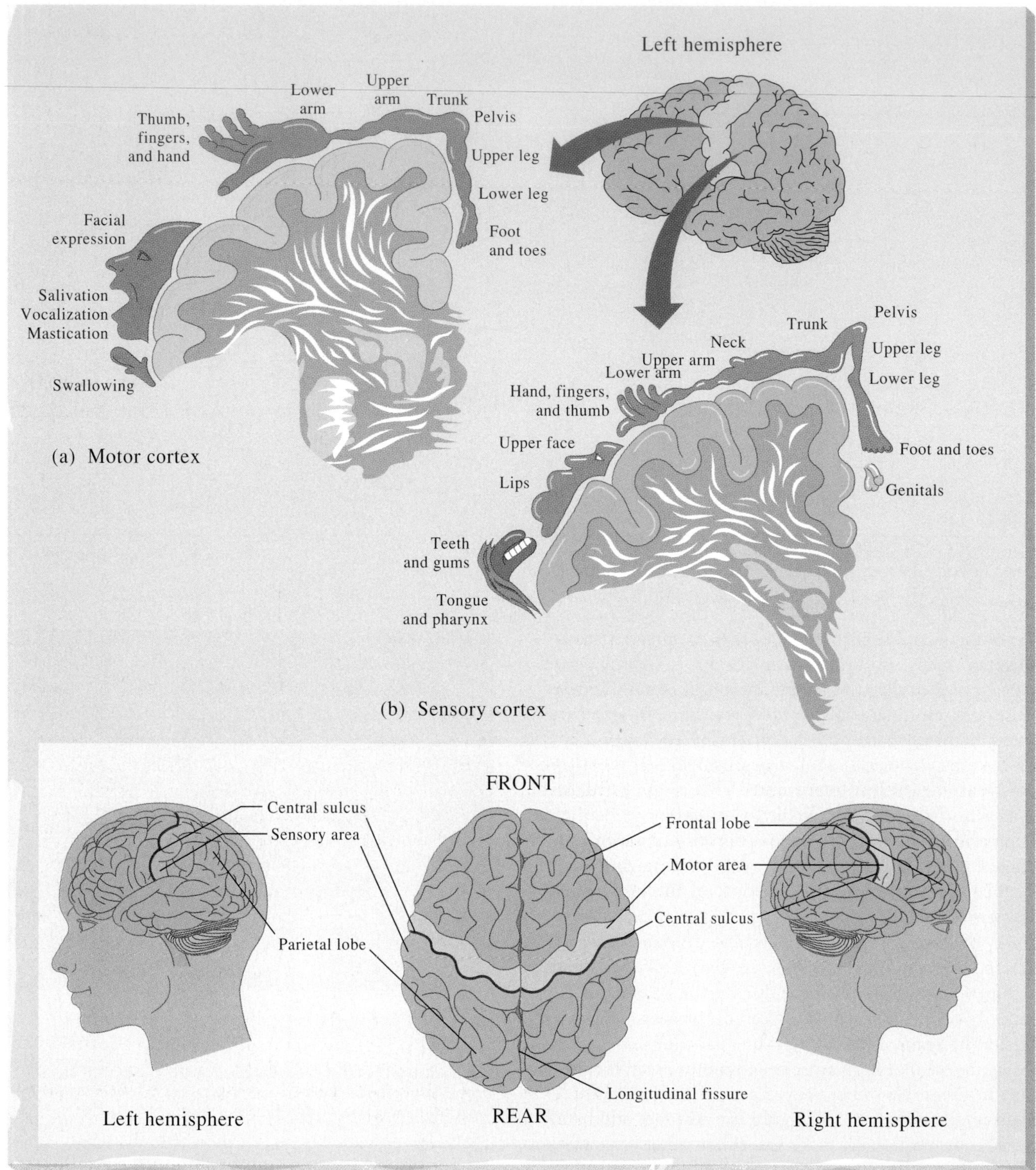

FIGURE 21

Locations of the Motor and Sensory Areas on the Cerebral Cortex

This figure shows (*a*) the motor areas involved with the control of the voluntary muscles and (*b*) the sensory areas involved with cutaneous and certain other senses. The body is disproportionately represented on the parietal and frontal lobes, with the hands and face receiving the most representation. Organization in inverse-functions represented at the top of the parietal lobe occurs in the lower regions of the body, for example.

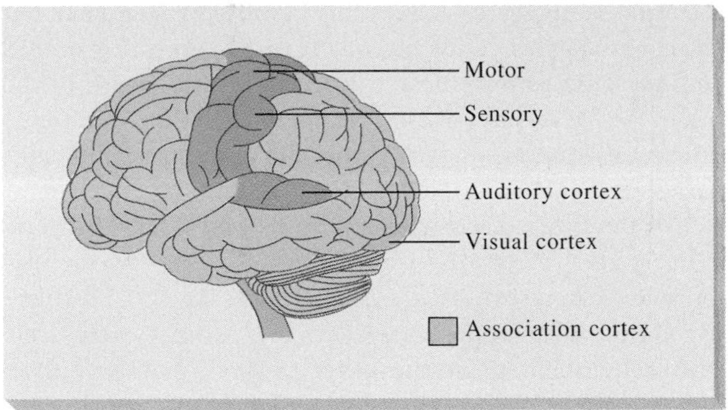

FIGURE 22

Association Cortex
The very large areas of the cerebral cortex, called the association cortex or association areas, do not respond when electrically stimulated, unlike the motor and sensory areas. Neurons in the association cortex communicate with neurons in other areas of the association cortex and with sensory and motor areas. Neuroscientists believe that the association areas are involved in thinking and problem solving.

country. Which phone was ringing would indicate which country (which part of the sensory field) had a message to convey.

One familiar example of what happens when these neural hot lines get connected the wrong way is seen in Siamese cats. Many Siamese cats have a genetic defect that causes the pathways from the eyes to connect to the wrong parts of the visual cortex during development. The result is that these cats spend their lives looking at things cross-eyed in an effort to "straighten out" the visual image of their visual cortex.

So far our description of the neocortex has focused on sensory and motor areas, but more than 75 percent of the neocortex is made up of areas called the association cortex (see figure 22). The **association cortex (or association areas)** *is the region of the neocortex involved in our highest intellectual functions, such as thinking and problem solving.* The neurons in the association cortex communicate with each other and with neurons in the motor area of the cortex.

Of special interest is the finding that damage to a specific part of the association cortex often does not result in a specific loss of function. With the exception of language areas (which are localized), loss of function seems to depend more on the extent of damage to the association areas than to the specific location of the damage. By observing brain-damaged individuals and using the mapping technique, scientists have found that the association cortex is involved in linguistic and perceptual functioning. The largest portion of association areas is located in the frontal lobe, directly under the forehead. Damage to this area does not lead to sensory or motor loss. Indeed, it is this area that may be most directly related to thinking and problem solving. Early experimentation even referred to the frontal lobe as the center of intelligence, but research suggests that frontal lobe damage may not result in a lowering of intelligence. Planning and judgment are characteristics often associated with the frontal lobe. Personality also may be linked with the frontal lobe. Recall the misfortune of Phineas Gage, whose personality radically changed after he experienced frontal lobe damage.

One of the truly fascinating areas of inquiry in contemporary neuroscience concerns the nature of cortical column function in the association cortex. Neuroscientist Vernon Mountcastle (1986) has speculated that individual columns in the association cortex might carry out specific functions such as planning new skeletal movements and shifting attention to new things. The coming decades likely will witness expansions on these themes. Imagine the behavioral result if some individuals had a genetic miswiring of association cortex columns similar to the miswiring of visual columns that occurs in some Siamese cats.

You have learned that the neocortex is divided into two hemispheres. The fascinating story of information processing in the neocortex involves lobes, maps, and columns, but it could not be completely told without knowing more about how the two sides, or hemispheres, of the brain work.

Split-Brain Research and the Cerebral Hemispheres

For many years scientists speculated that the **corpus callosum,** *a large bundle of axons that connects the brain's two hemispheres,* had something to do with relaying information between the two sides. Roger Sperry (1974) confirmed this in an experiment in which he cut the corpus callosum in cats. He also severed certain nerves leading from the eyes to the brain. After the operation, Sperry trained the cats to solve a series of visual problems with one eye blindfolded. After the cat learned the task, say with only its left eye uncovered, its other eye was blindfolded and the animal was tested again. The "split-brain" cat behaved as if it had never learned the task. It seems that the memory was stored only in the left hemisphere, which could no longer directly communicate with the right hemisphere.

Further evidence of the corpus callosum's function has come from experiments with patients who have severe, even life-threatening, forms of epilepsy. Epilepsy is caused by electrical "brainstorms" that flash uncontrollably across the corpus callosum. W. J. is one of the most famous cases. Neurosurgeons severed the corpus callosum of an epileptic patient now known as W. J. in a final attempt to reduce his unbearable seizures. Sperry (1968) examined W. J. and found that the corpus callosum functions the same in humans as in animals—cutting the corpus callosum seemed to leave the patient with "two separate minds" that learned and operated independently.

The right hemisphere, it turns out, receives information only from the left side of the body, and the left hemisphere receives information only from the right side of the body. When you hold an object in your left hand,

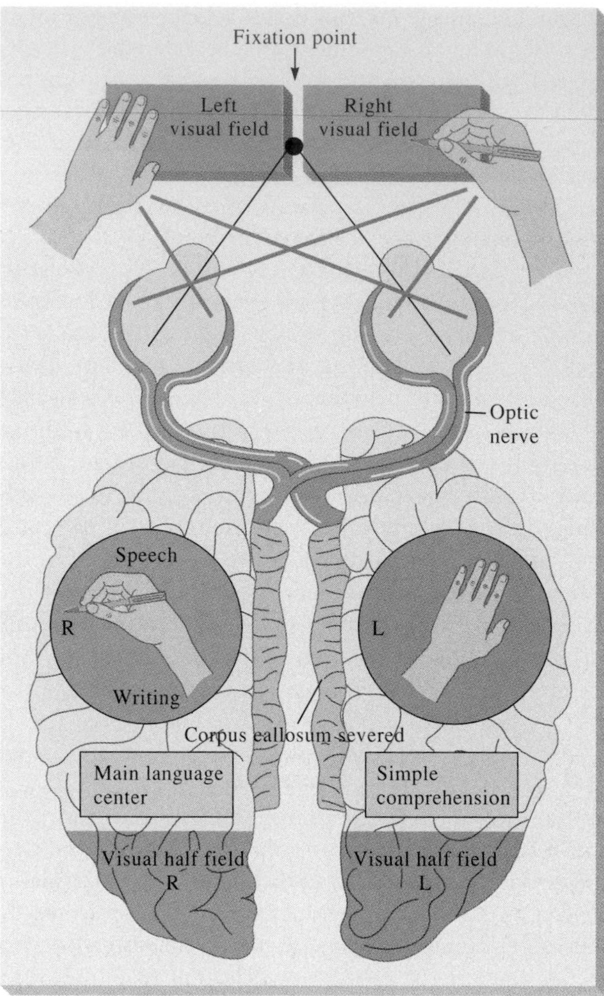

FIGURE 23

Visual Information in the Split Brain
In a split-brain patient, information from the visual field's left side projects only to the right hemisphere. Information from the visual field's right side projects only to the left hemisphere. Because of these projections, stimuli can be presented to only one of a split-brain patient's hemispheres.

for example, only the right hemisphere of your brain detects the object. When you hold an object in your right hand, only the left hemisphere of the brain detects the object (see figure 23). Because you have a normal corpus callosum, both hemispheres receive this information.

The most extensive and consistent research findings on the brain's two hemispheres involve language. The left hemisphere controls the ability to use language while the right hemisphere is unable to translate sensations into words. The split-brain patients in Sperry's experiments, such as W. J., could verbally describe sensations that were received by the left hemisphere—that is, a stimulus in the right visual field (Sperry & Gazzaniga, 1967). But they could not verbally describe sensations that were received by the right hemisphere—a stimulus in the left visual field. Because the corpus callosum was severed, the information could not be communicated from one hemisphere to the other. More recent investigations of split-brain patients document that language is rarely processed in the right hemisphere (Gazzaniga, 1983).

Speculation continues about the brain's hemispheric specialization—the notion that the two hemispheres function in different ways and that some psychological processes are restricted almost exclusively to one hemisphere or the other (Saravi, 1993). In fact, people commonly use the phrases *left-brained* and *right-brained* to say which hemisphere is dominant. Explorations in Psychology 1 addresses the nature of hemispheric specialization and separates fact from fantasy regarding a number of related myths.

Integration of Function in the Brain

How do all of the various brain regions cooperate to produce the wondrous complexity of thought and behavior that characterize humans? Part of the answer to this question, such as how the brain solves a murder mystery or writes a poetic essay, is beyond the grasp of neuroscience. Still, we can get a sense of integrative brain function by considering something like the act of escaping from a burning building. Gall and his phrenologists might have argued that such behavior was controlled by an "escaping from danger" center in the brain. Let's compare that view with a more contemporary one.

Imagine you are sitting at your desk writing letters when fire breaks out behind you. The sound of crackling flames is relayed from your ear, through the thalamus, to your auditory cortex, and on to the auditory association cortex. At each stage, the stimulus energy has been processed to extract information, and at some stage, probably at the association cortex level, the sounds are finally matched with something like a neural memory representing previous sounds of fires you have heard. The association "fire" sets new machinery in motion. Your attention (guided in part by the reticular formation) swings to the auditory signal being held in your association cortex, and simultaneously (again guided by reticular systems) your head turns toward the noise. Now your visual association cortex reports in: "Objects matching flames are present." In other association regions, the visual and auditory reports are synthesized ("We have things that look and sound like fire"), and neural associations representing potential actions ("flee") are activated. However, firing the neurons that code the plan to flee will not get you out of the chair. The basal ganglia must become engaged, and from there the commands will arise to set the brain stem, motor cortex, and cerebellum to the task of actually transporting you out of the room.

Actress Patricia Neal suffered a stroke when she was 39 years of age. The stroke paralyzed one of her legs and left her unable to read, write, or speak. However, an intensive rehabilitation program and the human brain's plasticity allowed her to recover her functioning to the point where she resumed her career as an actress four years later.

Which part of your brain did you use to escape? Virtually all systems had a role; each was quite specific, and together they generated the behavior. By the way, you would probably remember an event such as a fire in your room. That is because your limbic circuitry would have likely issued the "start print" command when the significant association "fire" was first triggered. The next time the sounds of crackling flames reach your auditory association cortex, the associations triggered will include those of this most recent escape. In sum, there is considerable integration of function in the brain.

Exploring the Brain

Other topics important for understanding the brain include these: What is the nature of brain damage, plasticity, and repair? What techniques can be used to study the brain? How do the brain and endocrine system work? What is the relation between brain and mind?

Brain Damage, Plasticity, and Repair

If the brain is damaged through injury or illness, does it have the capacity to repair itself? Are there external ways we can restore some or all of the brain's functioning after it has been damaged?

The Brain's Plasticity and Capacity for Repair

Brain damage can produce horrific effects, including paralysis, sensory loss, memory loss, and personality deterioration. When such damage occurs, can the brain recover some or all of its functions? Recovery from brain damage varies considerably (Garraghty, 1996).

Plasticity *is the brain's capacity to modify and reorganize itself following damage.* In one study, researchers surgically removed part of the monkeys' somatosensory cortex. Later the somatosensory cortical map shifted to intact adjacent parts of the parietal lobes, restoring the body's ability to experience sensations (Fox, 1984).

The human brain shows the most plasticity in young children before the functions of the cortical regions become entirely fixed (Kolb, 1989). For example, if the speech areas in an infant's left hemisphere are damaged, the right hemisphere assumes much of this language function. However, after age 5, permanent damage to the left hemisphere can permanently disrupt language ability.

A key factor in recovery is whether some, or all, of the neurons in an affected area are just damaged or completely destroyed. If the neurons are not completely destroyed, brain function often becomes restored over time. Unlike some fish and amphibians who can regenerate neurons, our central nervous system cannot. Once a human neuron is lost, it is gone forever.

Even though new neurons can't be regenerated in humans, other mechanisms of repair exist (Azar, 1996). One is **collateral sprouting,** *in which the axons of some healthy neurons adjacent to damaged cells will grow new branches.* The new branches may over time attach themselves to the synapses left vacant by the cells through damage (Veraa & Grafstein, 1981). Another way the brain can repair itself is through **substitution of function,** *in which the function of a damaged region is taken over by another area, or areas, of the brain.* This is what happened in our earlier example of the right hemisphere taking over the speech function of the damaged left hemisphere in infants. To read further about brain plasticity, turn to Explorations in Psychology 2.

Brain Tissue Transplants

The brain's capacity to repair itself may restore some lost functions following damage, but not in all cases. In recent years, considerable excitement has been generated about **brain grafts,** *which involve transplanting healthy tissue into damaged brains.* The potential success of brain grafts is much better with brain tissue from the

EXPLORATIONS IN PSYCHOLOGY 1

Left-Brain, Right-Brain Myths

You've probably seen James Garner on TV advertising beef. "Ya heard about the left brain/right brain stuff? The logical left brain understands nutrition," Garner explains, "but the right brain just knows it's good." Garner's pitch, and that of others in the media and popular books, is that the left hemisphere is rational, logical, and Western, while the brain's right hemisphere is creative, intuitive, and Eastern.

Everyone seems to accept this; everyone that is, except the scientists who have researched left- and right-hemisphere functions. To them, the concept of the brain as split into two tidy halves—one being the source of creativity, the other the source of logical thinking—is simplistic. Jerre Levy, a neuroscientist at the University of Chicago, points out that no complex function—music, art, reading, or whatever—can be assigned to one single hemisphere or the other. Complex thinking in normal people involves communication between both sides of the brain.

How did the left brain/right brain myth get started? It had its origin in Roger Sperry's classic studies of split-brain patients. Remember that Sperry examined people whose corpus callosum had been severed and found that after surgery the two sides of the brain learned and operated independently. As his findings made their way into the media, the complexity of Sperry's findings became oversimplified. Media reports indicated that when you worked on a novel, your left hemisphere was busy while your right was silent. Switch to creating an oil painting and your right brain is working while your left is quiet. People became either right-brained (and artistic) or left-brained (and logical). An example of the either/or oversimplification of the brain's left and right hemispheres is shown in the *Newsweek* drawing of how the brain divides its work (see figure A).

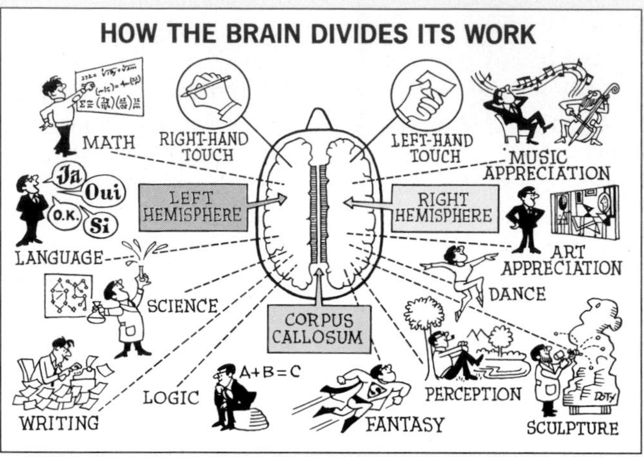

FIGURE A

Stereotyped Myths About Left Brain, Right Brain
Is left-brain, right-brain specialization all-or-none, as this drawing implies? No.

Roger Sperry did discover that the left hemisphere is superior in the kind of logic used to prove geometric theorems. But in the logic of everyday life, our problems involve integrating information and drawing conclusions. In these instances, the right brain's functions are crucial. In virtually all activities, there is an interplay between the

fetal stage (an early stage in prenatal development). The neurons of the fetus are still growing at that stage and are more likely than an adult's neurons to make connections with other neurons.

Most animal studies of brain grafts are done on rats. Researchers damage part of the rat's brain, wait until the animal recovers as much as possible by itself, and then assess its behavioral deficits. Then they take tissue from the corresponding area of a fetal rat's brain and transplant it into the damaged brain of the adult rat. In these studies, the rats that received the brain transplants demonstrated considerable behavioral recovery (Dunnett, 1989; Gash, Collier, & Sladek, 1985).

Might such brain grafts be successful with humans suffering from brain damage? One problem is finding donors. Aborted fetuses are a possibility, but they raise ethical issues. Another possibility has been attempted with individuals who have Parkinson's disease. This neurological disorder, which affects about a million people in the United States, greatly impairs coordinated movement, making even a walk across a room into a major ordeal. For individuals with this disease, brain grafters have tried to substitute adrenal gland tissue for brain tissue. Why adrenal gland tissue? Parkinson's disease damages neurons in the substantia nigra, an area of the brain that secretes the neurotransmitter dopamine.

Neuroscientist Jerre Levy has conducted extensive research on the nature of hemispheric function in the brain.

brain's two hemispheres (Hoptman & Davidson, 1994). For example, in reading, the left hemisphere comprehends syntax and grammar, which the right does not. However, the right brain is better at understanding a story's intonation and emotion. The same is true for music and art. Pop psychology assigns both to the right brain. In some musical skills, such as recognizing chords, the right hemisphere is better. In others, such as distinguishing which of two sounds came first, the left hemisphere takes over. Enjoying or creating music requires the use of both hemispheres.

Another offshoot of the left-brain, right-brain hoopla is speculation that more right-brain activities and exercises should be incorporated into our nation's schools (Edwards, 1979). In schools that rely heavily on rote learning to instruct students, children probably would benefit from exercises in intuitive thought and holistic thinking. But this deficiency in school curricula has *nothing at all* to do with left-brain, right-brain specialization.

There is so much more to understanding brain function and organization than to characterize people as right- or left-brained. After all, we are trying to understand the most complex piece of matter in the known universe.

Popular visions of right-brain, left-brain specialization suggest that Andy Warhol's (a) and Aretha Franklin's (b) right brains are responsible for their artistic and musical talents, and that Stewart Bulford's (c) and Albert Einstein's left (d) brains are responsible for their scientific giftedness. Is this popular vision overdramatized? Yes, extensively.

Adrenal gland cells produce dopamine. Early reports of adrenal gland transplants in Parkinson's patients were promising, but the long-term effects have been less so (Lewin, 1988).

The potential for brain grafts also exists for individuals with Alzheimer's disease, which is characterized by a progressive decline in intellectual functioning. Alzheimer's destruction of the brain involves the pathways of acetylcholine-releasing neurons involved in memory. Such degenerative changes can be reversed in rats (Gage & Bjorklund, 1986), but as yet no evidence of success has been found for such acetylcholine pathway transplants in humans. Nonetheless, the future holds promise that such transplants of brain tissue will be able to restore the functioning of damaged brains in humans.

Techniques to Study the Brain

Neuroscientists no longer have to perform surgery on living patients or cadavers to study the brain. Sophisticated techniques—such as high-powered microscopes, the electroencephalograph, single-unit recordings, the CAT scan, the PET scan, magnetic resonance imaging (MRI), and SQUID—allow researchers to "peer" into the brain while it's at work, without ruffling a hair (Brodic, 1996). We will consider each of these in turn.

Explorations in Psychology 2

The Brains of the Mankato Nuns

Nearly 700 nuns in a convent in Mankato, Minnesota, are the largest group of brain donors in the world. By examining the nuns' donated brains, as well as others, neuroscientists are beginning to understand that the brain has a remarkable capacity to change and grow, even in old age. The Sisters of Mankato lead an intellectually challenging life, and brain researchers recently have found that stimulating the brain with mental exercises can cause neurons to increase their dendritic branching (Snowden, 1995) (see figure B).

The capacity of the brain to change offers new possibilities for preventing and treating brain diseases, helping to explain why some individuals can

- Delay the onset of Alzheimer's disease symptoms for years; the more educated people are, the less likely they are to develop Alzheimer's, probably because intellectual activity develops surplus brain tissue that compensates for tissue damaged by the disease.
- Recover better from strokes. Researchers have found that even when areas of the brain are permanently damaged by stroke, new message routes can be created to get around the blockage or to resume the function of that area.
- Feel sensation in missing limbs. Scientists no longer believe that the complaints of pain in amputated body parts are psychosomatic. The sensations, which eventually fade, likely are the brain's way of keeping once-busy neurons active, providing evidence that areas of the brain no longer useful can be taken over by nearby regions of the cortex.

Figure B

The Brains of the Mankato Nuns
Sister Marcella Zachman (*inset, left*) finally stopped teaching at age 97. Now, at 99, she helps ailing nuns exercise their brains by quizzing them on vocabulary or playing a card game called Skip-Bo, at which she deliberately loses. Sister Mary Esther Boor (*inset, right*), also 99 years of age, is a former teacher who keeps alert by doing puzzles and volunteering to work the front desk. *Large photo:* A technician holds the brain of a deceased Mankato nun. The nuns donate their brains for research that explores the effects of stimulation on brain growth. This research is supported by the National Institutes of Aging.

High-powered microscopes are widely used in neuroscience research. Neurons are stained with the salts of various heavy metals such as silver and lead. These stains coat only a small portion of any group of neurons. The stains allow neuroscientists to view and study every part of a neuron in microscopic detail.

Also widely used, the **electroencephalograph (EEG)** *records the electrical activity of the brain. Electrodes placed on the scalp detect brain-wave activity, which is recorded on a chart known as an electroencephalogram* (see figure 24). This device has been used to assess brain damage, epilepsy, and other problems.

Not every recording of brain activity is made with electrodes. In single-unit recording, a portrayal of a single neuron's electrical activity, a thin wire or needle is inserted in or near an individual neuron. The wire or needle transmits the neuron's electrical activity to an amplifier.

For years X rays have been used to determine damage inside or outside our bodies, both in the brain and in other locations. But a single X ray of the brain is hard to interpret because it shows the three-dimensional nature of the brain's interior in a two-dimensional image. **Computer-assisted axial tomography (CAT scan)** *is three-dimensional imaging obtained from X rays of the head that are assembled into a composite image by computer.* The CAT scan provides valuable information about the location of damage due to a stroke, language disorder, or loss of memory.

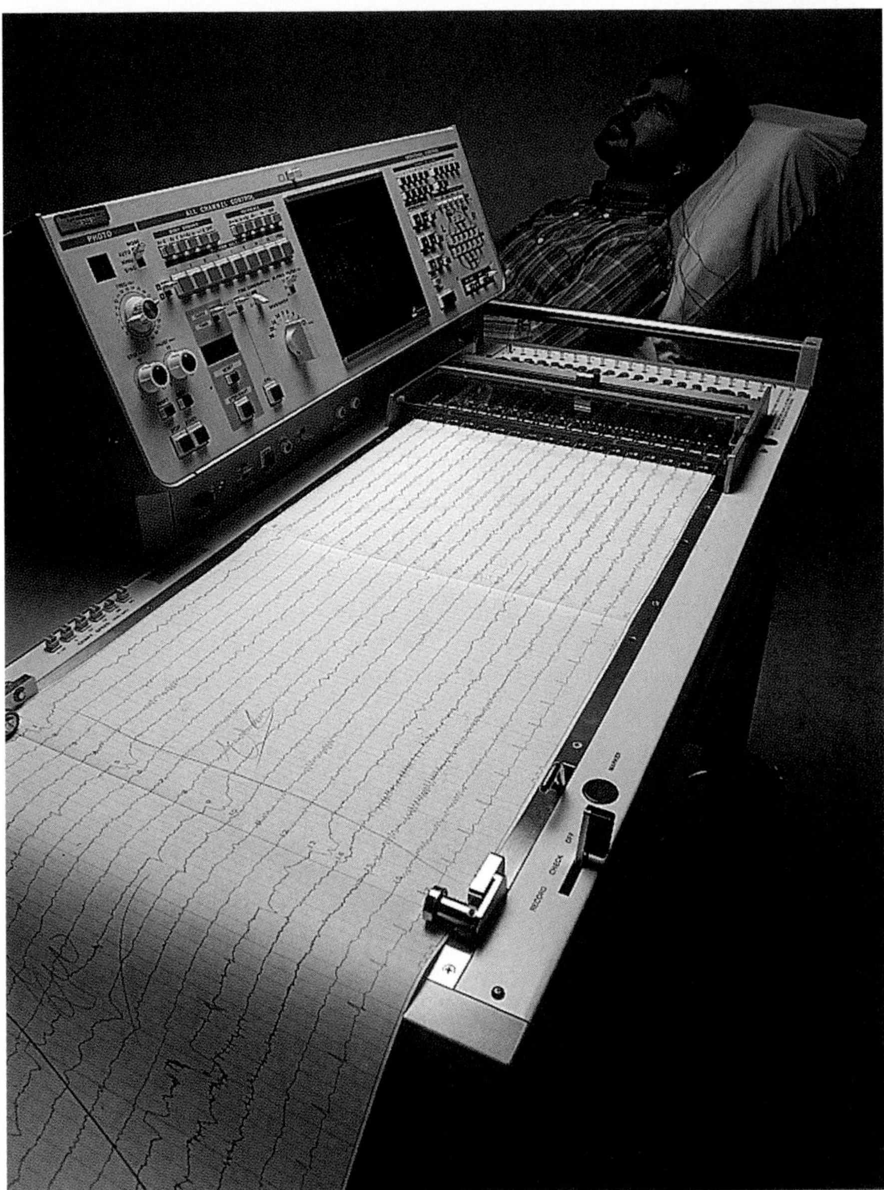

FIGURE 24

An EEG Recording
The electroencephalogram (EEG) is widely used in sleep research. Its use led to some major breakthroughs in understanding sleep by showing how the brain's electrical activity changes during sleep.

Positron-emission tomography (PET scan) *measures the amount of glucose in various areas of the brain, then sends this information to a computer.* Because glucose levels vary with the levels of activity throughout the brain, tracing the amounts of glucose generates a picture of activity level throughout the brain (Fiez & others, 1996; Zatorre & others, 1996). PET scans of people's brain activity while they are hearing, seeing, speaking, and thinking are shown in figure 25.

Another technique is **magnetic resonance imaging (MRI),** *which involves creating a magnetic field around a person's body and using radio waves to construct images of the person's brain tissues and biochemical activities.* MRI provides very clear pictures of the brain's interior, does not require injecting the brain with a substance, and does not pose a problem of radiation overexposure.

The **superconducting quantum interference device (SQUID)** *is a brain-scanning device that senses tiny changes in magnetic fields.* When neurons fire, they create an electrical current; electrical fields include magnetic fields, so magnetic changes indicate neural activity. Figure 26 displays images created by three of the brain-scanning instruments we have discussed—MRI, PET, and SQUID.

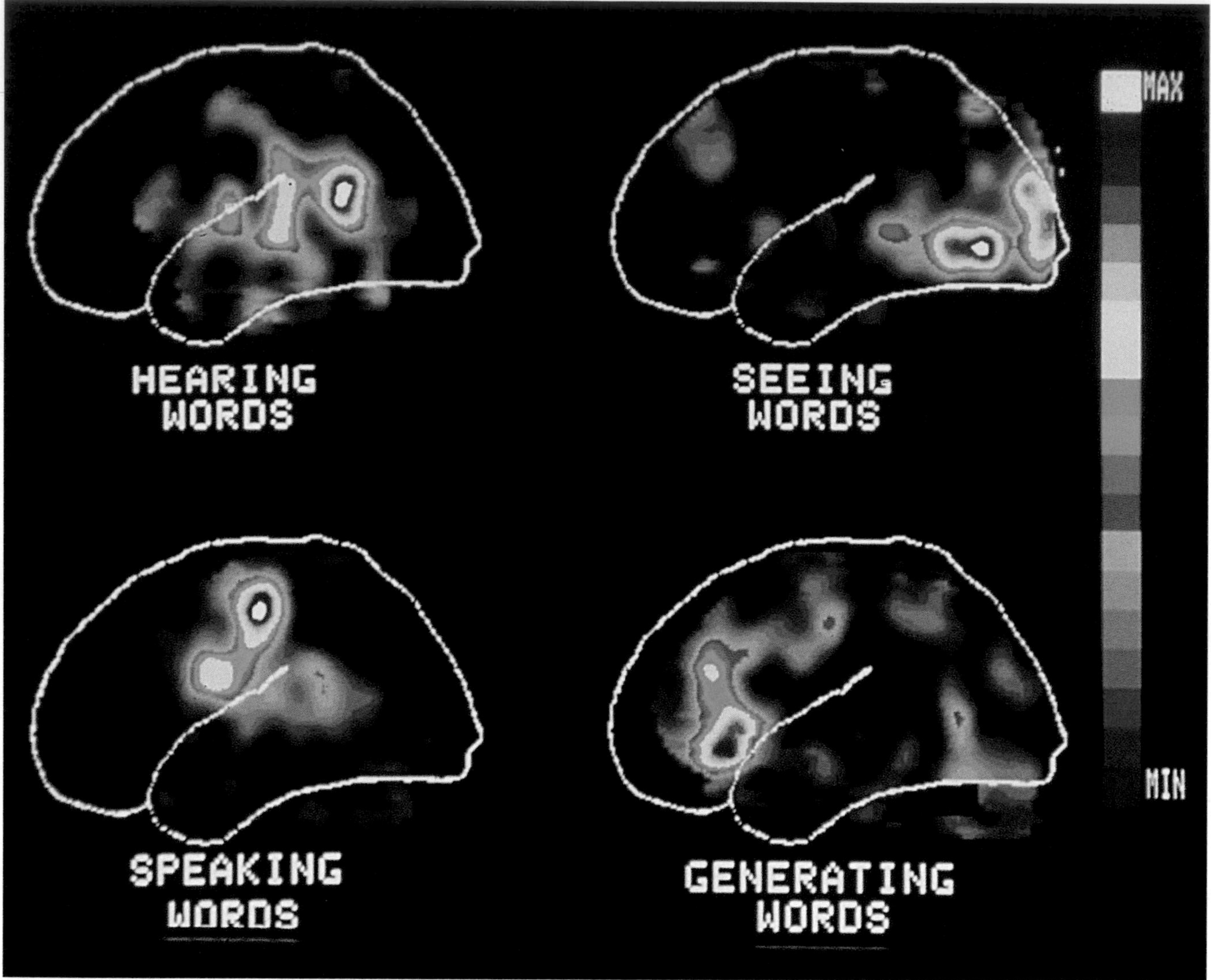

FIGURE 25

PET Scan
This PET scan of the left hemisphere of the brain contrasts the different areas used in aspects of language activity: hearing, seeing, speaking, and thinking.

At this point we have discussed many different aspects of the brain and techniques for studying it. One more important aspect of the body's biological makeup deserves further attention—the endocrine system.

The Brain and Endocrine System

Recall that the autonomic nervous system involves connections with internal organs, regulating processes like respiration, heart rate, and digestion. The autonomic nervous system acts on the endocrine glands to produce a number of important physiological reactions to strong emotions such as rage and fear.

The **endocrine glands** *are a set of glands that release their chemical products directly into the bloodstream. Hormones are chemical messengers manufactured by the endocrine glands.* Hormones travel more slowly than nerve impulses. The bloodstream conveys hormones to all parts of the body, and the membrane of every cell has receptors for one or more hormones.

The endocrine glands consist of the hypothalamus and the pituitary gland at the base of the brain, the thyroid and parathyroid glands at the front of the neck, the adrenal glands just above the kidneys, the pancreas in the abdomen, and the ovaries in the female's pelvis and the testes in the male's scrotum (see figure 27). Other hormones are produced as well, including several in the gastrointestinal tract that control digestion. In much the same way that the brain's control of muscular activity is constantly monitored and altered to suit the information received by the brain, the action of the endocrine glands is continuously

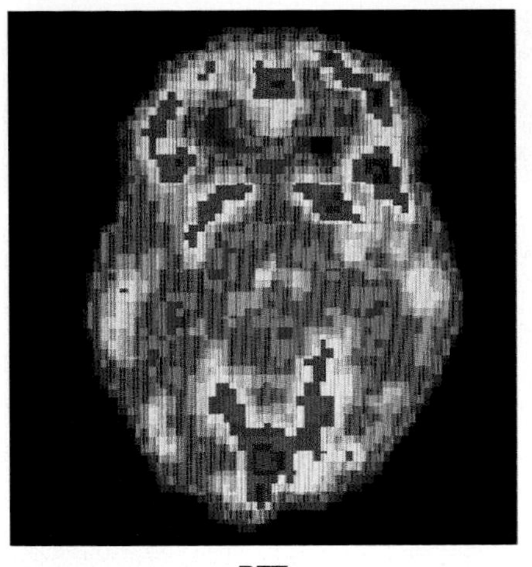

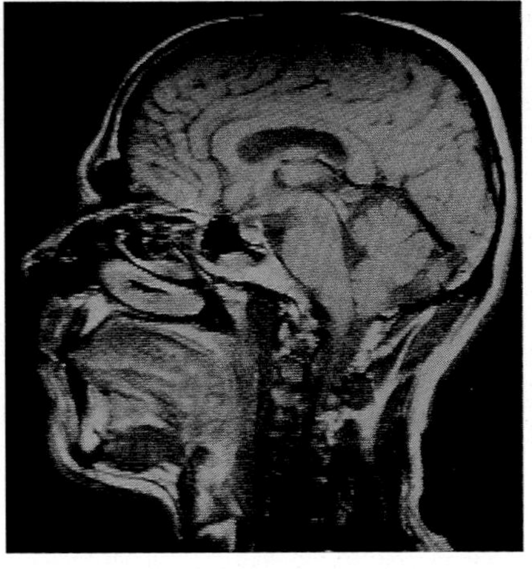

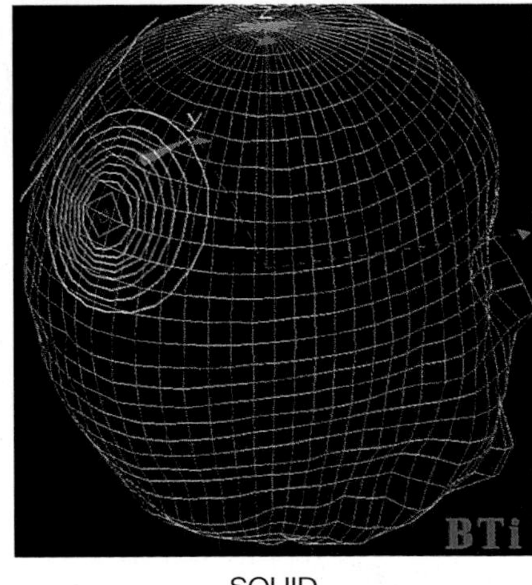

FIGURE 26

Contemporary Scanning Devices for Examining the Brain
Each scanning device has its strengths and weaknesses. For example, PET accurately tracks brain function, but can't resolve structures less than 0.5 inches apart. MRI can't detect functions, but can distinguish structures even 0.05 inches apart.

monitored and changed by the nervous, hormonal, and chemical information sent to them.

The **pituitary gland** *is an important endocrine gland that sits at the base of the skull and is about the size of a pea; the pituitary gland controls growth and regulates other glands.* The anterior (front) part of the pituitary is known as the master gland, because almost all of its hormones direct the activity of target glands elsewhere in the body. For example, follicle-stimulating hormone (FSH) produced by the pituitary monitors the level of sex hormones in the ovaries of females and testes of males. Though most pituitary hormones influence a specific organ, growth hormone (GH) acts on all tissues to produce growth during childhood and adolescence. Dwarfs have too little of this hormone, giants too much (see figure 28).

The **adrenal glands** *play an important role in our moods, our energy level, and our ability to cope with stress. Each adrenal gland secretes epinephrine (also called adrenaline) and norepinephrine (also called noradrenaline).* While most hormones travel rather slowly, epinephrine and norepinephrine do their work quickly. Epinephrine helps a person get ready for an emergency by acting on smooth muscles, the heart, stomach, intestines, and sweat glands. Epinephrine also stimulates the reticular formation, which in turn arouses the sympathetic nervous system, and this system subsequently excites the adrenal glands to produce more epinephrine. Norepinephrine also alerts the individual for emergency situations by interacting with the pituitary and the liver. You may remember that norepinephrine also functions as a neurotransmitter when released by neurons. In the case of the adrenal glands, norepinephrine is released as a hormone. In both instances, norepinephrine conveys information—in the first instance to neurons, in the second to glands (Raven & Johnson, 1996).

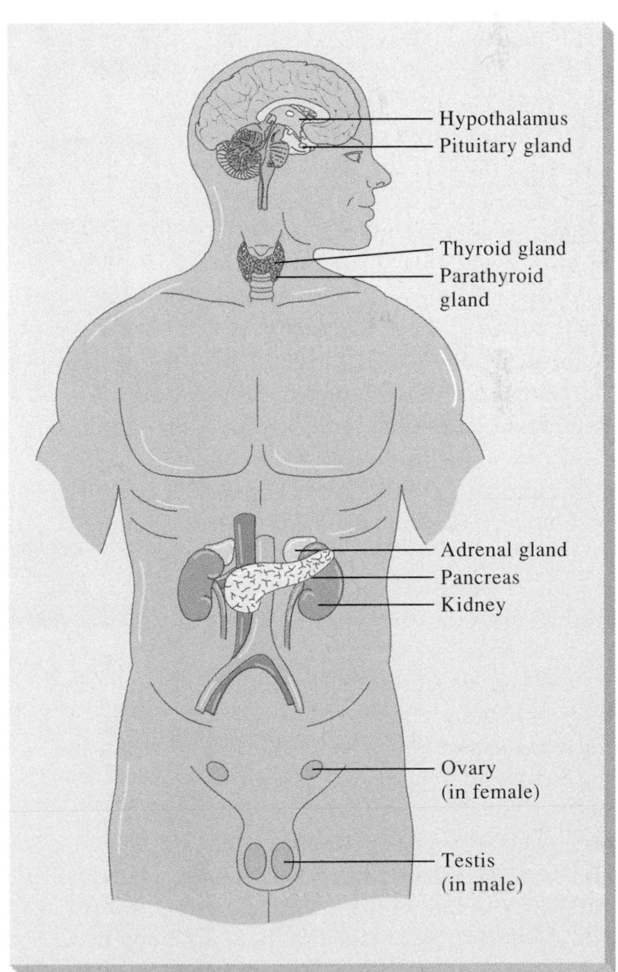

FIGURE 27

The Major Endocrine Glands
The pituitary gland releases hormones that regulate the hormone secretions of the other glands. The pituitary gland is itself regulated by the hypothalamus.

Brain and Mind

Is everything that makes us human no more than the interaction of chemicals and electrical charges inside the labyrinth of the brain, or is there something more? A popular joke told by Thomas Hewitt Key in the nineteenth century went like this:

> What's the matter?
> Never mind.
> What is mind?
> No matter.

Though the Victorians may have believed that mind is mind and matter is matter and the two never meet, psychologists today are not so sure.

Two prominent positions on the mind-body issue are monism and dualism. **Monism** *stresses a single substance underlying the existence of mind and body—in other words, mind and body are inseparable.* In this view, mind is brain and brain is mind. By contrast, **dualism** *stresses that mind and body are separate, the mind being nonphysical and the brain being physical.* In one version of dualism, proposed by philosopher René Descartes, mind and body exist separately but can interact.

Interest in the relation of mind and brain has increased in the last several decades due to surges of interest in the neurosciences and cognitive psychology. The philosopher Popper and the scientist Eccles (Popper & Eccles, 1977) put their minds (brains?) together, agreeing with Descartes that mind and brain are separate but interact. The neuroscientist Sperry and the philosopher Searle declare themselves clearly on the side of mind, believing that mind moves and controls matter (Searle, 1984; Sperry, 1976). By contrast, the famous behaviorist B. F. Skinner (1987) gave up hope for a science of mental life.

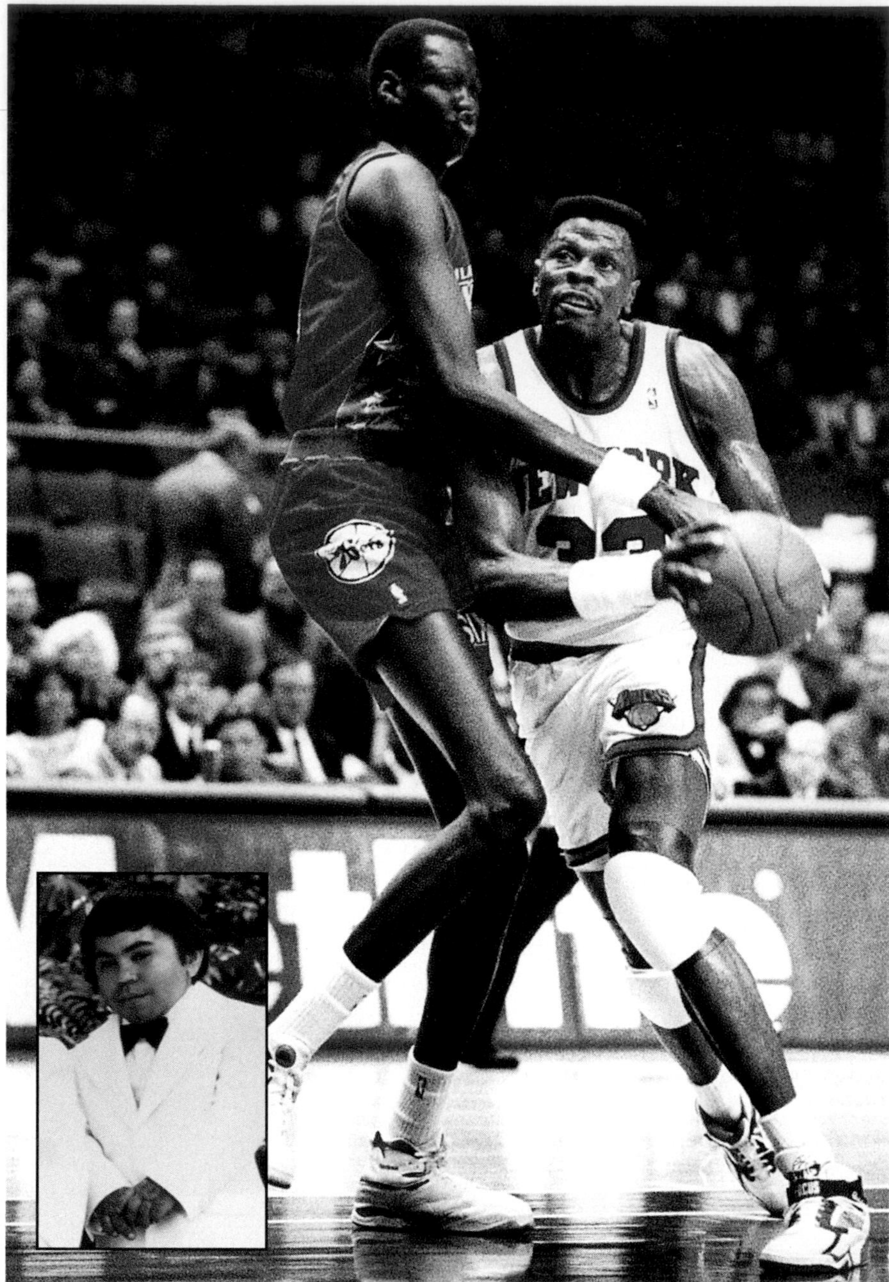

FIGURE 28

Giants and Dwarfs
The height of former NBA player Manute Bol (*at left in large photo*) is 7′6¼″ due to a higher-than-usual amount of growth hormone, produced by the anterior pituitary gland. (*Inset*) Dwarfs, such as Herve Villechaize, who starred as Tattoo on the television show "Fantasy Island," have less than the usual amount of growth hormone.

There is no known scientific method to help choose among the possible answers to the mind-body issue. Some brain researchers, though, believe that the concept of mind is headed for a fateful death as they chip away at the depths of the brain and uncover more information about its electrochemical basis. Still, there are skeptics who argue that such human characteristics as will and consciousness will forever elude brain researchers.

At this point, we have discussed many ideas about the brain, the endocrine system, and the relation between brain and mind. A summary of these ideas is presented in concept table 3.

Concept Table 3

Brain Structure and Function, and Exploring the Brain

Concept	Processes/Related Ideas	Characteristics/Description
Brain Structure and Function	Embryological development	A neural tube develops into the hindbrain (lowest level), midbrain (middle level), and forebrain (highest level).
	Hindbrain, midbrain, and forebrain	The main structures of the hindbrain are the medulla, cerebellum, and pons. The midbrain's major structure is the reticular formation; many fiber systems ascend and descend in the midbrain. Among the forebrain's main structures are the limbic system (which also runs through the midbrain), thalamus, basal ganglia, hypothalamus, and neocortex. Each is specialized to perform certain information-processing jobs.
	Neocortex	The neocortex is a vast sheet of neural tissue in the forebrain. The wrinkled surface of the cortex is divided into two hemispheres (left and right) and four lobes (frontal, parietal, temporal, and occipital). Topographic mapping has helped scientists determine the neocortex's role in different behaviors. The neocortex also can be divided into sensory areas, motor areas, and association areas.
	Split-brain research and the cerebral hemispheres	Pioneered by Sperry, split-brain research involves severing the corpus callosum. Such research has revealed that language is primarily a left-hemisphere function. In normal individuals, the two hemispheres work together to process information. A number of myths have developed that exaggerate left-brain and right-brain functions.
	Integration of function in the brain	Most psychological functions do not involve a single structure in the brain, but rather, the integration of information by a number of structures.
Exploring the Brain	Brain damage, plasticity, and repair	Recovery from brain damage varies considerably. Plasticity is the brain's capacity for modification and reorganization following damage. If neurons in the central nervous system are destroyed, they cannot be regenerated. Plasticity is greater in young children than in adults. Collateral sprouting and substitution of function are two mechanisms of repair in the brain. Brain grafts involve transplanting healthy tissue into damaged brains. The most successful brain grafts involve the use of fetal brain tissue, but this procedure raises ethical issues. The potential for brain tissue transplants exists for individuals with Parkinson's disease and with Alzheimer's disease. Brain grafts have been much more successful with rats than with humans.
	Techniques to study the brain	Among the most widely used techniques are high-powered microscopes, the electroencephalograph, single-unit recordings, the CAT scan, the PET scan, magnetic resonance imaging (MRI), and SQUID.
	The brain and endocrine system	The endocrine glands discharge their chemical products directly into the bloodstream. These chemical products, called hormones, can travel to all parts of the body. The pituitary gland and the adrenal glands are important parts of the endocrine system.
	Brain and mind	Philosophers and scientists have speculated about the relation of mind and brain (or mind and body) for centuries. Two prominent views are monism and dualism. There is no known scientific method to examine the mind-body issue.

Critical Thinking About Behavior

The Romance of Simplicity

> *Things should be as simple as possible, not simpler.*
>
> **Albert Einstein**

If you are like many introductory students, you may have found the contents of this chapter to be especially challenging. Many terms and processes in the neurobiological arena are difficult to grasp from two-dimensional illustrations or text descriptions. Yet a thorough understanding of the contributions of biology to behavior is an important foundation for the rest of your study in this course. In addition, as the science of psychology continues to grow through research, the neurobiological area will grow in complexity. If you return to this area of study 10 years from now, you likely will be impressed to see how many more details and concepts have been added to come progressively closer to a complete picture of how the body works.

Yearning for less-complex explanations might be a routine part of the human condition. If the brain happened to come with an owner's manual, it would need to contain this warning: "Your brain might interpret things as being simpler than they really are." We can find several examples of this tendency in the history of research in this area.

One of the first attempts to explain brain function was a curious approach called phrenology, which we briefly discussed early in this chapter (see figure C). A German physician named Franz Joseph Gall developed this approach, in which various bumps and indentations on the skull were interpreted as providing a map of character. A bump corresponded to an excess of the characteristic. An indentation signified a deficiency. A phrenological reading might describe you as generous or stingy, based on whether you had a bump or an indentation at the particular site believed to correspond to this trait. This simplistic system of connecting characteristics of the skull to specialized features had some merit—it anticipated the more extensive brain-localization studies of scientists such as Wilder Penfield—but the content of phrenology was wrong. However, phrenology was widely appealing because it presented such a simple system of explanation.

Identifying specific structures responsible for brain functions has also proved to be a difficult problem. Unlike the helpful color graphics in this book, the brain tends to be a uniform color, so differentiating brain structures has not been easy. In addition, most behaviors are complex events that involve many brain functions and structures simultaneously. Isolating causal relationships requires sophisticated medical techniques. As you also studied in this chapter, the distinction between left and right hemispheric function is a simplification that has been enthusiastically and erroneously adopted by many in our culture. Attributions about race as a cause of behavior are also oversimplifications that are likely to create even more complex problems in our adaptation to an increasingly diverse world.

Simple explanations might be very compelling, but when it comes to behavior, simple explanations are rarely very satisfying. Have you experienced situations in which a simple solution fell short because it underestimated the complexity of the problem? Can you think of behaviors that you interpreted in a simple manner that turned out to be far more complicated? Your awareness of this interpretive bias can help you overcome the tendency to draw premature conclusions. This awareness will also assist you to pursue alternative explanations to promote comprehensive explanations.

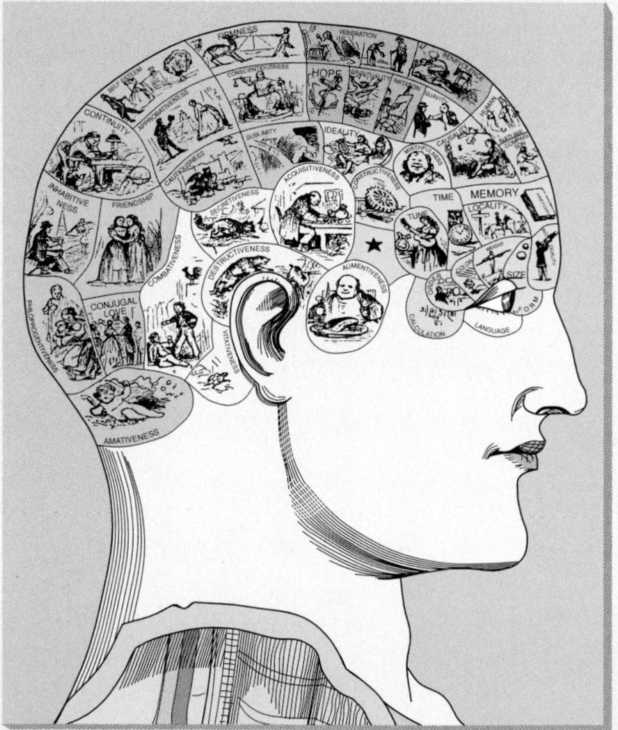

Figure C

Phrenology Map Based on Gall's System
Gall was the father of the pseudoscience of phrenology. He believed that the brain was made up of about 30 "organs," each responsible for a single trait. Phrenology swept the United States and Europe, spawning phrenological societies, books, pamphlets, and sideshows. The craze attracted Edgar Allan Poe, Karl Marx, and Queen Victoria, who got a phrenologist to examine the royal children's cranial knobs. One fanatic proclaimed, "Phrenologist after phrenologist may die, but phrenology will never perish"; perish it did, however, under the onslaught of reason and ridicule.

Overview

We began this chapter by exploring the nature of heredity, the evolutionary perspective, and nature/nurture. Next, we studied the brain and nervous system, including early approaches, the elegant organization of the nervous system, neurons, and glial cells. Then we turned our attention to brain structure and function, evaluating embryological development, the hindbrain, the midbrain, the forebrain, the neocortex, split-brain research and the cerebral hemispheres, and integration of function in the brain. We also read about brain damage, plasticity and repair, techniques to study the brain, the brain and the endocrine system, and brain and mind. Don't forget that you can obtain an overall summary of the chapter by again studying the concept tables on pages 56, 64, and 81.

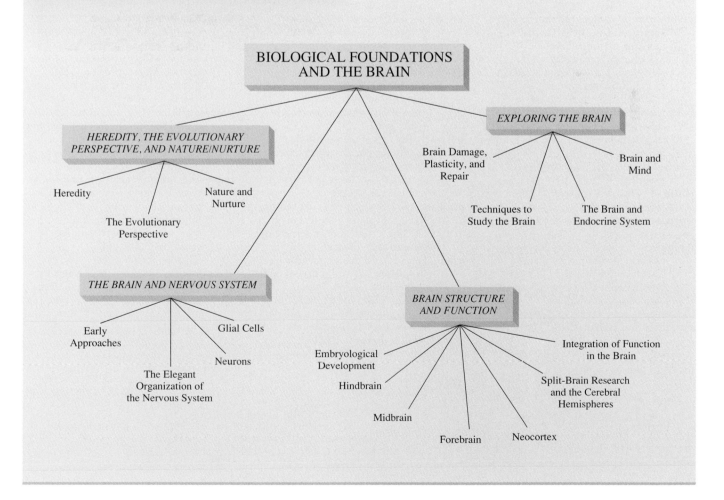

BIOLOGICAL FOUNDATIONS AND THE BRAIN

- *HEREDITY, THE EVOLUTIONARY PERSPECTIVE, AND NATURE/NURTURE*
  - Heredity
  - The Evolutionary Perspective
  - Nature and Nurture
- *EXPLORING THE BRAIN*
  - Brain Damage, Plasticity, and Repair
  - Techniques to Study the Brain
  - The Brain and Endocrine System
  - Brain and Mind
- *THE BRAIN AND NERVOUS SYSTEM*
  - Early Approaches
  - The Elegant Organization of the Nervous System
  - Neurons
  - Glial Cells
- *BRAIN STRUCTURE AND FUNCTION*
  - Embryological Development
  - Hindbrain
  - Midbrain
  - Forebrain
  - Neocortex
  - Split-Brain Research and the Cerebral Hemispheres
  - Integration of Function in the Brain

Key Terms

chromosomes Threadlike structures that come in 23 pairs, one member of each pair coming from each parent; chromosomes contain DNA. p. 52

deoxyribonucleic acid (DNA) A complex molecule that contains genetic information. p. 52

genes Short segments of chromosomes that are the units of hereditary information and are composed of DNA. p. 52

dominant-recessive genes principle The principle that if one gene of a pair is dominant and the other is recessive, the dominant gene exerts its effect, overriding the potential influence of the recessive gene. A recessive gene exerts its influence only if both genes in the pair are recessive. p. 52

natural selection The evolutionary process that favors genes that code for design features that are most likely to lead to reproduction and survival. p. 53

sociobiology A view that relies on evolutionary biology to explain social behavior. p. 54

evolutionary psychology A contemporary approach that emphasizes that behavior is a function of mechanisms, requires input for activation, and is ultimately related to successful survival and reproduction. p. 55

environment All of the surrounding conditions and influences that affect the development of living things. p. 55

nurture An organism's environmental experiences. p. 55

nature An organism's biological inheritance. p. 55

neurons Nerve cells, the basic units of the nervous system. p. 56

phrenology An approach developed by a German physician named Franz Joseph Gall, who argued that the bumps on the skull were associated with personality and intelligence. p. 57

central nervous system (CNS) The brain and spinal cord. p. 58

peripheral nervous system A network of nerves that connects the brain and spinal cord to other parts of the body. The peripheral nervous system takes information to and from the brain and spinal cord and carries out the commands of the CNS to execute various muscular and glandular activities. p. 58

somatic nervous system The sensory nerves, which convey information from the skin and muscle to the CNS about such matters as pain and temperature, and the motor nerves, which tell muscles when to act. p. 58

autonomic nervous system The system of nerves that take messages to and from the body's internal organs, monitoring such processes as breathing, heart rate, and digestion. p. 59

sympathetic nervous system The division of the autonomic nervous system that arouses the body. p. 59

parasympathetic nervous system The division of the autonomic nervous system that calms the body. p. 59

afferent nerves Sensory nerves that carry information to the brain. p. 60

efferent nerves Motor nerves that carry the brain's output. p. 60

interneurons Central nervous system neurons that go between sensory input and motor output. Interneurons make up most of the brain. p. 60

cell body The part of the neuron that contains the nucleus, which directs the manufacture of the substances the neuron uses for its growth and maintenance. p. 60

dendrite The receiving part of the neuron, serving the important function of collecting information and orienting it toward the cell body. p. 60

axon The part of the neuron that carries information away from the cell body to other cells. p. 60

myelin sheath A layer of fat cells that encases most axons; this sheath not only insulates the axon but also helps the nerve impulse travel faster. p. 61

all-or-none principle The principle that once the electrical impulse reaches a certain level of intensity, it fires and moves all the way down the axon, remaining at the same strength throughout its travel. p. 61

ions Electrically charged particles, including sodium (Na) chloride (C1) and potassium (K). The neuron creates electrical signals by moving these charged ions back and forth through its membrane; the waves of electricity that are created sweep along the membrane. p. 61

resting potential The stable, negative charge of an inactive neuron. p. 61

action potential The brief wave of electrical charge that sweeps down the axon. p. 61

synapses Tiny gaps between neurons. Most synapses are between the axon of one neuron and the dendrites or cell body of another neuron. p. 62

neurotransmitters Chemical substances that carry information across the synaptic gap to the next neuron. p. 62

GABA Gamma aminobutyric acid, a neurotransmitter that inhibits the firing of motor neurons. p. 62

acetylcholine (ACh) A neurotransmitter that produces contractions of skeletal muscles by acting on motor nerves. p. 62

norepinephrine A neurotransmitter that usually inhibits the firing of neurons in the brain and spinal cord but excites the heart muscles, intestines, and urogenital tract. p. 62

dopamine An inhibitory neurotransmitter related to movement, attention, learning, and mental health; too much dopamine in the brain's synapses is associated with the severe mental disorder schizophrenia. p. 62

serotonin An inhibitory neurotransmitter involved in the regulation of sleep and depression. p. 62

endorphins Natural opiates that are neurotransmitters; endorphins are involved in pleasure and the control of pain. p. 63

glial cells Non-neuron cells that provide supportive and nutritive functions. p. 63

hindbrain The lowest portion of the brain, located at the skull's rear. It consists of the spinal cord, lower brain stem (pons and medulla), and cerebellum. p. 65

medulla The portion of the brain located where the spinal cord enters the skull. It helps control breathing and regulates a portion of the reflexes that allow us to maintain an upright posture. p. 65

cerebellum A part of the brain that extends from the rear of the hindbrain, above the medulla. It consists of two rounded structures thought to play important roles in motor control. p. 65

pons A bridge in the hindbrain that contains several clusters of fibers involved in sleep and arousal. p. 65

midbrain Located between the hindbrain and forebrain, this is an area where many nerve-fiber systems ascend and descend to connect lower and higher portions of the brain; in particular, the midbrain relays information between the brain and the eyes and ears. p. 65

reticular formation A diffuse collection of neurons involved in stereotyped patterns of behavior such as walking, sleeping, or turning to attend to a sudden noise. p. 65

forebrain The highest region of the brain; among its important structures are the thalamus, the hypothalamus and endocrine system, the limbic system, and the cerebrum. p. 66

limbic system A loosely connected network of structures under the cerebral cortex that plays an important role in both memory and emotion. p. 66

amygdala A limbic system structure located within the base of the temporal lobe. It is involved in the discrimination of objects that are important for an organism's survival, such as appropriate food, mates, and social rivals. p. 66

hippocampus A limbic system structure that has a special role in the storage of memories. p. 66

thalamus A portion of the brain that sits at the top of the brain stem in the central core of the brain. It serves as an important relay station, functioning much like a telephone switchboard between the diverse areas of the cortex and the reticular formation. p. 67

basal ganglia Forebrain structures essential to starting and stopping voluntary movements. p. 67

hypothalamus Located just below the thalamus, the hypothalamus monitors three enjoyable activities—eating, drinking, and sex. It also helps to direct the endocrine system through the pituitary gland, and is involved in emotion, stress, and reward. p. 67

neocortex The most recently evolved part of the brain; covering the rest of the brain almost like a cap, it is the largest part of the brain and makes up about 80 percent of its volume. p. 67

occipital lobe The portion of the cerebral cortex at the back of the head that is involved in vision. p. 68

temporal lobe A portion of the neocortex that is just above the ears and is involved in hearing. p. 68

frontal lobe A portion of the cerebral cortex that is behind the forehead and is involved in the control of voluntary muscles and in intelligence. p. 68

parietal lobe A portion of the cerebral cortex at the top of the head, and toward the rear, that is involved in processing bodily sensations. p. 68

association cortex (association areas) The region of the neocortex involved in the highest intellectual functions, such as problem solving and thinking. p. 71

corpus callosum A large bundle of axons that connects the brain's two hemispheres. p. 71

plasticity The brain's capacity to modify and reorganize itself following damage. p. 73

collateral sprouting A form of regeneration in which the axons of some healthy neurons adjacent to damaged cells will grow new branches. p. 73

substitution of function A form of brain repair in which the function of the damaged region is taken over by another area of the brain. p. 73

brain graft The transplantation of healthy tissue into a damaged brain. p. 73

electroencephalograph (EEG) A machine that records the electrical activity of the brain. Electrodes placed on an individual's scalp record brain-wave activity, which is reproduced on a chart known as an electroencephalogram. p. 77

computer-assisted axial tomography (CAT scan) Three-dimensional imaging obtained from X rays of the head that are assembled into a composite image by computer. p. 77

positron-emission tomography (PET scan) A technology in which the amount of specially treated glucose in various areas of the brain is measured and then analyzed by computer. p. 77

magnetic resonance imaging (MRI) A technology in which a magnetic field is created around a person's body and radio waves are used to construct images of the person's brain tissues and biochemical activity. p. 77

superconducting quantum interference device (SQUID) A brain-scanning device that senses tiny changes in magnetic fields. p. 77

endocrine glands Glands that release their chemical products, called hormones, directly into the bloodstream. p. 78

pituitary gland An important endocrine gland that sits at the base of the skull and is about the size of a pea; it controls growth and regulates other glands. p. 79

adrenal glands Glands that play an important role in our moods, energy level, and ability to cope with stress; each adrenal gland secretes epinephrine (also called adrenaline) and norepinephrine (also called noradrenaline). p. 79

monism The view that a single substance underlies mind and body, and that therefore mind and body are inseparable. p. 80

dualism The view that mind and body are separate, the mind being nonphysical, the brain being physical. p. 80

Resources and Readings in Psychology

Brain, Mind, and Behavior (1988, 2nd ed.)
by F. E. Bloom, A. Lazerson, and L. Hofstader
New York: W. H. Freeman

This book is part of a multimedia teaching package involving the Public Broadcasting System's eight-part series "The Brain." The beauty of the brain is captured in both photographs and well-written essays on its many facets.

Classic Cases in Neuropsychology (1996)
by Chris Code, Claus Wallesch, Yves Joanette, and Andres Lecours
Hillsdale NJ: Erlbaum

This book explores classic case studies that have shaped our knowledge about the way the brain works. Among the cases examined are Broca's first two cases, Phineas Gage, H.M.: The medical temporal lobes and memory, and many others.

The Diversity of Life (1992)
by E. O. Wilson
New York: W. W. Norton

E. O. Wilson's 1975 *Sociobiology* is the landmark book that stimulated considerable interest in the field of sociobiology. *The Diversity of Life* presents Wilson's most recent sociobiological views.

The Double Helix (1968)
by J. D. Watson
New York: New American Library

This is a personalized account of the research leading up to one of the most provocative discoveries of the twentieth century—the DNA molecule. Reading like a mystery novel, it illustrates the exciting discovery process in science.

The Evolution of Desire (1994)
by David Buss
New York: Basic Books

David Buss, one of evolutionary psychology's architects, weaves a fascinating account of how our evolutionary past shapes human sexuality and love.

Human Growth Foundation
7777 Leesburg Pike
Falls Church, VA 22043
703–883–1773

This organization seeks to promote better understanding of human growth problems caused by pituitary gland irregularities. Information about hormone-related problems is available as well as recommendations for educational programs.

Left Brain, Right Brain (1994)
by S. P. Springer and G. Deutsch
New York: W. H. Freeman

This book includes an up-to-date description of research on the roles of the brain's two hemispheres in a number of areas, such as handedness, learning disabilities, and consciousness.

Parkinson's Educational Program
3900 Birch Street
Newport Beach, CA 92660

This program serves as a clearinghouse for information about Parkinson's disease, a neurological disorder. It assists in establishing support groups throughout the world. Educational materials are available.

Parkinson Foundation of Canada
710-390 Bay Street
Toronto, ON M5H 2V2 CANADA
416–366–0099
1–800–565–3000

This foundation is dedicated to heightening public awareness, raising funds for research, developing literature and materials and distributing them to individuals and organizations across Canada, and providing services to support persons with Parkinson's and their families and caregivers. Their newsletter *Network* is published five times a year.

The Science of Mind (1989)
by Kenneth Klivington
New York: Cambridge University Press

This beautifully illustrated book describes how intelligence, love, hate, daily body rhythms, sleep and dreams, schizophrenia, and drug addictions are linked to functions in the brain. Information about brain implants is also provided.

CHAPTER

S&P

Sensation and Perception

JOHN W. SANTROCK
China Odyssey, detail

CHAPTER

S&P

Sensation and Perception

with Alice O'Toole

Chapter Outline

Chapter Boxes

The setting sun, and music at close,
As the last taste of sweets, is sweetest last,
Writ in remembrance more than
things long past.

—**William Shakespeare**

Minds that have nothing to confer
find little to perceive.

—William Wordsworth

IMAGES OF PSYCHOLOGY

The Man Who Mistook His Wife for a Hat

Dr. P. was a distinguished musician, being an accomplished singer and teacher. However, he began to have difficulty in perceiving his world. It was his music students who first recognized his problem. Sometimes he would fail to recognize students he had known for a long time. However, the moment the students spoke, Dr. P. knew who they were by their voices. Becoming aware that something was wrong with the way he was seeing his world, Dr. P. went to see an ophthalmologist. Following a careful examination, Dr. P. was told there was nothing wrong with his eyes, but that he should see a neurologist.

Dr. P. was referred to a neurologist, Oliver Sacks (1985), who wrote about him in a book, *The Man Who Mistook His Wife for a Hat.* Dr. P. saw nothing as familiar, even confusing his wife for a hat. When shown a glove, Dr. P. said it was a container of some sort, maybe a change-purse. Visually, he was lost in a world of lifeless abstractions.

What would it be like to live in Dr. P.'s world, surrounded by a visual world that can never be put together into coherent objects and events? People like Dr. P., who suffer from brain trauma, strokes, or tumors, lose function in a part of their visual system that we sometimes forget exists—the brain. The eyes are just the beginning of visual perception. By themselves, our eyes provide little more than a faithful image of the world. It is only when we consider both what the eyes see and what the brain interprets that we can fully understand how we visually perceive our world.

PREVIEW

Each of us has a number of sensory and perceptual systems to detect, process, and interpret what we experience in our environment. Sensing and perceiving involve a complex and sophisticated visual system; an auditory system that is an elaborate engineering marvel compacted into a space the size of an Oreo cookie; and other processes that inform us about soft caresses and excruciating pain, sweet and sour tastes, floral and peppermint odors, and whether our world is upside down or right side up. Before we tackle each of the senses in greater detail, we need to know more about the nature of sensation and perception.

DETECTING AND PERCEIVING THE WORLD

How can sensation and perception be defined? How do we detect the sensory world?

Defining Sensation and Perception

How do you know the color of grass, that a smell is sweet, that a sound is a sigh, and that the lights around the shore are dim? You know these things because of your *senses.* All outside information comes into us through our senses. Without vision, hearing, touch, taste, smell, and other senses, your brain would be isolated from the world: you would live in a dark silence—a tasteless, colorless, feelingless void.

Sensation *is the process of detecting and encoding stimulus energy in the world.* Stimuli emit physical energy—light, sound, and heat, for example. The sense organs detect this energy and then transform it into a code that can be transmitted to the brain. The first step in "sensing" the world is the work of receptor cells, which respond to certain forms of energy. The retina of the eye is sensitive to light, and special cells in the ear are sensitive to sound, for example. This physical energy is transformed into electrical impulses; the information carried by these electrical impulses travels through nerve fibers that connect the sense organs with the central nervous system. Once in the brain, information about the external world travels to the appropriate area of the cerebral cortex.

Perception *is the brain's process of organizing and interpreting sensory information to give it meaning.* The retinas of our eyes record a fast-moving silver object in the sky, but they do not "see" a passenger jet: our eardrum vibrates in a particular way, but it does not "hear" a Beethoven symphony. Organizing and interpreting what is sensed—"seeing" and "hearing" meaningful patterns in sensory information—is perception.

In our everyday lives, the two processes of sensation and perception are virtually inseparable. When the brain receives information, for example, it automatically interprets and responds to the information. Because of this, most contemporary psychologists refer to sensation and perception as a unified information-processing system (Goldstein, 1996).

Thresholds

How close does an approaching bumblebee have to be before you can hear its buzzing? How far away does a brewing coffeepot have to be for you to detect the smell of coffee? How different does the percentage of fat have to be for you to taste a difference between the "low-fat" and "regular" versions of your favorite ice cream?

Absolute Threshold

A basic problem for any sensory system is its ability to detect varying degrees of energy in the environment. This energy can take the form of light, sound, chemical, or mechanical stimulation. How much of a stimulus is necessary for you to see, hear, taste, smell, or feel something? One way to address these questions is to assume that each of us has an **absolute threshold,** *or minimum amount of energy that we can detect.* When a stimulus has less energy than this absolute threshold, we cannot detect its presence; when the stimulus has more energy than the absolute threshold, we can detect the stimulus. An experiment with a wristwatch or a clock will help you understand the principle of absolute threshold. Find a wristwatch or clock that ticks; put it on a table and walk far enough across the room so that you no longer hear the ticking. Then gradually move toward the wristwatch or clock. At some point you will begin to hear the ticking. Hold your position and notice that occasionally the ticking fades and you may have to move forward to reach the threshold; at other times it may become loud and you can move backward.

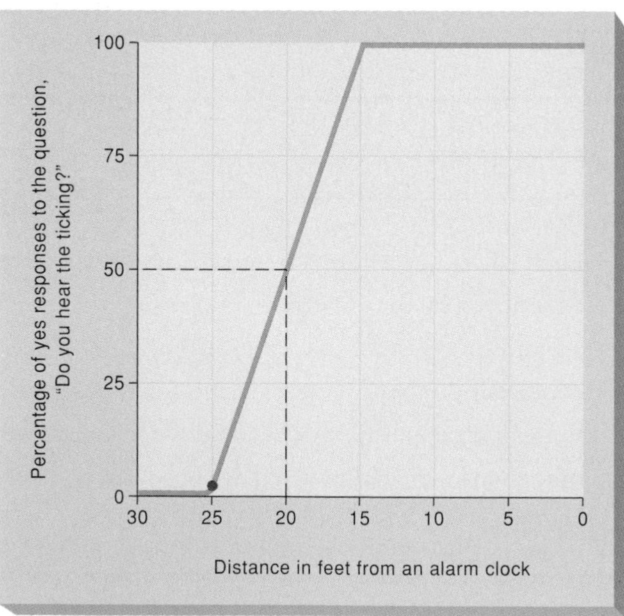

FIGURE 1

Determining Absolute Threshold
Absolute threshold is the stimulus value a person detects 50 percent of the time. Here the individual's absolute threshold for detecting the ticking of a clock is 20 feet. People have different absolute thresholds. Another individual tested with the ticking clock might have an absolute threshold of 22 feet, for example.

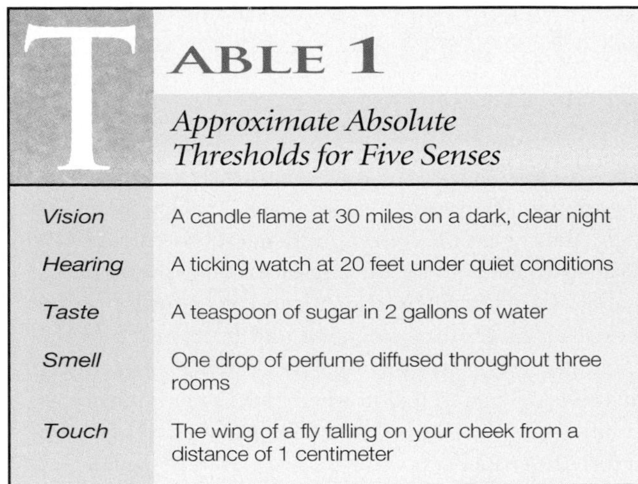

TABLE 1

Approximate Absolute Thresholds for Five Senses

Vision	A candle flame at 30 miles on a dark, clear night
Hearing	A ticking watch at 20 feet under quiet conditions
Taste	A teaspoon of sugar in 2 gallons of water
Smell	One drop of perfume diffused throughout three rooms
Touch	The wing of a fly falling on your cheek from a distance of 1 centimeter

Source: Adapted from Galatner, 1962.

In this experiment, the absolute threshold is not always what you expect it to be. If you conduct the experiment a number of times, you will record several different distances as the absolute threshold. For example, the first time you try it, you might hear the ticking at 25 feet from the clock. But you probably won't hear it every time at 25 feet. Maybe you hear it ticking at 25 feet only 38 percent of the time. You might hear the ticking at 20 feet 50 percent of the time and at 15 feet 65 percent of the time. People have different thresholds, because some people have better hearing than others, and some people have better vision than others. Figure 1 shows one person's absolute threshold for detecting a clock's ticking sound. Generally, the absolute threshold is described as the point at which the observer begins detecting the stimulus 50 percent of the time. Using the same clock, another person might have an absolute threshold of 26 feet, another at 22 feet, another yet at 17 feet. To learn about the approximate absolute threshold of five senses, see table 1.

Under ideal circumstances, our senses have very low absolute thresholds, and so we can be remarkably good at detecting small amounts of stimulus energy. You can demonstrate this to yourself by using a sharp pencil point to carefully lift a single hair on your forearm. You will probably be surprised to realize that for most of us this tiny bit of pressure on the skin is easily detectable. You might also be surprised to learn in table 1 that the human eye can see a candle flame at 30 miles on a dark, clear night. But our environment seldom gives us ideal conditions to detect stimuli. If the night is cloudy and the air is polluted, for example, you would have to be much closer to see the flicker of a candle flame. And other lights on the horizon—car or house lights—might hinder your ability to detect the candle's flame. **Noise** *is the term given to irrelevant and competing stimuli.* For example, suppose someone speaks to you from the doorway of the room where you are sitting. You might fail to respond because your roommate is talking on the phone and a CD player is blaring out your favorite song. We usually think of noise as being auditory, but the psychological meaning of the term *noise* also involves other senses. The pollution, cloudiness, car lights, and house lights are forms of visual noise that hamper your ability to see a candle flame from a great distance.

We have discussed sensations that are above an individual's threshold of awareness, but what about the possibility that we experience the sensory world at levels below our conscious detection? To learn more about this controversial possibility, turn to Explorations in Psychology 1.

Difference Threshold

In addition to studying the amount of stimulation required for a stimulus to be detected, psychologists investigate the degree of difference that must exist between two stimuli before this difference is detected. This **difference threshold,** *or just noticeable difference (jnd), is the smallest difference in stimulation required to discriminate one stimulus from another 50 percent of the time.* An artist might detect the difference between two similar shades of color. A tailor might determine a difference in the texture of two fabrics by feeling them. How different must the colors and textures be for these people to determine the difference? Just as the absolute threshold is determined by a 50 percent detection rate, the difference threshold is the point at which a person reports that two stimuli are different 50 percent of the time.

An important aspect of difference thresholds is that the threshold increases with the magnitude of the stimulus. You may notice when your roommate turns up the volume on the stereo by even a small amount when the music is playing softly. But if he or she turns the volume up an equal amount when the music is playing very loudly, you may not notice. More than 150 years ago, E. H. Weber, a German psychologist, noticed that, regardless of their magnitude, two stimuli must differ by a constant proportion to be detected. **Weber's law** *states that the difference threshold is a constant percentage of the magnitude of the comparison stimulus rather than a constant amount. Weber's law generally holds true.* For example, we add 1 candle to 60 candles and notice a difference in the brightness of the candles; we add 1 candle to 120 candles and do not notice a difference. We discover, though, that adding 2 candles to 120 candles does produce a difference in brightness. Adding 2 candles to 120 candles is the same proportionately as adding 1 candle to 60 candles. The exact proportion varies with the stimulus involved. For example, a change in a tone's pitch of 3 percent can be detected, but in taste a 20 percent change is required for a person to detect a difference, and in smell a 25 percent change is required.

Signal Detection Theory

To measure absolute and difference thresholds, we need to ask people to tell us about their sensations. Can you taste sugar in this iced tea? Can you smell a difference

Explorations in Psychology 1

Subliminal Perception—From Cokes to Rock Music

Subliminal perception fascinates us. After all, aren't you curious about whether you can be influenced by messages you are not even aware of? Two widely publicized claims of subliminal perception involve a commercial firm's claim in the 1950s that very brief presentations of the words *Drink Coca-Cola* and *Eat popcorn* dramatically increased the sales of these items and the current belief by some that satanic messages are embedded in rock music.

Some years ago *Life* magazine reported that more than 45,000 unknowing movie viewers were exposed to very brief flashes of the words *Drink Coca-Cola* while they were watching movie screens. The article stated that Coke sales rose 18 percent and popcorn sales soared more than 50 percent because of the subliminal messages (Brean, 1958). Scientists criticized the claims of the subliminal perception enthusiasts and asked if the messages enhanced an already existing but weak desire for Coke, if they induced a drive that had not existed, and if individuals rose from their seats and marched like robots to the concession stand or bought Coke on the way home from the movie. In a later experiment, individuals who were exposed to "Drink Coke" subliminal messages did rate themselves as thirstier than a control group (Hawkins, 1970). Such results suggest the possible existence of subliminal perception, but they do not tell if we would buy Coke over another drink. They clearly do not support claims that advertisers can make us buy whatever they desire.

An experiment by Carol Fowler and her colleagues (1981) provides some evidence that we process information from our sensory world at a level beneath our awareness. In this experiment, words were shown on a screen so rapidly that the subjects could not tell what they were seeing. Subsequently, the subjects were shown two words (such as *hotel* and *book*) and asked which was most like the subliminally presented word (*lodge*). Somewhat amazingly, the subjects answered most questions correctly. A possible explanation for these results is that sensory information too faint to be recognized consciously may be picked up by sensory receptors and transmitted to the brain at a level beneath conscious awareness. Advertisers continue to be interested in whether they can influence us to buy their products by embedding subliminal messages in their advertisements.

Another area involving subliminal perception that has generated considerable controversy is whether subliminal messages are embedded in rock music. Some rock groups allegedly have inserted satanic messages played backward in their records and tapes. According to this theory, when the record is played normally (forward), the messages cannot be consciously perceived, but they influence our behavior in a subliminal way. The backward messages *supposedly* embedded in songs include these:

- "Satan, move in our voices" in a song by Styx about cocaine
- "Son of Satan" in "A Child Is Coming" by Jefferson Starship
- "I love you said the Devil" in a song by the Rolling Stones
- "Backward mask where are you, oh. Lost in error, Satan" in Mötley Crue's *Shout at the Devil* album

Researchers have been unable to find any evidence whatsoever that these and other backward satanic messages exist or, if they do, that they influence our behavior

between an expensive perfume and a cheaper cologne version of the same scent? Did you hear something go bump in the night? Thinking about detection and discrimination in terms of absolute thresholds assumes that people *can and do* report their sensations faithfully, regardless of other factors. Let's consider the hypothetical case of two people with exactly the same sensory ability to detect blips indicating hostile aircraft on a radar screen; one is monitoring the radar screen in wartime and the other in peacetime. We would expect that the wartime operator would be very likely to report *anything* that might possibly be an enemy aircraft. The peacetime operator, on the other hand, would not be especially prone to report hostile aircraft. If we tested the two radar operators on a threshold task, the wartime radar operator might report seeing blips much more often than the peacetime operator and we might mistakenly conclude that the wartime operator was a better detector of hostile aircraft than the peacetime operator.

To accurately characterize the detection of even very simple sensory stimuli, we need to take all of these contextual factors into account. **Signal detection theory** *is the theory that sensitivity to sensory stimuli depends on a variety of factors besides the physical intensity of the stimulus and the sensory abilities of the observer* (Swets, 1964). According to this theory, responding to a stimulus is a process that relies not only on our ability to detect the stimulus, but also on the way we make decisions about reporting the

(McIver, 1988). Even if we were to take a very clearly recorded sentence and play it backward, no one could tell what it said. Investigators have found that people's perceptions of whether or not these messages exist is largely a function of what they expect to hear. In one experiment, when told beforehand that a message of satanic quality would influence them, subjects were more likely to hear the message. With no such expectation, subjects did not hear the message (Vokey & Read, 1985). And in a recent study, individuals failed to perceptually detect any information in subliminal self-help auditory tapes (Moore, 1995).

What can we make of the claims of subliminal perception enthusiasts and the research conducted by experimental psychologists? First, weak sensory stimuli can be registered by sensory receptors and is possibly encoded in the brain at a level beneath conscious awareness. Second, no evidence supports the claims of advertisers and rock music critics that such sensory registry and neural encoding have any substantial impact on our thoughts and behavior. Rather, evidence suggests that we are influenced extensively by those sounds and views we are consciously aware of and can attend to efficiently (Smith & Rogers, 1994).

Mötley Crue's Shout at the Devil *album has been one of the targets of groups who believe that backward messages are embedded in songs. The protesters say that this album has the phrase* Backward mask where are you, oh. Lost in error, Satan. *However, researchers have been unable to find any evidence whatsoever that these and other satanic messages are encoded in the music or that, if they are, they can influence behavior.*

stimulus. Some of us "feel" pain when the dentist drills deeply into a cavity, while others of us begin to "feel" pain the second the drill touches the surface of the tooth. In terms of an absolute pain threshold, we would explain this by saying that some of us, unfortunately, need less pressure on the nerves in our teeth to feel pain than others do. Signal detection theory, on the other hand, holds that while there are certainly differences in how sensitive individuals are to a stimulus (for example, pain), there is no absolute detection threshold. Instead, signal detection theory assumes that there is a continuum of sensory activation. The task of detection involves making a decision about how much sensory activation we need to experience before we report the existence of a stimulus.

At this point you should have a basic understanding of sensation and perception, the thresholds of sensory awareness, and signal detection theory. A summary of these ideas is presented in concept table 1. Now we'll turn our attention to each of the senses in more detail. We begin with the sense we know the most about—vision.

The Visual System

We see a world of shapes and sizes—some stationary, others moving, some in black and white, others in color. But how do we see all of this? What is the machinery that enables us to experience this marvelous landscape?

Concept Table 1

Detecting and Perceiving the World

Concept	Processes/Related Ideas	Characteristics/Description
What Are Sensation and Perception?	Sensation	This refers to the process of detecting and encoding stimulus energy in the world.
	Perception	This refers to the process of organizing and interpreting sensory information. Most contemporary psychologists refer to sensation and perception as a unified information-processing system.
Thresholds	Absolute threshold	A basic problem for any sensory system is to detect varying degrees of energy in the environment. One way to cope with this problem is to assume that each of us has an absolute threshold, or minimum amount of energy we can detect.
	Difference threshold	Also, the difference threshold, or just noticeable difference (jnd), is the smallest difference in stimulation required to discriminate one stimulus from another 50 percent of the time. Weber's law states that the difference threshold is a constant percentage of the magnitude of the comparison stimulus rather than a constant amount.
Signal Detection Theory	Its nature	This is the theory that sensitivity to stimuli depends on a variety of factors besides the physical intensity of the stimulus and the sensory abilities of the observer. In this theory, we rely not only on our ability to detect the stimulus, but also on the way we make decisions about reporting the stimulus.

The Visual Stimulus and the Eye

Light *is a form of electromagnetic energy that can be described in terms of wavelengths.* Waves of light are much like the waves formed when a pebble is tossed into a lake. The **wavelength** *is the distance from the peak of one wave to the peak of the next.* The human visual system can detect electromagnetic energy with wavelengths ranging from about 400 to 700 nanometers (a nanometer is one billionth of a meter and is abbreviated *nm*). Outside of this range are longer radio and infrared radiation waves, and shorter ultraviolet and X rays (see figure 2). These other wavelengths can bombard us, but we do not *see* them, though we can be affected by them. X rays, for example, can be damaging to our bodies without being detected by our senses. Why do we see only the narrow band of the electromagnetic spectrum between 400 and 700 nanometers? The most likely answer is that our visual system evolved in the sun's light. Thus, our visual system is able to perceive the spectrum of energy emitted by the sun. By the time sunlight reaches the earth's surface, it is strongest in the 400–700 nanometer range.

The purpose of the eye is not unlike that of a camera: to get the best possible "picture" of the world. A good picture is one that is in focus, is not too dark or too light, and has good contrast between the dark and light parts. Each of several structures in the eye plays an important role in this process. By looking closely at your eyes in the mirror, you notice three parts—the *sclera, iris,* and *pupil* (figure 3). The **sclera** *is the white outer part of the eye that helps to maintain the shape of the eye and to protect it from injury.* The **iris** *is the colored part of the eye, which can range from light blue to dark brown.* The **pupil,** *which appears black, is the opening in the center of the iris. The iris contains muscles that function to control the size of the pupil and, hence, the amount of light that gets into the eye.* This allows the eye to function optimally under different conditions of illumination, which can range in the course of a normal day from the darkest of basements to the brightest of summer sunshine. To get a good "picture" of the world, the amount of light that enters the eye needs to be adjustable. In this sense, the pupil acts like the aperture of a camera, opening to let in more light when it is needed and closing to let in less light when there is too much.

You can demonstrate changes in the size of your own pupil by looking at your eyes in the mirror and turning the room lights up and down. (You obviously need to try this in a room with sufficient light to see your eyes even when the lights are turned all the way down.) As you turn down the room light, the pupil will begin to enlarge to let in more light; as you turn the room lights back up, the pupil opening will shrink to let in less light.

If the eye is to act like a camera, in addition to having the right amount of light, the image has to be in focus at the back of the eye. Two structures serve this purpose: the **cornea,** *which is a clear membrane just in front of the*

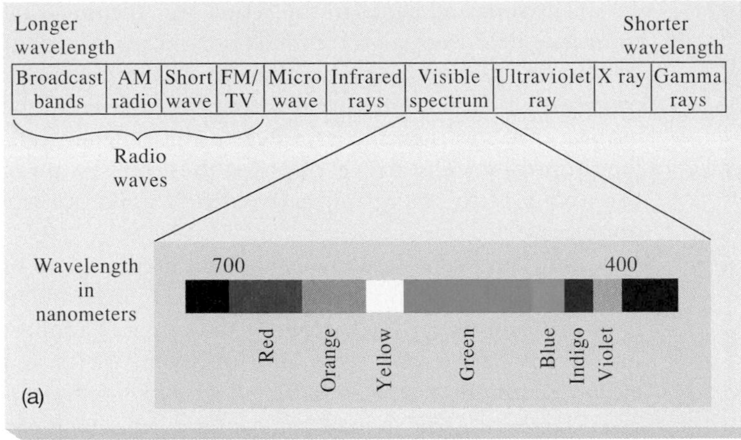

FIGURE 2

Electromagnetic Spectrum and Visible Light
(*a*) Visible light is only a narrow bank in the electromagnetic spectrum. Visible light's wavelengths range from about 400 to 700 nanometers. X rays are much shorter and radio waves are much longer. (*b*) Ultraviolet: Most ultraviolet rays are absorbed by the ozone in the earth's upper atmosphere. The small fraction that reaches the earth is the ingredient in sunlight that tans the skin and can cause skin cancer. (*c*) Infrared: The electromagnetic radiation just beyond red in the spectrum is felt as heat by receptors in the skin.

eye, and the **lens of the eye,** *which is a transparent and somewhat flexible ball-like entity filled with a gelatinous material. The function of both of these structures is to bend the light falling on the surface of the eye just enough to focus it at the back of the eye.* The curved surface of the cornea does most of this bending, while the lens "fine-tunes" the focus as needed. When you are looking at far-away objects, the lens has a relatively flat shape. This is because the light reaching the eye from far-away objects is parallel and the bending power of the cornea is sufficient to keep things in focus. The light reaching the eye from objects that are close, however, is more scattered and so more bending of the light is required to achieve focus. This focusing is done by a process called **accommodation,** *in which the lens changes its curvature.* Without this fine-tuning ability, it would be difficult to focus on objects that are close to us, like needlework or reading. As we get older, the lens of our eye begins to lose its flexibility and, hence, its ability to change from its normal flattened shape to the rounder shape needed to bring close objects into focus. This is why many people with normal vision throughout their young adult life require reading glasses when they get older.

The parts of the eye that we have discussed so far work together to get the best possible picture of the world. All of this effort, however, would be for naught without a method for keeping or "recording" the images we take of the world. In a camera, film serves just such a purpose. Film is made of a material that responds to light. Likewise, the **retina** *is the light-sensitive surface in the back of the eye that houses light receptors called rods and cones.* Making an analogy between the film of a camera and the retina, however, vastly underestimates the complexity and elegance of the retina's design. Even after decades of intense study, the full marvel of this structure is far from understood.

Because the retina is so important to vision, we need to study its makeup more closely. There are two kinds of receptors in the retina: rods and cones. They serve to turn the electromagnetic energy of light into a form of energy that can be processed by the nervous system. This process is referred to as transduction. **Rods** *are receptors in the retina that are exquisitely sensitive to light but are not very useful for color vision.* Thus, they function well under low illumination; as you might expect, they are hard at work at night. **Cones** *are the receptors that we use for color perception.* There are three types of

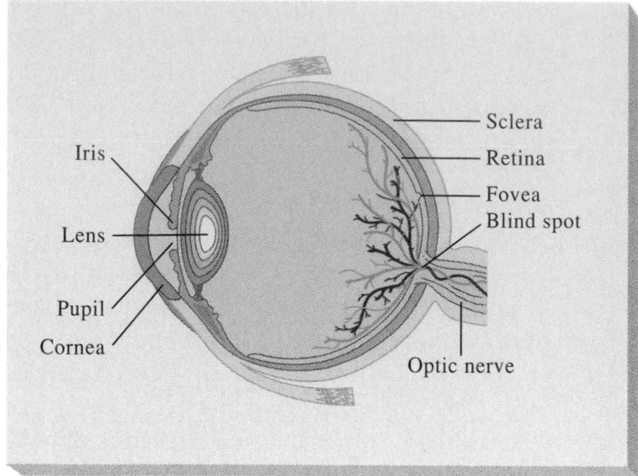

FIGURE 3

Main Structures of the Eye

cones, each maximally sensitive to a different range of wavelengths or hues. As we will see shortly, our color perception operates by being able to compare the responses of these three cone systems to a stimulus. Like the rods, cones are light sensitive. However, they require a larger amount of light than the rods do to respond, and so they operate best in daylight or under high illumination.

The rods and cones in the retina are receptors that transduce light into neural impulses by means of a photochemical reaction. The breakdown of the chemicals produces a neural impulse that is first transmitted to the bipolar cells and then moves down to the ganglion cells (see figure 4). The nerve impulse then passes along the axons of the ganglion cells, which make up the optic nerve.

Rods and cones are involved in different aspects of vision and differ both in how they respond to light and in their distribution on the surface of the retina. The most important part of the retina is the **fovea,** *which is a minute area in the center of the retina where vision is at its best. The fovea is able to resolve much finer detail than any other part of the retina and contains only cones.* The fovea is vitally important to many visual tasks (try reading out of the corner of your eye!). By contrast, rods are found almost everywhere on the retina except in the fovea. As their name suggests, rods are long and cylindrical. Since they require little light to respond, they work best under conditions of low illumination. Because of this light sensitivity and the rods' location on the retina, we are able to detect fainter spots of light on the peripheral retina than at the fovea. It has been known for centuries that if you want to see a very faint star, you should gaze slightly to the right or left of the star. A more modern example of

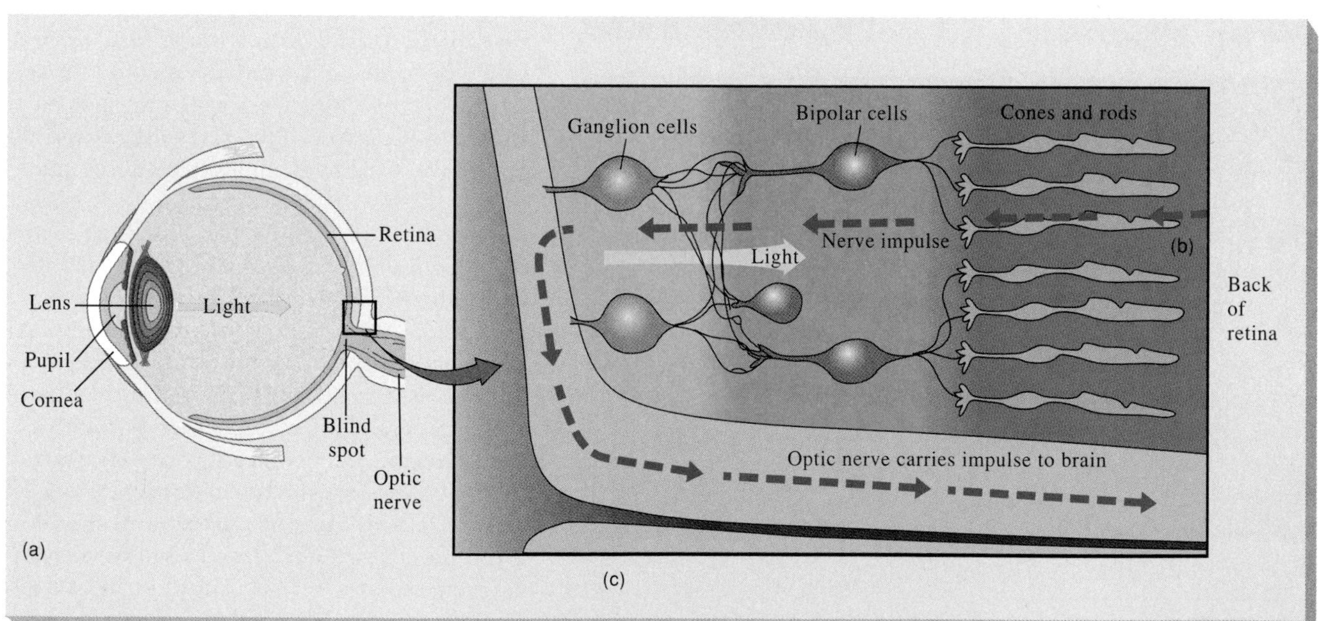

FIGURE 4

Transmission of Light Information Through the Eye

(*a*) Light passes through the cornea, pupil, and lens and then falls on the retina, a light-sensitive surface. (*b*) In the retina, light first triggers a photochemical reaction in the rods and cones. The photochemical reaction of the rods and cones activates the bipolar cells, which in turn activate the ganglion cells. (*c*) This drawing shows the direction of light information in the retina. The ganglion cells intersect to become the optic nerve, which carries information to the brain.

the peripheral retina's greater light sensitivity is the fact that the annoying flicker of a dying fluorescent light can be detected easily when you are not gazing at the light but seemingly disappears when you look directly at the light. The rods throughout the peripheral retina are sensitive enough to detect these small fluctuations in the intensity of the dying light when the less-sensitive cones on the fovea fail to.

Cones are shorter and fatter than rods and are concentrated in the fovea, but they can also be found on the peripheral retina. The three receptor types respond best to colors that correspond roughly to blue (around 435 nm), green (around 535 nm), and red (around 565 nm). While each of the three types responds best to one of these colors, each also responds to a range of wavelengths around these "best colors." We will discuss the properties of color vision shortly, but note for now that the color-sensitive properties of these three kinds of cones form the basis of our color perception abilities. Given these properties, we can say a bit more about the differences in our visual abilities in the fovea and the peripheral retina. First, because we know that rods are used in poorly lit conditions and that the fovea has no rods, we can conclude that vision is poor for objects registered on the fovea at night. Second, because color perception works by comparing the responses of the three types of cones and because there is only one type of rod, rods are not very useful for color perception. Thus, third, it is easy to see why we have difficulty seeing color at night.

Finally, there is one place on the retina that contains neither rods nor cones. Not surprisingly, this area is called the **blind spot;** *it is the place on the retina where the optic nerve leaves the eye on its way to the brain.* We cannot see anything that reaches only this part of the retina. To experience your blind spot, see figure 5.

A summary of some of the main characteristics of rods and cones is presented in table 2. So far we have studied the importance of light and structures of the eyes. The journey of vision now leads us to the brain and how it processes visual information.

FIGURE 5

The Eye's Blind Spot
There is a normal blind spot in your eye, a small area where the optic nerve leads to the brain. To find your blind spot, hold this book at arm's length, cover your left eye, and stare at the red pepper on the left with your right eye. Move the book slowly toward you until the yellow pepper disappears. To find the blind spot in your left eye, cover your right eye, concentrate on the yellow pepper, and adjust the book until the red pepper disappears.

TABLE 2

Characteristics of Rods and Cones

Characteristics	Rods	Cones
Type of vision	Black and white	Color
Light conditions	Dimly lit	Well lit
Shape	Thin and long	Short and fat
Distribution	Not on fovea	On fovea and scattered outside of fovea

From Eye to Brain and Neural-Visual Processing

The optic nerve leads out of the eye toward the brain carrying information about light. The optic chiasm is the point at which approximately half of the optic nerve fibers cross over the midline of the brain. Before reaching the optic chiasm, stimuli in the left visual field were registered in the right half of the retina in both eyes, and stimuli in the right visual field were registered in the left half of the retina in both eyes. At the optic chiasm the optic nerve fibers divide. The visual information originating in the right halves of the two retinae is then transmitted to the left side of the occipital lobe in the back of the brain; the visual information originating in the left halves of the retinae is transmitted to the right side of the occipital lobe. What all of these crossings mean is that what we see in the left side of our visual field ends up in the right side of our brain, and what we see in the right visual field ends up in the left side of our brain (see figure 6).

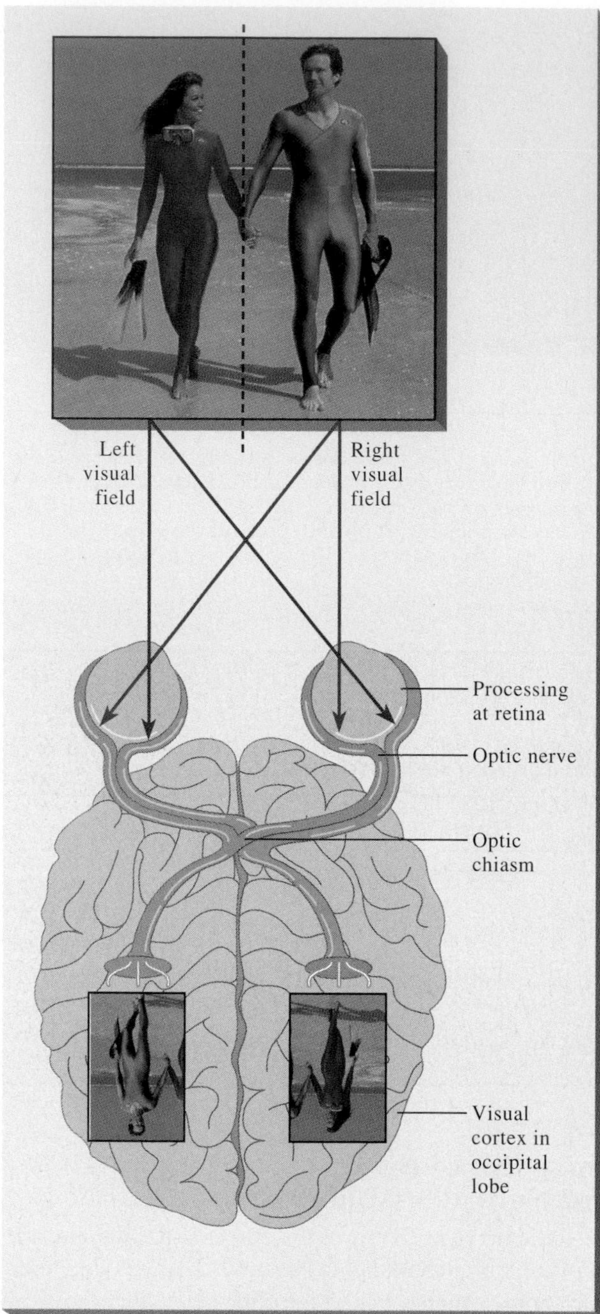

FIGURE 6

Visual Pathways to and Through the Brain
Light from each side of the visual field falls on the opposite side of each eye's retina. Visual information then travels along the optic nerve to the optic chiasm, where most of the visual information crosses over to the other side of the brain. From there visual information goes to the occipital lobe at the rear of the brain. What all of the crossings mean is that what we see in the left side of our visual field (in this figure, the woman) ends up in the right side of our brain, and what we see in the right visual field (the man) ends up in the left side of our brain.

The visual cortex in the occipital lobe combines information from both eyes and is responsible for higher levels of visual processing. David Hubel and Torsten Wiesel (1965) won a Nobel Prize for their discovery that some neurons detect different features of the visual field. By recording the activity of a *single* neuron in a cat while it looked at patterns that varied in size, shape, color, and movement, the researchers found that the visual cortex has neurons that are individually sensitive to different types of lines and angles. For example, one neuron might show a sudden burst of activity when stimulated by lines of a particular angle; another neuron might fire only when moving stimuli appear; yet another neuron might be stimulated when the object in the visual field has a combination of certain angles, sizes, and shapes (see figure 7).

Sensory Adaptation

Turning out the lights in your bedroom at night, you stumble across the room to your bed, completely blind to the objects around you. Gradually, the objects in your room reappear and become more and more clear. The ability of the visual system to adjust to the darkened room is an example of the principle of **sensory adaptation**—*a change in the responsiveness of the sensory system based on the average level of surrounding stimulation.* You have experienced sensory adaptation countless times in your life—adapting to the temperature of a shower, to the water in an initially "freezing" swimming pool, or to the smell of the Thanksgiving dinner that is wonderful to the arriving guests but almost undetectable to the cook who slaved over it all day. These are examples of sensory adaptation. While all senses adapt to prolonged stimulation, we will take up this topic using vision as an example since you have just learned about the mechanisms involved in adapting to light.

Let's return to our example of adapting to the dark. When you turn out the lights, everything is black. Conversely, when you step out into the bright sunshine after spending some time in a dark basement, your eyes are flooded with light and everything appears light. When we talked about the purpose of the eye, we said that the eye needs to get a good picture of the world. Good pictures have sharp contrasts between dark and light parts. We have already seen that the pupil serves an important function in adjusting the amount of light that gets into the eye and therefore helping to preserve the contrast between dark and light in our picture. Additionally, structures throughout the visual system also adapt. You may have noticed that the change in the size of the pupil as you dim or brighten the lights happens very quickly. You also may have noticed that when you turn out the lights in your bedroom, the contrast between dark and light continues to improve for nearly 20 minutes. This is because both the rods and the cones in the visual system adapt or adjust their response rates on the basis of the average light level of the surrounding room. This adaptation takes longer than the pupil adjustment. All of these mechanisms allow the visual system to preserve the contrast in the images it takes of the world over an extremely large range of background illumination conditions. The price we pay for our ability to adapt to the mean light level is *time.* Driving out of a dark tunnel under a mountain into the glistening and blinding reflection of the sun off the snow reminds us that our ability to adapt does have a price.

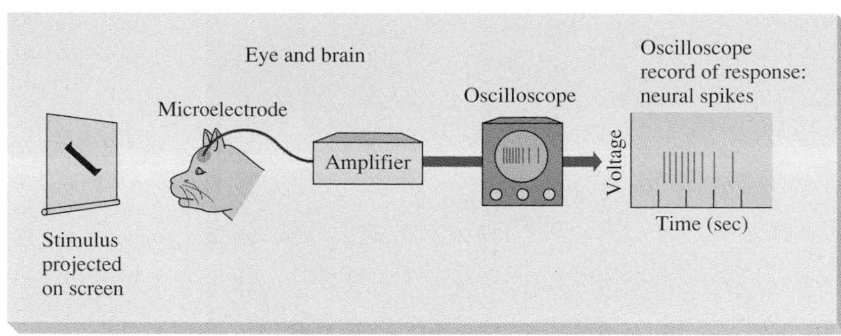

FIGURE 7

Hubel and Wiesel's Research on Visual Information Processing
An electrode is inserted into a cell at a point in the visual system of an experimental animal. Various light stimuli are projected onto a screen in front of the animal's eyes. The burst of activity by an individual cell in response to the stimuli (shown on the oscilloscope) indicates the cell's action.

From H. R. Schiffman, *Sensation and Perception,* 2d ed. Copyright © 1982 John Wiley & Sons, Inc.

Color Vision

We spend a lot of time thinking about color—the color of the car we want to buy, the color we are going to paint the walls of our room, the color of the clothes we wear. We can change our hair color or even the color of our eyes to make us look more attractive.

What Is Color?

As we mentioned before, the human eye registers wavelengths between 400 and 700 nm (shown in figure 2). Light waves themselves have no color. The sensations of color reside in the visual system of the observer. So, if we talk about red light, we refer to the wavelengths of light that evoke the sensation of red. Objects appear a certain color to us because they reflect specific wavelengths of light to our eyes. These wavelengths are split apart into a spectrum of colors when the light passes through a prism, as in the formation of a rainbow.

We can remember the colors of the light spectrum by thinking of an imaginary man named ROY G. BIV, for the colors red, orange, yellow, green, blue, indigo, and violet.

If you go into a paint store and ask the salesperson for some red paint, the salesperson will probably ask you what kind of paint you want, such as dark or light, pinkish or more crimson, pastel or deep, and so on. A color's **hue** *is based on its wavelength content,* a color's **saturation** *on its purity,* and a color's **brightness** *on its intensity* (see figure 8). The longest wavelengths seen by the human eye (about 700 nm) appear as red, the shortest (about 400 nm) appear as violet. Hue is what we commonly think of color to be. The purity of a color is determined by the amount of white light added to a single wavelength of color. When we vary the saturation of a hue, we see a much larger range of colors—pink and crimson, as well as a basic red, for example. But one more dimension also is involved in color—brightness, which is the intensity of light.

FIGURE 8

A Color Tree Showing Color's Three Dimensions: Hue, Saturation, and Brightness
Hue is represented around the color tree, saturation horizontally, and brightness vertically.

When we mix colors we get different results depending on whether we mix light or pigments (see figure 9). An **additive mixture** *of colors is a mixing of beams of lights from different parts of the color spectrum.* Through additive mixing we can produce virtually the entire color circle by using any three widely spaced colors. Television is an example of additive mixing—only three colors are involved—red, blue, and green. If you look at a color television screen through a magnifying glass, you will notice that a yellow patch of light is actually a combination of tiny red and green dots. Look at the other patches of color on a television screen with a magnifying glass to observe their composition.

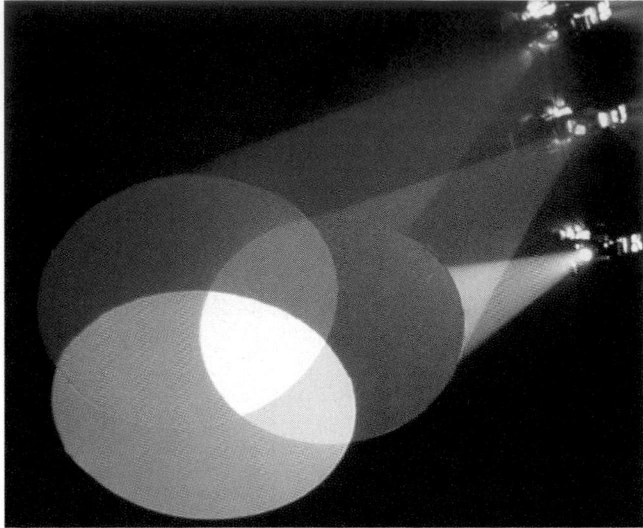

(a)

(b)

FIGURE 9

Comparing the Mixing of Light with the Mixing of Pigments
(*a*) Additive color mixtures occur when lights are mixed. For example, red and green lights when combined yield yellow. The three colors together give white. (*b*) Subtractive color mixtures occur when pigments are mixed or light is shown through colored filters placed over one another. Most of the time, a mixture of blue-green and yellow produces green, and a mixture of complementary colors produces black.

By contrast, a **subtractive mixture** *of color is a mixing of pigments rather than beams of light.* An artist's painting is an example of subtractive mixing. When blue and yellow are mixed on the television screen, a gray or white appears. But when the artist mixes a dab of blue paint with a dab of yellow paint, the color green is produced. In a subtractive color mixture each pigment absorbs (subtracts) some of the light falling on it and reflects the rest of the light. When two pigments are mixed, only the wavelengths that are not absorbed or subtracted from either one emerges.

Theories of Color Vision

The study of human color vision using psychological methods has a long and distinguished history. A full century before the methods existed to study the anatomical and neurophysiological basis of color perception, psychological studies had discovered many of these basic principles of our color vision system. These studies resulted in two main theories, each of which turned out to be correct.

The first color vision theory we discuss is based on what you just learned about the three kinds of cone receptors in the retina. The **trichromatic theory** *states that color perception is based on the existence of three types of receptors that are maximally sensitive to different, but overlapping, ranges of wavelengths.* The trichromatic theory of color vision was proposed by Thomas Young in 1802 and extended by Hermann von Helmholtz in 1952. The theory is based on the results of experiments on human color-matching abilities. These experiments show that a person with normal vision can match any color in the spectrum by combining three other wavelengths. In this type of experiment, individuals are given a light of a single wavelength and are asked to combine three other single-wavelength lights to match the first light. They can do this by changing the relative intensities of three lights until the color of the combination light is indistinguishable from the color of the first light. Young and Helmholtz reasoned that if the combination of any three wavelengths in different intensities is indistinguishable from any single pure wavelength, the visual system must be basing its perception of color on the relative responses of three receptor systems. To understand how this works, imagine that we have one kind of receptor mechanism for each wavelength in the spectrum of visible light and that each receptor responds to only one wavelength. The color represented by a wavelength of 550 nm would be registered in our visual system whenever the receptor type that was sensitive to 550 nm responded. With this system there is no way to perceptually match any color with any other set of colors, since only one type of receptor response could signal that color. By contrast, with three kinds of receptors that respond best to different overlapping ranges of wavelengths, by adjusting the relative intensities of any combination of three wavelengths we can exactly match the response that is produced for any single wavelength.

These color-matching experiments were carried out long before anything was known about the physiological properties of receptors in the retina. The existence of three types of color receptors, or cones, with different color-sensitive properties was confirmed in the 1960s, over 100 years after the proposal of the trichromatic theory of color perception (Wald & Brown, 1964)!

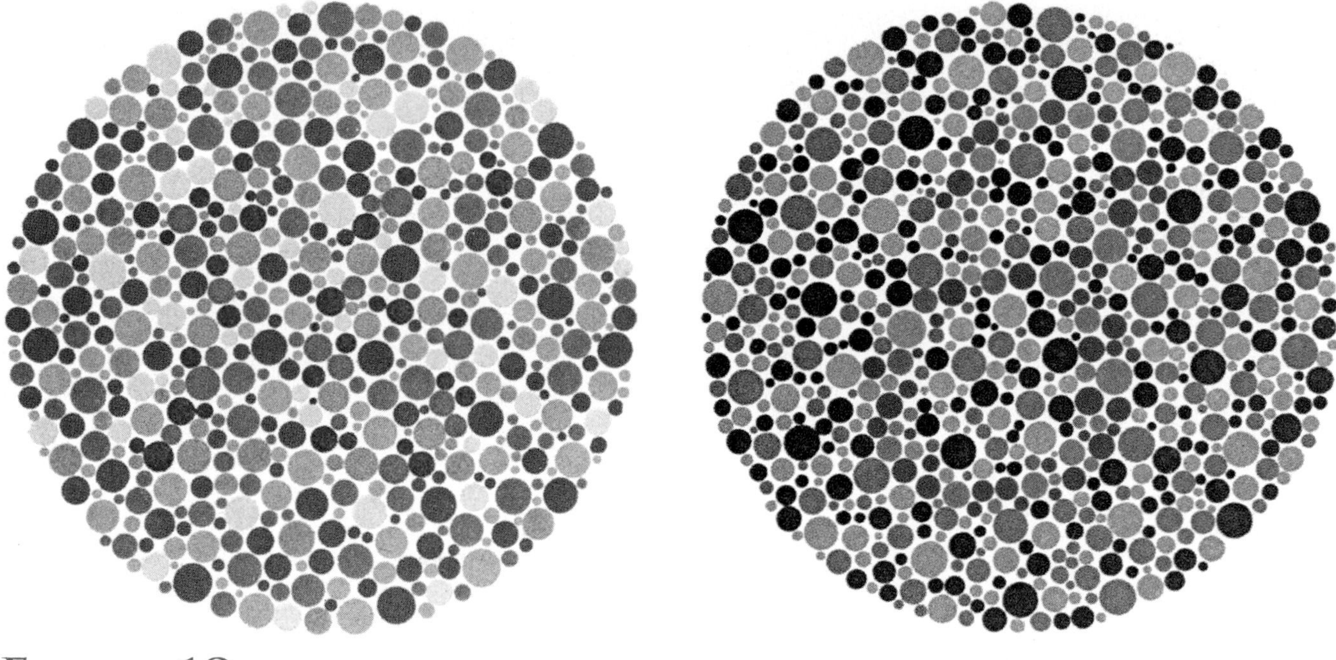

FIGURE 10

Examples of Stimuli Used to Test for Color Blindness
In the left circle, people with normal vision see the number 16, but people with red-green color blindness do not. In the right circle, people with normal vision detect the number 8, but those with red-green color blindness see one number or none. A complete color blindness assessment involves the use of fifteen stimuli.

Further convincing support for the trichromatic theory is found in the study of defective color vision (see figure 10). The term *color blind* is somewhat misleading because it suggests that a color-blind person cannot see color at all. Complete color blindness is rare; most people who are color blind, the vast majority of whom are men, can see some colors but not others. The nature of color blindness depends on which of the three kinds of cones is inoperative. For example, in the most common form of color blindness, the green cone system malfunctions in some way. Green is indistinguishable from certain combinations of blue and red. Color-matching experiments performed by people with this form of color blindness show that they need only two other colors to match a pure color and hence have dichromatic color perception. **Dichromats** *are people with only two kinds of cones.* **Trichromats** *are people with normal color vision, having three kinds of cone receptors.*

The German physiologist Ewald Hering was not completely satisfied with the trichromatic theory of color vision. Hering observed that some colors cannot exist together whereas others can. For example, it is easy to imagine a greenish-blue or a reddish-yellow, but nearly impossible to imagine a reddish-green or a bluish-yellow. Hering also observed that trichromatic theory could not adequately explain **afterimages,** *sensations that remain after a stimulus is removed.* Color afterimages are common and they involve complementary colors (to experience an afterimage, turn to figure 11). One example of afterimages that many people are familiar with occurs after prolonged exposure to a computer terminal screen with green lettering, such as those used in many businesses. After working with a computer like this all day, it is not unusual for white objects and walls to appear reddish. Conversely, if you look at red long enough, eventually a green afterimage will appear; if you look at yellow long enough, eventually a blue afterimage will appear. Such information led Hering to propose that the visual system treats colors as complementary pairs—red-green and blue-yellow.

Hering's view is called **opponent-process theory,** *which states that cells in the visual system respond to red-green and blue-yellow colors; a given cell might be excited by red and inhibited by green, while another cell might be excited by yellow and inhibited by blue.* Researchers have found that opponent-process theory does explain afterimages (Hurvich & Jameson, 1969; Jameson & Hurvich, 1989). If you stare at red, for instance, your red-green system seems to "tire," and when you look away, it rebounds and gives you a green afterimage. Also, if you mix equal amounts of opponent colors, such as blue and yellow, you see gray; figure 12 illustrates this principle.

We have seen that the trichromatic theory of color perception is correct in that we do in fact have three kinds of cone receptors like those predicted by Young and Helmholtz. Then how can the opponent-process theory

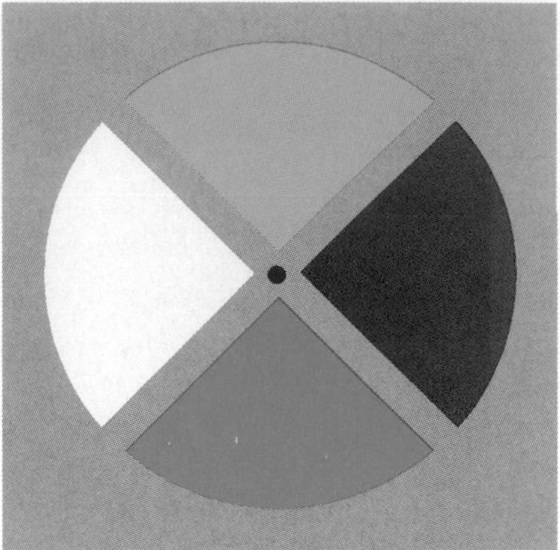

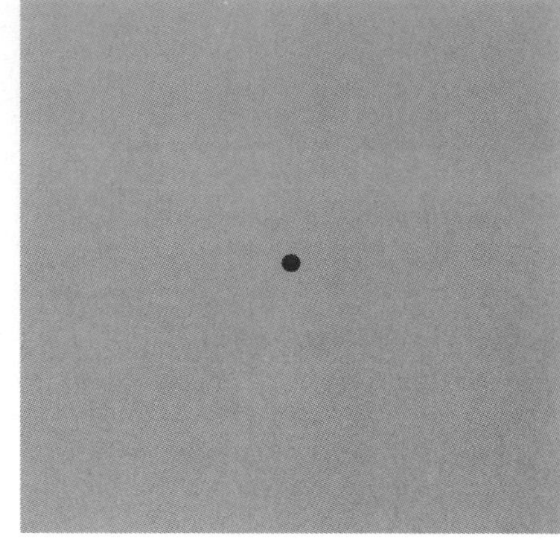

FIGURE 11

Negative Afterimage—Complementary Colors
If you gaze steadily at the dot in the colored panel on the left for a few moments, then shift your gaze to the gray box on the right, you will see the original hues change into their complementary colors. The blue appears as yellow, the red as green, the green as red, and the yellow as blue. This pairing of colors has to do with the fact that color receptors in the eye are apparently sensitive as pairs; when one color is turned off (when you stop staring at the panel), the other color in the receptor is briefly "turned on." The afterimage effect is especially noticeable when you spend time painting walls or objects in bright colors.

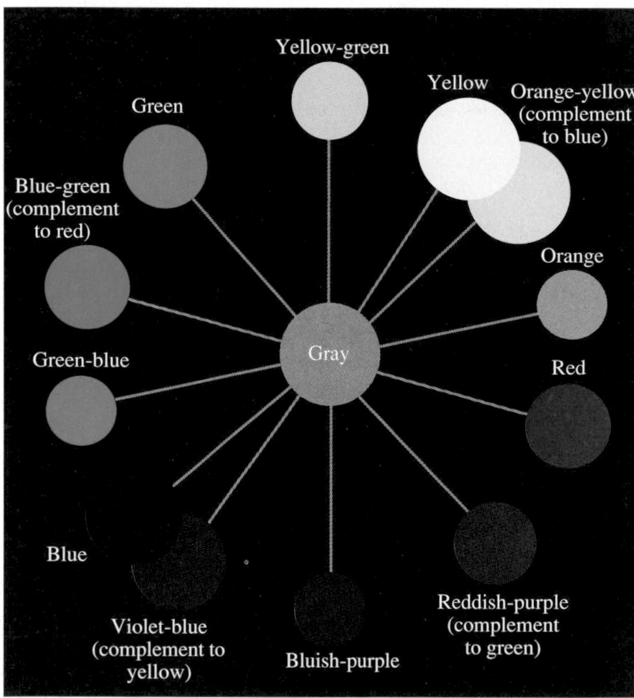

FIGURE 12

Color Wheel
Colors opposite each other produce the neutral gray in the center when they are mixed. For instance, blue-green is the complement of red.

also be correct? The answer is that the red, blue, and green cones in the retina are connected to retinal ganglion cells in such a way that the three-color code is immediately translated into the opponent-process code. For example, a green cone might inhibit and a red cone might excite a particular ganglion cell. Thus, *both* the trichromatic and opponent-process theory are correct—the eye and the brain use both methods to code colors.

Our tour of the visual system has been an extensive one—you have read about the light spectrum, the structures of the eye, neural-visual processing, and the marvels of color vision. To help you remember the main themes of the visual system, see concept table 2. Next you will study the second most researched sensory system—hearing.

THE AUDITORY SYSTEM

Just as light provides us with information about the environment, so does sound. Think about what life would be like without music, the rushing sound of ocean waves, or the gentle voice of someone you love. Sounds in the world tell us about the approach of a person behind us, an approaching car, the force of the wind outside, the mischief of a 2-year-old, and, perhaps most importantly, the kinds of information that we transmit through language and song.

The Nature of Sound and How We Experience It

At a rock concert you may have felt the throbbing pulse of loud sounds or sensed that the air around you was vibrating. Bass instruments are especially effective at creating mechanical pulsations, even causing the floor or a seat to vibrate on occasion. When a bass is played loudly we can sense air molecules being pushed forward in waves from the speaker. **Sounds,** *or sound waves, are vibrations in the air that are processed by our auditory (or hearing) system.*

Concept Table 2

Vision

Concept	Processes/Related Ideas	Characteristics/Description
The Visual Stimulus and the Eye	The visual stimulus	Light is a form of electromagnetic energy that can be described in terms of wavelengths. The wavelength is the distance from the peak of one wave of light to the next. The receptors in the human eye are sensitive to wavelengths from 400 to 700 nm.
	The eye	Key external parts are the sclera, the iris, the pupil, and the cornea. The lens and the cornea bend the light falling on the surface of the eye just enough to focus it on the back of the eye. The retina is the light-sensitive surface in the back of the eye, consisting of light receptors called rods (which function well under low illumination), cones (which function in color vision), and different neurons.
From Eye to Brain and Neural-Visual Processing	The nature of transmission	The optic nerve transmits neural impulses to the brain. Because of crossovers of nerve fibers, what we see in the left visual field is registered in the right side of the brain and vice versa. Visual information reaches the occipital lobe of the brain, where it is further integrated. Hubel and Wiesel discovered that neurons in the visual cortex can detect features of our visual world such as line, angle, and size.
Sensory Adaptation	Its nature	Sensory adaptation involves weakened sensory response after prolonged stimulation.
Color Vision	The nature of color	Objects appear in color because they reflect certain wavelengths of light between 400 and 700 nm. Important properties of color are hue (based on wavelength content), saturation (based on purity), and brightness (based on intensity). Mixing colors of light involves an additive mixture; mixing pigments involves a subtractive mixture.
	Theories of color vision	Scientists have found support for two theories. The trichromatic theory states that color perception is based on the existence of three types of receptors, which are maximally sensitive to different, but overlapping, ranges of wavelengths. This theory is also called the Young-Helmholtz theory and emphasizes the colors of red, green, and blue. The trichromatic theory explains color blindness but not afterimages. The opponent-process theory does explain afterimages. The opponent-process theory, developed by Hering, states that cells in the visual system respond to red-green and blue-yellow colors. Researchers have found that the red, blue, and green cones are connected to the retinal ganglion cells in such a way that the three-color code is translated into the opponent-process code. Thus, both theories are right—the eye and the brain use both methods to code colors.

Remember that we described light waves as being much like the waves fanned when a pebble is tossed into a lake, with concentric circles moving outward from where the pebble entered the water. Sound waves are similar. They vary in wavelength, which determines the **frequency** *of the sound wave or the number of cycles (or full wavelengths) that pass through a point in a given time* (see figure 13). **Pitch** *is the perceptual interpretation of the frequency of sound.* High-frequency sounds are perceived as having a high pitch, low-frequency sounds are perceived as having a low pitch. A soprano voice sounds high-pitched, a bass voice sounds low-pitched. As with the wavelength of light, human sensitivity is limited to a range of sound frequencies. It is common knowledge that dogs, for example, can hear higher frequencies than can humans.

Sound waves vary not only in frequency but also in amplitude. The sound wave's **amplitude** *is measured in decibels (dB), the amount of pressure produced by a sound wave relative to a standard;* the typical standard is the weakest sound the human ear can detect. Thus, zero decibels

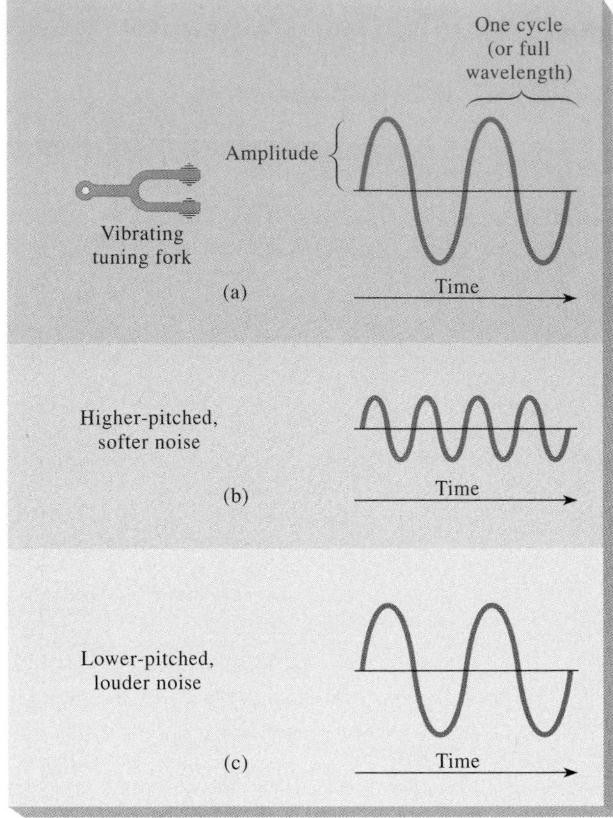

FIGURE 13

Frequency and Amplitude of Sound Waves
(*a*) A tuning fork is an instrument with two prongs that produces a tone when struck. You may have seen one in a music classroom or science laboratory. The vibrations of the tuning fork cause air molecules to vibrate like a musical instrument, producing a sound-wave pattern like the one shown. (*b*) Wavelength determines the frequency of the sound wave, which is the number of cycles, or full wavelengths, that can pass through a point in a given time. In the tuning fork example, two cycles (full wavelengths) have occurred in the time frame shown. In the sound waves shown here, four cycles have occurred in this time frame, so this sound wave has a higher frequency than the sound wave with the tuning fork; hence, it has a higher pitch. (*c*) The amplitude of the sound wave is the change in pressure created by the sound wave and is reflected in the sound wave's height. This sound wave has a smaller amplitude than the sound wave shown with the tuning fork; thus, it does not sound as loud.

would be the softest noise detectable by humans. Noise rated at 80 decibels or higher, if heard for prolonged periods of time, can cause permanent hearing loss. A quiet library is about 40 decibels, a car horn about 90 decibels, a rock band at close range 120 decibels, and a rocket launching 180 decibels. Noise levels have risen in recent years (Staples, 1996).The decibel levels of various sounds are shown in figure 14. **Loudness** *is the perception of a sound wave's amplitude.* In general, the higher the amplitude of the sound wave, the louder the sound is perceived to be. In the world of amplitude, this means that air is moving rapidly for loud sounds and slowly for soft sounds.

So far we have been describing a single sound wave with just one frequency. This is similar to the single wavelength or pure colored light we just discussed in the context of color matching. Most sounds, however, including those of speech and music, are complex sounds. **Complex sounds** *are those in which numerous frequencies of sound blend together.* **Timbre** *is the tone color or perceptual quality of a sound.* Timbre differences are what make the difference between a trumpet and a trombone playing the same note, and are also responsible for the quality differences we hear between human voices.

Structures and Functions of the Ear

What happens to sound waves once they reach your ear? How do various structures of the ear transform sound waves of expanded and compressed air so they can be understood by the brain as sound? The function of the ear is analogous to the function of the eye. The ear serves the purpose of transmitting a high-fidelity version of sounds in the world to the brain for analysis and interpretation. Just as an image needs to be in focus and sufficiently bright for the brain to interpret it, a sound needs to be transmitted in a way that preserves information about its location (think how confusing life would be if you could hear sounds without being able to determine where they are coming from!); its frequency, which helps us distinguish the voice of a child from that of an adult; and its timbre, which allows us to identify the voice of a friend on the telephone.

The ear is divided into the *outer ear, middle ear,* and *inner ear* (the major structures of the ear are shown in figure 15). The **outer ear** *consists of the pinna and the external auditory canal.* The pinna is the outer visible part of the ear (elephants have very large ones). Its shape helps us to localize sounds by making the sound different in front of us than behind us. The pinnae of many animals such as dogs are movable and serve a more important role in sound localization than do the pinnae of humans. Dogs will prick up their ears toward the direction of a faint and interesting sound.

After passing the pinna, sound waves are then funneled through the external auditory canal to the middle ear. The **middle ear** *has four main parts: eardrum, hammer, anvil, and stirrup.* The eardrum is the first structure that sound touches in the middle ear. The **eardrum** *is a membrane that vibrates in response to a sound. The sound is then transmitted by the three smallest bones in the human body—the hammer, anvil, and stirrup—to the inner ear.* The middle ear bones translate the sound waves in air into sound waves in water (lymph) so they can be processed further in the inner ear. Most of us know that sound travels far more easily in air than in water. When we are swimming underwater, loud shouts from the side of the pool are barely detectable to us. Sound waves entering the ear travel in air up until they reach the inner

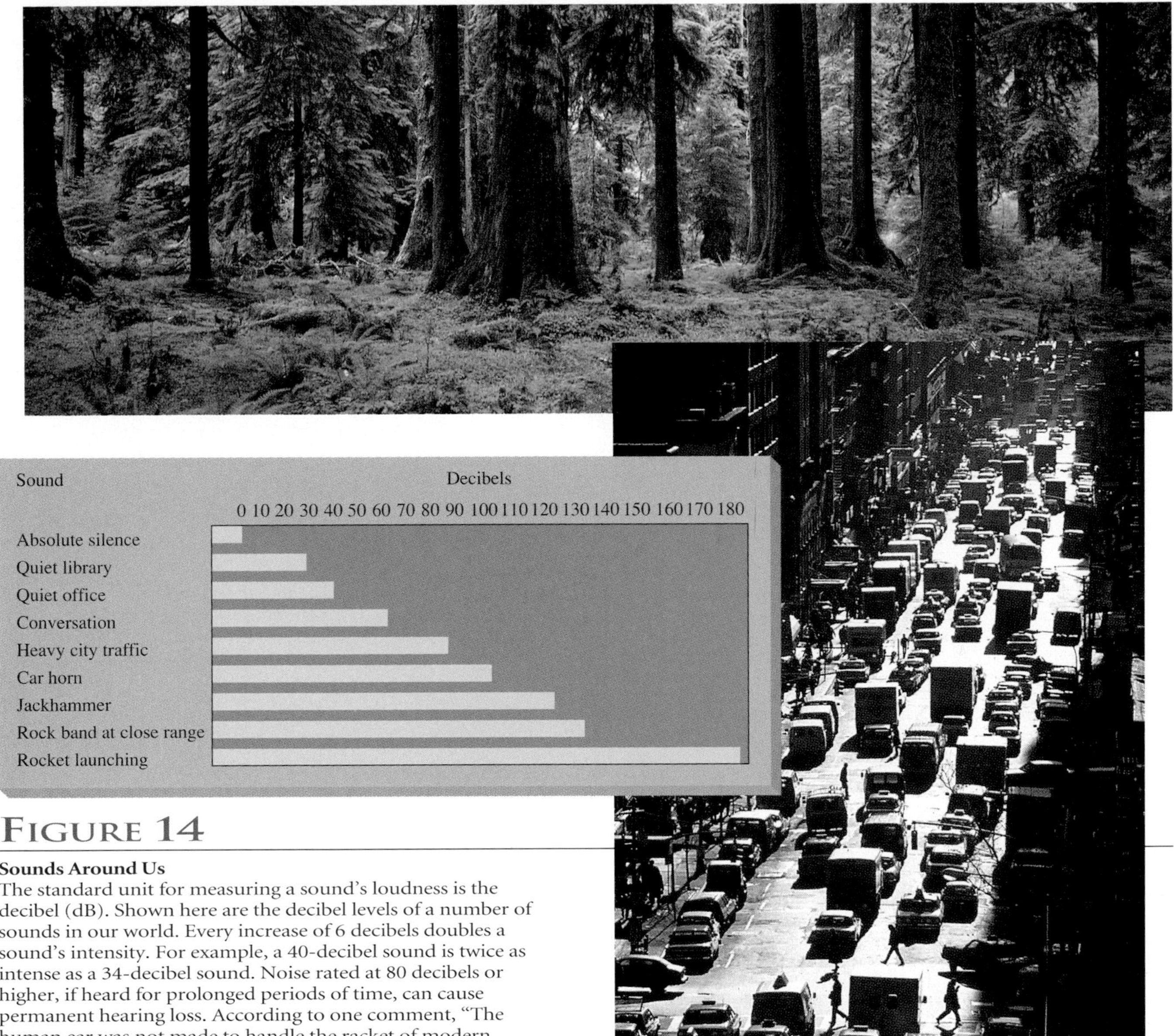

FIGURE 14

Sounds Around Us
The standard unit for measuring a sound's loudness is the decibel (dB). Shown here are the decibel levels of a number of sounds in our world. Every increase of 6 decibels doubles a sound's intensity. For example, a 40-decibel sound is twice as intense as a 34-decibel sound. Noise rated at 80 decibels or higher, if heard for prolonged periods of time, can cause permanent hearing loss. According to one comment, "The human ear was not made to handle the racket of modern civilization." By one estimate, machinery is making the Western world noisier by about 1 decibel a year.

ear, at which point they will begin to be transmitted through body fluids. At this border between air and fluid, sounds meet the same kind of resistance that shouts directed at an underwater swimmer meet when they hit the surface of the water. The hammer, anvil, and stirrup form a connected chain of bones that act like a lever to amplify the sound waves before they reach the liquid-filled inner ear.

The main parts of the **inner ear** *are the oval window, cochlea, and the organ of Corti.* The stirrup is connected to the *oval window,* which is a membrane like the ear drum and transmits the waves to the cochlea. The **cochlea** *is a long tubular fluid-filled structure that is coiled up like a snail.* The **basilar membrane** *is housed inside the cochlea and runs its entire length.* The **organ of Corti,** *also running the length of the cochlea, sits on the basilar membrane and contains the ear's sensory receptors, which change the energy of the sound waves into nerve impulses that can be processed by the brain.* Hairlike sensory receptors in the organ of Corti are stimulated by vibrations of the basilar membrane. Sound waves traveling in the fluid of the inner ear cause these hairlike receptors to move. The movement generates nerve impulses, which vary with the frequency and extent of the membrane's vibrations.

One of the auditory system's mysteries is how the inner ear registers the frequency of sound. Two theories

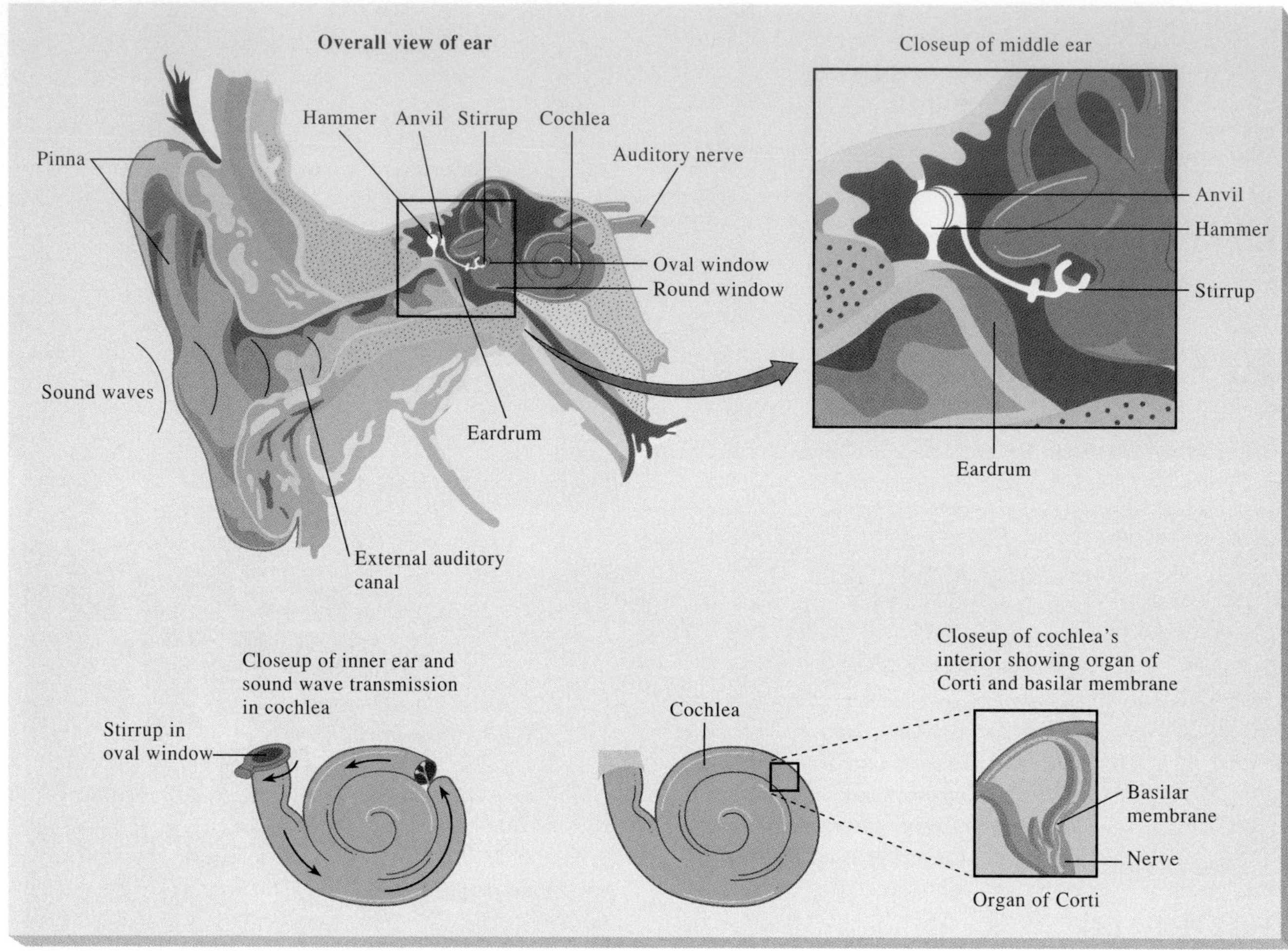

FIGURE 15

Major Structures of the Human Ear and the Transmission of Sound Waves
Sound waves are funneled through the external auditory canal to the eardrum in the middle ear. Three bony structures in the middle ear—hammer, anvil, and stirrup—concentrate sound waves so they can be further processed in the inner ear. The stirrup relays the eardrum's vibrations through the oval window to the cochlea, a snaillike, fluid-filled structure, where sound waves are further processed before the auditory information moves on to the auditory nerve to be transmitted to the brain. The organ of Corti runs the entire length of the cochlea and contains the basilar membrane at its base. The movement of sound waves in the cochlear fluid causes the basilar membrane to vibrate and its hair cells to bend. The vibrating hair cells stimulate nearby nerve cells, which join to form the auditory nerve.

have been proposed to explain this mystery: place theory and frequency theory. **Place theory** *is a theory of hearing which states that each frequency produces vibrations at a particular spot on the basilar membrane.* Georg von Békésy won a Nobel Prize in 1961 for his research on the basilar membrane. Von Békésy (1960) studied the effects of vibration applied at the oval window on the basilar membrane of human cadavers. Through a microscope, he saw that this stimulation produced a traveling wave on the basilar membrane. A traveling wave is like the ripples that appear in a pond when you throw in a stone. However, since the cochlea is a long tube, the ripples can travel in only one direction, from the end of the cochlea where the oval window is placed to the far tip of the cochlea. High-frequency vibrations create traveling waves that maximally displace (or move) the area of the basilar membrane next to the oval window; low-frequency vibrations maximally displace areas of the membrane closer to the tip of the cochlea.

Place theory adequately explains high-frequency sounds but fares poorly with low-frequency sounds. A high-frequency sound stimulates a very precise area on the basilar membrane. By contrast, a low-frequency sound causes a large part of the basilar membrane to be displaced, so it is hard to localize the "maximal displacement" of the basilar membrane. Because humans can hear low-frequency sounds better than predicted by looking at the precision of the basilar membrane's response to these sounds, some other factors must be involved. **Frequency theory** *states that the perception of a sound's frequency is due to how often the auditory nerve fires.* One problem with frequency theory is that a single neuron has a maximum firing rate of about 1,000 times per second. Because of this limitation, frequency theory cannot be applied to tones with frequencies that would require a neuron to fire more than 1,000 times per second. To deal with this limitation, a modification of place theory called **volley theory** *states that high frequencies can be signaled by teams of neurons that fire at different offset times to create an overall firing rate that could signal a very high frequency.* The term *volley* was used because the neurons fire in a sequence of rhythmic volleys at higher frequencies. The alteration in neural firing makes possible frequencies above 1,000 times per second. Thus, frequency theory can better explain the perception of low-frequency sounds and place theory can better explain the perception of high-frequency sounds. There is some evidence that the auditory system is correctly described by both place and frequency theory. And so, it is possible that both are correct but that sounds of high and low frequencies may be signaled with different coding schemes.

Neural-Auditory Processing

As we saw in the visual system, once energy from the environment is picked up by our receptors, it must be transmitted to the brain for processing and interpretation. An image on the retina does not a Picasso make—likewise, a pattern of receptor responses in the cochlea does not a symphony make! In the retina, we saw that the responses of the rod and cone receptors feed into ganglion cells in the retina and leave the eye via the optic nerve. In the auditory system, the **auditory nerve** *carries neural impulses to the brain's auditory areas.* Auditory information moves up the auditory pathway in a more complex manner than does visual information in the visual pathway. Many synapses occur in the ascending auditory pathway, with some fibers crossing over the midline and others proceeding directly to the hemisphere on the same side as the ear of reception. The auditory nerve extends from the cochlea to the brain stem, with some fibers crossing over the midline. The cortical destination of most of these fibers is the temporal lobes of the brain (beneath the temples of the head).

Now that we have described the visual and auditory systems in some detail, we turn to a number of other sensory systems—the skin senses, the chemical senses (smell and taste), and the kinesthetic and vestibular senses. As you can tell, we have more than the traditional five senses of sight, hearing, taste, touch, and smell.

Other Senses

In addition to our visual and auditory senses, we also have other senses that detect information in the environment. They include the skin senses, the chemical senses, and the kinesthetic and vestibular senses.

The Skin Senses

We know when a friend has a fever by putting our hand to her head; we know how to find our way to the light switch in a darkened room by groping along the wall; and we know whether or not a pair of shoes is too tight by the way the shoes touch different parts of our feet when we walk. Many of us think of our skin as a canvas rather than a sense. We color it with cosmetics, dyes, and tatoos. But the skin is our largest sensory system, draped over the body with receptors for touch, temperature, and pain. These three kinds of receptors form the cutaneous senses. A large variety of important information comes to us through our ability to detect touch.

Touch

Touch is one of the senses that we most often take for granted. As we saw in the earlier discussion on detection, our ability to respond to touch is astounding. Raising a single hair on your forearm with the sharp point of a pencil should be enough to convince you of this. What do we detect when we feel "touch"? What kind of energy does our sense of touch pick up from our external environment? In vision, we detect electromagnetic energy or light. In audition, we detect the vibrations of air or soundwaves pressing against our eardrum. In touch, we detect mechanical energy, or pressure against the skin. The lifting of a single hair causes pressure on the skin around the shaft of hair. This tiny bit of mechanical pressure at the base of the hair is sufficient for us to detect the "touch" of the pencil point! More commonly, we detect the mechanical energy of the pressure of a car seat against our buttocks, or the pressure of a pencil in our hands. Is this kind of energy so different than the kind of energy we detect in vision or audition? Sometimes the only difference is one of intensity—the sound of a rock band playing softly is auditory stimulus, but at the high volumes that make a concert hall reverberate, such an auditory stimulus is *felt* as mechanical energy pressing against your skin.

Just as our visual system is more sensitive to images on the fovea than to images in the peripheral retina, our sensitivity to touch is not equally good across all areas of the skin. As you might expect, human toolmakers need to have excellent touch discrimination in their hands, but much less touch discrimination in other parts of the body such as the torso or legs. What this amounts to is having more space in the brain to analyze touch signals coming from the hands than from the legs.

Temperature

Beyond the need to sense physical pressure on the skin, we need to detect temperature, even in the absence of direct contact with the skin. We can immediately sense the temperature of water in a bathtub or swimming pool by submerging the tips of our toes. We can also warm ourselves at a safe distance from a roaring campfire. **Thermoreceptors,** *which are receptors located under the skin, respond to increases and decreases in temperature.* Thermoreceptors not only serve a general function of sensing temperature changes at or near our skin, but also serve as input to our body's temperature regulation system, whose job is to keep our bodies at a constant 98.6 degrees Fahrenheit.

Pain

When contact with the skin takes the form of a sharp pinch, our sensation of mechanical pressure changes from touch to pain. When a pot handle is so hot that it burns your hand, your sensation of temperature becomes one of pain. Many kinds of stimuli can cause pain. Intense stimulation of any one of the senses can produce pain—too much light, very loud sounds, very spicy food, for example. Our ability to sense pain is vital for our survival as a species. **Pain** *is the sensation that warns us that damage to our bodies is occurring.* It functions as a quick-acting system that tells the motor systems of the brain that they must act to minimize or eliminate this damage. A hand touching a hot stove must be pulled away; ears should be covered up when one walks by a loud pavement drill; chili should be buffered with some crackers.

While we have seen that all sensations are affected by factors such as motivation, expectation, and other related decision factors, the sensation of pain is especially susceptible to these factors (Philips & Rachman, 1996). Cultural and ethnic contexts, also, can greatly determine the degree to which an individual experiences pain. For example, one pain researcher described a ritual performed in India in which a chosen person travels from town to town delivering blessings to the children and the crops while suspended from metal hooks embedded in his back (Melzak, 1973). The chosen person apparently reports no sensation of pain and appears to be in ecstasy.

One theory of pain perception that offers insight into how cognitive and emotional factors might exert such dramatic influences on the experience of pain was developed by Ronald Melzak and Patricia Wall (1965, 1983). They proposed the **gate-control theory,** *which states that the spinal column contains a neural gate that can be opened (allowing the perception of pain) or closed (blocking the perception of pain).* In this account, the brain can send signals downward to the spinal cord to close the gate, and hence suppress the sensation of pain (see figure 16). The gate-control theory has also been proposed as an explanation for the effects of **acupuncture,** *a technique in which thin needles are inserted at specific points in the body to produce various effects, such as local anesthesia* (figure 17). The gate-control theory of pain assumes that the presence of acupuncture needles somehow manages to shut the pain gate, inhibiting the experience of pain. Gate-control theory may also explain the fact that gentle pressure on the skin, such as lightly rubbing the skin, seems to inhibit the pain signal.

The Chemical Senses

We've seen that the information impinging on our senses comes in many diverse forms: electromagnetic energy in vision, soundwaves in audition, and mechanical pressure and temperature in the cutaneous senses. The last two senses we will study are responsible for processing chemicals in our environment. With the sense of smell we detect airborne chemicals, and with taste we detect chemicals that have been dissolved in saliva. Taste and smell are frequently stimulated simultaneously. We sometimes only realize the strong links between the two senses when a nasty cold and nasal congestion seem to take the pleasure out of eating. Our favorite foods become "tasteless" without the smells that characterize them. Despite this link, we will see that our senses of taste and smell have lives and functions all their own.

Taste

What would life be with no sense of taste? For anyone who has tried to diet, "not worth living" is an all-too-often way of responding. The thought of giving up a favorite taste, such as chocolate or butter, can be a very depressing thought. We use our sense of taste to select food and to regulate food intake. While it is not so easy to see or smell mold on a blueberry, a small taste is enough to prompt you to sense that the fruit is no longer fit for consumption. Beyond that, the pleasure associated with the taste of food depends on many aspects of our body's need for a particular food (Bartoshuk & Beauchamp, 1994). The taste of devil's food cake can be very pleasurable when we are hungry yet almost revolting after eating a banana split.

It is not the prettiest sight you've ever seen, but try this anyway. Take a drink of milk and allow it to coat your tongue. Then go to a mirror, stick out your tongue, and look carefully at its surface. You should be able to see rounded bumps above the surface of your tongue. Those bumps, called **papillae,** *contain your taste buds, which are the receptors for your taste.* About 10,000 of these taste buds are located on your tongue. As in all of the other sensory systems we have discussed, the information picked up by these receptors is transmitted to the brain for analysis and response (spitting something out, for example) when it is necessary.

The taste qualities we respond to can be categorized as sweet, sour, bitter, and salty. Though all areas of the tongue can detect each of the four tastes, different regions of the tongue are more sensitive to one taste than another. The tip of the tongue is the most sensitive to sweet; the rear of the tongue is the most sensitive to bitter; just behind the area for sweet is the area most sensitive for salt; and just behind that is the most sensitive area for sour. While the tastes we experience can be categorized along these dimensions, our tasting ability goes far beyond them. Most of us pride ourselves on being able to discriminate different brands of ice cream; caffeinated and decaffeinated soda, coffee, and tea; and the many variations of

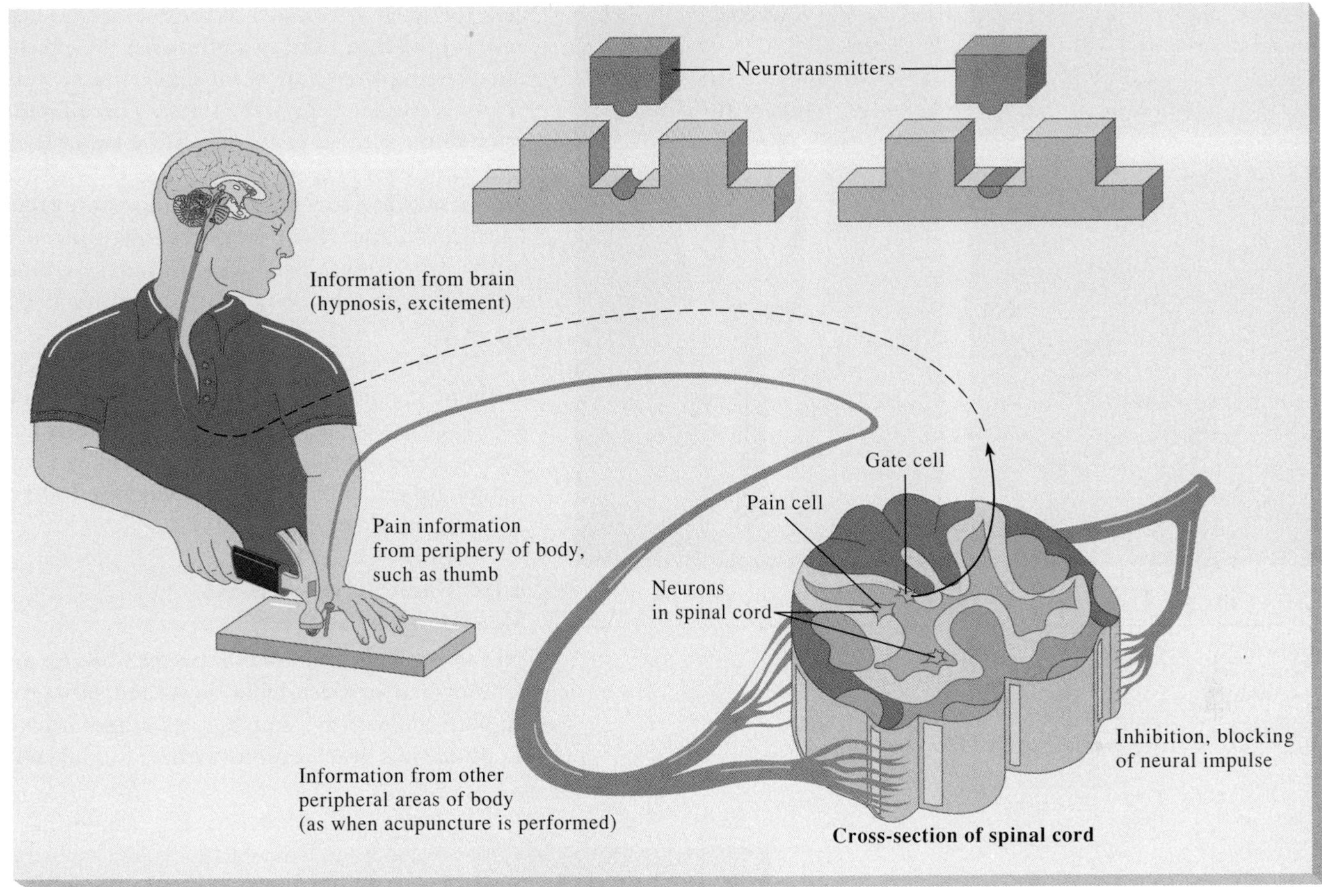

FIGURE 16

Gate-Control Theory of Pain
In the case of hitting your thumb with a hammer, pain signals initially go through the spinal cord and then to the brain. Gate-control theory states that pain information can be blocked in the spinal cord. Pain pathways from the periphery of the body (thumb, foot, etc.) make a synaptic connection in the spinal cord and then ascend to the brain. Interneurons can inhibit transmission through these pathways, as shown in the drawing on the right. When a strong peripheral stimulus (as applied during acupuncture) comes into the spinal cord, this can turn on the interneuron and close the gate in the pain pathway. Also, when a signal comes down from the brain (during hypnosis or the excitement of athletic competition), it, too, can turn on the interneuron and close the gate. The gate is not a physical structure that actually opens and shuts; rather, the gate is the inhibition of neural impulses. Neurotransmitters (the tiny circles in the synapse between the pain cell and the gate cell) are involved in gate control, but much is yet to be known about their identity.

product substitutes that are supposed to be better for us than the standard high-cholesterol, high-sugar, and high-fat culinary pleasures.

Smell

A good way to begin our discussion of smell is to consider the many functions it serves. It is often easier to understand the importance of smell when we think about animals with more sophisticated senses of smell than our own. A dog, for example, can use its sense of smell to find its way back from a lone stroll, distinguish friend from foe, or even (with some practice!) detect illegal drugs concealed in a suitcase. In fact, dogs can detect odors in concentrations 100 times lower than those detectable by humans. In comparison to the nasal feats of the average dog, we might be tempted to believe that the sense of smell has outlived its usefulness in humans. What do *we* use smell for? For one, humans need the sense of smell to decide what to eat. We can distinguish rotten food from fresh food, and remember (all too well) which foods have made us ill in the past. The smell of a food that has previously made us ill is often, by itself, enough to make us feel nauseous. Second, while tracking is a function of smell that we often associate only with animals, humans are competent odor trackers. We can follow the smell of gas to a leak, the smell of smoke to a fire, or the smell of a hot apple pie to a windowsill.

What physical equipment do we use to process odor information? Just as the eyes scan the visual field for objects of interest, and the pinnae prick up to direct attention to sounds of interest, the nose is not a passive instrument. We actively sniff when we are trying to track down the source of a fire, or of a burned-out fluorescent light. The receptor

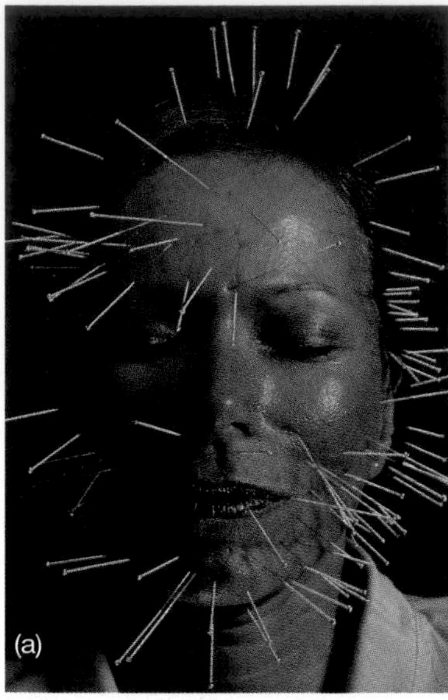

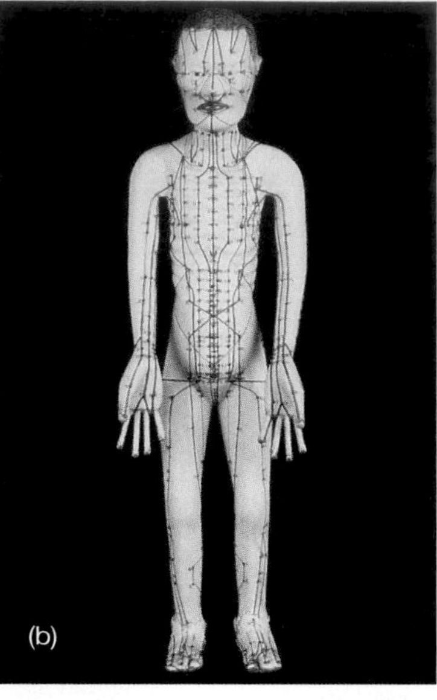

FIGURE 17

Acupuncture
(*a*) This woman is being treated for pain by an acupuncturist.
(*b*) Acupuncture points are carefully noted on this nineteenth-century Japanese papier-mâché figure. In their adaptation of the Chinese methodology, the Japanese identified 660 points.

cells for smell are located in the roof of the nasal cavity (see figure 18*a*), so sniffing has the effect of maximizing the chances of detecting an odor (Doty & Muller-Schwarze, 1992). The **olfactory epithelium,** *located at the top of the nasal cavity, contains a sheet of receptor cells for smell.* These receptor sites are covered with millions of minute hairlike antennae that project through the mucus in the top of the nasal cavity and make contact with air on its way to the throat and lungs (see figure 18*b*).

How good are you at identifying smells? Without practice, most people do a rather poor job of identifying odors. But the human olfactory sense can be improved. Perfumers, as perfume testers are called, can identify between 100 and 200 different fragrances.

The Kinesthetic and Vestibular Senses

You know the difference between walking and running and between lying down and sitting up. To perform even the simplest acts of motor coordination, like reaching out to take a book off a

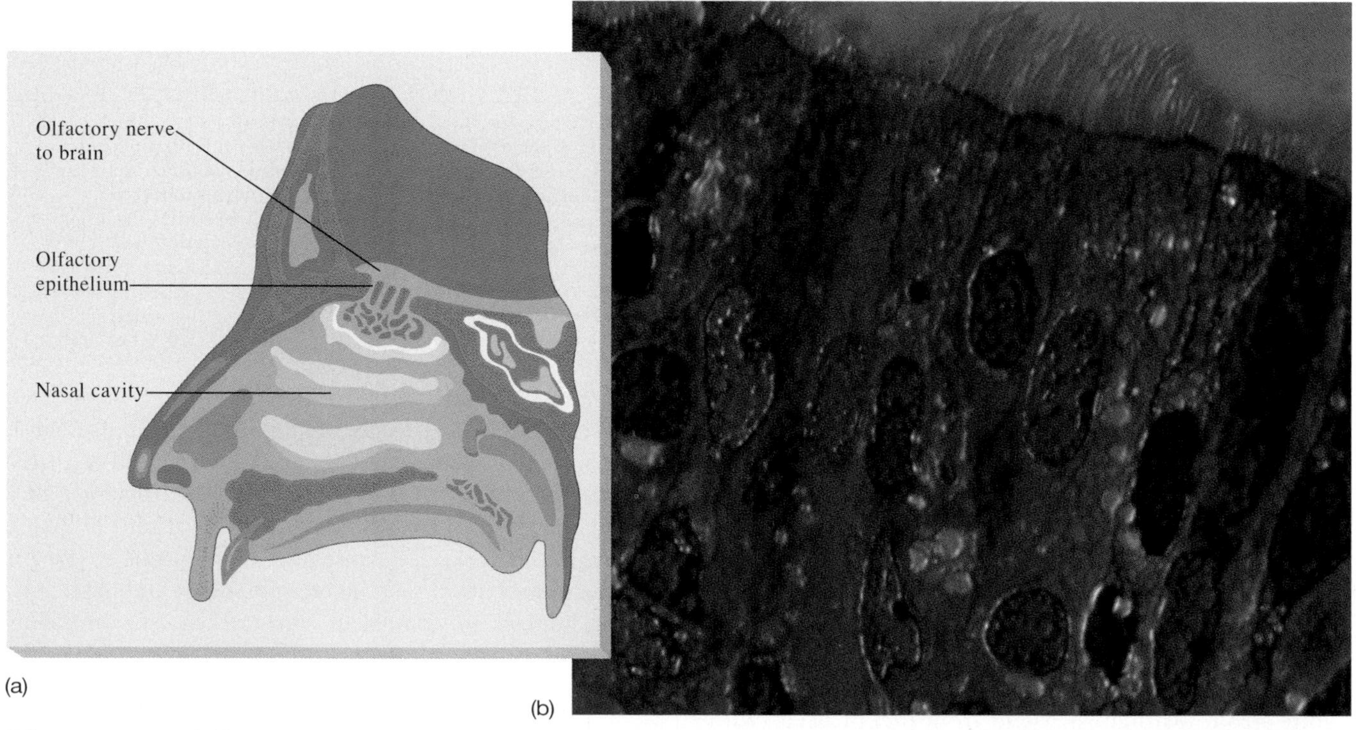

FIGURE 18

Olfactory Sense
(*a*) Airborne molecules of an odor reach tiny receptor cells in the roof of the nasal cavity. The receptor cells form a mucous-covered membrane called the olfactory epithelium. Then the olfactory nerve carries information about the odor to the brain for further processing. (*b*) Shown here is a microphotograph of the olfactory epithelium with the minute, hairlike antennae at the bottom.

library shelf or getting up out of a chair, the brain must be constantly receiving and coordinating information from every part of the body. Your body has two kinds of senses that provide information about your movement and orientation in space: the **kinesthetic senses** *provide information about movement, posture, and orientation,* and the **vestibular sense** *provides information about balance and movement.*

No specific organ contains the kinesthetic senses. Instead, they are embedded in muscle fibers and joints. As we stretch and move, these receptors signal the state of the muscle. Kinesthesia is a sense that you often don't even notice until it is gone. Try walking when your leg "is asleep," or smiling (never mind talking) when you've just come from a dentist's office and you are still under the effects of novocaine. Perhaps the sophistication of kinesthesis can be best appreciated when we think in terms of memory. Even a mediocre typist can bang out twenty words per minute—but how many of us could write down the order of the letters on a keyboard without looking? We say that our fingers remember the positions of the keys. Typing is a skill that relies on very coordinated sensitivity to the orientation, position, and movements of our fingers. Likewise, the complicated movements a pitcher uses to throw a ball cannot be written down or communicated easily using language. They involve nearly every muscle and joint in the body.

FIGURE 19

The Semicircular Canals and Vestibular Sense
(*a*) This is a photograph of the semicircular canals located in the ear. The semicircular canals play an important role in the vestibular sense. The three canals are roughly perpendicular to each other in the three planes of space. Any angle of head rotation is registered by hair cells in one or more semicircular canals in both ears. (*b*) The semicircular canals provide feedback to the gymnast's brain as her body and head tilt in different directions.

The vestibular sense tells us whether our head (and hence usually our body) is tilted, moving, slowing down, or speeding up. It works in concert with the kinesthetic senses to coordinate our proprioceptive feedback, which is information about the position of our limbs and body parts in relation to other body parts. Consider the combination of sensory abilities involved in the motion of ice hockey players skating down the ice with the puck cradled and pushed forward with the hockey stick. The hockey players are responding simultaneously to a multitude of sensations including those produced by the slickness of the ice, the position of the puck, the speed and momentum of the forward progression, and the requirements of the play to turn and to track the other players on the ice.

The **semicircular canals,** *located in the inner ear, contain the sensory receptors that detect head motion that is caused when we tilt or move our heads and/or bodies* (see figure 19). These canals consist of three fluid-filled circular tubes that lie in the three planes of the body—right-left, front-back, and up-down. We can picture these as three intersecting hoola-hoops.

As you move your head, the fluid of the semicircular canals flows in different directions and at different speeds (depending upon the force of the head movement), and the cupula gets pulled to and fro with the fluid flow. Our perception of head movement and position is determined by the movements of these receptor cells. This ingenious system of using the motion of fluid in tubes to sense head position is not unlike the system we learned about in audition. In audition, though, the fluid movement in the cochlear is caused by the pressure sound exerts on the oval window, whereas in the vestibular sense the movements we sense are real movements of the head and body.

The combination of kinesthetic and vestibular senses is supplemented by information from vision. This simple principle has made many an amusement park and large-screen movie theater profitable. When films are shown on screens that are large enough to fill our visual field, such as those found in many theme parks, the motion you perceive on the screen can make you feel like *you* are moving. This is the same principle that causes motorists to slam on the brakes in their tiny little sports car when the big truck next to them starts to move forward. When everything in our visual field is moving, it is generally because we are moving.

At this point we have described a number of ideas about the auditory, skin, chemical, kinesthetic, and vestibular senses. A summary of these ideas is presented in concept table 3.

PERCEPTION

Earlier in this chapter we said that perception is the brain's process of organizing and interpreting sensory information to give it meaning. When perception goes to work, sensory receptors have received energy from stimuli in the external world and sensory organs have processed and transformed the information so it can be transmitted to the brain. Perception is a creation of the brain; it is based on input extracted from sensory organs, such as the eye, ear, and nose. But perception goes beyond this input. The brain uses information previously extracted as a basis for making educated guesses, or interpretations, about the state of the outside world. Usually the interpretations are correct and useful. For example, on the basis of a change in color or texture, we can conclude that a dog is on the rug. On the basis of a continuous increase in size, we can conclude that a train is coming toward us. Sometimes, though, the interpretations or inferences are wrong; the result is an illusion—when we see something that is not there. Our exploration of perceptual worlds evaluates the following questions: What are some approaches to explaining why we perceive the world the way we do? How do we perceive shape, depth, motion, and constancy? What are perceptual illusions, and why do we see these illusions? Is perception learned, or is it innate? What is extrasensory perception, and is it real?

Approaches to Perception

Two important approaches address how we perceive the world the way we do: the information-processing and ecological approaches.

The Information-Processing Approach

Some of the most useful insights concerning the nature of perception have emerged in recent years as a result of asking some simple but long-neglected questions. One such question was posed by David Marr (1982). He asked, "What is the purpose of vision?" Stop for a moment to consider how you would answer such a seemingly simple question. Marr pointed out problems associated with survival of the species and adaptation to the environment. The visual system in its current form is evolution's solution to a subset of these problems. Understanding the nature of these problems will surely help us to understand the nature of visual perception.

Let's return to Marr's question about the purpose of vision. You may have come up with answers to this question such as "The purpose of vision is to move around the world without bumping into things," "The purpose of vision is to be able to recognize people and objects," or "The purpose of vision is to be able to coordinate actions, like catching a ball, picking up a baby, or finding your mouth with a fork." Marr's answer to this question is simpler than these answers but general enough to encompass all of them. He proposed that the purpose of vision is to create a three-dimensional representation or map of the world in the brain. This means that we use vision to internalize the shapes, sizes, and positions of the objects in the visual field. An **information-processing approach** *states that perception is the process of representing information from the world internally. As information from the world is processed, it undergoes a series of internal manipulations.* We need this representation for all of the purposes of vision that you may have thought of in answering Marr's question: to navigate through our environment without bumping into things, to be able to grasp and manipulate objects, and eventually to create a representation of visual objects that you can compare with the representations in your memory.

The lesson we learn from asking questions about the purpose of our perceptual systems is that perception is a problem for which there are potentially many solutions. The solution that our brain has happened upon is the result of millions of years of evolution, shaped by the problems humans and their ancestors overcame to survive. You may wonder how else, but with two eyes and a brain, we could solve the problem Marr believes we solve with vision (that is, the creation of a three-dimensional map of the visual world). A careful look at some of our distant relatives in the animal kingdom is enough to humble the human ego on the marvels of its visual system. Vision is not the only solution to the problem of creating a three-dimensional map of the world in the brain. Bats, for example, solve the "vision"

Concept Table 3

The Auditory, Skin, Chemical, Kinesthetic, and Vestibular Senses

Concept	Processes/Related Ideas	Characteristics/Description
The Auditory System	The nature of sound and how we experience it	Sounds or sound waves are vibrations in the air that are processed by the auditory (or hearing) system. Sound waves vary in wavelength, which determines the frequency of the sound wave or the number of cycles (or full wavelengths) that pass through a point in a given time. Pitch is the perceptual interpretation of the frequency of sound. Amplitude is measured in decibels (dB), the amount of pressure produced by a sound wave relative to a standard. Loudness is the perception of a sound wave's amplitude. Complex sounds are those in which numerous frequencies of sound blend together. We experience the particular combination of frequencies in a sound as the quality or timbre of a sound.
	Structures and functions of the ear	The ear serves the function of transmitting a high-fidelity version of sounds in the world to the brain for analysis and interpretation. The ear is divided into the outer ear, middle ear, and inner ear. The outer ear consists of the pinna and the external auditory canal. The middle ear consists of the eardrum, hammer, anvil, and stirrup. The main parts of the inner ear are the oval window, cochlea, and the organ of Corti. The basilar membrane, located inside the cochlea, is where vibrations are changed into nerve impulses.
	Theories of hearing	Place theory states that each frequency produces vibrations at a particular spot on the basilar membrane. Frequency theory states that the perception of a sound's frequency is due to how often the auditory nerve fires. Volley theory is a modification of place theory, stating that high frequencies can be signaled by teams of neurons that fire at different offset times to create an overall firing rate that could signal a very high frequency. Frequency theory is better at explaining lower-frequency sounds, volley and place theories higher-frequency sounds.
	Neural-auditory processing	Information about sound is carried from the cochlea to the brain by the auditory nerve. Information is integrated in the temporal lobe.
The Skin Senses	Touch	In touch, we detect mechanical energy, or pressure against the skin.
	Temperature	Thermoreceptors, which are receptors located under the skin, respond to increases and decreases in temperature.
	Pain	Pain is the sensation that warns us that damage to our bodies is occurring. Gate-control theory states that the spinal column contains a neural gate that can be opened (allowing the perception of pain) or closed (blocking the perception of pain). Gate-control theory has been proposed as one explanation of acupuncture, a technique in which thin needles are inserted at specific points in the body to produce various effects, including local anesthesia. Gate-control theory does not completely explain how we experience pain.
The Chemical Senses	Taste	We use our sense of taste to select food and to regulate food intake. Papillae are rounded bumps above the surface of the tongue that contain taste buds, the receptors for taste. The taste qualities we can respond to are classified as sweet, sour, bitter, and salty.
	Smell	The functions of smell include deciding what to eat, tracking, and communication. The olfactory epithelium, located at the top of the nasal cavity, contains a sheet of receptor cells for smell.
The Kinesthetic and Vestibular Senses	Their nature	The kinesthetic senses provide information about movement, posture, and orientation, while the vestibular sense provides information about balance and movement. The semicircular canals, located in the inner ear, contain the sensory receptors that detect head motion that is caused when we tilt or move our heads and/or bodies.

problem with their ears and their voices. They use a system called **echolocation,** *in which they produce loud sounds (too high in frequency to be heard by the human ear) that travel through the environment hitting objects and echoing back to the bat's ear.* By comparing the time the sound was produced with the time it echoes back to the bat's ear, the bat is able to ascertain useful information about the distance between itself and objects in the world. Using this system, the bat is competent to fly through its environment at high speeds, avoid predators, and find prey. Why has evolution gone to such trouble in the case of the bat? The answer is simple. Vision requires light, and bats are nocturnal animals—wakeful and hunting at night. Any method of building internal representations of the environment that requires light would not be an effective system for the bat.

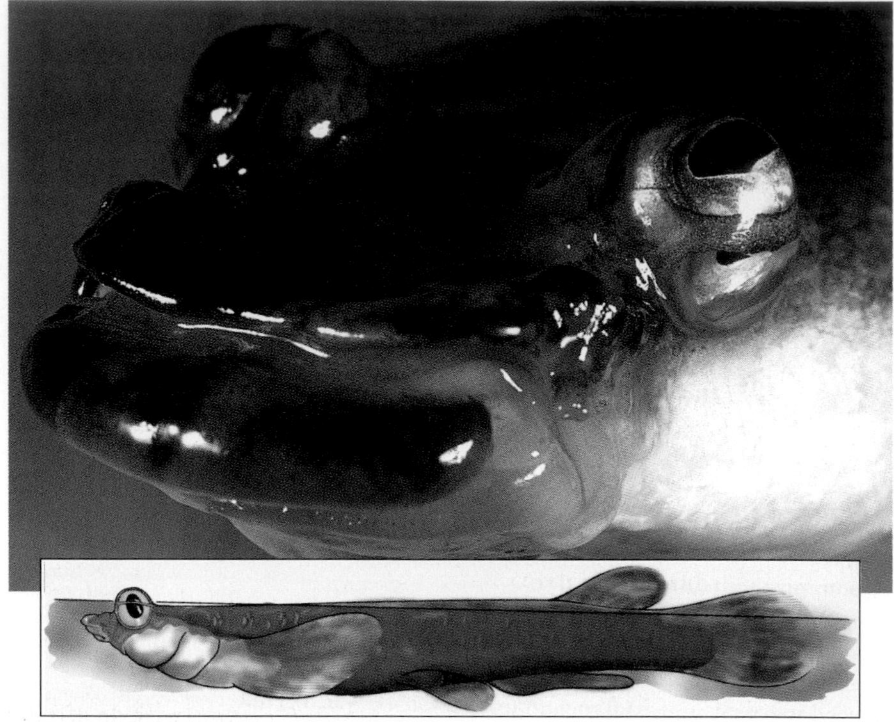

FIGURE 20

Anableps Microlepis
This fish can control its visual system so that it effectively has four eyes. The light-adapted condition shown here allows it to simultaneously view prey both above and below the water line.

The visual systems of our ancestors shaped many of the basic principles of our perceptual systems; organisms from the smallest of goldfish to the largest of elephants have eyes, and something similar to ears. This is because most animals need to be sensitive to events in their environments that affect the pattern of light, sound, and chemicals, around them. Predators, prey, and potential mates can be heard, seen, and perhaps smelled from a distance. When we think of the day-to-day life challenges of a squirrel, a bird, or a cat, the similarity of the human perceptual system to the perceptual systems of these animals is striking. However, when we look closely at the visual systems of animals, despite basic similarities to our own, each is exquisitely tailored to the environmental niche in which it evolved. A marvelous example of the exquisite accomplishments of evolution can be seen in a fish called *Anableps microlepis* (see figure 20), which has four eyes! To survive, this fish must monitor visual events both above and below the surface of the water. *Anableps microlepis* can swim just at the surface of the water, with its two aerial eyes surveying the visual field above the water while its two aquatic eyes monitor visual happenings underwater. As any swimmer knows, the properties of light traveling in water and in air are quite different, so it is not surprising that the kind of eye that sees best above the surface of the water is a very different eye than one tailored to see underwater. The visual system of *Anableps microlepis* solves this difficult problem by simply having both kinds of eyes, with a strong muscle for moving the lenses of the visual system back and forth between the aerial and the aquatic eyes!

The Ecological Approach

By asking questions about what we use vision for, we can take a more principled approach to studying the information we extract from our visual world to succeed at the perceptual tasks we need to accomplish. While Marr's statement about the purpose of vision defines a research agenda, not everyone agrees with such an agenda. J. J. Gibson (1966), in studying the perceptual challenges faced by pilots flying during World War II, proposed an **ecological approach,** *a view of perception that stresses an active perceiver exploring and moving about the environment.* In this approach, perception is an active interaction between the perceiver and the environment. An ecological approach to the study of perception assumes that the purpose of vision is to detect perceptual invariants. These invariants are abstracted from complex moving visual scenes. Gibson called this the **optic array,** *which is the constantly changing pattern of light that specifies the environment.*

Let's take an example that illustrates the difference between an approach that follows Marr's idea that the purpose of vision is to create a three-dimensional map of the world in the brain and one that follows Gibson's ecological approach. To create a three-dimensional map of the world, the distances of each object in the visual world must be ascertained. As we will see shortly, there are many cues to the size and distance of an object. For example, the size of the object on the retina and what you know about the size of a particular kind of object are both important cues to an object's actual size. However, these cues alone do not provide perfect information: The light reflected from a toy car will make a very small image on the retina. Combining this information with your experiences of the average-sized car, these cues alone would lead you to interpret the pattern of light created by the toy car as a real car that is very far away. So to perceive the actual size of the toy car, your perceptual system must make use of other cues to its real size, such as the sizes of other objects around the toy car (for example, your hand). In Marr's approach, this complex problem is divided into modules, each of which evaluates the information from a single cue to distance. Because no one cue alone is sufficient, the brain must combine the information from all of these modules to estimate the actual size of the object.

In the ecological theory of perception, on the other hand, the brain tries to determine very different kinds of information about the visual world. For example, in an environment with an object in motion, such as a baseball, what the brain detects or picks up is "time-to-contact," or, in other words, "how much time do I have before I need to put up my glove to intercept the ball?" Gibson's approach contains a very different answer to Marr's question. For Gibson, *perception is for action.* Where navigation through the environment is concerned, the ecological theory asserts that perception tells us things like when to duck, when to turn your body to fit through a narrow passageway, and when to put your hand up to catch something. Where object recognition is concerned, perception provides us with information about the function(s) of objects. In the ecological view, an object *is* what you can do with it—anything you can sit on is a chair, anything you can drink from is a cup. The purpose of vision is to detect the complex set of invariants that specify the information we need to move about our world and effectively interact with the environment.

Although Marr's approach has been more dominant in the study of perception, Gibson's ecological approach is becoming increasingly influential (Nakayama, 1994). Both approaches have contributed to our understanding of perception, and talk between psychologists from the two approaches is beginning to further increase our knowledge of why we perceive the world the way we do.

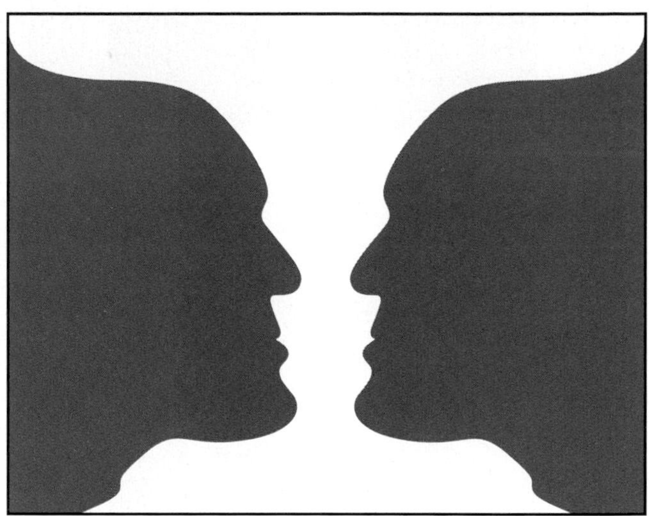

FIGURE 21

Reversible Figure-Ground Pattern
Either a goblet or a pair of silhouetted faces in profile is seen.

FIGURE 22

Sophisticated Use of the Figure-Ground Relationship in Escher's Woodcut *Relativity* (1938)

Shape Perception

Think about the world you see and its shapes—buildings against the sky, boats on the horizon, letters on this page. We see these shapes because they are marked off from the rest of what we see by **contour,** *a location at which a sudden change of brightness occurs.* Think about the letters on this page again. As you look at the page, you see letters, which are shapes, in a field or background, the white page. The **figure-ground relationship** *is the principle by which we organize the perceptual field into stimuli that stand out (figure) and those that are leftover (ground).* Some figure-ground relationships, though, are highly ambiguous, and it is difficult to tell what is figure and what is ground. A well-known ambiguous figure-ground relationship is shown in figure 21. As you look at the figure, your perception is likely to shift between seeing two faces or seeing a single goblet. Another example of figure-ground ambiguity is found in the work of artist M. C. Escher, which keeps us from favoring one figure over another seemingly because spatial location and depth cues are not provided (see figure 22).

One group of psychologists—the Gestalt psychologists—has been especially intrigued by how we perceive shapes. According to **Gestalt psychology,** *people naturally organize their perceptions according to certain patterns;* Gestalt *is a German word that means "configuration" or "form." One of*

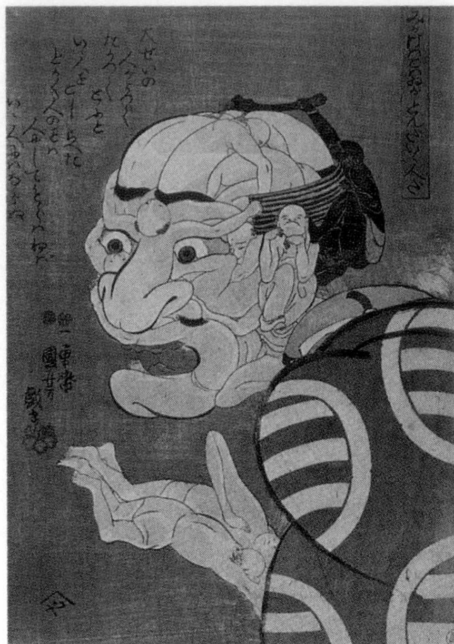

FIGURE 23

The Whole Does Not Equal the Sum of Its Parts
The configuration of the whole in Kuniyoshi Ichiyusai's *A Kindly Man* is clearly different from the sum of its parts.

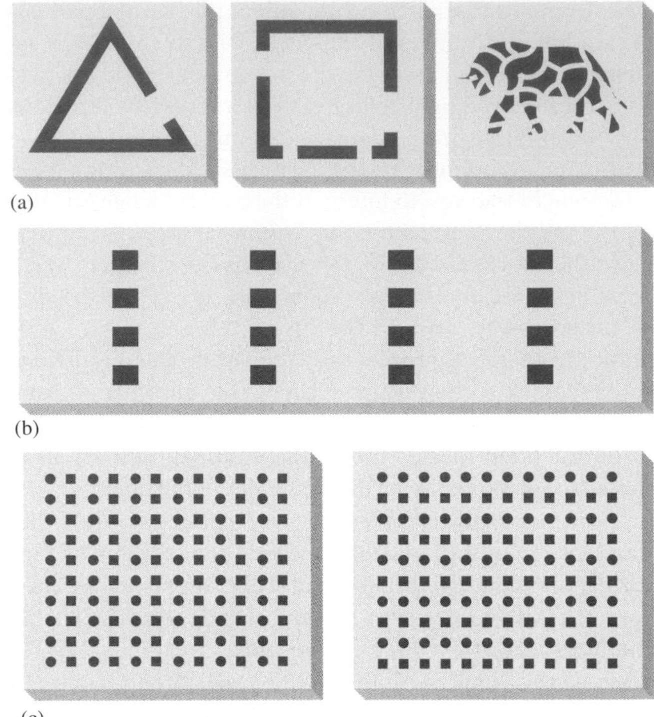

FIGURE 24

Gestalt Principles of Closure, Proximity, and Similarity
(*a*) Closure: When we see disconnected or incomplete figures, we fill in the spaces and see them as complete figures.
(*b*) Proximity: When we see objects that are near each other, they tend to be seen as a unit. You are likely to perceive the grouping as 4 columns of 4 squares, not 1 set of 16 squares.
(*c*) Similarity: When we see objects that are similar to each other, they tend to be seen as a unit. In this display, you are likely to see vertical columns of circles and squares in the left box but horizontal rows of circles and squares in the right box.

Gestalt psychology's main principles is that the whole is not equal to the sum of its parts. For example, when you watch a movie, the "motion" you see in the film cannot be found in the film itself; if you examine it, you see only separate frames at a rate of many per second. When you watch the film you perceive a whole that is very different from the separate individual pictures that are the whole's parts. Figure 23 also illustrates this fundamental principle of Gestalt psychology.

The figure-ground relationship just described is another Gestalt principle. Three other Gestalt principles are closure, proximity, and similarity. The principle of *closure* states that when individuals see a disconnected or incomplete figure, they fill in the spaces and see it as a complete figure (see figure 24*a*). The principle of *proximity* states that when individuals see objects closer to each other, they tend to group them together (see figure 24*b*). The principle of *similarity* states that the more similar objects are, the more likely we are to group them together (see figure 24*c*).

Depth Perception

The images of the world we see appear on our retinas in two-dimensional form, yet we see a three-dimensional world. **Depth perception** *is the ability to perceive objects three-dimensionally.* Look at the setting where you are. You don't see it as flat. You see some objects farther away, some closer. Some objects overlap each other. The scene and objects that you are looking at have depth. How do you see depth? To see a world of depth, we use two kinds of information, or cues—binocular and monocular. We have two eyes, which view the world from slightly different places. **Binocular cues** *are depth cues that are based on the combination of the images on the left and right eyes and on the way the two eyes work together.* **Monocular cues** *are depth cues that can be extracted from the image in one eye, either the left or the right eye.*

Because we have two eyes, we get two views of the world, one from each eye. The pictures are slightly different because the eyes are in slightly different positions. Try holding your hand about 10 inches from your face. Alternately close and open your left and right eyes, so that only one eye is open at a time. The image of your left hand will appear to jump back and forth. This is because the image of your hand is in a slightly different place on the left and right retinas. The **disparity,** *or difference of the image in the two eyes, is the binocular cue the brain uses to determine the depth or distance of an object.* Both images are combined in the brain, and the disparities between the images of objects in the two eyes gives us information about the three-dimensionality of the world.

The perception of depth from disparity can be demonstrated as in figure 25, based on a principle for presenting

FIGURE 25

A Stereogram

Seen in the right way, this figure contains 3 three-dimensional objects: a sphere in the top left, a pyramid in the top right, and a curved pointed conical figure in the center at the bottom. They may take a moment or two to see, but when you see them, they will be astoundingly clear and three-dimensional. There are two ways to see the three-dimensional objects in this figure. Technique 1: Cross your eyes by holding your finger up between your face and the figure. Look at the tip of your finger, and then slowly move your finger back and forth, toward and away from the figure, being careful to maintain focus on your finger. When the correct distance is reached, the three-dimensional objects will pop out at you. Technique 2: Put your face very close to the figure, so that it is difficult to focus or converge your eyes. Wait a moment, and begin to pull your face very slowly back from the figure. The picture should appear blurred for a bit, but when a good distance is reached should snap into three-dimensionality. Regardless of the technique you try, be patient! You may have to try one or both of these techniques a few times. The difficulty is that your eyes will try to converge at the distance of the page (very sensible of them!)—but you will be able to perceive this illusion only if you can trick them into converging elsewhere, either in front of the page, as will happen in technique 1, or perfectly parallel and unconverged, as will happen in technique 2. Note: Some people will not be able to see the three-dimensionality in these figures at all, for one of several reasons. First, some of us have eyes much too well adapted to the real world to be convinced to converge in the "wrong place," given the image data appearing on the retinas! Second, some very common visual deficits that can yield appreciable differences between the quality of the image on the left and right retinas can affect the development of normal binocular vision. The brain requires comparable image quality from the two eyes in the first few years of life to develop a high degree of stereoacuity. When this is not the case, the development of binocular neural mechanisms, which need to compare information in the two eyes, can be affected and can pose problems in processing the *pure* stereoscopic information in this figure. The information in this figure is purely stereoscopic because other kinds of cues to depth, like shading and perspective, are not available.

FIGURE 26

An Artist's Use of the Monocular Cue of Linear Perspective
Famous landscape artist J. M. W. Turner used linear perspective to give the perception of depth to his painting *Rain, Steam, and Speed.*

stereoscopic information from a single two-dimensional image (Tyler, 1983). These kinds of displays have become extremely popular in recent years and can now be found in art books, on greeting cards, and on posters in specialty shops; around the turn of the century, stereograms were similarly popular when stereoviewers became easily available.

In addition to having an indication of the depth of objects from the difference between the two-eye images, our perception of depth also makes use of a number of monocular cues, or cues available from a single-eye image. These are powerful cues and under normal circumstances can provide a very compelling impression of depth. Try closing one eye—your perception of the world still retains many of its three-dimensional qualities. Some examples of monocular cues are as follows:

1. *Aerial perspective.* Pollution and water vapor in the air scatter light waves, giving distant objects a hazy appearance.
2. *Familiar size.* This cue to the depth and distance of objects is based on what we have learned from experience about the standard sizes of objects. We know how large oranges tend to be, so we can tell something about how far away an orange is likely to be by the size of its image on the retina.
3. *Height in the field of view.* All other things being equal, objects that are higher in a picture are seen as farther away.
4. *Linear perspective.* This cue is based on the fact that objects farther away take up less space on the retina. As shown in figure 26, as an object recedes into the distance, parallel lines in the scene appear to converge.
5. *Overlap.* An object that partially conceals or overlaps another object is perceived as closer.
6. *Shadowing.* The shadow of an object provides cues to its depth.
7. *Size in the field of view.* All other things being equal, objects that are smaller are seen to be farther away.

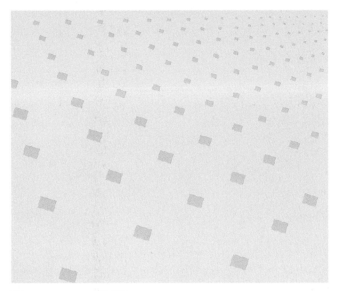

FIGURE 27

Texture Gradient
The gradients of texture create an impression of depth on a flat surface.

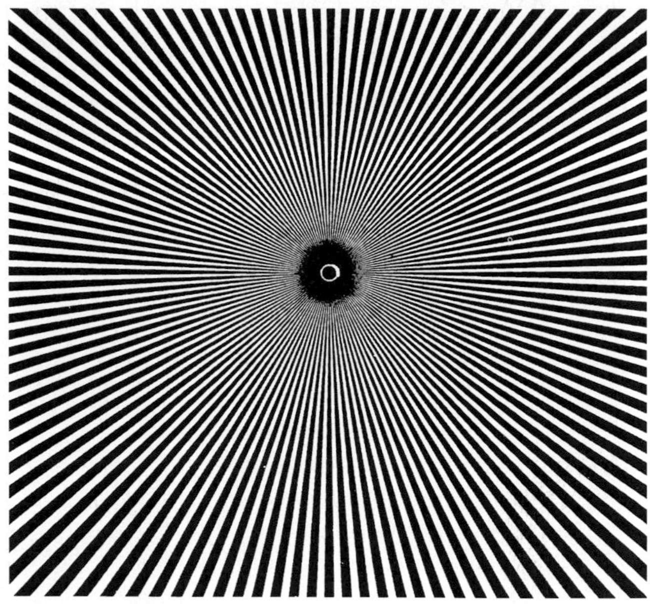

FIGURE 28

Movement Aftereffects
This is an example of a geometric pattern that produces afterimages in which motion can be perceived. If the center of the pattern is fixated for approximately 10 seconds and then the afterimage is projected on a plain white surface, rotary motion is usually perceived.

8. *Texture gradient.* Texture becomes more dense and finer, the farther away it is from the viewer (see figure 27).

Depth perception is especially intriguing to artists. They face a problem because the real world is three-dimensional and they have to paint on a two-dimensional canvas. Artists often use monocular cues to give the feeling of depth to their paintings. Indeed, monocular cues have become so widely used by artists that they have also been called *pictorial cues.* To learn more about art and perception, turn to Explorations in Psychology 2.

Motion Perception

During the course of each day, we perceive objects that move—other people, cars, planes, animals. Why are we able to perceive motion? First, we have neurons that are specialized to detect motion. Second, feedback from our body tells us whether we are moving or someone or an object is moving. For example, you move your eye muscles as you watch a ball coming toward you. Third, the environment we see is rich in cues that give us information about movement. For example, when we run, we can tell that the background is moving.

Psychologists are interested in both real movement and **apparent movement,** *which occurs when an object is stationary but we perceive it to be moving.* An example of apparent movement can be experienced at Disneyland. Bell Telephone mounted nine cameras on an airplane to obtain nine different perspectives on a number of sights around the United States; the films are shown at a Disneyland attraction. The motion pictures are shown on nine screens that surround the viewers, who stand in the middle of the room, a setting that simulates the view from an airplane. Viewers are warned to hold the handrail because perceived movement is so realistic it is easy to fall while experiencing the "movement."

Two forms of apparent motion are stroboscopic motion and movement aftereffects. **Stroboscopic motion** *is the illusion of movement created when a rapid stimulation of different parts of the retina occurs*—motion pictures are a form of stroboscopic motion. **Movement aftereffects** *happen when we watch continuous movement and then look at another surface, which then appears to move in the opposite direction.* Figure 28 provides an opportunity to experience movement aftereffects.

Perceptual Constancy

Retinal images are constantly changing as we experience our world. Even though the stimuli that fall on the retinas of our eyes change as we move closer or farther away from objects, or look at objects from different orientations and in light or dark settings, we perceive objects as constant and unchanging. We experience three types of perceptual constancies: size constancy, shape constancy, and brightness constancy. **Size constancy** *is the recognition that an object remains the same size even though the retinal image of the object changes* (see figure 29). **Shape**

Explorations in Psychology 2

The Perceptual Worlds of Art

Look at figure A. If you stood very close to this painting and looked at one area, you would see only daubs of colored pigments on a canvas. If you stood back and considered the whole painting, however, you would see the brilliantly colored landscape with a tree, a village, a church, and a turbulent sky. The painting is nineteenth-century Dutch artist Vincent van Gogh's masterpiece *Starry Night.* This is not likely the scene most of us would paint if we were trying to recreate the real world. Stars do not race about in frenzied whirlpools. What caused van Gogh to paint *Starry Night* the way he did? For one thing, he was a tormented, intense, mystical man. Some of the torment, and a kind of ecstasy, are built into the painting. Another artist, not experiencing van Gogh's mental anguish, would likely have painted the same starry night very differently.

Figure A

Vincent van Gogh's *Starry Night*

Was van Gogh painting what he actually saw? We don't know the answer to that question, but we do know that, at some points in history, artists have strived to mirror the world just as it appears to their eyes; at others they have deliberately distorted reality. The Renaissance masters tried to paint the world as accurately as possible, as if their canvas were a photograph (see figure B). They relied on many of the cues for depth perception to portray three-dimensional reality on a flat surface.

Figure B

Raphael's *Fire in the Borgo*

The Renaissance masters used depth cues to give their paintings three-dimensional appearance. Notice the detailed attention to perspective, such as how the roofs above the columns extend backward. Notice also the smaller size of the people in the distance and the overlapping of people and buildings.

Whereas the Renaissance artists tried to paint the world as their eyes saw it, other schools of art strove for something different. For example, the nineteenth-century French Impressionists focused on the *impression* a scene makes on the observer instead of trying to paint the scene as accurately as possible. They strove to capture the viewer's perception of nature's fleeting sensations of light. Their technique involved the creation of a patchwork of varying daubs of brightly colored paint (see figure C). When you look at a French Impressionist painting up close, you see individual patches of color; however, when you stand away from the painting, the individual patches of color blur and mix together.

Many modern painters moved even further away from recreating the world we actually see. In the twentieth century, Pablo Picasso liked to place varying geometrical forms (circles, triangles, rectangles, for example) together and challenge observers to interpret what he had painted. Look at Picasso's painting in figure D. Can you tell what it is without looking at the figure legend?

As can be seen, understanding perception's role in art is complex, involving not only the artist's perceptions but also the perceptions of the art's observers. Artists paint not only what they see but also what they know, and what observers perceive a painting to be is influenced by their experiences. Van Gogh's *Starry Night* might be perceived as a bombing raid by a Londoner who experienced the German blitz in World War II; as a hallucinatory vision by someone under the influence of drugs or a fever; as the way the sky always looks by someone with a particular visual disorder; and as weird or bizarre by someone who views nature in meticulous, ordered ways. Above all else, art is artist, observer, and communication, not unlike a "perceptual conversation" between one person's view of the world and another person's view of the world.

FIGURE D

Picasso's *Nude Woman*
Look at the painting and think about the way some of the Gestalt principles of perception are incorporated. The nude is an incomplete figure. You have to fill in the spaces to make it complete. Remember that this is the principle of closure. The principles of proximity and similarity cause you to see the two objects toward the bottom of the painting as feet.

FIGURE C

What Is the Nature of Impressionist Art?

FIGURE 29

Size Constancy
Even though our retinal image of the hot air balloons changes, we still perceive the different balloons as being approximately the same size. This illustrates the principle of size constancy.

constancy *is the recognition that an object remains the same shape even though its orientation to us changes.* Look around the room in which you are reading this book. You probably see objects of various shapes—chairs and tables, for example. If you walk around the room, you will see these objects from different sides and angles. Even though the retinal image of the object changes as you walk, you still perceive the objects as being the same shape (see figure 30). **Brightness constancy** *is the recognition that an object retains the same degree of brightness even though different amounts of light fall on it.* For example, regardless of whether you are reading this book indoors or outdoors, the white pages and the black print do not look any different to you in terms of their whiteness or blackness.

FIGURE 30

Shape Constancy
The various projected images from an opening door are quite different, yet you perceive a rectangular door.

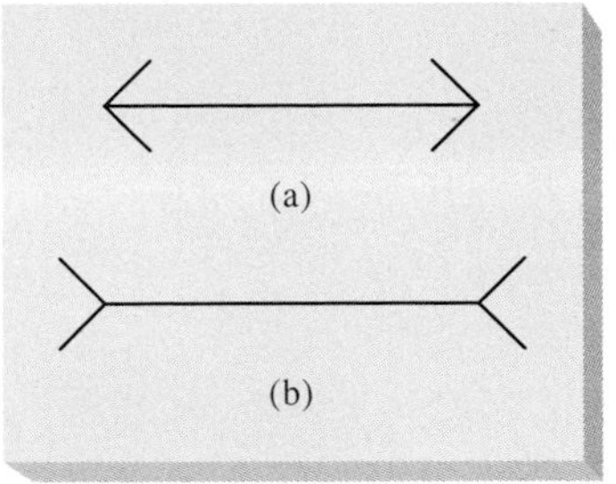

FIGURE 31

Müller-Lyer Illusion
The two lines are exactly the same length, although (*b*) looks longer than (*a*).

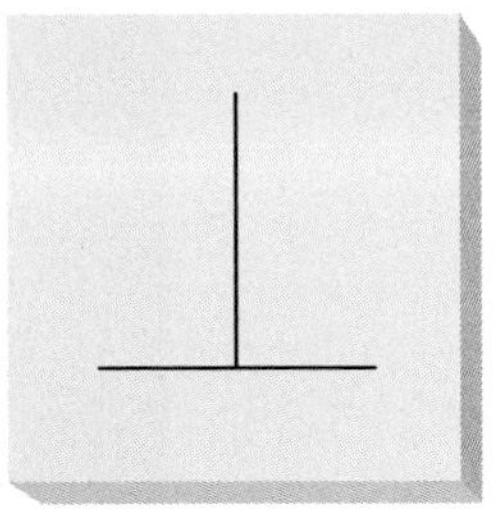

FIGURE 32

The Horizontal-Vertical Illusion
The vertical line looks longer than the horizontal line, but they are the same length.

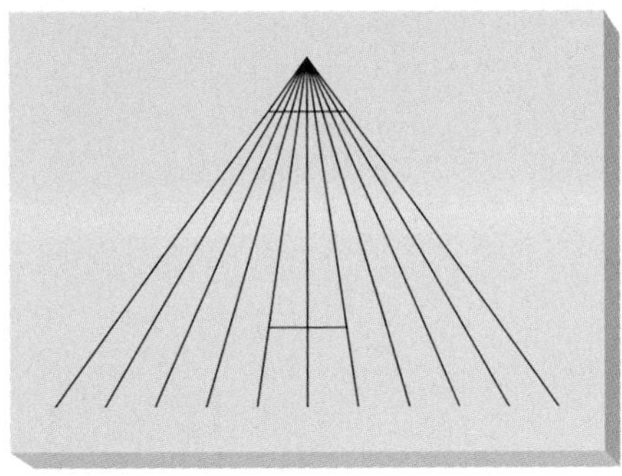

FIGURE 33

Ponzo Illusion
The top line looks much longer than the bottom line, but they are equal in length.

How are we able to resolve the discrepancy between a retinal image of an object and its actual size, shape, and brightness? Experience is important. For example, no matter how far away you are from your car, you know how large it is. Not only is familiarity important in size constancy, but so are binocular and monocular distance cues. Even if we have never previously seen an object, these cues provide us with information about an object's size. Many visual illusions are influenced by our perception of size constancy.

FIGURE 34

Moon Illusion
When the moon is on the horizon, it looks much larger than when it is high in the sky, directly above us. Why does the moon look so much larger on the horizon?

Illusions

A **visual illusion** *occurs when two objects produce exactly the same retinal image but are perceived as different images.* Illusions are incorrect, but they are not abnormal. They can provide insight into how our perceptual processes work. More than two hundred different types of illusions have been discovered; we will study five.

One of the most famous is the Müller-Lyer illusion, illustrated in figure 31. The two lines are exactly the same length, although *b* looks longer than *a*. Another illusion is the horizontal-vertical illusion in which a vertical line looks longer than a horizontal line even though the two are equal (see figure 32). In the Ponzo illusion (see figure 33), the top line looks much longer than the bottom line.

Why do these illusions trick us? One reason is that we mistakenly use certain cues for maintaining size constancy. For example, in the Ponzo illusion we see the upper line as being farther away (remember that objects higher in a picture are perceived as being farther away). The Müller-Lyer illusion, though, is not so easily explained. We might make our judgments about the lines by comparing incorrect parts of the figures. For example, when people were shown the Müller-Lyer illusion with the wings painted a different color than the horizontal lines, the illusion was greatly reduced (Coren & Girus, 1972). Shortly we also will discuss how cultural experiences influence an individual's perception of the Müller-Lyer illusion.

Another well-known illusion is the moon illusion (see figure 34). The moon is 2,000 miles in diameter and 289,000 miles away. Since both the moon's size and its distance from us are beyond our own experience, we have difficulty judging just how far away it really is. When the moon is high in the sky, directly above us, little information is present to help us judge its distance—no texture gradients or stereoscopic cues exist, for example. But when the moon is on the horizon, we can judge its distance in

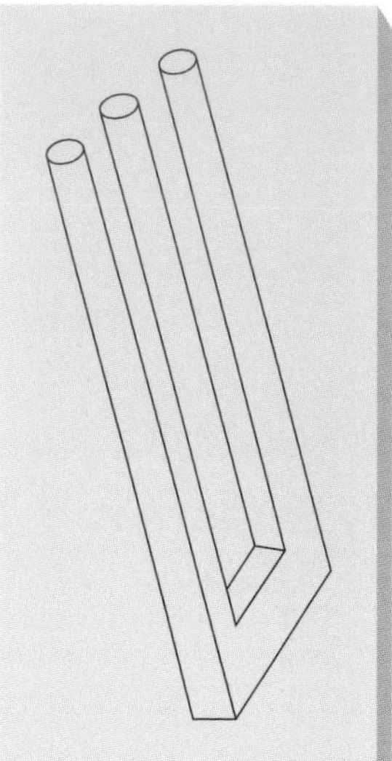

FIGURE 35

Devil's Tuning Fork

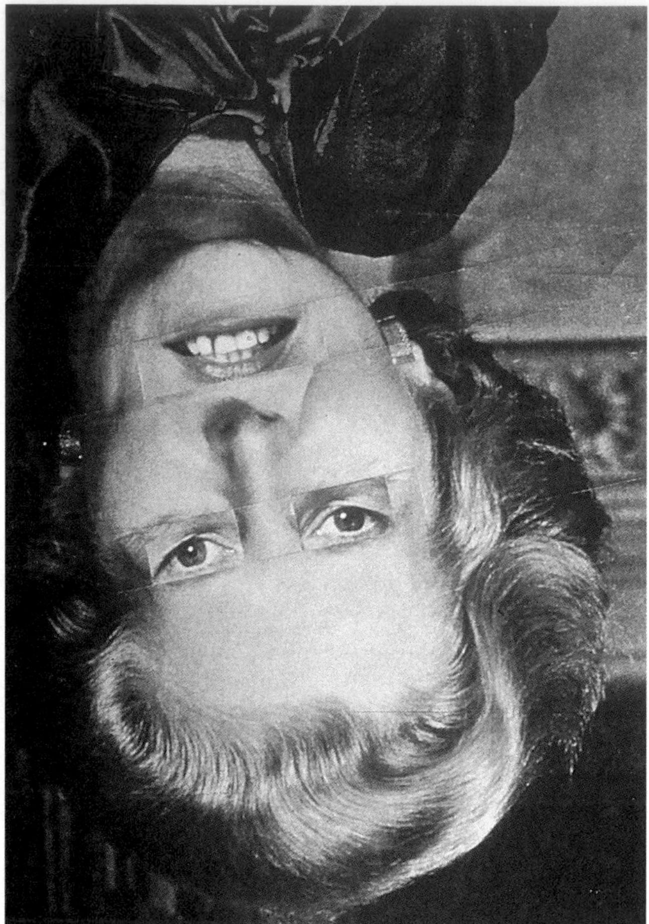

FIGURE 36

Why Does This Famous Face Look So Different When You Turn the Book Upside Down?

relation to familiar objects—trees and buildings, for example—which makes it appear farther away. The result is that we estimate the size of the moon as much larger when it is on the horizon than when it is overhead.

The devil's tuning fork is another fascinating illusion. Look at figure 35 for about 30 seconds, then close the book. Now try to draw the tuning fork. You undoubtedly found this a difficult, if not impossible, task. Why? Since the figure's depth cues are ambiguous, you had problems correctly interpreting it.

In our final example of an illusion, a "doctored" horrific face seen upside down goes unnoticed. Look at figure 36—you probably recognize this famous face as Margaret Thatcher. What seems to be an ordinary portrait is actually doctored. The mouth and eyes have been cut out from the original and pasted back on upside down. If you turn this book upside down, the horrific look is easily seen. The "Thatcher" illusion may take place because the mouth is so far out of alignment that we simply cannot respond to its expression; it is still a fearsome face, but we do not see that, and we may have a difficult time telling what really is the top of the mouth in the picture.

Is Perception Learned or Innate?

One long-standing question in psychology is whether or not perception is learned or innate (inborn, unlearned). Researchers have tried to unravel this nature/nurture question on depth perception in a number of ways: experiments with infants, studies of individuals who recover from blindness, and cross-cultural studies about how people perceive their world.

The Visual Cliff

An experiment by Eleanor Gibson and Richard Walk (1960) indicates that by at least 6 months of age infants have an understanding of depth. Gibson and Walk constructed a miniature cliff with a shallow side and a drop-off that was covered by firm glass (see figure 37). This structure is known as a *visual cliff.* Infants old enough to crawl (6 months and older) were placed on the shallow side. The infants stayed in place rather than venture out onto the glass-covered drop-off, indicating that they perceived depth. However, infants at 6 months are old enough to have encountered many situations where they could have *learned* to perceive death, so the visual cliff experiment failed to provide convincing evidence that depth perception is innate. Whether or not infants younger than 6 months perceive depth is controversial.

Other studies have shown that during the first month of life, human infants turn away to avoid objects that move directly toward them, but do not turn away when objects move toward them at angles that would not collide with

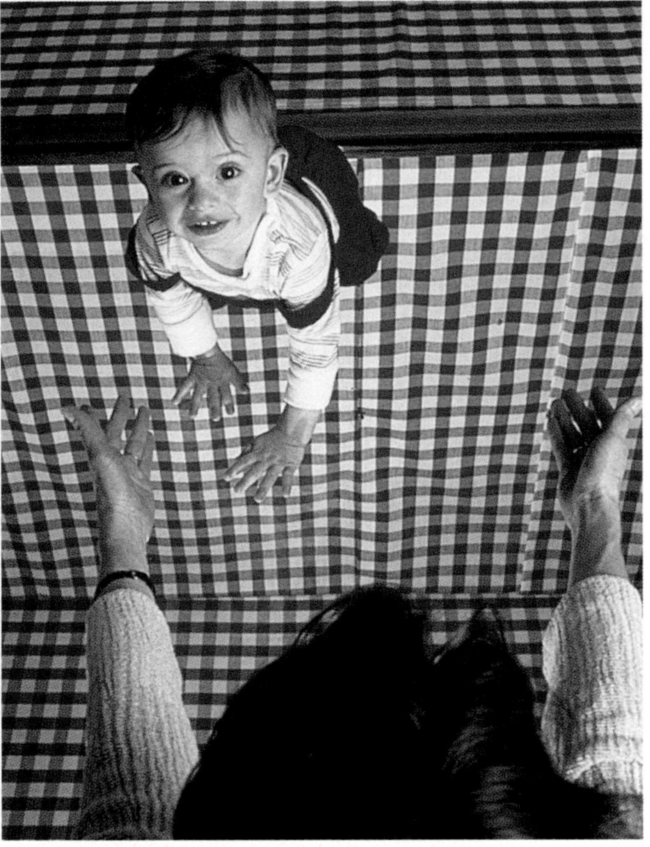

FIGURE 37

The Visual Cliff
The visual cliff was developed by Eleanor Gibson and Richard Walk (1960). The infant shown here hesitates as he moves onto the glass-covered drop-off, the deep side of the visual cliff. Even when coaxed by their mothers, infants are still reluctant to venture out onto the deep drop-off, indicating they can perceive depth.

FIGURE 38

S. B.'s Drawing of a Bus After Recovering from Blindness
S. B. drew the bus at the top 48 days after a corneal transplant restored his vision, and he drew the bus at the bottom a year after the operation. Both drawings reflect more detail for the parts of the bus S. B. used or touched while he was blind than the parts he did not use or touch. In the bottom drawing, notice the absence of the front of the bus, which S. B. never touched.

them (Ball & Tronick, 1971). And animals with little visual experience—including day-old goats and just-hatched chicks—respond just as 6-month-old human infants do; they remain on the visual cliff's shallow side and do not venture out onto the glass-covered drop-off. These studies suggest that some of the ability to perceive depth is innate.

Recovery from Blindness

In further attempts to determine whether or not depth perception is innate, psychologists have also studied people who were born blind, or became blind shortly after birth, and whose sight later was restored by medical procedures. If the ability to interpret sensory information is innate, such people should be able to see their world clearly after they recover from the operation. Consider S. B., blind since birth, who had a successful corneal transplant at the age of 52 (Gregory, 1978). Soon after S. B.'s bandages were removed, he was able to recognize common objects, identify the letters of the alphabet, and tell time from a clock. However, S. B. had some perceptual deficiencies. While his eyes functioned effectively, S. B. had difficulty perceiving objects he had not previously touched (see figure 38).

The findings for formerly blind persons also do not answer the question of whether or not perception is innate or learned. Some people recognize objects soon after their bandages are removed; others require weeks of training before they recognize such simple shapes as a triangle. Neural connections, such as those between the eyes and the brain, can deteriorate from disuse. So a person whose sight has been restored after a lifetime of blindness may have an impaired ability to perceive visual information. Further, previously blind adults, unlike infants, have already experienced the world through their nonvisual senses, such as touch and hearing, and those perceptual systems may continue to contribute to their perception after they regain their vision.

Culture and Perception

While our biological inheritance equips us with some elegant perceptual capabilities, our experiences also contribute to how we perceive the world. Some cross-cultural

FIGURE 39

The Carpentered-World Hypothesis
The Zulu live in isolated regions of southeastern Africa in a world of open spaces and curves. Their huts are round with round doors, and they even plow their fields in curved, rather than straight, furrows. How does their environment influence their responses to the Müller-Lyer illusion?

psychologists have proposed that the demands of different cultures lead to greater emphasis on certain senses (Wober, 1966). For example, hunters who have to stalk small game animals may develop their kinesthetic senses more than office workers in highly industrialized nations.

Cross-cultural psychologists have been especially interested in how people from different cultures perceive visual illusions (Segall & others, 1990). The **carpentered-world hypothesis** *states that people who live in cultures in which straight lines, right angles, and rectangles predominate (for instance, in which most rooms and buildings are rectangular and many objects, such as city streets, have right angles) should be more susceptible to illusions involving straight lines, right angles, and rectangles than are people who live in noncarpentered cultures* (figure 39). This tendency enhances the Müller-Lyer illusion and makes people from carpentered environments more susceptible to it than people from noncarpentered environments are. For example, the Zulu in isolated regions of southeastern Africa live in a world of open spaces and curves. Their huts are round with round doors, and they even plow their fields in curved, rather than straight, furrows. According to the carpentered-world hypothesis, the Zulu would not be very susceptible to the Müller-Lyer illusion. Cross-cultural psychologists have found this to be the case (Segall, Campbell, & Herskovits, 1963).

Another example in which culture shapes perception is found in the Pygmies who live in the dense rain forests of the African Congo. Because of the thick vegetation, the Pygmies rarely see objects at great distances. Anthropologist Colin Turnbull (1961) observed that when Pygmies traveled to the African plains and saw buffalo on the horizon, they thought the animals were tiny "insects" and not huge buffalo. The Pygmies' lack of experience with distant objects probably accounts for their inability to perceive size constancy.

It seems that both nature and nurture are responsible for the way we perceive the world. One view of how the two influences interact to shape perception is that all people, regardless of culture, have the same perceptual processes and the same potential for perceptual development, but cultural factors determine what is learned and at what age (Kagitcibasi, 1995). So far we have discussed perception in terms

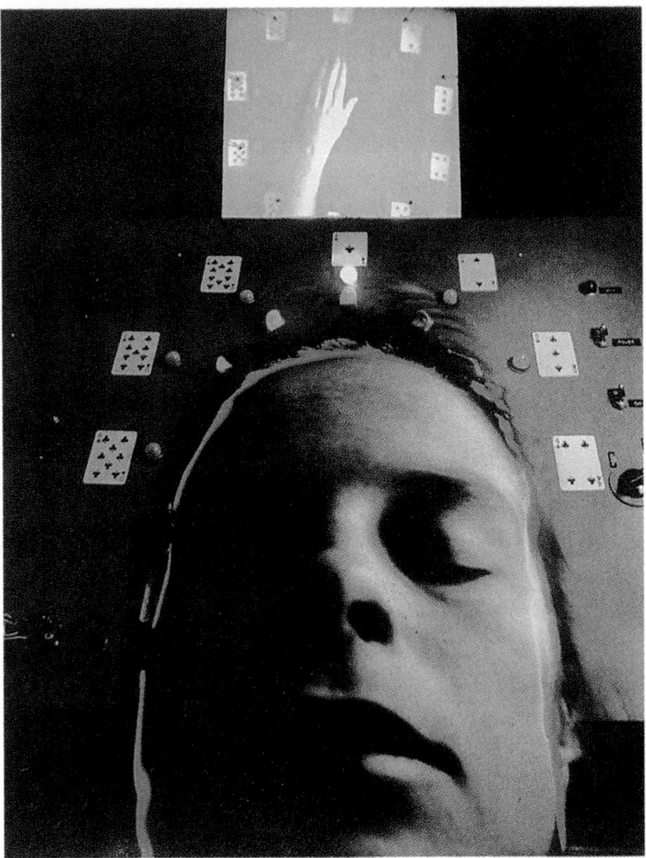

FIGURE 40

An Experimental Situation Involving an Attempt to Demonstrate Telepathy

At the top (*blue insert*), a person in one room tries to "send" a message through thought to a person (the subject) in another room. The sender selects a card and then attempts to relay the information mentally to the subject. The subject then selects a card, and it is compared to the one previously chosen by the sender to see if the cards match. If the mind-to-mind communication occurs beyond levels of chance, then it would be argued that telepathy has taken place.

of shape, depth, constancy, illusion, and whether or not perception is innate or learned. But we'll also briefly discuss another, curious realm of perceptual phenomena—extrasensory perception.

Extrasensory Perception

Our eyes, ears, mouth, nose, and skin provide us with sensory information about the external world. Our perceptions are based on our interpretation of this sensory information. Some people, though, claim they can perceive the world through something other than normal sensory pathways. **Extrasensory perception (ESP)** *is perception that occurs without the use of any known sensory process.* Most psychologists do not believe in ESP; however, a few of them investigate it.

Extrasensory experiences fall into three main categories. The first is **telepathy,** *which involves the transfer of thought from one person to another.* For example, this skill is supposedly possessed by people who can "read" another person's mind. If two people are playing cards and one person can tell what cards the other person picked up, telepathy is taking place (see figure 40). **Precognition** *involves "knowing" events before they happen.* For example, a fortuneteller might claim to see into the future and tell you what will happen to you in the coming year. Or an astrologer might predict that a major earthquake will take place in Los Angeles in June of next year. **Clairvoyance** *involves the ability to perceive remote events that are not in sight.* For example, a person at a movie theatre senses a burglar breaking into his house at that moment. **Psychokinesis,** *closely associated with ESP, is the mind-over-matter phenomenon of being able to move objects without touching them, such as mentally getting a chair to rise off the floor or shattering a glass merely by staring at it.*

One of the most famous claims of ESP involved Uri Geller, a psychic who supposedly performed mind-boggling feats. Observers saw Geller correctly predict the number on a die rolled in a closed box eight out of eight times, reproduce drawings that were hidden in sealed envelopes, bend forks without touching them, and start broken watches. While he had worked as a magician, Geller claimed his supernatural powers were created by energy sent from another universe. Careful investigation of Geller's feats revealed they were nothing more than a magician's tricks. For example, in the case of the die, Geller was allowed to shake the box and open it himself, giving him an opportunity to manipulate the die (Randi, 1980).

Through their astonishing stage performances, many psychics are very convincing. They seemingly are able to levitate tables, communicate with spirits, and read an audience member's mind. Many psychics, like Uri Geller, are also magicians who have the ability to perform sleight-of-hand maneuvers and dramatic manipulations that go unnoticed by most human eyes. One magician's personal goal, though, is to expose the hoaxes of the psychics. James Randi (1980) has investigated a number of psychics' claims and publicized their failures. More about Randi's debunking of supposed psychic powers is presented in Explorations in Psychology 3.

Not only have magicians such as Randi investigated psychics' claims, but scientists have also examined ESP in experimental contexts. Some ESP enthusiasts believe the phenomena are more likely to occur when a subject is totally relaxed and deprived of sensory input. In this kind of ESP experiment, the subject lies down and half a Ping-Pong ball is placed over each eye, affixed with cotton and tape. An experimenter watches through a one-way mirror from an adjacent room, listening to and recording the subject's statements. At an agreed-upon time someone from another location concentrates on the message to be sent mind to mind.

Carl Sargent (1987) has used this procedure in a number of telepathy experiments and reported a great deal of ESP success. In one experiment, Sargent has a "sender" mentally transmit an image of one of four

EXPLORATIONS IN PSYCHOLOGY 3

Debunking Psychics' Claims

A woman reports that she has power over the goldfish in a huge 50-gallon tank. She claims that she can will them to swim to either end of the tank. As soon as she wills it, the fish takes off.

Under the careful scrutiny of James Randi, this woman's account turned out to be just another fish story. The woman had written Randi, a professional magician, who has a standing offer of $10,000 to anyone whose psychic claims withstand his analysis. In the case of the woman and her goldfish, Randi received a letter from her priest validating her extraordinary power. Randi talked with the priest, who told him that the woman would put her hands in front of her body and then run to one end of the tank. The fish soon followed. Since the fish could see out of the tank just as we can see into it, Randi suggested that she put opaque brown wrapping paper over one end of the tank and then try her powers. The woman did and called Randi about the result, informing him that she had discovered something new about her powers: that her mind could not penetrate the brown paper. The woman believed that she had magical powers and completely misunderstood why Randi had asked her to place the brown paper over the fish tank.

No one has claimed Randi's $10,000 prize, but he has been called to investigate several hundred reports of supernatural and occult powers. Faith healers have been among those he has evaluated. Randi has witnessed individuals yelling and dancing up and down, saying they are healed of such maladies as cancer and diabetes. When asked how they know they are healed, they usually say it is because they no longer have the disease or because the faith healer told them so. On checking back with the "healed" a week later, Randi has found diabetics taking insulin and a cancer patient resuming radiation therapy. In some cases, their health has dramatically worsened, as in the case of a diabetic who had to be taken to the hospital because he had stopped his insulin treatment. When asked if they still believed in the faith healer's treatment, it is not unusual to hear these individuals say that they just did not believe strongly enough.

Randi makes the distinction between the tricks of magicians, such as himself, and the work of psychics and faith healers. He says that magic is done for entertainment, the other for swindling.

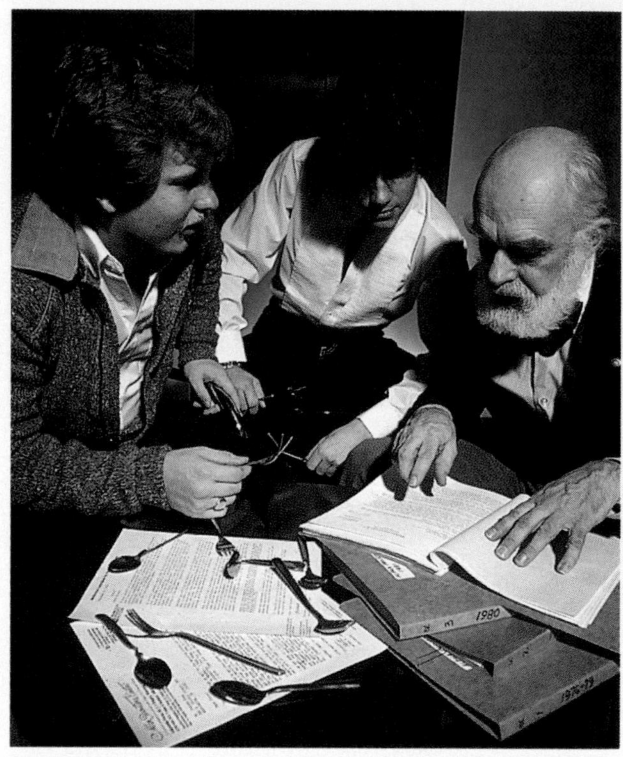

Magician James Randi (right) has investigated a large number of psychics' claims. No one has yet won Randi's standing offer of $10,000 to anyone whose psychic claims withstand his analysis.

pictures selected from one of 27 randomly selected sets of four pictures. Immediately afterward, the experimenter and the subject examined a duplicate set of four pictures and together judged and ranked their degree of correspondence with the subject's recorded impression. Experimental psychologist Susan Blackmore (1987) was skeptical about Sargent's success in ESP experiments, so she visited his laboratory at Cambridge University in England and observed a number of his telepathy sessions. With the subject shown four pictures, the success rate expected by chance was 25 percent (one of four pictures). In the experimental sessions observed by Blackmore, the subjects' hit rate was 50 percent, far exceeding chance.

Sargent supposedly invokes a number of elaborate procedures to protect randomization, experimenter bias, unbiased selection by the subject, and so on. Blackmore was still skeptical, finding some disturbing flaws in the way Sargent's experiments were conducted. In some sessions, he did the randomization of the picture himself, putting himself where he could manipulate the ordering of the pictures. In other sessions, he came in while the subject was judging the pictures and "pushed" the subject toward the picture that had been "transmitted" by the "sender."

Concept Table 4

Perception

Concept	Processes/Related Ideas	Characteristics/Description
Two Theories of Perception	The information-processing approach	This approach states that perception is the process of representing information from the world internally. As information from the world is processed, it undergoes a series of internal manipulations. Marr's view reflects the information-processing approach.
	The ecological approach	Developed by J. J. Gibson, this approach stresses the active perceiver exploring and moving about the environment. Perception is viewed as an active interaction between the perceiver and the environment. In this approach, the purpose of vision is to detect perceptual invariants that are abstracted over time from the changing visual scene.
Shape Perception, Depth Perception, Motion Perception, and Perceptual Constancy	Shape perception	Shape is perceived because it is marked off by contour. Gestalt psychologists developed a number of principles of perceptual organization, a fundamental one being that the whole is not equal to the sum of its parts.
	Depth perception	Depth perception is our ability to perceive objects as three-dimensional. To see a world of depth, we use binocular cues, such as retinal disparity and convergence, and monocular cues (also called pictorial cues), such as linear perspective, texture gradient, relative size, interposition, shadowing, and aerial perspective.
	Motion perception	Motion perception focuses on both real movement and apparent movement. Stroboscopic motion and movement aftereffects are two prominent forms of apparent movement.
	Perceptual constancy	This concept includes size, shape, and brightness constancy. Experience with objects and distance cues help us to see objects as unchanging.
Illusions	Their nature	Illusions occur when two objects produce exactly the same retinal image but are perceived as different images. Among the more than 200 different illusions are the Müller-Lyer illusion and the moon illusion. Perceptual constancies and cultural experiences are among the factors thought to be responsible for illusions.
Is Perception Innate or Learned?	The visual cliff	Experiments using the visual cliff with young infants and animals indicate that some of the ability to perceive depth is innate.
	Recovery from blindness	Investigations of formerly blind adults are inconclusive with regard to whether perception is innate or learned.
	Culture	Our experiences contribute to how we perceive the world. People in different cultures do not always perceive the world in the same way. The carpentered-world hypothesis reveals how experiences influence perception.
Extrasensory Perception	Its nature	Perception that does not occur through normal sensory channels. Three main forms are telepathy, precognition, and clairvoyance. Psychokinesis is a closely related phenomenon. The claims of ESP enthusiasts have not held up to scientific scrutiny.

No one has been able to replicate the high hit rates in Sargent's experiments. Proponents of ESP, such as Sargent, claim they have demonstrated the existence of ESP, but critics such as Blackmore, demand to see or experience the same phenomena themselves. Replication is one of the hallmarks of scientific investigation, yet replication has been a major thorn in the side of ESP researchers. ESP phenomena have not been reproducible when rigorous experimental standards are applied (Bates, 1995; Hines, 1988).

At this point, we have discussed a number of ideas about perception. To help you sort out the main concepts in this discussion, turn to concept table 4.

Critical Thinking About Behavior

The Creative Brain

> *Imagination frames events unknown,*
> *In wild, fantastic shapes of hideous ruin,*
> *And what it fears, creates.*
>
> **Hannah More**

In chapters MET (Methods) and BFB (Biological Foundations and the Brain), you have studied the impressive abilities of the brain, the command center of the central nervous system. There is much we can marvel at about the brain. It weighs only 3 pounds. It never rests. It seems to have an unlimited capacity for performance. We use only a portion of its potential.

One of the most interesting features of the brain and the perceptual systems within it is our capacity to fill in missing information. The simplest example of this phenomenon is the blind spot. You have two holes in your visual field, corresponding to where the optic nerve attaches to the back of the retina in each eye, yet you do not see these holes. You see a unified field of vision because the brain creatively fills in the holes to be consistent with the surrounding information.

However, the same creative ability that assists our adaptation can also make life more complicated. For example, many of us commonly experience a perceptual illusion that is most annoying, due to the brain's capacity to create explanations. Have you ever heard the phone ringing after you have stepped into the shower, only to find that it stopped as soon as you left the shower? Someone might have been trying to get in touch with you; however, it is more likely that you suffered a hallucination. The phone-ringing hallucination is a compelling one that illustrates the extent to which the brain automatically processes information and creates text to explain perceptions.

Let's examine a second example. You are home alone. You begin to hear odd noises. The floorboards of the house creak. The wind howls. You begin to consider all the possibilities that would explain this set of disturbances. It gets worse. You feel a cold wind across your cheek. You might hear your name spoken. The curtain moves suddenly. Is it an intruder? Is it a ghost? Your active imagination creates an explanatory text that gives you a sense of control over the environment and may prompt you to take some self-protective action even if the explanation isn't valid.

A final example of the brain's creativity involves grief. A surprising number of people report that when a loved one dies, they experience some unsettling perceptions. Mourning individuals sometimes report that they hear the voice of the loved one. Some see the loved one. These hallucinations appear to be a normal part of grieving, enhanced by a brain and its perceptual systems eager to make comforting interpretations.

How might our brain's creativity be related to convictions about extrasensory perception? If we are convinced that extrasensory phenomena are real, then we are more likely to experience events that support the beliefs. In contrast, if we are disbelievers, our perceptual set is likely to encourage different interpretations of the same perceptual cues.

How many of these circumstances have you experienced? You might have thought yourself a bit mad at the time, but these experiences simply attest to the brain's power to interpret perceptual experiences creatively. Psychologists believe that maintaining a skeptical outlook is probably one of the best ways to overcome our tendencies to arrive at inappropriate conclusions about our own experiences. Practicing skepticism encourages making accurate observations, descriptions, and inferences.

Overview

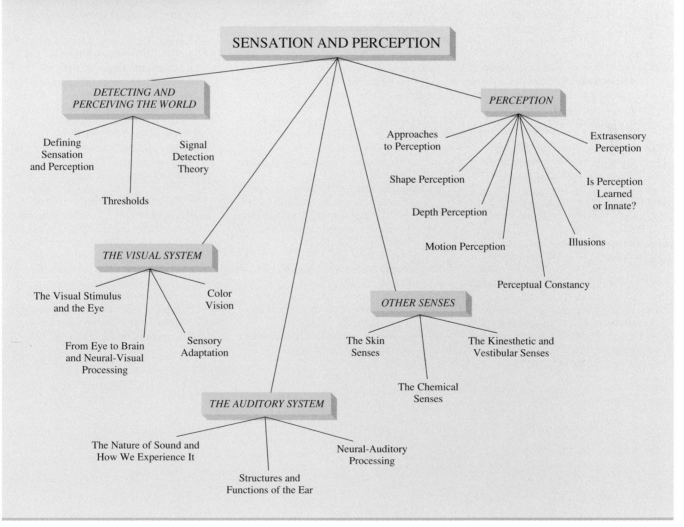

We began this chapter by evaluating how people detect and perceive the world; we defined sensation and perception and also discussed thresholds and signal detection theory. Next we read about the visual sense—the visual stimulus and the eye, from eye to brain, and neural-visual processing; and the auditory sense—the nature of sound and how we experience it, structures and functions of the ear, and neural-auditory processing. We also learned about the skin, chemical, kinesthetic, and vestibular senses. Our coverage of perception focused on two theories of perception, shape perception, depth perception, motion perception, perceptual constancy, illusions, whether perception is innate or learned, and extrasensory perception. Don't forget that you can obtain an overall summary of these ideas by again studying the concept tables on pages 94, 103, 113, and 129.

Key Terms

sensation The process of detecting and encoding stimulus energy in the world. p. 89

perception The brain's process of organizing and interpreting sensory information to give it meaning. p. 90

absolute threshold The minimum amount of energy that we can detect. p. 90

noise Irrelevant and competing stimuli. p. 91

difference threshold The smallest difference in stimulation required to discriminate one stimulus from another 50 percent of the time. Also called the just noticeable difference (jnd). p. 91

Weber's law This law states that the difference threshold is a constant percentage of the magnitude of the comparison stimulus rather than a constant amount. Weber's law generally holds true. p. 91

signal detection theory The theory that sensitivity to sensory stimuli depends on a variety of factors besides the physical intensity of the stimulus and the sensory abilities of the observer. p. 92

light A form of electromagnetic energy that can be described in terms of wavelengths. p. 94

wavelength The distance from the peak of one wave to the peak of the next. p. 94

sclera The white outer part of the eye that helps maintain the shape of the eye and protect it from injury. p. 94

iris The colored part of the eye, which can range from light blue to dark brown. p. 94

pupil The opening in the center of the iris; it appears black. The iris contains muscles that control the size of the pupil and, hence, the amount of light that enters the eye. p. 94

cornea A clear membrane on the front surface of the eye. Its function is to bend the light falling on the surface of the eye just enough to focus it at the back of the eye. p. 94

lens of the eye A transparent and somewhat flexible ball-like entity at the front of the pupil, filled with a gelatinous material; its function is to bend the light falling on the surface of the eye just enough to focus it at the back of the eye. p. 95

accommodation Adjustment of the eye lens to change its curvature. p. 95

retina The light-sensitive surface at the back of the eye that houses light receptors called rods and cones. p. 95

rods The receptors in the retina that are exquisitely sensitive to light but are not very useful for color vision. p. 95

cones Receptors in the retina for color perception. p. 95

fovea A minute area in the center of the retina where vision is at its best. p. 96

blind spot The area of the retina where the optic nerve leaves the eye on its way to the brain. p. 97

sensory adaptation A change in the responsiveness of the sensory system based on the average level of surrounding stimulation. p. 98

hue A characteristic of color based on its wavelength content. p. 99

saturation A characteristic of color based on its purity. p. 99

brightness A characteristic of color based on its intensity. p. 99

additive mixture The mixing of beams of light from different parts of the color spectrum. p. 99

subtractive mixture The mixing of pigments of different colors. p. 100

trichromatic theory The theory that color perception is based on the existence of three types of receptors that are maximally sensitive to different, but overlapping, ranges of wavelengths. p. 100

dichromats People with only two kinds of cones. p. 101

trichromats People with normal color vision—they have three kinds of cone receptors. p. 101

afterimages Sensations that remain after a stimulus is removed. p. 101

opponent-process theory The theory that cells in the visual system respond to red-green and blue-yellow colors; a given cell might be excited by red and inhibited by green, while another cell might be excited by yellow and inhibited by blue. p. 101

sounds Vibrations of air that are processed by the auditory (hearing) system; also called sound waves. p. 102

frequency The number of cycles (or full wavelengths) that pass through a point in a given time. p. 103

pitch The perceptual interpretation of a sound's frequency. p. 103

amplitude The amount of pressure produced by a sound wave relative to a standard, measured in decibels (dB). p. 103

loudness The perception of a sound wave's amplitude. p. 104

complex sounds Sounds in which sound waves of numerous frequencies blend together. p. 104

timbre The tone color or perceptual quality of a sound. p. 104

outer ear The pinna and the external auditory canal. p. 104

middle ear The section of the ear consisting primarily of the eardrum, hammer, anvil, and stirrup. p. 104

eardrum A membrane in the middle ear that vibrates in response to sound. The sound is then transmitted by the hammer, anvil, and stirrup to the inner ear. p. 104

inner ear The oval window, cochlea, and the organ of Corti. p. 105

cochlea A long tubular fluid-filled structure in the inner ear that is coiled up like a snail. p. 105

basilar membrane A membrane housed inside the cochlea that runs its entire length. p. 105

organ of Corti A tissue that runs the length of the cochlea and sits on the basilar membrane. It contains the ear's sensory receptors, which change the energy of sound waves into nerve impulses that can be processed by the brain. p. 105

place theory The theory that each frequency of sound waves produces vibrations at a particular spot on the basilar membrane. p. 106

frequency theory The theory that the perception of a sound's frequency is due to how often the auditory nerve fires. p. 106

volley theory The theory that high frequencies can be signaled by teams of neurons that fire at different offset times to create an overall firing rate that could signal a very high frequency. p. 107

auditory nerve The nerve that carries neural impulses to the brain's auditory areas. p. 107

thermoreceptors Receptors located under the skin that respond to changes in temperature. p. 108

pain The sensation that warns us that damage is occurring to our bodies. p. 108

gate-control theory The theory that the spinal column contains a neural gate that can be opened (allowing the perception of pain) or closed (blocking the perception of pain). p. 108

acupuncture A technique in which thin needles are inserted at specific points in the body to produce various effects, such as local anesthesia. p. 108

papillae Bumps on the surface of the tongue that contain taste buds, the receptors for taste. p. 108

olfactory epithelium Tissue located at the top of the nasal cavity that contains a sheet of receptor cells for smell. p. 110

kinesthetic sense The sense that provides information about movement, posture, and orientation. p. 111

vestibular sense The sense that provides information about balance and movement. p. 111

semicircular canals Canals in the inner ear that contain the sensory receptors that detect head motion caused by tilting the head or other bodily motion. p. 111

information-processing approach The view that perception is the process of internally representing information from the world, subjecting it to a series of internal manipulations. p. 112

echolocation A system, used by animals like bats, in which the animal emits loud sounds (too high in frequency for humans to hear) that travel through the environment, hitting objects and echoing back to the animal's ears or other auditory receptors. p. 114

ecological approach A view of perception that stresses an active perceiver exploring and moving about the environment. p. 114

optic array The constantly changing pattern of light that specifies the environment. p. 114

contour A location on a surface at which a sudden change of brightness occurs. p. 115

figure-ground relationship The principle by which we organize the perceptual field into stimuli that stand out (figure) and those that are left over (ground). p. 115

Gestalt psychology An approach that states that people naturally organize their perceptions according to certain patterns. *Gestalt* is a German word that means "configuration" or "form." One of Gestalt psychology's main principles is that the whole is not equal to the sum of its parts. p. 115

depth perception The ability to perceive objects three-dimensionally. p. 116

binocular cues Depth cues that are based on both eyes working together. p. 116

monocular cues Depth cues based on each eye working independently. p. 116

disparity The difference between the images from the left and right eye that the brain uses as a binocular cue to determine the depth or distance of an object. p. 116

apparent movement Our perception of a stationary object as being in motion. p. 119

stroboscopic motion The illusion of movement created by a rapid stimulation of different parts of the retina. p. 119

movement aftereffects An illusion of movement that occurs when people watch continuous movement and then look at another surface, which then appears to move in the opposite direction. p. 119

size constancy Recognition that an object remains the same size even though the retinal image of the object changes. p. 119

shape constancy Recognition that an object remains the same shape even though its orientation to us changes. p. 119

brightness constancy Recognition that an object retains the same degree of brightness even when different amounts of light fall on it. p. 122

visual illusion Illusion that occurs when two objects produce exactly the same retinal image but are perceived as different images. p. 123

carpentered-world hypothesis The hypothesis that people who live in cultures in which straight lines, right angles, and rectangles predominate (for instance, in which most rooms and buildings are rectangular and many things, such as city streets, have right-angled corners) should be more susceptible to illusions involving straight lines, right angles, and rectangles (such as the Müller-Lyer illusion) than are people who live in noncarpentered cultures. p. 126

extrasensory perception (ESP) Perception that occurs without the use of any known sensory process. p. 127

telepathy The extrasensory transfer of thought from one person to another. p. 127

precognition "Knowing" events before they occur. p. 127

clairvoyance The ability to perceive remote events that are out of view. p. 127

psychokinesis Closely associated with ESP, the mind-over-matter phenomenon of being able to move objects without touching them, such as mentally getting a chair to rise off the floor or shattering a glass merely by staring at it. p. 127

Resources and Readings in Psychology

Canadian Association of the Deaf/
Association des sourds du Canada

2435 Holly Lane, #205
Ottawa, ON K1V 7P2 Canada
613–526–4785

This association protects and promotes the rights, needs, and concerns of deaf Canadians.

The Canadian Council of the Blind/
Le conseil canadien des aveugles

396 Cooper Street, #405
Ottawa, ON K2P 2H7 Canada
613–567–0311

This council is a nonprofit, nationally based center for advocacy, consumerism, peer support, and social and recreational activities for blind Canadians. It maintains contact with divisional offices across Canada.

Human Behavior in Global Perspective (1990)

by Marshall Segall, Pierre Dasen, John Berry, and Ype Poortinga
New York: Pergamon

Segall's research has made important contributions to an understanding of cultural influences on perception. An entire chapter of this book is devoted to how culture affects our perception of visual illusions.

National Alliance of Blind Students

1115 15th Street, NW, Suite 720
Washington, DC 20005
800–424–8666

This is an organization for postsecondary blind students that seeks to improve their educational opportunities and protect their rights.

National Association of the Deaf

814 Thayer Avenue
Silver Spring, MD 20910
301–587–1788

This association serves adult deaf persons, parents of deaf children, professionals, students, and others interested in deafness. The group publishes *Deaf American* and provides information about various books on American Sign Language.

National Federation of the Blind

1320 Johnston Street
Baltimore, MD 21230
410–659–9314

This organization seeks to establish the complete equality and integration of the blind into society. It publishes *Braille Monitor,* a monthly magazine, and a number of educational brochures. Job opportunities for the blind are listed.

Pseudoscience and the Paranormal (1988)

by Terence Hines
Buffalo, NY: Prometheus Books

This comprehensive book examines the empirical evidence behind virtually all forms of alleged paranormal and pseudoscientific phenomena, including biorhythms, graphology, plant perception, subliminal perception, astrology, and UFO abductions. The author analyzes the puzzling question of why people continue to believe in the reality of the supernatural in spite of overwhelming evidence against it.

Seeing: Illusion, Brain, and Mind (1980)

by J. P. Frisby
New York: Oxford University Press

This fascinating book presents many illusions and describes attempts to explain them.

The Story of My Life (1970)

by Helen Keller
New York: Airmont

This fascinating portrayal of Helen Keller's life as a blind person provides insights into blind people's perception of the world and how they use other senses.

C H A P T E R

SOC

States of Consciousness and Drugs

JOHN W. SANTROCK
Hypnogogic State, detail

CHAPTER

SOC

States of Consciousness and Drugs

Chapter Outline

Chapter Boxes

The ultimate gift of conscious life is a sense of the mystery that encompasses it.

—Lewis Mumford

Sleep that knits up the ravelled sleave of care . . .
Balm of hurt minds,
nature's second course,
Chief nourisher in life's feast.

—**William Shakespeare**

Images of Psychology

Colin Kemp's Tragic Night Terror

It was August 1985, and Colin Kemp, a 33-year-old salesman in Caterham, England, went to sleep as usual. About 2 hours later, he was confronted by two Japanese soldiers in his bedroom. They started to chase him. One soldier had a knife, the other a gun. Kemp ran away from them as fast as he could, but he wasn't fast enough. Kemp wrestled with the knife-wielding soldier. The other soldier aimed his gun at Kemp's head. Kemp tripped him, gripped his neck, and began choking him, but he slipped away. He turned, aimed the gun at Kemp, and fired. Kemp awoke in a state of panic, sweat pouring down his head. In a frenzy of terror, he turned to his wife, who was lying next to him in bed. She was dead. Kemp had strangled her, not the Japanese soldier.

A trial was held 9 months later. Kemp said he was asleep when he killed his wife, pleading not guilty to the murder charge because he had intended to kill the Japanese solider, not his wife. Psychiatrists testified on Kemp's behalf, instructing the jury that Kemp was having a night terror at the time he killed his wife. A **night terror** *is characterized by sudden arousal from sleep and intense fear, usually accompanied by a number of physiological reactions such as rapid heart rate and breathing, loud screams, heavy perspiration, and physical movement.* In most instances, the individual has little or no memory of what happened during the night terror.

Kemp experienced night terrors on two occasions prior to the fatal event. Both times he was being chased during his sleep. In one of the night terrors, he punched at his wife. She awakened and asked what was happening. The second time he kicked her in the back. Strangling someone to death is a much more elaborate and sustained activity than kicking an individual in the back. Is it possible that an action like Kemp's—strangling someone to death—could actually take place during sleep? The jury apparently thought so. They acquitted Kemp.

His act was viewed as an *automatic* one. That is, although Kemp was capable of action, the jury concluded he was not *conscious* of what he was doing (Restak, 1988).

Preview

Most of us take for granted our nightly sojourn into the realm of sleep. But Colin Kemp's experiences stimulate us to wonder about the nature of sleep and our states of consciousness. What is consciousness? What are sleep and dreams really like? In this chapter, we will explore these fascinating questions as well as the intriguing topics of hypnosis and how drugs alter states of consciousness.

FIGURE 1

Conscious and Subconscious Processing of Information
A number of contemporary cognitive psychologists believe that conscious awareness is only the tip of the iceberg in processing information. If you are looking out over the ocean and see this whale diving and cavorting in the water, how is your conscious and subconscious processing of information likely to unfold? Some psychologists argue that your conscious awareness of the whale is preceded by individual brain events.

What Is Consciousness?

For much of the twentieth century, psychologists shunned the slippery, subjective trappings of consciousness that intrigued their predecessors in the late nineteenth century. Instead, they focused on overt behaviors and the rewards and punishments that determined those behaviors (Skinner, 1938; Watson, 1913). Only recently, though, has the study of consciousness gained widespread respectability in cognitive science (Nelson, 1996). For the first time in many decades, psychologists from many different fields are interested in consciousness, including its relation to unconsciousness (Baars & McGovern, 1994; Cohen & Schooler, 1996; Pribram, 1995).

As we go through our lives, we process information at different levels of awareness. We are aware of some of the processing, unaware of other processing. Conscious awareness allows us to have voluntary control and to communicate our mental states to others. Conscious awareness occurs in sequence (that is, in a serial manner) at a relatively slow pace and has a limited capacity.

A number of contemporary cognitive psychologists believe that conscious awareness is only the tip of the iceberg in processing information. Unlike the serial processing of conscious information, subconscious processing of information occurs simultaneously along many different pathways (Baars, 1989). Imagine that you are looking out over the ocean and see a whale. As you look at the whale diving and cavorting in the water, you are consciously aware of the result of your cognitive processing but not of your subprocessing of information about the animal's size, color, movements, identity, and so on. Some cognitive psychologists argue that consciousness is formed by the individual brain events that immediately preceded it (in the case of the whale, your immediately preceding brain processing of its size, movement, distance, identity, and the like) (see figure 1).

Although there is still disagreement about the nature of consciousness, we can define **consciousness** *as awareness of both external and internal stimuli or events.* The external events include what you attend to as you go through your day—the comment your best friend just made about your new hairstyle, the car in front of you that just swerved to miss a dog, the music you are listening to on your Walkman, for example. Internal events include your awareness of your sensations—my headache just returned, I'm breathing too fast, my stomach's rumbling—as well as your thoughts and feelings—I'm really having trouble in biology this semester, I'm anxious about the exam next week, I'm happy Marsha is coming with me to the game tonight.

The contents of our awareness may change from one moment to the next, since information can move rapidly in and out of consciousness. Many years ago, William James (1890) described the mind as a **stream of consciousness**—*a continuous flow of changing sensations, images, thoughts, and feelings.* Our minds race from one topic to the next—from thinking about the person who is approaching us, to how well we feel, to what we are going to do tomorrow, to where we are going for lunch.

While William James was interested in charting the shifting nature of our stream of consciousness, remember that Sigmund Freud (1900/1953) believed that most of our thoughts are unconscious. **Unconscious thought,** *according to Freud, is a reservoir of unacceptable wishes, feelings, and thoughts that are beyond conscious awareness.* Unconscious thought has nothing to do with being unconscious after being knocked out by a blow on the head in a boxing match, being anesthetized, or falling into a coma.

According to Freud, unconscious thoughts are too laden with sexual and aggressive meaning for consciousness to admit them. For example, a young man who is nervous around women breaks into a cold sweat as a woman approaches him. He is unconscious that his fear of women springs from the cold, punitive way his mother treated him when he was a child. Freud believed that one of psychotherapy's main goals was to bring unconscious thoughts into conscious awareness so they can be addressed and dealt with.

Freud accurately recognized the complexity of consciousness. It is not simply a matter of being aware or unaware. Consciousness comes in different forms and levels. Sometimes consciousness is highly focused and alert, at other times it is more passive. Even sleep, once thought to be completely passive and unconscious, is now known to have active and at least minimally conscious properties. **Controlled processes** *represent the most alert states of consciousness, in which individuals actively focus their efforts toward a goal.* Controlled processes require focused attention and interfere with other ongoing activities. Consider Anne, who is learning how to use her new personal computer. She is completely absorbed in reading the tutorial manual that accompanies the computer—she doesn't hear her roommate humming to herself or the song on the radio. This state of focused awareness is what is meant by controlled processes.

Once Anne learns how to use the software, maneuvers on the computer keyboard become almost automatic; that is, she doesn't have to concentrate so hard on how to perform each of the steps required to get the computer to do something. Two weeks ago she had to stop and concentrate on which keys to press to move a paragraph from one page to another. Now her fingers fly across the computer keyboard when she needs to move a block of material. This kind of consciousness involves automatic processes. **Automatic processes** *are forms of consciousness that require minimal attention and do not interfere with other ongoing activities.* Automatic processes require less conscious effort than controlled processes. Remember that the jury acquitted Colin Kemp because they reasoned that he acted automatically rather than consciously. When we are awake, our automatic behaviors should be thought of as lower in awareness than controlled processes, rather than not conscious at all. Since Anne pushed the right keys at the right time on her computer keyboard, she apparently was aware of what she was doing, at some level.

Daydreaming *is another form of consciousness that involves a low level of conscious effort.* Daydreaming lies somewhere between active consciousness and dreaming while we are asleep. It is a little like dreaming when we are awake. Daydreams usually start spontaneously when what we are doing requires less than our full attention. Mind-wandering is probably the most obvious type of daydreaming. We regularly take brief side trips into our own private kingdoms of imagery and memory even as we read, listen, or work. When we daydream we often drift off into a world of fantasy. We imagine ourselves on dates, at parties, on television, at faraway places, at another time in our lives. Sometimes our daydreams are about ordinary, everyday events, such as paying the rent, getting our hair done, or dealing with someone at work. This semiautomatic thought flow can be useful. As you daydream while you shave, iron a pair of pants, or walk to the store, you may be making plans or solving a problem. Daydreams can remind us of important things ahead. Daydreaming keeps our minds active while helping us to cope, to create, and to fantasize.

When we sleep and dream, our level of awareness is lower than when we daydream, but remember that we no longer think of being asleep as the complete absence of consciousness. Sleep and dreams, though, are at very low levels of consciousness. How is sleep different from being in a coma? Sleep differs from being in a coma in that it is periodic, natural, and reversible.

So far the states of consciousness we have described are normal, everyday occurrences in each of our lives. An **altered state of consciousness** *occurs when a person is in a mental state that noticeably differs from normal awareness. Drugs, meditation, traumas, fatigue, hypnosis, and sensory deprivation produce altered states of consciousness.* Whether a state of consciousness is described as normal or altered depends on how the word *normal* is defined. Someone who drinks a caffeinated soda to increase their alertness, for instance, is considered to be in a normal state of consciousness. But someone who takes a drug that induces hallucinations, such as LSD, is considered to be in an altered state of consciousness. In Explorations in Psychology 1, we discuss the role that altered states of consciousness played in the origin of some of the world's great religions.

Explorations in Psychology 1

Altered States of Consciousness and the World's Great Religions

- Yemenite Jews in a Jerusalem synagogue—wrapped in their prayer shawls, barefoot, sitting cross-legged, and swaying back and forth—recite the Torah.
- Dar Jo and Lai Sarr, Zen monks, explore the Buddha-nature at the center of their beings through zazen meditation, meditative walking, and chanting sutras.
- Coptic Christians in Cairo, Egypt, emit an eerie and spine-tingling cry of spiritual fervor.
- Muslims in Pakistan fast from dawn to dusk during the month of Ramadan, consistent with the fourth pillar of Islam.

Today billions of people around the world guide their lives by the tenets of Judaism, Christianity, Islam, and Buddhism (Hood, 1995). Most religions involve the practice of altered states of consciousness as expected parts of religious ritual, whether the altered state is derived through meditation, prayer, fasting, or substance use.

Many of the world's great religions began with a moment of revelation, an ecstatic moment infused with such mystery, power, and beauty that it forever altered the founding prophet's consciousness (Paloutzian, 1996). God called Abraham, bidding him to leave his homeland in Mesopotamia to seek a promised land known as Canaan. There he founded a religious faith, Judaism, whose followers were to enjoy a special relationship with the creator of heaven and earth. In the Christian religion, death could not vanquish Jesus in A.D. 29; following his death, Jesus appeared in a revelation to Paul, who then became a believer in Christ's resurrection and traveled widely to preach Christianity. In the Islamic religion, Mohammed saw a vision and heard a voice in the year 610 B.C. that would alter his life; the angel Gabriel came to Mohammed and said, "Mohammed, thou art a messenger of God."

Mystical revelation did not play a role in the creation of Buddhism. In the late sixth century B.C., Siddhartha Gautama (Buddha) developed enlightenment without assistance from any teachers or divine revelation. The Buddhist path to enlightenment involves meditating—turning inward to discover that within oneself is the origin of the world, the end of the world, and the way to all goals.

Regardless of whether you believe in the teachings of one or more of the world's religions, you can recognize the importance of altered states of consciousness as a critical component in the foundation or practice of the religions of the world. Can you identify how altered states of consciousness might play a role in your own religious tradition?

Among those who practice altered states of consciousness in the world's religions are (a) Zen monks who explore the Buddha-nature at the center of their beings and (b) Muslims in Pakistan who fast from dawn to dusk during the month of Ramadan as the fourth pillar of Islam.

Level	Form	Description	Image	Example
HIGH-LEVEL AWARENESS	Controlled processes	High level of awareness, focused attention required		This student is using controlled processes that require focused concentration.
LOWER-LEVEL AWARENESS	Automatic processes	Awareness, but minimal attention required		This woman is an experienced computer operator. Her maneuvers with the keyboard are automatic, requiring minimal awareness.
	Daydreaming	Low level of awareness and conscious effort, somewhere between active consciousness and dreaming while asleep		Our daydreams often start spontaneously when what we are doing requires less than our full attention.
	Altered states of consciousness	A mental state noticeably different from normal awareness; produced by drugs, trauma, fatigue, hypnosis, meditation, and sensory deprivation		Shown here is a woman being hypnotized.
	Sleep and dreams	No longer thought of as the absence of consciousness, but they are at very low levels of consciousness	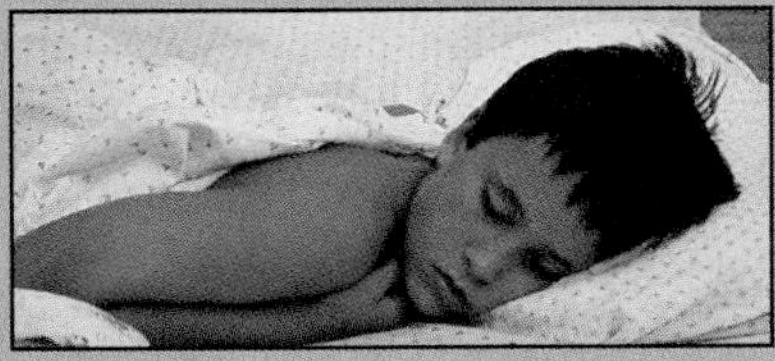	All of us dream while we sleep, but some of us dream more than others.
NO AWARENESS	Unconscious mind (Freudian)	Reservoir of unacceptable wishes, feelings, and memories, often with sexual and aggressive overtones, that are too anxiety provoking to be admitted to consciousness		The woman shown lying on the couch is undergoing psychoanalytic therapy to reveal her unconscious thoughts.
	Unconscious (non-Freudian)	Being knocked unconscious by a blow or when we are anesthetized; deep prolonged unconciousness characterizes individuals who go into a coma as the result of injury, disease, or poison		Unconsciousness can result from an injury, such as a blow to the head.

FIGURE 2

Forms of Consciousness and Levels of Awareness and Unawareness

As you can see, our states of consciousness are many, varied, and complex. A summary of some of the main forms of consciousness and their level of awareness or unawareness is presented in figure 2. Now we turn our attention to the fascinating world of sleep and dreams.

SLEEP AND DREAMS

Each night something lures us from work, from play, and from our loved ones into a solitary state. It is sleep, which claims about one-third of the time in our lives, more than

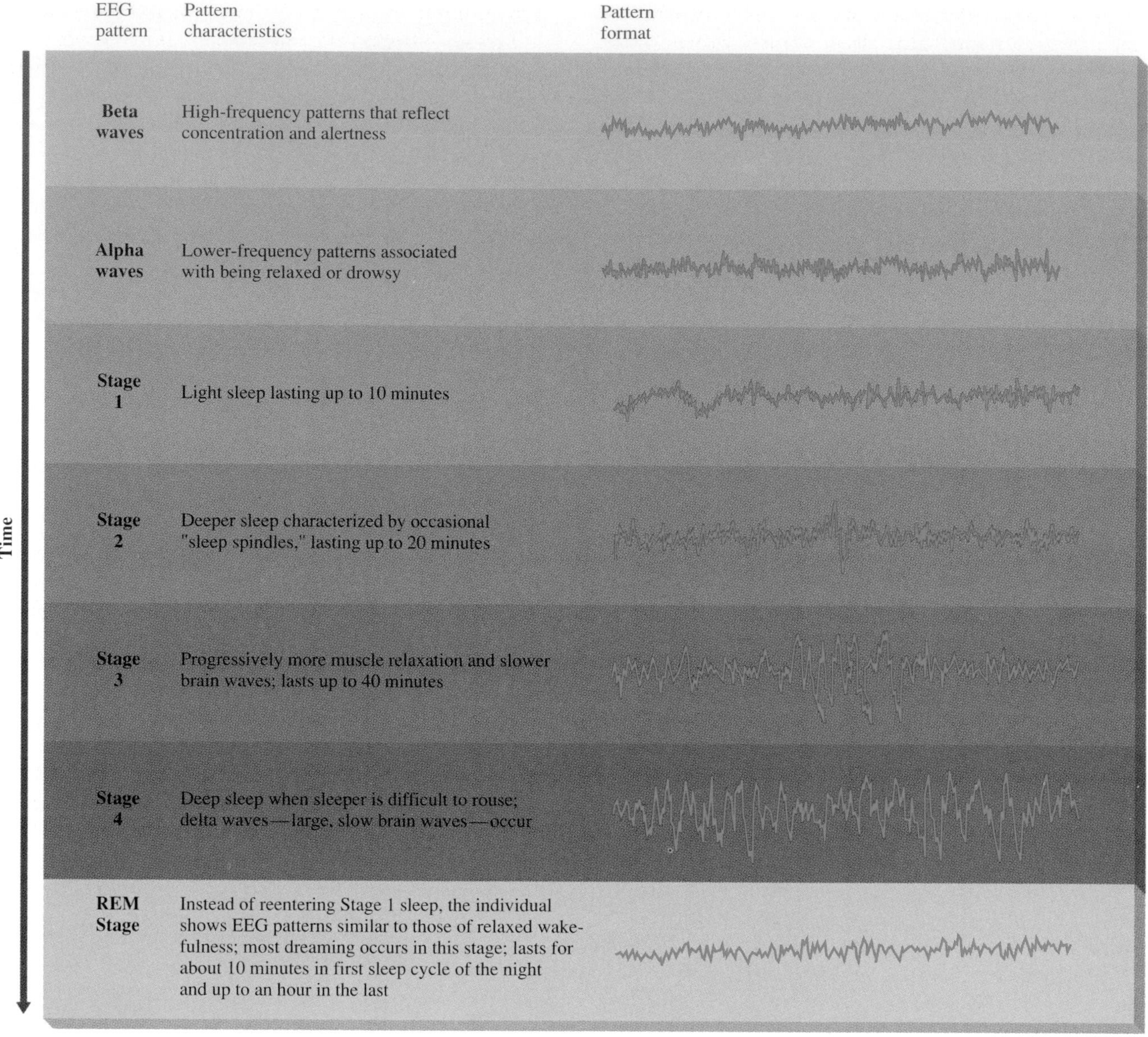

EEG pattern
Pattern characteristics
Pattern format
Beta waves
High-frequency patterns that reflect concentration and alertness
Alpha waves
Lower-frequency patterns associated with being relaxed or drowsy
Stage 1
Light sleep lasting up to 10 minutes
Stage 2
Deeper sleep characterized by occasional "sleep spindles," lasting up to 20 minutes
Stage 3
Progressively more muscle relaxation and slower brain waves; lasts up to 40 minutes
Stage 4
Deep sleep when sleeper is difficult to rouse; delta waves—large, slow brain waves—occur
REM Stage
Instead of reentering Stage 1 sleep, the individual shows EEG patterns similar to those of relaxed wakefulness; most dreaming occurs in this stage; lasts for about 10 minutes in first sleep cycle of the night and up to an hour in the last
Time

FIGURE 3

Characteristics and Format of EEG Recordings During Stages of Wakefulness and Sleep

any other pursuit. This alluring realm of mental escapades we enter each night has intrigued philosophers and scientists for centuries. Those who investigated sleep were primarily interested in its role as a springboard for dreams. We no longer regard sleep as the complete absence of consciousness. Now we know that sleep involves much more.

Stages of Sleep

The stunning stages of sleep correspond to massive electrophysical changes throughout the brain, as the fast, irregular, and low-amplitude activity of wakefulness is replaced by the regular, slow, high-amplitude waves of deep sleep. The invention of the electroencephalograph (EEG) led to some major breakthroughs in understanding sleep by revealing how the brain's electrical activity changes during sleep. Figure 3 shows the EEG patterns for various sleep stages.

Alpha waves *make up the EEG pattern of individuals who are awake but relaxed.* As your breathing slows and your brain waves slow further, you enter the somewhat irregular wave pattern of stage 1 sleep. **Sleep spindles** *are brief bursts of higher-frequency waves that periodically occur during stage 2 sleep.* Stage 2 lasts up to 20 minutes. Beginning in stage 3 and increasingly in stage 4, **delta waves,** *which are large, slow brain waves associated with deep sleep,* appear. Together, stages 3 and 4 are often referred to as "deep sleep." The sleeper who awakens during deep sleep often appears confused, and it is during stage 4 sleep that sleepwalking, sleeptalking, and bed-wetting most often occur.

After about 90 minutes of sleep, much of which is spent in stages 3 and 4, the sleeper moves restlessly and drifts up through the sleep stages toward wakefulness. But instead of reentering stage 1, the person enters a different form of sleep called "rapid eye movement" (REM) sleep. **REM sleep** *is a periodic, active stage of sleep during which dreaming occurs.* During REM sleep, the EEG pattern shows fast waves similar to those of relaxed wakefulness and the sleeper's eyeballs move up and down and from left to right (see figure 4).

A person who is awakened during REM sleep is more likely to report having dreamed than when awakened at any other stage. Even people who claim they rarely dream frequently report dreaming when they are awakened during REM sleep. The longer the period of REM sleep, the more likely a person will report dreaming. Dreams do occur during slow-wave or non-REM sleep, but the frequency of dreams in the other stages is relatively low.

So far we have described a normal cycle of sleep, which consists of four stages, plus REM sleep. There are several important points to remember about the nature of these stages (see figure 5). One of these cycles lasts about 90 minutes and recurs several times during the night. The amount of deep sleep (stage 4) is much greater in the first half of a night's sleep than in the second half. The majority of REM sleep takes place during the latter part of a night's sleep, when the REM period becomes progressively longer. The night's first REM period might last for only 10 minutes, the final REM period for as long as an hour.

Sleep and Circadian Rhythms

We are unaware of most of our body's rhythms—for example, the rise and fall of hormones in the bloodstream, accelerated and decelerated cycles of brain activity, high and lows in body temperature. Some rhythms are *circadian* (from the Latin word *circa* meaning "about" and *dies* meaning "day"). A **circadian rhythm** *is a daily behavioral or physiological cycle; an example is the 24-hour sleep/wake cycle.*

One circumstance in which the circadian rhythm of the human sleep/wake cycle may become desynchronized is when we take a long cross-country or transoceanic flight. If you fly from Los Angeles to New York and then go to bed at 11 P.M. eastern standard time, you may have trouble falling asleep because your body is still on Pacific time. Even if you sleep for 8 hours that night, you may find it hard to wake up at 7 A.M. eastern time, because your body thinks it is 4 A.M. If you stay in New York for several days, your body will adjust to the new schedule.

The phase shift that occurred when you flew from Los Angeles to New York means your body time is out of phase, or synchronization, with clock time. When jet lag occurs, it is the result of two or more body rhythms being out of sync. You usually go to bed when your body temperature begins to drop, but, in your new location, you may be trying to go to bed when it is rising. When you wake up in the morning, your adrenal glands release large doses of cortisol. In your new geographical location, the glands may be releasing this chemical just as you are getting ready for bed at night.

Another circumstance in which circadian rhythms may become desynchronized is when shift workers change their work hours. A number of near-accidents in air travel

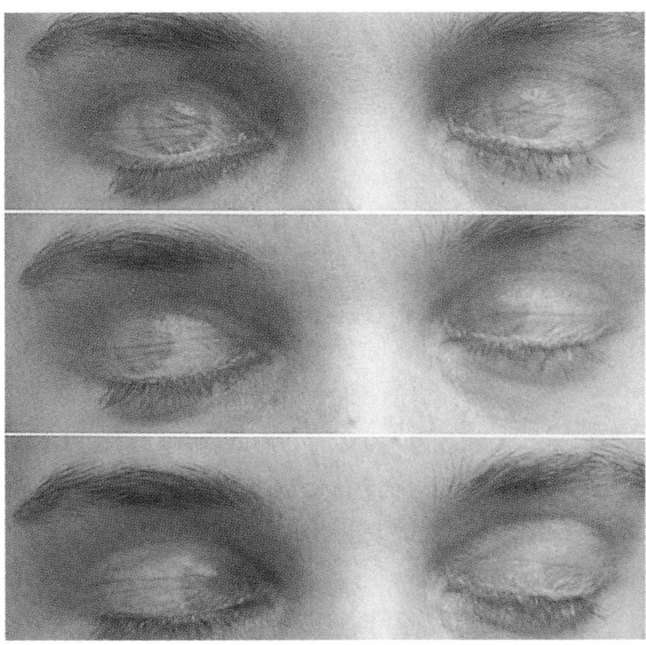

FIGURE 4

REM Sleep
During REM sleep, our eyes move rapidly as if we were observing the images we see moving in our dreams.

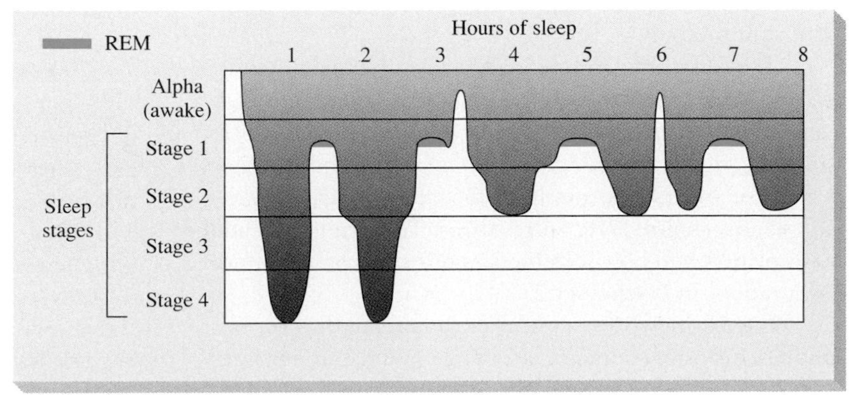

FIGURE 5

Normal Sleep Patterns of Young Adults
Notice the reduction of slow-wave sleep, especially stage 4 sleep, during the latter part of the night, and notice the increase of REM sleep in the latter part of the night.

EXPLORATIONS IN PSYCHOLOGY 2

Cave Days and Calendar Days

French scientist Michel Siffre entered Midnight Cave near Del Rio, Texas, on February 14, 1972. A small nylon tent deep within the cave was Siffre's home for 6 months. Because Siffre could not see or sense the sun rising and setting in the cave, he began to live by biological cycles instead of by days. When Siffre wanted to go to sleep, he called the support crew outside and told them to turn off the lights in the cave. Just before he went to sleep, he attached electrodes to his scalp so his sleep cycles could be recorded. When he woke up, he called the support crew and asked them to turn on the cave's lights.

The photograph shows the interior of the cave where Michel Siffre lived for six months.

Siffre referred to each one of his sleep/wake cycles as a day. Siffre's days closely resembled a 24-hour cycle throughout the 6 months in the cave, although they were slightly longer and more varied toward the end of the 6 months. Near the end of his stay in the cave, occasionally Siffre's days were very long, but most still averaged about 28 hours.

After 6 months, Siffre misjudged which month it was. It was August, but he thought it was only July. On day 151 of Siffre's cave experience, the caveman made this entry into a diary:

> Gerard tells me it is August 10 . . . and the experiment is concluded; I am confused; I believed it to be mid-July. Then, as the truth sinks in, comes a flood of relief.

Siffre's comments about life in the cave reflect the cave's eeriness and the confusion such experiences create:

> You live following your mind . . . you have not the alternance of day and night. . . . It's all in your brain . . . no sound, nothing . . . darkness completely.

have been associated with pilots who have not yet become synchronized to their new shift and are not working as efficiently as usual. Shift rotation might have been one of the causes of the nuclear accident at Three Mile Island (Moore-Ede, Sulzman, & Fuller, 1982). The team of workers monitoring the nuclear plant when the incident took place had been placed on night shift just after a 6-week period of constant shift rotation.

As researchers became intrigued by the role of biological rhythms, they naturally were curious about what happens when an individual is completely isolated from clocks, calendars, night, the moon, the sun, and all indices of time. A number of experiments have focused on such isolation experiences (Kales, 1970; Siffre, 1975). To learn more about this isolation and how it influences our sleep patterns, read Explorations in Psychology 2.

Interestingly, the natural circadian rhythm of most animals, including humans, is 25 to 26 hours, but our internal clocks easily adapt to the 24-hour rhythms (light, sounds, warmth) of the turning earth. When we are isolated from environmental cues, our sleep-wake cycles continue to be rather constant but typically longer than 24 hours, as the experience of Michel Siffre showed.

Why Do We Sleep?

There are two main theories about why we sleep—repair theory and ecological theory. **Repair theory** *states that sleep restores, replenishes, and rebuilds our brains and bodies, which somehow are worn out or used up by the day's waking activities.* This idea fits with the feeling of being "worn out" before we sleep and "restored" when we wake. Aristotle proposed a repair theory of sleep centuries ago, and most experts today believe in some version of repair.

But how much sleep do we need each night? Some of us can get by on an average of 5 to 6 hours of sleep, others may need 9 to 10 hours to function effectively. The idea that each of us needs 8 hours of sleep each night is a myth.

How long can people go without sleep and still function? The effects of profound sleep loss have been difficult to study because preventing a person from sleeping causes stress. After 2 or 3 days without sleep, people tend to become irritable, lose concentration, and show other signs of stress (Webb, 1978). As people become more motivated to sleep, they may snatch bits of sleep while standing up. However, people who are highly motivated and able to cope with the stress can function surprisingly well after as many as 8 to 10 days without sleep (Dement, 1978).

Ecological theory *is a relatively recent view of why we sleep. This evolutionary-based approach argues that the main purpose of sleep is to prevent animals from wasting their energy and harming themselves during those parts of the day or night to which they have not adapted.* For example, it was not adaptive for our ancestors to fumble around in the dark, risking accidents or attack by large predators such as lions and tigers. So, like the chimpanzees who slept safely in treetops, our ancestors presumably hid and slept through the night.

Both repair theory and ecological theory have some merit. Perhaps sleep was most important originally for keeping us out of trouble, but has evolved since to allow for certain repair processes.

The Neural Basis of Sleep

For many years researchers thought sleep occurred in the absence of enough sensory stimulation to keep the brain awake. Without stimuli, the brain was believed to just "slow down," producing sleep. But researchers realized that sleep comes and goes without any obvious change in the amount of environmental stimulation. Theorists suggested we might have an internal "activating system" in the reticular formation that keeps the brain activated, or awake, all day (Hobson & McCarley, 1977). According to this theory, "fatigue" of the so-called activating system, or an accumulation of some "sleep toxin" that chemically depressed the activating system, induced sleep.

The contemporary view of sleep is radically different. As you have learned, the brain does not "stop" during sleep, but instead carries out complex processes that produce both REM and non-REM sleep behaviors. In fact, at the cellular level, many neurons fire faster during sleep than in a waking state.

The puzzle is not completely solved, but some of the major pieces of the brain's machinery involved in sleep have been identified. Non-REM sleep, for example, requires the participation of neurons in both the forebrain and the medulla. REM sleep is a period of especially intense brain activity, also requiring the cooperation of a number of brain systems. To read further about the brain's role in sleep and in learning, turn to Explorations in Psychology 3.

So far we have discussed normal aspects of sleep. Next we'll see that sleep is not always predictable; there are many ways sleep can go awry.

Sleep Disorders

Most people go to bed, fall asleep, and have a restful night. But some people have fitful nights and want to sleep much of the day. Others sleepwalk, sleeptalk, or have nightmares or night terrors, and some have breathing problems while they sleep.

Insomnia

Insomnia *is a common sleep problem; put simply, it is the inability to sleep.* Insomnia may involve a problem in falling asleep, waking up during the night, or waking up too early. As many as one in five Americans has insomnia. It is more common among women, older adults, thin people, depressed or stressed people, and people who are poor.

We spend large sums of money, especially for drugs, trying to sleep better. Many sleep experts now believe that physicians have been too quick to prescribe sedatives for insomniacs. Sedatives reduce the amount of time a person spends in stage 4 and REM sleep, and may disrupt the restfulness of sleep. There is some danger of overdose, and over time sedatives lose their effectiveness, requiring ever greater dosages to achieve the same effect. Sedatives and nonprescription sleeping pills should be used with caution and only for short-term sleep problems.

Caffeine and nicotine may be the culprits in some cases of insomnia. Experts recommend decreasing their use if you are having sleep problems. Avoid large quantities of alcohol before going to bed. Drinking before going to bed may initially help you to fall asleep, but after the sedative effects wear off you probably will have difficulty staying asleep. Other suggested remedies for insomniacs include adopting a regular schedule so that you go to sleep and wake up at approximately the same time each day; do something relaxing before you go to bed, such as listening to soft music; avoid discussing highly stressful issues, such as money or dating problems, just before you go to bed; and adopt a regular exercise program (but don't exercise just before going to bed, because that increases your energy and alertness).

Sleepwalking and Sleeptalking

Somnambulism *is the formal term for sleepwalking, which occurs during the deepest stages of sleep.* For many years experts believed somnambulists were acting out their dreams. But somnambulism occurs during stages 3 and 4 of sleep, the times when a person usually does not dream. Sleepwalking is most common in children, although some adults also sleepwalk. Most children outgrow the problem without having to seek professional help. Except for the danger of accidents while wandering about in the dark, there is nothing really abnormal about sleepwalking. It is safe to awaken sleepwalkers, and it's probably a good idea since they might harm themselves as they roam through the night.

Another quirky night behavior is sleeptalking. Most sleeptalkers are young adults, but sleeptalkers come in all ages. If you interrogated a sleeptalker, could you find out what he did last Thursday night? Probably not. Although he may speak to you and make fairly coherent statements, the sleeptalker is soundly asleep. Most likely the sleeptalker will mumble some response to your question, but don't count on its accuracy.

Nightmares and Night Terrors

A **nightmare** *is a frightening dream that awakens the sleeper from REM sleep.* The nightmare's content invariably involves some danger—the dreamer is chased, robbed, raped, murdered, or thrown off a cliff. Nightmares are common. Most of us have had them, especially when we were young

Explorations in Psychology 3

Can We Learn While We Are Asleep?

King Henry IV of France once said, "Great eaters and great sleepers are incapable of anything else that's great." But King Henry had not seen the recent sleep research that raises the possibility that learning might take place while we are asleep.

Two recent studies, one on rats and one on college students, demonstrated the value of sleep in strengthening memories from the previous day. To remember where you have been or learn a new skill, sleep seems to help.

In one of the studies, researchers fitted rats with recording devices that detected simultaneous firings of nerve cells in the hippocampus, a brain structure involved in remembering a new place (Wilson & McNaughton, 1994). When the rats were allowed to explore new locations, different hippocampus cells fired electrical impulses. The researchers found that the nerve cells most likely to fire together during sleep were the ones that fired together during daytime exploration. Apparently, the rat's brain uses sleep as an opportunity to strengthen memories from the previous day's activities.

This type of memory—of places, events, or facts—is called *declarative memory.* Neuroscientists have documented that the hippocampus plays an important role in declarative memory. Another type of memory, *procedural memory,* which involves learning skills or habits, like driving a car, does not seem to be based in the hippocampus. Rather, such repetition of tasks trains the brain's outer layer of "thinking" nerve cells to perform the job more automatically.

Researchers had thought that sleep strengthens declarative memory, but they saw no reason why sleep should improve procedural memory. However, in one recent study the results suggested otherwise (Karni & others, 1994). College students were trained to recognize subtle differences in visual patterns: to identify the shape of a figure in a pattern. They improved their performance with practice, and performed the task better after a good night's sleep than at the end of the previous day's practice session, suggesting that their brains were doing something during sleep to enhance the newly learned skill. Actually, earlier research had shown that performance improves after an 8- to 10-hour lag, even if the lag is during the day and the performers are awake during it. The new study documented that the improvement also occurs during sleep.

In this chapter, we have learned that all sleep is not alike—for example, some is slow-wave sleep, other involves REM sleep. Might one phase of sleep enhance learning more than others? In the learning task–sleep study, the researchers monitored the students' brain waves to detect when REM sleep was occurring and rang a bell anytime they began to drift off into REM sleep (Karni & others, 1994). In another trial, the bell went off only during slow-wave sleep.

Apart from the obvious results—such as the students' being a little testy the next day from having their sleep interrupted—some interesting findings emerged in their ability to tell the shape of a pattern. If slow-wave sleep was disrupted, the students still scored better on the tasks than they had the previous day. But if REM sleep was disrupted, the sleep did the students no good and their skill was not improved. Thus, something about REM sleep might hold a key to strengthening this type of memory. Old skills, in which memories are presumably already strong enough, were not diminished by REM sleep deprivation in this study. So, presumably, REM sleep facilitates the learning of new skills (Siegried, 1994).

But what about material that is presented to individuals during sleep? Could you possibly enhance your performance on tests or learn a foreign language by being presented with information while you are sleeping? The research evidence suggests that sleep learning is ineffective when measured in terms of an individual's ability to consciously remember material presented during sleep (Druckman & Bjork, 1994). So playing back a tape recording of your professor's lecture while you are sleeping will not improve your knowledge of the material.

---

children. Even most adults experience an occasional nightmare. Nightmares are usually so vivid that we can remember them if someone awakens us, although they account for only a small portion of our dream world.

Recall from the opening of the chapter that *night terrors* are characterized by sudden arousal from sleep and intense fear, usually accompanied by a number of physiological reactions such as rapid heart rate and breathing, loud screams, heavy perspiration, and physical movement. Night terrors are less common than nightmares, and the person usually has little or no recall of an accompanying dream. Also unlike nightmares, night terrors occur in slow-wave, non-REM sleep.

Narcolepsy

Narcolepsy *is the overpowering urge to fall asleep.* The urge is so strong that the person may fall asleep while talking or standing up. Narcoleptics immediately enter REM sleep rather than moving through the first four sleep stages. Researchers suspect that narcolepsy is inherited since it runs in families.

FIGURE 6

Artists' Portrayals of Dreams
Through the centuries, artists have been adept at capturing the enchanting or nightmarish characteristics of our dreams. (*Left*) Dutch painter Hieronymus Bosch (1450–1516) captured both the enchanting and frightening world of dreams in *The Garden of Delights.* (*Above*) In *The Nightmare,* Henry Fuseli (1741–1825) portrayed the frightening world of nightmarish dreams by showing a demon sitting on a woman having a nightmare.

Sleep Apnea

Sleep apnea *is a sleep disorder in which individuals stop breathing because the windpipe fails to open or brain processes involved in respiration fail to work properly.* Individuals with sleep apnea wake up periodically during the night so they can breathe better, although they are not usually aware of their awakened state. During the day these people may feel sleepy because they were deprived of sleep at night. This disorder is most common among infants and people over the age of sixty-five.

In our tour of sleep we have seen that dreams usually occur during REM sleep. Let's now explore the fascinating world of dreams in greater detail.

Dreams

Ever since the dawn of language, dreams have been imbued with historical, personal, and religious significance. As early as 5000 B.C. Babylonians recorded and interpreted their dreams on clay tablets. Egyptians built temples in honor of Serapis, the god of dreams. People occasionally slept in these temples in the hope that Serapis would appear in their dreams and either heal them or tell them what to do to be healed. Dreams are described at length in more than seventy passages in the Bible, and in many primitive cultures dreams are an extension of reality. For example, there is an account of an African chief who dreamed that he had visited England. On awakening, he ordered a wardrobe of European clothes. As he walked through the village in his new wardrobe, he was congratulated for having made the trip. Similarly, Cherokee Indians who dreamed of being bitten by a snake were treated for the snakebite.

Today, we still try to figure out what dreams mean (see figure 6). Much of the interest stems from psychoanalysts who have probed the unconscious mind to understand the symbolic content of dreams. While we do have concrete information regarding sleep stages, there is very little scientific data to explain why we dream or what the dreams mean.

The Interpretation of Dreams

Many of us dismiss the nightly excursion into the world of dreams as a second-rate mental activity, unworthy of our rational selves. By focusing only on the less mysterious waking world, we deny ourselves the opportunity of chance encounters with distant friends, remote places, dead relatives, gods, and demons.

Freud's Theory In Freud's (1900) theory, the reason we dream is *wish fulfillment.* After analyzing clients' dreams in therapy, Freud concluded that dreams are unconscious attempts to fulfill needs, especially those involving sex and aggression, that cannot be expressed or go ungratified during waking hours. For example, people who are sexually inhibited while awake would likely have dreams with erotic content; those who have strong aggressive tendencies and hold in anger while awake would likely have dreams filled with violence and hostility. Freud also stressed that dreams often contain memories of infancy and childhood experiences, and especially of events associated with parents. And he said our dreams frequently contain information from the day or two preceding the dream. In his view, many of our dreams consist of combinations of these distant early experiences with our parents and more recent daily events. He emphasized that the task of dream interpretation is complicated because we successfully disguise our wish fulfillment in our dreams.

In disguising our wish fulfillment, Freud believed that our dreams contain a great deal of symbolism. Do you dream about elongated objects, including sticks, tree trunks, umbrellas, neckties, and snakes? If so, Freud would have said you are dreaming about male genitals. Do you dream about small boxes, ovens, cavities, ships, and rooms? Freud would have claimed your dreams were about female genitals. Freud thought that once the therapist understood a client's symbolism, the nature of the dream could then be interpreted. However, critics of Freud's dream theory of unconscious dream fulfillment argue that there is no scientific evidence for it.

Problem-Solving Theory Rather than being an arena in which to play out our unsatisfied needs, dreams might be a mental realm where we can solve problems and think creatively. The Scottish author Robert Louis Stevenson (1850–1894), for example, claimed he got the idea for Dr. Jekyll and Mr. Hyde in a dream. Elias Howe, attempting to invent a machine that sewed, reportedly dreamed he was captured by savages carrying spears with holes in their tips. Upon waking, Howe realized he should place the hole for the thread at the end of the needle, not the middle. Dreams may spark such gifts of inspiration because, in unique and creative ways, they weave together current experiences with the past.

Rosalind Cartwright (1978) studied the role of dreaming in problem solving. Participants in her study were awakened just after they had completed a period of REM sleep and then questioned about their dreams. The first dream of the night, it turns out, often reflects a realistic view of a problem. The second dream usually deals with a similar experience in the recent past. Frequently, the third dream goes back to an earlier point in the dreamer's life. The next several dreams often take place in the future. It is at this point, Cartwright says, that problem solving begins. However, many sleepers never get this far in a night's dreaming, and others just keep repeating the problem.

Activation-Synthesis Theory Possibly psychological explanations of dreams are inadequate. Possibly physiological events during REM sleep explain the occurrence and unique characteristics of dreams. In **activation-synthesis theory,** *dreams have no inherent meaning. Rather, they reflect the brain's efforts to make sense out of or find meaning in the neural activity that takes place during REM sleep. In this view, the brain's activity involves a great deal of random activity during REM sleep and dreams are an attempt to synthesize this chaos* (Hobson & McCarley, 1977).

More About Dreams

The world of dreams raises some intriguing questions. For instance, Do we dream in color? Do animals dream? Why can't we remember all of our dreams? Can we influence what we dream about?

Some people say they dream only in black and white, but virtually everyone's dreams contain color. However, we often forget the color by the time we awaken and recall the dream. Some people claim that certain colors have fixed meanings in their dreams—white for purity, red for passion, green for vitality, black for evil or death, for example. However, no evidence has been found to support this belief. Red may stand for passion in one dream, danger in another, and anger in yet another dream.

It is impossible to say for certain whether or not animals dream; we know they have periods of REM sleep, so it is possible that they do. But dogs' twitching and howling during sleep, for instance, should not be taken as evidence that they necessarily are dreaming.

Everyone dreams, but some of us remember our dreams better than others. It's not surprising that no one remembers all their dreams, since dreaming occurs at such a low level of consciousness. Psychoanalytic theory suggests we forget most of our dreams because they are threatening, but there is no evidence to support this belief. We remember our dreams best when we are awakened during or just after a dream. Similarly, the dreams we have just before we awaken are the ones we are most likely to remember. People whose sleep cycles have long periods between their last REM stage and awakening are more likely to report they don't dream at all or rarely remember their dreams.

Can we banish evil, fly high and fast, or create a happy ending for our dreams at will? According to Stanford researcher Stephen LaBerge (1985), in the landscape of "lucid dreams," you can actually learn to take control of your dreams. **Lucid dreaming** *is dreaming while knowing one is dreaming.* During the lucid dream, the sleeper is consciously aware that the dream is taking place and can gain some control over the dream's content.

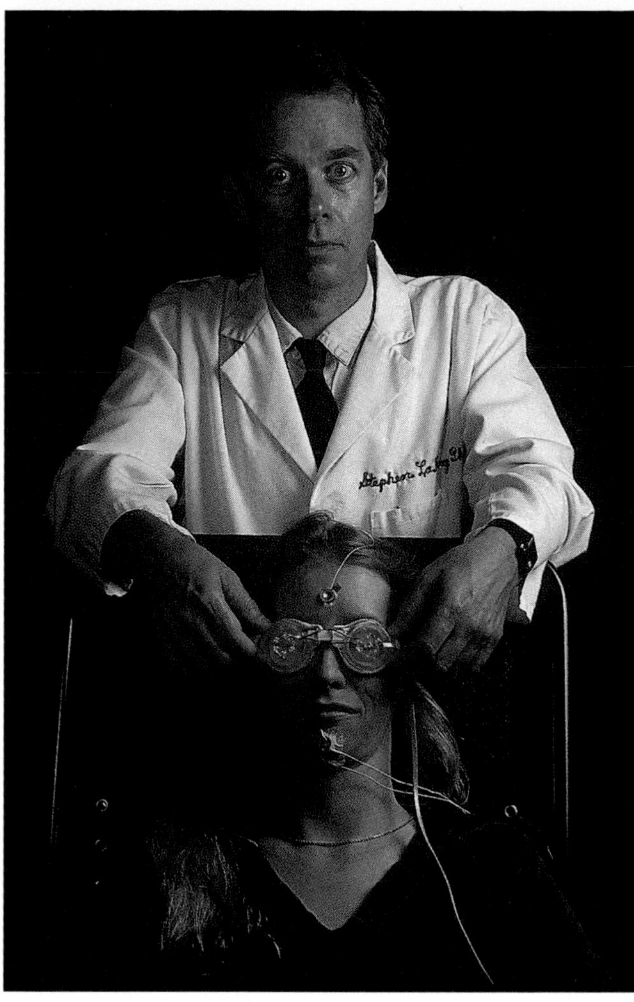

One of Stephen LaBerge's strategies for studying lucid dreaming is to ask volunteers to wear goggles that flash during REM sleep, cueing the person to recognize that dreaming is occurring and thus have a lucid dream.

Our tour of states of consciousness, and of sleep and dreams, has held some fascinating moments. A summary of the main themes of this discussion appears in concept table 1. Next, we turn our attention to hypnosis and altered states of consciousness.

Hypnosis

A young cancer patient is about to undergo a painful bone-marrow transplant procedure. A man directs the boy's attention, asking him to breathe with him and listen carefully. The boy becomes absorbed in a pleasant fantasy—he is riding a motorcycle over a huge pizza, dodging anchovies and maneuvering around chunks of mozzarella. Minutes later the procedure is over. The boy is relaxed and feels good about his self-control.

The doctor successfully used hypnosis as a technique to help the young cancer patient control pain. **Hypnosis** *is a psychological state of altered attention and awareness in which the individual is unusually receptive to suggestions.* Hypnosis has been used since the beginning of recorded history. It has been associated with religious ceremonies, magic, the supernatural, and many erroneous theories. Today hypnosis is recognized as a legitimate process in psychology and medicine, although much is yet to be learned about how it works.

In the eighteenth century the Austrian physician Friedrich Anton Mesmer cured his patients by passing magnets over their bodies. Mesmer said the problems were cured by "animal magnetism," an intangible force that passes from therapist to patient. In reality, the cures were due to some form of hypnotic suggestion. Mesmer's claims were investigated by a committee appointed by the French Academy of Science. The committee agreed that Mesmer's treatment was effective; however, they disputed his theoretical claims about animal magnetism and prohibited him from practicing in Paris. Mesmer's theory of animal magnetism was called mesmerism, and even today we use the term *mesmerized* to mean hypnotized or enthralled.

Features of the Hypnotic State

There are four requirements for hypnosis to succeed. First, distractions are minimized and the person to be hypnotized is made comfortable. Second, the subject is told to concentrate on something specific, such as an imagined scene or the ticking of a watch. Third, the subject is told what to expect in the hypnotic state (such as relaxation or a pleasant floating sensation). Fourth, the hypnotist suggests certain events or feelings that he knows will occur or observes occurring (such as "Your eyes are getting tired"). When the suggested effects occur, the subject interprets them as being caused by the hypnotist's suggestions and accepts them as an indication that something is happening. This increases the subject's expectations that the hypnotism will make things happen in the future and makes him even more suggestible.

Individual Differences in Hypnosis

Do you think you could be hypnotized? What about your friends—are they more or less likely to be influenced by hypnosis than you? For as long as hypnosis has been studied, about 200 years, we've known that some people are more easily hypnotized than others. In fact, about 10 to 20 percent of the population are very susceptible to hypnosis, 10 percent or less cannot be hypnotized at all, and the remainder fall somewhere in between (Hilgard, 1965). There is no simple way to tell whether you can be hypnotized. But if you have the capacity to immerse yourself in imaginative activities—listening to a favorite piece of music or reading a novel, for example—you are a likely candidate. People susceptible to hypnosis become completely absorbed in what they are doing, removing the boundaries between themselves and what they are experiencing in their environment.

Concept Table 1

States of Consciousness, Sleep, and Dreams

Concept	Processes/Related Ideas	Characteristics/Description
States of Consciousness	Their nature	Conscious processing of information is serial and involves a limited capacity, while subconscious information processing is simultaneous and involves unlimited capacity. Consciousness is awareness of both external and internal stimuli and events. Consciousness is a rich, complex landscape of the mind, consisting of processes at varying levels of awareness. Among the many forms of consciousness are controlled processes, automatic processes, daydreaming, altered states of consciousness, sleep and dreams, unconscious thought (Freudian), and unconsciousness (non-Freudian, such as an anesthetized state).
Sleep	Stages of sleep	Different stages of sleep are measured by the electroencephalograph (EEG), which measures the brain's electrical activity. Alpha waves occur when we are in a relaxed state. When we sleep we move from light sleep in stage 1 to deep sleep in stage 4 (delta waves). Then we go directly into REM sleep, where dreams occur. Each night we go through a number of these sleep cycles.
	Sleep and circadian rhythms	A circadian rhythm is a cycle of about 24 hours. The human sleep/wake cycle is an important circadian rhythm. This cycle can become desynchronized. Individuals isolated in caves for months continue to approximate a 24-hour cycle, although at times the cycle is slightly longer. There is no set amount of sleep we need each night.
	Why do we sleep?	We sleep for restoration and repair (repair theory) and to keep us from wasting energy and risking harm during the time of day or night to which we are not adapted (ecological theory).
	The neural basis of sleep	Early views emphasized environmental stimulation and subsequently an internal activating system in the reticular formation. The contemporary view states that the brain is actively engaged in producing sleep behaviors, and different neurotransmitters are involved.
	Sleep disorders	Among the most prominent are insomnia, sleepwalking and sleeptalking, nightmares and night terrors, narcolepsy, and sleep apnea.
Dreams	The interpretation of dreams	Freud's psychoanalytic view states that dreams are the unconscious wish fulfillment of needs unmet in our waking state. Freud believed that dreams often involve a combination of daily residue and early childhood experiences. He stressed that dreams have rich, symbolic content. A second view of dreams states that dreams are thinking activities and attempts to solve problems. A third view, the activation-synthesis view, states that dreams are the brain's way of trying to make sense out of its neural activity during REM sleep.
	More about dreams	We usually dream in color but often don't remember that we do. We don't know whether animals dream but they may, since they experience REM sleep. Everyone dreams, but some of us remember our dreams better than others. No evidence exists that dreams are prophetic. Although it is not easy, some individuals have been able to influence their dreams, especially their ability to have lucid dreams.

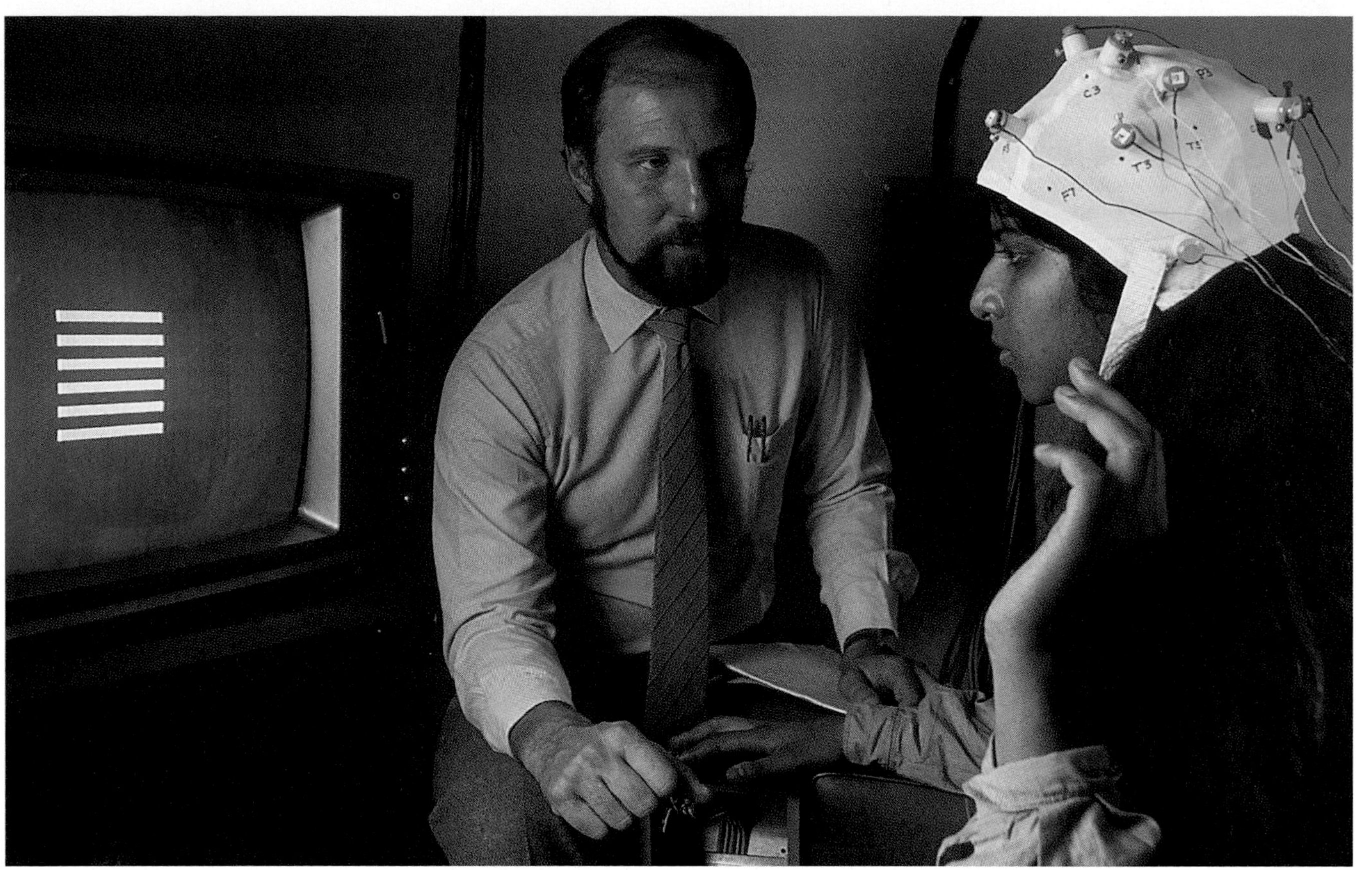

In the special process theory, hypnotic responses, elicited by suggestions, are involuntary. In the situation shown here, the brain activity of a hypnotized subject is being monitored.

Theories of Hypnosis

Ever since Anton Mesmer proposed his theory of "animal magnetism," we have been trying to figure out why hypnosis works. Contemporary theorists are divided as to whether hypnosis produces a special cognitive process or is simply a form of learned social behavior.

In the **special process theory,** *hypnotic behavior is different from nonhypnotic behavior. Hypnotic responses elicited by suggestions are involuntary, rather than voluntary, reactions. Dissociations in cognitive systems take place and amnesic barriers are formed.* **Hidden observer** *is the term used by Ernest Hilgard for the part of the hypnotized individual's mind that is aware of what is happening. This part remains a passive, or hidden, observer until called upon to comment.* Hilgard (1977) discovered this double train of thought in hypnosis during a class demonstration with a student who was blind. Hilgard, the hypnotist, induced deafness in the blind student and demonstrated that the subject was completely unresponsive to what was going on around him. A student asked whether the subject really was as unresponsive as he seemed. Hilgard, being a flexible teacher, asked the subject if there was a part of him that could hear. If so, he was told to raise a finger. Surprisingly, the finger rose. Hilgard asked the subject to report from the part that was listening and made his finger rise; at the same time, he told the subject that he would not be able to hear what this part of himself said. The second part of the individual's awareness, indeed, had heard all that went on and reported it. Further inquiry by Hilgard revealed that approximately half of a group of highly hypnotizable subjects had a hidden observer but were unaware of it until they went through a procedure similar to the blind individual's.

Psychologist Ernest Hilgard developed the hidden observer theory of hypnosis, which stresses that part of a hypnotized individual's mind is aware of what is happening; that part remains a passive, or hidden, observer until called on to comment.

A conflicting perspective, the **nonstate view,** *says that hypnotic behavior is similar to other forms of social behavior and can be explained without resorting to special processes. According to this* *perspective, hypnotic behavior is purposeful, goal-directed action that is best understood by the way subjects interpret their situation and how they try to present themselves.* The nonstate view recognizes that "good" hypnotic subjects often act as if they have lost control over their behavior. But these aspects of behavior are interpreted as voluntary rather than automatic (Spanos, 1988).

Applications of Hypnosis

Hypnosis is widely used in psychotherapy, medicine and dentistry, criminal investigation, and sports. Hypnosis has been used in psychotherapy to treat alcoholism, somnambulism, suicidal tendencies, overeating, and smoking. One of the least effective, but most common, applications of hypnosis is to help people stop overeating and quit smoking. Hypnotists direct their patient to stop these behaviors, but dramatic results rarely are achieved unless the patient is already highly motivated to change. The most effective use of hypnosis is as an adjunct to different forms of psychotherapy.

A long history of research and practice clearly has demonstrated that hypnosis can reduce the experience of pain (Crasilneck, 1995). However, not everyone is hypnotizable enough to experience this effect. The effectiveness of hypnosis in increasing muscular strength and endurance, as well as sensory thresholds, has not been demonstrated (Druckman & Bjork, 1994).

There is also considerable interest today in the application of hypnosis to help people recall forgotten events. To read about this fascinating topic, turn to Explorations in Psychology 4.

In our discussion of hypnosis, we have seen that, in the special process view, hypnosis alters the person's state of consciousness. Next we will see that ever since the dawn of human history people have used drugs to alter consciousness, to "get high."

Psychoactive Drugs

When Sigmund Freud began to experiment with cocaine, he was looking for possible medical applications, such as a painkiller in eye surgery. He soon found that the drug induced ecstasy. He even wrote to his fiancée and told her how just a small dose of cocaine produced lofty, wonderful sensations. As it became apparent that some people became psychologically addicted to cocaine and several died from overdoses, Freud quit using the drug. Cocaine is just one of many drugs taken to alter consciousness.

The Uses of Psychoactive Drugs

Psychoactive drugs *act on the nervous system to alter our state of consciousness, modify our perceptions, and change our moods.* Ever since the ancients first sat entranced in front of the communal fire, humans have searched for substances they hoped would produce pleasurable sensations and alter their state of consciousness. Among the substances that alter consciousness are alcohol, hemp and cactus plants, mushrooms, poppies, and tobacco, an herb that has been smoked and sniffed for more than 400 centuries.

Human beings are attracted to psychoactive substances because they help them adapt to an ever-changing environment. Smoking, drinking, and taking drugs reduce tension and frustration, relieve boredom and fatigue, and in some cases help us escape from the harsh realities of the world. Psychoactive drugs provide us with pleasure by giving us inner peace, joy, relaxation, kaleidoscopic perceptions, surges of exhilaration, and prolonged heightened sensation. They may be useful in helping us to get along in our world. For example, amphetamines may keep us awake all night so we can study for an exam. We may also take drugs because we are curious about their effects, in some cases because of sensationalistic accounts in the media. We may wonder if the drugs described can provide us with unique, profound experiences. We also take drugs for social reasons, hoping they will make us feel more at ease and happier in our interactions and relationships with others.

The use of psychoactive drugs for such personal gratification and temporary adaptation, however, carries a high price tag: drug dependence, personal and social disorganization, and a predisposition to serious and sometimes fatal diseases. What was initially intended as enjoyment and adaptation can eventually turn into sorrow and maladaptation. For example, drinking may initially help people relax and forget about their worries. But then they may begin to drink more and more, until the drinking becomes an addiction that destroys relationships and careers, and leads to physical and psychological damage, including permanent liver damage and major depression.

Addiction

What is the nature of addiction? Are addictions diseases? What is the range of activities to which people can become addicted?

The Nature of Addiction

As a person continues to take a psychoactive drug, the body develops a **tolerance,** *which means that a greater amount of the drug is needed to produce the same effect.* The first time someone takes 5 milligrams of Valium, for example, the drug will make them feel very relaxed. But after taking the pill every day for 6 months, the person may need to take 10 milligrams to achieve the same calming effect.

Physical dependence *is the physical need for a drug that is accompanied by unpleasant withdrawal symptoms when the drug is discontinued.* **Psychological dependence** *is the subjective feeling of craving and perceived need for a drug.* Due to both physical and psychological dependence, the psychoactive drug plays a powerful role in the user's life (Doweiko, 1996).

Explorations in Psychology 4

Is Hypnosis a Window to Forgotten Events?

Hypnosis has sometimes been used in an attempt to enhance people's ability to accurately recall forgotten events. For example, police departments sometimes arrange to have eyewitnesses to crimes hypnotized, in the hope that this will significantly improve their recall.

Most research now indicates that hypnosis does not dramatically improve the accuracy of recall and does not increase the accuracy with which witnesses identify perpetrators whom they have observed commit mock crimes (Lynn, Rhue, & Spanos, 1994). Although subjects do sometimes recall new information following an hypnotic interview, they may also recall much new information when motivated by nonhypnotic instructions (Frischholtz, 1995; Kluft, 1995). Also, when hypnotic (and sometimes nonhypnotic) procedures are used to obtain new information from witnesses, the new information is often inaccurate. And in most real-life circumstances, there is nothing that enables either the witnesses or the interviewer to discriminate between accurate and inaccurate aspects of recall.

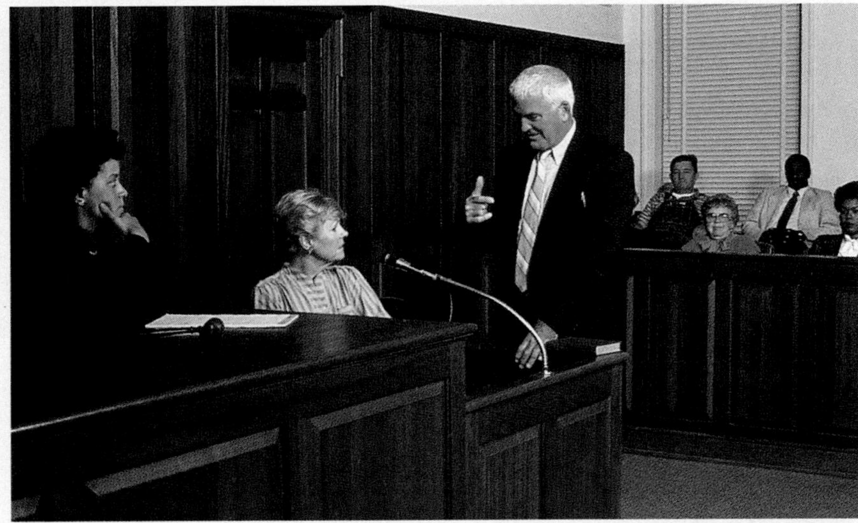

Why should extreme caution be exercised when evaluating memories generated by hypnotic testimony?

Hypnotic subjects can be influenced by leading questions. For example, hypnotic subjects might be asked, "What color was the subject's mustache?" The subjects then often create an image of the suspect they saw and supply the suspect with a mustache, even though the actual suspect did not have a mustache. If these witnesses later see a police lineup that has a suspect with a mustache, they might misidentify that suspect as the perpetrator.

In a number of studies, witnesses who have been given hypnotic interviews are more confident about the inaccurate aspects of their recall or about misidentifications than are nonhypnotized witnesses. On the basis of such findings, as well as research revealing that hypnotic subjects are susceptible to leading questions, Martin Orne (1959) proposed that the recall of hypnotic witnesses might reflect *pseudomemories*—false memories that are confidently believed in as real memories. Orne further stressed that because hypnotic witnesses have so much confidence in their pseudomemories, they are effectively immunized against cross-examination.

However, other researchers have found that pseudomemories occur as frequently in nonhypnotic subjects as in hypnotic subjects. And several studies have reported that hypnotic testimony is no more resistant to cross-examination than nonhypnotic testimony.

Hypnotic testimony in the courtroom has been banned in some states. Because of the mixed research evidence, the issue of whether to admit hypnotic testimony in the courtroom still has no easy answer. If hypnotic testimony is admitted, extreme caution needs to be exercised in administering hypnotic procedures to victims and witnesses.

Are Addictions Diseases?

Controversy continues about whether addictions are diseases. The **disease model of addiction** *describes addictions as biologically based, lifelong diseases that involve a loss of control over behavior and require medical and/or spiritual treatment for recovery.* In the disease model, addiction is either inherited or bred into a person early in life. Current or recent problems or relationships are not believed to be causes of the disease. Once involved in the disease, you can never completely rid yourself of it, according to this model. The disease model has been strongly promoted and supported by the medical profession and Alcoholics Anonymous.

Critics of the disease approach argue that the disease approach is not the best one because the biological mechanisms that might account for addictive behavior have not been identified, it keeps people from developing self-control, it stigmatizes people with labels such as *addict* and *alcoholic*—in some cases for life, it dispenses a rigid program of therapy rather than advocating more flexible approaches, and addiction is not necessarily lifelong. Two critics of the disease model, Stanton Peele and Archie Brodsky (1991), believe that addiction is a habitual response and a source of gratification or security. They say that an addiction can involve *any* attachment or sensations that grow to such proportions that they impair the person's life—including drugs, food, gambling, shopping, love, and sex. In this view, the "hook" of the addiction—what keeps people coming back to it—is that it provides people with feelings and gratifying sensations they are not able to get in other ways. Peele and Brodsky believe that understanding addiction requires that it be placed in the proper context, as part of people's lives, their personalities, their relationships, their environments, and their perspectives. They call their model the "life-process" model. In sum, the **life-process model of addiction** *argues that addiction is not a disease but rather a habitual response and a source of gratification or security that can be understood only in the context of social relationships and experiences.*

Each of these views of addiction—the disease model and the nondisease, life-process model—has its supporters.

Alcohol

We do not always think of alcohol as a drug, but it is an extremely potent one. Alcohol acts upon the body primarily as a depressant and slows down the brain's activities. This may seem surprising since people who normally tend to be inhibited may begin to talk, dance, or socialize after a couple of drinks. People "loosen up" after one or two drinks because the areas in the brain involved in controlling inhibition and judgment *slow down.* As people drink more, their inhibitions become reduced even further and their judgment becomes increasingly impaired. Activities requiring skill, such as driving, and intellectual functioning become impaired as more alcohol is consumed. Eventually the drinker becomes drowsy and falls asleep. With extreme intoxication, a person may even lapse into a coma and die. Each of these effects varies with how the person's body metabolizes alcohol, body weight, the amount of alcohol consumed, and whether previous drinking has led to tolerance.

Alcohol is the most widely used drug in our society. A 1992 Gallup poll revealed that 64 percent of American adults drank beer, wine, or liquor at least occasionally—down from 71 percent in the late 1970s. More than 13 million people in the United States call themselves alcoholics. Alcoholism is the third leading killer in the United States. Each year approximately 25,000 people are killed and 1.5 million are injured by drunk drivers. More than 60 percent of homicides involve the use of alcohol by either the offender or the victim, while 65 percent of aggressive sexual acts against women involve the use of alcohol by the offender. Alcohol costs the United States more than $40 billion each year in health costs, lost productivity, accidents, and crimes.

The number one substance-abuse problem among adolescents is alcohol abuse. These adolescents are attending an antidrug rally in Pasadena, California.

Many alcoholics show a tolerance to alcohol and are physically and psychologically dependent on it. **Alcoholism** *is a disorder that involves long-term, repeated, uncontrolled, compulsive, and excessive use of alcoholic beverages, impairing the drinker's health and interpersonal relationships.* Estimates indicate that approximately 10 percent of all adult drinkers are likely to experience either alcoholism or problem drinking at some point in their lives.

A special concern that recently has surfaced is an increase in drug use, including alcohol consumption, by young adolescents. While the gradual decline in drinking by high school seniors continued, the decline did not occur for eighth graders; in fact, eighth graders showed a slight increase in drinking (Johnston, O'Malley, & Bachman, 1995).

It is often difficult to distinguish between alcoholism and problem drinking. Even professionals in the field of drug abuse have difficulty determining whether an individual is an alcoholic or just has a drinking problem. For example, consider recent data that 44 percent of college students regularly consume four or more drinks in a row (Wechsler & others, 1994). In this study a drink was defined as 12 ounces of beer or wine cooler, 4 ounces of wine, or 1.25 ounces of liquor. Are binge-drinking college students alcoholics or merely problem drinkers? Experts have not been able to agree on an answer to this question.

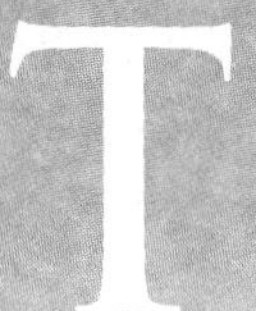

TABLE 1

Items on the Rutgers Collegiate Substance Abuse Screening Test That Were Most Likely to Identify Young Adult Substance Abusers

1. Have you gotten into financial difficulties as a result of drinking or using other drugs?
2. Is alcohol or other drug use making your college life unhappy?
3. Has drinking alcohol or using other drugs ever been behind your losing a job?
4. Has alcohol ever interfered with your preparation for exams?
5. Has your efficiency decreased since drinking and/or using other drugs?
6. Is your drinking and/or drug use jeopardizing your academic performance?
7. Has your ambition decreased since drinking and/or drug using?
8. Does drinking or using other drugs cause you to have difficulty sleeping?
9. Have you ever felt remorse after drinking and/or using other drugs?
10. Do you crave a drink or other drug at a definite time daily?
11. Do you want a drink or other drug the next morning?
12. Have you ever had a complete or partial loss of memory as a result of drinking or using other drugs?
13. Is drinking or using other drugs affecting your reputation?
14. Does drinking and/or using other drugs make you careless of your family's welfare?
15. Have you ever been to a hospital or institution on account of drinking or other drug use?

Note: Young adults who answered "yes" to these questions were more likely to be substance abusers than those who answered "no."
This should be used only as part of a complete assessment battery, as more research still needs to be done.
From M. E. Bennett et al., "Identifying Young Adult Substance Abusers" in *Journal of Studies on Alcohol,* 54:526.

In the recent national study on college drinking patterns that surveyed 17,592 college students on 140 campuses, 47 percent of the binge drinkers reported problems such as missing classes, injuries, troubles with police, or having unprotected sex. For example, the binge drinkers were eleven times more likely to fall behind in school, ten times more likely to drive after drinking, and several times more likely to have unprotected sex than were their non-binge-drinking counterparts.

The assumption among many college students that "everyone" is getting drunk, or wishes they were, might increase alcohol abuse. In one recent series of studies, students systematically overestimated their fellow students' support for heavy drinking (Prentice & Miller, 1993). Thus, many college students are under the false impression that everyone else approves of heavy drinking, and they don't want to appear "uncool." See table 1 for some questions that often identify young adult substance abusers.

People in many other countries actually drink more than Americans do. More than 90 percent of the adults in Belgium, England, Czech Republic, and Hungary drink; and more than 85 percent of the adults in Australia, Norway, and Spain drink (compared to 64 percent of adults in the United States). Some ethnic groups have higher rates of alcoholism than others. Irish and Native Americans, as well as people in many European countries, such as France, have high rates of alcoholism. Jews, Greeks, and Chinese have low rates of alcoholism.

The widespread problem of alcohol abuse has led to a search for its cause and cure. There is increasing evidence of a genetic predisposition to alcoholism, although it is important to remember that both genetic and environmental factors are involved (Oosteen, Knibbe, & deVries, 1996).

Is there a personality profile that accurately predicts who will become an alcoholic and who will not? No, but researchers have discovered several traits linked to the risk of alcohol addiction (Cloninger, 1988). The first trait is called *harm avoidance,* characteristic of individuals who try to avoid potentially harmful activity. They have a high anxiety level and drink to relax or "drown their sorrows." The second characteristic linked to the risk of alcohol addiction is shown by individuals with a high rating on a personality trait called *novelty seeking.* These individuals are risk takers, such as high school or college students who drink excessively and "raise hell" on weekends.

Barbiturates and Tranquilizers

Barbiturates, *such as Nembutal and Seconal, are depressant drugs that induce sleep or reduce anxiety.* In heavy dosages, they can lead to impaired memory and decision making. When combined with alcohol, as when taking sleeping pills after a night of binge drinking, the result can be lethal. Barbiturates by themselves also can produce death in heavy dosages, which makes them the drug most often chosen in suicide attempts.

Tranquilizers, *such as Valium and Xanax, are depressant drugs that reduce anxiety and induce relaxation.* They are among the most widely used drugs in the United States and can produce withdrawal symptoms when a person stops taking them.

Opiates

Opiates, *which consist of opium and its derivatives, depress the central nervous system's activity.* The most common opiate drugs—morphine and heroin—affect synapses in the brain that use endorphins as their neurotransmitter. When these drugs leave the brain, the affected synapses become understimulated. For several hours after taking an opiate, a person feels euphoric, is relieved of pain, and has an increased appetite for food and sex. But the opiates are among the most physically addictive drugs, leading to a craving and painful withdrawal when the drug becomes unavailable. Morphine is sometimes used medically as a painkiller. Indeed, opiates—synthetic or otherwise—are the standard in treating severe pain.

Recently, another hazardous consequence of opiate addiction has surfaced: AIDS. Most heroin addicts inject the drug intravenously. When they share their needles, blood from the needles may be passed on. When this blood comes from someone with AIDS, the virus can spread from the infected user to the uninfected user.

Stimulants

Stimulants *are psychoactive drugs that increase the central nervous system's activity.* The most widely used stimulants are caffeine, nicotine (in cigarettes), amphetamines, and cocaine. Coffee, tea, and caffeinated soft drinks are mild stimulants. Amphetamines and cocaine are much stronger stimulants.

Amphetamines are widely prescribed, often in the form of diet pills. They are also called pep pills and uppers. Amphetamines increase the release of the neurotransmitter dopamine, which increases activity level and pleasurable feelings.

Cocaine comes from the coca plant, native to Bolivia and Peru. For centuries, Bolivians and Peruvians chewed on the plant to increase their stamina. Today cocaine is either snorted in the form of crystals or powder or injected. The effect is a rush of euphoria, which eventually wears off, followed by depression, lethargy, insomnia, and irritability. Cocaine can even trigger a heart attack, stroke, or brain seizure.

When animals and humans chew coca leaves, small amounts of cocaine enter the bloodstream gradually without any apparent adverse effects. However, when extracted cocaine is sniffed, smoked, or injected, it enters the bloodstream very rapidly, producing a rush of euphoric feelings that lasts for about 15 to 30 minutes. Because the rush depletes the supply of the neurotransmitters dopamine and norepinephrine in the brain, an agitated, depressed mood usually follows as the drug's effects decline.

Crack *is an intensified form of cocaine, consisting of chips of pure cocaine that are smoked.* Crack is believed to be one of the most addictive substances known, much more so than heroin, barbiturates, and alcohol. Emergency-room admissions related to crack soared from less than 600 cases in 1985 to more than 15,000 a year in the early nineties.

Treating cocaine addiction has not been very successful. Cocaine's addictive properties are so strong that 6 months after treatment, more than 50 percent of cocaine abusers return to the drug. Researchers have found that monkeys will press a lever more than 12,000 times to obtain each injection of cocaine, a testimony to cocaine's addictive qualities (Siegel, 1990). Experts on drug abuse believe the best approach to reduce cocaine addiction is through prevention programs.

Marijuana

Marijuana comes from the hemp plant, *Cannabis sativa,* which originated in central Asia but is now grown in most parts of the world. Marijuana is made of the hemp plant's dry leaves; its dried resin is known as hashish. The active ingredient in marijuana is THC, which stands for the chemical delta-9-tetrahydrocannabinol. This ingredient does not resemble the chemicals of other psychoactive drugs and does not affect a specific neurotransmitter. Rather, marijuana disrupts the membranes of neurons and affects the functioning of a variety of neurotransmitters and hormones.

The physical effects of marijuana include increases in pulse rate and blood pressure, reddening of the eyes, coughing, and dryness of the mouth. Psychological effects include a mixture of excitatory, depressive, and mildly hallucinatory characteristics, making it difficult to classify the drug. Marijuana can trigger spontaneous unrelated ideas, distorted perceptions of time and place, increased sensitivity to sounds and colors, and erratic verbal behavior. Marijuana can also impair attention and memory. When used daily in large amounts, marijuana can also alter sperm count and change hormonal cycles, and it may be involved in some birth defects. Marijuana use declined during the 1980s, but a recent increase in use has occurred (Johnston, Bachman, & O'Malley, 1995).

Hallucinogens

Hallucinogens *are psychoactive drugs that modify a person's perceptual experiences and produce visual images that are not real. Hallucinogens are also called psychedelic ("mind altering") drugs.* LSD, PCP, and mescaline are examples of hallucinogens.

LSD, lysergic acid diethylamide, is a hallucinogen that, even in low doses, produces striking perceptual changes. Objects change their shape and glow. Colors become kaleidoscopic, fabulous images unfold as users close their eyes. Designs swirl, colors shimmer, bizarre scenes appear. Sometimes the images are pleasurable; sometimes they are grotesque. Figure 7 shows one kind of

FIGURE 7

LSD-Induced Hallucination
Under the influence of hallucinogenic drugs, such as LSD, several users have reported seeing images that have a tunnel effect like the one shown here.

perceptual experience that a number of LSD users have reported. LSD can influence the user's perception of time as well. Time often seems to slow down dramatically, so that brief glances at objects are experienced as deep, penetrating, and lengthy examinations, and minutes often turn into hours or days.

LSD's effects on the body may include dizziness, nausea, and tremors. LSD acts primarily on the neurotransmitter serotonin in the brain, though it can affect dopamine as well. Emotional and cognitive effects may include rapid mood swings or impaired attention and memory. LSD's popularity in the late 1960s and early 1970s dropped after its unpredictable effects became well publicized. However, a recent increase in LSD use by high school and college students has been reported (Johnston, Bachman, & O'Malley, 1995). LSD may be a prime example of generational forgetting. Today's youth don't hear what an earlier generation heard—that LSD can cause bad trips and undesirable flashbacks.

At this point we have discussed a number of drugs and their effects. A summary of the main types of drugs we have studied is presented in figure 8.

Drug-Abuse Prevention and Education

Drug-abuse prevention is an admirable goal and the ideal way to prevent the damaging effects of drug abuse. However, decreasing substance abuse through prevention and education has been an elusive goal.

Prevention programs have focused on three goals: primary, secondary, and tertiary prevention, with the greatest emphasis being targeted at primary and tertiary prevention. **Primary prevention** *is prevention that attempts to stop people from taking drugs by helping them to not start.* Primary prevention programs are increasingly being initiated with elementary school children. The most recent primary prevention models are based on the belief that early prevention works best, especially through the influence of respected role models who advocate abstinence from drugs and through peer pressure (Pentz, 1993).

Secondary prevention *is an attempt to minimize the harm caused by drug use with a high-risk population or with a group that is involved in experimental or occasional use.* In high schools, secondary prevention often involves attempts to reduce alcohol or tobacco use. Recognizing that a majority of high school students drink at least occasionally, secondary prevention programs focus on the hazardous consequences of drinking and driving. Other secondary prevention programs include crisis counseling and drug-abuse counseling for individuals whose drug use has gone beyond experimental or occasional use.

Tertiary prevention *consists of treatment for people who abuse drugs.* Tertiary prevention programs include medical treatment, residential facilities, and rehabilitation.

Two factors stand out when the successful components of drug-abuse prevention are analyzed: intensive individualized attention and community-wide, multiagency collaboration (Dryfoos, 1990). Children who grow up in families in which they are given considerable nurturance and support are less likely to become drug abusers than are children who are neglected and not given adequate support and attention from their parents (Brook & others, 1990). When high-risk children or adolescents become attached to a responsible adult who gives them attention and responds to their needs, their risk status declines. In one successful substance-abuse program, a student assistance counselor was available full-time for individual counseling and referral for treatment.

The basic philosophy of community-wide programs is that a number of different programs have to be in place. The Midwestern Prevention Program developed by Mary Ann Pentz (1993) implemented a community-wide health promotion campaign that used local media, community education, and parent programs in concert with a substance-abuse curriculum in the schools. An evaluation of the program after 18 months and after 4 years in use revealed significantly lower rates of alcohol and marijuana use by adolescents than their counterparts in areas of the city where the program was not in operation.

At this point we have discussed a number of ideas about hypnosis and psychoactive drugs. A summary of these ideas is presented in concept table 2.

One glass of wine equals one can of beer in alcoholic content.

Cocaine is extracted from coca plants.

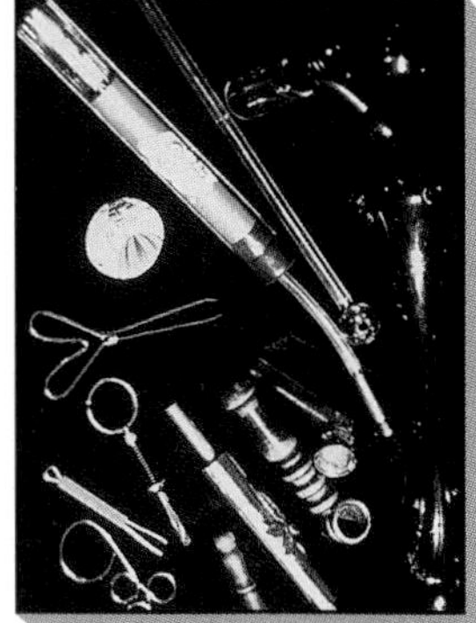

Cannabis paraphernalia, drug equipment or gadgets, is usually sold in "head shops" for use in smoking marijuana.

Drug classification	Medical uses	Short-term effects
Depressants		
Alcohol	Pain relief	Relaxation, depressed brain activity, slowed behavior, reduced inhibitions
Barbiturates	Sleeping pill	Relaxation, sleep
Tranquilizers	Anxiety reduction	Relaxation, slowed behavior
Opiates (narcotics)	Pain relief	Euphoric feelings, drowsiness, nausea
Stimulants		
Amphetamines	Weight control	Increased alertness, excitability; decreased fatigue, irritability
Cocaine	Local anesthetic	Increased alertness, excitability, euphoric feelings; decreased fatigue, irritability

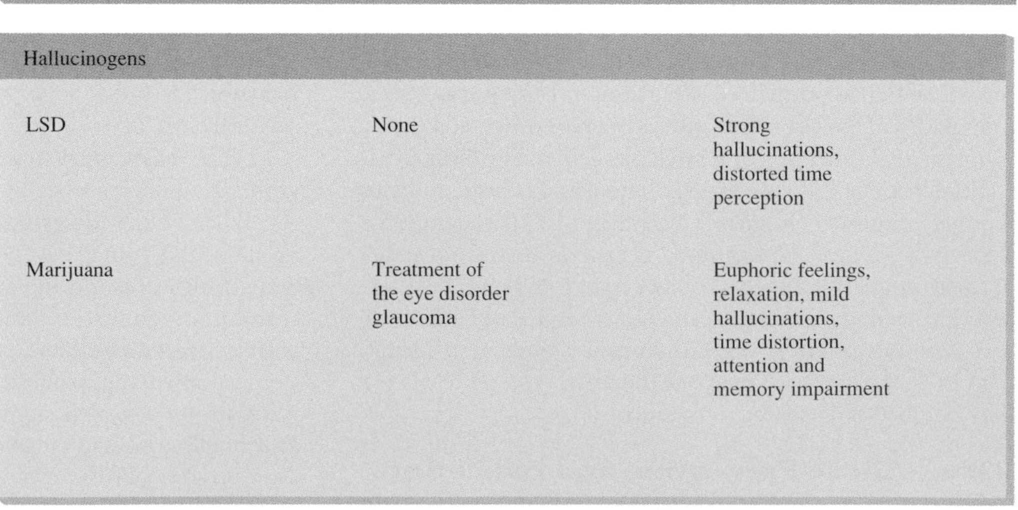

Drug classification	Medical uses	Short-term effects
Hallucinogens		
LSD	None	Strong hallucinations, distorted time perception
Marijuana	Treatment of the eye disorder glaucoma	Euphoric feelings, relaxation, mild hallucinations, time distortion, attention and memory impairment

FIGURE 8

Drugs—Their Use, Effects, and Addictive Characteristics

Overdose	Health risks	Risk of psychological dependence
Disorientation, loss of consciousness, even death at high blood-alcohol levels	Accidents, brain damage, liver disease, heart disease, ulcers, birth defects	Moderate
Breathing difficulty, coma, possible death	Accidents, coma, possible death	High
Breathing difficulty, coma, possible death	Accidents, coma, possible death	Low–moderate
Convulsions, coma, possible death	Accidents, infectious diseases such as AIDS	Very high
Extreme irritability, feelings of persecution, convulsions	Insomnia, hypertension, malnutrition, possible death	High
Extreme irritability, feelings of persecution, convulsions, cardiac arrest, possible death	Insomnia, hypertension, malnutrition, possible death	High
Severe mental disturbance, loss of contact with reality	Accidents	Very low
Fatigue, disoriented behavior	Accidents, respiratory disease	Low–moderate

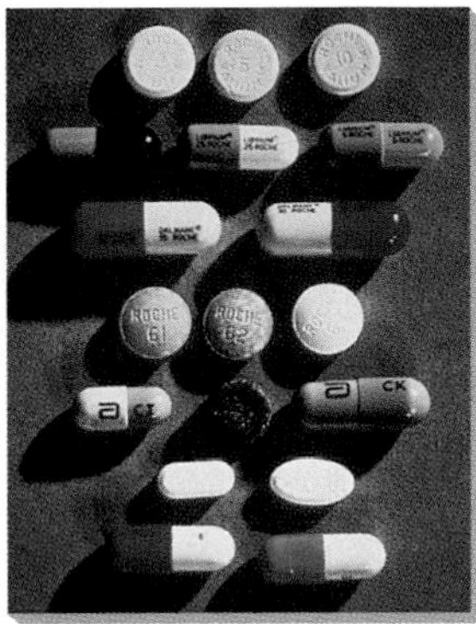

Tranquilizers are used for reducing anxiety and inducing relaxation.

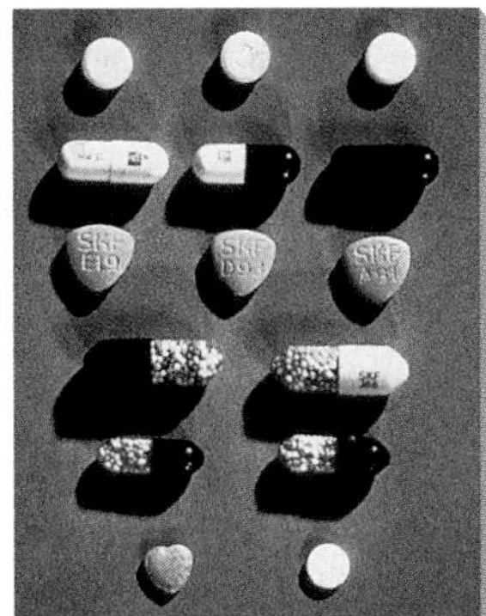

Amphetamines are stimulants used to increase alertness and energy.

Shown here is a private, illegal laboratory for manufacturing LSD.

Concept Table 2

Hypnosis and Psychoactive Drugs

Concept	Processes/Related Ideas	Characteristics/Description
Hypnosis	Its nature and history	Hypnosis is a psychological state of altered consciousness in which the subject is unusually receptive to suggestion. The history of hypnosis began with Friedrich Anton Mesmer and his belief in animal magnetism and moves to the present view of the hidden observer.
	Induction, common features, and individual differences	Hypnosis involves reducing distracting stimuli and making the subject comfortable, getting the individual to concentrate, and suggesting what is to be experienced in the hypnotic state. About 10 to 20 percent of the population is highly susceptible to hypnosis, about 10 percent cannot be hypnotized at all, and the remainder fall in between.
	Theories of hypnosis	There are two broad, competing frameworks. In the special process view, hypnotic behavior is qualitatively different. It is involuntary and dissociation among cognitive systems and amnesic barriers are believed to be involved. Special attention has been given to Hilgard's hidden observer perspective. The alternative nonstate view argues that hypnotic behavior is similar to other forms of social behavior. From this perspective, hypnotic behavior is purposeful, goal-directed action that is understood by focusing on the way subjects interpret their role and the way they try to present themselves.
	Applications	Hypnosis has been widely applied with mixed results to a variety of circumstances, including psychotherapy, medicine, dentistry, criminal trials, and sports.
Psychoactive Drugs	Their nature and uses	They act on the central nervous system to alter one's state of consciousness, modify perceptions, and alter mood. Psychoactive substances have been used since the beginning of recorded history for pleasure, utility, curiosity, and social reasons.
	Addiction	Tolerance for psychoactive drugs develops when a greater amount of the drug is needed to produce the same effect. Physical withdrawal is the physical need for a drug that is accompanied by unpleasant withdrawal symptoms when the drug is discontinued. Psychological dependence is the need to take a drug to cope with problems and stress. The disease model of addiction describes addictions as biologically based, lifelong diseases that involve a loss of control over behavior and require medical and/or spiritual treatment for recovery. Critics argue that the biological mechanisms of alcoholism have not been identified, alcoholism is not necessarily lifelong, that the disease model stigmatizes people with labels such as "addict" and "alcoholic," and that it advocates a rigid program of therapy. In the life-process model, addiction is not a disease but rather a habitual response and a source of gratification or security that can only be understood and treated in the context of social relationships and experience.

Concept	Processes/Related Ideas	Characteristics/Description
Psychoactive Drugs—(continued)	Alcohol	Alcohol is an extremely powerful drug, acting on the body primarily as a depressant. Drinking makes people less inhibited and impairs their judgment, motor skills, and intellectual functioning. With extreme intoxification, the drinker may lapse into a coma and even die. Effects of alcohol vary according to a number of factors. Alcohol is the most widely used drug in America and the third leading killer. A special concern is the high rate of alcohol consumption by high school and college students. People in many countries drink more than people in the United States. Alcoholism is a disorder that involves long-term, repeated, uncontrolled, compulsive, and excessive use of alcoholic beverages that impair the drinker's health and interpersonal relationships.
	Barbiturates and tranquilizers	Barbiturates are depressant drugs that induce sleep or reduce anxiety. Tranquilizers are depressant drugs that reduce anxiety and induce relaxation.
	Opiates	Opiates, which consist of opium and its derivatives, depress the central nervous system's activity. Both methadone and opiate antagonists have been used to treat heroin addicts with the results often not very encouraging.
	Stimulants	Stimulants are psychoactive drugs that increase central nervous system activity. The most widely used stimulants are caffeine, nicotine, amphetamines, and cocaine. Cocaine provides a euphoric rush that is followed by depression, lethargy, insomnia, and irritability. Cocaine can even trigger a heart attack, stroke, or brain seizure. Crack is an intensified form of cocaine and is believed to be one of the most addictive drugs. Treating cocaine addiction has not been very successful.
	Marijuana	Marijuana's psychological effects include a mixture of excitatory, depressive, and mildly hallucinatory characteristics, making the drug difficult to classify. Marijuana affects a number of neurotransmitters and hormones, and can cause impaired attention and memory.
	Hallucinogens	Hallucinogens are psychoactive drugs that modify a person's perceptual experiences and produce visual images that are not real. Hallucinogens are also called psychedelic drugs, which means mind altering. LSD, PCP, and mescaline are examples of hallucinogens. There has been a recent increase in use of LSD.
	Drug-abuse prevention and education	Three forms of prevention are: primary, secondary, and tertiary. Primary prevention is prevention that attempts to stop people from taking drugs by helping them not to start. Primary prevention programs are increasingly being used with elementary school children. The most recent primary prevention models are based on modeling and peer pressure and emphasize the importance of the media and role models. Secondary prevention is an attempt to minimize the harm caused by drug use with high-risk populations or with groups that are involved in experimental or occasional use. Tertiary prevention consists of treatment for people who have been affected by drug use. Two factors stand out when the successful components of drug abuse prevention are analyzed: intensive individualized attention and community-wide, multiagency collaboration.

Critical Thinking About Behavior

Critical Thinking as a Controlled Process

> *To be uncertain is to be uncomfortable, but to be certain is to be ridiculous.*
>
> **Chinese proverb**

As you have gathered by now, critical thinking can be a complex activity. How does the topic of consciousness relate to critical thinking? You learned in this chapter that human abilities allow us to function consciously at different levels of attention. The first distinction we discussed in this chapter emphasized the difference between automatic and controlled processes. In the early stages of learning an activity, we focus our attention. We concentrate hard to master the skills involved. As we become experienced and skilled in the activity, our actions become more automatic and we can reduce the conscious attention we pay to it. This process is much like being on "automatic pilot." We are free to direct our conscious attention elsewhere and still do a reasonable job at the task at hand.

Critical-thinking processes may be similar. We might struggle at first to learn the component skills, but then we can ease up. Or can we? It is fairly easy to be a lazy or uncritical thinker—one who engages in experience without analyzing it very much. We can invest very little energy in thinking and still "get by." We can stop paying attention in such concentrated ways and function on automatic pilot as a thinker. We can formulate opinions, express ideas, and even advocate action without necessarily demonstrating critical-thinking skills. We can give in to the forces that encourage us to think of our environment as unchallenging, stable, and certain.

How can we ward off these automatizing influences and maximize our critical-thinking skills? We can promote critical thinking as a controlled and purposeful process by adopting the following attitudes or skills:

- *Observe carefully.*
  Scrutinize the phenomenon or argument carefully so you understand it as completely as possible. Careful observation can help you identify some new features that eluded you at first glance.
- *Look for discrepancies.*
  It sometimes helps to ask, "What's missing from this picture?" Are there elements that should be present? How well do all the pieces fit together?
- *Expect that criticism will be appropriate.*
  Almost any argument will have a flaw or a special advantage.
  Almost any work of art or thought will have aspects to criticize.
  Almost any product or creation could be improved or refined.
- *Examine assumptions that underlie any position.*
  What would you have to believe in order to endorse the position?
  Are the values consistent with or discrepant from your own?
- *Adopt a skeptical stance.*
  If you are skeptical, it will be easier to ask meaningful questions about any phenomenon. Question even the obvious.
- *Tolerate uncertainty.*
  We might not be able to explain any behavior completely; but this doesn't justify withdrawing from critical analysis. Grappling with complex, incomplete ideas can be a very rewarding and adaptive activity.

If you notice that your critical-thinking experiences start to become easy or less frequent, be on your guard. Automatizing forces can rob you of some meaningful critical-thinking activities.

Overview

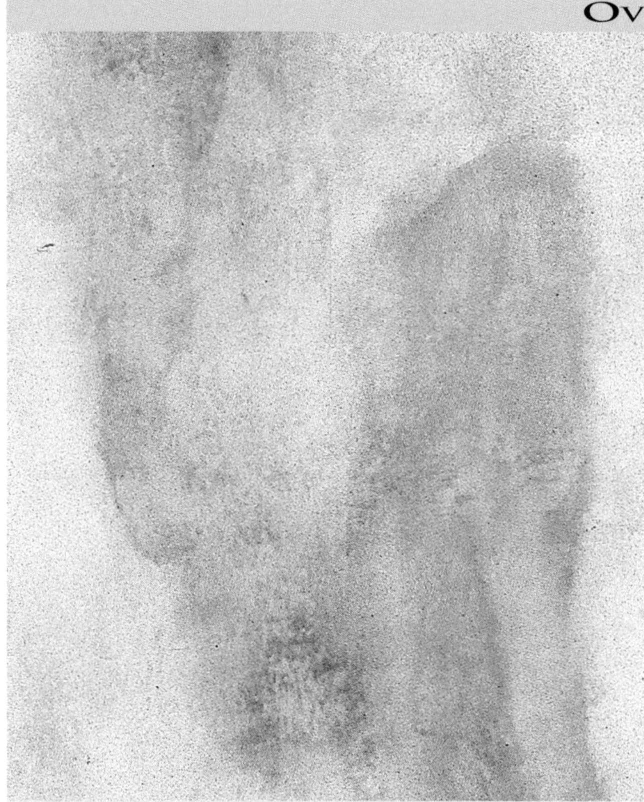

We began this chapter by discussing the nature of consciousness. Then we explored sleep and dreams, evaluating stages of sleep, sleep and circadian rhythms, why we sleep, the neural basis of sleep, sleep disorders, as well as how dreams are interpreted and a variety of other interesting questions about dreams. Our coverage of hypnosis focused on features of the hypnotic state, individual differences in hypnosis, theories of hypnosis, and applications of hypnosis. Our portrayal of psychoactive drugs included the uses of psychoactive drugs, addiction, alcohol, barbiturates and tranquilizers, opiates, stimulants, marijuana, hallucinogens, and drug-abuse prevention and education. Remember that you can obtain an overall summary of the chapter by again studying the concept tables on pages 150 and 160.

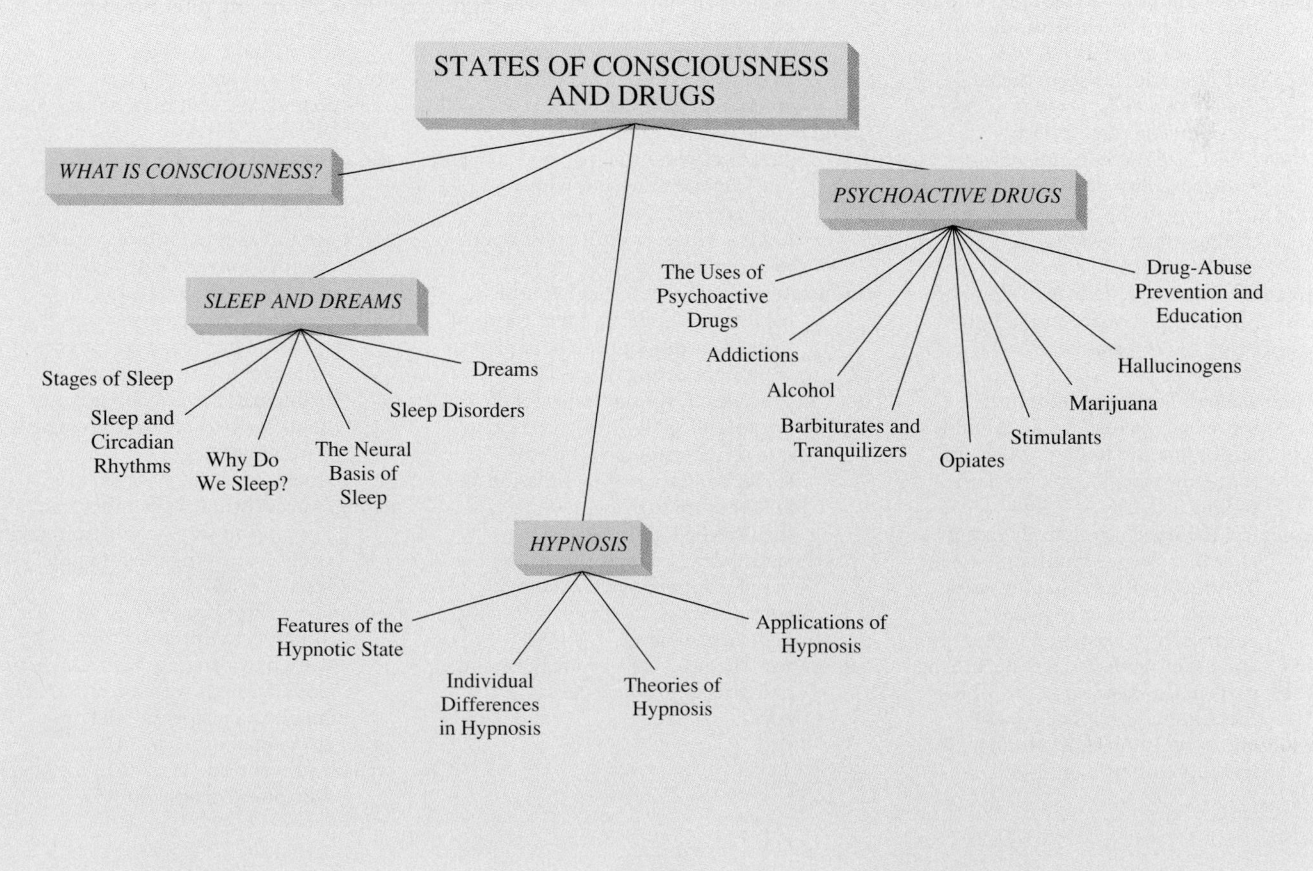

Key Terms

night terror Sudden arousal from sleep, with intense fear, usually accompanied by a number of physiological reactions. p. 137

consciousness Awareness of both external and internal stimuli or events. p. 138

stream of consciousness A continuous flow of changing sensations, images, thoughts, and feelings. p. 139

unconscious thought According to Freud, a reservoir of unacceptable wishes, feelings, and thoughts that we are not consciously aware of. p. 139

controlled processes The most alert states of consciousness, in which individuals actively focus their efforts toward a goal. p. 139

automatic processes Forms of consciousness that require minimal attention and do not interfere with other ongoing activities. p. 139

daydreaming A form of consciousness that involves a low level of conscious effort. p. 139

altered states of consciousness Mental states that noticeably differ from normal awareness. Drugs, meditation, fatigue, hypnosis, and sensory deprivation can produce altered states of consciousness. p. 139

alpha waves Brain waves that make up the EEG pattern of a person who is awake but relaxed. p. 142

sleep spindles Brief bursts of higher-frequency waves that periodically occur during stage 2 sleep. p. 142

delta waves Large, slow brain waves associated with deep sleep. p. 142

REM sleep A periodic, active stage of sleep during which dreaming occurs. p. 143

circadian rhythm A daily behavioral or physiological cycle, an example being the 24-hour sleep/wake cycle. p. 143

repair theory The theory that sleep restores, replenishes, and rebuilds our brains and bodies, which are somehow worn out by the day's waking activities. p. 144

ecological theory The relatively recent view that sleep is evolution based. This theory argues that the main purpose of sleep is to prevent animals from wasting their energy and harming themselves during the parts of the day or night to which they have not adapted. p. 145

insomnia A common sleep problem; the inability to sleep. p. 145

somnambulism The formal term for sleepwalking; somnambulism occurs during the deepest stages of sleep. p. 145

nightmare A frightening dream that awakens the sleeper from REM sleep. p. 145

narcolepsy The overpowering urge to fall asleep. p. 146

sleep apnea A sleep disorder in which the sleeper stops breathing because the windpipe fails to open or brain processes involved in respiration fail to work properly. p. 147

activation-synthesis view The view that dreams have no inherent meaning but, rather, reflect the brain's efforts to make sense out of or find meaning in the neural activity that takes place during REM sleep. In this view, the brain has considerable random activity during REM sleep, and dreams are an attempt to synthesize the chaos. p. 148

lucid dreaming Dreaming while knowing that one is dreaming. p. 148

hypnosis A psychological state of altered attention and awareness in which the individual is unusually receptive to suggestions. p. 149

special process theory A view that hypnotic behavior is different from nonhypnotic behavior, and that hypnotic responses are elicited by suggestion rather than being voluntary reactions. p. 151

hidden observer Hilgard's term for the part of a hypnotized person's mind that is aware of what is happening. This part remains a passive, or hidden, observer until called upon to comment. p. 151

nonstate view The view that hypnotic behavior is similar to other forms of social behavior and can be explained without resorting to special processes. Hypnotic behavior is purposeful, goal-directed action that is best understood by the way subjects interpret their situation and how they try to present themselves. p. 151

psychoactive drugs Drugs that act on the nervous system to alter states of consciousness, modify perceptions, and change moods. p. 152

tolerance The need for a greater amount of a drug to produce the same effect. p. 152

physical dependence The physical need for a drug that is accompanied by unpleasant withdrawal symptoms when the drug is discontinued. p. 152

psychological dependence The subjective feeling of craving and perceived need for a drug. p. 152

disease model of addiction The view that addictions are biologically based, lifelong diseases that involve a loss of control over behavior and require medical and/or spiritual treatment for recovery. p. 153

life-process model of addiction The view that addiction is not a disease but rather a habitual response and a source of gratification and security that can be understood only in the context of social relationships and experiences. p. 154

alcoholism A disorder that involves long-term, repeated, uncontrolled, compulsive, and excessive use of alcoholic beverages, impairing the drinker's health and interpersonal relationships. p. 154

barbiturates Depressant drugs, such as Nembutal and Seconal, that induce sleep or reduce anxiety. p. 155

tranquilizers Depressant drugs, such as Valium and Xanax, that reduce anxiety and induce relaxation. p. 156

opiates Opium and its derivatives; these depress the central nervous system's activity. p. 156

stimulants Psychoactive drugs that increase the central nervous system's activity. p. 156

crack An intensified form of cocaine; chips of pure cocaine that are usually smoked. p. 156

hallucinogens Psychoactive drugs that modify a person's perceptual experiences and produce hallucinatory visual images; hallucinogens are called psychedelic ("mind altering") drugs. p. 156

primary prevention Prevention that attempts to stop people from taking drugs by helping them to not start. p. 157

secondary prevention Prevention that attempts to minimize the harm caused by drug use with a high-risk population or with a group that is involved in experimental or occasional use. p. 157

tertiary prevention Treatment for people who abuse drugs. p. 157

Resources and Readings in Psychology

Addiction Research Foundation/Fondation de la recherche sur la toxomanie

33 Russell Street
Toronto ON M5S 2S1 Canada
416–595–6111
800–387–2916 (in Canada)

This foundation's information line offers a tape on drug and alcohol abuse. The staff will discuss substance-abuse issues. They maintain a reference library, an audiovisual desk, and a pharmacy, and they provide educational materials, including information on treatment programs. They have information available in English, French, Cantonese, Greek, Hindi, Italian, Mandarin, Polish, Portuguese, Punjabi, Spanish, and Urdu.

Alcoholics Anonymous World Services

475 Riverside Drive
New York, NY
212–878–3400

Alcoholics Anonymous (AA) provides support groups for individuals with drinking problems or other addictive behaviors. Most communities have local chapters of AA.

Alcoholism and Other Drug Problems (1996)

by James Royce and David Scratchley
New York: The Free Press

This book provides broad coverage of alcoholism and related drug problems. Drug prevention and intervention programs are evaluated.

Alliance for a Drug-Free Canada/Alliance pour un canada sans drogues

P.O. Box 355, Station A
Toronto ON M5W 1C5 Canada
416–730–4217
800–563–5000 (in Canada)

This group has resources and information available to help prevent drug use.

Association for the Study of Dreams

P.O. Box 1600
Vienna, VA 22183
703–242–8889

This association provides an international, interdisciplinary forum for furthering knowledge about dreams. Medical professionals, psychologists, educators, and students are welcomed as members. The group publishes a quarterly newsletter.

The Chemistry of Consciousness (1994)

by J. A. Hobson
Boston: Little, Brown

This book on the neurobiological basis of dreaming is written by one of the field's leading researchers.

Cocaine Helpline

800–COCAINE (262–2463)

This hot line is open 24 hours a day and is answered by former cocaine addicts. It refers cocaine users, including parents of adolescents who use cocaine, to treatment centers in many areas of the United States.

Concepts of Chemical Dependency (3rd ed., 1996)

by Harold Doweiko
Pacific Grove, CA: Brooks/Cole

This is an informative, up-to-date book on drug abuse and treatment. Topics include the scope of abuse, cocaine, marijuana, nicotine, the hidden faces of abuse, and addiction and the family.

Consciousness Explained (1991)

by Daniel Dennett
Boston: Little, Brown

This witty, intellectual book provides an in-depth look at contemporary thinking about the nature of consciousness. The author draws on the fields of psychology, philosophy, neuroscience, and artificial intelligence to portray how consciousness works. Dennett criticizes a number of simpleminded commonsense views of consciousness and explains how we feel sensations and have conscious experiences.

Encyclopedia of Sleep and Dreaming (1993)

edited by Mary Carskadon
New York: Macmillan

This book contains entries for virtually every imaginable aspect of sleep and dreaming, with contributions from a number of leading experts.

Handbook of Clinical Hypnosis (1993)

edited by Judith Rhue and colleagues
Washington, DC: American Psychological Association

This volume focuses on applications of hypnosis in clinical settings and provides contemporary coverage of a number of research issues.

Hypnosis: Questions and Answers (1986)

by B. Zilbergeld, M. Edelstein, and D. Araoz
New York: Norton

The authors queried eighty-five experts on hypnosis and asked them a wide array of questions about hypnosis.

Intoxification (1990)

by R. K. Siegel
New York: Pocket Books

This easy-to-read book tours the many drugs of intoxification and includes commentary on how people use drugs and what effects the drugs have on individuals.

Lucid Dreaming (1988)
by Stephen LaBerge
Los Angeles: Tarcher

If you want to try to increase your lucid dreaming, this book will tell you how. Easy-to-follow instructions are included, along with an examination of the nature of dreaming.

The Lucidity Institute
2555 Park Boulevard, #2
Palo Alto, CA 94306
800–GO–LUCID

This institute offers books, courses, and biofeedback devices for lucid dreaming.

National Clearinghouse for Alcohol and Drug Information
P.O. Box 2345
Rockville, MD 20847-2345
800–729–6686
800–662–HELP (4357)

This government information center refers individuals to programs that seek to prevent adolescents from using alcohol and drugs. It also provides videotapes, brochures, and other publications.

Our Dreaming Mind (1994)
by Robert Van de Castle
New York: Ballantine

This extensive volume delves into a number of provocative issues in dreaming, taking the reader on a tour of the dreaming mind that emphasizes psychoanalytic interpretations of dreaming.

Rational Recovery Systems
P.O. Box 800
Lotus, CA 95651
916–621–4374

This organization uses the techniques of Albert Ellis' rational-emotive therapy to teach individuals how to eliminate their addictive behavior. An increasing number of cities have Rational Recovery programs.

Sleep/Wake Disorders Canada/Affections du sommeil/eveil Canada
3089 Bathurst Street, Suite 304
Toronto ON M6A 2A4 Canada
416–787–5374
800–387–9253 (in Canada)

Sleep/Wake Disorders Canada is a national self-help registered charity dedicated to helping the thousands of Canadians suffering from sleep/wake disorders. There are chapters across the country, and members work to improve the quality of life, alertness, and productivity of persons with sleep/wake disorders. SWDC offers informational brochures, articles, booklets, and videos and publishes a quarterly newsletter, *Good/Night Good/Day.*

The Truth About Addiction and Recovery (1991)
by Stanton Peele and Archie Brodsky
New York: Simon & Schuster

Drawing on recent research and detailed case studies, the authors conclude that addictions—whether to food, cigarettes, alcohol, or drugs—are not diseases and are not necessarily lifelong problems. Instead of twelve-step treatment programs like AA, Peele and Brodsky recommend their "life-process program," which emphasizes coping with stress and achieving one's goals.

CHAPTER

LRN

Learning

RAPHAEL 1509–1511
The School of Athens, detail

Learning

Chapter Outline

Chapter Boxes

We are born capable of learning.

—Jean-Jacques Rousseau

To learn is a natural pleasure.

—**Aristotle**

Images of Psychology

"Sesame Street" Around the World

Much of what we do results from what we have *learned*. If you had grown up in another part of the world, you would speak a different language, would like different foods and clothing, and would behave in ways characteristic of that culture. Why? Because the content of your *learning* experiences in that culture would have been different.

One way we learn is by watching what other people do and say. This kind of learning is called *observational learning*. Observational learning has changed dramatically in the twentieth century because of the introduction and pervasive use of television, which has touched virtually every American's life. Television has been called a lot of names, not all of them good—the "one-eyed monster" and the "boob tube," for example. Television has been accused of interfering with children's learning; critics say television lures children from schoolwork and books, and makes them passive learners. Rarely does television require active responses from its observers.

Television can also contribute to children's learning. For example, it can introduce children to worlds that are different from the one they live in. "Sesame Street" was specifically designed to improve children's cognitive and social skills (Green, 1995; Wright, 1995). Almost half of America's 2- to 5-year-olds watch it regularly (Condry, 1989). Highly successful at teaching kids, "Sesame Street" uses fast-paced action, sound effects, music, and humorous characters to grab the attention of its young audience. With their eyes "glued" to the screen, young children learn basic academic skills like letter and number recognition.

When "Sesame Street" first appeared in 1969, its creators had no idea that this "street" would lead to locations as distant as Kuwait, Israel, Latin America, and the Philippines. Since "Sesame Street" first aired in the United States, it has been televised in eighty-four countries and thirteen foreign-language versions have been produced. "Barrio Sesamo" is shown in seventeen South and Central American countries, as well as Puerto Rico. It emphasizes learning about the diversity of cultures and lifestyles in South America. "Rechov Sumsum" is shown in Israel; it especially encourages children to learn how people from different ethnic and religious backgrounds can live in harmony. When children in the Netherlands watch "Sesamstraat," they learn about the concept of school, and a 7-foot-tall blue bird named Pino is always eager to learn.

In Spain, children watch Barrio Sesamo—the Spanish version of Sesame Street. The bakery is Barrio Sesamo's central meeting place. The residents include two full-size puppets. Espinete, a special friend of the children, is a hedgehog who tries to get the cast members to play games whenever possible. Don Pimpon (shown above) is a shaggy old codger, at times a bit absent-minded, who has traveled extensively and entertains with stories of his adventures.

Preview

The ability to learn is a remarkable and enchanting gift. When we think about learning, we might come up with an image of someone sitting at a desk and studying a book. Studying does involve learning, but learning is much more than just studying. You will see in this chapter that learning applies to many domains of acquiring new behaviors and skills, as well as knowledge. Our coverage of learning begins with an evaluation of what learning is, followed by an exploration of three main forms of learning: classical conditioning, operant conditioning, and observational learning. Next, we will discuss the increased attention being given to cognitive factors in learning and conclude with the roles that biological and cultural factors play in learning.

What Is Learning?

In learning how to use a computer, you might make some mistakes along the way, but at some point you will get the knack of how to use it. You will change from being someone who could not operate a computer to being one who can. Learning anything new involves change. Once you have learned to use a computer, the skill usually does not leave you. Once you learn how to drive a car, you do not have to go through the process again at a later time. Learning involves a relatively permanent influence on behavior. You learned how to use a computer through experience with the machine. Through experience you also learned that you have to study to do well on a test, that when you go to a rock concert there is usually a warm-up act, and that a field goal in American football scores three points. Putting these pieces together, we arrive at a definition of **learning:** *a relatively permanent change in behavior that occurs through experience.*

Psychologists explain our many experiences with a few basic learning processes. We respond to things that happen to us, we act and experience consequences for our behavior, and we observe what others say and do. These three aspects of experiences form the three main types of learning we will study in this chapter—classical conditioning (responding), operant conditioning (acting), and observational learning (observing). As we study the nature of learning, you will discover that early approaches investigated the way experience and behavior are connected without referring to cognitive or mental processes. In recent years, cognitive processes have assumed a more important role in learning. We will discuss more recent cognitive approaches to learning later in the chapter, but first we will examine classical conditioning.

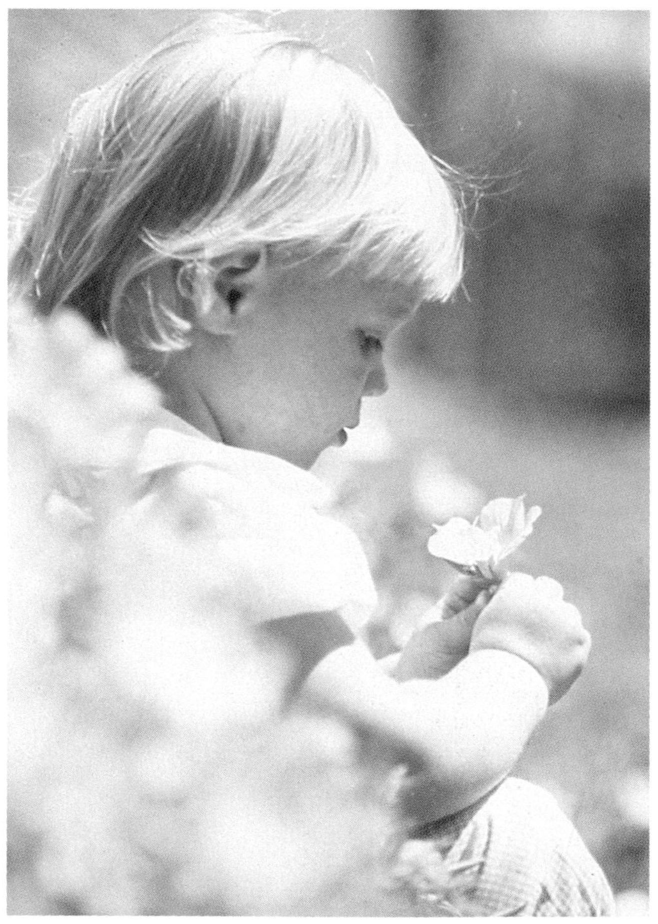

If a bee stings this young girl while she is holding a pink flower, how would classical conditioning explain her panic at the sight of pink flowers in the future?

Classical Conditioning

It is a nice spring day. A father takes his baby out for a walk. The baby reaches over to touch a pink flower and is badly stung by the bumblebee sitting on the petals. The next day, the baby's mother brings home some pink flowers. She removes a flower from the arrangement and takes it over for her baby to smell. The baby cries loudly as soon as she sees the pink flower. The baby's panic at the sight of the pink flower illustrates the learning process of **classical**

conditioning, *in which a neutral stimulus becomes associated with a meaningful stimulus and acquires the capacity to elicit a similar response.*

Pavlovian Conditioning

In the early 1900s, the Russian physiologist Ivan Pavlov investigated the way the body digests food. As part of his experiments, he routinely placed meat powder in a dog's mouth, causing the dog to salivate. Pavlov began to notice that the meat powder was not the only stimulus that caused the dog to salivate. The dog would salivate in response to a number of stimuli associated with the food, such as the sight of the food dish, the sight of the individual who brought the food into the room, and the sound of the door closing when the food arrived. Pavlov recognized that the dog's association of these sights and sounds with the food was an important type of learning, which came to be called classical conditioning.

Pavlov wanted to know *why* the dog salivated to various sights and sounds before eating the meat powder. He observed that the dog's behavior included both learned and unlearned components. The "unlearned" part of classical conditioning is based on the fact that some stimuli automatically produce certain responses apart from any prior learning; in other words they are inborn or innate. **Reflexes** *are automatic stimulus-response connections.* They include salivation in response to food, nausea in response to bad food, shivering in response to low temperature, coughing in response to the throat being clogged, pupil constriction in response to light, and withdrawal in response to blows or burns. An **unconditioned stimulus (US)** *is a stimulus that produces a response without prior learning; food was the US in Pavlov's experiments.* An **unconditioned response (UR)** *is an unlearned response that is automatically elicited by the US.* In Pavlov's experiments, the saliva that flowed from the dog's mouth in response to food was the UR. In the case of the baby and the flower, the baby's learning and experience did not cause her to cry when the bee stung her. Her crying was unlearned and occurred automatically. The bee's sting was the US and the crying was the UR.

In classical conditioning, the **conditioned stimulus (CS)** *is a previously neutral stimulus that eventually elicits the conditioned response after being associated with the unconditioned stimulus.* The **conditioned response (CR)** *is the learned response to the conditioned stimulus that occurs after CS-US pairing* (Pavlov, 1927). In studying a dog's response to various stimuli associated with meat powder, Pavlov rang a bell before giving meat powder to the dog. Until then, ringing the bell did not have a particular effect on the dog, except perhaps to wake the dog from a nap. The bell was a neutral stimulus. But the dog began to associate the sound of the bell with the food and salivated when it heard the bell. The bell had become a conditioned (learned) stimulus (CS) and the salivation a conditioned response (CR). Before conditioning (or learning), the bell and the food were not related. After their association, the conditioned stimulus (the bell) produced a conditioned response (salivation). For the unhappy baby, the flower was the baby's bell, or CS, crying was the CR after the sting (US) and the flower (CS) were paired. Figure 1 shows Pavlov's laboratory setting for studying classical conditioning and Pavlov demonstrating the procedure of classical conditioning. A summary of how classical conditioning works is shown in figure 2.

The interval between the CS and the US is one of the most important aspects of classical conditioning (DeCola & Fanselow, 1995). It is important because it defines the degree of association or *contiguity* of the stimuli. Conditioned responses develop when the interval between the CS and US is very short, as in a matter of seconds. In many instances optimal spacing is a fraction of a second (Kimble, 1961).

Generalization, Discrimination, and Extinction

After a time Pavlov found that the dog also responded by salivating to other sounds, such as a whistle. The more bell-like the noise, the stronger the dog's response. Similarly, the baby cried not only at the sight of pink flowers, but also at the sight of red and orange flowers. **Generalization** *in classical conditioning is the tendency of a new stimulus that is similar to the original conditioned stimulus to produce a response that is similar to the conditioned response.*

Stimulus generalization is not always beneficial. For example, the cat who generalizes from a minnow to a piranha has a major problem; therefore it is important to discriminate between stimuli. **Discrimination** *in classical conditioning is the process of learning to respond to certain stimuli and not to respond to others.* To produce discrimination, Pavlov gave food to the dog only after ringing the bell and not after any other sounds. In this way, the dog learned to distinguish between the bell and other sounds. Similarly, the baby did not cry at the sight of blue flowers, thus discriminating between them and pink flowers.

Pavlov rang the bell repeatedly in a single session and did not give the dog any food. Eventually the dog stopped salivating. This result is **extinction,** *which in classical conditioning is the weakening of the conditioned response in the absence of the unconditioned stimulus.* Without continued association with the unconditioned stimulus (US), the conditioned stimulus (CS) loses its power to elicit the conditioned response (CR). Over time, after her bee sting, the baby encountered many pink flowers and was not stung by a bee. Consequently, her fear of pink flowers subsided and eventually disappeared. The pink flower (CS) lost its capacity to elicit fear (CR) when the flower was no longer associated with bee stings (US) and the pain and fear they cause (UR).

Extinction is not always the end of the conditioned response. The day after Pavlov extinguished the conditioned salivation at the sound of a bell, he took the dog to the laboratory and rang the bell, still not giving the dog any

FIGURE 1

Pavlov's Experimentation
(*a*) Surgical preparation for studying the salivary reflex: when the dog salivated, the saliva collected in a glass funnel attached to the dog's cheek. This way the strength of the salivary response could be measured precisely. (*b*) Shown here is Pavlov's experimental apparatus used to examine classical conditioning. (*c*) Pavlov (the white-bearded gentleman in the center) is shown demonstrating the nature of classical conditioning to students at the Military Medical Academy in the Soviet Union.

meat powder. The dog salivated, indicating that an extinguished response can spontaneously recur. **Spontaneous recovery** *is the process in classical conditioning by which a conditioned response can recur after a time delay without further conditioning.* In the case of the baby, even though she saw many pink flowers after her first painful encounter and was not "stung" by them, she showed some signs of fear from time to time. Over time her conditioned fear (CR) to pink flowers (CS) diminished; she showed less tendency to recover her fear of pink flowers spontaneously, especially since she did not experience further painful stings (US). Figure 3 shows the sequence of acquisition, extinction, and spontaneous recovery. Spontaneous recovery can occur several times, but as long as the conditioned stimulus is presented alone, spontaneous recovery becomes weaker and eventually ceases to occur.

How Classical Conditioning Works: Pavlov and the Contemporary Perspective

Stimulus substitution *was Pavlov's theory of how classical conditioning works; it states that the nervous system is structured in such a way that the CS and US bond together and eventually the CS substitutes for the US.* However, if the CS substitutes for the US, the two stimuli should produce similar responses. This does not always happen. Using a

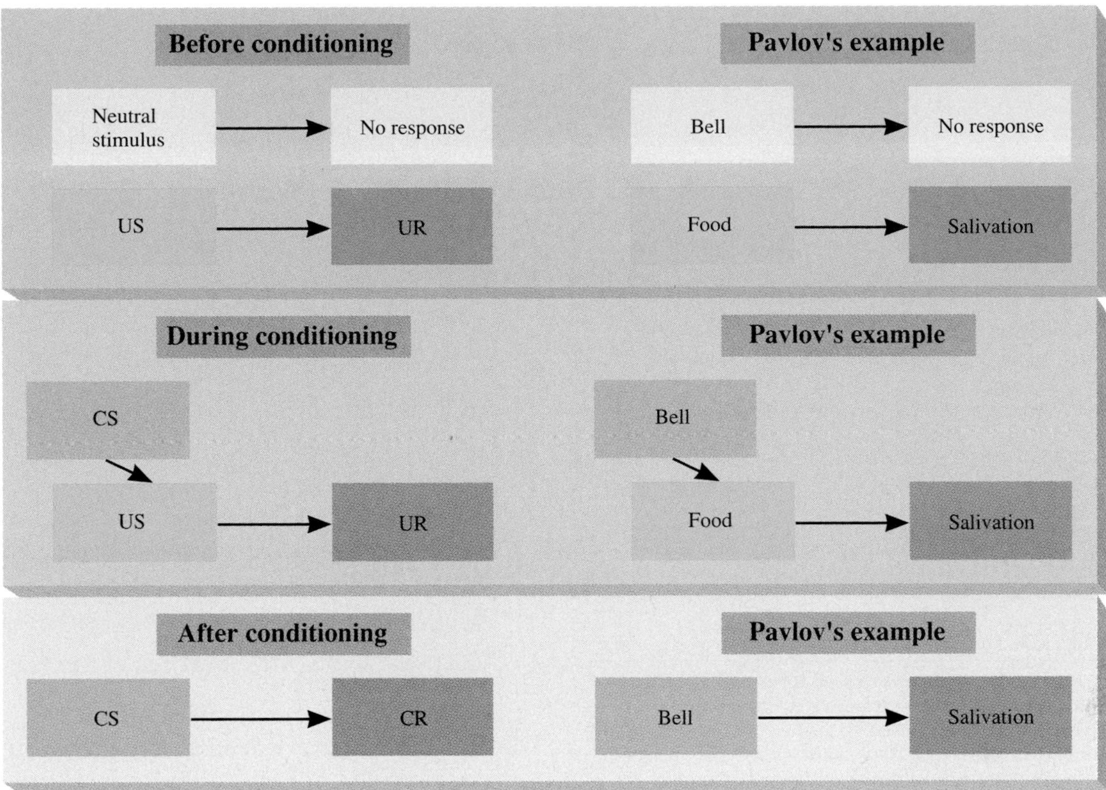

FIGURE 2

Classical Conditioning Procedure
At the start of conditioning, the US will evoke the UR, but the CS does not have this capacity. During conditioning, the CS and US are associated so that the CS comes to elicit the response. The key learning ingredient is the association of the US and CS.

shock as a US often elicits flinching and jumping, whereas a light (CS) paired with a shock may cause the organism to be immobile, for example.

Information theory *is one contemporary explanation of why classical conditioning works; it stresses that the key to understanding classical conditioning focuses on the information an organism gets from the situation.* Some years ago, E. C. Tolman (1932) said the information value of the CS is important in telling the organism what will follow. In Tolman's words, the organism uses the CS as a sign or expectation that a US will follow. Tolman's belief that the information the CS provides is the key to understanding classical conditioning was a forerunner of contemporary thinking.

In one contemporary view of classical conditioning, an organism is seen as an information seeker using logical and perceptual relations among events, along with preconceptions, to form a representation of the world (Rescorla, 1988, 1996). The contemporary view still recognizes contiguity between the CS and US as important in classical conditioning, but it emphasizes that what is important about the CS-US connection is the information the stimuli give the organism (Kohn & Kalat, 1995). A classic experiment conducted by Leon Kamin (1968) illustrates the importance of an organism's history and the information provided by a conditioned stimulus in classical conditioning. A rat was conditioned by repeatedly pairing a tone (CS) and a shock (US), until the tone alone produced a strong conditioned response (fear). The tone continued to be paired with the shock, but a light (a second CS) was turned on each time the tone was sounded. Even though the light (a CS) and the shock (US) were repeatedly paired, the rat showed no conditioning to the light. The light by itself produced no CR. Conditioning to the light was blocked, almost as if the rat had not attended to it. The rat apparently used the tone as a signal to predict that a shock would be forthcoming; it did not need to learn information about the light's pairing with the shock, because that information was redundant with the information already learned in the pairing of the tone and the shock. In this experiment, conditioning was governed not by the contiguity of the CS and US but, rather, by the rat's history and the information it received. Contemporary classical conditioning researchers are exploring further the role of information in an organism's learning (Domjan, 1996; Fanselow, DeCola, & Young, 1993).

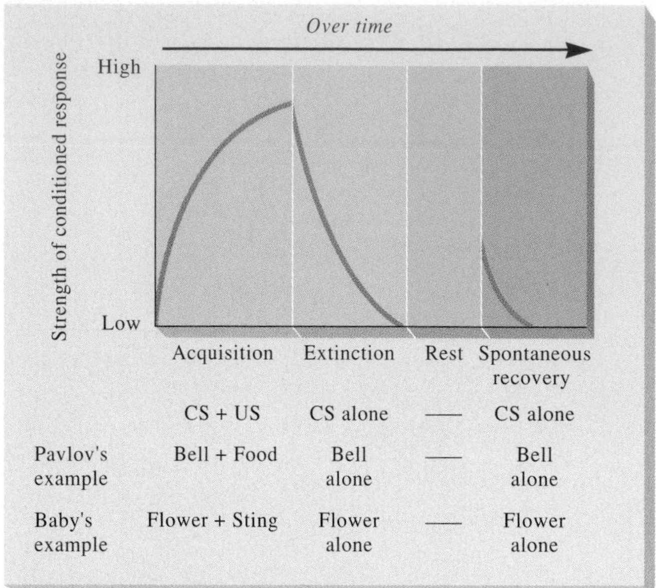

FIGURE 3

The Strength of a Classically Conditioned Response During Acquisition, Extinction, and Spontaneous Recovery
During acquisition the conditioned stimulus and unconditioned stimulus are associated. As seen in the graph, when this occurs, the strength of the conditioned response increases. During extinction the conditioned stimulus is presented alone, and, as can be seen, this results in a decrease of the conditioned response. After a rest period, spontaneous recovery appears, although the strength of the conditioned response is not nearly as great at this point as it was after a number of CS-US pairings. When the CS is presented alone again after spontaneous recovery, the response is extinguished rapidly.

You will note that their ability to comprehend, assess and process information increases dramatically when Professor Podhertz throws in the cat.

Classical Conditioning in Humans

Since Pavlov's experiments, individuals have been conditioned to respond to the sound of a buzzer, a glimpse of light, or the touch of a hand. Classical conditioning has a great deal of survival value for the individual (Kimmel, 1989; Vernoy, 1995). Because of classical conditioning, we jerk our hands away before they are burned by fire. Classical conditioning also is at work when a tranquil scene—such as an empty beach with waves lapping onto the sand—is described and the harried executive relaxes as if she were actually lying on that beach.

Phobias *are irrational fears.* Classical conditioning provides an explanation of these and other fears. The famous behaviorist John Watson conducted an investigation to demonstrate classical conditioning's role in phobias. A little boy named Albert was shown a white laboratory rat to see if he was afraid of it. He was not. As Albert played with the rat a loud noise was sounded behind his head. As you might imagine, the noise caused little Albert to cry. After only seven pairings of the loud noise with the white rat, Albert began to fear the rat even when the noise was not sounded. Albert's fear was generalized to a rabbit, a dog, and a sealskin coat (see figure 4). Today we could not ethically conduct such an experiment. Especially noteworthy is the fact that Watson and his associate (Watson & Raynor, 1920) did not remove Albert's fear of rats, so presumably this phobia remained with him after the experiment. Many of our fears—fear of the dentist after a painful experience, fear of driving after having been in an automobile accident, fear of dogs after having been bitten, for example—can be learned through classical conditioning.

If we can produce fears by classical conditioning, we should be able to eliminate them using conditioning procedures. **Counterconditioning** *is a classical conditioning procedure for weakening a CR by associating the fear-provoking stimulus with a new response incompatible with the fear.* Though Watson did not eliminate little Albert's fear of white rats, an associate of Watson's, Mary Cover Jones (1924), did eliminate the fears of a 3-year-old boy named Peter. Peter had many of the same fears as Albert; however, Peter's fears were not produced by Jones. Among Peter's fears were white rats, fur coats, frogs, fish, and mechanical toys. To eliminate these fears, a rabbit was brought into Peter's view but kept far enough away that it would not upset him. At the same time the rabbit was brought into view, Peter was fed crackers and milk. On each successive day the rabbit was moved closer to Peter as he ate crackers and milk. Eventually Peter reached the point where he would eat the food with one hand and pet the rabbit with the other.

Some of the behaviors we associate with health problems or mental disorders can involve classical conditioning. Certain physical complaints—asthma, headaches,

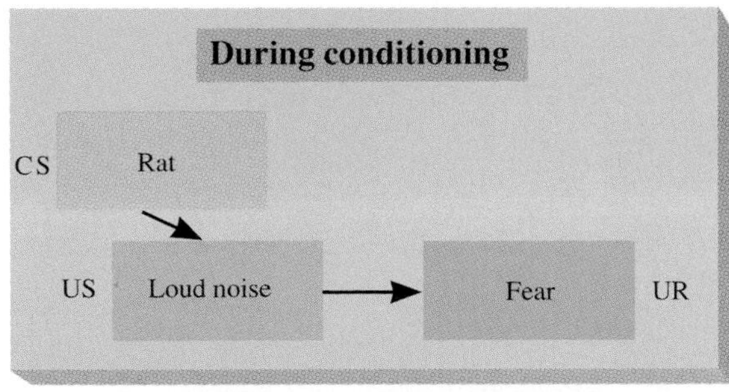

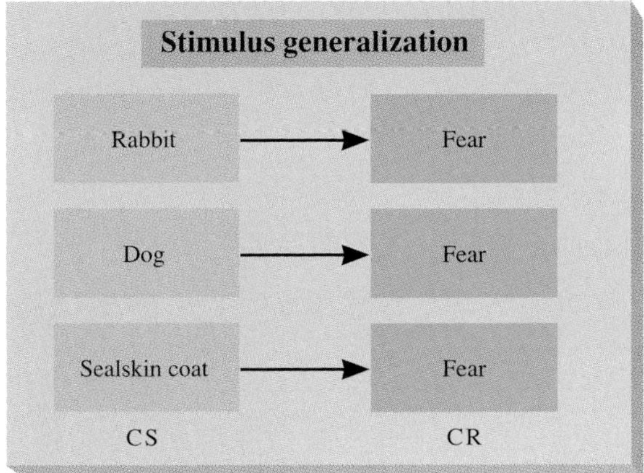

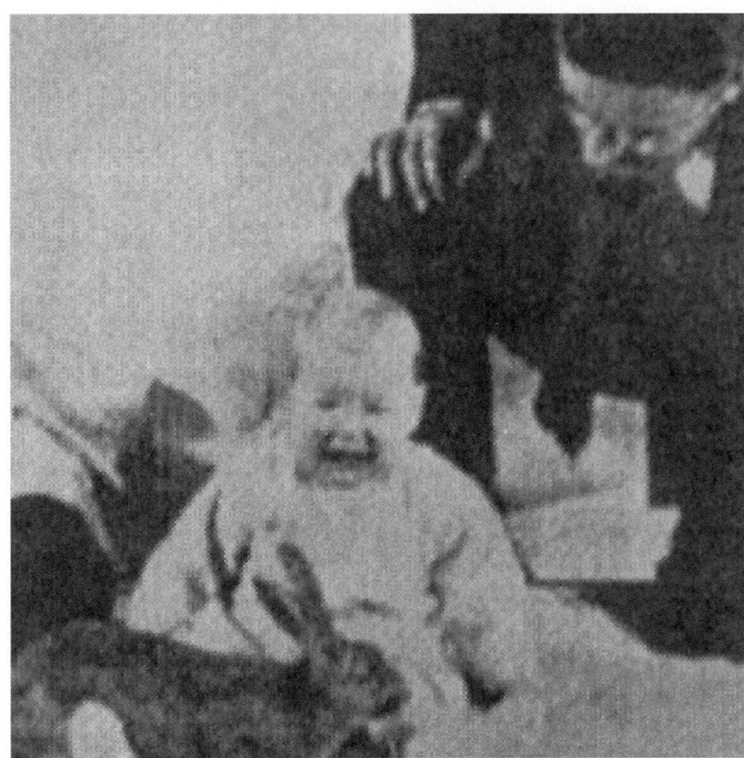

FIGURE 4

Little Albert's Generalized Fear
In 1920, 9-month-old little Albert was conditioned to fear a white rat by pairing the rat with a loud noise. When little Albert was subsequently placed with other stimuli similar to the white rat, such as the rabbit shown here with little Albert, he was afraid of them too. This illustrates the principle of stimulus generalization in classical conditioning.

ulcers, and high blood pressure, for example—may partly be the products of classical conditioning. We usually say that such health problems are caused by stress, but often what happened is that certain stimuli, such as a boss' critical attitude or a wife's threat of divorce, are conditioned stimuli for physiological responses. Over time, the frequent presence of the physiological responses may produce a health problem or disorder. A boss' persistent criticism may cause an employee to develop muscle tension, headaches, or high blood pressure. Anything associated with the boss, such as work itself, can then trigger stress in the employee (see figure 5).

Classical conditioning is not restricted to unpleasant emotions. Among the things in our life that produce pleasure because they have become conditioned might be the sight of a rainbow, a sunny day, or a favorite song. If you have a positive romantic experience, the location where that experience took place can become a conditioned stimulus. This is the result of the pairing of a place (CS) with the event (US). Sometimes, though, classical conditioning involves an experience that is both pleasant and deviant from the norm. Consider a fetishist who becomes sexually aroused by the sight and touch of certain clothing, such as undergarments or shoes. The fetish may have developed when the fetish object (undergarment, shoe) was associated with sexual arousal, especially when the individual was young. The fetish object becomes a conditioned stimulus that can produce sexual arousal by itself (Chance, 1979).

Evaluation of Classical Conditioning

Pavlov described learning in terms of classical conditioning. While classical conditioning helps us to learn about our environment, we learn about our world in other ways, too. Classical conditioning describes the organism as *responding* to the environment, a view that fails to capture the active nature of the organism and its influence on the environment. Next, we study a major form of learning that places more emphasis on the organism's *activity* in the environment—operant conditioning.

Before turning to that discussion, however, let's review the main themes of classical conditioning. Concept table 1 will help you with this review and will provide information about the basic nature of learning.

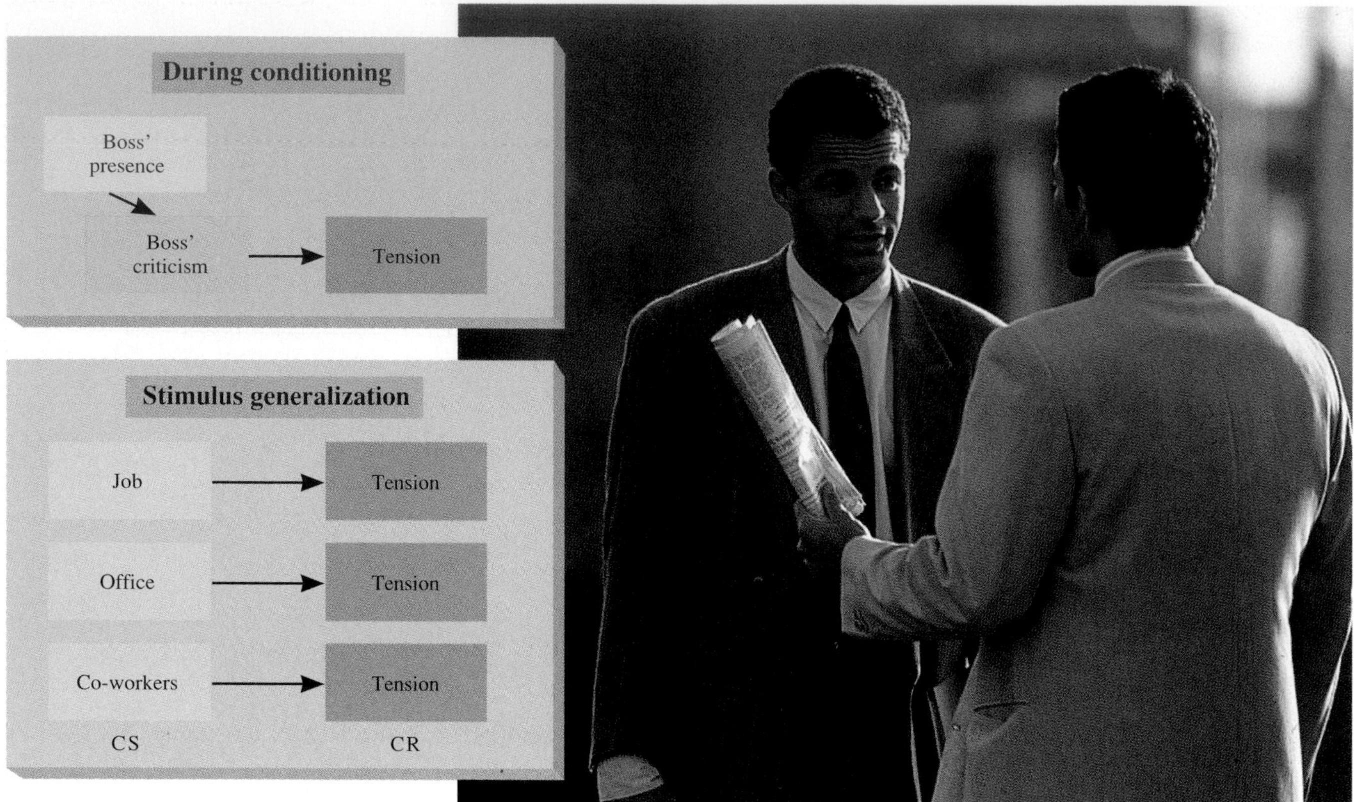

FIGURE 5

Classical Conditioning: Boss' Criticism and High Blood Pressure

Operant Conditioning

Classical conditioning excels at explaining how neutral stimuli become associated with unlearned, involuntary responses, but it might not be as effective in explaining voluntary behaviors, such as studying hard for a test, playing slot machines in Las Vegas, or teaching a pigeon to play Ping-Pong. Operant conditioning is usually better than classical conditioning at explaining *voluntary* behavior. The concept of operant conditioning was developed by the American psychologist B. F. Skinner (1938). **Operant conditioning** *(or instrumental conditioning) is a form of learning in which the consequences of behavior produce changes in the probability of the behavior's occurrence.* Skinner chose the term *operant* to describe the behavior of the organism—the behavior operates on the environment, and the environment in turn operates on the behavior. The consequences are *contingent,* or dependent, on the organism's behavior. For example, a simple operant might be pressing a lever that leads to the delivery of food; the delivery of food is contingent on pressing the lever.

We have mentioned one main difference between classical and operant conditioning—that classical conditioning is better at explaining involuntary responding, while operant conditioning is better at explaining voluntary responding. A second difference is that the stimuli that govern behavior in classical conditioning precede the behavior; the stimuli that govern behavior in operant conditioning *follow* the behavior.

Thorndike's Law of Effect

Although B. F. Skinner has emerged as the primary figure in operant conditioning, E. L. Thorndike's experiments established the power of consequences in determining voluntary behavior. At about the same time Ivan Pavlov was conducting classical conditioning experiments with salivating dogs, American psychologist E. L. Thorndike was studying cats in puzzle boxes. Thorndike put a hungry cat inside a box and a piece of fish outside. To escape from the box, the cat had to learn how to open the latch inside the box. At first the cat made a number of ineffective responses. It clawed or bit at the bars and thrust its paw through the openings. Eventually the cat accidentally stepped on the treadle that released the door bolt. When the cat returned to the box, it went through the same random activity until it stepped on the treadle once more. On subsequent trials, the cat made fewer and fewer random movements, until it immediately clawed the treadle to

Concept Table 1

The Nature of Learning and Classical Conditioning

Concept	Processes/Related Ideas	Characteristics/Description
Learning	Its nature	Learning is a relatively permanent change in behavior due to experience. How we respond to the environment (classical conditioning), how we act in the environment (operant conditioning), and how we observe the environment (observational learning) are the most important ways in which we experience. Early approaches emphasized connections between environment and behavior; many contemporary approaches stress that cognitive factors mediate environment-behavior connections.
Classical Conditioning	The basic features	Pavlov discovered that an organism learns the association between an unconditioned stimulus (US) and a conditioned stimulus (CS). The US automatically produces the UR (unconditioned response). After conditioning (CS-US pairing), the CS elicits the CR (conditioned response) by itself. Generalization, discrimination, and extinction also are involved.
	How classical conditioning works: Pavlov and the contemporary perspective	Pavlov explained classical conditioning in terms of stimulus substitution but one modern explanation is based on information theory.
	Classical conditioning in humans	Classical conditioning has survival value for humans, as when we develop a fear of hazardous conditions. Irrational fears are explained by classical conditioning. Counterconditioning has been used to eliminate fears.
	Evaluation of classical conditioning	Classical conditioning is important in explaining the way learning in animals occurs. It is not the only way humans learn and fails to capture the active nature of an organism in the environment.

open the door (see figure 6). The **law of effect,** *developed by Thorndike, states that behaviors followed by positive outcomes are strengthened, whereas behaviors followed by negative outcomes are weakened.*

The key question for Thorndike was how the correct stimulus-response bond strengthens and eventually dominates incorrect stimulus-response bonds. According to Thorndike, the correct S-R association strengthens and the incorrect association weakens because of the *consequences* of the organism's actions. Thorndike's view is called *S-R theory* because the organism's behavior is due to a connection between a stimulus and a response. As we see next, Skinner's operant conditioning approach expanded Thorndike's basic ideas.

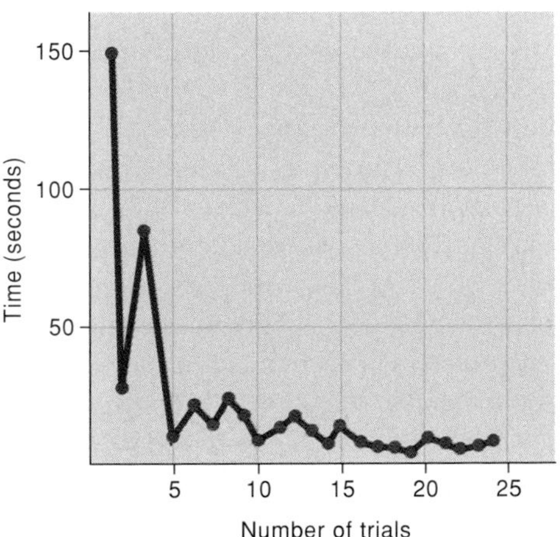

FIGURE 6

Learning Curve of One Cat's Escape Time
This learning curve shows the time required by one cat to escape from the puzzle box on 24 separate trials. Notice how the cat learned to escape much more quickly after about 5 trials.

Skinner's Operant Conditioning

Earlier we indicated that Skinner describes operant conditioning as a form of learning in which the consequences of behavior lead to changes in the probability of that behavior's occurrence. The consequences—rewards or

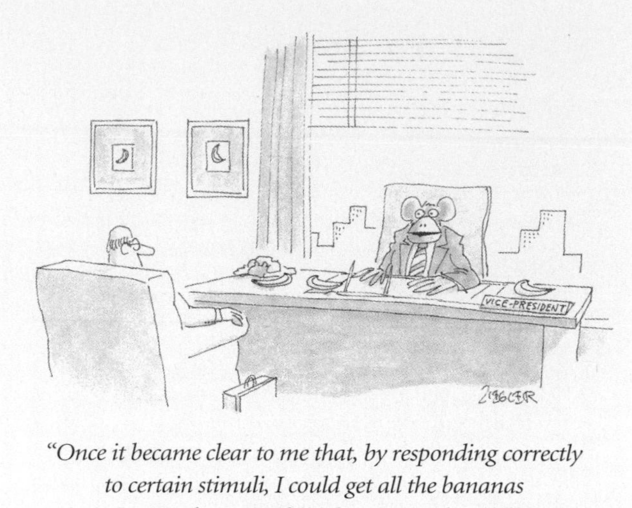

"Once it became clear to me that, by responding correctly to certain stimuli, I could get all the bananas I wanted, getting this job was a pushover."

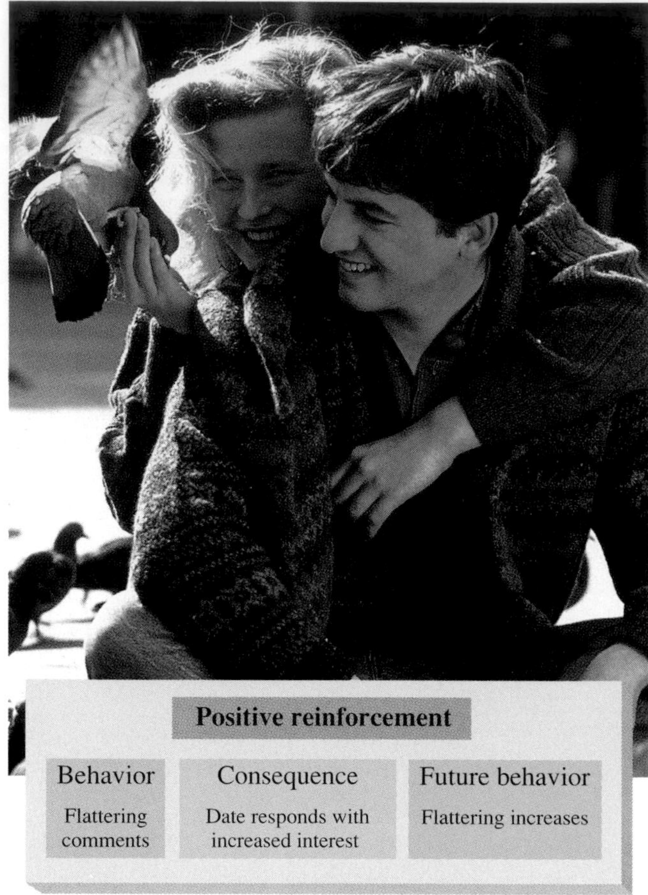

Positive reinforcement
Behavior
Flattering comments
Consequence
Date responds with increased interest
Future behavior
Flattering increases

FIGURE 7

Positive Reinforcement
In positive reinforcement, the frequency of a response increases because it is followed by a stimulus. For example, in this stimulus situation, a male's flattering comments to a female have positive consequences, increasing the male's chances of getting to know the female better.

punishments—are contingent on the organism's behavior. More needs to be said about rewards and punishments. **Reinforcement** *(reward) is a consequence that increases the probability that a behavior will occur.* In contrast, **punishment** *is a consequence that decreases the probability that a behavior will occur.* For example, if someone you meet smiles at you and the two of you continue talking for some time, the smile has reinforced your talking. However, if someone you meet frowns at you and you quickly leave the situation, then the frown has punished your talking with the individual.

Reinforcement can be complex. *Reinforcement* means "to strengthen." In **positive reinforcement** *the frequency of a response increases because it is followed by a stimulus,* as in our example of the smile increasing talking. Similarly, complimenting someone you are attracted to might make that person more receptive to your advances and increase the probability that you will get to know the person better (see figure 7). The same principle of positive reinforcement is at work when an animal trainer teaches a dog to "shake hands" by giving it a piece of food when it lifts its paw. Positive reinforcement strengthens a behavior by the response-contingent presentation of a stimulus. Positive reinforcement can be pleasant (such as praise from a parent) *or* unpleasant (such as working at something you don't want to do, in order to get fed). Conversely, in **negative reinforcement** *the frequency of a response increases because the response either removes a stimulus or involves avoiding the stimulus.* For example, your father nags at you to clean out the garage. He keeps nagging. Finally you get tired of the nagging and clean out the garage. Your response (cleaning out the garage) removed the unpleasant stimulus (nagging).

Taking aspirin works the same way. Taking aspirin is reinforced when this behavior is followed by a reduction of pain (see figure 8). Thus, negative reinforcement strengthens behaviors by the response-contingent withdrawal of a stimulus. Negative reinforcement can be pleasant (such as emptying the bladder) or unpleasant (such as turning down a loud stereo). Thus, in relation to reinforcement, "positive" and "negative" refer to stimulus operations, not to perceived effects of stimuli (Tauber, 1995).

Another way to remember the distinction between positive and negative reinforcement is that in positive reinforcement something is added, or obtained; in negative reinforcement something is subtracted, avoided, or escaped. For example, if you receive a sweater as a graduation present something has been added to increase your achievement behavior. But consider the situation when your parents criticize you for not studying hard enough. As you study harder, they stop criticizing you—something has been subtracted, in this case their criticism.

Negative reinforcement
Behavior
Taking aspirin
Consequence
Pain removed
Future behavior
Taking aspirin increases

FIGURE 8

Negative Reinforcement
In negative reinforcement, the frequency of a response increases because the response either removes a stimulus or involves avoiding the stimulus. For example, in a torture situation, if you talk, the interrogator stops torturing you.

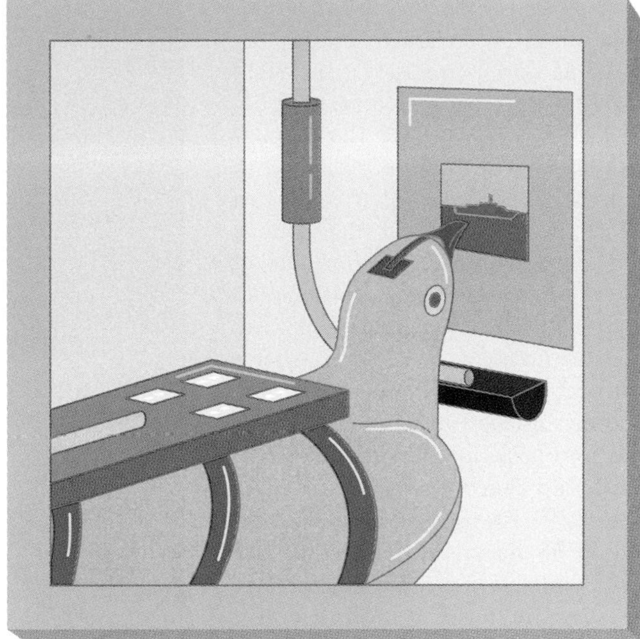

FIGURE 9

Skinner's Pigeon-Guided Missile
Skinner wanted to assist the military by using pigeons' tracking behavior. A gold electrode covered the tip of the pigeons' beaks. Contact with the screen on which the image of the target was projected sent a signal informing the missile's control mechanism of the target's location. A few grains of food occasionally given to the pigeons maintained their tracking behavior.

Negative reinforcement and punishment are easily confused. To keep them straight, remember that negative reinforcement increases the probability a response will occur, whereas punishment decreases the probability a response will occur. When an alcoholic consumes liquor to alleviate uncomfortable withdrawal symptoms, the probability of future alcohol use is increased. The reduction of the withdrawal symptoms is a negative reinforcer for drinking. But if an inebriated alcoholic is seriously injured in a car wreck in which his drinking was a factor and he subsequently stops drinking, then punishment is involved because a behavior—drinking—was decreased.

Now that you know the basic concepts of operant conditioning, several additional points will help you understand how behaviorists study operant conditioning. One of Skinner's basic beliefs was that the mechanisms of learning are the same for all species. This belief led him to an extensive study of animals in the hope that the basic mechanisms of learning could be understood with organisms more simple than humans.

For example, during World War II, Skinner constructed a rather strange project—a pigeon-guided missile. A pigeon in the warhead of the missile operated the flaps on the missile and guided it home by pecking at an image of a target. How could this possibly work? When the missile was in flight, the pigeon pecked the moving image on a screen. This produced corrective signals to keep the missile on its course. The pigeons did their job well in trial runs, but top Navy officials just could not accept pigeons piloting their missiles in a war. Skinner, however, congratulated himself on the degree of control he was able to exercise over the pigeons (see figure 9).

Following the pigeon experiment, Skinner (1948) wrote *Walden Two,* a novel in which he presented his ideas about building a scientifically managed society. Skinner envisioned a utopian society that could be engineered through behavioral control. Skinner viewed existing societies as poorly managed because people believe in myths such as free will. He pointed out that humans are no more free than pigeons are; denying that our behavior is controlled by environmental forces is to ignore science and reality, he argued. Skinner believed that in the long run we would be much happier when we recognized such truths, especially his concept that we could live a prosperous life under the control of positive reinforcement.

Skinner and other behaviorists have made every effort to study organisms under precisely controlled conditions so that the connection between the operant and the specific consequences could be examined in minute detail. One of the ways in which Skinner achieved such control was the development in the 1930s of the Skinner box (see figure 10). A device in the box would deliver food pellets into a tray at random. After a rat became accustomed to the box, Skinner installed a lever and observed the rat's behavior. As the hungry rat explored the box, it occasionally pressed the lever and a food pellet would be dispensed. Soon after, the rat learned that the consequences of pressing the lever were positive—it would be fed. Further control was achieved by soundproofing the box to ensure that the experimenter was the only influence on the organism. In many experiments the responses were mechanically recorded by a cumulative recorder and the food (the stimulus) was dispensed automatically. Such precautions were designed to avoid human error.

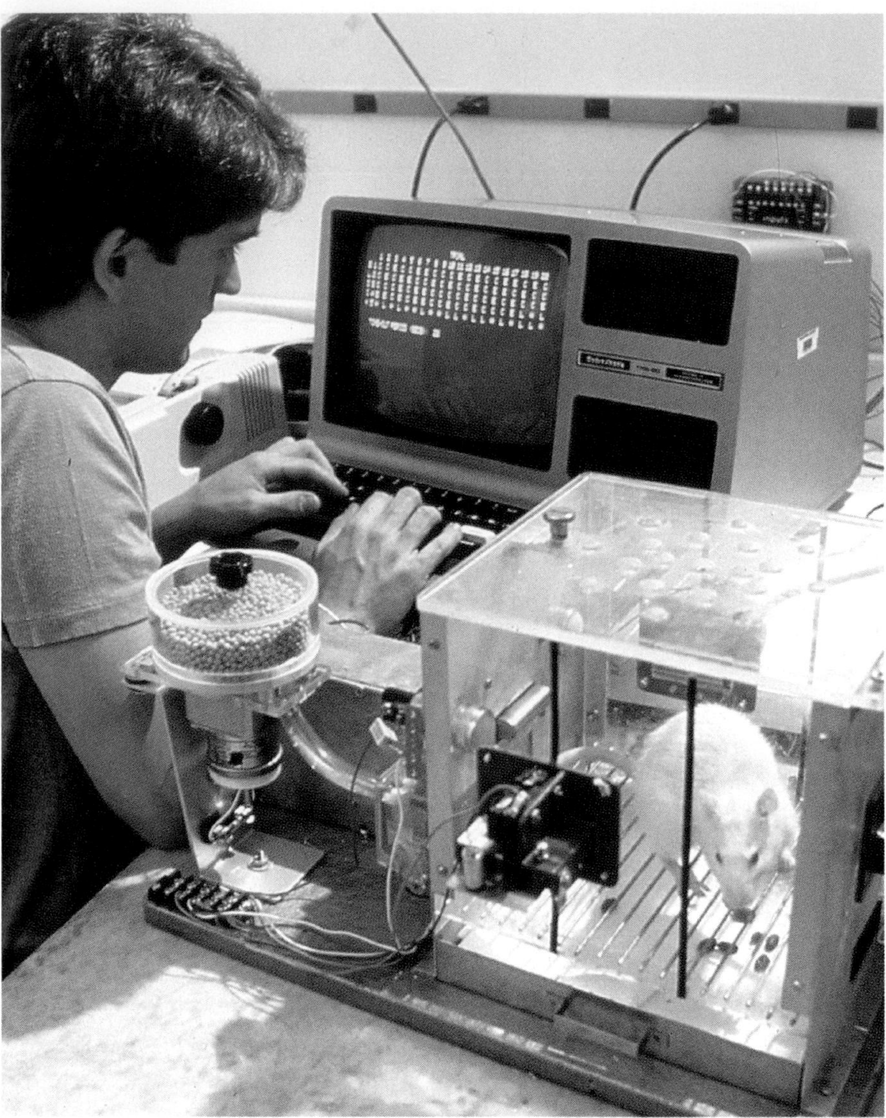

FIGURE 10

Operant Conditioning in a Behavioral Laboratory
Shown here is a rat being conditioned in a Skinner box. Notice the elaborate machinery used to deliver food pellets as reinforcers and to keep track of the rat's behavior.

Some Principles of Operant Conditioning

As Skinner searched for a more precise analysis of behavior and its controlling conditions, he developed a number of concepts. Among the questions to which he sought answers were these: When is the most efficient time for consequences to be experienced? How can you shorten the learning process if it takes a long time for a behavior to occur before it can be rewarded? Are there distinctions between reinforcements that acquire their value through experience, compared to those that are biologically based? How does operant conditioning proceed when we are not reinforced every time we make a response? How can behavior be eliminated, generalized, and discriminated? We consider each of these questions in turn.

Time Interval

As with classical conditioning, learning is more efficient in operant conditioning when the interval between response and reinforcement is a few seconds rather than minutes or hours. An especially important distinction to remember is that learning is more efficient under *immediate* rather than delayed consequences (Holland, 1996). Information about the importance of this distinction in our everyday lives is presented in Explorations in Psychology 1.

Shaping and Chaining

When a behavior takes time to occur, the learning process in operant conditioning may be shortened if an *approximation* of the desired behavior is rewarded. **Shaping** *is the process of rewarding approximations of desired behavior.* In one situation, parents used shaping to toilet train their 2-year-old son. The parents knew all too well that the grunting sound the child made signaled he was about to fill his diaper. In the first week they gave him candy if they heard the sound

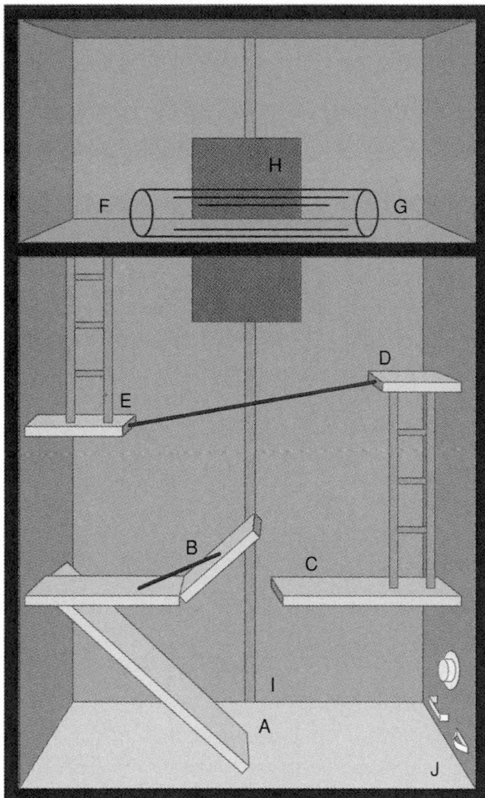

FIGURE 11

An Example of Chaining
Starting at A, the rat climbs the ramp to B, crosses the drawbridge to C, climbs the ladder to D, crosses the tightrope to E, climbs the ladder to F, crawls through the tunnel to G, enters the elevator at H, descends to I, presses the lever at J, and then receives food. In chaining, the experimenter would reinforce lever pressing at J first, then movement from I to J, then descending from H to I to J and so on.

within 20 feet of the bathroom. The second week he was given candy only if he grunted within 10 feet of the bathroom, the third week only if he was in the bathroom, and the fourth week, he had to use the toilet to get the candy (Fischer & Gochros, 1975). It worked!

Chaining *is an operant conditioning technique used to teach a complex sequence, or chain, of behaviors. The procedure begins by shaping the final response in the sequence. Then you work backward until a chain of behaviors is learned.* For example, after the final response is learned, the next-to-last response is reinforced, and so on. Both shaping and chaining are used extensively by animal trainers to teach complex or unusual sequences of behavior. A dolphin that does three back flips, throws a ball through a hoop, places a hat on its head, and finally applauds itself learned the sequence of tricks in reverse order if its trainer used chaining. Figure 11 shows a sequence of behaviors a rat learned through the process of chaining.

Primary and Secondary Reinforcement

Positive reinforcement can be classified as primary reinforcement or secondary reinforcement, which focuses on a distinction between inborn, unlearned, and learned aspects of behavior. **Primary reinforcement** *involves the use of reinforcers that are innately satisfying, that is, they do not take any learning on the organism's part to make them pleasurable.* Food, water, and sexual satisfaction are primary reinforcers.

Secondary reinforcement *acquires its positive value through experience; secondary reinforcers are learned or conditioned reinforcers.* Hundreds of secondary reinforcers characterize our lives. For example, secondary reinforcers include such social situations as getting a pat on the back, praise, and eye contact. One popular story in psychology focuses on the use of eye contact as a secondary reinforcer to shape the behavior of a famous university professor, an expert on operant conditioning. Some students decided to train the professor to lecture from one corner of the classroom. They used eye contact as a reinforcer and began reinforcing successive approximations to the desired response. Each time the professor moved toward the appropriate corner, the students would look at him. If he moved in another direction, they looked away. By gradually rewarding successive approximations to the desired response, the students were able to get the professor to deliver his lecture from just one corner of the classroom. The well-known operant conditioning expert denies that this shaping ever took place. Whether it did or not, the story provides an excellent example of how secondary reinforcers can be used to shape behavior in real life circumstances (Chance, 1979).

Another example also helps to understand the importance of secondary reinforcement in our everyday lives. When a student is given $25 for an A on her report card, the $25 is a secondary reinforcer. It is not innate, and it increases the likelihood the student will work to get another A in the future. Money is often referred to as a *token reinforcer.* When an object can be exchanged for some other reinforcer, the object may have reinforcing value itself, so it is called a token reinforcer. Gift certificates and poker chips are other token reinforcers.

Schedules of Reinforcement

In most of life's experiences, we are not reinforced every time we make a response. A golfer does not win every tournament she enters; a chess whiz does not win every match he plays; a student is not patted on the back each time she solves a problem. **Partial reinforcement** *(or intermittent reinforcement) simply means that responses are not reinforced each time they occur.* **Schedules of reinforcement** *are "timetables" that determine when a response will be reinforced.* The four main schedules of reinforcement are fixed-ratio, variable-ratio, fixed-interval, and variable-interval.

Explorations in Psychology 1

The Role of Immediate and Delayed Consequences in Developing Self-Control

- "That double-dutch chocolate dessert is just too good to pass up."
- "I know I should start exercising more but I guess I'm just too lazy to get started."
- "I've got an important paper due tomorrow morning. Why am I here at this party? Why aren't I home writing the paper?"

If you are like most people, self-control problems like these crop up in your life, unfortunately all too frequently. We often describe ourselves as not having enough willpower to handle these situations. Actually, many of these situations reflect a conflict between immediate and delayed consequences of behavior involving various combinations of reinforcers and punishers (Martin & Pear, 1996).

Immediate Small Reinforcers Versus Delayed Strong Punishers

One reason obesity is a major health problem is that eating is a behavior with immediate positive consequences—food tastes very good and quickly provides a pleasurable feeling. Although the potential delayed consequences of overeating are negative (obesity and other possible health risks), immediate consequences are difficult to override. When the delayed consequences of behavior are punishing and the immediate consequences are reinforcing, the immediate consequences usually win, even when the immediate consequences are small reinforcers and the delayed consequences are major punishers. Smoking and drinking follow a similar pattern. The immediate consequences of smoking are reinforcing for most smokers—the powerful combination of positive reinforcement (tension relief, energy boost) and negative reinforcement (removal of craving, "nicotine fit"). The punishing aspects of smoking are primarily long-term, including shortness of breath, a sore throat, coughing, emphysema, heart disease, lung cancer, and other cancers. The immediate pleasurable consequences of drinking override the delayed consequences of a hangover or even alcoholism.

Immediate Small Reinforcers Versus Delayed Stronger Reinforcers

Self-control problems also are brought about by the choice we face when we can obtain a small immediate reinforcer or wait for a delayed but much-higher-valued reinforcer. For example, you can spend your money now on clothes, trinkets, parties, and the like or save your money and buy a house or car later. In another circumstance, you can play around now and enjoy yourself, which produces immediate small reinforcers, or you can study hard over a long period of time, which can produce delayed stronger reinforcers such as good grades, scholarships to graduate school, and better jobs.

Immediate Punishers Versus Delayed Reinforcers

Why are some of us so reluctant to take up a new sport? To try a new dance step? To go to a social gathering? To do something different? One reason is that learning new skills often involves minor punishing consequences, such as initially looking stupid, not knowing what to do, having to put up with sarcastic comments from onlookers, and so on. In these circumstances, reinforcing consequences are often delayed. For example, it takes us a long time to become a good golfer or a good dancer and enjoy ourselves in these activities.

Immediate Weak Punishers Versus Strong Delayed Punishers

Why do so many of us postpone such activities as going to the dentist, scheduling minor surgery, or paying campus parking fines? In this kind of self-control problem, if we act immediately we experience a weak punisher—it hurts to get our teeth drilled, it is painful to have minor surgery, and it is not very pleasurable to pay a campus parking fine. However, the delayed consequences can be more punishing—our teeth can fall out, we might need major surgery, and our car might get towed away or we might get thrown in jail. All too often, though, immediate consequences win out in these self-control situations.

In these examples of different combinations of immediate and delayed consequences of our behavior, we have seen that immediate consequences often interfere with our ability to control our behavior. Later in the chapter you will find some suggestions for ways to improve self-control through behavioral strategies.

A **fixed-ratio schedule** *reinforces a behavior after a set number of responses.* For example, if you are playing the slot machines in Atlantic City and they are on a fixed-ratio schedule, you might get $5 back every 20 times you put money in the machine. It wouldn't take long to figure out that if you watched someone else play the machine 18 or 19 times, not get any money back, and then walk away, you should step up, insert your coin, and get back $5.

Consequently, slot machines are on a **variable-ratio schedule,** *a timetable in which responses are rewarded an average number of times, but on an unpredictable basis.* For example, a slot machine might pay off an average of every twentieth time, but unlike the fixed-ratio schedule, the gambler does not know when this payoff will be. The slot machine might pay off twice in a row and then not again until after 58 coins have been inserted, which averages out to a reward for every 20 responses, but when the reward is given is unpredictable.

The remaining two reinforcement schedules are determined by *time elapsed* since the last behavior was rewarded. A **fixed-interval schedule** *reinforces the first appropriate response after a fixed amount of time has elapsed.* For example, you might get a reward the first time you put money in a slot machine after every 10-minute period has elapsed. A **variable-interval schedule** *is a timetable in which a response is reinforced after a variable amount of time has elapsed.* On this schedule, the slot machines might reward you after 10 minutes, then after 2 minutes, then after 18 minutes, and so forth.

Which of these schedules is the most effective? The closer a schedule is to continuous reinforcement, the faster the individual learns. However, once behavior is learned, the intermittent schedules can be effective in maintaining behavior. The rate of behavior varies from one schedule to the next (Skinner, 1961). The fixed-ratio schedule produces a high rate of behavior with a pause occurring between the reinforcer and the behavior. This type of schedule is used widely in our lives. For example, if an individual is paid $100 for every ten lawns he mows, then he is on a fixed-ratio schedule. The variable-ratio schedule also elicits a high rate of behavior when the pause after the reinforcement is eliminated. This schedule usually elicits the highest response rate of all four schedules.

The interval schedules produce behavior at a lower rate than the ratio schedules do. The fixed-interval schedule stimulates a low rate of behavior at the start of an interval and a somewhat faster rate toward the end. This happens because the organism apparently recognizes that the behavior early in the interval will not be rewarded but that later behavior will be rewarded. A scallop-shaped curve characterizes the behavior pattern of an organism on a fixed-interval schedule. The variable-interval schedule produces a slow, consistent rate of behavior.

Slot machines are on a variable-ratio schedule of reinforcement. What does this mean?

Extinction, Generalization, and Discrimination

Remember from our discussion of classical conditioning that extinction is the weakening of the CS's tendency to elicit the CR by unreinforced presentations of the CS. **Extinction** *in operant conditioning occurs when a previously reinforced response is no longer reinforced and there is a decreased tendency to perform the response.* Spontaneous recovery also characterizes the operant form of extinction. For example, a factory worker gets a monthly bonus for producing more than her quota. Then, as a part of economic tightening, the company decides that it can no longer afford the bonuses. When bonuses were given, the worker's productivity was above quota every month; once the bonus was removed, performance decreased.

In classical conditioning, generalization is the tendency of a stimulus similar to the conditioned stimulus to produce a response similar to the conditioned response. **Generalization** *in operant conditioning means giving the same response to similar stimuli.* For example, in one study pigeons were reinforced for pecking at a disc of a particular color (Guttman & Kalish, 1956). Stimulus generalization was tested by presenting the pigeons with discs of varying

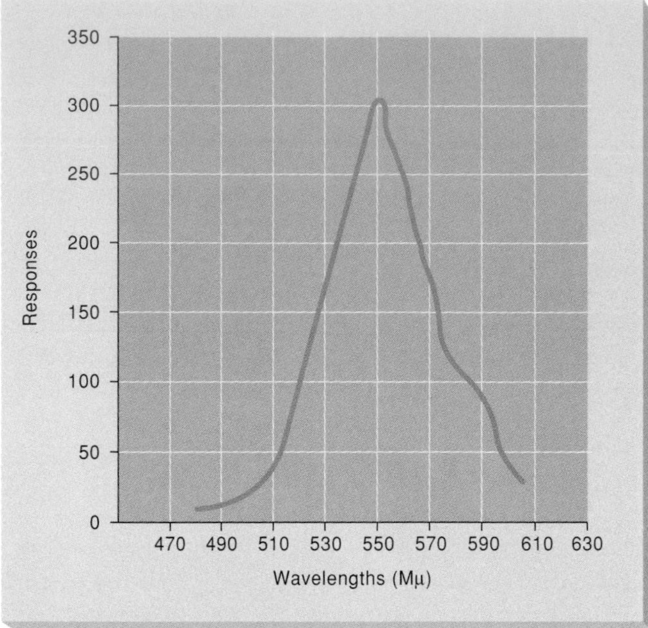

FIGURE 12

Stimulus Generalization
In the experiment by Guttman and Kalish (1956), pigeons initially pecked a disc of a particular color (in this graph, a color with a wavelength of 550 Mμ) after they had been reinforced for this wavelength. Subsequently, when the pigeons were presented discs of colors with varying wavelengths, they were more likely to peck discs that were similar to the original disc.

Stimulus situation			
R	S^D	R	S^R
Spout water	Whistle	Approach feeding platform	Receive food

FIGURE 13

Teaching Behavior to a Killer Whale
When spouting water was followed by a whistle, it reinforced spouting and provided the signal for approaching the feeding platform to receive the reinforcing stimulus (S^R) of food.

colors. As shown in figure 12, the pigeons were most likely to peck at the disc closest in color to the original. An example of stimulus generalization in everyday life that is familiar to many parents involves an infant learning to say "doggie" to a hairy, four-legged creature with floppy ears and a friendly bark (Martin & Pear, 1996). Later, the infant sees a different kind of dog and says "doggie." This is an example of stimulus generalization because a previously reinforced response ("doggie") appeared in the presence of a new stimulus (a new kind of dog). Later, the infant sees a horse and says "doggie." This is another example of stimulus generalization, even though the infant's labeling is incorrect, which indicates that not all instances of stimulus generalization are favorable and illustrates why discriminations need to be taught.

In classical conditioning, discrimination is the process of learning to respond to certain stimuli and not to others. **Discrimination** *in operant conditioning is the tendency to respond only to those stimuli that are correlated with reinforcement.* For example, you might look at two street signs, both made of metal, both the same color, and both with words on them. However, one sign says "Enter at your own risk," and the other reads "Please walk this way." The words serve as discriminative stimuli because the sign that says "Please walk this way" indicates that you will be rewarded for doing so, whereas the sign that says "Enter at your own risk," suggests that the consequences may not be positive. **Discriminative stimuli** *signal that a response will be reinforced.* Discrimination is one of the techniques used to teach animals to perform tricks. When Kent Burgess (1968) wanted to teach a killer whale tricks, he used a whistle as the discriminative stimulus. Whenever the whistle sounded, the killer whale got fed. Burgess would blow the whistle immediately after a correct response and the killer whale would approach the feeding platform where she would be fed. Using this tactic, Burgess taught the killer whale to spout water, leap in the air, and so on (see figure 13).

Applications of Operant Conditioning

A preschool child repeatedly throws his glasses and breaks them. A high school student and her parents have intense arguments. A college student is deeply depressed. An elderly woman is incontinent. Operant conditioning procedures have helped people such as these to adapt more successfully and cope more effectively with their problems (Herson & Miller, 1996).

Applied behavior analysis (behavior modification) *is the application of operant conditioning principles to change human behavior.* Consequences for behavior are established to ensure that more-adaptive actions are reinforced and less-adaptive ones are not (Kohlenberg, Tsai, & Kohlenberg, 1996; Pierce & Epling, 1995). Advocates of behavior modification believe that many emotional and behavior problems are caused by inadequate (or inappropriate) response consequences. The child who throws down his glasses and breaks them may be receiving too much attention from his teacher and peers for his behavior; they unwittingly reinforce an unacceptable behavior. In this instance, the parents and teachers would be instructed to divert attention from the destructive behavior and transfer it to a more constructive behavior, such as working quietly or playing cooperatively with peers (Harris, Wolf, & Baer, 1964).

Consider another circumstance. Barbara and her parents were on a collision course. Things got so bad that her parents decided to see a clinical psychologist. The psychologist, who had a behavioral orientation, talked with each family member, trying to get them to pinpoint the problem. The psychologist got the family to sign a behavioral contract that spelled out what everyone needed to do to reduce the conflict. Barbara agreed to (1) be home before 11 P.M. on weeknights; (2) look for a part-time job so she could begin to pay for some of her activities; and (3) refrain from calling her parents insulting names. Her parents agreed to (1) talk to Barbara in a low tone of voice rather than yell if they were angry; (2) refrain from criticizing teenagers, especially Barbara's friends; and (3) give Barbara a small sum of money each week for gas, makeup, and socializing, but only until she found a job.

Also consider Sam, a 19-year-old college student, who has been deeply depressed lately. His girlfriend broke off their relationship of 2 years, and his grades have been dropping. He decides to go to a psychologist who has a behavioral orientation. The psychologist enrolls him in the Coping with Depression course developed by Peter Lewinsohn (1987). Sam learns to monitor his daily moods and increase his ratio of positive to negative life events. The psychologist trains Sam to develop more efficient coping skills and gets Sam to agree to a behavioral contract, just as the psychologist did with Barbara and her parents.

Mary is an elderly woman who lives in a nursing home. In recent months she has become incontinent and is increasingly dependent on the staff for help with her daily activities. The behavioral treatment designed for Mary's problem involves teaching her to monitor her behavior and schedule going to the toilet. She is also required to do pelvic exercises. The program for decreasing Mary's dependence requires that the staff attend more to her independent behavior when it occurs and remove attention from dependent behavior whenever possible. Such strategies with the elderly have been effective in reducing problems with incontinence and dependence.

Behavior modification is used to teach couples to communicate more effectively, to encourage fathers to engage in more competent caregiving with their infants, to train autistic children's interpersonal skills, to help individuals lose weight, and to reduce an individual's fear of social situations. Another effective use of behavior modification is to improve an individual's self-control (Logue, 1995). Information about how this is accomplished is described in Explorations in Psychology 2.

Behavior modification not only is effective in therapy, but it has also been applied to the world of computers to promote better instruction. Some years ago, Skinner developed a machine to help teachers instruct students. The teaching machine engaged the student in a learning activity, paced the material at the student's rate, tested the student's knowledge of the material, and provided immediate feedback about correct and incorrect answers. Skinner hoped that the machine would revolutionize learning in schools, but the revolution never took place.

Today the idea behind Skinner's teaching machine is applied to computers, which help teachers instruct students. Research comparisons of computer-assisted instruction with traditional teacher-based instruction suggest that, in some areas, such as drill and practice on math problems, computer-assisted instruction may produce superior results (Kulik, Kulik, & Bangert-Drowns, 1985).

By now you should have a good feel for how operant conditioning works. A summary of the main themes of operant conditioning is presented in concept table 2.

Observational Learning

Would it make sense to teach a 15-year-old boy how to drive by either classical conditioning or operant conditioning procedures? Driving a car is a voluntary behavior, so classical conditioning doesn't really apply. In terms of operant conditioning, we would ask him to drive down the road and then reward his positive behaviors. Not many of us would want to be on the road, though, when some of his disastrous mistakes occur. Albert Bandura (1986, 1994) believes that if we learned only in such a trial-and-error fashion, it would be exceedingly tedious and at times hazardous. Instead, many of our complex behaviors are the result of exposure to competent models who display appropriate behavior in solving problems and coping with their world.

Observational learning, *also called imitation or modeling, is learning that occurs when a person observes and imitates someone's behavior.* The capacity to learn behavior patterns by observation eliminates tedious trial-and-error learning. In many instances observational learning takes less time than operant conditioning.

The following experiment by Bandura (1965) illustrates how observational learning can occur by watching a model who is neither reinforced nor punished. The only requirement for learning is that the individual be connected in time and space with the model. The experiment also illustrates an important distinction between learning and performance.

An equal number of boys and girls of nursery-school age watched one of three films in which someone beat up an adult-sized plastic toy called a Bobo doll (see figure 14). In the first film, the aggressor was rewarded with candy, soft drinks, and praise for aggressive behavior; in the second film, the aggressor was criticized and spanked for the aggressive behavior; and in the third film, there were no consequences to the aggressor for the behavior. Subsequently, each child was left alone in a room filled with toys, including a Bobo doll. The child's behavior was observed through a one-way mirror. As shown in figure 15, children who watched the film where the aggressive behavior was reinforced or went unpunished imitated the

Explorations in Psychology 2

Using Behavior Modification to Improve Self-Control

Chances are each of us could stand to change something about our lives. What would you like to change? What would you like to be able to control more effectively in your life? To answer these questions, you first have to specify your problem in a concrete way. For Al, this is easy—he is overweight and wants to lose 30 pounds. Stated even more precisely, he wants to consume about 1,000 fewer calories per day than he uses to give him a weight loss of about 2 pounds per week. Some problems are more difficult to specify, such as "wasting time," "having a bad attitude toward school," "having a poor relationship with ———," or "being too nervous and worrying a lot." These types of problems have been called "fuzzies" because of their abstract nature (Mager, 1972). It is important to "unfuzzify" these abstract problems and make them more specific and concrete. Problems can be made more precise by writing out your goal and listing the things that would give you clear evidence that you have reached your goal.

A second important step in a self-control program is to make a *commitment* to change (Martin & Pear, 1988). Both a commitment to change and a knowledge of change techniques have been shown to help college students become more effective self-managers of their smoking, eating, studying, and relationship problems. Building a commitment to change requires you to do things that increase the likelihood you will stick to your project. First, tell others about your commitment to change—they will remind you to stick to your program. Second, rearrange your environment to provide frequent reminders of your goal, making sure the reminders are associated with the positive benefits of reaching your goal. Third, put in a lot of time and energy in planning your project. Make a list of statements about your project, such as "I've put a lot of time into this project; I am certainly not going to waste all of this effort now." Fourth, because you will invariably face temptations to backslide or quit your project, plan ahead for ways you can deal with temptation, tailoring these plans to your problem.

A third major step in developing a self-control program is to collect data about your behavior. This is especially important in decreasing excessive behaviors such as overeating and frequent smoking. One of the reasons for tracking your behavior is that it provides a reference point for evaluating your progress. When recording the frequency of a problem during initial observations, you should examine the immediate consequences that could be maintaining the problem (Martin & Pear, 1996). Consider Al's situation. When first asked why he eats so much, Al said, "Because I like the taste, and eating makes me feel comfortable." However, when Al began evaluating the circumstances in which he usually snacks, he noticed that usually when he eats, reinforcement follows: After eating a candy bar, he meets his girlfriend; after potato chips, his favorite basketball star scores another basket; after a beer, his fraternity brothers laugh at his jokes. Al eats while getting ready to meet his girlfriend, while watching television, while socializing with his fraternity brothers, and in many other social situations during which he comes into contact with a variety of reinforcing events in the environment. No wonder Al has trouble with his weight.

A fourth important step in improving your self-control is to design a program. There are many different strategies you can follow. Virtually every self-control program incorporates self-instruction or self-talk (Meichenbaum, 1986). Consider the self-instruction program followed by a Canadian psychologist to improve his running (Martin & Pear, 1996). During the winter, he started an exercise program that consisted of running 2 miles (14 laps) at the university's indoor track. He found that, after 9 or 10 laps, fatiguing thoughts set in, and he often talked himself out of completing the last few laps, saying something like, "I've done pretty good today by running 9 laps." He decided to start a self-reinforcement program to increase his antifatigue thoughts in the last few laps of his running regimen. Specifically, during the 10th to 14th laps, he thought an antifatigue thought and followed it with a pleasurable thought. The antifatigue thought he chose was about a TV fitness commercial claiming that the average 60-year-old Swede is in the same physical condition as the average 30-year-old Canadian (the claim is actually false, but this is not important to this example). Each time the psychologist got to a certain place on the track, he thought about a healthy Swede jogging smoothly

behavior more than the children who saw that aggressive behavior was punished. As might be expected, boys were more aggressive than girls. The important point about these results is that observational learning occurred just as extensively when modeled aggressive behavior was not reinforced as when it was reinforced.

A second important point focuses on the distinction between *learning* and *performance.* Just because an organism does not perform a response does not mean it was not learned. When children were rewarded (in the form of stickers or fruit juice) for imitating the model, differences in the imitative behavior among the children

(a)

(b)

Behavioral strategies for improving self-control have been effectively applied to college students' (a) studying and (b) relationships. For ways to tailor a self-control program to your needs, you might want to contact the counseling center at your college or university.

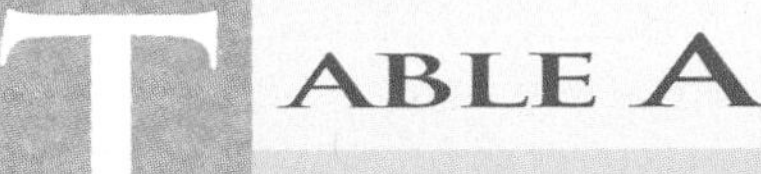

TABLE A

Five Steps in Developing a Self-Control Program

1. Define the problem
2. Commit to change
3. Collect data about yourself
4. Design a self-control program
5. Make the program last—maintenance

along the track. At the next turn, he thought about something enjoyable, such as going to the beach or to a party where others complimented him on his healthy appearance. After practicing this sequence of thoughts for about 2 weeks during his running, he was able to eliminate his fatiguing thoughts and complete his 2-mile runs.

A fifth important aspect of improving your self-control is to make it last. One strategy is to establish specific dates for postchecks and to plan a course of action if your postchecks are not favorable. For instance, if your self-control program involves weight reduction, you might want to weigh yourself once a week. If your weight increases to a certain level, then you immediately go back on your self-control program.

Another strategy is to establish a buddy system by finding a friend or someone with a similar problem. The two of you set mutual maintenance goals. Once a month, get together and check each other's behavior. If your goals have been maintained, get together and celebrate in an agreed-upon way. Table A summarizes the main steps in the self-control program we have described.

For other ideas on how to establish an effective self-control program tailored to your needs, you might want to contact the counseling center at your college or university. A good book on behavior modification or self-control also can be helpful—one is described in the suggested readings at the end of the chapter (Martin & Pear, 1996).

in the three conditions were eliminated. In this experiment, all of the children learned about the model's behavior, but the performance of the behavior did not occur for some children until reinforcement was presented. Bandura believes that when an individual observes behavior but makes no observable response, the individual still may have acquired the modeled response in cognitive form.

Since his early experiments, Bandura (1986) has focused on some of the specific processes that influence an observer's behavior following exposure to a model. One of these is attention. Before a person can reproduce a

CONCEPT TABLE 2

Operant Conditioning

Concept	Processes/Related Ideas	Characteristics/Description
Thorndike's Law of Effect	Its nature	This law states that behaviors followed by a positive outcome are strengthened, whereas those followed by a negative outcome are weakened. Referred to as S-R theory.
Skinner's Operant Conditioning	What operant conditioning is	An organism's behavior operates in the environment to produce change that will lead to reinforcement. This is a form of learning in which the consequences of the behavior lead to changes in the probability of its occurrence.
	Comparison with classical conditioning	Operant conditioning focuses on what happens after a response is made; classical conditioning emphasizes what occurs before a response is made. The key connection in classical conditioning is between two stimuli; in operant conditioning, it is between the organism's response and its consequences. Operant conditioning mainly involves voluntary behavior; classical conditioning, involuntary behavior.
	Positive reinforcement, negative reinforcement, and punishment	Positive reinforcement occurs when the frequency of a response increases because it is followed by a stimulus. Positive reinforcement strengthens behavior by the response-contingent presentation of a stimulus. Negative reinforcement occurs when the frequency of a response increases because the response either removes a stimulus or involves avoiding the stimulus. Punishment is a consequence that decreases the probability a behavior will occur.
Some Principles of Operant Conditioning	Time interval	Immediate consequences are more effective than delayed consequences.
	Shaping and chaining	Shaping is the process of rewarding approximations of the desired behavior. Chaining involves establishing a complex chain of responses. The final response in the sequence is learned first, then the next to the last, and so on.
	Primary and secondary reinforcement	Primary reinforcement refers to innate reinforcers (food, water, sex): secondary reinforcement refers to reinforcers that acquire positive value through experience (money, smiles).
	Schedules of reinforcement	A response will be reinforced on a fixed-ratio schedule, a variable-ratio schedule, a fixed-interval schedule, or a variable-interval schedule. These schedules have varying degrees of effectiveness.
	Extinction, generalization, and discrimination	Extinction is a decrease in the tendency to perform the response brought about by unreinforced consequences of that response. Generalization means giving the same response to similar stimuli. Discrimination is the process of responding in the presence of one stimulus that is reinforced but not in the presence of another stimulus that is not reinforced.
Applications of Operant Conditioning	Behavior modification	This refers to the use of learning principles to change maladaptive or abnormal behavior; focuses on changing behavior by following it with reinforcement.
	Application	Behavior modification is used widely to reduce maladaptive behavior. Among its applications are controlling aggressive behavior, reducing conflicts between parents and adolescents, coping with depression, helping elderly individuals function more independently, teaching by computer-assisted instruction, and improving self-control.

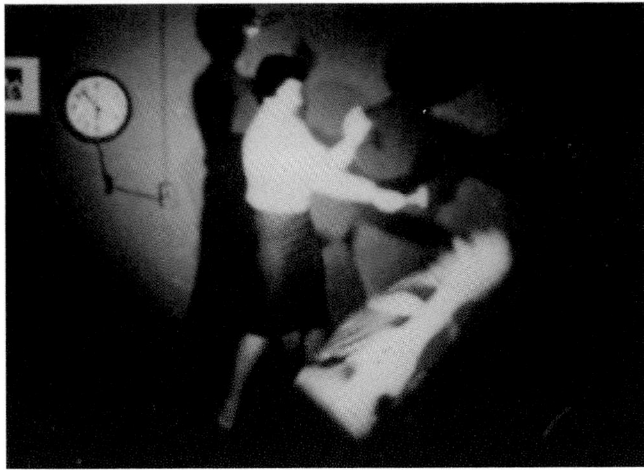

FIGURE 14

Bandura's Experiment on Imitation and Aggression
In the frame on the left, an adult model aggressively attacks a Bobo doll. In the frame on the right, the preschool-aged girl who has observed the adult model's aggressive actions follows suit.

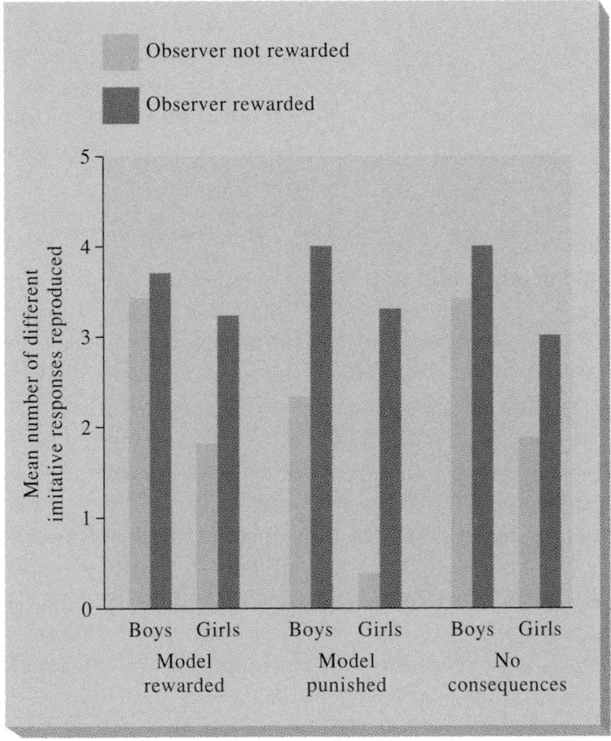

FIGURE 15

Results of Bandura's Experiment on Observational Learning and Aggression
Children who watched an aggressor be reinforced or experience no consequences for aggressive behavior imitated the aggressive behavior more than children who watched the aggressor be punished. Boys were more aggressive than girls. When children were offered rewards for imitating the aggressive model's behavior, even those children who had seen the model punished demonstrated they had learned the model's behavior by behaving aggressively.

model's actions, she must attend to what the model is doing or saying. You might not hear what a friend says if the stereo is blaring or you might miss the teacher's analysis of a problem if you are admiring someone sitting in the next row. Attention to the model is influenced by a host of characteristics. For example, warm, powerful, atypical people command more attention than do cold, weak, typical people.

Retention is considered next. To reproduce a model's actions, you must code the information and keep it in memory so that it can be retrieved. A simple verbal description or a vivid image of what the model did assists retention. Memory is such an important cognitive process that the next chapter is devoted exclusively to it.

Another process involved in observational learning is motor reproduction. People may attend to a model and code in memory what they have seen, but because of limitations in motor development they may not be able to reproduce the model's action. Thirteen-year-olds may see Michael Jordan do a reverse two-handed dunk but be unable to reproduce the pro's actions.

A final process in Bandura's conception of observational learning involves reinforcement or incentive conditions. On many occasions we may attend to what a model says or does, retain the information in memory, and possess the motor capabilities to perform the action, but we might fail to repeat the behavior because of inadequate reinforcement. This was demonstrated in Bandura's (1965) study when those children who had seen a model punished for aggression reproduced the model's aggression only when they were offered an incentive to do so. A summary of Bandura's model of observational learning is shown in figure 16.

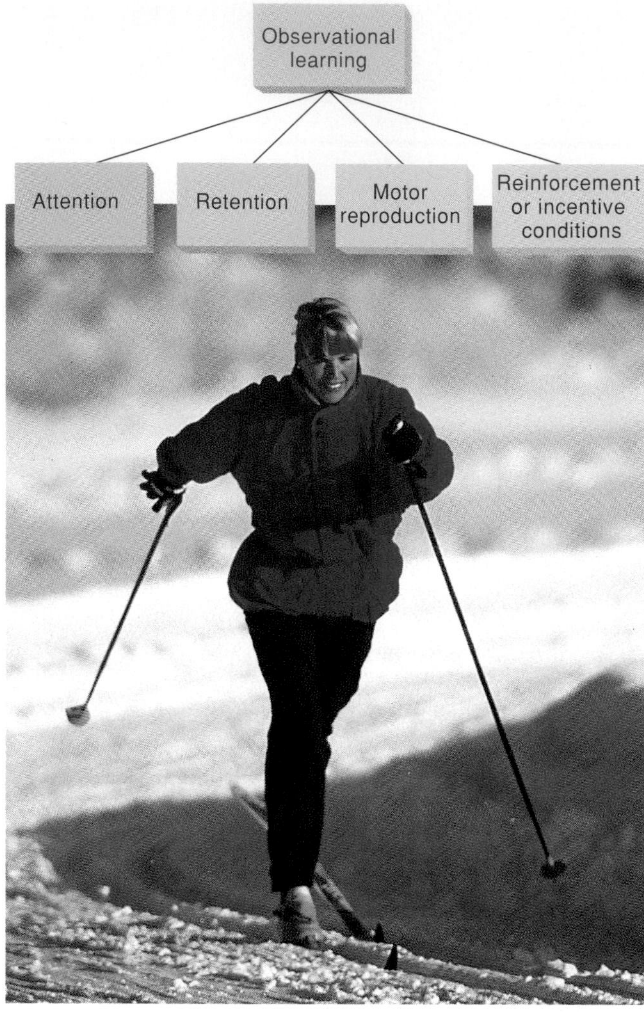

FIGURE 16

Bandura's Model of Observational Learning
Bandura argues that observational learning consists of four main processes: attention, retention, motor reproduction, and reinforcement or incentive conditions. Consider a circumstance involving learning to ski. You need to attend to the instructor's words and demonstrations. You need to remember what the instructor did and her tips for avoiding disasters. You also need the motor abilities to reproduce what the instructor has shown you, and praise from the instructor after you have completed a few moves on the slopes should improve your motivation to continue skiing.

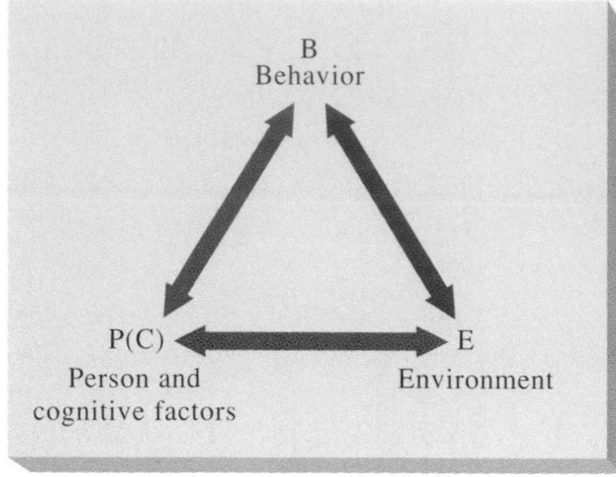

FIGURE 17

Bandura's Model of Reciprocal Influences on Behavior, Person and Cognitive Factors, and Environment
In this figure, *B* is behavior, *P(C)* is person and cognitive factors, and *E* is environment. The arrows reflect how relations between these factors are reciprocal rather than unidirectional. Examples of person factors include intelligence, skills, and self-control.

Bandura views observational learning as an information-processing activity. As a person observes, information about the world is transformed into cognitive representations that serve as guides for action. As we see next, interest in the cognitive factors of learning has increased dramatically in recent years.

COGNITIVE FACTORS IN LEARNING

When we learn, we often cognitively represent or transform our experiences. In our excursion through learning we have had little to say about these cognitive processes, except in our description of observational learning. In the operant conditioning view of Skinner and the classical conditioning view of Pavlov, no room is given to the possibility that cognitive factors such as memory, thinking, planning, or expectations might be important in the learning process. Skinnerians point out that they do not deny the existence of thinking processes, but since they cannot be observed they may interfere with the discovery of important environmental conditions that govern behavior.

Many contemporary psychologists, including behavioral revisionists who recognize that cognition should not have been ignored in classical and operant conditioning, believe that learning involves much more than stimulus-response connections. The **S-O-R model** *is a model of learning that gives some importance to cognitive factors. S* stands for stimulus, *O* for organism, and *R* for response. The *O* sometimes is referred to as the "black box," because the mental activities of the organism cannot be seen and, therefore, must be inferred.

Bandura (1994) described another model of learning that involves behavior, person, and environment. As shown in figure 17, behavior, person and cognitive factors, and environmental influences operate interactively. Behavior influences cognition and vice versa; the person's cognitive activities influence the environment; environmental experiences change the person's thought; and so on.

Let's consider how Bandura's model might work in the case of a college student's achievement behavior. As the student studies diligently and gets good grades, her behavior produces in her positive thoughts about her abilities. As part of her effort to make good grades, she plans and develops a number of strategies to make her studying more efficient. In these ways her behavior has influenced her thought, and her thought has influenced her behavior. At the beginning of the semester, her college made a special effort to involve students in a study skills program. She decided to join. Her success, along with that of other students who attended the program, has led the college to expand the program next semester. In these ways, environment influenced behavior, and behavior changed the environment. And the expectations of the college administrators that the study skills program would work made it possible in the first place. The program's success has spurred expectations that this type of program could work in other colleges. In these ways cognition changed environment, and the environment changed cognition. Expectations are an important variable in Bandura's model. How might expectations be further involved in understanding learning?

Expectations and Cognitive Maps

E. C. Tolman says that when classical and operant conditioning occur the organism acquires certain expectations. In classical conditioning the young boy fears the rabbit because he expects it will hurt him. In operant conditioning a woman works hard all week because she expects to be paid on Friday.

In 1946, Tolman and his colleagues conducted a classic experiment to demonstrate the power of expectations in learning. Initially, rats ran on an elevated maze (see figure 18*a*). The rats started at *A*, ran across the circular table at *B*, through an alley at *CD*, then along the path to the food box at *G*. *H* represents a light that illuminated the path from *F* to *G*.

This maze was replaced by one with several false runways (see figure 18*b*). The rats ran down what had been the correct path before but found that it was blocked. Which of the remaining paths would the rats choose? We might anticipate that they would choose paths 9 and 10 because those were nearest the path that led to success. Instead, the rats explored several paths, running along one for a short distance, returning to the table, then trying out another one, and so on. Eventually, the rats ran along one path all the way to the end. This path was number 6, not 9 or 10. Path 6 ran to a point about 4 inches short of where the food box had been located previously. According to Tolman, the rats not only had learned how to run the original maze, they also had learned to expect food upon reaching a specific place.

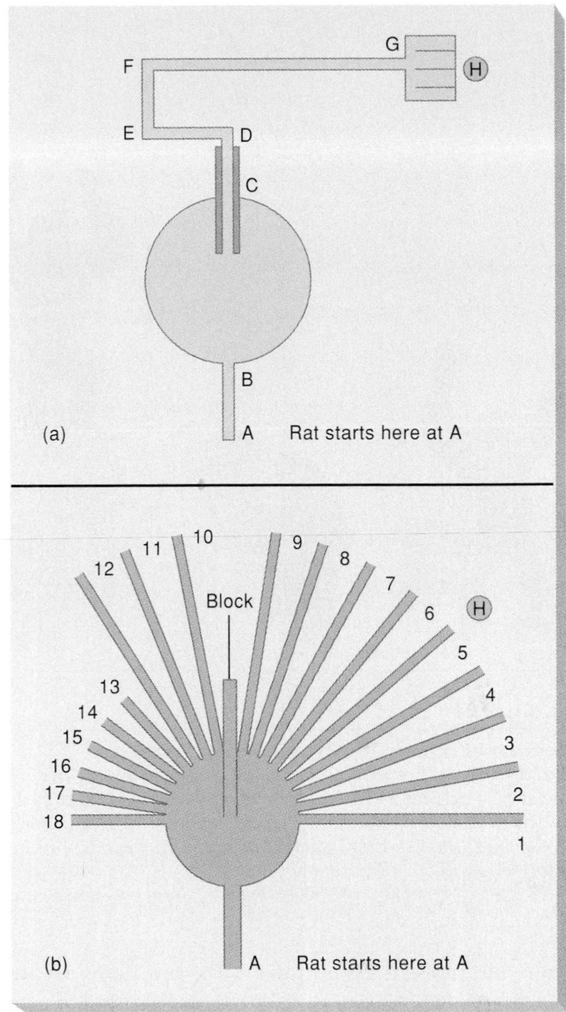

FIGURE 18

Tolman's Experiment on Expectations in Learning
In Tolman's classic experiment on the role of expectations in learning, initially rats ran on this elevated maze from A through G, with H representing a light that illuminated the path from F to G. After the rats ran the maze in (*a*), they were placed in the maze shown in (*b*). What path did the rats follow in (*b*)? Why?

In his paper "Cognitive Maps in Rats and Men," Tolman (1948) articulated his belief that organisms select information from the environment and construct a cognitive map of their experiences. A **cognitive map** *is an organism's mental representation of the structure of physical space.* In Tolman's maze experiment just described, the rats had developed a mental awareness of physical space and the elements in it. The rats used this cognitive map to find where the food was located.

Tolman's idea of cognitive maps is alive and well today. When we move around in our environment, we develop a cognitive map of where things are located, on both small and large scales. We have a cognitive map of where rooms are located in our house or apartment, and we have a cognitive map of where we are located in the United States, for example. A popular tradition is to draw a cognitive map reflecting our perception of the city or state in which we live, relative to the rest of the United States. Texans, for example, usually draw the state of Texas as about three-fourths the size of the entire United States. In Manhattan, "The City" is often drawn about nine-tenths the size of the United States. Of course, such cognitive maps deliberately distort the physical world, reflecting the perceivers' egocentric interest in their city or state.

Tolman was not the only psychologist who was dissatisfied with the S-R view of learning. Gestalt psychologist Wolfgang Kohler thought that the cognitive process of insight learning was also an important form of learning.

Insight Learning

Wolfgang Kohler, a German psychologist, spent 4 months in the Canary Islands during World War I observing the behavior of apes. While there he conducted two fascinating experiments. One is called the "stick problem," the other the "box problem." Though these two experiments are

FIGURE 19

Kohler's Box Problem Involving Insight Learning
Sultan, one of Kohler's brightest chimps, is faced with the problem of reaching a cluster of bananas overhead. Suddenly he solves the problem by stacking boxes on top of one another to reach the bananas. Kohler called this type of problem solving "insight learning."

basically the same, the solutions to the problems are different. In both situations, the ape discovers that it cannot reach an alluring piece of fruit, either because the fruit is too high or it is outside of the ape's cage and beyond its reach. To solve the stick problem, the ape has to insert a small stick inside a larger stick to reach the fruit. To master the box problem, the ape must stack several boxes to reach the fruit (see figure 19).

According to Kohler (1925), solving these problems does not involve trial and error or mere connections between stimuli and responses. Rather, when the ape realizes that his customary actions are not going to get the fruit, he often sits for a period of time and appears to ponder how to solve the problem. Then he quickly gets up, as if he had a sudden flash of insight, piles the boxes on top of one another, and gets the fruit. **Insight learning** *is a form of problem solving in which the organism develops a sudden insight or understanding of a problem's solution.*

Biological and Cultural Factors in Learning

Albert Einstein had many special talents. He combined enormous creativity with great analytic ability to develop some of this century's most important insights about the nature of matter and the universe. Genes obviously provided Einstein extraordinary intellectual skills to think and reason on a very high plane, but cultural factors also undoubtedly contributed to Einstein's genius. Einstein received an excellent, rigorous European education, and later in the United States he experienced the freedom and support believed to be important in creative exploration. Would Einstein have been able to fully develop his intellectual skills and make such brilliant insights if he had grown up in the more primitive cultures of his time or even in a Third World country today? Unlikely. Quite clearly both biological *and* cultural factors contribute to learning.

Biological Factors

We can't breathe under water, fish can't play Ping-Pong, and cows can't solve math problems. The structure of an organism's body permits certain kinds of learning and inhibits others. For example, chimpanzees cannot learn to speak English because they lack the necessary vocal equipment. Some of us cannot solve difficult calculus problems, others of us can, and the differences do not all seem to be the result of experiences.

Some animals also learn readily in one situation but have difficulty learning in slightly different circumstances. The difficulty might not result from some aspect of the learning situation but from the predisposition of the organism (Seligman, 1970). **Preparedness** *is the species-specific biological predisposition to learn in certain ways but not in others.* For example, cats can escape from a cage by pulling a string to open the door or by pushing the door, but if they have to lick, their escape ability is greatly reduced. In most situations humans are prepared to walk and talk.

Another example of biological influences on learning is **instinctive drift,** *the tendency of animals to revert to instinctive behavior that interferes with learning.* Consider the situation of Keller and Marion Breland (1961), students of B. F. Skinner, who used operant conditioning to train animals to perform at fairs, conventions, and in television advertisements. They used Skinner's techniques of shaping, chaining, and discrimination to teach pigs to cart large wooden nickels to a piggy bank and deposit them. They also trained raccoons to pick up a coin and place it in a metal tray. Although the pigs and raccoons, as well as other animals such as chickens, performed well at most of the tasks (raccoons became adept basketball players, for example—see figure 20), some of the animals began acting strangely. Instead of picking up the large wooden nickel and carrying it to the piggy bank, the pigs would drop the nickel on the ground, shove it with their snouts, toss it in the air, and then repeat these actions. The raccoons began to hold onto their coin rather than dropping it into the metal container. When two coins were introduced, the raccoons rubbed them together in a miserly fashion. Somehow these behaviors overwhelmed the strength of the reinforcement that was given at the end of the day. Why were the pigs and the raccoons misbehaving? The pigs were rooting, an instinct which is used to uncover edible roots. The raccoons engaged in an instinctive food-washing response. Their instinctive drift interfered with learning.

FIGURE 20

Instinctive Drift
This raccoon's skill in using its hands made it an excellent basketball player, but because of instinctive drift, the raccoon had a much more difficult time taking money to the bank.

A psychologist went to dinner with his wife and ordered filet mignon with Bérnaise sauce, his favorite dish. Afterward they went to the opera. Several hours later, he became very ill with stomach pains and nausea. Several weeks later, he tried to eat Bérnaise sauce but couldn't bear it. The psychologist's experience involves *taste aversion,* another biological constraint on learning (Alvarez & Lopez, 1996; Espinet & others, 1995; Garcia, Ervin, & Koelling, 1966 Kling, 1995).

If an organism ingests a substance that poisons but does not kill it, the organism often develops considerable distaste for that substance. Rats that experience low levels of radiation after eating show a strong aversion to the food they were eating when the radiation made them ill. This aversion has been shown to last for as long as 32 days. Such long-term effects cannot be accounted for by classical conditioning, which would argue that a single pairing of the conditioned and unconditioned stimuli would not last that long. Radiation and chemical treatment of cancer often produces nausea in patients, and the resulting pattern of aversions often resembles those shown by laboratory animals.

Knowledge about taste aversion has been applied to balancing the ecological worlds of animals. For example, the livestock of farmers and ranchers may be threatened by wolves or coyotes. Instead of killing the pests or predators, the farmers feed them poisoned meat of their prey (cattle, sheep). The wolves and coyotes, poisoned but not killed, develop a taste aversion for cattle or sheep and, hence, are less of a threat to the farmers and ranchers. In this way, ranchers, farmers, cattle, sheep, wolves, and coyotes can live in a semblance of ecological balance.

Cultural Factors

In traditional views of learning, concepts such as culture have been given little or no attention. The behavioral orientation that dominated American psychology for much of the twentieth century does focus on the cultural contexts of learning, but the organisms in those contexts have often been animals. When humans have been the subjects, there has been little or no interest in the cultural context.

How does culture influence learning? Most psychologists agree that the principles of classical conditioning, operant conditioning, and observational learning are universal and are powerful learning processes in every culture. However, culture can influence the *degree* to which these learning processes are used, and it often determines the *content* of learning. For example, punishment is a universal learning process, but as we see next, its use and type show considerable sociocultural variation.

When behaviorism was dominant in the United States between 1910 and 1930, child-rearing experts regarded the infant as capable of being shaped into almost any child. Desirable social behavior could be achieved if the child's antisocial behaviors were always punished and never indulged, and if positive behaviors were carefully conditioned and rewarded in a highly controlled and structured child-rearing regimen. The famous behaviorist John Watson (1928) authored a publication, *Infant Care,* that was the official government booklet for parents. This booklet advocated never letting children suck their thumb, and, if necessary, restraining the child by tying her hands to the crib at night and painting her fingers with foul-tasting liquids. Parents were advised to let infants "cry themselves out" rather than reinforce this unacceptable behavior by picking them up to rock and soothe them.

However, from the 1930s to 1960s, a more permissive attitude prevailed and parents were advised to be concerned with the feelings and capacities of the child. Since the 1960s there has been a continued emphasis on the role of parental love in children's socialization, but experts now advise parents to play a less permissive and more active role in shaping children's behavior. Experts stress that parents should set limits and make authoritative decisions in areas where the child is not capable of reasonable judgment. However, they should listen and adapt to the child's point of view, should explain their restrictions and discipline, but they should not discipline the child in a hostile, punitive manner.

Most child-rearing experts in the United States today do not advocate the physical punishment of children, but the United States does not have a law that prohibits parents

Concept Table 3

Observational Learning, Cognitive Factors, and Biological/Cultural Factors

Concept	Processes/Related Ideas	Characteristics/Description
Observational Learning	Its nature	Occurs when an individual observes someone else's behavior. Also called imitation or modeling. It is important to distinguish between what is learned and whether it is performed.
	Processes	Bandura believes that observational learning involves attention, retention, motor reproduction, and reinforcement or incentive conditions.
Cognitive Factors in Learning	Models	Many psychologists recognize the importance of studying how cognitive factors mediate environment-behavior connections. The S-O-R model reflects this, as does Bandura's contemporary model, which emphasizes reciprocal connections between behavior, person (cognition), and environment.
	Expectations and cognitive maps	Tolman reinterpreted classical and operant conditioning in terms of expectations. We construct cognitive maps of our experiences that guide our behavior; psychologists still study the nature of cognitive maps.
	Insight learning	Kohler, like Tolman, was dissatisfied with the S-R view of learning. He believed that organisms reflect and suddenly gain insight into how a problem should be solved.
Biological and Cultural Factors	Biological factors	Biological factors restrict what an organism can learn from experience. These constraints include physical characteristics, preparedness, instinctive drift, and taste aversion.
	Cultural factors	While most psychologists agree that the principles of classical conditioning, operant conditioning, and observational learning are universal, cultural customs can influence the degree these learning processes are used and culture often determines the content of learning.

from spanking their children. In 1979 Sweden passed a law forbidding parents from using physical punishment, including spanking and slapping, when disciplining their children (Ziegert, 1983). Physical punishment of children is treated as a punishable offense, just like any other attack on a person. The law is especially designed to curb child abuse. Sweden is the only industrial country in the world to pass such a law.

The United States probably could not pass this type of law. Many Americans would view such a law as totalitarian, and the law would likely stimulate protest from civil libertarians and others. An important factor in Sweden's " antispanking" law is its attitude toward rule of law. The United States enforces laws through punishment, but Sweden takes a softer approach, encouraging respect for law through education designed to change attitudes and behavior. When people, often teachers or doctors, suspect that a parent has spanked a child, they often will report the incident because they know that the state will try to provide the parent with emotional and educational support rather than assessing a fine or sending the parent to jail. Accompanying the antispanking law was a parenting guide—*Can One Manage to Raise Children Without Spanking or Slapping?*—that was widely available at day-care centers, preschool programs, physicians' offices, and other similar locations. The publication includes advice about why physical punishment is not a good strategy for disciplining children, along with specific information about better ways to handle children's problems.

The content of learning is also influenced by culture (Cole & Cole, 1996). We cannot learn about something we do not experience. The 4-year-old who grows up among the Bushmen of the Kalahari desert is unlikely to learn about taking baths or pouring water from one glass into another. Similarly, a child growing up in Chicago is unlikely to be skilled at tracking animals or finding water-bearing roots in the desert. Learning often requires practice, and certain behaviors are practiced much more often in some cultures than others. In Bali many children are skilled dancers by the age of 6, while Norwegian children are much more likely to be good skiers and skaters by that age. Children growing up in a Mexican village famous for its pottery may work with clay day after day, while children in a nearby village famous for its woven rugs and sweaters rarely become experts at making clay pots.

Since our last review, we have studied a number of ideas about observational learning, cognitive factors in learning, and biological/cultural factors in learning. A summary of these ideas is presented in concept table 3.

Critical Thinking About Behavior

Operant Solutions to Grocery Store Nightmares

Can you see how applying operant conditioning principles enhances your personal adaptation and can enhance the well-being of others?

Behavior modification has become a popular resource for parents who find themselves struggling with misbehaving children in grocery stores. If you think about it, children in grocery stores are at the mercy of an environment that is not particularly conducive to good behavior. The store is filled with all kinds of stimulating sights, smells, and sounds. Advertisers have gone to great lengths to encourage customers to reach out and pluck their product from the shelves. Why shouldn't such inducements also appeal to children? They do.

Unfortunately, it is very easy to teach children to misbehave in this setting. As the shopper in charge, you probably have a keen sense of the amount of time you wish to spend in the store, and it might be far longer than your child's attention span. How to fix this problem? Some shoppers offer candy as a diversionary tactic when the child gets fussy or feisty. An operant perspective shows how foolhardy this practice can be. In the short run, the child might be quieted for as long as the candy lasts. In the long run, the shopper has taught the child that the way to get candy is to be fussy, whiny, or obnoxious.

What suggestions from the principles of behavior modification would help reduce the stress involved in a trip to the grocery store? Which principle of operant behavior would be most effective in curbing children's misbehavior and in helping the beleaguered shopper—positive reinforcement, negative reinforcement, punishment, or extinction?

If you answered punishment, guess again. Skinner and other behavior modification theorists believe that punishment may be ineffective in the long run in reducing the frequency of an undesirable behavior. Punishment has many side effects that make its use unattractive. It might be too easy for the punisher to overuse punishment to get the intended effect; the punisher risks becoming abusive. The child might learn to behave in the presence of the punisher but continue the behavior when the punisher is not around. Children dislike the punisher, and punishers might not like themselves too much, either. Most of all, punishment discourages undesirable behavior but doesn't teach appropriate behavior in its place. However, many parents have found some success in managing children with time-out consequences (removing the child from the environment for short periods of time as a consequence to each onset of inappropriate behavior).

If you guessed extinction, you are on target. The parent would identify the specific kind of misbehavior to be suppressed. For instance, suppose the child whines. Rather than pay attention to or punish the child, the parent ignores the child, waiting for more appropriate behavior before attending to the child again. As you can easily imagine, there are some problems with this technique. Because extinction can take a long time, it is sometimes tempting to return to old methods out of fatigue. These lapses have the additional danger of intermittently reinforcing the behavior that preceded. We know from reading about schedules of reinforcement earlier in the chapter that intermittent reinforcement can encourage resistance to extinction. Therefore, once you begin operant conditioning by extinction, you must stay with the plan in order for the child to learn the inappropriateness of acting out in the grocery store.

If you guessed positive reinforcement, you could be right. However, you would need to positively reinforce the appropriate behavior of nonwhining rather than reinforce whining. Behavior modification theorists point out that the longer the period in which children manage themselves well, the less time available to be spent in misbehavior. Yet it can feel awkward to compliment children on controlling their behavior.

What about negative reinforcement? Most whining children are not really in real distress; they have learned to whine because it so often pays off in candy and attention from the caregiver. Therefore, negative reinforcement doesn't really apply to the child's situation. However, negative reinforcement explains well how the caregiver's behavior of doling out candy developed originally in response to the child's distress. The noise and embarrassment caused by an acting-out child is hard to bear. When a child embarks on this strategy, the parent might offer candy as way to escape or avoid the problem.

Overview

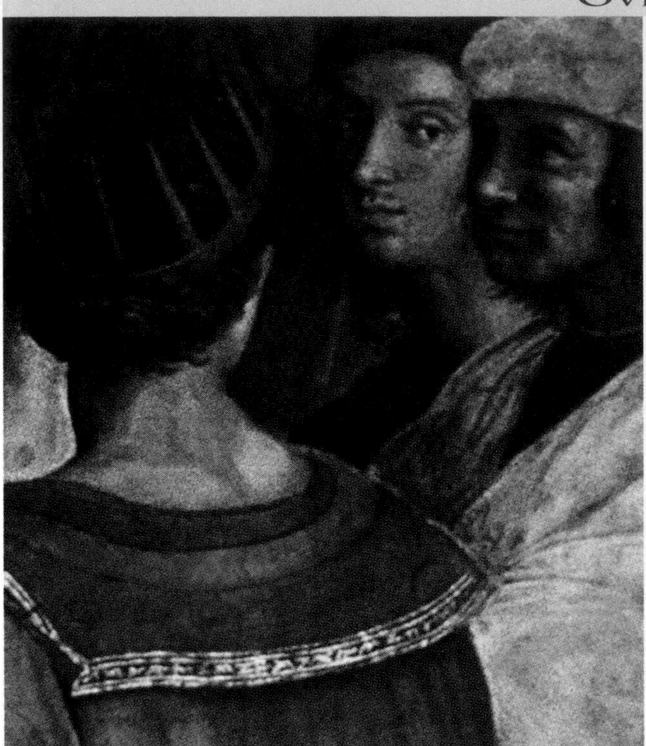

We began this chapter by defining learning and then turned our attention to three main forms of learning—classical conditioning, operant conditioning, and observational learning. Our coverage of classical conditioning focused on Pavlovian conditioning, generalization, discrimination, and extinction, how classical conditioning works, classical conditioning in humans, and an evaluation of classical conditioning. Our discussion of operant conditioning emphasized Thorndike's law of effect, Skinner's operant conditioning, some principles of operant conditioning, extinction, generalization, and discrimination, and applications of operant conditioning. In the final main part of the chapter we explored the nature of observational learning, cognitive factors, and biological and cultural factors in learning. Don't forget that you can obtain an overall summary of the chapter by again studying the three concept tables on pages 177, 188, and 194.

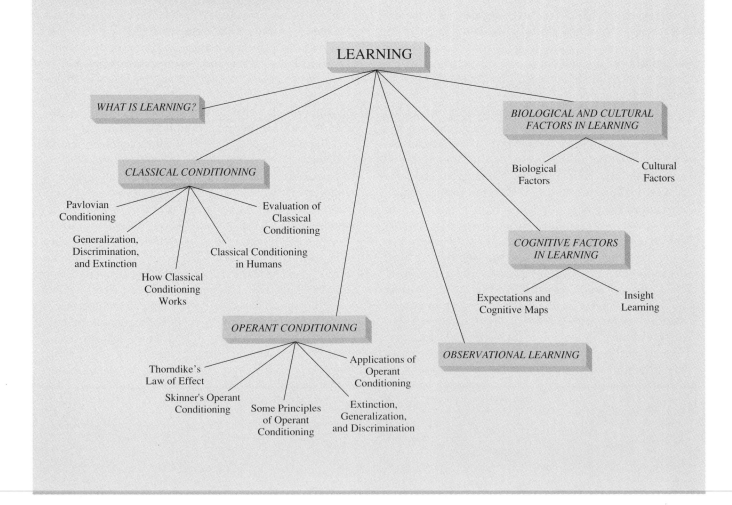

LEARNING

- *WHAT IS LEARNING?*
- *CLASSICAL CONDITIONING*
  - Pavlovian Conditioning
  - Generalization, Discrimination, and Extinction
  - How Classical Conditioning Works
  - Classical Conditioning in Humans
  - Evaluation of Classical Conditioning
- *OPERANT CONDITIONING*
  - Thorndike's Law of Effect
  - Skinner's Operant Conditioning
  - Some Principles of Operant Conditioning
  - Extinction, Generalization, and Discrimination
  - Applications of Operant Conditioning
- *OBSERVATIONAL LEARNING*
- *COGNITIVE FACTORS IN LEARNING*
  - Expectations and Cognitive Maps
  - Insight Learning
- *BIOLOGICAL AND CULTURAL FACTORS IN LEARNING*
  - Biological Factors
  - Cultural Factors

Key Terms

learning A relatively permanent change in behavior that occurs through experience. p. 170

classical conditioning A form of learning in which a neutral stimulus becomes associated with a meaningful stimulus and acquires the capacity to elicit a similar response. p. 170

reflexes Automatic stimulus-response connections that are "hardwired" into the brain. p. 171

unconditioned stimulus (US) A stimulus that produces a response without prior learning. p. 171

unconditioned response (UR) An unlearned response that is automatically associated with the unconditioned stimulus. p. 171

conditioned stimulus (CS) A previously neutral stimulus that elicits the conditioned response after being paired with the unconditioned stimulus. p. 171

conditioned response (CR) The learned response to the conditioned stimulus that occurs after CS-US association. p. 171

generalization In classical conditioning, the tendency of a new stimulus that is similar to the original conditioned stimulus to elicit a response that is similar to the conditioned response. p. 171

discrimination In classical conditioning, the process of learning to respond to certain stimuli and not to respond to others. p. 171

extinction In classical conditioning, the weakening of the conditioned response in the absence of the unconditioned stimulus. p. 171

spontaneous recovery The process in classical conditioning by which a conditioned response can appear again after a time delay without further conditioning. p. 172

stimulus substitution Pavlov's theory of how classical conditioning works: The nervous system is structured in such a way that the CS and US bond together and eventually the CS substitutes for the US. p. 172

information theory The contemporary explanation of how classical conditioning works: The key to understanding classical conditioning is the information the organism obtains from the situation. p. 173

phobias Irrational fears. p. 174

counterconditioning A classical conditioning procedure for weakening a conditioned response of fear by associating the fear-provoking stimulus with a new response that is incompatible with the fear. p. 174

operant conditioning (instrumental conditioning) A form of learning in which the consequences of behavior produce changes in the probability of the behavior's occurrence. p. 176

law of effect Developed by Robert Thorndike, this law states that behaviors followed by positive outcomes are strengthened, whereas behaviors followed by negative outcomes are weakened. p. 177

reinforcement (reward) A consequence that increases the probability that a behavior will occur. p. 178

punishment A consequence that decreases the probability that a behavior will occur. p. 178

positive reinforcement Reinforcement in which the frequency of a response increases because the response is followed by a stimulus. p. 178

negative reinforcement Reinforcement in which the frequency of a response increases because the response either removes a stimulus or involves avoiding the stimulus. p. 178

shaping The process of rewarding approximations of desired behavior. p. 180

chaining An operant conditioning technique used to teach a complex sequence, or chain, of behaviors. The procedure begins by shaping the final response in the sequence, then working backward until a chain of behaviors is learned. p. 181

primary reinforcement The use of reinforcers that are innately satisfying (that is, they do not require any learning on the organism's part to make them pleasurable). p. 181

secondary reinforcement Reinforcement that acquires its positive value through experience; secondary reinforcers are learned, or conditioned, reinforcers. p. 181

partial reinforcement Intermittent reinforcement; responses are not reinforced every time they occur. p. 181

schedules of reinforcement Timetables that determine when a response will be reinforced. p. 181

fixed-ratio schedule Reinforcement of a behavior after a set number of responses. p. 183

variable-ratio schedule A timetable in which responses are rewarded an average number of times, but on an unpredictable basis. p. 183

fixed-interval schedule Reinforcement of the first appropriate response after a fixed amount of time has elapsed. p. 183

variable-interval schedule Reinforcement of a response after a variable amount of time has elapsed. p. 183

extinction In operant conditioning, a decrease in the tendency to perform a behavior that no longer receives either positive or negative reinforcement. p. 183

generalization In operant conditioning, giving the same response to similar stimuli. p. 183

discrimination In operant conditioning, the tendency to respond only to those stimuli that are correlated with reinforcement. p. 184

discriminative stimuli Stimuli that signal that a response will be reinforced. p. 184

applied behavior analysis (behavior modification) The application of operant conditioning principles to change human behavior. p. 184

observational learning Learning that occurs when a person observes and imitates someone else's behavior; also called imitation or modeling. p. 185

S-O-R model A model of learning that gives some importance to cognitive factors. *S* stands for stimulus, *O* for organism, and *R* for response. p. 190

cognitive map An organism's mental representation of the structure of physical space. p. 191

insight learning A form of problem solving in which an organism develops a sudden understanding of a problem's solution. p. 192

preparedness The species-specific biological predisposition to learn in certain ways but not in others. p. 192

instinctive drift The tendency of animals to revert to instinctive behavior that interferes with learning. p. 192

Resources and Readings in Psychology

Behavior Modification: What It Is and How to Do It (1996, 5th ed.)
by G. Martin and R. Pear
Engelwood Cliffs, NJ: Prentice Hall

This excellent, easy-to-read book provides guidelines for using behavior modification to change behavior.

Conditioning and Learning (1996)
by Michael Domjan
Pacific Grove, CA: Brooks/Cole

A leading researcher in learning and conditioning, Domjan discusses contemporary perspectives with special emphasis on classical and instrumental conditioning. Chapter topics include stimilus control of behavior, avoidance learning, and punishment.

Don't Shoot the Dog (1991)
by K. Pryor
New York: Simon & Schuster

This is a practical guide for applying the principles of reinforcement to everyday life. Topics include training animals, managing employees, coping with intrusive roommates, and improving self-control.

Families (1975)
by Gerald Patterson
Champaign, IL: Research Press

Families presents a behavior modification approach that parents can use to correct children's problem behaviors. A step-by-step reinforcement management program is presented. The book is especially helpful for learning how to modify the behavior of aggressive boys whose behavior is out of control.

Learning Disabilities Association of America
4156 Library Road
Pittsburgh, PA 15234
412–341–1515

This organization provides education and support for parents of children with learning disabilities and interested professionals and others. More than 500 chapters are in operation nationwide. Information services, pamphlets, and book recommendations are available.

Learning Disabilities Association of Canada/Troubles d'apprentissage-association canadienne
323 Chapel Street, Suite 200
Ottawa ON KIN 7Z2 Canada
613–238–5721

This association works to advance the education, employment, social development, legal rights, and general well-being of people with learning disabilities. They publish many handbooks for parents, children, and adults with learning disabilities, including *Together for Success: A Road Map for Secondary Students with Learning Disabilities* and their quarterly newsletter, *National.*

Mentors (1992)
by T. Evans
Princeton, NJ: Peterson's Guides

This book describes how mentors can make a difference in children's lives, especially as a tutor in a one-to-one relationship.

National Center for the Study of Corporal Punishment
Temple University
253 Ritter Annex
Philadelphia, PA 19122
215–787–6091

This center provides information about the psychological and educational aspects of school discipline. It also provides legal advocacy to protest the use of corporal punishment and psychological abuse in schools. Consultation service for parents and teachers is available.

Self-Control (1995)
by Alexandra Logue
Upper Saddle River, NJ: Prentice-Hall

This leading researcher evaluates specific areas of concern regarding self control—eating, drug abuse, education, money, lying, depression, suicide, and aggression. Logue also lists places to contact for further information about some of the clinical problems covered in the text.

Social Foundations of Thought (1986)
by Albert Bandura
Englewood Cliffs, NJ: Prentice Hall

This book presents Bandura's cognitive social learning theory, which emphasizes reciprocal connections between behavior, environment, and person (cognition). Extensive coverage of observational learning is included.

Through Mentors
202–393–0512

This organization recruits mentors from corporations, government agencies, universities, and professional firms. The goal is to provide every youth in the District of Columbia with a mentor through high school. To learn how to become involved in a mentoring program or to start such a program, call the number above. Also, the National One to One Partnership Kit guides businesses in establishing mentoring programs (call 202–338–3844).

Walden Two (1948)
by B. F. Skinner
New York: Macmillan

Skinner once entertained the possibility of a career as a writer. In this provocative book, he outlines his ideas on how a more complete understanding of the principles of operant conditioning can produce a happier life. Critics argue that his approach is too manipulative.

C H A P T E R

MEM

Memory

John W. Santrock
Istanbul After Dark, detail

CHAPTER

Memory

with James C. Bartlett

Chapter Outline

Chapter Boxes

> *I come into the fields and spacious*
> *palaces of my memory, where*
> *are treasures of countless images*
> *of things of every manner.*
>
> —**St. Augustine**

Life is all memory, except for the one present moment that goes by so quick you hardly catch it going.

—Tennessee Williams

Images of Psychology

M. K. and the Russian, S.

How important is memory to us? Consider the unfortunate case of M. K., a high school teacher who at the age of 43 was stricken with an acute episode of encephalitis. Within hours he lost access to almost all the memories he had formed during the previous 5 years. Worse still, he had virtually no memory of anything that happened to him after the onset of the encephalitis. Since the illness began, M. K. has learned a few names and a few major events over the years, and he can get around the hospital. M. K.'s tragic circumstance, in which a microscopic viral agent rendered him memoryless, conveys the emptiness of a life without memory.

The power of memory is also revealed in another, very different case. A Russian known only by the initial S. could remember a list of seventy items without making an error, and he had no difficulty recalling the list backward. S. once was asked to remember the following formula:

$$N \cdot \sqrt{d^2 \cdot \frac{85}{VX}} \cdot 3\sqrt{\frac{276^2 \cdot 86x}{n^2V \cdot \pi 264}}\, n^2b = sv\,\frac{1624}{32^2} \cdot r^2s$$

S. studied the formula for 7 minutes and then reported how he memorized it. The following portion of his response reveals how he made up stories to aid his memory:

> Neiman (N) came out and jabbed at the ground with his cane ($\cdot$). He looked up at a tall tree, which resembled the square-root sign ($\sqrt{}$), and thought to himself: "No wonder this tree has withered and begun to expose its roots. After all, it was here when I built these two houses" (d^2). Once again he poked his cane ($\cdot$). Then he said: "The houses are old, I'll have to get rid of them; the sale will bring in far more money." He had originally invested 85,000 in them (85).

S.'s complete story was four times this length. It must have been a powerful one, because 15 years later with no advance notice he recalled the formula perfectly.

Envious as we might be of S.'s remarkable memory, especially when taking college exams, S. suffered from it. He had to devise techniques for forgetting because he remembered virtually everything, no matter how trivial. He once commented that each word called up images, which collided with one another—the result sometimes was chaos. Forgetting was M. K.'s curse, but it was S.'s salvation. It should be noted that individuals like S., who are extremely good at remembering vast amounts of material, are somewhat rare.

Preview

There are few moments when we are not steeped in memory. Memory can quietly stir, or spin off, with each step we take, each thought we think, each word we utter. Memory is the skein of private images that weaves the past into the present. It anchors the self in continuity. In this chapter we will explore many facets of memory, including the nature of memory, memory processes, how knowledge is represented in memory, the neurobiological basis of memory, and mnemonics and memory strategies.

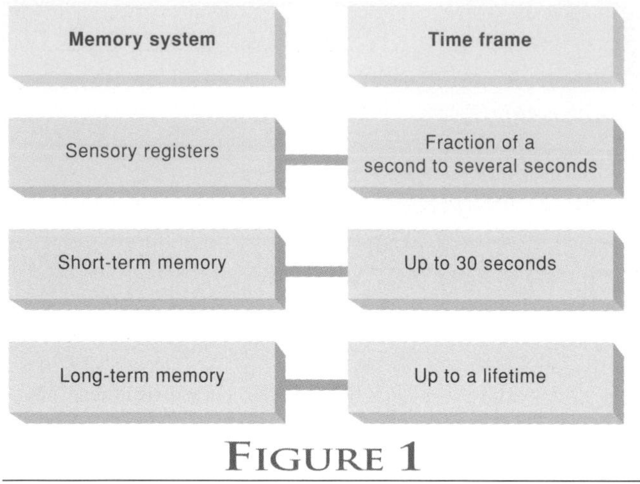

FIGURE 1

Memory Systems

FIGURE 2

Auditory and Visual Sensory Registers
If you hear this bird's call while walking through the woods, your auditory sensory registers hold the information for several seconds. If you see the bird, your visual sensory registers hold the information for only about one-quarter of a second.

THE NATURE OF MEMORY

Memory *is the retention of information over time. Psychologists study how information is initially placed, or encoded into memory, how it is retained, or stored, after being encoded, and how it is found, or retrieved, for a certain purpose later.* To learn about the nature of memory, we will examine memory's time frames and contents.

Time Frames of Memory

We remember some information for less than a second, some for half a minute, and other information for minutes, hours, years, even a lifetime. Since memory often functions differently across these varied time intervals, we can distinguish among different types of memory partly on the basis of their differing time frames. The three types of memory that vary according to their time frames are *sensory memory,* with time frames of a fraction of a second to several seconds; *working memory* (also often called short-term memory), with time frames of up to 30 seconds; and *long-term memory,* with time frames of up to a lifetime (see figure 1). Let's now examine in greater detail each of these three important types of memory that are linked to the time frames of their existence.

Sensory Memory

Sensory memory *holds information from the world in its original sensory form for only an instant, not much longer than the brief time it is exposed to the visual, auditory, and other senses.* Sensory memory is very rich and detailed, but the information in it is very quickly lost unless certain processes are engaged in that transfer it into working or long-term memory.

Think about all the sights and sounds you encounter as you walk to class on a typical morning. Literally thousands of stimuli come into your fields of vision and hearing—cracks in the sidewalk, chirping birds, a noisy motorcycle, the blue sky, faces of hundreds of people. We do not process all of these stimuli, but we do process a number of them. In general, you process many more stimuli at the sensory level than you consciously notice. The sensory registers retain this information from your senses, including a large portion of what you think you ignore. But the sensory registers do not retain the information very long. **Echoic memory** *(from the word* echo*) is the name given to auditory sensory memory in which information is retained up to several seconds.* **Iconic memory** *(from the word* icon, *which means* "image"*) is the name given to visual sensory memory in which information is retained only for about 1/4 second* (see figure 2). The sensory memory for other senses, such as smell and touch, has received little attention.

Though the way sensory memory functions is difficult to detect, several common experiences reveal its existence. Consider the "What-did-you-say-Oh-never-mind"

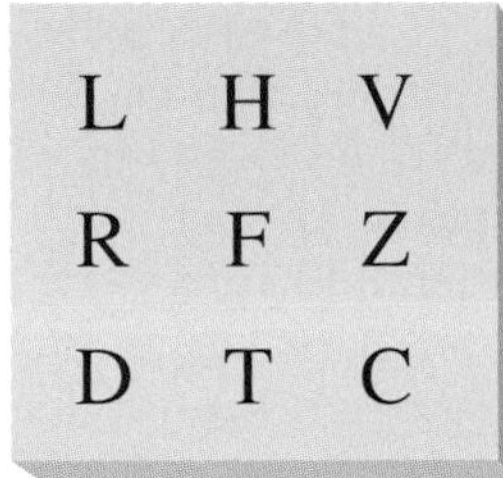

FIGURE 3

Sperling's Sensory Registers Experiment
This array of stimuli is similar to those flashed for about 1/20 second to subjects in Sperling's experiment.

phenomena that can occur when you are reading. You are engrossed in a book when someone walks into the room and asks you a question. You notice they are speaking, but since your attention is focused on your book, you do not comprehend the message. You experience the *sound* but not the *sense.* Looking up, you ask, "What did you say?" Before the person can answer, though, you somehow just "know." Then you say, "Oh, never mind," and respond to their question because you now understand. The sensory features of the spoken message made it to your echoic sensory memory, but initially they made it no further. Looking up, you switched your attention, retrieving the information from echoic memory and sending it "upstream" for higher-level analysis (comprehension).

The "What-did-you-say-Oh-never-mind" phenomenon involves echoic memory. The first scientific research on sensory memory, however, focused on iconic memory. In George Sperling's (1960) classic study, subjects were presented with patterns of stimuli such as those in figure 3. As you look at the letters, you have no trouble recognizing them. But Sperling flashed the letters on a screen for only very brief intervals, about 1/20 second. After a pattern was flashed on the screen, the subjects could report only 4 or 5 letters. With such short exposure, reporting all 9 letters was impossible.

But some of the participants in Sperling's study reported feeling that, for an instant, they could *see* all 9 letters within a briefly flashed pattern. But they ran into trouble when they tried to *name* all the letters they had initially *seen.* One hypothesis to explain this experience is that all 9 letters were initially processed as far as iconic sensory memory. This is why all 9 letters were *seen.* However, forgetting was so rapid that the subjects could name only a handful of letters before they were lost from sensory memory.

Sperling decided to test this hypothesis. He reasoned that if all 9 letters were actually processed in sensory memory, they should all be available for a brief time. To test this possibility, Sperling sounded a low, medium, or high tone just after a pattern of letters was shown. The subjects were told that the tone was a signal to report only the letters from the bottom, middle, or top row, respectively. Under these conditions, the subjects performed much better, suggesting a brief memory for most or all of the letters.

Working Memory

Working memory, *also sometimes called short-term memory, is a limited-capacity memory system in which information is retained for as long as 30 seconds, unless the information is rehearsed, in which case it can be retained longer.* Compared to sensory memory, working memory is limited in capacity but is relatively longer in duration. Its limited capacity was examined by George Miller (1956) in a classic paper with a catchy title, "The Magical Number Seven, Plus or Minus Two." Miller pointed out that on many tasks individuals are limited in how much information they can keep track of without external aids. Usually the limit is in the range of 7 ± 2 items. The most widely cited example of the 7 ± 2 phenomenon involves **memory span,** *which is the number of digits an individual can report back in order after a single presentation of them.* Most college students can handle lists of 8 or 9 digits without making any errors. Longer lists, however, pose problems because they exceed your working memory capacity. If you rely on simple working memory to retain longer lists of items you probably will make errors.

Of course, there are many examples where working memory seems to hold much more than 5 or 6 units. For instance, consider a simple list of words: *hot, city, book, time, forget, tomorrow,* and *smile.* Try to hold these words in memory for a moment, then write them down. If you recalled all seven words, you succeeded in holding 34 letters in your working memory. Does this make you a genius with outrageous working memory skills? Or does it disprove the idea of limited capacity? The answer is neither. **Chunking** *is the grouping or "packing" of information into higher-order units that can be remembered as single units. Chunking expands working memory by making large amounts of information more manageable.* In demonstrating working memory for 34 letters, you "chunked" the letters into 7 meaningful words. Since your working memory can handle seven chunks, you were successful in remembering 34 letters. Although working memory has limited capacity, chunking lets you make the most of it.

Maintenance rehearsal *is the conscious repetition of information that increases the length of time it stays in working memory* (Craik & Lockhart, 1972). To understand what we mean by maintenance rehearsal, imagine you are looking up a telephone number. If you can directly reach for the telephone, you will probably have no trouble dialing the number, because the entire combined action of looking up the number and dialing it can take place in the 30-second time frame of your working memory. But what if the telephone is not right by the phone book? Perhaps the phone book is in the kitchen and you want to talk privately on the extension in the den. You will probably *rehearse* the number as you walk from the kitchen to the den. Most of us experience a kind of "inner voice" that repeats the number again and again until we finally dial it. If someone or something interrupts our maintenance rehearsal, we may lose the information from short-term memory.

Working memory without maintenance rehearsal lasts half a minute or less, but if rehearsal is not interrupted, information can be retained indefinitely. Our rehearsal is often verbal, giving the impression of an inner voice, but it can also be visual or spatial, giving the impression of a private inner eye. One way to use your visualization skills is to maintain the appearance of an object or scene for a period of time after you have viewed it. People who are unusually good at this task are said to have *eidetic imagery,* or a photographic memory. All of us can do this to some degree, but a small number of individuals may be so good at maintaining an image they literally "see" the page of a textbook as they try to remember information during a test. However, eidetic imagery is so rare it has been difficult to study; some psychologists even doubt its existence (Gray & Gummerman, 1975).

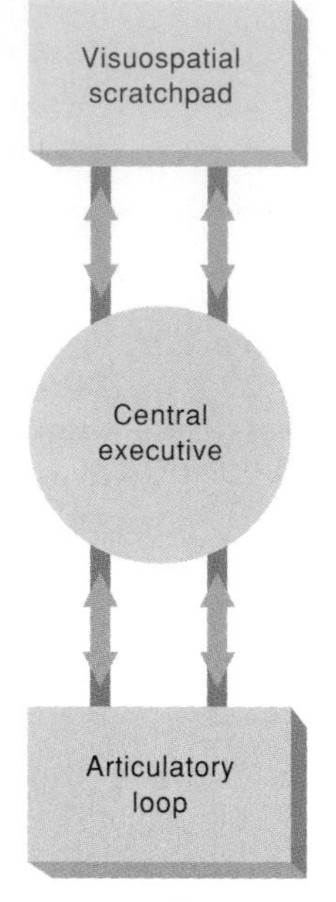

FIGURE 4

A Model of Working Memory
In this model, the two slave systems—the visuospatial scratchpad and phonological loop—help the executive do its job. The visuospatial scratchpad involves our spatial imagery skills, the phonological loop our language skills.

Rehearsal is an important aspect of working memory, but there is much more we need to know about this type of memory. Working memory is a kind of mental "workbench" that lets us manipulate and assemble information when we make decisions, solve problems, and comprehend written and spoken language (Klatsky, 1984). For example, in one study, young children who were accurate readers but had trouble comprehending what they had read were studied (Yuill, Oakhill, & Parkin, 1989). Why couldn't this group of children comprehend what they read? Examination of their cognitive skills revealed that their poor working memory was responsible for their poor comprehension.

One model of working memory is shown in figure 4 (Baddeley, 1990, 1993, 1995). In this model, working memory consists of a general "executive" and two "slave" systems that help the executive do its job. One of the slave systems is the phonological loop, which is specialized to process language information. This is where maintenance rehearsal occurs. The other slave system is the visuospatial scratchpad, which includes some of our spatial imagery skills, such as visualizing an object or a scene. We will soon see that such visualization has powerful effects when we learn new information.

To gain a better grasp of the working memory system, imagine that a friend is giving you directions to a party, telling you to head north on Central Expressway, turn right at Renner, turn left at Shiloh, and then left again on Leon Drive. Having nothing to write on, you might try to hold this information in memory through maintenance rehearsal. This would involve your phonological loop. But an additional strategy is to picture the route using your visuospatial scratchpad. In using this tactic, you notice the route follows a zigzag pattern going generally northeast until the last turn, which goes west. Although you still want to remember the sequence of street names, you no longer have to worry about the left and right turns—your image captured this information. The phonological loop and the visuospatial scratchpad often work in concert like this to help us process information more efficiently.

Working memory has a wide range of functions that affect many aspects of our lives (Ericsson & Kintsch, 1995; Wenger & Payne, 1996). For example, we all admire people with elaborate vocabularies, and many individuals spend considerable time trying to increase their vocabulary. Some persons seem to learn new words with little effort; for others, increasing their vocabulary is extremely hard work. In one study, the talent some individuals have in easily improving their vocabulary was located in the phonological loop (Gathercole & Baddeley, 1989). In this study, 4- and 5-year-old children were tested for their ability to repeat back nonsense words, which reflects the functioning of the phonological loop. The children's performance on this task was a good predictor of their vocabulary 1 year later.

Working memory can also help us understand how brain damage influences cognitive skills. For example, some types of amnesiacs perform well on working memory tasks, but show gross deficits in learning new information in long-term memory tasks. Another group of patients have normal long-term memory abilities, yet do very poorly on working memory tasks. One such patient had good long-term memory despite having a memory span of only two digits (Baddeley, 1992)! Working memory deficits also are involved in Alzheimer's disease—a progressive, irreversible brain disorder in older adults. Baddeley and his colleagues (in press) believe the central executive of the working memory model is the culprit, because Alzheimer's patients have great difficulty coordinating different mental activities, one of the central executive's functions.

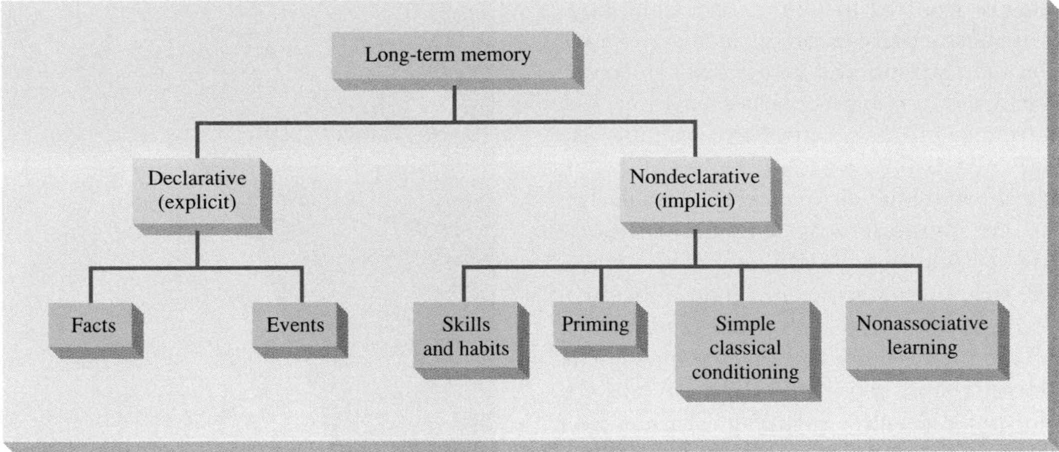

FIGURE 5

A Hierarchical Organization of Long-Term Memory's Contents

Long-Term Memory

Long-term memory *is a relatively permanent type of memory that holds huge amounts of information for a long period of time.* In one study, people remembered the names and faces of their high school classmates with considerable accuracy for at least 25 years (Bahrick, Bahrick, & Whitlinger, 1975). The storehouse of long-term memory is indeed staggering. John von Neumann, a distinguished computer scientist, put the size at 2.8×10^{20} (280 quintillion) bits, which in practical terms means that our storage capacity is virtually unlimited. Von Neumann assumed we never forget anything, but even considering that we do forget things, we can hold several billion times more information than a large computer. Even more impressive is the efficiency with which we retrieve information. It usually takes only a moment to search through this vast storehouse to find the information we want. Who discovered America? What was the name of your first date? When were you born? Who developed the first psychology laboratory? You can, of course, answer these questions instantly.

Contents of Memory

Just as different types of memory can be distinguished by how long they last—time frames of memory—memories within each time frame can be distinguished by their *content.* As we discussed earlier, the contents of sensory memory consist of memory for audition (echoic memory) and vision (iconic memory). Similarly, we learned that the contents of working memory vary according to at least two kinds of content—the articulatory loop, which holds information about speech, and the visuospatial scratchpad, which holds mental images. Therefore, it should be no surprise that the contents of long-term memory can also be differentiated. Indeed, many psychologists today accept the three-level hierarchy of long-term memory contents shown in figure 5 (Squire, 1987). In this hierarchical organization of long-term memory's contents, long-term memory is divided into the subtypes of declarative and nondeclarative memory. Declarative memory is subdivided into episodic memory and semantic memory, while nondeclarative memory is subdivided into skills and habits, priming, classical conditioning, and nonassociative learning.

Declarative and Nondeclarative Memory

Declarative memory *is the conscious recollection of information, such as specific facts or events, and, at least in humans, information that can be verbally communicated. Because of its conscious and verbalizable nature, declarative memory has been called "explicit memory."* Examples of declarative (or explicit) memory include recounting the events of a movie you have seen and describing a basic principle of psychology to someone. However, you do not need to be talking to be using declarative memory. Simply sitting and consciously reflecting about Einstein's theory of relativity, or the date you had last weekend, involves declarative memory.

Nondeclarative memory *refers to a variety of phenomena of memory in which behavior is affected by prior experience without that experience being consciously recollected. Because nondeclarative memory cannot be verbalized or consciously recollected, at least not in the form of specific events or facts, it also is called "implicit memory."*

Examples of nondeclarative (implicit) memory include the skills of playing tennis, riding a bicycle, and typing. They also include perceptual abilities, often called "priming," such as finding a product on a grocery store shelf. The first time you purchase a certain kind of product, it often takes a while to find it on the shelf, even if you know what aisle to walk down. But with practice the product "pops out" perceptually as you scan down the aisle. Another example of nondeclarative memory is classical conditioning, as when a dog (or even you, yourself) begin to salivate after hearing the dinner bell. Conditioning is thought of as associative learning (such as, learning associations between stimuli and responses). However, more complex forms of nonassociative learning, like learning the grammar of one's native language, are also nondeclarative.

To further illustrate the distinction between declarative (explicit) and nondeclarative (implicit) memory, imagine you are at Wimbledon: Steffi Graf moves gracefully for a wide forehand, finishes her follow-through, runs quickly back to the center of the court, pushes off for a short ball, and volleys the ball for a winner. If we asked her about this rapid sequence of movements, she probably would have difficulty explaining each move. In contrast, if we asked her who is her toughest opponent, she might quickly respond, "Sanchez-Vicario." In the first instance, she was unable to verbally describe exactly what she had done. In the second, she had no problem answering our question.

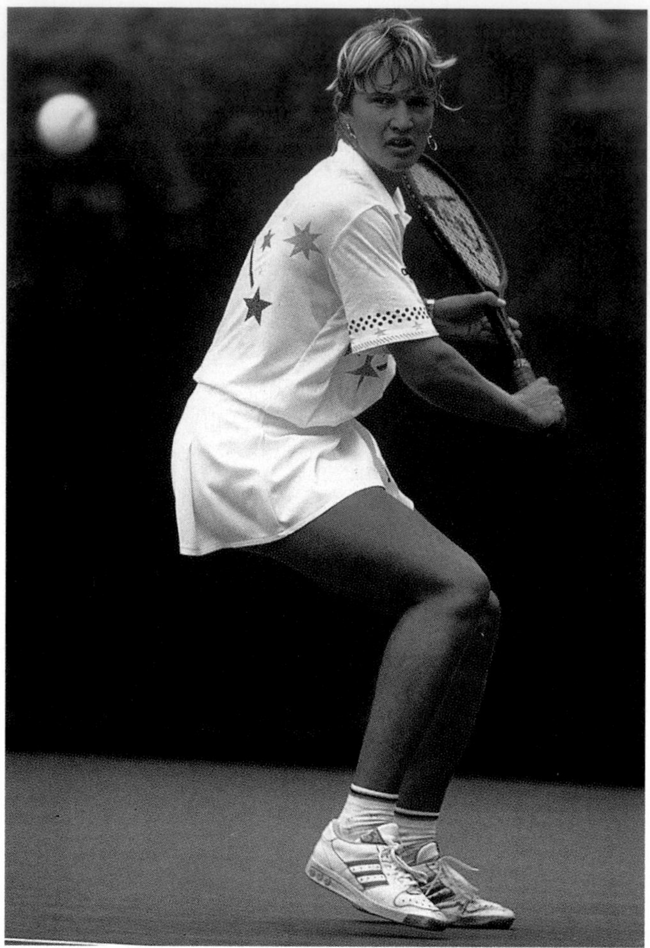

What kind of knowledge is involved when Steffi Graf hits a tennis ball?

Episodic and Semantic Memory

Canadian cognitive psychologist Endel Tulving (1972) has been the foremost advocate of distinguishing between two subtypes of declarative memory: episodic and semantic (see figure 5). **Episodic memory** *is the retention of information about the where and when of life's happenings—what it was like when your younger brother or sister was born, what happened to you on your first date, what you were doing when you heard Desert Storm had begun in the Persian Gulf, and what you had for breakfast this morning.*

Semantic memory *is a person's knowledge about the world. It includes a person's fields of expertise (knowledge of chess for a skilled chess player, for example); general academic knowledge of the sort learned in school (knowledge of geometry, for example); and "everyday" knowledge about meanings of words, famous individuals, important places, and common things (who Nelson Mandela and Mahatma Gandhi are, for example). A critical characteristic of semantic memory knowledge is that it appears to be independent of the individual's personal identity with the past.* You can access a fact—such as "Lima is the capital of Peru"—and not have the foggiest notion of when and where you learned it.

Several examples help to clarify the distinction between episodic and semantic memory. In a certain type of amnesiac state, a person might forget entirely who she is—her name, family, career, and all other personal information about herself—yet she can talk and demonstrate general knowledge about the world. Her episodic memory is impaired, but her semantic memory is functioning. An especially dramatic case of this type, a young man named K. C., was reported by Endel Tulving (1989). After suffering a motorcycle accident, K. C. lost virtually all use of his episodic memory. The loss was so profound that he was unable to consciously recollect a single thing that had ever happened to him. At the same time, K. C.'s semantic memory was sufficiently preserved that he could learn about his past as a set of facts, just as he would learn about another person's life. He could report, for example, that the saddest day of his life was when his brother died of drowning about 10 years before. This sounds as if K. C. has episodic memory, but further questioning revealed that he had no conscious memory of the drowning event. He simply knew about the drowning because he was able to recall—apparently through use of his semantic memory—what he had been told about his brother by other members of his family.

Some aspects of the episodic/semantic memory distinction are summarized in table 1. Although the distinctions listed have attracted considerable attention, they remain controversial. One criticism is that many cases of declarative memory are neither purely episodic nor purely semantic but fall in a gray area in between. Consider your memory for what you studied last night. You probably added knowledge to your semantic memory—that was,

TABLE 1

Some Characteristics That Differentiate Episodic and Semantic Memory

Characteristic	Episodic Memory	Semantic Memory
Units	Events, episodes	Facts, ideas, concepts
Organization	Temporal	Conceptual
Affect	More important	Less important
Retrieval process	Deliberate (effortful)	Automatic
Retrieval report	"I remember"	"I know"
Education	Irrelevant	Relevant
Intelligence	Irrelevant	Relevant
Legal testimony	Admissible in court	Inadmissible in court

Source: From E. Tulving, *Elements of Episodic Memory*, p. 35.

after all, the reason you were studying. You probably remember where you were studying, as well as when you started and about when you stopped. You probably also can remember some minor occurrences, such as a burst of loud laughter from the room next door or the coffee you spilled on the desk. Is episodic or semantic memory involved here? Tulving (1983) argues that semantic and episodic systems often work together in forming new memories. In such cases, the memory that ultimately is formed might consist of an autobiographical episode *and* semantic information.

Priming

Until very recently, nondeclarative (or implicit) memory had been given little attention in comparison to declarative (or explicit) memory. However, today there is a flurry of research interest in one type of nondeclarative memory—priming (Bowers & Schacter, 1993; Reinitz & Alexander, 1996; Rybash, 1996). **Priming** *is the facilitation in responding to a stimulus that immediately follows a related stimulus.* An example of priming is the perceptual experience of improving your ability to find a product on a grocery-store shelf. Another example involves trying to complete the following word fragments to make English words:

_SS_SS_N
A_PI__N
Y_GH_R_
R_I_I_
R_M_UN_TI_US

If you had some difficulty completing the words, you are not alone. But what if before doing the fragment completion you had seen the following words: *assassin, aspirin, yogurt, raisin,* and *rambunctious?* You might suspect that your performance in completing the fragments would have been much better. Memory researchers have found that such prior exposure to stimuli often improves people's performance on fragment completion tasks (Tulving, Schacter, & Stark, 1982).

Priming is clearly different from declarative types of memory—both episodic and semantic—because it does not involve explicit or conscious recollection of previous experiences. Tests of priming require individuals to identify, reproduce, or judge stimuli in some way, not to decide if the stimuli were previously studied (Wippich, 1995). In fact, priming occurs regardless of whether a person consciously remembers having previously seen the stimuli. Some memory experts, such as Daniel Schacter and Endel Tulving (1994), believe that priming involves a different memory system than other types of nondeclarative memory. Specifically, they suggest that the nondeclarative abilities of skill-acquisition and conditioning involve a system called **procedural memory,** *which deals with gradual, incremental forms of learning (such as learning to ride a bicycle or ice skate).* In contrast, many phenomena of priming are based on a **perceptual representation system (PRS),** *which is important in the perceptual identification of words, objects, faces, and other important types of stimuli in our world.* Unlike procedural memory, the PRS exhibits rapid learning: Even one exposure to ASSASSIN may improve your ability to complete the fragment, _SS_SS_N, even though one full week has gone by (Tulving, Schacter, & Stark, 1982). Perhaps the most impressive evidence that procedural memory and PRS are separate memory systems comes from studies of patients with different types of brain disease. Patients with Huntington's disease suffer on procedural memory tasks such as motor-skill learning, but their priming appears to be intact. In contrast, patients with Alzheimer's disease appear normal in simple motor-skill learning, but their priming is impaired (Butters, Heindel & Salmon, 1990). Research is ongoing, but these findings suggest motor-skill learning and some types of priming are based on different circuits in the brain. The basal ganglia damaged in Huntington's disease may be critical for motor-skill learning, whereas certain areas of the cerebral cortex which tend to atrophy in Alzheimer's disease may be essential for priming.

Interactions Between Types of Memory

Although there are several types of memory, they often work together when we perform tasks. The traditional information-processing model was developed in the late 1960s by Richardson Atkinson and Richard Shiffrin (1968) (see figure 6). In the **traditional information-processing model,** *memory involves a sequence of three stages—sensory registers, short-term memory, and long-term memory.* Much information makes it no further than the sensory registers, which means that it is retained for only a few seconds at most. However, some information—that to which we pay attention—is transferred into short-term (or working) memory. Information in short-term memory is retained for somewhat longer than that in sensory memory; but without the aid of "control processes," such as rehearsal (what we called "maintenance rehearsal" earlier), its life is still short—about 30 seconds. Atkinson and Shiffrin claimed that the longer information was maintained in short-term memory through rehearsal, the greater the likelihood that it would be transferred to long-term memory. Retrieval involves searching long-term memory and taking the information we find in this search back to short-term memory. In sum, in the traditional information-processing model, retaining information for more than a few seconds required that it be transferred into short-term memory by paying attention to it, and that it then be transferred to long-term memory through rehearsal or other control processes.

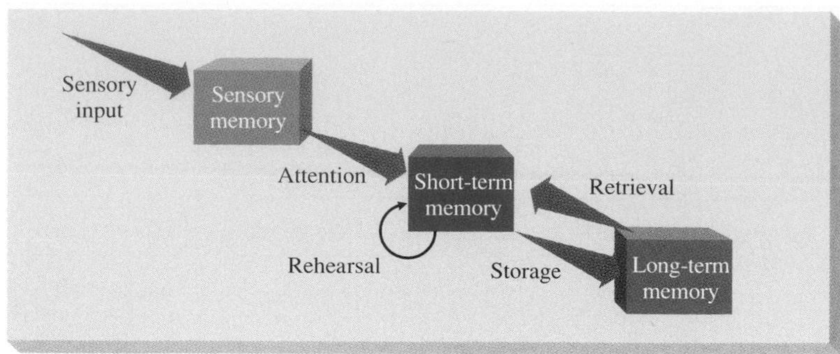

FIGURE 6

The Traditional Information-Processing Model of Memory

Although the influential traditional information-processing model of memory captures some important aspects of memory, it does not adequately distinguish different contents (such as semantic, episodic, and nondeclarative) of long-term memory and does not do justice to the complex nature of working memory, with its executive and slave systems (see figure 4). Another limitation of the traditional model is its failure to explain the kind of brain-damaged patient we described earlier, one who has a good long-term memory but a memory span of only two digits. If learning involves transfer from short-term memory to long-term memory, an impaired short-term memory would create a bottleneck by greatly reducing storage of new information into long-term memory. Thus, having a good long-term memory and a poor short-term memory just would not be possible. We previously described how the letters of a word are chunked together as a single unit in short-term memory. How could we chunk the letters correctly unless we used long-term memory to recognize the word?

A more contemporary model is the **working memory model,** *which states that long-term memory precedes working memory, and that working memory uses long-term memory in a variety of flexible ways* (see figure 7). To get a better sense of the working memory model, consider the situation you are in right now—reading this textbook for your introductory psychology class. Information flows into your sensory memory, activating knowledge of visual features, words, and word meanings in declarative memory. Some of this activated knowledge reaches working memory, where the phonological loop and visuospatial scratchpad can be brought into play to help comprehension. For example, in tackling a tough section of this book, you might find yourself proceeding very slowly through a sentence, using maintenance rehearsal (in the phonological loop) to "hold on" to the first words while you "take in" words that follow. Alternately, when studying a book with rich spatial content (such as architecture or astronomy), you might visualize the meaning of the sentences you are reading using the visuospatial scratchpad. The comprehension you achieve through such working memory processes, results in new learning, which is represented by the arrow from working memory back to the declarative portion of long-term memory in figure 7.

The arrows in figure 7 between working memory and declarative memory represent retrieval as well as comprehension. The executive formulates a retrieval strategy and starts a search of declarative memory (right-to-left arrow). If appropriate information is found, a copy of the declarative information is sent back to the executive component, where conscious recollection takes place (left-to-right arrow).

The important role of nondeclarative memory is again illustrated in tasks such as reading (Carpenter & Just, 1981). Activated knowledge in the working memory system can trigger small units of nondeclarative knowledge, often called "procedures." These procedures detect

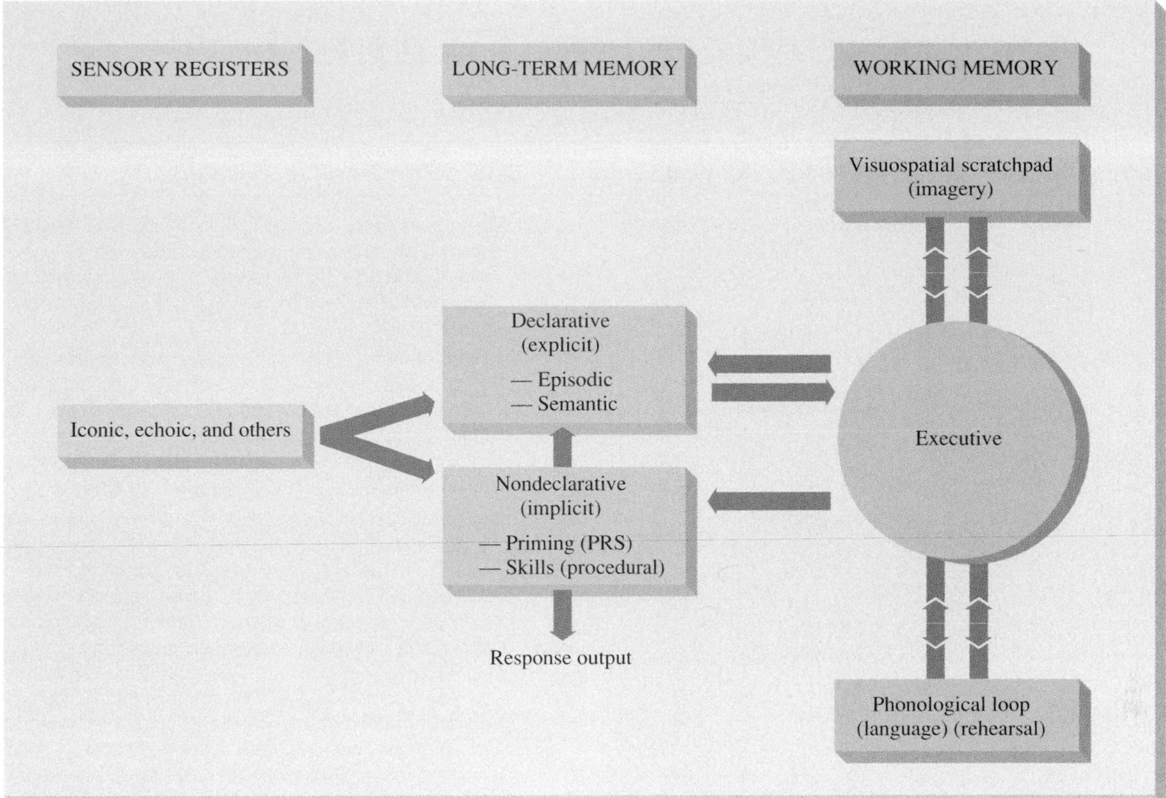

FIGURE 7

The Contemporary Working Memory Model

information in working memory and replace it with new knowledge drawn from semantic memory—this would involve following the arrows in figure 7 from working memory to nondeclarative memory, from nondeclarative memory to declarative (semantic) memory, and from declarative memory back to working memory. Some of these procedures apply to language rules. For example, if you had just read the words *Susan, hit, John,* and representations of these words were placed in working memory, a procedure that interrogates semantic memory might add the semantic information that *Susan* was an agent, *hit* was an action, and *John* was an object of the action. If the words had been *Susan, was, hit, by,* and *John,* another procedure might interrogate semantic memory to add the information that *John* was the agent and *Susan* was the object. Note that there is no direct arrow from nondeclarative memory to working memory. This reflects the fact that nondeclarative knowledge cannot be consciously recollected or verbalized. However, it can and does affect conscious recollection and verbal behavior by activating knowledge stored in the declarative component of long-term memory.

At this point, we have discussed a number of ideas about what memory is, time frames of memory, subtypes of memory within time frames, and relations among different types of memory. A summary of these ideas is presented in concept table 1.

Memory Processes

Psychologists who study memory are especially interested in **memory processes,** *which involve the encoding of new information into memory and to the retrieval of what was previously stored.*

Encoding

Encoding *is the transformation and/or transfer of information into a memory system.* Information can be encoded into sensory memory and short-term or working memory, but here our main focus is on encoding information into long-term memory. In everyday language, encoding has much in common with learning. When you are listening to a lecture, watching a movie, listening to music, or

Concept Table 1

The Nature of Memory

Concept	Processes/Related Ideas	Characteristics/Description
What Is Memory?	Its nature	Memory is the retention of information over time. Psychologists study how information is encoded into memory, how it is stored, and how it is retrieved for some purpose later. Two important ways memory varies are in its time frame and in its contents.
Time Frames of Memory	Sensory memory	This type of memory holds information from the world in its original sensory form only for an instant, not much longer than the brief time it is exposed to the visual, auditory, and other senses. Visual sensory memory (iconic memory) retains information for about 1/4 second, auditory sensory memory (echoic memory) for several seconds.
	Working memory	This type of memory, also called short-term memory, is a limited-capacity memory system in which information is retained for as long as 30 seconds, unless the information is rehearsed, in which case it can be retained longer. Compared to sensory memory, working memory is limited in capacity but has a relatively long duration—up to about 30 seconds. According to George Miller, the limitation of working memory is 7±2 units of information. Chunking can expand working memory and maintenance rehearsal keeps information in working memory longer. In one model of working memory, an executive plus two slave systems—the phonological loop (which holds speech information) and the visuospatial scratchpad (which holds mental images) are involved.
	Long-term memory	This type of memory is a relatively permanent type of memory that holds huge amounts of information for a long period of time.
Contents of Memory	Declarative (explicit) and nondeclarative (implicit) memory	Many psychologists accept a three-level hierarchical organization of memory in which long-term memory is divided into declarative and nondeclarative memory. Declarative memory is subdivided into episodic and semantic memory, and nondeclarative memory is subdivided into skills (procedural memory) and priming (perceptual representation system [PRS]), classical conditioning, and other types of nonconscious knowledge. Declarative memory, which has been called “explicit memory,” is the conscious recollection of information, such as specific facts or events, and, at least in humans, information that can be verbally communicated. Nondeclarative memory, which has been called “implicit memory,” refers to knowledge in the form of skills, habits, and cognitive operations. Nondeclarative memory cannot be consciously recollected, at least not in the form of specific events or facts, and this makes such memory difficult, if not impossible, to communicate verbally.
	Episodic and semantic memory	Episodic memory is the retention of information about the where and when of life’s happenings. Semantic memory is a person’s knowledge about the world.
	Priming	This refers to a type of nondeclarative memory that involves improvement in the ability to identify objects or to make perceptual judgments about objects due to prior experiences with these objects.
Interactions Between Types of Memory	Their nature	The traditional information-processing model involves a sequence of three stages—sensory registers, short-term memory, and long-term memory. The working memory model is the most widely accepted contemporary model of memory. It emphasizes that long-term memory precedes working memory, and that, in general, memory consists of complex interactions between different types of memory.

talking to a friend, you are encoding information into long-term memory. It is unlikely, though, that you are encoding all the information you receive. Psychologists are interested not only in how much encoding takes place, but also in the types of processes involved and their operating principles. Among the processes believed to be extremely important in encoding are automatic and effortful processing, depth of processing and elaboration of information, imagery, and organization, each of which we consider in turn.

Depth of processing ↓		
SHALLOW PROCESSING	Physical and perceptual features are analyzed.	The lines, angles, and contour that make up the physical appearance of an object, such as a car, are detected.
INTERMEDIATE PROCESSING	Stimulus is recognized and labeled.	The object is recognized as a car.
DEEP PROCESSING	Semantic, meaningful, symbolic characteristics are used.	Associations connected with car are brought to mind—you think about the Porsche or Ferrari you hope to buy or the fun you and friends had on spring break when you drove a car to the beach.

FIGURE 8

Depth of Processing
According to the levels of processing theory of memory, deep processing of stimuli produces better memory of them.

Automatic and Effortful Processing

Encoding processes differ in how much effort they require. For example, imagine you are driving down a street and chatting with a friend. You're fine as long as the driving is easy and the conversation involves an everyday topic, such as gossip about a mutual acquaintance. But what if the streets are icy, or if the conversation turns serious and you find yourself in an intense argument? Something probably has to give—the driving or the talking. If two or more activities are somewhat difficult, it is almost impossible to perform them simultaneously without causing a problem, such as an increase in errors. Because of this fact, many cognitive psychologists believe in the existence of a kind of mental energy for doing mental work. They believe that the amount of this energy is limited, and that therefore overload can occur. This mental energy is defined as *capacity, cognitive resources,* or simply *effort.* Using this concept, psychologists distinguish effortful processing and automatic processing. **Effortful processing** *requires capacity or resources to encode information into memory.* **Automatic processing** *does not require capacity, resources, or effort to encode information into memory.* Automatic processing occurs regardless of how people focus their attention (Hasher & Zacks, 1979).

Information about spatial aspects of the environment or frequency of events can be encoded automatically. For example, many students who are taking a test remember reading a certain piece of information on a specific page of the text. Such memory for location of written information is not based on conscious memorization strategies, but rather automatic memory processes. However, many activities that are important for memory do require mental effort—organization, rehearsal, visualization, and elaboration, for example. In a number of studies, this allocation of capacity, or effort, was related to good memory (Ellis, Thomas, & Rodriguez, 1984; O'Brien & Myers, 1985).

Where do effortful processes take place within our memory systems? Return to figure 7 and take another look at the portion labeled working memory. Effortful processing takes place mainly in working memory. Now we consider some of the most important effortful processes—depth of processing and elaboration, mental imagery, and organization.

Depth of Processing and Elaboration

Following the discovery that maintenance rehearsal was not an efficient way to improve long-term memory, Fergus Craik and Robert Lockhart (1972) developed a new model of memory. **Levels of processing** *is Craik and Lockhart's theory that memory is on a continuum from shallow to deep; in this theory, deeper processing produces better memory.* The sensory or physical features of stimuli are analyzed first at a *shallow* level. This might involve detecting the lines, angles, and contours of a printed word's letters, or a spoken word's frequency, duration, and loudness. At an *intermediate* level of processing, the stimulus is recognized and given a label. For example, a four-legged, barking object is identified as a dog. Then, at the *deepest* level, information is processed semantically, in terms of its meaning. For example, if you saw the word *boat,* at the shallow level you might notice the shapes of the letters, at the intermediate level you might think of characteristics of the word (such as it rhymes with *coat*), and at deepest level you might think about the kind of boat you would like to own and the last time you went fishing. Figure 8 depicts the levels of processing theory of memory. A number of studies have shown that people's memories improve when they make semantic associations to stimuli, as opposed to attending just to their physical aspects. In other words, you're more

The more you elaborate about an event, the better your memory for the event will be. For example, if you encode information about how large the crowd was, the people with you, the songs you heard, their performers, and how much money was raised, you probably will remember a concert—such as the Farm Aid Benefit, shown here—more vividly.

likely to remember something when you process information at a deep, rather than a shallow, level (Chaffin & Hermann, 1995; Parkin, 1984).

However, cognitive psychologists soon recognized that there was more to a good memory than "depth." Within deep, semantic processing, psychologists discovered that the more extensive the processing, the better the memory (Craik & Tulving, 1975). **Elaboration** *is the extensiveness of processing at any given depth in memory.* For instance, rather than memorizing the definition of *memory,* you would do better to learn the concept of memory by coming up with examples of how information enters your mind, how it is stored, and how you can retrieve it. Thinking of examples of a concept is a good way to understand it. Self-reference is another effective way to elaborate information. For example, if the word *win* is on a list of words to remember, you might think of the last time you won a bicycle race, or if the word *cook* appears, you might imagine the last time you cooked dinner. In general, deep elaboration—elaborate processing of meaningful information—is an excellent way to remember (Schacter & McGlynn, 1989).

One reason that elaboration produces good memory is that it adds to the *distinctiveness* of the "memory codes" (Ellis, 1987). To remember a piece of information, such as a name, an experience, or a fact about geography, you need to search for the code that contains this information among the mass of codes contained in long-term memory. The search process is easier if the memory code is somehow unique (Hunt & Kelly, 1996). The situation is not unlike searching for a friend at a crowded airport. If your friend is 6 feet tall and has flaming red hair, it will be easier to find him or her in the crowd. Similarly, highly distinctive memory codes can be more easily differentiated. Also, as encoding becomes more elaborate, more information is stored. And as more information is stored, the more likely it is that this highly distinctive code will be easy to differentiate from other memory codes. For example, if you witness a bank robbery and observe that the getaway car is a red 1987 or 1988 Pontiac with tinted windows and spinners on the wheels, your memory of the car is more distinctive than that of a person who notices only that the getaway car is red.

Before leaving the topic of depth and elaboration of processing, we need to consider an important new discovery concerning the type of memory called priming, which we discussed earlier in the chapter. Although deep and elaborate processing generally benefit memory, priming or perceptual learning—such as that involved in the fragment completion task we mentioned earlier—is not improved by deep or elaborative processing. The positive effects of deep, elaborative processing are likely restricted to declarative memory—that is, episodic and semantic memory. That priming is not influenced by deep, elaborative processing is one of the key findings that supports the conclusion that priming might be a unique type of memory.

Copyright © Bob Thaves.

Imagery

How many windows are in your apartment or house? If you live in a dorm room with only one or two windows, this question may be too easy. If so, how many windows are in your parents' apartment or house? Few of us have ever memorized this information, but many of us believe we can come up with a good answer, especially if we use imagery to "reconstruct" each room. We take a mental walk through the house, counting windows as we go.

For many years psychologists ignored the role of imagery in memory because it was believed to be too mentalistic by behaviorists. But the studies of Allan Paivio (1971, 1986) documented how imagery can improve memory. Paivio argued that memory is stored in one of two ways: as a verbal code or as an image code. For example, a picture can be remembered by a label (verbal code) or by a mental image. Paivio thinks that the image code, which is highly detailed and distinctive, produces better memory. Although imagery is widely accepted as an important aspect of memory, there is controversy over whether we have separate codes for words and images. More about imagery appears later in the chapter when we discuss strategies for improving memory. For now, just keep in mind that if you need to remember a list of things, forming mental images will help you out (Shepard, 1996).

Organization

Recall the 12 months of the year as quickly as you can. How long did it take you? What was the order of your recall? The answers to these questions probably are "four to six seconds," and "natural order" (January, February, March, etc.). Now try to remember the months in alphabetical order. Did you make any errors? How long did it take you? There is a clear distinction between recalling the months naturally and alphabetically. This demonstration makes it easy to see that your memory for the months of the year is organized. Indeed, one of memory's most distinctive features is its organization.

An important feature of memory's organization is that sometimes it is hierarchical. A *hierarchy* is a system in which items are organized from general classes to more specific classes. Gordon Bower and his colleagues (1969) showed the importance of organization in memory. Subjects who were presented the words in hierarchies remembered the words much better than those who were given the words in random groupings. Other studies have revealed that, if people are simply encouraged to organize material, their memory of the material improves, even if no warning is given that memory will be tested (Mandler, 1980).

We have seen that semantic elaboration, organization, and imagery are effective ways to encode information for long-term memory storage but that maintenance rehearsal is not. Now we turn our attention to the ways we can retrieve information from memory storage.

Retrieval and Forgetting

Have you ever forgotten where you parked your car, your mother's birthday, or the time you were supposed to meet a friend to study? Have you ever sat in class taking an exam, unable to remember the answer to a question? Psychologists have developed a number of ideas about why we forget information and how we retrieve it.

Ebbinghaus' Pioneering Research

One of psychology's pioneers, Hermann Ebbinghaus (1850–1909), was the first individual to conduct scientific research on forgetting. In 1855, Ebbinghaus studied his own forgetting. He invented *nonsense syllables,* meaningless materials that are uncontaminated by prior learning. Examples of these consonant-vowel-consonant nonsense syllables include: *zeq, xid, lek, vut,* and *riy.* Ebbinghaus memorized a list of thirteen such nonsense syllables and then assessed how many of them he could remember. Even just one day later, he could only recall a few of the syllables. Ebbinghaus concluded that the most forgetting takes place soon after we learn something.

If we forget so quickly, why put effort into learning something? Fortunately, researchers have demonstrated that forgetting is not so extensive as Ebbinghaus envisioned (Baddeley, 1992). Ebbinghaus studied meaningless nonsense syllables. When we memorize more meaningful material, such as poetry, history, or the type of material in this text, forgetting is not so rapid and extensive. Let's now turn to how we actually retrieve information from our long-term memory.

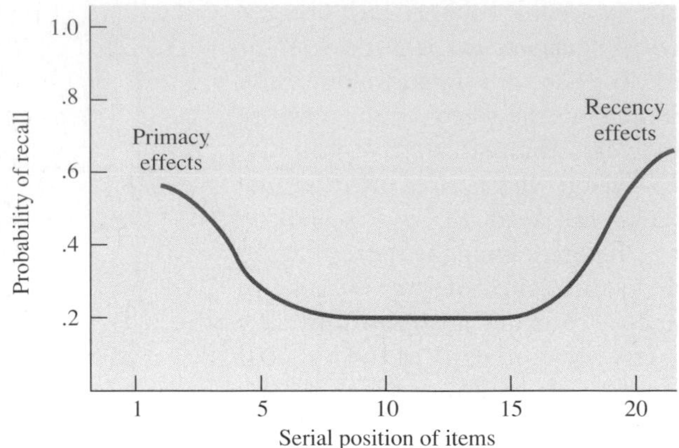

FIGURE 9

Serial Position Effect
When a person is asked to memorize a list of words, the words memorized last usually are recalled best, those at the beginning next best, and those in the middle least efficiently.

Retrieval from Long-Term Memory

To retrieve something from our mental "data bank," we search our store of memory to find the relevant information. Just as with encoding, this search can be virtually automatic or it can require effort. For example, if someone asks you what your mother's first name is, the answer immediately springs to your lips; that is, retrieval is automatic. But if someone asks you the name of your first-grade teacher, it may take some time to dredge up the answer; that is, retrieval requires more effort. As appropriate information is found, it is pulled together to guide and direct a person's verbal and motor responses.

One glitch in retrieving information that we're all familiar with is the **tip-of-the-tongue phenomenon,** or **TOT state.** *It is a type of "effortful retrieval" that occurs when people are confident they know something but just can't quite seem to pull it out of memory* (Brown & Nix, 1996). In one study on the TOT state, participants were shown photographs of famous people and asked to say their names (Yarmey, 1973). The researcher found that people tended to use two strategies to try to retrieve the name of a person they thought they knew. One strategy was to pinpoint the person's profession. For example, one participant correctly identified the famous person as an artist but the artist's name, Picasso, remained elusive. Another retrieval strategy was to repeat initial letters or syllables—such as *Monetti, Mona, Magett, Spaghetti,* and *Bogette* in the attempt to identify Liza Minelli. The tip-of-the-tongue phenomena suggests that without good retrieval cues, information encoded in memory may be difficult to find.

Understanding how retrieval works also requires knowledge of the **serial position effect**—*that recall is superior for items at the beginning and at the end of a list.* If someone gave you the directions "Left on Mockingbird, right on Central, right on Stemmons, left on Balboa, and right on Parkside," you probably would remember "Left on Mockingbird" and "right on Parkside" more easily than the turns and streets in the middle. The **primacy effect** *refers to superior recall for items at the beginning of a list.* The **recency effect** *refers to superior recall for items at the end of the list.* Together with the relatively low recall of items from the middle of the list, this pattern makes up the serial position effect. See figure 9 for a typical serial position effect that shows a weaker primacy effect and a stronger recency effect.

How can primacy and recency effects be explained? The first few items in the list are easily remembered because they are rehearsed more often than later items (Atkinson & Shiffrin, 1968). Working memory is relatively empty when they enter, so there is little competition for rehearsal time. And since they get more rehearsal, they stay in working memory longer, and are more likely to be successfully encoded into long-term memory. In contrast, many items from the middle of the list drop out of working memory before being encoded into long-term memory. The last several items are remembered for different reasons. First, at the time these items are recalled, they may still be in working memory. Second, even if these items are not in working memory, their relative recency, compared to other list items, makes them easier to recall. For example, if you are a sports fan, try remembering football games you have seen at the end of the football season, or baseball games you have seen at the end of the baseball season. You probably will find that the more recent games are easier to remember than less recent games. This represents a recency effect that extends far beyond the time span of working memory.

Two other factors involved in retrieval are (a) the nature of the cues that can prompt your memory, and (b) the retrieval task that you set for yourself. If effective cues for what you are trying to remember do not seem to be available, you need to create them—a process that takes place in working memory. For example, if you have a "block" about remembering a new friend's name, you might go through the alphabet, generating names that begin with each letter. If you manage to stumble across the right name, you'll probably recognize it.

While cues help, your success in retrieving information also depends on the task you set for yourself. For instance, if you're simply trying to decide if something seems familiar, retrieval is probably a snap. Let's say you see a short, dark-haired woman walking toward you. You quickly decide she's someone who lives in the next dorm. But remembering her name or a precise detail, such as when you met her, can be harder. Such findings have implications for police investigations: A witness might be certain she has previously seen a face, yet she might have a hard time deciding if it was at the scene of the crime or in a mugshot.

The two factors just discussed—the presence or absence of good cues, and the retrieval task required—are involved in an important memory distinction: recall versus recognition memory. **Recall** *is a memory measure in which the individual must retrieve previously learned information, as on an essay test.* **Recognition** *is a memory measure in which the individual only has to identify ("recognize") learned items, as on multiple-choice tests.* Most college students prefer multiple-choice tests because they're easier than essay tests or fill-in-the blank tests. Recall tests, such as fill-in-the-blank tests, have poor retrieval cues. You are told to try to recall a certain class of information ("Discuss the factors that caused World War II"). In multiple-choice "recognition" tests, you merely judge whether a stimulus is familiar or not (Does it match something you experienced in the past?).

You have probably heard people say they are terrible at remembering names but they "never forget a face." If you have made that claim yourself, try to actually *recall* a face. It's not so easy. Police officers know that witnesses can be terrible at describing a suspect, so they often bring in an artist to reconstruct the suspect's face. Recalling faces is difficult. If you think you are better at remembering faces rather than names, it is probably because you generally are better at recognition than recall.

Although it often is the case that people are better at recognition than recall, there are exceptions to this rule. Fortunately, Endel Tulving (1983) uncovered a much more powerful rule for explaining why retrieval sometimes succeeds and sometimes fails, in recognition memory as well as recall. This rule is the **encoding specificity principle,** *which states that remembering depends on your processing of a retrieval cue, as well as the contents of the record or "trace" that you previously stored in memory. The key factor is the similarity or match between your processing of the cue and the memory trace. If the match is good, retrieval probably will succeed, but if the match is poor, retrieval probably will fail.*

In a typical example of recognition memory, you see a face at a party that you have seen around campus, and you get a feeling that the person is familiar to you. Note that the retrieval cue (the face at the party) is close to something you saw before (the face around campus), and so there is likely to be a good match between your processing of the cue (you might notice the big ears), and information in your memory trace (you probably noticed the big ears before and stored this observation in memory). Recognition of the face is likely to succeed. However, suppose that the person has long hair that she combs back when on campus, but wears "down" when at parties. You might not notice the big ears in this case, and so your processing of the cue (the face with hair down) provides a poor match with your memory trace (an internal image of the face with hair up and ears showing). In this case, recognition is likely to fail.

In the preceding example, a physical change produced a poor match between the processing of a cue and a memory trace. But a change in the context can do so as well. Imagine you are a subject in a memory experiment, and you are shown the word "jam" with "raspberry" to its left. Later you take a recognition test in which the word "jam" appears again. Will you recognize that "jam" is a word that you saw earlier? Many studies have shown that it depends on whether the context has changed (Light & Carter-Sobell, 1970). If "jam" once again has "raspberry" to its left, you will probably have no trouble. But if "jam" is presented with "traffic" to its left, you are likely to judge that you did not see "jam" before. Why? According to the principle of encoding specificity, the reason is that successful retrieval depends on the match between your processing of the cue and your memory trace (Thieman, 1995). Your memory trace probably contains information about the kinds of jam that you get out of jars and spread on toast in the morning. For example, if you thought of a visual image of a child licking jam off of a knife, this would be part of your memory trace. If your encoding of the cue contains similar information, recognition will be easy. But if your encoding of the cue contains information about backed-up cars on a freeway, with angry drivers breathing carbon monoxide fumes, recognition will be hard.

Just like recognition memory, recall memory also depends on the goodness of match between a memory trace and the processing of retrieval cues. In the case of recall, however, it is often much less obvious just what these cues are. Some intriguing research suggests that the cues that we use for recall memory include the environmental context as well as our own moods. The strongest evidence for environmental context as a cue comes from a study in which scuba divers learned information both on land and under water (Godden & Baddeley, 1975). They were then asked to recall the information. The scuba divers' recall was much better when the encoding and retrieval locations were constant (both on land or both under water) (see figure 10). Although changing from land to under water or vice versa adversely affects one's memory, less dramatic changes in environmental context, such as moving to a new room to take an exam, show weaker effects. Even changing one's mood (from happy to sad or vice versa) can impair recall memory,

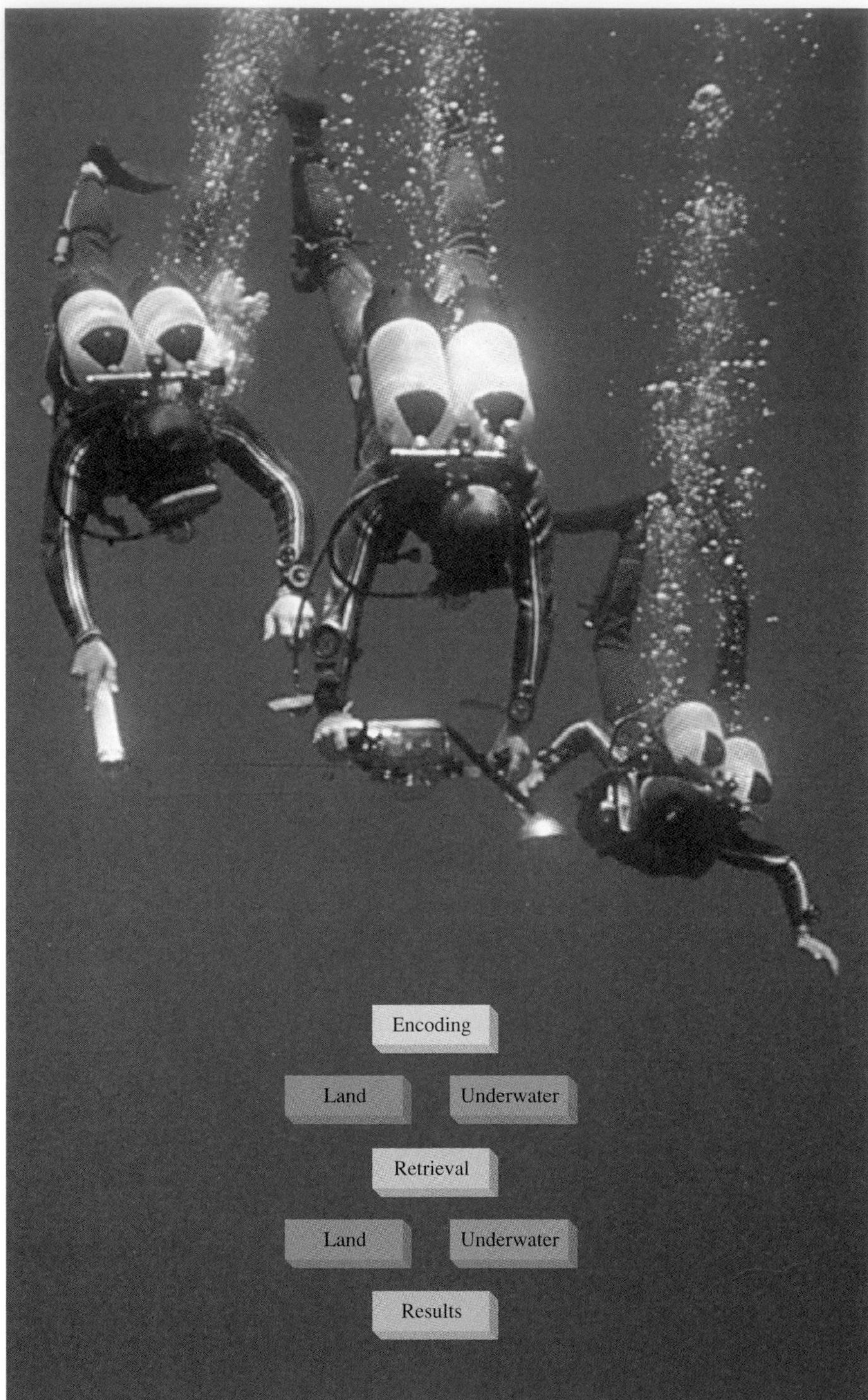

FIGURE 10

Experiment by Godden and Baddeley on Encoding and Retrieval Cues
Divers recalled information better when encoding and retrieval locations were constant (both on land, both under water).

though these effects are restricted to certain conditions (Eich, 1995; Hertel, 1995). You probably do not need to worry very much if your exam in a course is moved to a new room, or if you are a bit less happy while taking the exam than you were during the lectures and when studying at home. However, if the professor announces that the exam will be taken under 20 feet of water, there may be cause for concern!

Cue-dependent forgetting *is a form of forgetting information because of failure to use effective retrieval cues.* Cue-dependent forgetting can explain why we sometimes fail to retrieve a needed fact on an exam even when we "know" that piece of information. These failures to retrieve what is stored in memory occur because we do not use the right cues. For example, you might forget the point of Sperling's experiment if "Sperling's experiment" is your only cue. But if you also use the cue of "sensory memory" or "iconic memory," you might suddenly recollect what Sperling did and what he discovered.

Some important retrieval processes are clearly revealed in the study of autobiographical memory—a person's memory for events in his or her personal life (Conway, 1995; Sehulster, 1996). In one study of autobiographical memory, students were asked to think out loud as they remembered a specific event, such as going to the zoo, feeling sad, or being turned down for a date (Reiser, Black, & Abelson, 1985). The students called on several strategies to remember such events. They often used the particular activity, person, or time period they thought was involved to establish the general context of memory, as well as to limit their search process. When asked about the circumstances that made them sad, for example, they searched for activities in which they felt sad. In another study, both emotional reactions to an event and many rehearsals of the event were required to maintain details of the event over a long period of time (Bohannon, 1988). A common strategy for remembering certain information is to think about events in a given time period. We tend to remember something that happened about the same time as, before, or after a particular event (Conway & Rubin, 1993; Thompson & others, 1996). To read about a special type of autobiographical memory, turn to Explorations in Psychology 1, where you will learn about the nature of flashbulb memories.

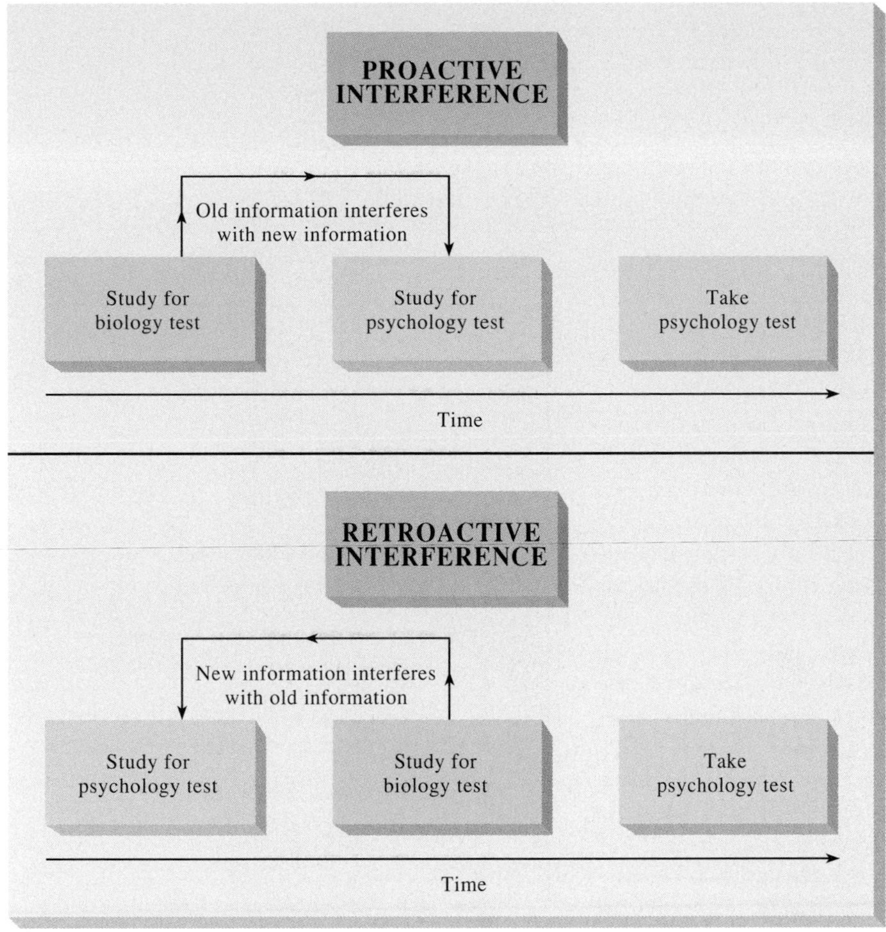

FIGURE 11

Proactive and Retroactive Interference
Pro- means "forward"; in proactive interference, old information has a forward influence by getting in the way of new material learned. *Retro-* means "backward"; in retroactive interference, new information has a backward influence by getting in the way of material learned earlier.

Interference and Decay

The principle of cue-dependent forgetting is consistent with a previously developed view of forgetting—**interference theory,** *which states that we forget not because memories are actually lost from storage, but because other information gets in the way of what we want to remember.* There are two kinds of interference: proactive and retroactive.

Proactive interference *occurs when material that was learned earlier disrupts the recall of material learned later.* Remember that *pro-* means "forward in time." For example, suppose you had a good friend 10 years ago named *Mary,* and last night you met someone at a party named *Marie.* You might find yourself calling your new friend *Mary* because the old information (*Mary*) interferes with retrieval of new information (*Marie*). **Retroactive interference** *occurs when material learned later disrupts retrieval of information learned earlier.* Remember that *retro-* means "backward in time." Suppose you have become friends with *Marie* (and finally have gotten her name straight). If you find yourself sending a letter to your old friend *Mary,* you might address it to *Marie* because the new information (*Marie*) interferes with the old information (*Mary*) (see figure 11).

Proactive and retroactive interference *both* might be explained by cue-dependent forgetting. The reason that *Mary* interferes with *Marie,* and that the name *Marie* interferes with the name *Mary* might be that the cue you are using to remember does not distinguish between the two memories. For example, if the cue you were using was "my good friend," it might evoke both names. This could result in retrieving the wrong name, or in a kind of blocking in which each name interferes with the other and neither comes to mind. Memory researchers have shown that retrieval cues (like *friend* in our example) can become overloaded, and when that happens we are likely to forget.

Although interference is involved in forgetting, it is not the whole story. **Decay theory** *states that when something new is learned a neurochemical "memory trace" is formed, but*

EXPLORATIONS IN PSYCHOLOGY 1

Flashbulb Memories

Flashbulb memories are memories of emotionally significant events that people often recall with considerable accuracy and vivid imagery (Weaver, 1993). Perhaps you remember where you were when the space shuttle *Challenger* exploded. Such flashbulb memories are characterized by their surprise occurrence and the extensive attention they are accorded. What is intriguing about flashbulb memories is that several decades later people often remember where they were and what was going on in their lives at the time of such an event. Some psychologists believe that these memories are part of an adaptive system that fixes in memory the details that accompany important events so that they can be interpreted at a later time.

In one study of flashbulb memories, the types of events that make up flashbulb memories were studied (Rubin & Kozin, 1984). College students were asked to report the three most vivid memories in their lives. Virtually all of these memories were of a personal nature rather than nationally significant events or circumstances. The memories tended to center around an injury or accident, sports, members of the opposite sex, animals, deaths, the first week of college, and vacations. The students also answered questions about their memories of 20 events likely to produce flashbulb memories. As shown in table A, 85 percent of the students said a car accident they had witnessed was of the flashbulb type (meaning it was surprising, consequential, emotional, and vivid), whereas only 12 percent reported their thirteenth birthday as being this way.

TABLE A
Flashbulb Memories

Cues	Percent*
A car accident you were in or witnessed	85
When you first met your roommate at Duke	82
The night of your high school graduation	81
The night of your senior prom (if you went or not)	78
An early romantic experience	77
A time you had to speak in front of an audience	72
When you got your admissions letter from Duke	65
Your first date—the moment you met him/her	57
When President Reagan was shot in Washington	52
The night President Nixon resigned	41
The first time you flew in an airplane	40
The moment you opened your SAT scores	33
Your 17th birthday	30
The day of the first space shuttle flight	24
The last time you ate a holiday dinner at home	23
Your first class at Duke	21
When you heard that President Sadat of Egypt had been shot	21
When you heard that the Pope had been shot	21
The first time your parents left you alone for some time	19
Your 13th birthday	12

*Percent of Duke students who reported the events were of flashbulb quality.

From D. C. Rubin and M. Kozin, "Vivid Memories" in *Cognition,* 16:81–95. Copyright © 1984, Associated Scientific Publishers, Amsterdam, Netherlands.

A critical question about flashbulb memories is, Are they accurate? There is no doubt that such memories seem to be accurate, probably because they are so vivid. However, just because they are vivid does not necessarily mean they are accurate. For example, cognitive psychologist Ulric Neisser (1982) reported that for many years he had a flashbulb memory of hearing the news about the bombing of Pearl Harbor in December 1941. In his flashbulb memory, Neisser recalled that

over time this trace tends to disintegrate. Decay theory suggests that the passage of time always increases forgetting. However, there is one circumstance in which older memories can be stronger than more recent ones. Older memories are sometimes more resistant to shocks or physical assaults on the brain than recent memories.

Consider the case of H. M. At the age of 10, H. M. underwent surgery to stop his epileptic seizures and emerged with his intelligence and most of his mental abilities intact, but the part of his brain that was responsible for laying down new memories was damaged beyond repair. **Amnesia** *is the loss of memory.* Although some types he was listening to a baseball game on the radio at home during the bombing. He also recollected that upon hearing the news he ran upstairs to tell his mother. All of this seems plausible until we think of one simple fact—no baseball games are broadcast in December! Football games were not even broadcast by radio in December 1941. Thus, Neisser's flashbulb memory was vivid but inaccurate, possibly something he constructed at some point after the bombing of Pearl Harbor.

Are flashbulb memories always this inaccurate? No, sometimes they can be impressively true to fact. Flashbulb memories are often very accurate when they focus on events that we personally experienced, as opposed to events such as the *Challenger* disaster, that most of us learned about through the media. Two research teams—one at Emory University and one at the University of California studied flashbulb memories related to the California earthquake that occurred in 1989 (Neisser, Winograd, & Weldon, 1991; Palmer, Schreiber, & Fox, 1991). Shortly after the earthquake, the researchers contacted students at Georgia (Emory) and California campuses and questioned them about their experiences. Then, approximately 18 months later, the researchers tested the students' recall of what they reported the first time. The California students—who had experienced the earthquake—showed excellent recall of their personal experiences and somewhat poorer recall of other information not personally experienced (such as the collapsing of the Bay Bridge). The Georgia students—whose knowledge of the earthquake came solely from the media—had much poorer recall. Indeed, they frequently recalled erroneous material with a very high degree of confidence. Whatever the mechanisms of flashbulb memories, they apparently are more accurate when "real-life" experiences are involved than when information is acquired secondhand.

(a)

(b)

Do you have a flashbulb memory for (a) the night of your senior prom in high school, and (b) the California earthquake of 1989? If so, what are these flashbulb memories like?

of amnesia clear up over time, H. M.'s amnesia endured. In the years following surgery, H. M.'s memory showed no improvement. The amnesia suffered by H. M. was primarily anterograde in nature. **Anterograde amnesia** *is a memory disorder that prevents the retention of new information or events. What was learned before the onset of the condition is not affected.* For example, H. M. could identify his friends, recall their names, and even tell stories about them—but only if he had known them before surgery. Anyone H. M. met after surgery remained a virtual stranger, even if they spent thousands of hours with him. The vast majority of H. M.'s experiences were never encoded in his long-term memory. H. M.'s short-term memory remained unchanged, and as indicated earlier, his overall intelligence, which was above average, remained intact.

Contrary to common sense, although anterograde amnesiacs cannot remember new information, this deficit primarily affects declarative memory (that is, episodic and semantic memory) rather than nondeclarative memory. These patients can learn new skills, and in many instances they show normal priming (Squire, 1987). One especially intriguing case involves a patient with severe amnesia who acquired the necessary skills to perform a complex data entry job (Glisky & Schacter, 1987). Just like any normal person, the patient became more adept at her job with time. But it was as though each day was her first day because she could never remember having learned her job. This finding supports the distinction between declarative memory and nondeclarative memory made earlier in the chapter. In addition, some case studies of amnesiacs support the distinction within declarative memory between episodic and semantic memory. One amnesiac could learn new facts and semantic information (semantic memory) despite gross impairments in remembering events (episodic memory).

Amnesia also occurs in a second form known as **retrograde amnesia,** *which involves memory loss for a segment of the past but not for new events.* It is much more common than anterograde amnesia, and, in fact, most patients who suffer anterograde amnesia suffer from retrograde amnesia as well (this includes H. M., though his retrograde amnesia is relatively mild compared to his anterograde amnesia). A common cause of retrograde amnesia is an assault on the brain, in the form of a physical blow or electrical shock. For example, a football player might suffer retrograde amnesia after a head injury in a game. The key difference from anterograde amnesia is that the forgotten information is *old* (prior to the event that caused the amnesia), and the person's ability to acquire new memories is not affected.

Repression and Memory

Repression is one of psychology's most controversial concepts. Long the province of clinical psychology, repression of threatening, anxiety-laden unconscious thoughts has caught the eye of memory researchers in cognitive psychology. Repression takes place when something shocking happens and the mind pushes all memory of the occurrence into some inaccessible part of the unconscious mind. At some later point in time, the memory might emerge into consciousness. Repression is one of the foundations on which the field of psychoanalysis rests. To read further about the nature of repressed memories, turn to Explorations in Psychology 2.

At this point, we have discussed a number of ideas about the memory processes of encoding and retrieval. A summary of these ideas is presented in concept table 2. Now we turn our attention to the ways in which knowledge is represented in memory.

The Representation of Knowledge in Memory

While we have talked about time frames of memory, and about the processes of encoding and retrieval, we haven't tackled the questions of how knowledge is represented in memory. Three approaches have addressed this issue: network theories, schema theories, and connectionist theories.

Network Theories

One of the first network theories claimed that our memories consist of a complex network of nodes that stand for labels or concepts. The network was assumed to be hierarchically arranged with more concrete concepts (*canary,* for example) nestled under more abstract concepts (*bird*). More recently, cognitive psychologists realized such hierarchical networks were too neat and regular to fit the way human cognition actually works (Shanks, 1991). For example, people take longer to answer true or false to the statement *An ostrich is a bird* than they do to the statement *A canary is a bird.* Memory researchers now envision the network as more irregular and distorted: a *typical* bird, such as a canary, is closer to the node or center of the category *bird* than the atypical ostrich. The revised model allows for the typicality of information while retaining the original notion of node and network.

We add new material to this network by placing it in the middle of the appropriate region. The new material is gradually tied in—by meaningful connections—to the appropriate nodes in the surrounding network. That is why if you cram for a test, you will not remember the information over the long term. The new material is not knit into the long-term web. In contrast, discussing the material or incorporating it into a research paper interweaves it and connects it to other knowledge you have. These multiple connections increase the probability you can retrieve the information many months or even years later.

Schema Theories

Long-term memory has been compared to a library. Your memory stores information just as a library stores books. We retrieve information in a fashion similar to the process we use to locate and check out a book. But the process of retrieving information from long-term memory is not as precise as the library analogy suggests. When we search through our long-term memory storehouse we don't always find the *exact* "book" we want, or we might find the book we want but discover that only several pages are intact. We have to *reconstruct* the rest.

When we reconstruct information, we often fit it into information that already exists in our mind. A **schema** *is information—concepts, events, and knowledge—that already exists in a person's mind.* Schemas from prior encounters with the environment influence the way we code, make inferences about, and retrieve information (Jou, Shanteau, & Harris, 1996). Unlike network theories, which assume that

EXPLORATIONS IN PSYCHOLOGY 2

Repressed Memories, Child Abuse, and Reality

Recently there has been a dramatic increase in reported memories of childhood sexual abuse that were allegedly repressed for many years. With recent changes in legislation, people with recently discovered memories are suing alleged perpetrators for events that occurred 20, 30, even 40 or more years earlier. Memory researcher Elizabeth Loftus (1993) recently analyzed the nature of repressed memories, child abuse, and reality.

In 1991, popular actress Roseanne's story was on the cover of *People* magazine. She reported that her mother had abused her from the time she was an infant until she was 6 or 7 years of age, only becoming aware of the abuse recently during therapy. Other highly publicized cases of repressed memories of child abuse coming into awareness during therapy dot the pages of large numbers of popular magazines, and many self-help books encourage readers to uncover repressed memories of childhood abuse.

Roseanne said that her mother abused her from the time she was an infant until she was 6 or 7 years old. Why have many psychologists questioned some of the reports of activation of repressed memories, such as Roseanne's?

There is little doubt that actual childhood abuse is tragically common. Loftus (1993) and others (Kutchinsky, 1992) don't dispute that child abuse is a serious social problem. What Loftus does take issue with is how the abuse is recalled in the minds of adults. Despite the belief on the part of many in the therapeutic community that childhood repression of abuse is very common, few research studies provide evidence about the extent to which repression occurs. At present, there aren't any completely satisfying methods for discovering the answer to how common repressed abuse is. Repression researchers are in the unenviable position of asking people about a memory for a forgotten memory. In the studies that have been conducted, from 18 to 59 percent of therapists' clients have reported having repressed memories of child abuse and then becoming aware of the incidents as an adult. As Loftus (1993) points out, this is a large range and hardly suggestive of an accurate, agreed-upon incidence of repressed memories of child abuse.

Repressed memories of abuse often return in therapy, in some cases after suggestive probing by the therapist. This raises several issues (Schacter, 1995). First, is it possible that false recollections of childhood abuse can originate in therapy? In light of the highly suggestive and potentially biasing nature of many therapeutic memory-recovery techniques—which include hypnosis and guided visualization—and also in view of many laboratory studies that show that leading questions and other forms of suggestion can lead to significant distortions in memory, the answer to this question is probably yes. At the same time, there are cases known as "psychogenic amnesia" in which traumatic events appear to lead to forgetting, and such cases suggest that instances of childhood sexual abuse—which must surely be traumatic—could be forgotten as well. This is especially likely in the case of single, individual instances of abuse. In cases of repeated abuse occurring over many years (such as Roseanne's case), we currently lack any scientifically sound evidence that complete forgetting is probable, let alone that such forgetting could be followed by recovery such that the previously forgotten memories can be recollected in detail.

Perhaps memory for highly traumatic events operates through different processes than ordinary memory, in which case laboratory studies of human memory—which neither can nor should deal with highly traumatic experiences—will shed little light on whether true repression and recovery can occur. This troubling possibility cannot be ruled out, but recent neurophysiological research with human beings as well as animals suggests that while there may be special circuits involved in the storage of emotionally charged memories, these circuits lead to enhancements of memory, not repression or even rapid forgetting (Cahill, Prins, Weber, & McGaugh, 1995). Perhaps the most important point to make at this juncture is that we must keep open the door to research, including not only experiments with normal human subjects, but also clinical case studies of unfortunate individuals who have experienced traumas much too terrible to bring into the lab. Laboratory studies conducted with animals will also be useful in illuminating the physiological and neural mechanisms underlying retention as well as forgetting of emotionally charged events. It is only through careful scientific research that we ever will be able to resolve the complex issues surrounding repression, recovery, and the doubtlessly serious psychological repercussions of childhood sexual abuse (Conway & others, 1996; Kuyken & Brewin, 1995).

One final tragic risk of neglecting science in this area is that, ultimately, the uncritical acceptance of all allegations made by clients will be replaced by uncritical denial, and that society in general will come to disbelieve the actual cases of child abuse that deserve extensive attention and evaluation. In general, any careless or uncritical acceptance of unreplicated findings in psychology, especially when they have a colorful element that attracts media attention, harms public attitudes toward the contributions of psychological research (Howe, 1995; Ornstein, 1995).

Concept Table 2

Memory Processes: Encoding and Retrieval

Concept	Processes/Related Ideas	Characteristics/Description
Encoding	Its nature	The transformation and/or transfer of information into a memory system. Information can be encoded into sensory memory and short-term, or working, memory, but the main focus is on encoding information into long-term memory.
	Automatic and effortful processing	Automatic processes do not require capacity or resources; effortful processes require capacity or resources to take place. Effortful processing includes depth of processing and elaboration, imagery, and organization.
	Depth of processing and elaboration	Craik and Lockhart developed the levels of processing view of memory, which stresses that memory is on a continuum from shallow to deep. In this view, deeper processing produces better memory. Elaboration refers to the extensiveness of processing at any depth and it leads to improved memory, making encoding more distinctive.
	Imagery	Imagery involves sensations without a corresponding external stimulus. Paivio argues that we have separate verbal and image codes, but this is controversial. Imagery often improves memory.
	Organization	One of the most pervasive aspects of memory. Involves grouping or combining items. Often information is organized hierarchically.
Retrieval and Forgetting	Ebbinghaus' pioneering research	In 1855, Herman Ebbinghaus tested his own memory of nonsense syllables he had learned. He discovered that his forgetting was rapid and extensive. However, researchers have found that we forget less than Ebbinghaus envisioned, especially when we learn meaningful material.
	Retrieval from long-term memory	This involves getting information out of long-term memory. The search can be automatic or effortful. An interesting aspect is the tip-of-the-tongue phenomenon (TOT state), which occurs when we can't quite pull something out of memory. The implication of TOT is that, without good retrieval cues, information stored in memory is difficult to find. The serial position effect influences retrieval—retrieval is superior for items at the beginning of a list (primacy effect) and at the end of a list (recency effect). One key factor that makes retrieval effortful is the absence of effective cues. A second factor is the nature of the retrieval task, which, along with the presence or absence of retrieval cues, distinguishes recall and recognition memory. Failure to use effective retrieval cues is one reason we forget, a phenomenon known as cue-dependent forgetting.
	Interference and decay	The principle of cue-dependent forgetting is consistent with a previously developed view of forgetting—interference theory, the belief that we forget not because memories are actually lost from storage but because other information gets in the way of what we want to remember. Proactive interference is when material that was learned earlier disrupts the recall of material learned later. Retroactive interference occurs when material learned later disrupts retrieval of information learned earlier. Decay theory argues that, when something new is learned, a memory trace is formed but, as time passes, this trace tends to disintegrate.
	Amnesia	This involves extreme memory deficits and comes in two forms. Anterograde amnesia is a memory disorder that prevents the retention of new information and events. Retrograde amnesia is a memory disorder that involves memory loss for a segment of the past but not for new events. However, skill learning and priming can be normal in amnesiacs.
	Repression	Memory researchers have recently become interested in repression, long a province of clinical psychology.

retrieval involves specific facts, schema theory claims that long-term memory search is not very exact. We seldom find precisely what we want, or at least not all of what we want; hence, we have to reconstruct the rest. Our schemas support this reconstruction process, helping us fill in the gaps between our fragmented memories.

The schema theory of memory began with Sir Frederick Bartlett's (1932) studies of how people remember stories. Bartlett was concerned about how a person's background determines what they encode and remember about stories. Bartlett chose stories that sounded strange and were difficult to understand. He reasoned that a person's background, which is encoded in schemas, would reveal itself in the person's reconstruction (modification and distortion) of the story's content. For example, one of Bartlett's stories was called "War of the Ghosts," an English translation of an American Indian folktale. The story contained events that were completely foreign to the experiences of the middle-class British research participants.

Summarized, the story goes like this: An Indian joins a war party that turns out to consist entirely of ghosts. They go off to fight some other Indians, and the main character gets hit but feels no pain. He returns to his people, describes his adventure, and goes to sleep. But in the morning he dies as something black comes out of his mouth.

What interested Bartlett was how differently the participants might reconstruct this and other stories from the original versions. The British participants used both their general schemas for daily experiences, and their schemas for adventurous ghost stories in particular, to reconstruct "War of the Ghosts." Familiar details from the story that "fit into" the participant's schemas were successfully recalled. But details that departed from the person's schemas were often extensively distorted. For example, the "something black" that came out of the Indian's mouth became blood in one reconstruction and condensed air in another.

There has been a flurry of interest in reconstructive memory, especially in the way people recall stories, give eyewitness testimony, remember their past, and recall conversations (Fivush, 1995; Howe, 1995). To learn more about the nature of reconstructive memory in eyewitness testimony turn to Explorations in Psychology 3.

We have schemas not only for stories but also for scenes or spatial layouts (a beach, a bathroom), as well as for common events (going to a restaurant, playing football, writing a term paper). A **script** *is a schema for an event* (Schank & Abelson, 1977). Scripts often have information about physical features, people, and typical occurrences. This kind of information is helpful when people need to figure out what is happening around them. For example, if you are enjoying your after-dinner coffee in a restaurant and a man in a tuxedo comes over and puts a piece of paper on the table, your script tells you that the man probably is a waiter who has just given you the check.

Connectionist Theories

When students learn about network theories and schema theories, they often wonder how networks of concepts and abstract schemas are stored in the human brain. Most network and schema theories have little or nothing to say about the role of the physical brain in memory. A new wave of excitement in memory research has been generated over a theory called *connectionism,* or sometimes *parallel distributed processing (PDP).* Unlike network and schema theories, connectionist theories are inspired by the brain's physical structure (Gluck & Granger, 1993; MacWhinney & Chang, 1995). We know that the human cerebral cortex contains millions of neurons richly interconnected through hundreds of millions of synapses. Because of these synaptic connections, which can be excitatory or inhibitory, the activity of one neuron is influenced by many others. For example, if there is an excitatory connection between neurons A and B, activity in neuron A will tend to increase activity in neuron B. If the connection is inhibitory, activity in neuron A will tend to reduce activity in neuron B. The strength of both excitatory and inhibitory connections can vary. Thus, the level of activity in neuron A can have a strong effect on neuron B (if the connection is strong) or a weak effect on neuron B (if the connection is weak).

Because of these simple facts, connectionist models claim that changes in the strength of synaptic connections, both excitatory and inhibitory, are the fundamental bases of memory (Kosslyn, Chabris, & Baker, 1995; Parkin, 1996). Units for concepts and abstract schemas do not exist in this model, only neurons and the connections between them. Any piece of knowledge—such as the name of your dog, *Fido*—is embedded in the strengths of hundreds or even thousands of connections between neurons. Memory occurs on the basis of the connection strengths. In sum, the basic idea in **connectionism, or parallel distributed processing (PDP),** *is that memory is stored in a distributed fashion over a wide range of connections between neurons. Memory occurs or does not occur because of the extent, inhibitory or excitatory nature, and strength of neuron connections.* Figure 12 provides a comparison of the network, schema, and connectionist models of memory.

Let's see how the connectionist model explains a typical memory, such as remembering the name of a new friend. Initially your processing of the new friend's face might activate a small number of weak neuron connections that make you remember only a general category ("interesting looking woman" or "handsome young man"). However, after more extensive and stronger neuron connections have taken place, you remember the person's name.

Part of the appeal of connectionist models is that they are consistent with what we know about the brain's structure (Wiles & Humphreys, 1993). Another part of their appeal is that they can actually mimic some of our most complex human behaviors. When programmed on computers, the connectionist models have successfully predicted the results of some memory experiments (McClelland & Rumelhart, 1986).

Explorations in Psychology 3

Eyewitness Testimony

At times, one person's memories can take on national importance. This was true for John Dean in the Watergate cover-up. It is in the legal arena, especially, that one person's memory of events given as testimony can be crucial in determining a defendant's, or a nation's, future. Much of the interest in eyewitness testimony has focused on distortion, bias, and inaccuracy in memory (Loftus, 1979, 1993; Sporer, Malpass, & Koehnken, 1995; Wells, 1993).

Memory fades over time. That's why the amount of time that has passed between an incident and a person's recollection of it becomes a critical factor in eyewitness testimony (Chance & Goldstein, 1995). In one study, people were able to identify pictures with 100 percent accuracy after a 2-hour time lapse. But 4 months later they achieved an accuracy of only 57 percent; remember that chance alone accounts for 50 percent accuracy (Shepard, 1967).

Unlike a videotape, memory can be altered by new information. In one study, students were shown a film of an automobile accident (Loftus, 1975). Some of the students were asked how fast the white sports car was going when it passed the barn. Other students were asked the same question without any mention of a barn. In fact, there was no barn in the film. Yet 17 percent of the students who heard the question which included the barn mentioned it in their answer; only 3 percent of those whose question did not include the barn mentioned that they saw it. New information, then, can add or even replace existing information in our memory.

Studies have shown that people of one ethnic group are less likely to recognize individual differences in people of another ethnic group (Brewer, 1996). Latino eyewitnesses, for example, may have trouble distinguishing among several Asian suspects. This makes identifying individuals from a police lineup or photographs an unreliable tool. In one investigation, clerks in small stores were asked to identify photographs of customers who had shopped there two hours earlier (Brigham & others, 1982). Only 33 percent of the customers were correctly identified. In another experiment, a mugging was shown on a television news program. Immediately after, a lineup of six suspects was broadcast and viewers were asked to phone in and identify which of the six individuals they thought committed the robbery. Of the 2,000 callers, more than 1,800 identified the wrong person. In addition, even though the robber was White, one-third of the viewers identified an African American or Latino suspect as the criminal.

Identification of individuals from police lineups or photographs is not always reliable. Individuals from one race or ethnic group often have difficulty recognizing differences among people of another race or ethnic background.

The connectionist models are not without their critics. Some say that the models are almost *too* good, meaning they can perform many memory tasks expertly but do not take into account the errors and misjudgments that plague human cognition. Another criticism is that they handle lower-level cognition, such as simple forms of perception and learning, better than higher-level, abstract thought. Perhaps models of knowledge that are developed in the future will consist of a connectionist component for perception and low-level cognition and a network and/or schema component for abstract reasoning.

The Neurobiological Basis of Memory

Regardless of the connectionist models' fate, the study of how knowledge can be stored in the brain will continue (Milner, 1996). Karl Lashley (1950) spent a lifetime looking for a location in the brain where memories are stored. He trained rats to discover the correct pathway in a maze and then cut out a portion of the animals' brains and retested their memory of the maze pathway. After experimenting with thousands of rats, Lashley found that the loss of various cortical areas did not affect rats' ability to remember the maze's path. Lashley concluded that memories are not stored in a specific location in the brain.

Many neuroscientists believe that memory is located in discrete sets or circuits of neurons. Brain researcher Larry Squire (1990; Squire, Knowlton, & Musen, 1993), for example, says that most memories are probably clustered in groups of about 1,000 neurons. He points out that memory is distributed throughout the brain in the sense that no specific memory center exists. Many parts of the brain and nervous system participate in the memory of a particular event. Yet memory is localized in the sense that a limited number of brain systems and pathways are involved, and each probably contributes in different ways (Lynch, 1990).

	Theory		
	Semantic network	Schema	Connectionist
Nature of memory units	Abstract concepts ("bird")	Large knowledge structures (e.g., going to a restaurant)	Small units, connections among neurons
Number of units	Tens of thousands	Unknown	Tens of millions
Formation of new memories	Form new nodes	Form new schemas or modify old ones	Increased strength of excitatory connections among neurons
Attention to brain structure	Little	Little	Extensive

FIGURE 12

Key Features of Network, Schema, and Connectionist Theories

Single neurons, of course, are at work in memory. Researchers who measure the electrical activity of single cells have found that some respond to faces, others to eye or hair color, for example. But for you to recognize your Uncle Albert, individual neurons that provide information about hair color, size, and other characteristics must act together.

Ironically, some of the answers to the complex questions about the neural mechanics of memory come from studies on a very simple experimental animal—the inelegant sea slug. Eric Kandel and James Schwartz (1982) chose this large snail-without-a-shell because of the simple architecture of its nervous system, which consists of only about 10,000 neurons.

The sea slug can hardly be called a quick learner or an animal with a good memory, but it is equipped with a reliable reflex. When anything touches the gill on its back, it quickly withdraws it. First the researchers habituated the sea slug to having its gill prodded. After a while, it ignored the prod and stopped withdrawing its gill. Next the researchers applied an electric shock to its tail when they touched the gill. After many rounds of the shock-accompanied prod, the sea slug violently withdrew its gill at the slightest touch. The researchers found that the sea slug remembered this message for hours or even weeks.

More important than the discovery that sea slugs had memories was the finding that memory seems to be written in chemicals. Shocking the sea slug's gill releases the neurotransmitter serotonin at the synapses, and this chemical release basically provides a reminder that the gill was shocked. This "memory" informs the nerve cell to send out chemical commands to retract the gill the next time it is touched. If nature builds complexity out of simplicity, then the mechanism used by the sea slug may work in the human brain as well. Chemicals, then, may be the ink with which memories are written.

While some neuroscientists are unveiling the cellular basis of memory, others are examining the broadscale architecture of memory in the brain. In a series of studies, Mortimer Mishkin and his colleagues (Mishkin & Appenzellar, 1987) examined the role of brain structures in the memories of monkeys. They assume that the same brain structures that are responsible for memory in monkeys are also responsible for memory in humans, an assumption that generates spirited debate.

In a typical experiment, Mishkin and his colleagues compare the memory of monkeys who have an intact brain with the memory of monkeys who have undergone surgery that has impaired some part of their brain. Impairment at any point in the "memory circuit" can produce deficits in memory. Damage to the amygdala and the hippocampus, two brain regions deep inside the brain at the tip of the brain stem, cause the most serious deficits in memory. However, damage to the thalamus and the mammillary body cause deficits as well, as does damage to the basal forebrain and the prefrontal cortex. Figure 13 shows the location of these six brain structures that are involved in monkeys' memory.

Is there any evidence that these brain structures are responsible for memory in humans? Researchers have found that humans who have brain damage due to strokes, Alzheimer's disease, Korsakoff's syndrome, and operations intended to cure epilepsy implicate the same brain structures in human memory. Recall the case of H. M., who was virtually unable to recall events that had occurred since his operation for epilepsy. H. M.'s hippocampus had been destroyed.

The "memory circuit" outlined by Mishkin and his colleagues appears to be involved in declarative memory only, not being responsible for nondeclarative memory. The nondeclarative memory of human amnesiacs such as H. M. also is preserved, which means that nondeclarative memory likely has a memory circuit somewhere else in the brain. Ultimately, researchers may be able to link each type and subtype of memory we have discussed (episodic, semantic, priming, sensory memory, and working memory) to discrete brain circuits.

Researchers also are using brain imaging techniques to reveal which areas of the brain are active when individuals are engaging in various memory activities. Using such

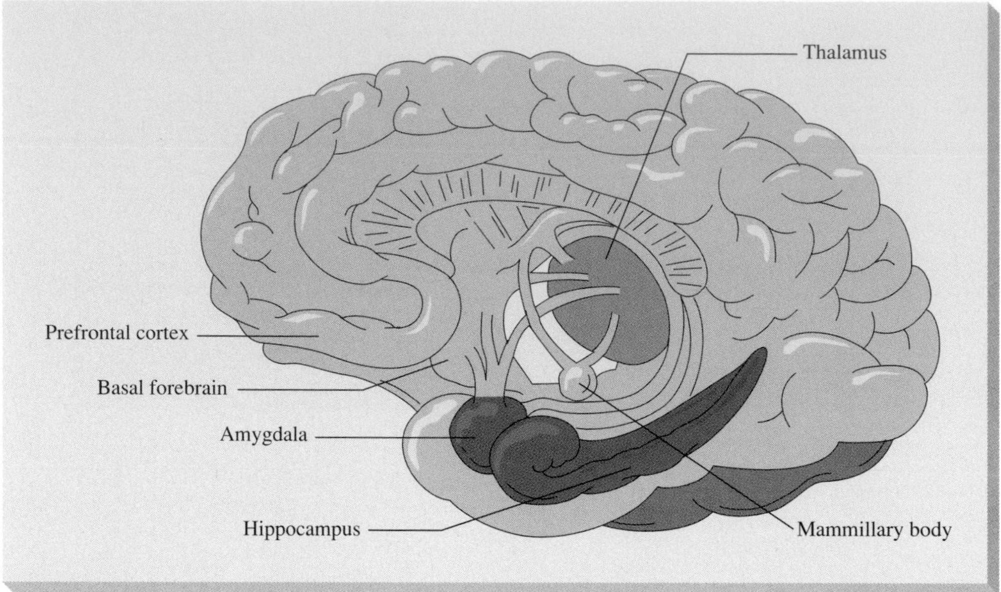

FIGURE 13

Memory Circuit Involved in Declarative Memory
Mortimer Mishkin and his colleagues have demonstrated that the amygdala, hippocampus, thalamus, mammillary body, basal forebrain, and prefrontal cortex are involved in declarative memory. Neuroscientists refer to the combination of brain structures involved in memory as "memory circuit."

memory imaging techniques as PET (positron emission tomograph, which depicts the activity of different brain regions by showing each area's consumption of sugar glucose), they have shown that:

- Deep encoding is specifically associated with activity in the brain's frontal lobe (Kapur & others, 1994)
- The parietal lobe is involved in the phonological loop of working memory (Paleus & others, 1993)
- The temporal lobe is linked with priming of structurally visible objects, whereas the hippocampus is associated with the episodic recognition of these objects (Schacter, 1995; Zola, 1996). This finding relates to our earlier discussion of priming and the removal of the hippocampus from the patient H. M.

As neuroscientists discover the identity of memory circuits in the brain, might we reach a point at which the psychological study of memory becomes unimportant? That's unlikely. First, we are far from working out all of the complexities of the neurochemical underpinnings in human memory. And second, even if we were successful in unraveling the neurochemical mystery of memory, each person's private kingdom of memories will remain intact.

Mnemonics and Memory Strategies

In the fifth century B.C., the Greek poet Simonides attended a banquet. After he left, the building collapsed, crushing the guests and maiming their bodies beyond recognition. Simonides was able to identify the bodies by using a memory technique. He generated vivid images of each individual and mentally pictured where they had sat at the banquet table. Specific techniques such as this, many of which involve imagery, have been used to improve memory. **Mnemonics** *is the term used to denote the techniques designed to make memory more efficient.*

Imagery

The memory technique Simonides used is called the *method of loci.* It is an imagery technique you can apply to memory problems of your own. Suppose you have a list of chores to do. To ensure that you remember them all, first associate a concrete object with each chore. A trip to the store becomes a dollar bill, a telephone call to a friend becomes a telephone, cleanup duty becomes a broom, and so on. Then produce an image of each object so you can imagine it in a particular location in a familiar building, such as your house. You might imagine the dollar bill in the kitchen, the telephone in the dining room, and so on. The vividness of the image and the unusual placement virtually guarantee recollection. It also helps if you mentally move logically through the house as you place the images.

A second imagery strategy is the *peg method,* in which a set of mental pegs, such as numbers, have items attached to them. For instance, you might begin with something like: "One is a bun, two is a shoe, three is a tree," and so forth up to as many as 10 to 20 numbers. Once you can readily reproduce these rhymes, you can use them as mental pegs. For example, if you were required to remember a list of items in a specific order—such as the directions to someone's

CONCEPT TABLE 3

The Representation of Knowledge in Memory, Neurobiological Factors, and Mnemonics and Memory Strategies

Concept	Processes/Related Ideas	Characteristics/Description
Representation of Knowledge in Memory	Network theories	Early network theories stressed that memories consist of a complex network of nodes that are hierarchically arranged. More recent network theories stress the role of meaningful nodes in the surrounding network.
	Schema theories	The concept of schema refers to information we have about various concepts, events, and knowledge. Schema theory claims that long-term memory is not very exact and that we construct our past. Schemas for events are called scripts.
	Connectionist theories	The basic idea of the connectionist, or parallel distributed processing (PDP), theory is that memory is stored in a distributed fashion over a wide range of connections of neurons. Memory occurs or does not occur because of the extent, inhibitory or excitatory nature, and strength of neuron connections.
The Neurobiological Basis of Memory	Its nature	A main issue is the extent to which memory is localized or distributed. Single neurons are involved in memory, but some neuroscientists believe that most memories are stored in circuits of about 1,000 neurons. There is no specific memory center in the brain; many parts of the brain participate in the memory for an event. However, researchers have found the brain circuit that underlies declarative memory.
Mnemonics and Memory Strategies	Imagery	Mnemonics are techniques that improve memory. Many of these involve imagery, including the method of loci and peg method.
	Systematic memory and study strategies	Systems based on a number of aspects of our knowledge about memory have been developed, including ARESIDORI and SQ3R.

house—you would use the following mental pegs: one-bun-left on Market; two-shoe-right on Sandstone; three-tree-right on Balboa, and so on. Then develop an image for each direction: I left the bun at the market; my right shoe got caught in the sand and stone; there's a tree right on Balboa. When you have to retrieve the directions, you select the appropriate cue word, such as *bun* or *shoe,* and this should stimulate the production of the compound image with the correct response. Researchers have been encouraged by the effectiveness of such strategies in improving memory (Cornoldi & DeBeni, 1996).

Systematic Memory and Study Strategies

Techniques such as the method of loci and the peg method can be used to improve memory, but strategies that incorporate an understanding of how we remember are especially helpful (Intons-Peterson, 1993, 1996; McDaniel, Waddill, & Skakesby, 1995; Pressley, 1996). One such strategy is denoted ARESIDORI, a simple mnemonic code for (1) Attention, (2) Rehearsal, (3) Elaboration, (4) Semantic processing, (5) Imagery, (6) Distinctiveness, (7) Organization, (8) Retrieval, (9) Interest (Ellis, 1987). Most of the components of ARESIDORI have been discussed in this chapter and are basic to memory. Note that number 9, interest, essentially refers to motivation. It is helpful to determine which of the principles of ARESIDORI you already use effectively and which you could use more often in order to improve your study habits.

Many different approaches to study exist and many of them include some basic principles of memory. The most widely used system is SQ3R (Robinson, 1961) *S* stands for Survey, *Q* for Question, and *3R* for Read, Recite, Review. To use this system in the next chapter, you might do the following. To survey, glance over the headings to find the main points of the chapter (the chapter outline helps in this regard). To question, turn each heading into a question, and continue to ask yourself questions throughout the chapter. To accomplish the 3R part of the system, start reading the chapter as you normally would, recite information periodically as you go through the chapter, and then review the material you have read several times before you take a test. The concept tables and summary will help you with the review process.

Concept table 3 reviews the main ideas in our discussion of how knowledge is represented in memory, as well as mnemonics and memory strategies.

Critical Thinking About Behavior

"Are You Sure About That?": Declarative Memory and Confidence

> *It isn't so astonishing the number of things that I can remember, as the number of things I remember that aren't so.*
>
> **Mark Twain**

Think back to the last time you had an argument with someone whom you cared about, an argument that centered on whose memory was most accurate. Your serious disagreement probably reflected different "realities" constructed out of the same experience. Let's explore systematically many of the ways in which two individuals can disagree about what constitutes the "truth" of any situation. In how many ways can individual differences affect common understanding?

1. *Differences in attention at the level of the sensory register and working memory.* Just because two people share the same physical space doesn't mean they "take in" the same sensory data. Whether the stimulus is visual or auditory, two people might extract different elements of the experience for further processing in working memory.
2. *Differences in the quality of working memory.* Individuals differ in the efficiency and effectiveness of their working memory. Some people seem to process information quickly; others labor harder to convert working memory contents into long-term memory.
3. *Differences in the strength of semantic long-term memory.* People differ in the kinds of ready access they have to different ideas in long-term memory. For example, some people readily learn a variety of facts about art or gardening or sports. Some have a big investment in developing expertise in specific areas; others find such endeavors boring or foolish. These areas of specialty in semantic memory can be a source of differences in different people's memories.
4. *Differences in schemas as a basis for attention and reconstruction.* We enter into situations with different schemas in different stages of development that shape our expectations about how things will work. Schemas filter out what we do not find to be important and can influence what we recall through reconstruction. We might believe our memories to be accurate not because they are accurate but because they seem to fit best with our general expectations about how things *should have been.*
5. *Differences in the quality (and quantity) of episodic recall.* Some people seem to have a knack for describing details of interpersonal discussions. Others seem to extract only larger details. These differences in ability show up in partners with maddening frequency.

Reexamine your own position in your argument with your friend. What elements were produced by your own episodic memory? Do any of these elements explain how your disagreement with your friend might have arisen?

- Did you both process the same elements of the situation?
- Did you both process working memory efficiently?
- Did differences in semantic memory affect your position?
- Could different scripts influence attention?
- Could aspects of the problem have been reconstructed?
- Did you both pay attention to the same details of the episode?

So who was wrong and who was right? Regardless of how convinced we are that we have a handle on the truth and that our friend is wrong (deluded, stupid, misguided, or mentally unbalanced), we have to conclude that there might be other interpretations. The number of points in the memory process that are vulnerable to error should temper our convictions about the accuracy of our own recall and help us have a more open-minded stance toward resolving differences of opinion. The analysis also supports the importance of actively taking the perspective of others in solving problems, even when we run the risk of demonstrating our own fallibility.

Overview

We began this chapter by exploring the nature of memory—what it is, time frames of memory (sensory memory, working memory, and long-term memory), contents of memory (declarative and nondeclarative memory, episodic and semantic memory, and priming), and interactions between types of memory. Our coverage of memory processes focused on encoding and retrieval and forgetting. We also studied how knowledge is represented in memory—network theories, schema theories, and connectionist theories. You also read about the neurobiological basis of memory as well as mnemonics and memory strategies. Don't forget that you can obtain an overall summary of the chapter by again studying the concept tables on pages 210, 222, and 227.

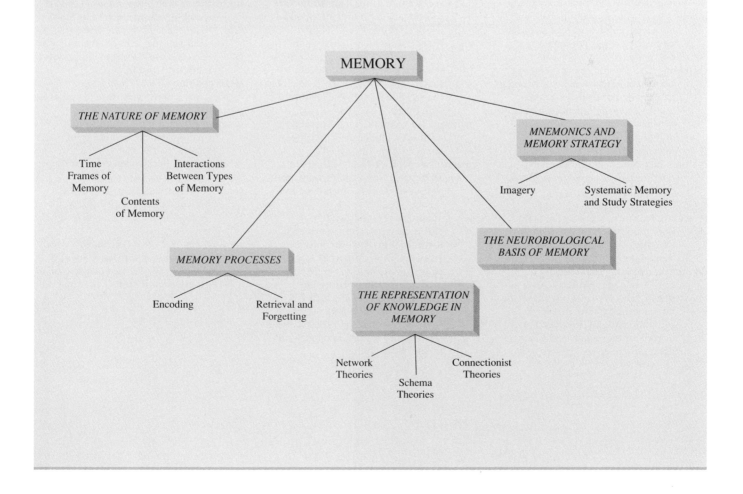

MEMORY

- *THE NATURE OF MEMORY*
  - Time Frames of Memory
  - Contents of Memory
  - Interactions Between Types of Memory
- *MEMORY PROCESSES*
  - Encoding
  - Retrieval and Forgetting
- *THE REPRESENTATION OF KNOWLEDGE IN MEMORY*
  - Network Theories
  - Schema Theories
  - Connectionist Theories
- *THE NEUROBIOLOGICAL BASIS OF MEMORY*
- *MNEMONICS AND MEMORY STRATEGY*
  - Imagery
  - Systematic Memory and Study Strategies

Key Terms

memory The retention of information over time. Psychologists study how information is initially placed, or encoded into memory; how it is retained, or stored, after being encoded; and how it is found, or retrieved, for a certain purpose later. p. 202

sensory memory This form of memory holds information from the world in its original sensory form for only an instant, not much longer than it is exposed to the visual, auditory, and other senses. p. 202

echoic memory The auditory sensory registers, in which information is retained for up to several seconds. p. 202

iconic memory The visual sensory memory in which information is retained for about 1/4 second. p. 202

working memory A limited-capacity memory system in which information is retained for as long as 30 seconds, unless the information is rehearsed, in which case it can be retained longer. Also sometimes called short-term memory. p. 203

memory span The number of digits an individual can report back in order following a single presentation of them. p. 203

chunking The grouping or "packing" of information into higher-order units that can be remembered as single units. Chunking expands working memory by making large amounts of information more manageable. p. 203

maintenance rehearsal The conscious repetition of information to increase the length of time it stays in working memory. p. 203

long-term memory Memory that holds huge amounts of information for a long period of time, relatively permanently. p. 205

declarative memory The conscious recollection of information, such as specific facts or events, and at least in humans, information that can be verbally communicated. Because of its conscious and verbalizable nature, declarative memory has been called "explicit memory." p. 205

nondeclarative memory Refers to a variety of phenomena of memory in which behavior is affected by prior experience without that experience being consciously recollected. Because nondeclarative memory cannot be verbalized or consciously recollected, at least not in the form of specific events or facts, it also is called "implicit memory." p. 205

episodic memory The retention of information about the where and when of life's happenings—what it was like when your younger brother or sister was born, what happened to you on your first date, what you were doing when you heard Desert Storm had begun in the Persian Gulf, and what you had for breakfast this morning. p. 206

semantic memory A person's knowledge about the world. It includes a person's field of expertise (knowledge of chess for a skilled chess player, for example); general academic knowledge of the sort learned in school (knowledge of geometry, for example); and "everyday" knowledge about meanings of words, famous individuals, important places, and common things (who Nelson Mandela and Mahatman Gandhi are, for exampe). A critical characteristic of semantic memory knowledge is that it appears to be independent of the individual's personal identity with the past. p. 206

priming The facilitation in responding to a stimulus that immediately follows a related stimulus. p. 207

procedural memory Deals with gradual, incremental forms of learning (such as learning to ride a bicycle or ice skate). p. 207

perceptual representation system (PRS) Important in the perceptual identification of words, objects, faces, and other important types of stimuli in our world. p. 207

traditional information-processing model The model in which memory involves a sequence of three stages—sensory registers, short-term memory, and long-term memory. p. 208

working memory model The model in which long-term memory precedes working memory, and working memory uses long-term memory in a variety of flexible ways (such as rehearsal and imagery). p. 208

memory processes The encoding of new information into memory and the retrieval of what was previously stored. p. 209

encoding The transformation and/or transfer of information into a memory system. p. 209

effortful processing Processing that requires capacity or resources to encode information in memory. p. 211

automatic processing Processing that does not require capacity, resources, or effort to encode information into memory. p. 211

levels of processing In Craik and Lockhart's theory, memory's continuum from shallow to deep; in this theory, deeper processing produces better memory. p. 211

elaboration The extensiveness of processing at any given depth in memory. p. 212

tip-of-the-tongue phenomenon (or TOT state) A type of effortful retrieval that occurs when people are confident they know something but just can't quite seem to pull it out of memory. p. 214

serial position effect Recall is superior for items at the beginning and end of a list. p. 214

primacy effect Recall is superior for items at the beginning of a list. p. 214

recency effect Recall is superior for items at the end of a list. p. 214

recall A memory measure in which the individual must retrieve previously learned information, as on an essay test. p. 215

recognition A memory measure in which the individual only has to identify ("recognize") learned items, as on a multiple-choice test. p. 215

encoding specificity principle States that remembering depends on your processing of a retrieval cue, as well as the contents of the record or "trace" that you previously stored in memory. The key factor is the similarity or match between your processing of the cue and the memory trace. If the match is good, retrieval probably will succeed, but if the match is poor, retrieval will probably fail. p. 215

cue-dependent forgetting A form of forgetting information because of failure to use effective retrieval cues. p. 216

interference theory The theory that we forget, not because memories are actually lost from storage, but because other information gets in the way of what we want to remember. p. 217

proactive interference The interference caused when material that was learned earlier disrupts the recall of material learned later. p. 217

retroactive interference The interference caused when material learned later disrupts material learned earlier. p. 217

decay theory The theory that when something new is learned, a neurochemical "memory trace" is formed, but over time this trace tends to disintegrate. p. 217

amnesia The loss of memory. p. 218

anterograde amnesia A memory disorder that prevents the retention of new information or events. p. 219

retrograde amnesia Memory loss for a segment of the past but not for new events. p. 220

schema Information—about concepts, events, and knowledge—that already exists in a person's mind. p. 220

script A schema for an event. p. 223

connectionism (or parallel distributed processing [PDP]) The idea that memory is stored in a distributed fashion over a wide range of connections between neurons. Memory occurs or does not occur because of the extent, inhibitory or excitatory nature, and strength of neuron connections. p. 223

mnemonics Techniques designed to make memory more efficient. p. 226

Resources and Readings in Psychology

Basic and Applied Memory Research, Vols. I and II (1996)
by Douglas Hermann, Cathy McEvoy, Chris Hertzog, Paula Hertel, and Marcia Johnson (eds.)
Hillsdale, NJ: Erlbaum

A wide array of topics in basic and applied memory research are evaluated, including the practical application of memory research, memory and clinical problems, memory and study strategies, eyewitness memory, memory for faces, memory aids, amnesia, drugs and memory, and aging.

Human Memory (1990)
by A. Baddeley
Boston: Allyn & Bacon

The chapter you have just read highlighted Baddeley's contemporary working memory model. In his book, Baddeley extensively reviews research on memory to support the development of his memory model.

Memory and Cognition
edited by Gregory Loftus, U. of Washington

This research journal publishes articles on many aspects of memory and cognition. Topics of articles in recent issues of the journal include priming, distinctiveness, organization, autobiographical memory, schema theory, face processing, working memory, and retrieval processes.

The 36-Hour Day (1981)
by Nancy Mace and Peter Rabins
Baltimore: Johns Hopkins University Press

Alzheimer's is a widespread disorder in aging individuals. Its symptoms include memory loss. This book is a family guide to caring for persons with Alzheimer's.

Psychological Factors in Eyewitness Identification (1995)
by Siegried Sporer, Roy Malpass, and Guenter Koehnken (eds.)
Hillsdale, NJ: Erlbaum

Researchers from different fields address a variety of issues involving eye witness identification. Among the topics discussed are voice recognition by humans and computers, children's memories, cross-racial identification, facial image reconstruction techniques, and person descriptions.

Remembering Our Past (1995)
by David Rubin (ed.)
New York: Cambridge

Currently, there is increased interest in autobiographical memory. In this book, a number of contributors describe many dimensions of autobiographical memory.

Total Recall (1984)
by Joan Minninger
New York: Pocket Books

This book is full of helpful techniques for improving your memory. The author has given seminars on improving memory to a number of corporations, including IBM and General Electric. Tips on how to improve your memory draw on such important dimensions of memory as retrieval cues, depth of processing, linkages between short-term and long-term memory, episodic memory, and semantic memory. You also learn how to remember what you read, how to remember names and faces, how to remember dates and numbers, how to remember what you hear, and effective study strategies.

Your Memory: How It Works and How to Improve It (1988)
by K. L. Higbee
Englewood Cliffs, NJ: Prentice Hall

This practical book outlines strategies for using the principles of memory to remember all sorts of things in your personal life.

CHAPTER

T&L

Thinking and Language

PABLO PICASSO
Young Boy with Dog, detail

Thinking and Language

with James C. Bartlett, Barry S. Stein, and William F. Katz

Chapter Outline

Chapter Boxes

The mind is an enchanting thing.

—Marianne Moore

> **I** *think, therefore I am.*
>
> —**Descartes**

Images of Psychology

Explorations in Thought and Language

It's a beautiful thing, the destruction of words. . . . If you have a word like "good," what need is there for a word like "bad"? "Ungood" will do just as well. . . . It was B. B.'s (Big Brother's) idea originally, of course. . . . Do you know that Newspeak is the only language in the world whose vocabulary gets smaller every year? . . . Don't you see that the whole aim of Newspeak is to narrow the range of thought? In the end we shall make thought crime literally impossible, because there will be no words in which to express it. . . . Every year fewer and fewer words, and the range of consciousness always a little smaller.

So says a colleague at the Ministry of Truth to Winston Smith in George Orwell's novel *Nineteen Eighty-four,* published in 1949. The novel is about the life of an intelligent man who lives under absolute totalitarian control. The government regulates every facet of life and, above all, corrupts language in its pursuit of power. The purpose of Newspeak was not only to provide a means of expressing "appropriate" thoughts, but to make all other modes of thought impossible.

While the year 1984 is long gone and the English language is still overflowingly rich, some of Orwell's predictions have an eerily familiar ring. In recent years politicians illegally funded mercenaries, called "freedom fighters," to overthrow the Nicaraguan government, referred to nuclear warheads as "peacemakers," and forbade federally funded clinics to counsel pregnant women about the option of abortion.

Preview

We will have much more to say about how thought and language influence each other later in the chapter. Among the topics we will explore in this chapter on thinking and language are the cognitive revolution in psychology, problem solving, reasoning and judgment, and many dimensions of language, including its biological and environmental determinants as well as how children's language develops and whether animals have language.

The Cognitive Revolution in Psychology

Behaviorism was a dominant force in psychology until the late 1950s and 1960s, when many psychologists began to realize that they could not understand or explain human behavior without making reference to mental processes. The term *cognitive psychology* became a label for approaches that sought to explain observable behavior by investigating mental processes and structures that cannot be directly observed (Hassebrock, 1995).

Although behaviorists like John B. Watson had argued that psychology could not be a legitimate "scientific" discipline unless it restricted itself to the study and description of directly observable events, proponents of the cognitive revolution argued that scientific explanations usually explain the observable using terms or concepts that cannot be directly observed. For example, Isaac Newton explained the behavior of falling objects using a concept called gravitational force, a force that could not be directly observed.

Although the term *introspection* is seldom seen in contemporary psychological research, cognitive psychologists still use subjective descriptions of thinking as one source of information about thought processes. These

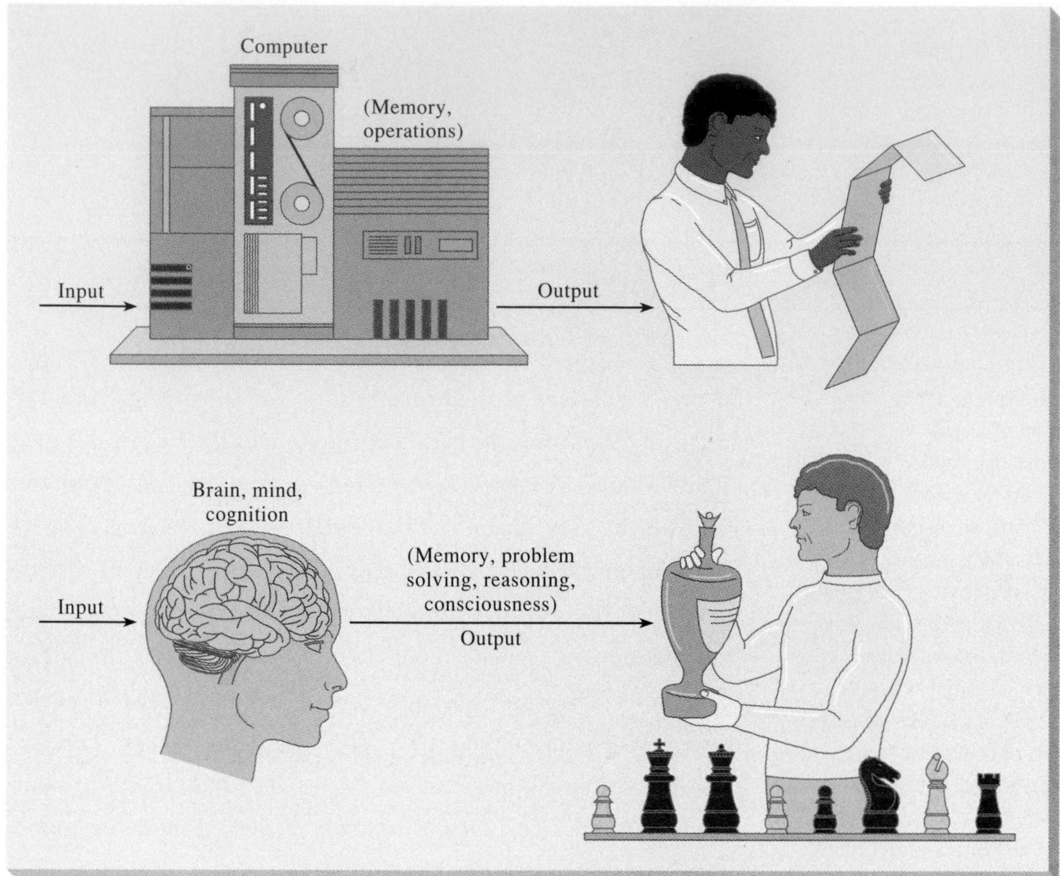

FIGURE 1

Computers and Cognition: An Analogy
The physical brain is described as analogous to a computer's hardware; cognition is described as analogous to a computer's software.

subjective descriptions are sometimes referred to as *problem-solving protocols.* Unlike earlier research that was based primarily on subjective reports, cognitive psychologists realize the limitations of subjective reports and use a variety of other measures to explore thinking and mental processes. For example, cognitive psychologists might examine the precise time taken to make decisions, the accuracy of decisions, the type of information used by a person to make a decision, or even the ability to transfer thinking skills from one context to another. Indeed, most current investigations of thinking use a combination of measures to explore thinking and mental processes. Although a variety of factors stimulated the growth of cognitive psychology, perhaps one of the more important was the development of computers (Reed, 1996).

The first modern computer, developed by John von Neumann in the late 1940s, showed that inanimate machines could perform logical operations. This indicated that some mental operations might be modeled by computers, possibly telling us something about the way cognition works. Cognitive psychologists often use the computer as an analogy to help explain the relation between cognition and the brain. The physical brain is described as the computer's hardware and cognition as its software (see figure 1).

While the development of computers played an important role in psychology's cognitive revolution, it is important to realize that inanimate computers and human brains function quite differently in some respects. For example, each brain cell, or neuron, is alive and can be altered in its functioning by many types of events in its biological environment. Current attempts to simulate neural networks greatly simplify the behavior of neurons. The brain derives information about the world through a rich system of visual, auditory, olfactory, gustatory, tactile, and vestibular sensory receptors that operate on analog signals. Most computers receive information from a human who has already digitally coded the information and represented it in a way that removes much of the ambiguity in the natural world. Attempts to use computers to process visual information or spoken language have only achieved limited success in highly constrained situations where much of the natural ambiguity is removed. The human brain also has an incredible ability to learn new rules, relationships, concepts, and patterns that it can generalize to novel situations. In comparison, current approaches to artificial intelligence are quite limited in their ability to learn and generalize.

The differences between computers and brains are reflected in the fact that computers can do some things better than humans, and humans can do some things better than computers. Computers can perform complex numerical calculations much faster and more accurately than humans could ever hope to. Computers can also apply and follow rules more consistently and with fewer errors than humans and represent complex mathematical patterns better than humans. Although a computer can simulate certain types of learning that may improve its ability to recognize patterns or use rules of thumb to make decisions, it does not have the means to develop new learning goals. Furthermore, the human mind is aware of itself; the computer is not. Indeed, no computer is likely to approach the richness of human consciousness. In short, the brain's extraordinary capabilities will probably not be mimicked by computers anytime in the near future.

Expert systems are used for advances in medical diagnosis and treatment, weather prediction, analysis of geological formations, and automobile construction.

The computer's role in cognitive psychology continues to increase, giving rise in recent years to a field called **artificial intelligence (AI),** *the science of creating machines capable of performing activities that require intelligence when they are done by people.* AI is especially helpful in tasks requiring speed, persistence, and a vast memory (Boden, 1996; Jacquette, 1996). For example, today we have chess-playing programs that can beat everyone but the best players our species has to offer.

These so-called **expert systems,** *computer-based systems for assessing knowledge and making decisions in advanced skill areas,* not only have been applied to playing chess, but have been designed to assist in the diagnosis of medical illnesses, diagnosing equipment failures, developing integrated circuits, evaluating loan applicants, advising students about what courses to take, and a broad range of other problems. These programs are especially beneficial when human experts are in short supply or are not available in the locations where they are needed. Expert systems also might help to preserve the expertise of talented individuals when they retire or die.

Whereas expert systems require the identification of relevant facts and rules to make decisions, neural networks learn patterns and relationships from a set of training data. These patterns or relationships can involve voices, images, or even complex numerical patterns. Unlike expert systems, neural networks can generalize (within limits) to new situations. Although these predictions may not have high accuracy, they are often much faster than other techniques. Consequently, many scientists are using neural networks to find patterns in historical or experimental data that would allow them to predict new economic trends, the effects of new chemical combinations, or the properties of new engineering designs.

Problem Solving

The study of thinking spans two broad areas: problem solving, and reasoning and judgment. We will first consider problem solving, focusing on the general characteristics of problem solving and different kinds of problems that people try to solve. We then will turn to some techniques used by experts and novices to solve problems in different fields, and consider some ways we can improve our problem solving.

Characteristics of Problem Solving

According to Allan Newell and Herbert Simon (1972), a **problem** *is something you experience when you have a goal but do not know immediately what you must do to reach it.* Breaking this idea down, problem solving must be directed toward a *goal,* and a person who is solving the problem must engage in some *sequence of operations* in order to achieve this goal (Ashcraft, 1994). Some of these operations are behavioral in nature (such as writing something down, or moving a piece in a puzzle or game). Others are cognitive and harder to observe. For example, in working a math problem you might subtract or multiply some numbers "in your head," without necessarily saying or writing anything. Fortunately, psychologists have a method for exploring such mental operations. The method is **protocol analysis,** *the procedure of having subjects talk aloud while solving a problem and recording and analyzing everything they say.* Since problem solving is goal directed and involves sequences of operations, there are many kinds of thinking that are not problem solving. For example, idle daydreaming is not problem solving, because there is no true goal. And recalling your birthday or telephone number is not problem solving either, because it is easy for you to recall the information without going through a sequence of steps.

Another characteristic of many problem-solving efforts is that people engage in strategies called heuristics and algorithms. **Heuristics** *are strategies or rules of thumb that can suggest a solution to a problem but do not guarantee a solution.* Let's say you have the problem of driving to a friend's house and you have never been there before. You are driving in an unfamiliar part of town, and after a while you realize that you are lost. If you know your destination is north, you might use the heuristic of turning onto a road that heads in that direction. This procedure might work, but it also might fail—the road might end or turn off to the east. In contrast to heuristics, **algorithms** *are procedures that guarantee an answer to a problem.* When you solve a multiplication problem, you are using an algorithm—you learned this algorithm as part of your schooling. When you follow the directions for putting together a lawn chair, you are using an algorithm. It would be nice if all of our problems in life could be solved by algorithms that would guarantee correct solutions, but life is not always so straightforward. Most problem solving involves the use of heuristics.

One important problem-solving heuristic is the **means-end strategy,** *finding the biggest difference between where you are now in your work on a problem and where you want to be, and then trying to find an operation that can reduce this difference.* Another name for the means-end strategy is simply "difference reduction" (Haberlandt, 1994). A second heuristic is the **subgoal strategy,** *finding an intermediate goal that will put you in a better position to reach the final goal.* Subgoals are important because one or more operations that can take you to your goal may be blocked by an obstacle. A good strategy in such situations is to set a subgoal of removing the obstacle (Ashcraft, 1994).

One way to visualize the means-end strategy and the use of subgoals and other heuristics is shown in figure 2. The figure illustrates a **problem space,** *a representation of the possible states of work on a problem and the sequence of operations that will lead to these states.* Problem spaces come in differing forms, but all have a start state that represents the "givens" of a problem, as well as a goal state that represents the solution. In addition, there are intermediate states on the path to the goal and other intermediate states on the path to one or more "dead ends."

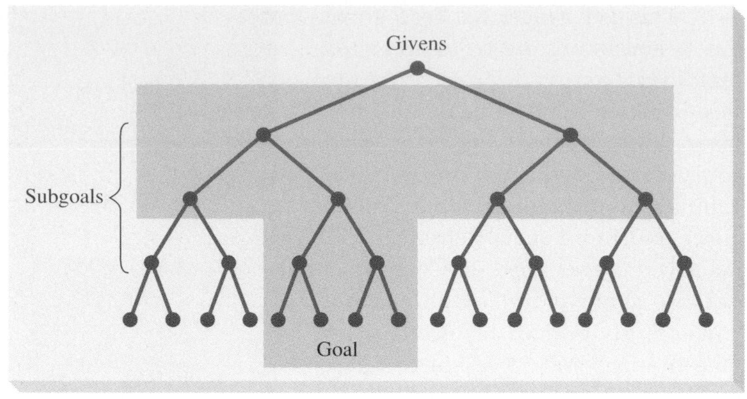

FIGURE 2

A General Diagram of a Problem Space, with Various Branches of the Space Illustrated

Often a hint or an inference can prune the search tree, restricting the search to just one portion. This idea is represented by the shaded area of the figure. Note that in most problems the problem-space tree is much larger, so the benefits of pruning are far greater.

For some problems the problem space takes the form of an upside-down tree; the start state is at the trunk of the tree, and the goal state is at the end of one twig. The treelike structure reflects the fact that for many problems there are many possible sequences of operations leading away from the start state, but only one sequence leading straight to the goal. The importance of a subgoal is to reduce the number of sequences to consider; subgoals allow you to "prune" the "tree" of your problem space.

The means-end and subgoal strategies are only two of the heuristics used in solving problems, but they are perhaps the most important because of their wide applicability. As an example, consider the real-world problem of finding yourself at school in Atlanta and wanting to go to Chicago for spring break (Haberlandt, 1994). If you follow the means-end strategy of removing the biggest difference between your start state (being in Atlanta) and your goal state (being in Chicago), you might decide that the best operation to reduce this difference is to get on an airplane and fly. But there is an obstacle; you do not have an airline ticket. Thinking over this obstacle, you set the subgoal of going to the airport and buying the ticket. But now there is another obstacle; you don't have enough money for an airline ticket. So now you form still another subgoal, that of getting enough money. Reaching this subgoal might involve still more operations, such as offering to type a friend's term paper, or asking someone for a loan. Will you make it to Chicago? That depends on your choice of subgoals and your ability to reach them. Problem solving sometimes fails!

Perhaps the most general characteristic of problems is that they are around us throughout our lives. Fortunately, we have impressive skills for solving these problems even at a very young age. Consider 2-year-old Georgie, who wants to throw some rocks out the kitchen window (Waters, 1989). His father says he can't do that because the lawnmower is just outside the window and the rocks might break it. So Georgie "has an idea." He runs outside to get some green peaches he had been playing with earlier and says, "They won't break the lawnmower." Although Georgie is very young, he formed a goal and engaged in a sequence of operations that allowed him to achieve this goal.

How Problems Differ

Even though there are general characteristics of how we solve problems, it is important to remember that not all problems are alike. In fact, there are different kinds of problems that must be solved in different ways. No single technique for improving problem solving is likely to be effective with all types of problems. Different types of problems require different techniques.

Knowledge-Lean and Knowledge-Rich Problems

One way problems differ is in how much education or knowledge is required to solve them. Many problems in puzzle books and on IQ tests are **knowledge-lean problems,** *problems that can be solved with little or no background knowledge.*

Although many problems are knowledge-lean, others are **knowledge-rich problems**—*problems whose solution depends on considerable knowledge in a particular domain.* The field of medicine is an excellent source for knowledge-rich problems. Consider the problem of diagnosing a young man who is complaining of shaking chills and fever combined with sweating, a feeling of exhaustion, and shortness of breath. He has also experienced temporary losses of vision in his right eye. Your physical exam confirms the fever, the patient's temperature is 104 degrees Fahrenheit, and his blood pressure is 110/40. His mucous membranes are pink, and he has puncture wounds in his left arm. The patient's pulse is 120 per minute but collapsing. He has a heart murmur and a flame-shaped hemorrhage in the left eye.

It turns out that this patient contracted bacterial endocarditis from a contaminated needle, possibly from intravenous drug use (Patel & Green, 1986). However, it is obvious that no one without medical training or experience could hope to solve this problem—indeed, few people other than doctors could understand the solution; do you even know what bacterial endocarditis is?

Well-Defined Versus Ill-Defined Problems

The distinction between knowledge-lean and knowledge-rich problems is related to another difference between problems, a difference in how well they are defined. **Well-defined problems** *are problems whose initial states, goal states, and permissible operations are clearly specified.* However, real life presents us with many **ill-defined problems,** *whose initial states, goal states, and/or permissible operations are only vaguely specified or not specified at all.* Extreme examples of ill-defined problems are the existential questions we put to ourselves in life: How can I be happy? What can I do to find a good relationship? How can I be more creative in my work? Less extreme examples abound in the areas of law, medicine, and the social sciences. The diagnosis problem we considered has well-specified start and goal states, but the operations used in solving the problem are not clear at all. Here is another example of a rather ill-defined problem (Voss & Post, 1988):

> Imagine you are the minister for agriculture in Russia. The crop yield has been low for several years and the country faces severe food shortages. How would you go about increasing agricultural productivity in the country?

The start state and goal state are both reasonably clear, but the possible operations are left open. This is a far cry from a knowledge-lean problem like working a puzzle toy where the only possible operations consist of moving disks from one post to another!

In one study, the crop production problem was investigated using the method of protocol analysis—subjects talked aloud as they worked on the task (Voss & Post, 1988). An interesting feature of this study is that two kinds of subjects were compared, experts and novices. The experts were professors of agriculture and political science; the novices were undergraduate students and professors in distant fields such as chemistry. The experts spent much of their time turning this ill-defined problem into a better-defined problem. They accomplished this feat by considering constraints on how a solution could be reached. For example, one expert considered that only about 10 percent of the land in Russia is arable, and that what can be grown on this 10 percent is limited by climate. This narrowed down his choice of operations for working on the problem, which made it better defined. Novices paid less attention to constraints, examining the problem in general terms so that it remained quite ill defined. As you might expect, the experts' solutions appeared to be better.

Problem Solving in Experts and Novices

As we considered some different classes of problems, we began to think about how different classes of people—experts versus novices—might approach problem solving differently. Psychologists are eagerly pursuing the question of why experts are so much better than novices at solving tough problems in particular domains.

Knowledge Base

Experts have broad and highly organized knowledge about their field, which allows them to solve a problem from memory without going through a tedious problem-solving

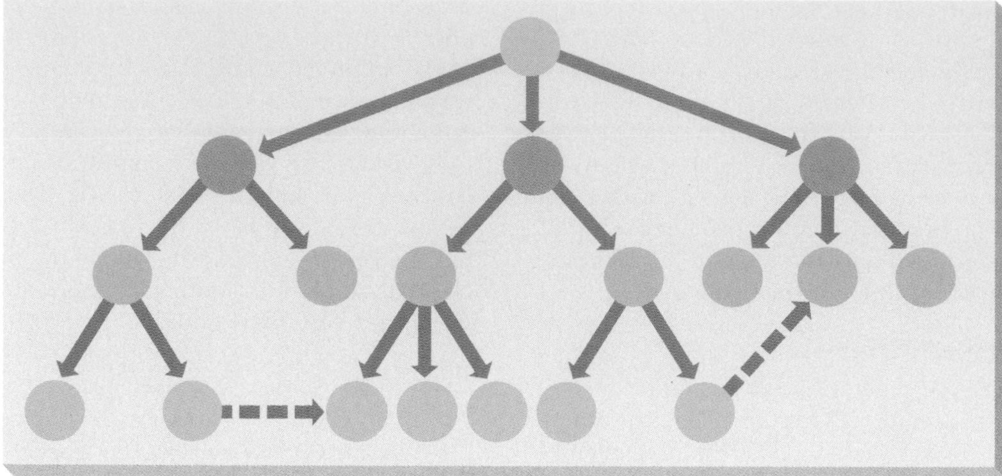

FIGURE 3

How Information About a Physics Problem Was Organized in an Expert's Mind
An expert's knowledge is based on many years of experience in which small bits of information have been linked with other small pieces, which together are placed into a more general category. This category in turn is placed in an even more general category of knowledge. The dotted lines are used as pointers, associations between specific elements of knowledge that connect the lower branches and provide mental shortcuts in the expert's mind.

effort (Wilding & Valentine, 1995). An expert organizes knowledge hierarchically. In the expert's mind, specific details are grouped into chunks, which in turn are grouped into more general topics, which in turn come under the heading of even more general topics, and so on.

Figure 3 shows the hierarchical arrangement one physicist used to organize the knowledge needed to solve a physics problem. The dotted lines are associations made by experience that lead directly from one specific point to another. These *pointers* connect the smaller branches of the "concept tree" and possibly produce shortcuts in solving the problem. An example of how a novice might solve the same problem is shown in figure 4. Notice the absence of pointers and the smaller number of levels and interconnections. Experts seem to have many interconnections in their storehouse of knowledge.

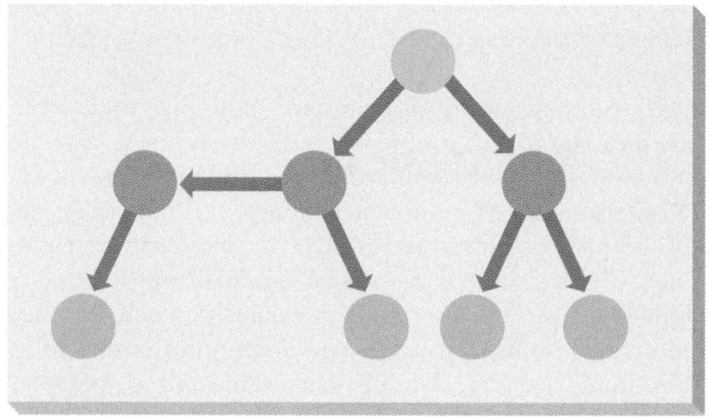

FIGURE 4

How Information About a Physics Problem Might Be Organized in a Novice's Mind
The novice's knowledge shows far fewer connections, shortcuts, and levels than the expert's knowledge.

How do experts achieve this storehouse of knowledge, with all of its interconnections and shortcuts? It takes experience and effort, gradually built up over many years. Experts develop efficient strategies for accomplishing tasks, they are capable of quickly and accurately evaluating alternative ideas, and they acquire tailored "tricks" (associations and networks of ideas that make things work) that make problems more manageable. Whether the field is cardiology, commodities trading, chemical engineering, law, or gardening, many of these characteristics distinguish experts from novices (Johnson, 1979).

Internal Representation

A second important difference between novices and experts is in the *internal representation of problems,* or how problems are interpreted and classified in one's mind. An expert who encounters a problem is able to put it into a class of problems that can be solved in certain ways. Hence, while a novice must often think through various approaches to a problem, the expert can simply *recall* the best approach for problems in that class. When novices at physics are asked to look through a set of physics problems and to sort them into categories, they tend to group the problems based on superficial characteristics. For example, they might group together problems that have something rotating, or that have something to do with an incline plane. They are strongly influenced by pictorial details of illustrations that accompany the problems; it is as if they classify problems based on visual appearance, instead of abstract principles of physics.

Experts are entirely different. Ignoring superficial aspects, such as details of illustrations that accompany a

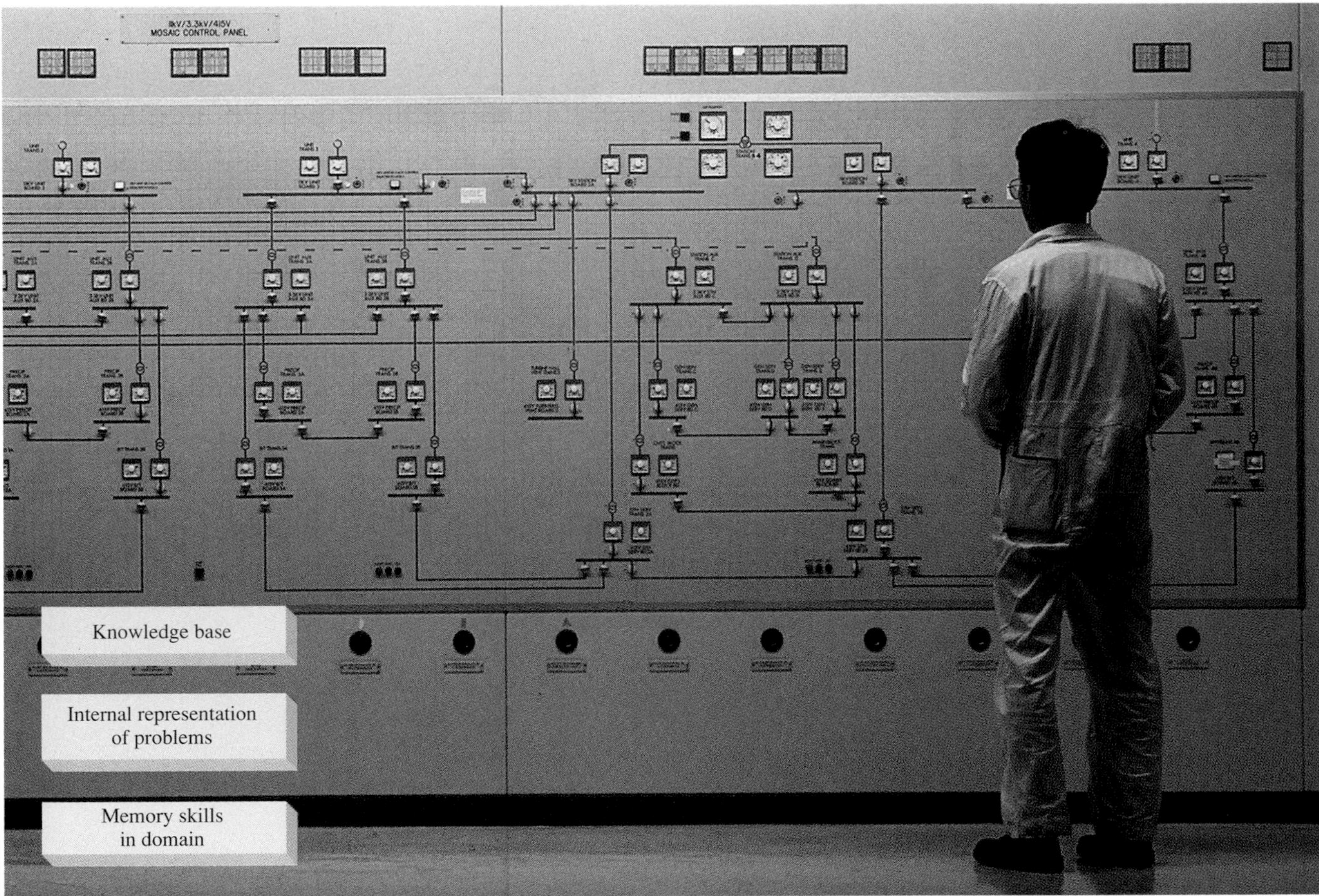

FIGURE 5

Three Main Differences Between Novices and Experts

problem, they classify problems based on principles of physics, such as conservation of energy and Newton's second law. It is not hard to understand why such grouping is important. When experts in physics see a new physics problem, they think immediately of other physics problems that require the same principles for their solutions. The novice, in contrast, thinks about problems whose appearance might be similar but that do not necessarily require the same principles, and this can interfere with finding a solution.

Domain Memory Skills

The third difference between novices and experts involves *domain memory skills* (see figure 5). Experts generally are much better than novices at remembering information in their domain of expertise. It is not that their memories are better in general; it is just that they use their vast storehouse of knowledge to organize and chunk information in ways that make it memorable. This can be helpful because good memory for relevant information in a problem can often help you solve it.

All three of these differences between novices and experts are revealed very clearly in chess. In fact, several studies have shown that experts exceed even well-practiced players in their knowledge base, their representations of chess problems, and their skills in remembering chessboard displays (Chase & Simon, 1973; deGroot, 1965). In one study, chess masters competed with class A players (the next lower rank) in several tasks aimed at determining the nature of expert play in chess (de Groot, 1965). In one task, chess masters and class A players examined a chessboard display and thought aloud while deciding on the best next move. Using the technique of protocol analysis, the researcher tape-recorded everything that was said, and then studied the tapes to find out what the players were thinking step by step. As anyone who has played chess would expect, the players would pick a possible next move, think about how the opponent would respond, think about how they themselves would then respond, and so on for several moves. They then would pick another next move, considering its consequences for the next several plays. This was not surprising, but there was an important new finding as well: When the researcher examined how many next moves the players considered, he found that the chess masters considered *fewer* next moves than the class A players did. It was as if the better experts knew which possible next moves were worth thinking about, and which could be ignored.

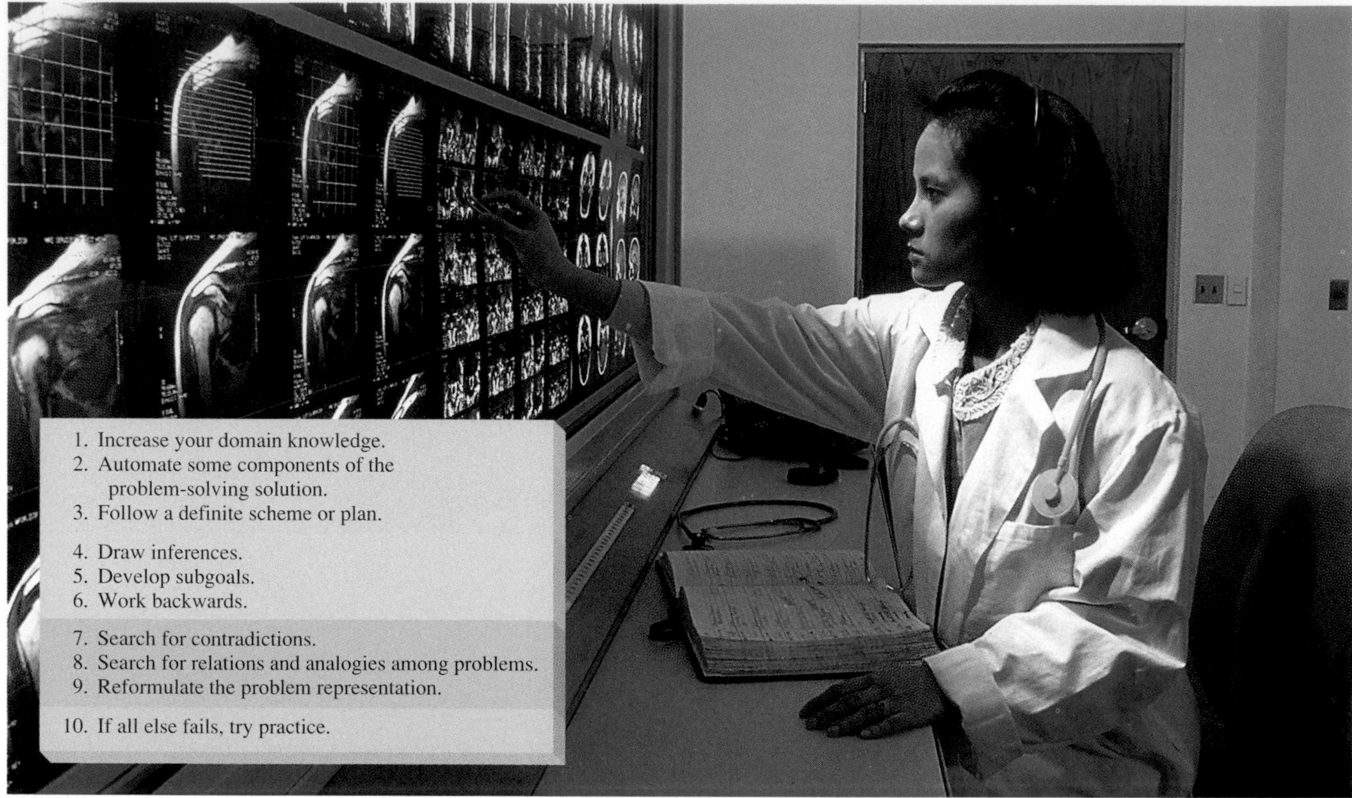

1. Increase your domain knowledge.
2. Automate some components of the problem-solving solution.
3. Follow a definite scheme or plan.
4. Draw inferences.
5. Develop subgoals.
6. Work backwards.
7. Search for contradictions.
8. Search for relations and analogies among problems.
9. Reformulate the problem representation.
10. If all else fails, try practice.

FIGURE 6

Ashcraft's Strategies for Improving Problem Solving

How was this possible? Apparently the masters' richer store of knowledge about chess allowed them to interpret and organize the displays in ways that suggested the best next moves to consider. For example, while a novice or even a class A player might form an internal representation consisting of various chess pieces in various positions, the master might form an internal representation in which subsets of several pieces are "chunked" into higher-order units or patterns that suggest the possibility of a particular response. Since chunking is known to benefit memory, it became important to study whether masters have better memory for chessboard displays than do persons of lesser skill.

In another study, experts who had spent from 10,000 to 50,000 hours playing chess—the equivalent of about 1 to 4 hours a day for 30 years—were studied (Chase & Simon, 1973). These experts were compared to novice players who had spent less than a total of 100 hours playing chess. The expert chess players were much better than the novices at remembering chessboard configurations. However, it was unclear from the initial observations whether the experts generally had better memories than the novices, or whether the experts' greater exposure to chess improved their chunking of the displays. To investigate this issue, the researchers presented subjects with chessboard configurations that did not illustrate a meaningful game of chess. Such meaningless configurations cannot be chunked based upon a person's knowledge of chess. If chess experts really do have better short-term memories than other chess players, they should remember these random chess patterns better than novices do. However, if the experts' superior memory performance depends on their ability to chunk information based on previous experience, then they should do no better than the novices at remembering random chess patterns. In fact, experts did no better than novices when they were asked to remember random chess configurations. These findings showed that experts are not better at memory *in general.* Rather, their greater knowledge base in chess helps them to form representations of meaningful chess patterns, organizing these patterns in terms of chunks. These chunks are associated with good ideas for next moves, and they also improve memory.

Improving Problem-Solving Skills

Life is filled with problems—trying to figure out why your car won't start, planning how to get enough money to buy a stereo, working on a jigsaw puzzle, or estimating your chances of winning at blackjack. How can we go about solving such problems? Mark Ashcraft (1994) discussed ways to improve your problem solving, each of which we will discuss in turn (see figure 6).

Increasing Your Domain Knowledge

Increasing your domain knowledge is one of the best strategies. We have already discussed research on chess and physics problems that reveals that experts perform much better than novices in their domain of expertise. Unfortunately, acquiring expertise takes time. In many areas it appears that at least 10 years of concentrated work are required before a significant level of expertise is obtained.

Automating Some Components of the Problem-Solving Process

Automating some components may also take considerable time, but much less than 10 years. If you repeat an operation or sequence of operations for a period of time, it becomes automated at least to a degree. This means that you can perform the process with very little attention or use of short-term memory. This is important, because many problems place demands upon memory—if you are able to perform more elementary operations without overloading memory, you can use your memory for more complex operations, such as formulating subgoals or forming visual images.

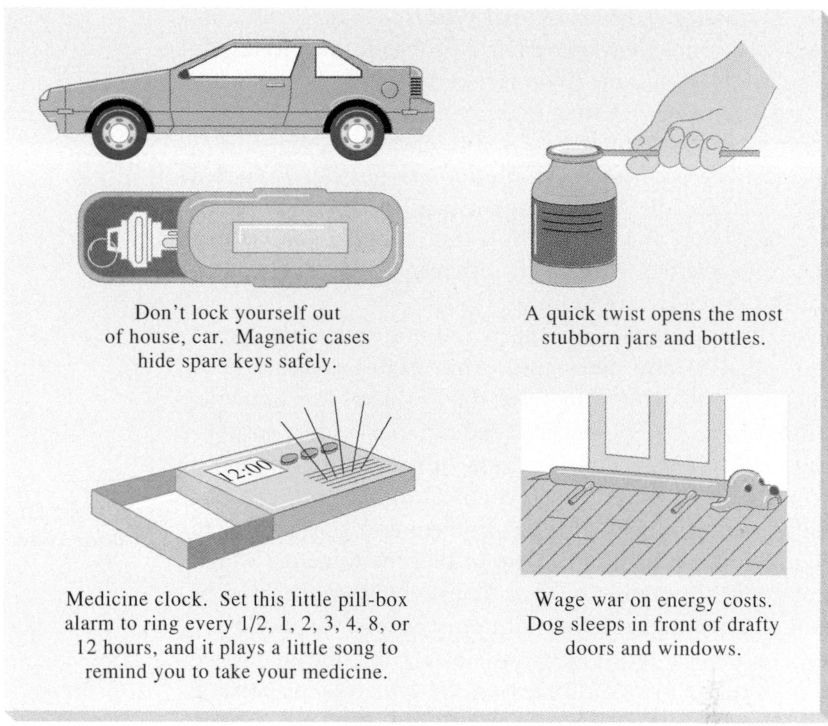

Don't lock yourself out of house, car. Magnetic cases hide spare keys safely.
A quick twist opens the most stubborn jars and bottles.
12:00
Medicine clock. Set this little pill-box alarm to ring every 1/2, 1, 2, 3, 4, 8, or 12 hours, and it plays a little song to remind you to take your medicine.
Wage war on energy costs. Dog sleeps in front of drafty doors and windows.

FIGURE 7

Inventions Designed to Solve Some Common Problems

Following a Systematic Plan

The technique of following a systematic plan was developed by John Bransford and Barry Stein (1993), who developed a system called the IDEAL problem solver. The IDEAL system consists of five components:

- Identifying problems (I)
- Defining and representing problems (D)
- Exploring possible strategies (E)
- Acting on the strategies (A)
- Looking back and evaluating the effects (L)

I: Identifying Problems Before a problem can be solved it first needs to be recognized and identified. Consider the real-life problem two brothers faced. Ladislao and George Biro were proofreaders who spent a lot of their time correcting spelling mistakes and typographical errors in the days before computers. They used fountain pens to record the errors they found, because pencil faded; but fountain pen ink was messy. The Biro brothers recognized they had a problem. So they came up with a solution—they invented the ballpoint pen. Their original company is now part of a corporation known as Bic.

The next time you receive a mail-order catalog, sit down and peruse it. Depending on the catalog, you'll find everything from "continuous-feed" pet food bowls to inflatable bathtub pillows. Most of the gadgets are good examples of clever solutions to common problems (see figure 7). The first step the inventors of these objects took was to identify a problem.

Problem identification is clearly one of the most important steps in the invention process and underlies many creative acts (Getzels & Csikszentmihalyi, 1975). Unfortunately, all too often our society discourages people from identifying problems. For instance, many businesses and government agencies discourage or even fire people who identify problems in the workplace. Accidents such as the crash of the space shuttle *Challenger* and increased incidents of cancer from asbestos may have been avoided if problems that employees had identified were acknowledged and acted on by those in positions of authority. The pressure to ignore problems in business and government agencies is strong enough that Congress eventually passed a bill that provided some protection for people who were brave enough to persist in their fight to be heard, a bill known as the Whistle-Blowers Protection Act.

Fortunately, however, there is an increasing awareness in some businesses and organizations that encouraging employees to identify problems and develop solutions can improve productivity and prevent those problems from becoming more costly later on. Clearly, our educational systems need to place more emphasis on encouraging students to identify problems instead of just trying to solve well-defined problems that are presented in textbooks.

D: Defining Problems and Goals Many people assume that once they encounter a problem, they need only search for a solution. However, earlier in this chapter we considered the fact that many problems are *ill-defined;* their start states, their goal states, and/or the operations that may be used for their solution are not clearly spelled out. For example, many students assume that their goals are clear when they study for a test. Unfortunately, when they take the test, they might discover that they prepared for the wrong type of exam.

How we define a problem and our goals in the problem situation also determines what strategies and experiences we will explore to solve the problem. For example, John Adams (1979) described the experiences of a consulting team hired to develop ways of preventing tomatoes from being damaged by mechanical tomato pickers. Initially, the team defined their problem and goal as how to modify the mechanical pickers so that the tomatoes would not get bruised and damaged. This definition of the problem and goal focused the team on strategies for modifying the mechanical picker, such as slowing the machine down to reduce the force of impact on the tomatoes, or padding the arms of the mechanical picker. It wasn't until the group considered alternative ways of defining the problem and their goals that they realized it would be better to modify the tomatoes than to modify the mechanical picker. The group then explored strategies such as breeding tomatoes that would be less likely to be damaged by the mechanical pickers. How people define their goals in problem situations can directly affect the creativity of their solutions.

E: Exploring Alternative Approaches The third component of the IDEAL framework is to explore alternative approaches and strategies for solving the problem. The strategies that you consider will be determined in part by how you defined the problem and goal. If you are solving a physics problem, then concepts and equations from the domain of physics will certainly be relevant. Earlier in the chapter, we mentioned that there are general-purpose *heuristics* that can help you solve problems in many domains. In fact, items 4 through 10 in figure 6 all are examples of problem-solving heuristics that can work in a variety of situations.

A and L: Acting on a Plan and Looking Back at the Effects We can't know if we have correctly identified, defined, and explored strategies to a problem until we act on them to see if they really work. The final two steps (acting on and looking at the effects of a strategy) are closely related. Figure 6 illustrates the importance of acting on the strategies and looking at the effects. This item was invented to solve the problem of following a recipe in a cookbook while your hands are busy chopping vegetables and measuring spices.

Let's say you invented this apparatus. You probably would want to try it out and see if it works. As you use it,

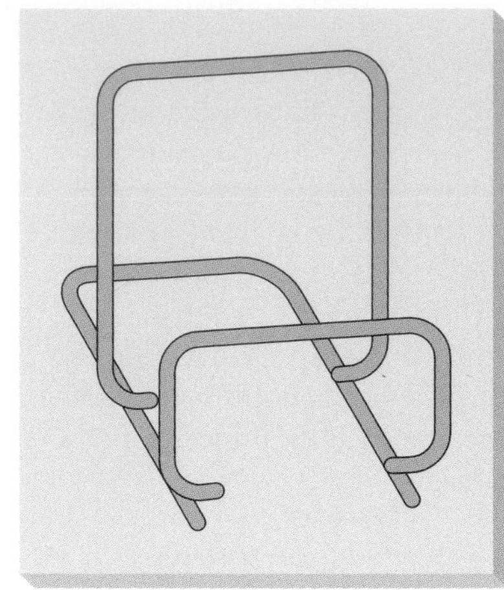

FIGURE 8

Book Holder

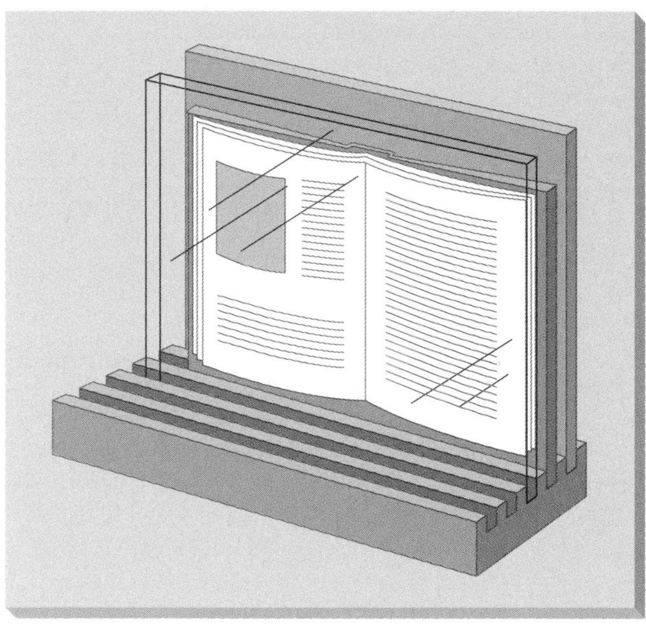

FIGURE 9

Book Holder That Guards Against Stains

you would soon see that there's a problem—the cookbook is not protected from spilled or splattered food. Looking at these effects, you might revise the apparatus to look like the holder shown in figure 9. Without acting on your plan and evaluating the effects, you might not have improved your invention. A summary of the steps in the IDEAL problem solver is shown in figure 10.

Drawing Inferences

Returning to the list of problem-solving strategies (figure 6), we come next to *drawing inferences.* **Inferring** *is the process of taking the information that is given in a problem*

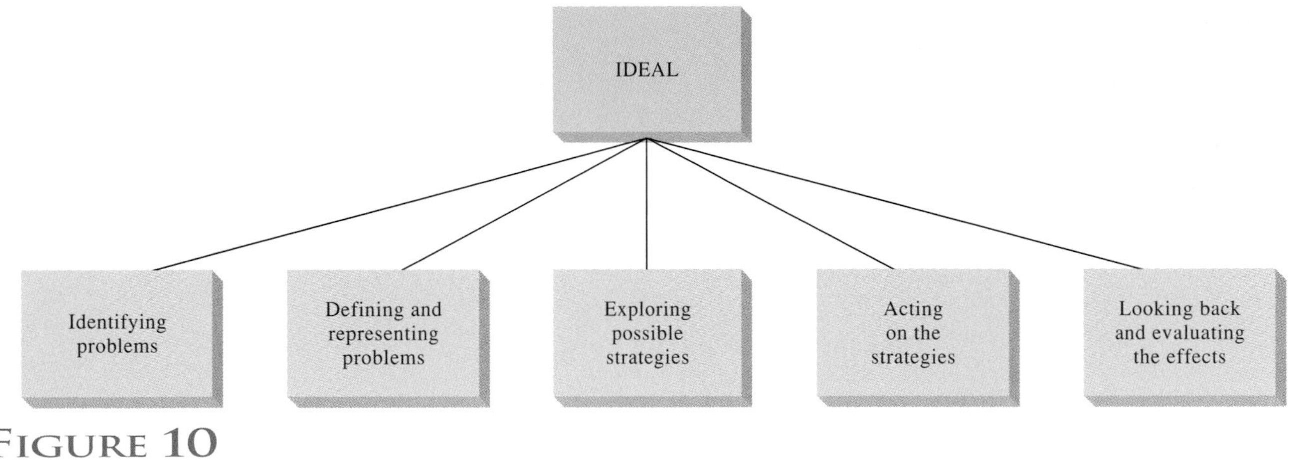

FIGURE 10

IDEAL Problem Solver
According to Bransford and Stein's model of the IDEAL problem solver, problem solving can be divided into five main steps, as shown here.

and considering what this information implies beyond what is explicitly stated; it involves going beyond the information given. If you do not know how to even start on a problem, the strategy of drawing inferences can be a significant help (Wickelgren, 1974).

An important part of the strategy of drawing inferences is to *evaluate* your inferences to determine if they are valid. In many cases we fail to solve problems because we make inferences that are *invalid.* Reexamining the inferences we have made about a problem can point the way to progress.

One type of inference that people frequently make, and that limits their problem solving, is that an object or procedure can be used only for its most common function. For example, in one investigation people were presented with two cords suspended from the ceiling just far enough apart that they could not hold one and reach the other (figure 11) (Maier, 1931). People were asked to find a way to tie the two cords together. The participants were free to use anything they found in the room. On a table were several objects, including a pliers. Can you solve the problem? Even when given hints beforehand, many people failed to realize that the pliers could be used as a weight to create a pendulum. By swinging the string with the pliers attached to it, they would be able to grasp it while holding the other string (see figure 12). People failed to use the pliers as a weight because of **functional fixedness,** *the inability to solve a problem because something is viewed only in terms of its usual function.* A person who needs to raise a slide projector and sees the books on the table next to it only as things to read is missing sight of tools ready at hand to solve the problem. To see a new function for a familiar object is to triumph over functional fixedness. With regard to the pliers, the subjects in that experiment viewed the pliers only in terms of their common function. Incidently, can you think of another way of solving this problem without removing the cords or tying an object to one cord? If you thought of moving the table near the second cord and standing on it to reach the second cord, then you have mastered another strategy that is often overlooked because of functional fixedness.

Each of us occasionally gets into the mental rut of solving problems with a particular strategy. A **learning set** *is the tendency to solve all problems with the same strategy.* Learning sets often serve us efficiently. Without them, we would waste time looking for the solution to a problem we already know. You may have encountered a problem with learning sets in your college classes. Let's say several of your professors base their exams primarily on lecture materials. You pore over your lecture notes and ace the exams. So you follow the same strategy for your Psych. 1 class and spend very little time studying the textbook. When you see the first exam in this class, you learn that the strategy is inappropriate—this exam has a number of questions based only on the text.

Here's a puzzle that is often used to demonstrate the concept of a learning set. It's called the nine-dot problem. Take out a piece of paper and copy the arrangement of the following dots:

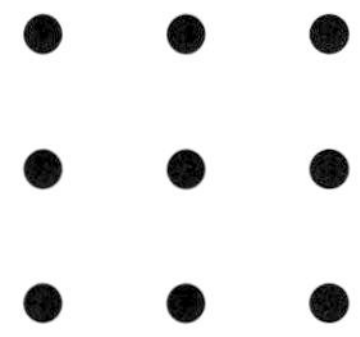

Without lifting your pencil connect the dots using only four straight lines. Most people have difficulty—and lots just give up on—finding a solution to the nine-dot problem. Part of the difficulty is that we have a learning set that tells us to think of the nine-dot configuration as a square. We consider the outer dots as the boundary and do not extend the lines beyond them. Yet the solution to the nine-dot

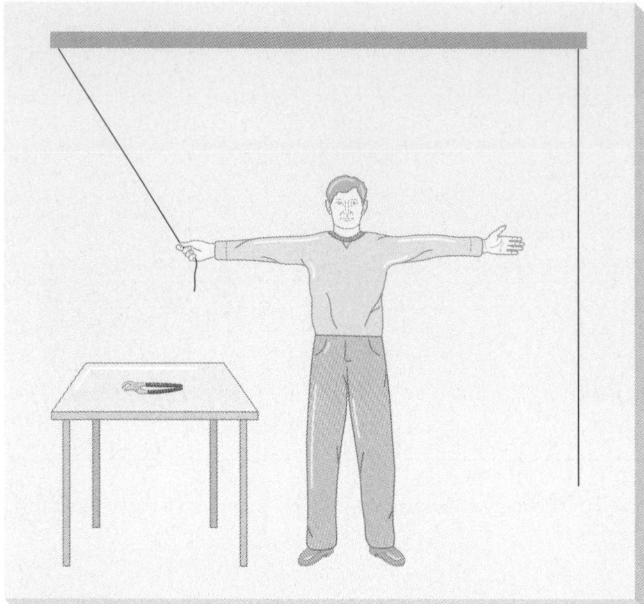

FIGURE 11

Maier String Problem
How can you tie the two strings together if you cannot reach them both at the same time?

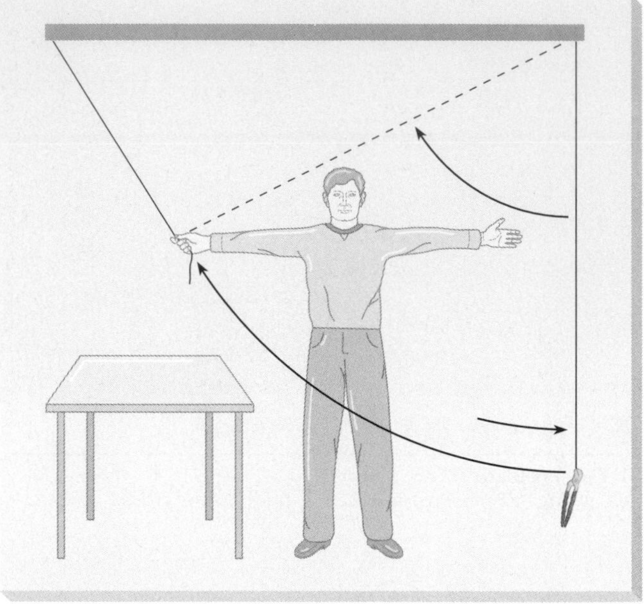

FIGURE 12

Solution to the Maier String Problem
Use the pliers as a weight to create a pendulum motion that brings the second string closer.

problem, shown at the end of this chapter, requires going outside the square. One interesting study explored the effects of telling subjects, after they had spent a period of time on the problem, that they could go outside the square (Weisberg & Alba, 1981). The instruction helped, but the effect was rather small. Unfortunately, it seems that, for many problems, we need other heuristics besides that of making and evaluating inferences.

Developing Subgoals

We considered the heuristic of developing subgoals earlier in the chapter. An important point about the subgoaling heuristic is that it is critical for many real-world problems too. For example, imagine you are faced with the problem of coordinating a fund-raising banquet. This is a complex problem that can be broken down into a number of smaller problems, such as finding a suitable location, arranging decorations, notifying and inviting guests, arranging entertainment, selecting a menu and preparing food, serving food, and cleaning up. The complexity of this problem also requires an effective scheme for representing and coordinating information among these tasks. For example, the number of people needed to serve the food will depend, in part, on the menu and the size of the guest list. Furthermore, certain tasks need to be accomplished before others can be started. For instance, sending out invitations or announcements requires information about the time and place for the event as well as the menu and entertainment. The invitations will also take time to print and mail; thus, the timing of each subtask must be carefully scheduled if the event is to be successful.

Problems of such complexity are quite common whenever new products are being developed, large buildings are being constructed, or political campaigns are being organized. These problems frequently involve many individuals working on many different subproblems. In recent years computer technology has aided in the solution of such problems with project management software. These programs help represent and analyze the temporal sequence and interdependence of different tasks. This software often makes it easier to identify potential time conflicts or resource allocation conflicts so the project coordinator can correct them early in the problem-solving process.

Working Backward

The heuristic of working backward can help you solve mazes. Many mazes have numerous routes away from the start box but only one that reaches the goal. If you start at the goal and move backward, the successful route can suddenly become quite obvious to you. In general, working backward should be attempted whenever the end state of a problem is well defined but the start state is not. For example, imagine that you need to meet someone across town for dinner and you don't want to be late. You know where and when you want to arrive but you don't know exactly when you need to leave. If you consider that your dinner date is for 6:00 P.M., that you will need about 10 minutes to find a parking place, and that the drive across town will take about 30 minutes, you can work backward to solve the problem (6:00 P.M. – 10 minutes – 30 minutes = 5:20 P.M. departure).

Searching for Contradictions

The heuristic of searching for contradictions can help you with the multiple-choice exams used in some college courses. Often the incorrect choices in a multiple-choice question contradict information that is stated in the question or in prior questions. For example, if one question asks you to choose a reason why *heuristics* sometimes fail (and none of the options is that they never do), and one of the choices for another question is that heuristics always produce a correct result, you have good reason to believe that that choice is wrong.

Searching for Relations Among Problems

Searching for relations among problems can help you when a current problem can be solved through analogy to one you have encountered in the past. In the research on transferring one's knowledge to new problems, it has been found that subjects who have relevant knowledge often fail to use this knowledge unless they are given a hint to use it. In your own problem solving, you can give such hints to yourself. The next time you are stumped on a problem, ask yourself if you can recall similar types of problems you have worked on in the past. If you can recall such problems, you might be able to employ the same solution, or an analogous solution, to solve the problem you are struggling with now.

Reformulating the Representation of the Problem

Reformulating your representation of a problem can be a great aid in solving tough problems. Earlier we discussed how experts in a field differ from novices in their representations of problems. But even a novice working on knowledge-lean problems can try different types of representation.

A useful type of representation for a great many problems is a "vivid representation" (Holyoak & Spellman, 1993), such as a visual image or graph. Consider the Buddhist Monk problem (Matlin, 1989):

> Exactly at sunrise one morning, a Buddhist monk set out to climb a tall mountain. The narrow path was not more than a foot or two wide, and it wound around the mountain to a beautiful, glittering temple at the mountain peak.
>
> The monk climbed the path at varying rates of speed. He stopped many times along the way to rest and to eat the fruit he carried with him. He reached the temple just before sunset. At the temple, he fasted and meditated for several days. Then he began his journey back along the same path, starting at sunrise and walking, as before, at variable speeds with many stops along the way. However, his average speed going down the hill was greater than his average climbing speed.
>
> Prove that there must be a spot along the path that the monk will pass on both trips at exactly the same time.

This can be a difficult problem, until it is represented as shown in figure 13. If we graph altitude as a function of time of day, we see that regardless of the factor of speed, there must be some time at which the monk was at the same spot going up the mountain as he was when he was coming down.

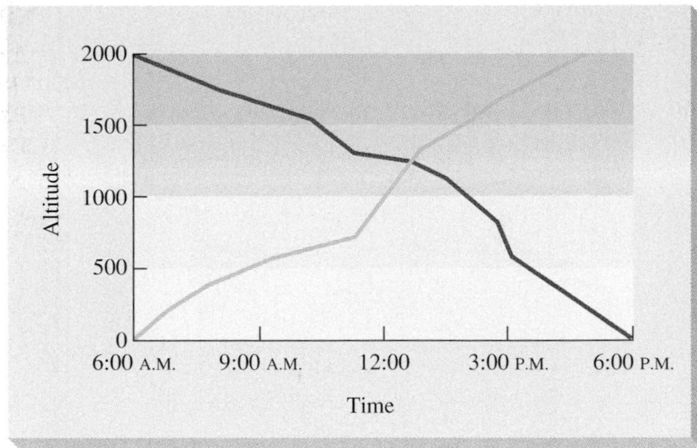

FIGURE 13

The Buddhist Monk Problem

Practicing

Practicing might not always be fun, but you can be sure of one thing: No one gets better at problem solving without solving problems (Ashcraft, 1994). If you practice working problems in an area, you will build up your knowledge base and also begin to "automate" certain processes.

At this point we have discussed a number of ideas about the cognitive revolution in psychology and about problem solving. Next, we turn to the second main area of thinking—reasoning and judgment.

REASONING AND JUDGMENT

Aside from solving problems, a second broad area of thought is reasoning and judgment. Our discussion of this topic will begin with the nature of inductive and deductive reasoning, focusing on how context and content influence reasoning. We will then consider how people make decisions and estimate probabilities, reviewing how their use of heuristics can lead to poor judgments. Next we will cover a topic of considerable interest to educators as well as psychologists: critical thinking. We will conclude with an evaluation of research on the nature of conceptual knowledge, including formal and everyday concepts.

Inductive and Deductive Reasoning

"Elementary, my dear Watson," Sherlock Holmes, the master detective, would say to his baffled companion. Holmes would then go on to explain how he had solved a particularly difficult case. No matter how tough the problem, Holmes always came up with the right solution. Dr. Watson would listen in amazement at how Holmes had spotted all the clues and made sense of them, while he had either missed them or

What was the nature of Sherlock Holmes' reasoning in solving a particularly difficult case?

misinterpreted them. Holmes' adventures, written by Sir Arthur Conan Doyle, all involve intricate problems that Holmes solves with amazing powers of reasoning.

The fictional character, Sherlock Holmes, used a combination of thinking skills known as inductive and deductive reasoning. **Inductive reasoning** *refers to the process of deriving abstract principles, concepts, or hypotheses from specific observations.* For example, when we take our car to a mechanic, he may listen to our description of the car's symptoms and provide us with a hypothesis about the underlying cause of our problem. The mechanic may also suggest that an inspection and/or tests be conducted to confirm his hypothesis. In the latter situation the mechanic is using **deductive reasoning,** *that is, reasoning from the general to the specific. Deductive reasoning involves working with more abstract information or statements, usually called "premises," and deriving a conclusion.* Many types of problem-solving tasks, such as diagnosing a car problem or conducting scientific research, involve a combination of inductive and deductive reasoning skills.

Inductive Reasoning and Intuition

Although psychologists have conducted numerous studies involving inductive reasoning (we will consider some of these studies later in this chapter when we explore concept formation), little is understood about the process. Our failure to identify any systematic rules or strategies that could help us make inductive inferences is, perhaps, one reason that we are so amazed by Sherlock Holmes' ability to develop crime theories using such a limited number of observations. In fact, the inductive reasoning skills of this fictional character are not unlike those of other experts.

Experts' impressive ability to formulate and identify abstract relationships is undoubtedly the result of the extensive experience they have had working similar problems. One reason these skills may be difficult to understand is that they may have more to do with the way we perceive information than with the way we strategically use information. Indeed, psychologists such as James Gibson (1966) have argued that much of what we attribute to complex thought processes might actually be explained by changes in the sensitivity of our perceptual systems to information around us (Mace, 1974). For example, the expert wine taster is much better than the novice at discriminating different wines, because the expert has learned to differentiate a much richer array of smell and taste patterns in wine than the novice has. Chess experts also seem to have much richer vocabularies for identifying and remembering chess patterns than novices do. If inductive reasoning depends more on changes in perceptual experience than on changes in strategic thinking, that might be related to what is often called intuition.

Hypothesis Testing and Deductive Reasoning

The discussion above suggests that our ability to identify abstract relationships might depend more on an intuitive perceptual process than on systematic logical reasoning. How is this perceptual skill developed and refined? Although experience plays an important role in this process, we must refine these skills by evaluating our ideas and correcting them when we are wrong. For example, when Sherlock Holmes formulated a theory of a crime, he frequently sought additional information that would test his idea. **Hypothesis testing** *is the process of using our theories and intuitions to make predictions and then evaluating those predictions with further observations.* For example, suppose that our car won't start and the symptoms appear to indicate that the cause of the problem is a faulty battery. We might test our idea by conducting further observations or tests. For example, we might reason: "If our intuition is correct and the battery is dead, then installing a new battery will allow the car to start." Our subsequent observations may help us decide if our intuition was correct. This process of conducting systematic observations and tests to evaluate our intuitions and theories is also the basis for scientific research.

Philosophers and scientists often compare the hypothesis-testing process described above to more formal systems of deductive reasoning. For instance, in conditional reasoning tasks, a statement (premise) is presented that relates two events in a sentence of the form *If A, then B.* For example, consider this premise: *If it is raining, then the streets are wet.* Each if-then premise includes an antecedent *(If. . .)* and a consequent *(then . . .).* In our example, the antecedent is *If it is raining,* and the consequent is *then the streets are wet.* In conditional reasoning, a second premise is also provided, which either affirms or denies the antecedent or the consequent. Consider the following two premises and conclusion:

If it is raining, then the streets are wet.
It is raining.
Therefore, the streets are wet.

Does the conclusion follow from the premises? If you agreed with the conclusion, you used a valid form of logical reasoning known as affirming the antecedent. Now consider another example:

If it is raining, then the streets are wet.
The streets are wet.
Therefore, it is raining.

Does the conclusion follow from the premise? If you agreed with the conclusion, you used an invalid form of reasoning known as the fallacy of affirming the consequent. We cannot conclude that it rained, because the streets might be wet for another reason, such as a broken water main or someone washing her car. This second example illustrates one of the limitations of using deductive reasoning to evaluate our intuitions or theories: We cannot prove that our intuitions or theories are correct simply by finding empirical evidence that is consistent with our predictions, because there will always be alternative theories that can explain the same observations. Figure 14 displays four possible ways of drawing inferences in conditional reasoning. Two of these are logically valid, and the other two are invalid. If you reason in a valid way, then you know that your conclusion is true—*provided* that you know that all your premises are true. On the other hand, invalid reasoning can produce false conclusions even when all the premises are true.

Do people reason logically (validly)? According to research on conditional reasoning problems, the answer is no, or at least "often not." Even intelligent adults make the error of accepting conclusions based on denying the antecedent and affirming the consequent (see items II and III in figure 14). Moreover, people often fail to accept perfectly logical conclusions based on denying the consequent (see item IV in figure 14). Do you understand the logic of denying the consequent? If not, you have a good deal of company. But don't worry—just read on.

Research on conditional reasoning has produced a remarkable finding: People appear to be more logical if reasoning problems draw on their knowledge of familiar everyday rules, such as giving permission or obeying the law (Cheng & others, 1986; Griggs & Cox, 1982). After you have worked through the examples in figure 14, try the examples in figure 15. Was it easier in figure 15 to see that items I and IV are valid, and that items II and III are not? For most people it is. We know about laws regarding underage drinking, and because of this it is obvious that if someone is drinking beer legally, they are 18 years old or older (item I), and that if they are *under* 18 years old (that is, they are *not* 18 years old or older) and they are drinking beer, they are *not* drinking the beer legally (item IV).

First premise:

The antecedent: If this book is great,
The consequent: then it will sell a zillion copies.

Possible second premises and conclusions:

I. Affirming the antecedent (valid reasoning):
This book is great.
Therefore, it will sell a zillion copies.

II. Denying the antecedent (invalid reasoning):
This book is not great.
Therefore, it will not sell a zillion copies.

III. Affirming the consequent (invalid reasoning):
This book will sell a zillion copies.
Therefore, it is great.

IV. Denying the consequent (valid reasoning):
This book will not sell a zillion copies.
Therefore, it is not great.

FIGURE 14

Four Ways of Drawing Conclusions in Conditional Reasoning Problems

First premise:

The antecedent: If a person is drinking beer legally,
The consequent: then she or he is 18 years old or older.

Possible second premises and conclusions:

I. Affirming the antecedent (valid reasoning):
This person is drinking beer legally.
Therefore, she or he is 18 years old or older.

II. Denying the antecedent (invalid reasoning):
This person is not drinking beer legally.
Therefore, she or he is not 18 years old or older.

III. Affirming the consequent (invalid reasoning):
This person is 18 years old or older.
Therefore, she or he is drinking beer legally.

IV. Denying the consequent (valid reasoning):
This person is not 18 years old or older.
Therefore, she or he is not drinking beer legally.

FIGURE 15

Four Ways of Drawing Conclusions in Conditional Reasoning Problem Drawing on Background Knowledge

EXPLORATIONS IN PSYCHOLOGY 1

Can Reasoning Be Taught?

An important issue in philosophy and education is whether schools can help students learn to reason better, making them more sophisticated voters, wiser consumers, more productive employees, and better parents (Nisbett & others, 1987). The idea that formal training in an academic discipline can improve the mind's functioning in everyday life has an early historical origin. The Greek philosopher Plato claimed that exposure to arithmetic and geometry benefits reasoning, and went on to argue that future leaders of the state should be strongly encouraged to study these subjects so that they will govern more effectively. Philosophers in ancient Rome recommended the study of grammar and memory to improve mental functioning in life, while medieval scholars stressed the benefits of training in the formal rules of logic. More recently, humanists argued that the study of Latin and Greek improves the mind, if only because of the great discipline required to master these difficult subjects.

What does psychology have to say on this point? Surprisingly, much writing by psychologists over the last 90 years has been pessimistic on the issue of whether good thinking can be taught. The famous learning theorist Edward Thorndike (1906) approached this issue in his large-scale project on "transfer" effects in learning. He examined whether training in various tasks could improve subsequent performance in other tasks, and discovered that generally there is very little transfer except when two tasks have many elements in common. For example, he found very little transfer between two tasks of estimating the areas of rectangles, though the only difference between the two tasks was in the shapes and sizes of the rectangles. Apparently, the effects of practice in estimating areas are specific to particular shapes and delimited ranges of size.

The famous Swiss developmental psychologist Jean Piaget (1952) also questioned the benefits of teaching people how to think. Piaget argued that the rules of abstract thought, which he called "formal operations," were acquired spontaneously in early adolescence through an active process of self-discovery. Attempts to teach such rules to speed their acquisition were hopeless, in his view.

Despite this history of pessimistic views, research suggests that formal training in school—or in laboratory experiments—can indeed improve our reasoning. The key is to teach the kinds of thinking rules that actually are useful in our everyday lives. It also is helpful if the rules that are taught are already known in an elementary way, so that the training can build on preexisting knowledge instead of beginning from "scratch."

According to psychologist Richard Nisbett and his colleagues (1987), one set of rules that are teachable in school are "statistical heuristics," rules concerning randomness and probability such as those you might learn in a class on statistics (required for psychology majors in many universities). You might not think that statistical principles have much use in everyday thought, but consider a fact that many sports fans have pondered: Two weeks into the major league baseball season, the top hitter's batting average often is as high as .450. And yet no one has attained such a high batting average by the end of the baseball season. Or, if you love food, consider this situation, all too common in an epicure's life: After experiencing a fabulous meal on your first visit to a restaurant, you are disappointed time and time again on subsequent visits (often to your considerable embarrassment, having raved about the restaurant to friends).

Many factors can contribute to these types of experiences, but one of them is a statistics law called the "law of large numbers." This law applies to all situations in which individuals try to judge a group or individual based on a sample of observations of this group or individual. In essence, the law simply states that the larger the sample, the better the sample; small samples can be misleading.

According to the law of large numbers, a small sample of performance of any individual—a batter on a baseball team or a chef in a restaurant—often is *not* a reliable guide for predicting their performance in future situations. Good predictions of performance depend on adequate samples, and one meal in a restaurant or two weeks of baseball are just not adequate to do the job.

Can training in statistics help people understand the statistical factors involved in prediction? Yes. Using everyday problems like those discussed above, researchers conducted a

As for item II in figure 15, the premise *This person is not drinking beer legally* is ambiguous. Suppose you take it to mean that the person is *drinking beer illegally.* Well, there can be other reasons, apart from age, why a person's drinking beer would be illegal—the person might be drinking it while driving an automobile, or drinking it in public in a "dry" town, for instance. Or suppose you take the other possible meaning of the premise: that the person *is not drinking beer* (and therefore not drinking it "illegally"). Now it's even more obvious that the conclusion doesn't follow—people don't start drinking beer incessantly when they turn 18 (even the ones you'd like to offer as counterexamples have to sleep sometimes). You can use the same common knowledge to explain why item III is invalid. (Now you'll see, though, that item IV is valid only if we take the conclusion as meaning that the person *is drinking beer illegally.* It would not be valid to conclude that the person *is not drinking beer.* Such matters of telephone survey of college students who were enrolled in a course on statistics (Fong, Krantz, & Nisbett, 1986). Some students were interviewed near the start of the semester, while others were interviewed near the end. The students were not told that the telephone interview had anything to do with the course they were taking. Nonetheless, the students interviewed near the end of the semester gave more and better statistical answers using the law of large numbers and similar principles, as compared to the students interviewed at the start. Going through a course on statistics appeared to improve students' statistical reasoning outside the classroom context. Even a 30-minute training session dealing with statistical principles, or with examples of these principles at work, improves subjects' statistical reasoning in problems of this type.

Nisbett and his colleagues (1987) examined the effects of training on other types of reasoning and concluded that these effects are not always strong. For example, training in the logic of conditional reasoning has only limited effects, perhaps because people have no preexisting knowledge of the logical rules involved in such reasoning (Cheng & others, 1986). To be effective, training in how to reason should build upon rules people already know—trying to teach people entirely new rules of thought will be difficult at best.

(left) Tony Gwynn of the San Diego Padres, one of baseball's leading hitters. Why might a two week sample of Gwynn's hitting performance not be a good indicator of his batting average at the end of the season? (right) Why are you often disappointed on subsequent visits to a resaurant you initially raved about?

ambiguity show that it is very important to be clear about meanings if you are going to learn to think clearly. Ambiguity is a natural part of natural language in everyday life; learning to disambiguate is a natural part of learning to reason well.)

People *appear* to reason much more logically when they can draw on their knowledge about everyday rules they are familiar with. Whether they *actually* do *reason* better, though, is a matter of debate. Perhaps they simply *remember* how these rules are applied and don't do the work of actually thinking through the logic that underlies those applications of the rules.

An important issue in philosophy and education is whether schools can help students learn to reason better, making them more sophisticated voters, more productive employees, and better parents (Nisbett & others, 1987). To read further about this important issue, turn to Explorations in Psychology 1.

Estimating Probabilities

We judge probabilities in many situations. A personnel officer interviewing a job applicant must judge the probability that this person will meet the demands of the position. A homeowner considering flood insurance must judge the probability that a major flood will occur. In such cases, there is no procedure that guarantees a good estimate; a judgment of probabilities is required.

To understand the nature of judging probabilities, remember the distinction we made between *algorithms* and *heuristics*. Algorithms are procedures guaranteed to produce an answer to a problem, whereas heuristics are rules of thumb that can suggest a solution but do not ensure that it will work. Three heuristics that individuals use in estimating probabilities are the availability, simulation, and representativeness heuristics (Kahneman & Tversky, 1982; Tversky & Kahneman, 1973.).

The **availability heuristic** *is the strategy of judging the probability of an event by the ease with which prior occurrences come to mind.* Thus, we might assess the probability of a space vehicle falling in a particular area by recalling whether any other space materials had fallen there. Other factors involved in the availability heuristic are our familiarity with the information and the vividness of the possible event. Because the media tend to overexpose us to information about such things as tornadoes, cancer, and accidents, we might overestimate their occurrence.

A variant of the availability heuristic has important effects on our emotional lives; it determines our sense of frustration or bad luck when things don't work out as we would like. This is the **simulation heuristic,** *the strategy of judging the probability of an event by the ease of imagining or constructing scenarios that would cause it to occur.* Consider for a moment whether you would enjoy receiving a gift of a million dollars. Most people would enjoy this. Do you feel frustrated by the fact that you have *not* received such a gift? It's to be hoped that you don't spend much time thinking about it and that, no, you're not really frustrated. Now consider how you would feel if an eccentric billionaire had decided to pick someone at random and give them a million dollars. He stood outside the university you attend and decided to give the money to the 23rd person who passed his way. You were the 22nd; the person walking behind you got the check. Would you be upset?

A study conducted by Daniel Kahneman and Amos Tversky (1982), using stories similar to that sketched above, provides evidence that you would. In fact, you probably would feel *more* upset if you were the 22nd passerby than if you were the 1st or 2nd, or had decided to skip class that day and didn't go to campus. *Just missing* receiving a million dollars seems much more disappointing than missing it "by miles." The reason is that, having just missed the gift, it is easy to imagine alternative scenarios that would make you the lucky one. If only you had stopped to say "Hi" to those friends; if only you hadn't been walking so fast; if only the billionaire had reached campus a little earlier. If it is easy to construct a certain scenario, its outcome becomes highly available in your mind. Hence, you feel that the outcome is very highly probable. Because it is highly probable, you might tend to feel that it should have occurred, but that, instead, fate snatched it away. In contrast, if you weren't even close to being the winner, it is harder to come up with such "if only" scenarios. Being the winner seems much less probable and *not* being the winner seems much less disappointing.

The **representativeness heuristic** *is the strategy of judging the probability of an event based on how well it matches a prototype (the most common or representative example).* Consider the following description of an individual's dinner companion: skilled at carpentry, proficient at wrestling, owns a pet snake, knows how to repair motorcycles, and has been arrested for beating someone with a chain. What is the probability that this person is male? Most likely, the description fits your prototype of a man more than your prototype of a woman, so you might estimate that there is a 9 in 10 chance the dinner companion is male.

In this example, your prototype served you well because there are far more men than women in the population who fit the description. Sometimes, however, our prototypes do not take into account the frequency of events in a total population. For example, suppose that the dinner companion is a man. Which would you say has a greater probability: that he is a member of an outlawed motorcycle gang, or that he is a salesman? You probably answered something like, "There is a much greater chance that he is a member of an outlawed motorcycle gang," in which case you would be wrong. Why? Although only a very small percentage of the millions of salesmen in the world fit the description of the dinner companion, the total number represented by this percentage is greater than the total number of outlawed motorcycle gang members who fit the description. Let's assume there are 10,000 members of violent motorcycle gangs in the world and 100 million salesmen. Even if 1 of every 100 motorcycle gang members fits our description, there would be only 100 of them. If just 1 of every 100,000 salesmen fits our description, their total would number 1,000, so the probability is 10 times greater that the dinner companion is a salesman than a member of a motorcycle gang. Our lives involve many such instances in which we judge probabilities based on representativeness while failing to consider the population from which a sample is drawn.

Another problem with the representativeness heuristic is known to affect gamblers. This problem, called the **gamblers' fallacy,** *is the tendency to underestimate the probability of long runs of similar events.* A common scenario in a gambling casino is the naive tourist at the roulette table betting on red and winning several rounds in a row. At this point the tourist decides to stop playing—or to bet on black because "it must be time for black after all those reds

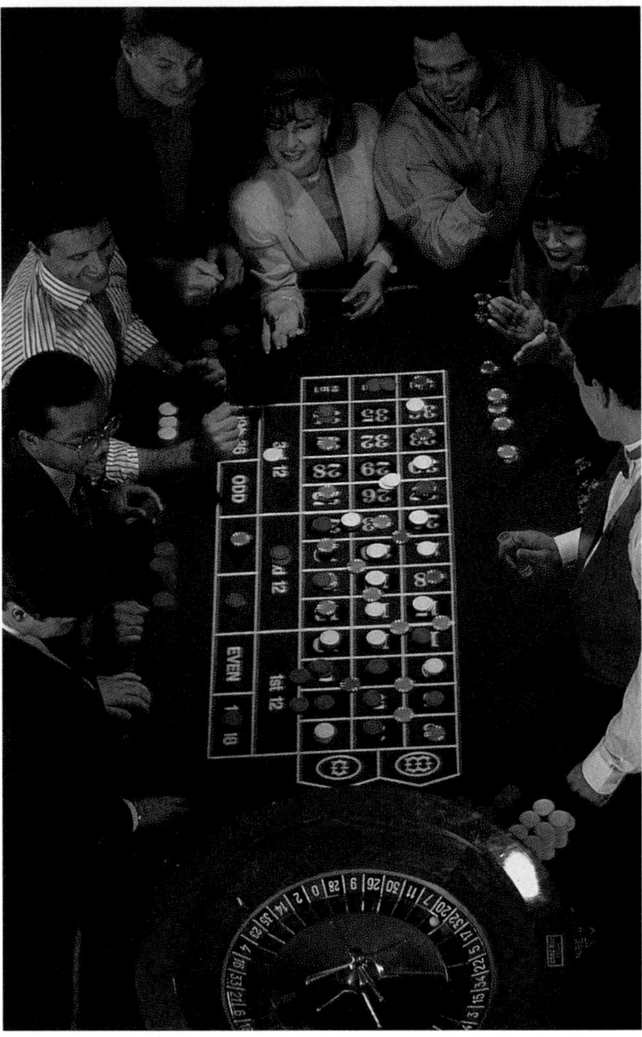

What is the nature of the gamblers' fallacy?

in a row." A more frightening example of the gamblers' fallacy is tourists who think they invented a fail-proof "system" for winning or at least breaking even. It goes like this: First bet a dollar on red; and if you lose, then bet two dollars on red; and if you lose again, bet four dollars on red; and if you still lose, bet eight dollars on red . . . and so on. Red will win at some point, and then all losses will be recouped, right?

Wrong! The problem with this system is that long strings of blacks (or any other outcome) are not as rare as many people suppose, and if a long string occurs, you might wind up making larger and larger bets ($16, $32, $64, $128, $256, . . .) until you hit the house limit or simply go broke. Not a happy outcome.

What is behind the gamblers' fallacy? The representativeness heuristic: believing that a sequence of events produced through a roulette wheel or some other random process should have a random-looking appearance (such as red, black, black, red, red, red, black, red, . . .). Hence, individuals judge a random-looking sequence as much more likely than a "run" of like events. What people forget is that any *particular* sequence is just as unlikely as any other particular sequence—red, black, black, red, red, red has the same probability as red, red, red, red, red, red. What color comes up on any spin of the roulette wheel is always about a 50–50 proposition (not quite 50–50, because the 0 and 00 slots on the roulette wheel are neither red nor black). After all, the roulette wheel has no memory; it doesn't know what sequence outcomes preceded any particular spin.

Critical Thinking

Currently there is considerable interest in critical thinking among both psychologists and educators, although it is not a completely new idea. Educator John Dewey (1933) was working with a similar idea when he contrasted "reflective thinking" with "nonreflective thinking in the use of formulas or rules to achieve goals." So was Gestalt psychologist Max Wertheimer (1945) when he distinguished between "productive thinking" and "blind induction." Although today's definitions of **critical thinking** vary, they have in common the notions of *grasping the deeper meaning of problems, of keeping an open mind about different approaches and perspectives, and of deciding for oneself what to believe or do.* Another, often implicit, assumption is that critical thinking is a very important aspect of everyday reasoning (Galotti, 1989). Critical thinking can and should be used, not just in the classroom but outside it as well (Halpern, 1995; McBurney, 1996).

Considerable interest has recently developed in teaching critical thinking in our schools (Halonen, 1995). One goal of this book is to teach critical thinking about psychology.

Robert J. Sternberg (1985) believes that most school programs that teach critical thinking are basically flawed. He thinks that schools focus too much on formal reasoning tasks and not enough on the critical-thinking skills needed in everyday life. What are these critical-thinking skills we need in everyday life? Sternberg lists ten. The first three skills involve (1) recognizing that problems exist, (2) defining problems more precisely, and (3) coping with poorly structured problems. These skills map onto steps 1 and 2 in the IDEAL problem solver discussed earlier in the chapter (see figure 10).

Three additional skills listed by Sternberg pertain to some of the basic differences between formal and everyday reasoning tasks: People need to develop skills to (4) deal with problems that are *not* self-contained (such as deciding on a college when that bears on your marriage plans), (5) handle problems with no single right answer or any clear criteria for the point at which the problem is solved (such as finding a rewarding career), and (6) make decisions on issues of personal relevance (such as deciding to have a risky operation).

Finally, Sternberg cites four additional critical-thinking skills on which, to date, there has been little research. These involve (7) obtaining information, (8) using informal knowledge, (9) thinking in groups, and (10) developing long-term approaches to long-term problems.

Conceptual Knowledge

There remains to be considered one final important piece of the thinking puzzle—that of conceptual knowledge. Indeed, it would be impossible to solve problems and think without using concepts. Think about driving, something most of us do every day. Signs and traffic signals every few blocks tell us to stop, yield, or proceed apace. Usually we don't think of these signs and signals as solutions to problems, but they are (Bransford & Stein, 1993). Most of the symbols that keep traffic moving so smoothly are the brainchild of William Eno, the "father of traffic safety." Eno, born in New York City in 1858, became concerned about the horrendous traffic jams in the city. The horsedrawn vehicles were making street traffic dangerous. Eno published a paper about the urgency of street traffic reform. His concept proposed solutions to the problem—stop signs, one-way streets, and pedestrian safety islands—ideas that affect our behavior today.

We have a special ability for categorizing things. We know that apples and oranges are fruits, but we know that they have different tastes and colors, too. We know that Porsches and Yugos are both automobiles, but we also know that they differ in cost, speed, and prestige. How do we know that apples and oranges are fruits and that Porsches and Yugos are automobiles despite their differences? The answer lies in our ability to ignore their different forms and group them on the basis of some feature(s). For example, all Porsches and Yugos have four wheels and a steering wheel and provide a means of transportation. In other words we have a concept of what an automobile is. A **concept** *is a category used to group objects, events, and characteristics on the basis of common properties.*

Why are concepts important? Without concepts, each object and event in our world would be unique to us. Any kind of generalization would be impossible for us. Concepts allow us to relate experiences and objects. The Chicago Cubs, Atlanta Braves, and Milwaukee Brewers are professional baseball teams. Without the concept of a baseball team, we would be unable to compare these teams.

Concepts grease the wheels of memory, making it more efficient. When we group objects to form a concept, we remember the characteristics associated with the concept rather than each object or experience. When one stockbroker tells another stockbroker that the Dow Jones Industrial Average went up today, the second broker knows that there is a good chance that IBM, Exxon, and General Motors, whose stocks contribute to the average, increased in value. The use of the concept of the Dow made communication more efficient and probably jogged memory as well.

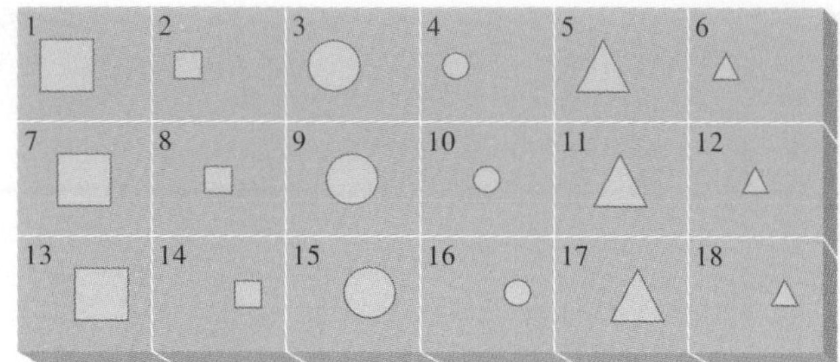

FIGURE 16

Typical Concept Formation Task
This array of cards might be presented to a number of subjects. The experimenter arbitrarily chooses the correct concept, such as "large circles," and then the subject tries to discover the rule that defines the concept.

Concepts also keep us from "reinventing the wheel" each time we come across a piece of information. For example, we don't have to relearn what the Dow Jones Industrial Average is each time we pick up a newspaper. We already know what the concept means. Concepts also provide clues about how to react to an object or experience. For example, if we see a dish of pretzels, our concept of food lets us know it's okay to eat them. Concepts allow us to associate classes of objects or events. Some classes of objects are associated in structured patterns. For example, Dennis Conner won the America's Cup; the America's Cup is given to the winner of an international yachting competition; yachting is a sport.

Because concepts are so critical to our ability to make sense of the world around us, researchers have spent a lot of time studying the process of concept formation. In studying concept formation, psychologists have investigated an individual's ability to discover a rule for why some objects fall within a concept while others do not (Keil, 1989). These rules are based on features or combinations of features. For example, a rule for a concept might be "all stimuli that are triangles (but not circles or squares)," or "all stimuli that are circles," or "all stimuli that are colored red," or "stimuli that are both circles and red (all that are circles and red)."

To get a better sense of cognition, let's examine more closely how an experiment on concept formation might proceed. Figure 16 displays a number of cards shown to the person in a typical concept formation study (Moates & Schumacher, 1980). The shapes (square, circle, or triangle), sizes (small, large), and positions (left, middle, or right) of the figures on the cards vary. The experimenter arbitrarily chooses a concept, such as "large circles," and asks the individual to discover it. Subjects are shown an example of the concept (such as card 3) and asked to choose other cards until they discover the nature of the concept. After each choice, the subject is told whether or not the chosen card is an example of the concept.

An important process in concept formation is to develop hypotheses about what defines the concept and to test these hypotheses in new examples. Suppose you are an avid tennis player but feel you are losing too many matches because your serve is weak. Despite hours of practice, your serve just isn't getting any better. Your problem might be that you have only a vague concept of what a "killer" serve is really like. In order to get a feel for the concept and to see how the best players serve, you head for the tennis courts. Based on your observations, you develop a hypothesis about the mechanics of an excellent serve. For example, after hours of watching the "weekend pros" ace their opponents, you decide that the ball must be tossed high so the server has to stretch to reach it, and that the server needs to swing the racket just like a baseball pitcher throws a ball. You might want to scrutinize the serves of more skilled players to see if they confirm your hypothesis. You'll also want to test the hypothesis in your own game to see if the two aspects of the hypothesis—that good servers toss the ball high and swing the racket like a baseball player throws a ball—improve your serve.

At this point we have discussed a number of ideas about the cognitive revolution in psychology, problem solving, and reasoning and judgment. A summary of these ideas is presented in concept table 1.

Language

Language is an elegant system of communication. Let's explore just what this system is like.

Exploring the Nature of Language

Every human society has language. There are thousands of human languages, and they differ so dramatically that many individuals despair of ever mastering more than one. However, all human languages have some common characteristics.

First, language consists of a sequence of words (Miller, 1981). This description of language has two parts—the presence of words and sequencing. It might seem obvious that all languages have words, but think for a moment about what words are. We produce and perceive words every day; yet words have an almost magical quality. They stand for, or symbolize, things. We use words to refer to objects, people, actions, events, and even abstract ideas. What a word refers to is arbitrary, in the sense that it is based on convention; what a word symbolizes is something agreed upon by a group of language users. To understand this point, consider that different languages have different names for the same thing. What we call a "house" is called "casa" in Spanish and "maison" in French. Since different languages have different words, we are forced to conclude that words are linked arbitrarily and by convention to their referents.

Although words are important in language, the mere presence of words is not enough to make a language. Sequencing of the words is also required. Can you imagine a language with one-word utterances? A 13-month-old infant might use one-word utterances, but as we will see later in the chapter, experts stress that the infant has whole sentences in mind when uttering a single word.

Why is sequencing important for language? The answer leads to another important characteristic of language—**infinite generativity,** *an individual's ability to generate an infinite number of meaningful sentences using a finite set of words and rules, which makes language a highly creative enterprise.* It is possible for us to say things never before said by anyone else.

Yet another characteristic of language is **displacement,** *the use of language to communicate information about another place and time,* although we also use language to describe what is currently happening in our immediate environment. Anyone who reads fiction can attest to the power of displacement in language. However, reading fiction is just one example of how language gives secondhand experience. Consider the everyday experience of being told what happened elsewhere or what someone else said. Language contributes to the transmission of knowledge not only from one individual to another but also from one generation to the next.

Language's role in communication needs to be underscored. Indeed, above all else, language enables humans to communicate. We speak to others, listen to others, and write something that others will read, all as part of using language to communicate.

Another property of language is *signal simultaneity and overlap.* Unlike simple signaling systems (such as a traffic signal or a doorbell), language transmits several aspects of information simultaneously. Each bit of spoken language is packed with information about word- and sentence-level meaning, as well as speaker identity and emotion. In addition, language is not discrete and sequential like beads on a string, but instead is compressed and overlapped. For example, try saying the words *see* and *sue.* Notice that the *s-* portion of the word *see* already sounds higher and more *ee-*like than the *s-* of *sue.* In other words, part of the vowel sound is already present in the consonant part of the word. This type of signal overlap is common in language.

A final important aspect of language is that it is characterized by rule systems, which are studied as phonology, morphology, syntax, semantics, and pragmatics. We will discuss these rule systems shortly.

In summary, we can define **language** *as a system of symbol (word) sequences used to communicate with others; this system involves infinite generativity, displacement, signal simultaneity and overlap, and rule systems.* One of the truly remarkable aspects of language is how children acquire this complex system, especially how they acquire it so quickly. Let's now explore the important rule systems of language.

Concept Table 1

The Cognitive Revolution in Psychology, Problem Solving, Reasoning, and Judgment

Concept	Processes/Related Ideas	Characteristics/Description
The Cognitive Revolution in Psychology	Its nature	This revolution occurred in the last half-century. The computer has played an important role, stimulating the model of the mind as an information-processing system. Artificial intelligence (AI) is the science of creating machines capable of performing activities that require intelligence when they are done by people. Expert systems, computer-based systems for accessing knowledge and making decisions in advanced-skill areas, have been applied to many domains.
Problem Solving	Characteristics of problem solving	A problem is something you experience when you have a goal but you do not know immediately what you must do to reach it. Problem solving is goal-directed and involves a sequence of operations. Problem solving also often involves heuristics or algorithms. Two heuristics with widespread applications are the means-end strategy and the subgoal strategy.
	How problems differ	Different types of problems often require different problem-solving techniques. Problems differ in regard to how much education or knowledge is required to solve them (a distinction is made between knowledge-lean and knowledge-rich problems), and how well they are defined (a distinction is made between well-defined and ill-defined problems).
	Problem solving in experts and novices	Three important differences between the problem solving of experts and that of novices involve one's knowledge base, internal representations (how problems are interpreted and classified), and domain memory skills.
	Improving problem-solving skills	The following strategies can help: Increase your domain knowledge; follow a definite scheme or plan; automate some components of the problem-soving solution; draw inferences; develop subgoals; work backward; search for contradictions; search for relations and analogies among problems; reformulate the problem representation; and, if all else fails, try practice.
Inductive and Deductive Reasoning	Inductive reasoning	Inductive reasoning is reasoning from the specific to the general. Hypothesis testing is an important aspect of inductive reasoning. Inductive reasoning is not well understood.
	Deductive reasoning	Deductive reasoning is reasoning from the general to the specific. Many people do not reason logically. People reason better when they can draw on their knowledge about the rules of everyday life.
Estimating Probabilities	Heuristics	The availability and representativeness heuristics help us to estimate probabilities. A variant of the availability heuristic is the simulation heuristic. One problem with the representativeness heuristic is the gamblers' fallacy.
Critical Thinking	Its nature	Much interest has recently developed in the concept of critical thinking, which involves grasping the deeper meaning of problems, keeping an open mind about different approaches, and deciding for oneself what to believe or do. Sternberg believes that when schools teach critical thinking, they rely too much on formal logic; instead, they should spend more time teaching critical-thinking skills needed in everyday life.
Conceptual Knowledge	The nature of concepts and concept formation	A concept is used to group objects, events, or characteristics. Concepts help us generalize, improve our memory, keep us from constantly needing to learn, have informational value, and improve our association skills. Psychologists have often investigated individuals' ability to detect why an object is included in a particular concept. Developing hypotheses about concepts is important in thinking.

The Rule Systems and Units of Language

Researchers have divided the study of language into several levels. It is important to keep in mind that these divisions are made chiefly for purposes of study; in actual language use, all of these levels are accessed simultaneously.

Phonology

The vast majority of the world's languages have a sound-based organization. **Phonology** *is the study of the sound systems of language.*

How can we describe the sounds of language? It is tempting to try to "spell out" these sounds using the English alphabet, but this would present difficulties. For example, the letter *a* is pronounced differently in the words *apple, date,* and *ball.* We would therefore have to substitute groups of letters (such as *aa, ey,* and *aw*) to stand for these vowels.

Phonological rules ensure that certain sound sequences occur (for example, *sp, ba,* or *ar*) and others do not (for example, *zx* or *qp*). A good example of a phoneme in the English language is /k/, the sound represented by the letter *k* in the word *ski* and the letter *c* in the word *cat.* Although the /k/ sound is slightly different in these two words, the variation is not distinguished and the /k/ sound is described as a single phoneme. In some languages, such as Arabic, this kind of variation represents separate phonemes.

Imagine what languages would be like if there were no *phonemes,* or basic sounds. Each word in the language would have to be represented by a signal—a sound, for example—that differed from the signals of all other words. Speakers and listeners would therefore have to memorize sound patterns for thousands (or tens of thousands) of words, and there would be no way of recognizing that a sound found in one word (such as /k/) was related to the same sound found in another word. Humans can construct a large and expandable set of words out of two or three dozen signal elements (Dresher & van der Hulst, 1994). We do not need 500,000 signal elements.

Morphology

Morphology *is the study of the rules for combining* morphemes, *meaningful units of sound that contain no smaller meaningful parts.* Although it might seem that *words* are the smallest units of meaning in language, this is not the case. Every word in the English language is made up of one or more morphemes. Some words consist of a single morpheme (such as *help*), while others are made up of more than one morpheme. For instance, *helper* has two morphemes (*help* and *-er*), with the suffix *-er* meaning "one who does ____." Notice that not all morphemes are words (for example, *pre-, -er,* and *-ing*). Just as the rules that govern phonemes ensure that certain sound sequences occur, the rules that govern morphemes ensure that phonemes occur in particular sequences (we would not reorder *helper* as *erhelp,* for instance).

Syntax

Syntax *involves the ways words are combined to form acceptable phrases and sentences.* For example, *He didn't stay, did he?* is a grammatical sentence, but *He didn't stay, didn't he?* is unacceptable and ambiguous. Similarly, if I say to you, "Bob slugged Tom" and "Bob was slugged by Tom," you know who did the slugging and who was slugged in each case, because we share the same syntactic understanding of sentence structure. This concept of "who does what to whom" is called *grammatical relations,* and it is an important type of syntactic information.

Semantics

The term **semantics** *refers to the meanings of words and sentences.* Every word has a set of semantic features. *Girl* and *woman,* for instance, both have some of the semantic features of the words *female* and *human,* but they also differ in meaning (for instance, regarding age). Words have semantic restrictions on how they can be used in sentences. The sentence *The bicycle talked the boy into buying a candy bar* is syntactically correct but semantically incorrect. The sentence violates our semantic knowledge that bicycles do not talk.

Pragmatics

A final set of language rules involves **pragmatics,** *which is the use of appropriate conversation and the study and knowledge of the rules underlying the use of language in context.* The domain of pragmatics is broad, covering such circumstances as (a) taking turns in discussions instead of everyone talking at once, (b) using questions to convey commands ("Why don't you be quiet?"), (c) using words like *the* and *a* in a way that enhances understanding ("I read a book last night. The plot was boring"), (d) using polite language in appropriate situations (for example, when talking to one's teacher, and (e) telling stories that are interesting, jokes that are funny, and lies that convince (Ninio & Snow, 1996).

Biological and Cultural/ Environmental Influences

To what extent is language rooted in biology and evolution? How much of language is due to sociocultural/environmental influences?

Biological Influences

Language has strong biological underpinnings (Rice, 1996; Scott, 1997). One of the strongest arguments for biology's influence on language is that children all over the world acquire language milestones at about the same time developmentally and in about the same order, despite the vast variation in the language input they receive. For example, in some cultures adults never talk to children under 1 year of age, yet these infants still acquire language. Also, there is no other convincing way to explain how *quickly* children learn language than through biological foundations.

With these thoughts in mind, let's now explore these questions about biological influences on language: What is the role of biological evolution in language? What is the brain's role in language? Is there a "grammar gene"? Are children biologically prewired to learn language?

Biological Evolution The brain, nervous system, and vocal system changed over hundreds of thousands of years. Prior to *Homo sapiens,* the physical equipment to produce spoken language did not exist; *Homo sapiens* went beyond the simple signaling system of their predecessors to develop abstract speech. Estimates vary as to how long ago humans acquired language: from about 100,000 to 250,000 years ago. In evolutionary time, then, language is a very recent acquisition.

Many theorists stress language's biological basis. They believe that human infants are like newborn birds, who come into the world biologically prepared to sing the song of their species. For example, the famous linguist Noam Chomsky (1975) has referred to a "language organ" that is uniquely human and that "unfolds" during a child's development. Other researchers take a more indirect approach and suggest that while the physical precursors for speech and language production (for example, the brain and vocal tract) have clearly evolved, the structure of language itself is shaped more by social and cultural constraints. This spirited debate on the nature-versus-nurture controversy has been of key importance to linguistics and psychology.

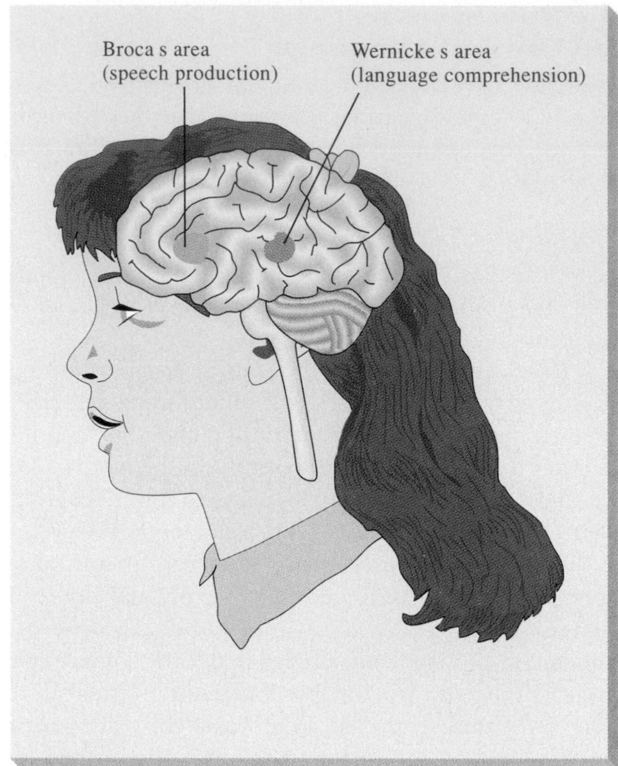

FIGURE 17

Broca's Area and Wernicke's Area
Damage to Broca's area and surrounding tissue often causes problems in speech production, whereas damage to Wernicke's area often causes problems in language comprehension. These areas are in the left hemisphere of the brain.

Language and the Brain Another aspect of biology's role in language involves the accumulating evidence that language is controlled by particular regions of the brain. In 1861, Paul Broca, a French surgeon and anthropologist, examined a 52-year-old man who had received an injury to the left side of his brain. The patient was nicknamed "Tan" because although he seemed to understand what was said to him, he could respond only with the single syllable *tan* (along with some hand gestures and an occasional swear word). Tan suffered from **aphasia,** *specific language loss resulting from brain damage.* Aphasia is not due to any general cognitive or intellectual impairments, and it does not result from deficits in the nerves or muscles of the vocal tract or auditory system. Rather, aphasic damage has to do only with the production and understanding of spoken language.

Tan died several days after Broca evaluated him, and an autopsy revealed the location of the injury. Over the next 7 years, Broca studied twenty similar cases and consistently found damage to a specific frontal region of the left hemisphere. Today we refer to this part of the brain as **Broca's area,** *an area of the left frontal lobe of the brain that is involved in speech motor output* (see figure 17). People with damage to left frontal tissue often end up with *nonfluent aphasia,* a condition in which language understanding is good but speech production is halting and labored. One patient with nonfluent aphasia made the following comments about her hobbies: "I . . . um . . . art! You know . . . I'm gonna be, um, . . . famous painter." Notice that some function words are missing (*a,* and the helping verb *do*). The fact that function words are compromised in nonfluent aphasia provides important evidence that aphasia does not result from simple memory deficits, because such function words are some of the most common words in language.

Another place in the brain where an injury can seriously impair language is **Wernicke's area,** *a region of the brain's left hemisphere involved in language comprehension* (see figure 17). This region of the brain was named after the German neurologist Karl Wernicke (1848–1904). People with damage to Wernicke's area generally have *fluent aphasia,* involving poor language understanding and well-formed but semantically impoverished speech output. Fluent aphasic subjects generally understand others, but their scrambled speech content often resembles a "word salad." One patient gave the following answer to a question about the nature of his business: "I just sold my uh uh. . . . Right now I work for these other people . . . er, my verinol . . . I'm into me vehaul. I help en . . . whatever, but I'm not." This speech shows some examples of *jargon aphasia,* which is the substitution of one phoneme for another (as in "vehaul" and "verinaul").

Cultural and Environmental Influences

What is the role of cultural and social evolution in language? How does environment influence language?

Cultural and Social Evolution Anthropologists have speculated about the social conditions that led to the development of language. Social forces may have pushed humans to develop abstract reasoning and to create an efficient system for communicating with others (Crick, 1977). For example, early humans probably developed complex plans and strategies for hunting. If hunters can verbally signal one another about changes in strategies for hunting big game, the hunt is much more likely to be successful. In addition, elaborate burial sites, some 100,000 years old, suggest that early humans may have used language for developing religious and moral codes. Language clearly gave humans an enormous edge over other animals and increased their chances of survival.

Environmental Influences

Today most language acquisition researchers believe that children from a wide variety of cultural contexts acquire their native language without explicit teaching, in some cases without apparent encouragement.

Language researcher Roger Brown (1973) wondered how parents might help their children learn language. He was especially interested in whether parents reinforce their children for speaking in grammatical ways, as behavioral theories predict. After spending many hours observing parents and their young children, he found that parents sometimes smiled and praised their children for correct sentences, but they also reinforced many ungrammatical sentences. Brown concluded that learning grammar is not based on reinforcement.

One intriguing element of the environment in a young child's language acquisition is called **motherese,** *the way mothers and others often talk to babies in a higher pitch than normal and with simple words and sentences.* It is hard to talk in motherese when not in the presence of a baby, but many people immediately shift into it when they start talking to a baby. Much of this is automatic and something most parents are not aware that they are doing. Motherese has the important functions of capturing the infant's attention and maintaining communication. When parents are asked why they use motherese, they point out that it is designed to teach their baby to talk. Older peers also talk motherese to infants (Dunn & Kendrick, 1982).

Other than motherese, are there other strategies adults use to enhance the child's acquisition of language? Four candidates are recasting, echoing, expanding, and labeling. **Recasting** *is phrasing the same or a similar meaning of a sentence in a different way, perhaps turning it into a question.* For example, if a child says, "The dog was barking," the adult can respond by asking, "When was the dog barking?" The effects of recasting fit with suggestions that "following in order to lead" helps a child learn language. That is, letting a child initially indicate an interest and then proceeding to elaborate that interest—commenting, demonstrating, and explaining—may enhance communication and help language acquisition. In contrast, an overly active, directive approach to communicating with the child may be harmful. **Echoing** *is repeating what the child says to you, especially if it is an incomplete phrase or sentence.* **Expanding** *is restating, in a linguistically sophisticated form, what the child has said.* **Labeling** *is identifying the names of objects.* Young children are forever being asked to identify the names of objects. Roger Brown (1986) identified this as the great word game and claimed that much of the early vocabulary acquired by children is motivated by this adult pressure to identify the words associated with objects.

The strategies we have just described—recasting, echoing, expanding, and labeling—are used naturally in meaningful conversations. Parents do not (and should not) teach their children to talk in any deliberate way. Even for children who are slow in learning language, the experts agree that intervention should occur in natural ways, with the goal being to convey meaning (Kapur, 1994; Snow, 1996).

It is important to recognize that children differ in their ability to acquire language and that this variation cannot be readily explained by differences in environmental input alone. For children who are slow to develop language skills, opportunities to talk and be talked with are important. But remember that encouragement of language development, not drill and practice, is the key (deVilliers, 1996). Language development is not a simple matter of imitation and reinforcement—even most behaviorists acknowledge this fact today.

Language Development

In the thirteenth century, Holy Roman Emperor Frederick II had a cruel idea. He wanted to know what language children would speak if no one talked to them. He selected several newborns and threatened their caregivers with death if they ever talked to the infants. Frederick never found out what language the children spoke because they all died. As we move toward the twenty-first century, we are still curious about infants' development of language, although our experiments and observations are, to say the least, far more humane than the evil Frederick's.

Is There A Critical Period for Learning Language?

Have you ever encountered young children serving as unofficial "translators" for their non-English-speaking parents? This is a scene that doctors or nurses sometimes report while admitting patients to a hospital. Why would this be? Would this indicate that young children are able to easily learn language, while their parents have somehow missed out? Such an explanation would fit the concept of a

critical period, *a period in which there is a learning readiness; beyond this period learning is difficult or impossible.* The notion of a critical period applies nicely to certain varieties of songbirds. For example, baby white-crowned sparrows learn the song of their species quite well if they are exposed during a specific time as a chick; after this time they can never develop a fully formed song pattern (Marler & Mundinger, 1971). But whether this notion applies to language learning by humans is much less certain.

Almost all children learn one or more languages during their early years of development, so it is difficult to determine whether there is a critical period for language development (Obler, 1993). In the 1960s, Eric Lenneberg (1967) proposed a biological theory of language acquisition. He said that language is a maturational process and that there is a critical period between about 18 months of age and puberty during which a first language can be acquired. Central to Lenneberg's thesis is the idea that language develops rapidly and easily during the preschool years as a result of maturation. Lenneberg provided support for the critical-period concept from studies of several atypical populations, including children with damage in the left hemisphere of the brain, deaf children, and children with mental retardation (Tager-Flusberg, 1994). With regard to brain damage, Lenneberg believed that adults had already passed the critical period during which plasticity of brain functioning allows reassignment and relearning of language skills.

The stunted language development of a modern "wild child" supports the idea that there is a critical period for language acquisition (see figure 18). In 1970, a California social worker made a routine visit to the home of a partially blind woman who had applied for public assistance. The social worker discovered that the woman and her husband kept their 13-year-old daughter, Genie, locked away from the world. Genie's parents had kept her in almost total isolation during her childhood. Genie could not speak or stand erect. During the day she was forced to sit naked on a child's potty seat, bound to it by a harness her father had made—she could move only her hands and feet. At night she was placed in a kind of straitjacket and caged in a crib with wire mesh sides and a cover. Whenever Genie made a noise, her father beat her. He never communicated with her in words but growled and barked at her instead (Rymer, 1993).

Genie spent a number of years in extensive rehabilitation programs such as speech and physical therapy (Curtiss, 1977). She eventually learned to walk with a jerky motion and to use the toilet. Genie also learned to recognize many words and to speak in rudimentary sentences. At first she spoke in one-word utterances. Later she was able to string together and create two-word combinations such as *Big teeth, Little marble,* and *Two hand.* Consistent with the language development of most children, three-word combinations followed—for example, *Small two cup.* Unlike normal children, Genie never learned how to ask questions and she never understood grammar. She was never able to distinguish between pronouns or passive and active verbs. Four years after she had begun stringing words together, her speech still sounded like a garbled telegram. And as an adult she speaks in short, mangled sentences, such as *Father hit leg, Big wood,* and *Genie hurt.*

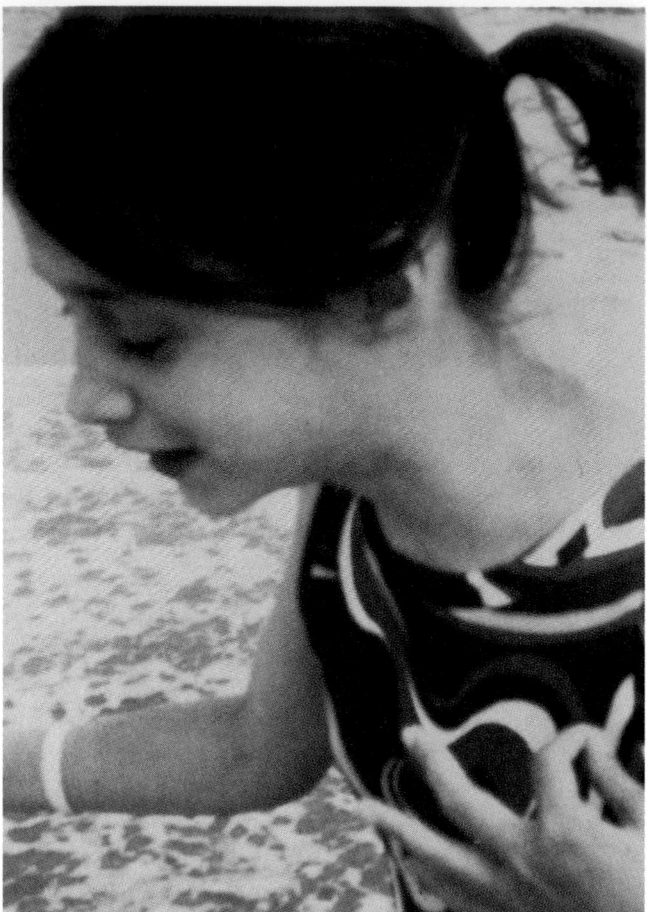

FIGURE 18

Genie
What was the nature of Genie's experiences, and what implications do they have for language acquisition?

Children like Genie, "Wild" Peter of Germany, and Kamala the "wolfgirl," who are abandoned, abused, and not exposed to language for years, rarely speak normally. Such tragic evidence supports the critical-period hypothesis in language development. However, because these children also suffer severe emotional trauma and possible neurological deficits, the issue is still far from clear.

Let's go back to our "child translator" example. Why is it that children seem to do better than older people in learning language? Many researchers have proposed that the first 5 years of life may be a critical period for language acquisition. Evidence for this notion comes from studies of brain development in young children, and from the amount of language learned by preschool children. However, other evidence suggests that such a critical period might not be so "hard and fast." First of all, although much language learning takes place during the preschool years, learning continues well into the later school years and adulthood. Also, with respect to second-language learning, adults can do as well as or better than young children, provided they are motivated and spend equivalent amounts of time at it. In other words, young children's proficiency in language, while impressive, does not seem to involve a biologically salient critical period that older children and adults have missed out on.

Around the world, young children learn to speak in two-word utterances, in most cases at about 18 to 24 months of age.

Language Development in Infants

Before babies ever say their first words, at the age of 10 to 12 months, they babble. Babbling—endlessly repeating sounds and syllables such as *goo-goo* and *ga-ga*—begins at about the age of 3 to 6 months and is determined by biological readiness, not reinforcement or the ability to hear. Babbling probably allows the baby to exercise its vocal chords and helps develop articulation. Babbling seems to appear in stages: The first stage, from around 2 to 6 months, is called *reduplicative babbling,* consisting of repeated syllables such as *ga-ga* or *da-da.* For many babies, there is a second stage, called *variegated (or jargon) babbling,* in which a variety of sounds are produced with very convincing prosody. For some children, jargon babbling might continue well into the development of actual speech, whereas other children never produce jargon babbling but instead seem to carefully produce one word at a time.

Even deaf babies babble for a time (Lenneberg, Rebelsky, & Nichols, 1965). This suggests that all children have an innate predisposition to discover the units of language. The babbling of deaf babies is rather flat and random compared to that of hearing children, although deaf babies are much more proficient in producing manual babbling (Pettito & Marentette, 1991). This suggests that infants babble based on the type of language input they receive.

Between 10 and 12 months of age, children utter their first words, and over the next few months they show a steady increase in vocabulary. A child's first words name important people *(dada),* familiar animals (*kitty*), vehicles *(car),* toys (*ball*), food (*milk*), body parts (*eye*), clothes (*hat*), household items (*clock*), or greetings (*bye*). These were babies' first words 50 years ago, and they are babies' first words today (Clark, 1983). During this time, children's meanings do not always match those of adults. The **holophrase hypothesis** *is the concept that a single word can be used to imply a complete sentence; an infant's first words characteristically are holophrastic.* For example, the demand "Milk!" might mean "I'm hungry and want to eat now." Another type of meaning mismatch, **overextension,** *involves using a name too broadly* (such as using *doggy* for all animals). Children also demonstrate meaning **underextension,** *in which a name is used to apply too narrowly,* as when a child will say "muffin" only for blueberry muffins but not other types of muffins.

By the time children reach the age of 18 to 24 months, they usually utter two-word statements. They quickly grasp the importance of expressing concepts and the role that language plays in communicating with others. To convey meaning in two-word statements, the child relies heavily on gesture, tone, and context. Children can communicate a wealth of meaning with two words; for instance:

Identification:	See doggie.
Location:	Book there.
Repetition:	More milk.
Nonexistence:	Allgone thing.
Negation:	Not wolf.
Possession:	My candy.
Attribution:	Big car.
Agent-action:	Mama walk.
Action-direct-object:	Hit you.
Action-indirect-object:	Give papa.
Action-instrument:	Cut knife.
Question:	Where ball? (Slobin, 1972)

These examples are from children whose first languages were English, German, Russian, Finnish, Turkish, and Samoan. Although these two-word sentences omit many parts of speech, they are remarkably succinct in conveying many messages. In fact, a child's first combination of words has this economical quality in every language. **Telegraphic speech** *is the use of short and precise words to communicate; it is characteristic of young children's two- or three-word combinations.* When we send a telegram, we try to be short and precise, excluding any unnecessary words. As a result, articles, auxiliary verbs, and other connectives usually are omitted. Of course, telegraphic speech is not limited to two-word phrases. *Mommy give ice cream* or *Mommy give Tommy ice cream* also are examples of telegraphic speech. As children leave the two-word stage, they move rather quickly into three-, four-, and five-word combinations.

In expanding this concept of classifying children's language development in terms of number of utterances, Roger Brown (1973) proposed that **mean length of utterance (MLU),** *an index of language development based on the number of morphemes per sentence a child produces in a sample of about 50 to 100 sentences,* is a good index of language maturity. Brown identified five stages based on MLU:

Stage	MLU
1	1+ to 2.0
2	2.5
3	3.0
4	3.5
5	4.0

The first stage begins when a child generates sentences consisting of more than one word, such as the examples of two-word utterances mentioned earlier. The 1+ designation suggests that the average number of morphemes in each utterance is greater than one but not yet two, because some of the child's utterances are still holophrases. This stage continues until the child averages two morphemes per utterance. Subsequent stages are marked by increments of 0.5 in mean length of utterance. Figure 19 shows Roger Brown's examination of MLU in three children.

As we have just seen, language unfolds in a sequence. At every point in development, the child's linguistic interaction with parents and others obeys certain principles. Not only is this development strongly influenced by the child's biological wiring, but the language environment is more complex than behaviorists such as Skinner imagined.

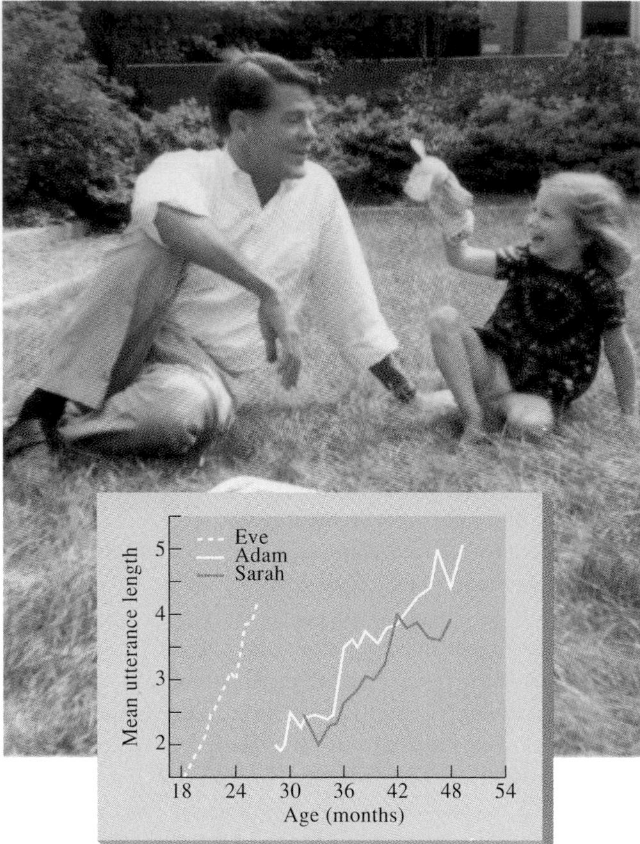

FIGURE 19

Roger Brown and His Examination of MLU in Three Children
The graph shows the average length of utterances generated by three children ranging in age from 1 1/2 to just over 4 years. The photograph shows Roger Brown talking with a young girl. Brown has been a pioneer in providing rich insights about children's language development. Among his contributions is the concept of MLU, or mean length of utterance, which has been documented as a good index of a child's language maturity.

Bilingualism

A hot debate in many school districts, especially in Florida, Texas, California, New Mexico, and Arizona, is how best to educate children whose first language is not English. Today educators realize that such children have a difficult time in English-speaking classes. As bilingual education researchers Kenji Hakuta and Eugene Garcia (1989) point out, the ultimate goal of mainstreaming students into English-speaking classrooms is widely shared, but the question of how to achieve this goal has both parents and educators up in arms.

One camp favors native-language instruction. According to proponents of this approach, mainstreaming should be deferred until a child has mastered her or his native language. They argue that developing competence in fundamental skills, such as reading and writing in the student's native tongue, provides a basic foundation for learning all academic subjects, such as math and science, as well as English.

In contrast, opponents of this strategy argue that the first step toward mainstreaming a non-native speaker should be to teach the child English. Once the child is fluent in English, the child is ready to go into a standard classroom. When these children find themselves behind in subjects, catching up should be relatively easy if they have mastered English. The approach advocated by the all-English theory is that classes should be taught in English—simplified English if necessary—from the very start. This English-only approach to education can be coupled with instruction in English as a second language to speed the child's progress.

Unfortunately, even after 20 years of debate and research, psychologists still have little wisdom to offer on this subject. Although there have been many studies on bilingual education, the methods have often been weak and the outcomes inconclusive. One persistent problem is that too many studies have focused on only one measure, such as the children's competence in English. These studies have overlooked how well the children are doing in other subjects, such as math and science. In addition, these studies have not considered such critical factors as how well the children are coping with school and developing positive social relationships.

Even so, research has shed light on at least one aspect of the bilingual education debate. At one time bilingualism was believed to be detrimental. Educators reasoned that a child's first language would interfere with learning a second language. But research has shown that children can learn a second language without being hampered by their first (Anderson, 1996; McLaughlin, 1987; NAEYC, 1996).

In one recent study, Kimbrough Oller (1995) compared a group of children from bilingual families, where they grew up speaking both English and Spanish, with a group of children from families that spoke only English. As infants, both groups began making simple speech sounds, such as *da* and *ba,* at about the same age. At 3 years of age, bilingual children performed as well in Spanish as children who spoke only that language. The results apply only to children who learn English and Spanish simultaneously from a young age. Latino children who begin learning English in kindergarten may be handicapped in school because they have not yet developed needed English skills.

The linguistic relativity hypothesis states that our cultural experiences for a particular concept shape a catalog of names that can be either rich or poor. Consider how different your mental library of names for camel *might be if you had extensive experience with camels in a desert world and how different your mental library of names for* snow *might be if you lived in an arctic world of ice and cold. Despite its intriguing appeal, the linguistic relativity concept is controversial and many psychologists do not believe it plays a pivotal role in shaping thought.*

In another investigation, Grace Yeni-Komshian (1995) studied individuals who had moved from Korea to the United States between 2 and 24 years of age. She found that individuals who began speaking English at 6 to 8 years of age were proficient in neither Korean nor English. One recommendation for kindergarten and school-age children living in the United States who have not yet learned English is a two-way program in which bilingual children learn in their native language half a day and in English the other half. There are about 200 two-way programs in the United States, and these usually continue through elementary school.

Language, Culture, and Cognition

Take a moment and reflect on several questions. Did the culture in which you grew up influence your language? Does language influence the way you think? Does thinking influence the nature of your language?

Language and Culture

Linguist Benjamin Whorf (1956) argued that language actually determines the way we think. Whorf and his student Edward Sapir were specialists in Native American languages, and they were fascinated by the possibility that speakers of different languages might view the world differently as the result of the languages they speak. Whorf's **linguistic relativity hypothesis** *states that language determines the structure of thinking and shapes our basic ideas.* The Inuit in Alaska, for instance, have a dozen or more words to describe the various textures, colors, and physical states of snow. Hopi Indians have no words for past and future. And Arabs have 6,000 words for aspects of the camel.

Our cultural experiences for a particular concept shape a catalog of names that can be either rich or poor. For example, if the *camel* part of your mental library of names is the product of years of experience with camels, you probably will see and think about this desert animal in finer gradations than someone who has no experience with camels. In this way, language acts as a window that filters the amount and nature of information passed on for further processing.

Critics of Whorf's theory say that words merely reflect, rather than cause, the way we think. The Inuits' adaptability and livelihood in Alaska depend on their capacity to recognize various conditions of snow and ice. A professional skier who is not Inuit might also know numerous words for snow, far more than the average person; and a person who doesn't know the words for the different types of snow might still be able to perceive these differences.

Eleanor Rosch (1973) found just that. She studied the effect of language on color perception among the Dani in New Guinea. The Dani have only two words for color—one that approximately means "white" and one that approximately means "black." If the linguistic relativity hypothesis were correct, the Dani would lack the ability to tell the difference between colors such as green, blue, red, yellow, and purple. But Rosch found that the Dani perceived colors just as we perceive them. As we know, color perception is biologically determined by receptors in the retinas in the eyes.

Even though Whorf's linguistic relativity hypothesis missed the mark, researchers agree that although language does not determine thought, it can influence it.

Language and Cognition

What about our memory and problem solving? What role does language play in these important cognitive activities? Memory is stored not only in terms of sounds and images, but also in words. When words are stored in memory, their processing often is deep and their retrieval more effortful.

Language helps us think, make inferences, tackle difficult decisions, and solve problems. Language can be thought of as a tool for representing ideas. Some psychologists have argued that we cannot think without language, a proposition that has produced heated controversy. Is thought dependent on language, or is language dependent on thought? Language does provide a medium for representing abstract ideas. Our language rules are more sophisticated than thought at an earlier point in our development, suggesting that language is not always dependent on thought (Bruner, 1964).

Cognition also might be an important foundation for language (Berninger, 1993). Evidence that cognition is separate from language comes from studies of deaf children. On a variety of thinking and problem-solving tasks, deaf children perform at the same level as children of the same age who have no hearing problems. Some of the deaf children in these studies do not even have command of written or sign language (Furth, 1971).

So, thought can direct language, and language can direct thought (Jenkins, 1969). Language is virtually an unbounded symbol system, capable of expressing most thoughts, and language is the way we humans communicate most of our thoughts to each other. We do not always think in words, but undoubtedly our thinking would be greatly impoverished without them.

Our coverage of language has taken us down many roads. However, the remarkable story of language would not be complete without considering whether animals have language.

The Rumbaughs (Sue and Duane) of the Yerkes Primate Center and Georgia State University have studied the basic question of whether chimps understand symbols. Their research evidence suggests chimps can understand symbols.

Do Animals Have Language?

Many animal species do have complex and ingenious ways to signal danger and to communicate about basic needs such as food and sex. For example, in one species of firefly the female has learned to imitate the flashing signal of another species to lure the aliens into her territory. Then she eats them. But is this language in the human sense? And what about the animals who are our closest relatives, the great apes?

Chimpanzees and *Homo sapiens* have 98 percent of their genetic material in common. Chimpanzee behavior includes hunting, toolmaking, embracing, back patting,

Explorations in Psychology 2

In Pursuit of Language in Animals: Observations of Ake and Phoenix

In quick succession, a trainer forms four hand signals that mean "basket," "right," "Frisbee," and "fetch." A female dolphin named Ake has been taught the meaning of each sign but has never before been given this particular combination of signs. Nonetheless, Ake understands that this command tells her to go to the Frisbee to her right and take it to the basket. Ignoring a Frisbee floating at the left side of the pool, Ake moves to her right and scoops up the Frisbee floating there. She nudges it along the water's surface to a basket floating 30 feet away and flips it in. A shrill whistle tells her she has successfully completed her task, and she swims over to the trainer for a plump herring and a hug.

Ake is a seasoned veteran at the University of Hawaii Mammal Laboratory, directed by psychologist Louis Herman. Another veteran in Herman's lab is a dolphin named Phoenix, who, like Ake, has been trained and observed since 1979 (see figure A). Herman wanted to discover whether the dolphins could master word order and syntax. Phoenix learned an acoustic language made up of computer-generated sounds, whereas Ake learned a visual system of hand signals. Phoenix's system involved a left-to-right grammar in which, for example, "Frisbee, in, basket" means "Place the Frisbee in the basket." In contrast, Ake learned an inverse grammar in which "basket, Frisbee, in" means the same thing—"Place the Frisbee in the basket." After receiving a message to place the Frisbee in the basket, as described at the beginning of this boxed feature, the dolphins will swim past other objects, retrieve the Frisbee, and place it as directed. The dolphins are even learning how to answer their trainers. When asked if a certain object is in their tank, the animals can answer by pressing one of two paddles for a yes or no response.

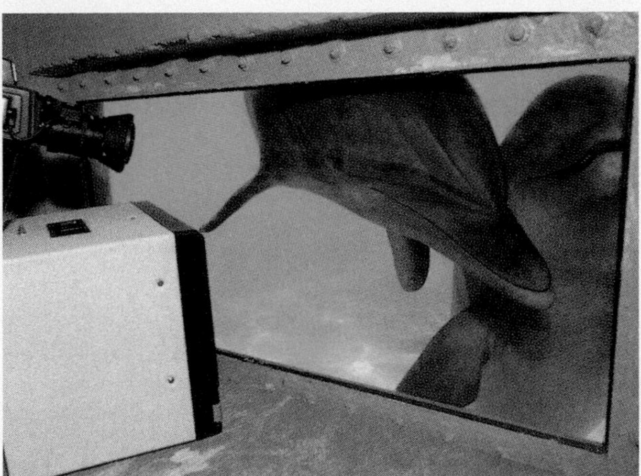

Figure A

Phoenix and Ake, Two Dolphins in Herman's Studies
A TV monitor and camera near their tank's underwater window allows Phoenix (*left*) and Ake to be observed by psychologists.

If animals like dolphins can be trained to communicate with a language-like system, do they use such a system in nature? Recently biologists and psychologists have carefully analyzed recordings of dolphins' whistles in the sea. Their findings reveal that each dolphin has a signature whistle that identifies it to others. The whistle also expresses emotional states—under stress, a dolphin's signature whistle changes pitch and duration. At present, though, there have been no data collected to support the contention that dolphins, chimpanzees, or any other nonhuman creatures use abstract symbols or syntax in the wild.

kissing, and holding hands. Do animals this closely related to us have language? Can we teach human language to them?

Some researchers believe apes can learn language. One celebrity in this field is a chimp named Washoe, who was adopted when she was about 10 months old (Gardner & Gardner, 1971). Since apes do not have the vocal apparatus to speak, the researchers tried to teach Washoe the American Sign Language, which is one of the sign languages of the deaf. Washoe used sign language during everyday activities, such as meals, play, and car rides. In 2 years, Washoe learned 38 different signs, and by the age of 5 she had a vocabulary of 160 signs. Washoe learned how to put signs together in novel ways, such as *You drink* and *You me tickle.* A number of other efforts to teach language to chimps have had similar results (Premack, 1986).

The debate about chimpanzees' ability to use language focuses on two key issues: Can apes understand the meaning of symbols—that is, can they comprehend that one thing stands for another? And can apes learn syntax—that is, can they learn the kinds of mechanics and rules that give human language its creative productivity? The first of these issues may have been settled recently by Sue Savage-Rumbaugh and her colleagues (1993). These researchers found strong evidence that the chimps Sherman and Austin can understand symbols. For example, if Sherman

CONCEPT TABLE 2

Language

Concept	Processes/Related Ideas	Characteristics/Description
What Is Language?	Exploring the nature of language	We can define language as a system of symbol (word) sequences used to communicate with others that involves infinite generativity, displacement, signal simultaneity and overlap, and rule systems.
	Language's rule systems and units	These include phonology, morphology, syntax, semantics, and pragmatics. Phonology is the study of the sound systems of language. Phonological rules ensure that certain sound sequences occur. Morphology refers to the rules for combining morphemes, meaningful units of sounds that contain no smaller meaningful parts. Syntax involves the way words are combined to form acceptable phrases and sentences. Semantics refers to the meaning of words, phrases, and sentences. Pragmatics involves the use of appropriate conversation and knowledge of the rules underlying the use of language in context.
Biological and Cultural/Environmental Influences	Biological influences	Among the strongest arguments for biology's influence on language is that children all over the world acquire language milestones at about the same time developmentally and in about the same order, despite the vast variation in the language input they receive. There also is no other convincing way to explain how quickly children learn language than through biological foundations. Many theorists stress language's biological basis. Another aspect of biology's role in language involves the accumulating evidence that language is controlled by particular regions in the brain. Aphasia is a specific language loss resulting from brain damage. Language is chiefly controlled by the brain's left hemisphere. Broca's area is involved in speech motor output. Wernicke's area is involved in language comprehension.
	Cultural/environmental influences	Sociocultural conditions may have pushed humans to develop abstract reasoning and to create an economical system for communicating with others. Today most language acquisition researchers believe that children from a wide variety of cultures acquire their native language without explicit teaching, in some cases without apparent encouragement. Among the social supports for language acquisition in children are motherese, recasting, echoing, expanding, and labeling.

or Austin is sitting in a room, and a symbol for an object is displayed on a screen, he will go into another room, find the object, and bring it back. If the object is not there, he will come back empty-handed (Cowley, 1988). Austin and Sherman can play a game in which one chimp points to a symbol for food (such as M&Ms), and the other chimp selects the food from a tray, then they both eat it. These observations are clear evidence that chimps can understand symbols.

Chimps' ability to learn syntax is still being debated. Study of the common chimpanzee (*Pan troglodytes*) indicates that the syntax of their productions never reaches much beyond that of 2-year-old children (Gardner and Gardner, 1978). From such findings, some researchers have concluded that chimpanzees' syntactic abilities constitute little more than imitation, and that chimps do not have humanlike syntax (Terrace, 1979). However, others have been impressed with how humanlike chimps' utterances are.

Recent evidence concerning chimps' syntactic ability has come from study of rare pygmy chimpanzees (*Pan paniscus*), also known as "bonobos." These chimps are friendlier and brighter than their cousins, and show some remarkable language abilities. For example, star pupil Kanzi is very good at understanding spoken English and has been shown to comprehend over 600 sentences, such as *Can you*

Concept	Processes/Related Ideas	Characteristics/Description
Language Development	Is there a critical period for learning language?	A critical period is a period when there is learning readiness; beyond this period learning is difficult or impossible. The stunted growth of children such as Genie supports the notion of a critical period for language acquisition. However, the critical-period concept is still controversial.
	Language development in infants	Before babies ever say their first words, they babble. Between 10 to 12 months, children say their first words. The holophrase hypothesis is the concept that a single word can be used to imply a complete sentence; infants' first words characteristically are holophrastic. Overextension and underextension also characterize early language development, as does telegraphic speech—the use of short and precise words to communicate—which is characteristic of young children's two- or three-word combinations. Roger Brown proposed the concept of MLU (mean length of utterance), which is a good indicator of language development.
	Bilingualism	This has become a major issue in our nation's schools, with debate raging over the best way to conduct bilingual education. No negative effects of bilingualism have been found, and bilingual education is often associated with positive outcomes. Increasingly, researchers are emphasizing the complexity of bilingual education.
Language, Culture, and Cognition	Language and culture	Whorf's linguistic relativity hypothesis states that language determines the structure of thinking and shapes our basic ideas. Whorf's ideas are controversial.
	Language and cognition	Thoughts and ideas are associated with words and ideas, and different languages promote different ways of thinking. Language does not completely determine thought, but does influence it. Language is important in many cognitive activities, among them memory and thinking. Cognitive activities also influence language.
Do Animals Have Language?	The nature of the issue	Animals clearly can communicate, and chimpanzees can be taught to use symbols. Whether animals have the same language abilities as humans continues to be debated.

make the bunny eat the sweet potato? Kanzi also produces fairly complex sentences using a response board hooked to a speech synthesizer. To read further about language in animals, turn to Explorations in Psychology 2.

The debate over whether or not animals can use language to express thoughts is far from resolved. Researchers agree that animals can communicate with each other and that some can manipulate language-like symbols with syntax that resembles that of young children. At the same time, it is clear that their language abilities do not show the same degree of generativity and complexity as adult human language. As this research progresses, investigators have begun to rethink the questions they started out with. In addition to the general issue of whether apes can learn language, researchers are now asking a host of specific questions: When animals use symbols in ways similar to our word use, do they know and mean what they are saying? Can apes use language to communicate among themselves? What is ape communication like in the wild? Can language training itself increase intelligence? The future will hold fascinating answers concerning the role of language in distinguishing humans from our fellow creatures on the earth.

At this point we have discussed a number of ideas about language. A summary of these ideas is presented in concept table 2.

Critical Thinking About Behavior

What's in a Name?

> *What's in a name? that which we call a rose by any other name would smell as sweet.*
>
> **Juliet, in *Romeo and Juliet,* act 2, scene 2**

Not many people in today's heated sociopolitical climate are as nonchalant about the process of labeling as Juliet indicated in the famous balcony scene from *Romeo and Juliet.* It seems as though controversy attaches to nearly every reference that labels some aspect of our identity. For example, if you are in your first year of college, are you a freshman? A freshperson? A first-year student? Some individuals believe the choice of term may reflect the value system of the user. The term *freshman* might disenfranchise the majority of students, who are women. Although the term *freshperson* might be more "politically correct," many people believe that the term is awkward. Using the term *first-year student* might avoid the dilemmas associated with the other terms.

A similar evolution in language has taken place in relation to describing people who perform poorly in intelligence testing. Alfred Binet's early diagnostic efforts distinguished "imbeciles" and "morons" from people of normal intelligence. Eventually these terms became popularly used as insults, to such a degree that psychologists developed a different labeling system, referring to "retardates" who experienced varying degrees of "retardation." A more recent refinement in educational systems now labels such individuals as "cognitively different." Similarly, learning-disabled children are now referred to as children with a "learning difference."

The evolution of language has also complicated matters among ethnic groups. For example, African Americans appear to be divided on a preferred designation for themselves. Some prefer to be referred to as African Americans. Some prefer to be referred to as Black Americans. Some find the argument profound. Some find it silly. Some find it overwhelming to consider the possibility of hyphenating references to identity, particularly when the identity may be unknown.

Why do language and labeling have the power to create such strong feelings? The answer lies in the distinction between connotation and denotation. Language is very flexible. It can be used to refer to specific qualities (denotation), or it can be used to imply other characteristics (connotation), sometimes favorable and sometimes unfavorable. Labels can make it easier to identify some important characteristics. They can also be used to disparage others. People can be offended by a label they regard as inappropriate, whether or not offense was intended.

Let's take the example of the use of the term *girl* to denote women. One of the major accomplishments of the women's movement was to develop some general sensitivity in society to the connotations of the term *girl.* For instance, must a female have children before she "earns" the designation *woman?* Does it make sense to refer to the "girls" in the office when most of them are over 40? Why is there no comparable confusion in the distinction between boys and men?

How do we minimize the problems associated with inappropriate or offensive use of language? One way is to determine whether the label you have in mind is truly necessary to get your communication across. Another is to pay specific attention to the evolution of language use. Popular usage is often reflected in the media. A final method is to embark on a frank discussion with people of different backgrounds (for instance, persons of different gender or ethnicity) whose opinions matter to you, to see if you have been using language that has negative connotations to them. Your own sensitivity to the power of language will demonstrate your ability to use psychological knowledge to promote human welfare.

OVERVIEW

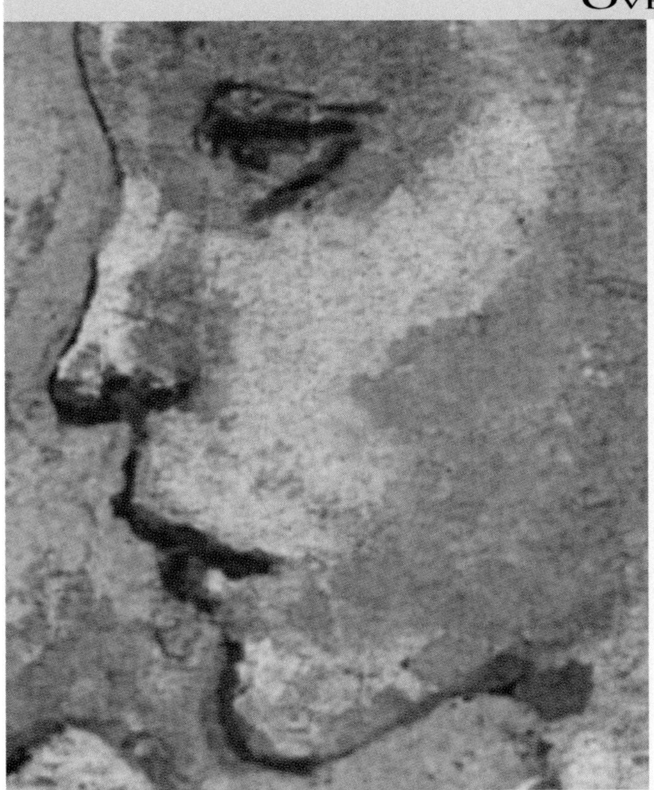

We began this chapter by exploring the nature of thinking, especially focusing on the cognitive revolution in psychology. Then we turned our attention to problem solving, including its characteristics, how problems differ, problem solving by experts and novices, and improving problem-solving skills. Our coverage of reasoning and judgment involved inductive and deductive reasoning, estimating probabilities, critical thinking, and conceptual knowledge. We also learned about the nature of language, including its characteristics, rule systems and the units of language, biological and cultural/environmental influences, language development, the relations between language, culture, and cognition, and whether animals have language. Remember that you can obtain an overall summary of the chapter by again studying the concept tables on pages 256 and 266.

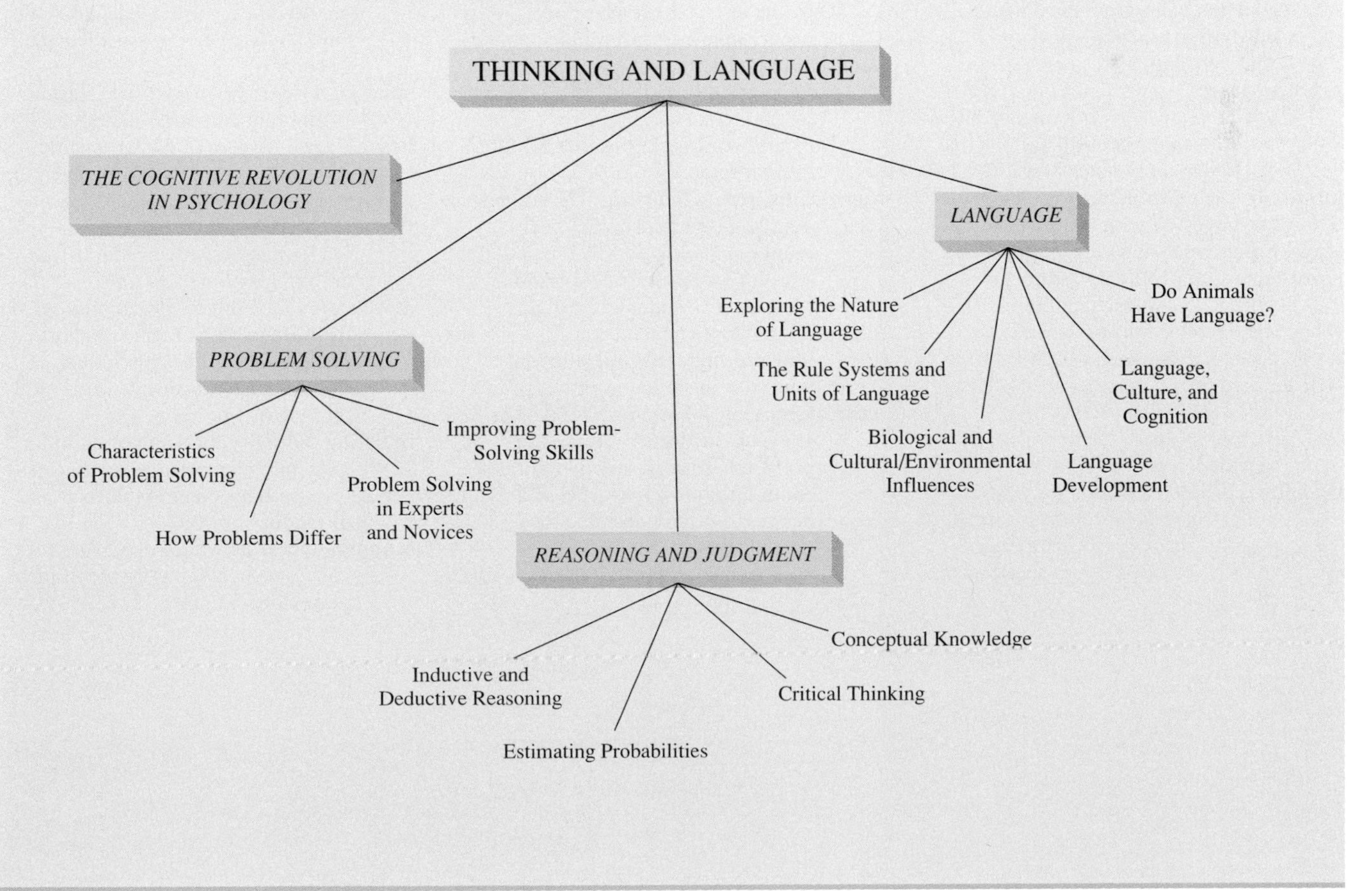

Key Terms

artificial intelligence (AI) The science of creating machines capable of performing activities that require intelligence when they are done by people. p. 237

expert systems Computer-based systems for assessing knowledge and making decisions in advanced skill areas. p. 237

problem Something you experience when you have a goal but do not know immediately what you must do to reach it. p. 237

protocol analysis The procedure of having subjects talk out loud while solving a problem and recording and analyzing everything they say. p. 238

heuristics Strategies or rules of thumb that can suggest a solution to a problem but do not ensure that the solution will work. p. 238

algorithms Procedures that guarantee an answer to a problem. p. 238

means-end strategy Finding the biggest difference between where you are now in your work on a problem and where you want to be, and then trying to find an operation that can reduce this difference. p. 238

subgoal strategy Finding an intermediate goal that will put you in a better position to reach the final goal. p. 238

problem space A representation of the possible states of work on a problem and the sequence of operations that will lead to those states. p. 238

knowledge-lean problems Problems that can be solved with little or no background knowledge. p. 239

knowledge-rich problems Problems whose solutions depend on considerable knowledge in a particular domain. p. 239

well-defined problems Problems whose initial states, goal states, and permissible operations are clearly specified. p. 239

ill-defined problems Problems whose initial states, goal states, and/or permissible operations are only vaguely specified or not specified at all. p. 239

inferring The process of taking information that is given in a problem and considering what this information implies beyond what is explicitly stated; it involves going beyond the information given. p. 244

functional fixedness The inability to solve a problem because something is viewed only in terms of its usual function. p. 245

learning set The tendency to solve all problems with the same strategy. p. 245

inductive reasoning The process of deriving abstract principles, concepts, or hypotheses from specific observations. p. 248

deductive reasoning Reasoning from the general to the specific; this often involves working with more abstract information or statements, usually called "premises," and deriving conclusions. p. 248

hypothesis testing The process of using our theories and intuitions to make predictions and then evaluating those predictions with further observations. p. 248

availability heuristic The strategy of judging the probability of an event by the ease with which prior occurrences come to mind. p. 252

simulation heuristic The strategy of judging the probability of an event by the ease of imagining or constructing scenarios that would cause it to occur. p. 252

representativeness heuristic The strategy of judging the probability of an event based on how well it matches a prototype (the most common or representative example). p. 252

gamblers' fallacy The tendency to underestimate the probability of long runs of similar events. p. 252

critical thinking Thinking that involves grasping the deeper meaning of problems, keeping an open mind about different approaches and perspectives, and deciding for oneself what to believe or do. p. 253

concept A category used to group objects, events, and characteristics based on common properties. p. 254

infinite generativity An individual's ability to generate an infinite number of meaningful sentences using a finite set of words and rules, which makes language a highly creative enterprise. p. 255

displacement The use of language to communicate information about another place and time. p. 255

language A system of symbol (word) sequences used to communicate with others that involves infinite generativity, displacement, signal simultaneity and overlap, and rule systems. p. 255

phonology The study of the sound systems of language. p. 257

morphology The study of the rules for combining morphemes, meaningful units of sound that contain no smaller meaningful parts. p. 257

syntax The ways words are combined to form acceptable phrases and sentences in a language. p. 257

semantics The study of the meanings of words, phrases, and sentences. p. 257

pragmatics The use of appropriate conversation and knowledge of the rules underlying the use of language in context. p. 257

aphasia Specific language loss resulting from brain damage. p. 258

Broca's area An area of the left frontal lobe of the brain that is involved in speech motor output. p. 258

Wernicke's area A region of the brain's left hemisphere involved in language comprehension. p. 258

motherese The kind of speech often used by mothers and others to talk to babies—in a higher pitch than normal and with simple words and sentences. p. 259

recasting Phrasing the same or a similar meaning of a sentence in a different way, perhaps turning it into a question. p. 259

echoing Repeating what a child says to you, especially if it is an incomplete phrase or sentence. p. 259

expanding Restating, in linguistically sophisticated form, what a child has said. p. 259

labeling Identifying the names of objects. p. 259

critical period A period in which there is learning readiness; beyond this period learning is difficult or impossible. p. 260

holophrase hypothesis The concept that a single word can be used to imply a complete sentence; an infant's first words characteristically are holophrastic. p. 261

overextension Using a name too broadly; characteristic of young children's language use. p. 261

underextension Using a name too narrowly; characteristic of young children's language use. p. 261

telegraphic speech The use of short and precise words to communicate; characteristic of young children's two- or three-word combinations. p. 261

mean length of utterance (MLU) An index of language development based on the number of morphemes per sentence a child produces in a sample of about 50 to 100 sentences. p. 262

linguistic relativity hypothesis Whorf's hypothesis that language determines the structure of thinking and shapes our basic ideas. p. 263

Resources and Readings in Psychology

Alexander Graham Bell Association for the Deaf
3417 Volta Place, N.W.
Washington, DC
202–337–5220

This is an organization for teachers of the hearing impaired, speech-language specialists, and other professionals and laypersons interested in the problems of the hearing impaired. The organization publishes a newsletter for parents of hearing-impaired children.

The American Speech-Language Hearing Association
10801 Rockville Pike
Rockville, MD 20852
301–897–5700

This is the national professional organization of speech-language pathologists and audiologists. The association issues a number of publications, certifies programs, and assesses community needs.

The Cambridge Encyclopedia of Language (1987)
edited by D. Crystal
Cambridge: Cambridge University Press

This encyclopedia gives a comprehensive account of the variety of modern languages, as well as critical information concerning their history, structure, and processing.

Choosing Books for Kids (1986)
by Joanne Oppenheim, Barbara Brenner, and Betty Boegehold
New York: Ballantine

This is an excellent book on how to choose the right book for the right child at the right time.

Contact Center, Inc.
P.O. Box 81826
Lincoln, NE 68501
402–464–0602
National Hot Line: 800–228–8813

This organization is devoted to eliminating illiteracy in the United States. The center provides tips for encouraging children to read, as well as lists of magazines for children. Books that help literate adults help their children also are available.

Feral Children and Clever Animals: Reflections on Human Nature (1993)
by D. K. Candland
New York: Oxford University Press

Candland reviews extraordinary cases of feral children and relates them to current issues in the animal language controversy.

Genie (1993)
by Russ Rymer
New York: HarperCollins

In this book, Russ Rymer tells the poignant story of Genie, a child who grew up without language or any form of social training. Rymer skillfully interweaves the tale of Genie's hesitant progress toward adulthood with the tale of the bitter ethical debates that raged over her treatment by the professionals who studied her after she was rescued from her parents. Rymer also explores how theories of language development can be used to address Genie's case. This eye-opening biography reveals how personal squabbles and the research bureaucracy may have impeded Genie's development.

Growing Up With Language (1992)
by Naomi Baron
Reading, MA: Addison-Wesley

This book does an excellent job of conveying the appropriate role of parents in children's language development. The author focuses on three representative children and their families, exploring how children put their first words together, how they struggle to understand meaning, and how they come to use language as a creative tool. She shows parents how their own attitudes about language are extremely important in the child's language development.

The IDEAL Problem Solver (1994, 2nd ed.)
by John Bransford and Barry Stein
New York: W. H. Freeman

This book discusses hundreds of fascinating problems and ways to effectively solve them.

National Aphasia Association
P.O. Box 1887
Murray Hill Station
New York, NY 10156–0611
800–922–4622

The NAA is a nonprofit organization dedicated to meeting the needs of people with aphasia and their families. The NAA's goals include raising public awareness of the condition of aphasia and its impact on the person, the family, and society; providing a public resource for information on current research and clinical issues; and facilitating the development of community programs designed to meet the specific needs of people with aphasia and their families.

The Orton Dyslexia Society, Inc.
80 Fifth Avenue, Room 903
New York, NY 10011
212–691–1930

This nonprofit organization is concerned with the many children and adults who experience difficulty in learning such skills as speaking, reading, writing, spelling, and mathematics.

Teaching Thinking Skills (1987)
edited by J. B. Baron and R. J. Sternberg
New York: W. H. Freeman

Twelve eminent psychologists, educators, and philosophers contribute information about the latest approaches to teaching thinking skills. Descriptions of promising training programs are provided.

Solution to Nine-Dot Problem

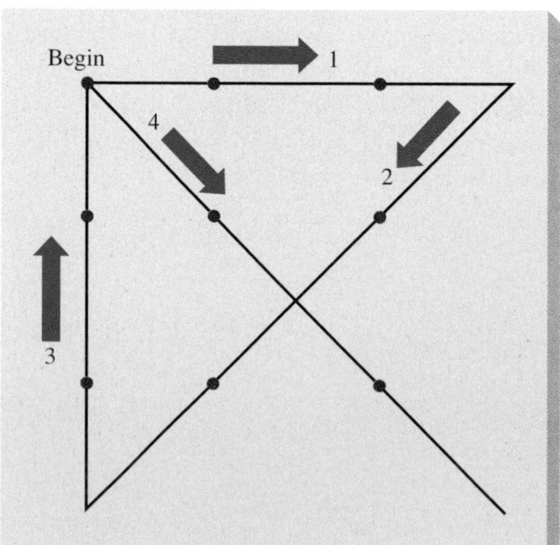

CHAPTER

INT

Intelligence

CAMILLE PISSARRO
Self-Portrait, detail

C H A P T E R

INT

Intelligence

Chapter Outline

Chapter Boxes

The thirst to know and understand . . . these are the goods in life's rich hand.

—Sir William Watson, 1905

What a piece of work is a man!
How noble in reason! how infinite
in faculty! in form, in moving,
how express and admirable! in
action how like an angel! in
apprehension how like a god!

—Shakespeare

Images of Psychology

Intelligence Controversies

Intelligence and intelligence tests frequently make the news. The following two stories appeared in the *Los Angeles Times:*

> IQ testing that leads to the placement of an unusually large number of black children in so-called mentally retarded classes has been ruled unconstitutional by a federal judge. On behalf of five black children, Chief District Court Judge Robert Peckham said the use of standardized IQ tests to place children in educable mentally retarded (EMR) classes violated recently enacted federal laws and the state and federal constitutions. . . . Peckham said the history of IQ testing and special education in California "revealed an unlawful discriminatory intent . . . not necessarily to hurt black children, but it was an intent to assign a grossly disproportionate number of black children to the special, inferior and dead-end EMR classes" (October 18, 1979).

> A controversial Escondido sperm bank for superbrains has produced its first baby—a healthy, nine-pound girl born to a woman identified only as a small-town resident in "a sparsely populated state." . . . Founded by inventor Robert K. Graham of Escondido in 1979, the facility contains sperm donated by at least three Nobel Prize winners, plus other prominent researchers. . . . The sperm bank was founded to breed children of higher intelligence. The goal has been denounced by many critics, who say that a child's intelligence is not determined so much by his genes as by his upbringing and environment (May 25, 1982).

As you might expect, these stories sparked impassioned debate (Kail & Pellegrino, 1985). Some arguments focus on the ethical and moral implications of selective breeding of bright children and selective placement of children in special classes. Other arguments concern the statistical basis of conclusions, such as whether the tests are really biased if the data are analyzed properly.

Preview

The field of intelligence has its share of controversies, as we just witnessed. Later in the chapter we will explore other controversies in intelligence, as well as the history of interest in intelligence and intelligence tests, and the extremes of intelligence and creativity. But to begin we will examine the nature of intelligence and its measurement.

The Nature of Intelligence and Its Measurement

What is intelligence? How are tests, such as intelligence tests, constructed and evaluated?

What Is Intelligence?

Intelligence is a possession that most of us value highly, yet its concept is abstract, with few agreed-upon referents. You would agree on referents for such characteristics as height, weight, and age, but if asked to agree on referents for, perhaps, an individual's size, there is less certainty. Size is a more *abstract* notion than height or weight. Also, size is more difficult to measure directly than height or weight. We can only estimate size from a set of empirical measures of height and weight. Measuring intelligence is much the same as measuring size, though *much more* abstract. That is, we believe intelligence exists, but we do not measure intelligence directly. We cannot peel back an individual's scalp and observe intellectual processes in action. The only way we can study these intellectual processes is *indirectly,* by evaluating the intelligent acts that an individual generates. For the most part, psychologists have relied on intelligence tests to provide an estimate of these intellectual processes.

Throughout much of the history of Western civilization, intelligence has been described in terms of knowledge and reasoning (Kail & Pellegrino, 1985). Today most of us view intelligence in a similar light. In one investigation, individuals were asked to judge which of 250 behaviors were typical of an intelligent individual (Sternberg & others, 1981). Both experts (psychologists researching intelligence) and lay individuals (people of various backgrounds and education) judged the behaviors similarly. The two groups agreed that intelligence can be divided into two main categories. The first is *verbal ability,* reflected in such behaviors as "displays a good vocabulary," "reads with high comprehension," "is knowledgeable about a particular field of knowledge," and "displays curiosity." The second category is *problem-solving skills,* reflected in such behaviors as "reasons logically and well," "is able to apply knowledge to problems at hand," and "makes good decisions."

Thus, the primary components of intelligence are very close to the mental processes—thinking and language. The differences between how we discussed thinking and language and how we will discuss intelligence lies in the concepts of individual differences and assessment. **Individual differences** *are the consistent, stable ways in which people are different from each other.* The study of intelligence in psychology has focused extensively on individual differences and their assessment (Blades, 1997). We can talk about individual differences in personality, or in any other domain in psychology, but it is in the area of intelligence that the most attention is given to individual differences. For example, an intelligence test will tell if you can logically reason better than most others who have taken the test.

Psychometrics *is the field that involves the assessment of individual differences.* In a few moments, we will go on a brief historical tour of individual differences and intelligence tests, but first we need to know something very important in the field of psychometrics—how tests are constructed and evaluated.

How Tests Are Constructed and Evaluated

Measurement and testing have been involved in human decision making for centuries. Our ancestors used principles of measurement to build shelter, hunt prey, and fashion clothing long before the appearance of psychological tests. The Chinese first developed formal oral tests of knowledge as early as 2200 B.C. The Chinese emperor Ta Yü conducted a 3-year cycle of "competency testing" of government officials. After three examinations, the officials were either promoted or fired (Sax, 1989). Tests have become commonplace in today's world as psychologists have sought more precise measurement of psychology's concepts. Any good test must meet three criteria—it must be reliable, it must be valid, and it must be standardized. We will consider each of these criteria in turn.

Reliability

If a test that measures a characteristic is a stable and consistent test, scores should not significantly fluctuate because of chance factors, such as how much sleep you get the night before the test, who the examiner is, the temperature in the room where you take the test, and so on. **Reliability** *is the extent to which a test yields a consistent, reproducible measure of performance.* Reliability can be measured in several ways. **Test-retest reliability** *is the extent to which a test yields the same measure of performance when an individual is given the same test on two different occasions.* Thus, if we gave an intelligence test to a group of high school students today and then gave them the same test in 6 months, the test would be considered reliable if those who scored high on the test today generally score high on the test in 6 months. One negative feature of test-retest reliability is that individuals sometimes do better the second time they take the test because they are familiar with it.

A second method of measuring reliability is to give alternate forms of the same test on two different occasions. The test items on the two forms of the test are similar but not identical. This strategy eliminates the chance of individuals performing better due to familiarity with the items, but it does not eliminate an individual's familiarity with the procedures and strategies involved in the testing.

A third method of measuring reliability is **split-half reliability.** *With this method, test items are divided into two halves, such as the odd-numbered items and the even-numbered items. The items are different, and the two scores are compared to determine how consistently an individual performed.* When split-half reliability is high, we say that a test is *internally consistent.* For example, if we gave an intelligence test that included vocabulary items on one-half of the test and logical reasoning items on the other half, we would expect the total scores of the individuals taking the test to be similar to their scores on each half of the test.

Validity

A test may consistently measure an attribute, such as intelligence or personality, but this consistency does not ensure that we are measuring the attribute we want to measure. A test of intelligence might actually measure something else, such as anxiety. The test might consistently measure how anxious you are and, thus, have high reliability but not measure your intelligence, which it purports to measure. **Validity** *is the extent to which a test measures what it is intended to measure.*

Like reliability, there are a number of methods to measure validity. One method is **content validity,** *which* *refers to the test's ability to test a broad range of the content that is to be measured.* For example, a final test in this class, if it is over the entire book, should sample items from each of the chapters rather than just two or three chapters. If an intelligence test purports to measure both verbal ability and problem-solving ability, the items should include a liberal sampling of items that reflects both of these domains. The test would not have high content validity if it asked you to define several vocabulary items but did not require you to reason logically in solving a number of problems.

One of the most important methods of measuring validity is **criterion validity,** *which is the test's ability to predict an individual's performance when measured by other measures, or criteria, of the attribute.* For example, a psychologist might validate an intelligence test by asking the employers of the individuals who took the intelligence test how intelligent they are at work. The employers' perceptions would be another criterion for measuring intelligence. It is not unusual for the validation of an intelligence test to be another intelligence test. When the scores on the two measures overlap substantially, we say the test has high criterion validity. Of course, we may use more than one other measure to establish criterion validity. We might give the individuals a second intelligence test, get their employers' perceptions of their intelligence, and observe their behavior in problem-solving situations ourselves.

Criterion validity can follow one of two courses, concurrent or predictive. **Concurrent validity** *is a form of criterion validity that assesses the relation of a test's scores to a criterion that is presently available (concurrent).* For example, a test might assess children's intelligence. Concurrent validity might be established by analyzing how the scores on the intelligence test correspond to the children's grades in school at this time.

Predictive validity *is a form of criterion validity that assesses the relation of a test's scores to an individual's performance at a point in the future.* For example, scores on an intelligence test might be used to predict whether the individual will be successful in college. Likewise, the SAT test is used for a similar purpose. Tests might also be developed to determine success as a police officer or pilot. Individuals take the test and then are evaluated later to see if they are indeed able to perform effectively in these jobs.

Standardization

Good tests are not only reliable and valid, they are standardized as well (Aiken, 1996). **Standardization** *involves developing uniform procedures for administering and scoring a test, and it also involves developing norms for the test.* Uniform testing procedures require that the testing environment be as similar as possible for all individuals. The test directions and the amount of time allowed to complete the test should be the same, for example. **Norms** *are established standards of performance for a test. Norms are established by giving the test to a large group of individuals representative of the population for whom the test is intended, which allows the test constructor to determine the distribution of test scores. Norms inform us which scores are considered high, low, or average.* For example, suppose you receive a score of 120 on an intelligence test; that number alone has little meaning. The score takes on meaning when we compare it with the other scores. If only 20 percent of the standardized group scored above 120, then we can interpret your score as high rather than low or average. Many tests of intelligence are designed for individuals from diverse groups. So that the tests are applicable to such different groups, many of them have norms—established standards of performance for individuals of different ages, social classes, and ethnic groups (Cohen, Swerdlik, & Phillips, 1996; Saklofske & Zeidner, 1995). Figure 1 summarizes the main topics in our discussion of test construction and evaluation.

Standardization of tests requires that uniform procedures be followed. For example, the test directions and the amount of time allowed to complete the test should be the same for all individuals.

The History of Interest in Intelligence and Intelligence Tests

Robert J. Sternberg recalls being terrified of taking IQ tests as a child. He literally froze, he says, when the time came to take such tests. Even as an adult, Sternberg stings with humiliation when he recalls being in sixth grade and taking an IQ test with the fifth graders. Sternberg finally overcame his anxieties about IQ tests and not only performed much better on them, he even devised his own IQ test at the age of thirteen and began assessing his classmates—until the school psychologist found out and scolded him. In fact, Sternberg became so fascinated with the topic he's made it a lifelong pursuit. Sternberg's theory of intelligence, which we will discuss later in the chapter, has received considerable attention recently.

Earlier we indicated that intelligence is often defined in terms of verbal ability and problem-solving skills. We also indicated, however, that intelligence is an abstract

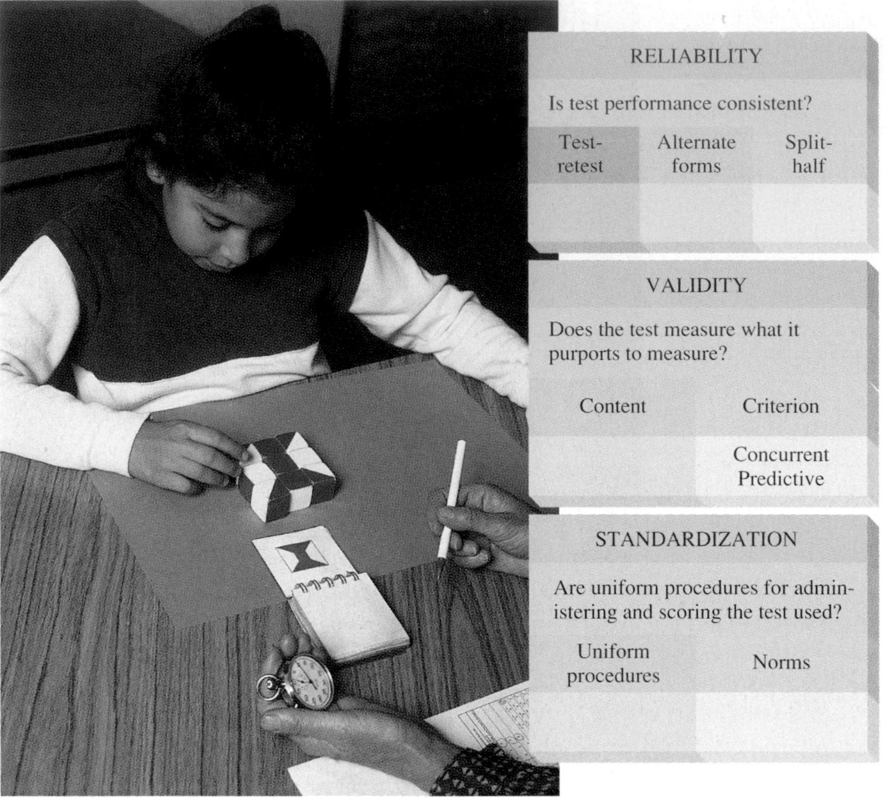

FIGURE 1

Test Construction and Evaluation

concept that is difficult to define. Whereas many psychologists and lay people equate intelligence with verbal ability and problem-solving skills, others prefer to define it as the individual's ability to learn from and adapt to the experiences of everyday life. If we were to settle on a definition of intelligence based on these criteria, it would be that **intelligence** *is verbal ability, problem-solving skills, and the ability to learn from and adapt to the experiences of everyday life* (see figure 2). As we discuss the measurement of intelligence throughout history, you will discover, however, that psychologists have debated the nature of intelligence.

Early History

The German psychologists who created psychology as a separate discipline, especially Wilhelm Wundt, were not interested in intelligence and its assessment. For them, psychology's appropriate subject matter was sensation and perception. They completely ignored the "higher mental processes," such as thinking and problem solving, that we equate with intelligence today. The early German psychologists were interested in the general laws of behavior; any differences between individuals were thought to be mistakes in measurements reflective of a young science. Before the close of the nineteenth century, however, proposals were made for a psychology of intelligence and individual differences.

In 1884 visitors to the International Health Exhibition at London's South Kensington Museum were invited to pay 3 pence each to enter Sir Francis Galton's "Anthropomorphic Laboratory" (Fancher, 1990). Galton tempted the visitors by offering them a partial view of what was happening behind the trellised wall. Observers could see that each paying customer manipulated a number of interesting contrivances while an attendant wrote down information about their performance. By the exhibition's end, more than 9,000 men and women had been enticed into the laboratory. Without knowing it, they constituted the first large sample to take an intelligence test, though the term was not used at that time and a modern observer would find little similarity between the "tests" they took and the ones in use today. The battery of tests Galton administered measured such characteristics as head size, strength of hand grip, breathing capacity, reaction time, visual acuity, and memory for visual forms.

Sir Francis Galton is considered the father of mental tests (Boring, 1950). Like the early German psychologists, Galton believed that simple sensory, perceptual, and motor responses were the key dimensions of intelligence. In his laboratory, he attempted to discover systematic individual differences in these processes; however, his efforts produced no important findings about individual differences, possibly because of the sheer amount of data he collected. Although his research provided few conclusive results, Galton raised many important questions about intelligence—how it should be measured, what its components are, and the degree to which it is inherited—that we continue to study today.

The first North American psychologist to study individual differences was James McKeen Cattell. His most notable work was in the last decade of the nineteenth century. Like Galton, Cattell thought that sensory, perceptual, and motor processes represented the heart of intelligence. Cattell's battery of tests included asking college students to select the heavier of two weights and evaluating the speed with which they responded to a tone. He sought to discover a relation between these responses and achievement in college, but the results were disappointing. Cattell is credited with developing the label *mental test.* His research, like Galton's, provided few important conclusions about intelligence, but he, too, developed a tradition that paved the way for further studies of individual differences in intelligence.

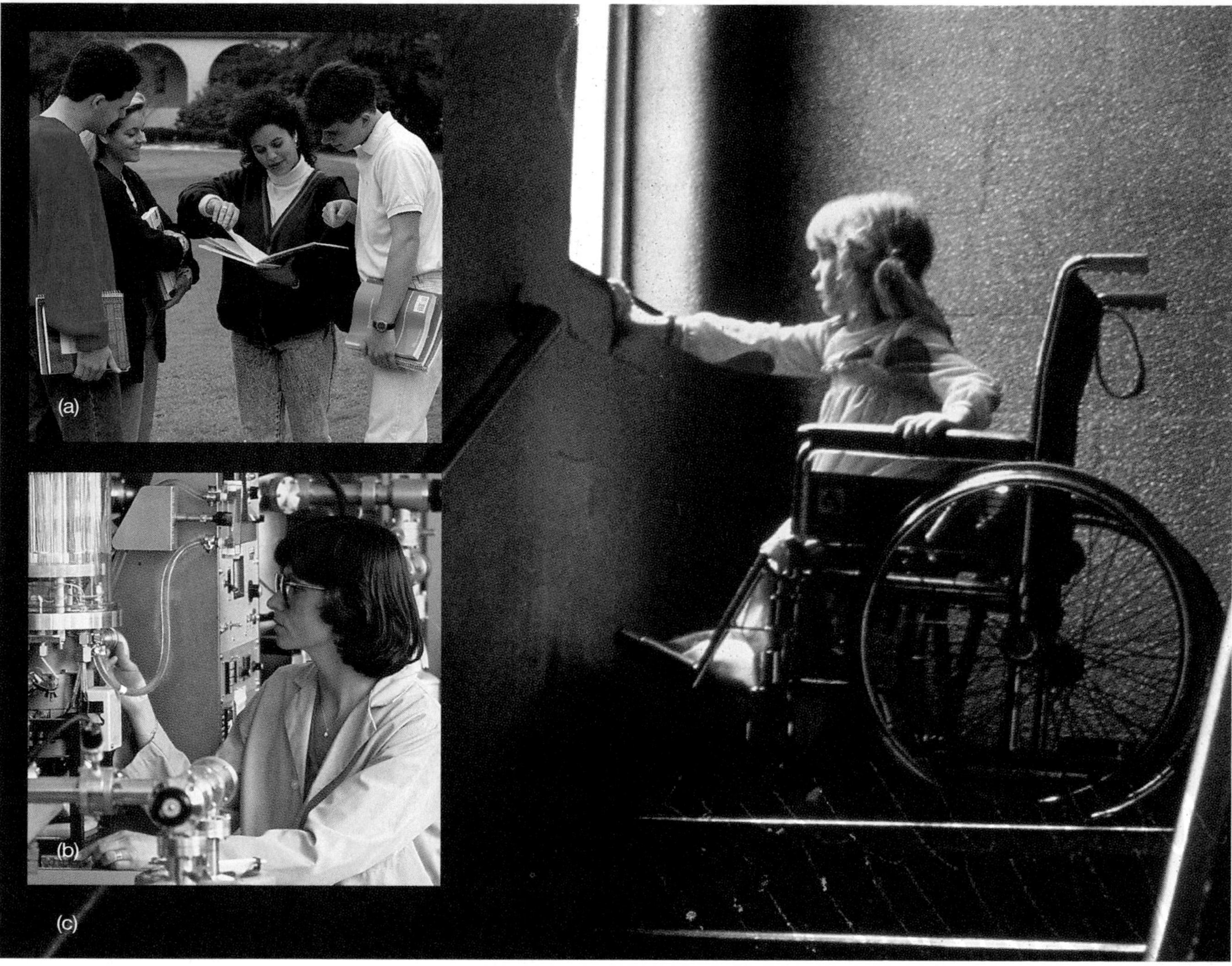

FIGURE 2

Defining Intelligence
Intelligence is an abstract concept that has been defined in various ways. The three most commonly agreed-upon aspects of intelligence are the following: (*a*) verbal ability, as reflected in the verbal skills of these college students faced with the task of writing a paper for tomorrow morning's class; (*b*) problem-solving skills, as reflected in this scientist's search for an AIDS cure; and (*c*) the ability to learn from and adapt to experiences of everyday life, as reflected in this handicapped child's adaptation to her inability to walk.

Alfred Binet and the Binet Tests

In 1904 the French Ministry of Education asked psychologist Alfred Binet to devise a method that would determine which students did not profit from typical school instruction. School officials wanted to reduce overcrowding by placing those who did not benefit from regular classroom teaching in special schools. Binet and his student Theophile Simon developed an intelligence test to meet this request. The test is referred to as the 1905 Scale and consisted of 30 items ranging from the ability to touch one's nose or ear when asked to the ability to draw designs from memory and define abstract concepts.

Binet developed the concept of **mental age (MA)**, *which is an individual's level of mental development relative to others.* Binet reasoned that a mentally retarded child would perform like a normal child of a younger age. He developed norms for intelligence by testing 50 nonretarded children from the ages of 3 to 11. Children suspected of mental retardation were given the test and their performance was compared with children of the same chronological age in the normal sample. Average mental age (MA) scores correspond to chronological age (CA), which is age from birth. A bright child has an MA considerably above CA; a dull child has an MA considerably below CA.

The term **intelligence quotient (IQ)** *was devised in 1912 by William Stern. IQ consists of an individual's mental age divided by chronological age multiplied by 100:*

$$IQ = \frac{MA}{CA} \Xi \; 100$$

If mental age is the same as chronological age, then the individual's IQ is 100; if mental age is above chronological

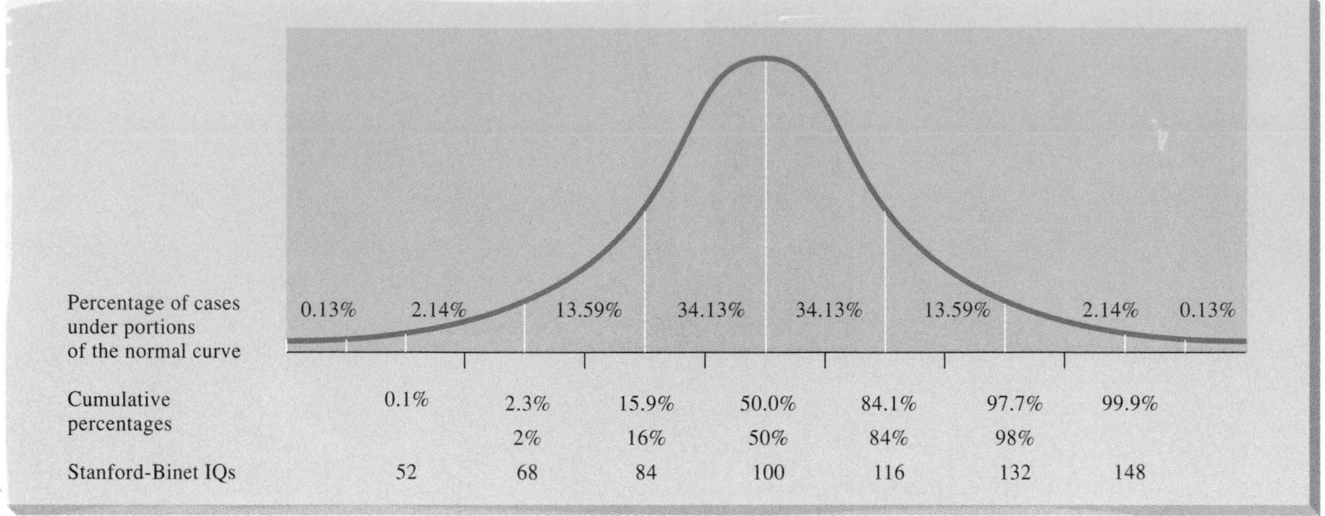

FIGURE 3

The Normal Curve and Stanford-Binet IQ Scores
The distribution of IQ scores approximates a normal curve. Most of the population falls in the middle range of scores. Notice that extremely high and extremely low scores are very rare. Slightly more than two-thirds of the scores fall between 84 and 116. Only about 1 in 50 individuals has an IQ of more than 132 and only about 1 in 50 individuals has an IQ of less than 68.

age, the IQ is more than 100; if mental age is below chronological age, the IQ is less than 100. Scores noticeably above 100 are considered above average; those considerably below are considered below average. For example, a 6-year-old child with a mental age of 8 would have an IQ of 133, whereas a 6-year-old child with a mental age of 5 would have an IQ of 83.

Over the years, extensive effort has been expended to standardize the Binet test, which has been given to thousands of children and adults of different ages selected at random from different parts of the United States. By administering the test to large numbers of individuals and recording the results, it has been found that intelligence measured by the Binet approximates a normal distribution (see figure 3). A **normal distribution** *is symmetrical, with a majority of cases falling in the middle of the possible range of scores and few scores appearing toward the extremes of the range.*

The Binet test has been revised many times to incorporate advances in the understanding of intelligence and intelligence testing. The many revisions are called the Stanford-Binet tests (Stanford University is where the revisions were done). Many of the revisions were carried out by Lewis Terman, who applied Stern's IQ concept to the test, developed extensive norms, and provided detailed, clear instructions for each problem on the test.

Why were the Binet scales such a major advance over the earlier efforts of Galton and Cattell? Binet argued that intelligence could not be reduced to sensory, perceptual, and motor processes, as Galton and Cattell believed. Binet stressed that the core of intelligence consists of more complex mental processes such as memory, imagery, comprehension, and judgment. Galton and Cattell thought that children were untrustworthy subjects in psychological research, but Binet believed that a developmental approach was crucial for understanding the concept of intelligence. The developmental interest was underscored by the emphasis on the child's mental age in comparison to chronological age.

The current Stanford-Binet is given to individuals from the age of 2 through adulthood. It includes a wide variety of items, some requiring verbal responses, others nonverbal responses. For example, items that characterize a 6-year-old's performance on the test include the verbal ability to define at least six words, such as *orange* and *envelope,* and the nonverbal ability to trace a path through a maze. Items that reflect the average adult's intelligence include defining such words as *disproportionate* and *regard,* explaining a proverb, and comparing idleness and laziness.

The fourth edition of the Stanford-Binet was published in 1985. One important addition to this version is the analysis of the individual's responses in terms of four content areas: verbal reasoning, quantitative reasoning, abstract/visual reasoning, and short-term memory. A general composite score also is obtained to reflect overall intelligence. The Stanford-Binet continues to be one of the most widely used individual tests of intelligence.

The Wechsler Scales

Besides the Stanford-Binet, the other most widely used intelligence tests are the Wechsler scales, developed by David Wechsler. They include the Wechsler Adult Intelligence Scale—Revised (WAIS-R); the Wechsler Intelligence Scale for Children—Revised (WISC-R), to test children between the ages of 6 and 16; and the Wechsler Preschool and

VERBAL SUBSCALES

SIMILARITIES

An individual must think logically and abstractly to answer a number of questions about how things might be similar.

For example, "In what ways are boats and trains the same?"

COMPREHENSION

This subscale is designed to measure an individual's judgment and common sense.

For example, "Why do individuals buy automobile insurance?"

PERFORMANCE SUBSCALES

PICTURE ARRANGEMENT

A series of pictures out of sequence is shown to an individual, who is asked to place them in their proper order to tell an appropriate story. This subscale evaluates how individuals integrate information to make it logical and meaningful.

For example, "The pictures below need to be placed in an appropriate order to tell a story."

BLOCK DESIGN

An individual must assemble a set of multicolored blocks to match designs that the examiner shows. Visual-motor coordination, perceptual organization, and the ability to visualize spatially are assessed.

For example, "Use the four blocks on the left to make the pattern at the right."

Remember that the Wechsler includes 11 subscales, 6 verbal and 5 nonverbal. Four of the subscales are shown here.

FIGURE 4

Sample Subscales of the Wechsler Adult Intelligence Scale—Revised

Primary Scale of Intelligence (WPPSI), to test children from the ages of 4 to 6½ (Wechsler, 1949, 1955, 1967, 1974, 1981).

The Wechsler scales not only provide an overall IQ score but the items are grouped according to eleven subscales, six of which are verbal and five of which are nonverbal. This allows the examiner to obtain separate verbal and nonverbal IQ scores and to see quickly the areas of mental performance in which the individual is below average, average, or above average. The inclusion of a number of nonverbal subscales makes the Wechsler test more representative of verbal and nonverbal intelligence; the Binet test includes some nonverbal items but not as many as the Wechsler scales. Several of the Wechsler subscales are shown in figure 4.

Does Intelligence Have a Single Nature?

Is it more appropriate to think of intelligence as a general term that can peg people in terms of how "smart" or "dumb" they are? Or is it a number of specific abilities?

Early Pioneers

Long before David Wechsler analyzed intelligence in terms of general and specific abilities (giving the individual an overall IQ but also providing information about specific subcomponents of intelligence), Charles Spearman (1927) proposed that intelligence has two factors. **Two-factor theory** *is Spearman's theory that individuals have both general intelligence, which he called* g, *and a number of specific intelligences, which he called* s. Spearman believed that these two factors accounted for a person's performance on an intelligence test.

However, some researchers abandoned the idea of a general intelligence and searched for specific factors only. **Multiple-factor theory** *is L.L. Thurstone's (1938) theory that intelligence consists of seven primary mental abilities: verbal comprehension, number ability, word fluency, spatial visualization, associative memory, reasoning, and perceptual speed.*

We have seen that Spearman, Thurstone, and many others were pioneers in the development of tests to assess individual differences in intelligence. Figure 5 summarizes the contributions of these pioneers.

1880 — 1880s: Sir Francis Galton, the father of "mental tests," sets out to measure individual differences in sensory, perceptual, and motor processes, which he believes are the core of intelligence.

Sir Francis Galton

1890 — 1890s: J. McKeen Cattell becomes the first North American to study individual differences; he also thought intelligence consisted of sensory, perceptual, and motor processes. He developed the concept of mental tests.

J. McKeen Cattell

1900 — 1900s: Alfred Binet develops the first intelligence test after being asked to develop a measure that would determine which children could benefit from instruction in schools and which could not. Binet's 1905 scale measured more complex mental processes than the tests of Galton and Cattell.

1910

Alfred Binet

1920 — 1920s: Charles Spearman stresses that we possess both a general intelligence and a number of specific abilities. His theory is called the two-factor theory (one for general abilities, the other for specific abilities).

1930 — 1930s: L. L. Thurstone emphasizes that we have a number of primary mental abilities.

Charles Spearman

1940 — 1940s: David Wechsler constructs the Wechsler Intelligence Scale for Children and the Wechsler Adult Intelligence Scale, which provide separate scores for verbal and performance intelligence. His work continues into the 1950s.

L. L. Thurstone

1950

1960

David Wechsler

FIGURE 5

Pioneers in the Construction of Tests to Measure Individual Differences in Intelligence

Contemporary Perspectives

Two modern efforts to pin down the components of intelligence have been proposed by Howard Gardner and Robert J. Sternberg.

Gardner's Seven Frames of Mind A recent attempt to classify intelligence, developed by Howard Gardner (1983, 1989), includes seven components, although they are not the same as Thurstone's seven factors. The talents of Michael Jordan and Ludwig von Beethoven reflect the diversity of Gardner's concept of intelligence. Jordan, the 6′6″ superstar of the Chicago Bulls, springs into motion. Grabbing a rebound off the defensive board, he quickly moves across two-thirds the length of the 94-foot basketball court, all the while processing the whereabouts of his five opponents and four teammates. As the crowd screams, Jordan calmly looks one way, finesses his way past a defender, and whirls a behind-the-back pass to a fastbreaking teammate, who dunks the

Verbal skills *Math skills* *Spatial skills* *Movement skills*

Musical skills *Insight about self* *Insight about others*

FIGURE 6

Gardner's Seven Frames of Mind

ball for two points. Is there specific intelligence to Jordan's movement and perception of the spatial layout of the basketball court? Now we turn the clock back 200 years. A tiny boy just 4 years old is standing on the footstool in front of a piano keyboard practicing. At the age of 6, the young boy has been given the honor of playing concertos and trios at a concert. The young boy is Ludwig von Beethoven, whose musical genius was evident at a young age. Did Beethoven have a specific type of intelligence, one we might call musical intelligence?

Jordan and Beethoven are two different types of individuals with different types of abilities. Gardner argues that Jordan's talent reflects his movement intelligence and his ability to analyze the world spatially, and that Beethoven's talent reflects his musical intelligence. Beyond these three forms of intelligence, Gardner argues that we have four other main forms: verbal intelligence, mathematical intelligence, insightful skills for analyzing ourselves, and insightful skills for analyzing others (see figure 6).

Gardner believes that each of the seven intelligences can be destroyed by brain damage, that each involves unique cognitive skills, and that each shows up in exaggerated fashion in both the gifted and in *idiots savants,* which is the French label for individuals who are mentally retarded but who have unbelievable skill in a particular domain, such as drawing, music, or computing. For example, an individual may be mentally retarded but be able to respond instantaneously with the correct day of the week (for example, Tuesday or Saturday) when given any date in history (such as June 4, 1926, or December 15, 1746).

Sternberg's Triarchic Theory While Gardner believes there are seven types of intelligence, Robert J. Sternberg (1986) thinks there are three. **Triarchic theory** *is Sternberg's theory that intelligence consists of componential intelligence, experiential intelligence, and contextual intelligence.* Consider Ann, who scores high on traditional intelligence tests such as the Stanford-Binet and is a star analytical thinker. Consider Todd, who does not have the best test scores but has an insightful and creative mind. And consider Art, a street-smart person who has learned to deal in practical ways with his world, although his scores on traditional IQ tests are low.

Sternberg calls Ann's analytical thinking and abstract reasoning "componential intelligence"; it is the closest to what we call intelligence in this chapter and what is commonly measured by intelligence tests. Todd's insightful and creative thinking is called "experiential intelligence" by Sternberg. And Art's street smarts and practical know-how is called "contextual intelligence" by Sternberg (see figure 7).

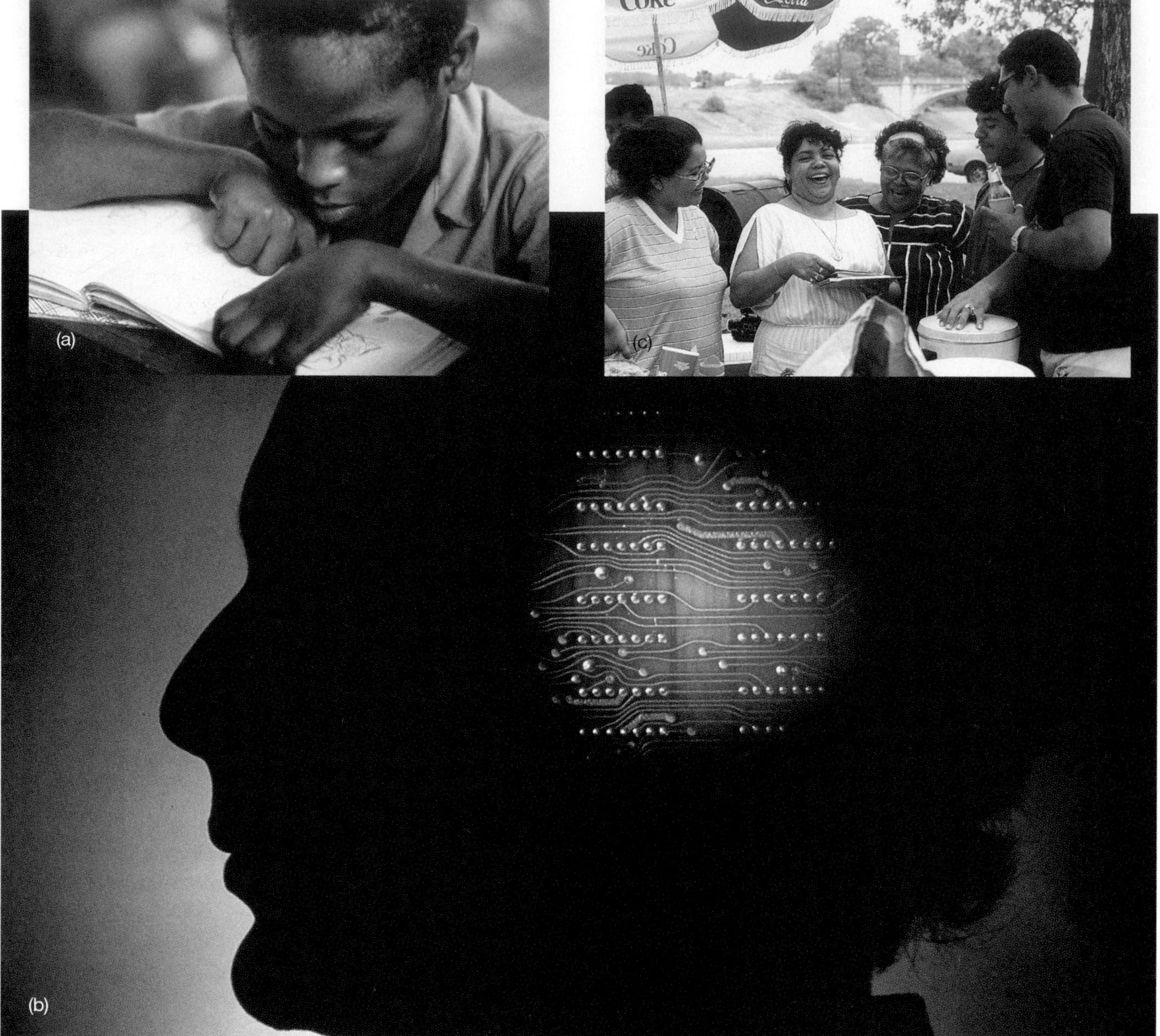

FIGURE 7

Sternberg's Triarchic Model of Intelligence

(*a*) Componential intelligence is the closest to what is commonly measured on intelligence tests and is reflected in the ability to process information as we read. (*b*) Photographer Mieke Maas showed experiential intelligence in creating this unique image of a printed circuit board inside an individual's head. Experiential intelligence involves creativity and insight. (*c*) Contextual intelligence refers to practical knowledge, especially "street smarts."

In Sternberg's view of componential intelligence, the basic unit in intelligence is a component, simply defined as a basic unit of information processing. Sternberg believes such components include the ability to acquire or store information; to retain or retrieve information; to transfer information; to plan, make decisions, and solve problems; and to translate our thoughts into performance.

The second part of Sternberg's model focuses on experience. According to Sternberg, intellectual people have the ability to solve new problems quickly, but they also learn how to solve familiar problems in an automatic, rote way so their minds are free to handle other problems that require insight and creativity.

The third part of the model involves practical intelligence—such as how to get out of trouble, how to replace a fuse, and how to get along with people. Sternberg describes this practical or contextual intelligence as all of the important information about getting along in the real world that you are not taught in school. He believes contextual intelligence is sometimes more important than the "book knowledge" that is often taught in school.

"You're wise, but you lack tree smarts."

Group Tests

The Stanford-Binet and Wechsler tests are individually administered intelligence tests. A psychologist approaches the testing situation as a structured interaction between the psychologist and the individual being tested. This provides an opportunity to sample the individual's behavior. During testing the psychologist observes the ease with which rapport is established, the level of energy and enthusiasm the individual expresses, and the degree of frustration tolerance and persistence the individual shows in performing difficult tasks. Each of these observations helps the psychologist understand the individual.

On some occasions, though, it is necessary to administer group intelligence tests, which are more convenient and economical than individual tests. For example, when World War I began, Binet's test was already popular, and the idea of using tests to measure intelligence was generally accepted. The armed services thought it would be beneficial to know the intellectual abilities of its thousands of recruits. All of these people clearly could not be tested individually. The result was the publication of the Army Alpha Test in 1917 to measure the intelligence of this large number of individuals on a group basis. In the same year, the Army Beta Test, mainly a performance test given orally, was designed for illiterate individuals who could not read the Army Alpha Test.

Though economical and convenient, group tests have some significant disadvantages. When a test is given to a large group, the examiner cannot establish rapport, determine the level of anxiety, and so on. Most testing experts recommend that, when important decisions are to be made about an individual, a group intelligence test should be supplemented by other information about the individual's abilities. For example, many children take ability tests at school in a large group. If a decision is to be made about placing a child in a special education class, it should not be based on such group tests alone. The psychologist should administer an individual intelligence test, such as Stanford-Binet or Wechsler, and collect an extensive amount of additional information about the child's abilities outside of the testing situation.

A group test that many of you have taken in recent years is the Scholastic Aptitude Test (SAT). This test, taken each year by more than 1 million high school seniors, measures some of the same abilities as intelligence tests. However, it does not yield an overall IQ score; rather, the SAT provides separate scores for verbal and mathematical ability. The SAT is similar to the original Binet test in that it was developed to predict success in school.

The SAT is used widely as a predictor of success in college, but it is only one of many pieces of information that determines whether a college admits a student. High school grades, the quality of the student's high school, letters of recommendation, individual interviews with the student, and special circumstances in the student's life that might have impeded academic ability are taken into account along with the SAT scores.

In recent years, a controversy has developed over whether private coaching can raise a student's SAT scores. The student's verbal and mathematical abilities, which the SAT assesses, have been built over years of experience and instruction. Research shows that private coaching on a short-term basis cannot help raise SAT scores substantially. Researchers have found that, on the average, SAT preparation courses raise a student's scores only 15 points on the SAT's 200 to 800 scale (Kulik, Bangert-Drowns, & Kulik, 1984).

The latest controversy to hit the SAT is the discovery that certain items favor males. In one recent study, the answers of 100,000 students were analyzed. On 23 of 145 questions, one sex did better than the other. Males did better on all but two. Examples of questions that favored males included:

- "Dividends are to stockholders as. . . ." The answer is "royalties are to writers." Fifteen percent more males than females answered this item correctly.
- "The opposite of stamina is. . . ." The answer is "lack of endurance." Twelve percent more males answered this item correctly.

Educational Testing Service, responsible for the SAT's content, is revising the test by throwing out questions that are unusually difficult for females or males.

Aptitude Tests and Achievement Tests

Psychologists distinguish between an **aptitude test,** *which predicts an individual's ability to learn a skill or what the individual can accomplish with training,* and an **achievement test,** *which measures what has been learned or what skills have been mastered.* The distinction between these two types of tests is sometimes blurred, however. Both tests assess an individual's current status, both include similar types of questions, and both produce results that usually are highly correlated.

In each of your psychology classes, you will take tests to measure your mastery of the class's content. These tests are achievement tests. If you major in psychology and decide to apply for graduate school, you may take the Graduate Record Exam Subject Test in Psychology, which would be used with other information (such as college grades; interviews; scores on the verbal, math, and analytical sections of the Graduate Record Exam; and so on) to predict whether you will be successful at graduate work in psychology. The Graduate Record Exam Subject Test in Psychology may contain questions similar to those from various psychology tests in undergraduate school, but this time the test items are being used to predict your performance in graduate school, so it would fall into the category of aptitude test. The test's *purpose,* not its *content,* determines whether it is an aptitude or an achievement test.

The SAT has the ingredients of both an aptitude test and an achievement test. It is an achievement test in the sense that it measures what you have learned in terms of vocabulary, reading comprehension, algebraic skills, and so on; it is an aptitude test in the sense that it is used to predict your performance in college.

At this point, we have covered many different facets of test construction and the nature of intelligence tests. To help your study of the main points of this discussion, turn to concept table 1.

Controversies and Issues in Intelligence

We have seen that intelligence is a complex and slippery concept with many competing definitions, theories, and tests. It is not surprising, therefore, that attempts to understand the nature of intelligence have been filled with controversy. Three controversies that currently share the spotlight are the following: (1) the degree to which intelligence is due to heredity or to environment, (2) the extent of ethnic differences and the role of culture in intelligence, and (3) the use and misuse of intelligence tests. We will consider each of these in turn and then discuss some of the uses and misuses of intelligence tests.

The Heredity-Environment Controversy

Arthur Jensen (1969) sparked lively and, at times, hostile debate when he stated his theory that intelligence is primarily inherited and that environment and culture play only a minimal role in intelligence. In one of his most provocative statements, Jensen claimed that genetics account for clear-cut differences in the average intelligence between races, nationalities, and social classes. When Jensen published an article in the *Harvard Educational Review* stating that lower intelligence probably was the reason that African Americans do not perform as well in school as Whites, he was called naive and racist. He received hate mail by the bushel, and police had to escort him to his classes at the University of California at Berkeley.

Jensen reviewed the research on intelligence, much of which involved comparisons of identical and fraternal twins. Identical twins have exactly the same genetic makeup. If intelligence is genetically determined, Jensen reasoned, identical twins' IQs should be similar. Fraternal twins and ordinary siblings are less similar genetically, so their IQs should be less similar. Jensen found support for his argument.

The studies on intelligence in identical twins that Jensen examined showed an average correlation of .82, a very high positive association. Investigations of fraternal twins, however, produced an average correlation of .50, a moderately high positive correlation. Note the substantial difference of .32. To show that genetic factors are more important than environmental factors, Jensen compared identical twins reared together with those reared apart. The correlation for those reared together was .89, and for those reared apart it was .78, a difference of .11. Jensen argued that if environmental factors were more important than genetic factors, siblings reared apart, who experienced different environments, should have IQs that differed more than .11. Jensen places heredity's influence on intelligence at about 80 percent. To read further about the role of heredity in intelligence, turn to Explorations in Psychology 1.

Today, most researchers agree that genetics do not determine intelligence to the extent Jensen envisioned (Ceci, 1996). For most people, this means that modifying their environment can change their IQ scores considerably (Campbell & Ramey, 1993). It also means that programs designed to enrich a person's environment can have a considerable impact, improving school achievement and the acquisition of skills needed for employability. While genetic endowment may always influence a person's intellectual ability, the environmental influences and opportunities we provide children and adults do make a difference.

Keep in mind, though, that environmental influences are complex (Neisser & others, 1996). Growing up with all the "advantages," for example, does not necessarily guarantee success. Children from wealthy families may have easy access to excellent schools, books, travel, and tutoring, but they may take such opportunities for granted and fail to develop the motivation to learn and to achieve. In the same way, "poor" or "disadvantaged" does not automatically equal "doomed."

Some years ago I knocked on the door of a house in a low-income area of a large city. The father came to the door and invited me into the living room. Even though it was getting dark outside, no lights were on inside the house. The father excused himself, then returned with a lightbulb, which he screwed into the lamp socket. He said that he could barely pay his monthly mortgage and that the electric company had threatened to turn off his electricity, so he was carefully monitoring how much electricity his family used.

There were seven children in the family, ranging in age from 2 to 16 years old. Neither the father nor his wife had completed high school. He worked as a bricklayer when he could find work, and his wife ironed clothes in a laundry. The parents wanted their children to pursue education and to have more opportunities in life than they had had.

The children from this inner-city family were exposed to both positive and negative influences. On the one hand,

CONCEPT TABLE 1

Intelligence, Test Construction, and Intelligence Tests

Concept	Processes/Related Ideas	Characteristics/Description
What Is Intelligence?	Its nature	An abstract concept that is measured indirectly. Psychologists rely on intelligence tests to estimate intellectual processes. Verbal ability and problem-solving skills are included in a definition of intelligence. Some psychologists believe that intelligence includes an ability to learn from and adapt to everyday life. Extensive effort is given to assessing individual differences in intelligence. This is called psychometrics.
How Tests Are Constructed and Evaluated	Reliability	How consistently an individual performs on a test. Three forms of reliability are test-retest, alternate forms, and split-half.
	Validity	The extent to which a test measures what it is intended to measure. Two methods of assessing validity are content validity and criterion validity. Criterion validity involves either concurrent or predictive validity.
	Standardization	Involves uniform procedures for administering and scoring a test; it also involves norms.
The Measurement and Nature of Intelligence	Early history	Sir Francis Galton is the father of mental tests. He believed that sensory, perceptual, and motor processes were the core of intelligence; he tried to measure individual differences but found no formidable conclusions. James McKeen Cattell was the first North American to study individual differences; he developed the label of mental test.
	Alfred Binet and the Binet tests	Alfred Binet developed the first intelligence test, known as the 1905 Scale. He developed the concept of mental age, whereas William Stern developed the concept of IQ. The Binet has been standardized and revised a number of times. The many revisions are called the Stanford-Binet tests. The test approximates a normal distribution and assesses more complex mental processes than those of Galton and Cattell. The current test is given to individuals from the age of 2 through adulthood.
	The Wechsler scales	Besides the Binet, the Wechsler scales are the most widely used intelligence tests. They include the WAIS-R, the WISC-R, and the WPPSI. These tests provide an overall IQ, verbal and performance IQ, and information about eleven subtests.
	Does intelligence have a single nature?	Psychologists debate whether intelligence is a general ability or a number of specific abilities. Spearman's two-factor theory and Thurstone's multiple-factor theory state that a number of specific factors are involved. So do Gardner's contemporary theory of seven types of intelligence and Sternberg's triarchic theory.
	Group tests	Convenient and economical, but they do not allow an examiner to monitor the testing and personally interact with the subject. The Army Alpha and Beta tests were the first widely used group intelligence tests. The SAT is a group test used in conjunction with other information to predict academic success in college.
	Aptitude tests and achievement tests	Aptitude tests predict an individual's ability to learn a skill or the individual's future performance; achievement tests assess what an individual already knows. The distinction between these tests is sometimes blurred; the SAT has the ingredients of both.

they were growing up in an intact family where education was encouraged, and their parents provided a model of the work ethic. On the other hand, they were being short-changed by society and had few opportunities to develop their intellectual abilities.

Researchers increasingly are interested in manipulating the early environment of children who are at risk for impoverished intelligence (Blair & Ramey, 1996; Feldman, 1996). The emphasis is on prevention rather than remediation. Many low-income parents have difficulty providing an

Explorations in Psychology 1

The Bell-Curve Controversy

In *The Bell Curve: Intelligence and Class Structure in Modern Life,* Richard Hernstein and Charles Murray (1994) argued that America is rapidly evolving a huge underclass of intellectually deprived individuals whose cognitive abilities will never match the future needs of most employers. The authors believe that this underclass, a large proportion of which is African American, may be doomed by their shortcomings to welfare dependency, poverty, crime, and lives void of any hope of ever reaching the American dream.

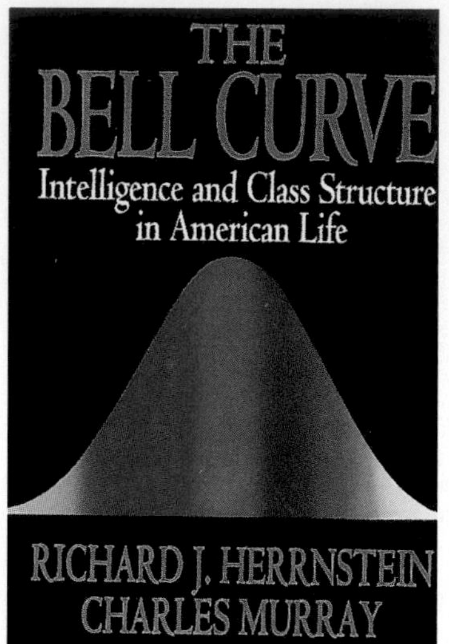

Hernstein and Murray believe that IQ can be quantitatively measured and that IQ test scores vary across ethnic groups. They point out that in the United States, Asian Americans score several points higher than Whites, while African Americans score about 15 points lower than Whites. They also argue that these IQ differences are at least partly due to heredity. The authors say that government money spent on education programs such as Project Head Start is wasted, helping only the government's bloated bureaucracy.

Why do Hernstein and Murray call their book *The Bell Curve?* The term *bell curve* refers to the shape of a normal distribution graph (discussed earlier in this chapter), which looks like a bell, bulging in the middle and thinning out at the edges. The normal distribution graph is used to represent large numbers of people who are sorted according to some shared characteristic, such as weight, exposure to asbestos, taste in clothes, or IQ.

Hernstein and Murray often refer to bell curves to make a point: that predictions about any individual based exclusively on the person's IQ are virtually useless. It is only when weak correlations between intelligence and job success are applied to large groups of people that they have predictive value. Within such large groups, say Hernstein and Murray, the pervasive influence of IQ on human society becomes apparent (Browne, 1994).

Significant criticisms have been leveled at *The Bell Curve.* Experts on intelligence generally agree with Hernstein and Murray that African Americans score lower than Whites on IQ tests. However, many of these experts raise serious questions about the ability of IQ tests to accurately measure a person's intelligence. Among the criticisms of IQ tests is that the tests are culturally biased against African Americans and Latinos. In 1971, the Supreme Court endorsed such criticisms and ruled that tests of general intelligence, in contrast to tests that solely measure fitness for a particular job, are discriminatory and cannot be administered as a condition of employment.

A final criticism is that most investigations of heredity and environment do not include environments that differ radically. Thus, it is not surprising that many genetic studies show environment to be a fairly weak influence (Fraser, 1995).

---

intellectually stimulating environment for their children. Programs that educate parents to be more sensitive caregivers and train them to be better teachers, as well as support services such as Head Start, can make a difference in a child's intellectual development.

Culture and Ethnicity

Are there cultural and ethnic differences in intelligence? How does adaptation affect the role culture plays in understanding intelligence? Are standard intelligence tests biased? If so, can we develop tests that are fair?

Cultural and Ethnic Comparisons

In the United States, children from African American and Latino families score below children from White families on standardized intelligence tests. On the average, African American schoolchildren score 10 to 15 points lower on standardized intelligence tests than White American schoolchildren (Anastasi, 1988). But we are talking about average scores here. Estimates also indicate that 15 to 25 percent of African American schoolchildren score higher than half of all White schoolchildren. And many Whites score lower than most African Americans. This is because the distribution of scores for African Americans and Whites overlap.

How extensively are ethnic differences in intelligence influenced by heredity and environment? There is no evidence to support a genetic interpretation. For example, as African Americans gain social, economic, and educational opportunities, the gap between White and African American children on standardized intelligence tests has begun to narrow. And when children from disadvantaged African

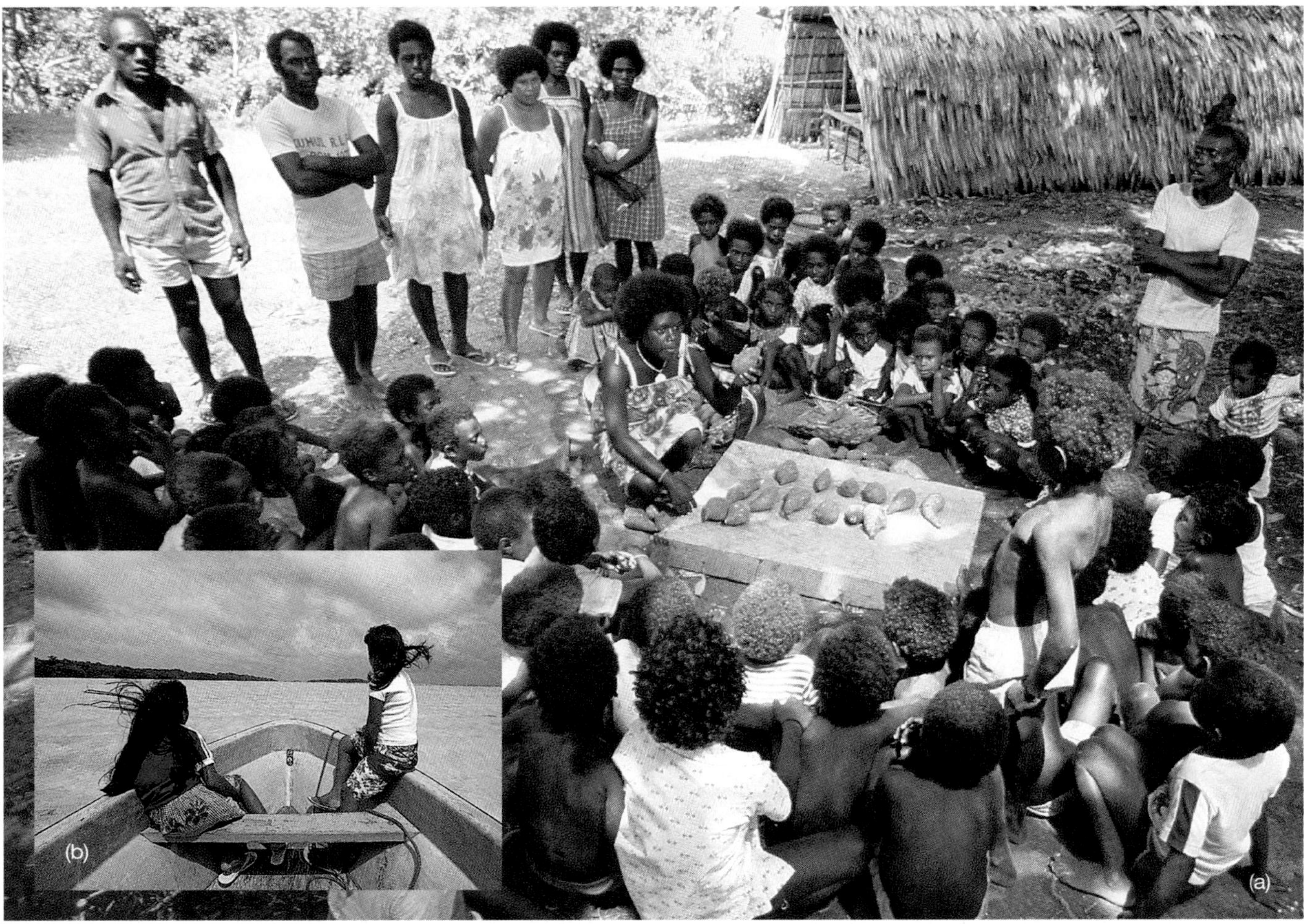

FIGURE 8

Iatmul and Caroline Islander Intelligence
(*a*) The intelligence of the Iatmul people of Papua, New Guinea, involves the ability to remember the names of many clans. (*b*) The Caroline Islands number 680 in the Pacific Ocean east of the Philippines. The intelligence of their inhabitants includes the ability to navigate by the stars.

American families are adopted into more advantaged middle-class families, their scores on intelligence tests more closely resemble national averages for middle-class than for lower-class children (Scarr, 1991).

Cultural Bias and Culture-Fair Tests

Many of the early intelligence tests were culturally biased, favoring people who were from urban rather than rural environments, middle-class rather than lower-class, and White rather than African American (Miller-Jones, 1989). For example, a question on an early test asked what should be done if you find a 3-year-old child in the street. The correct answer was "call the police." But children from inner-city families who perceive the police as adversaries are unlikely to choose this answer. Similarly, children from rural areas might not choose this answer if there is no police force nearby. Such questions clearly do not measure the knowledge necessary to adapt to one's environment or to be "intelligent" in an inner-city neighborhood or in rural America (Scarr, 1984). Also, members of minority groups often do not speak English or may speak nonstandard English. Consequently, they may be at a disadvantage understanding verbal questions that are framed in standard English, even if the content of the test is appropriate.

Cultures also vary in the way they define intelligence. Most European Americans, for example, think of intelligence in terms of technical skills. But people in Kenya consider responsible participation in family and social life an integral part of intelligence. Similarly, an intelligent person in Uganda is someone who knows what to do, and who then follows through with appropriate action. Intelligence to the Iatmul people of Papua, New Guinea, involves the ability to remember the names of some 10,000 to 20,000 clans. And the islanders in the widely dispersed Caroline Islands incorporate the talent of navigating by the stars in their definition of intelligence (see figure 8).

An example of possible cultural bias in intelligence tests can be seen in the life of Gregory Ochoa. When Gregory was a high school student, he and his classmates took an IQ test. But when Gregory looked at the test questions he understood only

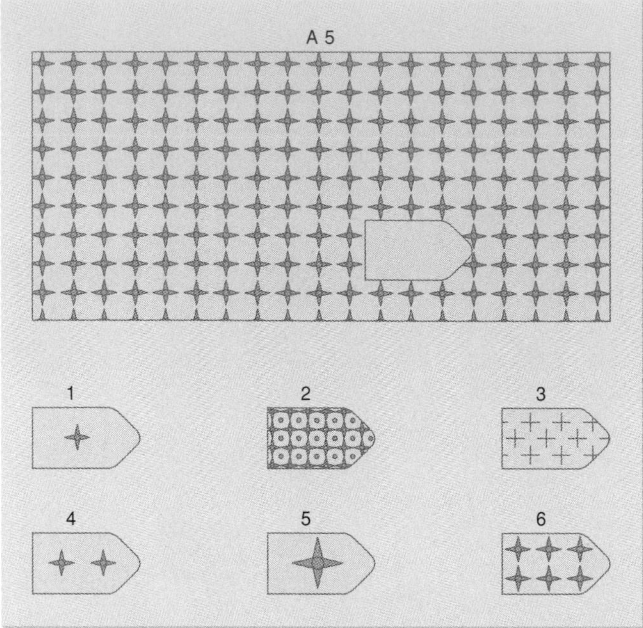

FIGURE 9

Sample Item from the Raven Progressive Matrices Test
Individuals are presented with a matrix arrangement of symbols, such as the one at the top of this figure, and must then complete the matrix by selecting the appropriate missing symbol from a group of symbols.

a few words, since he did not speak English very well and spoke Spanish at home. Several weeks later Gregory was placed in a special class for mentally retarded students. Many of the students in the class, it turns out, had last names like Ramirez and Gonzales. Gregory lost interest in school, dropped out, and eventually joined the Navy. In the Navy, Gregory took high school courses and earned enough credits to attend college later. He graduated from San Jose City College as an honor student, continued his education, and wound up as a professor of social work at the University of Washington in Seattle.

As a result of such cases, researchers have tried to develop tests that accurately reflect a person's intelligence. **Culture-fair tests** *are intelligence tests that are intended to not be culturally biased.* Two types of culture-fair tests have been devised. The first includes questions that are familiar to people from all socioeconomic and ethnic backgrounds. For example, a child might be asked how a bird and a dog are different, on the assumption that virtually all children are familiar with dogs and birds.

The second type of culture-fair test removes all verbal questions. Figure 9 shows a sample item from the Raven Progressive Matrices Test. Even though tests such as the Raven Progressive Matrices are designed to be culture-fair, people with more education still score higher than those with less education.

One test that considers the socioeconomic background of children is the SOMPA, which stands for System of Multicultural Pluralistic Assessment (Mercer & Lewis, 1978). This test can be given to children from 5 to 11 years of age, and was especially designed for children from low-income families. Instead of relying on a single test, SOMPA is based on information from four different areas of the child's life: (1) verbal and nonverbal intelligence, assessed by the WISC-R; (2) social and economic background, obtained through a one-hour parent interview; (3) social adjustment to school, determined through a questionnaire that parents complete; and (4) physical health, assessed by a medical examination.

Most researchers agree that traditional intelligence tests are probably culturally biased, but efforts to develop culture-fair tests so far have yielded unsatisfactory results.

Culture, Intelligence, and Adaptation

People adapt to their environment, and what's appropriate in one environment may not be appropriate in another. As mentioned earlier in the chapter, intelligence is expressed differently in different cultures (Berry & others, 1992). In one study, the researcher asked members of the Kpelle in Liberia (located on the western coast of Africa) to sort twenty objects (Glick, 1975). Rather than sort the objects into the "appropriate" categories the researcher had predicted, the Kpelle sorted the objects into functional groups—such as a knife with an apple and a potato with a hoe. Surprised by the answers, the researcher asked the Kpelle to explain their reasoning. The Kpelle responded that that was the way a wise person would group things. When the researcher asked how a fool would classify the objects, the Kpelle answered that four neat piles of food in one category, four tools in another category, and so on was the fool's way. The Kpelle were not lacking in intelligence; the researcher lacked an understanding of the Kpelle culture. The Kpelle sorted the items in ways that were adaptive for their culture.

Another example of human adaptability involves spatial ability. One study showed that people who live in hunter-gatherer societies score higher on spatial ability tests than do people from industrialized societies (Berry, 1971). People who must hunt to eat depend on their spatial skills for survival.

Few of us will ever have firsthand experience with hunter-gatherer societies, but many of us know people who are adaptable, savvy, and successful yet do not score correspondingly high on intelligence tests. Canadian cross-cultural psychologist John Berry (1983) has an explanation for this gap between intelligence exhibited in one's own culture and intelligence displayed in a formal testing situation. He describes people as being embedded in four levels of environmental contexts. Level 1, the ecological context, is an individual's natural habitat. Level 2, the experiential context, is the pattern of recurring experiences from which the individual regularly learns. Level 3, the performance context, is the limited set of circumstances in which the individual's natural behavior is observed. Level 4, the experimental

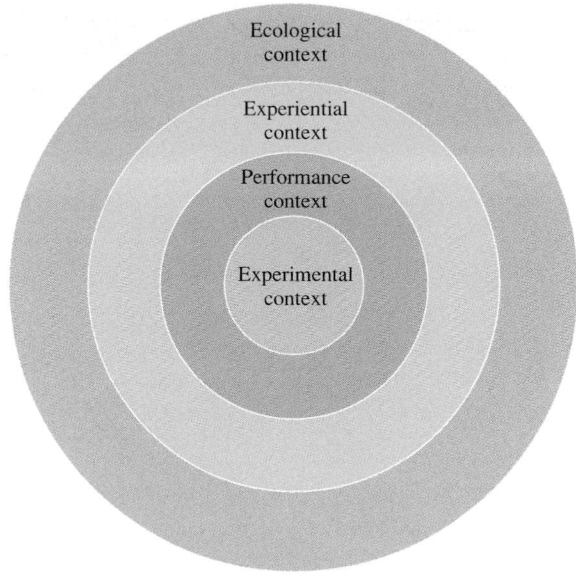

FIGURE 10

Berry's Model of the Contexts of Intelligence
In this model of the contexts of intelligence, there is much more to consider than the actual context in which a test is being administered (the experimental context). In addition, it is also important to consider three other contextual levels—the performance context, experiential context, and ecological context.

context, is the set of environmental circumstances under which test scores are actually generated (Berry's model is presented in figure 10).

When the experimental context differs considerably from the ecological or experiential context, Berry says, the individuals being tested are at a disadvantage. Presumably, the greater the difference, the greater the disadvantage. However, relations among contexts change. If an individual has been given the same test previously, some of the gap between the experiential and experimental contexts closes, resulting in higher test scores.

The Use and Misuse of Intelligence Tests

Psychological tests are tools. Like all tools, their effectiveness depends on the knowledge, skill, and integrity of the user. A hammer can be used to build a beautiful kitchen cabinet or it can be used as a weapon of assault. Like a hammer, psychological tests can be used for positive purposes or they can be badly abused. It is important for both the test constructor and the test examiner to be familiar with the current state of scientific knowledge about intelligence and intelligence tests (Anastasi, 1988).

Even though they have limitations, tests of intelligence are among psychology's most widely used tools. To be effective, though, intelligence tests must be viewed realistically. They should not be thought of as a fixed, unchanging indicator of an individual's intelligence. They should be used in conjunction with other information about an individual and not relied on as the sole indicator of intelligence. For example, an intelligence test should not solely determine whether a child is placed in a special education or gifted class. The child's developmental history, medical background, performance in school, social competencies, and family experiences should be taken into account too.

The single number provided by many IQ tests can easily lead to stereotypes and expectations about an individual. Many people do not know how to interpret the results of intelligence tests, and sweeping generalizations are too often made on the basis of an IQ score. For example, imagine that you are a teacher in the teacher's lounge the day after school has started in the fall. You mention a student—Johnny Jones—and a fellow teacher remarks that she had Johnny in class last year; she comments that he was a real dunce and points out that his IQ is 78. You cannot help but remember this information, and it may lead you to think that Johnny Jones is not very bright so it is useless to spend much time teaching him. In this way, IQ scores are misused and stereotypes are formed (Rosenthal & Jacobsen, 1968).

Ability tests can help a teacher divide children into homogeneous groups who function at roughly the same level in math or reading so they can be taught the same concepts together. However, when children are placed in tracks, such as "advanced," "intermediate," and "low," extreme caution needs to be taken. Periodic assessment of the groups is needed, especially with the "low" group. Ability tests measure *current* performance, and maturational changes or enriched environmental experiences may produce advances in a child's intelligence that require she be moved to a higher group.

Despite their limitations, when used judiciously by a competent examiner, intelligence tests do provide valuable information about individuals. There are not many alternatives to these tests. Subjective judgments about individuals simply reintroduce the bias the tests were designed to eliminate.

The Extremes of Intelligence and Creativity

Intelligence tests have been used to discover indications of mental retardation or intellectual giftedness—the extremes of intelligence. As we just learned, though, at times intelligence tests have been misused for this purpose. Continuing the theme that an intelligence test should not be used as the sole indicator of mental retardation or giftedness, we will explore the nature of these intellectual extremes, as well as creativity.

Mental Retardation

The most distinctive feature of mental retardation is inadequate intellectual functioning. Long before formal tests were developed to assess intelligence, the mentally retarded were identified by a lack of age-appropriate skills in learning and caring for themselves. Once intelligence tests were developed, numbers were assigned to indicate the degree of mental retardation. But it is not unusual to find two retarded people with the same low IQ, one of whom is married, employed, and involved in the community and the other of whom requires constant supervision in an institution. These differences in social competence led psychologists to include deficits in adaptive behavior in their definition of mental retardation. **Mental retardation** *is a condition of limited mental ability in which the individual has low IQ, usually below 70 on a traditional intelligence test, and has difficulty adapting to everyday life.* About 5 million Americans fit this definition of mental retardation.

There are different classifications of mental retardation. About 89 percent of the mentally retarded fall into the mild category, with IQs of 55 to 70. About 6 percent are classified as moderately retarded, with IQs of 40 to 54; these people can attain a second-grade level of skills and may be able to support themselves as adults through some type of labor. About 3.5 percent of the mentally retarded are in the severe category, with IQs of 25 to 39; these individuals learn to talk and engage in very simple tasks, but require extensive supervision. Less than 1 percent have IQs below 25; they fall into the profoundly mentally retarded classification and are in constant need of supervision.

Mental retardation may have an organic cause, or it may be social and cultural in origin. **Organic retardation** *is mental retardation caused by a genetic disorder or by brain damage;* organic *refers to the tissues or organs of the body, so there is some physical damage in organic retardation.* Down syndrome, one form of mental retardation, occurs when an extra chromosome is present in the individual's genetic makeup (see figure 11). It is not known why the extra chromosome is present, but it may involve the health or age of the female ovum or male sperm. Most people who suffer from organic retardation have IQs that range between 0 and 50.

Cultural-familial retardation *is a mental deficit in which no evidence of organic brain damage can be found; individuals' IQs range from 50 to 70.* Psychologists suspect that such mental deficits result from the normal genetic variation that distributes people along the range of intelligence scores above 50, combined with growing up in a below-average intellectual environment. As children, those who are familially retarded can be detected in schools, where they are likely to fail; need tangible rewards (candy rather than praise); and are highly sensitive to what others—both peers and adults—want from them. However, as adults the familially retarded are usually invisible perhaps because adult settings don't tax their cognitive tasks as severely. It also may be that the familially retarded increase their intelligence as they move toward adulthood.

FIGURE 11

A Down Syndrome Child
What causes a child to develop Down syndrome? In which major classification of mental retardation does the condition fall?

Giftedness

There have always been people who in their abilities and accomplishments outshine others—the whiz kid in class, the star athlete, the natural musician. **Giftedness** *means having above-average intelligence (an IQ of 120 or higher) and/or a superior talent for something.* When it comes to programs for the gifted, most school systems select children who have intellectual superiority and academic aptitude. Children who are talented in the visual and performing arts (arts, drama, dance); athletics; or other special aptitudes tend to be overlooked.

Until recently giftedness and emotional distress were thought to go hand in hand. The English novelist Virginia Woolf suffered from severe depression, for example, and eventually committed suicide. And Sir Isaac Newton, Vincent van Gogh, Ann Sexton, Socrates, and Edgar Allan Poe all had emotional problems. But these are the exception rather than the rule; in general, no relation between giftedness and mental disorders has been found. A number of studies support the conclusion that gifted people tend to be more mature and have fewer emotional problems than others (Janos & Robinson, 1985).

Lewis Terman (1925), one of the pioneers in research on intelligence, is still engaged in a study of gifted people he began more than 60 years ago. Terman has followed the lives of approximately 1,500 children whose Stanford-Binet IQs averaged 150 into adulthood; the study will not be complete until the year 2010. Terman has found that this remarkable group is an accomplished lot: Of the 800 males, 78 have obtained doctorates (they include two past presidents of the American Psychological Association), 48 have earned MDs, and 85 have been granted law degrees. Most of these figures are 10 to 30 times greater than those found among the 800 men of the same age chosen randomly as a comparison group. These findings challenge the commonly held belief that the intellectually gifted are emotionally disturbed or socially maladjusted.

The 672 gifted women studied by Terman (Terman & Oden, 1959) underscore the importance of relationships and intimacy in women's lives. Two-thirds of these exceptional women graduated from college in the 1930s, and one-fourth attended graduate school. Despite their impressive educational achievements, when asked to order their life's priorities, the gifted women placed families first, friendships second, and careers last. For these women, having a career often meant not having children. Of the 30 most successful women, 25 did not have any children. Such undivided commitments to the family are less true of women today. Many of the highly gifted women in Terman's study questioned their intelligence and concluded that their cognitive skills had waned in adulthood. Studies of gifted women today reveal that they have a stronger confidence in their cognitive skills and intellectual abilities than did the gifted women in Terman's study (Tomlinson-Keasey, 1990). Terman's gifted women represented a cohort who reached midlife prior to the women's movement and the pervasiveness of the dual-career couple and the single-parent family (Tomlinson-Keasey, 1993).

In the most recent analysis of Terman's gifted children, two factors predicted longevity: personality and family stability (Friedman & others, 1995). With regard to personality, children who were conscientious and less impulsive lived significantly longer. With regard to family stability, children whose parents divorced before the children reached age 21 faced a one-third greater mortality risk than did their nondivorced counterparts. Individuals who became divorced themselves also faced a shorter life. And not marriage itself, but rather a stable marriage history, was linked with increased longevity.

In another study, 120 individuals with exceptional talents as adults were interviewed about what they believe contributed to their giftedness (Bloom, 1985). The individuals had excelled in six fields—concert pianists and sculptors (arts), Olympic swimmers and tennis champions (psychomotor), and research mathematicians and research neurologists (cognitive). They said the development of their exceptional accomplishments required special environmental support, excellent teaching, and motivational encouragement. Each experienced years of special attention under the tutelage and supervision of a remarkable series of teachers and coaches. All of these stars devoted exceptional amounts of time to practice and training, easily outdistancing the amount of time spent in all other activities combined. Nine-year-old Robert, a violin prodigy, had little time for television, sports, or other activities, for example. He practiced his talent several hours each day after school and spent weekends taking lessons and going to concerts. The stars also received extensive support and encouragement from their parents. Most stars had at least one parent who devoted a considerable part of each day to developing the child's talents. Raising a star requires levels of energy, commitment, sensitivity, and patience that go beyond what most parents are willing to give (Feldman, 1989). Of course, not all parents want to raise stars, but some who do put unbearable pressure on their children, expecting achievements that far exceed their talents. For every Chris Evert, there are thousands of girls with only mediocre tennis talent whose parents want them to become "another Chris Evert." Such unrealistic expectations always meet with failure and can produce considerable stress in children's lives, and all too often, parents push children into activities that bore them rather than excite them (Feldman & Piirto, 1995).

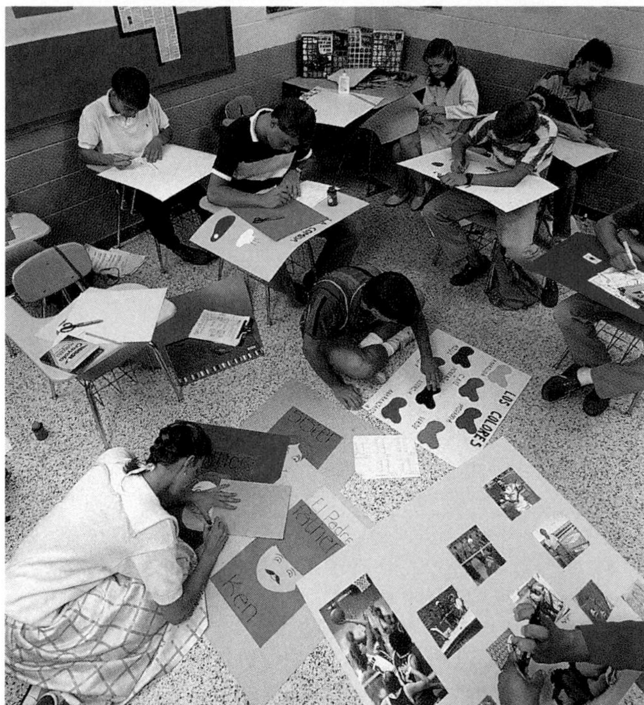

Creativity involves thinking about something in novel and unusual ways and coming up with unique solutions to problems. Creativity is enhanced when individuals have the time and independence to entertain a wide range of possible solutions in an enjoyable setting.

Creativity

Most of us would like to be both gifted and creative. Why was Thomas Edison able to invent so many things? Was he simply more intelligent than most people? Did he spend long hours toiling away in private? Surprisingly, when Edison was a young boy, his teacher told him he was too dumb to learn anything. Other famous people experienced unpleasantness in their lives despite their creativity, including Katharine Hepburn, whose genius for acting failed to protect her from criticism about her nonconformist behavior; Walt Disney, who was fired from a newspaper job because he did not have any good ideas; Enrico Caruso, whose music teacher told him that his voice was terrible; and Winston Churchill, who failed a year of secondary school.

Explorations in Psychology 2

The Snowflake Model of Creativity

Daniel Perkins (1984) describes his view as the *snowflake model of creativity.* Like the six sides of a snowflake, each with its own complex structure, Perkins' model consists of six characteristics common to highly creative individuals (see figure A). People who are creative may not have all six characteristics, but the more they have, the more creative they tend to be, says Perkins.

The first characteristic is a *strong commitment to a personal aesthetic.* This refers to the drive to impart order, simplicity, meaning, and powerful expression to what is seemingly chaos. For example, Albert Einstein's life was full of circumstances reflecting his powerful motivation for simplicity. Someone once asked him why he used hand soap for shaving instead of shaving cream. He replied that two soaps were too complicated. As part of their personal aesthetic, creative individuals have a high tolerance for complexity or ambiguity, disorganization, and asymmetry. They seem to thrive on the challenge of producing order out of chaos and struggling toward a synthesis of unlike elements. In science, for example, the core challenge is often to deal with a maze of ambiguities to come up with a unique solution.

The second characteristic of creative individuals in Perkins' model is the ability to *excel in finding problems.* Creative people spend an unusual amount of time thinking about problems. They also explore a number of options in solving a particular problem before choosing which solution to pursue. Creative individuals value good questions because they can produce discoveries and creative answers. A student once asked Nobel laureate Linus Pauling how he came up with good ideas. Pauling said he developed a lot of ideas and threw away the bad ones.

The third characteristic in the creative model is *mental mobility,* which allows individuals to find new perspectives and approaches to problems. One example of mental mobility is being able to think in terms of opposites and contraries while seeking a new solution.

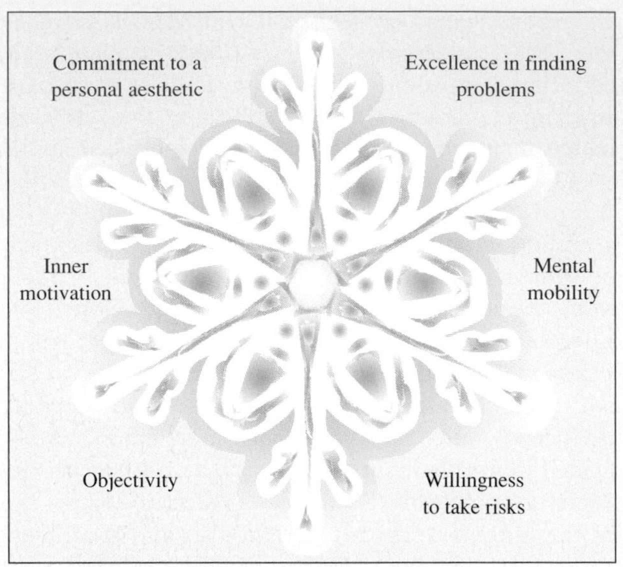

Figure A

The Snowflake Model of Creativity
Like a snowflake, Perkins' model of creativity has six parts: commitment to a personal aesthetic, excellence in finding problems, mental mobility, willingness to take risks, objectivity, and inner motivation.

The fourth characteristic is a *willingness to take risks.* Accompanying risk taking is the acceptance of failure as part of the creative quest and the ability to learn from failures. Creative geniuses don't always produce masterpieces. For example, Picasso produced more than 20,000 works of art, but much of it was mediocre. The more you produce, the better your chance of creating something important.

The fifth characteristic is *objectivity.* The popular image of creative individuals usually highlights their subjective, personal

Edison, Hepburn, Disney, Caruso, and Churchill were all intelligent, but experts on creativity believe that intelligence and creativity are not the same thing. One common distinction is between **convergent thinking,** *which produces one correct answer and is characteristic of the kind of thinking on standardized intelligence tests,* and **divergent thinking,** *which produces many different answers to the same question and is more characteristic of creativity* (Guilford, 1967). For example, this is a typical problem on an intelligence test that requires convergent thinking: "How many quarters will you get in return for 60 dimes?" But the following question has many possible answers: What image comes to mind when you hear the phrase "sitting alone in a dark room?" Responses such as "the sound of a violin with no strings" and "patience" are considered creative answers. Conversely, common answers, such as "a person in a crowd" or "insomnia" are not very creative (Baron, 1989).

Creativity *is the ability to think about something in novel and unusual ways, and to come up with unique solutions to problems.* When creative people such as artists and scientists are asked what enables them to solve problems in novel ways, they say that the ability to find affinities between seemingly unrelated elements plays a key role. They also say they have time and independence in an enjoyable setting to entertain a wide range of possible solutions to a problem. How strongly is creativity related to intelligence?

One of Albert Einstein's (left) main motivations in life was to find simplicity. Linus Pauling (middle) had many ideas that never worked out at all, and Pablo Picasso (right) produced more than 20,000 paintings, many of which were mediocre. Three important characteristics of creative individuals are a strong commitment to a personal aesthetic, which, for some creative people, involves the search for simplicity; excellence in finding problems, which includes discarding the ones that aren't worth working on or are bad ideas; and the willingness to take risks, which often involves putting out a lot of works or ideas and learning from failures.

insights and commitments; however, without some objectivity and feedback from others, they would create a private world that is distant from reality and could not be shared or appreciated by others. Creative individuals not only criticize their own works, they also seek criticism from others. Contrary to the popular image, a creative individual is not a self-absorbed loner. For example, in studying both amateur and professional poets, Perkins found that those who sought feedback produced poetry that a panel of experts judged to be superior to the poetry of those who did not seek criticism. Objectivity involves more than luck or talent. It means seeking advice from others and testing ideas in the real world.

The sixth characteristic in Perkins' model is a very important one—*inner motivation.* Creative individuals are motivated to produce something for its own sake, not for school grades or money. Their catalyst is the challenge, enjoyment, and satisfaction of the work itself. Researchers have found that individuals ranging from preschool children through adults are more creative when they are internally rather than externally motivated. Work evaluation, competition for prizes, and supervision tend to undermine internal motivation and diminish creativity (Amabile, 1990; Amabile, Phillips, & Collins, 1993).

While most creative people are quite intelligent, the reverse is not necessarily true. Many highly intelligent people (as measured by IQ tests) are not very creative.

Some experts remain skeptical that we will ever fully understand the creative process. Others believe that a psychology of creativity is in reach. Most experts do agree that the concept of creativity as spontaneously bubbling up from a magical well is a myth. Momentary flashes of insight, accompanied by images, make up only a small part of the creative process. At the heart of creativity lies ability and sustained effort. As Edison supposedly put it, "Genius is one-tenth inspiration and nine-tenths perspiration."

Based on his own research and analysis of the creativity literature, Daniel Perkins (1984) has developed a model that considers the complexity of the creative process. An overview of Perkins' model is presented in Explorations in Psychology 2. As we learn more about creativity, we come to understand its importance as a human resource, truly being one of life's wondrous gifts.

At this point we have studied controversies and issues in intelligence, as well as the extremes of intelligence. A summary of the main ideas in this discussion is presented in concept table 2.

Concept Table 2

Controversies and Issues in Intelligence and the Extremes of Intelligence

Concept	Processes/Related Ideas	Characteristics/Description
Controversies and Issues in Intelligence	The heredity-environment controversy	In the late 1960s, Jensen argued that intelligence is approximately 80 percent hereditary and that genetic differences exist in the average intelligence of races, nationalities, and social classes. Intelligence *is* influenced by heredity, but not as strongly as Jensen believed. The environments we provide children and adults do make a difference.
	Culture and ethnicity	There are cultural and ethnic differences on intelligence tests, but the evidence suggests they are not genetically based. In recent decades, the gap between African Americans and Whites on intelligence tests has diminished as African Americans have experienced more socioeconomic opportunities. Early intelligence tests favored White, middle-class individuals. Current tests try to reduce this bias. Culture-fair tests are an alternative to traditional tests; most psychologists believe they cannot completely replace the traditional tests.
	The use and misuse of intelligence tests	Despite limitations, when used by a judicious examiner, tests can be valuable tools for determining individual differences in intelligence. The tests should be used with other information about the individual. IQ scores can produce unfortunate stereotypes and expectations. Ability tests can help divide children into homogeneous groups; however, periodic testing should be done. Intelligence or a high IQ is not necessarily the ultimate human value.
The Extremes of Intelligence	Mental retardation	A mentally retarded individual has a low IQ, usually below 70 on a traditional IQ test, and has difficulty adapting to everyday life. Different classifications of mental retardation have been made. The two main causes of retardation are organic and cultural-familial.
	Giftedness and creativity	A gifted individual has above-average intelligence (an IQ of 120 or more) and/or superior talent for something. Creativity is the ability to think about something in a novel or unusual way and to come up with unique solutions to problems.

Critical Thinking About Behavior

Triangulating and Framing Your Own Intelligence

Both Robert Sternberg and Howard Gardner have proposed interesting theories to explain human intelligence. If you adopt Sternberg's triarchic model, which aspect of the triangle would you consider to be your relative strength—the componential (analytic and abstract reasoning), the experiential (insightful and creative thinking), or the contextual (practical intelligence or street smarts)? Which would be your relative weakness?

If you adopt Gardner's approach, in which of the seven frames of intelligence do your intellectual strengths mostly clearly lie?

- Are you mathematically inclined?
- Do you seem to have special gifts in understanding spatial relations?
- Do you show comfort and confidence in moving your body through space?
- Do you have special artistic talents?
- Are words and languages your forte?
- Do you have special abilities in understanding other people?
- Do you show unusual insights about your own self?

Which of these frames is least comfortable for you?

Now that you have applied two theoretical frameworks to your own abilities, which framework do you prefer? Why does this framework appeal more to you? Your ability to apply these psychological concepts to enhance personal adaptation may have some implications for the course of study you select and the future career path you choose.

OVERVIEW

We began this chapter by evaluating the nature of intelligence and its measurement, studying what intelligence is and how tests are constructed and evaluated. Then we read about the history of interest in intelligence and intelligence tests, learning about early history, Alfred Binet and the Binet tests, the Wechsler scales, whether intelligence has a single nature, group tests, and aptitude tests and achievement tests. Our coverage of controversies and issues in intelligence focused on the heredity-environment controversy, culture and ethnicity, and the use and misuse of intelligence tests. We also explored the nature of mental retardation, giftedness, and creativity. Remember that you can obtain an overall summary of the chapter by again studying the concept tables on pages 287 and 296.

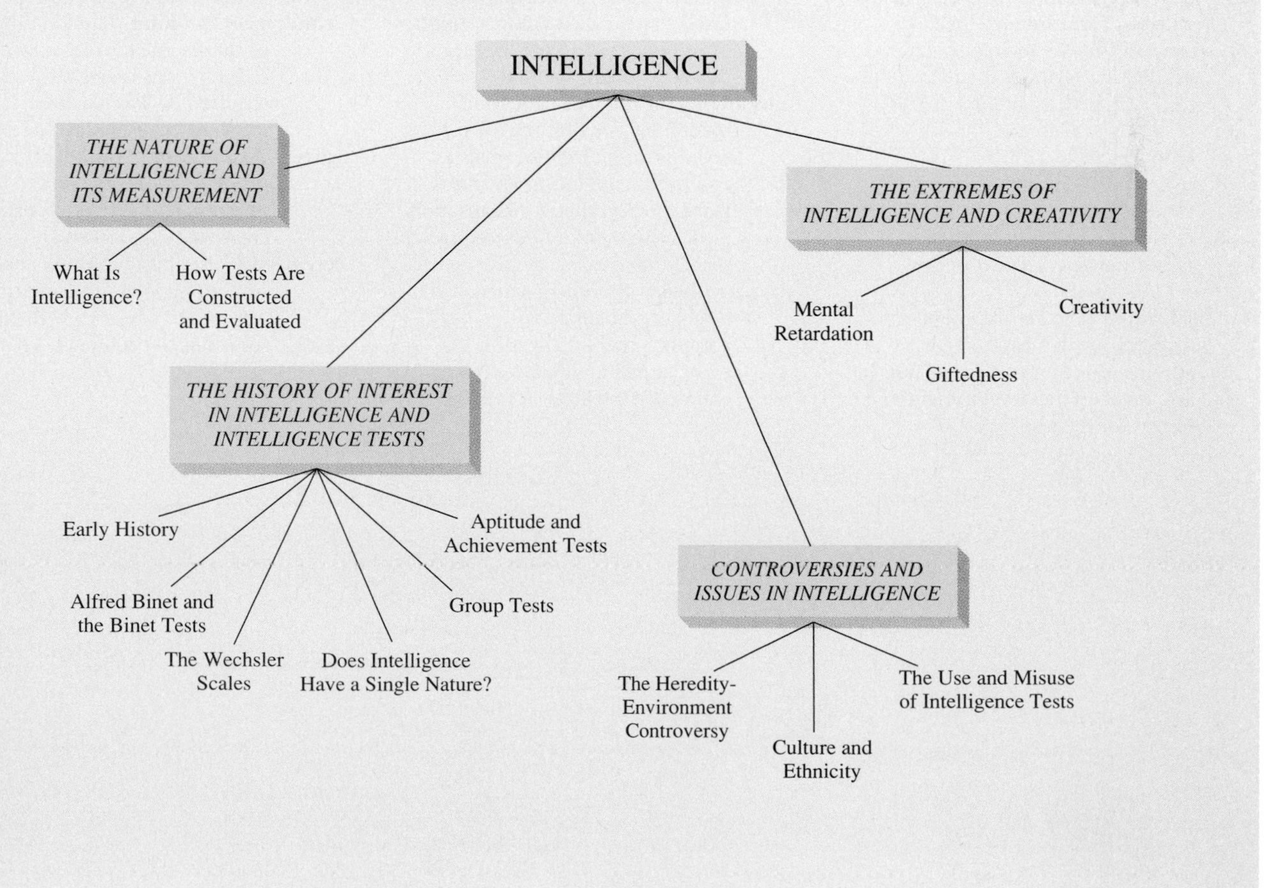

Key Terms

individual differences The stable, consistent ways in which people are different from one another. p. 276

psychometrics The field that involves assessment of individual differences. p. 276

reliability The extent to which a test yields a consistent, reproducible measure of performance. p. 276

test-retest reliability The extent to which a test yields the same measure of performance when an individual is given the same test on two different occasions. p. 276

split-half reliability A method in which test items are divided into two halves, such as odd-numbered items and even-numbered items. The items are different, and the two scores are compared to determine how consistently an individual performed. p. 276

validity The extent to which a test measures what it is intended to measure. p. 276

content validity A test's ability to test a broad range of the content that is to be measured. p. 276

criterion validity A test's ability to predict an individual's performance when measured by other measures, or criteria, of an attribute. p. 277

concurrent validity A form of criterion validity that assesses the relation of a test's scores to a criterion that is presently available (concurrent). p. 277

predictive validity A form of criterion validity that assesses the relation of a test's scores to an individual's performance at a point in the future. p. 277

standardization The development of uniform procedures for administering and scoring a test. It also involves the development of norms for the test. p. 277

norms Established standards of performance for a test. Norms are established by giving the test to a large group of individuals representative of the population for whom the test is intended, which allows the test constructor to determine the distribution of test scores. Norms inform us which scores are considered high, low, or average. p. 277

intelligence Verbal ability, problem-solving skills, and the ability to learn from and adapt to the experiences of everyday life. p. 278

mental age (MA) An individual's level of mental development relative to others. p. 279

intelligence quotient (IQ) Devised in 1912 by William Stern, IQ consists of mental age divided by chronological age, multiplied by 17. p. 279

normal distribution A symmetrical configuration of scores, with most cases falling in the middle of the possible range of scores and few scores appearing toward the extremes of the range. p. 280

two-factor theory Spearman's theory that individuals have both general intelligence, called *g*, and a number of specific types of intelligence, called *s*. p. 282

multiple-factor theory Thurstone's theory that intelligence consists of seven primary abilities: verbal comprehension, number ability, word fluency, spatial visualization, associative memory, reasoning, and perceptual speed. p. 282

triarchic theory Sternberg's theory that intelligence consists of componential intelligence, experiential intelligence, and contextual intelligence. p. 283

aptitude test A test that predicts an individual's ability to learn a skill or what the individual can accomplish with training. p. 285

achievement test A test that measures what has been learned or what skills have been mastered. p. 285

culture-fair tests Intelligence tests that are intended to not be culturally biased. p. 290

mental retardation A condition of limited mental ability in which individuals have a low IQ, usually below 70 on a traditional test of intelligence, and have difficulty adapting to everyday life. p. 292

organic retardation Mental retardation caused by a genetic disorder or brain damage; *organic* refers to the tissue or organs of the body, so there is some physical damage in organic retardation. p. 292

cultural-familial retardation Mental retardation in which there is no evidence of organic brain damage; individuals' IQs range from 50 to 70. p. 292

giftedness Having above-average intelligence (an IQ of 120 or higher) or a superior talent for something, or both. p. 292

convergent thinking Thinking that produces one correct answer and is characteristic of the kind of thinking required on standardized intelligence tests. p. 294

divergent thinking Thinking that produces many answers to a question and is characteristic of creativity. p. 294

creativity The ability to think about something in a novel and unusual way and to come up with unique solutions to problems. p. 294

Resources and Readings in Psychology

American Association on Mental Retardation
1719 Kalorama Road, NW
Washington, DC 20009
202–387–1968
800–424–3688

This organization works to promote the well-being of mentally retarded children and adults. Among the materials they have available is *Parents for Children, and Children for Parents: The Adoption Alternative.*

Assessment of Intellectual Functioning (1996, 2nd Ed.)
by Lewis Aiken
New York: Plenum

This volume includes discussion of new tests and revisions of tests for assessing intelligence, testing in other countries and cultures, case materials and related psychological testing reports, and testing disabled individuals.

Canadian Down Syndrome Society/Société canadienne de syndrome de Down
12837 76th Avenue, #206
Surrey, BC V3W 2V3, Canada

This society works to improve the lives of Canadians with Down syndrome and to educate the public about Down syndrome.

Creating Minds (1993)
by Howard Gardner
New York: Basic Books

Building on his framework of seven intelligences, ranging from musical intelligence to intelligence involved in understanding oneself, Gardner explores the lives of seven extraordinary individuals—Sigmund Freud, Albert Einstein, Pablo Picasso, Igor Stravinsky, T. S. Eliot, Martha Graham, and Mahatma Gandhi—each an outstanding exemplar of one kind of intelligence. In analyzing their lives, Gardner describes patterns crucial to understanding how people can become more creative. He believes it takes at least 10 years to make the initial creative breakthrough and another 10 years for subsequent breakthroughs. Gardner argues that an essential element in the creative process is the support of caring individuals who believe in the revolutionary ideas of their creators.

Intelligence: Knowns and Unknowns
by Ulric Neisser and others
American Psychologist, 51, 77–102

This outstanding overview of what we know and don't know about intelligence is based on the input of a task force established by the Board of Scientific Affairs of the American Psychological Association. The task force concluded that much is known about intelligence but that many critical questions remain unanswered including the pathway which genes produce their effects and the specific environmental factors that contribute to intelligence.

The Intelligence Men: Makers of the IQ Controversy (1985)
by R. E. Fancher
New York: W. W. Norton

Fancher's book includes an extensive portrayal of the history of intelligence testing—many insights and detailed descriptions of the lives of the intelligence test makers are provided.

Manual of Diagnosis and Professional Practice in Mental Retardation (1996)
by John Jacobson and James Mulik (eds.)
Washington, DC: American Psychological Association

Contributing experts address such mental retardation topics as adaptive behavior, neuropsychology, biological factors in prevention and treatment, cultural contexts, and sexuality.

National Association for Gifted Children
1155 15th Street NW, #1002
Washington, DC 20005
202–785–4268

This is an association of academicians, educators, and librarians. The organization's goal is to improve the education of gifted children. They provide periodic reports on the education of gifted children and publish the journal *Gifted Children Quarterly.*

Parents Guide to Raising a Gifted Child (1985)
by James Alvino
New York: Ballantine

This is a practical, informative book on how to raise and educate gifted children. How to assess whether a child is gifted or not is covered, along with how to select a day-care center, a school, and a home reference library. The book includes a list of recommended readings and sections on the roles of computers and television in gifted children's lives.

Special Olympics International
13150 New York Avenue, NW, Suite 500
Washington, DC 20005
202–628–3630

This international organization is dedicated to sponsoring year-round sports training and athletic competition in a variety of Olympic-type events for mentally retarded children and adults.

Testing and Your Child (1992)
by Virginia McCullough
New York: Plume

Written for parents, this comprehensive guide describes 150 of the most common educational, psychological, and medical tests, explaining who administers the tests, what the tests test for, what they cannot reveal, what preparation is required, what influences scoring, and what follow-up testing might be recommended. The tests include tests of intelligence, giftedness, achievement, and personality.

Chapter

HMD

Human Development

Edouard Vuillard
The Luncheon at Vasouy, 1901–1903, detail

CHAPTER

HMD

Human Development

Chapter Outline

Chapter Boxes

Explorations in Psychology

In every child who is born, Under no
matter what circumstances,
And of no matter what parents,
The potentiality of the human race
Is born again.

—James Agee

The first cry of a newborn baby in Chicago or Zamboango, in Amsterdam or Rangoon, has the same pitch and key, each saying, "I am! I have come through! I belong! I am a member of the Family." . . . Babies arriving, suckling, growing into youths restless and questioning. Then as grown-ups they seek and hope. They mate, toil, fish, quarrel, sing, fight, pray.

—**Carl Sandburg**

Images of Psychology

The Best of Times and the Worst of Times for Today's Children

It is both the best of times and the worst of times for today's children. Their world possesses powers and perspectives inconceivable 50 years ago: computers; longer life expectancies; and the entire planet accessible through television, satellites, and air travel. So much knowledge, though, can be chaotic, even dangerous. School curricula have been adapted to teach new topics, such as AIDS, suicide, drug and alcohol abuse, and incest. Children want to trust, but the world has become untrustworthy. The adult world's hazards—its sometimes fatal temptations—descend on children so early that their ideals become tarnished. Crack cocaine is far more addictive and deadly than marijuana, the drug of an earlier generation. Strange fragments of violence and sex come flashing out of television sets and lodge in the minds of children. The messages are powerful and contradictory. Rock videos suggest orgiastic sex. Public health officials counsel safe sex. Oprah Winfrey and Phil Donahue conduct seminars on lesbian nuns, exotic drugs, transsexual surgery, and serial murders. Television pours a bizarre version of reality into children's imaginations. In New York City, two 5-year-olds argue about (1) whether there is a Santa Claus and (2) what Liberace died of. In New Orleans, a first-grader shaves chalk and passes it around the classroom, pretending it is cocaine.

Every stable society transmits values from one generation to the next. That is civilization's work. In today's world, the transmission of values is not easy. Parents are raising children in a world far removed from Ozzie and Harriet's era of the 1950s, when two of three American families consisted of a breadwinner (the father), a mother, and the children they were raising. Today fewer than one in five families fits that description. Such phrases as *quality time* have found their way into the American vocabulary. A motif of absence plays in the lives of many children. It may be an absence of authority and limits, or of emotional commitment (Morrow, 1988).

Preview

As the twenty-first century approaches, children's well-being is one of our most important concerns. Development does not end with childhood, though, and intriguing questions are being raised about how much people can continue to change even when they are old. In this chapter we will explore the following topics: the nature of development, development during the childhood years, adolescence, late adulthood and aging, and death and dying.

What Is Development?

Each of us develops somewhat like *all* other individuals, like *some* other individuals and like *no* other individuals. Most of the time, our attention is directed to an individual's uniqueness; however, child developmentalists are drawn to children's communalities as well. As children, each of us traveled some common paths. Each of us—Leonardo da Vinci, Joan of Arc, George Washington, Martin Luther King, Jr., your author, and you—walked at about the age of 1, talked at about the age of 2, engaged in fantasy play as a young child, and became more independent as an adolescent. Yet we are also unique. No one else in the world, for example, has the same set of fingerprints as you. Researchers who study child development are intrigued by children's universal characteristics as well as by their idiosyncracies.

When we speak of **development,** we mean *a pattern of movement or change that begins at conception and continues throughout the life span.* Most development involves growth, although it also consists of decay (as in death). The pattern of change is complex because it is the product of several processes—biological, cognitive, and socioemotional.

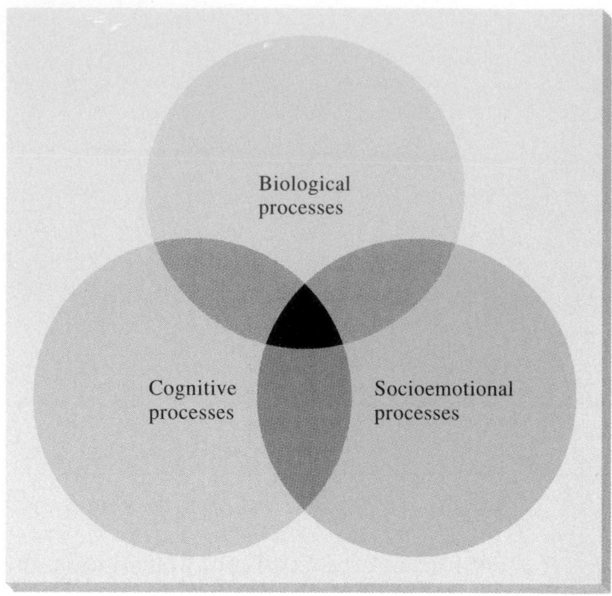

FIGURE 1

Changes in Development Are the Result of Biological, Cognitive, and Socioemotional Processes
These processes are interwoven as individuals develop.

Biological, Cognitive, and Socioemotional Processes

Biological processes *involve changes in an individual's physical nature.* Genes inherited from parents, the development of the brain, height and weight gains, motor skills, and the hormonal changes of puberty all reflect the role of biological processes in development.

Cognitive processes *involve changes in an individual's thought, intelligence, and language.* The tasks of watching a colorful mobile swinging above a crib, putting together a two-word sentence, memorizing a poem, solving a math problem, and imagining what it would be like to be a movie star all reflect the role of cognitive processes in children's development.

Socioemotional processes *involve changes in an individual's relationships with other people, changes in emotions, and changes in personality.* An infant's smile in response to her mother's touch, a young boy's aggressive attack on a playmate, a girl's development of assertiveness, and an adolescent's joy at the senior prom all reflect the role of socioemotional processes in children's development.

Remember as you read about biological, cognitive, and socioemotional processes that they are intricately interwoven. You will read about how socioemotional processes shape cognitive processes, how cognitive processes promote or restrict socioemotional processes, and how biological processes influence cognitive processes. Although it is helpful to study the various processes involved in children's development in separate sections of the chapter, keep in mind that you are studying the development of an integrated human child in whom mind and body are interdependent (see figure 1).

Periods of Development

For the purposes of organization and understanding, we commonly describe development in terms of periods. The most widely used classification of developmental periods involves the following sequence: prenatal period, infancy, early childhood, middle and late childhood, adolescence, early adulthood, middle adulthood, and late adulthood. Approximate age ranges are placed on the periods to provide a general idea of when a period first appears and when it ends.

The **prenatal period** *is the time from conception to birth.* It is a time of tremendous growth—from a single cell to an organism complete with a brain and behavioral capabilities, produced in approximately a 9-month period.

Infancy *is the developmental period that extends from birth to 18 or 24 months.* Infancy is a time of extreme dependence on adults. Many psychological activities are just beginning—language, symbolic thought, sensorimotor coordination, and social learning, for example.

Early childhood *is the developmental period that extends from the end of infancy to about 5 or 6 years; sometimes the period is called the preschool years.* During this time, young children learn to become more self-sufficient and to care for themselves, develop school readiness skills (following instructions, identifying letters), and spend many hours in play and with peers. First grade typically marks the end of this period.

Middle and late childhood *is the developmental period that extends from about 6 to 11 years of age, approximately corresponding to the elementary school years; sometimes the period is called the elementary school years.* Children master the fundamental skills of reading, writing, and arithmetic, and they are formally exposed to the larger world and its culture. Achievement becomes a more central theme of the child's world, and self-control increases.

Adolescence *is the developmental period of transition from childhood to early adulthood, entered approximately at 10 to 12 years of age and ending at 18 to 22 years of age.* Adolescence begins with rapid physical changes—dramatic gains in height and weight; changes in body contour; and the development of sexual characteristics such as enlargement of the breasts, development of pubic and facial hair, and deepening of the voice. At this point in development, the pursuit of independence and an identity are prominent. Thought is more logical, abstract, and idealistic. More and more time is spent outside of the family during this period.

Early adulthood *is the developmental period that begins in the late teens or early twenties and lasts through the thirties.* It is a time of establishing personal and economic independence; a time of career development; and for many a time of selecting a mate, learning to live with someone in an intimate way, starting a family, and rearing children.

Middle adulthood *is the developmental period that begins at approximately 35 to 45 years of age and extends into the sixties.* It is a time of expanding personal and social involvement and responsibility; of assisting the next generation in becoming competent, mature individuals; and of reaching and maintaining satisfaction in one's career.

Late adulthood *is the developmental period that begins in the sixties or seventies and lasts until death.* It is a time of adjustment to decreasing strength and health, life review, retirement, and adjustment to new social roles.

The periods of the human life span are shown in figure 2, along with the processes of development—biological, cognitive, and socioemotional. As can be seen in figure 2, the interplay of biological, cognitive, and socioemotional processes produces the periods of the human life span.

In our description of the life span's periods, we placed approximate age bands on the periods; however, one expert on life span development, Bernice Neugarten (1980), believes that we rapidly are becoming an age-irrelevant society. She says we are already familiar with the 28-year-old mayor, the 35-year-old grandmother, the 65-year-old father of a preschooler, the 55-year-old widow who starts a business, and the 70-year-old student. Neugarten says that she has had difficulty clustering adults into age brackets that are characterized by particular issues. She stresses that choices and dilemmas do not spring forth at 10-year intervals, and decisions are not made and then left behind as if they were merely beads on a chain. Neugarten argues that most adulthood themes appear and reappear throughout the human life span. The issues of intimacy and freedom can haunt couples throughout their relationship. Feeling the pressure of time, reformulating goals, and coping with success and failure are not the exclusive property of adults of any age.

Maturation and Experience (Nature and Nurture)

We can think of development as produced not only by the interplay of biological, cognitive, and socioemotional processes, but also by the interplay of maturation and experience. **Maturation** *is the orderly sequence of changes dictated by each person's genetic blueprint.* Just as a sunflower grows in an orderly way—unless defeated by an unfriendly environment—so does the human grow in an orderly way, according to the maturational view. The range of environments can be vast, but, the maturational approach argues, the genetic blueprint produces communalities in our growth and development. We walk before we talk, speak one word before two words, grow rapidly in infancy and less so in early childhood, experience a rush of sexual hormones in puberty after a lull in childhood, reach the peak of our physical strength in late adolescence and early adulthood and then decline, and so on. The maturationists acknowledge that extreme environments—those that are psychologically barren or hostile—can depress development, but they believe basic growth tendencies are genetically wired into the human.

By contrast, other psychologists emphasize the importance of experiences in life-span development. Experiences run the gamut from the individual's biological environment (nutrition, medical care, drugs, and physical accidents) to the social environment (family, peers, schools, community, media, and culture).

The debate about whether development is primarily influenced by maturation or by experience has been a part of psychology since its beginning. This debate is often referred to as the **nature/nurture controversy.** Nature *refers to an organism's biological inheritance,* nurture *to environmental experiences. The "nature" proponents claim biological inheritance is the most important influence on development, and the "nurture" proponents claim that environmental experiences are the most important.*

Continuity and Discontinuity

Think for a moment about who you are. Did you become this person gradually, like the slow, cumulative growth of a seedling into a giant oak? Or did you experience sudden, distinct changes in your development, the way a caterpillar changes into a butterfly? For the most part, developmental psychologists who emphasize experience have described

Periods of Development

Late adulthood

Middle adulthood

Early adulthood

Adolescence

Middle and late childhood

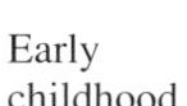

Early childhood

Infancy

Prenatal period

Processes of development

Biological processes

Cognitive processes

Socioemotional processes

FIGURE 2

Processes and Periods of Life-Span Development

The unfolding of the life span's periods of development is influenced by the interplay of biological, cognitive, and socioemotional processes.

(a)

(b)

(c)

FIGURE 3

Metaphors for Development
Three metaphors that have been used to describe the nature of development are (*a*) a staircase, (*b*) a seedling in a greenhouse, and (*c*) a strand of ivy in a forest.

development as a gradual, continuous process; those who emphasize maturation have described development as a series of distinct stages.

The view that stresses **continuity of development** argues that *development involves gradual, cumulative change from conception to death.* A child's first word, while seemingly an abrupt, discrete event, is actually the result of months of growth and practice. Similarly, while puberty might seem to happen overnight, it is actually a gradual process that occurs over several years.

The view that stresses **discontinuity of development** argues that *development involves distinct stages in the life span.* In this view, each of us passes through a sequence of stages that are qualitatively, rather than quantitatively, different. As a caterpillar changes into a butterfly, it does not become more caterpillar; it becomes a different kind of organism. Its development is discontinuous. Similarly, a child who earlier could think only in concrete terms becomes capable of thinking abstractly about the world. This is a qualitative, discontinuous change in development, not a continuous, quantitative change.

Metaphors for Development

Many metaphors have been used to describe the nature of development, including the metaphors of (1) a staircase, (2) a seedling in a greenhouse, and (3) a strand of ivy in a forest. The staircase metaphor is directly related to the stage (discontinuity) view of development. Recently, cognitive developmentalist Robbie Case (1992) even titled a book *The Mind's Staircase* to emphasize the staircase-like nature of children's cognitive development.

The metaphor of the seedling in a greenhouse has been popular for many years in developmental psychology. In this view, the child is acted upon by the environment (according to the behavioral perspective of Watson and Skinner) or the child acts on the world (in Piaget's prose). This metaphor emphasizes the child as the primary unit of development.

The contemporary metaphor of the strand of ivy in a forest stresses the many different paths development can take and the importance of contextual factors in that development (Kagan, 1992). In this metaphor, development is not portrayed as consistently stagelike as in the staircase analogy, and the child is not seen as a solitary young scientist as in Piaget's view. An important dimension of this metaphor is its emphasis on the child's reciprocal encounters with others—adults and children—and the changing symbolic construction of these relationships.

Which of these metaphors best reflects the way development actually occurs? As with virtually all theories and metaphors, each has its adherents, although the ivy metaphor has become increasingly popular in recent years. A visual image of the three metaphors is shown in figure 3.

Child Development

In this section we journey from the beginning of human life through the childhood years. Along the way we will study prenatal development and birth, infancy, early childhood, and middle and late childhood.

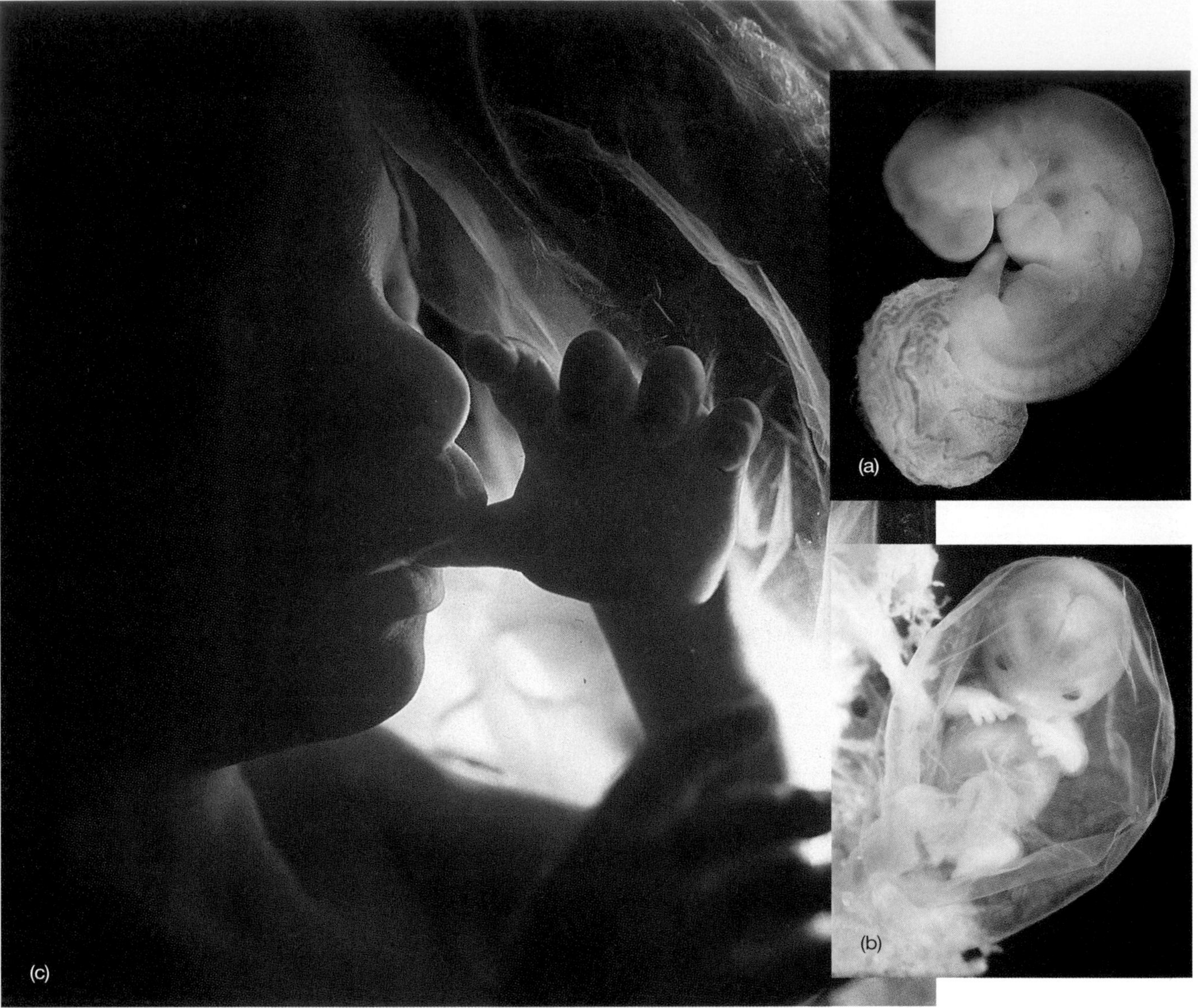

FIGURE 4

Embryonic Period
(*a*) Embryo at 4 weeks. At about 4 weeks, an embryo is about 0.2 inches in length. The head, eyes, and ears begin to show. The head and neck are half the body length; the shoulders will be located where the whitish arm buds are attached. (*b*) Embryo at 8 weeks. At 8 weeks and 4 centimeters (1.6 inches), the developing individual is no longer an embryo, but a fetus. Everything that will be found in the fully developed human being has now begun to form. The fetal stage is a period of growth and perfection of detail. The heart has been beating for a month, and the muscles have just begun their first exercises. (*c*) Fetus at 4½ months. At 4½ months, the fetus is about 18 cm (just over 7 inches). When the thumb comes close to the mouth, the head may turn, and lips and tongue begin their sucking motions—a reflex for survival.

Prenatal Development and Birth

Within a matter of hours after fertilization, a human egg divides, becomes a system of cells, and continues this mapping of cells at an astonishing rate. In a mere 9 months, there is a squalling bundle of energy that has its grandmother's nose, its father's eyes, and its mother's abundant hair.

The Course of Prenatal Development

Conception *occurs when a single sperm cell from the male penetrates the female's ovum (egg). This process also is called fertilization.* A **zygote** *is a fertilized egg.* It receives one-half of its chromosomes from the mother, the other half from the father. The zygote begins as a single cell. After 1 week and many cell divisions, the zygote is made up of 100 to 150 cells. By the end of 2 weeks, the mass of cells attaches to the uterine wall. The **germinal period** *is these first 2 weeks after conception.*

During the **embryonic period,** *weeks 3 through 8 after conception,* some remarkable developments unfold (see figure 4). Before most women even know they are pregnant, the rate of cell differentiation intensifies, support systems for the cells form, and the beginnings of organs appear. In the third week the neural tube that eventually becomes the spinal cord is forming. At about 21 days, eyes begin to appear, and by 24 days the cells of the heart begin to differentiate. During the fourth week, arm and leg buds emerge. At 5 to 8 weeks, arms and legs become more differentiated, the face starts to form, and the intestinal tract appears. All of this is happening in an organism that by 8 weeks weighs only 1/30 ounce and is just over 1 inch long.

The **fetal period** *begins 2 months after conception and lasts, on the average, for 7 months.* Growth and development continue their dramatic course, and organs mature to the point where life can be sustained outside the womb. At 4 months after conception, the fetus is about 6 inches long and weighs 4 to 7 ounces. Prenatal reflexes become more apparent, and the mother feels the fetus move for the first time. At 6 months after conception, the eyes and eyelids are completely formed, a fine layer of hair covers the fetus, the grasping reflex appears, and irregular breathing begins. By 7 to 9 months, the fetus is much longer and weighs considerably more. In addition, the functioning of various organs steps up.

As these massive changes take place during prenatal development, some pregnant women tiptoe about in the belief that everything they do has a direct effect on the unborn child. Others behave more casually, assuming their experiences have little impact. The truth lies somewhere between these extremes. Although it floats in a comfortable, well-protected environment, the fetus is not totally immune to the larger environment surrounding the mother (Kopp, 1994).

A **teratogen** (the word comes from the Greek word *tera,* meaning "monster") *is any agent that causes a birth defect.* Rarely do specific teratogens, such as drugs, link up with specific birth defects, such as leg malformation, but the drug thalidomide is an exception. During the late 1950s several hundred women took thalidomide early in pregnancy to prevent morning sickness and insomnia. Tragically, babies born to these mothers had arms and legs that had not developed beyond stumps. Heavy drinking by pregnant women can also have devastating effects on offspring (Abel, 1984). **Fetal alcohol syndrome (FAS)** *is a cluster of abnormalities that occur in children born to mothers who are heavy drinkers.* These abnormalities include a small head (microencephaly) and defective limbs, face, and heart. Most of these children are also below average in intelligence. Recently concern has increased about the well-being of the fetus when pregnant women drink even small amounts of alcohol. In one study, infants whose mothers drank moderately during pregnancy (for example, one to two drinks a day) were less attentive and alert, with the effects still present at 4 years of age (Streissguth & others, 1984). Cocaine and its newest form, crack, can also harm the developing fetus (Dow-Edwards, 1995; Lester, Freier, & LeGasse, 1995). When taken by pregnant women, crack can cause infant hypertension and damage to the offspring's heart.

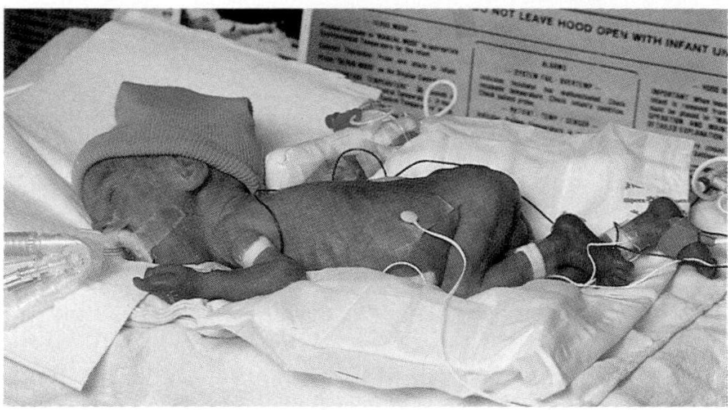

This baby was born addicted to cocaine because its mother was a cocaine addict. Researchers have found that the offspring of women who use cocaine during pregnancy often have hypertension and heart damage. Many of these infants face a childhood full of medical problems.

Birth and the Newborn

The newborn is on a threshold between two worlds. In the womb the fetus exists in a dark, free-floating, low-gravity environment with a relatively warm, constant temperature. At birth, the newborn must quickly adapt to light, gravity, cold, and a buzzing array of changing stimuli.

A full-term infant has grown in the womb for the full 38 to 42 weeks between conception and delivery. A **preterm infant** *(also called a premature infant) is an infant born prior to 38 weeks after conception.* Whether a preterm infant will have developmental problems is a complex issue. Very small preterm infants are more likely than their larger counterparts to have developmental problems. Also, preterm infants who grow up in conditions of poverty are more likely to have developmental problems than are those who live in middle-class surroundings. Indeed, many larger preterm infants from middle-class families do not have developmental problems. Nonetheless, more preterm infants than full-term babies have learning disorders (Kopp, 1994).

Researchers are continuing to unveil new ideas for improving the lives of preterm infants. One increasingly used technique is to regularly massage and gently exercise preterm infants; this technique is described in Explorations in Psychology 1.

Children's Physical Development

At no other time in a person's life will there be so many changes occurring so fast as during the first few years. During infancy, we change from virtually immobile, helpless beings to insatiably curious, talking creatures who toddle as fast as our legs can carry us.

Infancy

The newborn is not an empty-headed organism. It comes into the world already equipped with several genetically "wired" reflexes. For example, the newborn has no fear of water, naturally holding its breath and contracting its throat

Explorations in Psychology 1

The Power of Touch and Massage in Development

There has been great interest recently in the roles of touch and massage in improving the growth, health, and well-being of infants and children. This interest has especially been stimulated by a number of research investigations by Tiffany Field (1995), director of the Touch Research Institute at the University of Miami School of Medicine. In one study, 40 preterm infants who had just been released from an intensive care unit and placed in a transitional nursery were studied (Field, Scafidi, & Schanberg, 1987). Twenty of the preterm babies were given special stimulation with massage and exercise for three 15-minute periods at the beginning of 3 consecutive hours every morning for 10 weekdays. For example, each infant was placed on its stomach and gently stroked. The massage began with the head and neck and moved downward to the feet. It also moved from the shoulders down to the hands. The infant was then rolled over. Each arm and leg was flexed and extended; then both legs were flexed and extended. Next, the massage was repeated.

The massaged and exercised preterm babies gained 47 percent more weight than their preterm counterparts who were not massaged and exercised, even though both groups had the same number of feedings per day and averaged the same intake of formula. The increased activity of the massaged, exercised infants would seem to work against weight gain. However, similar findings have been discovered with animals. The increased activity may increase gastrointestinal and metabolic efficiency. The massaged infants were more active and alert, and they performed better on developmental tests. Also, their hospital stays were about 6 days shorter than those of the nonmassaged, nonexercised group, which saved about $3,000 per preterm infant. Field has recently replicated these findings with preterm infants in another study.

In another study, Field (1992) gave the same kind of massage (firm stroking with the palms of the hands) to preterm infants who had been exposed to cocaine in utero. The infants also showed significant weight gain and improved scores on developmental tests. Currently, Field is using massage therapy with HIV-exposed preterm infants with the hope that their immune system functioning will be improved. Others she has targeted include infants of depressed mothers, infants with colic, infants and children with sleep problems, as well as children who have diabetes, asthma, and juvenile arthritis.

Field also reports that touch has been helpful with children and adolescents who have touch aversions, such as children who have been sexually abused, autistic children, and adolescents with eating disorders. Field also is studying the amount of touch a child normally receives during school activities. She hopes that positive forms of touch will return to school systems, where touching has been outlawed because of potential sexual-abuse lawsuits.

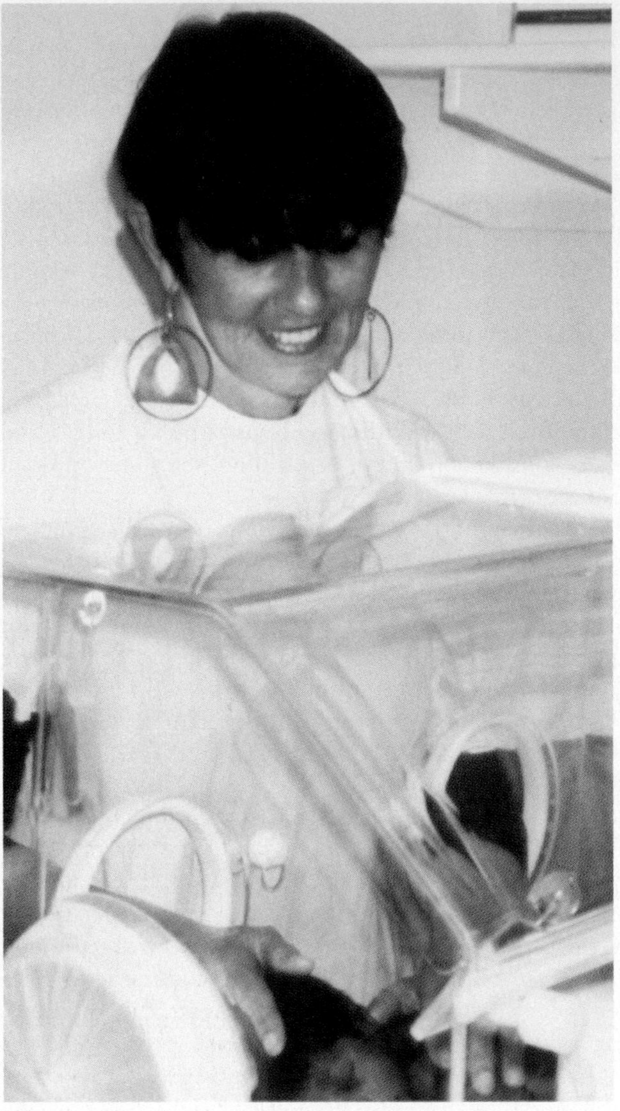

Shown here is Dr. Tiffany Field massaging a newborn infant. Dr. Field's research has clearly demonstrated the power of massage in improving the developmental outcome of at-risk infants. Under her direction the Touch Research Institute in Miami, Florida, was recently developed to investigate the role of touch in a number of domains of health and well-being.

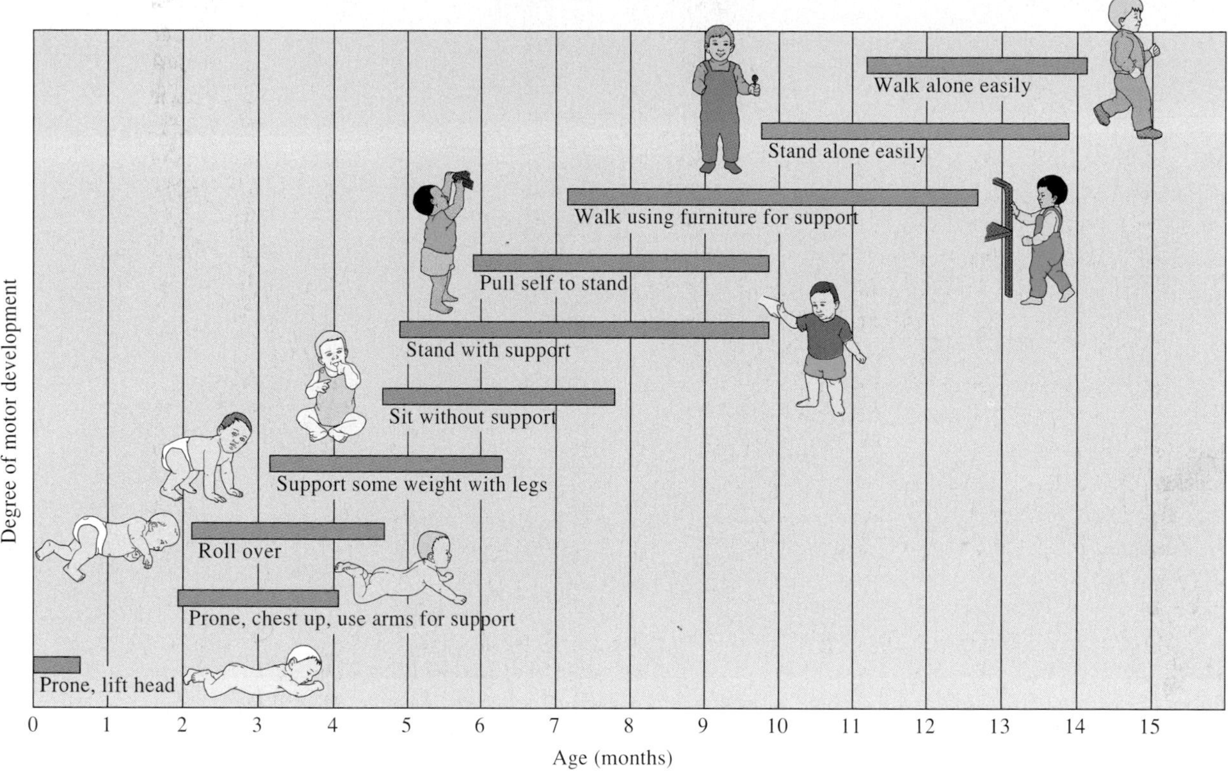

FIGURE 5

Developmental Accomplishments in Gross Motor Skills During the First 15 Months

to keep water out. Some of the reflexes we possess as newborns persist throughout our lives—coughing, blinking, and yawning, for example. Others disappear in the months following birth as higher brain functions mature and we develop voluntary control over many behaviors. One of the most dramatic reflexes of the newborn is the Moro reflex. When a newborn is roughly handled, hears a loud noise, sees a bright light, or feels a sudden change of position, it becomes startled, arches its back, and throws back its head. At the same time, the newborn flings its arms and legs out and then rapidly closes them to the center of the body as if falling. The Moro reflex disappears by 3 to 4 months of age.

The infant's physical development in the first 2 years of life is dramatic. At birth, the newborn (neonate) has a gigantic head (relative to the rest of the body) that flops around uncontrollably. In the span of 12 months, the infant becomes capable of sitting anywhere, standing, stooping, climbing, and often walking. During the second year, growth decelerates, but rapid increases in such activities as running and climbing take place. Figure 5 shows the average ages at which infants accomplish various motor milestones.

As an infant walks, talks, runs, shakes a rattle, smiles, and frowns, changes in its brain are occurring. Consider that the infant began life as a single cell and 9 months later was born with a brain and nervous system that contained approximately 100 billion nerve cells. Indeed, at birth the infant has virtually all of the nerve cells (neurons) it is going to have in its entire life. However, at birth and in early infancy, the connectedness of these neurons is impoverished. As the infant ages from birth to 2 years, the interconnection of neurons increases dramatically as the dendrites (the receiving parts) of the neurons branch out.

Childhood

By their third birthday, children are full of new tricks such as climbing, skipping, and jumping. They are beginning to be able to make their body do what they want it to do, giving them a greater sense of self-control.

Catching, throwing, kicking, balancing, rolling, cutting, stacking, snapping, pushing, dancing, and swimming—preschool children perform these special feats and many, many more. As the poet Dylan Thomas put it, "All the sun long they were running." The growth rate slows down in early childhood. Otherwise, we would be a species of giants. The growth and development of the brain underlie the young child's improvement in motor skills, reflected in activities such as the ability to hold a pencil and make increasingly efficient marks with it. A child's brain is closer to full growth than the rest of its body, attaining 75 percent of its adult weight by the age of 3 and 90 percent by age 5.

In middle and late childhood, motor development is much smoother and more coordinated than in early childhood. While a preschool child can zip, cut, latch, and dance, an elementary school child can zip, cut, latch, and dance

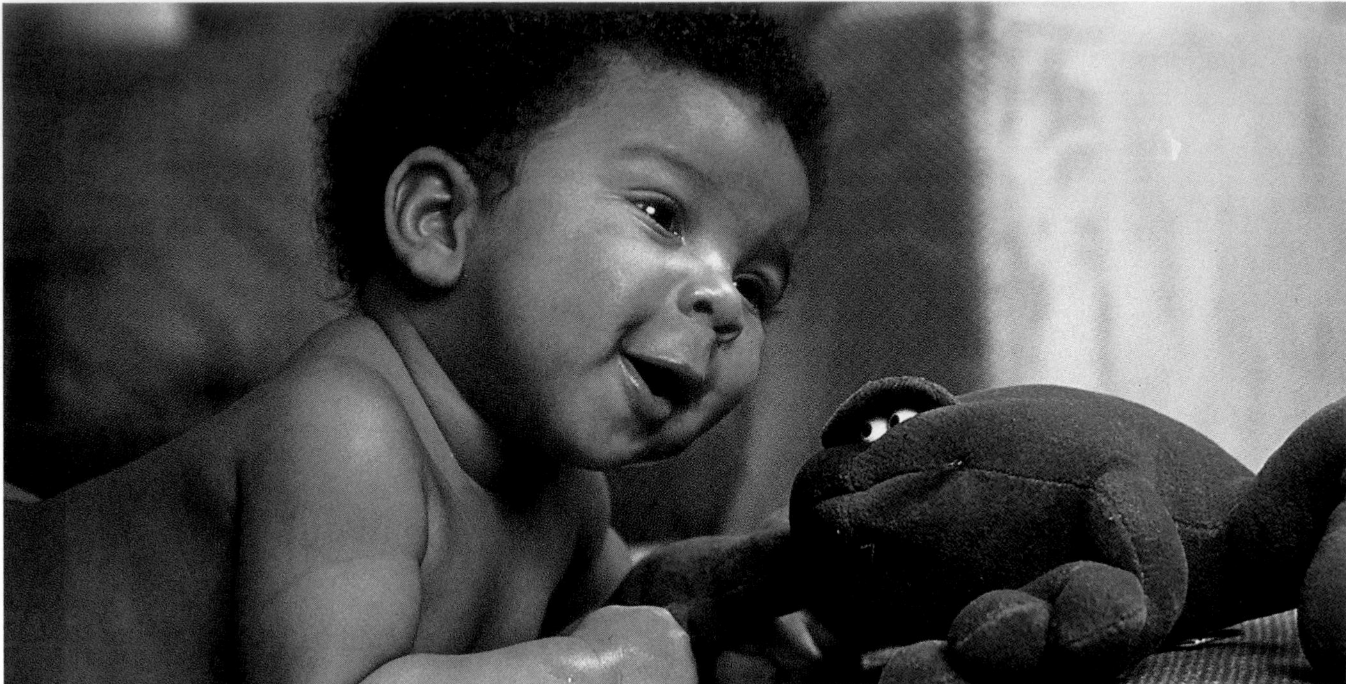

According to Piaget, infants are in the sensorimotor stage of cognitive development. What does that mean?

more efficiently and with more flair. Physical activities are essential for children to refine their developing skills. Child development experts believe children should be *active,* rather than passive, and should be able to plan and select many of their own activities. An ideal elementary school, for example, would include a gym and a safe, elaborate outdoor play area where students can participate in a variety of games and sports; a classroom with a fully equipped publishing center, complete with materials for writing, typing, illustrating, and binding student-made books; and a science area with animals and plants for observation and books to study. Children also need to "just" play. Education experts recognize that spontaneous play provides additional opportunities for children to learn. Schools that offer children many opportunities to engage in a wide range of self-initiated activities, such as the ideal school we just described, considerably enhance their students' physical development.

At this point, we have discussed a number of ideas about what development is, the prenatal period and birth, and children's physical development. In the school atmosphere just described, in which children's education involves many opportunities for physical and self-initiated activities, not only is physical development enhanced, so is cognitive development, the topic to which we now turn.

Children's Cognitive Development

Jean Piaget, the famous Swiss developmental psychologist, was a meticulous observer of his three children—Laurent, Lucienne, and Jacqueline (Piaget, 1952). At 21 days of age, Laurent finds his thumb after three attempts; once he finds his thumb, he sucks it for several minutes. But when he is placed on his back, he does not know how to coordinate the movement of his arms with that of his mouth; his hands draw back even when his lips seek them.

Toward the end of her fourth month, Lucienne is lying in her crib. Piaget hangs a doll over her feet. Lucienne thrusts her feet at the doll and makes it move. Afterward she looks at it, then kicks at it again. She has no visual control of her foot because her movements are the same whether she only looks at the doll or whether it is placed over her head.

At 1 year, 2 months, Jacqueline holds an object in her hands that is new to her: a round, flat box that she turns over and shakes; then she rubs it against her crib. She lets it go and tries to pick it up. She only succeeds in touching it with her index finger, being unable to fully reach and grasp it. She makes the box tilt up but it falls over again. Jacqueline shows an interest in this result and studies the fallen box.

For Piaget, such observations reflect the infant's cognitive development. Let's further explore the nature of Piaget's theory.

Piaget's Theory

Piaget (1896–1980) stressed that children do not just passively receive information from their environment, they actively construct their own cognitive world. Two processes underlie a child's mental construction of the world—organization and adaptation. To make sense of our world, we organize our experiences. For example, we separate important ideas from less important ones. We connect one idea to another. But not only do we organize our observations and experiences, we also *adapt* our thinking to include those new ideas. Piaget (1960) believed we adapt in two ways: assimilation and accommodation.

Jean Piaget, the famous Swiss developmental psychologist, changed the way we think about the development of a child's mind. For Piaget, a child's mental development is a continuous creation of increasingly complex forms.

Assimilation *is the incorporation of new information into one's existing knowledge.* **Accommodation** *is an individual's adjustment to new information.* Imagine that a 5-year-old girl is given a hammer and some nails, and asked to hang a picture on the wall. She has never used a hammer, but from experience and observation she realizes that a hammer is an object to be held, that to hit the nail she must swing the hammer by the handle, and that she probably will need to swing it a number of times. Recognizing each of these things, she fits her behavior into information she already has (assimilation). However, the hammer is heavy, so she holds it near the top. She swings too hard and the nail bends, so she adjusts the pressure of her strikes. These adjustments reveal her ability to alter slightly her conception of the world (accommodation).

Piaget thought that even young infants are capable of assimilation and accommodation. Newborns reflexively suck everything that touches their lips (assimilation), but after several months they come to a new understanding of their world. Some objects, such as fingers and the mother's breast, can be sucked, and others, such as fuzzy blankets, should not be (accommodation).

Piaget also believed that we go through four stages in understanding the world. Each of the stages is age related and consists of distinct ways of thinking. Remember, it is the *different* way of understanding the world that makes one stage more advanced than another; knowing *more* information does not make the child's thinking more advanced, in Piaget's view. This is what Piaget meant when he said that the child's cognition is *qualitatively* different in one stage compared to another. Let's turn now to Piaget's first three stages: sensorimotor thought, preoperational thought, and concrete operational thought.

Sensorimotor Thought

Sensorimotor thought *is the first Piagetian stage of development, lasting from birth to about 2 years of age, corresponding to the period of infancy. In this stage, the infant constructs an understanding of the world by coordinating sensory experiences (such as seeing and hearing) with physical (motor) actions—hence the term* sensorimotor. At the beginning of this stage, the newborn engages with its environment with little more than reflexive patterns; at the end of the stage, the 2-year-old has complex sensorimotor patterns and is beginning to use primitive symbols in thinking.

We live in a world of objects. Imagine yourself as a 5-month-old infant and how you might experience the world. You are in a playpen filled with toys. One of the toys, a monkey, falls out of your grasp and rolls behind a larger toy, a hippopotamus. Would you know the monkey is behind the hippopotamus, or would you think it is completely gone? Piaget believed that "out of sight" literally was "out of mind" for young infants; at 5 months of age, then, you would not have reached for the monkey when it fell behind the hippopotamus. By 8 months of age, though, the infant begins to understand that out of sight is not out of mind; at this point, you probably would have reached behind the hippopotamus to search for the monkey, coordinating your senses with your movements.

Object permanence *is Piaget's term for one of the infant's most important accomplishments: understanding that objects and events continue to exist even when they cannot directly be seen, heard, or touched.* The most common way to study object permanence is to show an infant an interesting toy and then cover the toy with a sheet or a blanket. If infants understand that the toy still exists, they try to uncover it (see figure 6). Object permanence continues to develop throughout the sensorimotor period. For example, when infants initially understand that objects exist even when out of sight, they look for them only briefly. By the end of the sensorimotor period, infants engage in a more prolonged and sophisticated search for an object.

Object permanence is also important in the infant's social world. Infants develop a sense that people are permanent, just as they come to understand that toys are permanent. Five-month-old infants do not sense that

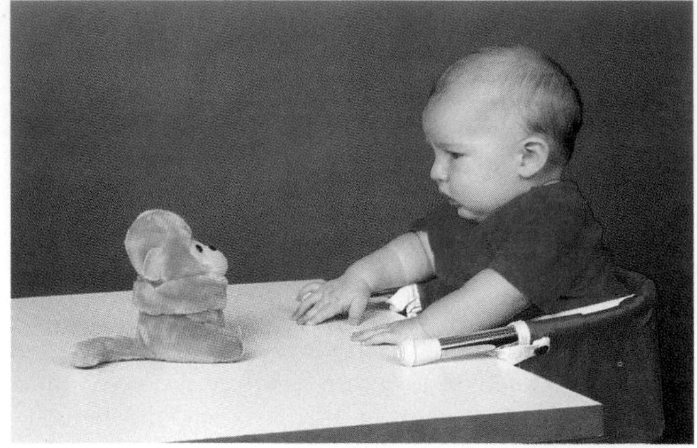

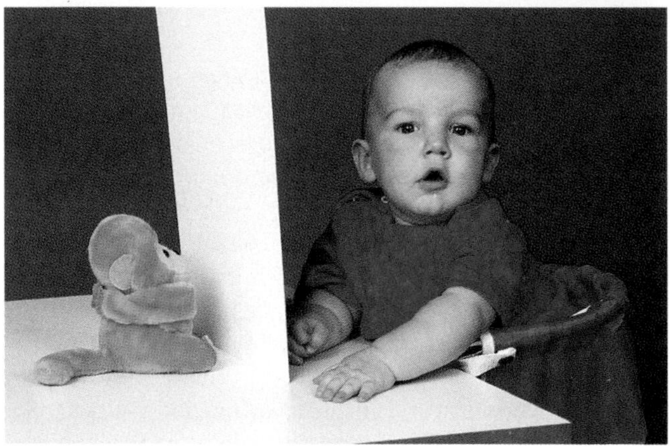

FIGURE 6

Object Permanence
Piaget thought that object permanence was one of infancy's landmark cognitive accomplishments. For this 5-month-old boy, "out of sight" is literally out of mind. The infant looks at the toy monkey (*top*), but when his view of the toy is blocked (*bottom*), he does not search for it. Eventually, he will search for the hidden toy monkey, reflecting the presence of object permanence.

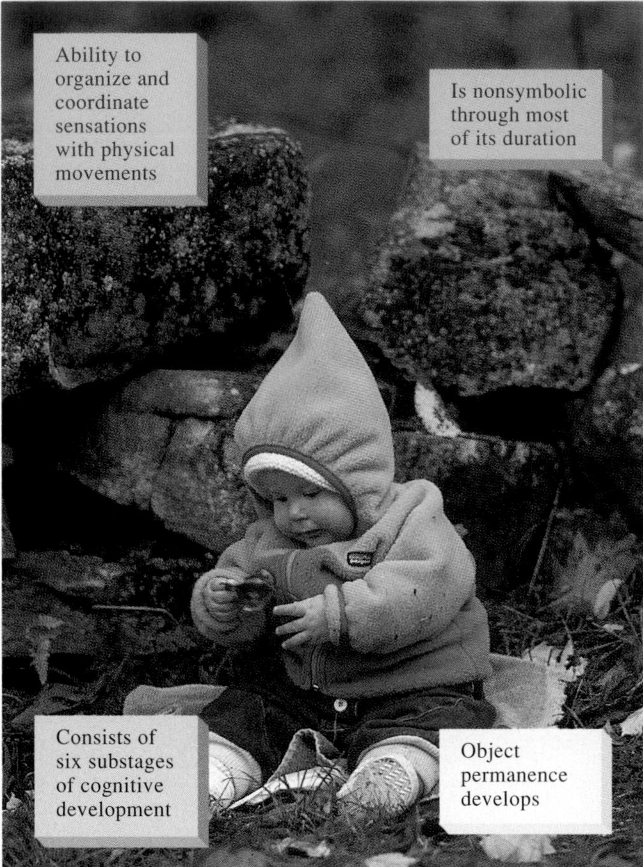
Ability to organize and coordinate sensations with physical movements
Is nonsymbolic through most of its duration
Consists of six substages of cognitive development
Object permanence develops

FIGURE 7

The Main Characteristics of Sensorimotor Thought, According to Piaget

caregivers exist beyond moment-to-moment encounters, but by 8 months of age they do. Infants' cognitive accomplishments, then, tell us not only how infants understand a world of blocks, toys, and playpens, but also how they construct a world of relationships with people. A summary of the main characteristics of sensorimotor thought is presented in figure 7.

In the past decade, a new understanding of infants' cognitive development has been occurring. To read about the "new look" in infant cognition, turn to Explorations in Psychology 2.

Preoperational and Concrete Operational Thought

Possibly because young children are not very concerned about reality, their drawings are fanciful and inventive. Suns are blue, skies are yellow, and cars float on clouds in their symbolic, imaginative world. One 3½-year-old child looked at the scribble he had just drawn and described it as a pelican kissing a seal (see figure 8*a*). The symbolism is simple but strong, like the abstractions found in some modern art. As Picasso once commented, "I used to draw like Raphael but it has taken me a lifetime to draw like young children." In the elementary school years, the child's drawings become more realistic, neat, and precise (see figure 8*b*). Suns are yellow, skies are blue, and cars travel on roads.

Preschool children begin to represent their world with words, images, and drawings. Symbolic thoughts go beyond simple connections of sensorimotor information and physical action. While preschool children can symbolically represent the world, they still cannot perform operations. **Operations,** *in Piaget's theory, are mental representations that are reversible.* Preschool children have difficulty understanding that reversing an action brings about the original conditions from which the action began. This sounds rather complicated, but stay with us. The following two examples will help you to understand Piaget's concept of reversibility. The preschool child may know that 4 + 2 = 6 but not understand that the reverse, 6 − 2 = 4, is true. Or let's say a preschooler walks to his friend's house each day but always gets a ride home. If you asked him to walk home one day he would probably reply that he didn't know the way since he

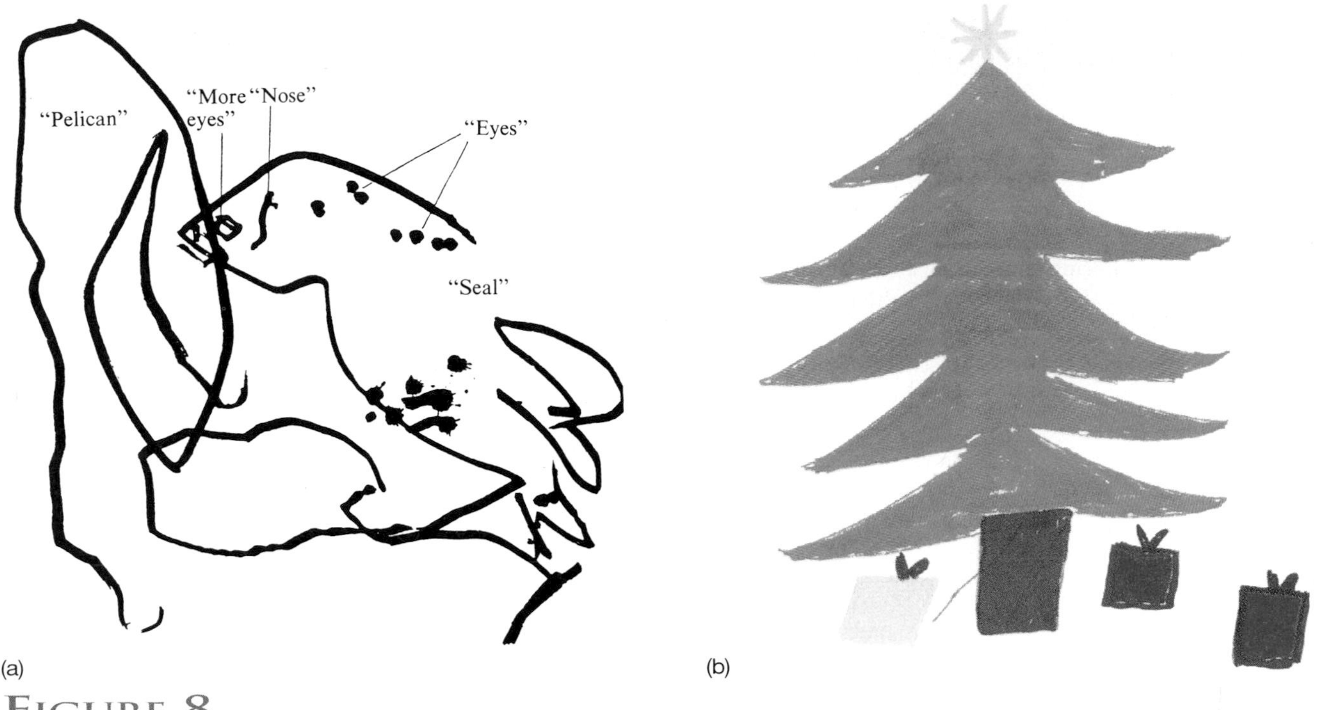

FIGURE 8

Developmental Changes in Artistic Drawings
(*a*) A 3½-year-old's symbolic drawing. Halfway into this drawing, the 3½-year-old artist said it was "a pelican kissing a seal." (*b*) An 11-year-old's drawing. An 11-year-old's drawing is neater and more realistic but also less inventive.

had never walked home before. **Preoperational thought** *is the term Piaget gave to the 2- to 7-year-old child's understanding of the world. Children at this stage of reasoning cannot understand such logical operations as the reversibility of mental representations.*

A well-known test of whether a child can think "operationally" is to present a child with two identical beakers, A and B, filled with liquid to the same height (see figure 9). Next to them is a third beaker, C. Beaker C is tall and thin, while beakers A and B are wide and short. The liquid is poured from B into C, and the child is asked whether the amounts in A and C are the same. The 4-year-old child invariably says that the amount of liquid in the tall, thin beaker (C) is greater than that in the short, fat beaker (A).

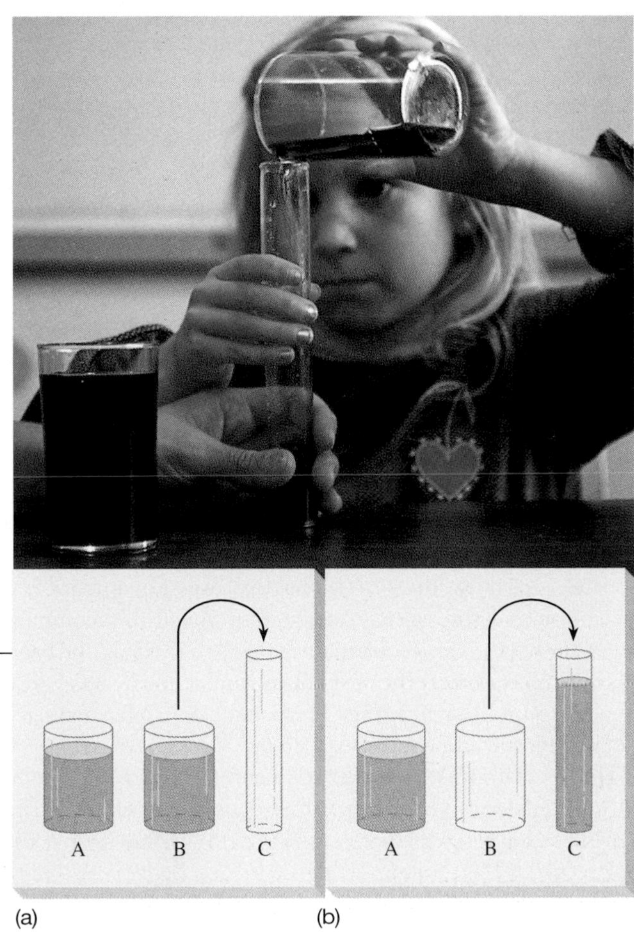

FIGURE 9

Piaget's Conservation Task
The beaker test is a well-known Piagetian test to determine whether a child can think operationally—that is, can mentally reverse actions and show conservation of the substance. (*a*) Two identical beakers are presented to the child. Then, the experimenter pours the liquid from B into C, which is taller and thinner than A or B. (*b*) The child is asked if these beakers (A and C) have the same amount of liquid. The preoperational child says no. When asked to point to the beaker that has more liquid, the preoperational child points to the tall, thin beaker.

EXPLORATIONS IN PSYCHOLOGY 2

The "New Look" in Infant Cognition

For many years, Piaget's ideas were so widely known and respected that, to many psychologists, one aspect of development seemed certain: Human infants go through a long, protracted period during which they cannot think (Mandler, 1990). They can learn to recognize things and smile at them, to crawl, and to manipulate objects, but they do not yet have concepts and ideas. Piaget believed that only near the end of the sensorimotor stage of development, at about 1½ to 2 years of age, do infants learn how to represent the world in a symbolic, conceptual manner.

Piaget constructed his view of infancy mainly by observing the development of his own three children. Very few laboratory techniques were available at the time. Recently, however, sophisticated experimental techniques have been devised to study infants, and a large number of research studies on infant cognitive development have accumulated. Much of the new research suggests that Piaget's theory of sensorimotor development will have to be modified substantially.

Piaget's theory of sensorimotor development has been attacked from two sources. First, extensive research in the area of infant perceptual development suggests that a stable and differentiated perceptual world is established much earlier in infancy than Piaget envisioned. Second, researchers recently have found that memory and other forms of symbolic activity occur by at least the second half of the first year. Let's now look in greater detail at research strategies for studying infants' memories.

Popular child-rearing expert Penelope Leach (1990) tells parents that 6- to 8-month-old babies cannot hold in their mind a picture of their mother or father. And historically, psychologists have believed that infants cannot store memories until they have the language skills required to form them and retrieve them. Recently, though, child development experts have developed ingenious strategies that reveal that infants as young as 3 months of age have memory skills (Grunwald & others, 1993).

In one study, infants were placed in large black boxes where they looked up at television screens, viewing a sequence of colorful objects that appeared repeatedly (Canfield & Haith, 1991). The babies' eye movements were monitored with an infrared camera linked to a computer. After having viewed the sequence only five times, the babies anticipated where the next object would appear. With just a little more practice, they predicted a four-step sequence, and most could remember it up to 2 weeks later!

In another type of experiment, Carolyn Rovee-Collier (1987) placed a baby in a crib underneath an elaborate mobile, tied one of the baby's ankles to the mobile with a satin ribbon, then observed as the baby kicked and made the mobile move. Weeks later, when the baby's feet were left untied and the mobile was returned to the crib, the baby would kick again, apparently remembering when earlier kicking had made the mobile move (see figure A). However, if the mobile's makeup was changed even slightly, the baby did not kick at it. As soon as the familiar and expected were brought back into the context, the baby began kicking again.

Nancy Myers and her colleagues (1987) found that an infant's experiences at 6 months of age can be remembered by the infants 2 years later. They placed 6-month-old babies (the experimental group) in a dark room with objects that made different sounds. Using infrared cameras, they observed how and when the infants reached for objects. Two years later, the same children were brought back into the laboratory, along with a control group of 16 other 2½-year-old children (Perris & others, 1990). The experimental-group children revealed the same behavior they had shown at 6 months of age, reaching for the objects and displaying no fear, but fewer control-group children reached for the objects, and many of them cried. The experiment demonstrates that young children can remember experiences that occurred up to 2 years earlier when they are placed in the same context as the earlier experiences occurred in.

In sum, the capacity for memory appears much earlier in infancy than was once believed, and it is also more precise than earlier conclusions suggested. Figure A shows some of the techniques researchers are using to unveil the nature of infants' perceptual and cognitive development.

FIGURE A

Research on Infant Cognition
(*a*) A 4-month-old in Elizabeth Spelke's infant perception laboratory is tested to determine if it knows that an object in motion will not stop in midair. Spelke believes that the young infant's knowledge about how the perceptual world works is innate. (*b*) In Rovee-Collier's investigation of infant memory, the mobile is connected to the infant's ankle by the ribbon and moves in direct proportion to the frequency and vigor of the infant's kick. This infant is in a reinforcement period. During this period the infant can see the mobile, but because the ribbon is attached to a different stand, she cannot make the mobile move. Baseline activity is assessed during a nonreinforcement period prior to training, and all retention tests are also conducted during periods of nonreinforcement. As can be seen, this infant has already learned and is attempting to make the mobile move by kicking her leg with the ribbon attachments. (*c*) Researchers use a variety of ingenious techniques to study the infant's cognitive development. In researcher Mark Johnson's laboratory, at Carnegie Mellon University, babies have shown an ability to organize their world and to anticipate future events by learning and remembering sequences of colorful images on TV monitors.

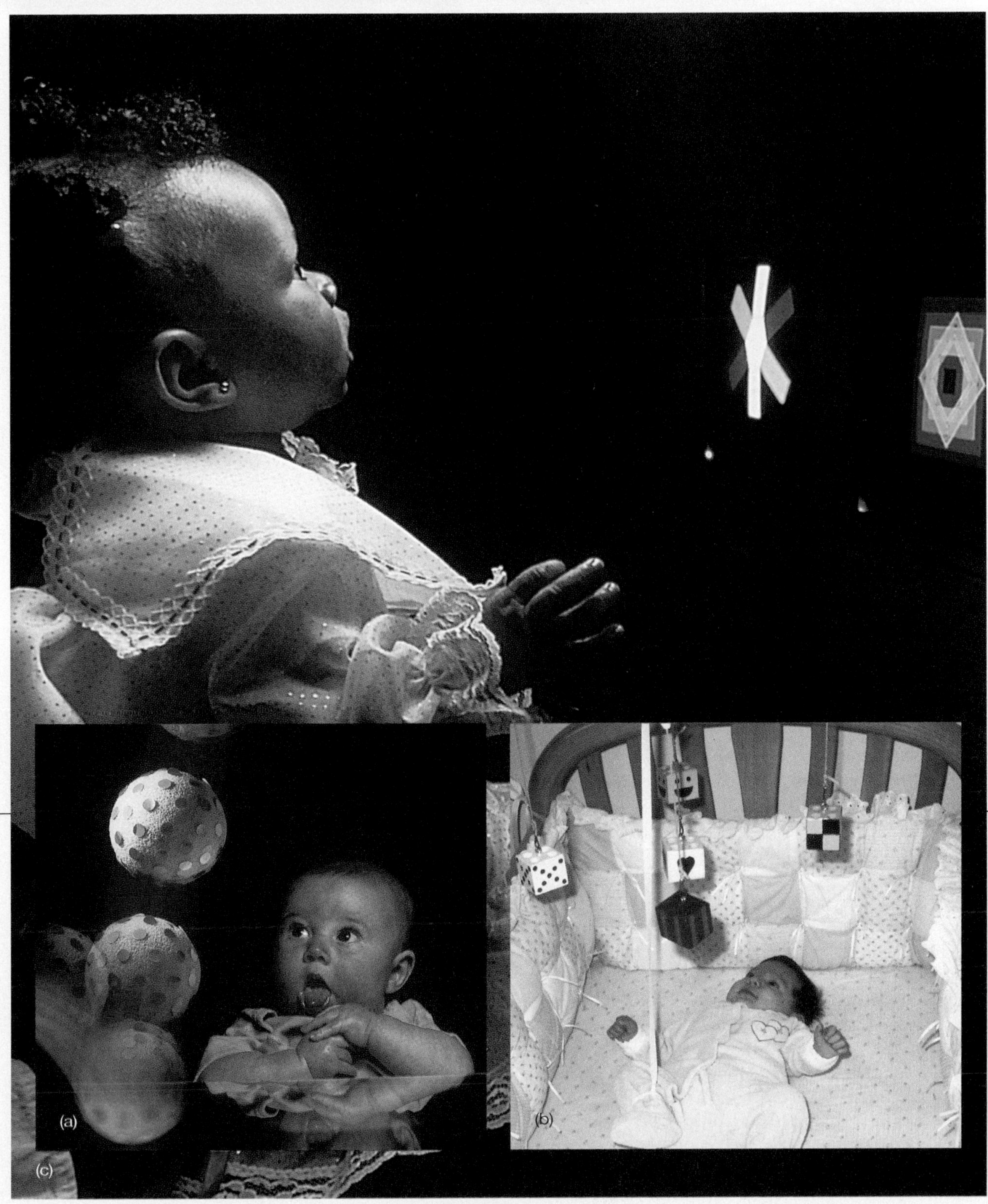
(a)
(b)
(c)

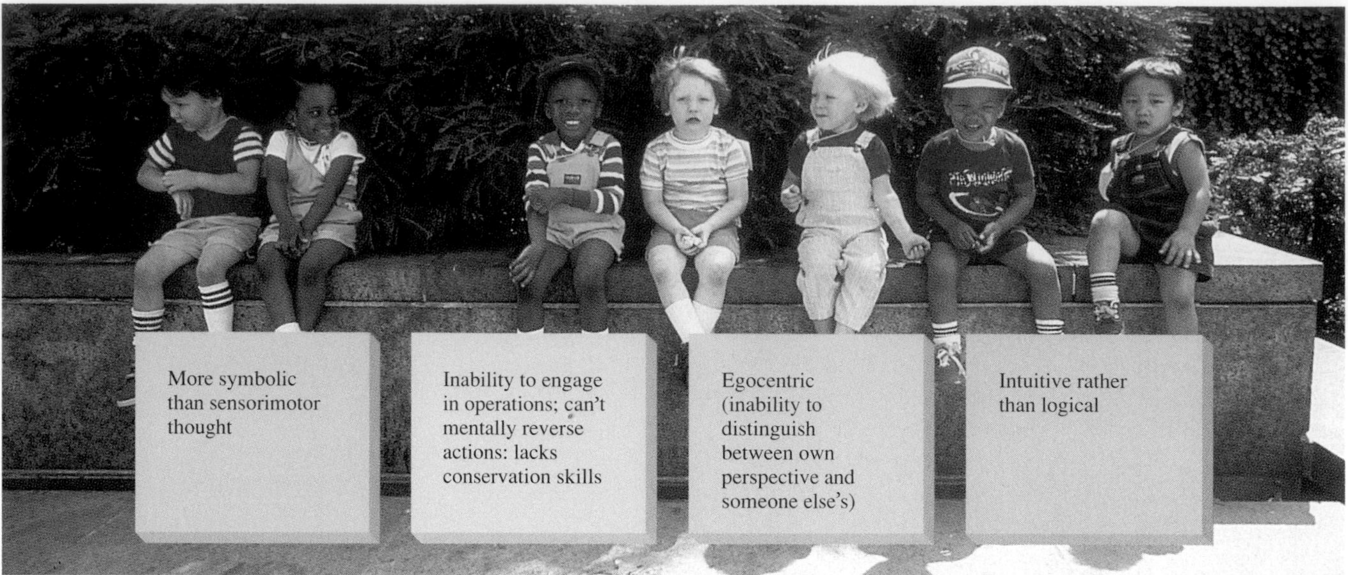

More symbolic than sensorimotor thought
Inability to engage in operations; can't mentally reverse actions: lacks conservation skills
Egocentric (inability to distinguish between own perspective and someone else's)
Intuitive rather than logical

FIGURE 10

Characteristics of Preoperational Thought

The 8-year-old child consistently says the amounts are the same. The 4-year-old child, a preoperational thinker, cannot mentally reverse the pouring action; that is, she cannot imagine the liquid going back from container C to container B. Piaget said that children such as this 4-year-old girl have not grasped the concept of **conservation,** *a belief in the permanence of certain attributes of objects or situations in spite of superficial changes.*

The child's thought in the preoperational stage also is egocentric. By **egocentrism,** *Piaget meant the inability to distinguish between one's own perspective and someone else's perspective.* The following telephone conversation between 4-year-old Mary, who is at home, and her father, who is at work, typifies Mary's egocentric thought:

Father: Mary, is mommy there?
Mary: (silently nods)
Father: Mary, may I speak to mommy?
Mary: (nods again silently)

Piaget also called preoperational thought *intuitive,* because when he asked children why they knew something, they often did not give logical answers, but offered personal insights or guesses instead. Yet, as Piaget observed, young children seem so sure that they know something, even though they do not use logical reasoning to arrive at the answer. Young children also have an insatiable desire to know their world, and they ask a lot of questions:

"Why does a lady have to be married to have a baby?"
"Who was the mother when everybody was the baby?"

"Why do leaves fall?"
"Why does the sun shine?"

"Mrs. Hammond! I'd know you anywhere from little Billy's portrait of you."

At this point we have discussed four main characteristics of preoperational thought. A summary of these is presented in figure 10.

Concrete operational thought *is the term Piaget gave to the 7- to 11-year-old child's understanding of the world. At this stage of thought children can use operations. Logical reasoning replaces intuitive thought as long as the principles are applied to concrete examples.* For instance, the concrete operational thinker cannot imagine the steps necessary to complete an algebraic equation, which is too abstract at this stage of children's development.

Earlier we described a beaker task that was too difficult for a child who had not yet reached the stage of operational thought. Another well-known task to demonstrate

Piaget's concrete operational thought involves two equal amounts of clay. The experimenter shows the child two identical balls of clay and then rolls one ball into a long, thin shape. The other is retained in its original ball shape. The child is then asked if there is more clay in the ball or in the long, thin piece of clay. By the time children reach 7 to 8 years of age, most answer that the amount of clay is the same. To solve this problem correctly, children have to imagine that the clay ball is rolled out into a long, thin strip and then returned to its original round shape—imagination that involves a reversible mental action. Concrete operations allow the child to coordinate several characteristics rather than focusing on a single property of an object. In the clay example, the preoperational child is likely to focus on height *or* width. The child who has reached the stage of concrete operational thought coordinates information about both dimensions.

Many of the concrete operations identified by Piaget focus on the way children think about the properties of objects. One important skill at this stage of reasoning is the ability to classify or divide things into different sets or subsets and to consider their interrelations. One way to see if a child possesses this ability is to see if he or she can understand a family tree of four generations (see figure 11) (Furth & Wachs, 1975). This family tree suggests that the grandfather (A) has three sons (B, C, and D), each of whom has two sons (E through J), and that one of these sons (J) has three sons (K, L, and M). A child who comprehends the classification system can move up and down a level (vertically), across a level (horizontally), and up and down and across a level (obliquely) within the system. The child who grasps concrete operational thought understands that person J can at the same time be father, brother, and grandson, for example. A preoperational child cannot perform this classification and says that a father cannot fulfill these other roles.

We have discussed four main characteristics of concrete operational thought. A summary of these characteristics is presented in figure 12.

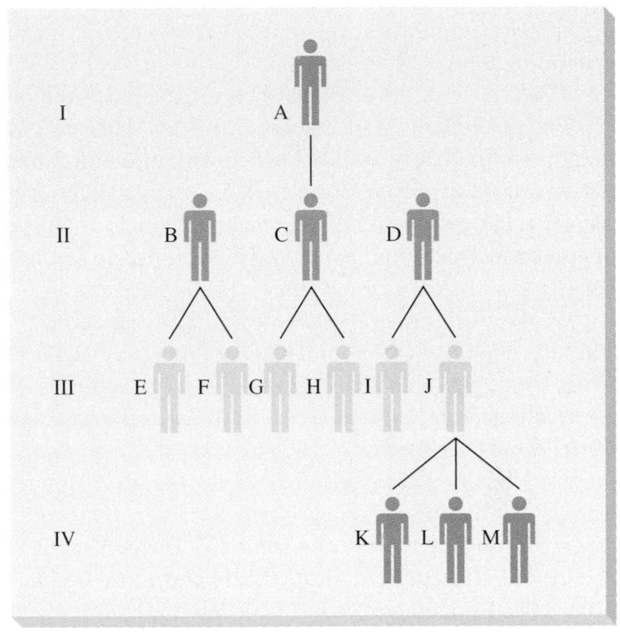

FIGURE 11

Classification: An Important Ability in Concrete Operational Thought

A family tree of four generations (I to IV): The preoperational child has trouble classifying the members of the four generations; the concrete operational child can classify the members vertically, horizontally, and obliquely (up and down and across).

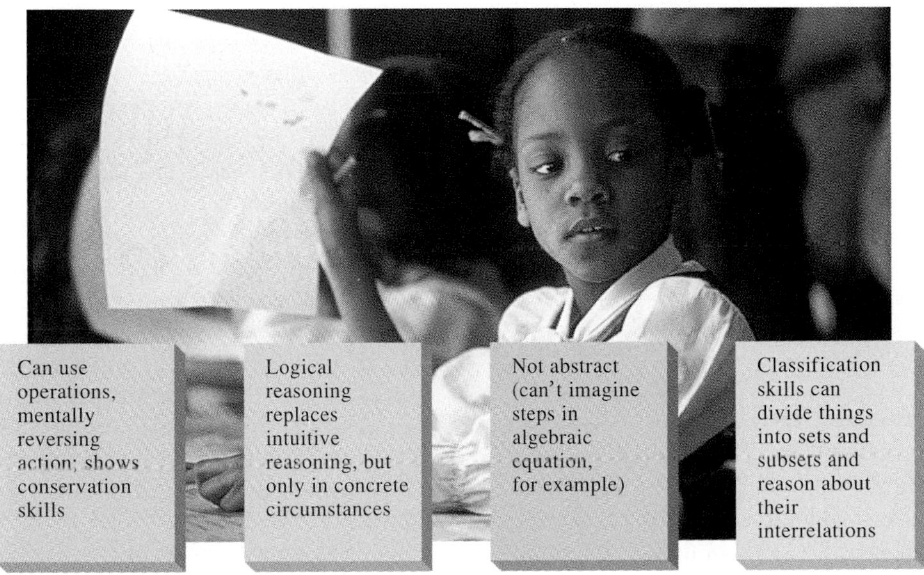

Can use operations, mentally reversing action; shows conservation skills
Logical reasoning replaces intuitive reasoning, but only in concrete circumstances
Not abstract (can't imagine steps in algebraic equation, for example)
Classification skills can divide things into sets and subsets and reason about their interrelations

FIGURE 12

Characteristics of Concrete Operational Thought

Evaluating Piaget

Piaget was a genius at observing children, and his insights are often surprisingly easy to verify. Piaget showed us some important things to look for in cognitive development, such as object permanence in infancy, egocentrism in early childhood, and operational thought in middle and late childhood. He also told us how we must make experiences fit our cognitive framework, yet simultaneously adapt our understanding to new experiences.

Piaget's views, however, have been criticized and modified. Piaget conceived of stages as unitary structures of thought, so his theory assumes synchrony in development. That is, various aspects of a stage would emerge at about the same time. However, several concrete operational concepts do not appear in synchrony. For example, children do not learn to conserve at the same time as they learn to cross-classify.

Most contemporary developmentalists agree that children's cognitive development is not as grand-stage-like as Piaget thought. **Neo-Piagetians** *are developmentalists who have elaborated on Piaget's theory, believing children's cognitive development is more specific in many respects than he thought.* Neo-Piagetians don't believe that all of Piaget's ideas should be junked. They argue, however, that a more accurate vision of the child's cognitive development involves fewer references to grand stages and more emphasis on the roles of strategies, skills, how fast and automatically children can process information, the task-specific nature of children's cognition, and the importance of dividing cognitive problems into smaller, more precise steps (Gelman & Au, 1996; Gouin–Decarie, 1996).

Neo-Piagetians still believe that children's cognitive development contains some general properties (Flavell, 1992). They stress that there is a regular, maturation-based increase with age in some aspects of the child's information-processing capacity, such as how fast or efficiently the child processes information. As the child's information-processing capacity increases with increasing age, new and more complex forms of cognition in all content domains are possible because the child can now hold more information in mind and think about more things at once. For example, Canadian developmentalist Robbie Case (1985) argues that adolescents have increasingly more available cognitive resources than they did as children because they can process information more automatically, they have more information-processing capacity, and they are more familiar with a range of content knowledge.

Children's Socioemotional Development

As children grow and develop, they are socialized by and socialize others—parents, siblings, peers, and teachers, for example. Their small world widens as they discover new refuges and new challenges. To begin, we will examine Erik Erikson's masterpiece on how we develop socially.

Erikson's Theory of Socioemotional Development

Erik Erikson (1902–1994) spent his childhood and adolescence in Europe. After working as a psychoanalyst under Freud's direction, Erikson came to the United States in 1933. He became a United States citizen and taught at Harvard University.

Erikson recognized Freud's contributions to our understanding of human development, but he broke rank with some of Freud's basic tenets. In contrast to Freud's psychosexual stages, for instance, Erikson (1950, 1968) argues that we develop in *psychosocial stages.* In addition, Freud believed that our basic personality is shaped in the first 5 years of life, but Erikson emphasizes developmental change throughout the life span. In Erikson's view, everyone must pass through eight stages of development on the way to maturity and wisdom. The first four of these stages occur in childhood (see figure 13), the last four in adolescence and adulthood (these last four stages are discussed later in this chapter). Each stage is precipitated by a "crisis" that requires a person to grapple with a unique developmental task. For Erikson, this crisis is not a catastrophe, but a turning point of increased vulnerability or enhanced potential. The more successfully a person resolves the crises, the more complete a human being he or she will become.

Trust versus mistrust, *which occurs during the baby's first year, is Erikson's first psychosocial stage. Trust is built when an infant's basic needs—such as comfort, food, and warmth—are met.* Trust in infancy sets the stage of a lifelong expectation that the world will be a good and pleasant place to live.

Erikson's second stage of development, **autonomy versus shame and doubt,** *occurs around the age of 2. After developing trust, infants begin to discover that their behavior is their own. They start to assert their sense of independence or autonomy; they realize their will.* If infants are overly restrained or punished too harshly, they are likely to develop a sense of shame and doubt.

Initiative versus guilt, *Erikson's third stage of development, occurs during the preschool years. As preschool children encounter a widening social world, they are challenged more than they were as infants. Active, purposeful behavior is needed to cope with these challenges. Children are asked to assume responsibility for their bodies, their behavior, their toys, and their pets.* Developing a sense of responsibility increases initiative. Uncomfortable guilt feelings may arise, though, if the child is irresponsible and is made to feel too anxious. Erikson has a positive outlook on this stage. He believes most guilt is quickly compensated for by a sense of accomplishment.

Sometime during the elementary school years children go through Erikson's fourth developmental stage, **industry versus inferiority.** *Children's initiative brings*

Erikson's stages	Developmental period	Characteristics
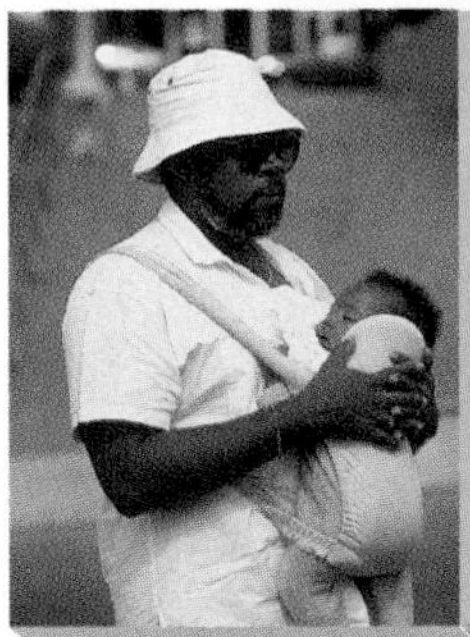 Trust versus mistrust	Infancy (first year)	A sense of trust requires a feeling of physical comfort and a minimal amount of fear about the future. Infants basic needs are met by responsive, sensitive caregivers.
 Autonomy versus shame and doubt	Infancy (second year)	After gaining trust in caregivers, infants start to discover that they have a will of their own. They assert their sense of autonomy, or independence. They realize their will. If infants are restrained too much or punished too harshly, they are likely to develop a sense of shame and doubt.
 Initiative versus guilt	Early childhood (preschool years, ages 3–5)	As preschool children encounter a widening social world, they are challenged more and need to develop more purposeful behavior to cope with these challenges. Children are now asked to assume more responsibility. Uncomfortable guilt feelings may arise, though, if the children are irresponsible and are made to feel too anxious.
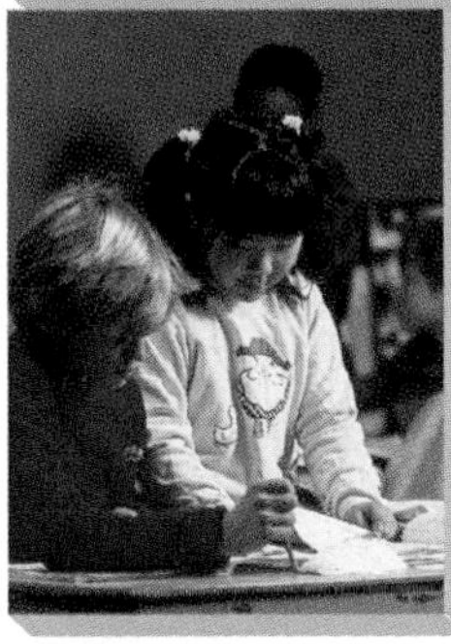 Industry versus inferiority	Middle and late childhood (elementary school years, 6 years–puberty)	At no other time are children more enthusiastic than at the end of early childhood's period of expansive imagination. As children move into the elementary school years, they direct their energy toward mastering knowledge and intellectual skills. The danger at this stage involves feeling incompetent and unproductive.

FIGURE 13

Erikson's First Four Stages of Development

them into contact with a wealth of new experiences. As they move into middle and late childhood, they direct their energy toward mastering knowledge and intellectual skills. With their expansive imaginations, children at this stage are thirsty to learn. The danger in the elementary school years is a sense of inferiority—feeling incompetent and inadequate. Erikson believes teachers have a special responsibility to help children develop a sense of competence and achievement. They should "mildly but firmly coerce children into the adventure of finding out that one can learn to accomplish things which one would never have thought of by oneself" (Erikson, 1968).

Attachment

Erikson (1968) believes that the caregiver's responsive and sensitive behavior toward the infant during its first year provides an important foundation for later development. A number of contemporary developmental psychologists who study the process of "attachment" during infancy agree. Attachment usually refers to a strong relationship between two people in which each person does a number of things to continue the relationship. Many types of people are attached: relatives, lovers, a teacher and a student. In the language of developmental psychology, **attachment** *is the close emotional bond between the infant and its caregiver.*

Theories about infant attachment abound. Freud believed that the infant becomes attached to the person or object that provides oral satisfaction. For most infants, this is the mother, since she is most likely to feed the infant.

But researchers have questioned the importance of feeding in attachment. Harry Harlow and Robert Zimmerman (1959) evaluated whether feeding or contact comfort was more important to infant attachment. The researchers separated infant monkeys from their mothers at birth and placed them in cages where they had access to two artificial "mothers." One of the mothers was made of wire, the other of cloth. Half of the infant monkeys were fed by the wire mother, half by the cloth mother. The infant monkeys nestled close to the cloth mother and spent little time on the wire one, even when it was the wire mother that gave milk. This study clearly demonstrates that contact comfort, not feeding, is the crucial element in the attachment process (see figure 14).

FIGURE 14

Harlow's Classic "Contact Comfort" Study
Regardless of whether they were fed by a wire mother or by a cloth mother, the infant monkeys overwhelmingly preferred to be in contact with the cloth mother, demonstrating the importance of contact comfort in attachment.

In a famous study, Konrad Lorenz (1965) illustrated attachment behavior in geese. Lorenz separated the eggs laid by one goose into two groups. He returned one group to the goose to be hatched; the other group was hatched in an incubator. The goslings in the first group performed as predicted; they followed their mother as soon as they hatched. But those in the second group, who first saw Lorenz after hatching, followed him everywhere as if he were their mother. Lorenz marked the goslings and then placed both groups under a box. Mother goose and "mother" Lorenz stood aside as the box was lifted. Each group of goslings went directly to its "mother" (see figure 15). Lorenz called this process **imprinting,** *the tendency of an infant animal to form an attachment to the first moving object it sees and/or hears.*

For goslings, the critical period for imprinting is the first 36 hours after birth. There also appears to be a longer, more flexible "sensitive" period for attachment in human infants. A number of developmental psychologists believe that attachment to the caregiver in humans during the *first year* provides an important foundation for later development. This view has been especially emphasized by John Bowlby (1969, 1989) and Mary Ainsworth (1979). Bowlby believes the infant and the mother instinctively form an attachment. He believes the newborn is innately equipped to elicit the mother's attachment behavior; it cries, clings, smiles, and coos. Later the infant crawls, walks, and follows the mother. The infant's goal is to keep the mother nearby. Research on attachment supports Bowlby's view that the infant's attachment to its caregiver intensifies at about 6 to 7 months (Ainsworth, 1967; Schaffer & Emerson, 1964).

Some babies have a more positive attachment experience than others. Ainsworth (1979) believes that the difference depends on how sensitive the caregiver is to the infant's signals. Ainsworth says that in **secure attachment** *infants use the caregiver, usually the mother, as a secure base from which to explore the environment.* Infants who are securely

FIGURE 15

Konrad Lorenz, a Pioneering Student of Animal Behavior, Is Followed Through the Water by Three Imprinted Greylag Geese
Lorenz described imprinting as rapid, innate learning within a critical period that involves attachment to the first moving object seen. For goslings, the critical period is the first 36 hours after birth.

attached are more likely to have mothers who are more sensitive, accepting, and expressive of affection toward them than those who are insecurely attached (Waters, 1991; Waters & others, 1995).

The securely attached infant moves freely away from the mother but also keeps tabs on her location by periodically glancing at her. The securely attached infant responds positively to being picked up by others, and when put back down, happily moves away to play. An insecurely attached infant, in contrast, avoids the mother or is ambivalent toward her. The insecurely attached infant fears strangers and is upset by minor, everyday sensations.

Many researchers, such as Ainsworth and Bowlby, believe secure attachment during the infant's first year provides an important foundation for psychological development later in life (Bretherton, 1996; Sroufe, 1996). For example, in one study, researchers found that infants who were securely attached to their mothers were less frustrated and happier at 2 years of age than their insecurely attached counterparts (Matas, Arend, & Sroufe, 1978).

Not all developmentalists believe that a secure attachment in infancy is the only path to competence in life. Some developmentalists believe that too much emphasis is placed on the importance of the attachment bond in infancy (Young & Shahinfar, 1995). Jerome Kagan (1992), for example, believes that infants are highly resilient and adaptive; he argues that they are evolutionarily equipped to stay on a positive developmental course even in the face of wide variations in parenting. Kagan and others stress that genetic and temperament characteristics play more important roles in a child's social competence than the attachment theorists, such as Bowlby, Ainsworth, and Sroufe, are willing to acknowledge (DiBiase, 1993). For example, infants may have inherited a low tolerance for stress; this, rather than an insecure attachment bond, may be responsible for their inability to get along with peers.

Another criticism of attachment theory is that it ignores the diversity of socializing agents and contexts that exist in an infant's world (Thompson, 1991). In some cultures, infants show attachments to many people. In the Hausa culture in Nigeria, both grandmothers and siblings provide a significant amount of care to infants (Super, 1980). Infants in agricultural societies tend to form attachments to older siblings, who are assigned a major responsibility for younger siblings' care. The attachments formed by infants in group care in Israeli kibbutzim provide another challenge to the singular attachment thesis.

Researchers recognize the importance of competent, nurturant caregivers in an infant's development—at issue, though, is whether or not secure attachment, especially to a single caregiver, is critical.

Parenting Styles

While many children spend a great deal of time in child-care situations away from the home, parents are still the main caregivers for the vast majority of the world's children. And parents have always wondered what is the best way to rear their children. "Spare the rod and spoil the

From the notebook of a printer: "The frightening part about heredity and environment is that we parents provide both." Developmental psychologists have been especially interested in pinning down the aspects of parenting that contribute to children's social competence. Diana Baumrind believes a cluster of characteristics she calls authoritative parenting is the best parenting strategy. What does authoritative parenting involve?

child." "Children are to be seen and not heard." There was a time when parents took those adages seriously. But our attitudes toward children—and parenting techniques—have changed.

Diana Baumrind (1971, 1991) believes parents interact with their children in one of four basic ways. She classifies these parenting styles as authoritarian, authoritative, neglectful, and indulgent.

Authoritarian parenting *is a restrictive, punitive style that exhorts the child to follow the parent's directions and to respect work and effort. The authoritarian parent firmly limits and controls the child with little verbal exchange.* Authoritarian parenting is associated with children's social incompetence. In a difference of opinion about how to do something, for example, the authoritarian parent might say, "You do it my way or else. . . . There will be no discussion!" Children of authoritarian parents often are anxious about social comparison, fail to initiate activity, and have poor communication skills.

Authoritative parenting *encourages children to be independent but still places limits and controls on their behavior. Extensive verbal give-and-take is allowed and parents are warm and nurturant toward the child. Authoritative parenting is associated with children's social competence.* An authoritative parent might put his arm around the child in a comforting way and say, "You know you should not have done that; let's talk about how you can handle the situation better next time." Children whose parents are authoritative tend to be socially competent, self-reliant, and socially responsible.

Parents who use a **neglectful** *style are very uninvolved in their child's life; this style is associated with the child's social incompetence, especially a lack of self-control.* This parent cannot give an affirmative answer to the question "It's 10 P.M. Do you know where your child is?" Children have a strong need for their parents to care about them; children whose parents are neglectful might develop a sense that other aspects of the parents' lives are more important than they are. Children whose parents are neglectful tend to show poor self-control and do not handle independence well.

Parents who use an **indulgent** *style are highly involved with their children but place few demands or controls on them. Indulgent parenting is associated with children's social incompetence, especially a lack of self-control.* Such parents let their children do what they want, and the result is the children never learn to control their own behavior and always expect to get their way. Some parents deliberately rear their children in this way because they believe the combination of warm involvement with few restraints will produce a creative, confident child. One boy whose parents deliberately reared him in an indulgent manner moved his parents out of their bedroom suite and took it over for himself. He is almost 18 years old and still has not learned to control his behavior; when he can't get something he wants, he throws temper tantrums. As you might expect, he is not very popular with his peers. Children whose parents are indulgent never learn respect for others and have difficulty controlling their behavior.

Children's Games *by Pieter Breughel, 1560. Is the play of today's children different than the play of children in collective village life?*

American children's play once took place in the rural fields and city streets. Today play is often confined to backyards, basements, playrooms, and bedrooms. The content of children's play today is often derived from video games, television dramas, and Saturday-morning cartoons.

There is more to understanding parent-child relationships than parenting style. For many years the socialization of children was viewed as a straightforward, one-way matter of indoctrination—telling small children about the use of spoons and potties, the importance of saying thank you, and not killing the baby brother. The basic philosophy was that children had to be trained to fit into the social world, so their behavior had to be shaped into that of a mature adult. The young child is not like the inanimate blob of clay the sculptor forms into a polished statue. **Reciprocal socialization** *is the process by which children socialize parents just as parents socialize children.*

As developmental psychologists probe the nature of reciprocal socialization, they are impressed with the importance of synchrony in parent-child relationships (Stenhouse, 1996). **Synchrony** *refers to carefully coordinated interaction between the parent and child in which, often unknowingly, they are attuned to each other's behavior.* The turn-taking that takes place in a number of enjoyable parent-infant games reflects the reciprocal, synchronous nature of some parent-child relationships.

Another factor that shapes the parent-child relationship is the child's developmental status. A competent parent does not interact with a 10-year-old child in the same way as with a 2-year-old child (Maccoby, 1980; Santrock, 1996). Parents usually discipline a toddler by some form of physical manipulation—the child is carried away from mischievous activity, fragile objects are placed out of reach, or sometimes the child is spanked. As the child grows older, parents turn more to reasoning, lecturing, and giving or withholding privileges. Parents also spend less time with older children and monitor their activities more indirectly.

Peers and Play

If you think back to your childhood, some of the first memories that spring to mind may be of the times you spent hanging out with friends. You learned all sorts of things about the world outside your family through your peers. All children do. By talking to a friend, a child may learn that another child's parents argue all the time, make him go to bed early, or give him an allowance. Many children get their first information (much of it wrong) about sex from friends. And children frequently compare themselves with their peers: Are they better than, about the same as, or worse than their peers at skateboarding, math, or making friends?

Most children want to have friends and be popular. Children who are happy, enthusiastic, show concern for others, and have good conversational skills tend to be popular and make friends easily (Parker & Gottman, 1989). In fact, peer relations have been found to be important predictors of children's adjustment and future competence. For example, children who are rejected by their peers tend to have more problems than children who are popular.

It is largely through play that children forge the bonds of friendship. The word *play* is a conspicuous part of children's conversations: "What can we play now?" "Let's play hide-and-seek." "Let's play outside." Most young children spend a good deal of their day playing. Children learn to cooperate with their peers, set and follow rules, work off frustrations, and explore the world around them through play.

Gender

What exactly do we mean by gender? **Gender** *refers to the sociocultural dimension of being female or male.* Two aspects of gender bear special mention: gender identity and gender role. **Gender identity** *is the sense of being female or male, which most children acquire by the time they are 3-year-olds.* A **gender role** *is a set of expectations that prescribe how females or males should think, act, and feel.*

Biological, Social, and Cognitive Influences

To understand how gender develops in our lives, we need to learn about biological, social, and cognitive influences.

Biological Influences on Gender It was not until the 1920s that researchers confirmed the existence of human sex chromosomes, the genetic material that determines our sex. Humans normally have 46 chromosomes arranged in pairs. The 23rd pair may have two X-shaped chromosomes to produce a female, or it may have both an X-shaped and a Y-shaped chromosome to produce a male.

In the first few weeks of gestation, female and male embryos look alike. Male sex organs start to differ from female sex organs when the Y chromosome in the male embryo triggers the secretion of **androgens,** *the main class of male sex hormones.* Low levels of androgen in a female embryo allow the normal development of female sex organs. **Estrogen** *is the main class of female sex hormones.*

Sex hormone levels are related to some cognitive abilities in females and males, especially spatial ability. For example, girls whose glands overproduce testosterone have spatial abilities more similar to those of the average boy than to those of the average girl (Hines, 1990). Also, boys whose glands underproduce testosterone, and thus are late maturing, have spatial abilities more similar to those of the average girl than to those of the average boy (Kimura, 1989).

Sex hormones also are related to aggression. Violent male criminals have above-average levels of testosterone (Dabbs & others, 1987), and professional football players have higher levels of testosterone than ministers do (Dabbs & Morris, 1990). Researchers have been able to increase the aggressiveness of animals in different species by giving them testosterone.

Social Influences In our culture, adults discriminate between the sexes shortly after the infant's birth. The "pink and blue" treatment may be applied to boys and girls before they leave the hospital. Soon afterward, differences in hairstyles, clothes, and toys become obvious. Adults and peers reward these differences throughout development. And girls and boys learn gender roles through imitation or observational learning by watching what other people say and do. In recent years, the idea that parents are the critical agents in gender-role development has come under fire. Culture, schools, peers, the media, and other family members also influence gender behavior (Maccoby, 1993). Yet it is important to guard against swinging too far in this direction, because—especially in the early years of development—parents are important influences on gender development.

Two prominent theories address the way children acquire masculine and feminine attitudes and behaviors from their parents: identification theory and social learning theory of gender. **Identification theory** *stems from Freud's view that the preschool child develops a sexual attraction to the parent of the opposite sex. At about the age of 5 or 6, Freud theorized, the child renounces this attraction because of anxious feelings and identifies with the same-sex parent, unconsciously adopting this parent's behavior.* Today, however, many experts do not believe that sexual attraction is involved in children's gender development. Children become masculine or feminine much earlier than 5 to 6 years of age, even when the same-sex parent is absent from the family.

The **social learning theory of gender** *emphasizes that children learn maleness and femaleness by observing and imitating masculine and feminine behavior, as well as through rewards and punishments for what is considered appropriate and inappropriate gender behavior.* For example, parents teach gender behavior when they praise their daughters for playing with dolls or when they reproach their sons for crying. (A comparison of the identification and social learning theories is presented in figure 16.)

Although parents provide children with the first models of gender roles, children also learn from observing other adults in the neighborhood and on television. As children get older, peers become increasingly important influences. For example, when children play in ways that our culture says are sex-appropriate, they tend to be rewarded by their peers. Those who engage in activities that are considered inappropriate tend to be criticized or abandoned by their peers. Children show a clear preference for same-sex peers. Critics of the social learning view argue that gender roles are not as passively acquired as it suggests. Another view, known as cognitive developmental theory, argues that individuals actively construct their gender world.

Theory	Processes	Emphasis
Freud's identification theory	Sexual attraction to opposite-sex parent at 3–5 years of age; anxiety about sexual attraction and subsequent identification with same-sex parent at 5–6 years of age.	Gender behavior similar to same-sex parent
Social learning theory	Rewards and punishments of gender-appropriate and inappropriate behavior by adults and peers; observation and imitation of models' masculine and feminine behavior	Gender behavior

FIGURE 16

Social Theories of Gender Development
Parents influence their children's gender development by action and example.

Cognitive Influences Two prominent theories have addressed the role of cognitive influences on gender: cognitive developmental theory and gender schema theory.

In the **cognitive developmental theory of gender,** *children's gender typing occurs after they have developed a concept of gender. Once they consistently conceive of themselves as female or male, children often organize their world on the basis of gender.* Initially developed by psychologist Lawrence Kohlberg (1966), this theory argues that gender development proceeds in the following way: "I am a girl, I want to do girl things; therefore, the opportunity to do girl things is rewarding." Kohlberg based his ideas on Piaget's cognitive developmental theory, which emphasizes that once they have acquired the ability to categorize things, children strive toward consistency in their use of categories and behavior. Therefore, as children's cognitive development matures, so does their understanding of gender. Two-year-olds can apply the labels *boy* and *girl* correctly to themselves and others; their concept of gender is simple and concrete. Preschool children rely on physical features such as dress and hairstyle to decide who falls into each gender category. Girls are people with long hair; boys are people who never wear dresses. Some preschool children believe that people can change their gender by getting a haircut or a new outfit. Obviously they do not yet have the cognitive machinery to think of gender as adults do. According to Kohlberg, all the reinforcement in the world won't modify that fact.

However, by the concrete operational stage (Piaget's third stage, which begins around the age of 6 or 7 years), children understand gender constancy. They know, for example, that a male is still a male regardless of whether he is wearing pants or a skirt or an earring, or whether his hair is short or long (Tavris & Wade, 1984). Now that their concept of gender constancy is clearly established, school-age children become motivated to become a competent, or "proper," boy or girl. Consequently, the child finds same-sex activities rewarding and imitates the behavior of same-sex models.

A **schema** *is a cognitive structure, a network of associations that organizes and guides an individual's perceptions.* A **gender schema** *organizes the world in terms of female and male.* **Gender schema theory** *states that an individual's attention and behavior are guided by an internal motivation to conform to gender-based sociocultural standards and stereotypes.* Gender schema theory suggests that "gender typing" occurs when individuals are ready to encode and organize information along the lines of what is considered appropriate or typical for males and females in a society (Martin, 1993). Whereas Kohlberg's cognitive developmental theory argues that a particular cognitive prerequisite—gender constancy—is necessary for gender typing, gender schema theory states that a general readiness to respond to and categorize information on the basis of culturally defined gender roles fuels children's gender-typing activities. A comparison of the cognitive developmental and gender schema theories is presented in figure 17.

Gender Similarities and Differences

Some experts believe that differences between the sexes have been exaggerated. Statements such as the following are not unusual: "While only 32 percent of the women were found to . . . , fully 37 percent of the men were. . . ." This difference of 5 percent is probably a very small difference, and might not even be statistically significant or capable of being replicated in a separate study (Denmark & others, 1988). Similarly, statements that make comparisons between females and males usually are not making claims about all females versus all males. For example, consider the claim that "males outperform females in math." This does not mean that all males outperform all females at math. Rather, it usually means that the average math achievement scores for males at certain ages are higher than the average math achievement scores for females at those ages. The math achievement scores of males and females overlap. An average difference might favor males, but many females have higher math achievement scores than many males. Further, there is a tendency to think of such differences between females and males as being biologically based. Remember, though, that such differences can be influenced by society and culture.

Let's now examine some of the differences between the sexes, keeping in mind that (a) the differences are averages; (b) even when differences are reported, there is overlap between the sexes; and (c) the differences might be due primarily to biological factors, sociocultural factors,

Theory	Processes	Emphasis
Cognitive developmental theory	Development of gender constancy, especially around 6–7 years of age, when conservation skills develop; after children develop the ability to consistently conceive of themselves as male or female, children often organize their world on the basis of gender, such as selecting same-sex models to imitate	Cognitive readiness facilitates sex typing
Gender schema theory	Sociocultural emphasis on gender-based standards and stereotypes; children's attention and behavior are guided by an internal motivation to conform to these gender-based standards and stereotypes, allowing children to interpret the world through a network of gender-organized thoughts	Gender schemas reinforce gender typing

FIGURE 17

Cognitive Developmental and Gender Schema Theories of Gender Development

or both. We will first examine physical and biological differences, then turn to cognitive and social differences.

Females, on the average, live longer than males. Females are also less likely than males to develop certain physical disorders. Estrogen strengthens the immune system, making females more resistant to some kinds of infection, for example, and female hormones signal the liver to produce more "good" cholesterol, which makes their blood vessels more "elastic." Testosterone triggers the production of low-density lipoprotein, which clogs blood vessels, and as a result males have twice the risk of coronary disease as females. Higher levels of stress hormones cause faster clotting in males, and also higher blood pressure. Adult females have about twice the body fat of their male counterparts, most of which is concentrated around breasts and hips; in males, fat is more likely to go to the abdomen. Males grow about 10 percent taller than females, on the average. Male hormones promote the growth of long bones; female hormones stop such growth at puberty. In short, there are many physical differences between females and males.

However, similarity rather than dissimilarity was the rule rather than the exception in a recent study of metabolic activity in the brains of females and males (Gur & others, 1995). The exceptions involved emotional and physical expressiveness (for both of which there was more activity in the related regions of the brain in females). Next we will see that there is considerable similarity in the cognitive performances of females and males.

In a classic review of gender differences in 1974, Eleanor Maccoby and Carol Jacklin concluded that males have better math skills and better visual and spatial ability (the kinds of skills an architect would need to design a building's angles and dimensions), while females have better verbal abilities. Maccoby (1990) later revised her conclusions about several gender dimensions. Verbal differences between the sexes have virtually disappeared, she now says, though the math and spatial differences still exist.

Males are more active and aggressive than females. The consistent difference in aggression often appears in children's development as early as 2 years of age. Although males and females do not experience different emotions, they frequently differ in the emotions they feel free to express in public and how they express those emotions (Paludi, 1995). Females tend to be better at "reading" emotions (Malatesta, 1990). With regard to helping behavior, social psychologists Alice Eagly and Maureen Crowley (1986) argue that the female gender role fosters behavior that is nurturant and caring, while the male gender role promotes behavior that is heroic and chivalrous. They found that males were more likely to help in situations in which there was a perceived danger and in which males felt most competent to help. For example, males are more likely than females to help when a person is standing by the roadside with a flat tire, a situation involving some danger and a circumstance in which many males feel a sense of competence—automobile problems. In contrast, if the situation involves volunteering time to help a problem child, most researchers have found more helping by females because there is little danger present for the helper and because females feel more competent in nurturing (Hyde, 1990).

These findings illustrate an important point about gender. To fully understand gender, it is important to consider the *context* in which gender is involved.

Not all psychologists agree that sex differences between females and males are rare or small. Alice Eagly (1995, 1996) stated that the belief that such differences are rare or small came about because of a feminist commitment to gender similarity as a route to political equality, and that it also arose from piecemeal and inadequate interpretations of relevant empirical research. Many feminists express a fear that differences will be interpreted as deficiencies on the part of females and as biologically based, which could produce a portrayal of women as innately inferior to men (Unger & Crawford, 1992). Eagly (1995, 1996) argues that contemporary psychology has produced a large body of research that reveals that behavior is sex-differentiated to varying extents.

Evolutionary psychologist David Buss (1995, 1996; Buss & Malamuth, 1996) argues that men and women differ in those psychological domains in which they have faced different adaptive problems across their evolutionary history. In all other domains, predicts Buss, the sexes are psychologically similar. He cites a sex difference in the cognitive domain that favors males—spatial rotation. This ability is essential for hunting, in which the trajectory of a spear must anticipate the trajectory of an animal as each moves through space and time. Buss also cites a sex difference in casual sex, with men engaging in this behavior more than women. In one study, men said they would like to ideally have more than eighteen sex partners in their lifetime, whereas women stated they ideally would like to have only four or five (Buss & Schmitt, 1993). In another study, 75 percent of the men but none of the women approached by an attractive stranger of the opposite sex consented to a request for sex (Clark & Hatfield, 1989). Such sex differences, says Buss, are exactly the type predicted by evolutionary psychology.

In sum, current controversy swirls about the issue of whether sex differences are rare and small or frequent and large (Derry, 1996; Hyde & Plant, 1995; Maracek, 1995; Silverstein, 1996). The controversy documents that negotiating the science and politics of gender is not an easy task (Eagly, 1995).

How Can Gender Roles Be Classified?

In the past, the well-adjusted female was expected to be dependent, nurturant, and uninterested in power. The well-adjusted male was expected to be independent, aggressive, and power-oriented. Further, feminine characteristics were considered undesirable by society; male characteristics were considered healthy and good. In a classic study in the early 1970s, the traits and behaviors that college students believed were characteristic of females and those they believed were characteristic of males were assessed (Broverman & others, 1972). The traits clustered into two groups, labeled "expressive" and "instrumental." The expressive traits paralleled the female's responsibility to be warm and emotional in the home. The instrumental traits paralleled the male's purposeful, competent entry into the outside world to gain goods for his family. Such stereotypes are more harmful to females than to males because the characteristics assigned to males are more valued by society than those assigned to females.

In the 1970s, as both females and males became dissatisfied with the burdens imposed by their strictly stereotyped roles, alternatives to "femininity" and "masculinity" were explored. Instead of thinking of femininity and masculinity as a continuum, with more of one meaning less of the other, feminists argued that people could show *both expressive and instrumental* traits. This thinking led to the concept of **androgyny,** *the presence of desirable feminine and masculine characteristics in the same individual* (Bem, 1977; Spence & Helmreich, 1978). The androgynous individual might be a female who is nurturant (feminine) and assertive (masculine), or a male who is dominant (masculine) and sensitive to others' feelings (feminine).

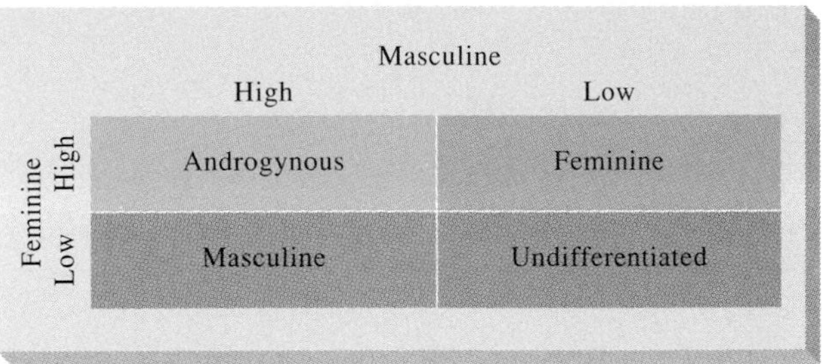

FIGURE 18

Gender-Role Classification

Psychological measures have been developed to assess androgyny. One of the most widely used gender measures is the Bem sex-role inventory, developed by a leading early proponent of androgyny, Sandra Bem. According to Bem (1977), individuals can be classified as having one of four gender-role orientations: feminine, masculine, androgynous, or undifferentiated (see figure 18). The androgynous individual is simply a female or male who has a high degree of both feminine (expressive) and masculine (instrumental) traits. An undifferentiated individual is high on neither masculine nor feminine traits. Androgynous women and men, according to Bem, are described as more flexible and more mentally healthy than either masculine or feminine individuals, while undifferentiated individuals are the least competent. To some degree, though, context influences which gender role is most adaptive. In close relationships, a feminine or androgynous gender role may be more desirable because of the expressive nature of close relationships. However, a masculine or androgynous gender role may be more desirable in academic and work settings because of their demands for action and assertiveness. And the culture in which individuals live also plays an important role in determining what is adaptive. On the one hand, increasing numbers of children in the United States and other modernized countries such as Sweden are being raised to behave in androgynous ways. But traditional gender roles continue to dominate the cultures of many countries around the world.

Children: Our Nation's Future

As the twenty-first century approaches, the well-being of children is one of America's foremost concerns. Children are the future of any society. Those who do not reach their potential, who are destined to make fewer contributions to society than society needs, and who do not take their place as productive adults diminish that society's future.

At this point, we have discussed a number of ideas about children's social development. A summary of these ideas is presented in concept table 1. Next, we continue our journey through life-span development, moving into the adolescent years.

Concept Table 1

Children's Development

Concept	Processes/Related Ideas	Characteristics/Description
What Is Development?	Its nature	Development is a pattern of movement or change that occurs throughout the life span.
	Biological, cognitive, and socioemotional processes	Development is influenced by an interplay of biological, cognitive, and socioemotional processes.
	Periods of development	The life span is commonly divided into the following periods of development: prenatal, infancy, early childhood, middle and late childhood, adolescence, early adulthood, middle adulthood, and late adulthood. Some experts on life-span development, however, believe too much emphasis is placed on age; Neugarten believes we are moving toward a society in which age is a weaker predictor of development in adulthood.
	Maturation and experience	Development is influenced by the interaction of maturation and experience. The debate over the role of maturation and experience is another version of the nature/nurture controversy.
	Continuity and discontinuity	Development may be described as either continuous (gradual, cumulative change) or discontinuous (abrupt, sequence of stages).
	Metaphors for development	Three such metaphors are (1) a staircase, (2) a seedling in a greenhouse, and (3) a strand of ivy in a forest.
Prenatal Development and Birth	Course of prenatal development	Conception occurs when a sperm unites with an ovum. The fertilized egg is the zygote. The first 2 weeks after conception is the germinal period, weeks 3 through 8 is the embryonic period, and the next 2 to 9 months is the fetal period. Teratogens are agents that cause birth defects. Drugs and maternal diseases are examples of teratogens.
	Birth and the newborn	Birth marks a dramatic transition for the fetus. Special interest focuses on preterm infants. Social class and ethnicity are factors affecting the preterm infant's development.
Children's Physical Development	Its nature	Infants come into the world equipped with a number of reflexes. Physical development slows during the childhood years, although motor development becomes smoother and more coordinated.
Children's Cognitive Development	Basic ideas in Piaget's theory	Piaget stressed that children actively construct their cognitive world. Piaget believed we adapt our thinking in two ways: through assimilation and accommodation. Piaget also theorized that individuals go through four cognitive stages of development: sensorimotor, preoperational, concrete operational, and formal operational.
	Sensorimotor thought	This stage refers to Piaget's belief that from birth to about 2 years of age infants construct an understanding of the world by coordinating sensory experiences with physical/motor actions. Piaget believed that sensorimotor thought is nonsymbolic and that an important milestone in sensorimotor thought is the development of object permanence.
	Preoperational and concrete operational thought	Preoperational thought is the term Piaget gave to the 2- to 7-year-old child's understanding of the world. Children at this stage cannot understand such logical operations as the reversibility of mental representations. Piaget also argued that the preoperational child does not have an understanding of conservation. Preoperational thought is

Concept	Processes/Related Ideas	Characteristics/Description
Children's Cognitive Development (continued)	Preoperational and concrete operational thought (continued)	more symbolic than sensorimotor thought, egocentric (showing an inability to distinguish between one's own perspective and someone else's), and intuitive rather than logical. Concrete operational thought is the term Piaget gave to the 7- to 11-year-old child's understanding of the world. The concrete operational child can use operations, replaces intuitive thinking with logical thinking but only in concrete circumstances, does not think abstractly, and develops classification skills.
	Evaluating Piaget	Piaget was a genius at observing children. He changed forever the way we view a child's understanding of the world. His views have not gone uncriticized, especially his concept of age-related stages. Neo-Piagetians have significantly revised Piaget's theory.
Children's Socioemotional Development	Erikson's theory	Erikson proposed eight stages of psychosocial development. Erikson's four childhood stages are trust versus mistrust (first year); autonomy versus shame, doubt (second year); initiative versus guilt (3–5 years); and industry versus inferiority (6 years–puberty).
	Attachment	Attachment is a close bond between an infant and its caregiver(s). A number of theories of attachment have been developed. Feeding is not critical in attachment (which does not support Freud's view), but contact comfort (supported by Harlow's research), familiarity (supported by Lorenz's research), and the caregiver's sensitivity and responsiveness are. Many developmentalists, especially Bowlby and Ainsworth, believe that the development of a secure attachment in the first year of life is a key developmental task. Ainsworth stresses that secure attachment is critical for competent development, although some other theorists and researchers do not.
	Parenting styles	Baumrind's parenting styles—authoritarian, authoritative, neglectful, and indulgent—are widely used classifications. Socially competent children are more likely to have authoritative parents. However, the socialization of children is a reciprocal process; children also socialize parents. Synchrony is an important aspect of this reciprocal parent-child interaction. Another factor that shapes the parent-child relationship is the child's developmental status. Competent parents adapt their behavior to the child's changing status.
	Peers and play	Peers and play are important dimensions of children's development. Psychologists study the factors that contribute to peer popularity and friendship. Play takes up a major portion of many young children's days and serves many functions.
	Gender	Understanding gender involves knowing what gender is; biological, cognitive, and social influences on gender; gender similarities and differences (currently controversy swirls about the issue of how rare and small versus how frequent and large gender differences really are); and gender-role classification.
Children: Our Nation's Future	Nature	Children are the future of any society.

Adolescence

Twentieth-century poet-essayist Roger Allen once remarked, "In case you are worried about what's going to become of the younger generation, it's going to grow up and start worrying about the younger generation." Virtually every society has worried about its younger generation, but it was not until the beginning of the twentieth century that the scientific study of adolescence began.

Historical Beginnings and the Nature of Adolescence

In 1904, psychologist G. Stanley Hall wrote the first scientific book on adolescence. Hall referred to the adolescent years as a time of "storm and stress." The **storm-and-stress view** *is Hall's concept that adolescence is a turbulent time charged with conflict and mood swings.* Thoughts, feelings, and actions oscillate between conceit and humility, good and temptation, happiness and sadness. The adolescent may be nasty to a peer one moment and kind the next moment. At one time the adolescent may want to be alone, yet seconds later seek companionship.

During most of the twentieth century, American adolescents have been described as abnormal and deviant. In addition to Hall, Freud described adolescents as sexually driven and conflicted. And media portrayals of adolescents—*Rebel Without a Cause* in the late 1950s, *Easy Rider* in the 1960s, for example—portrayed adolescents as rebellious, conflicted, faddish, delinquent, and self-centered. Consider also the current image of adolescents as stressed and disturbed, from *Sixteen Candles* and *The Breakfast Club* in the 1980s to *Boyz in the Hood* in the 1990s.

Adults probably forget their own adolescence. Most adults can with a little effort recall things they did that stretched—even shocked—the patience of their own parents. In matters of taste and manners, young people of every generation have seemed radical, unnerving, and different to adults—different in how they look, how they behave, the music they enjoy. But it is an enormous error to confuse the adolescent's enthusiasm for trying on new identities and enjoying moderate amounts of outrageous behavior with hostility toward parental and societal standards. Acting out and boundary testing are time-honored ways in which adolescents move toward accepting, rather than rejecting, parental values.

It does little good, and can do considerable disservice, to think of adolescence as a time of rebellion, crisis, pathology, and deviation. It's far more accurate to view adolescence as a time of evaluation, a time of decision making, a time of commitment as young people carve out their place in the world. How competent they will become often depends on their access to a range of legitimate opportunities and long-term support from adults who deeply care about them.

As we move toward the close of the twentieth century, experts on adolescence are trying to dispel the myth that adolescents are a sorry lot. That stereotype is usually based on a small group of highly visible adolescents. A study by Daniel Offer and his colleagues (1988) showed that the vast majority of adolescents are competent human beings who are not experiencing deep emotional turmoil. He sampled the self-images of adolescents around the world—in the United States, Australia, Bangladesh, Hungary, Israel, Japan, Taiwan, Turkey, and West Germany—and found that three out of four had a positive self-image. They were moving toward adulthood in generally healthy ways, happy most of the time, enjoying life, valuing work and school, having positive feelings about their family and friends, expressing confidence in their sexual selves, and believing they have the ability to cope with life's stresses—not exactly in the throes of storm and stress.

At the same time, adolescents have not experienced an improvement in health over the past 30 years, largely as a result of a new group of dangers called the "new morbidity." These include problems such as accidents, suicide, homicide, substance abuse, sexual diseases including AIDS, delinquency, and emotional difficulties.

Our discussion underscores an important point about adolescents: They do not make up a homogeneous group. The majority of adolescents negotiate the lengthy path to adult maturity successfully, but too large a group does not. Ethnic, cultural, gender, socioeconomic, age, and lifestyle differences influence the actual life trajectory of every adolescent. Different portrayals of adolescents emerge, depending on the particular group of adolescents being described (Brooks-Gunn, 1996; Feldman & Elliott, 1990). The complex relationships among physical, cognitive, and socioemotional development that influence rates of health and emotional problems make it important for us to understand these aspects of adolescent development. Let's examine physical development first.

Physical Development

Imagine a toddler displaying all the features of puberty—a 3-year-old girl with fully developed breasts or a boy just slightly older with a deep male voice. We would see this by the year 2250 if the age of puberty were to continue to decrease at its present pace. Menarche (the first menstruation) has declined from 14.2 years in 1900 to about 12.45 years today. Age of menarche has been declining an average of about 4 months a decade for the last century. We are unlikely, though, to see pubescent toddlers in the future because what happened in the last century is special. That something special is a higher level of nutrition and health. A lower age of menarche is associated with higher standards of living (Petersen, 1979).

Menarche is one event that characterizes puberty, but there are others as well. **Puberty** *is a period of rapid skeletal and sexual maturation that occurs mainly in early adolescence.* However, it is not a single, sudden event. We know when a young person is going through puberty, but pinpointing its beginning and its end is difficult. Except for menarche,

Adults often have short memories about their adolescence. With a little effort, most adults can remember behavior that stretched, or even broke, the patience of their elders. Acting out and boundary testing are time-honored methods that move adolescents toward an identity of their own. Adolescence should not be viewed as a time of crisis, rebellion, pathology, and deviation. Far more accurate is a vision of adolescence as a time of evaluation, decision making, and commitment as adolescents seek to find out who they are and carve out a place for themselves in the world.

which occurs rather late in puberty, no single marker heralds puberty. For boys, the first whisker or first wet dream could mark its appearance, but both may go unnoticed.

Hormonal changes characterize pubertal development. Hormones are powerful chemical substances secreted by the endocrine glands and carried through the body in the bloodstream. The concentrations of certain hormones increase dramatically during puberty (Dorn & Chrousos, 1996). **Testosterone** *is a hormone associated in boys with the development of genitals, an increase in height, and a change in voice.* **Estradiol** *is a hormone associated in girls with breast, uterine, and skeletal development.* In one study, testosterone levels doubled in girls but increased eighteenfold in boys during puberty; similarly, estradiol doubled in boys but increased eightfold in girls (Nottelmann & others, 1987). These hormonal and body changes occur on the average about two years earlier in females (10½ years) than in males (12½ years).

Some researchers now question whether the effects of puberty are as strong as once believed. Puberty affects some adolescents more strongly than others, and some behaviors more strongly than others. Body image, interest in dating, and sexual behavior are clearly affected by pubertal change. If we look at overall development and adjustment in the human life cycle, pubertal variations (such as early and late maturation) are less dramatic than is commonly thought. In thinking about puberty's effects, keep in mind that the adolescent's world involves cognitive and socioemotional changes, as well as physical changes. As with all periods of development, these processes work in concert to produce who we are in adolescence (Graber, Petersen, & Brooks–Gunn, 1996).

Cognitive Development

Aristotle once remarked that adolescents think they know everything and are quite sure about it. We will examine this egocentrism of adolescence shortly, but first let's see what Piaget had to say about cognitive development in adolescence. **Formal operational thought** *is Piaget's name for the fourth stage of cognitive development, which appears between 11 and 15 years of age. Formal operational thought is abstract, idealistic, and logical.* Unlike elementary school children, adolescents are no longer limited to actual concrete experience as the anchor of thought. They can conceive make-believe situations, hypothetical possibilities, or purely abstract propositions. Thought also becomes more idealistic. Adolescents often compare themselves and others to ideal standards. And they think about what an ideal world would be like, wondering if they couldn't carve out a better world than the one the adult generation has handed to them.

At the same time adolescents think more abstractly and idealistically, they also think more logically. Adolescents begin to think more like a scientist thinks, devising plans to solve problems and systematically testing solutions. This type

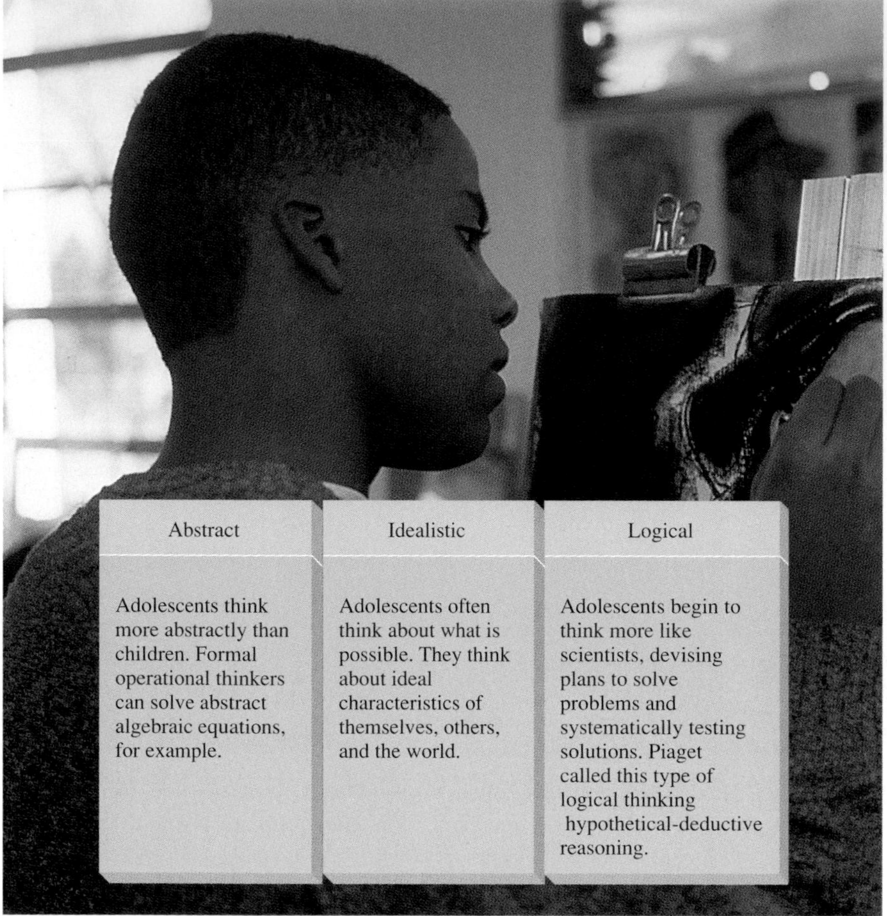

Abstract
Adolescents think more abstractly than children. Formal operational thinkers can solve abstract algebraic equations, for example.
Idealistic
Adolescents often think about what is possible. They think about ideal characteristics of themselves, others, and the world.
Logical
Adolescents begin to think more like scientists, devising plans to solve problems and systematically testing solutions. Piaget called this type of logical thinking hypothetical-deductive reasoning.

FIGURE 19

Characteristics of Formal Operational Thought
Adolescents begin to think in more abstract, idealistic, and logical ways than when they were children.

of problem solving has an imposing name. **Hypothetical-deductive reasoning** *is Piaget's name for adolescents' ability to develop hypotheses, or best hunches, about ways to solve problems, such as an algebraic equation. They then systematically deduce, or conclude, which is the best path to follow to solve the problem.* By contrast, children are more likely to solve problems in a trial-and-error fashion. Figure 19 summarizes the main features of formal operational thought.

Some of Piaget's ideas on formal operational thought are currently being challenged. There is more individual variation in formal operational thought than Piaget envisioned. Only about one in three young adolescents is a formal operational thinker.

Adolescent thought, especially in early adolescence, is also egocentric. **Adolescent egocentrism** *involves the belief that others are as preoccupied with the adolescent as she herself is, the belief that one is unique, and the belief that one is indestructible* (Elkind, 1978). Attention-getting behavior, so common in adolescence, reflects egocentrism and the desire to be onstage, noticed, and visible. Imagine the eighth-grade boy who feels as if all eyes are riveted on his tiny facial blemish. Imagine also the sense of uniqueness felt by the following adolescent girl: "My mother has no idea about how much pain I'm going through. She has never been hurt like I have. Why did Bob break up with me?" And imagine the sense of indestructibility of two adolescent males drag racing down a city street. This sense of indestructibility may lead to drug use and suicide attempts.

Socioemotional Development

Mark Twain, reflecting on his youth commented, "When I was a boy of 14 my father was so ignorant I could hardly stand to have the man around. But when I got to be 21, I was astonished how much he learnt in seven years." Let's explore the world of parent-adolescent relationships Twain spoke about.

Parent-Adolescent Relationships

There are many myths about parent-adolescent relationships, including the following: (1) Adolescents detach themselves from parents and move into an isolated world of peers. (2) Throughout adolescence, parent-adolescent relationships are intense, filled with conflict, and highly stressful.

Adolescents do not simply move away from parental influence into a decision-making world all their own. As adolescents move toward becoming more autonomous, it is healthy for them to continue to be attached to their parents. Just as they did in infancy and childhood, parents continue to provide an important support system that helps the adolescent explore a wider, more complex social world full of uncertainties, challenges, and stresses. Although adolescents show a strong desire to spend more time with their peers, they do not necessarily isolate themselves (Ladd & Le Sieur, 1995). In one study, adolescents who were securely attached to their parents were also securely attached to their peers; those who were insecurely attached to their parents were also insecurely attached to their peers (Armsden & Greenberg, 1984). Of course, there are times when adolescents reject this closeness, connection, and attachment as they pursue a more autonomous life. But for the most part, the adolescent's worlds of parents and peers are coordinated and connected, not uncoordinated and disconnected (Allen & Bell, 1995; Bell, 1995). For example, parents' choices of

Old model of parent-adolescent relationships

- Autonomy, detachment from parents; parent and peer worlds isolated
- Intense conflict throughout adolescence; stormy and stressful on a daily basis

New model of parent-adolescent relationships

- Autonomy, but attachment to parents; adolescent-parent and adolescent-peer worlds interconnected
- Moderate conflict promotes growth; conflict greater in early adolescence

FIGURE 20

Old and New Models of Parent-Adolescent Relationships

neighborhoods, churches, schools, and their own friends influence the pool from which their adolescents select possible friends (Cooper & Ayers-Lopez, 1985).

Adolescence is a period of development when individuals push for autonomy, but the development of mature autonomy is a lengthy process, taking place over 10 to 15 years. As adolescents pursue a more autonomous life, many parents perceive them as changing from compliant children to noncompliant adolescents. Parents tend to adopt one of two strategies to handle the noncompliance: They clamp down and put more pressure on the adolescents to conform to parental standards, or they become more permissive and let the adolescents do as they please. Neither is a wise overall strategy. Rather a more flexible, adaptive approach is called for. At the onset of adolescence, the average boy or girl does not have the knowledge to make appropriate decisions in all areas of life. As adolescents push for autonomy, the wise parent relinquishes control in areas where adolescents can make mature decisions. The wise parent also calmly communicates with the adolescent and tries to help the adolescent make reasonable decisions in areas where he or she shows less mature behavior.

Conflict with parents does increase in adolescence, but it does not reach the tumultuous proportions described by G. Stanley Hall, and it is not uniformly intense throughout adolescence (Holmbeck, 1996; Holmbeck, Paikoff, & Brooks-Gunn, 1995). Rather, much of the conflict involves the everyday events of family life, such as keeping a bedroom clean, dressing neatly, getting home by a certain hour, not talking on the phone forever, and so on. Such conflicts with parents are more common in early adolescence, especially during the apex of pubertal change, than in late adolescence. The conflicts usually do not involve major dilemmas such as drugs and delinquency. The everyday negotiations and conflicts that characterize parent-adolescent relationships can even serve a positive developmental function. These minor disputes and negotiations facilitate the adolescent's transition from being dependent on parents to being more autonomous. For example, in one study, adolescents who disagreed with their parents also explored identity issues more actively than adolescents who consistently agreed with their parents (Cooper & others, 1982).

In sum, the old model of parent-adolescent relationships suggested that as adolescents mature they detach themselves from parents and move into a world of autonomy apart from parents. The old model suggested that parent-adolescent conflict is intense and stressful throughout adolescence. The new model emphasizes that parents serve as important attachment figures and support systems as adolescents explore a wider, more complex social world (Cohen & Beckwith, 1996). The new model also emphasizes that in the majority of families, parent-adolescent conflict is moderate rather than severe, and that the everyday negotiations and minor disputes can serve the positive developmental function of helping the adolescent make the transition from childhood dependency to adult independence (see figure 20).

Peers

Imagine you are back in junior or senior high school: friends, cliques, parties, and clubs probably come to mind. During adolescence, especially early adolescence, we conform more than we did in childhood. Conformity to peers, especially their antisocial standards, often peaks around the eighth or ninth grade, a time when teenagers might join a peer in stealing hubcaps from a car, drawing graffiti on a wall, or harassing a teacher (Berndt & Perry, 1990).

Dating also takes on added importance during adolescence. As Dick Cavett (1974) remembers, the thought of an upcoming dance or sock hop was absolute agony: "I knew I'd never get a date. There seemed to be only this limited set of girls I could and should be seen with, and they were all taken by the jocks." Adolescents spend considerable time either dating or thinking about dating, which has gone far beyond its original courtship function to a form of recreation, a source of status and achievement, and a setting for learning about close relationships. Dating is but one of a number of circumstances that signal the development of an identity in adolescence that is different from the identity formed in childhood.

Our discussion of adolescents' social development so far has taken us through families and peers—two of the most important social contexts in the adolescent's development. Experiences in these social settings, as well as other settings such as schools, influence one of the most dramatic changes in the adolescent's life—identity development.

Identity Development

Identity versus identity confusion *is the fifth of Erikson's (1968) stages of human development, occurring primarily in the adolescent years. The development of identity involves finding out who we are, what we are all about, and where we are headed in life.* Seeking an identity is about trying on one face after another, trying to find one's own.

During adolescence, individuals enter what Erikson calls a "psychological moratorium"—a gap between the security of childhood and the autonomy of adulthood. In their search for identity, adolescents experiment with different roles. Those who successfully explore a number of alternatives emerge with a new sense of self that is both refreshing and acceptable; those who do not successfully resolve the identity crisis are confused, suffering what Erikson calls identity confusion. This confusion takes one of two courses: Individuals withdraw, isolating themselves from peers and family, or they lose themselves in the crowd. Adolescents want to decide freely for themselves such matters as what careers they will pursue, whether they will go to college, and whether they will marry. In other words, they want to free themselves from the shackles of their parents and other adults and make their own choices. At the same time, many adolescents have a deep fear of making the wrong decision and of failing. But as adolescents pursue their identity and their thoughts become more abstract and logical, they reason in more sophisticated ways. They are better able to judge what is morally right and wrong and become capable decision makers.

Finding out who you are, what you are all about, and where you are going—the search for identity—is an important developmental task for every human being. As we see next, another important developmental task involves developing a system of moral standards.

Moral Development

In Europe a woman was near death from a special kind of cancer. There was one drug that the doctors thought might save her. It was a form of radium that a druggist in the same town had recently discovered. The drug was expensive to make, but the druggist was charging ten times what the drug cost him to make. He paid $200 for the radium and charged $2,000 for a small dose of the drug. The sick woman's husband, Heinz, went to everyone he knew to borrow the money, but he could get together only $1,000. He told the druggist that his wife was dying and asked him to sell it cheaper or let him pay later. But the druggist said, "No. I discovered the drug, and I am going to make money from it." Desperate, Heinz broke into the man's store to steal the drug for his wife (Kohlberg, 1969).

This story is one of eleven devised by Lawrence Kohlberg (1986) to investigate the nature of moral thought. After reading the story, the interviewee answers a series of questions about the moral dilemma. Should Heinz have done that? Was it right or wrong? Why? Is it a husband's duty to steal the drug for his wife if he can get it in no other way? Would a good husband do it? Did the druggist have the right to charge that much when there was no law actually setting a limit on the price? Why?

Based on the answers that individuals have given to questions about this and other moral dilemmas, Kohlberg believes that three levels of moral development exist, each of which is characterized by two stages. A key concept in understanding moral development, especially Kohlberg's theory, is **internalization,** *the developmental change from behavior that is externally controlled to behavior that is controlled by internal, self-generated standards and principles.*

1. The **preconventional level** *is Kohlberg's lowest level of moral thinking, in which the individual shows no internalization of moral values—moral thinking is based on punishments (stage 1) or rewards (stage 2) that come from the external world.* In regard to the story about Heinz and the druggist, at stage 1 an individual might say he should not steal the drug because it is a big crime; at stage 2, an individual might say he shouldn't steal the drug because the druggist needs to make a profit.
2. The **conventional level** *is Kohlberg's second level of moral thinking, in which the individual has an intermediate level of internalization. The individual abides by certain standards (internal), but they are the standards of others (external), such as parents (stage 3) or the laws of society (stage 4).* At stage 3, an individual might say that Heinz should steal the drug for his wife because that is what society expects a good husband would do; at stage 4, an individual might say that it is natural to want to save his wife but that it still is always wrong to steal.

3. The **postconventional level** *is Kohlberg's highest level of moral thinking; moral development is completely internalized and not based on others' standards. The individual recognizes alternative moral courses, explores the options, and then develops a personal moral code. The code is among the principles generally accepted by the community (stage 5) or it is more individualized (stage 6).* At stage 5, an individual might say that the law was not set up for these circumstances so Heinz can steal the drug; it is not really right, but he is justified in doing it. At stage 6, the individual is faced with the decision of whether to consider the other people who need the drug just as badly as his wife. Heinz should consider the value of all lives involved.

Kohlberg believed these levels and stages occur in a sequence and are age-related. Some evidence for Kohlberg's theory has been found, although few people reach stages 5 and 6 (Colby & others, 1983). Kohlberg thought moral development occurs through maturation of thought, the mutual give-and-take of peer relations, and opportunities for role taking. Parent-child relationships do not contribute to moral thought in Kohlberg's view because they are too dominated by their parents' moral values, with little opportunity for the youth to experiment with alternative moral values.

Kohlberg's provocative view continues to generate considerable research on moral development, but critics challenge his theory. One criticism of Kohlberg's view is that moral reasons are often a shelter for immoral behavior. When bank embezzlers and presidents are asked about their moral reasoning, it may be advanced, even at Kohlberg's postconventional level, but when their own behavior is examined it may be filled with cheating, lying, and stealing. The cheaters, liars, and thieves may know what is right and what is wrong, but still do what is wrong.

A second major criticism of Kohlberg's view is that it does not adequately reflect relationships and concerns for others. The **justice perspective** *is a theory of moral development that focuses on the rights of the individual; individuals stand alone and independently make moral decisions. Kohlberg's theory is a justice perspective.* By contrast, the **care perspective** *is Carol Gilligan's (1982) theory of moral development that sees people in terms of their connectedness with others and focuses on interpersonal communication, relationships with others, and concern for others.* According to Gilligan, Kohlberg greatly underplayed the care perspective in moral development. She believes this may have happened because he was a male, most of his research was with males rather than females, and he used male responses as a model for his theory.

Gilligan (1992, 1996) also believes that girls reach a critical juncture in their development when they reach adolescence. Gilligan says that at the edge of adolescence, at about 11 or 12 years of age, girls become aware that their intense interest in intimacy is not prized by the male-dominated culture, even though society values females as caring and altruistic. The dilemma, says Gilligan, is that girls are presented with a choice that makes them appear either self-

Carol Gilligan with some of the students she has interviewed about the importance of relationships in a female's development. According to Gilligan (center), the sense of relationships and connectedness is at the heart of a female's development.

ish (if they become independent and self-sufficient) or selfless (if they remain responsive to others). Gilligan states that as young adolescent girls experience this dilemma, they increasingly "silence" their distinctive voice. They become less confident and more tentative in offering their opinions, which often persists into adulthood. Some researchers believe this self-doubt and ambivalence too often translates into depression and eating disorders among adolescent girls.

A third criticism of Kohlberg's view is that it is culturally biased (Jensen, 1995; Miller, 1995). One review of research on moral development in 27 countries found that moral reasoning appears to be more culture-specific than Kohlberg envisioned and that Kohlberg's scoring system does not recognize higher-level moral reasoning in certain cultural groups (Snarey, 1987). Kohlberg did not recognize values such as communal equity and collective happiness in Israel, the unity and

CONCEPT TABLE 2

Adolescence

Concept	Processes/Related Ideas	Characteristics/Description
Historical Beginnings and the Nature of Adolescence	Historical beginnings	G. Stanley Hall is the father of the scientific study of adolescence. In the early 1900s, he proposed the storm-and-stress view.
	Nature of adolescence	Adolescence is a transition between childhood and adulthood. Adolescence is best viewed as a time of evaluation, decision making, and commitment rather than as a time of rebellion, crisis, and pathology. Different portrayals of adolescents emerge, depending on the particular group of adolescents being described.
Physical Development	Nature of puberty	Puberty is a rapid change in maturation occurring mainly in early adolescence, which has been arriving earlier in recent years. Hormonal changes are prominent. Puberty occurs roughly 2 years earlier for girls than for boys, although its normal range is large. Some experts believe that puberty's effects are overstated.
Cognitive Development	Its nature	Piaget argued that formal operational thought appears between 7 and 11 years of age. Thought is abstract and idealistic but includes planning and logical analysis. Some of Piaget's ideas on formal operational thought are being challenged. Egocentrism also characterizes adolescent thought.
Socioemotional Development	Parent-adolescent relationships	The old model emphasized autonomy and detachment from parents, as well as intense, stressful conflict throughout adolescence. The new model emphasizes both attachment and autonomy, with parents acting as important support systems and attachment figures for adolescents; the new model also emphasizes that moderate, rather than severe, conflict is common, and it can serve a positive developmental function. Conflict with parents is greater in early adolescence, especially during the apex of puberty, than in late adolescence.
	Peers	Adolescents spend increased time with peers. Conformity to antisocial peer standards peaks about the eighth and ninth grades. Dating is a major interest.
	Identity development	Erikson believes that adolescence is characterized by the fifth stage of the human life cycle, identity versus identity confusion. Adolescents enter a psychological moratorium between childhood dependency and adult independence, seeking to find out who they are and where they are going in life.
	Moral development	Kohlberg proposed three levels (each with two stages) of moral development, which vary in the degree to which moral development is internalized—preconventional, conventional, and postconventional. Criticisms of Kohlberg's theory include the belief that his theory does not pay adequate attention to moral behavior, that moral development is more culture-specific than he believed, and that his theory places too much importance on the justice of the individual and not enough on close relationships and connectedness to others. The latter criticism has been made by Gilligan, who also believes that early adolescence is a critical juncture in the development of females.

sacredness of all life forms in India, or the relation of the individual to the community in New Guinea as examples of higher-level moral reasoning. Kohlberg's system would not score these values at the highest level of moral reasoning because they do not emphasize the individual's rights and abstract principles of justice. In summary, moral reasoning is shaped more by the values and beliefs of a culture than Kohlberg acknowledged.

At this point we have discussed a number of ideas about adolescence. A summary of these ideas is presented in concept table 2. Now we turn our attention to adult development and aging.

Adult Development and Aging

Just as the years from conception to adulthood are identified by certain periods, so too are the adult years. Let's explore developmental changes in the early, middle, and late adulthood periods.

Early and Middle Adulthood

Changes continue in the physical, cognitive, and socioemotional dimensions of adulthood. To begin, we will explore the physical changes that take place in early and middle adulthood.

Physical Development

Athletes keep getting better. They run faster, jump higher, lift more weight today than they did in years past. Despite this steady improvement, the age at which athletes are at their best has stayed virtually the same. In one study, researchers analyzed records from track and field, swimming, baseball, and golf to learn at what ages athletes truly hit their stride (Schulz & Curnow, 1988). They found that most athletes reach their peak performance under the age of 30, often between the ages of 19 and 26. Athletes who specialize in the strength and speed events peak relatively early, golf stars around the age of 31. In recent years though, the "biological window" of peak performance has widened even in the strength and speed events. Weight training, once unthinkable for women, has become standard procedure for star athletes. Florence Griffith Joyner's ability to lift 320 pounds helped build the strength behind her explosive start and leg drive that won world records in the 100 and 200 meters in the 1988 Olympics.

Not only do we reach our peak performance during early adulthood, we also are the healthiest. Few young adults have chronic health problems, and they have fewer colds and respiratory problems than they had as children. But young adults rarely recognize that bad eating habits, heavy drinking, and smoking in early adulthood can impair their health as they age. Despite warnings on packages and in advertisements that cigarettes are hazardous to health, individuals actually increase their use of cigarettes as they enter early adulthood (Bachman, O'Malley, & Johnston, 1978). They also increase their use of alcohol, marijuana, amphetamines, barbiturates, and hallucinogens (Bachman & others, 1996).

As we enter middle adulthood we are more acutely concerned about our health status. We experience a general decline in physical fitness throughout middle adulthood and some deterioration in health. The three greatest health concerns at this age are heart disease, cancer, and weight. Cancer related to smoking often surfaces for the first time in middle adulthood.

The *Harvard Medical School Newsletter* reports that about 20 million Americans are on a "serious" diet at any particular moment. Being overweight is a critical health problem, especially in middle adulthood. For individuals who are 30 percent or more overweight, the probability of dying in middle adulthood increases by 40 percent. Obesity also increases the probability an individual will suffer other ailments, including hypertension, digestive disorders, and diabetes.

Because our culture stresses a youthful appearance, physical deterioration—the graying hair, wrinkling skin, and sagging body—in middle adulthood is difficult to handle. Many middle-aged adults dye their hair and join weight reduction programs; some even undergo cosmetic surgery to look young. In one study, middle-aged women focused more attention on their facial attractiveness than older or younger women did. The middle-aged women also perceived that the signs of aging had a more detrimental effect on their appearance (Novak, 1977).

Cognitive Development

Piaget believed that adults and adolescents think in the same way but some developmental psychologists believe it is not until adulthood that individuals consolidate their formal operational thinking. That is, they may begin to plan and hypothesize about problems as adolescents, but they become more systematic in approaching problems as adults. Although some adults are more proficient than adolescents at developing hypotheses and deducing solutions to problems, remember from our earlier discussion that many adults do not think in formal operational ways at all (Keating, 1991).

Other psychologists believe that the absolute nature of adolescent logic and youth's buoyant optimism diminish in early adulthood (Labouvie-Vief, 1986). They argue that competent young adults are less caught up in idealism and tend to think logically and to adapt to life as circumstances demand. Less clear is whether our mental skills, especially memory, actually decline with age. Putting together the pieces of the research puzzle, memory appears to decline more often when long-term rather than short-term memory is involved. For example, middle-aged individuals can remember a phone number they heard 30 seconds ago, but they probably won't remember the number as efficiently the next day. Memory is also more likely to decline when organization and imagery are not used. In addition, memory tends to decline when the information to be recalled is recently acquired or when the information is not used often. For example, middle-aged adults probably won't remember the rules to a new game after only a lesson or two, and they are unlikely to know the new fall television schedule after its first week. And finally, memory tends to decline if recall rather than recognition is required. Middle-aged individuals can more efficiently select a phone number they heard yesterday if they are shown a list of phone numbers (recognition) rather than having to simply recall the number off the top of their head. Memory in middle adulthood also declines if the individual's health is poor (Rybash, Roodin, & Hoyer, 1995).

Socioemotional Development

As both Sigmund Freud and the Russian novelist Leo Tolstoy observed, adulthood is a time for work and a time for love. For some of us, though, finding our place in society and committing ourselves to a stable relationship take longer than we would have imagined. Among the socioemotional changes in early and middle adulthood are those involving careers and work, lifestyles, marriage, and other life events.

Careers and Work At age 21, Thomas Smith graduated from college and accepted a job as a science teacher at a high school in Boston. At age 26, Sally Caruthers graduated from medical school and took a job as an intern at a hospital in Los Angeles. At age 20, Barbara Breck finished her training at a vocational school and went to work as a computer programmer for an engineering firm in Chicago. Earning a living, choosing an occupation, establishing a career, and developing a career—these are important themes of adulthood.

By the end of adolescence or the beginning of early adulthood, most people have "an occupation." A few people seem to have known what they wanted to be ever since they were a little kid. But for many people, "getting there" may seem more like a time of floundering, ambiguity, and stress. Career counselors widely recommend exploring a variety of career options.

Career interests continue to be an important aspect of life for many middle-aged adults. A popular notion about midlife is that it is a time when people carefully examine their career, evaluate what they have accomplished, and seriously consider a change. However, only about 10 percent of Americans change careers in midlife. And only some do so because they seek greater fulfillment; others do so because they get laid off or fired.

Lifestyles Should I get married? If I wait any longer, will it be too late? Will I get left out? Should I stay single or is it too lonely a life? If I get married, do I want to have children? How will it affect my marriage? These are questions that many young adults ask themselves as they try to figure out what they want their life to be about.

Until about 1930, the goal of a stable marriage was accepted as a legitimate endpoint of adult development. In the last 60 years, however, we have seen the emergence of the desire for personal fulfillment—both inside and outside a marriage—as a force that can compete with marriage's stability. The changing norm of male-female equality in marriage has produced relationships that are more fragile and intense than they were earlier in the twentieth century. More adults are remaining single longer in the 1990s, and the average duration of a marriage in the United States currently is just over 9 years. The divorce rate, which increased astronomically in the 1970s, has finally begun to slow down, although it still remains alarmingly high. Even with adults remaining single for longer and divorce a frequent occurrence, Americans still show a strong preference for marriage—the proportion of women who never marry has remained at about 7 percent throughout the twentieth century, for example (Hernandez, 1988).

We often have idealistic expectations of marriage, which helps to explain our nation's high divorce rate and dissatisfaction in marriage (Notarius, 1996). We expect our spouse to simultaneously be a lover, a friend, a confidant, a counselor, a career person, and a parent. Many myths about marriage contribute to these unrealistic expectations (Rice, 1996).

Many myths also are associated with being single, ranging from "the swinging single" to "the desperately lonely, suicidal single." Most singles are somewhere between these two extremes. The pluses of being single include time to make decisions about one's life, time to develop personal resources to meet goals, freedom to make autonomous decisions and pursue one's own schedule and interests, opportunities to explore new places and try out new things, and privacy. Common problems of single adults include a lack of intimate relationships with others, loneliness, and finding a niche in a marriage-oriented society. Some single adults would rather remain single; others would rather be married.

Stage Theories of Adult Personality Development Psychologists have proposed different theories about adult development. Most theories address themes of work and love, career and intimacy. One set of theories proposes that adult development unfolds in stages.

Erikson's eight stages of the human life span include one stage for early adulthood and one stage for middle adulthood. Erikson believes that only after identity is well developed can true intimacy occur. **Intimacy versus isolation** *is Erikson's sixth stage of development, occurring mainly in early adulthood. Intimacy is the ability to develop close, loving relationships.* Intimacy helps us to form our identity because, in Erikson's words, "We are what we love." If intimacy does not develop, Erikson argues that a deep sense of isolation and impersonal feelings overcome the individual.

Generativity versus stagnation *is Erikson's seventh stage of development, occurring mainly in middle adulthood. Middle-aged adults need to assist the younger generation in leading useful lives.* Competent child rearing is one way to achieve generativity. However, adults can also satisfy this need through guardianship or a close relationship with the children of friends and relatives. The positive side of this stage—generativity—reflects an ability to positively shape the next generation. The negative side—stagnation—leaves the individual with a feeling of having done nothing for the next generation. As Erikson (1968) put it, "Generations will depend on the ability of all procreating individuals to face their children."

In *The Seasons of a Man's Life,* Daniel Levinson (1978) also described adult development as a series of stages. He extensively interviewed middle-aged male hourly workers, academic biologists, business executives, and novelists and concluded that developmental tasks must be mastered at a number of different points in adulthood (see figure 21).

In early adulthood, the two major tasks are exploring the possibilities for adult living and developing a stable life structure. The twenties represent the novice phase of adult

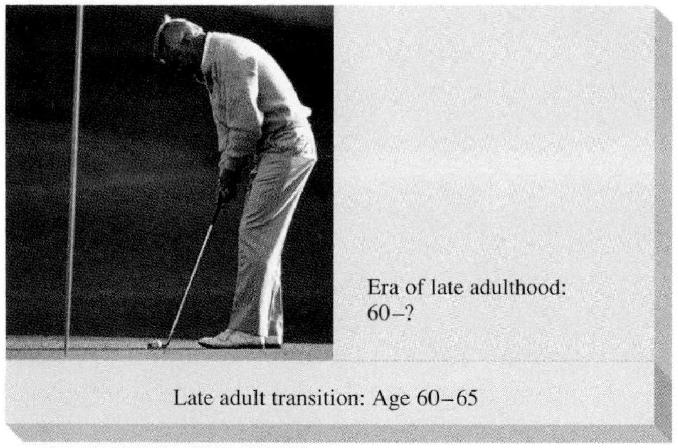

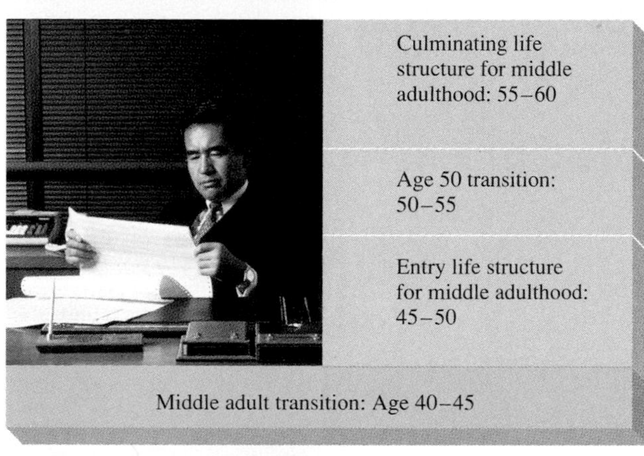

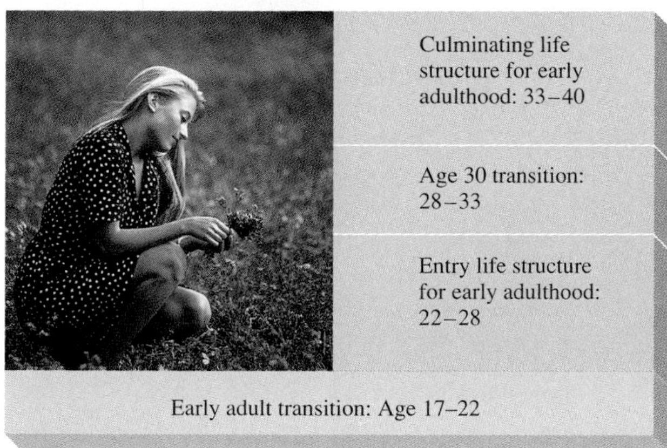

FIGURE 21

Levinson's Periods of Adult Development

development. By the end of a boy's teens, a transition from dependence to independence should occur. This transition is marked by a dream—an image of the kind of life the young man wants, especially in terms of marriage and a career. The novice phase is a time of experimenting and testing the dream in the real world.

Men actually determine their goals by the age of 28 to 33. During the thirties, a man usually works to develop his family life and career. In the late thirties, he enters a phase of becoming his own man (or BOOM, becoming one's own man, as Levinson calls it). By age 40, he reaches a stable point in his career; outgrows his earlier, more tenuous status as an adult; and now looks forward to the kind of life he will lead as a middle-aged adult.

In Levinson's view, the change to middle adulthood lasts about 5 years and requires that adults come to grips with four major conflicts that have existed since adolescence: (1) being young versus being old; (2) being destructive versus being constructive; (3) being masculine versus being feminine; and (4) being attached to others versus being separated from them. The success of the midlife transition depends on how effectively they can reduce these polarities and accept each of them as a part of their being. Levinson's original subjects were all males, but more recently he reported that these midlife issues hold for females as well (Levinson, 1978).

Erikson and Levinson emphasize that we go through a number of adult stages of development. In evaluating these stage theories, several points need to be kept in mind. First, the research on which they are based is not empirically sound—much of it involves clinical observations rather than rigorous, controlled observations. Second, the perspectives tend to describe the stages as crises, especially in the case of the midlife stage. Research on middle-aged adults reveals that few adults experience midlife in the tumultuous way described by the stage-crisis views: individuals vary extensively in how they cope with and perceive midlife (Vaillant, 1977).

Life Events, Cohort Effects, and Social Clocks

Life events rather than stages may be responsible for changes in our adult lives. Events such as marriage, divorce, the death of a spouse, a job promotion, and being fired from a job involve varying degrees of stress and influence our development as adults (Holmes & Rahe, 1967). However, we also need to know about the many factors that mediate the influence of life events on adult development—physical health, intelligence, personality, family support, and income, for example (Hultsch & Plemons, 1979). In addition, we need to know how a person perceives the life events and how he or she copes with the stress involved. For instance, one person may perceive a divorce as highly stressful, whereas another person may perceive the same life event as a challenge. We also need to consider the person's life stage and circumstances. Divorce may be more stressful for an individual in his fifties who has been married for many years, for example, than for someone in her twenties who has been married only a few years. Individuals may cope with divorce more effectively in the 1990s than people did in the 1890s because divorce has become more commonplace and accepted in today's society.

An increasing number of developmental psychologists stress that changing social expectations influence how different **cohorts**—*groups of individuals born in the same year or time period*—move through the life cycle. For example, people born during the Depression may have a different outlook on life than those born during the optimistic 1950s.

Bernice Neugarten (1980) believes that the social environment of a particular age group can alter its "social clock"—the timetable according to which individuals are expected to accomplish life's tasks, such as getting married, having children, and establishing themselves in a career. Social clocks act as guides for our lives. People who are somehow "out of sync" with these social clocks find their lives more stressful than those who are on schedule, says Neugarten. One study found that between the late 1950s and the late 1970s there was a dramatic decline in adults' beliefs that there is a "right age" for major life events and achievements (Passuth, Maines, & Neugarten, 1984).

Continuity and Discontinuity Richard Alpert, an achievement-oriented, hardworking college professor in the 1960s, suddenly became Ram Dass, a free-spirited guru in search of an expanded state of consciousness, in the 1970s. It would seem as though Richard Alpert and Ram Dass were two very different people; but Harvard psychologist David McClelland, who knows Ram Dass well, says that he is the same old Richard—still charming, still concerned with inner experience, and still power hungry.

Jerry Rubin views his own transformation from yippie to Wall Street businessman in a way that underscores continuity in personality. Rubin says that he discovered his identity in a typical Jerry Rubin fashion—trying out anything and everything, behaving in a wild and crazy manner. Whether yippie or Wall Street yuppie, Rubin approached life with enthusiasm and curiosity.

William James (1890) said that our basic personality is like plaster, set by the time we are 30. James believed that our bodies and attitudes may change through the adult years—as did Richard Alpert's and Jerry Rubin's—but the basic core of our personality remains the same. Some modern researchers, such as Paul Costa (1988; Costa & McRae, 1995), also believe that traits such as how extraverted we are, how well-adjusted we are, and our openness to new experiences do not change much during our adult lives. Costa says that a person who is shy and quiet at age 25 will basically be that same shy and quiet person at age 50. Yet other psychologists are enthusiastic about our capacity for change as adults, arguing that too much importance is attached to personality change in childhood and not enough to change in adulthood.

A more moderate view of the stability-change issue comes from the architects of the California Longitudinal Study, which now spans more than 50 years (Eichorn & others, 1981). These researchers believe some stability exists over the long course of adult development, but that adults are more capable of changing than Costa thinks. For example, a person who is shy and introverted at age 25 may not be completely extraverted at age 50 but may be less introverted than at 25. This person may have married someone who encouraged him to be more outgoing and supported his efforts to socialize; perhaps he changed jobs at age 30 and became a salesman, placing him in a situation where he was required to develop his social skills.

(a)

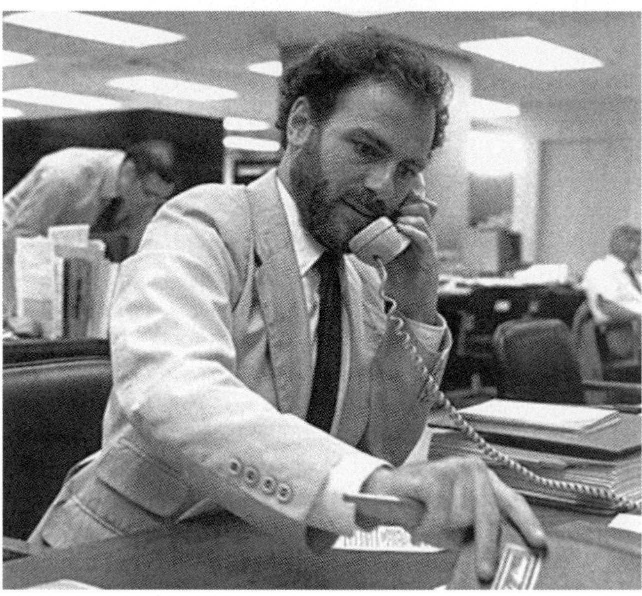

(b)

How much does personality change and how much does it stay the same through adulthood? In the early 1970s, Jerry Rubin was a yippie demonstrator (a), but, in the 1980s, Rubin became a Wall Street businessman (b).

Humans are adaptive beings. We are resilient throughout our adult lives, but we do not acquire entirely new personalities (Bengtson, 1996). In a sense we change but remain the same—underlying the change is coherence and stability.

Late Adulthood and Aging

In the words of twentieth-century Italian poet Salvatore Quasimodo, "Each of us stands alone at the heart of the earth pierced through by a ray of sunlight: And suddenly

Eighty-five-year-old Sadie Halperin doubled her strength in exercise after just 11 months. Before developing an exercise routine, she felt wobbly and often had to hold on to a wall when she walked. Now she walks down the middle of hallways and says she feels wonderful.

it is evening." While we may be in the evening of our lives in late adulthood, we are not meant to live out passively our remaining years.

Physical Development

Everything we know about older adults suggests that the more active they are, the healthier and happier they are (Birren & Schaie, 1996). John Pianfetti, age 70, and Madge Sharples, age 65, recently competed in the New York Marathon. Older adults don't have to run marathons to be healthy and happy; even moderate exercise benefits their health. One study over an 11-year period of more than 13,000 men and women at the Aerobics Institute in Dallas, Texas, found that sedentary participants were more than twice as likely to die during that period than those who were moderately fit (Blair & Kohl, 1989).

Jogging hogs have shown the dramatic effects of exercise on health. Colin Bloor and Frank White (1983) trained a group of hogs to run approximately 100 miles per week. Then they narrowed the arteries that supplied blood to the hogs' hearts. The hearts of these jogging hogs developed extensive alternate pathways for blood supply, and 42 percent of their threatened heart tissue was salvaged, compared to only 17 percent in a control group of hogs (see figure 22).

Exercise is an excellent way to maintain health in late adulthood and possibly increase our longevity. Just how long can we live, and what influences our longevity?

We are no longer a youthful society. As more people live to older ages, the proportion of individuals at different ages has become increasingly similar. Indeed, the concept of a period called late adulthood is a recent one. Until the twentieth century most people died before they were 65. In 1900 only 1 American in 25 was over 65. Today the figure is 1 in 9. By the middle of the twentieth-first century, 1 in 4 Americans will be 65 years of age or older (see figure 23).

FIGURE 22

Bloor and White's Study of Exercise and Health
Hogs, such as the one shown here, were trained to run approximately 100 miles per week. Then the experimenters narrowed the arteries that supplied blood to the hogs' hearts. The jogging hogs' hearts developed alternative pathways for blood supply, whereas a group of nonjogging hogs were less likely to recover.

The life span has remained virtually unchanged since the beginning of recorded history. What has changed is life expectancy, the number of people expected to reach what seems to be an unbudging end point (Birren, 1996). Even though improvements in medicine, nutrition, exercise, and lifestyle have given us, on the average, 22 additional years of life since 1900, few of us will live to be 100. In Explorations in Psychology 3, you will read about three areas of the world purported to have large numbers of inhabitants who live to be more than 100 years old.

Even if we are remarkably healthy through our adult years, we begin to age at some point. What are the biological explanations of aging? Virtually all biological theories of aging and life span assign an important role to genes (Schneider & others, 1996). Research demonstrates that the body's cells can divide only a limited number of times; cells from embryonic tissue can divide about fifty times, for example (Hayflick, 1977). Cells

FIGURE 23

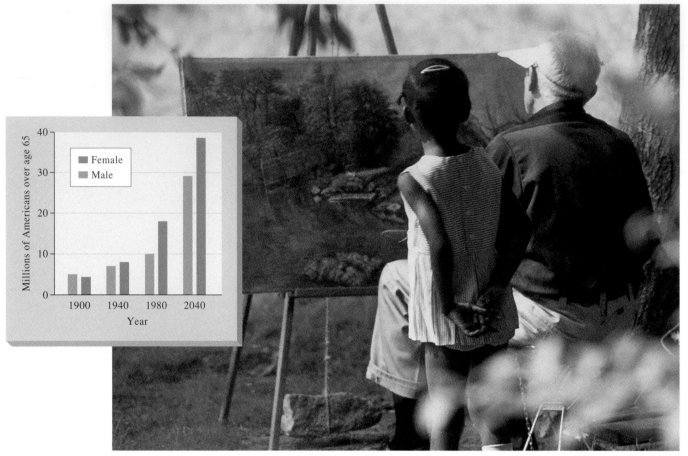

Millions of Americans Over Age 65 in 1900, 1940, and 1980, and Projected for the Year 2040

extracted from older adults divide fewer times than those taken from younger adults. The cells of elderly people still have dividing capability, although we rarely live to the end of our life-span potential. Based on the rate at which human cells divide, biologists place the upper limit of the human life cycle at about 120 years.

As we age in late adulthood the probability we will have a disease or become seriously ill increases (Whitbourne, 1996). For example, a majority of individuals who are alive at age 80 have some physical impairment. Alzheimer's disease is of special concern (Butters, Delis, & Lucas, 1995). **Alzheimer's disease** *is a degenerative, irreversible brain disorder that impairs memory and social behavior.* More than 2 million people over the age of 65 in the United States have Alzheimer's disease.

Older adults may not be as quick with their thoughts as younger adults, but wisdom may be an entirely different matter. This elderly woman shares the wisdom of her experiences with a classroom of children.

Cognitive Development

At age 70, Dr. John Rock developed the birth control pill. At age 89, Arthur Rubinstein gave one of his best performances at New York's Carnegie Hall. From 85 to 90 years of age, Pablo Picasso completed three sets of drawings. And at age 76, Anna Mary Robertson Moses took up painting. As Grandma Moses, she became internationally famous and staged fifteen one-woman shows throughout Europe. As Aeschylus said in the fifth century B.C., "It is always in season for the old to learn." But are the feats of Grandma Moses and others rare exceptions?

The issue of intellectual decline through the adult years is a provocative one. David Wechsler (1972) concluded

Explorations in Psychology 3

Aging in Russia, Ecuador, and Kashmir

Imagine that you are 120 years old. Would you still be able to write your name? Could you think clearly? What would your body look like? Would you be able to walk? To run? Could you still have sex? Would you have an interest in sex? Would your eyes and ears still function? Could you work?

Has anyone ever lived to be 120 years old? Supposedly. In three areas of the world, not just a single person but many people have reportedly lived more than 130 years. These areas are the Republic of Georgia in Russia, the Vilcabamba valley in Ecuador, and the province of Hunza in Kashmir (in Northern India). Three people over 100 years old (centenarians) per 100,000 people is considered normal. But in the Russian region where the Abkhasian people live, approximately 400 centenarians per 100,000 people have been reported. Some of the Abkhasians are said to be 120 to 170 years old (Benet, 1976).

However, there is reason to believe that some of these claims are false (Medvedev, 1974). Indeed, we really do not have sound documentation of anyone living more than 120 years. In the case of the Abkhasians, birth registrations and other documents, such as marriage certificates and military registrations, are not available. In most instances, the ages of the Abkhasians have been based on the individuals' recall of important historical events and interviews with other members of the village (Benet, 1976). In the Russian villages where people have been reported to live a long life, the elderly experience unparalleled esteem and honor. Centenarians are often given special positions in the community, such as being the leader of social celebrations. Thus there is a strong motivation to say that one is older than one really is. One individual who claimed to be 130 years of age was found to have used his father's birth certificate during World War I to escape army duty. Later it was discovered that he only was 78 years old (Hayflick, 1975).

(a) Selakh Butka, who says he is 113 years old, is shown with his wife, who says she is 101. The Butkas live in the Georgian Republic of Russia, where reports of unusual longevity have surfaced. Why are scientists skeptical about their age?
(b) Eighty-seven-year-old José Maria Rosa is from the Vilcabamba region of Ecuador, which also is renowned for the longevity of its inhabitants.

that the decline is simply part of the general aging process we all go through. But the issue seems more complex (Birren & others, 1996). Remember that we do not have just one type of intelligence; intelligence comes in different forms. Older adults do not score as high on intelligence tests as young adults when speed of processing is involved and this undoubtedly harms their performance on school-related tasks and traditional measures of intelligence. But when we consider general knowledge and wisdom, older adults often outperform younger adults.

Recently, Paul Baltes and his colleagues (Baltes & Baltes, 1990; Marsiske & others, 1995) further clarified the distinction between those aspects of the aging mind that show decline and those that do not, or even show some improvement. He makes a distinction between "cognitive mechanics" and "cognitive pragmatics." Using computer language as an analogy, **cognitive mechanics** *are the hardware of the mind and reflect the neurophysiological architecture of the brain as developed through evolution. At the operational level, cognitive mechanics involve speed and accuracy of the processes involving sensory input, visual and motor memory, discrimination, comparison, and categorization.* Because of the strong influence of biology, heredity, and health on cognitive mechanics, their decline with aging is likely. Conversely, **cognitive pragmatics** *refer to the culture-based "software" of the mind. At the operational level, cognitive pragmatics include reading and writing skills, language comprehension, educational qualifications, professional skills, and also the type of knowledge about the self and life skills that help us to master or cope with life.* Because of the strong influence of culture on cognitive pragmatics, their progress into old age is possible. Because of the enhancing and compensatory power of cognitive pragmatics, they may increase in old age even in the face of age-related decline in cognitive mechanics. For example, people who can read, a case of cognitive pragmatics, can outperform others who can't read, even if they have worse cognitive mechanics.

Ageism is one of our society's ugliest practices. Older adults may be shunned socially because they are perceived as senile or boring. Their children may edge them out of their lives. In these circumstances, a social network of friendships becomes an important support system for older adults. Researchers have found that close attachment to one or more individuals, whether friends or family, is associated with greater life satisfaction.

Socioemotional Development

In the past, the image of the older adult was of a person sitting in a rocking chair watching the world go by. Now we know that the most well-adjusted and satisfied older adults are active, not passive. **Activity theory** *states that the more active and involved older people are, the more satisfied they are and the more likely they will stay healthy.* Researchers have found that older people who go to church, attend meetings, take trips, and exercise are happier than those who simply sit at home. Predictably, the better the health and the higher the income, the more likely an older person is to be satisfied with life as well.

The elderly often face painful discrimination. A new word in our vocabulary is **ageism,** *which is prejudice against people because of their age, in particular prejudice against older people.* Older adults may be branded with a number of stereotypes—such as feebleminded, boring, ugly, parasitic. As a result they may be treated like children and described as cute and adorable. And far worse, they often are not hired for new jobs or are forced out of existing ones, they may be shunned, or they may even be edged out of their own families. The elderly who are poor or who are from ethnic minority backgrounds face special hardships (Aneshensel & others, 1996).

Life-span developmentalist Paul Baltes and his colleagues (Baltes & Baltes, 1990; Marsiske & others, 1995) believe that successful aging is related to three main factors: selection, optimization, and compensation. *Selection* is based on the concept that in old age there is a reduced capacity and loss of functioning, which mandates a reduction of performance in most domains of life. *Optimization* suggests that it is possible to maintain performance in some areas by practice and the use of new technologies. *Compensation* becomes relevant when life tasks require a level of capacity beyond the current level of the older adult's performance potential. Older adults especially need to compensate in circumstances with high mental or physical demands, such as when thinking about and memorizing new material, reacting quickly when driving a car, or running fast (Abraham & Hansson, 1995; Carstensen, Hanson, & Freund, 1995; Dixon & Backman, 1995). Illness in old age makes the need for compensation obvious.

Consider the late Arthur Rubinstein, who was interviewed when he was 80 years old. Rubinstein said that three factors were responsible for his ability to maintain his status as an admired concert pianist into old age. First, he mastered the weaknesses of old age by reducing the scope of his repertoire and playing fewer pieces (an example of selection). Second, he spent more time at practice than earlier in his life (an example of optimization). And third, he used special strategies such as slowing down before fast segments, thus creating the image of faster playing than was objectively true (an example of compensation).

"Life is lived forward, but understood backwards," said the Danish philosopher Søren Kierkegaard. This is truer of late adulthood than of any other life period. Kierkegaard's words reflect Erikson's final stage of development through the life span. Erikson called this eighth stage **integrity versus**

In late adulthood, we review our lives, looking backward and examining our journey through the human life cycle. The words of Sarah Teasdale in Dark of the Moon *(1926) capture our search for meaning in late adulthood:*

When I look life in the eyes
Grown calm and very coldly wise,
Life will have given me the truth,
And taken in exchange—my youth.

despair. *Occurring mainly in late adulthood, it is a time of looking back at what we have done with our lives.* If the older person has developed a positive outlook in each of the preceding periods of development, the retrospective glances and reminiscences will reveal a life well spent, and the individual will feel satisfied (integrity). But if the older adult has a negative outlook on life, the retrospective glances may produce doubt, gloom, and despair about the value of one's life. (For an overview of Erikson's eight stages of development, see figure 24.) As Erikson (1968) put it, "To whatever abyss ultimate concerns may lead individual men, man as a psychosocial creature will face, toward the end of his life, a new edition of the identity crisis, which we may state in the words, 'I am what survives of me.' "

Death and Dying

"I'd like to know what this show is all about before it's out," wrote the twentieth-century Dutch poet and inventor Piet Hein. Death may come at any time, but it is during late adulthood that we realize our days are literally numbered. Societies throughout history have had philosophical or religious beliefs about death (Petrinovich, 1996). And most have some form of ritual to mark the passing from life to death. Some cultures hold a ceremonial meal accompanied by festivities. In others, mourners wear a black armband. Figure 25 shows two rituals that reveal cultural variations in dealing with death.

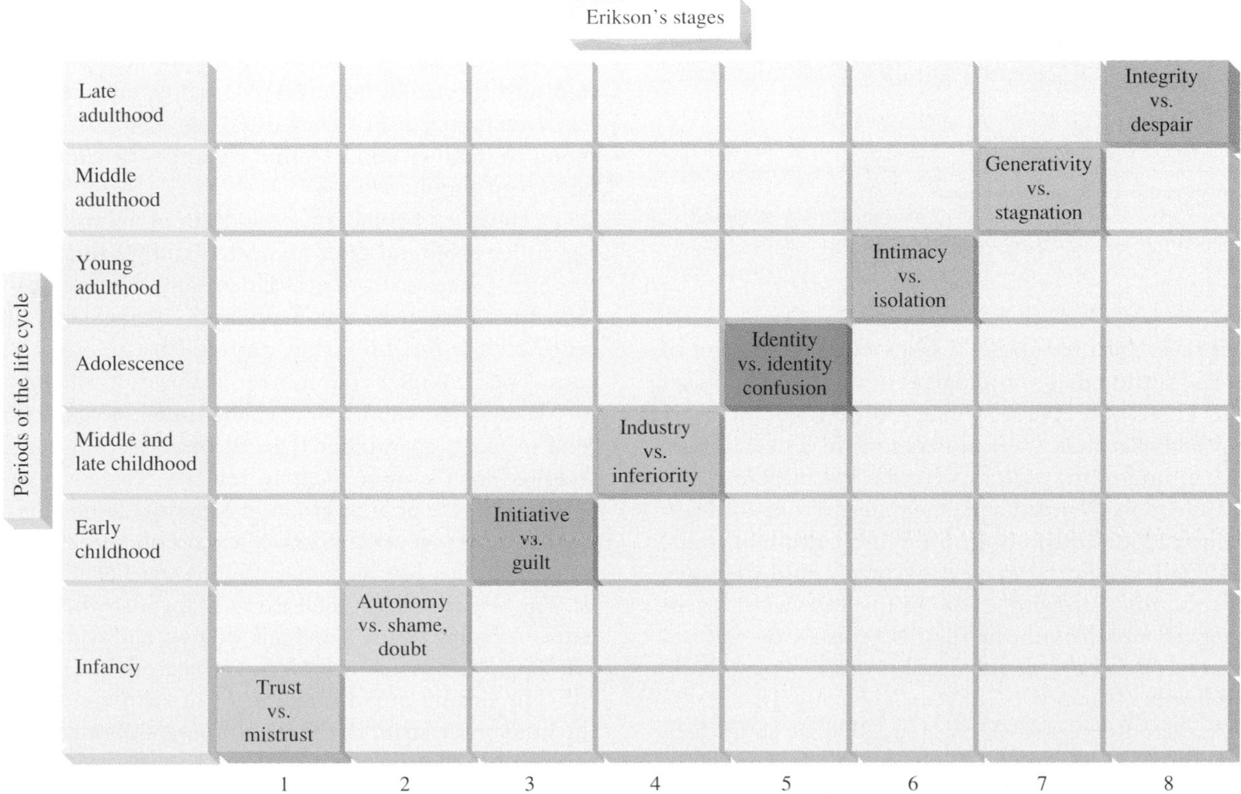

FIGURE 24

Erikson's Eight Stages of the Human Life Span

(a)

(b)

FIGURE 25

Cultural Variations Regarding Death

(*a*) A New Orleans street funeral is in progress. (*b*) A deceased person's belongings are left on a mountainside in Tibet.

In most cultures, death is not viewed as the end of existence—although the biological body dies, the spirit lives on. This belief is held by many Americans. Reincarnation, the belief that the soul is reborn in a new human body, is an important aspect of Hindu and Buddhist religions. Cultures often differ in their perception of death and their reaction to death. In the Gond culture of India, death is believed to be caused by magic and demons; Gonds react to death with anger. In the Tanala culture of Madagascar, death is thought to be caused by natural forces. The members of the Tanala culture peacefully react to death.

Elisabeth Kübler-Ross (1974) says that we go through five stages in facing death: denial and isolation, anger, bargaining, depression, and acceptance. Initially, the individual responds, "No, it can't be me. It's not possible." But denial is only a temporary defense. When the individual recognizes that denial no longer can be maintained, she often becomes angry and resentful. Now the individual's question becomes, "Why me?" Anger often is displaced onto physicians, nurses, family members, and even God. In the third stage, the dying person develops the hope that death can somehow be postponed or delayed. The individual now says, "Yes, me, but. . . ." The dying person bargains and negotiates, often with God, offering a reformed life dedicated to God and the service of others for a few more months of life.

As the dying individual comes to accept the certainty of her death, she often enters a period of preparatory grief, becoming silent, refusing visitors, and spending much of the time crying or grieving. This behavior is a normal effort to disconnect the self from all love objects. Kübler-Ross describes the final stage, characterized by peace and acceptance of one's fate, as the end of the struggle, the final resting stage before death.

Not everyone goes through the stages in the sequence Kübler-Ross proposed. Indeed, Kübler-Ross herself says she has been misread, pointing out that she never believed every individual copes with death in a specific sequence. But she does maintain that the optimal way to cope with death is through the stages she has outlined.

But some individuals struggle until the very end, angrily hanging onto their lives. They follow the encouragement of Dylan Thomas: "Do not go gentle into that good night. Old age should burn and rave at close of day . . . rage, rage against the dying of the light." In these instances, acceptance of death never comes. People die in different ways and experience different feelings and emotions in the process: hope, fear, curiosity, envy, apathy, relief, even anticipation. They often move rapidly from one mood to another and in some instances two moods may be present simultaneously.

Those left behind after the death of an intimate partner suffer profound grief and often endure financial loss, loneliness, increased physical illness, and increased psychological disorders including depression (DeSpelder & Strickland, 1996). But how they cope with the crisis varies considerably. Widows outnumber widowers by the ratio of 5 to 1 because women live longer than men, because women tend to marry men older than themselves, and because a widowed man is more likely to remarry. Widowed women are probably the poorest group in America, despite the myth of huge insurance settlements. Many are also lonely, and the poorer and less educated they are, the lonelier they tend to be. The bereaved are at increased risk for many health problems, including death. For both widows and widowers, social support helps them to adjust to the death of a spouse.

In closing our discussion of development through the human life span, think for a moment about Erik Erikson's words, "In the end, the power behind development is life." A summary of the main ideas in our discussion of adult development, aging, death, and dying is presented in concept table 3.

Concept Table 3

Adult Development and Aging

Concept	Processes/Related Ideas	Characteristics/Description
Adult Periods of Development	Early adulthood	Early adulthood begins in the late teens or early twenties and ends in the late thirties to early forties. It is a time when individuals establish personal and economic independence, pursue a career, and seek intimacy with one or more individuals.
	Middle adulthood	Middle adulthood begins at about 35 to 45 years of age and ends at 55 to 65 years of age. It is a time of expanding personal and social involvement, increased responsibility, adjustment to physical decline, and career satisfaction.
	Late adulthood	Late adulthood begins at 60 to 70 years of age and ends when an individual dies. It is a time of adjustment to decreased strength and health, retirement, reduced income, and new social roles.
Early and Middle Adulthood	Physical development	The peak of our physical skills and health usually comes in early adulthood, a time when it is easy to develop bad health habits. In middle adulthood, most individuals experience a decline in physical fitness, some deterioration in health, and an increased interest in health matters.
	Cognitive development	Some psychologists argue that cognition becomes more pragmatic in early adulthood. Cognitive skills are strong in early adulthood. In middle adulthood, memory may decline, but such strategies as organization can reduce the decline.
	Socioemotional development	Among the important aspects of career and work in early and middle adulthood are the increasing number of females in the workforce. Adults must choose the type of lifestyle they want to follow—single, married, or divorced, for example. One set of adult personality theories proposes that adult development unfolds in stages (Erikson, Levinson). Other theorists emphasize life events, social clocks, and cohort effects. The stage theorists have exaggerated the prevalence of a midlife crisis. There is both continuity and discontinuity in adult personality development.
Late Adulthood and Aging	Physical development	Everything we know about older adults suggests that the more physically active they are, the healthier and happier they are, and the longer they live. Life expectancy has increased dramatically, but the life span has remained virtually unchanged for centuries. Longevity is influenced by such factors as heredity, family, health, education, personality, and lifestyle. Virtually all biological theories of aging assign an important role to genes. Based on the rate at which cells divide, biologists place the upper limit on the human life span at about 120 years of age. As we grow old, the chances of becoming seriously ill increase. Alzheimer's disease is a degenerative brain disorder that impairs memory and social behavior.
	Cognitive development	There is extensive debate about whether intelligence declines in late adulthood. Recent naturalistic memory research suggests that the decline is exaggerated. Remember that we have many forms of intelligence, and the overall question of intellectual decline is a global one. As we age, speed of processing declines, but wisdom may increase. Baltes recently proposed a distinction between cognitive mechanics and cognitive pragmatics.
	Socioemotional development	Everything we know about late adulthood suggests that an active lifestyle is preferable to disengagement. Baltes believes successful aging is related to selection, optimization, and compensation. Erikson believes that the final issue in the life span to be negotiated is integrity versus despair, which involves a life review.
Death and Dying	Its nature	Death may come at any point in the life span, but in late adulthood we know it is near. Most societies have rituals that deal with death, although cultures vary in their orientation toward death. Kübler-Ross proposed five stages of coping with death.

Critical Thinking About Behavior

Moral Crimes and Misdemeanors

It is a good thing that we don't regularly have to face decisions as difficult as Heinz's about whether or not to steal a drug to save his wife's life. However, decisions about right and wrong regularly confront us on a much smaller scale. Examine the everyday moral dilemmas described below, decide on your likely course of action, and think about the reasons why you would act in that manner.

- Do you tell the waitress who has charged you an insufficient amount about her error, or do you pocket the difference?
- Do you comment to Don that his new hairstyle, which you find unflattering, is "different" or "awful"?
- Do you let your eyes wander to your neighbor's test paper to compare your answer, when the teacher is out of the room?
- At tax time are you scrupulous about reporting to the Internal Revenue Service every earned penny, or do you look for opportunities to misrepresent your income?
- Do you invite people to parties because you wish to be in their company, or do you sometimes ask people you don't like because you might lose some social status if you don't invite them?
- When you sell a car, do you identify every aspect of the car that will need repair?

Kohlberg was less interested in establishing moral absolutes in relation to the dilemmas he created than he was in the justifications or reasons that his interviewees provided to justify their actions. As you examine your responses to the small moral dilemmas described above, do any patterns emerge in your answers? Would you have been scrupulously honest in those circumstances? Or would you have acted according to self-protection or personal gain? Was there any variation in your responses?

Let's examine just one moral dilemma from Kohlberg's point of view to sort out the levels of moral reasoning that apply to the situation. This exercise will encourage the practice of ethical treatment toward individuals and groups. Suppose we examine the moral challenge of properly paying income taxes. Are you ever tempted to cheat, or do you consistently pay what the government says you owe? What is your justification?

You could pay your taxes out of fear of getting caught, or you could decide to take some inappropriate write-offs because you'd be willing to pay the penalty if you get caught. Both of these answers reflect a *preconventional* level of reasoning because a concern with the rewards and punishments is at the heart of your decision. At the *conventional* level, you might pay your taxes because everyone else does. You would not like to risk the disapproval of other good citizens. On the other hand, you might decide to misrepresent your tax debt, justifying your actions with your belief that most taxpayers engage in the same sort of tactics. You might even believe that you would lose others' approval by paying your appropriate amount. Finally, *postconventional* reasoning can also be present in justifying either course of action. You might choose fair payment because you believe democratic governments need to be well funded to function well and serve the citizenry effectively. You might even be proud to pay your fair share. On the other hand, the postconventional reasoner might justify nonpayment as withholding support from government activities that aren't humane. As you can see, the specific decision does not dictate whether an act is evaluated as moral or immoral. The complexity of the justification is what determines the level of reasoning, according to Kohlberg.

Overview

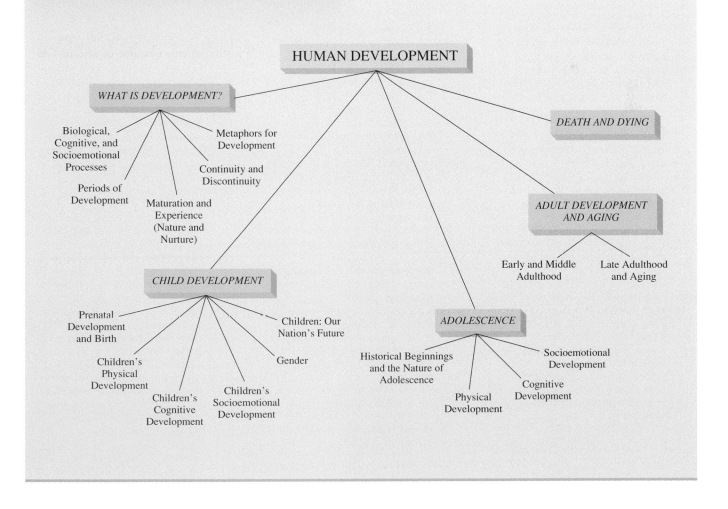

We began this chapter by exploring the nature of development, biological, cognitive, and socioemotional processes, periods of development, maturation and experience (nature and nurture), continuity and discontinuity, and metaphors for development. Then we studied children's development—physical, cognitive, and socioemotional—and considered the nature of gender and how children are the future of society. We evaluated adolescent development—physical, cognitive, and socioemotional. And we read about adulthood and aging, including early and middle adulthood, and late adulthood and aging. We concluded the chapter by examining death and dying. Don't forget that you can obtain an overall summary of the chapter by again studying the concept tables on pages 330, 338, and 349.

HUMAN DEVELOPMENT

- *WHAT IS DEVELOPMENT?*
  - Biological, Cognitive, and Socioemotional Processes
  - Periods of Development
  - Maturation and Experience (Nature and Nurture)
  - Continuity and Discontinuity
  - Metaphors for Development
- *CHILD DEVELOPMENT*
  - Prenatal Development and Birth
  - Children's Physical Development
  - Children's Cognitive Development
  - Children's Socioemotional Development
  - Gender
  - Children: Our Nation's Future
- *ADOLESCENCE*
  - Historical Beginnings and the Nature of Adolescence
  - Physical Development
  - Cognitive Development
  - Socioemotional Development
- *ADULT DEVELOPMENT AND AGING*
  - Early and Middle Adulthood
  - Late Adulthood and Aging
- *DEATH AND DYING*

Key Terms

development The pattern of movement or change that begins at conception and continues through the life span. p. 304

biological processes Processes that involve changes in an individual's physical nature. p. 304

cognitive processes Processes that involve changes in an individual's thought, intelligence, and language. p. 304

socioemotional processes Processes that involve changes in an individual's relationships with other people, changes in emotions, and changes in personality. p. 304

prenatal period The time from conception to birth. p. 304

infancy The developmental period that extends from birth to 18 or 24 months of age. p. 304

early childhood The developmental period that extends from the end of infancy to about 5 or 6 years; sometimes the period is called the preschool years. p. 304

middle and late childhood The developmental period that extends from about 6 to 11 years of age, approximately corresponding to the elementary school years; sometimes the period is called the elementary school years. p. 305

adolescence The transition from childhood to adulthood, which involves physical, cognitive, and socioemotional changes. In most cultures adolescence begins at about 10 to 13 years of age and ends at about 18 to 21 years of age. p. 305

early adulthood The developmental stage that begins in the late teens or early twenties and ends in the thirties. It is a time when individuals establish personal and economic independence, intensely pursue a career, and seek intimacy with one or more individuals. p. 305

middle adulthood The developmental stage that begins at about 35 to 45 years of age and ends at about 55 to 65 years of age. It is a time of expanding personal and social involvement, increased responsibility, adjustment to physical decline, and attainment and maintenance of career satisfaction. p. 305

late adulthood The developmental stage that begins around 60 to 70 years of age and ends when an individual dies. It is a time of adjustment to decreased strength and health, retirement, reduced income, new social roles, and learning how to age successfully. p. 305

maturation The orderly sequence of changes dictated by each person's genetic blueprint. p. 305

nature/nurture controversy *Nature* refers to an organism's biological inheritance, *nurture* to environmental experiences. The "nature" proponents claim biological inheritance is the most important influence on development, the "nurture" proponents claim that environmental experiences are the most important. p. 305

continuity of development The view that development involves gradual, cumulative change from conception to death. p. 307

discontinuity of development The view that development involves distinct stages in the life span. p. 307

conception The penetration of an ovum (egg) by a sperm cell; also called fertilization. p. 308

zygote A single cell formed through fertilization. p. 308

germinal period The period of prenatal development that takes place in the first 2 weeks after conception. It includes the creation of the zygote, continued cell division, and the attachment of the zygote to the uterine wall. p. 308

embryonic period The period of prenatal development that occurs from 3 to 8 weeks after conception. During the embryonic period, the rate of cell differentiation intensifies, support systems for the cells form, and the beginnings of organs appear. p. 308

fetal period The prenatal period of development that begins 2 months after conception and lasts for 7 months, on the average. p. 309

teratogen (The word comes from the Greek word *tera,* meaning "monster.") Any agent that causes a birth defect. The field of study that investigates the causes of birth defects is called teratology. p. 309

fetal alcohol syndrome (FAS) A cluster of abnormalities that appear in the offspring of mothers who drink alcohol heavily during pregnancy. p. 309

preterm infant An infant who is born prior to 38 weeks into the prenatal period; also called a premature infant. p. 309

assimilation The incorporation of new information into one's existing knowledge. p. 313

accommodation An individual's adjustment to new information. p. 313

sensorimotor thought The first Piagetian stage, lasting from birth to about 2 years of age. In this stage, infants construct an understanding of the world by coordinating sensory experiences (such as seeing and hearing) with physical (motor) actions—hence the term *sensorimotor.* p. 313

object permanence The Piagetian term for one of an infant's most important accomplishments: understanding that objects and events continue to exist even when they cannot directly be seen, heard, or touched. p. 313

operations In Piaget's theory, mental representations that are reversible; internalized sets of actions that allow the child to do mentally what was done physically before. p. 314

preoperational thought The term Piaget gave to the 2- to 7-year-old child's understanding of the world. Children at this stage of reasoning cannot understand such logical operations as the reversibility of mental representations. p. 315

conservation A belief in the permanence of certain attributes of objects or situations in spite of superficial changes. p. 318

egocentrism A salient feature of preoperational thought; the inability to distinguish between one's own perspective and someone else's perspective. p. 318

concrete operational thought The term Piaget gave to the 7- to 11-year-old child's understanding of the world. At this stage of thought children can use operations. Logical reasoning replaces intuitive thought as long as the principles are applied to concrete examples. p. 318

neo-Piagetians Developmentalists who have elaborated on Piaget's theory, believing that children's cognitive development is more specific in many respects than Piaget thought. p. 320

trust versus mistrust Erikson's first psychosocial stage, experienced in the first year of life. Trust is built when an infant's basic needs—such as needs for comfort, food, and warmth—are met. p. 320

autonomy versus shame and doubt Erikson's second psychosocial stage, occurring from about 1 to 3 years of age. After developing trust, infants begin to discover that their behavior is their own. They start to assert their sense of independence, or autonomy; they realize their will. p. 320

initiative versus guilt Erikson's third stage of development, occurring during the preschool years. As preschool children encounter a widening social world, they are challenged more than they were as infants. Active, purposeful behavior is needed to cope with these challenges. Children in this stage are asked to assume responsibility for their bodies, their behavior, their toys, and their pets. p. 320

industry versus inferiority Erikson's fourth stage of development, occurring during the elementary school years. In this stage, children's initiative brings them into contact with a wealth of new experiences. As they move into middle and late childhood, they direct their energy toward mastering knowledge and intellectual skills. With their expansive imaginations, children at this stage are eager to learn. p. 320

attachment A close emotional bond between the infant and its caregiver. p. 322

imprinting The tendency of an infant animal to form an attachment to the first moving object it sees or hears. p. 322

secure attachment Securely attached infants use the caregiver, usually the mother, as a secure base from which to explore the environment. Ainsworth believes that secure attachment in the first year of life provides an important foundation for psychological development later in life. p. 322

authoritarian parenting A restrictive, punitive style in which the parent exhorts the child to follow the parent's directions and to respect work and effort. The authoritarian parent places firm limits and controls on the child and allows little verbal exchange. Authoritarian parenting is associated with children's social incompetence. p. 324

authoritative parenting A style in which parents encourage children to be independent but still places limits and controls on their actions. Extensive verbal give-and-take is allowed, and parents are warm and nurturant toward the child. Authoritative parenting is associated with children's social competence. p. 324

neglectful parenting A style of parenting in which parents are very uninvolved in the child's life; it is associated with children's social incompetence, especially a lack of self-control. p. 324

indulgent parenting A style of parenting in which parents are very involved with their children but place few demands or controls on them; it is associated with children's social incompetence, especially a lack of self-control. p. 324

reciprocal socialization Bidirectional socialization, in which children socialize their parents just as parents socialize their children. p. 325

synchrony The carefully coordinated interaction between the parent and child in which, often unknowingly, they are attuned to each other's behavior. p. 325

gender The sociocultural dimension of being male or female. p. 326

gender identity The sense of being male or female, which most children begin to acquire by the time they are 3 years old. p. 326

gender role A set of expectations that prescribes how females or males should think, act, or feel. p. 326

androgens The main class of male sex hormones. p. 326

estrogen The main class of female sex hormones. p. 326

identification theory A theory that stems from Freud's view that preschool children develop a sexual attraction to the opposite-sex parent, then, at 5 to 6 years of age, renounce the attraction, due to anxiety, subsequently identifying with the same-sex parent and unconsciously adopting the same-sex parent's characteristics. p. 326

social learning theory of gender The theory that children's gender development occurs through observation and imitation of gender-related behavior, as well as through the rewards and punishments children experience for gender-appropriate and gender-inappropriate behaviors. p. 326

cognitive developmental theory of gender The view that children's gender typing occurs after they have developed a concept of gender. Once they begin to consistently conceive themselves as male or female, children often organize their world on the basis of gender. p. 327

schema A cognitive structure, or network of associations, that organizes and guides an individual's perception. p. 327

gender schema A cognitive structure that organizes the world in terms of female and male. p. 327

gender schema theory The theory that children's attention and behavior are guided by an internal motivation to conform to gender-based sociocultural standards and stereotypes. p. 327

androgyny The presence of desirable masculine and feminine characteristics in one individual. p. 329

storm-and-stress view G. Stanley Hall's view that adolescence is a turbulent time charged with conflict and mood swings. p. 332

puberty A period of rapid skeletal and sexual maturation that occurs in early adolescence. p. 332

testosterone A hormone associated in boys with development of the genitals, an increase in height, and a change of voice. p. 333

estradiol A hormone associated in girls with breast, uterine, and skeletal development. p. 333

formal operational thought Piaget's fourth stage of cognitive development, which appears between 11 and 15 years of age. Formal operational thought is abstract, idealistic, and logical. p. 333

hypothetical-deductive reasoning Piaget's name for adolescents' cognitive ability to develop hypotheses, or best guesses, about how to solve problems, such as algebraic equations. p. 334

adolescent egocentrism The adolescent's belief that others are as preoccupied with the adolescent as she is herself, that she is unique, and that she is indestructible. p. 334

identity versus identity confusion The fifth of Erikson's stages of human development, occurring primarily during the adolescent years. The development of identity involves finding out who we are, what we are all about, and where we are going in life. p. 336

internalization The developmental change from behavior that is externally controlled to behavior that is controlled by internal, self-generated standards and principles. p. 336

preconventional level Kohlberg's lowest level of moral thinking, in which an individual shows no internalization of moral values—moral thinking is based on punishments (stage 1) or rewards (stage 2) that come from the external world. p. 336

conventional level Kohlberg's second level of moral thinking, in which an individual shows an intermediate level of internalization. The individual abides by certain standards (internal), but they are the standards of others (external), such as parents' standards (stage 3) or society's laws (stage 4). p. 336

postconventional level Kohlberg's highest level of moral thinking; moral development is completely internalized and not based on others' standards. An individual recognizes alternative moral courses, explores the options, and then develops a personal moral code. The code is among the principles generally accepted by the community (stage 5) or it is more individualized (stage 6). p. 337

justice perspective A theory of moral development that focuses on the rights of the individual; individuals independently make moral decisions. Kohlberg's theory is a justice perspective. p. 337

care perspective In Carol Gilligan's theory of moral development, the care perspective focuses on people in terms of their connectedness with others, interpersonal communication, relationships with others, and concern for others. p. 337

intimacy versus isolation Erikson's sixth stage of development, occurring mainly in early adulthood. Intimacy is the ability to develop close, loving relationships. p. 340

generativity versus stagnation Erikson's seventh stage of development, occurring mainly in middle adulthood. Middle-aged adults need to assist the younger generation in leading useful lives. p. 340

cohorts Groups of individuals born in the same year or time period. p. 341

Alzheimer's disease A degenerative, irreversible brain disorder that impairs memory and social behavior. p. 344

cognitive mechanics The hardware of the mind, reflecting the neurophysiological architecture of the brain as developed through evolution. At the operational level, cognitive mechanics involve speed and accuracy of the processes involving sensory input, visual and motor memory, discrimination, comparison, and categorization. p. 345

cognitive pragmatics The culture-based "software" of the mind. At the operational level, cognitive pragmatics include reading and writing skills, language comprehension, educational qualifications, professional skills, and also the type of knowledge about the self and life skills that help us master or cope with life. p. 346

activity theory The theory that the more active and involved older people are, the more satisfied they will be with their lives and the more likely they will stay healthy. p. 346

ageism Prejudice against people based on their age; in particular, prejudice against older people. p. 346

integrity versus despair Erikson's eighth and final stage of human development, which occurs mainly in late adulthood. It is a time of looking back at what we have done with our lives. p. 346

Resources and Readings in Psychology

Baby Steps (1994)
by Claire Kopp
New York: W. H. Freeman

Baby Steps is a guide to physical, cognitive, and socioemotional development in the first 2 years of life.

The Carnegie Council on Adolescent Development
2400 N Street, NW
Washington, DC 20037
202–429–7979

The Carnegie Council on Adolescent Development is a program of the Carnegie Foundation of New York. Its goal is to improve the health and well-being of adolescents. The council has generated a number of task forces to improve education, reduce adolescent pregnancy, and reduce alcohol and drug use among adolescents.

Child Development, Developmental Psychology, Journal of Research on Adolescence, and Journal of Gerontology

These are leading research journals in human development and they publish a wide array of articles on biological, cognitive, and socioemotional dimensions of development.

Child Poverty Action Group
22 Wellesley Street, East
Toronto ON M4Y 1G3 Canada
416–922–3126

Among its other advocacy initiatives, this group sponsors a toll-free help line for children in trouble.

Foster Grandparent Program
ACTION, The National Volunteer Association
Washington, DC
202–634–9108

This program matches older Americans with special-needs children. Older adult volunteers work in many different settings, ranging from Head Start programs to foster-care homes. ACTION also runs the Senior Companion Program, which matches older adults with frail elderly persons. A special goal of this program is to help the homebound elderly gain the confidence needed for independent living.

Handbook of the Biology of Aging (1996, 4th ed.)
by Edward Schneider, John Rowe, Thomas Johnson, Nikki Holbrook, and John Morrison.
Orlando FL: Academic Press

This handbook provides an up-to-date look at the biological underpinnings of aging. Topics examined include genetic views of aging, menopause, and the aging of the brain and nervous system.

Handbook of Parenting, Vols I–IV (1995)
by Mark Bornstein (ed.)
Hillsdale NJ: Erlbaum

These four volumes provide a wealth of information on a wide variety of parenting issues. Leading researchers discuss such topics as divorce, adoption, gifted children, ethnicity, day care, moral development, and poverty.

How to Save the Children (1992)
by Amy Hatkoff and Karen Klopp
New York: Simon & Schuster

This innovative resource guide is filled with practical ideas about how volunteerism can help to counter the effects of poverty and neglect on America's children.

How to Survive the Loss of a Love (1991)
by Melba Colgrove, Harold Bloomfield, and Peter McWilliams
Los Angeles, CA: Prelude Press

This book provides messages about how to cope with the loss of a loved one. The authors address loss through death as well as other types of loss, such as divorce, rape, loss of long-term goals, and loss through aging.

The Measure of Our Success: A Letter to My Children and Yours (1992)
by Marian Wright Edelman
Boston: Beacon Press

Edelman's book stimulates thought about what kind of nation we want to be, what kind of values mean the most to us, and what we can do to improve the health and well-being of our nation's children and parents.

The Mismeasure of Woman (1992)
by Carol Tavris
New York: Touchstone

This is an excellent book on gender stereotyping, similarities and differences between the sexes, and how women should be measured by their own standards, not men's. It is well documented and captivating in presenting a witty portrayal of women's issues and dilemmas, and what can be done about them.

National Association for the Education of Young Children (NAEYC)
1834 Connecticut Avenue, NW
Washington, DC 20009–5786
202–232–8777
800–424–2460

NAEYC is a large organization that serves as an important advocacy group for young children, has developed guidelines for a number of dimensions of early childhood education, and publishes the excellent journal *Young Children.*

The National Council on Aging
1331 F Street, NW
Washington, DC 20005
202–347–8800

This organization is dedicated to increasing the well-being of older Americans. The council publishes a number of materials about aging and services available to older Americans.

Older Women's League (OWL)
666 11th Street NW, Suite 700
Washington, DC 20001
202–783–6686

The Older Women's League is for women of any age who support issues of concern to midlife and older women, including access to jobs and pensions for older women and maintaining self-sufficiency. The League publishes *Owl Observer.*

Touchpoints (1992)
by T. Berry Brazelton
Reading, MA: Addison-Wesley

Touchpoints is respected pediatrician T. Berry Brazelton's most recent book. Brazelton focuses on the concerns and questions that parents have about the child's feelings, behavior, and development from pregnancy to first grade.

Transitions Through Adolescence (1996)
by Julia Graber, Jeanne Brooks–Gunn, and Anne Petersen (eds.)
Hillsdale NJ: Erlbaum

There currently is increased interest in research on biological, cognitive, and socioemotional dimensions of adolescence. In this book, leading researchers evaluate such subjects as continuity and discontinuity, puberty, drug use, delinquency, parent-adolescent conflict, schools, and poverty.

You and Your Adolescent (1990)
by Laurence Steinberg and Ann Levine
New York: HarperPerennnial

This is an excellent book for parents of adolescents. It serves the dual purpose of educating parents about how adolescents develop and giving them valuable parenting strategies for coping with teenagers.

C H A P T E R

M&E

Motivation and Emotion

Bill Rane
Taos Window, detail

CHAPTER

M&E

Motivation and Emotion

with Laura King

Chapter Outline

Chapter Boxes

The passions and desires, like the two twists of a rope, mutually mix with the other, and twine inextricably round the heart; producing good, if moderately indulged; but certain destruction if suffered to become inordinate.

—**Robert Burton**

Whatever you can do, or dream you can, begin it. Boldness has genius, power, and magic in it.

—Johann Wolfgang von Goethe

Images of Psychology

Gerard d'Aboville

On July 11, 1991, a 45-year-old former French paratrooper cast off in his rowboat from the small fishing village Choshi, nestled on a peninsula east of Tokyo, and began rowing toward the United States. Gerard d'Aboville had made a name for himself 11 years earlier when he became the first person to row solo across the Atlantic Ocean from the mainland of the United States to the mainland of Europe. Afterward, he swore to his friends that he would never try such a challenge again. He wrote a book, designed motorboats for a race down the river Niger in Africa, and pursued catamaran and off-road racing as other accomplishments. Then, in spite of past vows, d'Aboville decided to try the transpacific crossing.

He created a specially designed half-ton rowboat, the *Sector*. It was equipped with a ham radio, dehydrated food, a gas stove, and a desalination pump activated by the motion of the boats oars that could turn sea water into drinking water. The *Sector* also had a watertight cabin for sleeping and eating behind the open cockpit. Although d'Aboville had hoped to leave in June, typhoons in the Pacific forced him to delay his launch until July, even though Japanese oceanographers warned him that further storms were likely. "Once I believed that maybe it was possible," d'Aboville said, "it was all over." He had planned to row 12 hours per day and progress slowly across the ocean, but a typhoon blew him back toward the Japanese coast just 5 days after he'd started, and another held him in place for over a week despite backbreaking rowing. One of his numerous capsizings resulted in a broken rib. Still, he rowed on and on and on, for 6,300 miles, until he finally reached the shore near Portland, Oregon—more than 4 months after he had started.

Overcoming wind, rain, unspeakable loneliness, physical exhaustion, and fears of dying at sea, d'Aboville overcame impossible odds to complete something that no one else had ever accomplished. He described his accomplishment by saying, "Whenever I felt that I could not go further, I just did something." Like Gerard d'Aboville, we all know people who have overcome great odds to accomplish something. What motivates great achievements? What motivates each of us to get out of bed each morning and work toward our own goals, like completing an introductory psychology course? Why do some people succeed while others fail or even give up on life altogether? The psychology of motivation tries to answer these and many other questions.

Gerard d'Aboville overcame wind, rain, unspeakable loneliness, physical exhaustion, and fears of dying at sea to accomplish something no one else ever had—crossing the Pacific Ocean from Japan to the United States in a rowboat. What motivates people like d'Aboville to overcome great odds to achieve something?

PREVIEW

What would motivate a person to attempt to cross the Pacific Ocean in a rowboat? In this chapter we will explore the "whys" of behavior—motivation—as well as the fascinating nature of our emotions.

SOME IDEAS BEHIND THE "WHYS" OF BEHAVIOR

Before his death in 1992, Sam Walton, the founder of Wal-Mart stores, was making as much as $6 billion a year. What motivated him to do this? "Every why hath a wherefore," said Shakespeare. Why are you so hungry? Why are you so interested in having sex? Why do you want to get an A in this class? Why do you want a change in your life? The answer: because you are motivated. **Motivation** *involves the question of "why" people behave, think, and feel the way they do.* Motivated behavior is energized, directed, and sustained. Motivation also determines when a type of behavior will stop.

If you are hungry, you will probably put this book down and go to the refrigerator. If you are sexually motivated, you might go to a party and flirt with someone you think is attractive. If you are motivated to achieve, you might stay in the library until midnight studying. When you are motivated, your behavior is energized and directed: you go to the refrigerator, to a party, to the library. Hunger, sex, and achievement are three important motivational areas of our lives—each of which we discuss in this chapter.

Motivations differ not only in kind, such as an individual's being motivated to eat rather than have sex, but also in intensity. We can speak of an individual as being more or less hungry, or more or less motivated to have sex. Let's now turn our attention to different ways psychologists conceptualize motivation, beginning with instincts.

Instincts

An **instinct** *is an innate, biological determinant of behavior.* Did Sam Walton have an instinct for acquisitiveness? Early in this century, interest in instincts flourished. Influenced by Darwin's evolutionary theory, American psychologist William McDougall (1908) argued that all behavior is determined by instincts. He said we have instincts for acquisitiveness, curiosity, gregariousness, pugnacity, and self-assertion. At about the same time, Sigmund Freud (1917) argued that behavior is instinctually based. He believed sex and aggression were especially powerful in motivating behavior.

It was not long before a number of psychologists had laundry lists of instincts. Psychologists thought that perhaps we have one instinct for physical aggression, one for assertive behavior, and yet another for competitive behavior. Instinct theory, though, did not really explain anything. The wherefore behind Shakespeare's why was not adequately explored. An instinct was invariably inferred from the behavior it was intended to explain. For example, if a person was aggressive, he had an instinct for aggression. If another person was sociable, she had an instinct for sociability. Instinct theory did call attention to the idea that some of our motivation is unlearned and involves physiological factors. This idea is important in our understanding of motivation today, but instinct theory itself landed in psychology's dustheap many years ago.

Needs and Drives

If you do not have an instinct for sex, maybe you have a need or a drive for it. A **drive** *is an aroused state that occurs because of a physiological need.* A **need** *is a deprivation that energizes the drive to eliminate or reduce the deprivation.* You might have a need for water, for food, or for sex. The need for food, for example, arouses your hunger drive. This motivates you to do something—to go to MacDonald's for a Big Mac, for example—to reduce the drive and satisfy the need. As a drive becomes stronger, we are motivated to reduce it. This explanation is known as *drive reduction theory.*

Usually, but not always, needs and drives are closely associated in time. For example, when your body needs food, your hunger drive will probably be aroused. An hour after you have eaten a Big Mac, you might still be hungry (thus, you need food), but your hunger drive might have subsided. From this example you can sense that drive pertains to a psychological state; need involves a physiological state.

The goal of drive reduction is **homeostasis,** *the body's tendency to maintain an equilibrium, or steady state.* Literally hundreds of biological states in our bodies must be maintained within a certain range: temperature, blood-sugar level, potassium and sodium levels, oxygen, and so on. When you dive into an icy swimming pool, your body heats up. When you walk out of an air-conditioned room into the heat of a summer day, your body begins to cool down. These changes occur automatically in an attempt to restore your body to its optimal state of functioning.

Homeostasis is achieved in our bodies much like a thermostat in a house keeps the temperature constant. For example, assume that the thermostat in your house is set at 68 degrees. The furnace heats the house until a temperature of 68 degrees is reached, then the furnace shuts off. Without a source of heat, the temperature in the house eventually falls below 68 degrees. The thermostat detects this and turns the furnace back on again. The cycle is repeated so that the temperature is maintained within narrow limits. Today homeostasis is used to explain both physiological and psychological imbalances.

Incentives

"If a man runs after money, he's money mad; if he keeps it, he's a capitalist; if he spends it, he's a playboy; if he doesn't try to get it, he lacks ambition; and if he accumulated it after a life-time of hard work, people call him a fool who never got anything out of life." These words of Vic Oliver suggest that something more than internal drives can sometimes motivate our behavior—something more external. Money is an example of an external stimulus that is a powerful motivator of behavior.

Incentives *are positive or negative external stimuli or events that motivate an individual's behavior.* For example, a lucrative income of $100,000+ is a positive incentive for becoming a physician; the threat of an intruder is a negative incentive for purchasing a security system for your home. By identifying the concept of incentives, psychologists expanded their definition of the why of behavior to include both internal (physiological needs and psychological drives) and external (incentives) factors.

Hierarchy of Motives

Is getting an A in this class more important to you than eating? If the person of your dreams told you that you were marvelous, would that motivate you to throw yourself in front of a car for her safety? According to Abraham Maslow (1954, 1971), our "basic" needs must be satisfied before our "higher" needs can be. According to Maslow's **hierarchy of motives,** *individuals' main kinds of needs must be satisfied in the following sequence: physiological needs, safety needs, the need for love and belongingness, the need for esteem, cognitive needs, aesthetic needs, and the need for self-actualization* (see figure 1). According to this hierarchy, people must satisfy their need for food before they can achieve, and they must satisfy their needs for safety before they can satisfy their needs for love.

It is the need for self-actualization that Maslow has described in the greatest detail. **Self-actualization,** *the highest and most elusive of Maslow's needs, is the motivation to develop one's full potential as a human being.* According to Maslow, self-actualization is possible only after the other needs in the hierarchy are met. Maslow cautions that most people stop maturing after they have developed a high level of esteem, and thus do not become self-actualized. Many of Maslow's writings focus on how people can reach the elusive motivational state of self-actualization.

The idea that human motives are hierarchically arranged is an appealing one. Maslow's theory stimulates us to think about the ordering of motives in our own lives. However, the ordering of the needs is somewhat subjective. Some people may seek greatness in a career to achieve self-esteem, for example, while putting their needs for love and belongingness on hold.

Motivation's Biological, Cognitive, and Sociocultural Dimensions

At this point we have discussed a number of approaches to understanding motivation. As we approach the twenty first century, what has had staying power in understanding motivation and what is being added today? Above all else, most psychologists today recognize that our behavior is energized and/or directed by a complex mix of biological, cognitive, and sociocultural processes.

Biological

While psychologists rejected the biological concept of instinct many years ago, biology's role in motivation continues to be strong. Konrad Lorenz (1965) conducted a classic study in which goslings became attached to Lorenz because he was the first moving object they saw shortly after they were born. Lorenz interpreted the goslings' behavior as evidence of rapid innate learning within a critical time period. Lorenz's field is **ethology,** *the study of the biological basis of behavior in natural habitats.* Ethology is sometimes referred to as modern instinct theory, although Lorenz and other ethologists have carefully avoided using the term *instinct* because of the taint it got earlier in psychology's history. Ethology emerged as an important theory because of the work of European zoologists such as Lorenz in the 1930s, who argued that behaviorism had gone too far in promoting the role of environmental experiences in motivation.

Like behaviorists, ethologists are careful observers of behavior. Unlike many behaviorists, though, ethologists believe laboratories are not good settings for observing behavior. They observe behavior in its natural surroundings instead, believing that behavior cannot be completely understood unless it is examined in the context in which it evolved. For example, ethologists have observed many species of animals in the wild, discovering their powerful motivation to stake out their own territory and band together to fight off any intruders (Lorenz, 1966).

Ethological theory reminds us of our biological origins and raises the issue of how strongly we are motivated by our biological makeup versus our experiences in life. Are we motivated to hurt someone else because we were born that way or because of our interactions with people who hit and yell, for example? As you can see, even though classical instinct theory bit the dust, the issue regarding whether motivation is innate or learned, biologically or experientially based is still alive and kicking.

Our body's physiological makeup—including brain structures, body organs, and hormones—also play an important role in contemporary views of motivation.

FIGURE 1

Maslow's Hierarchy of Motives
Abraham Maslow developed the hierarchy of human motives to show how we have to satisfy certain basic needs before we can satisfy higher needs. In the diagram, lower-level needs are shown toward the base of the pyramid, higher-level needs toward the peak. The lowest needs (those that must be satisfied first) are physiological—hunger, thirst, and sleep, for example. The next needs that must be satisfied are safety needs, which ensure our survival—we have to protect ourselves from crime and war, for example. Then we must satisfy love and belongingness needs—we need the security, affection, and attention of others, for example. Then, esteem needs have to be met—we need to feel good about ourselves, for example. Next in the hierarchy are cognitive needs—which involve a motivation for knowledge and understanding. Near the top of the hierarchy are aesthetic needs—which can involve order and beauty, for instance. Finally, at the top of the pyramid and the highest of Maslow's needs are self-actualization needs—which involve the realization of one's potential.

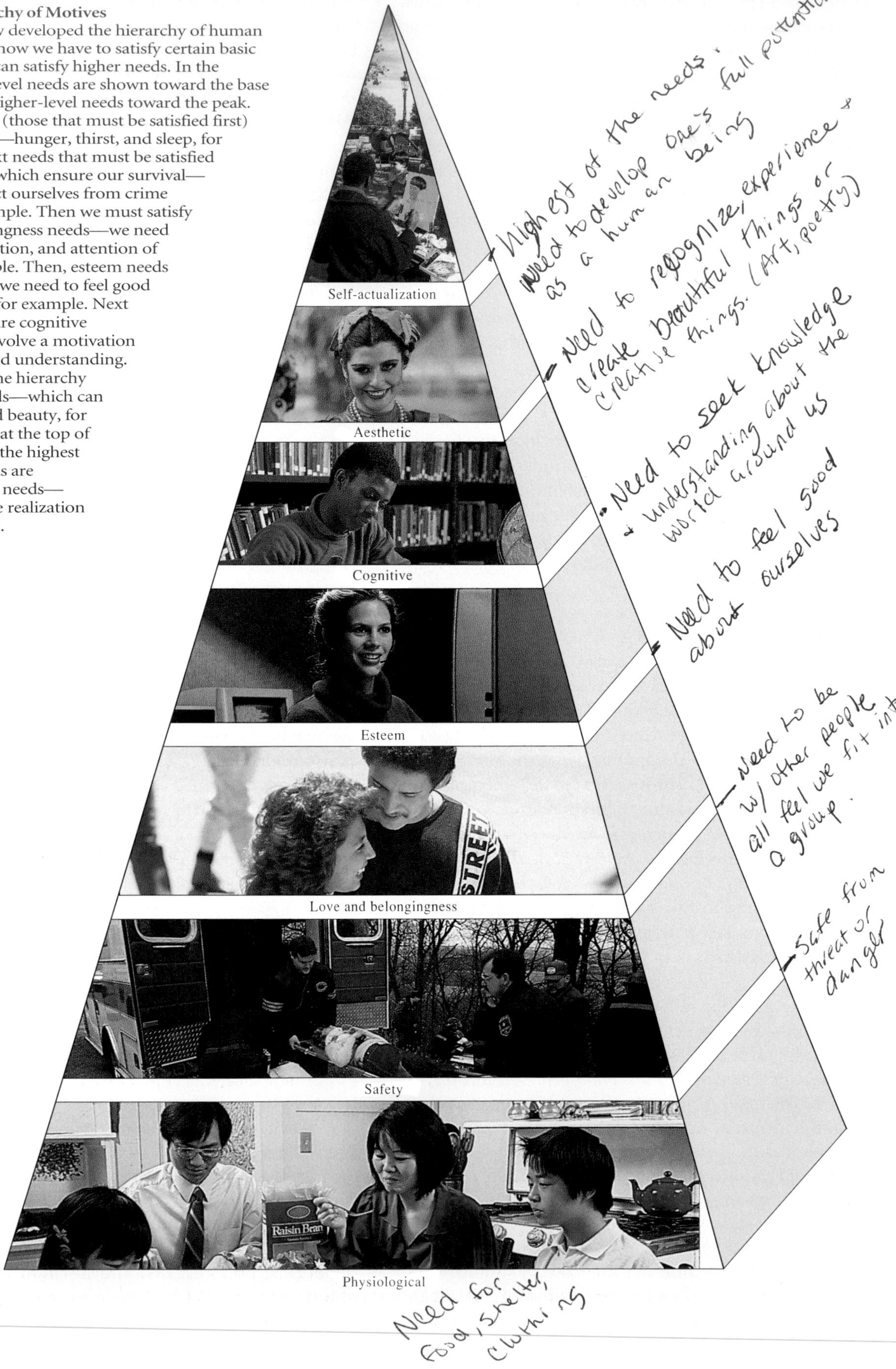

Self-actualization

Aesthetic

Cognitive

Esteem

Love and belongingness

Safety

Physiological

We'll discuss these physiological mechanisms in our discussion of hunger. But first we'll look at how thought influences motivation.

Cognitive

The contemporary view of motivation also emphasizes the importance of cognitive factors (Petri, 1996). Consider your motivation to do well in this class. Your confidence in your ability to do well and your expectation for success may help you to relax, concentrate better, and study more effectively. If you think too much about not doing well in the class and fear that you will fail, you may become too anxious and not perform as well. Your ability to consciously control your behavior and resist the temptation to party too much and avoid studying will improve your achievement, as will your ability to use your information-processing abilities of attention, memory, and problem solving as you study for and take tests.

Psychologists continue to debate the role of conscious versus unconscious thought in understanding motivation. Freud's legacy to contemporary psychoanalytic theory is the belief that we are largely unaware of why we behave the way we do. Psychoanalytic theorists argue that few of us know why we love someone, why we eat so much, why we are so aggressive, or why we are so shy. Although some cognitive psychologists have begun to study the role of the unconscious mind, for the most part they emphasize that human beings are rational and aware of their motivation. Humanistic theorists like Maslow also stress our ability to examine our lives and become aware of what motivates us.

Sociocultural

As is true of much human behavior, environmental and sociocultural influences play an important role in motivation. Even "biological" motives have environmental and sociocultural underpinnings. Why does the same meal—say, steak, baked potato, and salad—satisfy our hunger so much more when we are seated near someone we love in a candle-lit room than in a noisy school cafeteria, for example? And consider the social motive of achievement. To fully understand achievement, we need to examine how parents and children interact, examine how peers compare one another, and examine the people we look up to as models of success, along with the standards for achievement in different cultures.

The role of sociocultural and environmental factors raises another important issue regarding motivation: Are we internally motivated or externally motivated? Do we study hard because we have an internal standard that motivates us to do well or because of external factors such as wanting to get good grades so we can get into a doctoral program in psychology or medical school? As a rule, the study of biological and cognitive factors stresses the role of internal motivation, and the study of sociocultural and environmental factors stresses the role of external motivation. We'll get back to the internal—external issue in motivation later in the chapter in our discussion of achievement motivation.

In our description of motivation's biological, cognitive, and sociocultural underpinnings, we have encountered three important issues: (1) To what degree are we motivated by innate, unlearned, biological factors as opposed to learned, sociocultural, experientially based factors? (2) To what degree are we aware of what motivates us—that is, to what extent is our motivation conscious? (3) To what degree are we internally or externally motivated? These are issues that researchers continue to wrangle with and debate.

Keep in mind that, although we separated the biological, cognitive, and sociocultural underpinnings of motivation for the purpose of organization and clarification, in reality they are often interrelated (Mook, 1996). For example, in the study of social cognition, psychologists call attention to how contextual/social factors interact with thinking to determine our motivation. Next we will turn our attention to an important dimension of motivation—hunger.

HUNGER

Imagine that you live in the Bayambang area of the Philippines. You are very poor and have little food to eat. Hunger continuously gnaws at everyone in your village. Now imagine yourself as the typical American, eating not only breakfast, lunch, and dinner, but snacking along the way—and maybe even raiding the refrigerator at midnight.

Food is an important aspect of life in any culture. Whether we have very little or large amounts of food available to us, hunger influences our behavior. What mechanisms explain why we get hungry?

Physiological Factors

You are sitting in class and it is 2 P.M. You were so busy today that you skipped lunch. As the professor lectures, your stomach starts to growl. For many of us, a growling stomach is one of the main signs that we are hungry. Psychologists have wondered for many years about the role of peripheral factors—such as the stomach, liver, and blood chemistry—in hunger.

Peripheral Factors

In 1912, Walter Cannon and A. L. Washburn conducted an experiment that revealed a close association between stomach contractions and hunger (see figure 2). As part of the procedure, a partially inflated balloon was passed through a tube inserted in Washburn's mouth and pushed down into his stomach. A machine that measures air pressure was connected to the balloon to monitor Washburn's stomach contractions. Every time Washburn reported hunger pangs, his stomach was also contracting. This finding, which was confirmed in subsequent experiments with other volunteers, led the two to believe that gastric activity was *the* basis for hunger.

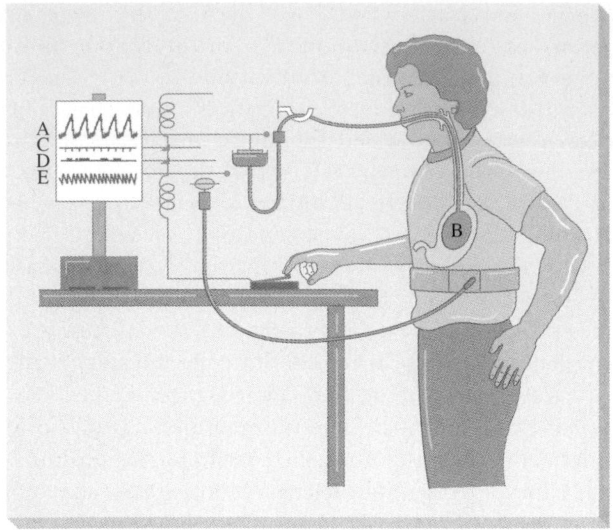

FIGURE 2

Cannon and Washburn's Classic Experiment on Hunger
Notice the letters A, B, C, D, and E in the drawing. A is the record of the increases and decreases in the volume of the balloon in the subject's stomach, B. The number of minutes elapsed is shown in at C. The subject's indication of feeling hungry is recorded at D. E is a reading of the movements of the abdominal wall to ensure that such movements are not the cause of changes in stomach volume.

Stomach signals are not the only factors that affect hunger. People whose stomachs have been surgically removed still get hunger pangs. Stomach contractions can be a signal for hunger, but the stomach also can send signals that stop hunger. We all know that a full stomach can decrease our appetite. In fact, the stomach actually tells the brain not only how full it is, but also how much nutrient is in the stomach load. That is why a stomach full of rich food stops your hunger faster than a stomach full of water. The same stomach hormone that helps start the digestion of food (called cholecystokinin, or CCK) reaches your brain through the bloodstream and signals you to stop eating.

Blood sugar (glucose) is an important factor in hunger, probably because the brain is critically dependent on sugar for energy. One set of sugar receptors is located in the brain itself, and these receptors trigger hunger when sugar levels get too low. Another set of sugar receptors is in the liver, which is the organ that stores excess sugar and releases it into the blood when needed. The sugar receptors in the liver signal the brain via the vagus nerve, and this signal also can make you hungry. Another important factor in blood-sugar control is the hormone insulin, which causes excess sugar in the blood to be stored in cells as fats and carbohydrates. Insulin injections cause profound hunger because they lower blood sugar drastically.

Psychologist Judith Rodin (1984) has further clarified the role of insulin and glucose in understanding hunger and eating behavior. She pointed out that when we eat complex carbohydrates such as cereals, bread, and pasta, insulin levels go up but then fall off gradually. When we consume simple sugars like candy bars and Cokes, insulin levels rise and then fall off sharply—the all-too-familiar "sugar low." Glucose levels in the blood are also affected by these complex carbohydrates and simple sugars in similar ways. The consequence is that we are more likely to eat within the next several hours after eating simple sugars than after eating complex carbohydrates. And the food we eat at one meal often influences how much we will eat at our next meal. So consuming doughnuts and candy bars, in addition to providing no nutritional value, set up an ongoing sequence of what and how much we probably will crave the next time we eat.

Brain Processes

So far we have been talking about peripheral factors in hunger. But the brain is also involved in hunger. The **ventromedial hypothalamus (VMH)** *is a region of the hypothalamus that plays an important role in controlling hunger.* When a rat's VMH is surgically destroyed, it immediately becomes hyperphagic (that is, it eats too much) and rapidly becomes obese. Researchers thought that the VMH was a "satiety center," and its destruction left animals unable to fully satisfy their hunger. The picture now emerging, however, suggests that the destruction causes a hormonal disorder (remember that the hypothalamus is the master control center for many hormones). After the VMH is destroyed, the rat's body cells act as if they are starving, constantly converting all nutrients from the blood into fat and never releasing them. That is the main reason the animals become obese (see figure 3). One of the fascinating aspects of this condition is that the animals stop gaining weight once they reach a certain weight, suggesting that hormones and body cells may control the body's overall "set point" for body weight. **Set point** *refers to the weight maintained when no effort is made to gain or lose weight.*

To summarize, we can see that the brain monitors both blood sugar levels and the condition of the stomach, then integrates this information (and probably other information as well) in the process of regulating hunger. Hypothalamic regions, especially VMH, are involved in integrating information about hunger.

Your internal physiological world is very much involved in whether or not you are hungry. But some external and cognitive factors are also involved.

External and Cognitive Factors

How might external cues stimulate hunger? Could a combination of external cues, set point, and brain processes give us a better explanation than external cues alone? What roles do self-control and exercise play in eating behavior? What is the nature of restrained eating and emotional distress?

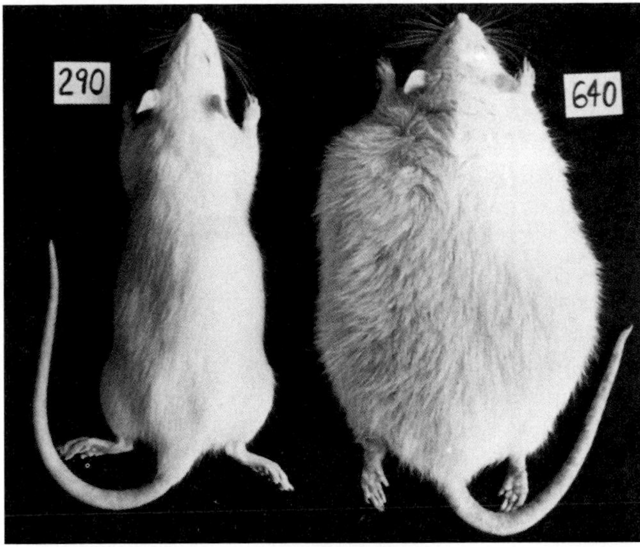

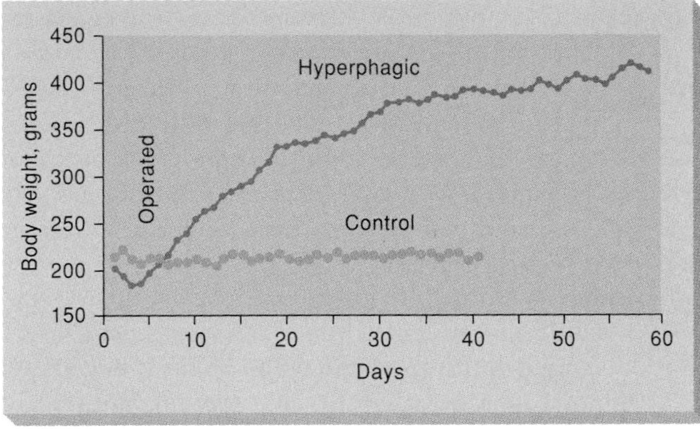

FIGURE 3

Role of the Ventromedial Hypothalamus (VMH) in the Obesity of Rats

(*top*) A hyperphagic rat gained three times its normal body weight after a lesion was made in its VMH. (*bottom*) This graph displays the weight gain by a group of rats in which lesions were made in the VMH (hyperphagic) and by a group of rats in which no lesions were made (control). Notice how quickly the hyperphagic rats gained weight but that, after about 1 month, they virtually stopped gaining weight. This suggests that hormones and body cells control the body's overall set point for weight.

External Cues

Psychologists are interested in how environmental cues might stimulate hunger. You may know someone who seems literally incapable of walking past an ice cream shop without stopping to eat a huge hot fudge sundae. Stanley Schachter (1971) believes that one of the main differences between obese and normal weight individuals is their attention to environmental cues for signals of when to eat. From this perspective, people of normal weight attend to internal cues for signals of when to eat—for example, when blood sugar level is low, hunger pangs are sensed in the stomach. In contrast, an obese person responds to external cues as signals of when to eat—how the food tastes, looks, and smells, for example. One problem that is left unresolved by Schachter's view is that not all people who have this special sensitivity to such cues are overweight (Rodin, 1984). Alternative perspectives have sought to integrate what we know about the importance of physiology and external cues in understanding obesity.

Combining External Cues, Set Point, and Brain Processes

Richard Nisbett (1972) has pointed out that one group of people who share obese individuals' sensitivity to external cues is people who are severely deprived of food. Nisbett has proposed an interesting view of obesity, based on the idea of set points, combining work on external cues with research on the brain's control of eating and weight gain. He believes that very obese and very hungry people are remarkably similar in a number of ways. Both groups have a heightened sensitivity to food cues, both tend to be easily frustrated and easily upset, and both have low energy levels and low interest in sex. Based on these similarities, Nisbett has suggested that the brains of obese people literally think that these people are *starving!* To understand this intriguing perspective, imagine that each person's brain perceives a particular level of fat as being normal for that person's body. Some people will have more fat and some less. The problem is that our society stresses that a thin body is the best type to have, so individuals who would naturally be heavy (or heavier than the average fashion model) are in a difficult position: They must lose weight that their brains consider to be natural for them. The brain considers their set point to be higher than the societal norm. So, when these people try to lose weight by restricting their eating, their fat cells become ravenous for food and their brain assumes that they are in a kind of "starvation mode" or a time of famine. In order to cope with the lack of nutrition, the fat cells become "selfish" and refuse to release nutrients into the body, causing these individuals to remain heavy—and hungry.

Self-Control and Exercise

Rodin (1984) points out that not too long ago we believed that obesity was caused by such factors as unhappiness or responding to external food cues. According to Rodin, a number of biological, cognitive, and social factors are more important. We already discussed some important biological factors, including the roles of complex carbohydrates and simple sugars in insulin and glucose levels. In regard to external cues, Rodin says that while obese persons are more responsive to external food cues than normal-weight persons are, there are individuals at all weight levels who respond more to external than to internal stimuli. Many persons who respond to external cues also have the conscious ability to control their behavior and keep environmental food cues from externally controlling their eating patterns.

Rodin believes not only that conscious self-control of eating patterns is important in weight control, but that exercise is also. No matter what your genetic background, aerobic exercise increases your metabolic rate, which helps to burn calories.

Restrained Eating and Emotional Distress

Another area of research relevant to the issues of hunger and eating behavior concerns "restrained eating." Many of us can view our lives as one long diet, interrupted by occasional hot fudge sundaes or chocolate chip cookies. **Restrained eaters** *are individuals who chronically restrict their food intake to control their weight. Restrained eaters are often on diets, are very conscious of what they eat, and tend to feel guilty after splurging on sweets.* One interesting characteristic of restrained eaters is that when they stop dieting, they tend to be more likely to binge eat—to eat large quantities of food in a short amount of time (Polivy, Heatherton, & Herman, 1988).

Even a largely physiologically controlled behavior like eating may have other, psychological motivations that modify it (Capaldi, 1996). For example, Shelley Chaiken and her colleagues (Chaiken & Pliner, 1987; Mori, Chaiken, & Pliner, 1987) have shown that individuals, especially women, will alter their eating behavior depending on the type of impression they are trying to make. A common source of humor among female college roommates is that some women will eat a full meal before going out to dinner with a man so that they can "eat like a bird" at dinner. Or they "eat like a bird" on a date, and then return home and clean out the refrigerator.

SEXUALITY

We do not need sex for everyday survival, the way we need food and water, but we do need it for the survival of the species. Some of the fascinating questions we will explore about our sexual lives are these: What roles do hormones and the brain play in our sexuality? What is the nature of the human sexual response pattern? How do psychosexual dysfunctions develop? What is the nature of heterosexuality? What is the nature of homosexuality?

Hormones and Brain Processes

Sex hormones are among the most powerful chemicals in nature. They are controlled by the master gland in the brain, the pituitary. **Estrogen** *is the main class of female sex hormones.* **Androgen** *is the main class of male sex hormones.*

By governing the secretion of androgen, genes direct the sexual development of the young fetus. When sufficiently high levels of androgen are present, as in normally developing boys, male organs and genitals form. When little androgen is present, as in normally developing girls, female organs and genitals form. When an intermediate level of androgen is present (insufficient androgen in a genetically male fetus, or excessive androgen in a genetically female fetus), the genitals become intermediate between male and female. Individuals with such characteristics are called *hermaphrodites.*

The secretion of sex hormones is regulated by a feedback system. The pituitary gland monitors hormone levels, but it is regulated by the hypothalamus. The pituitary gland sends out a signal to the testes or ovaries to manufacture the hormone. Then the pituitary gland, through interaction with the hypothalamus, detects when an optimal hormone level is reached and maintains this level.

The importance of the hypothalamus in sexual activity has been shown by electrically stimulating or surgically removing it. Electrical stimulation of certain hypothalamic areas increases sexual behavior; surgical removal of areas of the hypothalamus produces sexual inhibition. Electrical stimulation of the hypothalamus in a male can lead to as many as twenty ejaculations in 1 hour. The limbic system, which runs through the hypothalamus, also seems to be involved in sexual behavior. Its electrical stimulation can produce penile erection in males and orgasm in females.

In higher animals, the temporal lobes of the neocortex play an important role in moderating sexual arousal and directing it to an appropriate goal object. For example, temporal lobe damage in male cats impairs the animals' ability to select an appropriate partner. Male cats with temporal lobe damage try to copulate with everything in sight: teddy bears, chairs, even researchers. Temporal lobe damage in humans also has been associated with changes in sexual activity.

Although estrogen is the dominant sex hormone in females and androgen is the dominant sex hormone in males, each person's body contains both hormones. The amount of each hormone varies from one individual to the next. For example, among singers, basses have more androgen than tenors.

As we move from the lower to the higher animals, hormones have less influence on sexual behavior. When the testes of a male rat are removed (castration), sexual behavior declines and eventually ceases. In monkeys and humans, however, castration produces greater variation in sexual behavior. Some male monkeys and human males lose their sexual motivation rather quickly following castration, whereas others experience only a gradual decline over many years.

Might smell also be involved in sexual interest? **Pheromones** *are odorous substances released by animals that are powerful attractants.* Pheromones are involved when male guinea pigs are attracted by the urine of an ovulating female. They are at work when all the male cats in a neighborhood know that a female cat is in heat. Several years ago, Jōvan developed a fragrance they claimed would attract men to women who wore it. The company advertised that the perfume contained a pheromone derived from human sweat. It was designed to lure human males just as pheromones attract male guinea pigs and cats. The fragrance was not the smashing success the perfumery anticipated, however, indicating that there is more than smell involved in human sexual attraction.

The Human Sexual Response Cycle

How do humans respond physiologically during sexual activity? To answer this question, gynecologist William Masters and his colleague Virginia Johnson (1966) carefully observed and measured the physiological responses of 382 female and 312 male volunteers as they masturbated or had sexual intercourse. The **human sexual response pattern** *consists of four phases—excitement, plateau, orgasm, and resolution—as identified by Masters and Johnson* (see figure 4). The *excitement phase* begins erotic responsiveness; it lasts from several minutes to several hours, depending on the nature of the sex play involved. Engorgement of blood vessels and increased blood flow in genital areas and muscle tension characterize the excitement phase. The most obvious signs of response in this phase are lubrication of the vagina and partial erection of the penis.

The second phase of the human sexual response, called the *plateau phase,* is a continuation and heightening of the arousal begun in the excitement phase. The increases in breathing, pulse rate, and blood pressure that occurred during the excitement phase become more intense, penile erection and vaginal lubrication are more complete, and orgasm is closer.

The third phase of the human sexual response cycle is *orgasm.* How long does orgasm last? Some individuals sense that time is standing still when it takes place, but orgasm lasts for only about 3 to 15 seconds. Orgasm involves an explosive discharge of neuromuscular tension and an intense pleasurable feeling. However, not all orgasms are exactly alike. For example, females show three different patterns in the orgasm phase, as shown in figure 4: (a) multiple orgasms, (b) no orgasm, and (c) excitement rapidly leading to orgasm, bypassing the plateau phase; the third pattern most clearly corresponds to the male pattern in intensity and resolution.

Following orgasm, the individual enters the *resolution phase,* in which blood vessels return to their normal state. One difference between males and females in this phase is that females may be stimulated to orgasm again without delay. Males enter a refractory period, lasting anywhere from several minutes to an entire day, in which they cannot have another orgasm. The length of the refractory period increases as men age.

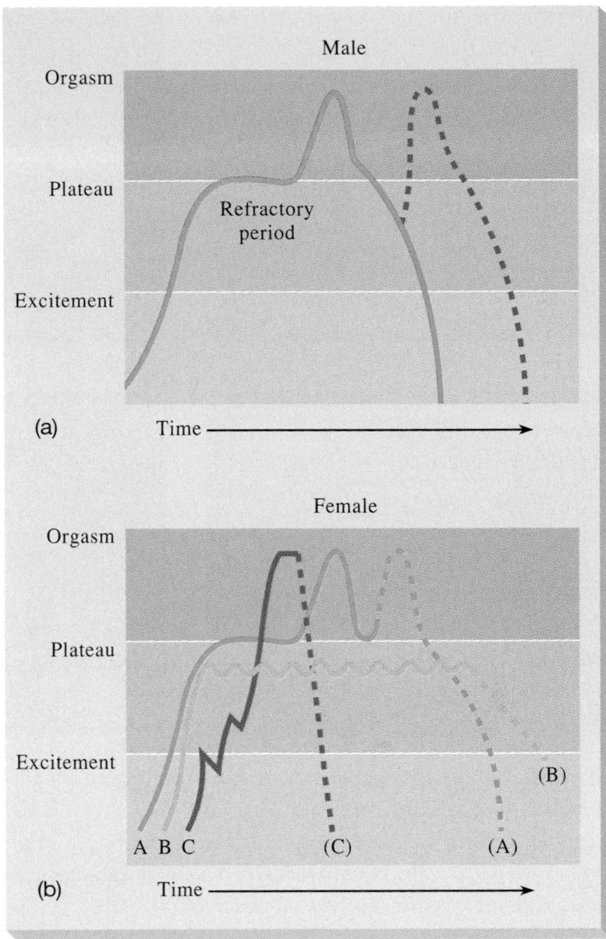

FIGURE 4

Male and Female Human Sexual Response Patterns
(*a*) This diagram shows the excitement, plateau, orgasm, and resolution phases of the human male sexual response pattern. Notice that males enter a refractory period, which lasts from several minutes up to a day, in which they cannot have another orgasm. (*b*) This diagram shows the excitement, plateau, orgasm, and resolution phases of the human female sexual response pattern. Notice that female sexual responses follow one of three basic patterns. Pattern A somewhat resembles the male pattern, except that pattern A includes the possibility of multiple orgasm (the second peak in pattern A) without falling below the plateau level. Pattern B represents nonorgasmic arousal. Pattern C represents intense female orgasm, which resembles the male pattern in its intensity and rapid resolution.

Psychosexual Dysfunctions

Myths about females and males would have us believe that many women are "frigid" and uninterested in sexual pleasure, while most men can hardly get enough. Both myths conceal the facts, revealed through the accumulating experience of sex therapy clinics (Crooks & Bauer, 1996). The facts are that both women and men have similar desires for sexual pleasure, but both sexes may experience psychological problems that interfere with the attainment of pleasure. **Psychosexual**

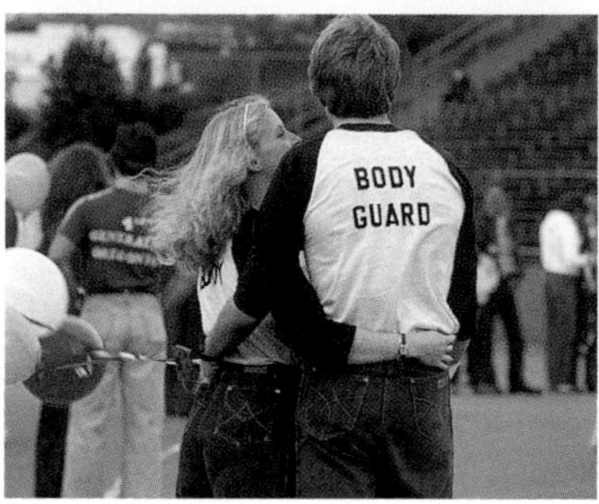

Sexual behavior has its magnificent moments throughout the animal kingdom. Insects mate in midair, peacocks display their plumage, and male elephant seals have prolific sex lives. Socioemotional experiences and cognitive interpretation play a more important role in human sexual behavior. We can talk about sex with each other, read about it in magazines, and watch it on television and the movie screen.

dysfunctions *are disorders that involve impairments in the sexual response pattern, either in the desire for gratification or in the inability to achieve it.* In disorders associated with the desire phase, both men and women show little or no sexual drive or interest. In disorders associated with the excitement phase, men may not be able to maintain an erection. In disorders associated with the orgasmic phase, both women and men reach orgasm too quickly or not at all. Premature ejaculation in men occurs when the time between the beginning of sexual stimulation and ejaculation is unsatisfactorily brief. Many women do not routinely experience orgasm in sexual intercourse, a pattern so common it can hardly be called dysfunctional. Inhibited male orgasm does occur, but it is much less common than inhibited female orgasm.

The treatment of psychosexual dysfunctions has undergone nothing short of a revolution in recent years. Once thought of as extremely difficult therapeutic challenges, most cases of psychosexual dysfunction now yield to techniques tailored to improve sexual functioning.

Attempts to treat psychosexual dysfunctions through traditional forms of psychotherapy, as if the dysfunctions were personality disorders, have not been very successful; however, new treatments that focus directly on each sexual dysfunction have reached success rates of 90 percent or more (McConaghy, 1993). For example, the success rate of a treatment that encourages women to enjoy their bodies and engage in self-stimulation to orgasm, with a vibrator if necessary, approaches 100 percent (Anderson, 1983). Some of these women subsequently transfer their newly developed sexual responsiveness to interactions with partners. Success rates also approach 100 percent in the treatment of premature ejaculation, but considerably lower success rates occur in the treatment of males who cannot maintain an erection.

Heterosexuality and Homosexuality

Gathering accurate information about sexual attitudes and behavior is a difficult task. Consider how you would respond if someone asked you the following questions: How often do you have sex? How many different sexual partners have you had? How often do you masturbate? The people most likely to respond to surveys about sexual behavior are those with liberal sexual attitudes who engage in liberal sexual behaviors. Thus, what we know is limited by the reluctance of some individuals to candidly answer questions about extremely personal matters, and by our inability to get any answer, candid or otherwise, from individuals who believe that they should not talk about sex with strangers. Researchers refer to this as a "volunteer bias." Imagine how challenging this problem would be with the additional complication of studying sexual practices in other cultures. With these cautions in mind, let's now turn to a discussion of sexual attitudes and behavior, primarily in the United States, beginning with heterosexual relations and then turning to homosexual relations.

Heterosexual Attitudes and Behavior

To explore heterosexual relations, we will examine a number of surveys of sexual attitudes and behavior at different points in the twentieth century, the frequency of sexual intercourse, and sexual scripts.

Had you been a college student in 1940, you probably would have had a very different attitude toward many aspects of sexuality than you do today, especially if you are a female. A review of college students' sexual practices and attitudes from 1900 through the 1990s reveals two important trends (Darling, Kallon, & Van Duesen, 1984; Robinson & others, 1991). First, more young people today are reporting having had sexual intercourse. Second, the gap between the proportion of sexually active males and sexually active females is narrowing. Prior to the 1970s, about twice as many college males as college females reported they had engaged in sexual intercourse, but since 1970 the proportion of males and females has become nearly equal. These changes suggest a major shift away from a double standard of sexual behavior, which held that it was more acceptable for unmarried males than for unmarried females to have sexual intercourse.

Two surveys that included wider age ranges of adults verified this shift in trends. In 1974 Morton Hunt surveyed more than 2,000 adult readers of *Playboy.* Although the magazine readership's bias might have led to an overestimation of sexual permissiveness, the results suggested movement toward increased sexual permissiveness when compared to the results of Alfred Kinsey's inquiries during the 1940s (Hunt, 1974; Kinsey, Pomeroy, & Martin, 1948). Kinsey's earlier survey found that foreplay consisted of a kiss or two, but by the 1970s Hunt had discovered that foreplay had lengthened, averaging 15 minutes. Hunt also found that individuals in the 1970s were using more varied sexual techniques in their lovemaking. For example, oral-genital sex, virtually taboo at the time of Kinsey's survey, was more accepted in the 1970s.

More than 40 years after Kinsey's famous study, Robert Michael and his colleagues (1994) conducted a comprehensive survey of American sexual patterns. The findings are based on face-to-face interviews with nearly 3,500 individuals from 18 to 50 years of age. The sample generated by Michael and his colleagues was randomly selected, unlike the flawed samples of Kinsey, Hunt, and others, which were based on unrepresentative groups of volunteers.

Among the key findings from the 1994 survey:

- Americans tend to fall into three categories: One-third have sex twice a week or more, one-third a few times a month, and one-third a few times a year or not at all.
- Married couples have sex the most and also are the most likely to have orgasms when they do.
- Most Americans do not engage in kinky sexual acts. When asked about their favorite sexual acts, the vast majority (96 percent) said that vaginal sex was "very" or "somewhat" appealing. Oral sex was in third place, after an activity that many have not labeled a sexual act—watching a partner undress.
- Adultery is clearly the exception rather than the rule. Nearly 75 percent of the married men and 85 percent of the married women indicated that they have never been unfaithful.
- Men think about sex far more than women do—54 percent of the men said they think about it every day or several times a day, whereas 67 percent of the women said they think about it only a few times a week or a few times a month.

The findings in the 1994 Sex in America survey contrast sharply with some magazine polls that portray Americans as engaging in virtually unending copulation. The magazine polls are inflated from the start by the individuals who fill them out, such as *Playboy* subscribers who want to brag about their sexual exploits. Even the famous Kinsey studies, which caused such a scandal in the 1940s and 1950s by indicating that half of American men had extramarital affairs, were flawed. Kinsey obtained his subjects where he could find them—in boarding houses, college fraternities, and even mental hospitals. He also quizzed hitchhikers who passed through town. Clearly, Kinsey's subjects were not even close to being a random sample of the population.

In sum, one of the most powerful messages in the 1994 survey was that Americans' sexual lives are more conservative than previously believed. Although 17 percent of the men and 3 percent of the women said they have had sex with at least 21 partners, the overall impression from the survey was that sexual behavior is ruled by marriage and monogamy for most Americans.

Sexual Scripts

As we explore our sexual identities, we often follow sexual scripts. Differences in female and male sexual scripts can cause problems for individuals as they work out their sexual identities and seek sexual fulfillment. Females learn to link sexual intercourse with love more than males do (Cassell, 1984). Therefore females are more likely than males to justify their sexual behavior by telling themselves that they were swept away by love. A number of investigators have found that females, more than males, cite being in love as the main reason for being sexually active. Far more females than males have intercourse only with partners they love and would like to marry. Other reasons females offer for having sexual intercourse include giving in to the male's desire for pleasure, gambling that sex is a way to get a boyfriend or husband, curiosity, and sexual desire unrelated to loving and caring. The male sexual script emphasizes sexual conquest; higher status tends to accrue to males who can claim substantial sexual activity. For males, sex and love might not be as intertwined as they are for females.

Although it has recently become acceptable for females to engage in premarital sex, there is still a **double standard,** *a belief that many sexual activities are acceptable for males but not for females.* The double standard can be hazardous because it encourages women to deny their sexuality and do minimal planning to ensure that their sexual encounters are safe. It can also lead females to think that males are more sexual than females, that males are less in control of their sexual behaviors, and that females must justify their sexual activity by claiming that they were swept away by the passion of the moment.

The double standard encourages males to dismiss or devalue their female partner's values and feelings, and it puts considerable pressure on males to be as sexually active as possible. As one male adolescent remarked, "I feel a lot of pressure from my buddies to go for the score." Further evidence of physical and emotional exploitation of females was found in a survey of 432 adolescents from 14 to 18 years old (Goodchilds & Zellman, 1984). Of the adolescents surveyed, both females and males accepted the view that the male adolescent had a right to be sexually aggressive and assigned to females the task of setting limits for the male's behavior. Males who accept the double standard might believe that touch and contact are not "manly," and sex with a woman might be the only experience of touch and bodily comfort acceptable to these "real men." The seemingly cold and uncaring concept of "scoring" might be the only option some males think they have to reduce their loneliness, have warmth with another person, and "let their guard down."

Homosexual Attitudes and Behavior

Until the end of the nineteenth century, it was generally believed that people were either heterosexual or homosexual. Today, many experts in the field of human sexuality view sexual orientation as a continuum ranging from exclusive heterosexuality to exclusive homosexuality. Pioneering this view were Alfred Kinsey and his associates (Kinsey, Pomeroy, & Martin, 1948), who described sexual orientation as a continuum of a six-point scale, with 0 signifying exclusive heterosexuality and 6 signifying exclusive homosexuality (see figure 5). Some individuals are *bisexual,* being sexually attracted to people of both sexes. In Kinsey's research, approximately 1 percent of individuals reported being bisexual (1.2 percent of males and 0.7 percent of females) and from 2 to 5 percent reported being homosexual (4.7 percent of males and 1.8 percent of females). The actual incidence of exclusive homosexuality continues to be debated; estimates range from approximately 1 percent (in a recent national survey, only 1.1 percent said they are exclusively gay) to 10 percent (Billy & others, 1993). In the 1994 Sex in America study, 2.7 percent of men and 1.3 percent of women reported that they had had homosexual sex in the past year (Michael & others, 1994).

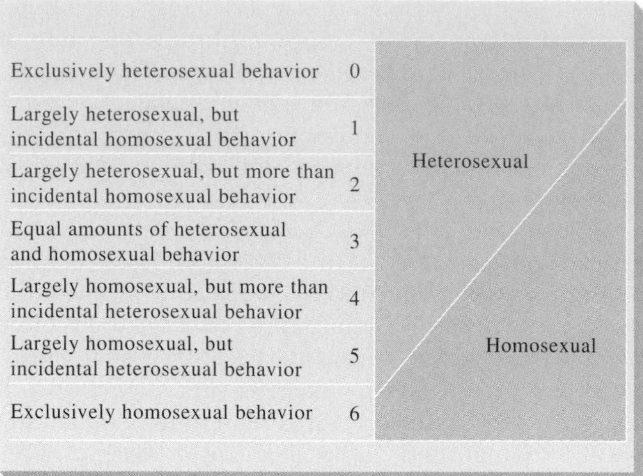

FIGURE 5

The Continuum of Sexual Orientation
The continuum ranges from exclusive heterosexuality, which Kinsey and associates (1948) rated as 0, to exclusive homosexuality (6). People who are about equally attracted to both sexes (ratings 2 to 4) are bisexual.

Although many people think of heterosexual and homosexual behavior as distinct patterns of behavior that are easy to define and composed of fixed decisions, orientation toward a sexual partner of the same or the opposite sex is not necessarily a fixed decision that is made once in life and adhered to forever. For example, it is not unusual for an individual, especially a male, to engage in homosexual experimentation in adolescence but not as an adult. Homosexual behavior is common among prisoners and others with no alternatives for intimate, enduring relationships. Kinsey's 1948 findings revealed that 37 percent of men and 13 percent of women had participated in some homosexual acts to orgasm between adolescence and old age.

Why are some individuals homosexual and others heterosexual? Speculation about this question has been extensive, but no firm answers are available. Homosexuals and heterosexuals have similar physiological responses during sexual arousal and seem to be aroused by the same types of tactile stimulation. Investigators find no differences between homosexuals and heterosexuals for a wide range of attitudes, behaviors, and adjustments (Bell, Weinberg, & Mammersmith, 1981). In the 1970s, recognizing that homosexuality is not a form of mental illness, both the American Psychiatric Association and the American Psychological Association discontinued their classification of homosexuality as a mental disorder.

Recently researchers have explored the possible biological basis of homosexuality by examining genetic factors, hormone levels, and differences in anatomical structures (Gladue, 1994). In one study of pairs of identical twins of which one of the twins was homosexual, over 50 percent of the other twins in the pairs were also homosexual. In contrast, only one-fourth of the fraternal twins of homosexuals were homosexual (Bailey & Pillard, 1991). (Fraternal twins are genetically no more similar than ordinary siblings, because they come from different eggs and sperm; identical twins develop from the same fertilized egg.) The results of hormone studies have been inconsistent. If male homosexuals are given male sex hormones (androgens), their sexual orientation does not change; their sexual desire simply increases. A critical period in fetal development might influence sexual orientation. In the second to fifth months after conception, exposure of the fetus to hormone levels characteristic of females might cause the individual (female or male) to become attracted to males (Ellis & Ames, 1987). If this critical-period hypothesis turns out to be correct, it would explain why clinicians have found that sexual orientation is difficult, if not impossible, to modify.

With regard to anatomical structures, neuroscientist Simon LeVay (1991) proposed, based on autopsy evidence, that an area of the hypothalamus that governs

What is the nature of homosexual behavior? Why are some individuals homosexual and others heterosexual?

sexual behavior is twice as large (about the size of a grain of sand) in heterosexual men as it is in homosexual men. In homosexual men, this part of the hypothalamus is about the same size as in heterosexual females. Critics of LeVay's work point out that many of the homosexuals in the study had AIDS and suggest that their brains could have been altered by the disease.

An individual's sexual orientation—homosexual, heterosexual, or bisexual—is most likely determined by a combination of genetic, hormonal, cognitive, and environmental factors (Whitman, Diamond, & Martin, 1993). Most experts on homosexuality believe that no one factor alone causes homosexuality and that the relative weight of each factor can vary from one individual to the next. In effect, no one knows exactly what causes an individual to be homosexual. Scientists have a clearer picture of what does *not* cause homosexuality. For example, children raised by gay or lesbian parents or couples are no more likely to be homosexual than are children raised by heterosexual parents (Patterson, 1995). There also is no evidence that male homosexuality is caused by a dominant mother or a weak father, or that female homosexuality is caused by girls' choosing male role models.

At this point we have discussed a number of ideas about the nature of motivation, hunger, and sexuality. Next we consider two other important dimensions of motivation—competence and achievement.

Competence and Achievement

We are a species motivated to gain mastery over our world, to explore unknown environments with enthusiasm and curiosity, and to achieve greatness. Unlike the motives of hunger and thirst, the social motives of competence and achievement are less likely to involve reduction of a drive or satisfaction of a need.

Competence Motivation

In the 1950s, psychologists recognized that our motivation involves much more than the reduction of biological needs. **Competence motivation** *is our motivation to deal effectively with the environment, to be adept at what we attempt, to process information efficiently, and to make the world a better place.* R. W. White (1959) said we do these things not because they serve biological needs, but because we have an internal motivation to effectively interact with our environment.

Among the research White used to support his concept of competence motivation were experiments that showed organisms are motivated to seek stimulation rather than to reduce a need. For example, monkeys solved simple problems just for the opportunity to watch a toy train (see figure 6) (Butler, 1953). Rats consistently chose a complex maze with a number of pathways over a simple maze with few pathways. And a series of experiments suggested that

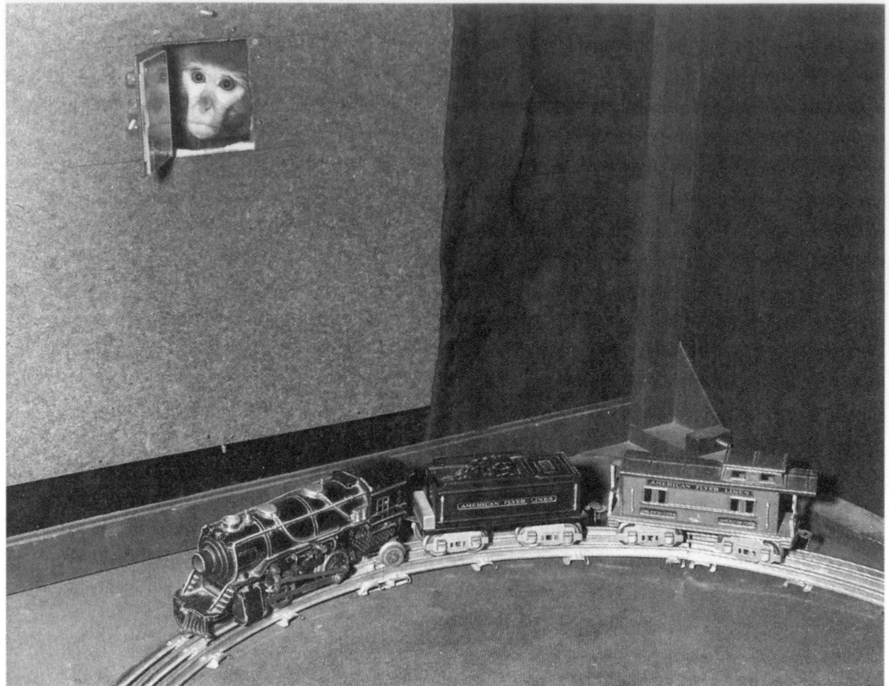

FIGURE 6

Motivation for Novel Stimulation
This monkey showed a motivation for novel stimulation and was willing to work just so he could unlock the window and watch a toy train go around in a circle.

college students could not tolerate sensory deprivation for more than 2 to 3 days (Bexton, Heron, & Scott, 1954). These students developed a strong motivation to quit the experiment even though they were getting paid to participate in it. They became bored, restless, and irritable.

Psychologists have investigated how shorter periods of sensory deprivation—such as spending time in a water immersion tank—can reduce stress (Suedfeld & Coren, 1989). Imagine that you have just stepped into a shallow pool of densely salted water. You close the hatch, then lie on your back and float. The tank is totally dark. The only sound is your own breathing, which is barely audible. Feeling suspended, you have no sense of temperature and little sense of time. Gradually your muscles relax. After 55 minutes, music is piped into the tank to signal the end of the session. The flotation tank experience is called restricted environmental stimulation therapy (REST). Researchers have documented that a series of about 20 REST sessions can significantly lower blood pressure in many individuals with hypertension (Fine & Turner, 1987). REST also has been found to improve athletic performance, creative thinking, and to reduce chronic pain (Suedfeld, Metcalfe, & Bluck, 1987). Researchers suspect that REST is effective because our fast-paced lives have become overstimulating and demanding. REST allows us to "get away from it all" in a dramatic way. In summary, sensory deprivation can both harm and help. It's harmful when we are deprived of sensory input for too long; it's helpful in short spurts.

Achievement Motivation

"Winning isn't everything, it is the *only* thing," exhorted Vince Lombardi, the former coach of the Green Bay Packers. We live in an achievement-oriented world with standards that tell us success is important. Some psychologists believe our world is too achievement-oriented. David Elkind (1981) said we are a nation of hurried, wired people who are too uptight about success and failure, and far too worried about what we accomplish in comparison to others.

Some people are highly motivated to succeed and expend a lot of effort striving to excel. Other people are not as motivated to succeed and don't work as hard to achieve. These two types of individuals vary in their **achievement motivation,** or **need for achievement,** *the desire to accomplish something, to reach a standard of excellence, and to expend effort to excel.* Borrowing from Henry Murray's (1938) theory and measurement of personality, psychologist David McClelland (1955) assessed achievement by showing individuals ambiguous pictures that were likely to stimulate achievement-related responses. The individuals were asked to tell a story about the picture, and their comments were scored according to how strongly they reflected achievement. Researchers have found that individuals whose stories reflect high achievement motivation have a stronger hope for success than fear of failure, are moderate rather than high or low risk takers, and persist with effort when tasks become difficult (Atkinson & Raynor, 1974).

McClelland (1978) also wondered if you could boost achievement behavior by increasing achievement motivation. To find out, he trained the businessmen in a village in India to become more achievement oriented, encouraging them to increase their hope for success, reduce their fear of failure, take moderate risks, and persist with a great deal of effort when tasks become difficult. Compared to village businessmen in a nearby town, the village businessmen who were trained by McClelland started more new businesses and employed more new people in the two years after the training.

Intrinsic and Extrinsic Motivation

Parents have always wanted their children to do their best. In the 1950s, McClelland argued that parents who wanted their children to be achievers should train them to become more independent. More recently, researchers have found that to increase their children's achievement motivation

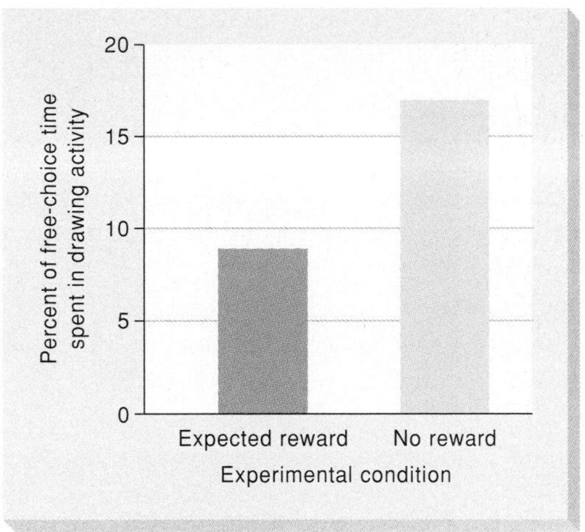

FIGURE 7

Intrinsic Motivation and Drawing Activity
Students with an initial high interest in art spent more time in art activity when no reward was mentioned than did students who expected a reward for their participation (Lepper, Greene, & Nisbett, 1973).

they need to set high standards for achievement, model achievement-oriented behavior, and reward their children's successes.

Our achievement motivation—whether in school, at work, or in sports—can be divided into two main types: **Intrinsic motivation,** *the desire to be competent and to do something for its own sake;* and **extrinsic motivation,** *which is influenced by external rewards and punishments.* If you work hard in college because a personal standard of excellence is important to you, intrinsic motivation is involved. But if you work hard in college because you know it will bring you a higher-paying job when you graduate, extrinsic motivation is at work.

Almost every boss, parent, or teacher has wondered whether or not to offer a reward to someone who does well (extrinsic motivation), or whether to let his or her internal, self-determined motivation operate (intrinsic motivation). If someone is producing shoddy work, seems bored, or has a negative attitude, offering incentives may improve his or her motivation. But there are times when external rewards can get in the way of achievement motivation. One study showed that students who already had a strong interest in art spent more time drawing when they didn't expect a reward than their counterparts who knew they would be rewarded (Lepper, Greene, & Nisbett, 1973) (see figure 7).

Some of the most achievement-oriented people are those who have a high personal standard for achievement (internal) and who also are highly competitive (external). In one study, students who had poor math skills but who set their own goals (internal) and received information about their peers' achievement (external) worked more math problems and got more of them correct than their counterparts who experienced either situation alone (Schunk, 1983). Other research suggests that social comparison by itself is not a wise strategy (Ames & Ames, 1989). The argument is that social comparison puts the individual in an ego-involved, threatening, self-focused state rather than a task-involved, effortful, strategy-focused state.

One of psychology's newest and most rapidly growing fields is sport psychology. Whether Little League baseball or Olympic competition, sports have become an integral part of our society. Do athletes become stars because they are internally motivated or externally motivated? Just as with other areas of life, both internal and external factors are involved. Star athletes experience a remarkable set of teachers, parents, and other external supports through their careers. Many are motivated by a desire for fame and fortune or by a competitive spirit; however, most top athletes also have a deep, burning desire to do their best, to reach a personal standard of excellence. To read more about the area of sport psychology and motivation, turn to Explorations in Psychology 1.

Mastery Versus Helpless and Performance Orientations

Closely related to an emphasis on intrinsic motivation, attributions of internal causes of behavior, and the importance of effort in achievement is a mastery orientation. Valanne Henderson and Carol Dweck (1990) have found that children and adolescents show two distinct responses to difficult or challenging circumstances. Individuals with a **helpless orientation** *seem trapped by the experience of difficulty, and they attribute their difficulty to lack of ability.* They frequently say things like "I'm not very good at this," even though they might earlier have demonstrated their ability through many successes. And once they view their behavior as failure, they often feel anxious, and their performance worsens even further. Individuals with a **mastery orientation** *are task oriented. Instead of focusing on their ability, they are concerned about their learning strategies and the process of achievement rather than outcomes.* Mastery-oriented individuals often instruct themselves to pay attention, to think carefully, and to remember strategies that have worked for them in previous situations. They frequently report feeling challenged and excited by difficult tasks, rather than being threatened by them.

What psychological factors have been found to undergird the mastery and helpless achievement orientations? In one recent investigation, students were followed over the first few months of the seventh grade, their first year of junior high school (Henderson & Dweck, 1990). Students who believed that their intelligence was malleable and who had confidence in their abilities earned significantly higher grades than their counterparts who believed that their intelligence was fixed and who did not have much confidence in their abilities. Students who believed that their intelligence was fixed also had higher levels of anxiety than students who believed that it was changeable. Apparently, then,

Explorations in Psychology 1

Sport Psychology and Motivation

The Houston Rockets trail the New York Knicks 102–101 with 10 seconds left in the game. Hakeem Olajuwon backs in against his defender, spins as if to shoot, but instead, through a swarm of Knicks players, threads a bullet pass to a teammate racing the baseline, who slams a dunk for the win. Nancy Lopez is tied for the lead in the Ladies' Professional Golf Championship. On the eighteenth hole of the final round, she sinks a birdie putt to win the championship. What psychological and motivational characteristics allow athletes like Olajuwon and Lopez to perform so well under pressure?

In one study, elite athletes—the stars in 23 sports—differed from lesser athletes in several important ways (Mahoney, Gabriel, Perkins, 1987). Although all professional athletes have innate physical gifts, the way elite athletes handle psychological matters—self-confidence, anxiety, concentration, and motivation—is what tips the balance and makes them great.

Self-confidence is a tricky area to study, partly because it is not simply the absence of self-doubt. And while it is a uniquely personal experience, there are also some characteristics common to all self-confident athletes (Mahoney, 1989). They show a willingness, sometimes even an eagerness to be under pressure, and the ability to remain focused on immediate demands. With 2 seconds to go in the game and down one point, they all want the ball.

Star athletes generally report that they have set reasonable and personally meaningful goals in training, but that sometimes pushing themselves too hard can harm their performance or lead to "burn out." Athletes who seek a balanced life, for example, tend to do better than those who spend all their time in training.

Top athletes also have the ability to control their emotions. In particular, they are able to control their anxiety. For many years sports psychologists thought that very low and very high levels of anxiety produced lower performances. That view is now seen as too simplistic. Top athletes say that what is more important is what anxiety means to them and what they do with it (Mahoney, 1989). Many get the jitters sometime before a game—maybe a week before, maybe just minutes before. Sometimes their anxiety even spills over into the first few minutes of the game. But once they are into the heat of competition they are able to get past their anxiety and become totally absorbed in the moment. When athletes let their anxiety get the upper hand, however, their muscles tense, their minds race, and they may "choke."

What psychological and motivational characteristics help basketball player Hakeem Olajuwon and golfer Nancy Lopez perform well under pressure?

the way students think about their intelligence and their confidence in their abilities may affect their ability and desire to master academic material. Believing that learning new material increases one's intelligence may actually promote academic mastery.

Another issue in motivation involves whether to adopt a mastery or a performance orientation. We have already described what a mastery orientation is like. A **performance orientation** *involves being concerned with outcomes—winning is what matters, and happiness is thought to result from winning.*

What sustains mastery-oriented individuals is the self-efficacy and satisfaction they feel from effectively dealing with the world in which they live. By contrast, what sustains performance-oriented individuals is winning. Although skills can be, and often are, involved in winning, performance-oriented individuals often do not view themselves as necessarily having skills. Rather, they see themselves as using tactics, such as undermining others, to get what they want.

Does all of this mean that mastery-oriented individuals do not like to win and that performance-oriented individuals are not motivated to experience the self-efficacy that comes from being able to take credit for one's accomplishments? No. A matter of emphasis or degree is involved, though. For mastery-oriented individuals, winning isn't everything, but winning is everything for their performance-oriented counterparts. And for performance-oriented individuals, skill development and self-efficacy take a back seat to winning.

Goal Setting and Self-Efficacy

The current position in the motivation field is that the self produces thoughts and images but not actions (Franken, 1994); it is goal setting that produces action (Locke & Latham, 1990). Goals help us reach our dreams, provide the focus needed for success, provide the basis for self-discipline, and maintain our interest (Emmons & Kaiser, 1995; King & Pennebaker, 1995).

It is often helpful to have both long-term and more immediate goals. Albert Bandura (1986) argues that having immediate goals (also called proximal goals or subgoals) can generate satisfaction based on personal accomplishment. Such immediate subgoals can provide a continuing source of motivation apart from loftier superordinate goals that often take a long time to accomplish. For example, an undergraduate student might have a superordinate goal of getting into a graduate program. The student can also set more immediate goals such as getting good grades this semester, on the next test, and so on.

Bandura (1994) stresses that another important dimension of achievement is **self-efficacy,** *a belief that one has mastery over a situation and the ability to produce positive outcomes.* Self-efficacy can help people adhere to behavior change programs, such as quitting smoking, and engage in competent decision making (Bandura & Jourden, 1991). As a part of self-efficacy, individuals learn the skills they need to deal with specific situations. For example, people who fear public speaking need to develop the skills to engage in effective public speaking. Such skills often increase individuals' sense of mastery over the situation.

Self-Esteem

Self-esteem *involves the evaluative and affective dimensions of self-concept. Self-esteem is also referred to as self-worth or self-image.* What are the consequences of having low self-esteem? Poor self-esteem has been implicated in low achievement, depression, and many other adjustment problems (Harter & Marold, 1992). Also, individuals with high self-esteem tend to focus on their strengths, whereas those with low self-esteem are more likely to dwell on their negative qualities or weaknesses (Showers, 1992).

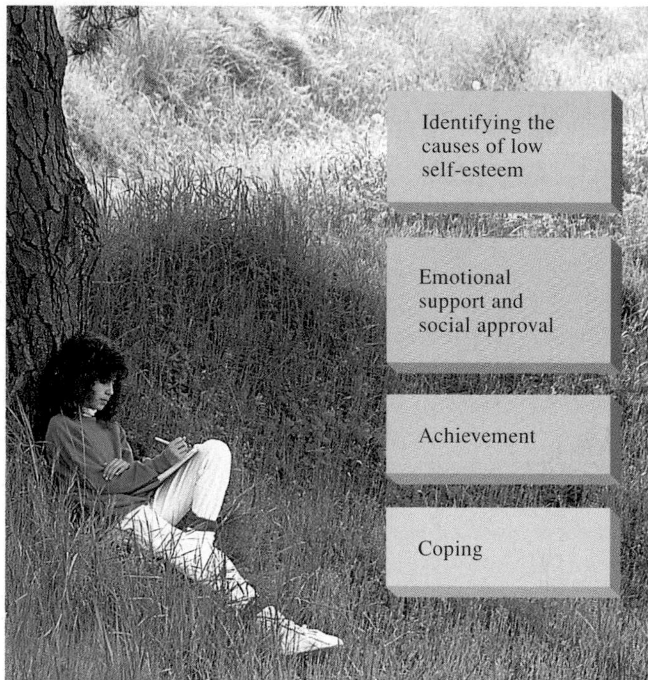

FIGURE 8

Four Main Ways to Improve Self-Esteem

How can an individual's self-esteem be improved? Four ways are (1) identifying the causes of low self-esteem, (2) emotional support and approval, (3) achievement, and (4) coping (see figure 8). Emphasis on achievement fits with Bandura's concept of self-efficacy. The straightforward teaching of real skills often results in increased achievement and, thus, in enhanced self-esteem. Individuals develop higher self-esteem because they know what tasks are important for achieving goals.

Self-esteem is also increased when individuals face a problem and try to cope with it rather than avoid it (Lazarus, 1993). Individuals who cope rather than avoid are more likely to face problems realistically, honestly, and nondefensively. The converse is true of low self-esteem. Unfavorable self-evaluations trigger denial, deception, and avoidance in an attempt to disavow that which has already been glimpsed as true. This process leads to self-generated disapproval as a form of feedback to the self about personal adequacy.

Cultural, Ethnic, and Social Class Variations in Achievement

People in the United States are often more achievement-oriented than people in many other countries. One study of 104 societies revealed that parents in nonindustrialized countries placed a lower value on achievement and independence in their children and a higher value on obedience and cooperation than parents in industrialized countries (Barry, Child, & Bacon, 1959). And in comparisons between White American children and Mexican and other

Latino children, White American children were more competitive and less cooperative. For example, one study found that White American children were more likely to keep other children from gaining when they could not realize those gains themselves (Kagan & Madsen, 1972). Another study showed that Mexican children were more family-oriented while White American children tended to be more concerned about themselves (Holtzmann, 1982).

Until recently, researchers studying achievement focused almost exclusively on White males. And when achievement in ethnic minority groups has been studied, the cultural differences have too often been viewed against standards of achievements for White males. As a result, many researchers have reached the conclusion that ethnic minorities are somehow deficient when it comes to achievement.

In addition, most studies on ethnic minorities do not consider socioeconomic status. Socioeconomic status (also called SES) is determined by some combination of occupation, education, and income. When both ethnicity and social class are considered in the same study, social class tends to be a far better predictor of achievement than ethnicity (Graham, 1986). For example, middle-class individuals, regardless of their ethnic background, have higher expectations for success and higher aspirations, and they recognize the importance of effort more than their lower-class counterparts do.

Psychologist Sandra Graham (1986, 1994), for example, has found that middle-class African American children do not fit our stereotype of either deviant or special populations. They, like their middle-class White counterparts, have high expectations for their own achievement and understand that failure is often due to lack of effort, rather than to luck.

And it's an indisputable fact that many people from ethnic minority backgrounds face educational, career, and social barriers. The Civil Rights Act of 1964 has made some progress chipping away at these barriers, but much more needs to be done. We do not have all of the answers to the problems of poverty and racism in this country, but as the Reverend Jesse Jackson commented, perhaps we have begun to ask some of the right questions.

At the same time that researchers are concerned about lower achievement levels of African American, Latino, and Native American children, they are intrigued by the high achievement of Japanese, Chinese, and Asian American children. To explore the reasons underlying such high achievement, Harold Stevenson and his colleagues (1995; Stevenson, Chen, & Lee, 1993) conducted extensive investigations of children's achievement in the United States, China, and Japan for almost two decades.

The stimulation for this research comes from the poor performance of American students on tests of mathematics and science in comparison to students in other countries. For example, in one cross-national study of math achievement, American eighth- and twelfth-grade students were below the national average in problem solving, geometry, algebra, calculus, and other areas of math (McKnight & others, 1987). In contrast, Japanese eighth-graders had the highest average scores of children from twenty countries, and in the twelfth grade, Japanese students were second only to Chinese students in Hong Kong. In a recent cross-national comparison of the math and science achievement of 9- to 13-year-olds, Korean and Taiwanese students placed first and second, respectively (Educational Testing Service, 1992). In this cross-national study, 9- to 13-year-old students in the United States finished 13th (out of 15) in science and 15th (out of 16) in math achievement.

UCLA psychologist Sandra Graham is shown here talking with a group of young boys about motivation. Dr. Graham has conducted research showing that middle-class African American children—like their White counterparts—have high achievement expectations and understand that their failure is often due to lack of effort rather than to lack of luck.

Stevenson's approach is to go beyond just describing American children's lower achievement and seek the answer to the all-important question, Why? He has found that, contrary to popular stereotypes, Asian children's and adolescents' high level of achievement does not result from rote learning and repeated drilling in tension-filled schools. Rather, these children and adolescents are motivated to learn, and teaching is innovative and interesting in many Asian schools. These children are not just force-fed knowledge, but rather they are encouraged to construct their own ways of representing knowledge. Long school days in Asia are punctuated with a number of breaks and recess periods. Asian schools embrace many of the ideals Americans have for their own schools, but are more successful in implementing them in interesting and productive ways that make learning more enjoyable for children and adolescents.

Harold Stevenson and his colleagues have found that Asian schools embrace many of the ideals Americans have for their own schools, but are more successful in implementing them in interesting and productive ways that make learning more enjoyable for children and adolescents.

These conclusions were reached by Stevenson and his colleagues after completing five different cross-national studies of children and adolescents in the United States, China, Taiwan, and Japan. In these studies, Asian children and adolescents consistently outperformed their U.S. counterparts in math. And the longer they were in school, the wider the gap between the Asian and American students' math scores became—the lowest differential was in first grade, the highest in eleventh grade.

To learn more about the reasons for these large cross-cultural differences, the researchers spent hundreds of hours observing in classrooms; interviewing teachers, students, and mothers; and giving questionnaires to fathers. They found that American parents were very satisfied with their children's achievement and education but that the parents' standards were low in comparison to Asian parents'. Also, American parents emphasize that their children's math achievement is mainly determined by innate ability, whereas Asian parents believe their children's math achievement is primarily due to effort and training.

In 1990, former President George Bush and the nation's governors adopted a well-publicized goal: to change American education in ways that will help students lead the world in math achievement by the year 2000. Stevenson (1995) says that is unlikely to happen because American standards and expectations for students' math achievement are too low by international standards.

As we have seen, Stevenson did not find that Asian students' math achievement hid a dark underside of great stress and tension in the students and their schools. Stevenson (1995) asked eleventh-grade students in Japan and the United States how often in the past month they had experienced feelings of stress, depression, aggression, and other problems, such as not being able to sleep well. He also asked them how often they felt nervous when they took tests. On all of these characteristics, the Japanese students expressed less distress and fewer problems than the American students did. Such findings do not support the Western stereotype that Asian students are tense, wired individuals driven by relentless pressures for academic excellence. However, these findings should be interpreted cautiously, because Asians tend not to disclose personal information, especially not about things of a stressful nature.

Critics of cross-national studies say that such comparisons are flawed because countries differ in curricula and in the percentage of adolescents who go to school. Even in the face of such criticism, there is a growing consensus, based on the findings of different research teams, that American adolescents' achievement is very low, that American educators' and parents' expectations for students' math achievement are too low, and that American schools are long overdue for an extensive overhaul.

At this point we have discussed many ideas about the nature of motivation. A summary of these ideas is presented in concept table 1. Next, we turn our attention to emotion.

EMOTION

Motivation and emotion are closely linked. Think about sex, which often is associated with joy; about aggression, which usually is associated with anger; and about achievement, which is associated with pride, joy, and anxiety. The terms *motivation* and *emotion* both come from the Latin word *movere,* which means "to move." Both motivation and emotion spur us into action.

Just as with motivation, there are different kinds and intensities of emotions. Not only can a person be motivated to eat rather than have sex, but be more or less hungry, or more or less interested in having sex. Similarly, a person can be happy or angry, and can be fairly happy or ecstatic, annoyed or fuming.

Defining emotion is difficult because it is not easy to tell when a person is in an emotional state. Are you in an

Concept Table 1

Principles of Motivation, Hunger, Sexuality, Competence, and Achievement

Concept	Processes/Related Ideas	Characteristics/Description
The "Whys" of Behavior	Motivation	Motivation involves the question of "why" people behave, think, and feel the way they do. Motivations vary not only in kind but also in intensity.
	Instincts, needs, and drives	Instinct theory flourished early in the twentieth century, but instincts do not adequately explain motivation. Drive theory emphasized a drive as an aroused state brought about by a physiological need. Reducing the drive satisfies the need. Drive-reduction theory stimulated an interest in homeostasis, an important motivational process.
	Incentives	Incentives are based on the belief that external factors are important in motivation.
	Hierarchy of motives	Maslow believed that some motives need to be satisfied before others. Self-actualization is given considerable importance.
	Biological, cognitive, and social dimensions	The contemporary view of motivation includes a focus on biological (especially physiological) factors, conscious thoughts and understanding, and social processes. Three important issues are the degree to which motivation is innate versus learned, conscious versus unconscious, and internal versus external.
Hunger	Physiological factors	The brain monitors both blood-sugar level and the condition of the stomach, then integrates this information. (Interest in the stomach was stimulated by Cannon's research.) Hypothalamic regions are important, especially the VMH, and the dopamine system helps activate feeding behavior.
	External and cognitive factors	Schachter's research suggested that environmental cues are involved in the control of eating. However, not all people equally sensitive to external cues are overweight. Nisbett's view combines information about external cues, set point, and brain processes to explaining eating behavior and hunger. Rodin argues that self-control and exercise are important in understanding eating behavior. The nature of restrained eating and emotional distress also contributes to our understanding of eating behavior.
Sexuality	Hormones and brain processes	Androgen in males and estrogen in females are the dominant sexual hormones. Hormonal control over the sex drive is stronger in lower animals than in humans. In humans, sexual activity is integrated into a number of brain systems.
	The human sexual response cycle	Masters and Johnson mapped out the nature of the human sexual response pattern, which consists of four phases—excitement, plateau, orgasm, and resolution.
	Psychosexual dysfunctions	Psychosexual dysfunctions involve impairments in the sexual response pattern, either in the desire for sexual gratification or in the ability to achieve it. Significant advances in the treatment of psychosexual dysfunctions have been made in recent years.
	Heterosexuality and homosexuality	Heterosexual attitudes and behavior have become more liberal in the twentieth century. The 1994 Sex in America survey was based on a more random sample of subjects than in previous studies, and portrayed Americans' sex lives more conservatively than previous studies. Today it is generally accepted to view sexual orientation as occurring along a continuum from exclusive heterosexuality to exclusive homosexuality rather than being an either/or proposition. About 1 percent of the population is bisexual. About 2 to 5 percent of individuals report being homosexual. Preference for same- or other-sex partners is not always a fixed decision. An individual's sexual orientation—heterosexual, homosexual, bisexual—is likely determined by a combination of genetic, hormonal, cognitive, and environmental factors.

Concept	Processes/Related Ideas	Characteristics/Description
Sexuality (continued)	Heterosexuality and homosexuality (continued)	Of special concern are the obstacles gays and lesbian couples must overcome to develop successful relationships and the general discrimination they experience.
Competence Motivation	Its nature	Competence motivation is the motivation to deal effectively with the environment, to be adept at what is attempted, to process information efficiently, and to make the world a better place. This concept recognizes that motivation is much more than simply reducing physiological needs.
Achievement Motivation	Definition and intrinsic/extrinsic motivation	Achievement motivation (or need for achievement) is the desire to accomplish something and to reach a standard of excellence. McClelland studied variations of achievement motivation by getting individuals to tell stories about achievement-related themes. Intrinsic motivation is the internal desire to be competent and to do something for its own sake. Extrinsic motivation is externally determined by rewards and punishments. In many instances, individuals' achievement motivation is influenced by both internal and external factors.
	Mastery orientation versus helpless and performance orientations	Individuals with a helpless orientation seem trapped by the experience of difficulty. They attribute their difficulty to lack of ability. Individuals with a mastery orientation are task oriented. Instead of focusing on their ability, they are concerned about their learning strategies, often instructing themselves to pay attention, to think carefully, and to remember strategies that have worked in previous situations. They frequently report feeling challenged and excited by difficult tasks, rather than being threatened by them. Students who believe that their intelligence is malleable and who have confidence in their abilities earn better grades than their counterparts who believe that their intelligence is fixed and who have low confidence in their abilities. Performance-oriented individuals are concerned with outcomes, whereas mastery-oriented individuals are concerned with process. In the performance orientation, winning is what matters most and happiness is thought to result from winning.
	Goal setting and self-efficacy	Goal setting is the action-producing dimension of achievement. Individuals should set goals; more immediate, proximal goals are especially helpful. Bandura stresses the importance of self-efficacy—the belief that one has mastery over a situation and the ability to produce positive outcomes—in achievement.
	Self-esteem	Self-esteem is the evaluative and affective dimension of self-concept; it is also called self-worth or self-image. Four ways to improve self-esteem are (1) identifying the causes of low self-esteem, (2) emotional support and approval, (3) achievement, and (4) coping.
	Cultural, ethnic, and social class variations in achievement	Individuals in the United States are more achievement motivated than individuals in most cultures. A special concern is the achievement of individuals from various ethnic groups. Too often ethnic differences are interpreted as "deficits" by middle-class White standards. When ethnicity and social class are considered in the same investigation, social class is often a better predictor of achievement. Middle-class individuals fare better than their lower-class counterparts in a variety of achievement situations. Psychologists are especially interested in the high-achievement levels of Japanese and Asian American individuals. Japanese schools and parents place a much stronger emphasis on education and achievement, especially math achievement, than their American counterparts.

emotional state when your heart beats fast, your palms sweat, and your stomach churns? Or are you in an emotional state when you think about how much you are in love with someone? Or when you smile or grimace? The body, the mind, and the face play important roles in understanding emotion. Psychologists debate how critical each is in determining whether we are in an emotional state. For our purposes, we will define **emotion** *as feeling, or affect, that involves a mixture of physiological arousal (a fast heartbeat, for example), conscious experience (thinking about being in love with someone, for example), and overt behavior (a smile or grimace, for example).*

Range and Classification of Emotions

When we think about emotions, a few dramatic feelings, such as rage, fear, and glorious joy, usually spring to mind. But emotions can be subtle as well—the feeling a mother has when she holds her baby, the mild irritation of boredom, the uneasiness of living in the nuclear age. And the kinds of emotions we can experience are legion. There are more than 200 words for emotions in the English language.

Psychologists have classified our many emotions. Robert Plutchik (1980), for example, believes emotions have four dimensions: (1) They are positive or negative; (2) they are primary or mixed; (3) many are polar opposites; and (4) they vary in intensity. Ecstasy and enthusiasm are positive emotions; grief and anger are negative emotions. For example, think about your ecstasy when you get an unexpected A on a test, or your enthusiasm about the football game this weekend—these are positive emotions. In contrast, think about negative emotions, such as your grief when someone close to you dies or your anger when someone verbally attacks you. Positive emotions enhance our self-esteem; negative emotions lower our self-esteem. Positive emotions improve our relationships with others; negative emotions depress the quality of those relationships.

Plutchik also believes that emotions are like colors. Every color of the spectrum can be produced by mixing the primary colors. Possibly some emotions are primary, and if mixed together, they combine to form all other emotions. Happiness, disgust, surprise, sadness, anger, and fear are candidates for primary emotions. For example, combining sadness and surprise gives disappointment. Jealousy is composed of love and anger. Plutchik developed the emotion wheel to show how primary emotions work. Mixtures of primary emotions adjacent to each other combine to produce other emotions. Some emotions are opposites—love and remorse, optimism and disappointment. Plutchik believes we cannot experience simultaneously emotions that are polar opposites. You cannot feel sad at the same time you feel happy, he says. Imagine just getting a test back in this class. As you scan the paper for the grade, your emotional response is happy or sad, not both.

Happiness is an emotion we all seek. Like other emotions, its intensity varies. Sometimes we are incredibly happy; at other times, only a little happy. You might be overwhelmed with happiness if you get the highest grade on the next test in this class but only slightly happy if you get a B or a low A. Earlier we mentioned that Plutchik, like most psychologists, believes that emotions are experienced as positive or negative. To illustrate how positive emotions are involved in stress, we will examine the nature of happiness; then, to show how negative emotions function in stress, we will study the nature of anger.

Happiness

It was not until 1973 that *Psychological Abstracts,* the major source of psychological research summaries, included *happiness* as an index term. Interest in happiness focuses on positive ways we experience our lives, including cognitive judgments of our well-being (Parducci, 1996). That is, psychologists want to know what makes you happy and how you perceive your happiness. Many years ago, French philosopher Jean-Jacques Rousseau described the subjective nature of happiness this way: "Happiness is a good bank account, a good cook, and a good digestion."

In a recent review of research on happiness, being a good cook and having a good digestion were not on the list of factors that contribute to our happiness, but four other factors were (Myers & Diener, 1995):

- Psychological and personality characteristics of high self-esteem, optimism, extraversion, and personal control
- A supportive network of close relationships
- A culture that offers positive interpretations of most daily events
- Being engaged by work and leisure
- A faith that embodies social support, purpose, and hope

Some factors that many people believe are involved in happiness, such as age and gender, are not.

But what about Rousseau's "good bank account"? Can we buy happiness? One study tried to find out if lottery winners are happier than people who have not received a landslide of money (Brickman, Coates, & Janoff-Bulman, 1978). Twenty-two major lottery winners were compared with twenty-two people living in the same area of the city. The general happiness of the two groups did not differ when they were asked about the past, present, and the future. The people who hadn't won a lottery were happier than the winners at doing life's mundane things such as watching television, buying clothes, and talking with a friend.

Winning a lottery does not appear to be the key to happiness. What is important, though, is having enough money to buy life's necessities. Extremely wealthy people are not happier than people who can purchase the necessities. People in wealthy countries are not happier than people in poor countries. The message is clear: If you believe money buys happiness, think again (Diener, 1984).

Psychologist Ed Diener (1984) agrees that intense positive emotions—such as the feelings you might have if you win a lottery or get a date with the person of your dreams—do not add much to a person's general sense of well-being, in part because they are rare, and because they can decrease the positive emotion and increase the negative emotion we feel in other circumstances. According to Diener, happiness boils down to the frequency of positive emotions and the infrequency of negative emotions. Diener's view flies in the face of common sense; you would think that frequent, intense positive emotions and minimal nonintense negative emotions produce the most happiness. But the commonsense view fails to consider that intense positive moments can diminish the sensation of future positive events. For example, if you shoot par in a round of golf, you will be overwhelmed with happiness at the time you perform this feat, but if you play golf a week later and do well but not great, the previous emotional high can diminish your positive emotion the next week. It is the rare, if nonexistent, human being who experiences intense positive emotions and infrequent negative emotions week after week after week.

Psychologist Mihaly Csikszentmihalyi (1990) has been studying the optimal experiences of emotion—those times when people report feelings of deep enjoyment and happiness—for more than two decades. According to Csikszentmihalyi, optimal experiences include what the sailor feels when the wind whips through her hair and the boat lunges through the waves—sails, hull, wind, and sea harmoniously vibrating in the sailor's body. Optimal experience is what an artist feels when the colors on a canvas begin to establish a magnetic relation with each other, and a new *thing* begins to take shape in front of the astonished creator. Optimal experience of emotions also is the feeling a father has when his child responds to his smile for the first time. Such events do not occur only when external conditions are favorable; however, people who have survived concentration camps or have lived through near-fatal dangers often recall that in the midst of their ordeal they experienced extraordinarily rich epiphanies of emotion in response to such simple events as hearing the song of a bird in the forest, completing a difficult task, or sharing a crust of bread with a friend.

Contrary to what we usually believe, says Csikszentmihalyi, moments like these, the best emotional moments of our lives, are not usually passive, relaxing times—although such experiences can also involve enjoyable emotions, if we have worked hard to attain them. The best emotional moments frequently occur when a person's body or mind is stretched to the limits in a voluntary effort to achieve something difficult and worthwhile. Thus, the optimal experience of emotion is something we *make* happen. For a child, it might be using trembling fingers to place a final block on a tower she has built, higher than any she has previously constructed; for a swimmer, it might be training extremely hard and then beating his best record; and for a violinist, it might be mastering an intricate musical passage. For each individual, there are thousands of opportunities, thousands of challenges, to expand ourselves and attain optimal emotional experiences.

Such experiences are not necessarily pleasant at the time they occur. The swimmer's muscles might have ached during training and even during his most memorable race; his lungs might have felt like they were exploding, and he might have been dizzy with fatigue—yet these could have been the best moments of his life. Gaining control over life is never easy, and sometimes it can be painful. But in the long run, optimal experiences of emotion add up to a sense of mastery—or, perhaps better, a sense of *participation* in determining the contents of life—that comes as close to what is usually meant by happiness as anything else we can conceivably imagine.

Flow, *according to Csikszentmihalyi, involves optimal experiences in life that are most likely to occur when people develop a sense of mastery. Flow involves a state of concentration in which an individual becomes absorbed while engaging in an activity.* Flow can be controlled and should not be left to chance. We can develop flow by setting challenges for ourselves—tasks that are neither too difficult nor too simple for our abilities. With such goals, we learn to order the information that enters consciousness and thereby the quality of our lives. To read further about flow, turn to Explorations in Psychology 2.

Anger

Anger is a powerful emotion. It has a strong impact not only on our social relationships, but also on the person experiencing the emotion (Lazarus, 1991). We can easily recount obvious examples of anger that often harm not only others but the angry individual as well—unrestrained and recurrent violence toward others, verbal and physical abuse of children, perpetual bitterness, the tendency to carry a "chip on the shoulder" in which a person overinterprets others' actions as demeaning, and the inability to inhibit the expression of anger.

What makes people angry? People often get angry when they feel they are not being treated fairly or when their expectations are violated. One researcher asked people to remember or keep records of their anger experiences (Averill, 1983). Most of the people said they became at least mildly angry several times a week; some said they became mildly angry several times a day. In many instances, the people said they got angry because they perceived that a

Explorations in Psychology 2

Flow

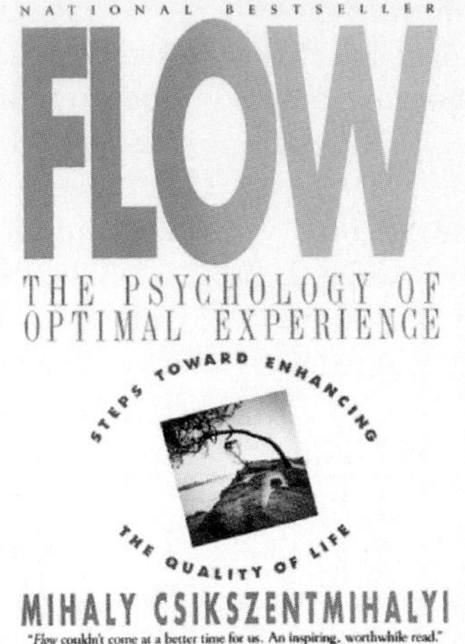

NATIONAL BESTSELLER
FLOW
THE PSYCHOLOGY OF OPTIMAL EXPERIENCE
STEPS TOWARD ENHANCING THE QUALITY OF LIFE
MIHALY CSIKSZENTMIHALYI

In the course of his research, Csikszentmihalyi (1990) tried to understand as precisely as possible how people felt when they most enjoyed themselves, and why. He began by studying several hundred "experts"—artists, athletes, musicians, chess masters, and surgeons—who seemed to spend their time in activities they preferred. From their accounts of what it felt like to do what they were doing, he developed a theory of optimal experience based on the concept of flow. Following the study of these several hundred "experts," Csikszentmihalyi and many colleagues around the world interviewed people from different walks of life. Optimal experiences were described in virtually the same way by females and males; young people and old people; and people in many different cities, countries, and cultures—Korea, Thailand, India, Tokyo, Navajo, Italy, and Chicago.

Csikszentmihalyi says that flow is the way people describe their state of mind and feeling when their consciousness is harmoniously ordered and they want to pursue whatever they are doing for its own sake. In reviewing some of the activities that consistently produce flow—such as sports, games, art, and hobbies—it becomes easier to understand what makes people happy. But we cannot rely completely on games and art for our happiness in life. To achieve control over what happens to our thoughts and feelings, we can draw on an almost infinite range of opportunities for enjoyment—the use of physical energy and sensory skills ranging from athletics to music to yoga, as well as the development of symbolic skills such as poetry, philosophy, or math, he says. Since most of us spend the largest part of our lives working and interacting with others, especially family members, it is important for us to transform jobs into flow-producing activities and to think of ways of making relations with parents, spouses, children, and friends more enjoyable.

Many of our lives are also punctured by tragic accidents, and even the most fortunate of us are subjected to stressors of many kinds. Yet such blows and stressors do not necessarily diminish a person's happiness, because it is how people respond to and cope with stress that determines whether they will profit from misfortune or be miserable. Thus, people who experience flow develop effective coping skills and manage to enjoy life despite adversities.

Csikszentmihalyi believes that the last step in achieving flow is joining all of life's experiences into a meaningful pattern. For example, it is not unusual for famous athletes to be deeply committed to their sport and to gain pleasure from playing but off the playing field to be morose and hostile. Picasso enjoyed painting, but as soon as he lay down his brushes he turned into a rather unpleasant man. Bobby Fischer, the chess genius, appeared to be helplessly inept except when his mind was on chess. These and many other examples remind us that having achieved flow in one activity does not guarantee that it will be carried over to the rest of life. However, when people can join all of their experiences into a meaningful pattern, they feel in control of their life and feel that it makes sense. The fact that they are not slim, rich, or powerful no longer matters. The tide of rising expectations is silenced, and unfulfilled needs no longer trouble them. Even humdrum experiences become enjoyment.

---

friend or a loved one performed a misdeed. They especially got angry when they perceived the other person's behavior as unjustified, avoidable, and willful.

Doesn't getting angry sometimes make us feel better and possibly help us cope better with our challenging lives? For example, Mark Twain once remarked, "When angry, count four; when very angry, swear." **Catharsis** *is the release of anger or aggressive energy by directly or vicariously engaging in anger or aggression; the catharsis hypothesis states that behaving angrily or watching others behave angrily reduces subsequent anger.*

Psychoanalytic theory promotes catharsis as an important way to reduce anger, arguing that people have a natural, biological tendency to display anger. From this perspective, taking out your anger on a friend or a loved one should reduce your subsequent tendency to display anger; so should heavy doses of anger on television and the anger we see in football, hockey, professional wrestling, and other aspects of our culture. Why? Because such experiences release pent-up anger.

Social learning theory argues strongly against this view. This theory states that by acting angrily, people

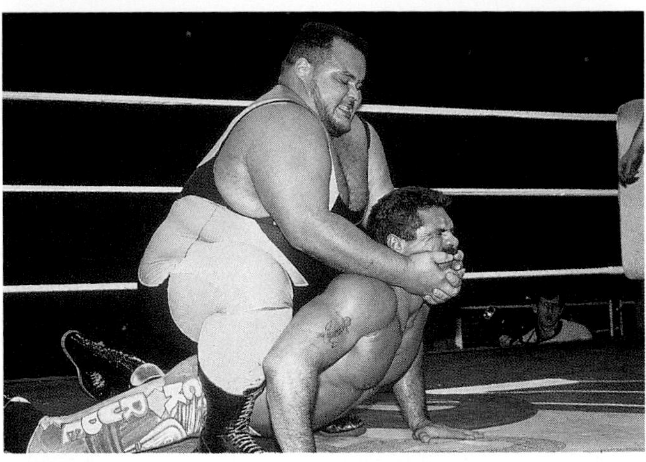

Is watching professional wrestling likely to have a cathartic effect?

often are rewarded for their anger, and that by watching others display anger, people learn how to be angry themselves. Which view is right? Research on catharsis suggests that acting angrily does not have any long-term power in reducing anger. If the catharsis hypothesis were correct, war should have a cathartic effect in reducing anger and aggression, but a study of wars in 110 countries since 1900 showed that warfare actually stimulated domestic violence (Archer & Gartner, 1976). Compared with nations that remained at peace, postwar nations had an increase in homicide rates. As psychologist Carol Tavris (1989) says in her book *Anger: The Misunderstood Emotion,* one of the main results of the ventilation approach to anger is to raise the noise level of our society, not to reduce anger or solve our problems. Individuals who are the most prone to anger get angrier, not less angry. Ventilating anger often follows this cycle: a precipitating event, an angry outburst, shouted recriminations, screaming or crying, a furious peak (sometimes accompanied by physical assault), exhaustion, and a sullen apology or just sullenness.

Every person gets angry at one time or another. How can we control our anger so it does not become destructive? Tavris (1989) makes the following recommendations:

1. When your anger starts to boil and your body is getting aroused, work on lowering the arousal by waiting. Emotional arousal will usually simmer down if you just wait long enough.
2. Cope with the anger in ways that involve neither being chronically angry over every little bothersome annoyance nor passively sulking, which simply rehearses your reasons for being angry.
3. Form a self-help group with others who have been through similar experiences with anger. The other people will likely know what you are feeling and together you might come up with some good solutions to anger problems.
4. Take action to help others, which can put your own miseries in perspective, as exemplified in the actions of the women who organized Mothers Against Drunk Drivers or any number of people who work to change conditions so that others will not suffer what they did.
5. Seek ways of breaking out of your usual perspective. Some people have been rehearsing their "story" for years, repeating over and over the reasons for their anger. Retelling the story from other participants' points of view often helps individuals to find routes to empathy.

When you are angry, are you aroused? What about when you are sad? Do you have to be aroused when you experience these and other emotions?

Physiological Arousal and Brain Processes in Emotion

Remember from our definition of emotion that it includes physiological arousal. Many psychologists argue that when you are in an emotional state, you are physiologically aroused.

The Nature of Arousal

As you drive down a highway, the fog thickens. Suddenly you see a pile of cars in front of you. Your mind temporarily freezes, your muscles tighten, your stomach becomes queasy, and your heart feels like it is going to pound out of your chest. You immediately slam on the brakes and try to veer away from the pile of cars. Tires screech, windshield glass flies, and metal smashes. Then all is quiet. After a few short seconds you realize you are alive. You find that you can walk out of the car. Your fear turns to joy, as you sense your luck in not being hurt. In a couple of seconds, the joy turns to anger. You loudly ask who caused the accident.

As you moved through the emotions of fear, joy, and anger, your body changed. During intense arousal your sympathetic nervous system was working. At the time of the accident your arousal decreased as the parasympathetic nervous system became more dominant: your heart rate, breathing rate, and blood sugar level decreased; your pupils constricted; and your stomach secretion and salivation increased.

Early in this century, two psychologists described the role of arousal in performance. What is now known as the **Yerkes-Dodson law** *states that performance is best under conditions of moderate rather than low or high arousal.* At the low end of arousal you might be too lethargic to perform tasks well; at the high end you may not be able to concentrate. Think about how aroused you were the last time you took a test. If your arousal was too high, your performance probably suffered.

Moderate arousal often serves us best in tackling life's tasks, but there are times when low or high arousal produces optimal performance. For well-learned or simple

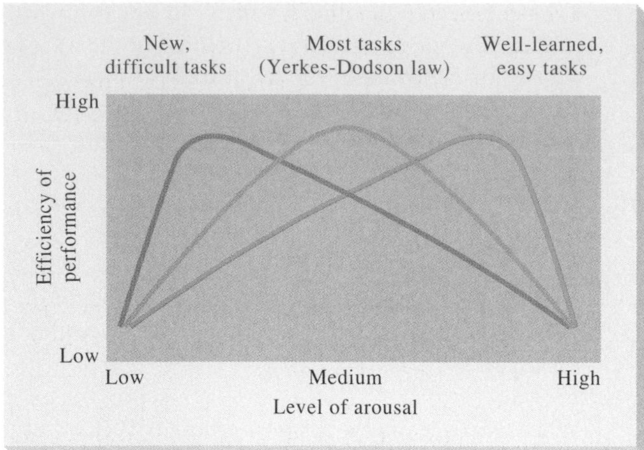

FIGURE 9

Arousal and Performance
The Yerkes-Dodson law states that optimal performance occurs under moderate arousal. However, for new or difficult tasks, low arousal may be best; for well-learned, easy tasks, high arousal can facilitate performance.

tasks (signing your name, pushing a button on request), optimal arousal can be quite high. By contrast, when learning a task (such as how to play tennis) or doing something complex (such as solving an algebraic equation), much lower arousal is preferred. Figure 9 projects how arousal might influence easy, moderate, and difficult tasks. As tasks become more difficult, the ability to be alert and attentive, but relaxed, is critical to optimal performance.

The Polygraph

You have been asked to think about your emotional states in the face of an automobile crash and a college exam. Now put yourself in the situation of lying to someone. Because body changes predictably accompany emotional states, it was reasoned that a machine might be able to determine if a person is lying. The **polygraph** *is a machine that tries to determine if someone is lying by monitoring changes in the body—heart rate, breathing, and electrodermal response (an index detecting skin resistance to passage of a weak electric current)—thought to be influenced by emotional states.* In a typical polygraph test, an individual is asked a number of neutral questions and several key, not so neutral, questions. If the individual's heart rate, breathing, and electrodermal response increase substantially when the key questions are asked, the individual is assumed to be lying. (See figure 10 to observe a polygraph testing situation.)

The polygraph has been widely used, especially in business, to screen new employees for honesty and to reveal employee theft. Following President Reagan's directive in 1983, the government increased their use of the polygraph to discover which individuals were leaking information to the media. Congressional hearings followed

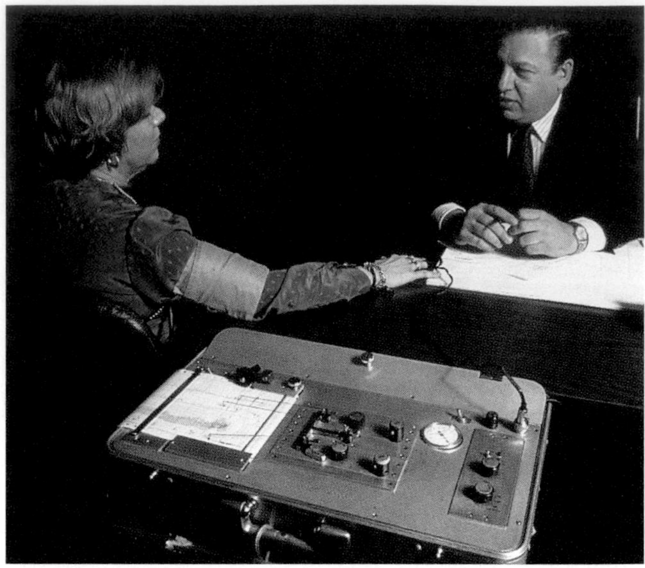

FIGURE 10

Polygraph Testing
A polygraph is supposed to tell whether someone is lying by monitoring changes in the body believed to be influenced by emotional states. Controversy has swirled about the polygraph's use. Because of the polygraph's inaccuracy, Congress passed the Employee Polygraph Protection Act of 1988, restricting the use of the polygraph in nongovernment settings.

and psychologists were called to testify about the polygraph's effectiveness (Saxe, Dougherty, & Cross, 1985). Testimony focused on how a standard lie detector situation does not exist. Inferring truth or deception based on physiological assessment of emotions requires a number of strategies. The complexity of the lie detector situation was brought out in testimony. Although the degree of arousal to a series of questions is measured through simple physiological changes, no unique physiological response to deception has been revealed (Lykken, 1987). Heart rate and breathing can increase for reasons other than lying, making interpretation of the physiological indicators of arousal complex.

Accurately identifying truth or deception rests on the skill of the examiner and the skill of the individual being examined. There are simple things people can do to avoid being detected of lying such as moving their body, taking drugs, and using various cognitive strategies or biofeedback techniques. Tensing your muscles, biting your tongue, squeezing your toes, and shifting your position in the chair can affect the polygraph's accuracy—examiners detect only about 50 to 75 percent of the countermeasures. Drugs, such as tranquilizers that have a calming effect on the individual, are more difficult to detect unless a test is conducted to reveal their use. Sometimes, though, the mere presence of the polygraph and the subject's belief it is accurate at detecting deception triggers confession. Police may use the polygraph in this way to get a criminal to confess. In such cases, the polygraph has served a positive purpose, but in too many instances it has been misused and misrepresented. Experts argue that the polygraph errs about one-third of the time, especially because it cannot distinguish between such feelings as anxiety and guilt. The testimony of psychologists that lie detectors are not always accurate led to the Employee Polygraph Protection Act of 1988, which restricts most nongovernment polygraph testing.

James-Lange and Cannon-Bard Theories

Psychologists have developed a number of theories about the role of arousal in emotion. Imagine that you and your date are enjoying a picnic in the country. As you prepare to eat, a bull runs across the field toward you. Why are you afraid? Two well-known theories of emotion provide answers to this question.

Common sense tells you that you are trembling and running away from the bull because you are afraid. But William James (1890/1950) and Carl Lange (1922) said emotion works in the opposite way. The **James-Lange theory** *suggests that emotion results from physiological states triggered by stimuli in the environment. Emotion occurs after physiological reactions.* You see the bull scratching his hoof, and you begin to run away. The aroused body then sends sensory messages to the brain, at which point emotion is perceived. According to this theory, you do not run away because you are afraid, rather you are afraid because you are running away. In other words, you perceive a stimulus in the environment, your body responds, and you interpret the body's reaction as emotion. In one of James' own examples, you perceive you have lost your fortune, you cry, and then interpret the crying as feeling sad. This goes against the commonsense sequence of losing your fortune, feeling sorry, and then crying.

Walter Cannon (1927) objected to the James-Lange theory. To understand his objection, imagine the bull and the picnic once again. Seeing the bull scratching its hooves causes the hypothalamus of your brain to do two things simultaneously: first, it stimulates your autonomic nervous system to produce the physiological changes involved in emotion (increased heart rate, rapid breathing); second, it sends messages to your cerebral cortex where the experience of emotion is perceived. Philip Bard (1934) supported this theory, and so the theory became known as the **Cannon-Bard theory,** *the theory that emotion and physiological reactions occur simultaneously.* In the Cannon-Bard theory, the body plays a less important role than in the James-Lange theory. Figure 11 shows how the James-Lange and Cannon-Bard theories differ.

As psychologists probed the elusive nature of emotion, they revealed the brain's important role. Next, we will examine a theory that opponent processes in the central nervous system are involved in emotion.

The Opponent-Process Theory

Richard Solomon (1980) developed a provocative view of the brain's role in emotion. He assumed the brain always seeks to maintain a state of equilibrium, just as in the concept of homeostasis discussed earlier in the chapter. **Opponent-process theory** *is Solomon's theory of emotion that pleasant or unpleasant stimuli can cause both a primary and a secondary process to occur in the brain. The secondary process is the central nervous system's reaction to the primary process of the autonomic nervous system. The secondary process reduces the intensity of a feeling and increases equilibrium; it strengthens with repeated stimulations.*

Parachute jumping and drug addiction provide examples of how the opponent-process theory works. Parachute jumpers experience a euphoric feeling after their jump. The euphoria opposes the high level of fear before the jump. After several jumps, the initial fear diminishes, but the euphoria remains strong so the person continues to jump. In this example, fear is the primary process and euphoria the secondary process (see figure 12). When a person takes opium, an intense rush occurs, followed by a less intense but pleasurable feeling. When the drug effects wear off, the user experiences discomfort and craves the drug, which leads to another dose. But the next dose produces a less intense rush and diminished pleasure. The aftereffects are more unpleasant—abstinence can cause sheer agony. The rush and pleasurable feelings represent the primary process of emotion; the unpleasurable feelings and craving, the secondary process.

Much of what we have said about emotion has focused on its physiological basis. While physiological factors play important roles in emotion, cognitive processes are at work as well.

Cognition and Emotion

Does emotion depend on the tides of the mind? Are we happy only when we think we are happy? Cognitive theories of emotion share an important point: emotion always has a cognitive component (Cornelius, 1996). Thinking is said to be responsible for feelings of love and hate, joy and sadness. While giving cognitive processes the main credit for emotion, the cognitive theories also recognize the role of the brain and body in emotion. That is, the hypothalamus and autonomic nervous system make connections with the peripheral areas of the body when emotion is experienced. According to cognitive theorists, body and thought are involved in emotion.

Schachter and Singer's View

Stanley Schachter and Jerome Singer (1962) developed a theory of emotion that gives cognition a strong role. They agree that emotional events produce internal, physiological arousal. As we sense the arousal, we look to the external

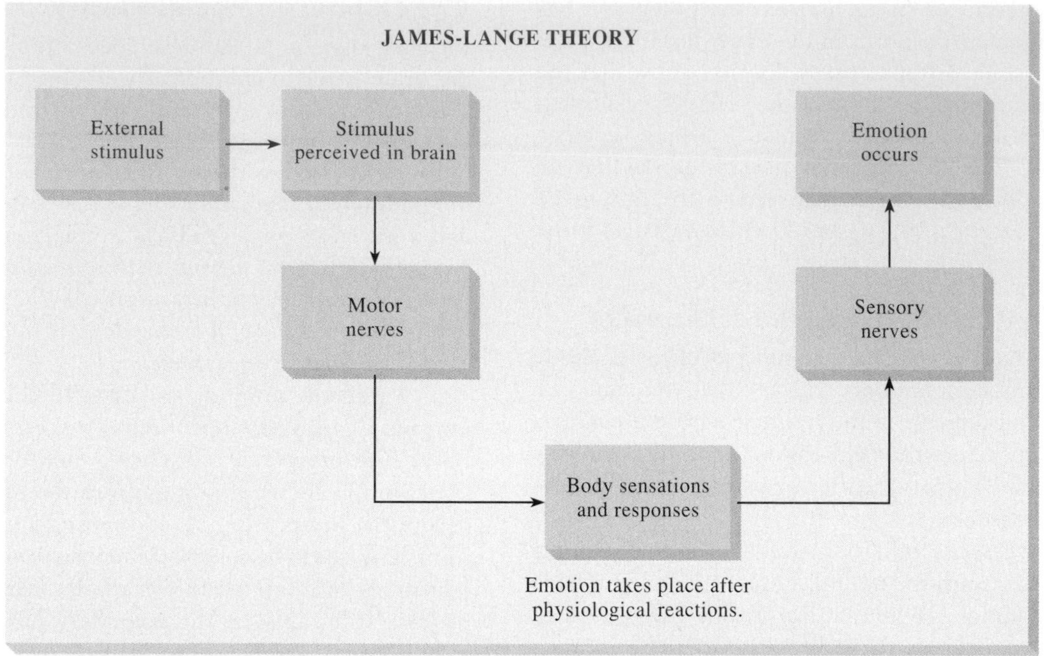

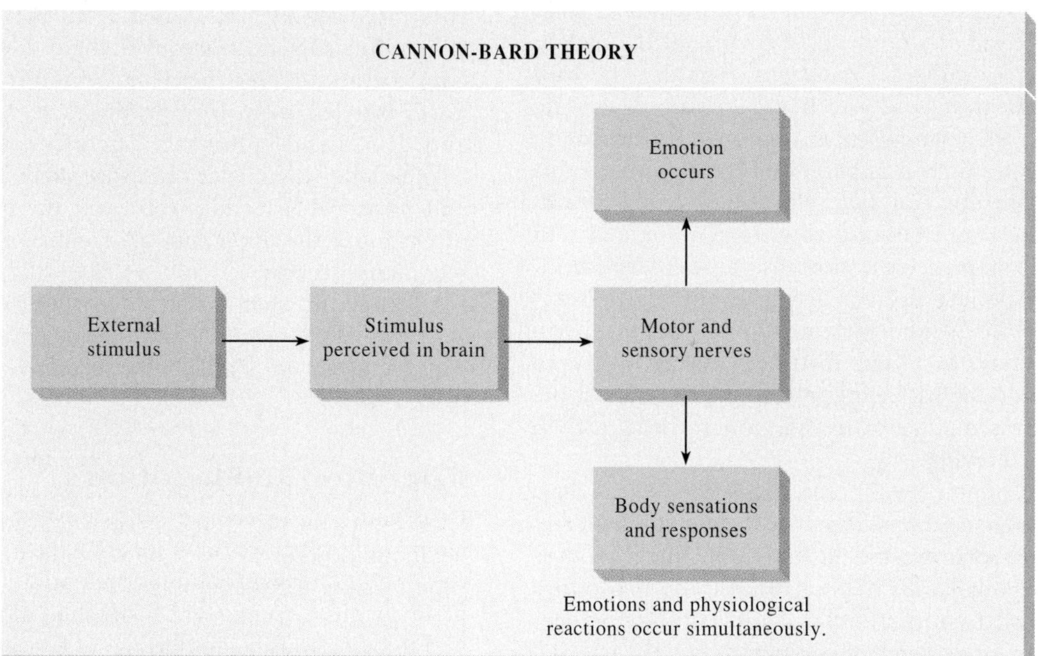

FIGURE 11

James-Lange and Cannon-Bard Theories of Emotion

world for an explanation of why we are aroused. We interpret the external cues present and then label the emotion. For example, if you feel good after someone has made a pleasant comment to you, you might label the emotion happy. If you feel bad after you have done something wrong, you may label the feeling guilty. Schachter and Singer believe much of our arousal is diffuse and not tied to specific emotions. Because the arousal is not instinctive, its meaning is easily misinterpreted.

To test their theory of emotion, Schachter and Singer (1962) injected subjects with epinephrine, a drug that produces high arousal. After volunteer subjects were given the drug, they observed someone else behave in either a euphoric way (shooting papers at a wastebasket) or an angry way (stomping out of the room). As predicted, the euphoric and angry behavior influenced the subjects' cognitive interpretation of their own arousal. When they were with a happy person, they rated themselves as happy; when they

FIGURE 12

Opponent Processes of Emotions in Parachute Jumping
How is parachute jumping an example of the way in which the opponent-process theory works? Parachute jumpers feel euphoric after a jump. The euphoria opposes the high level of fear that existed before the jump. After several jumps, the fear diminishes, but the euphoria remains strong, so the individual continues to jump. Fear is the primary process, and euphoria is the secondary process.

were with an angry person, they said they were angry. But this effect was found only when the subjects were not told about the true effects of the injection. When subjects were told that the drug would increase their heart rate and make them jittery, they said the reason for their own arousal was the drug, not the other person's behavior.

Psychologists have had difficulty replicating the Schachter and Singer experiment but, in general, research supports the belief that misinterpreted arousal intensifies emotional experiences (Leventhal & Tomarken, 1986). An intriguing study substantiates this belief. It went like this: An attractive woman approached men while they were crossing the Capilano River Bridge in British Columbia. Only those without a female companion were approached. The woman asked the men to make up a brief story for a project she was doing on creativity (Dutton & Aron, 1974). By the way, the Capilano River Bridge sways precariously more than 200 feet above rapids and rocks (see figure 13). The female interviewer made the same request of other men crossing a much safer, lower bridge. The men on the Capilano River Bridge told more sexually oriented stories and rated the female interviewer more attractive than did men on the lower, less frightening bridge.

The Primacy Debate: Cognition or Emotion?

Richard Lazarus (1991) believes cognitive activity is a precondition for emotion. He says we cognitively appraise ourselves and our social circumstances. These appraisals, which include values, goals, commitments, beliefs, and expectations, determine our emotions. People may feel happy because they have a deep religious commitment, angry because they did not get the raise they anticipated, or fearful because they expect to fail an exam.

Robert Zajonc (1984) disagrees with Lazarus. Emotions are primary, he says, and our thoughts are a result of them. Who is right? Both likely are correct. Lazarus refers mainly to a cluster of related events that occur over a period of time, whereas Zajonc describes single events or a simple preference for one stimulus over another. Lazarus speaks about love over the course of months and years, a sense of value to the community, and plans for retirement; Zajonc talks about a car accident, an encounter with a snake, and liking ice cream better than spinach. Some of our emotional reactions are virtually instantaneous and probably don't involve cognitive appraisal, such as a shriek on detecting a snake. Other emotional circumstances, especially those that occur over a long period of time, such as a depressed mood or anger toward a friend, are more likely to involve cognitive appraisal.

Developmental, Sociocultural, and Gender Influences

Many psychologists increasingly believe that emotions are not solely prewired, internal processes, but are influenced by development, sociocultural contexts, and gender.

Developmental Influences

How do emotions develop in infants? What is the nature of the new functionalist view of emotions in developmental psychology?

FIGURE 13

Capilano River Bridge Experiment: Misinterpreted Arousal Intensifies Emotional Experiences

The precarious Capilano River Bridge in British Columbia is shown at left; the experiment is shown in progress at right. An attractive woman approached men while they were crossing the 200-foot-high bridge; she asked them to make up a story to help her out. She also made the same request on a lower, much safer bridge. The men on the Capilano River Bridge told sexier stories, probably because they were aroused by the fear or excitement of being up so high on a swaying bridge. Apparently they interpreted their arousal as sexual attraction for the female interviewer.

The Development of Emotions in Infants We now know that interest, distress, and disgust are present early in infancy and can be communicated to parents. Much earlier than the arrival of language, infants add other emotions, such as joy, anger, surprise, shyness, and fear, to their repertoire (Izard, 1994).

What are the functions of emotions in infancy? Emotions are adaptive and promote survival, serve as a form of communication, and provide regulation (Teti & Teti, 1996). For example, various fears—such as fear of the dark and fear of sudden changes in the environment—are adaptive because there are clear links between such events and possible danger. Infants also use emotions to inform others about their feelings and needs. The infant who smiles probably is telling others that she is feeling pleasant; the infant who cries probably is communicating that something is unpleasant. Infants also use emotions to increase or decrease the distance between themselves and others. The infant who smiles may be encouraging someone to come closer; the infant who displays anger may be suggesting that an intruder should go away. Emotions also influence the information the infant selects from the perceptual world and the behaviors the infant displays. For example, an infant who is feeling pleasant may attend more efficiently to a mobile than would an infant who is crying uncontrollably.

How can we find out if the infant is displaying emotion? Carroll Izard (1982) developed a system for decoding the emotional expressions on infants' faces. Izard wanted to discover which emotions were inborn and which emerged later, and under which conditions they were displayed. The conditions included being given an ice cube, having tape put on the backs of their hands, being handed a favorite toy and then having it taken away, being separated from and reunited with their mothers, being approached by a stranger, having their heads gently restrained, having a ticking clock held next to their ears, having a balloon pop in front of their faces, and being given camphor to sniff and lemon rind and orange juice to taste.

Maximally Discriminative Facial Movement Coding System (MAX) *is Izard's system of coding infants' facial expressions related to emotion.* Using MAX, the coder watches slow-motion and stop-action videotapes of the infant's facial reactions to stimuli, such as the circumstances we described earlier. For example, anger is indicated when the brows are sharply lowered and drawn together, the eyes are narrowed or squinted, and the mouth is open in an angular, square shape. The developmental timetable of their emergence in infancy is shown in figure 14.

Although infants display a variety of their own emotions, can they also imitate someone else's emotional expressions? If an adult smiles, will a baby follow with a smile? If an adult protrudes her lower lip, wrinkles her forehead, and frowns, will the baby show a saddened look? If an adult opens her mouth, widens her eyes, and raises her eyebrows, will the baby follow suit? Can infants only 1 day old do these things? A number of researchers have found that young infants can imitate the facial expressions of another individual, but it is open to interpretation whether the imitation is learned or innate (Meltzoff & Kuhl, 1989) (see figure 15).

The New Functionalist View of Emotions in Developmental Psychology A number of developmentalists view the nature of emotion differently today than their predecessors did (Campos, 1994; Campos, Kermoian, & Witherington, 1995). The new view proposes that emotion is relational rather than intrapsychic, that there is a close link between emotion and the person's goals and effort, that emotional expressions can serve as social signals, and that the physiology of emotion involves much more than homeostasis and the person's interior—it also includes the ability to regulate and be regulated by social processes.

The new approach is called "functionalist," not because it focuses on evolutionary survival, but because it links emotion with what the person is trying to do. In this

Emotional Expression	Approximate Time of Emergence
Interest *Neonatal smile (a sort of half smile that appears spontaneously for no apparent reason) *Startled response *Distress Disgust	Present at birth
Social smile	4 to 6 weeks
Anger Surprise Sadness	3 to 4 months
Fear Shame/Shyness	5 to 7 months 6 to 8 months
Contempt Guilt	Second year of life

*The neonatal smile, the startled response, and distress in response to pain are precursors of the social smile and the emotions of surprise and sadness, which appear later. No evidence suggests that they are related to inner feelings when they are observed in the first few weeks of life.

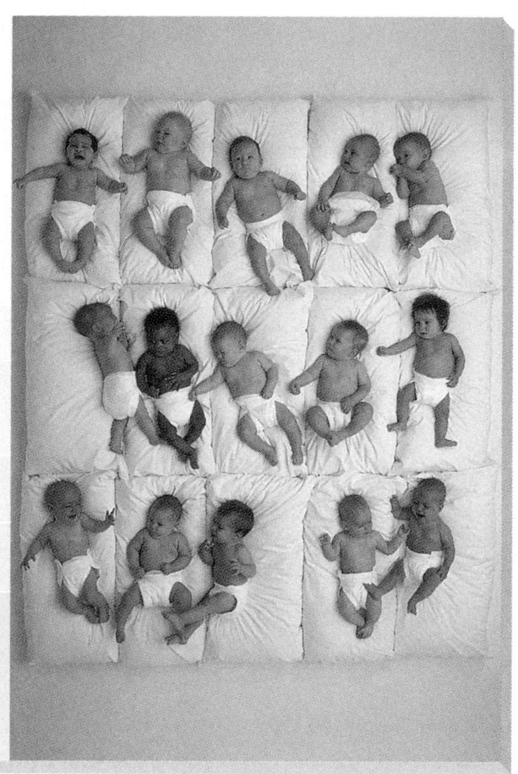

FIGURE 14

The Developmental Course of Infant Emotions

view, the person and an environmental event constitute a whole. Emotion thus involves person-event transactions, in this perspective (see figure 16).

The new functionalist approach does not diminish the importance of feelings, or the autonomic nervous system, but deals with such aspects of emotion differently than traditional theories do. What is new is the nesting of these factors—feelings and the body's physiology—within the description of the striving person's adaptation to the environment.

To learn how the new functionalists assess emotions, let's examine the concept of attachment. Advances in understanding attachment were made when researchers such as Alan Sroufe (1985) argued that "proximity seeking" and "felt security" could not be measured by concrete, observable behaviors like physical distance in meters. Sroufe proposed instead that researchers should investigate the functional dimensions of behaviors. For example, a child can show proximity seeking not only through a physical approach measured by actual distance but also by the child's attempts to be picked up, ease of soothing by the parent when distressed, or the smiles of delight when reunited with the parent. The extensive research literature on attachment in the last several decades contains many studies in which observers reliably made inferences about such functional properties of attachment instead of relying on discrete, concrete, observable behaviors (Sroufe, 1996).

More needs to be said about goals and emotion. Goals are related to emotion in a variety of ways. Regardless

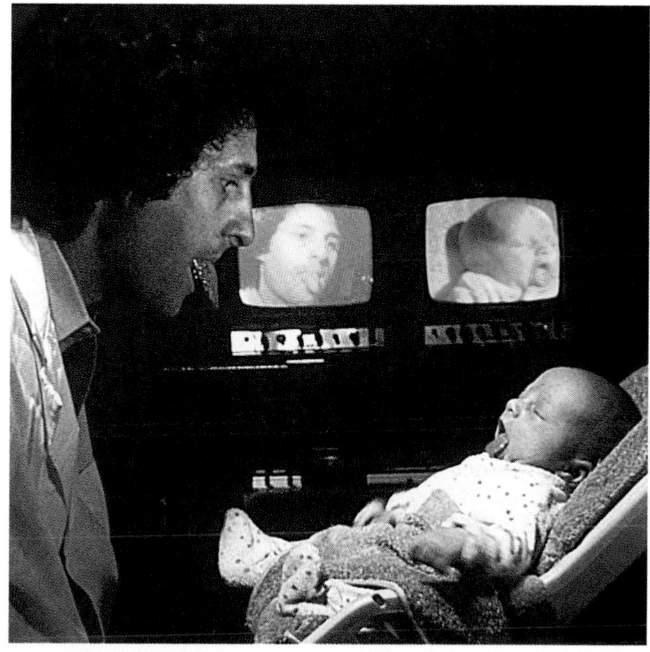

FIGURE 15

Infant Imitation

Infant development researcher Andrew Meltzoff displays tongue protrusion in an attempt to get the infant to imitate his behavior. Researchers have demonstrated that young infants can imitate adult behaviors far earlier than traditionally believed.

FIGURE 16

The New Functionalism in Emotions
Infant researcher Nathan Fox (in press) measures the brain waves of infants, like this 4-month-old, who have been shown toys to stimulate different emotional states. Fox has demonstrated that very inhibited babies show a distinctive brave-wave pattern (as measured by the electroencephalogram [EEG] helmet in the photograph). Fox's research fits within the new functionalist theories of emotion, which argue that the physiology of emotion involves much more than a homeostasis or an internal milieu. In the new functionalism, emotions are modes of adaptation to the environment.

of what the goal is, an individual who overcomes an obstacle to attain a goal experiences happiness. By contrast, a person who must relinquish a goal as unattainable experiences sadness. And a person who faces difficult obstacles in pursuing a goal often experiences anger. The specific nature of the goal can affect the experience of a given emotion. For example, avoidance of threat is linked with fear, desire to atone is related to guilt, and the wish to avoid the scrutiny of others is associated with shame. Many of the new functionalists focus their work on goal-related emotions.

Sociocultural Influences

How does culture influence the expression of emotions? What is the functionalist view of emotions from a cross-cultural perspective?

Culture and the Expression of Emotions In *The Expression of the Emotions in Man and Animals,* Charles Darwin (1872/1965) argued that the facial expressions of human beings are innate, not learned; are the same in all cultures around the world; and evolved from the emotions of animals. Darwin compared the similarity of human snarls of anger with the growls of dogs and the hisses of cats. He compared the giggling of chimpanzees when they are tickled under their arms with human laughter.

Today psychologists still believe that emotions, especially facial expressions of emotion, have strong biological ties. For example, children who are blind from birth and have never observed the smile or frown on another person's face, still smile or frown in the same way that children with normal vision do.

The universality of facial expressions and the ability of people from different cultures to accurately label the emotion that lies behind the facial expression has been extensively researched. Psychologist Paul Ekman's (1980, 1994, 1996) careful observations reveal that our many faces of emotion do not vary significantly from one culture to another. For example, Ekman and his colleague photographed people expressing emotions such as happiness, fear, surprise, disgust, and grief. They found that when they showed the photographs to other people from the United States, Chile, Japan, Brazil, and Borneo (an Indonesian island in the western Pacific Ocean), each person tended to label the same faces with the same emotions (Ekman & Friesen,

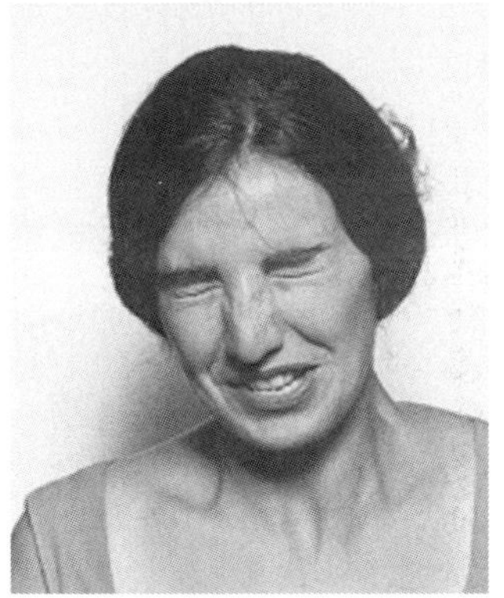
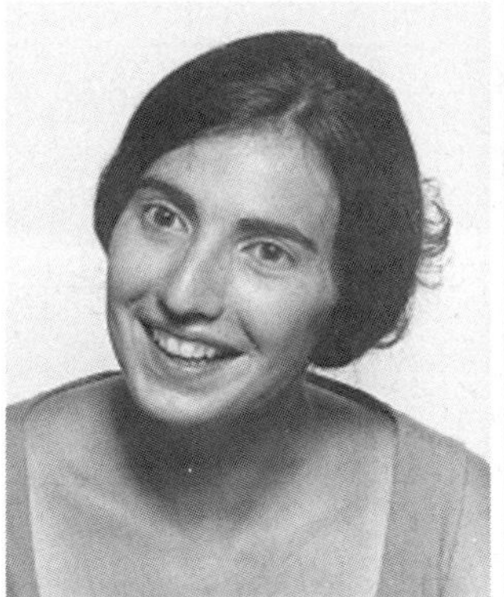

Figure 17

Emotional Expressions in the United States and New Guinea
At left is a woman from the United States; on the right are two men from the Fore tribe in New Guinea. Notice the similarity in their expressions of disgust and happiness. Psychologists believe that the facial expression of emotion is virtually the same in all cultures.

1968). In another study the focus was on the way the Fore tribe, an isolated Stone Age culture in New Guinea, matched descriptions of emotions with facial expressions (Ekman & Friesen, 1971). Before Ekman's visit, most of the Fore had never seen a Caucasian face. Ekman showed them photographs of American faces expressing emotions such as fear, happiness, anger, and surprise. Then he read stories about people in emotional situations. The Fore were able to match the descriptions of emotions with the facial expressions in the photographs. The similarity of facial expressions of emotions by persons in New Guinea and the United States is shown in figure 17.

While facial expressions of basic emotions appear to be universal across cultures, display rules for emotion are not culturally universal. **Display rules** *are sociocultural standards that determine when, where, and how emotions should be expressed.* For example, while happiness is a universally expressed emotion, when, where, and how it is displayed may vary from one culture to another. The same is true for other emotions such as fear, sadness, and anger. For example, members of the Utku culture in Alaska discourage anger by cultivating acceptance and by dissociating themselves from any display of anger. If a trip is hampered by an unexpected snowstorm, the Utku do not become frustrated, but accept the presence of the snowstorm and build an igloo. Most of us would not act as mildly in the face of subzero weather and barriers to our travel.

In addition to facial expressions, emotions are also expressed in many other nonverbal signals of body movement, posture, and gesture. Some basic nonverbal signals appear to be universal indicators of certain emotions, just as facial expressions are. For example, when people are depressed it shows not only in their sad facial expression, but also in their slow body movement, downturned head, and slumped posture.

Many nonverbal signals of emotion, though, vary from one culture to another (Cohen & Borsoi, 1996). For example, male-to-male kissing is commonplace in some cultures, such as Yemen (in the Middle East), but uncommon in other cultures, such as the United States. And the "thumb up" sign, which means either everything is OK or the desire to hitch a ride in most cultures, is an insult in Greece, similar to a raised third finger in the United States.

In the Middle Eastern country of Yemen, male-to-male kissing is commonplace, but in the United States it is very uncommon.

Gender Influences

Unless you've been isolated on a mountaintop away from people, television, magazines, and newspapers, you probably know the master stereotype about gender and emotion: She is emotional, he is not. This stereotype is a powerful and pervasive image in our culture (Shields, 1991).

Is this stereotype supported when researchers study the nature of emotional experiences in females and males? Researchers have found that females and males are often more alike in the way they experience emotion than the master stereotype would lead us to believe. Females and males often use the same facial expressions, adopt the same language, and describe their emotional experiences similarly when they keep diaries about their life experiences. Thus, the master stereotype that females are emotional and males are not is simply that—a stereotype. Given the complexity and vast territory of emotion—remember how many emotions we can experience from our earlier discussion of the

Concept Table 2

Emotion

Concept	Processes/Related Ideas	Characteristics/Description
Definition, Range, and Classification	Definition	Emotions are feelings, or affect, that involve a mixture of physiological arousal, conscious experience, and overt behavior.
	Range and classification	We experience a wide range. Plutchik believes that emotions are positive or negative, are primary or mixed, are bipolar opposites, and vary in intensity.
Happiness and Anger	Happiness	Self-esteem, a good marriage or love relationship, social contacts, regular exercise, the ability to sleep well, and religious faith are related to happiness. Positive emotions like happiness are more likely to increase generosity, eagerness, expansiveness, and free-flowing use of one's resources than negative emotions like sadness. People are the happiest when they develop a sense of mastery over their lives. In developing a sense of mastery, people often experience flow, a state of concentration that individuals reach when they become absorbed in an activity.
	Anger	Anger is a powerful emotion that not only has a strong influence on social relationships, but also on the person experiencing anger. Most psychologists consider catharsis to be an ineffective way of coping with angry feelings. Strategies for reducing anger include waiting, not being chronically angry over every little annoyance or passively sulking, forming a self-help group with others who have been through similar experiences with anger, taking action to help others, and seeking ways of breaking out of a usual perspective.
Arousal and Physiological Processes	Arousal	The sympathetic nervous system is involved in arousal; the parasympathetic system is involved when arousal decreases. Many aspects of our body are influenced by arousal. The Yerkes-Dodson law addresses the issue of arousal and performance. Polygraphs rest on the principle of arousal in emotion. The polygraph situation is complex and psychologists remain skeptical about its validity.
	James-Lange and Cannon-Bard theories	In the James-Lange view, we initially perceive a stimulus, our body responds, then we experience the emotion. By contrast, the Cannon-Bard theory plays down the body's role in emotion, saying we simultaneously experience an emotion and bodily changes. Dispute continues about whether the same body changes underlie all emotions.
	The opponent-process theory	In Solomon's view, every emotion has a primary and a secondary process. The secondary process is the central nervous system's reaction to the primary process of the autonomic nervous system. The secondary process reduces the intensity of an emotion and increases equilibrium; it strengthens with repeated stimulations.

classification of emotion; verbal and nonverbal dimensions of emotion; cognitive, behavioral, and physiological aspects of emotion; cultural experiences; and so on—we should not be surprised that this stereotype is not supported when actual emotional experiences are examined. Thus, for many emotional experiences, researchers do not find differences between females and males—both sexes are equally likely to experience love, jealousy, anxiety in new social situations, be angry when they are insulted, grieve when close relationships end, and be embarrassed when they make mistakes in public (Tavris & Wade, 1984).

When we go beyond the master stereotype and consider some specific emotional experiences, the context in which emotion is displayed, and certain beliefs about emotion, gender does matter in understanding emotion (Shields, 1991). Consider anger. Men are more likely to show anger toward strangers, especially other men, when they feel they have been challenged, and men are more likely to turn their anger into aggressive action than women are.

Differences between females and males regarding emotion are more likely to occur in contexts that highlight

Concept	Processes/Related Ideas	Characteristics/Description
Cognition and Emotion	Overview	Cognitive views argue that emotion always has a cognitive component and that, in most instances, cognition directs emotion.
	Schachter-Singer view	Emotional events produce emotional arousal. Arousal often is diffuse so we look to the external world to interpret. We label the emotion based on environmental cues.
	Primacy: Cognition or emotion?	Lazarus believes that cognition always directs emotion; Zajonc says emotion is dominant. Both probably are right.
Developmental, Sociocultural, and Gender Influences	Developmental influences	Infant emotions are adaptive, regulative, and communicative. Infants display a variety of emotions. Some appear earlier in development than others. Young infants can also imitate the emotional expressions of others. The new functionalist view emphasizes that emotion is relational rather than intrapsychic, that there is a close link between emotion and the person's goals and effort, that emotional expressions can serve as social signals, and that the physiology of emotion is much more than homeostasis and the person's interior—it also includes the ability to regulate and be regulated by social processes.
	Sociocultural influences	Emotions often involve social contexts and relationships. Most psychologists believe that the facial expression of basic emotions is universal across all cultures. While facial expressions of emotions are thought to be universal, display rules for emotions often vary from one culture to another. These display rules include nonverbal signals of body movement, posture, and gesture.
	Gender influences	The master stereotype of gender and emotion is that females are emotional, males are not. This is a stereotype; understanding emotion and gender is much more complex. When we go beyond the master stereotype and consider some specific aspects of emotional experiences, the context in which emotion is displayed, and certain beliefs about emotion, gender does matter in understanding emotion. Female—male differences in emotion are more likely to occur in contexts that highlight social roles and relationships.

social roles and relationships. For example, females are more likely than males to give accounts of emotion that include interpersonal relationships. And females are more likely to express fear and sadness than males, especially when communicating with their friends and family.

Beliefs about emotion play an important role in understanding how gender and emotion work in our culture. We often use beliefs about emotion to define the difference between what is masculine and feminine, male and female (Shields, 1991). For example, in one study, men were more likely to agree with the belief that men should conceal their feelings, but when reporting their own behavior, women more than men reported greater inhibition of emotional expression. Sex differences in self-reports tend to be consistent with emotion stereotypes, as if individuals compare themselves to a cultural standard when generating a response—"I must be emotional, after all I'm a woman," or "I must be inexpressive, after all I'm a man" (Shields, 1991).

At this point we have discussed a number of ideas about emotion. A summary of these ideas is presented in concept table 2.

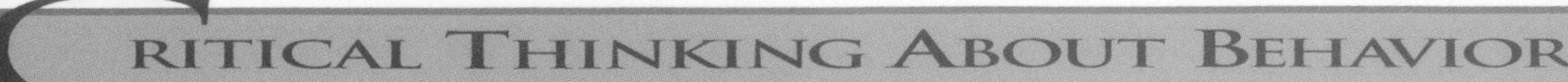

Critical Thinking About Behavior

The Value of Sexual Skepticism

One of the most important skills of good critical thinkers in psychology is *being able to evaluate how truthful claims are.* Because misinformation about sex is so widespread, it is especially important to adopt a skeptical attitude about many claims about sex until evidence confirms or disconfirms them.

Here is a sample of the myths that some psychology students have claimed to believe until they encountered disconfirming evidence:

- You can get pregnant most easily if you make love in water.
- If women don't achieve an orgasm during sex, then they won't get pregnant.
- A woman can prevent pregnancy by jumping up and down after sex.
- You can't get pregnant the first time you have intercourse.
- Women can't achieve orgasm without direct stimulation of the G-spot.
- The size of a man's penis determines how satisfying sex will be.
- The size of a man's penis corresponds to the size of his nose (foot, thumb).
- Simultaneous orgasm is the only acceptable form of satisfaction.
- Breast-feeding prevents pregnancy.
- If men can't ejaculate after a certain threshold of stimulation has been reached, they'll become sick.

Some of these myths are abandoned after experience provides (sometimes painful) disconfirmation. How can adolescents and adults learn to navigate the precarious waters of sexuality with a minimum of misinformation to make informed choices about their behavior? The following specific strategies can help protect you.

1. *Regard cause-and-effect claims about sexuality with suspicion.* Nature encourages behavior that will help living organisms reproduce. Pregnancy requires contact of an egg and a sperm. Measures that don't directly prevent that contact are not likely to be effective against pregnancy.
2. *Remember your own mortality.* It is relatively easy, especially in moments of passion, to abandon good judgment about self-protection. In such moments we tend to think of ourselves as immune to the laws of nature ("It won't happen to me"; "Just this once and never again"). Many carefree lovers end up very care-ridden by the biological consequences of impulsive unprotected sex.
3. *Evaluate the risk if the claim appears to be untrue.* Taking risks is part of life. However, sexual risk-taking in the absence of knowledge can result in dramatic life-changing outcomes. Where the risk is too great, restraint is the wiser course.
4. *Assess whether the source of the claims is trustworthy and astute.* Sometimes people promote myths as a strategy for getting a sexual relationship. Claims made by a person in the hopes of achieving intimacy could be manipulative; you need to establish whether you can trust a person you are considering becoming intimate with. People also sometimes pass along misguided sexual lore, with an intention not to take advantage but only to inform—but end up only misinforming. You need to establish whether the person you are discussing sexual lore with is likely to be well informed.
5. *Ask for evidence to support claims that are risk-promoting.* Always require evidence in support of any claim about a cause-and-effect relationship in behavior. This is imperative regarding claims that are relevant to the risks you might be taking by engaging in sexual activity. Questions to keep in mind include the following: *How did you learn about that? How much confidence do you have in the claim? What if you are wrong?*

Remembering the specific aspects of practicing sexual skepticism can help you make more responsible and reasonable sexual choices in an increasingly challenging world. Developing a skeptical attitude can assist you in evaluating the validity of claims about behavior.

Overview

To learn about motivation, we studied some ideas behind the "whys" of behavior—instincts, needs and drives, incentives, a hierarchy of motives, and motivation's biological, cognitive, and sociocultural dimensions. Our coverage of hunger focused on physiological factors, as well as external and cognitive factors. Our focus on sexuality emphasized hormones and the brain, the human sexual response cycle, psychosexual dysfunctions, and heterosexuality and homosexuality. We also discussed the nature of competence and achievement, exploring competence motivation, achievement motivation, intrinsic and extrinsic motivation, mastery versus helpless and performance orientations, goal setting and self-efficacy, self-esteem, and cultural, ethnic, and social class variations in achievement. To learn about emotion, we studied the range and classification of emotions, happiness, anger, physiological arousal and brain processes in emotion, cognition and emotion, and developmental, sociocultural, and gender influences. Remember that you can obtain an overall summary of the chapter by again studying the two concept tables on pages 378 and 392.

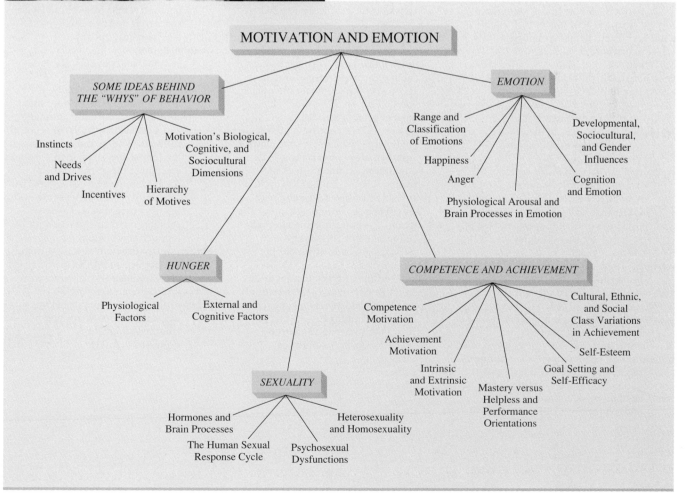

MOTIVATION AND EMOTION

- *SOME IDEAS BEHIND THE "WHYS" OF BEHAVIOR*
  - Instincts
  - Needs and Drives
  - Incentives
  - Hierarchy of Motives
  - Motivation's Biological, Cognitive, and Sociocultural Dimensions
- *HUNGER*
  - Physiological Factors
  - External and Cognitive Factors
- *SEXUALITY*
  - Hormones and Brain Processes
  - The Human Sexual Response Cycle
  - Psychosexual Dysfunctions
  - Heterosexuality and Homosexuality
- *COMPETENCE AND ACHIEVEMENT*
  - Competence Motivation
  - Achievement Motivation
  - Intrinsic and Extrinsic Motivation
  - Mastery versus Helpless and Performance Orientations
  - Goal Setting and Self-Efficacy
  - Self-Esteem
  - Cultural, Ethnic, and Social Class Variations in Achievement
- *EMOTION*
  - Range and Classification of Emotions
  - Happiness
  - Anger
  - Physiological Arousal and Brain Processes in Emotion
  - Cognition and Emotion
  - Developmental, Sociocultural, and Gender Influences

KEY TERMS

motivation Reasons why people behave, think, and feel the way they do. Motivated behavior is energized and directed. p. 360

instinct An innate, biological determinant of behavior. p. 360

drive An aroused state that occurs because of a physiological need. p. 360

need A deprivation that energizes the drive to eliminate or reduce the deprivation. p. 360

homeostasis The body's tendency to maintain an equilibrium, or steady state. p. 360

incentives Positive or negative external stimuli or events that motivate an individual's behavior. p. 361

hierarchy of motives According to Maslow, the main kinds of needs that each individual must satisfy, in this sequence: physiological needs, safety needs, the need for love and belongingness, the need for esteem, cognitive needs, aesthetic needs, and the need for self-actualization. p. 361

self-actualization The highest and most elusive human need, according to Maslow; the motivation to develop to one's full potential as a human being. p. 361

ethology The study of the biological basis of behavior in natural habitats. p. 361

ventromedial hypothalamus (VMH) A region of the hypothalamus that plays an important role in controlling hunger. p. 364

set point The body weight maintained when no effort is made to gain or lose weight. p. 364

restrained eaters Individuals who chronically restrict their food intake to control their weight. Restrained eaters are often on diets, are very conscious of what they eat, and tend to feel guilty after splurging on sweets. p. 366

estrogen The main class of female sex hormones. p. 366

androgen The main class of male sex hormones. p. 366

pheromones Odorous substances released by animals that are powerful attractants. p. 366

human sexual response pattern The four phases of human sexual response—excitement, plateau, orgasm, and resolution—identified by Masters and Johnson. p. 367

psychosexual dysfunctions Disorders that involve impairments in the sexual response cycle, either in the desire for gratification or in the ability to achieve it. p. 367

double standard The belief that many sexual activities are acceptable for males but not for females. p. 369

competence motivation Our motivation to deal effectively with the environment, to be adept at what we attempt, to process information efficiently, and to make the world a better place. p. 371

achievement motivation (need for achievement) The desire to accomplish something, to reach a standard of excellence, and to expend effort to excel. p. 372

intrinsic motivation The desire to be competent and to do something for its own sake. p. 373

extrinsic motivation Motivation produced by external rewards and punishments. p. 373

helpless orientation The orientation of individuals who feel trapped by the experience of difficulty. They attribute their difficulty to a lack of ability. p. 373

mastery orientation Being task oriented. Instead of focusing on their ability, such individuals are concerned about learning strategies and the process of achievement rather than outcomes. p. 373

performance orientation Being concerned with outcomes. For such individuals, winning is what matters most and happiness is thought to result from winning. p. 374

self-efficacy A belief that one has mastery over a situation and the ability to produce positive outcomes. p. 375

self-esteem The evaluative and affective dimensions of self-concept; also referred to as self-worth or self-image. p. 375

emotion Feeling, or affect, that involves a mixture of arousal (a fast heartbeat, for example), conscious experience (such as thinking about being in love with someone), and overt behavior (such as smiling or grimacing). p. 380

flow Optimal experiences in life that are most likely to occur when people develop a sense of mastery. Flow involves a state of concentration in which an individual becomes absorbed while engaging in an activity. p. 381

catharsis The release of anger or aggressive energy by directly or vicariously engaging in anger or aggression. The catharsis hypothesis states that behaving angrily or watching others behave angrily reduces subsequent anger. p. 382

Yerkes-Dodson law The law that performance is best under conditions of moderate rather than low or high arousal. p. 383

polygraph A machine that tries to determine if someone is lying by monitoring changes in the body—heart rate, breathing, and electrodermal response (an index that detects skin resistance to passage of a weak electric current)—thought to be influenced by emotional states. p. 384

James-Lange theory The theory that emotion results from physiological states triggered by stimuli in the environment. p. 385

Cannon-Bard theory The theory that emotions and physiological states occur simultaneously. p. 385

opponent-process theory Solomon's theory that pleasant or unpleasant stimuli can cause both a primary and a secondary process to occur in the brain. The secondary process is the central nervous system's reaction to the primary process of the autonomic nervous system. The secondary process reduces the intensity of feeling and increases equilibrium; it strengthens with repeated stimulation. p. 385

Maximally Discriminative Facial Movement Coding System (MAX) Izard's system of coding infants' facial expressions related to emotion. p. 388

display rules Sociocultural standards that determine when, where, and how emotions should be expressed. p. 391

Resources and Readings in Psychology

Aggressive Behavior (1994)
edited by Leonard Husemann
New York: Plenum

This up-to-date volume surveys a wide variety of topics on aggression.

Ambition (1992)
by Gilbert Brim
New York: Basic Books

The author tackles how humans experience—and must learn to handle—success and failure from birth to death. He evaluates how people can learn to manage their ambitions, develop strategies for coping with failure, and create plans for success.

Anger: The Misunderstood Emotion (1989)
by Carol Tavris
New York: Touchstone Books

Anger: The Misunderstood Emotion covers a wider terrain of anger. Indeed, it is hard to think of any facet of anger—from wrecked friendships to wars—that Tavris does not tackle. In addition to extensive coverage of anger between marital partners, she addresses highway anger, violence in sports, and young women's anger. Tavris debunks myths about anger, attacks the catharsis, ventilationist approach to anger, describes the toll of anger on the body, and tells readers how to rethink anger and make more adaptive choices.

Emotion (1995)
by Robert Kavanaugh, Betty Zimmberberg, and Steven Fein (eds.)
Hillsdale, NJ: Erlbaum

Experts discuss theoretical and applied issues involving emotion. Among the topics covered are the functional view of emtional development, neurobiological factors in emotion, and cognition and emotion.

Emotion and Culture (1994)
edited by Shinobu Kitayama and Hazel Markus
Washington, DC: American Psychological Association

This volume contains chapters by leading authorities in the field of emotion who believe that emotions are influenced and shaped by social and cultural experiences. Major book sections focus on emotion as a social product; emotion, language, and cognition; and emotion as moral category and phenomenon.

Flow (1990)
by Mihaly Csikszentmihalyi
New York: Harper & Row

Flow is about the optimal experiencing of life. Csikszentmihalyi (pronounced "chik-*sent*-me-high-yee") has been investigating the concept of flow for more than two decades. Earlier in the chapter we discussed the author's view of what flow is, namely a deep happiness people feel when they have a sense of mastering something.

For Yourself (1975)
by Lonnie Barbach
New York: Signet

For Yourself provides advice for women about how to achieve sexual fulfillment. Barbach addresses the worries that often distress nonorgasmic women and tells them how to achieve orgasm. Barbach attacks the negative cultural attitudes that say women should not enjoy sex.

The New Male Sexuality (1992)
by Bernie Zilbergeld
New York: Bantam

The New Male Sexuality is a very up-to-date, comprehensive book about male sexuality.

Permanent Partners (1988)
by Betty Berzon
New York: Plume

Permanent Partners presents the knowledge and understanding that will help gay and lesbian couples make their relationship work and last. Berzon examines the obstacles that same-sex couples face as they try to create a new life together.

Sex in America (1994)
by Robert Michael, John Gagnon, Edward Laumann, and Gina Kolata
Boston: Little, Brown

This book reveals the extensive, surprising results of a large-scale, random sample study of the sexual lives of Americans in the 1990s. The results suggest that Americans are more conservative in their sexual activities than previously was believed.

Striving and Feeling (1995)
by Leonard Martin and Abraham Tesser (eds.)
Hillsdale, NJ: Erlbaum

This volume focuses on the increased interest in how goals, affect, and self-regulation interact. Topics examined include goal orientation and emotional well-being, goal framing and performance, cognition and mood regulation, and emotion and communication.

Telling Lies: Clues to Deceit in the Marketplace, Politics, and Marriage (1985)
by Paul Ekman
New York: W. W. Norton

Ekman describes how to read facial expressions and gestures to determine whether people are lying.

Why We Eat What We Eat (1996)
by Elizabeth Capaldi (ed.)
Washington, DC: American Psychological Association

Experts cut through popular myths about eating to present the latest research on how eating patterns develop. Topics include the development of food preferences and aversions, how eating patterns develop in childhood, how biology affects eating behavior, and how social contexts influence eating patterns.

CHAPTER

PER

Personality

PAUL KLEE
Actor's Mask, detail

Personality

Chapter Outline

Chapter Boxes

Every person cries out to be read differently.

—Simone Weil

The living self has one purpose only:
to come into its own fullness of being,
as a tree comes into full blossom,
or a bird into spring beauty,
or a tiger into lustre.

—D. H. Lawrence

Images of Psychology

Everyday Descriptions of Personality

"She has a great personality."
"He has no personality."
"She is a personality."
"She has her mother's personality."

These statements reflect our everyday use of the term *personality*. You probably have used similar statements to describe someone you have known or known about. Let's look further at each of these statements (Peterson, 1988).

"She has a great personality." This statement is a positive evaluation. When you say this about a woman, it means you like something about her that does not involve looks, possessions, or status. There is something about her that makes you feel good when you are around her. Maybe it's the way she behaves, her attitude, her flair, her values, or even some of her quirks.

"He has no personality." This statement also is an evaluation, but it is a negative one. You do not really like this guy, but you might not dislike him either, unless you happen to be his college roommate or he is your boss. He makes your day boring. He has nothing unique that stamps him as very different from others: no passion, no weird hobby or unusual ability, and not much desire except just to schlepp through life unnoticed. He can take or leave Mexican food or Geraldo Rivera, he has no mismatched socks. He is almost like a piece of furniture.

"She is a personality." Andy Warhol once said that in the future everyone will be famous for 15 minutes. Then it will be someone else's turn. Some of us make *People* magazine; most of us don't. People write about celebrities so noncelebrities can read about them. Many celebrities have unique personalities and we call them "personalities." Roseanne, Whoopi Goldberg, and Eddie Murphy are celebrities we think of as personalities. They are well known not just for what they do, but for how they do it. They play a role in our culture that becomes identified with the personality they bring to the role.

"She has her mother's personality." Many statements about personality focus on distinctive characteristics, what makes us different from others in some way. Personality is also used to make comparisons among individuals, describing common characteristics and similarities. Most of us have talked about the way certain people remind us of someone else we have known. They may have similar mannerisms. She holds grudges just like her mother does, for example. They may have similar temperaments. She is the life of the party and loves to be around people, just like her father. Many people look at their family members and see certain similar personality characteristics. For example, someone may say, "My brother is an introvert just like my cousin Robert." Or "My sister has my grandmother's personality—she has a stubborn streak a mile long."

Many celebrities, such as Whoopi Goldberg, are called "personalities." They are well known not just for what they do, but also for how they do it. Whoopi Goldberg's outgoing personality is a property of Whoopi Goldberg and is related to how she functions in the world. Of course, it is not just celebrities who have a personality. Each of us has a personality that is our property and is related to how we function in the world.

Preview

How do the images of personality we use in our everyday conversations about people correspond to the way psychologists describe personality? The images suggest that personality is a property of the individual that is related to how the individual functions in the world. In this chapter's first topic of discussion—"What is personality?"—you will see that psychologists agree personality is a property of the individual, but that some disagreement exists about the nature of personality. In this chapter you will read about the main theories of personality: psychoanalytic, behavioral/social learning, phenomenological/humanistic, and trait. We also will evaluate the nature of personality research and how personality is assessed. Toward the end of the chapter we will examine some important issues that personality theories address and see how the main theories stack up against each other on these issues.

What Is Personality?

Think about yourself for a moment? What are you *really* like? Are you outgoing or shy? Aggressive or calm? Intellectual or nonintellectual? Considerate or uncaring? Try to come up with seven or eight of these traits that reflect the way you respond to your world. In compiling this list, you chose personality characteristics that you probably feel are an enduring part of your makeup as a person. For example, if you said that you are an outgoing person, wouldn't you also say that you were outgoing a year ago and that you will probably be an outgoing person 1 year, 5 years, and 10 years from now? Most of us believe that we do have some enduring personality characteristics. Psychologists define **personality** *as enduring, distinctive thoughts, emotions, and behaviors that characterize the way an individual adapts to the world.*

The theories we describe ask why individuals respond to the same situation in different ways. For example, *why* is Sam so talkative and gregarious, and Al so shy and quiet when they meet someone for the first time? *Why* is Gretchen so confident and Mary so insecure about upcoming job interviews? Some theorists believe that biological and genetic factors are responsible; others argue that life experiences are more important. Some theorists claim that the way we think about ourselves is the key to understanding personality, while others stress that the way we behave toward each other is more important.

The diversity of theories makes understanding personality a challenging undertaking (Maddi, 1996). Just when you think one theory has the correct explanation of personality, another theory will crop up and make you rethink your earlier conclusion. To keep from getting frustrated, remember that personality is a complex, multifaceted topic and no single theory has been able to account for all its aspects. Each theory has contributed an important piece to the personality puzzle. In fact, much of the information is *complementary* rather than contradictory. Together they let us see the total landscape of personality in all its richness (Mayer & Sutton, 1996).

Personality Perspectives

The field of personality includes a number of theoretical perspectives. The main perspectives we will discuss are the psychoanalytic, behavioral and social learning, phenomenological and humanistic, and trait theory and trait-situation interaction perspectives.

Psychoanalytic Perspectives

For psychoanalytic theorists, personality is mainly unconscious—that is, beyond awareness, and heavily colored by emotion. Psychoanalytic theorists believe that behavior is merely a surface characteristic and that to truly understand someone's personality we have to look at the symbolic meanings of behavior and the deep inner workings of the mind. Psychoanalysts also believe that early experiences with parents extensively shape our personalities. These characteristics were highlighted by the original psychoanalytic theorist, Sigmund Freud.

Freud's Theory

Loved and hated, respected and despised, Sigmund Freud, whether right or wrong in his views, has been one of the most influential thinkers of the twentieth century. Freud was a medical doctor who specialized in neurology. He developed his ideas about psychoanalytic theory from his work with psychiatric patients. He was born in Austria in 1856, and he died in London at the age of 83. Freud spent most of his life in Vienna, but he left the city near the end of his career to escape Nazi anti-Semitism.

As an eldest child, Freud was regarded as a genius by his brothers and sisters and doted on by his mother. Later we will see that one aspect of Freud's theory emphasizes a young boy's sexual attraction for his mother; it is possible that this aspect of his theory was derived from his own romantic attachment to his mother, who was beautiful and some 20 years younger than Freud's father.

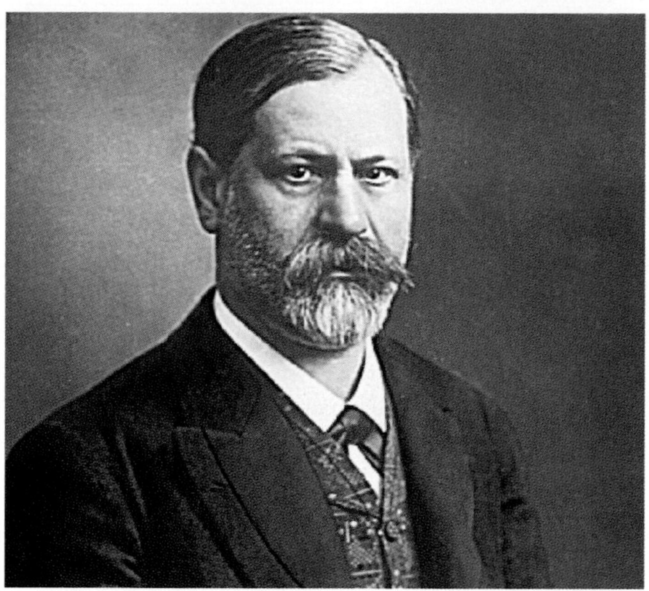

Sigmund Freud (1856–1939), the architect of psychoanalytic theory.

In Freud's view, much more of our mind is unconscious than conscious. He envisioned our mind as a huge iceberg, with the massive part below the surface of the water being the unconscious part. Freud said that each of our lives is filled with tension and conflict; to reduce this tension and conflict we keep information locked in our unconscious mind. For Freud, the unconscious mind held the key to understanding behavior. Freud believed that even trivial behaviors have special significance when the unconscious forces behind them are revealed. A twitch, a doodle, a joke, a smile, each may have an unconscious reason for appearing. They often slip into our lives without our awareness. For example, Barbara is kissing and hugging Tom, whom she is to marry in several weeks. She says, "Oh, *Jeff,* I love you so much." Tom pushes her away and says, "Why did you call me Jeff? I thought you didn't think about him anymore. We need to have a talk!" You probably can think of times when these so-called *Freudian slips* tumbled out of your own mouth.

Freud also believed that dreams hold important clues to our behavior. He said dreams are unconscious representations of the conflict and tension in our everyday lives. Since the conflict and tension are too painful to handle consciously, they come out in our dreams. Much of the dream content is disguised in symbolism, requiring extensive analysis and probing to be understood. Freud's view of the mind as unconscious and symbolic has played an important role in understanding some movements in art, as discussed in Explorations in Psychology 1.

The Structure of Personality Freud (1917) believed that personality has three structures: the id, the ego, and the superego. One way to understand the three structures is to consider them as three rulers of a country (Singer, 1984). The id is king or queen, the ego is prime minister, and the superego is high priest. The id is an absolute monarch, owed complete obedience; it is spoiled, willful, and self-centered. The id wants what it wants right now, not later. The ego as prime minister has the job of getting things done; it is tuned in to reality and is responsive to society's demands. The superego as high priest is concerned with right and wrong; the id may be greedy and needs to be told that nobler purposes should be pursued.

The **id** *is the Freudian structure of personality that consists of instincts, which are the individual's reservoir of psychic energy.* In Freud's view, the id is unconscious; it has no contact with reality. The id works according to the pleasure principle. The **pleasure principle** *is the Freudian concept that the id always seeks pleasure and avoids pain.*

It would be a dangerous and scary world if our personalities were all id. As young children mature, they learn they cannot slug other children in the face. They also learn they have to use the toilet instead of their diaper. As children experience the demands and constraints of reality, a new structure of personality is formed—the **ego,** *the Freudian structure of personality that deals with the demands of reality. The ego is called the executive branch of personality because it makes decisions based on rationality.* According to Freud, the ego abides by the **reality principle:** *It tries to bring the individual pleasure within the norms of society.* Few of us are cold-blooded killers or wild wheeler-dealers; we consider obstacles to our satisfaction that exist in our world. We recognize that our sexual and aggressive impulses cannot go unrestrained. The ego helps us to test reality, to see how far we can go without getting into trouble and hurting ourselves.

While the id is completely unconscious, the ego is partly conscious. It houses our higher mental functions—reasoning, problem solving, and decision making, for example. For this reason, the ego is referred to as the executive branch of the personality; like an executive in a company, it makes the rational decisions that help the company succeed.

The id and ego have no morality. They do not consider whether something is right or wrong. The **superego** *is the Freudian structure of personality that is the moral branch of personality. The superego considers whether something is right or wrong.* The superego is what we often refer to as our "conscience." Like the id, the superego does not consider reality; it doesn't deal with what is realistic, only with whether the id's sexual and aggressive impulses can be satisfied in moral terms. You probably are beginning to sense that both the id and the superego make life rough for the ego. Your ego might say, "I will have sex only occasionally and be sure to use an effective form of birth control." But your id is saying, "I want to be satisfied; sex feels so good." And your superego is at work too, "I feel guilty about having sex."

Remember that Freud considered personality to be like an iceberg; most of our personality exists below the

Explorations in Psychology 1

Freud, da Vinci, and Dali

Because of its emphasis on symbolic and unconscious thought, psychoanalytic theory has been extensively applied to art and literature. The psychoanalytic formula is that creative works of art satisfy unconscious wishes; because these wishes are often unacceptable, they have to be disguised. Artistic techniques are used for this purpose. Freud (1908) examined Leonardo da Vinci's life and art, concluding that da Vinci was a man of extreme sexual inhibition brought about by castration anxiety. According to Freud, da Vinci channeled his sexual energy into creating well-known works of art such as the *Mona Lisa* (see figure A). Freud believed that the Mona Lisa's mysterious smile was the smile of Leonardo's mother. How accurate was Freud's analysis of da Vinci and the Mona Lisa? As is the case for many ideas in psychoanalytic theory, we don't have a scientific way to examine Freud's ideas on the role of symbolic and unconscious thought in the creative works of artists.

Although psychologists and art critics debate whether many works of art are unconsciously based, there is general agreement that the twentieth-century art movement known as Surrealism was heavily influenced by Freud's ideas. The Surrealists saw Freud's concept of the unconscious mind as the true source of untainted creativity. They thought that the conscious mind was too warped by the conventions and constraints of society to produce truly great works. Surrealist artists used a number of techniques to tap unconscious thoughts they could turn into paintings: dream analysis, automatic writing and drawing, and hypnosis. They threw paint onto canvas at random. They imitated primitive art. They used rags instead of brushes.

Rene Magritte and Salvador Dali are two of the best-known Surrealist artists. Magritte painted memories of his dreams. He is famous for the distortion of perspective in his works. Dali used Freudian symbols to portray such sexual themes as guilt, masturbation, and intercourse (see figure B). The Surrealists made a conscious effort to apply their unconscious thoughts to canvas. As with Freud's conclusions about da Vinci's sexually repressed thoughts about his mother, it is open to debate whether the Surrealists' works support the psychoanalytic view of creativity (Peterson, 1988).

Figure A

The *Mona Lisa*. What was Freud's interpretation of her smile?

Figure B

Salvador Dali, *Illumined Pleasures (1929)*

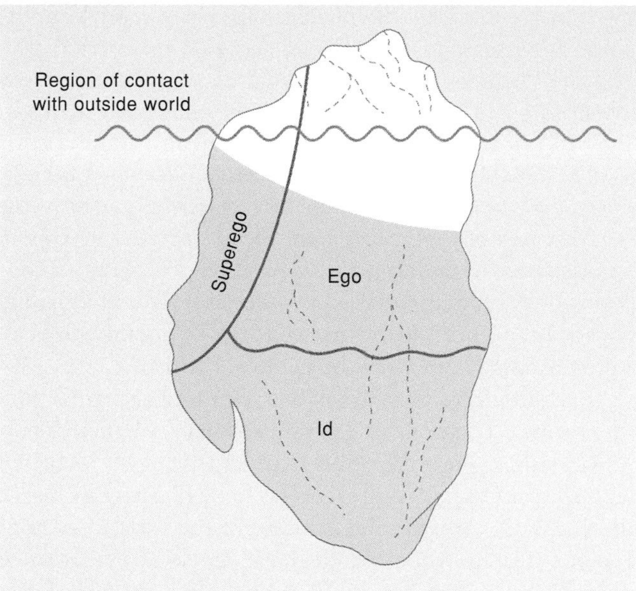

FIGURE 1

Conscious and Unconscious Processes: The Iceberg Analogy This rather odd-looking diagram illustrates Freud's belief that most of the important personality processes occur below the level of conscious awareness. In examining people's conscious thoughts and their behaviors, we can see some reflections of the ego and the superego. Whereas the ego and superego are partly conscious and partly unconscious, the primitive id is the unconscious, totally submerged part of the iceberg.

level of awareness, just as the massive part of an iceberg is beneath the surface of the water. Figure 1 illustrates this analogy and how extensive the unconscious part of our mind is in Freud's view.

Defense Mechanisms The ego calls upon a number of strategies to resolve the conflict between its demands for reality, the wishes of the id, and the constraints of the superego. Through **defense mechanisms,** *the psychoanalytic term for unconscious methods, the ego distorts reality, thereby protecting it from anxiety.* In Freud's view, the conflicting demands of the personality structures produce anxiety. For example, when the ego blocks the pleasurable pursuits of the id, a person feels inner anxiety. This diffuse, distressed state develops when the ego senses that the id is going to cause some harm. The anxiety alerts the ego to resolve the conflict by means of defense mechanisms.

Repression *is the most powerful and pervasive defense mechanism, according to Freud; it works to push unacceptable id impulses out of awareness and back into the unconscious mind.* Repression is the foundation from which all other defense mechanisms work; the goal of every psychological defense is to *repress* or push threatening impulses out of awareness. Freud said that our early childhood experiences, many of which he believed were sexually laden, are too threatening and stressful for us to deal with consciously. We reduce the anxiety of this conflict through repression.

Among the other defense mechanisms we use to protect the ego and reduce anxiety are rationalization, displacement, sublimation, projection, reaction formation, and regression. **Rationalization,** *according to psychoanalytic theory, is the defense mechanism that occurs when the real motive for an individual's behavior is not accepted by the ego and is replaced by a sort of cover motive.* For example, you are studying hard for an exam tomorrow. You are really getting into the material when a friend calls and says he is having a party in an hour. He tells you that a certain person you find attractive will be there. You know that if you don't stay in your room and study you will do poorly on tomorrow's exam. But you tell yourself, "I did well on the first test in this class and I have been studying hard all semester; it's time I have some fun." So you go to the party. The real motives are going to the party, having fun, and seeing the attractive person. But those reasons wouldn't justify doing poorly on the exam, so you think you should stay home and study. Your ego now steps in and comes up with a better motive. Your ego says that you have worked hard all semester and you need to unwind, and that you will probably do better on the exam if you relax a little—a rationale that is more acceptable than just going to have fun and meet the desirable other person.

Displacement *is the psychoanalytic defense mechanism that occurs when the individual shifts unacceptable feelings from one object to another, more acceptable object.* For example, a woman is harassed by her boss. She gets angry but she knows she can't take the anger out on the boss because she might get fired. When she gets home that evening, she yells at her husband, thus transferring her feelings toward her boss to her husband.

Sublimation *is the psychological defense mechanism in which a socially approved course of action replaces an unacceptable impulse.* Sublimation is actually a type of displacement. For example, an individual with strong sexual urges may turn them into socially approved behavior by becoming an artist who paints nudes.

Projection *is the psychoanalytic defense mechanism that occurs when we attribute our own shortcomings, problems, and faults to others.* For example, a man who has a strong desire to have an extramarital affair keeps accusing his wife of flirting with other men. The manipulative businesswoman who takes advantage of everyone to shove her way up the corporate ladder tells her associate, "Everybody around here is so manipulative; they never consider my feelings." When we can't face our own unwanted feelings, we *project* them onto others and see others as having the trait.

Reaction formation *is the psychoanalytic defense mechanism that occurs when we express an unacceptable impulse by transforming it into its opposite.* For example, an individual who is attracted to the brutality of war becomes a peace activist. Or a person who fears his sexual urges becomes a religious zealot.

Regression *is the psychoanalytic defense mechanism that occurs when we behave in a way characteristic of a previous developmental level.* When anxiety becomes too great for us, we revert to an early behavior that gave us pleasure. For example, a woman may run home to her mother every time she and her husband have a big argument.

Two final points about defense mechanisms need to be understood. First, they are unconscious; we are not aware we are calling on them to protect our ego and reduce anxiety. Second, when used in moderation or on a temporary basis, defense mechanisms are not necessarily unhealthy. For example, defense mechanisms such as denial can help a person cope with impending death. For the most part, though, we should not let defense mechanisms dominate our behavior and prevent us from facing life's demands.

The Development of Personality As Freud listened to, probed, and analyzed his patients, he became convinced that their problems were the result of experiences early in life. Freud believed that we go through five stages of psychosexual development, and that at each stage of development we experience pleasure in one part of the body more than in others. **Erogenous zones,** *according to Freud, are parts of the body that have especially strong pleasure-giving qualities at particular stages of development.*

Freud thought that our adult personality is determined by the way we resolve conflicts between these early sources of pleasure—the mouth, the anus, and then the genitals—and the demands of reality. When these conflicts are not resolved, the individual may become fixated at a particular stage of development. **Fixation** *is the psychoanalytic defense mechanism that occurs when the individual remains locked in an earlier developmental stage because needs are under- or overgratified.* For example, a parent may wean a child too early, be too strict in toilet training the child, punish the child for masturbation, or "smother" the child with too much attention. We will return to the idea of fixation and how it may show up in an adult's personality, but first we need to learn more about the early stages of personality development.

The **oral stage** *is the term Freud used to describe development during the first 18 months of life, in which the infant's pleasure centers on the mouth.* Chewing, sucking, and biting are chief sources of pleasure. These actions reduce tension in the infant.

The **anal stage** *is Freud's second stage of development, occurring between 1½ and 3 years of age, in which the child's greatest pleasure involves the anus or the eliminative functions associated with it.* In Freud's view, the exercise of anal muscles reduces tension.

The **phallic stage,** *Freud's third stage of development, occurs between the ages of 3 and 6. Its name comes from the Latin word* phallus, *which means "penis." During the phallic stage, pleasure focuses on the genitals as the child discovers that self-stimulation is enjoyable.*

In Freud's view the phallic stage has a special importance in personality development because this period triggers the Oedipus complex. This name comes from Greek mythology, in which Oedipus, the son of the King of Thebes, unwittingly killed his father and married his mother. The **Oedipus complex** *is Freud's idea that the young child develops an intense desire to replace the parent of the same sex and enjoy the affections of the opposite-sex parent.* As discussed in Explorations in Psychology 2, Freud's concept of the Oedipus complex was not as universal as he believed, being heavily influenced by the sociohistorical, cultural setting of turn-of-the-century Vienna.

At about 5 to 6 years of age, children recognize that their same-sex parent might punish them for their incestuous wishes. To reduce this conflict, the child identifies with the same-sex parent, striving to be like him or her. If the conflict is not resolved, though, the individual may become fixated at the phallic stage. Table 1 reveals some possible links between adult personality characteristics and fixation, sublimation, and reaction formation involving the phallic stage, as well as the oral and anal stage.

The **latency stage** *is the fourth Freudian stage of development, occurring approximately between 6 years of age and puberty; the child represses all interest in sexuality and develops social and intellectual skills.* This activity channels much of the child's energy into emotionally safe areas and aids the child in forgetting the highly stressful conflicts of the phallic stage.

The **genital stage** *is the fifth and final Freudian stage of development, occurring from puberty on. The genital stage is the time of sexual reawakening; the source of sexual pleasure now becomes someone outside of the family.* Freud believed that unresolved conflicts with parents reemerged during adolescence. Once resolved, Freud believed, the individual would become capable of developing a mature love relationship and functioning independently as an adult. Figure 2 summarizes Freud's psychosexual stages.

Psychoanalytic Dissenters and Revisionists

Because Freud was among the first theorists to explore many new and uncharted regions of personality, some of his ideas have needed to be updated, others revised, and some have been tossed out altogether. In particular, Freud's critics have said his ideas about sexuality, early experience, social factors, and the unconscious mind were misguided (Adler, 1927; Erikson, 1968; Fromm, 1947; Horney, 1945; Jung, 1917; Kohut, 1977; Rapaport, 1967; Sullivan, 1953). The critics stressed the following:

- Sexuality is not the pervasive underlying force behind personality that Freud believed it to be.
- The first 5 years of life are not as powerful in shaping adult personality as Freud thought; later experiences deserve more attention.

Explorations in Psychology 2

Freud's Oedipus Complex: Cultural and Gender Biases

The Oedipus complex was one of Freud's most influential concepts relating early psychosexual relationships to later personality development. Freud developed this aspect of his theory during the Victorian era of the late 1800s when sexual interests, especially the female's, were repressed.

According to Freud, the phallic stage begins for a girl when she realizes she has no penis. He also believed that she recognizes the superiority of the penis to her anatomy, and thus develops *penis envy.* Blaming her mother for her lack of a penis, the girl renounces her love for her mother and becomes intensely attached to her father. Since her desire for having a penis can never be satisfied directly, Freud speculated that the young girl yearns for a penis substitute, a baby (especially a male baby). This female version of the Oedipus complex is sometimes referred to as the *Electra complex.* Freud believed that the Electra complex is never fully resolved but merely dissipates over time as the girl begins to identify with her mother and take on similar values and feminine behavior. As a result, Freud assumed that women do not develop as strong a conscience (superego) as do men.

Many psychologists believe Freud placed far too much emphasis on anatomy's role in personality development. Freud concluded, for example, that boys are likely to develop a dominant, powerful personality because they have a penis; without a penis, girls are predisposed to become submissive and weak. In basing his view of male/female differences in personality development on anatomical differences, Freud ignored the enormous impact of culture and experience.

More than half a century ago, the English anthropologist Brownislaw Malinowski (1927) observed the family dynamics of the Trobriand islanders of the Western Pacific and found that the Oedipus complex is not universal. In the Trobriand Islands, the biological father is not the head of the household; that disciplinarian role is reserved for the mother's brother. In Freud's view, this family constellation would not alter the Oedipus complex; the young boy should still vie for his mother's love and perceive his father as the hated rival, but Malinowski found no such conflict between fathers and sons in the Trobriand islanders. He did observe, however, that young boys feared the authoritarian, maternal uncle and directed negative feelings toward him. Malinowski's finding undermined Freud's Oedipus complex because it showed that the sexual relations within the family did not always create conflict and fear for a child.

Bwaitalu village carvers in the Trobriand islands of New Guinea with children. In the Trobriand islands, the authoritarian figure in the young boy's life is the maternal uncle, not the father. The young boys in this culture fear the maternal uncle, not the father. Thus, it is not sexual relations in a family that create conflict and fear for a child, a damaging finding for Freud's Oedipus-complex theory.

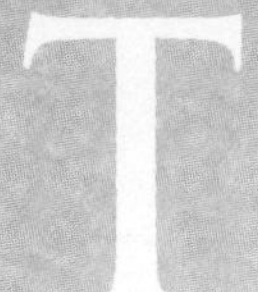

TABLE 1

Possible Links Between Adult Personality Characteristics and Fixation at Oral, Anal, and Phallic Stages

Stage	Adult Extensions	Sublimations	Reaction Formations
Oral	Smoking, eating, kissing, oral hygiene, drinking, chewing gum	Seeking knowledge, humor, wit, sarcasm, being a food or wine expert	Speech purist, food faddist, prohibitionist, dislike of milk
Anal	Notable interest in one's bowel movements, love of bathroom humor, extreme messiness	Interest in painting or sculpture, being overly giving, great interest in statistics	Extreme disgust with feces, fear of dirt, prudishness, irritability
Phallic	Heavy reliance on masturbation, flirtatiousness, expressions of virility	Interest in poetry, love of love, interest in acting, striving for success	Puritanical attitude toward sex, excessive modesty

Oral stage

Anal stage

Phallic stage

Latency stage

Genital stage

FIGURE 2

Freudian Psychosexual Stages

Freud said we go through five stages of psychosexual development. In the oral stage, pleasure centers around the mouth. In the anal stage, pleasure focuses on the anus—the nature of toilet training is important here. In the phallic stage, pleasure involves the genitals—the opposite-sex parent becomes a love object. In the latency stage, a child represses sexual urges—same-sex friendship is prominent. In the genital stage, sexual reawakening takes place—the source of pleasure now becomes someone outside the family.

Karen Horney developed the first feminist criticism of Freud's theory. Horney's model emphasizes women's positive qualities and self-evaluation.

Nancy Chodorow has developed an important contemporary feminist revision of psychoanalytic theory that emphasizes the meaningfulness of emotions for women.

- The ego and conscious thought processes play more dominant roles in our personality than Freud gave them credit for; we are not wed forever to the id and its instinctual, unconscious clutches. The ego has a separate line of development from the id; viewed in this way, achievement, thinking, and reasoning are not always tied to sexual impulses as Freud thought.
- Sociocultural factors are much more important than Freud believed. Freud placed more emphasis on the biological basis of personality by stressing the id's dominance.

Let's examine three theories by dissenters and revisionists of Freud's theory in greater detail—Horney's, Jung's, and Adler's theories.

Horney's Sociocultural Approach Karen Horney (1885–1952) rejected the classical psychoanalytic concept that "anatomy is destiny" in favor of an approach that emphasized the importance of sociocultural factors in development. She cautioned that ideas such as "penis envy" were only hypotheses. She insisted that these hypotheses should be supported with observable data before they were accepted as fact.

Horney pointed out that previous research about how women function was limited by the fact that those who described women, who influenced and represented the culture, and who determined the standards for suitable growth and development were men. She countered the notion of penis envy with the hypothesis that both sexes envy the attributes of the other, with men coveting women's reproductive capacities. She also argued that women who feel penis envy are desirous only of the status that men have in most societies.

Horney also believed that the need for security, not for sex or aggression, was the prime motive in human existence. Horney reasoned that when an individual's needs for security are met they should be able to develop their capacities to the fullest extent. She also suggested that people usually develop one of three strategies in their effort to cope with anxiety. First, individuals may *move toward* people, seeking love and support. Second, individuals may *move away* from people, becoming more independent. And third, individuals may *move against* people, becoming competitive and domineering. The secure individual uses these three ways of coping in moderation and balance, while the insecure individual often uses one or more of these strategies in an exaggerated fashion, becoming too dependent, too independent, or too aggressive.

Psychologists are still revamping psychoanalytic theory. Nancy Chodorow's (1978, 1989) feminist revision of psychoanalytic theory, for example, emphasizes that many more women than men define themselves in terms of their relationships, that many men use denial as a defense mechanism in regard to their relationships with others, and that emotions tend to be more salient to women's lives.

Jung's Depth Psychology Freud's contemporary Carl Jung (1875–1961) shared an interest in the unconscious, but he believed Freud underplayed the unconscious mind's role in our personality. Jung suspected that the roots of personality go back to the dawn of human existence. The **collective unconscious** *is the impersonal, deepest layer of the unconscious mind, shared by all human beings because of their common ancestral past.* These common experiences have made a deep, permanent impression on the human mind (Harris, 1996). **Archetype** *is the name Jung gave to the primordial*

FIGURE 3

Mandalas
Carl Jung believed that mandalas were so widely used to represent the self at different points in history that they were an archetype for the self.

Swiss psychoanalytic theorist Carl Jung developed the concepts of the collective unconscious and archetypes.

images in every individual's collective unconscious. Jung's psychoanalytic theory is often referred to as depth psychology because archetypes reside deep within the unconscious mind, far deeper than the Freudian personal unconscious.

Two common archetypes are *anima* (woman) and *animus* (man). Jung believed each of us has a passive "feminine" side and an assertive "masculine" side. We also have an archetype for self, which often is expressed in art. For example, the mandala, a figure within a circle, has been used so often Jung took it to represent the self (see figure 3). Another archetype is the shadow, our darker self. The shadow is evil and immoral. The shadow appears in many evil and immoral figures—Satan, Dracula, Mr. Hyde (of Jekyll and Hyde), Darth Vadar (of the *Star Wars* films), even J. R. Ewing (of the television show "Dallas") (Peterson, 1988).

Adler's Individual Psychology Alfred Adler (1870–1937) was another contemporary of Freud. **Individual psychology** *is the name Adler gave to his theory to emphasize the uniqueness of every individual.* Unlike Freud's belief in the power of the unconscious mind, Adler argued that we have the conscious ability to monitor and direct our lives; he also believed social factors are more important in shaping our personality than sexual motivation (Silverman & Corsini, 1984).

Adler thought that everyone strives for superiority. Adler's concept of **striving for superiority** *emphasizes the human motivation to adapt, improve, and master the environment.* Striving for superiority is our response to feelings of inferiority that we all experience as infants and young children when we interact with people who are bigger and more powerful. We strive to overcome these feelings of inferiority because they are uncomfortable. **Compensation** *is Adler's term for the individual's attempt to overcome imagined or real inferiorities or weaknesses by developing one's abilities.* Adler believed that compensation was normal, and he said we often make up for a weakness in one ability by excelling in a different ability. For example, one person may be a mediocre student but compensate for this by excelling in athletics. **Overcompensation** *is Adler's term for the individual's attempt to deny rather than acknowledge a real situation, or the exaggerated effort to conceal a weakness.* Adler described two patterns of overcompensation. **Inferiority complex** *is the name Adler gave to exaggerated feelings of inadequacy.* **Superiority complex** *is his concept for exaggerated self-importance designed to mask feelings of inferiority.*

In summary, Adler's theory emphasized that people are striving toward a positive being and that they create their own goals. Their adaptation is enhanced by developing social interests and reducing feelings of inferiority. Like Jung, Adler has a number of disciples today.

Evaluation of the Psychoanalytic Perspectives

Although psychoanalytic theories have diverged, they do share some core principles. Psychoanalytic theorists assert that our personality is determined both by current experiences and those from early in life. Two basic principles of psychoanalytic theory have withstood the test of time: early experiences do shape our personality, and personality can be better understood by examining it developmentally (Horowitz, 1989).

Another belief that continues to receive considerable attention is that we mentally transform environmental experiences. Psychologists also recognize that the mind is not all consciousness; unconscious motives lie behind some of our puzzling behavior. Psychoanalytic theorists' emphasis on conflict and anxiety leads us to consider the dark side of our existence, not just its bright side. Adjustment is not always an easy task, and the individual's inner world often conflicts with the outer demands of reality. And finally, psychoanalytic theories continue to force psychologists to study more than the experimental, laboratory topics of sensation, perception, and learning; personality and adjustment are rightful and important topics of psychological inquiry as well.

However, the main concepts of psychoanalytic theories have been difficult to test; they are largely matters of inference and interpretation. Researchers have not, for example, successfully investigated such key concepts as repression in the laboratory.

Much of the data used to support psychoanalytic theories have come from clinicians' subjective evaluations of clients; in such cases, it is easy for the clinician to see what she expects because of the theory she holds. Other data come from patients' recollections of the distant past (especially those from early childhood) and are of doubtful accuracy. And psychoanalytic theories place too much weight on these early experiences within the family to shape personality. We retain the capacity for change and adaptation throughout our lives.

Some psychologists object that Freud overemphasized the importance of sexuality in understanding personality, and that Freud and Jung placed too much faith in the unconscious mind's ability to control behavior. Others object that the psychoanalytic perspectives provide a model of the person that is too negative and pessimistic. We are not born into the world with only a bundle of sexual and aggressive instincts. The demands of reality do not always conflict with our biological needs.

Many psychoanalytic theories of personality have a male bias, especially Freud's. Although Horney's theory helped to correct this bias, psychoanalytic theory continues to be revised today.

You now should have a sense of what personality is and the themes of psychoanalytic theories. A summary of these ideas is presented in concept table 1. Next we will discuss a view of personality *very* different from the psychoanalytic theories.

Behavioral and Social Learning Perspectives

Tom is engaged to marry Ann. Both have warm, friendly personalities, and they enjoy being with each other. Psychoanalytic theorists would say that their personalities are derived from long-standing relationships with their parents, especially their early childhood experiences. They also would argue that the reason for their attraction is unconscious; they are unaware of how their biological heritage and early life experiences have been carried forward to influence their adult personalities.

Behaviorists and social learning theorists would observe Tom and Ann and see something quite different. They would examine their experiences, especially their most recent ones, to understand the reason for Tom and Ann's attraction to one another. Tom would be described as rewarding Ann's behavior, and vice versa, for example. No reference would be made to unconscious thoughts, the Oedipus complex, defense mechanisms, and so on.

Behaviorists believe psychology should examine only what can be directly observed and measured. At approximately the same time Freud was interpreting his patients' unconscious minds through their recollections of early childhood experiences, behaviorists such as Ivan Pavlov and John B. Watson were conducting detailed observations of behavior under controlled laboratory conditions. Out of the behavioral tradition grew the belief that personality is observable behavior, learned through experiences with the environment (Staats, 1996). The two versions of the behavioral approach today are the behavioral view of B. F. Skinner and social learning theory.

Skinner's Behaviorism

B. F. Skinner concluded that personality is the individual's *behavior,* which is determined by the *external environment.* Skinner believed we do not have to resort to biological or cognitive processes to explain personality (behavior). Some psychologists say that including Skinner among personality theorists is like inviting a wolf to a party of lambs because he took the "person" out of personality (Phares, 1984).

Behaviorists counter that you cannot pinpoint where personality is or how it is determined. In Skinner's view, personality simply consists of the collection of the person's observed, overt behaviors; it does not include internal traits or thoughts. For example, observations of Sam reveal that his behavior is shy, achievement-oriented, and caring. In short, these behaviors *are* his personality. According to Skinner, Sam is this way because the rewards and punishments in Sam's environment have shaped him into a shy, achievement-oriented, and caring person. Because of interactions with family members, friends, teachers, and others, Sam has *learned* to behave in this fashion.

Behaviorists who support Skinner's view would say that Sam's shy, achievement-oriented, and caring behavior may not be consistent and enduring. For example, Sam is uninhibited on Saturday night with friends at a bar, unmotivated to excel in English class, and occasionally nasty to his sister. In addition, Skinnerians' believe that consistency in behavior comes from consistency in environmental experiences. If Sam's shy, achievement-oriented, and caring behavior is consistently rewarded, his pattern of behavior likely will be consistent. However, Skinner stressed that our behavior always has the capacity for change if new experiences are encountered. The issue of consistency in personality is an important one. We will return to it on several occasions later in the chapter.

Since behaviorists believe that personality is learned and often changes according to environmental experiences and situations, it follows that by rearranging experiences and situations the individual's personality can be changed. For the behaviorist, shy behavior can be changed into outgoing behavior; aggressive behavior can be shaped into docile behavior; and lethargic, boring behavior can be shaped into enthusiastic, interesting behavior.

CONCEPT TABLE 1

The Nature of Personality and Psychoanalytic Perspectives

Concept	Processes/Related Ideas	Characteristics/Description
Personality	Its nature	Our enduring thoughts, emotions, and behaviors that characterize the way we adapt to the world. A key question is why individuals respond to the same situation in different ways.
Freud's Psychoanalytic Theory	Freud and the unconscious mind	Freud was one of the most influential thinkers in the twentieth century. He believed that most of the mind is unconscious.
	The structure of personality	Freud said personality has three structures: id, ego, and superego. The id is the reservoir of psychic energy that tries to satisfy our basic needs; it is unconscious and operates according to the pleasure principle. The ego tries to provide us with pleasure by operating within the boundaries of reality. The superego is the moral branch of personality.
	Defense mechanisms	The conflicting demands of personality structures produce anxiety; defense mechanisms protect the ego and reduce this anxiety. Repression, the most pervasive defense mechanism, pushes unacceptable id impulses back into the unconscious mind. Other defense mechanisms include rationalization, displacement, sublimation, projection, reaction formation, and regression. Defense mechanisms are unconscious.
	The development of personality	Freud was convinced that problems develop because of childhood experiences. He said we go through five psychosexual stages: oral, anal, phallic, latency, and genital. If our needs are under- or overgratified at a particular stage, we can become fixated at that stage. During the phallic stage, the Oedipus complex is a major source of conflict.
Psychoanalytic Dissenters and Revisionists	Criticisms of Freud's views	They stressed that Freud placed too much emphasis on sexuality and the first 5 years of life, and too little emphasis on the ego and conscious thought processes, as well as sociocultural factors.
	Horney	Karen Horney rejected the classical psychoanalytic concept of "anatomy is destiny," advocated by Freud, in favor of a sociocultural approach. She especially thought that Freud's theory is male biased. Horney said that need for security, not sex or aggression, is the prime motive in human existence. She also theorized that people usually develop one of three strategies to cope with anxiety—moving toward people, away from people, or against people. The rectification of male bias in psychoanalytic theory continues today through the efforts of individuals such as Nancy Chodorow.
	Jung and Adler	Jung thought Freud underplayed the role of the unconscious mind. He developed the concept of the collective unconscious, and his theory is often called depth psychology. Alfred Adler's theory is called individual psychology; it stresses every individual's uniqueness. Adler said people are striving toward a positive being and that they create their own goals. Their adaptation is enhanced by developing social interests and reducing feelings of inferiority.
Evaluating the Psychoanalytic Perspectives	Their nature	Strengths are an emphasis on the past, the developmental course of personality, mental representation of environment, unconscious mind, emphasis on conflict, and influence on psychology as a discipline. Weaknesses are the difficulty in testing main concepts, the lack of an empirical data base and overreliance on reports of the past, too much emphasis on sexuality and the unconscious mind, a negative view of human nature, too much power given to early experience, and a male bias.

Social Learning Theory

Some psychologists believe the behaviorists basically are right when they say that personality is learned and influenced strongly by environmental experiences. But they believe Skinner went too far in declaring that cognition is unimportant in understanding the nature of personality. The group of psychologists who emphasize behavior, environment, *and* cognition as the key factors in personality are called social learning theorists.

The social learning theorists say we are not mindless robots, responding mechanically to others in our environment. And we are not like weather vanes, behaving like a Communist in the presence of a Communist or like a John Bircher in the presence of a John Bircher. Rather, we think, reason, imagine, plan, expect, interpret, believe, value, and compare. When others try to control us, our values and beliefs allow us to resist their control.

Albert Bandura (1986, 1994) and Walter Mischel (1973, 1995) are the architects of social learning theory's contemporary version, which was labeled *cognitive* social learning theory by Mischel. Bandura believes much of our learning occurs by observing what others do. Through observational learning we form ideas about the behavior of others and then possibly adopt this behavior ourselves. For example, a young boy may observe his father's aggressive outbursts and hostile exchanges with people; when the boy is with his peers, he interacts in a highly aggressive way, showing the same characteristics as his father's behavior. Or a young executive adopts the dominant and sarcastic style of her boss. When this young woman interacts with one of her subordinates, she says, "I need this work immediately if not sooner; you are so far behind you think you are ahead!" Social learning theorists believe we acquire a wide range of such behaviors, thoughts, and feelings through observing others' behavior; these observations form an important part of our personality.

Social learning theorists also differ from the behavioral view of Skinner by emphasizing that we can regulate and control our own behavior, despite our changing environment. For example, another young executive who observed her boss behave in a dominant and sarcastic manner toward employees found the behavior distasteful and went out of her way to be encouraging and supportive of her subordinates. Someone tries to persuade you to join a particular social club on campus and makes you an enticing offer. You reflect about the offer, consider your interests and beliefs, and make the decision not to join. Your *cognition* (your thoughts) leads you to control your behavior and resist environmental influence in this instance.

Like the behavioral approach of Skinner, the social learning view emphasizes the importance of empirical research in studying personality. This research has focused on the processes that explain personality—the social and cognitive factors that influence what we are like as people. One process that Walter Mischel believes is important in understanding an individual's personality is delay of gratification,

Albert Bandura (left) and Walter Mischel (right) crafted social learning theory's contemporary version, which Mischel labeled cognitive social learning theory. Bandura's research has focused on observational learning, Mischel's on how we delay gratification.

which is the ability to defer immediate satisfaction for a more desirable future outcome. For example, when you are in school you resist the temptation to slack off and have a good time now so you will be rewarded with good grades later. Again, the point is that we are capable of controlling our behavior rather than always being influenced by others.

Mischel's research on delay of gratification addresses the issue of consistency in personality. Do we consistently delay gratification across many different situations? If we examine an individual's life across a span of 10 years, will the individual show similar delay of gratification tendencies? As discussed in Explorations in Psychology 3, Mischel believes that cognitive processes allow us to adapt to situations and that delay of gratification is consistent across time.

Evaluation of the Behavioral and Social Learning Perspectives

The behavioral and social learning theories emphasize that environmental experiences and situational influences determine personality. These approaches have fostered a scientific climate for understanding personality that highlights the observation of behavior. Social learning theory emphasizes both environmental influences and the "black box" of the human mind to explain personality; this theory also suggests that people have the ability to control their environment.

Critics of both the behavioral and social learning perspectives take issue with several aspects of both theorists. The behavioral view is criticized for ignoring the importance of cognition in personality and placing too much importance on the role of environmental experiences. Both approaches have been described as being too concerned with change and situational influences on personality and not paying adequate tribute to the enduring qualities of personality. Both views are said to ignore the

Explorations in Psychology 3

Delaying Gratification for Marshmallows and Pretzels

Four-year-old Barbara is told that she can have one marshmallow now or two marshmallows if she waits until the experimenter returns. What might influence Barbara's choice? Mischel believes that one factor is whether or not the rewards are visible. For example, in one investigation, preschool-age children were willing to wait 10 times longer when the rewards (such as marshmallows) were hidden from view than when they could be readily observed (Mischel, Ebbesen, & Zeiss, 1972) (see figure C). This suggests that children can gain control over their ability to delay gratification by keeping desired rewards out of sight.

Another way children might learn to delay gratification is to mentally represent the desired goal objects in different ways. For example, when children mentally represented the rewards in consummatory, or "hot," ways (such as focusing on their taste—thinking how yummy, crunchy, and tasty pretzels are), they delayed gratification much less than children who mentally represented the rewards in nonconsummatory, or "cold," ways (such as thinking of pretzels as sticks or tiny logs) (Mischel & Baker, 1975). These experiments showed that the way in which we mentally represent the outcomes of a situation influences our ability to delay gratification.

Social learning research focuses primarily on how cognitive and situational factors change an individual's behavior; the emphasis is on *change* and the processes responsible for the change, not on stable individual differences between people. Recently, though, Mischel has turned his attention to the important questions of how enduring is the ability to delay gratification and how stable are the differences between individuals.

Mischel and his colleagues have demonstrated that preschool children's ability to delay gratification for pretzels or marshmallows is related to their socially competent behavior 12 years later (Mischel, Peake, & Zeiss, 1984). For example, a preschool child who is willing to wait to get two marshmallows later instead of one right now is observed to be attentive and able to concentrate during adolescence. And seconds of delay time during the preschool years also significantly predicted verbal and math scores on the SAT taken in high school.

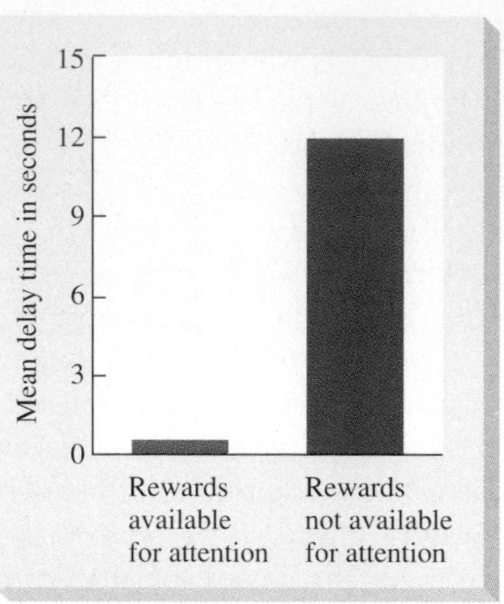

FIGURE C

Delay of Gratification as a Function of the Desired Goal Object's Being Available for Attention

Mischel points out that, although his research shows that a preschool child who delays behavior in one situation may not do so in even slightly different contexts (for example, if rewards are visible), this does not mean the child's tendency to delay gratification will not endure. The results of his laboratory research and his longitudinal investigation of individual differences portray personality as both adaptive to situations and consistent over time. Mischel's current conceptual and research interests continue to focus on the question of how the mental representation of a blocked goal (or outcome or reward) influences a person's motivation to continue to wait and work for the goal (Mischel, 1994; Mischel & Shoda, in press). That is, what cognitive processes enable individuals to delay gratification successfully? One such process is insight about the nature of delay of gratification and how it can provide benefits.

role biology plays in personality. Both are labeled reductionistic, which means they try to explain the complex concept of personality in terms of one or two factors. The critics charge that the behavioral and social learning views are too mechanical, missing the most exciting, rich dimensions of personality. This latter criticism—that the creative, spontaneous, human dimensions of personality are missing from the behavioral and social learning perspectives—has been made on numerous occasions by humanists, whose perspective we consider next.

Phenomenological and Humanistic Perspectives

Remember our example of the engaged couple, Tom and Ann, who were described as having warm, friendly personalities? Phenomenological and humanistic psychologists would say that Tom and Ann's warm, friendly personalities are a reflection of their inner self; they would emphasize that a key to understanding their attraction is their positive perception of each other. Tom and Ann are not viewed as controlling each other or each other's behavior; rather they have determined their own course of action and each has freely chosen to marry. No recourse to biological instincts or unconscious thoughts as reasons for their attraction occurs in the phenomenological and humanistic perspectives.

The **phenomenological perspective** *stresses the importance of our perceptions of ourselves and our world in understanding personality; this perspective emphasizes that for each individual, reality is what is perceived.* The **humanistic perspective** *is the most widely known phenomenological approach to personality. The humanistic perspective stresses the person's capacity for personal growth, freedom to choose one's own destiny, and positive qualities.* Humanistic psychologists believe each of us has the ability to cope with stress, control our lives, and achieve what we desire. Each of us has the ability to break through and understand ourselves and our world; we can burst the cocoon and become a butterfly, say the humanists.

You probably sense that the phenomenological and humanistic perspectives provide stark contrasts to the psychoanalytic perspective, which is based on conflict, destructive drives, and little faith in human nature, and to the behavioral perspective, which, at its extreme, seems to reduce human beings to mere puppets on the strings of rewards and punishments. Carl Rogers and Abraham Maslow were two of the leading architects of the humanistic perspective (Engler, 1995).

Carl Rogers was a pioneer in the development of the humanistic perspective.

Carl Rogers' Approach

Like Freud, Rogers (1902–1987) began his inquiry about human nature with people who were troubled. In the knotted, anxious, defensive verbal stream of his clients, Rogers (1961) examined the conditioned, controlling world that kept them from having positive self-concepts and reaching their full potential as human beings.

Our Conditioned, Controlling World Rogers believed that most people have considerable difficulty accepting their own true feelings, which are innately positive. As we grow up, people who are central to our lives condition us to move away from these positive feelings. Our parents, siblings, teachers, and peers place constraints and contingencies on our behavior; too often we hear people say things like "Don't do that," "You didn't do that right," and "How can you be so stupid?" When we don't do something right, we often get punished. And parents may even threaten to take away their love. **Conditional positive regard** *is Rogers' term for love and praise being withheld unless the individual conforms to parental or social standards.* The result is lower self-esteem.

These constraints and negative feedback continue during our adult lives. The result tends to be that our relationships either carry the dark cloud of conflict or we conform to what others want. As we struggle to live up to society's standards, we distort and devalue our true self. And we may even completely lose our sense of self by mirroring what others want.

The Self Through the individual's experiences with the world, a self emerges—this is the "I"or "me" of our existence. Rogers did not believe that all aspects of the self are conscious, but he did believe they are all accessible to consciousness. The self is a whole, consisting of one's self-perceptions (how attractive I am, how well I get along with others, how good an athlete I am) and the values we attach to these perceptions (good/bad, worthy/unworthy, for example). **Self-concept** *is a central theme in Rogers' and other humanists' views; self-concept refers to individuals' overall perceptions of their abilities, behavior, and personality.* In Rogers' view, a person who has a poor self-concept is likely to think, feel, and act negatively.

In discussing self-concept, Rogers distinguished between the real self—that is, the self as it really is as a result of our experiences—and the ideal self, which is the self we would like to be. The greater the discrepancy between the real self and the ideal self, said Rogers, the more maladjusted we will be. To improve our adjustment, we can develop more positive perceptions of our real self, not worry so much about what others want, and increase our positive experiences in the world.

Unconditional Positive Regard, Empathy, and Genuineness Rogers stressed that we can help a person develop a more positive self-concept through unconditional positive regard, empathy, and genuineness. Rogers said that we need to be accepted by others, regardless of what we do. **Unconditional positive regard** *is Rogers' term for accepting, valuing, and being positive toward another person regardless of the person's behavior.* Rogers recognized that when a person's behavior is below acceptable standards, inappropriate, or even obnoxious, the person still needs the respect, comfort, and love of others. Rogers strongly believed that unconditional positive regard elevates the person's self-worth. However, Rogers (1974) distinguished between unconditional positive regard directed at the individual as a person of worth and dignity and directed at the individual's behavior. For example, a therapist who adopts Rogers' view might say, "I don't like your behavior, but I accept you, value you, and care about you as a person."

Rogers also said we can help other people develop a more positive self-concept if we are *empathic* and *genuine.* Being empathic means being a sensitive listener and understanding another's true feelings. Being genuine means being open with our feelings and dropping our pretenses and facades. For Rogers, unconditional positive regard, empathy, and genuineness are three key ingredients of human relations. We can use these techniques to get other people to feel good about themselves and the techniques also help us to get along better with others.

The Fully Functioning Person Rogers (1980) stressed the importance of becoming a fully functioning person—someone who is open to experience, is not very defensive, is aware of and sensitive to the self and the external world, and for the most part has a harmonious relationship with others. A discrepancy between our real self and our ideal self may occur; others may try to control us; and our world may have too little unconditional positive regard. But Rogers believed that we are highly resilient and capable of becoming a fully functioning person.

This self-actualizing tendency of ours is reflected in Rogers' comparison of a person with a plant he once observed on the coastline of northern California. As Rogers looked out at the waves beating furiously against the jagged rocks and shooting mountains of spray into the air, he noticed the breakers pounding a sea palm (a kind of seaweed that looks like a 2- to 3-foot palm tree). The plant seemed fragile and top-heavy. The waves would crash against the plant, bending its slender trunk almost flat and whipping its leaves in a torrent of spray. Yet the moment the wave passed, the plant was erect, tough, and resilient once again. It was incredible that the plant could take this incessant pounding hour after hour, week after week, possibly even year after year, all the time nourishing itself, maintaining its position, and growing. In this palmlike seaweed, Rogers saw the tenacity and forward thrust of life, and the ability of a living thing to push into a hostile environment and not only hold its own, but adapt, develop, and become itself. So it is with each of us, in Rogers' view.

Abraham Maslow's Approach

Another theorist who made self-actualization the centerpiece of his humanistic philosophy was Abraham Maslow (1908–1970). Maslow was one of the most powerful forces behind the humanistic movement in psychology. He called the humanistic approach the "third force" in psychology—that is, an important alternative to the psychoanalytic and behavioral forces. Maslow pointed out that psychoanalytic theories place too much emphasis on disturbed individuals and their conflicts. Behaviorists ignore the person all together, he said.

Is getting an A in this class more important to you than eating? If the person of your dreams told you that you were marvelous would that motivate you to throw yourself in front of a car for her safety? According to Abraham Maslow (1954, 1971), our "basic" needs must be satisfied before our "higher" needs can be. According to Maslow's **hierarchy of motives,** *individuals' main kinds of needs must be satisfied in the following sequence: physiological needs, safety needs, the need for love and belongingness, the need for esteem, cognitive needs, aesthetic needs, and the need for self-actualization.* Accoring to this hierarchy, people must satisfy their need for food before they can achieve, and they must satisfy their needs for safety before they can satisfy their needs for love.

It is the need for self-actualization that Maslow has described in the greatest detail. The need for **self-actualization,** *the highest and most elusive of Maslow's needs, is the motivation to develop one's full potential as a human being.* According to Maslow, self-actualization is possible only after the other needs in the hierarchy are met. Maslow cautions that most people stop maturing after they have developed a high level of esteem, and thus do not become self-actualized. Many of Maslow's writings focus on how people can reach the elusive motivational state of self-actualization.

Maslow developed psychological profiles of famous people and concluded that such individuals as Eleanor Roosevelt, Albert Einstein, Abraham Lincoln, Walt Whitman, William James, and Ludwig van Beethoven were self-actualized. Table 2 lists Maslow's descriptions of the characteristics of self-actualized individuals. Everett Shostrum (1967) extended Maslow's ideas about self-actualization and described the self-actualizing tendencies of a number of famous individuals. To read about Shostrum's ideas, turn to Explorations in Psychology 4.

Evaluation of the Phenomenological and Humanistic Perspectives

The phenomenological and humanistic perspectives made psychologists aware that the way we perceive ourselves and the world around us are key elements of personality. Humanistic psychologists also reminded us that we need to consider the whole person and the positive bent of human nature. Their emphasis on conscious experience has given us the view that personality contains a well of "potential" that can be developed to its fullest.

A weakness of the humanistic perspective is that it is difficult to test. Self-actualization, for example, is not clearly defined. Psychologists are not certain how to study this concept empirically. Some humanists even scorn the

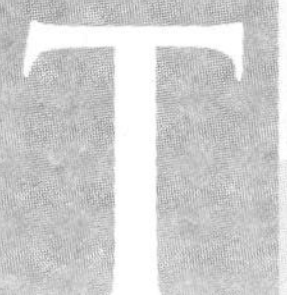

TABLE 2

Maslow's Characteristics of Self-Actualized Individuals

Characteristics
Realistic orientation
Self-acceptance and acceptance of others and the natural world as they are
Spontaneity
Problem-centered rather than self-centered
Air of detachment and need for privacy
Autonomous and independent
Fresh rather than stereotyped appreciation of people and things
Generally have had profound mystical or spiritual, though not necessarily religious, experiences
Identification with humankind and a strong social interest
Tendency to have strong intimate relationships with a few special, loved people rather than superficial relationships with many people
Democratic values and attitudes
No confusion of means with ends
Philosophical rather than hostile sense of humor
High degree of creativity
Resistance to cultural conformity
Transcendence of environment rather than always coping with it

Source: A. H. Maslow, *The Farther Reaches of Human Nature,* pp. 153–174. Copyright © 1971 Viking Press, NY.

experimental approach, preferring clinical interpretation as a data base. Verification of humanistic concepts has come mainly from clinical experiences rather than controlled, experimental studies. Some critics believe humanistic psychologists are too optimistic about human nature, overestimating the freedom and rationality of humans. And some critics say the humanists encourage self-love and narcissism.

We have seen that the behavioral and social learning perspectives, and the phenomenological and humanistic perspectives, take different paths to understanding personality. A summary of the main ideas in these perspectives is presented in concept table 2. Yet another important view of personality remains to be discussed—trait theory.

Trait Theory and Trait-Situation Interaction

Through the ages we have used an infinite variety of traits to describe ourselves and one another. More than 2,000 years ago Theophrastus described the stingy man, the liar, and the flatterer. A magazine article takes a modern swipe at the stingy man:

> Could a miser be lurking beneath the sensuous flesh and persuasive charm? Well, don't expect sapphires from him, dear, if he:
>
> - itemizes who owes what when you're out Dutch-treat rather than splitting the bill
> - washes plastic party cups to reuse them
> - steams uncanceled stamps from letters
> - reshapes bent paper clips
> - has a dozen recipes for chicken wings
> - cuts his own hair
> - wants rolls and butter included in his doggie bag. (*Cosmopolitan,* September 1976, p. 148)

Think about yourself and your friends. How would you describe yourself? You might say that you're outgoing and sociable and that, in contrast, one of your friends is shy and quiet. You might refer to yourself as emotionally stable and describe one of your other friends as a bit skittish. Part of our everyday existence involves describing ourselves and others in terms of traits.

Personality Type Theory

As early as 400 B.C. Hippocrates classified people's personalities according to their body type. Hippocrates thought that people with more yellow bile than others, for example, were "choleric"—easily angered—while people with an excess of blood were more "sanguine"—cheerful and buoyant. William Sheldon (1954) proposed a well-known

Explorations in Psychology 4

The Inner Journey from Manipulation to Self-Actualization

Everett Shostrum, former president of the Division of Humanistic Psychology in the American Psychological Association, was a strong advocate of Maslow's ideas on self-actualization. In his book *Man, the Manipulator* (subtitled *The Inner Journey from Manipulation to Actualization*), Shostrum (1967) described how each of us has manipulating tendencies that can be turned into self-actualizing ones. Figure D shows eight dimensions of personality that can turn toward either manipulation or self-actualization. For example, an individual may become a leader or a dictator, a bully or an assertor. Shostrum has listed famous individuals who, instead of following manipulating paths, chose self-actualizing courses.

From Dictator to Leader. The leader leads but does not dictate; he is forceful but not dominating. Winston Churchill exemplified this type of self-actualization; during World War II he evidenced a democratic form of leadership.

From Weakling to Empathizer. The empathizer not only talks but listens sensitively and is aware of weaknesses in the self. She requires competence but accepts the human tendency to err. Eleanor Roosevelt had this type of personality. While recognizing her personal limitations, she showed considerable empathy toward underdeveloped nations and impoverished people around the world.

From Calculator to Respecter. Instead of using or exploiting others, the self-actualizer respects others as people; they are not thought of as "things." This type of self-actualization was present in the personality of Mahatma Gandhi, a man whose nonviolent style always reflected a deep respect for others.

From Clinging Vine to Appreciator. The appreciator does not simply depend on others, like a clinging vine, but appreciates others' points of view. Pope John XXIII was an example of the appreciator through his role as ambassador to other religions of the world.

From Bully to Assertor. The assertor appreciates a worthy opponent but is direct and straightforward with adversaries. The assertor is not hostile and dominating like the bully. Abraham Lincoln was an assertor, as evidenced in the Lincoln-Douglas debates and his leadership during the Civil War.

From "Nice Guy" to Carer. The carer is not just a "goody-goody"; rather, he is affectionate, friendly, and deeply loving. Albert Schweitzer, through his sincere devotion to the people of Africa, exemplified the characteristics of the carer.

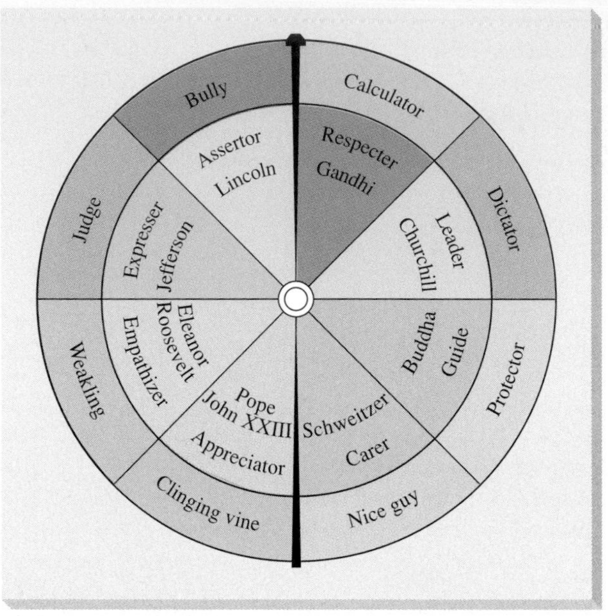

FIGURE D

Shostrum's Portrait of Manipulators and Self-Actualizers

From Judge to Expresser. The expresser is not judgmental of others; he is able to express his own convictions strongly, however. Thomas Jefferson revealed this type of personality in his presidential role.

From Protector to Guide. The guide does not protect or teach others; rather, she gently helps each person find a path of competence and identity. Buddha, the founder of the prominent Eastern religion of Buddhism, was such a person. He stressed that each person must find her own way up the mountain.

In some instances, self-actualizers integrate different characteristics. For example, Shostrum concluded that someone who combines expression and guidance does not think "for" others but "with" them. In this form of self-actualization, one's views are expressed but full decision making rests on the other person's shoulders. For example, Jesus expressed his views in the Sermon on the Mount but the decision to follow Jesus was with each individual; the same was true of the Beatitudes, which were invitations, not demands.

Concept Table 2

The Behavioral and Social Learning Perspectives and the Phenomenological and Humanistic Perspectives

Concept	Processes/Related Ideas	Characteristics/Description
The Behavioral and Social Learning Perspectives	Skinner's behaviorism	This view emphasizes that cognition is unimportant in personality; personality is observed behavior, which is influenced by the rewards and punishments in the environment. Personality often varies according to the situation.
	Social learning theory	The environment is an important determinant of personality, but so are cognitive processes. We can control our own behavior through thoughts, beliefs, and values. Bandura's emphasis on observational learning and Mischel's research on delay of gratification highlight the cognitive aspects of social learning theory.
	Evaluating the behavioral and social learning perspectives	Strengths of both perspectives include emphases on environmental determinants and a scientific climate for investigating personality, as well as a focus on cognitive processes and self-control in the social learning approach. The behavioral view has been criticized for taking the "person" out of personality and for ignoring cognition. These approaches have not given adequate attention to enduring individual differences, to biological factors, and to personality as a whole.
The Phenomenological and Humanistic Perspectives	Their nature	The phenomenological approach emphasizes our perceptions of ourselves and our world; it centers on the belief that reality is what is perceived. The humanistic approach is the most widely known phenomenological perspective.
	Carl Rogers' approach	Each of us is a victim of conditional positive regard. The result is that the real self is not valued. The self is the core of personality; it includes both the real and ideal self. Rogers said we can help others develop a more positive self-concept in three ways: unconditional positive regard, empathy, and genuineness. Rogers also stressed that each of us has the innate, inner capacity to become a fully functioning person.
	Abraham Maslow's approach	Maslow called the humanistic movement the "third force" in psychology. Maslow developed the hierarchy of needs concept with self-actualization being the highest human need.
	Evaluating the phenomenological and humanistic perspectives	They sensitized us to the importance of subjective experience, consciousness, self-conception, the whole person, and our innate, positive nature. Weaknesses focus on the absence of an empirical orientation, a tendency to be too optimistic, and an inclination to encourage self-love.

theory of body types and personality. He concluded that individuals basically are one of three types: **Endomorph** *was Sheldon's term for a soft, round, large-stomached person who is relaxed, gregarious, and food-loving.* **Mesomorph** *was Sheldon's term for a strong, athletic, and muscular person who is energetic, assertive, and courageous.* **Ectomorph** *was Sheldon's term for a tall, thin, fragile person who is fearful, introverted, and restrained.* **Somatotype theory** *was Sheldon's theory that precise charts of an individual's body reveal distinct body types, which in turn are associated with certain personality characteristics* (see figure 4).

Appealing as it was, somatotyping ran aground. For starters, research revealed there is no significant relation between body type and personality (Cortes & Gatti, 1970). And many people simply do not fit into a neatly packaged category. In addition, using one, two, or three categories to

(a)

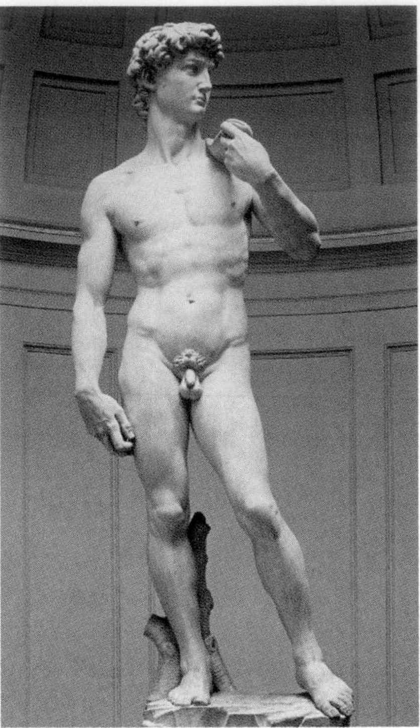
(b)

(c)

FIGURE 4

Artists' Portraits of Body Types and Accompanying Personality Characteristics
Shown here are (*a*) a gently endomorphic Venus by Titian; (*b*) a rugged, athletic mesomorphic David by Michelangelo; and (*c*) an anxious, ectomorphic actor by Picasso.

describe individuals ignores the rich diversity and complexity of human characteristics. Sheldon's somatotype theory is also biased. The theory especially reflects popular stereotypes about Caucasian male physiques. For example, a Vogue fashion model, a full-bodied Polynesian woman, a tall, thin African American man, and a sumo wrestler do not fit neatly into Sheldon's compartmentalization of human body types. Needless to say, Sheldon's somatotype theory is not popular today.

Trait Theories

Trait theories *state that personality consists of broad dispositions, called traits, that tend to lead to characteristic responses. In other words, people can be described in terms of the basic ways they behave, such as whether they are outgoing and friendly or whether they are dominant and assertive.* People who have a strong tendency to behave in these ways are described as high on the traits; those who have a weak tendency to behave in these ways are described as low on the traits. While trait theorists sometimes differ on which traits make up personality, they all agree that traits are the fundamental building blocks of personality (Cloninger, 1996).

Trying to pigeonhole the traits that make up personality is a herculean task. Gordon Allport (1937), for example, combed the dictionary and counted almost 18,000 words that could be used to describe people! Allport said that several overarching categories could be used to simplify the vast number of words to describe traits. One of Allport's trait categories was *individual traits,* the individual's unique way of dealing with the world.

Hans Eysenck (1967) also tackled the task of determining the basic traits of personality. He gave personality tests to large numbers of people and analyzed each person's response. Eysenck consistently found the traits of stability/instability and introversion/extraversion when the personalities of large numbers of individuals were assessed (see figure 5). An unstable personality is moody, anxious, restless, and touchy; a stable personality is calm, even-tempered, carefree, and has leadership qualities. An introverted personality is quiet, unsociable, passive, and careful; an extroverted personality is active, optimistic, sociable, and outgoing.

Recent Developments in Trait Psychology

Researchers continue to ferret out the basic traits of personality. Two areas of interest are known as the "basic five-factor structure of personality" and the "traits of individualism and collectivism."

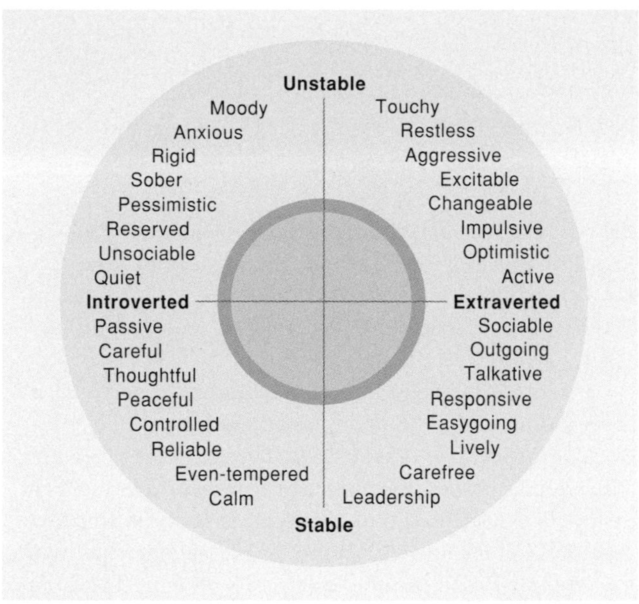

FIGURE 5

Eysenck's Dimensions of Personality
Eysenck concluded that personality consists of two basic dimensions: (1) stability-instability and (2) introversion-extraversion.

Five Basic Factors Trait psychologists are encouraged by evidence from a number of studies that reveals five basic dimensions of personality (Costa & McRae, 1995; Hogan, 1987). These are called the *big five factors in personality:*

- Emotional stability
- Extraversion
- Openness
- Agreeableness
- Conscientiousness

Emotional stability involves being calm rather than anxious, secure rather than insecure, and self-satisfied rather than self-pitying. Extraversion consists of being sociable instead of retiring, fun-loving instead of sober, and affectionate instead of reserved. Openness involves being imaginative rather than practical, preferring variety to routine, and being independent rather than conforming. Agreeableness consists of being softhearted, not ruthless; trusting, not suspicious; and helpful, not uncooperative. And conscientiousness involves being organized rather than disorganized, careful rather than careless, and disciplined, not impulsive. To read further about the "big five" factors in personality and their possible evolutionary significance, turn to Explorations in Psychology 5.

Individualism and Collectivism A small Texas corporation trying to improve productivity told its employees to look in the mirror and say "I am beautiful" one hundred times each day before coming to work. Employees of a Japanese supermarket that recently opened in New Jersey were told to begin the day by holding hands, telling each other that they are beautiful. In America, "the squeaky wheel gets the grease." In Japan, "the nail that stands out gets pounded down." Such anecdotes suggest that people in Japan and America have different views of the self and others (Markus & Kitayama, 1991).

How does the Eastern concept of personality differ from the Western concept?

In cross-cultural research, the search for basic traits has even extended to characteristics common to whole nations. In recent years, the most elaborate search for traits common to the inhabitants of a particular country has focused on the individualism/collectivism dichotomy (Hofstede, 1980; Kagitcibasi, 1995; Triandis, 1994). **Individualism** *involves giving priority to personal goals rather than to group goals; it emphasizes values that serve the self such as feeling good, personal distinction, and independence.* **Collectivism** *emphasizes values that serve the group by subordinating personal goals to preserve group integrity, interdependence of members, and harmonious relationships.*

As is true of a great deal of psychology's basic tenets, many of the assumptions about personality were developed in Western cultures, such as the United States, that emphasize the individual or self. Psychological terms about personality often include the word *self*—for example, *self-actualization, self-awareness, self-concept, self-efficacy, self-reinforcement, self-criticism, self-serving, selfishness,* and *self-doubt* (Lonner, 1988). Cross-cultural psychologists describe the cultures in many non-Western countries such as Russia, Japan, and India as more collectivistic than individualistic.

Critics of the Western notion of personality point out that human beings have always lived in groups, whether large or small, and have always needed one another for survival. They argue that the Western emphasis on individualism may undermine our species' basic need for relatedness (Kagitcibasi, 1995). Some social scientists believe that many of our

Explorations in Psychology 5

Evolutionary Psychology's Interpretation of the Big Five Personality Factors

There is an increasing interest in the biological dimensions of personality. One such interest stems from evolutionary psychology, which emphasizes that psychological mechanisms are the product of evolution (Buss, 1995; Symons, 1979). These psychological mechanisms owe their existence to successful solutions to adaptive problems faced in ancestral environments.

Personality psychology has always been concerned with the enduring ways in which individuals differ from one another. Evolutionary psychologists make the following points about personality and individual differences: (1) Stable individual differences can be caused by differences in recurrent adaptive problems to which individuals are exposed. (2) Complex species-typical mechanisms are necessary to explain individual differences, because without them the individual differences would not occur. And (3) the individual differences are outcomes of recurrently different input into species-typical mechanisms.

Evolutionary psychologist David Buss (1995) argues that the "big five" personality dimensions—emotional stability, extraversion, openness, agreeableness, and conscientiousness—might summarize the most important features of the social landscape that humans have had to adapt to. From this perspective, to know others is an adaptive necessity (Symons, 1979).

Evolutionary psychologists believe that personality traits summarize the most important features of the adaptive landscape (Buss, 1989, 1995). They provide a source for answering important life questions like these: Who is high or low in the social hierarchy? Who is likely to improve their status in the future? Who will make a good member of my coalition? Who has the resources I need? With whom should I share my resources, and who will share their resources with me? On whom can I depend when I am in need? With whom should I mate? Who might do me harm? Whom can I trust? To whom can I go to for competent advice? The evolutionary psychology thesis is that people have evolved psychological mechanisms sensitive to individual differences in others that are relevant to answering their critical adaptive questions.

problems, such as anxiety, depression, and shyness, are intensified by the emphasis on the self and independence in American culture (Munroe & Munroe, 1975). The pendulum may have swung too far toward individualism in Western cultures. We underscore the belief that people, regardless of their cultural background, need a positive sense of self *and* connectedness to others to fully develop as human beings.

As with other attempts to explain personality, the individualism—collectivism dichotomy has its detractors as well. They argue that describing entire nations of people as having a basic personality obscures the extensive diversity and individual variation that characterizes a nation's people. Also, certain values serve both individual and collective interests, such as wisdom, mature love, and tolerance (Schwartz, 1990).

The Attack on Traits In his landmark book *Personality and Assessment,* Walter Mischel (1968) criticized the trait view of personality as well as the psychoanalytic approach, both of which emphasize the internal organization of personality. Rather than viewing personality as consisting of broad, internal traits that are consistent across situations and time, Mischel said that personality often changes according to a given situation.

Mischel reviewed an array of studies and concluded that trait measures do a poor job of predicting actual behavior. For example, let's say Anne is described as an aggressive person. But when we observe her behavior we find that she is more or less aggressive depending on the situation—she may be aggressive with her boyfriend but almost submissive with her new boss. Mischel's view was called **situationism,** *which means that personality often varies considerably from one context to another.* Mischel's argument was an important one, but as we see next, many psychologists were not willing to abandon altogether the trait concept.

Trait-Situation Interaction

Today, most psychologists in the field of personality are interactionists, including Mischel. They believe both trait (person) and situation variables are necessary to understand personality. They also agree that the degree of consistency in personality depends on the kind of persons, situations, and behaviors sampled (Pervin, 1993; Mischel, 1995).

Suppose you want to assess the happiness of Bob, an introvert, and Jane an extrovert. According to trait-situation interaction theory, we cannot predict who will be happier unless we know something about the situations they are in. Imagine you get the opportunity to observe them in two situations, at a party and in a library. As described in figure 6, considering both the traits of the individuals and the settings they are in improves our ability to predict their happiness.

One outcome of the trait-situation controversy is that the link between traits and situations has been more

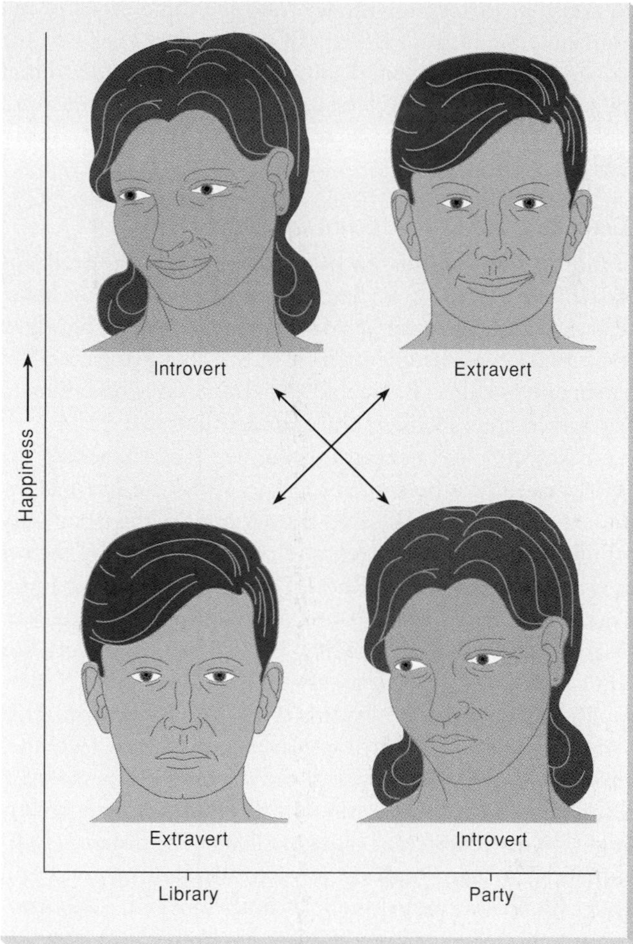

FIGURE 6

Trait-Situation Interaction
Who is happier, an introvert or an extravert? According to the concept of trait-situation interaction, we have to know the nature of the situation in which the introvert and extravert are behaving. At a party, the extravert probably will be happier than the introvert; at a library, the introvert probably will be happier than the extravert (Peterson, 1988).

precisely specified (Little, 1995; Walsh, 1995). For example, researchers have found that (1) the narrower and more limited a trait is, the more likely it will predict behavior; (2) some people are consistent on some traits and other people are consistent on other traits; and (3) personality traits exert a stronger influence on an individual's behavior when situational influences are less powerful.

Cross-cultural psychologists go several steps farther. They believe that considering both the immediate setting *and* the broader cultural context leads to a better understanding of the situation's role in the way personality is expressed (Katigbak, Church, & Akamine, 1996). For example, cross-cultural psychologists investigating certain aspects of personality and religion would observe a person's behavior in a chapel and put it in the context of social conventions regarding who should be in church, when, with whom, and how the person is expected to behave.

Personality Research

So far it might seem to you that the field of personality consists mainly of grand theoretical views. The theories we have discussed are an important dimension of understanding personality. However, there is another, equally important side to the field of personality—the empirical research side (Shrout & Fiske, 1995). Earlier in the chapter, we explored one aspect of personality research in some detail—Mischel's studies on the delay of gratification. The complex mosaic of the field of personality involves a myriad of research areas, including the biological and hereditary determinants of personality, cultural influences, repression, stability and change, cognitive processes, emotional processes, the role of individual differences, personality traits in social behavior, many dimensions of the self and identity, how personality develops, the role of family processes, and the search for the structure of personality. To sample the flavor of these empirical efforts, we will discuss three domains of personality research: self-esteem, the big five personality factors, and stability and change in personality over the human life span.

Self-Esteem

Self-esteem *is the evaluative and affective dimension of self-concept. Self-esteem is also referred to as self-worth or self-image.* Research on self-esteem covers a wide range of topics, among them the consequences of having low self-esteem and the multidimensional nature of self-esteem and whether some dimensions of self contribute more than others to overall self-esteem.

What are the consequences of having low self-esteem? Researchers have found that low self-esteem is implicated in low achievement, depression, and many other adjustment difficulties (Harter & Marold, 1992). Also, individuals with low self-esteem tend to focus on their weaknesses rather than their strengths (Showers, 1992).

Carolin Showers (1992) applied an information-processing approach to the compartmentalization of positive and negative self-knowledge. Consider two college students, both of whom have the same knowledge about themselves as students. Imagine that one student organizes this knowledge under two self-aspects—one that contains mainly positive information ("I see myself as a brilliant Renaissance scholar") and one that has primarily negative information ("I worry about tests and grades"). This student has compartmentalized positive and negative self-information into two separate categories. As long as the student's academic experiences mostly activate the first category, accessible self-information will be primarily positive. To the extent that the student can avoid activating the negative category (such as by not taking courses with high-pressure exams or by taking courses on a pass/fail basis), only the positive self-knowledge will be activated.

By contrast, consider that the same self-knowledge might be organized along different lines, unrelated to the positive or negative nature of the information. For example,

Compartmentalized Organization		Mixed Organization	
Renaissance scholar (+)	Taking tests, grades (–)	Humanities classes (+/–)	Science classes (+/–)
+ curious + disciplined + motivated + creative + analytical + expressive	– worrying – tense – distracted – insecure – competitive – moody	+ creative – insecure + motivated – distracted + expressive – moody	+ disciplined + analytical – competitive – worrying + curious – tense

Note. A positive (+) or negative (–) valence is indicated for each category and each item. The symbol (+/–) denotes a mixed-valence category.

FIGURE 7

Examples of Compartmentalized Organization and Mixed Organization for Identical Items of Information About Self as Student

a student might develop a mixed self-organization that consists of "myself in humanities classes" and "myself in science classes" (see figure 7).

Showers (1992) found that when subjects organized positive and negative aspects of the self into separate, evaluatively compartmentalized self-aspects, they were more likely to have high self-esteem and low depression scores than were their mixed-organization counterparts. She also revealed that when positive aspects of the self were perceived to be highly important (subjects used more positive adjectives—such as *energetic, creative, hard-working*—to describe themselves), compartmentalization was related to high self-esteem and low depression; when negative aspects were important (subjects used more negative adjectives—such as *insecure, lazy, irritable*—to describe themselves), compartmentalization was associated with low self-esteem and high depression scores. Thus, it is not just the content of knowledge about the self that is important, but also how the content is organized. Keeping one's "bad apples out of the bunch" may be advantageous as long as they do not represent important aspects of the self.

Another area of self-esteem research focuses on the multidimensional nature of self-esteem and whether some dimensions of self contribute more than others to overall self-esteem (Marsh, 1994). For example, some researchers assess an individual's self-evaluations in a set of specific domains and average across them (Pelham & Swann, 1989). Also, Susan Harter (1988) found that children with high global self-worth are successful in the domains they perceive to be important and are able to discount the importance of domains in which they feel less adequate. For instance, consider a child who is successful in academic and social domains, but not in the physical, athletic domain. This high-global-self-esteem child says that she knows she is not athletically talented and accepts the fact that she can't do everything exceptionally well. Which dimensions of self contribute the most to global self-esteem may vary with the individual's developmental status. Harter (1990) found that the self domains of perceived appearance and peer social acceptance were the most salient aspects of global self-esteem during adolescence.

The Big Five Factors in Personality

Earlier in this chapter, in our discussion of the trait approach to personality, we described the search for the cluster of basic traits in human personality. We indicated that there is currently considerable interest in the "big five factors" in personality—emotional stability, extraversion, openness to experience, agreeableness, and conscientiousness.

Research areas regarding the five factors include the development of a personality test to assess the five factors, the extent to which the five factors appear in personality profiles in different cultures, and the role of the five factors in predicting health and illness. Paul Costa and Robert McCrae (1992) constructed a test, the Neuroticism Extraversion Openness Personality Inventory, Revised (or *NEO-PI-R* for short), to assess the big five factors in personality. The test also evaluates six subdimensions that make up the five main factors. Costa and McRae (1989) believe that the test can improve the diagnosis of personality disorders and help therapists understand how therapy might influence different types of clients. For instance, individuals who score high on the extraversion factor might prefer group over individual psychotherapy, whereas introverts might do better in individual psychotherapy.

Do the five factors show up in the assessment of personality in cultures around the world? There is increasing evidence that they do (Ozer & Reise, 1994). Researchers have found that some version of the five factors appears in people in countries as diverse as Canada, Finland, Poland, China, and Japan (Paunonen & others, 1992; Yang & Bond, 1990).

The notion that personality characteristics might influence vulnerability to illness and illness progression continues to attract widespread research attention. Much of this research, though, is conducted without reference to a unified framework of personality. The big five trait structure offers the potential for such a unified framework.

In one recent study, Costa and McRae's big five personality test, along with representative personality scales from health psychology (such as scales for personal control and self-esteem, optimism and hope, negative affectivity, and emotional control) were administered to two samples of male military recruits (Marshall & others, 1994). Variations in many of the health-related personality scales could be moderately explained by the big five factors. In health psychology research, neuroticism and extraversion have been given disproportionate attention (not surprisingly, given the prominence of these factors

How much does personality change through adulthood? In the early 1970s, Jerry Rubin was a Yippie demonstrator (inset, top), but in the 1980s Rubin became a Wall Street businessman (inset, bottom). Rubin said that his transformation underscored continuity in personality: Whether Yippie or Wall Street yuppie, he approached life with curiosity and enthusiasm. In 1992, at age 55, Jack Nicholson (right) said, "I feel exactly the same as I've always felt: a slightly reined-in voracious beast." Remember that both stability and change can characterize our personality development.

in theories of arousal and stress). The factors of conscientiousness and openness to experience have especially been neglected in research on personality's role in health and illness.

Stability and Change in Personality Across the Life Span

How much does our personality change as we develop through the life span? Sigmund Freud (1917) argued that much of personality is formed in the first 5 years of life. William James (1890–1950) said that our personality is set in plaster by the time we are 30 and never softens again. Is our personality as stable in adulthood as Freud and James believed?

The best way to investigate stability and change in personality is through a **longitudinal study,** *a research strategy in which the same individuals are tested over a period of time, usually several years or more.* A number of longitudinal studies have assessed the personality development of individuals (Franz & McClelland, 1994; Helson & Roberts, 1994).

Using their five-factor personality test, Paul Costa and Robert McRae (1995) studied approximately a thousand college-educated men and women aged 20 to 96, assessing the same individuals over a period of many years. Data collection began in the 1950s to the mid 1960s and is ongoing. Costa and McRae concluded that considerable stability occurs in the five personality factors—emotional stability, extraversion, openness, agreeableness, and conscientiousness.

Another set of longitudinal investigations is called the Berkeley Longitudinal Studies. Initially, more than 500 children and their parents were studied in the late 1920s and early 1930s. John Clausen (1993) recently conducted in-depth life history interviews with 60 male and

In John Clausen's in-depth study, which spanned nearly 50 years of people's lives, planful competence in late adolescence was linked with occupational and family success in adult years.

female Berkeley Longitudinal subjects. Analyzing nearly 50 years of their lives, Clausen found that planful competence in late adolescence (based on personality trait ratings) was associated with occupational and family success in the adult years. What is planful competence? In Clausen's analysis, it consisted of three personal qualities—self-confidence, dependability, and intellectual investment. Planful competence, developed by the end of the high school years, influenced the scheduling of major social roles later occupied, the stability of role performance, and the person's attainment of life satisfaction over much of the life course. Individuals high in planful competence made more realistic educational, occupational, and marital choices, whereas their low-competence counterparts found less-satisfying jobs, shifted jobs (and spouses) more, and experienced more pressure to change themselves during the adult years. A few low-planful-competence adolescents became effective adults, and a few high-planful-competence adolescents had dismal adult lives, but they were the exceptions rather than the rule. Clausen concluded that personality development can involve stability and change—some people have stable, continuous lives and change little; others experience recurrent crises and change a great deal over the life course.

In summary, the longitudinal studies suggest that both stability and change can characterize personality. For many individuals, though, even amid change there is some underlying coherence. And some people, especially those who experience recurrent crises, change more than others.

Personality Assessment

"This line running this way indicates that you are a gregarious person, someone who really enjoys being around people. This division over here suggests that you are a risk taker; I bet you like to do things that are adventurous sometimes." These are the words you might hear from a palmist. Palmistry purports to "read" an individual's personality by interpreting the irregularities and folds in the skin of the hand. Each of these signs is interpreted in a precise manner. For example, a large mound of Saturn, the portion of the palm directly below the third joint of the middle finger, ostensibly relates to wisdom, good fortune, and prudence.

While palmists claim to provide a complete assessment of personality through reading lines in the hand, researchers debunk palmistry as quackery. Researchers argue that palmists give no reasonable explanation for their inferences about personality, and point out that the hand's characteristics can change through age and even exercise.

Even so, palmists manage to stay in business. They do so, in part, because they are keen observers—they respond to such cues as voice, general demeanor, and dress, which are more relevant signs of personality than the lines and folds on a person's palm. Palmists also are experts at offering general, trivial statements such as, "Although you usually are affectionate with others, sometimes you don't get along with people." This statement falls into the category of the **Barnum effect:** *If you make your predictions broad enough, any person can fit the description.* The effect was named after circus owner P. T. Barnum.

In contrast, psychologists use a number of scientifically developed tests and methods to evaluate personality (Walsh & Betz, 1995). And they assess personality for different reasons. Clinical and school psychologists assess personality to better understand an individual's psychological problems; they hope the assessment will improve their diagnosis and treatment of the individual. Industrial psychologists and vocational counselors assess personality to aid the individual's selection of a career. And research psychologists assess personality to investigate the theories and dimensions of personality we have discussed so far in this chapter. For example, if a psychologist wants to investigate self-concept, some measure of self-concept is needed.

Before we describe some specific personality tests, two more important points need to be made about the nature of personality assessment. First, the kinds of tests chosen by psychologists frequently depend on the psychologist's theoretical bent. And second, most personality tests are designed to assess stable, enduring characteristics, free of situational influence (Hy & Loeuinger, 1996).

Projective Tests

A **projective test** *presents individuals with an ambiguous stimulus and then asks them to describe it or tell a story about it. Projective tests are based on the assumption that the ambiguity of the stimulus allows individuals to project into it their feelings, desires, needs, and attitudes.* The test is especially designed to elicit the individual's unconscious feelings and conflicts, providing an assessment that goes deeper than the surface of personality. Projective tests attempt to get inside of your mind to discover how you really feel and think, going beyond the way you overtly present yourself.

The Rorschach Inkblot Test

The **Rorschach inkblot test,** *developed in 1921 by the Swiss psychiatrist Hermann Rorschach, is a widely used projective test; it uses an individual's perception of inkblots to determine his or her personality.* The test consists of ten cards, half in black and white and half in color, which are shown to the individual one at a time (see figure 8). The person taking the Rorschach test is asked to describe what he or she sees in each of the inkblots. For example, an individual may say, "That looks like two people fighting." After the individual has responded to all ten inkblots, the examiner presents each of the inkblots again and inquires about the individual's earlier response. For example, the examiner might ask, "*Where* did you see the two people fighting?" and "*What* about the inkblot made the two people look like they were fighting?" Besides recording the responses, the examiner notes the individual's mannerisms, gestures, and attitudes.

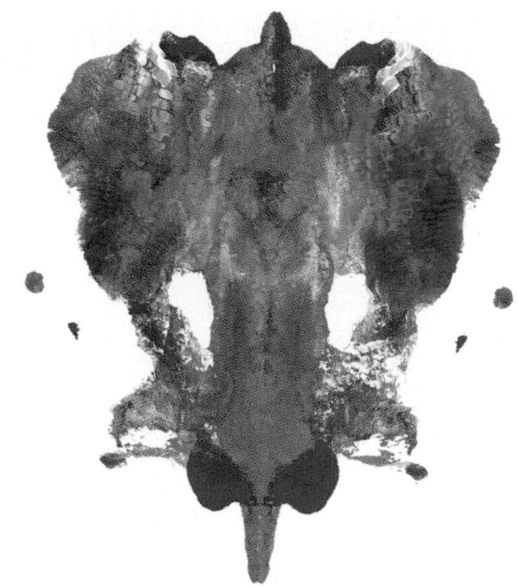

FIGURE 8

Type of Stimulus Used in the Rorschach Inkblot Test

How useful is the Rorschach in assessing personality? The answer to this question depends on one's perspective. From a scientific perspective, researchers are skeptical about the Rorschach (Feshbach & Weiner, 1996). Their disenchantment stems from the failure of the Rorschach to meet the criteria of reliability and validity. If the Rorschach were reliable, two different scorers should agree on the personality characteristics of the individual. If the Rorschach were valid, the individual's personality should predict behavior outside of the testing situation; that is, it should predict whether an individual will attempt suicide, become severely depressed, cope successfully with stress, or get along well with others. Conclusions based on research evidence suggest that the Rorschach does not meet these criteria of reliability and validity. This has led to serious reservations about the Rorschach's use in diagnosis and clinical practice.

Yet the Rorschach continues to enjoy widespread use in clinical circles; some clinicians swear by the Rorschach, saying it is better than any other measure at getting at the

FIGURE 9

Picture from the Thematic Apperception Test (TAT)

true, underlying core of the individual's personality (McDowell & Acklini, 1996; Sloan & others, 1996). They are not especially bothered by the Rorschach's low reliability and validity, pointing out that this is so because of the extensive freedom of response encouraged by the test. It is this freedom of response that makes the Rorschach such a rich clinical tool, say its advocates.

The Rorschach controversy continues (Murstein & Mathes, 1996; Wood, Nezworski, & Stejskal, 1996). And it probably will not subside in the near future. Research psychologists will continue to criticize the low reliability and validity of the Rorschach; many clinicians will continue to say that the Rorschach is a valuable clinical tool, providing insights about the unconscious mind that no other personality test can.

Other Projective Tests

The **Thematic Apperception Test (TAT),** *which was developed by Henry Murray and Christina Morgan in the 1930s, is an ambiguous projective test designed to elicit stories that reveal something about an individual's personality.* The TAT consists of a series of pictures, each on an individual card (see figure 9). The person taking the TAT is asked to tell a story about each of the pictures, including events leading up to the situation described, the characters' thoughts and feelings, and how the situation turns out. It is assumed that the person projects her own unconscious feelings and thoughts into the story she tells. In addition to being used as a projective test in clinical practice, the TAT is used in research of achievement motivation. Several of the TAT cards stimulate the telling of achievement-related stories, which enables the researcher to determine the person's need for achievement (McClelland & others, 1953).

Many other projective tests are used in clinical assessment. One test asks the individual to complete a sentence (for example "I often feel . . ." "I would like to . . ."); another test asks the individual to draw a person; and another test presents a word, such as *fear* or *happy,* and asks the individual to say the first thing that comes to mind. Like the Rorschach, these projective tests have their detractors and advocates; the detractors often criticize the tests' low reliability and validity, and the advocates describe the tests' abilities to reveal the underlying nature of the individual's personality better than more straightforward tests. Recently, another projective measure has generated considerable controversy—**graphology,** *the use of handwriting analysis to determine an individual's personality.* To read further about graphology and its lack of scientific status, turn to Explorations in Psychology 6.

Self-Report Tests

Self-report tests *assess your personality traits by asking you what they are; they are not designed to reveal your unconscious personality characteristics.* For example, self-report tests of personality include items such as the following:

- I am easily embarrassed.
- I love to go to parties.
- I like to watch cartoons on TV.

Self-report tests are questionnaires that include a large number of statements or questions like these. You respond with a limited number of choices (yes or no; true or false; agree or disagree). How do psychologists construct self-report tests of personality?

Constructing Self-Report Tests

Many of the early personality tests were based on **face validity,** *which is an assumption that the content of the test items is a good indicator of the individual's personality.* For example, if I developed a test item that asks you to respond whether or not you are introverted, and you answer, "I enjoy being with people," I accept your response as a straightforward indication that you are not introverted. Tests based on face validity assume that you are responding honestly and nondefensively, giving the examiner an accurate portrayal of your personality.

But not everyone is honest, especially when it concerns their own personality. Even if the individual basically

Explorations in Psychology 6

Being Skeptical About Graphology

Can the analysis of a person's handwriting provide insight into her personality? Examine the writing in figure E to see the kinds of interpretations graphologists make. At least 3,000 firms in the United States use graphology when hiring individuals. In other countries, such as Israel and Japan, the use of graphological analysis in hiring is even more widespread. One survey found that 85 percent of all European firms use graphology as part of their employee-selection process (Levy, 1979). The managing editor of the journal *United States Banker* commented, "Graphoanalysis [graphology] reveals capabilities and aptitudes in an individual, many of which the applicant may not be aware of" (Van Deventer, 1983). Given the recent popularity of handwriting analysis in business hiring, it is important to examine whether it really does reveal anything about an individual's personality characteristics (Hines, 1988).

The growing research literature on graphology is almost universally negative (Furnham, 1988; Nevo, 1986). One investigation typifies these negative results (Ben-Shakhar & others, 1986). Three professional graphologists agreed to rate handwriting samples from 52 bank employees. The graphologists were asked to assess the employees' competence at their jobs and the nature of their relationships with co-workers. The samples consisted of brief autobiographical essays and responses to a short biographical questionnaire. The researchers also used information from the samples, such as the employees' ages and job interests, the quality of their essays, and the attractiveness of their handwriting to make assessments about the employees' competence. The researchers' predictions and the graphologists' ratings were compared with the ratings by the employees' supervisors. The graphologists did no better than the researchers at matching the supervisors' ratings. A battery of personality tests were better at matching the supervisors' ratings. In a second study, five graphologists did no better than chance when asked to predict the occupations of 40 successful professional men based on several pages of their handwriting.

If the research investigation of graphological claims is so negative, why is graphology so widely used and accepted? Graphological analysis has a mysterious, powerful ring to it. People are easily impressed by confident, so-called experts and assume they know what they are talking about. Positive, unscientific reports of graphologists' abilities appear frequently in magazines and business commentaries. People are fascinated by graphology and want to believe that their handwriting, because it is highly individual, reveals something about themselves. Also, graphologists' predictions, like those of palmists and astrologers, are usually very general and difficult to disprove.

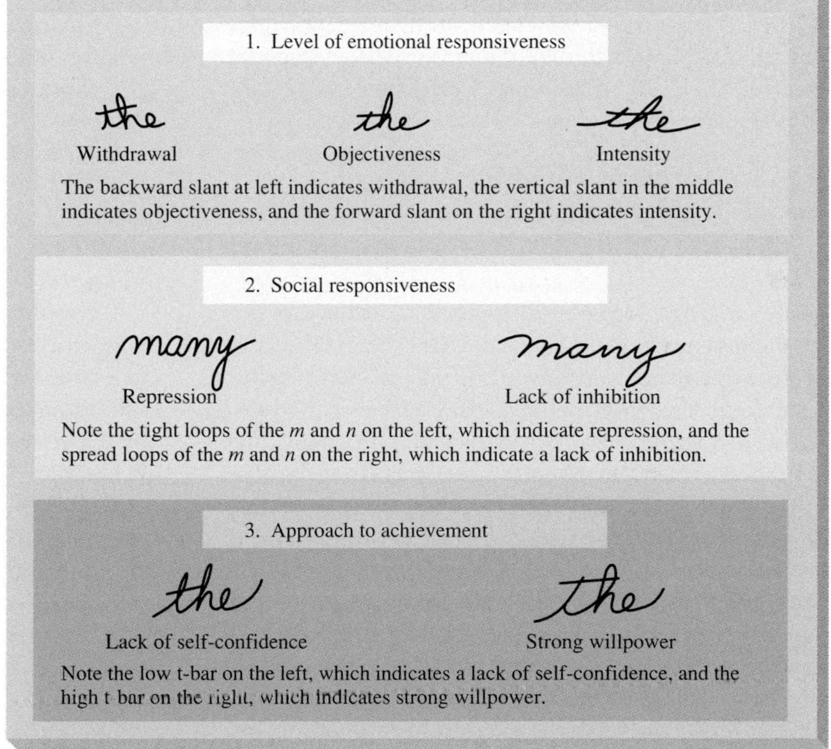

FIGURE E

Some Graphological Interpretations

is honest, he may be giving socially desirable answers. When motivated by **social desirability,** *individuals say what they think the interviewer wants to hear or what they think will make them look better.* For example, if I am basically a lazy person, I might not want you to know this, and I may try to present myself in a more positive way; therefore, I would respond negatively to the following item: "I fritter away time too much." Because of such responses psychologists realized they needed to go beyond face validity in constructing personality tests; they accomplished this by developing empirically keyed tests.

An **empirically keyed test** *relies on its items to predict some criterion. Unlike tests based on face validity, in which the content of the items is supposed to be a good indicator of what the individual's personality is like, empirically keyed tests make no assumptions about the nature of the items.* Imagine we want to develop a test that will determine whether or not applicants for a position as a police officer are likely to be competent at the job. We might ask a large number of questions of police officers, some of whom have excellent job records, others who have not performed as well. We would then use the questions that differentiate between competent and incompetent police officers on our test to screen job applicants. If the item, "I enjoyed reading poetry" predicts success as a police officer, then we would include it on the test even though it seems unrelated to police work. Next, we examine the most widely used empirically keyed personality test.

The Minnesota Multiphasic Personality Inventory

The **Minnesota Multiphasic Personality Inventory (MMPI)** *is the most widely used and researched self-report personality test.* The MMPI was originally developed to improve the diagnosis of mentally disturbed individuals. A thousand statements were given to both mental patients and apparently normal people. How often individuals agreed with each item was calculated; only the items that clearly differentiated the psychiatric patients from the normal individuals were retained. For example, a statement might be included on the depression scale of the MMPI if patients diagnosed with a depressive disorder agreed with the statement significantly more than did normal individuals. For example, a statement with little face validity, such as "I sometimes tease animals," might be included on the depression scale, or any other scale, of the MMPI.

The MMPI eventually was streamlined to 550 items, each of which can be answered true, false, or cannot say. The items vary widely in content and include such statements as the following:

- I like to read magazines.
- I never have trouble falling asleep.
- People are out to get me.

A person's answers are grouped according to ten clinical categories, or scales, that measure problems such as depression, psychopathic deviation, schizophrenia, and social introversion.

The MMPI includes four validity scales in addition to the ten clinical scales. The validity scales were designed to indicate whether an individual is lying, careless, defensive, or evasive when answering the test items. For example, if the individual responds "false" to a number of items, such as "I get angry sometimes," it would be interpreted that she is trying to make herself look better than she really is. The rationale for the lie scale is that each of us gets angry at least some of the time, so the individual who responds "false" to many such items is faking her responses.

For the first time in its approximately 40-year history, the MMPI was revised in 1989 (Butcher & others, 1989). The revision added new content scales and deleted some statements, including all items pertaining to religion and most of the questions about sexual practices. The revised MMPI has 567 items. Its basic clinical scales have not changed; however, content scales that relate to the broader interests of some clinicians and employers were added. The new content scales focus on substance abuse, eating disorders, Type A behavior, repression, anger, cynicism, low self-esteem, family problems, and inability to function in a job.

Thousands of research studies and many books have documented the ability of the MMPI to improve the diagnosis of mentally disordered individuals. The MMPI has been used in more than fifty countries, and more than 125 translations of the test are available. And increasingly, the MMPI has been used to assess normal rather than abnormal aspects of personality.

Despite its popularity and widespread use, critics believe the MMPI has a number of problems. For one, critics say the MMPI is biased in terms of culture, ethnicity, and gender. Cross-cultural psychologist Walter Lonner (1990) points out that the MMPI was developed by American psychologists and follows a Western view of mental health. Because it was standardized on a group of individuals in Minnesota, he recommends considerable caution when using the MMPI, as well as other personality tests, on people from other cultures. The MMPI also contains some outdated stereotypes regarding gender. For example, if a woman responds on the MMPI that she likes hunting and fishing, she might be labeled abnormally masculine simply because more men report enjoying hunting and fishing. Critics also believe the MMPI is less effective in diagnosing differences among normal than among abnormal individuals. They believe the MMPI is now being misused in business and education to predict which individual will make the best job candidate or which career an individual should pursue. Also, persons who are inadequately trained in psychological

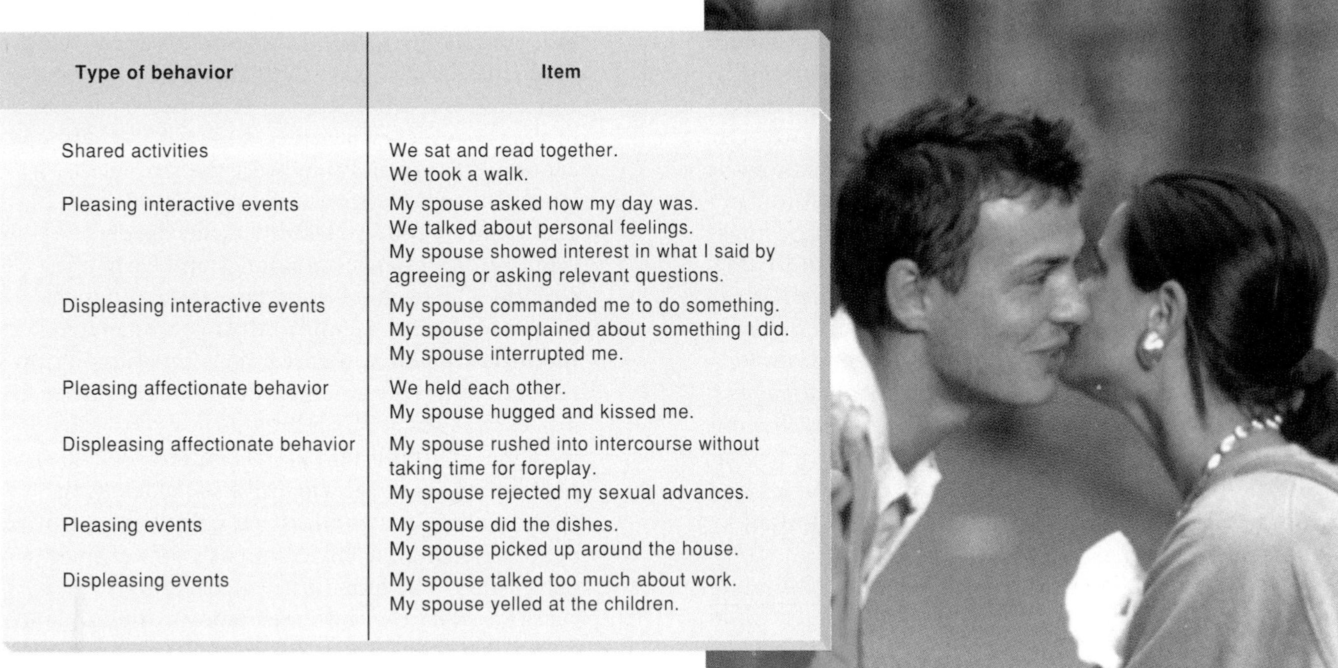

Type of behavior	Item
Shared activities	We sat and read together. We took a walk.
Pleasing interactive events	My spouse asked how my day was. We talked about personal feelings. My spouse showed interest in what I said by agreeing or asking relevant questions.
Displeasing interactive events	My spouse commanded me to do something. My spouse complained about something I did. My spouse interrupted me.
Pleasing affectionate behavior	We held each other. My spouse hugged and kissed me.
Displeasing affectionate behavior	My spouse rushed into intercourse without taking time for foreplay. My spouse rejected my sexual advances.
Pleasing events	My spouse did the dishes. My spouse picked up around the house.
Displeasing events	My spouse talked too much about work. My spouse yelled at the children.

FIGURE 10

Items from the Spouse Observation Checklist
Couples are instructed to complete a more extensive checklist for fifteen consecutive evenings. Spouses record their partner's behavior, and they make daily ratings of their overall satisfaction with the spouse's behavior.

testing and diagnosis sometimes both give and interpret the MMPI. In these cases, the MMPI is often used beyond its intent.

Evaluating Self-Report Tests

Adherents of the trait approach have strong faith in the utility of self-report tests. They point out that self-report tests have produced a better understanding of the nature of an individual's personality traits than can be derived from, for example, projective tests. However, some critics (especially psychoanalysts) believe the self-report measures do not get at the underlying core of personality and its unconscious determinants. Other critics (especially behaviorists) believe the self-report tests do not adequately capture the situational variation in personality and the ways personality changes as the individual interacts with the environment.

Behavioral Assessment

Behavioral assessment attempts to obtain more objective information about an individual's personality by observing the individual's behavior directly. Instead of removing situational influences from personality as projective tests and self-report measures do, behavioral assessment assumes that personality cannot be evaluated apart from the environment. Behavior modification is an attempt to apply learning principles to change maladaptive behavior. Behavioral assessment of personality emerged from this tradition. For example, recall that the observer often will make baseline observations of the frequency of the individual's behaviors. This might be accomplished under controlled laboratory conditions or in more naturalistic circumstances. The therapist then will modify some aspect of the environment, such as getting parents and the child's teacher to stop giving the child attention when he engages in the aggressive behavior. After a specified period of time, the therapist will observe the child again to determine if the changes in the environment were effective in reducing the child's maladaptive behavior.

Sometimes, though, direct observations are impractical. What does a psychologist with a behavioral orientation then do to assess personality? She might ask individuals to make their own assessments of behavior, encouraging them to be sensitive to the circumstances that produced the behavior and the outcomes or consequences of the behavior. For example, a therapist might want to know the course of marital conflict in the everyday experiences of a couple. Figure 10 shows a spouse observation checklist that couples can use to record their partner's behavior.

The influence of social learning theory has increased the use of cognitive assessment in personality evaluation. The strategy is to discover what thoughts underlie the individual's behavior; that is, how do individuals think about their problems? What kinds of thoughts precede maladaptive behavior, occur during its manifestation, and follow it? Cognitive processes such as expectations, planning, and memory are assessed, possibly by interviewing the individual or asking him or her to complete a questionnaire. For example, an interview might include questions that address whether the individual overexaggerates his faults and condemns himself more than is warranted. A questionnaire might ask a person what her thoughts are after an upsetting event or it might assess the way she thinks during tension-filled moments.

It has been some time since we considered the different theoretical approaches to personality. Next, to conclude the chapter, we return to those theories and compare their orientation on a number of important issues involving personality.

Comparing Personality Theories

Three important issues in personality are the degree to which it is innate or learned (biologically or experientially based); the degree to which it is conscious or unconscious; and the degree to which it is internally or externally determined.

1. *Innate versus learned.* Is personality due more to heredity and biological factors or more to learning and environmental experiences? Are individuals conceited and self-centered because they inherited the tendency to be conceited and self-centered from their parents or did they learn to be that way through experiences with other conceited, self-centered individuals? Freud's theory has a strong biogenetic foundation, although many psychoanalytic revisionists argued that he underestimated the power of environmental experiences and culture in determining personality. Behaviorism and humanism both endorse environment as a powerful determinant of personality, Skinner being the strongest advocate of environment's influence. However, humanistic theorists do believe that people have the innate ability to become self-actualized. Trait theorists vary in their emphasis on heredity and environment; Eysenck stressed the biological basis of personality, while Allport weighted biology and environment more equally.
2. *Conscious versus unconscious.* Is personality due more to conscious factors or more to unconscious factors? How aware are individuals that they are conceited and self-centered? How aware are they of the reasons they became conceited and self-centered? Freud and Jung were the strongest advocates of the unconscious mind's role in personality. Freud stressed that our deeply repressed experiences in infancy and early childhood determine what our personalities are like as adults, for example. Most psychoanalytic theorists argue that we are largely unaware of how our individual personalities developed. Skinner argues that neither unconscious nor conscious thoughts are important in determining personality, although cognitive social learning theorists Bandura and Mischel stress that cognitive factors mediate the environment's influence on personality. The humanists, such as Rogers and Maslow, stress the conscious aspects of personality, especially in the form of self-perception. Trait theorists pay little attention to the conscious-unconscious issue.
3. *Internal versus external determinants.* Is personality due more to an inner disposition or more to outer situations? Are individuals conceited and self-centered because of something inside themselves, a characteristic they have and carry around with them, or are they conceited and self-centered because of the situations they are in and the way they are influenced by people around them? Psychoanalytic theorists emphasize the internal dimensions of personality (Freud's internal structures of id, ego, and superego, for example). Trait theorists also stress internal determinants through their belief in the importance of self-concept and self-determination. By contrast, behaviorists emphasize personality's external, situational determinants, although cognitive social learning theorists examine both external and internal determinants.

A summary of personality theory comparisons on these three important issues—innate versus learned, conscious versus unconscious, and internal versus external determination—is presented in figure 11, along with a comparison of the methods advocated by the theorists.

At this point we have discussed a number of ideas about trait theory, trait-situation interaction, personality assessment, and comparing personality theories. A summary of these ideas is presented in concept table 3.

Issue	Personality theory			
	Psychoanalytic theory	Behavioral, social learning theory	Humanistic, phenomenological theory	Trait theory
Innate versus learned	Strong emphasis on biological foundations by Freud. Adler, Sullivan, and Erikson gave social experiences and culture more importance than Freud.	Skinner said personality is behavior that is environmentally determined. Social learning theorists also emphasize environmental experiences.	Humanistic theorists emphasize that personality is influenced by experience and can be changed.	Eysenck and Cattell stress personality's biological basis; Allport gave attention to both heredity and environment.
Conscious versus unconscious	Strong emphasis on unconscious thought, especially Freud and Jung	Skinner didn't think conscious or unconscious thought was important in personality. Bandura and Mischel emphasize cognitive process.	Stress conscious aspects of personality, especially self-concept, self-perception	Pay little attention to this issue
Internal versus external determinants	Emphasize internal determinants, personality structures	Emphasize external situational determinants of personality. Bandura and Mischel emphasize internal and external determinants, especially self-control.	Emphasize internal determinants of self-concept and self-determination	Stress internal, person variables
Personality measurement	Clinical interviews, unstructured personality tests, and psychohistorical analysis of lives	Observation, especially laboratory observation	Self-report measures and interviews. Clinical judgment more important than scientific measurement is view of many humanists.	Self-report tests such as MMPI

Sigmund Freud B. F. Skinner Carl Rogers Gordon Allport

FIGURE 11

Comparing Personality Theories

Concept Table 3

Trait Theory, Trait-Situation Interaction, Personality Research, Personality Assessment, and Comparison of Personality Theories

Concept	Processes/Related Ideas	Characteristics/Description
Trait Theory and Trait-Situation Interaction	Trait theory	Personality-type theory involves classifying an individual according to a particular type; Sheldon's somatotype theory is an example. This view has been heavily criticized. Trait theories emphasize that personality involves the organization of traits within the individual; these traits are assumed to be essentially stable over time and across situations. Allport stressed the individuality of traits; Eysenck sought to determine the traits common to all human beings. The search for basic trait dimensions continues; one contemporary view stresses that we have five basic traits. A contemporary interest in cross-cultural psychology is the individualism–collectivism dichotomy.
	Trait-situation interaction	Mischel's *Personality and Assessment* ushered in an attack on trait theory. Basically, the criticism was that personality varies according to the situation more than the trait theorists acknowledge. Today most personality psychologists are interactionists. They believe that personality is determined by a combination of traits or person variables and the situation. Cross-cultural psychologists believe the situation involves both the immediate setting and the broader cultural context.
Personality Research	Its nature	In addition to personality theories, the empirical research side of the field of personality is equally important. Personality research areas are far-ranging. These areas of personality research involve: self-esteem; the big five factors; and stability and change in personality across the life span.
Personality Assessment	Its nature	Psychologists use a number of tests and measures to assess personality. These measures are often tied to the psychologists' theoretical orientations. Personality tests were basically designed to measure stable, enduring aspects of personality.
	Types of measures	Projective tests use ambiguous stimuli to encourage an individual to project her personality into the stimuli. They are designed to assess the unconscious aspects of personality. The Rorschach is the most widely used projective test; its effectiveness is controversial. Self-report measures are designed to assess an individual's traits; the most widely used self-report measure is the MMPI, an empirically keyed test. Behavioral assessment tries to obtain more objective information about personality through observation of behavior and its environmental ties. Cognitive assessment increasingly is used as part of the behavioral assessment process.
Comparison of Personality Theories	Innate vs. learned, conscious vs. unconscious, and internally vs. externally determined	Three important issues addressed by personality theories are the degree to which personality is innate versus learned, conscious versus unconscious, and internally versus externally determined. Disagreements and agreements about these issues are found in psychoanalytic, behavioral, humanistic, and trait theories.

Critical Thinking About Behavior

Labeling and Justice

> *The very purpose of existence is to reconcile the glowing opinion we hold of ourselves with the appalling things that other people think about us.*
>
> **Quentin Crisp**

When you began this chapter, you constructed a list of characteristics that you thought captured your personality. You were challenged to think about whether the traits you selected were representative, enduring, consistent, and realistic. You were questioned about whether others would describe you in the same way.

Compassion could have been one of the traits you selected. Suppose we wanted to develop a simple self-report inventory that would allow the measurement of some aspects of compassion. Walter Mischel suggests that traits interact with situations. Suppose, to measure your compassion, we asked you which of the following acts you would perform:

- Agreeing to a request to sponsor a child in a technologically disadvantaged country
- Intervening in a friend's drug or alcohol problem
- Offering money to the homeless when they confront you personally
- Taking in stray animals
- Sacrificing your own plans to help a friend
- Volunteering assistance to a driver with a disabled car
- Alerting a friend who has some lunch stuck between his teeth
- Letting a sick friend copy your homework
- Giving away all your possessions to a needy organization

As you can see, measuring the trait of compassion with this inventory would be extremely difficult. The actions listed in this self-report checklist could all be compassionate in some circumstances, but it would certainly be difficult to evaluate a person's compassion using responses to this list. For example, you could endlessly adopt stray animals, but there are practical constraints on how much compassion you could show using this behavior. You could let a friend copy your homework in the compassion of the moment, but that judgment might be far from compassionate in the long run because your friend will be unlikely to learn something that could be useful in the future. Could we rule out your having any compassion if you indicated you wouldn't perform any of the actions on the list? Probably not. Although our compassion self-report checklist has face validity (that is, each item relates to compassion), it is unlikely that we could use it as it stands to conduct valid research on the trait.

Making judgments about traits is difficult not only in research situations; it can be surprisingly challenging in life. Although we regularly make trait attributions to help us understand situations, we might not sufficiently capture the complexity of the situation. The use of traits to explain behavior can help us be efficient processors of reality, but it is doubtful that it helps us make accurate or fair-minded interpretations. Sometimes the labels lead us to make premature judgments and turn our attention elsewhere—we assign a trait as the reason for an action and move on.

How can this knowledge help us to be more effective critical thinkers in relation to judgments about personality? We should be able to apply psychological concepts to enhance personal adaptation by incorporating the following skills:

Reserve judgment, especially when making negative attributions. How important is it to resolve a behavioral question by attributing someone's actions to a trait? In many situations, labeling requires making a judgment that we may later regret. In the tradition of Skinner, it may be more helpful to think about and describe specific behaviors involved in the situation than dispense with the situation by assigning dysfunctional traits as the cause. For example, marriage therapists often help couples learn to describe the behaviors that are upsetting to them rather than continue to use hurtful and unhelpful labeling (such as "You are inconsiderate and insecure").

Recognize the boundaries of labels. When we feel compelled to make trait judgments, it is still helpful to remember the context in which the behavior occurred and confine the judgment to that circumstance. For example, if you think of your father as "mean," it will be useful to identify the circumstances in which he is mean. He might be mean when he has not gotten enough sleep or when he is trying to watch his weight. This restricted use of the label recognizes that there are likely to be many circumstances in which he is not mean, which brings into question the fairness of the use of the term.

Abandon expectations about consistency. As you read in this chapter, many other cultures may be less intense about defining, categorizing, and judging personality features. This attitude may be a function of living in collectivistic cultures where there is no particular advantage in labeling others' traits. Richard Brislin (1993) believes that enduring relationships in collectivistic cultures may show greater tolerance about inconsistencies in human behavior. Even if we don't live in a collectivistic culture, we can save some frustration if, like collectivists, we do not expect human beings to be consistent across all situations.

Overview

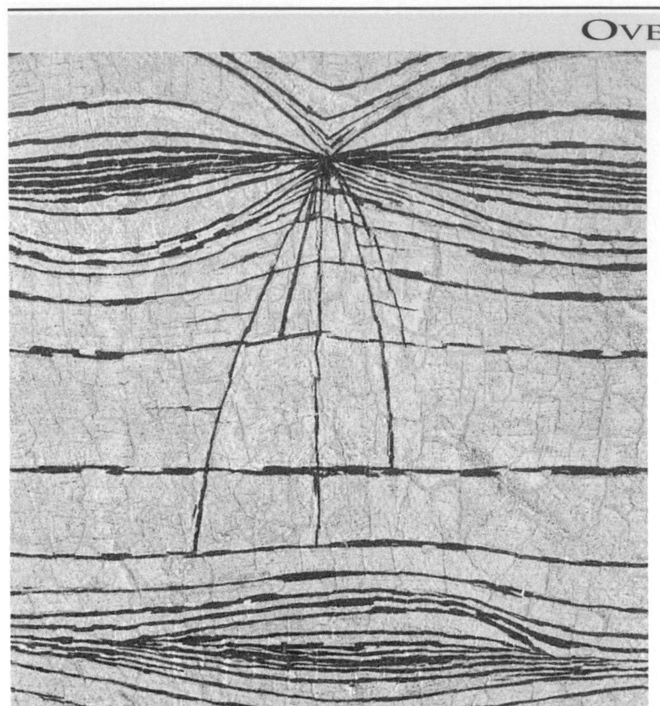

We began this chapter by evaluating what personality is and then considered a number of perspectives on personality. Our coverage of psychoanalytic perspectives focused on Freud's theory, psychoanalytic dissenters and revisionists, and an evaluation of the psychoanalytic perspectives. Our discussion of the behavioral and social learning perspectives included Skinner's behaviorism, social learning theory, and an evaluation. Our overview of the phenomenological and humanistic perspectives emphasized Rogers' approach and Maslow's approach, as well as an evaluation. We also described personality type theory, trait theories, recent developments in trait theory, and trait-situation interaction. We examined personality research by considering such topics as self-esteem, the big five factors in personality, and stability and change in personality across the life span. We studied how personality can be assessed, including projective tests, self-report tests, and behavioral assessment. Toward the end of the chapter we compared the main personality theories. Remember that you can obtain an overall summary of the chapter by again studying the concept tables on pages 412, 419, and 434.

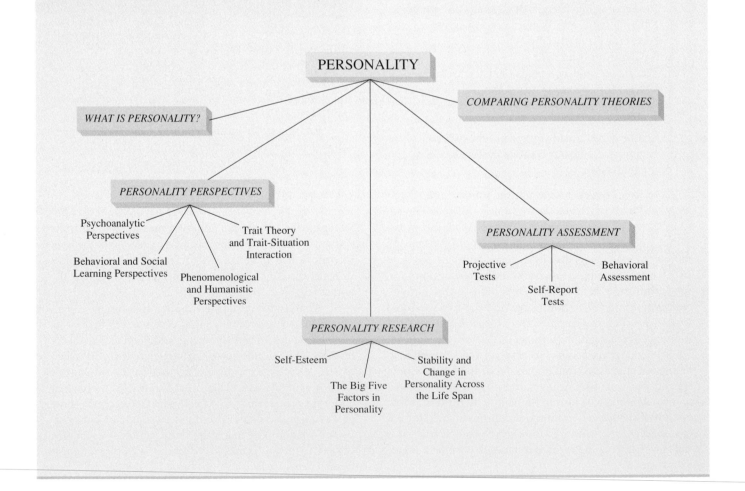

PERSONALITY

- *WHAT IS PERSONALITY?*
- *PERSONALITY PERSPECTIVES*
  - Psychoanalytic Perspectives
  - Behavioral and Social Learning Perspectives
  - Phenomenological and Humanistic Perspectives
  - Trait Theory and Trait-Situation Interaction
- *PERSONALITY RESEARCH*
  - Self-Esteem
  - The Big Five Factors in Personality
  - Stability and Change in Personality Across the Life Span
- *PERSONALITY ASSESSMENT*
  - Projective Tests
  - Self-Report Tests
  - Behavioral Assessment
- *COMPARING PERSONALITY THEORIES*

Key Terms

personality The enduring, distinctive thoughts, emotions, and behaviors that characterize the way an individual adapts to the world. p. 402

id The Freudian structure of personality that consists of instincts, which are the person's reservoir of psychic energy. p. 403

pleasure principle The Freudian concept that the id always seeks pleasure and avoids pain. p. 403

ego The Freudian structure of personality that deals with the demands of reality; the ego is called the executive branch of personality because it makes decisions based on rationality. p. 403

reality principle The Freudian principle that the ego tries to bring the individual pleasure within the norms of society. p. 403

superego The Freudian structure of personality that is the moral branch of personality. The superego takes into account whether something is right or wrong. p. 403

defense mechanisms According to psychoanalytic theory, unconscious methods of dealing with conflict; the ego distorts reality, thereby protecting itself from anxiety. p. 405

repression The most powerful and pervasive defense mechanism, according to Freud; it works to push unacceptable id impulses out of awareness and back into the unconscious mind. p. 405

rationalization According to psychoanalytic theory, the defense mechanism that occurs when the real motive for an individual's behavior is not accepted by the ego and is replaced by a sort of cover motive. p. 405

displacement The psychoanalytic defense mechanism that occurs when an individual shifts unacceptable feelings from one object to another, more acceptable object. p. 405

sublimation The psychoanalytic defense mechanism that occurs when a socially approved course of action replaces an unacceptable impulse. p. 405

projection The psychoanalytic defense mechanism that occurs when we attribute our own shortcomings, problems, and faults to others. p. 405

reaction formation The psychoanalytic defense mechanism that occurs when we express an unacceptable impulse by transforming it into its opposite. p. 405

regression The psychoanalytic defense mechanism that occurs when we behave in a way that is characteristic of a previous developmental level. p. 406

erogenous zones According to Freud, parts of the body that have especially strong pleasure-giving qualities at particular stages of development. p. 406

fixation The psychoanalytic defense mechanism that occurs when the individual remains locked in an earlier developmental stage because needs are under- or overgratified. p. 406

oral stage The term Freud used to describe development during the first 18 months of life, in which the infant's pleasure centers on the mouth. p. 406

anal stage Freud's second stage of development, occurring between 1½ and 3 years of age, in which the child's greatest pleasure involves the anus or the eliminative functions associated with it. p. 406

phallic stage Freud's third stage of development, which occurs between the ages of 3 and 6. Its name comes from the Latin word *phallus,* which means "penis." During the phallic stage, pleasure focuses on the genitals as the child discovers that self-stimulation is enjoyable. p. 406

Oedipus complex Freud's idea that the young child develops an intense desire to replace the parent of the same sex and to enjoy the affections of the opposite-sex parent. p. 406

latency stage The fourth Freudian stage of development, occurring approximately between 6 years of age and puberty; the child represses all interest in sexuality and develops social and intellectual skills. p. 406

genital stage The fifth Freudian stage of development, occurring from puberty on; the genital stage is the time of sexual reawakening, and the source of sexual pleasure now becomes someone outside of the family. p. 406

collective unconscious According to Jung, the impersonal, deepest layer of the unconscious mind, which is shared by all human beings because of their ancestral past. p. 409

archetype The primordial influences in every individual's collective unconscious; Jung's psychoanalytic theory is often referred to as "depth psychology" because archetypes rest deep within the unconscious mind, far deeper than the Freudian personal unconscious. p. 409

individual psychology The name Adler gave to his theory of psychology to emphasize the uniqueness of every individual. p. 410

striving for superiority According to Jung, the human motivation to adapt, improve, and master the environment. p. 410

compensation Adler's term for the individual's attempt to overcome imagined or real inferiorities or weaknesses by developing one's abilities. p. 410

overcompensation Adler's term for the individual's attempt to deny rather than acknowledge a real situation or the individual's exaggerated effort to conceal a weakness. p. 410

inferiority complex Adler's name for exaggerated feelings of inadequacy. p. 410

superiority complex Adler's concept of exaggerated self-importance designed to mask feelings of inferiority. p. 410

phenomenological perspective The perspective that stresses the importance of our perceptions of ourselves and our world in understanding personality; it emphasizes that for each individual, the world is what that individual perceives. p. 415

humanistic perspective The most widely adopted phenomenological approach to personality; it stresses personal growth, choosing one's own destiny, and positive qualities. p. 415

conditional positive regard Rogers's term for love and praise being withheld if the individual does not conform to parental or social standards. p. 415

self-concept A central theme in the views of Rogers and other humanists; individuals' overall perceptions of their abilities, behavior, and personality. p. 415

unconditional positive regard Rogers's term for accepting, valuing, and being positive toward another person regardless of the other person's behavior. p. 415

hierarchy of motives According to Maslow, the main kinds of needs that each individual must satisfy, in this sequence: physiological needs, safety needs, the need for love and belongingness, the need for esteem, cognitive needs, aesthetic needs, and the need for self-actualization. p. 416

self-actualization According to Maslow, the highest and most elusive human need; the motivation to develop to one's full potential as a human being. p. 416

endomorph Sheldon's term for a soft, round, large-stomached person who is relaxed, gregarious, and food loving. p. 419

mesomorph Sheldon's term for a strong, athletic, and muscular person who is energetic, assertive, and courageous. p. 419

ectomorph Sheldon's term for a tall, thin, fragile person who is fearful, introverted, and restrained. p. 419

somatotype theory Sheldon's theory that precise charts reveal distinct body types, which in turn are associated with certain personality characteristics. p. 419

trait theories Theories that propose that people have broad dispositions (traits) that are reflected in the basic ways they behave, such as whether they are outgoing and friendly or whether they are dominant and assertive. p. 420

individualism Giving priority to personal goals rather than group goals; emphasizing values that serve the self, such as feeling good, personal achievement and distinction, and independence. p. 421

collectivism Emphasizing values that serve the group by subordinating personal goals to preserve group integrity, interdependence of members, and harmonious relationships. p. 421

situationism Mischel's view that personality often varies from one context to another. p. 422

self-esteem The evaluative and affective dimension of self-concept, also referred to as self-worth or self-image. p. 423

longitudinal study A research strategy in which the same individuals are tested over a period of time, usually at least several years. p. 425

Barnum effect If you make your descriptions broad enough, any person can fit them. p. 427

projective test A test that presents individuals with an ambiguous stimulus and then asks them to describe it or tell a story about it. Projective tests are based on the assumption that the ambiguity of the stimulus allows individuals to project into it their feelings, desires, needs, and attitudes. p. 427

Rorschach inkblot test The most well known projective test, developed in 1921 by Swiss psychiatrist Hermann Rorschach. It uses individuals' perceptions of inkblots to determine their personality. p. 427

Thematic Apperception Test (TAT) A projective test designed to elicit stories that reveal something about an individual's personality; developed by Henry Murray and Christina Morgan in the 1930s. p. 428

graphology The use of handwriting analysis to determine an individual's personality. p. 428

self-report tests Tests that assess personality traits by asking what they are; these tests are not designed to reveal unconscious personality characteristics. p. 428

face validity An assumption that the content of test items is a good indicator of an individual's personality. p. 428

social desirability A factor that can motivate individuals to say what they think the interviewer wants to hear or what they think will make them look better. p. 430

empirically keyed test A test that relies on its items to predict a particular criterion; unlike tests based on face validity, empirically keyed tests make no assumptions about the nature of the items. p. 430

Minnesota Multiphasic Personality Inventory (MMPI) The self-report personality test most widely used in clinical and research settings. p. 430

Resources and Readings in Psychology

Control Your Depression (1992, rev. ed.)
by Peter Lewinsohn, Ricardo Muñoz, Mary Youngren, and Antonnete Zeiss
New York: Fireside

Control Your Depression tells you how to reduce your depression by learning self-control techniques, relaxation training, pleasant activities, planning ahead, modifying self-defeating thinking patterns, and other behavioral/cognitive strategies.

Gentle Roads to Survival (1991)
by Andre Auw
Lower Lake, CA: Aslan

In *Gentle Roads to Survival,* Auw presents a guide to making self-healing choices in difficult circumstances. Auw, a psychologist who was a close associate of Carl Rogers, tells you how to become a survivor.

Journal of Personality Assessment

This research journal publishes articles on many aspects of personality assessment, including empirically-keyed tests, such as the MMPI, and projective techniques, such as the Rorschach.

Journal of Personality and Social Psychology

This prestigious journal publishes research articles in the following areas: attitudes and cognition, interpersonal relations and group processes, and personality processes and individual differences.

Man and His Symbols (1964)
by Carl Jung
Garden City, NY: Doubleday

This book includes the writings of Jung and four of his disciples; Jung's ideas are applied to anthropology, literature, art, and dreams.

Man, the Manipulator (1972)
by Everett Shostrum
New York: Bantam

This paperback presents humanistic ideas about the route from manipulation to self-actualization. Many case studies are included.

Mental Measurements Yearbook (1992, 11th ed.)
edited by Jack Kramer and Jane Conoley
Lincoln: University of Nebraska Press

This voluminous resource provides details about a wide range of personality tests.

Personality (1992, 2nd ed.)
by Christopher Peterson
Fort Worth, TX: Harcourt Brace

This well-written textbook on personality includes many applications to real-world issues.

Personality Research, Methods, and Theory (1995)
Patrick Shrout and Susan Fiske (eds.)
Hillsdale, NJ.: Erlbaum

This volume examines current thinking about what can be known about personality, how concepts related to personality can best be measured, and how to approach research problems in specific areas of personality. Topics include the big-five trait factors, cultural dimensions, and conceptualizing and measuring self-esteem.

Psychological Testing of Hispanics (1992)
by Kurt Geisinger
Washington, DC: American Psychological Association

This book addresses a number of issues related to the psychological testing of Hispanics, including testing in clinical settings and the workplace.

Chapter

Abnormal Psychology

Paul Klee
Strange Garden, 1923, detail

Abnormal Psychology

Chapter Outline

Chapter Boxes

He raves; his words are loose as heaps of sand, and scattered from sense. So high he's mounted on his airy throne, that now the wind has got into his head, and turns his brain to frenzy.

—**John Dryden**

This wretched brain gave way, And I became a wreck, At random driven, Without one glimpse of reason.

—**Thomas Moore**

Images of Psychology

Hemingway's Depression and Suicide

Even before his father's suicide, the American author Ernest Hemingway seemed obsessed by the theme of self-destruction. As a young boy he enjoyed reading Stevenson's "The Suicide Club." At one point in his adult life, Hemingway said he would rather go out in a blaze of light than have his body worn out by age and his illusions shattered.

Hemingway's suicidal thoughts sometimes coincided with his marital crises. Just before marrying his first wife, Hadley, Hemingway became apprehensive about his new responsibilities and alarmed her by the mention of suicide. Five years later, during a crisis with his second wife, Pauline, he calmly told her he would have committed suicide if their love affair had not been resolved happily. Hemingway was strangely comforted by morbid thoughts of death. When he was feeling down and out, Hemingway would think about death and various ways of dying; the best way he thought, unless he could arrange to die in his sleep, would be to jump off an ocean liner at night.

Hemingway committed suicide in his sixties. His suicide made people wonder why a man with such good looks, sporting skills, friends, women, wealth, fame, genius, and a Nobel Prize would kill himself. His actual life did not reflect the glamorous one others assigned to him. Rather, Hemingway had developed a combination of physical and mental disorders. He had neglected his health for some years, suffering from weight loss, skin disease, alcoholism, diabetes, hypertension, and impotence. His body in a shambles, he dreaded becoming an invalid and the slow death this would bring. At this point, the severely depressed Hemingway was losing his memory and no longer could write. One month before his suicide, Hemingway said, "Staying healthy. Working good. Eating and drinking with friends. Enjoying myself in bed. I haven't any of them" (Meyer, 1985, p. 559).

Preview

Mental disorders know no social and economic boundaries. They find their way into the lives of the rich and famous and the poor and the unknown. In this chapter, we will study several mental disorders, including the depression that troubled the life of Ernest Hemingway. We begin by examining some basic questions about the nature of abnormal behavior, then turn our attention to the following mental disorders: anxiety, somatoform, dissociative, mood, schizophrenic, personality, and substance-use. To conclude, we will evaluate the legal aspects of mental disorders.

Abnormal Behavior: What Is It? What Causes It? How Can It Be Classified?

Were Hemingway's depression and suicide abnormal? If so, what made them abnormal? What causes abnormal behavior? How can we classify abnormal behavior? We will consider each of these important questions about abnormal behavior in turn.

What Is Abnormal Behavior?

Defining what is normal and what is abnormal is not an easy task. Is behavior abnormal when it is *atypical?* Consider Albert Einstein, Charles Barkley, and Barbara Walters, each of whom we think of as atypical. But we don't think Einstein was abnormal because he was a genius, or that Barkley is abnormal because he is such a masterful basketball player (although some might consider his temperamental outbursts unacceptable), or that Walters is abnormal because she is one of television's most talented interviewers.

Simply labeling behavior that is atypical as "abnormal" ignores the fact that what is atypical behavior at one point in history may be considered thoroughly acceptable at another, and that what is considered atypical behavior also varies from culture to culture. Early in this century, for example, many Americans believed masturbation was sinful and caused everything from warts to insanity. Today only a few people think of masturbation as wicked and most people accept it as part of normal sexuality. And women of the Mangaian culture in the South Sea Islands, for instance, initiate adolescent males in sexual techniques. These young men are then encouraged to practice their skills with adolescent females. But in the United States such behavior probably would be looked upon askance. In some cultures, people go about their daily activities with little or no clothes on. If we saw someone naked walking down a city street in the United States, we probably would consider such behavior inappropriate; we also might think that such behavior signaled that the person was in mental distress.

If being atypical does not make an individual abnormal, what does? **Abnormal behavior** *is behavior that is maladaptive and harmful.* Hemingway's suicide was maladaptive and harmful, and thus, was an abnormal behavior. Behavior that is *maladaptive* and *harmful* fails to promote the well-being, growth, and fulfillment of the person, and ultimately, others. The maladaptive and harmful behavior takes many forms—such as depression, having bizarre, irrational beliefs, assaulting others, and becoming addicted to drugs. These abnormal behaviors interfere with the ability to function effectively in the world, and can harm the well-being of others.

Shortly we will discuss how mental health professionals classify psychological disorders. You will learn that in the latest classification, some disorders were added and some were dropped, indicating changing standards of acceptability over time.

Maybe it's not me, y'know? . . . Maybe it's the rest of the herd that's gone insane."

What Causes Abnormal Behavior?

What causes people to become abnormal, to behave in maladaptive and harmful ways? The causes include biological, psychological, and sociocultural factors.

The Biological Approach

Proponents of the biological approach believe abnormal behavior is due to some physical malfunctioning in the body, especially the brain. If an individual behaves in an uncontrollable manner, is out of touch with reality, or is severely depressed, biological factors are the culprits. Today scientists and researchers who adopt the biological approach often focus on brain processes and genetic factors as the causes of abnormal behavior. In the biological approach, drug therapy is frequently used to treat abnormal behavior.

The **medical model,** *also called the disease model, was the forerunner of the biological approach; the medical model states that abnormality is a disease or illness precipitated by internal physical causes.* From this perspective, abnormalities are called mental *illnesses* and the individuals afflicted are *patients* in *hospitals* who are treated by *doctors.*

The Psychological and Sociocultural Approaches

While the biological approach provides an important perspective for understanding abnormal behavior, many psychologists believe it underestimates the importance of psychological and sociocultural factors such as emotional turmoil, inappropriate learning, distorted thoughts, and inadequate relationships (Gardner, 1995). Theories of personality—psychoanalytic, behavioral and social learning, and humanistic—provide insight about the nature of abnormal as well as normal behavior.

Most experts on abnormal behavior agree that many psychological disorders are universal, appearing in most cultures (Al-Issa, 1982). However, the frequency and intensity of abnormal behavior varies across cultures. Variations in disorders are related to social, economic, technological, religious, and other features of cultures (Draguns, 1990). Some disorders appear to be especially culture-bound. To learn about several of the more unusual culture-bound disorders, see table 1.

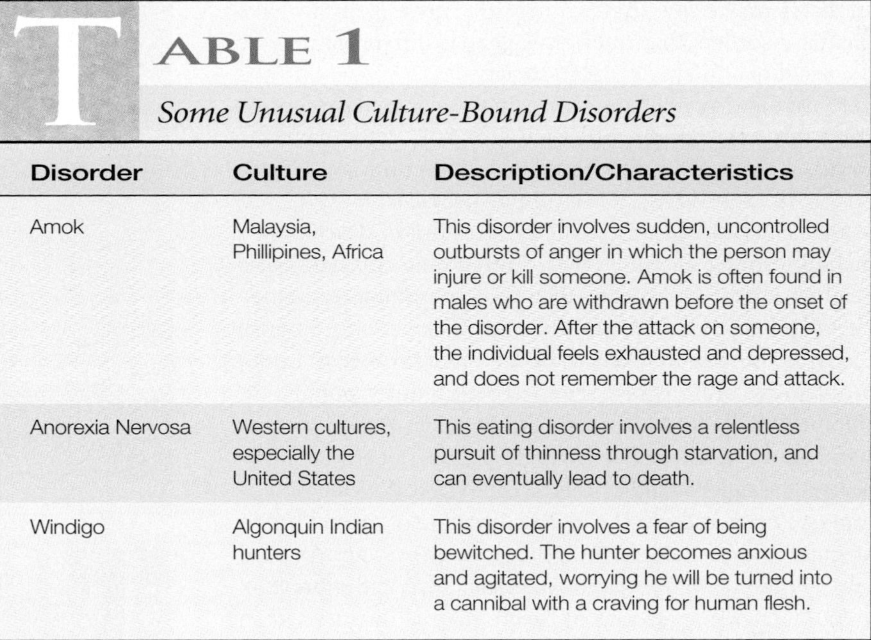

TABLE 1

Some Unusual Culture-Bound Disorders

Disorder	Culture	Description/Characteristics
Amok	Malaysia, Phillipines, Africa	This disorder involves sudden, uncontrolled outbursts of anger in which the person may injure or kill someone. Amok is often found in males who are withdrawn before the onset of the disorder. After the attack on someone, the individual feels exhausted and depressed, and does not remember the rage and attack.
Anorexia Nervosa	Western cultures, especially the United States	This eating disorder involves a relentless pursuit of thinness through starvation, and can eventually lead to death.
Windigo	Algonquin Indian hunters	This disorder involves a fear of being bewitched. The hunter becomes anxious and agitated, worrying he will be turned into a cannibal with a craving for human flesh.

How prevalent are mental disorders in the United States today? A study of 18,571 people randomly selected from five United States cities—New Haven, Connecticut; Baltimore, Maryland; St. Louis, Missouri; Piedmont, North Carolina; and Los Angeles, California—found that more than 15 percent had suffered from a mental disorder during the previous month (Robins & Regier, 1990).

For the 1-month incidence of mental disorders, data were also analyzed separately for men and women. Women had a slightly higher overall rate of mental disorders than men (16.6 percent versus 15.4 percent). Women had higher rates of mood disorders (for example, depression) (9.7 percent versus 4.7 percent); men had higher rates of substance-use disorders (6.3 percent versus 1.6 percent) and antisocial personality disorders (0.8 percent versus 0.2 percent).

Surprisingly, only one-third of the individuals reporting mental disorders had received treatment in the previous 6 months. The frequency of many mental disorders was much higher than anticipated because such a large percentage of individuals with a mental disorder had never gone for treatment (Robins & Regier, 1990).

Women tend to be diagnosed as having disorders that typify traditional stereotypes of females. In particular, women are more likely than men to suffer from anxiety disorders and depression, disorders with symptoms that are internalized, or turned inward. Conversely, men are socialized to direct their energy toward the outside world—that is, to externalize their feelings and thoughts—and are more likely to show disorders involving aggression and substance abuse.

More needs to be said about the finding mentioned above that women have higher overall rates of mental disorders than men. Several explanations have been given as to why today's women are diagnosed and treated for mental disorders at a higher rate than men (Paludi, 1995). One possibility is that women do not have more mental disorders than men do, but that women are simply more likely to behave in ways that others label as mental disorders. For example, women have been taught to express their emotions, while men have been trained to control them. If women express feelings of sorrow and sadness, some individuals may quickly conclude that women are more mentally disordered than men are. Thus, the difference in the rates of mental disorders could involve the possibility that women more freely display and discuss their emotional problems than men do. A second explanation of the gender difference in the diagnosis of mental disorders focuses on women's unequal social position and greater discrimination. Many women are more likely than men to experience certain trauma-inducing circumstances, such as incest, sexual harassment, rape, and marital abuse. The abuse many women experience may increase their emotional problems. A third explanation of the gender difference in the diagnosis of mental disorders is that women are often placed in a "double-bind" situation in our society. For example, women can be labeled as mentally disordered for either overconforming or underconforming to feminine gender-role stereotypes. That is, a woman who is overdependent, overly emotional, and less rational is overconforming to the traditional feminine gender-role stereotype. On the other hand, a woman who is independent, values her career more than her family, doesn't express emotions, and acts in a worldly and self-confident manner is underconforming to feminine gender-role stereotypes. In either case, the woman might be labeled mentally disordered. In sum, even though statistics may show that women are more likely to have mental disorders than men, this gender difference may be the result of antifemale bias in society.

In the United States, variations in mental disorders involve not only gender, but such factors as socioeconomic status, urbanization, neighborhood, and ethnicity (Neighbors & Jackson, 1996). For example, people who live closest to the center of a city have the greatest risk of developing a mental disorder (Suinn, 1984). Ethnic minority status also heightens the risk of mental distress. For example, one study on hospitalization rates found that persons with Spanish surnames were more likely to be admitted for mental health problems in areas where they were a minority population (Bloom, 1975). Another study conducted in New York City supports this finding: The fewer the number of ethnic members in an area—whether they were White, African American, or Puerto Rican—the higher their rate of mental health hospitalization (Rabkin, 1979). Yet another study revealed that Whites living in African American areas had more than a 300 percent higher rate of severe mental disorders than Whites living in White neighborhoods. Similarly, African Americans living in predominantly White areas had a 32 percent higher rate than African Americans living in African American neighborhoods (Mintz & Schwartz, 1964). All of these studies, however, are correlational in nature; they do not determine cause and effect. It is possible that people who are mentally disordered, or those predisposed to mental disorders, tend to choose communities in which they are the minority, or it may be that minority group status produces stress and its related disorders.

But knowing that people from poor minority neighborhoods have high rates of disorders does not tell us why they have such rates. Does poverty cause pathology? Or is poverty a form of pathology for middle-class diagnosticians who are unaware of what behaviors and self-protective beliefs are necessary to survive in harsh circumstances? Does racial discrimination cause individuals to become mentally disordered? Or does it make members of the majority group label the discriminated as mentally disordered in order to feel less guilty about discriminating against them? Researchers who are sensitive to, and comfortable with, these cultural dynamics are vital to the search for answers to these questions (Broman, 1996).

An Interactionist Approach

When considering an individual's behavior, whether abnormal or normal, it is important to remember the complexity of human nature and the multiple influences on behavior. Neither the biological nor the psychological and sociocultural approaches independently capture this complexity. Abnormal behavior is influenced by biological factors (brain processes and heredity, for example), by psychological factors (emotional turmoil and distorted thoughts, for example), and by social factors (inadequate relationships, for example). These factors often interact to produce abnormal behavior.

(a)

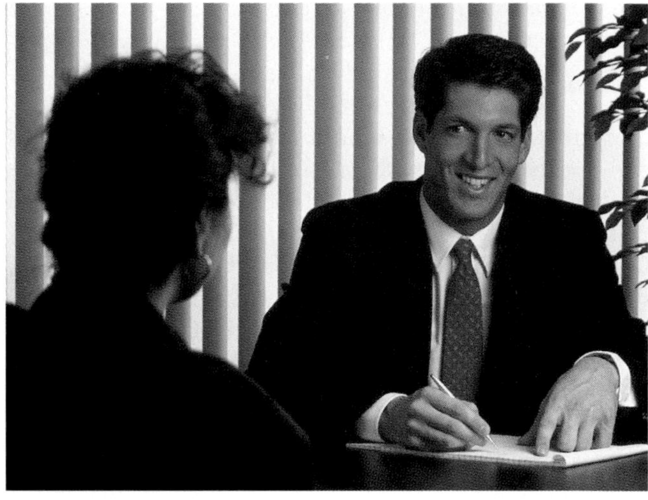

(b)

(a) People living in poor minority neighborhoods have high rates of mental disorders, but knowing this does not tell us why they have such high rates. Does poverty cause pathology, or is poverty a form of pathology for middle-class diagnosticians who are unaware of what behaviors and self-protective beliefs are necessary to survive in harsh contexts? Does racial discrimination cause individuals to develop mental disorders? (b) Effective therapy can take place when the client and therapist are from different sociocultural backgrounds. However, barriers to communication, which can develop in such circumstances, can destroy and undermine the effectiveness of therapy. Among the barriers are language differences, class-bound values, and culture-bound values.

How Can Abnormal Behavior Be Classified?

Ever since human history began, people have suffered from diseases, sadness, and bizarre behavior. And for almost as long, healers have tried to treat and cure them. The classification of mental disorders goes back to the ancient Egyptians and Greeks, and has its roots in biology and medicine.

The first classification of mental disorders in the United States, based on the census data of 1840, used one category for all mental disorders. This one category included both the mentally retarded and the insane.

In the twentieth century, the American Psychiatric Association (APA) developed the first major classification of mental disorders in the United States. The *Diagnostic and Statistical Manual of Mental Disorders,* first published in 1952, included better definitions of mental disorders than previous classification efforts. A revised edition, the DSM-II, with more systematic assistance from expert diagnosticians, appeared in 1968. The APA published a third edition, the DSM-III, in 1980, and a revision of that manual, the DSM-III-R, in 1987. Published in 1994, the current DSM-IV emphasizes refined empirical support of diagnostic categories (Wilson, 1993).

Before we discuss the system most widely used to classify mental disorders, we will explore the benefits of classifying mental disorders. First, a classification system gives professionals a shorthand system for communicating with each other. For example, if one psychologist says in a case review that her client has a panic disorder and another psychologist says that his client has a generalized anxiety disorder, the two psychologists understand which disorders these clients have been diagnosed as having. Second, a classification system can help psychologists make predictions about disorders; it provides information about the likelihood that a disorder will occur, which individuals are most susceptible to the disorder, progress of the disorder once it appears, and the prognosis for effective treatment (Meehl, 1986).

Using the DSM-IV

Continuing changes in the DSM reflect advancements in knowledge about the classification of mental disorders. On the basis of research and clinical experience, the DSM-IV added, dropped, or revised categories, sometimes generating controversy among the diagnosticians who rely on the classification system.

For example, the DSM-III dropped two important categories that have some historic importance: the categories of neurosis and psychosis. The term **neurotic** *refers to relatively mild mental disorders in which the individual has not lost contact with reality.* Individuals who are extremely anxious, troubled, and unhappy may still be able to carry out their everyday functions and have a clear perception of reality; these individuals would be classified as neurotic. The term **psychotic** *refers to severe mental disorders in which the individual has lost contact with reality.* The thinking and perception of psychotic individuals are so distorted that they live in a world far removed from others. Psychotic individuals might hear voices that are not present or think they are famous individuals, such as Jesus Christ or Napoleon. The DSM classification system dropped the terms *neurotic* and *psychotic* because they were too broad and ill-defined to be diagnostic labels. Although the DSM system dropped the labels, clinicians still sometimes use the labels as a convenient way of referring to relatively mild or relatively severe mental disorders, respectively.

The **DSM-IV** *(the* Diagnostic and Statistical Manual of Mental Disorders, *fourth edition) is the most recent major classification of mental disorders; it contains eighteen major classifications and describes more than 200 specific disorders.*

One feature of the DSM-IV is its **multiaxial system,** *which classifies individuals on the basis of five dimensions, or "axes," that include the individual's history and highest level of functioning in the last year. This system ensures that the individual will not merely be assigned to a mental disorder category, but instead will be characterized in terms of a number of clinical factors.* Following is a description of the axes:

Axis I: The primary classification or diagnosis of the disorder (for example, fear of people). This axis includes all disorders except for the personality disorders.

Axis II: Personality disorders, long-standing problems in relating to others (for example, a person with long-standing antisocial personality disorder), or developmental problems affecting the adjustment of children and adolescents.

Axis III: General medical conditions that might be relevant in understanding the mental disorder (for example, an individual's history of disease, such as a cardiovascular problem).

Axis IV: Psychosocial stressors in the individual's recent past that might have contributed to the mental problem (for example, divorce, death of a parent, or loss of job).

Axis V: Individual's highest level of functioning in the last year. For example, does the individual have a history of poor work and relationship patterns, or have there been times when the individual performed effectively at work and enjoyed positive interpersonal relationships? If functioning has been high at some point in the past, prognosis for recovery is enhanced.

What are some of the changes in the DSM-IV? The more than 200 mental health professionals who contributed to the development of the DSM-IV were a much more diverse group than their predecessors, who were mainly White male psychiatrists. More women, ethnic minorities, and nonpsychiatrists, such as clinical psychologists, were involved in the construction of the DSM-IV (Frances & Ross, 1996). (Nathan, 1994), and greater attention was given to gender- and ethnicity-related diagnosis. For example, the DSM-IV contains an appendix entitled "Guidelines for Cultural Formation and Glossary of Culture-Related Syndromes" (Mezzich, Fabegra, & Kleinman, in press). Also, the DSM-IV is accompanied by a number of sourcebooks that present the empirical base of the DSM-IV (Francis & Ross, 1996). In previous versions of the DSM, the reasons for diagnostic changes were not always explicit, so the evidence that led to their formulation was never available for public evaluation.

The Controversy Surrounding the DSM-IV

The most controversial aspect of the DSM-IV continues an issue that has been present since the publication of the DSM-I in 1952. Although more nonpsychiatrists than in previous editions were responsible for drafting the DSM-IV, it still reflects a medical, or disease, model (Clark, Watson, & Reynolds, 1995). Classifying individuals based on their symptoms and using medical terminology continues the dominance of the psychiatric tradition of thinking about mental disorders in terms of illness and disease. This strategy implies an internal cause that is more or less independent of external or environmental factors (Adams & Cassidy, 1993). Thus, even though researchers have begun to illuminate the complex interaction of genetic, neurobiological, cognitive, and environmental factors in the DSM disorders, the DSM-IV continues to espouse the medical/disease model of mental disorders (First, Frances, & Pincus, 1995; Frances, First, & Pincus, 1995; Nathan, 1994).

The DSM-IV is also controversial because it continues to label as mental disorders what are often thought of as everyday problems. For example, under learning or academic skills disorders, the DSM-IV includes the categories of reading disorder, mathematics disorder, and disorder of written expression. Under substance-related disorders, the DSM-IV includes the category of caffeine-use disorders. We don't usually think of these problems as mental disorders, but including them implies that such "normal behavior" should be treated as mental disorders. The developers of the DSM system argue that mental health providers have been treating many problems not included in earlier editions of DSM and that the classification system should be more comprehensive. One practical reason for including everyday problems in living in the DSM-IV is to help more individuals get their health insurance companies to pay for professional help. Most health insurance companies reimburse their clients only for disorders listed in the DSM-IV system.

Another issue frequently raised by the DSM's critics is that it is too responsive to changing political issues. One example is the decision by the DSM-III Task Force to endorse an earlier vote of the American Psychiatric Association to remove homosexuality from the nomenclature and replace it with a limited diagnosis applicable only to persons who are distressed by their homosexual orientation. Another example is the decision by the DSM-IV Task Force to rename late luteal phase dysphoric premenstrual dysphoric disorder, corresponding to premenstrual syndrome, and retain it in an appendix rather than incorporate it into the regular nomenclature.

Another criticism of the DSM-IV, and indeed of this type of classification system in general, is that the system focuses strictly on pathology and problems, with a bias toward finding something wrong with anyone who becomes the object of diagnostic study. A classic study by David Rosenhan (1973) demonstrated how strong the bias is toward attaching a label of mental disorder to someone. Rosenhan asked eight "normal" individuals to go to the admissions desk of a psychiatric hospital and complain that they heard an unidentified voice saying, "Empty," "Thud," and "Hollow." The psychiatric staff interviewed the eight individuals who were honest about their life histories. All eight of the "normal" individuals were immediately admitted by the hospitals. They behaved normally while in the psychiatric ward. Seven of the eight were diagnosed as schizophrenic, listed as such on their records, and labeled as schizophrenics in remission when they were discharged. Rosenhan concluded that normal people are not noticeably sane.

Because labels can become self-fulfilling prophecies, emphasizing strengths as well as weaknesses might help to destigmatize labels such as *borderline schizophrenic* or *ex-mental patient.* It would also help to provide clues to treatment that promote mental competence rather than working only to reduce mental distress.

The DSM-IV was developed by American mental health professionals. Most mental health professionals in other countries adopt the International Classification of Disease (ICD) guidelines established by the World Health Organization. The tenth edition of the ICD (ICD-10) was published in 1993. An effort was made to bring the DSM-IV into closer correspondence with the ICD-10, but substantial differences in categories still persist (Frances, Pincus, & Widiger, in press). Such differences ensure that American and non-American mental health professionals will continue to have problems communicating with each other.

Although psychologists usually go along with the DSM-IV, psychiatrists are more satisfied with it. Even though the DSM-IV has its critics, it is still the most comprehensive classification system available.

At this point, we have discussed a number of ideas about what abnormal behavior is, what causes abnormal behavior, and how abnormal behavior can be classified. A summary of these ideas is presented in concept table 1. Now we turn our attention to the specific diagnostic categories and the main types of mental disorders, beginning with the anxiety disorders.

Anxiety Disorders

Anxiety is a diffuse, vague, highly unpleasant feeling of fear and apprehension. People with high levels of anxiety worry a lot. **Anxiety disorders** *are psychological disorders that include the following main features: motor tension (jumpiness, trembling, inability to relax); hyperactivity (dizziness, a racing heart, or, possibly, perspiration); and apprehensive expectations and thoughts.* Five important types of anxiety disorders

Concept Table 1

Abnormal Behavior: What Is It, What Causes It, and How Can It Be Classified?

Concept	Processes/Related Ideas	Characteristics/Description
What Is Abnormal Behavior?	Its nature	It is behavior that is maladaptive and harmful. Atypical behavior is not always abnormal.
What Causes Abnormal Behavior?	The biological approach	Mental disorders have biological causes. The forerunner of this approach was the medical model, which describes individuals as patients with mental diseases in hospitals, where they are treated by doctors. Today's biological approach emphasizes the role of brain processes and heredity in mental disorders.
	The psychological and sociocultural approaches	Many psychologists believe that the biological approach understates the importance of psychological and sociocultural factors. They also emphasize that the medical model encourages the labeling of mental disorders. While many disorders are universal, the frequency of abnormal behavior varies across and within cultures. Such variations are related to socioeconomic status, ethnicity, technology, religion, gender, and urbanization.
	An interactionist approach	Biological, psychological, and social factors often interact to produce abnormal behavior.
How Can Abnormal Behavior Be Classified?	The DSM classifications	*DSM* stands for *Diagnostic and Statistical Manual of Mental Disorders.* The DSM-II included the categories of neurotic and psychotic behavior. Some mental health professionals still use these terms, but they have been dropped from the DSM classification. Mental disorder classification systems have advantages and disadvantages.
	DSM-IV	The most recent version of the DSM—DSM-IV—was published in 1994. One of the DSM-IV's features is its multiaxial system. The DSM-IV Task Force was made up of a much more diverse group of individuals than its predecessors, and the DSM-IV is more empirically based than earlier editions. The most controversial aspects of the DSM-IV continue to be the classification of individuals based on their symptoms and the use of medical terminology that perpetuates the medical or disease model of mental disorders. Another issue raised by critics is that the DSM-IV is too responsive to changing political times. Critics say that satisfactory mental health categories would reflect positive as well as negative characteristics. The DSM-IV and the ICD-10 (the International Classification of Disease) are still not completely compatible.

are: generalized anxiety disorder, panic disorder, phobic disorder, obsessive-compulsive disorder, and post-traumatic stress disorder, each of which we will discuss in turn.

Generalized Anxiety Disorder

Anna, who is 27 years old, had just arrived for her visit with the psychologist. She seemed very nervous and was wringing her hands, crossing and uncrossing her legs, and playing nervously with strands of her hair. She said her stomach felt like it was in knots, that her hands were cold, and that her neck muscles were so tight they hurt. She said that lately arguments with her husband had escalated. In recent weeks, Anna indicated she felt more and more nervous throughout the day as if something bad were about to happen. If the doorbell sounded or the phone rang, her heart beat rapidly and her breathing quickened. When she was around people she had a difficult time speaking. She began to isolate herself. Her husband became impatient with Anna, so she decided to see a psychologist (Goodstein & Calhoun, 1982).

Anna has a **generalized anxiety disorder,** *an anxiety disorder that consists of persistent anxiety for at least a month; the individual with a generalized anxiety disorder is unable to specify the reasons for the anxiety.* One study found that people with generalized anxiety disorder had higher degrees

Onset of attack	No. (%) of patients
Spontaneous	47 (78%)
Nonspontaneous, precipitated by	13 (22%)
Public speaking	3
Stimulant drug use	3
Family argument	2
Leaving home	2
Exercise (while pregnant)	1
Being frightened by a stranger	1
Fear of fainting	1

Stressful life events associated with attack	No. (%) of patients
No stressful life event within 6 months	22 (37%)
Stressful life event within 6 months*	38 (63%)
Threatened or actual separation from important person	11
Change in job, causing increased pressure	8
Pregnancy	7
Move	5
Marriage	3
Graduation	3
Death of close person	3
Physical illness	2

*Four patients had two concomitant stressful life events.

FIGURE 1

First Panic Attack, Precipitating Factors, and Associated Life Events
This table presents some of the data on first panic attacks, precipitating factors, and associated life events. The painting is Edvard Munch's *The Scream.* Experts often interpret Munch's painting as expressing the terror brought on by a panic attack.

of muscle tension and hyperactivity than people with other types of anxiety disorders. These individuals said they had been tense and anxious for more than half of their lives (Barlow & others, 1986).

Panic Disorder

Panic Disorder *is an anxiety disorder marked by the recurrent sudden onset of intense apprehension or terror.* The individual often has a feeling of impending doom but may not feel anxious all the time. Anxiety attacks often strike without warning and produce severe palpitations, extreme shortness of breath, chest pains, trembling, sweating, dizziness, and a feeling of helplessness. Victims are seized by fear that they will die, go crazy, or do something they cannot control (Asnis & van Praag, 1995).

What are some psychosocial and biological factors involved in panic disorder? As shown in figure 1, the majority of panic attacks are spontaneous; those that are not spontaneous are triggered by a variety of events (Breier, Charney, & Heninger, 1986). In many instances, a stressful life event has occurred in the last six months, most often a threatened or actual separation from a loved one or a change in job. Only recently have biological factors in panic disorder been explored (Abelson & Curtis, 1996; Beck, 1996).

Phobic Disorders

Agnes is an unmarried 30-year-old who had been unable to go higher than the second floor of any building for more than a year. When she tried to overcome her fear of heights by going up to the third, fourth, or fifth floor, she became overwhelmed by anxiety. She remembers how it all began. One evening she was working alone and was seized by an urge to jump out of an eighth-story window. She was so frightened by her impulse that she hid behind a file cabinet for more than 2 hours until she calmed down enough to gather her belongings and go home. As she reached the first floor of the building, her heart was pounding and she was perspiring heavily. After several months she gave up her position and became a lower-paid salesperson so she could work on the bottom floor of the store (Cameron, 1963).

A **phobic disorder,** *commonly called phobia, is an anxiety disorder in which the individual has an irrational, overwhelming, persistent fear of a particular object or situation.* Individuals with generalized anxiety disorder cannot pinpoint the cause of their nervous feelings; individuals with phobias can. A fear becomes a phobia when a situation is so dreaded that an individual goes to almost any length to avoid it. For example, Agnes quit her job to avoid being in high places. Some phobias are more debilitating

Agoraphobia is the fear of entering unfamiliar situations, especially open or public places. An individual with agoraphobia tries to avoid crowded situations, like the one shown here. They fear that escape would be difficult or impossible if they become highly anxious in such a crowd. Agoraphobic individuals also usually avoid standing in line and public transportation.

than others. An individual with a fear of automobiles has a more difficult time functioning in our society than a person with a fear of snakes, for example.

Phobias come in many forms. Some of the most common phobias involve height, open spaces, people, close spaces, dogs, dirt, the dark, and snakes. (See table 2 to read about a number of phobias.)

Agoraphobia, *the fear of entering unfamiliar situations, especially open or public spaces, is the most common type of phobic disorder.* It accounts for 50 to 80 percent of the phobic population, according to some estimates (Foa, Steketze, & Young, 1984). Women are far more likely than men to suffer from agoraphobia (Magee, 1996). One study found that 84 percent of the individuals being treated for agoraphobia were women, and almost 90 percent of those women were married (Al-Issa, 1982).

Psychologists have become increasingly interested in *social phobia,* the fear of social situations (Stein, 1995; Stemberger & others, 1995). Bashful or timid people often suffer from this phobia. Social phobia affects as many as 2 of every 100 Americans and tends to be evenly distributed between the sexes (Robins & others, 1984).

Why do people develop phobias? The answer often depends on the psychologist's perspective. Psychoanalytic theorists, for example, say phobias develop as defense mechanisms to ward off threatening or unacceptable impulses—Agnes hid behind a file cabinet because she feared she would jump out of an eighth-story window. Learning

TABLE 2
A Partial List of Phobias

Acrophobia	Fear of high places
Aerophobia	Fear of flying
Agoraphobia	Fear of open places
Ailurophobia	Fear of cats
Algophobia	Fear of pain
Amaxophobia	Fear of vehicles, driving
Arachnophobia	Fear of spiders
Astrapophobia	Fear of lightning
Claustrophobia	Fear of close places
Cynophobia	Fear of dogs
Gamophobia	Fear of marriage
Hydrophobia	Fear of water
Melissophobia	Fear of bees
Mysophobia	Fear of dirt
Nyctophobia	Fear of darkness
Ophidiophobia	Fear of nonpoisonous snakes
Thanatophobia	Fear of death
Xenophobia	Fear of strangers

theorists, however, explain phobias differently; they say phobias are learned fears. In Agnes' case, she may have fallen out of a window when she was a little girl. As a result, she associates falling with pain and now fears high places. Or she may have heard about or seen other people who were afraid of high places. These last two examples are classical conditioning and observational learning explanations for Agnes' phobia. Cross-cultural psychologists point out that phobias also are influenced by cultural factors. Agoraphobia, for example, is much more common in the United States and Europe than in other areas of the world (Kleinman, 1988).

Neuroscientists are finding that biological factors, such as greater blood flow and metabolism in the right side of the brain than in the left hemisphere, may also be involved in phobias. First-generation relatives of individuals suffering from agoraphobia and panic attacks have high rates of these disorders themselves, suggesting a possible genetic predisposition for phobias (d'Ansia, 1989). Others have found that identical twins reared apart sometimes develop the same phobias; one pair independently became claustrophobic, for example (Eckert, Heston, & Bouchard, 1981).

Obsessive-Compulsive Disorders

Bob is 27 years old and lives in a well-kept apartment. He has few friends and little social life. He was raised by a demanding mother and an aloof father. Bob is an accountant who spends long hours at work. He is a perfectionist. His demanding mother always nagged at him to improve himself, to keep the house spotless, and to be clean and neat. She made Bob wash his hands whenever he touched his genitals. As a young adult, Bob found himself ensnared in an exacting ritual in which he would remove his clothes in a prearranged sequence and then endlessly scrub every inch of his body from head to toe. He dressed himself in precisely the opposite way from which he took off his clothes. If he deviated from this order, he would *have* to start the sequence all over again. Sometimes Bob performed the cleansing ritual four to five times an evening. Even though he was aware that this ritual was absurd, he simply could not stop (Meyer & Osborne, 1982).

Obsessive-compulsive disorder (OCD) *is an anxiety disorder in which the individual has anxiety-provoking thoughts that will not go away (obsession) and/or urges to perform repetitive, ritualistic behaviors to prevent or produce some future situation (compulsion).* Obsessive-compulsives repeat and rehearse normal doubts and daily routines, sometimes hundreds of times a day. The basic difference between obsessives and compulsives is the difference between thought and action. Obsessives may be immobilized by horrifying yet irresistible thoughts of killing someone in a traffic accident, for instance, while some compulsives bloody their hands after 16 hours of washing away imaginary germs. Although obsessions and compulsions are different, a person afflicted with OCD may be caught in the relentless grip of both problems.

The most common compulsions are excessive checking, cleansing, and counting. For example, a young man feels he has to check his apartment for gas leaks and make sure the windows are locked. His behavior is not compulsive if he does this once, but if he goes back to check five or six times and then constantly worries that he may not have checked carefully enough once he has left the house, his behavior is compulsive. Most individuals do not enjoy their ritualistic behavior but feel anxious when they do not carry it out (Oldham, Hollander, & Skodol, 1996).

Positron emission tomography (PET) and other new brain-imaging techniques indicate a neurological basis for OCD. Irregularities in neurotransmitter systems, especially serotonin and dopamine, seem to be involved. And there may be a genetic basis for the disorder since OCD runs in families.

Post-Traumatic Stress Disorder

Post-traumatic stress disorder *is a mental disorder that develops through exposure to any of several traumatic events, such as war; severely oppressive situations, such as the holocaust; severe abuse, as in rape; natural disasters, such as floods and tornados; and accidental disasters, such as plane crashes. The disorder is characterized by anxiety symptoms that may immediately follow the trauma or be delayed by months or even years until onset.* The symptoms vary, but can include the following:

- "Flashbacks" in which the individual relives the event in nightmares, or in an awake, but dissociative-like state
- Constricted ability to feel emotions, often reported as feeling numb, resulting in an inability to experience happiness, sexual desire, or enjoyable interpersonal relationships
- Excessive arousal, resulting in an exaggerated startle response, or inability to sleep
- Difficulties with memory and concentration
- Feelings of apprehension, including nervous tremors
- Impulsive outbursts of behavior such as aggressiveness, or sudden changes in lifestyle

Not every individual exposed to the same disaster develops post-traumatic stress disorder, which overloads the individual's usual coping abilities (Boudewyns, 1996; Marsella & others, 1996; Shalev & others, 1996; Solomon, 1993). For example, it is estimated that 15 to 20 percent of Vietnam veterans experienced post-traumatic stress disorder. Vietnam veterans who had some autonomy and decision-making authority, such as Green Berets, were less likely to develop the disorder than soldiers who had no control over where they would be sent or when, and who had no option but to follow orders. Preparation for a trauma also makes a difference in whether an individual will develop the disorder. For example, emergency workers who are trained to cope with traumatic circumstances usually do not develop post-traumatic stress disorder. Some experts consider female sexual abuse and assault victims to be the single largest group of post-traumatic stress disorder sufferers (Koss, 1990).

Somatoform Disorders

"Look, I am having trouble breathing. You don't believe me. Nobody believes me. There are times when I can't stop coughing. I'm losing weight. I know I have cancer. My father died of cancer when I was twelve." Herb has been to six cancer specialists in the last 2 years; none can find anything wrong with him. Each doctor has taken X rays and conducted excessive laboratory tests, but Herb's test results do not indicate any illnesses. Might some psychological factors be responsible for Herb's sense that he is physically ailing?

Somatoform disorders *are mental disorders in which psychological symptoms take a physical, or somatic, form even though no physical causes can be found.* Although these symptoms are not caused physically, they are highly distressing for the individual; the symptoms are real, not faked. Two types of somatoform disorders are hypochondriasis and conversion disorder.

Hypochondriasis

Hypochondriacs always seem to overreact to a missed heartbeat, shortness of breath, or a slight chest pain, fearing that something is wrong with them. **Hypochondriasis** *is a somatoform disorder in which the individual has a pervasive fear of illness and disease.* At the first indication of something amiss in their bodies, hypochondriacs call a doctor. When a physical examination reveals no problems, hypochondriacs usually do not believe the doctor. They often change doctors, moving from one to another searching for a diagnosis that matches their own. Most hypochondriacs are pill enthusiasts, their medicine chests spill over with bottles of drugs that they hope will cure their imagined maladies.

Hypochondriasis is a difficult category to diagnose accurately. It is quite rare for it to occur without other mental disorders—for example, hypochondriacs often are depressed.

Conversion Disorder

Conversion disorder *is a somatoform disorder in which the individual experiences specific, genuine physical symptoms even though no physiological problems can be found. Conversion disorder received its name from psychoanalytic theory, which stressed that anxiety was "converted" into a specific physical symptom.* The hypochondriac has no physical disability; the individual with a conversion disorder does have some loss of motor or sensory ability. Individuals with a conversion disorder may be unable to speak, may faint, or they may even be deaf or blind.

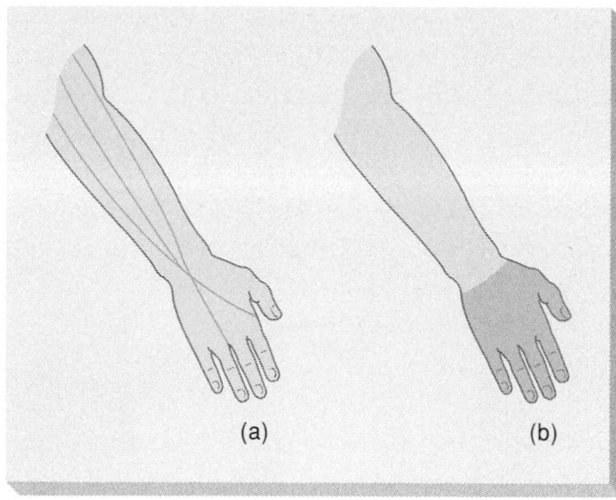

FIGURE 2

Glove Anesthesia

A patient who complains of numbness in the hand might be diagnosed as suffering from conversion disorder if the area of the hand affected showed that a disorder of the nervous system was not responsible. The skin areas served by nerves in the arm are shown in (*a*). The glove anesthesia shown in (*b*) could not result from damage to these nerves.

Conversion disorder was more common in Freud's time than today. Freud was especially interested in this disorder, in which physical symptoms made no neurological sense. For example, with *glove anesthesia* individuals report that their entire hand is numb from the tip of their fingers to a cutoff point at the wrist. As shown in figure 2, if these individuals were experiencing true physiological numbness, their symptoms would be very different. Like hypochondriasis, conversion disorder often appears in conjunction with other mental disorders. During long-term evaluation, conversion disorder turns out to be another mental or physical disorder.

Dissociative Disorders

Dissociative disorders *are psychological disorders that involve a sudden loss of memory or change in identity. Under extreme stress or shock, the individual's conscious awareness becomes dissociated (separated or split) from previous memories and thoughts.* Three kinds of dissociative disorders are amnesia, fugue, and multiple personality.

Amnesia and Fugue

Amnesia is the inability to recall important events. Amnesia can be caused by an injury to the head, for example. But **psychogenic amnesia** *is a dissociative disorder involving memory loss caused by extensive psychological stress.* For example, an individual showed up at a hospital and said he did not know who he was. After several days in the hospital, he awoke one morning and demanded to be released. Eventually he remembered that he had been involved in an automobile accident in which a pedestrian had been killed.

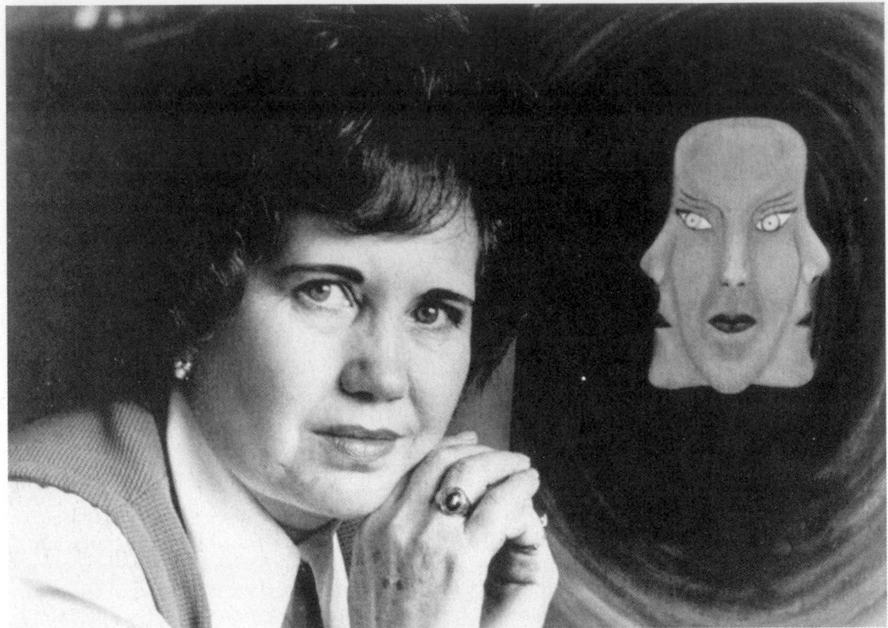

FIGURE 3

Multiple Personality: The Three Faces of Eve
Chris Sizemore, the subject of the book *The Three Faces of Eve,* is shown here with a work she painted, entitled *Three Faces in One.*

The extreme stress of the accident and the fear that he might be held responsible triggered the amnesia.

Fugue, *which means "flight," is a dissociative disorder in which the individual not only develops amnesia, but also unexpectedly travels away from home and assumes a new identity.* For example, one day a woman named Barbara vanished without a trace. Two weeks later, looking more like a teenager—with her hair in a ponytail and wearing bobby socks—than a 31-year-old woman, Barbara was picked up by police in a nearby city. When her husband came to see her, Barbara asked, "Who are you?" She could not remember anything about the last 2 weeks of her life. During psychotherapy, she gradually began to recall her past. She had left home with enough money to buy a bus ticket to the town where she grew up as a child. She spent days walking the streets and standing near a building where her father had worked. Later she went to a motel with a man; according to the motel manager, she entertained a series of men over a 3-day period (Goldstein & Palmer, 1975).

Multiple Personality

Multiple personality *is the most dramatic but least common dissociative disorder; individuals suffering from this disorder have two or more distinct personalities or selves, like the fictional Dr. Jekyl and Mr. Hyde of Robert Louis Stevenson's short story.* Each personality has its own memories, behaviors, and relationships; one personality dominates the individual at one point, another personality will take over at another time. The personalities are not aware of each other and the shift from one to the other usually occurs suddenly under distress.

One of the most famous cases of multiple personalities involves the "three faces of Eve" (Thigpen & Cleckley, 1957). Eve White was the original dominant personality. She had no knowledge of her second personality, Eve Black, although Eve Black had been alternating with Eve White for a number of years. Eve White was bland, quiet, and serious—a rather dull personality. Eve Black, by contrast, was carefree, mischievous, and uninhibited. She would "come out" at the most inappropriate times, leaving Eve White with hangovers, bills, and a reputation in local bars that she could not explain. During treatment, a third personality, Jane, emerged. More mature than the other two, Jane seemed to have developed as a result of therapy. (See figure 3 for a portrayal of the three faces of Eve.)

A summary of the research literature on multiple personality suggests that the most striking feature related to the disorder is an inordinately high rate of sexual or physical abuse during early childhood (Ludolph, 1982). Sexual abuse occurred in 56 percent of the reported cases, for example. Mothers tend to be rejecting and depressed; fathers distant, alcoholic, and abusive. Remember that while fascinating, multiple-personality disorder is rare. Until the 1980s approximately 300 cases had ever been reported (Suinn, 1984). In the last decade, hundreds more have been labeled "multiple-personality disorder," although some argue that the increase represents a diagnostic fad. Others believe that it is not so rare, but has been frequently misdiagnosed as schizophrenia. Improved techniques for assessing the physiological changes that occur when individuals change personalities increase the likelihood that more accurate rates can be determined.

At this point, we have considered three major types of mental disorders—anxiety, somatoform, and dissociative. A summary of the main ideas about these disorders is presented in concept table 2. Now we turn to a set of widespread disorders—mood disorders.

MOOD DISORDERS

The **mood disorders** *are psychological disorders characterized by wide emotional swings, ranging from deep depression to extreme euphoria and agitation. Depression can occur alone, as in major depression, or it can alternate*

Concept Table 2

The Anxiety, Somatoform, and Dissociative Disorders

Concept	Processes/Related Ideas	Characteristics/Description
Anxiety Disorders	Their nature	Anxiety is a diffuse, vague, highly unpleasant feeling of fear and apprehension. The main features of anxiety disorders are motor tension, hyperactivity, and apprehensive expectations and thoughts.
	Generalized anxiety disorder	This disorder consists of persistent anxiety for at least 1 month without being able to specify the reason for the anxiety.
	Panic disorder	Recurrent panic attacks marked by the sudden onset of intense apprehension or terror characterize a panic disorder.
	Phobic disorders	Commonly called phobias, they involve an irrational, overwhelming, persistent fear of a particular object or situation. Phobias come in many forms; the most common is agoraphobia. Psychoanalytic and learning explanations of phobias have been given; recently biological factors have been implicated, with individuals possibly having a genetic predisposition to develop a phobia.
	Obsessive-compulsive disorders	Recurrent obsessions or compulsions characterize these disorders. Obsessions are anxiety-provoking thoughts that won't go away. Compulsions are urges to perform repetitive, ritualistic behaviors that usually occur to prevent or produce a future situation.
	Post-traumatic stress disorder	This disorder develops through exposure to any of several traumatic events, such as war; severely oppressive situations, such as the holocaust; severe abuse, such as rape; natural disasters; and accidental disasters. Anxiety symptoms may immediately follow the trauma, or be delayed months or even years until onset.
Somatoform Disorders	Their nature	Psychological symptoms take a physical, or somatic, form, even though no physical cause can be found.
	Hypochondriasis	This disorder involves a pervasive fear of illness and disease. It rarely occurs alone; depression often accompanies hypochondriasis.
	Conversion disorder	This disorder occurs when an individual experiences specific, genuine symptoms even though no physiological problems can be found. Conversion disorder received its name from psychoanalytic theory, which stressed that anxiety was "converted" into a specific physical symptom. Some loss of motor or sensory ability occurs. The disorder was more common in Freud's time than today.
Dissociative Disorders	Their nature	Dissociative disorders occur when a person has a sudden loss of memory or change in identity. Under extreme stress or shock, conscious awareness becomes dissociated (separated or split) from previous memories and thoughts.
	Amnesia and fugue	Psychogenic amnesia involves memory loss caused by extensive psychological stress. Fugue also involves a loss of memory, but individuals unexpectedly travel away from home or work, assume a new identity, and do not remember their old one.
	Multiple personality	This disorder involves the presence of two or more distinct personalities in the same individual. The disorder is rare.

with mania, as in bipolar disorder. Depression is linked to the increasing rate of suicide. We consider each of these disorders in turn, and then examine the causes of the mood disorders.

Major Depression

Major depression *is a mood disorder in which the individual is deeply unhappy, demoralized, self-derogatory, and bored, showing changes in appetite and sleep patterns, decreased* *energy, feelings of worthlessness, concentration problems, and guilt feelings that might prompt thoughts of suicide.* For example, Peter had been depressed for several months. Nothing cheered him up. His depression began when the girl he wanted to marry decided marriage was not for her, at least not with Peter. Peter's emotional state deteriorated to the point where he didn't leave his room for days at a time, he kept the shades drawn and the room dark, and he could hardly get out of bed in the morning. When he managed to leave his room, he had trouble maintaining a conversation and he felt exhausted most of the time. By the time Peter finally contacted his college counseling center, he had gone from being mildly depressed to being in the grips of major depression.

Although most people don't spiral into major depression as Peter did, everyone feels "blue" sometimes. In our stress-filled world, people often use the term *depression* to describe brief bouts of normal sadness or discontent over life's problems. Perhaps you haven't done well in a class or things aren't working out in your love life. You feel down in the dumps and say you are depressed. In most instances, though, your depression won't last as long or be as intense as Peter's; after a few hours, days, or weeks, you snap out of your gloomy state and begin to cope more effectively with your problems. Nonetheless, depression is so widespread that it has been called the "common cold" of mental disorders; more than 250,000 individuals are hospitalized every year for the disorder. Students, professors, corporate executives, laborers—no one is immune to depression, not even F. Scott Fitzgerald, Ernest Hemingway, Virginia Woolf, Abraham Lincoln, or Winston Churchill—each of whom experienced major depression.

A man's lifetime risk of developing major depression is approximately 10 percent. The risk is much greater for a woman—almost 25 percent. In fact, the most common psychiatric diagnosis for African American and White women is depression (Russo, 1985).

In May 1988, the National Institute of Mental Health (NIMH) launched the public education phase of the first major program to communicate information about mood disorders (Regier & others, 1988). The inadequate care that results from a lack of understanding or a misunderstanding of depression is expensive and tragic. The annual cost of major depression to the nation is more than $16 billion. Given the existing range of psychological and pharmacological treatments, those individuals who go untreated suffer needlessly. To determine the extent to which you have shown depression tendencies in the last week, turn to table 3.

Bipolar Disorder

Bipolar disorder, *a mood disorder, is characterized by extreme mood swings; an individual with this disorder might be depressed, manic, or both.* We have described the symptoms of depression. In contrast, someone who is manic experiences elation, exuberance, and tireless stamina. They may be humorous, scheming, and have a tendency for excess. They also are relentless, irritable, and in almost constant motion. The type of mood swings that might occur in bipolar disorder are shown in figure 4, where they are contrasted with the mood swings of major depression.

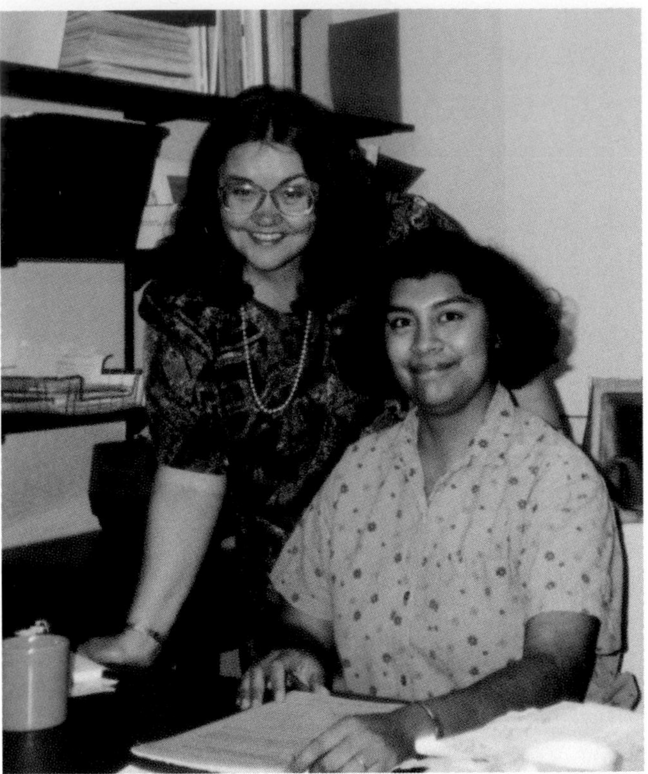

Nancy Felipe Russo (at left) has been instrumental in calling attention to the sociocultural factors involved in women's depression. She is the chair of the National Coalition of Women's Mental Health.

Consider Mrs. M. Although she had experienced extreme mood swings since she was a child, she was first admitted to a mental hospital at the age of 38. At 33, shortly before the birth of her first child, she became very depressed. One month after the baby was born she became agitated and euphoric. Mrs. M. signed a year's lease on an apartment, bought furniture, and piled up debts. Several years later other manic and depressive mood swings occurred. In one of her excitatory moods, Mrs. M. swore loudly and created a disturbance at a club where she was not a member. Several days later she began divorce proceedings. On the day prior to her admission to the mental hospital, she went on a spending spree and bought 57 hats. Several weeks later, she became despondent, saying "I have no energy. My brain doesn't work right. I have let my family down. I don't have anything to live for." In a subsequent manic bout, Mrs. M. pursued a romantic relationship with her doctor (Kolb, 1973).

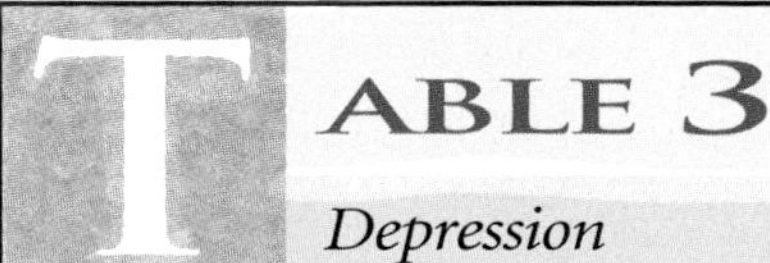

TABLE 3
Depression

Instructions

Following is a list of the ways you might have felt or behaved in the LAST WEEK.
Indicate what you felt by putting an X in the appropriate box for each item.

Items During the past week:	*Rarely or none of the time (Less than 1 day)*	*Some or a little of the time (1–2 days)*	*Occasionally or a moderate amount of the time (3–4 days)*	*Most or all of the time (5–7 days)*
1. I was bothered by things that usually don't bother me.	■	■	■	■
2. I did not feel like eating; my appetite was poor.	■	■	■	■
3. I felt that I could not shake off the blues even with help from my family and friends.	■	■	■	■
4. I felt that I was just as good as other people.	■	■	■	■
5. I had trouble keeping my mind on what I was doing.	■	■	■	■
6. I felt depressed.	■	■	■	■
7. I felt that everything I did was an effort.	■	■	■	■
8. I felt hopeful about the future.	■	■	■	■
9. I thought my life had been a failure.	■	■	■	■
10. I felt fearful.	■	■	■	■
11. My sleep was restless.	■	■	■	■
12. I was happy.	■	■	■	■
13. I talked less than usual.	■	■	■	■
14. I felt lonely.	■	■	■	■
15. People were unfriendly.	■	■	■	■
16. I enjoyed life.	■	■	■	■
17. I had crying spells.	■	■	■	■
18. I felt sad.	■	■	■	■
19. I felt that people disliked me.	■	■	■	■
20. I could not get going.	■	■	■	■

Turn to the end of the chapter to interpret your responses.

The lifetime risk of bipolar disorder is estimated at approximately 1 percent for both men and women (Weissman & Boyd, 1985). It is more common among divorced persons, although in such cases, bipolar disorder may be a cause rather than a consequence of the divorce. Bipolar disorder also occurs more frequently in close relatives of individuals with bipolar disorder than in close relatives of depressed, but nonbipolar disordered individuals.

Suicide

The rate of suicide has tripled since the 1950s in the United States. Each year about 25,000 people take their own lives. Beginning at about the age of 15, the suicide rate begins to rise rapidly. Suicide accounts for 12 percent of the mortality in the adolescent and young adult age group. Males are about three times more likely than women to succeed at committing suicide. This may be due to their more active methods for attempting suicide—shooting themselves, for example. By contrast, females more often use passive methods such as sleeping pills, which do not immediately cause death. Although males commit suicide more frequently, females attempt it more often (Meyer & others, 1996).

Estimates indicate that 6 to 10 suicide attempts occur for every successful suicide in the general population. For adolescents, the figure is as high as 50 attempts for every life taken. As many as 2 in every 3 college students have thought about suicide on at least one occasion.

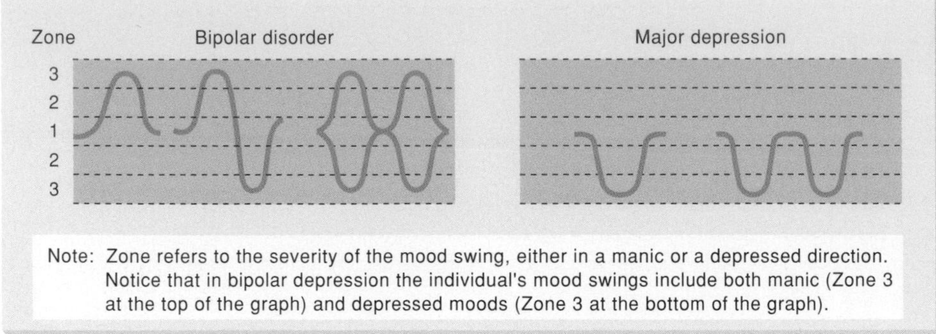
Zone
Bipolar disorder
Major depression
3
2
1
2
3
Note: Zone refers to the severity of the mood swing, either in a manic or a depressed direction. Notice that in bipolar depression the individual's mood swings include both manic (Zone 3 at the top of the graph) and depressed moods (Zone 3 at the bottom of the graph).

FIGURE 4

Comparison of Mood Swings in Bipolar and Major Depression

They have considered methods ranging from drugs to crashing into the White House in an airplane.

There is no simple answer to why people commit suicide (Gadpaille, 1996). Biological factors appear to be involved in suicide. Suicide, as with major depression, tends to run in families. Immediate and highly stressful circumstances such as the loss of a spouse or a job, flunking out of school, or an unwanted pregnancy can lead people, especially those who are genetically predisposed, to attempt suicide. Also, drug-related suicide attempts are more common now than in the past.

But earlier experiences, such as a long-standing history of family instability and unhappiness, can also play a role in why people attempt suicide. Studies of gifted men and women found several predictors of suicide, such as anxiety, conspicuous instability in work and relationships, depression, or alcoholism (Shneidman, 1971; Tomlinson-Keasey, Warren, & Elliott, 1986).

We do not have the complete answers for detecting when a person may be considering suicide or how to prevent it, but the advice offered in table 4 provides some valuable suggestions for communicating with someone you think may be contemplating suicide.

Causes of Mood Disorders

Explanations for mood disorders, such as Peter's depression and Mrs. M.'s bipolar disorder, come from psychoanalytic theory, cognitive and learning theories, biogenetic theories, and sociocultural theories.

Psychoanalytic Explanations

In 1917, Sigmund Freud published a paper called "Mourning and Melancholia," in which he described his view of depression. Freud believed depression was a turning inward of aggressive instincts. He theorized that the child's early attachment to a love object (usually the mother) contains a mixture of love and hate. When the child loses the love object or her dependency needs are frustrated, feelings of loss coexist with anger. Since the child cannot openly accept such angry feelings toward the individual she loves, the hostility is turned inward and experienced as depression. The unresolved mixture of anger and love is carried forward to adolescence and adulthood, where loss can bring back these early feelings of abandonment.

The British psychiatrist John Bowlby (1980, 1989) agrees with Freud that childhood experiences are an important determinant of depression in adulthood. He believes a combination of an insecure attachment to the mother, a lack of love and affection as a child, and the actual loss of a parent during childhood gives rise to a negative cognitive set, or schema. The schema built up during childhood causes the individual to interpret later losses as yet other failures in one's effort to establish enduring and close positive relationships.

One longitudinal study of depression found that parent's lack of affection, high control, and aggressive achievement orientation in early childhood were associated with depression among adolescent girls but not boys (Gjerde, 1985). The sex difference may have appeared because depression occurs more often in girls than boys.

Cognitive and Learning Explanations

Individuals who are depressed rarely think positive thoughts. They interpret their lives in self-defeating ways and have negative expectations about the future (Bradley, 1996). Psychologist Aaron Beck (1967) believes such negative thoughts reflect schemas that shape the depressed individual's experiences. These habitual negative thoughts magnify and expand a depressed person's negative experiences (Teasdale & others, 1995). The depressed person may overgeneralize about a minor occurrence and think that he is worthless because a work assignment was turned in late, his son was arrested for shoplifting, or a friend made a negative comment about his hair. Beck believes that depressed people blame themselves far more than is warranted. For example, an athlete

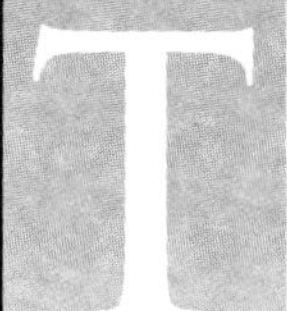

ABLE 4

What to Do and What Not to Do When You Suspect Someone Is Likely to Commit Suicide

What To Do
1. Ask direct, straightforward questions in a calm manner: "Are you thinking about hurting yourself?"
2. Assess the seriousness of the suicidal intent by asking questions about feelings, important relationships, others with whom the person has talked, and the amount of thought given to the means to be employed. If a gun, pills, rope, or other means has been procured and a specific plan has been developed, the situation is very dangerous. Stay with the person until help arrives.
3. Listen and be supportive, without giving false reassurances.
4. Encourage the young person to get professional help and provide assistance.

What Not To Do
1. Do not ignore warning signs.
2. Do not refuse to talk about suicide if a young person approaches you.
3. Do not react with horror, disapproval, or repulsion.
4. Do not offer false reassurances ("Everything will be all right.") or platitudes and simple answers ("You should be thankful for . . .").
5. Do not abandon the young person after the crisis has passed or after professional counseling has begun.

Reprinted from *Living with 10- to 15-Year-Olds: A Parent Education Curriculum.* Copyright 1992 by the Center for Early Adolescence, Carrboro, NC, 1982, rev. ed. 1987. Used with permission.

might accept complete blame for a team's loss when five or ten other teammates, the opposing team, and other factors were involved.

Self-defeating and sad thoughts fit the clinical picture of the depressed individual (Seligman, 1996). Whether these thoughts are the cause or the consequence of the depression, however, is controversial. Critics say that self-defeating thoughts are an outgrowth of biological and environmental conditions that produce depression. One of the environmental factors thought to be important in understanding depression is learned helplessness.

Some years ago, in the interest of science, a researcher drowned two rats. The first rat was dropped into a tank of warm water; it swam around for 60 hours before it drowned. The second rat was handled differently. The researcher held the rat tightly in his hand until it quit struggling to get loose. Then the rat was dropped into the tank; it swam around for several minutes before it drowned. The researcher concluded that the second rat drowned more quickly because its previous experiences told it to give up hope; the rat had developed a sense of helplessness (Richter, 1957).

Learned helplessness *occurs when individuals are exposed to aversive stimulation, such as prolonged stress or pain, over which they have no control. The inability to avoid such aversive stimulation produces an apathetic state of helplessness.* Martin Seligman (1975) argued that learned helplessness is one reason many individuals become depressed. When individuals encounter stress and pain over which they have no control, they eventually feel helpless and depressed. Recently, researchers proposed that the hopelessness characteristic of learned helplessness is often the result of a person's extremely negative, self-blaming attributions (Metalsky & others, 1993).

Biogenetic Explanations

Biological explanations of depression involve genetic inheritance and chemical changes in the brain (McGuffin, 1996; Miller, 1996). In a large twin study conducted in Denmark, identical twins were more likely to suffer from mood disorders than fraternal twins (Bertelson, 1979). If one identical twin developed a mood disorder, the other had a 70 percent chance of developing the disorder; a fraternal twin ran only a 13 percent risk. Another study revealed that biological relatives of an individual with a mood disorder were more likely to suffer from the disorder than adopted relatives (Wender & others, 1986). Neurotransmitters are chemical messengers that carry information from one neuron to the next. Two neurotransmitters involved in depression are norepinephrine and serotonin (Mann & others, 1996). Depressed individuals have decreased levels of norepinephrine, while individuals in a manic state have increased levels. Patients with unusually low serotonin levels are 10 times as likely to commit suicide than individuals with normal levels (Stanley & Stanley, 1989). The endocrine system also may be involved in depression—excessive secretion of cortisol from the adrenal gland occurs in depressed individuals, for example.

Sociocultural Explanations

Martin Seligman (1989) speculated that the reason so many young American adults are prone to depression is that our society's emphasis on self, independence, and individualism, coupled with an erosion of connectedness to others, family, and religion has spawned a widespread sense of hopelessness. Depressive disorders are found in virtually all cultures in the world, but their incidence, intensity, and components vary across cultures. A major difference in depression between Western and many non-Western cultures is the absence of guilt and self-deprecation in the non-Western cultures (Draguns, 1990).

Earlier in this chapter we mentioned that women run a far greater risk of depression than men—at a ratio of 2:1. Studies have shown that depression is especially high among single women who are the head of household and among young married women who work at unsatisfying, dead-end jobs (Russo, 1990). Such stressful circumstances, as well as others involving sexual abuse, sexual harassment, unwanted pregnancy, and powerlessness disproportionately affect women. These sociocultural factors may interact with biological and cognitive factors to increase women's rate of depression. However, in cultures where alcohol abuse and aggression are rare, such as the culturally homogeneous Amish community (a religious sect in Pennsylvania), the rate of depression for women and men is virtually equal.

Separating environmental, cognitive, biological, and sociocultural causes of depression is not easy. Whether neurotransmitters, cognitive factors, environmental factors, or cross-cultural factors are cause or effect is still unknown. Like most behaviors we have discussed, depression is best viewed as complex and multiple determined (Beckham & Leber, 1995).

Schizophrenic Disorders

Schizophrenia produces a bizarre set of symptoms and wreaks havoc on the individual's personality. **Schizophrenic disorders** *are severe psychological disorders characterized by distorted thoughts and perceptions, odd communication, inappropriate emotion, abnormal motor behavior, and social withdrawal. The term* schizophrenia *comes from the Latin words* schizo, *meaning "split," and* phrenia, *meaning "mind." The individual's mind is split from reality, and personality loses its unity.* Schizophrenia is not the same as multiple personality, which sometimes is called a "split personality." Schizophrenia involves the split of *one* personality from reality, not the coexistence of several personalities within one individual.

Characteristics of Schizophrenic Disorders

Bob began to miss work. He spent his time watching his house from a rental car parked inconspicuously down the street and following his fellow employees as they left work to see where they went and what they did. He kept a little black book in which he scribbled cryptic notes. When he went to the water cooler at work, he pretended to drink but instead looked carefully around the room to observe if anyone looked guilty or frightened.

Bob's world seemed to be closing in on him. After an explosive scene at the office one day, he became very agitated. He left and never returned. By the time Bob arrived at home, he was in a rage. He could not sleep that night and the next day he kept his children home from school; all day he kept the shades pulled on every window. The next night he maintained his vigil. At 4 A.M., he armed himself and burst out of the house, firing shots in the air while daring his enemies to come out (McNeil, 1967).

Bob is a paranoid schizophrenic, one of the schizophrenic disorders we will describe shortly. About 1 in every 100 Americans will be classified as schizophrenic in their lifetime (Gottesman, 1989). Schizophrenic disorders are serious, debilitating mental disorders; about one-half of all mental hospital patients in the United States are schizophrenics. More now than in the past, schizophrenics live in society and return for treatment at mental hospitals periodically (Kane & Barnes, 1995). Drug therapy is primarily responsible for fewer schizophrenics being hospitalized. About one-third of schizophrenics get better, about one-third get worse, and another third stay about the same once they develop this severe mental disorder. What are the symptoms of these individuals?

Many schizophrenics have *delusions,* or false beliefs—one individual may think he is Jesus Christ, another Napoleon, for example. The delusions are utterly implausible. One individual may think her thoughts are being broadcast over the radio, another may think that a double agent is controlling her every move. Schizophrenics also may hear, see, feel, smell, and taste things not there. These *hallucinations* often take the form of voices. The schizophrenic might think that he hears two people talking about him, for example. Or, on another occasion, he might say, "Hear that rumbling in the pipe. That is one of my men in there watching out for me."

Often schizophrenics do not make sense when they talk or write. Their language does not follow any rules. For example, one schizophrenic might say, "Well, Rocky, babe, help is out, happening, but where, when, up, top, side, over, you know, out of the way, that's it. Sign off." Such speech has no meaning. These incoherent, loose word associations are called *word salad.* As shown in figure 5, schizophrenics' paintings often have a bizarre quality, too.

The schizophrenic's motor behavior may be bizarre, sometimes taking the form of an odd appearance, pacing, statuelike postures, or strange mannerisms. Some schizophrenics withdraw from their social world; they become so insulated from others they seem totally absorbed in interior images and thoughts.

Forms of Schizophrenic Disorders

Schizophrenic disorders appear in four main forms; disorganized, catatonic, paranoid, and undifferentiated schizophrenia.

Disorganized schizophrenia *is a schizophrenic disorder in which an individual has delusions and hallucinations that have little or no recognizable meaning—hence, the label* disorganized. A disorganized schizophrenic withdraws from

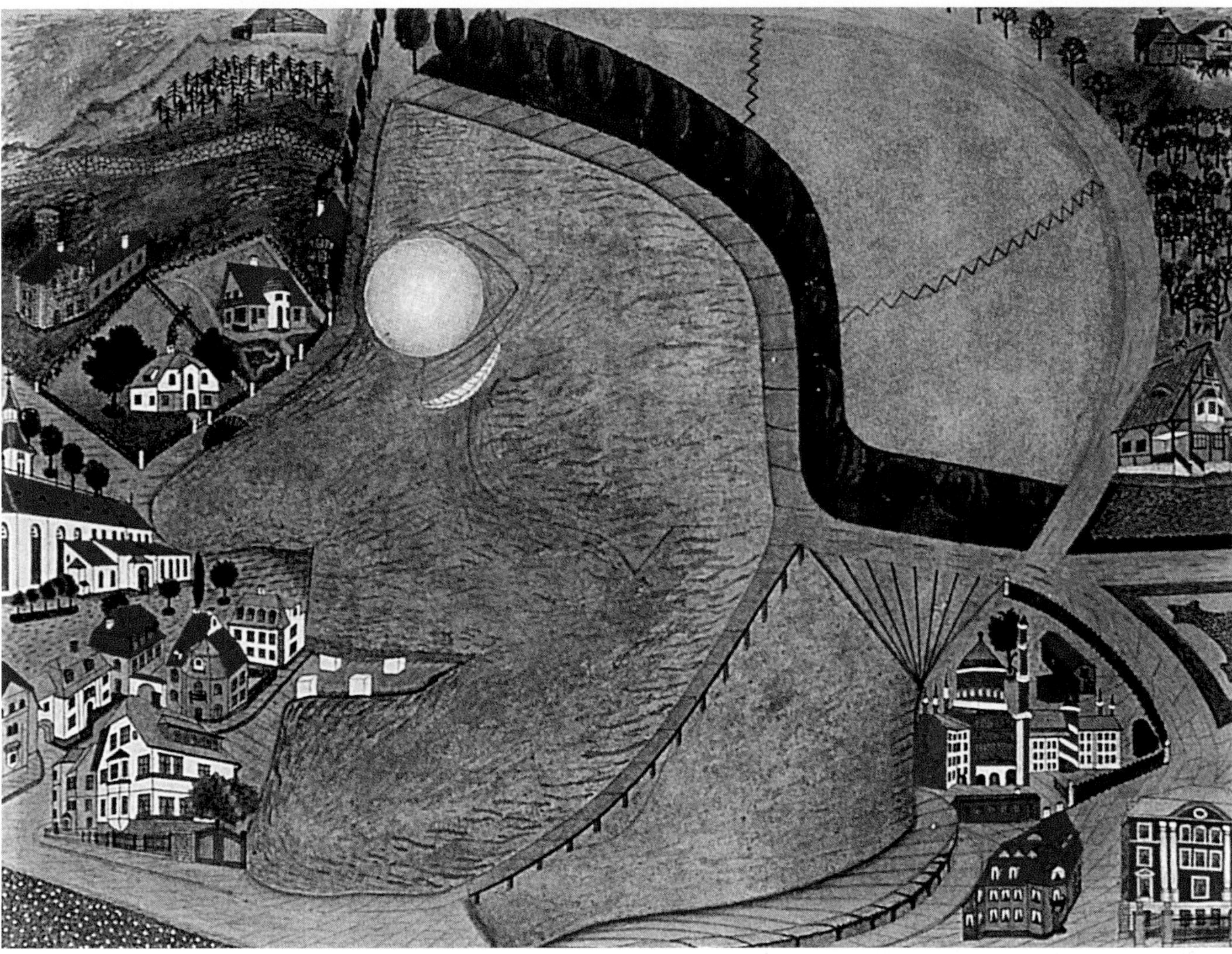

FIGURE 5

A Painting by a Schizophrenic
This painting is named *Landscape* and it is by August Neter, a successful nineteenth-century electrical engineer until he became schizophrenic in 1907. He lost interest in his work as an engineer as his mind became disorganized.

human contact and may regress to silly, childlike gestures and behavior. Many of these individuals were isolated or maladjusted during adolescence.

Catatonic schizophrenia *is a schizophrenic disorder characterized by bizarre motor behavior, which sometimes takes the form of a completely immobile stupor* (see figure 6). Even in this stupor, catatonic schizophrenics are completely conscious of what is happening around them. In a catatonic state, the individual sometimes shows *waxy flexibility;* for example, if the person's arm is raised and then allowed to fall, the arm stays in the new position.

Paranoid schizophrenia *is a schizophrenic disorder characterized by delusions of reference, grandeur, and persecution.* The delusions usually form a complex, elaborate system based on a complete misinterpretation of actual events. It is not unusual for schizophrenics to develop all three delusions in the following order. First, they sense they are special and have been singled out for attention (delusions of reference). Individuals with delusions of reference misinterpret chance events as being directly relevant to their own lives—a thunderstorm, for example, might be perceived as a personal message from God. Second, they believe that this special attention is the result of their admirable and special characteristics (delusions of grandeur). Individuals with delusions of grandeur think of themselves as exalted beings—the pope or the president, for example. Third, they think that others are so jealous and threatened by these characteristics that they spy and plot against them

FIGURE 6

A Catatonic Schizophrenic
Unusual motor behaviors are prominent symptoms in catatonic schizophrenia. Individuals may cease to move altogether, sometimes taking on bizzare postures.

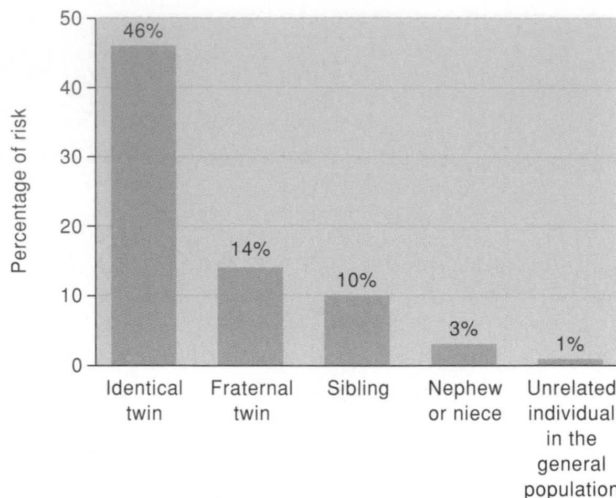

FIGURE 7

Lifetime Risk of Becoming Schizophrenic According to Genetic Relatedness
As your genetic relatedness to an individual with schizophrenia increases, so does your risk of becoming schizophrenic.

(delusions of persecution). Individuals with delusions of persecution often feel they are the target of a conspiracy—for example, recall Bob's situation described earlier.

Undifferentiated schizophrenia *is a schizophrenic disorder characterized by disorganized behavior, hallucinations, delusions, and incoherence.* This category of schizophrenia is used when an individual's symptoms either don't meet the criteria for the other types or they meet the criteria for more than one of the other types.

Causes of Schizophrenia

Schizophrenic disorders may be caused by genetic and biological factors, as well as environmental and sociocultural factors.

Genetic Factors

If you have a relative with schizophrenia, what are the chances you will develop schizophrenia? It depends on how closely you are related. As genetic similarity increases, so does your risk of becoming schizophrenic (Pritchard, 1996; Sasaki & Kennedy, 1995). As shown in figure 7, an identical twin of a schizophrenic has a 46 percent chance of developing the disorder, a fraternal twin 14 percent, a sibling 10 percent, a nephew or niece 3 percent, and an unrelated individual in the general population 1 percent (Gottesman & Shields, 1982). Such data strongly suggest that genetic factors are involved in schizophrenia, although the precise nature of the genetic influence is unknown. More about genetic and genetic-environmental influences on schizophrenia appears in Explorations in Psychology 1, which tells the fascinating story of quadruplets with schizophrenia.

Neurobiological factors

Many neuroscientists believe imbalances in brain chemistry, including deficits in brain metabolism, a malfunctioning dopamine system, and distorted cerebral blood flow, cause schizophrenia (Goldberg, Berman, & Weinberger, 1995). Imaging techniques, such as the PET scan, clearly show deficits in brain metabolism. Do these deficits cause the disorder, or are they simply symptoms of a disorder whose true origin lies deeper in the brain, in the genes, or in the environment? Whether cause or effect, information about neurobiological factors improves our knowledge of schizophrenia's nature. We do know that schizophrenics produce too much of the neurotransmitter, dopamine. Schizophrenics also have a reduced blood flow in the prefrontal cortex. For example, when scientists monitored the brains of schizophrenics as they performed a

EXPLORATIONS IN PSYCHOLOGY 1

NIMH—Nora, Iris, Myra, and Hester, the Schizophrenic Genain Quadruplets

The story of the Genain quadruplets began more than 50 years ago. Henry Genain had forgotten to buy his wife a birthday present, so she suggested he give her a child for their third wedding anniversary instead. The wish came true, but there were four presents instead of one (see figure A). The names given to the quadruplets by scientists—Nora, Iris, Myra, and Hester—come from the acronym for the National Institute of Mental Health (NIMH), where the quadruplets have been extensively studied.

Their birth was a celebrated occasion; one paper ran a contest to name the girls and received 12,000 entries. The city found a rent-free house for the unemployed father, a dairy company donated milk, and a baby carriage for four was given to the family. Newspaper stories appeared from time to time about the quadruplets, portraying their similarities, especially their drama talent and a song-and-dance routine they had developed.

However, a darker side to the quadruplets' story emerged by the time they reached high school. It became clear that the girls had serious mental problems. By the time they were in their twenties, each had been diagnosed as schizophrenic. A perceptive doctor recognized their symptoms and contacted NIMH. A research team led by David Rosenthal began extensive evaluation of the schizophrenic quadruplets (Rosenthal, 1963).

About 20 years later, psychologist Alan Mirksy invited the quadruplets back to NIMH to determine how they might have changed. The scientists also wanted to know if recently developed techniques could discover something special about their biological makeup.

PET scans revealed that sugar was used at an unusually high rate in the rear portion of the quadruplets' brains (see figure B). Their brains also showed much less alpha-wave activity than the brains of normal individuals. Remember that alpha-wave activity appears in individuals in a relaxed state; scientists speculate that the onset of hallucinations might possibly block alpha-wave activity.

Some environmental experiences probably contributed to the Genain quadruplets' schizophrenia as well. Their father placed strict demands on his daughters, delighted in watching them undress, and would not let them play with friends or participate in school or church activities. He refused to let the quadruplets participate in social activities even as adults, and he followed them to their jobs and opened their mail.

What makes the Genain quadruplets such fascinating cases is their uniqueness—identical quadruplets occur once in every 16 million births and only half survive to adulthood; only 1 in 100 become schizophrenic; and the chances of all of them being schizophrenic happens only once in tens of billions of births, a figure much greater than the current world population.

FIGURE A

The Genain Quadruplets as Children
All of the quadruplets had been diagnosed as schizophrenic by the time they were in their twenties.

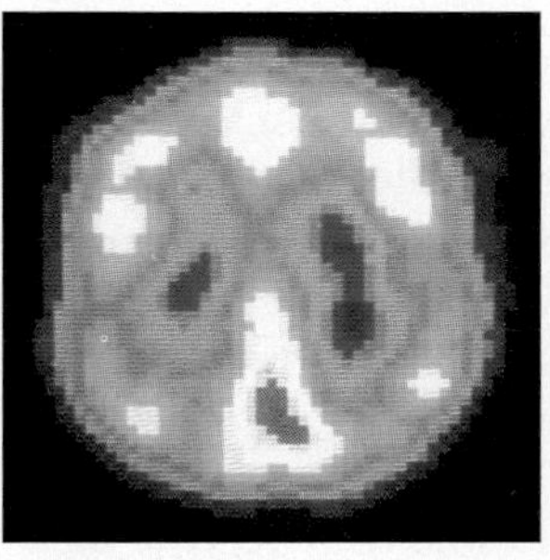

Nora

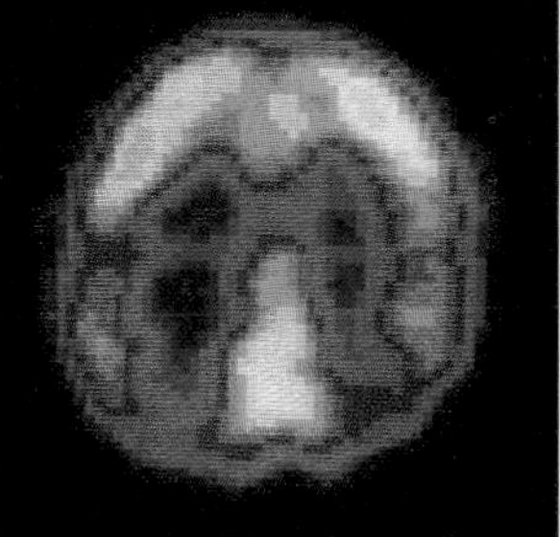

Normal Person

FIGURE B

PET Scans of the Genain Quadruplets
In a normal brain (*right photo*), the areas of high energy use are at the top (frontal lobes). The quadruplets all showed energy use in the visual areas at the bottom of their PET scan brain slices. Are these hallucinations? (Note: The other three sisters showed PET scans much more similar to Nora's than to a normal individual's.)

cardsorting task, blood did not adequately flow into the prefrontal region, where much of our advanced thinking takes place (Weinberger, Berman, & Zec, 1986).

Environmental Factors

As scientists understand schizophrenia's neurobiological basis, it is easy to lose sight of the fact that schizophrenia, like all other behavior, does not occur in an environmental vacuum. Some researchers believe environmental factors are important in schizophrenia (Goldstein, 1986), others believe genetic factors outweigh environmental factors (Gottesman & Shields, 1982).

Stress is the environmental factor given the most attention in understanding schizophrenia. The **diathesis-stress view** *argues that a combination of environmental stress and biogenetic disposition causes schizophrenia* (Meehl, 1962). A defective gene makeup may only produce schizophrenia when the individual lives in a stressful environment. Advocates of the diathesis-stress view emphasize the importance of stress reduction and family support in treating schizophrenia.

Sociocultural Factors

Disorders of thought and emotion are common to schizophrenia in all cultures, but the type and incidence of schizophrenic disorders may vary from culture to culture. For example, one of the more puzzling results is that the admission rates to mental health facilities for schizophrenia are very high for Irish Catholics in the Republic of Ireland (which is in southern Ireland) (Torrey & others, 1984), but not among Irish Catholics living elsewhere (Murphy, 1978). One reason for this difference could be that different diagnostic criteria are used in the Republic of Ireland, but this is not likely to be the complete answer. There are many areas of the world where the incidence of schizophrenia is considerably higher or lower than the worldwide incidence of just under 1 percent.

Rates of schizophrenia may also vary for different groups within a culture. For example, one study revealed that African Americans had higher rates of schizophrenia than Whites in both the United States and Great Britain (Bagley, 1984). The African Americans had a significantly greater number of life crises than Whites, which may have precipitated schizophrenic episodes. Also, the African Americans and African Britains who became schizophrenic had higher aspirations than those who did not. One explanation may be that the efforts of people of African descent to become assimilated into and achieve parity within a White mainstream society that is oppressively racist creates considerable stress.

In addition, the conditions of lower-class existence often restrict a person's ability to cope with many of life's stressors. Nonetheless, there are some individuals from lower class backgrounds who develop considerable resourcefulness and resilience. When supposed ethnic differences—comparing African Americans, Latinos, and Whites, for example—are examined in the context of socioeconomic status, the ethnic differences tend to vanish. Thus, it seems that poverty and the living conditions it engenders are much more likely to be associated with schizophrenia than ethnicity.

We have seen that the mood disorders and schizophrenic disorders are complex and often debilitating. A summary of the main ideas in our discussion of these disorders is presented in concept table 3. Next you will read about an intriguing set of disorders involving personality.

Personality Disorders

Personality disorders *are psychological disorders that develop when personality traits become inflexible and, thus, maladaptive.* Individuals with these maladaptive traits often do not recognize that they have a problem and may show little interest in changing. Personality disorders are notoriously difficult to treat therapeutically (Livesley, 1995).

Although there are eleven distinct personality disorder diagnoses described in the DSM-IV, clinicians think of the disorders as "clustered" around dominant characteristics. One cluster of personality disorders involves odd or eccentric behaviors. A second cluster emphasizes fear and anxiety. And a third cluster stresses dramatic, emotional, or erratic behaviors. We will describe one or more representative disorders from each cluster to illustrate their features. The complete list of personality disorders appears in table 5 (Halonen & Santrock, 1996).

Schizotypal Personality Disorder

Schizotypal personality disorder *is a personality disorder in the odd/eccentric cluster. Individuals with this disorder appear to be in contact with reality, but many aspects of their behavior are distasteful, which leads others to retreat or withdraw from them.* Individuals are likely to be diagnosed as having this disorder based on their eccentric patterns of behavior. Consider Bruce. Although he was able to hold a job, he associated little with his coworkers. He strongly preferred to spend his breaks and time away from work with a sketchpad, designing new flags for countries of the world. His geographic and political knowledge was impressive, but it was painful for him to engage in conversations with others. In contrast, when constructing new flags he hummed and talked to himself.

Obsessive-Compulsive Personality Disorder

Obsessive-compulsive personality disorder *is in the anxious/fearful cluster of personality disorders. Anxious adjustment is its primary feature.* Individuals with this disorder tend to be exacting, precise, and orderly. They generate discomfort in others by requiring the same precision from others. They pay attention to each detail as a means of warding off anxiety. Individuals who show obsessive-compulsive style often are successfully adjusted to positions that require

Concept Table 3

Mood Disorders and Schizophrenic Disorders

Concept	Processes/Related Ideas	Characteristics/Description
Mood Disorders	Their nature	Mood disorders are characterized by wide emotional swings, ranging from deep depression to great euphoria and agitation. Depression can occur alone, as in major depression, or it can alternate with mania, as in bipolar disorder.
	Major depression	Individuals with major depression are sad, demoralized, bored, and self-derogatory. They often do not feel well, lose stamina easily, have a poor appetite, and are listless and unmotivated. Depression is so widespread that it is called the common cold of mental disorders. Major depression sometimes leads to suicide, which has increased dramatically since the 1950s. Both immediate and earlier experiences are related to suicide.
	Bipolar disorder	This disorder is characterized by extreme mood swings; an individual with this disorder might be depressed, manic, or both. In the manic phase, individuals' moods are elated, humorous, and scheming. Manic individuals are exuberant, have tireless stamina, and have a tendency for excess. They also are restless, irritable, and in constant motion.
	Suicide	The suicide rate has increased in the United States in recent decades. Both recent stressful experiences and early experiences are related to suicide.
	Causes of mood disorders	Explanations of mood disorders come from psychoanalytic theory, cognitive and social learning theories, and biogenetic theories.
Schizophrenic Disorders	Their nature	Schizophrenic disorders are severe mental disorders characterized by distorted thoughts and perceptions, odd communication , inappropriate emotion, abnormal motor behavior, and social withdrawal. The mind splits from reality, and personality loses its unity.
	Characteristics of schizophrenic disorders	About 1 in 100 Americans becomes schizophrenic and schizophrenia accounts for approximately one-half of all mental hospital patients. Many schizophrenics have delusions, or false beliefs, and hallucinations They often do not make sense when they talk or write. A schizophrenic's motor behavior may be bizarre and the schizophrenic may withdraw from social relationships.
	Forms of schizophrenic disorders	Schizophrenic disorders appear in four main forms: disorganized, catatonic, paranoid, and undifferentiated.
	Causes of schizophrenia disorders	Proposed causes include genetic and biological factors, as well as environmental factors. Many neuroscientists believe imbalances in brain chemistry cause schizophrenia. The diathesis-stress model emphasizes both biogenetic disposition and environmental stress. Cognitive and emotional disorders of thought are common in schizophrenia in all cultures, but the type and incidence of schizophrenic disorders may vary cross-culturally and across social classes.

careful execution of details. For instance, Alex is a police officer in charge of preparing and maintaining evidence for trials. He repeatedly checks his files for completeness and order. Although well respected by his fellow officers for the quality of his work, he becomes enraged when they alter his meticulous organization.

Borderline Personality Disorder

Borderline personality disorder *is in the dramatic/emotional/erratic cluster of personality disorders.* Individuals with borderline tendencies often view the world as neatly divided into good and bad features. Their tolerance of frustration is very limited, as is their capacity to trust

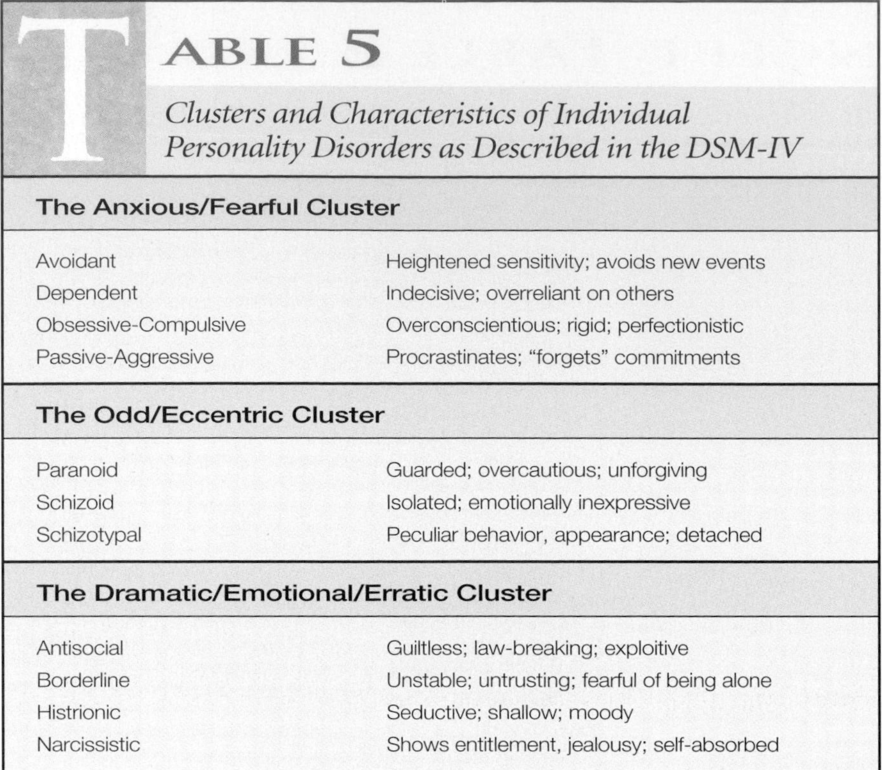

TABLE 5

Clusters and Characteristics of Individual Personality Disorders as Described in the DSM-IV

The Anxious/Fearful Cluster	
Avoidant	Heightened sensitivity; avoids new events
Dependent	Indecisive; overreliant on others
Obsessive-Compulsive	Overconscientious; rigid; perfectionistic
Passive-Aggressive	Procrastinates; "forgets" commitments
The Odd/Eccentric Cluster	
Paranoid	Guarded; overcautious; unforgiving
Schizoid	Isolated; emotionally inexpressive
Schizotypal	Peculiar behavior, appearance; detached
The Dramatic/Emotional/Erratic Cluster	
Antisocial	Guiltless; law-breaking; exploitive
Borderline	Unstable; untrusting; fearful of being alone
Histrionic	Seductive; shallow; moody
Narcissistic	Shows entitlement, jealousy; self-absorbed

others(Goldstein, 1995). Individuals with borderline personality disorder use dramatic, attention-seeking acts as a means of controlling others (Horwitz & others, 1996). Consider Pam, who could not manage to keep a college roommate. Each relationship would start off with promise. Pam spoke enthusiastically about each new prospect as "different from all the others." She would buy her new roommates presents and almost court their friendship. However, within a few weeks Pam would wildly criticize a new roommate, accusing her of poor hygiene, a preference for "low-life" acquaintances, and impossible housekeeping habits. In desperation, she would threaten to kill herself if someone more caring and sensitive were not assigned to her immediately.

Antisocial Personality Disorder

Antisocial personality disorder *is also in the dramatic/emotional/erratic cluster of personality disorders. It is the most problematic personality disorder for society. Individuals with antisocial personality disorder often resort to crime, violence, and delinquency.* These individuals (who used to be called psychopaths or sociopaths) regularly violate the rights of others. This disorder begins before the age of 15 and continues into adulthood; it is much more typical of males than of females. Tiffany demonstrates many antisocial characteristics already in high school: truancy, school suspension, running away from home, stealing, vandalism, drug use, sexual acting-out, and violation of rules at home and school. Such behaviors are commonplace among young adults afflicted with antisocial personality disorder. Consider Martin, who shows many of the behaviors typical of adults with antisocial personality. He cannot maintain a consistent work record. He steals, and he harasses others. Martin rarely plans ahead, and he fails to uphold financial obligations. He repeatedly gets into fights and shows little remorse when he has harmed someone.

The Controversy About Personality Disorders

The general category of personality disorders is perhaps the most controversial of the diagnostic areas in the DSM-IV. Many scholars believe that we should not regard challenging personality styles as equivalent to other diagnostic categories that may have a clearer medical origin. Some have suggested that personality disorders represent a "wastebasket diagnosis—any individual whose problems do not fit into a more precise diagnosis might end up labeled with a personality disorder. Finally, some scholars believe that personality disorders may serve as political conveniences to dismiss those whose behavior is troublesome, confusing, or irritating (Landrine, 1995).

Substance-Use Disorders

A problem associated with drug use is called a **substance-use disorder,** *which is characterized by one or more of the following features: (1) a pattern of pathological use that involves frequent intoxication, a need for daily use, and an inability to control use—in a sense, psychological dependence; (2) a significant impairment of social or occupational functioning attributed to the drug use; and (3) physical dependence that involves serious withdrawal problems.* Alcohol, barbiturates, and opium derivatives all are capable of producing either physical or psychological dependence. Alcoholism is an especially widespread substance-use disorder; it has been estimated that 6 to 8 million Americans are alcoholics. Although substantial numbers of women abuse alcohol, more men are alcoholics than women. Among African Americans, the male–female alcoholic ratio is 3:2; among Whites the ratio is approximately 4:1 (Russo, 1990).

Many individuals are often surprised to learn that substantial numbers of women are alcoholics or abusers of other drugs. While most research on drug abuse had been directed toward males, females are just as likely to be treated for drug-related problems in emergency rooms. Without a more intense research effort directed at

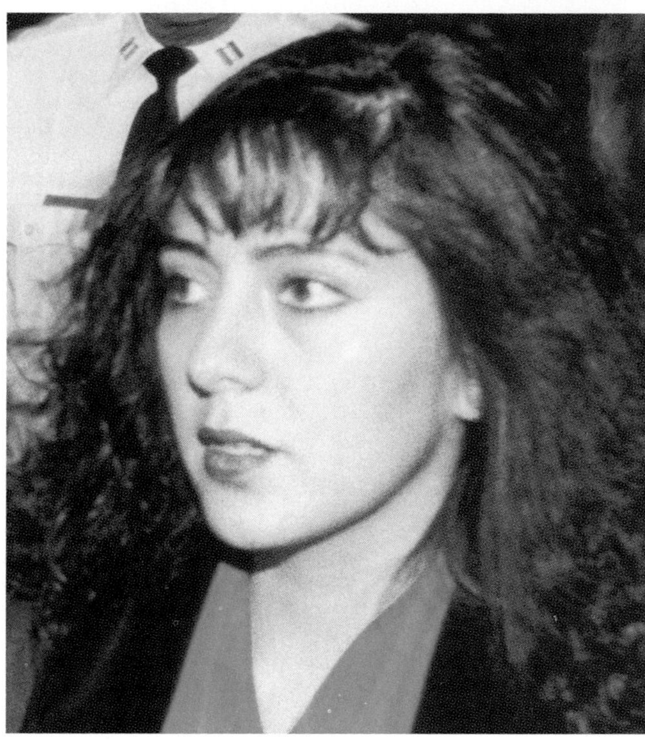

Two famous cases involving the insanity plea resulted in different outcomes. Before his murder in 1994, Jeffrey Dahmer's insanity defense for murder and cannibalism was unsuccessful. In contrast, a jury found Lorena Bobbitt "innocent by reason of insanity" in her sexual assault on her husband.

female drug abusers, the unique facets of their drug abuse will go uncharted. For both male and female drug abusers, biogenetic, psychological, and sociocultural factors may all be involved.

Legal Aspects of Mental Disorders

The legal status of the mentally disordered raises a number of controversial issues, including these: What is involved in committing disordered and dangerous individuals to mental institutions? What is the status of using the insanity defense for capital crimes?

Commitment and Dangerousness

The behavior of some mentally disordered individuals is so severe and extreme that they are a threat to themselves and/or to others, and they may need protective confinement. Being mentally disordered in itself is not adequate grounds for placing individuals in a mental institution against their will. While procedures vary somewhat from state to state, certain conditions usually need to be met before a person can be formally committed to a mental institution: Individuals must either be dangerous to themselves or to other people. Determining whether a mentally disordered individual is dangerous is not easy even for mental health professionals. Nonetheless, there are times when professionals have to make "dangerousness" judgments (Slobogin, 1996). Recent court decisions held mental health professionals liable when unconfined clients they were treating caused harm to others. Therapists are required to warn potential victims if their patients threaten to kill someone.

The Insanity Defense

Insanity *is a legal term, not a psychological term; individuals labeled "insane" are deemed mentally disordered and incapable of being responsible for their actions.* The **insanity defense** *is a plea of "innocent by reason of insanity" used as a legal defense in criminal trials.* In our culture, guilt implies responsibility and intent—to be guilty of a crime, an individual has to have knowingly and intentionally committed it. The jury determines whether the defendant is capable of such legally defined criteria. Controversy swirls about the concept of insanity because of concerns that criminals will unfairly use this plea to avoid prosecution.

In recent years, two publicized cases employing the insanity defense led to different outcomes (Halonen & Santrock, 1996). In 1992 Jeffrey Dahmer's attorneys were unable to persuade the jury that Dahmer's murdering and ritual cannibalism of fifteen young men had resulted from insanity. The prosecution pointed to his skilled execution and coverup of the crimes as evidence that he was rational and should be held responsible. The jury found Dahmer guilty and sane at the time

Concept Table 4

Personality Disorders, Substance-Use Disorders, and the Legal Aspects of Mental Disorders

Concept	Processes/Related Ideas	Characteristics/Description
Personality Disorders	Their nature	Personality disorders are psychological disorders that develop when personality traits become inflexible and, thus, maladaptive. Individuals with a personality disorder often do not recognize that they have a problem and show little interest in changing their behavior. Three clusters of personality disorders are the anxious/fearful cluster, the odd/eccentric cluster, and the dramatic/emotional/erratic cluster. The schizotypal personality is in the odd/eccentric cluster; obsessive-compulsive personality disorder is in the anxious/fearful cluster; borderline personality disorder and antisocial personality disorder are in the dramatic/emotion/erratic cluster. Personality disorders are a controversial category of mental disorders.
Substance-Use Disorders	Their nature	Substance-use disorders focus on individuals with problems associated with drug use. The disorder may involve psychological dependence, physical dependence, and impairment of social or occupational functioning. Alcoholism is an especially widespread substance-abuse disorder.
Legal Aspects of Mental Disorders	Their nature	Mentally disordered individuals must be either dangerous to themselves or others for formal commitment to a mental institution. Judgments about "dangerousness" are not easy. Mental health professionals have been held accountable when their clients caused harm to others. Insanity is a legal term, not a psychological term, that implies individuals are mentally disordered and incapable of being responsible for their actions. The insanity defense is a plea of "innocent by reason of insanity," used as legal defense in criminal trials. Controversy swirls around the insanity defense.

he committed the crimes and ordered him to serve fifteen life terms without the chance of parole.

In contrast, in 1994 Lorena Bobbitt's attorneys were successful in employing the insanity defense. Lorena Bobbitt claimed that she had suffered years of physical and sexual abuse from her husband, John. According to Bobbitt's defense attorneys, after an incident of particularly severe abuse by her husband, Bobbitt experienced an irresistible impulse. She waited for her husband to fall asleep, and then she cut off his penis, drove away from the house, and threw his penis out the car window. Although her trial was controversial, the jury found her guilty, but insane, at the time she committed the crime. After several weeks of confinement in a mental hospital, Lorena Bobbitt was able to return to the community.

The appropriateness of the insanity defense remains highly controversial (Perlin, 1996; Slovenko, 1995). Successful insanity defense is relatively rare because juries struggle with applying the legal criteria to complex situations. Some experts recommend changes in the defense, arguing that the determination of guilt should be independent of the court's determination of the defendant's sanity status (Steadman & others, 1989). Many states have moved to adopt this approach. In addition, the Supreme Court reviewed a case in 1994 that opened the opportunity for states to revisit their insanity plea practices.

At this point we have discussed a number of ideas about personality disorders, substance-use disorders, and the legal aspects of mental disorders. A summary of these ideas is presented in concept table 4.

Critical Thinking About Behavior

Mental Disorders, Biology, and Social Class

A classic study in the 1950s showed that schizophrenia appears to have a "downward drift" according to socio-economic class (Hollingshead & Redlich, 1958). Studying institutionalization patterns across multiple hospitals, the researchers suggested that being a member of a lower socioeconomic class enhances your risk of schizophrenia in your lifetime.

The usual degree of risk cited for schizophrenia is close to 1 percent, meaning that 1 out of every 100 individuals in the culture will become schizophrenic. However, a number of factors appear to be related to increasing the risk for schizophrenia. Although the presence of these factors does not guarantee the development of schizophrenia, they enhance the risk for the individual with these characteristics.

We can find a good example of increased risk in genetic studies (Gottesman & Shields, 1982). Blood relation to a diagnosed schizophrenic increases risk. Your risk of schizophrenia increases from 1.0 percent to 4.4 percent if you have a schizophrenic parent, to 13.7 percent if your fraternal twin has schizophrenia, and to 46.0 percent if your identical twin has schizophrenia. Thus, biological factors contribute to risk in substantial ways but do not completely account for the development of schizophrenia. If they did, we would expect that identical twins would virtually always avoid or succumb to schizophrenia together.

If living in lower socioeconomic classes does seem to enhance risk, can you identify possible variables that could account for this explanation? What specific factors might account for risk that can be more directly linked to the limited resources families have in lower socioeconomic existence?

One longitudinal study identified many "markers" for increased schizophrenic risk (Watt, 1984). These included

- Low birthweight and challenging birth conditions
- Absence of a close relationship with the mother early in life
- Underdeveloped infant motor coordination
- Being raised in an institution or foster home
- Underdeveloped intelligence skills, particularly verbal skills
- Distractibilty and attention problems
- Aggressiveness and anger
- Confusing parent-child communication

Did you think of other variables that could be associated with lower socioeconomic conditions?

Despite the restrictions that lower-class existence can impose on a person's ability to cope with life's stressors, there are, nonetheless, some individuals from lower-class backgrounds who develop considerable resourcefulness and resilience.

When supposed ethnic differences in schizophrenia are examined in the context of socioeconomic status—comparing African Americans, Latinos, and Whites, for example—the ethnic differences tend to vanish. Thus, it seems that poverty and the living conditions poverty engenders are much more likely to be associated with schizophrenia than is ethnicity. This research serves as a powerful reminder to pursue alternative explanations to explain behavior comprehensively.

Overview

We began this chapter by examining what abnormal behavior is, its causes, and its classification. Our coverage of anxiety disorders focused on generalized anxiety disorder, panic disorder, phobic disorders, obsessive-compulsive disorders, and post-traumatic stress disorder. We also studied somatoform disorders—hypochondriasis and conversion disorder—and dissociative disorders—amnesia and fugue, as well as multiple personality. We explored the nature of mood disorders, evaluating major depression, bipolar disorder, suicide, and causes of mood disorders. We read about schizophrenic disorders, including their characteristics, forms, and causes. We also studied personality disorders, substance-use, and the legal aspects of disorders. Remember that you can obtain an overall summary of the chapter by again studying the concept tables on pages 449, 455, 465, and 468.

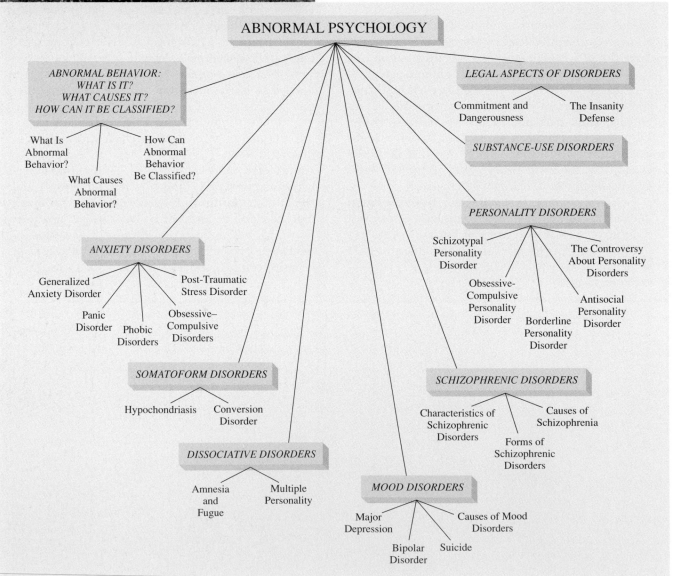

Key Terms

abnormal behavior Behavior that is maladaptive and harmful. p. 444

medical model The model that states that abnormal behavior is a disease or illness precipitated by internal physical causes; also called the disease model; the forerunner of the biological approach. p. 444

neurotic A term for relatively mild mental disorders in which the individual has not lost contact with reality. p. 447

psychotic A term for severe mental disorders in which the individual has lost contact with reality. p. 447

DSM-IV The *Diagnostic and Statistical Manual of Mental Disorders,* fourth edition. The DSM-IV is the most recent major classification of mental disorders and contains eighteen major classifications and more than 200 specific disorders. p. 447

multiaxial system A feature of DSM-IV in which individuals are classified on the basis of five dimensions or "axes" that include the individual's history and highest level of functioning in the last year. This system ensures that the individual will not be merely assigned to a mental disorder category, but instead will be characterized by a number of clinical factors. p. 447

anxiety disorders Psychological disorders that include the following main features: motor tension (jumpiness, trembling, inability to relax), hyperactivity (dizziness, racing heart, or perspiration), and apprehensive expectations and thoughts. p. 448

generalized anxiety disorder An anxiety disorder that consists of persistent anxiety for at least 1 month; an individual with this disorder is unable to specify the reasons for the anxiety. p. 449

panic disorder An anxiety disorder that is marked by the recurrent sudden onset of apprehension or terror. p. 450

phobic disorder An anxiety disorder in which the individual has an irrational, overwhelming, persistent fear of a particular object or situation; commonly called a phobia. p. 450

agoraphobia The fear of entering unfamiliar situations, especially open or public spaces; the most common phobic disorder. p. 451

obsessive-compulsive disorder (OCD) An anxiety disorder in which the individual has anxiety-provoking thoughts that will not go away (obsession) and/or urges to perform repetitive, ritualistic behaviors to prevent or produce a future situation (compulsion). p. 452

post-traumatic stress disorder A mental disorder that develops through exposure to any of several traumatic events—such as war; severely oppressive situations, such as the holocaust; severe abuse, as in rape; natural disasters, such as floods and tornados; and accidental disasters, such as plane crashes. The disorder is characterized by anxiety symptoms that may be apparent immediately after the trauma, or their onset might be delayed by months or even years. p. 452

somatoform disorders Mental disorders in which psychological symptoms take a physical, or somatic, form, even though no physical causes can be found. p. 453

hypochondriasis A somatoform disorder in which the individual has a pervasive fear of illness and disease. p. 453

conversion disorder A somatoform disorder in which an individual experiences genuine physical symptoms, even though no physiological problems can be found. Conversion disorder received its name from psychoanalytic theory, which stressed that anxiety is "converted" into a physical symptom. p. 453

dissociative disorders Psychological disorders that involve a sudden loss of memory or change in identity. Under extreme stress or shock, an individual's conscious awareness becomes dissociated (separated or split) from previous memories and thoughts. p. 453

psychogenic amnesia A dissociative disorder involving memory loss caused by extensive psychological stress. p. 453

fugue A dissociative disorder in which the individual not only develops amnesia but also unexpectedly travels away from home and establishes a new identity; *fugue* means "flight." p. 454

multiple personality The most dramatic but least common dissociative disorder; individuals with this disorder have two or more distinct personalities. p. 454

mood disorders Psychological disorders characterized by wide emotional swings, ranging from deep depression to extreme euphoria and agitation. Depression can occur alone, as in major depression, or it can alternate with mania, as in bipolar disorder. p. 454

major depression A mood disorder in which the individual is deeply unhappy, demoralized, self-derogatory, and bored, showing changes in appetite and sleep patterns, decreased energy, feelings of worthlessness, concentration problems, and guilt feelings that may prompt thoughts of suicide. p. 455

bipolar disorder A mood disorder characterized by extreme mood swings; an individual with this disorder might be depressed, manic, or both. p. 456

learned helplessness A product of exposure to aversive stimulation, such as prolonged stress or pain, over which one has no control. The inability to avoid such aversive stimulation produces an apathetic state of helplessness. p. 459

schizophrenic disorders Severe psychological disorders characterized by distorted thoughts and perceptions, odd communication, inappropriate emotion, abnormal motor behavior, and social withdrawal. The term *schizophrenia* comes from the Latin words *schizo,* meaning "split," and *phrenia,* meaning "mind." The individual's mind is split from reality, and personality loses it unity. p. 460

disorganized schizophrenia A schizophrenic disorder in which an individual has delusions and hallucinations that have little or no recognizable meaning—hence the label *disorganized.* p. 460

catatonic schizophrenia A schizophrenic disorder characterized by bizarre motor behavior, which sometimes takes the form of an immobile stupor. p. 461

paranoid schizophrenia A schizophrenic disorder characterized by delusions of reference, grandeur, and persecution. p. 461

undifferentiated schizophrenia A schizophrenic disorder characterized by disorganized behavior, hallucinations, delusions, and incoherence. p. 462

diathesis-stress view The view that schizophrenia is caused by a combination of environmental stress and biogenetic disposition. p. 464

personality disorders Psychological disorders that develop when personality traits become inflexible, and thus, maladaptive. p. 464

schizotypal personality disorder A personality disorder in the odd/eccentric cluster. Individuals with this disorder appear to be in contact with reality, but many aspects of their behavior are distasteful, which leads others to retreat or withdraw from them. p. 464

obsessive-compulsive personality disorder A disorder in the anxious/fearful cluster of personality disorders; anxious adjustment is the primary feature. Individuals with this disorder tend to be exacting, precise, and orderly. p. 464

borderline personality disorder A disorder in the dramatic/emotional/erratic cluster; behavior reflects these characteristics. p. 465

antisocial personality disorder A disorder in the dramatic/emotional/erratic cluster; the most problematic personality disorder for society. Individuals with this disorder often resort to crime, violence, and delinquency. p. 466

substance-use disorder A disorder characterized by one or more of the following features: (1) a pattern of pathological use that involves frequent intoxication, a need for daily use, and an inability to control use—in a sense, psychological dependence; (2) a significant impairment of social or occupational functioning attributed to drug use; and (3) physical dependence that involves serious withdrawal problems. p. 466

insanity A legal term, not a psychological term. Individuals who are labeled "insane" are deemed mentally disordered and incapable of being responsible for their actions. p. 467

insanity defense A plea of "innocent by reason of insanity," used as a legal defense in criminal trials. p. 467

Resources and Readings in Psychology

Anxiety Disorders and Phobias: A Cognitive Perspective (1985)

by Aaron Beck and Gary Emery
New York: Basic Books

This book provides information about different types of anxiety and how people can change their thinking to overcome the anxiety that is overwhelming them.

Depression and Related Affective Disorders

Johns Hopkins Hospital Meyer 3–181
600 N. Wolfe Street
Baltimore, MD 21205
410–955–4647

This is an organization for individuals with affective disorders and their families, friends, and mental health professionals. The organization provides support, referrals, and educational programs and publishes a quarterly newsletter, *Smooth Sailing.*

Don't Panic (1986)

by Reid Wilson
New York: HarperPerennial

Wilson presents a self-help program for coping with panic attacks. The book explains what panic attacks are, how it feels when you are undergoing one, what type of people are prone to having panic attacks, and how to sort through the physical and psychological aspects of panic attacks. You also learn how to conquer panic attacks, especially through the use of self-monitoring, breathing exercises, focused thinking, mental imagery, and deep muscle relaxation.

Feeling Good (1980)
by David Burns
New York: Avon

Feeling Good is a cognitive therapy approach to coping with depression. Cognitive therapists like Burns, who trained and continues to work with Aaron Beck at the University of Pennsylvania School of Medicine, argue that the key to coping with depression is to identify and restructure faulty negative thinking. In *Feeling Good,* Burns outlines the techniques people can use to identify and combat false assumptions that underlie their flawed negative thinking. Burns' easy-to-read style, extensive use of examples and charts, and enthusiasm give readers a clear understanding of cognitive therapy and the confidence to try out its techniques. Another good choice is Burns' *The Feeling Good Handbook,* which applies cognitive therapy to depression and other problems, including anxiety and those involving relationships.

International Society for the Study of Multiple Personality and Dissociation
5700 Old Orchard Road, 1st Floor
Skokie, IL 60077–1024
708–966–4322

This organization of mental health professionals and students promotes a greater understanding of dissociation.

Journal of Abnormal Psychology

This longstanding journal publishes articles on many different topics in abnormal psychology, including depression, schizophrenia, anxiety disorders, and the nature of abnormal behavior.

Law, Mental Health, and Mental Disorder (1996)
by Bruce Sales and Daniel Shuman (eds.)
Pacific Grove, CA: Brooks/Cole

Comprehensive and detailed coverage of mental health and the law is provided. Topics include newly emerging mental health laws, sex offenders, child abuse, child custody, malpractice, and ethnic minority individuals.

National Foundation for Depressive Illness
P.O. Box 2257
New York, NY 10116
800–248–4344

This foundation provides information and education about recent medical advances in affective mood disorders; it also has a referral service.

National Mental Health Association
1021 Prince Street
Alexandria, VA 22314–2971
800–969–NMHA

This consumer advocacy organization is devoted to promoting mental health and improving the lives of individuals with a mental disorder. It publishes *NMHA Focus* four times a year, as well as pamphlets on mental health issues.

National Mental Health Consumers Association
P.O. Box 1166
Madison, WI 53701

This organization seeks to protect the rights of mental health clients in housing, employment, and public benefits; it encourages the creation of self-help groups and aids them in acquiring funding and networking with other organizations.

Seeing Both Sides: Controversies in Abnormal Psychology (1995)
by Scott Lilienfeld
Pacific Grove, CA: Brooks/Cole

This book presents the pros and cons of nineteen controversial issues in abnormal psychology. The issues include whether psychotherapy is effective, whether psychiatric patients should be hospitalized against their will, and whether the diagnostic system is biased against females.

Youth Suicide National Center
204 E. 2nd Avenue, Suite 203
San Mateo, CA 94401
415–347–3961

This national clearinghouse develops and distributes educational materials on suicide and reviews current youth suicide prevention and support programs. Publications include *Suicide in Youth and What You Can Do About It* and *Helping Your Child Choose Life: A Parent's Guide to Youth Suicide.*

Scoring of the Depression Rating Scale

After completing the Depression Scale (Table 3), use the chart below to assign points to your answers. Add up all the points.

Interpretation

If your score is around 7, then you are like the average male in terms of how much depression you experienced in the last week. If your score is around 8–9, then your score is similar to how much depression the average female experienced in the last week. If your score is 16 or more, you might benefit from professional help for the depression you have been experiencing.

	Rarely or none of the time (Less than 1 day)	*Some or a little of the time (1–2 days)*	*Occasionally or a moderate amount of the time (3–4 days)*	*Most or all of the time (5–7 days)*
1.	0	1	2	3
2.	0	1	2	3
3.	0	1	2	3
4.	3	2	1	0
5.	0	1	3	3
6.	0	1	2	3
7.	0	1	2	3
8.	3	2	1	0
9.	0	1	2	3
10.	0	1	2	3
11.	0	1	2	3
12.	3	2	1	0
13.	0	1	2	3
14.	0	1	2	3
15.	0	1	2	3
16.	3	2	1	0
17.	0	1	2	3
18.	0	1	2	3
19.	0	1	2	3
20.	0	1	2	3

Total Number of Points: ______

CHAPTER

THR

Therapies

John W. Santrock
In Search of More Insight

Therapies

Chapter Outline

Chapter Boxes

EXPLORATIONS IN PSYCHOLOGY

Nothing can be changed until it's faced.

—James Baldwin

Every forward step we take we leave some phantom of ourselves behind.

—John Lancaster Spalding

Images of Psychology

Barbara and Tom's Therapy

Barbara and Tom married right after they graduated from college. She worked to help put him through graduate school. When their first child was born, she stayed home to be a full-time mother. After two more children and 15 years of being a chauffeur and cook for the family, she felt inadequate and unhappy. She decided to seek psychotherapy.

In the first several months of therapy, Barbara talked mainly about herself. As therapy continued she increasingly talked about Tom, often with emotional intensity. After 6 months of therapy, Barbara concluded that while she had made many of her problems, Tom had often made them worse; he treated her only as a housewife and mother, not as someone with a separate identity. Tom felt that Barbara's place was in the home. When she talked about working again or going back to school, he made derogatory comments.

As a result of therapy, Barbara developed enough self-confidence to finally confront Tom about his demeaning remarks and unwillingness to let her do something that would make her feel good about herself. After several months of working through her difficulties with her psychotherapist and trying to get Tom to be more flexible about her interests, Barbara asked Tom to move out. She got a job and eventually divorced Tom. She felt considerable pain and guilt over the decision, mainly because of her fear that it might have a negative impact on the children. Barbara hoped eventually to meet a man who would both love her *and* value her as an individual with her own identity (Sarason & Sarason, 1996).

Was the outcome of Barbara's therapy positive or negative? The answer obviously depends on your own values. Some people might insist that Barbara had an obligation to her husband and should not have confronted him. Others would vehemently disagree; they would say that therapy had been positive because it allowed Barbara to understand herself and develop her own identity, even though it led to divorce.

Preview

Many people today seek therapy. Some, like Barbara, want to gain insight into themselves and improve their lives. Others may need help overcoming trauma, such as physical or sexual abuse in childhood. And others may find themselves in the immobilizing grip of fears such as agoraphobia or the delusions of schizophrenia. Whatever the reason may be that people seek therapy, there are many different therapeutic approaches to help them—at last count there were more than 450. We will explore the most widely practiced therapies and give you an understanding for what it would be like to go to a therapist with a particular orientation. But before we study today's therapies, let's go back in time to discover how the mentally disordered were dealt with at different points in history.

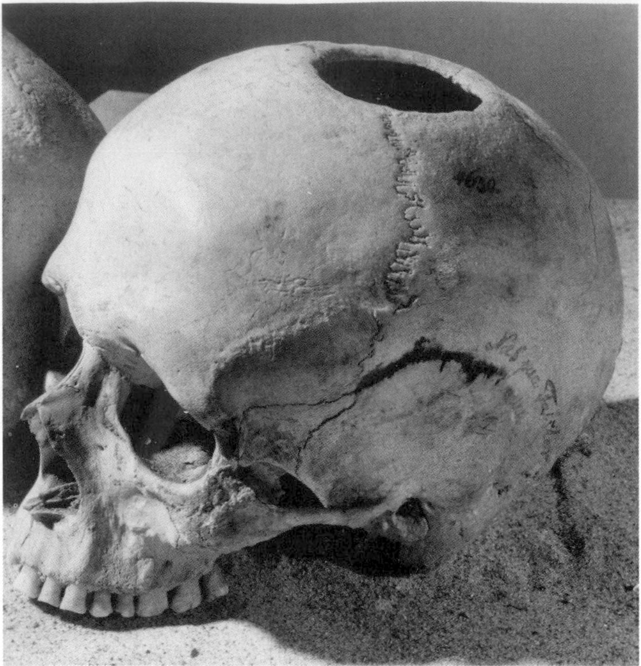

FIGURE 1

Trephining
The technique of trephining involved chipping a hole in the skull through which an evil spirit, believed to be the source of the person's abnormal behavior, might escape. The fact that some people actually survived the operation is shown by this skull. The bone had had time to heal considerably before the individual died.

FIGURE 2

Mentally Disordered People as Witches
Many mentally disordered individuals were thought to be witches in the fourteenth to seventeenth centuries. As many as 500,000 people were burned at the stake because they were believed to be witches, who were thought to have supernatural powers deriving from contact with the devil. This painting by Francisco Goya (1746–1828) is an image of the devil and the "witches" he had possessed.

Historical Perspective

In primitive societies, abnormal behavior was thought to be caused by evil spirits residing within the afflicted person. *Trephining,* which involved chipping a hole in the skull, was one early method of letting the evil spirit escape (see figure 1). The Greek physician Hippocrates, however, believed that mental problems and abnormal behavior were the result of brain damage or an imbalance of body chemicals. In the fourth century B.C., Hippocrates prescribed rest, exercise, a bland diet, and abstinence from sex and alcohol as cures for depression.

Over time, Hippocrates' ideas were lost. In the Middle Ages, theories of "possession" by evil spirits or the devil again became popular. People who simply were "different" or who suffered from neurological disorders such as Tourette's syndrome or epilepsy were thought to be possessed or witches. *Exorcism,* a religious rite that involved prayer, starvation, beatings, and various forms of torture, was used to cast out evil spirits. The notion behind exorcism was to make the mentally disordered people so physically uncomfortable that no devil would want to stay in their bodies. If that didn't work, the only "cure" left was to get rid of the body altogether. Between the fourteenth and seventeenth centuries, 200,000 to 500,000 people thought to be witches were either hanged or burned at the stake (see figure 2).

During the Renaissance, *asylums* (*asylum* means "sanctuary") were built to house the mentally disordered. Mentally disordered people were placed in an asylum to protect them from the exploitation they experienced on the streets. But the asylums were not much better; the mentally disordered often were chained to walls, caged, or fed sparingly.

Fortunately, Philippe Pinel (1745–1826), the head physician at a large asylum in Paris, initiated a significant change in the treatment of the mentally disordered. Pinel described them as ordinary people who could not reason well because of their serious personal problems. He believed that treating the mentally disordered like animals was not only inhumane but also hindered their recovery. Pinel convinced the French government to unchain large numbers of patients, some of whom had not been outside of the asylum for 30 to 40 years (see figure 3). He replaced the dungeons with bright rooms and spent long hours talking with patients, listening to their problems and giving advice.

Although Pinel's efforts led to reform, it was slow. Even as late as the nineteenth century in the United States, the mentally disordered were kept alongside criminals in

FIGURE 3

Pinel Unchaining Mentally Disordered Individuals
In this painting, Philippe Pinel is shown unchaining the inmates at La Bicêtre Hospital. Pinel's efforts led to widespread reform and more humane treatment of mentally disordered individuals.

prisons. Dorothea Dix, a nurse who had taken a position at a prison in the middle of the nineteenth century, was instrumental in getting the mentally disordered separated from criminals. She embarked on a state-to-state campaign to upgrade prisons and persuaded officials to use better judgement in deciding which individuals should be placed in prisons. State governments began building large asylums for the mentally disordered because of Dix's efforts, although the conditions in the asylums often were no better than in the prisons.

In the twentieth century, significant advances in how we view and treat the mentally disordered have taken place. The importance of humane treatment, concern for preventing mental disorders, and improved methods of therapy characterize the modern view.

The Nature of Psychotherapy

Psychotherapy *is the process used by mental health professionals to help individuals recognize, define, and overcome their psychological and interpersonal difficulties and improve their adjustment.* Psychotherapists use a number of strategies to accomplish these goals: talking, interpreting, listening, rewarding, and modeling, for example. Psychotherapy *does not* include biomedical treatment, such as drugs or surgery.

Theories of personality are the basis for a number of important approaches to psychotherapy. The psychoanalytic theories of Freud as well as his dissenters and revisionists underlie the psychodynamic therapies. The humanistic theories of Rogers and Maslow provide an important foundation for the humanistic therapies. The term **insight therapy** *characterizes both the psychodynamic and humanistic therapies because their goal is to encourage insight and awareness of oneself.* The behavioral and social learning theories of Skinner and Bandura, respectively, stimulated the development of the behavioral therapies. Other important approaches to therapy include cognitive therapies, couple and family therapy, group therapy, and the community mental health approach. We will consider each of these therapies, as well as biomedical treatment, later in the chapter.

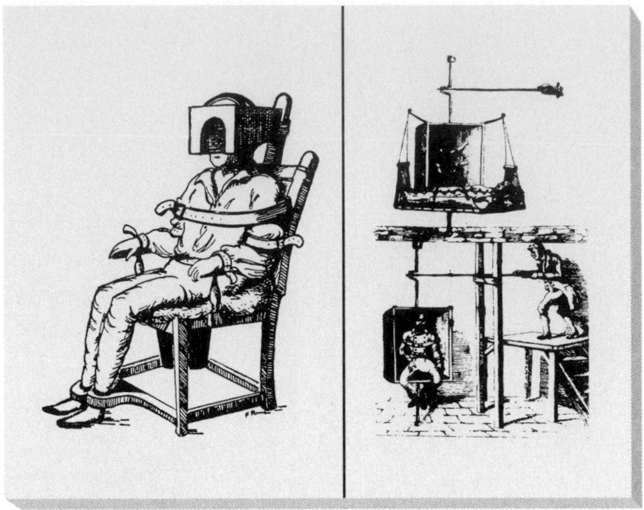

Even after Pinel and others reformed mental institutions, some rather strange techniques were invented to control the most difficult mentally disordered individuals. The tranquilizing chair (left) and circulating swing (right) were used to calm mentally disordered individuals at the beginning of the nineteenth century. Fortunately, their use was soon abandoned.

Most contemporary therapists do not use one form of therapy exclusively with their clients. The majority of today's therapists are *eclectic.* That is, they use a variety of approaches to therapy. Often a therapist will tailor the therapeutic approach to the client's needs. Even a therapist with a psychodynamic orientation might use humanistic approaches, or a family therapist might use behavioral techniques, for example.

Psychotherapy is practiced by a variety of mental health professionals, including clinical psychologists, psychiatrists, and counselors. Psychiatrists have a medical degree and can prescribe drugs for mental disorders. Clinical psychologists, by contrast, are trained in graduate programs of psychology and use psychotherapy rather than drugs to treat mental problems. Table 1 lists the main types of mental health professionals, their degrees, years of education required, and the nature of their training.

Just as there is a variety of mental health professionals, there is a variety of settings in which therapy takes place. During the first half of this century, psychotherapists primarily practiced in mental hospitals, where individuals remained for months and even years. During the last several decades, psychologists have recognized that psychotherapy is not just for those who are so disturbed they cannot live in society. Today, people who seek counseling and psychotherapy may go to a community health center, an outpatient facility of a hospital, or to the private office of a mental health practitioner.

Psychotherapy can be expensive. Even though reduced fees, and occasionally free services, can be arranged in public hospitals for those who are poor, many people who are most in need of psychotherapy do not get it. Psychotherapists have been criticized for preferring to work with young, attractive, verbal, intelligent, and successful clients (called YAVISes) rather than quiet, ugly, old, institutionalized, and different clients (called QUOIDs). Mental health professionals have become increasingly sensitive to such problems, but a national sample of clinical psychologists concluded that (a) the poorest and least educated clients have poor prognoses for successful therapy, and (b) psychologists are much less interested in treating this type of client than people from higher socioeconomic classes (Sutton & Kessler, 1986).

The challenge involved in paying for psychotherapeutic services has led to dramatic changes in mental health care delivery in recent years (Halonen & Santrock, 1996). Concerned by mounting mental health costs that seemed to be derived from protracted psychotherapy with questionable gains, health insurance companies began to seek new delivery systems. **Managed health care,** *a system in which external reviewers approve the type and length of treatment to justify insurance reimbursement,* has grown rapidly. Therapists whose clients participate in managed health care must confer with an external agent about their treatment goals and make systematic reports about client progress to secure continued insurance funding.

Many problems have surfaced with this practice (Broskowski, 1995; Fox, 1995; Glueckauf & others, 1996). Although managed health care has promoted the development of more explicit and measurable treatment plans, the emphasis on cost management clearly favors short-term over long-term therapy methods. This emphasis can shift some treatment inappropriately to superficial interventions when the clinical problem requires more depth and more time than the health care managers allow. Both clients and therapists report discomfort with the potential violation of confidentiality and privacy when reporting therapy details to a third party. Some research suggests that the bureaucracy involved in setting up the watchdog system may absorb the savings that were gained through the implementation of the system. Insurance reimbursement and managed health care will both be significantly affected by implementation of national health care mandates (Hersch, 1995; Karon, 1995).

Those who seek treatment from qualified mental health care practitioners can feel some reassurance that their problems will be addressed professionally and ethically, based on the systems used in certifying practitioners. Licensing and certificate practices require mental health care providers to know relevant state and professional ethical codes before their credentials are granted. Most of

TABLE 1

Main Types of Mental Health Professionals

Professional Type	Degree	Experience Beyond Bachelor's Degree	Nature of Training
Clinical psychologist and counseling psychologist	Ph.D.	5–7 years	Includes both clinical and research training. Involves a 1-year internship in a psychiatric hospital or mental health facility. Recently some universities have developed Psy.D. programs, which lead to a professional degree with a stronger clinical than research emphasis. The Psy.D. training program takes about the same number of years as the clinical psychology Ph.D. program and also requires a 1-year internship.
Psychiatrist	M.D.	7–9 years	Four years of medical school, plus an internship and residency in psychiatry are required. A psychiatry residency involves supervision in therapies, including psychotherapy and biomedical therapy.
Social worker	M.S.W. or Ph.D.	2–5 years	Graduate work in a school of social work that includes specialized clinical training in mental health facilities.
Psychiatric nurse	R.N., M.A., or Ph.D.	0–5 years	Graduate work in a school of nursing with special emphasis on care of mentally disturbed individuals in hospital settings and mental health facilities.
Occupational therapist	B.S., M.A., or Ph.D.	0–5 years	Emphasis on occupational training with focus on physically or psychologically handicapped individuals. Stresses getting individuals back into the mainstream of work.
Pastoral counselor	None to Ph.D. or D.D. (Doctor of Divinity)	0–5 years	Requires ministerial background and training in psychology. An internship in a mental health facility as a chaplin is recommended.
Counselor	M.A.	2 years	Graduate work in a department of psychology or department of education with specialized training in counseling techniques.

Note: The above list refers to the mental health professionals who go through formal training at recognized academic and medical institutions. The government commonly licenses these professionals and certifies their skills. Professional organizations regulate their activities.

these codes require ethical practice as well as vigilance about unethical practice from others in the field. The codes typically address the importance of doing no harm to clients, protecting the privacy of clients, avoiding dual relationships with clients, and staying updated in contemporary practices. Violations of ethical codes can result in loss of license to practice.

So far we have glimpsed the history of psychotherapy and the basic nature of psychotherapy. Contemporary psychotherapies include a number of diverse approaches to working with people to reduce their problems and improve their adjustment. We will begin our survey of psychotherapies with the insight therapies, first describing psychodynamic therapies, and then turning to the humanistic therapies.

PSYCHODYNAMIC THERAPIES

The **psychodynamic therapies** *stress the importance of the unconscious mind, extensive interpretation by the therapist, and the role of infant and early childhood experiences.* Many psychodynamic approaches have grown out of Freud's psychoanalytic theory of personality. Today some therapists with a psychodynamic perspective show allegiance to Freud, others do not.

Freud's Psychoanalysis

Psychoanalysis *is Freud's therapeutic technique for analyzing an individual's unconscious thought.* Freud believed that clients' current problems could be traced to childhood experiences, many of which involved conflicts about sexuality. He also recognized that the early experiences were not

To encourage his patients to relax, Freud had them recline on the couch while he sat in the chair on the left, out of their view.

readily available to the individual's conscious mind. Only through extensive questioning, probing, and analyzing was Freud able to put the pieces of the individual's personality together and help the individual become aware of how these early experiences were affecting present adult behavior. To reach the shadowy world of the unconscious, psychoanalytic therapists often use the following therapeutic techniques: free association, catharsis, interpretation, dream analysis, transference, and resistance, each of which we discuss in turn.

In psychoanalysis, the therapist uses **free association,** *the technique of encouraging individuals to say aloud whatever comes to mind no matter how trivial or embarrassing.* When Freud detected a person resisting the spontaneous flow of thoughts, he probed further. He believed that the crux of the person's emotional problem probably lurked below this point of resistance. By encouraging clients to talk freely, Freud thought that emotional feelings would emerge. **Catharsis** *is the psychoanalytic term for clients' release of emotional tension when they relive an emotionally charged and conflicted experience.*

Interpretation plays an important role in psychoanalysis. As the therapist interprets free association and dreams, the client's statements and behavior are not taken at face value. To understand what is truly causing the client's conflicts, the therapist constantly searches for symbolic, hidden meanings in what the individual says and does. From time to time the therapist suggests possible meanings of the client's statements and behavior. Explorations in Psychology 1 provides an example of how a psychoanalyst used interpretation to improve a client's understanding of her problems.

Dream analysis *is the psychotherapeutic technique used by psychoanalysts to interpret a client's dream. Psychoanalysts believe dreams contain information about the individual's unconscious thoughts and conflicts.* Freud distinguished between the dream's manifest and latent content. **Manifest content** *is the psychoanalytic term for the conscious, remembered aspects of a dream.* **Latent content** *is the psychoanalytic term for the unconscious, unremembered, symbolic aspects of a dream.* The psychoanalyst interprets the dream by analyzing the manifest content for disguised unconscious wishes and needs, especially those that are sexual

Explorations in Psychology 1

Penetrating Mrs. A. H.'s Unconscious Thoughts

Mrs. A. H. began her session with a psychoanalyst by describing how her husband, a businessman, had been caught in a financial squeeze and had anxiously gone to the bank to raise additional funds. She was in a state of panic, even though there was a good probability her husband would be able to obtain a loan from the bank. The previous night she had had diarrhea and had dreamed that her two sisters were discussing her mother, saying that she seldom did all that she had promised to others. Mrs. A. H. then commented that her mother had been wealthy and could have provided all the money her husband needed. Her father could have too, she said, but he was hard to deal with. She went on to recall her mother's involvement with another man and the illness her mother had had when Mrs. A. H. was an infant. Her sisters, who were considerably older, had taken care of their mother, but Mrs. A. H. wondered why they criticized their mother, who had been briefly hospitalized. They tended to blame poor health habits for her illness. Mrs. A. H. also reviewed her adolescent years, during which her mother denied the impact of her absence. She thought her mother's attitude was rather bizarre.

The psychoanalytic session seemed to be prompted by the husband's financial crisis and the repercussions it had for Mrs. A. H.'s longings for her mother, who would rescue her and her husband; her rage at her mother for her absence and possible unfaithfulness; and some implied concerns regarding her husband's ability to handle the business situation. There was little in the session to suggest what unconscious thoughts were evoking the gastrointestinal symptoms.

However, this session is intriguing in light of the next session that took place. In that session, Mrs. A. H. revealed she inadvertently had not mentioned an incident that had occurred prior to the previous session. One of her girlfriends had seen her husband having a drink with an attractive woman at a local restaurant. In this context, the psychoanalyst was able to gain more insight into what Mrs. A. H. had said in the previous session. In fact, she had used the past to conceal the present. She had used her mother as a screen to hide her most active and meaningful conflicts and unconscious fantasies about her husband. In the second session, her free associations related to fears of finding out that her husband was having an affair, to her dread of confronting him, and to her anxiety that others would be talking about his having an affair. The associations revealed her rage, her wishes to publicly humiliate him, and her death wishes toward him. The sister in the dream had also been suspected of having an affair. The bowel symptoms actually related to fantasies of defecating on and soiling her husband in an uncontrolled release of aggression, according to the analyst (Langs, 1978).

---

and aggressive in nature. For some examples of the sexual symbols psychoanalysts use to interpret dreams, turn to figure 4. But even Freud cautioned against over-interpreting. As he once quipped, "Sometimes a cigar is just a cigar."

Freud believed transference was an inevitable and essential aspect of the analyst-client relationship. **Transference** *is the psychoanalytic term for a client's relating to the analyst in ways that reproduce or relive important relationships in the client's life.* A client might interact with an analyst as if the analyst were a parent or lover, for example. When transference dominates therapy, the client's comments may become directed toward the analyst's personal life. Transference is often difficult to overcome in psychotherapy. However, transference can be used therapeutically as a model of how clients relate to important people in their lives.

Resistance *is the psychoanalytic term for the client's unconscious defense strategies that prevent the analyst from understanding the client's problems.* Resistance occurs because it is painful to bring conflicts into conscious awareness. By resisting therapy, individuals do not have to face their problems. Showing up late or missing sessions, arguing with the psychoanalyst, or faking free associations are examples of resistance. Some clients go on endlessly about a trivial matter to avoid facing their conflicts. A major goal of the analyst is to break through this resistance (Rosenthal, 1996; Strean, 1996).

Contemporary Psychodynamic Therapies

Although the face of psychodynamic therapy has changed extensively since its inception almost a century ago, many contemporary psychodynamic therapists still probe a client's unconscious thoughts about their earliest childhood experiences to provide clues to the client's current problems. Many contemporary psychodynamic therapists also try to help clients gain insight into their emotionally laden, repressed conflicts.

However, only a small percentage of contemporary psychodynamic therapists rigorously follow Freud's guidelines. Although many psychodynamic therapists still

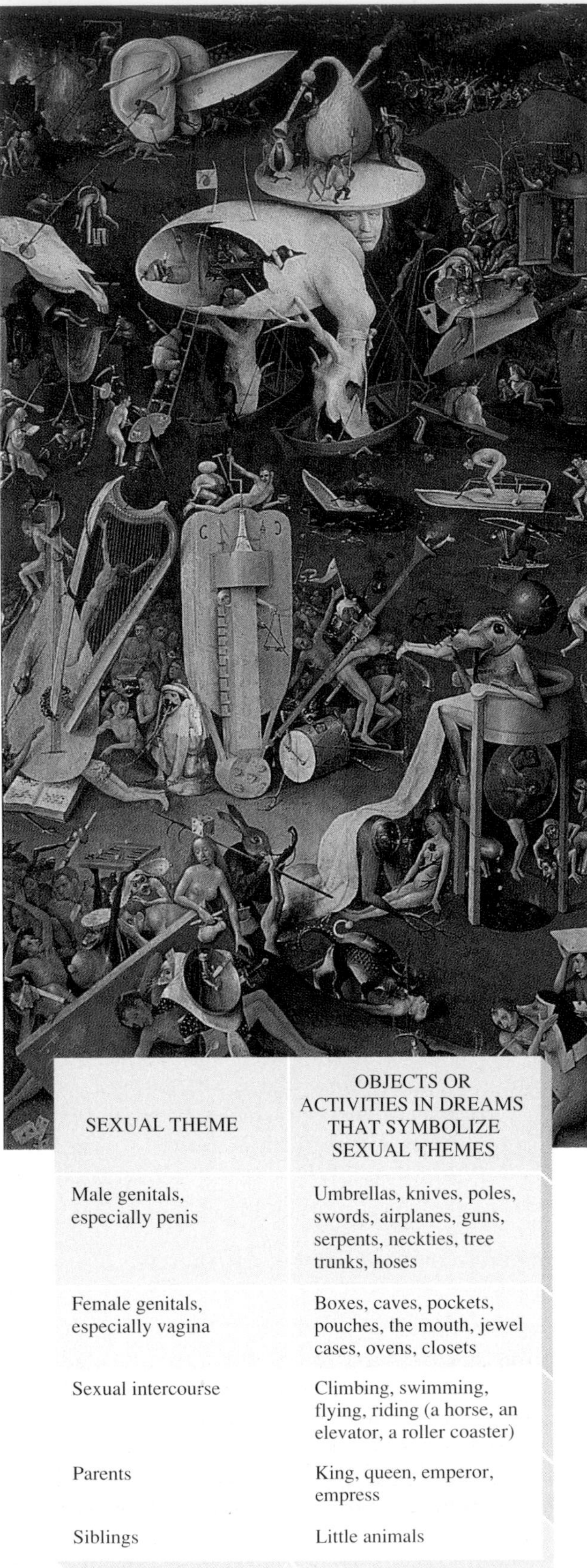

SEXUAL THEME	OBJECTS OR ACTIVITIES IN DREAMS THAT SYMBOLIZE SEXUAL THEMES
Male genitals, especially penis	Umbrellas, knives, poles, swords, airplanes, guns, serpents, neckties, tree trunks, hoses
Female genitals, especially vagina	Boxes, caves, pockets, pouches, the mouth, jewel cases, ovens, closets
Sexual intercourse	Climbing, swimming, flying, riding (a horse, an elevator, a roller coaster)
Parents	King, queen, emperor, empress
Siblings	Little animals

FIGURE 4

The Psychoanalyst's Interpretation of Sexual Symbolism in Dreams

emphasize the importance of unconscious thought and early family experiences, they also accord more power to the conscious mind and current relationships in understanding a client's problems. Clients rarely lie on a couch or see their therapist several times a week. Now clients usually have weekly appointments and sit in a comfortable chair facing their therapist.

Contemporary psychodynamic approaches emphasize the development of the self in social contexts (Erikson, 1968; Kohut, 1977; St Clair, 1996). In Heinz Kohut's view, early relationships with attachment figures, such as one's parents, are critical. As we develop we do not relinquish these attachments; we continue to need them. Kohut's prescription for therapy involves getting the patient to identify and seek out appropriate relationships with others. He also wants patients to develop more realistic appraisals of relationships. Kohut believes therapists need to interact with their clients in ways that are empathic and understanding. As we will see next, empathy and understanding are absolute cornerstones for humanistics therapists as they encourage their clients to further their sense of self.

HUMANISTIC THERAPIES

In the **humanistic psychotherapies** *clients are encouraged to understand themselves and to grow personally. In contrast to psychodynamic therapies, humanistic therapies emphasize conscious thoughts rather than unconscious thoughts, the present rather than the past, and growth and fulfillment rather than curing an illness.* Two main forms of the humanistic psychotherapies are person-centered therapy and Gestalt therapy.

Person-Centered Therapy

Person-centered therapy *is a form of humanistic therapy developed by Carl Rogers (1961, 1980) in which the therapist provides a warm, supportive atmosphere to improve the client's self-concept and encourage the client to gain insight about problems.* Rogers' therapy was initially called client-centered therapy, but he rechristened it person-centered therapy to underscore his deep belief that every person has the ability to grow. The relationship between the therapist and the person is an important aspect of Rogers' therapy. The therapist must enter into an intensely personal relationship with the client, not as a physician diagnosing a disease, but as one human being to another. Notice that Rogers referred to the "client" and then the "person" rather than the "patient."

Rogers believed each of us grew up in a world filled with *conditions of worth,* the positive regard we received from others had strings attached. We usually did not receive love and praise unless we conformed to the standards and demands of others. This causes us to be unhappy and have low self-esteem as adults; rarely do we feel that we measure up to such standards or feel that we are as good as others expect us to be.

To free the person from worry about the demands of society, the therapist creates a warm and caring environment

Frederick (Fritz) Perls was the founder of Gestalt therapy.

(Cain, 1996). The Rogerian therapist never disapproves of what the client says or does. Rogers believed this *unconditional positive regard* improved the person's self-esteem. The therapist's role is "nondirective"; that is, he or she does not try to lead the client to any particular revelation. The therapist is there to listen sympathetically to the clients' problems and to encourage greater self-regard, independent self-appraisal, and decision making.

Rogers advocated other techniques in addition to unconditional positive regard. **Genuineness** *is the Rogerian technique of being genuine and not hiding behind a facade. Therapists must let clients know their feelings.* **Accurate empathy** *is Rogers' term for the therapist's identification with client.* Rogers believed therapists must sense what it is like to be the client at any moment in the client-therapist relationship. **Active listening** *is Rogers' term for listening to another person with total attention to what that person says and means.* One way therapists improve active listening is by restating and supporting what the client has said and done.

Gestalt Therapy

Gestalt therapy *is a humanistic therapy developed by Fritz Perls (1893–1970) in which the therapist questions and challenges clients to help clients become more aware of their feelings and face their problems.* Perls was trained in Europe as a Freudian psychoanalyst, but as his career developed, his ideas became noticeably different from Freud's. Perls (1969) agreed with Freud that psychological problems originate in unresolved past conflicts and that these conflicts need to be acknowledged and worked through. Also like Freud, Perls stressed that interpretation of dreams is an important aspect of therapy.

But in other ways, Perls and Freud were miles apart. Perls believed that unresolved conflicts should be brought to bear on the here and now of the individual's life. The therapist *pushes* clients into deciding whether they will continue to allow the past to control their future or whether they will choose *right now* what they want to be in the future. To this end, Perls *confronted* individuals and encouraged them to actively control their lives and be open about their feelings.

Gestalt therapists use a number of techniques to encourage individuals to be open about their feelings, to develop self-awareness, and to actively control their lives. The therapist sets examples, encourages congruence between verbal and nonverbal behavior, and uses role playing. To demonstrate an important point to a client, the Gestalt therapist might exaggerate a client's characteristic. To stimulate change, the therapist often will openly confront the client.

Another technique of Gestalt therapy is role playing, either by the client, the therapist, or both. For example, if an individual is bothered by conflict with her mother, the therapist might play the role of the mother and reopen the quarrel. The therapist may encourage the individual to act out her hostile feelings toward her mother by yelling, swearing, or kicking the couch, for example. In this way, Gestalt therapists hope to help individuals better manage their feelings instead of letting their feelings control them.

As you probably noticed, the Gestalt therapist is much more directive than the nondirective, person-centered therapist. By being more directive, the Gestalt therapist provides more interpretation and feedback. Nonetheless, both of these humanistic therapies encourage individuals to take responsibility for their feelings and actions, to truly be themselves, to understand themselves, to develop a sense of freedom, and to look at what they are doing with their lives.

At this point we have studied a number of ideas about the history of psychotherapy, the nature of psychotherapy, the psychoanalytic therapies, and the humanistic therapies. A summary of these ideas is presented in concept table 1. Now that we have studied the insight therapies, we turn our attention to the therapies that take a very different approach to working with individuals to reduce their problems and improve their adjustment—the behavior therapies.

Behavior Therapies

Behavior therapies *use principles of learning to reduce or eliminate maladaptive behavior.* Behavior therapies are based on the behavioral and social learning theories of learning and personality. Behavior therapists do not search for unconscious conflicts like psychodynamic therapists or encourage individuals to develop accurate perceptions of their feelings and self like humanistic therapists. Insight and self-awareness are not the keys to helping individuals develop more adaptive behavior patterns, say the behavior therapists. The insight therapies—psychodynamic and humanistic—treat maladaptive symptoms as signs of underlying,

CONCEPT TABLE 1

Historical Perspective, the Nature of Psychotherapy, Psychodynamic Therapies, and Humanistic Therapies

Concept	Processes/Related Ideas	Characteristics/Description
Historical Perspective	Its nature	Many early treatments of mental disorders were inhumane. Asylums were built during the Renaissance. Pinel's efforts led to extensive reform. Dix's efforts helped separate the mentally disordered individuals from prisoners.
The Nature of Psychotherapy	What is psychotherapy?	Psychotherapy is a process to reduce individuals' problems and improve adjustment. Approaches include psychodynamic, humanistic, and behavioral and social learning. The term *insight therapy* is used to describe both the psychodynamic and humanistic therapies. Many therapists take an eclectic approach to therapy. Practitioners include clinical psychologists, counseling psychologists, psychiatrists, and social workers. Psychotherapy takes place in a greater variety of settings today than it did in the past. Lower socioeconomic-status individuals are less likely to receive therapy than higher socioeconomic-status individuals. Managed health care has increased dramatically in recent years, although not without problems. Psychotherapists are supposed to adhere to certain ethical standards.
Psychodynamic Therapies	Their nature	They stress the importance of the unconscious mind, early family experiences, and extensive interpretation by therapists.
	Freud's psychoanalysis	Mental disorders are caused by unresolved unconscious conflicts between the id, ego, and superego; the conflicts originate in early childhood family experiences. A therapist's interpretation of free association, dreams, transference, and resistance provides tools for understanding a client's unconscious conflicts.
	Contemporary psychodynamic therapies	Although psychodynamic therapy has changed, many contemporary psychodynamic therapists still probe the unconscious mind for early family experiences that might provide clues to clients' current problems. The development of the self in social contexts is an important theme in Kohut's contemporary approach.
Humanistic Therapies	Their nature	Clients are encouraged to understand themselves and to grow personally. The humanistic therapies emphasize conscious thoughts, the present, and growth and fulfillment.
	Person-centered therapy	This therapy was developed by Carl Rogers; a therapist provides a warm, supportive atmosphere to improve a client's self-concept and to encourage the client to gain insight into problems. The therapist replaces conditions of worth with unconditional positive regard and uses genuineness, accurate empathy, and active listening to raise the client's self-esteem.
	Gestalt therapy	This therapy was developed by Fritz Perls. In this approach, therapists question and challenge clients to help them become more aware of their feelings and face their problems. This approach is more directive than person-centered therapy.

internal problems. Behavior therapists, however, assume that the overt maladaptive symptoms are the problem. Individuals can become aware of why they are depressed and still be depressed, say the behavior therapists. The behavior therapist tries to eliminate the depressed symptoms or behaviors themselves rather than trying to get individuals to gain insight or awareness of why they are depressed (Lazarus, 1996; O'Donahue & Krasner, 1995).

The behavior therapies were initially based almost exclusively on the learning principles of classical and operant

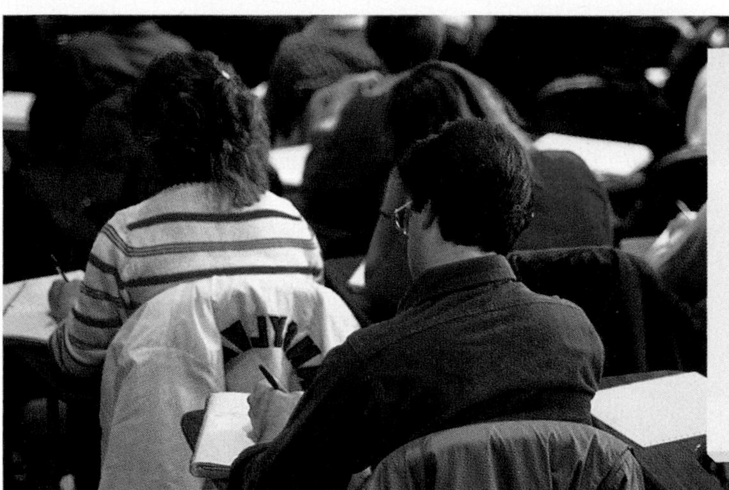

1. On the way to the university on the day of an examination
2. In the process of answering an examination paper
3. Before the unopened doors of the examination room
4. Awaiting the distribution of examination papers
5. The examination paper lies face down before her
6. The night before an examination
7. One day before an examination
8. Two days before an examination
9. Three days before an examination
10. Four days before an examination
11. Five days before an examination
12. A week before an examination
13. Two weeks before an examination
14. A month before an examination

FIGURE 5

A Desensitization Hierarchy from Most to Least Fearsome Circumstances
Systematic desensitization has been especially helpful in reducing anxiety in tension-producing situations.

conditioning, but behavior therapies have become more diverse in recent years. As social learning theory grew in popularity and the cognitive approach became more prominent in psychology, behavior therapists increasingly included cognitive factors in their therapy. First, we will discuss the classical and operant conditioning approaches, then turn to the cognitive behavior therapies.

Classical Conditioning Approaches

Some behaviors, especially fears, are acquired or learned through classical conditioning. If such fears can be learned, possibly they can be unlearned as well. If an individual has learned to fear snakes or heights through classical conditioning, perhaps the individual can unlearn the fear. Two procedures based on classical conditioning that are used in behavior therapy are systematic desensitization and aversive conditioning.

Systematic Desensitization

Systematic desensitization *is a method of behavior therapy that treats anxiety by associating deep relaxation with successive visualizations of increasingly intense anxiety-producing situations; this technique is based on classical conditioning* (Wolpe, 1963). Consider the common fear of giving a speech. Using systematic desensitization, the behavior therapist first asks the client which aspects of the feared situation—in this case, giving a speech—are the most and least frightening. Then, the behavior therapist arranges these circumstances in order from most to least frightening. An example of this type of desensitization hierarchy is shown in figure 5.

The next step is to teach individuals to relax. Clients are taught to recognize the presence of muscular contractions or tensions in various parts of their bodies and then how to contract and relax different muscles. Once individuals are relaxed, the therapist asks them to imagine the least fearful stimulus in the hierarchy. Subsequently, the therapist moves up the list of items from least to most fearful while clients remain relaxed. Eventually, individuals are able to imagine the most fearsome circumstance without being afraid—in our example, on the way to the university the day of the oral exam. In this manner, individuals learn to relax while thinking about the speech instead of feeling anxious.

Researchers have found that systematic desensitization is often an effective treatment for a number of phobias, such as fear of giving a speech, fear of heights, fear of flying, fear of dogs, and fear of snakes. If you were afraid of snakes, for instance, the therapist might initially have you watch someone handle a snake. Then the therapist would ask you to engage in increasingly more feared behaviors—you might first just go into the same room with the snake, next you would approach the snake, subsequently you'd touch the snake, and eventually you would play with the snake (Bandura, Blanchard, & Ritter, 1969). Figure 6 shows a desensitization treatment with individuals who were afraid of snakes.

Aversive Conditioning

Aversive conditioning *is an approach to behavior therapy that involves repeated pairings of the undesirable behavior with aversive stimuli to decrease the behavior's rewards so the individual will stop doing it; this technique is also based on classical conditioning.* Aversive conditioning is used to teach people to avoid such behaviors as smoking, eating, and drinking. Electric shocks, nausea-inducing substances, and verbal insults are some of the noxious stimuli used in aversive conditioning.

How could aversive conditioning be used to reduce a person's alcohol consumption? Every time a person drank

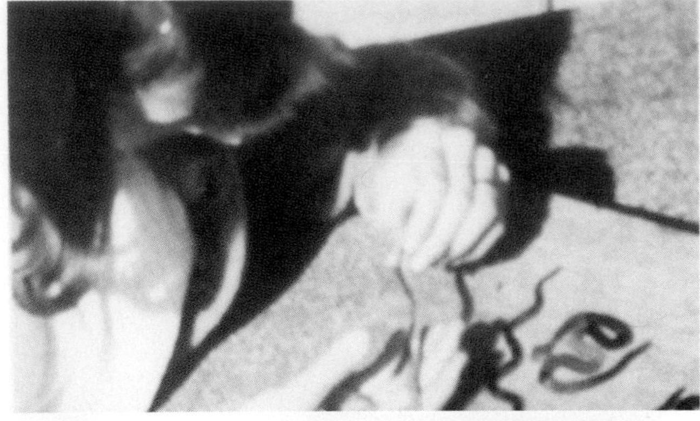

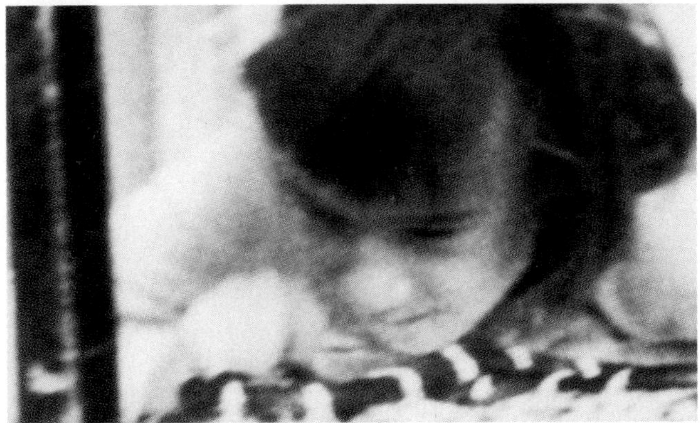

FIGURE 6

Systematic Desensitization
Systematic desensitization is often used to help eliminate phobias. In this systematic desensitization treatment, individuals have progressed from handling rubber snakes (*top*), to peering at snakes in an aquarium (*second from top*), to handling snakes with rubber gloves (*second from bottom*), to handling live but harmless snakes (*bottom*).

an alcoholic beverage, he or she also would consume a mixture that induced nausea. In classical conditioning terminology, the alcoholic beverage is the conditioned stimulus and the nausea-inducing agent is the unconditioned stimulus. By repeatedly pairing alcohol with the nausea-inducing agent, alcohol becomes the conditioned stimulus that elicits nausea, the conditioned response. As a consequence, alcohol no longer is associated with something pleasant, but rather something highly unpleasant.

Operant Conditioning Approaches

Andy is a college student who has difficulty studying. He complains that he always starts to fall asleep when he goes to his desk to study. He decided to see a therapist about how he might improve his studying because his grades were deteriorating. The behavior therapist's first recommendation was to replace his 40-watt bulb with a brighter one. The second recommendation was to turn his desk away from his bed. The third recommendation was to do only schoolwork at his desk; he was not allowed to write a letter, read a magazine, or daydream while at the desk. If he wanted to do any of these other things, he was told to leave his desk.

To help Andy improve his study habits the behavior therapist first evaluated Andy's responses to the stimuli in his room. Then the therapist gave Andy direct and precise suggestions about what to do. The therapist did not spend time analyzing his unconscious conflicts or encouraging him to "get in touch with his feelings." Rather, the therapist wanted to change Andy's responses to the stimuli in his environment that were causing the problem.

Behavior modification *is the application of operant conditioning principles to change human behavior; its main goal is to replace unacceptable responses with acceptable, adaptive ones.* Consequences for behavior are established to ensure that acceptable actions are reinforced and unacceptable ones are not. Advocates of behavior modification believe that many emotional and behavioral problems are caused by inadequate (or inappropriate) response consequences (Stanley & Turner, 1995). Consider the circumstance in which Barbara and her parents are on a collision course. Things get so bad that her parents decide to see a clinical psychologist. The psychologist, who has a behavioral orientation, talks with each family member, trying to get them to pinpoint the problem. The psychologist gets the family to sign a behavioral contract that spells out what everyone needs to do to reduce the conflict. Barbara agrees to (1) be home before 11 P.M. on weeknights; (2) look for a part-time job so she can begin to pay for some of her activities; and (3) refrain from calling her parents insulting names. Her parents agree to (1) talk to Barbara in a low tone of voice rather than yell if they are angry; (2) refrain from criticizing young people, especially Barbara's friends; and (3) give Barbara a small sum of money each week for gas, makeup, and socializing, but only until she has found a job.

A **token economy** *is a behavior modification system in which behaviors are reinforced with tokens (such as poker chips)* *that later can be exchanged for desired rewards (such as candy, money, or going to a movie).* Token economies have been established in a number of classrooms, institutions for the mentally retarded, homes for delinquents, and mental hospitals with schizophrenics.

In some instances, behavior modification works, in others it does not. One person may become so wedded to the tokens that when they are removed, the positive behavior associated with the tokens may disappear. Yet another person might continue the positive behavior after the tokens are removed. Some critics object to behavior modification because they believe such extensive control of another person's behavior unethically infringes on the individual's rights. But as with the college student who could not study, maladaptive responses can be turned into adaptive ones through behavior modification.

The behavior therapies you have just read about do not include cognitive processes in their effort to modify the behavior of individuals with problems. As we see next, cognitive behavior therapy gives thought processes a more prominent role in helping individuals reduce their problems and improve their adjustment.

Cognitive Behavior Therapy

Cognitive behavior therapy *is an approach to behavior therapy that tries to help individuals behave more adaptively by modifying their thoughts. Cognitive behavior therapy stems from both cognitive psychology, with its emphasis on the effect of thoughts on behavior, and behaviorism, with is emphasis on behavior-change techniques.* Cognitive behavior therapists strive to change misconceptions, strengthen coping skills, increase self-control, and encourage constructive self-reflection (Meichenbaum, 1993; Rosen, Orosan, & Reiter, 1995).

An important aspect of cognitive behavior therapy is **self-efficacy,** *the belief that one can master a situation and produce positive outcomes.* Self-efficacy is especially important in developing adaptive behavior according to social learning therapist Albert Bandura. Moreover, Bandura (1986, 1994) believes that self-efficacy is the key to successful therapy. At each step of the therapy process, people need to bolster their confidence by telling themselves, "I'm going to master this problem," "I can do it," "I'm improving; I'm getting better," and so on. As people gain confidence and engage in adaptive behavior, the successes become intrinsically motivating. Before long, individuals persist with considerable effort in their attempts to solve their problems because of the positive outcomes that were set in motion by self-efficacy.

Self-instructional methods *are cognitive behavior techniques aimed at teaching individuals to modify their own behavior* (Meichenbaum, 1977). Using self-instructional methods, cognitive behavior therapists try to get clients to change what they say to themselves. The therapist gives the client examples of constructive statements, known as "reinforcing self-statements," that the client can repeat in order to take positive steps to handle stress or meet a goal. The therapist will also encourage the client to practice the statements through role playing, and will strengthen the client's newly acquired skills through reinforcements. Following is a series of examples of self-instructional methods that can be used to cope with stressful situations (Meichenbaum, Turk, & Burstein, 1975):

Preparing for anxiety or stress
What do I have to do?
I'm going to map out a plan to deal with it.
I'll just think about what I have to do.
I won't worry; doesn't help anything.
I have a lot of different strategies to call on.
Confronting and handling the anxiety or stress
I can meet the challenge.
I'll keep on taking just one step at a time.
I can handle it. I'll just relax, breathe deeply, and use one of the strategies.
I won't think about the pain; I'll think about what I have to do.
Coping with feelings at critical moments
What is it I have to do?
I was supposed to expect the pain to increase; I just have to keep myself in control.
When the pain comes, I'll just pause and keep focusing on what I have to do.
Reinforcing self-statements
Good, I did it.
I handled it well.
I knew I could do it.
Wait until I tell other people how I did it!

The Widespread Use of Behavior Therapy

As the field of psychology has become more "cognitive" and as drugs have been used more often to treat mental disorders, the behavioral approach has lost some of its popularity. Nonetheless, behavior therapy is still used on a widespread basis (Bergin & Garfield, 1994; Follette, 1996). Some examples of recent applications include treating panic disorder, reducing compulsive hand washing, extinguishing a choking phobia, decreasing stuttering, and training developmentally disabled individuals to prepare a meal. Behavior therapy has also been used in treating schizophrenia and depression, a noteworthy achievement because it is commonly believed that behavior therapies are ineffective with more severe, psychotic disorders. To learn more about the use of behavior therapy in treating major depression, read Explorations in Psychology 2.

The cognitive behavior therapies are not the only therapists to emphasize thought processes. As we see next, the cognitive therapists also believe that changing the way people think about their problems is a key to helping people reduce their difficulties and better adjust to life's demands.

Explorations in Psychology 2

Contemporary Behavior Therapy and the Treatment of Depression—the Lewinsohn Approach

Henry Greene is a 36-year-old lawyer who wrestled with depression for months before finally seeking psychotherapy. His initial complaints were physical—fitful sleep, often ending at 3 A.M.; lack of appetite; weight loss of 15 pounds; and a disinterest in sex. Henry began to move more slowly and his voice became monotonous. He reached the point where he could barely cope with life. Henry finally let his guard down and confessed that, although he looked successful on the outside, he felt like a failure on the inside. He said he actually was a third-rate lawyer, husband, lover, and father—he felt he was bound to remain that way. Henry perceived life as a treadmill of duty and guilt; he felt exhausted and saw no reason to continue (Rosenfeld, 1985).

How would a contemporary behaviorist treat someone like Henry Greene? Peter Lewinsohn and his colleagues developed the "Coping with Depression Course" (Lewinsohn & others, 1984), a program that is receiving increased attention. A basic principle of the program is that feelings are caused by behavior. Therapists encourage people to increase the ratio of positive life events to negative life events to improve mood. To accomplish the desired ratio, most individuals require a variety of skill training exercises.

Someone like Henry Greene would first be assigned to monitor his moods. This would force him to pay attention to his daily mood changes; this information is used to determine which events are associated with which moods. Relaxation training would follow, because relaxation skills improve an individual's sense of well-being. Along with the direct benefits of relaxation, clients experience an enhanced sense of self-efficacy by mastering a new skill.

The next step for Henry Greene would be to determine how his moods are associated with pleasant and unpleasant events in his life. Henry would be asked to fill out a "Pleasant Events Schedule" and an "Unpleasant Events Schedule." Each week, Henry would complete a graph showing the number of pleasant and unpleasant events, as well as his mood, for each day. Henry probably would see a close relation between unpleasant events and negative moods, and between pleasant events and positive moods. The therapist would encourage Henry to increase the time he spends in pleasant activities with the hope that more positive moods will follow. The outcome should be that Henry gains control over his moods.

Some people require individually tailored approaches. For example, some people need training in social skills to improve their social relationships. Others need more work in changing their thoughts. In Lewinsohn's approach, thoughts are treated as behaviors to be modified; for example, positive thoughts are reinforced or a specified period is set aside for "worry time."

The final stage in this approach is maintenance planning. Henry would be asked to identify the components of the behavioral therapy that were the most successful in changing his maladaptive behavior; once they have been identified, Henry would be encouraged to continue their use. He also would be required to develop emergency plans for those times when stress overwhelms him. Henry would continue to go to follow-up sessions for 6 months after his treatment.

Cognitive Therapies

D., a 21-year-old single, undergraduate student has delusions that he is evil. He perceives himself as a failure in school and a failure to his parents. He is preoccupied with negative thoughts, dwells on his problems, and exaggerates his faults. Such thinking is common among depressed individuals, and suggests that cognitive therapy might be a viable approach to treat D.'s depression. The **cognitive therapies** *emphasize that the individual's cognitions or thoughts are the main source of abnormal behavior. Cognitive therapies attempt to change the individual's feelings and behaviors by changing cognitions.* Cognitive therapies differ from psychoanalytic therapies by focusing more on overt symptoms instead of deep-seated unconscious thoughts, by providing more structure to the individual's thoughts, and by being less concerned about the origin of the problem. However, the cognitive therapies are less likely than the cognitive behavior therapies to use structured training sessions that require the individual to practice prescribed exercises. Instead the cognitive therapies are more likely to adhere to a conversational format. The cognitive therapies also are less interested than the cognitive behavior therapies in manipulating the environment to increase adaptive behavior.

In recent years many therapists have focused more strongly on the cognitive perspective in their practices (Mahoney, 1993). Two of the most important cognitive therapies are Albert Ellis' rational emotive therapy and Aaron Beck's cognitive therapy.

Rational-Emotive Therapy

Rational-emotive therapy *is based on Albert Ellis' assertion that individuals become psychologically disordered because of their beliefs, especially those that are irrational*

Explorations in Psychology 3

"My Work Is Boring and I Resent It"

The following case illustrates the nature of rational emotive therapy. You will notice that this type of therapy is a forceful type of therapeutic persuasion.

Client: I know that I should do the inventory before it piles up to enormous proportions, but I just keep putting it off. To be honest, I guess it's because I resent it so much.

Therapist: But why do you resent it so much?

Client: It's boring; I just don't like it.

Therapist: So it's boring. That's a good reason for disliking this work, but is it an equally good reason for resenting it?

Client: Aren't the two the same thing?

Therapist: By no means. Dislike equals the sentence, "I don't enjoy this thing; therefore, I don't want to do it." That's a perfectly sane sentence in most instances, but resentment is the sentence, "*Because* I dislike doing this thing, I shouldn't *have* to do it," and that's invariably a very crazy sentence.

Client: Why is it so crazy to resent something that you don't like to do?

Therapist: There are several reasons. First of all, from a purely logical standpoint, it just makes no sense at all to say to yourself, "Because I dislike doing this thing, I shouldn't *have* to do it." The second part of this sentence just doesn't follow in any way from the first part. Your reasoning goes something like this: "Because I dislike doing this thing, *other people* and the *universe* should be so considerate of me that they should never make me do what I dislike," but, of course, this doesn't make any sense. Why *should* other people and the universe be that considerate of you? It might be nice if they were, but why the devil *should* they be? In order for your reasoning to be true, the entire universe, and all the people in it, would really have to revolve around and be uniquely considerate of you (Ellis, 1962).

The therapist has directly attacked the client's belief and forcefully told him that his thoughts are irrational. This represents an important distinction between cognitive therapists, such as Ellis, and behavioral or psychodynamic therapists. Behavioral and psychodynamic therapists might describe this client's behavior and attitudes as maladaptive and self-defeating, but Ellis points out that they are irrational and illogical as well.

---

and self-defeating. Ellis (1962, 1993, 1996) says that we usually talk to ourselves when we experience stress; too often the statements are irrational, making them more harmful than helpful.

Ellis abbreviated the therapy process into the letters *A, B, C, D, E.* Therapy usually starts at C, the individual's upsetting emotional *C*onsequence; this might involve depression, anxiety, or a feeling of worthlessness. The individual often says that C was caused by A, the *A*ctivating Experience, such as a blowup in marital relations, loss of job, or failure in school. The therapist works with the individual to show that an intervening factor, B, the individual's *B*elief System, is actually responsible for why he moved from A to C. Then the therapist goes on to D, which stands for *D*isputation; at this point, the individual's irrational beliefs are disputed or contested by the therapist. Finally, E is reached, which stands for *E*ffects or outcomes of the rational-emotive therapy, as when individuals put their changed beliefs to work. A summary of the A–E steps is presented in figure 7. To learn more about Ellis' rational-emotive therapy, read Explorations in Psychology 3.

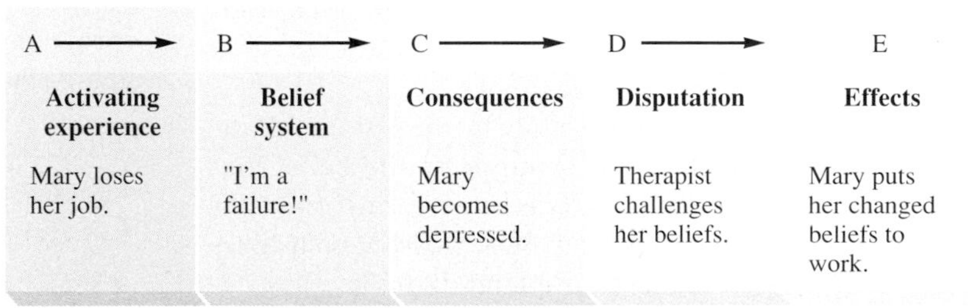

FIGURE 7

A–E Steps in Ellis' Rational-Emotive Therapy

Topic	Psychodynamic approach	Humanistic approach	Behavior approach	Cognitive approach
Cause of problem	Client's problems are symptoms of deep-seated, unresolved unconscious conflicts.	Client is not functioning at an optimal level of development.	Client has learned maladaptive behavior patterns.	Client has developed inappropriate thoughts.
Therapy emphasis	Discover underlying unconscious conflicts and work with client to develop insight.	Develop awareness of inherent potential for growth.	Learn adaptive behavior patterns through changes in the environment or cognitive processes.	Change feelings and behaviors by changing cognitions.
Nature of therapy and techniques	Psychoanalysis, including free association, dream analysis, resistance, and transference; therapist interprets heavily.	Person-centered therapy, including unconditional positive regard, genuineness, accurate empathy, and active listening; Gestalt therapy including confrontation to encourage honest expression of feelings; self-appreciation emphasized.	Observation of behavior and its controlling conditions; specific advice given about what should be done; therapies based on classical conditioning, operant conditioning; therapies emphasizing self-efficacy and self-instruction.	Conversation with client designed to get him or her to change irrational and self-defeating beliefs.

FIGURE 8

Comparison of Psychotherapies

Beck's Cognitive Therapy

Aaron Beck (1976, 1993) developed a form of cognitive therapy to treat psychological dysfunctions, especially depression. He believes the most effective therapy with depressed individuals involves four phases: (1) The depressed clients are shown how to identify self-labels—that is, how they view themselves. (2) They are taught to notice when they are thinking distorted or irrational thoughts. (3) They learn how to substitute appropriate thoughts for inappropriate ones. (4) They are given feedback and motivating comments from the therapist to stimulate their use of these techniques.

Results from a large-scale study by the National Institute of Mental Health (NIMH) supports the belief that Beck's cognitive therapy is an effective treatment for depression (Mervis, 1986). Aaron Beck and his colleagues conducted this therapy with moderately to severely depressed individuals for 16 weeks at three different sites. The symptoms of depression were eliminated completely in more than 50 percent of the individuals receiving Beck's cognitive therapy, compared to only 29 percent in a comparison group (Clark & Beck, 1989).

A comparison group is an important feature in most psychological research. Without a comparison group the researchers in the NIMH study would have had no way of knowing if the symptoms of depression in the experimental group would have disappeared even without therapy. That is, it is possible that in any random sample of depressed individuals, more than 50 percent show a remission of symptoms over a 16-week period, regardless of whether or not they receive therapy. Because only 29 percent of the depressed individuals in the comparison group were free of their symptoms, the researchers had good reason to believe that the cognitive therapy—which produced more than a 50 percent remission of symptoms—was effective.

At this point we have discussed four major approaches to therapy—psychodynamic, humanistic, behavioral, and cognitive. Figure 8 will help you keep the approaches straight in your mind.

Group Therapies and Community Psychology

A major issue in therapy is how it can be structured to reach more people and at less cost. One way to address this problem is for the therapist to see clients in a group rather than individually. A second way is through community psychology.

Group Therapies

Nine people make their way into a room, each looking tentatively at the others. Although each person has met the therapist during a diagnostic interview, no one knows any of the other clients. Some of the people seem reluctant,

Because many psychological problems develop in the context of interpersonal relationships and group experiences—within one's family, marriage, or peer group—group therapy can be an important context for learning how to cope more effectively with these problems.

others enthusiastic. All are willing to follow the therapist's recommendation that group therapy might help each of them learn to cope better with their problems. As they sit down and wait for the session to begin, one thinks, "Will they really understand me?" Another thinks, "Do the others have problems like mine?" Yet another thinks, "How can I stick my neck out with these people?"

Individual therapy is often expensive and time consuming. Freud believed that therapy is a long process and saw clients as often as three to five times a week for a number of years. Advocates of group therapy stress that individual therapy is limited because the client is seen outside the normal context of relationships, relationships that may hold the key to successful therapy (Gladding, 1995). Many psychological problems develop in the context of interpersonal relationships—within one's family, marriage, or peer group, for example. By seeing individuals in the context of these important groups, therapy may be more successful (Fuhrman & Burlingame, 1995).

Group therapy is diversified (Andronico, 1996; O'Neil, 1996). Psychodynamic, humanistic, behavior, or cognitive therapy is practiced by some therapists. Others use group approaches that are not based on the major psychotherapeutic perspectives. Six features make group therapy an attractive format (Yalom, 1975, 1995):

1. *Information.* The individual receives information about his problem from either the group leader or other group members.
2. *Universality.* Many individuals develop the sense that they are the only person who has such frightening and unacceptable impulses. In the group, individuals observe that others feel anguish and suffering as well.
3. *Altruism.* Group members support one another with advice and sympathy and learn that they have something to offer others.
4. *Corrective recapitulation of the family group.* A therapy group often resembles a family (and in family therapy the group *is* a family), with the leaders representing parents and the other members siblings. In this "new" family, old wounds may be healed and new, more positive "family" ties made.
5. *Development of social skills.* Corrective feedback from peers may correct flaws in the individual's interpersonal skills. A self-centered individual may see that he is self-centered if five other group members inform him about his self-centeredness; in individual therapy he may not believe the therapist.
6. *Interpersonal learning.* The group can serve as a training ground for practicing new behaviors and relationships. A hostile woman may learn that she can get along better with others by not behaving so aggressively, for example.

Family and Couple Therapy

"A friend loves you for your intelligence, a mistress for your charm, but your family's love is unreasoning; you were born into it and are of its flesh and blood. Nevertheless, it can irritate you more than any group of people in the world," commented the French biographer Andre Maurois. His statement suggests that the family may be the source of the individual's problems. **Family therapy** *is group therapy with family members.* **Couple therapy** *is group therapy with married or unmarried couples whose major problem is their relationship.* These approaches stress that while one person may have some abnormal symptoms, the symptoms are a function of family or couple relationships (Davis, 1996; Goldenberg, 1996; Lebow & Gurman, 1995). Psychodynamic, humanistic, or behavior therapies may be used in family or couple therapy, but the main form of family therapy is family systems therapy.

Family systems therapy *is a form of therapy based on the assumption that psychological adjustment is related to patterns of interaction within the family unit.* Families who do not function well together foster abnormal behavior on the part of one or more of their members (Haley, 1976; Minuchin, 1985; Satir, 1964). Four of the most widely used family systems techniques follow:

1. *Validation.* The therapist expresses an understanding and acceptance of each family member's feelings and beliefs, and thus validates the person. When the therapist talks with each family member, she finds something positive to say.
2. *Reframing.* The therapist teaches families to reframe problems; problems are cast as a family problem, not an individual's problem. A delinquent adolescent boy's problems are reframed in terms of how each family member contributed to the situation. The father's lack of attention to his son and marital conflict may be involved, for example.

Family systems therapy has become increasingly popular in recent years. In family systems therapy, the assumption is that psychological adjustment is related to patterns of interaction within the family unit.

3. *Structural change.* The family systems therapist tries to *restructure* the coalitions in a family. In a mother-son coalition, the therapist might suggest that the father take a stronger disciplinarian role to relieve some of the burden from the mother. Restructuring might be as simple as suggesting that parents explore satisfying ways to be together; the therapist may recommend that once a week the parents go out for a quiet dinner together, for example.
4. *Detriangulation.* In some families, one member is the scapegoat for two other members who are in conflict but pretend not to be. For example, in the triangle of two parents and one child, the parents may insist that their marriage is fine but find themselves in subtle conflict over how to handle the child. The therapist tries to disentangle, or *detriangulate,* this situation by shifting attention away from the child to the conflict between the parents.

While many of the principles of family therapy can be applied to most families, psychologists increasingly agree that the unique sociohistorical, cultural circumstances experienced by different ethnic minority groups require certain considerations. To read about some of the considerations regarding family therapy in African American families, turn to Explorations in Psychology 4.

Couples therapy proceeds in much the same way as family therapy. Conflict in marriages and in relationships between unmarried individuals frequently involves poor communication. In some instances, communication has broken down entirely. The therapist tries to improve the communication between the partners. In some cases, she will focus on the roles partners play: one may be "strong," the other "weak"; one may be "responsible," the other "spoiled," for example. Couples therapy addresses diverse problems such as jealousy, sexual messages, delayed childbearing, infidelity, gender roles, two-career families, divorce, and remarriage. Now we turn our attention to other forms of group therapy—personal growth and self-help groups.

Personal Growth and Self-Help Groups

A number of group therapies in recent years has focused on people whose lives are lacking in intimacy, intensity, and accomplishment. **Personal growth groups** *have their roots in the humanistic therapies; they emphasize personal growth and increased openness and honesty in interpersonal relations.*

An **encounter group** *is a personal growth group designed to promote self-understanding through candid group interaction.* For example, one member of the assembled group thinks he is better than everyone else. After several minutes of listening to the guy's insufferable bragging, one group member says, "Look, jerk, nobody here likes you; I would like to sell you for what you think you are worth and buy you for what you are actually worth!" Other members of the group might also criticize the braggart. Outside of an encounter group, most people probably would not confront someone about bragging; in the encounter group, they may feel free to express their true feelings about each other.

Encounter groups improve the psychological adjustment of some individuals, but not others. For example, one study showed that the majority of college students who were members of an encounter group felt better about themselves and got along better with others than their counterparts who were not involved in an encounter group (Lieberman, Yalom, & Miles, 1973). However, 8 percent of the participants in the encounter group felt that the experience was harmful. For the most part, they blamed the group leader for intensifying their problems; they said the leader's remarks were so personally devastating they could not handle them.

Although encounter groups are not as popular today as they were in the 1970s, they were the forerunners of today's self-help groups. **Self-help groups** *are voluntary organizations of individuals who get together on a regular basis to discuss topics of common interest. The group leader and members give support to help individuals with their problems. Self-help groups are called "self-help" because they*

Explorations in Psychology 4

African American Families in Therapy

The family therapist who works with African American families is often called on to fulfill various roles, such as educator, director, advocate, problem solver, and role model (Grevious, 1985). As the therapist takes on these roles he or she must recognize that the clients are members of a community, as well as individuals or members of families (Aponte, 1979). The following case study illustrates some of the multiple roles and the community orientation that a therapist must be aware of in working with African American families (Grevious, 1985).

Mrs. B. entered family therapy because her 11-year-old son Todd was disruptive in school and falling behind in his work. She complained of feeling overwhelmed and not being able to cope with the situation. The therapist later conducted a home visit and observed that the family lived in a run-down building in a poor neighborhood. Even so, the therapist found that Mrs. B.'s apartment was immaculate, work and sleep space had been set aside for Todd, and it was obvious from several religious paintings and a well-worn Bible lying on a table that Mrs. B. had strong religious convictions. The therapist discovered that Mrs. B.'s strong-willed mother recently had moved into the apartment after an incapacitating leg operation. The grandmother's diabetes created additional stress in the home. Despite her illness, the grandmother tried to exercise considerable control over Mrs. B. and Todd, causing a power struggle in the family. The therapist also learned that Mrs. B. had recently stopped attending church. After the therapist encouraged her to attend church again, Mrs. B.'s spirits improved considerably. In addition, the grandmother joined a senior citizens' program that transported her to the center three times a week and to church two Sundays a month. These increased community activities for the grandmother had a positive impact on the family.

Family therapists who see African American clients also believe it is important to provide concrete advice or assistance (Foley, 1975). If the problem is a parent-child relationship, for example, the family therapist might recommend that the parents participate in a parent-training program, rather than conduct insight therapy. Also, therapists may occasionally need to educate African American families about social service programs and the difficulties they might encounter gaining access to those programs.

The family therapist who works with African American families also needs to emphasize their strengths, such as pride in being African American, the extended family, and religion, as well as consider their vulnerabilities, such as the impact of racism, discrimination, and victimization (Boyd-Franklin, 1989).

are conducted without a professional therapist. Self-help groups play an important role in our nation's mental health—approximately 6.25 million people participate in such groups each year.

In addition to reaching so many people in need of help, these groups are important because they use community resources and are relatively inexpensive. They also serve people who are less likely to receive help otherwise, such as less educated, middle-aged adults, homemakers, and blue-collar workers.

Founded in 1930 by a reformed alcoholic, Alcoholics Anonymous (AA) is one of the best-known self-help groups. Mental health professionals often recommend AA for their alcoholic clients. Weight Watchers and TOPS (Take Off Pounds Sensibly) are also self-help groups. There

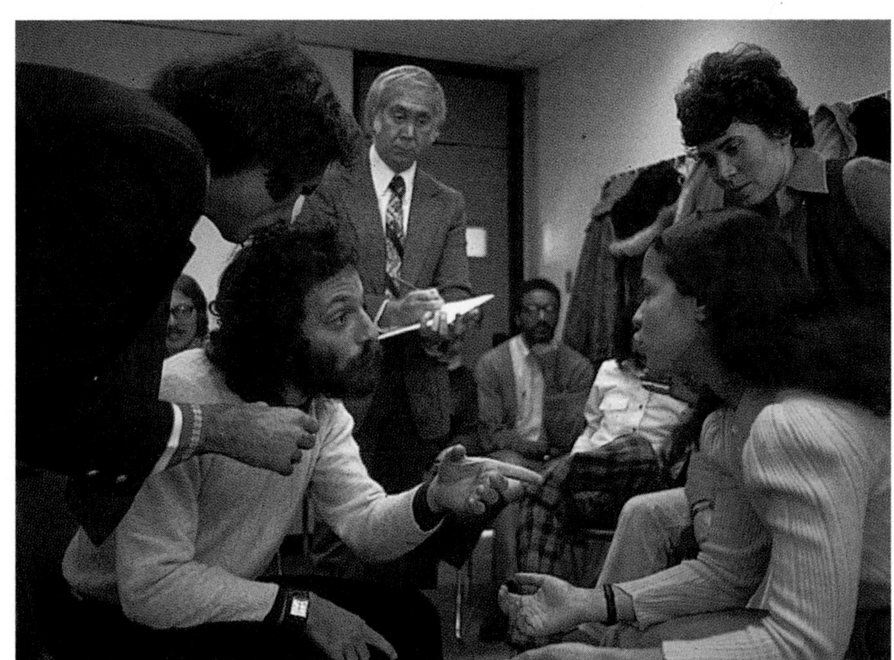

Encounter groups are personal growth groups designed to promote self-understanding through candid group interaction.

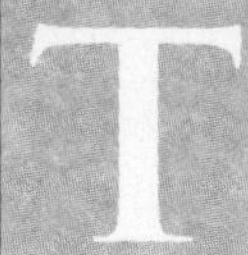

TABLE 2

A Potpourri of Self-Help Groups

A recent listing of self-help groups in a Tulsa, Oklahoma, Sunday newspaper included more than 200 entries. Among the wide variety of self-help groups listed were the following.

Social Concerns	
Tulsa Society for Depressed Women	Relocated Corporate Wives
Love Without Shame	Rebuilders: For Divorces
Gamblers Anonymous	Sex Addicts: Anonymous
Phobia Society of Tulsa	Rap Group and Caring and Coping Partners of Vietnam Veterans
Eating/Weight Disorders	
Movers and Shapers	TOPS (Take Off Pounds Sensibly)
Overeaters Anonymous	
Alcohol/Substance Abuse	
Students Against Drugs and Alcohol	Alcoholics Anonymous
Alcoholics Victorious	Teen Awareness Group
How to Cope with a Dependent Person	Cocaine Anonymous
Adult Children of Alcoholic Parents	
Parenting	
Single Working Mothers	Happier Home Parents
Tulsa Adoptive Parents	Stepparents Group
Parents Without Partners	Sooner Parents of Twins
After Baby Comes	
Health	
Resolve of Tulsa (an infertility group)	SHHH (Self-Help for the Hard of Hearing)
Group for Alzheimer's Caregivers	Families of Children with Diabetes
AIDS Support Program	Indian Health Care Resource Center
ENCORE (for breast cancer patients)	Families of Nursing Home Residents
Mended Hearts (for those who have had open-heart surgery)	LITHIUM Group (for those with bipolar disorder)

are myriad self-help groups such as Parents Without Partners, lesbian and gay support groups, cocaine-abuse support groups, and child-abuse support groups. Table 2 lists a sampling of the variety of self-help groups available in one city.

You may be wondering how a group of people with the same problem can come together and do one another any good. You might be asking yourself why don't they just help themselves and eliminate the need for the group all together? In fact, seeing that others share the same burden makes people feel less isolated, less like freaks of nature, increases a psychological sense of community or belonging, and can give hope where there might have been none before.

Self-help groups also provide an ideology or set of beliefs that members can use as a guide. These groups provide members with a sympathetic audience for confession, sharing, and emotional release. The social support, role modeling, and sharing of concrete strategies for solving problems that unfolds in self-help groups adds to their effectiveness. A woman who has been raped may not believe a male counselor, for instance, who tells her that, with time, she will be able to put back together the pieces of her life and work through much of the psychological pain. But the same message from another rape survivor—someone who has had to work through the same feelings of rage, fear, and violation—may be more believable.

Community Psychology

The community psychology movement was born in the early 1960s when it became apparent to mental health practitioners, including clinical psychologists, that our mental health care system was woefully inadequate. The system was not reaching the poor. And many of those who could afford help often did not seek therapy because of its social stigma. As a result, deinstitutionalization became a major thrust of the community mental health movement. **Deinstitutionalization** *is the movement to transfer the treatment of mental disorders from inpatient mental institutions to community-based facilities that stress outpatient care.* New drugs for treating the severely mentally disordered, such as schizophrenics, meant that large numbers of people could be released from mental institutions and treated in community-based centers.

In 1963, Congress passed the Community Mental Health Center Act, which provided funds for establishing one facility for every 50,000 individuals in the nation. The centers were designed to meet two basic goals—to provide community-based mental health services and to commit resources that help to *prevent* disorders as well as treat them. Outpatient care is one of the important services that

Coinciding with the increased use of drug therapy in mental institutions was the transfer of many mental patients back to the community. It was believed that these individuals could be given medication to keep them stabilized until they could find continuing care. However, many residents of mental health institutions have no families or homes to go to, and community mental health facilities are not adequately equipped to deal with the severe cases. Many individuals who are discharged from state mental hospitals join the ranks of "the homeless." Of course, though, not all homeless people are former mental patients. Controversy continues about whether individuals should be discharged so readily from state mental institutions.

community mental centers provide. Individuals can attend therapy sessions at a center, and still keep their job and live with their family. Another important innovation that grew out of the community mental health movement is called outreach services. Rather than expecting people with mental or emotional problems to make an appointment at the mental health center, mental health care workers in this program go to community locations, such as storefront clinics, where they are accessible and needed most. Community-based mental health services stay open 24 hours a day, often handling emergencies such as suicide attempts and drug overdoses.

The philosophy of community-based services also includes training teachers, ministers, family physicians, and others who directly interact with community members to offer lay counseling and various workshops such as assertiveness training or coping with stress. This broadens mental health resources, allowing an increased number of people to receive help in settings where they are more likely to be comfortable than in traditional mental health centers.

Borrowing from the field of public health, community psychology adopted the belief that the best way to treat a mental disorder is to prevent it from happening in the first place. Prevention takes one of three courses: primary prevention, secondary prevention, and tertiary prevention.

Primary prevention *involves efforts to reduce the number of new cases of mental disorders.* By definition, primary prevention programs are offered to populations completely free of a disorder. Like immunization in public health, primary prevention programs try to identify and "inoculate" populations against the development of mental disorders. Primary prevention programs tend to follow one of three strategies: community-wide, milestone, or high-risk (Bloom, 1985).

In the *community-wide approach,* programs are available to everyone in a given geographic area. Washington, D.C.'s "Beautiful Babies Right from the Start," for example, provides free prenatal care and well-baby care for the first 18 months to women and their infants in the poorest communities. This program attempts to avert behaviors, such as substance abuse or poor nutrition, by pregnant women that put infants at risk for premature birth, low birthweight, and disorders such as hyperactivity, impaired memory, and disorganized thinking. In the milestone approach, the target group is every person in a population who reaches a certain hurdle or critical life transition, such as being fired, becoming a parent for the first time, or going away to college. Counseling for fired employees and orientation programs for college students are just two examples of milestone programs. In the high-risk program, the focus is on specific groups of people, such as children of alcoholics, children with chronic illnesses, and ethnic minority children, whose chances of developing mental disorders are extremely high.

Secondary prevention *involves screening for early detection of problems, as well as early intervention.* A major goal of secondary prevention programs is to reach large numbers of potential clients. These programs often use *paraprofessionals,* volunteers without formal mental health training who work closely with psychologists, to meet this goal. One approach to secondary prevention involves teaching coping skills to people under high levels of stress, the bereaved, the newly employed, and prospective parents. Another type involves screening groups of individuals, such as schoolchildren, to find those who show early signs of problems and provide them with mental health services.

Tertiary prevention *involves efforts to reduce mental health disorders that were not prevented or arrested early in the course of the disorder.* Tertiary prevention programs are geared toward people who once required long-term care or hospitalization and provide services that can reduce the probability that they will become so debilitated again. Halfway houses (community residences for individuals who no longer require institutionalization but who still need some support in readjusting to the community) for formerly hospitalized schizophrenics are an example of tertiary prevention. Such programs seek to increase individuals' coping skills by reducing their social isolation, increasing their social skills, and by developing educational strategies tailored to their needs.

Community psychology has successfully reached large numbers of mentally and emotionally distressed people, not only through prevention but also through intervention (McMillan & others, 1995). Unfortunately, strong cutbacks in federal funding of community mental health centers in the 1980s have diminished their effectiveness and stalled their expansion.

Because programs such as outreach services may be the only mental health care available to those who are poor or who are from ethnic minority backgrounds, community psychology approaches are especially important (Marin, 1993; Maton & Salem, 1995; Perkins & Zimmerman, 1995). Remember from our earlier comments that psychotherapy has been more available to the wealthy. An explicit value of community psychology is to assist people who are disenfranchised from society to lead happier, more productive lives. **Empowerment** *refers to the importance of assisting individuals to develop skills they need to control their own lives.*

At this point we have discussed a number of ideas about behavior therapies, cognitive therapies, group therapies, and community psychology. A summary of these ideas is presented in concept table 2.

Is Psychotherapy Effective?

Do individuals who go through therapy get better? Are some approaches more effective than others? Or is the situation similar to that of the Dodo in *Alice's Adventures in Wonderland?* Dodo was asked to judge the winner of a race; he decided, "Everybody has won and all must have prizes." And how would we evaluate the effectiveness of psychotherapy? Would we take the client's word? The therapist's word? What would be our criteria for effectiveness? Would it be "feeling good," "adaptive behavior," "improved interpersonal relationships," "autonomous decision making," or "more positive self-concept," for example? During the last several decades an extensive amount of thought and research has addressed these questions.

Research on the Effectiveness of Psychotherapy

Four decades ago, Hans Eysenck (1952) shocked the pundits in the field of psychotherapy by concluding that treatment is ineffective. Eysenck analyzed twenty-four studies of psychotherapy and found that approximately two-thirds of the individuals with neurotic symptoms improved. Sounds impressive so far. But Eysenck also found that a similar percentage of neurotic individuals on waiting lists to see a psychotherapist also showed marked improvement even though they were not given any psychotherapy at all.

Eysenck's pronouncement prompted a flurry of research on psychotherapy's effectiveness. Hundreds of studies on the outcome of psychotherapy have now been conducted (Sanderson, 1995; Whiston & Sexton, 1993). One strategy for analyzing these diverse studies is called **meta-analysis,** *in which the researcher statistically combines the results of many different studies.* In one meta-analysis of psychotherapy research, 475 studies were statistically combined (Smith, Glass, & Miller, 1980). Only those studies in which a therapy group had been compared with an untreated control group were compared. The results showed greater psychotherapy effectiveness than Eysenck's earlier results: On 88 percent of the measures, individuals who received therapy improved more than those who did not. This meta-analysis and others (Lipsey & Wilson, 1993) document that psychotherapy is effective in general, but they do not inform us about the specific ways in which different therapies might be effective.

Concept Table 2

Behavior Therapies, Cognitive Therapies, Group Therapies, and Community Psychology

Concept	Processes/Related Ideas	Characteristics/Description
Behavior Therapies	Their nature	They use principles of learning to reduce or eliminate maladaptive behavior. Behavior therapies are based on behavioral and social learning theories of learning and personality. Behavior therapists try to eliminate the symptoms or behaviors rather than trying to get individuals to gain insight into their problems.
	Classical conditioning approaches	Two procedures are systematic desensitization and aversive conditioning.
	Operant conditioning approaches	Emphasis is placed on modifying individuals' maladaptive responses to the environment. The idea behind behavior modification is to replace unacceptable, maladaptive responses with acceptable, adaptive ones. Consequences are set up to ensure that acceptable responses are reinforced and unacceptable ones are not. A token economy is an example of behavior modification.
	Cognitive behavior therapy	This is behavior therapy that tries to help individuals behave more adaptively by modifying their thoughts. Cognitive behavior therapists strive to change misconceptions, strengthen coping skills, increase self-control, and encourage constructive self-talk.
	The widespread use of behavior therapy	Although behavior therapy has become less popular, it is still widely used in treating a number of psychological disorders, including the severe disorders of major depression and schizophrenia.
Cognitive Therapies	Their nature	They emphasize that individuals' thoughts, or cognitions, are the main sources of abnormal behavior. Cognitive therapies attempt to change feelings and behaviors by changing cognitions.
	Rational-emotive therapy	This is a cognitive therapy developed by Albert Ellis. It is based on the idea that individuals become psychologically disordered because of their beliefs, especially those that are irrational and self-defeating; therapy is designed to change these beliefs.
	Beck's cognitive therapy	Aaron Beck developed a form of cognitive therapy to treat psychological disorders, especially depression. The therapy involves identifying self-labels, detecting irrational thoughts, substituting appropriate for inappropriate thoughts, and receiving feedback from the therapist to stimulate these cognitive changes.
Group Therapies and Community Psychology	Group therapies	Social relationships hold the key to successful therapy; therefore, therapy involving group interactions may be more beneficial than individual therapy. Family therapy and couple therapy, as well as personal growth and self-help groups, are common.
	Community psychology	Community psychology was born in the 1960s. Deinstitutionalization, in which the treatment of mental disorders is transferred from inpatient mental institutions to outpatient community health facilities, has been especially important in community psychology. As a result, mental health services are more accessible to individuals from low-income and ethnic minority backgrounds. Three community psychology approaches are primary prevention, secondary prevention, and tertiary prevention. Empowerment is a key concept in community psychology that refers to the importance of assisting people to develop skills they need to control their own lives.

People who are thinking about seeing a psychotherapist not only want to know whether psychotherapy in general is effective, but they would especially like to know which form of psychotherapy is effective for their particular problem. In the meta-analysis conducted by Mary Lee Smith and her colleagues (Smith, Glass, & Miller, 1980), comparisons of different types of psychotherapy were also made. For example, behavior therapies were compared with insight therapies (psychodynamic, humanistic). Both the behavior and insight therapies were superior to no treatment at all, but they did not differ from each other in effectiveness. While no particular therapy was the best in the study by Smith and her colleagues, some therapies do seem to be more effective in treating some disorders than others. The behavior therapies have been most successful in treating specific behavioral problems, such as phobias and sexual dysfunctions (Bowers & Clum, 1988; Sanderson, 1995). The cognitive therapies have been most successful in treating depression (Butler & others, 1991; Clark & Beck, 1989). Also, many therapies have their maximum benefit early in treatment with less improvement occurring as the individual remains in therapy (Karasu, 1986).

The informed consumer also needs to be aware of some evidence that in certain cases psychotherapy can actually be harmful. For example, people who have a low tolerance of anxiety, low motivation, and strong signs of psychological deterioration may worsen as therapy progresses. Characteristics of the therapist also have been related to a worsening of the client's status as therapy progresses. Therapists who are aggressive, who try to get clients to disclose personal information too quickly, and who are impatient with the process of change may exacerbate their clients' problems (Suinn, 1984). Therapist bias can be harmful when the therapist does not understand ethnic, religious, gender, or other cultural differences, but instead pressures such clients to conform to White, middle-class norms. Finally, therapists who engage in sex with a client harm the client; such behavior is absolutely unethical.

While incompetent and unethical therapists do exist, there are many impeccable therapists who successfully help their clients. Like jazz musicians, psychotherapists must be capable of improvising, gracefully. As psychologist Jerome Frank put it, "Successful therapy is not just a scientific process, it is a healing art as well."

Common Themes and Specificity in Psychotherapy

After carefully studying the nature of psychotherapy for more than 25 years, Jerome Frank (1982) concluded that effective psychotherapies have the common elements of expectations, mastery, and emotional arousal. By inspiring an expectation of help, the therapist motivates the client to continue coming to therapy. These expectations are powerful morale builders and symptom relievers in themselves. The therapist also increases the client's sense of mastery and competence. For example, clients begin to feel that they can cope effectively with their world. Therapy also arouses the individual's emotions, essential to motivating behavioral change, according to Frank.

The therapeutic relationship is another important ingredient in successful psychotherapy (Strupp, 1989, 1995). A relationship in which the client has confidence and trust in the therapist is essential to effective psychotherapy (Walborn, 1996). In one study, the most common ingredient in the success of different psychotherapies was the therapist's supportiveness of the client (Wallerstein, 1989). The client and therapist engage in a "healing ritual," which requires the active participation of both the client and the therapist. As part of this ritual, the client gains hope and becomes less alienated.

But while psychotherapies have common themes, some critics worry about carrying this commonality too far. Specificity in psychotherapy still needs careful attention—we need to understand "*what* treatment is most effective for *this* individual with *that* specific problem, and under *which* circumstances" (Paul, 1967). At this time, however, we do not know which approach works best in which situation with which therapist. Some therapists are better trained than others, some are more sensitive to a person's feelings, some are more introverted, and some are more conservative. Because of the myriad ways we differ as human beings, the ideal "fit" of therapist and client is difficult to pinpoint scientifically. To read about guidelines for seeking professional help, turn to Explorations in Psychology 5.

Culture and Ethnicity

Only in the last two decades have psychologists become sensitive to the concerns of culture and ethnicity in psychotherapy. For far too long, psychotherapists were concerned almost exclusively with helping middle- and upper-class individuals cope with their problems while ignoring the needs of people who were poor or from ethnic minority backgrounds (Ponterotto & others, 1995; Reid & Bing, 1996; Sue, 1996).

Orientation of Ethnic Minority Individuals to Therapy

As part of their history of being ignored by psychotherapists, ethnic minority individuals have developed a preference for discussing problems with parents, friends, and relatives rather than mental health professionals. Another reason why they turn to family and friends when they are in emotional or mental distress is that there are so few ethnic minority psychotherapists (Sue, Ivey, & Pedersen, 1996). For example, in one study, African American college students were more likely to use the college's mental health facilities if an African American clinician or counselor were available than if only White counselors were available (Thompson & Cimbolic, 1978). However, therapy can be effective when the therapist and client are from different cultural backgrounds if the therapist has excellent clinical skills and is culturally sensitive. Researchers have also found that Asian Americans, African Americans, Latinos, and Native

EXPLORATIONS IN PSYCHOLOGY 5

Guidelines for Seeking Professional Help

Marcia felt anxious most of the time. But what caused her the greatest difficulty was that she became so anxious during exams in her classes that she would nearly freeze. Her mind would go blank and she would begin to sweat and shake all over. It was such a problem that she was failing her classes. She told one of her professors that this was the problem with her grades. He told her that it sounded like she had a serious case of test anxiety, and that she should get some help. Marcia decided that she better take his advice and wanted to find a psychotherapist. How would she go about finding a therapist? Are certain professionals more qualified than others? How could she know that she was going to see someone who could help her, as opposed to a professional who would not be helpful, or perhaps even make things worse? These are only a few of the questions people commonly have when they seek to find a therapist.

When trying to find a therapist, Marcia could consider a psychologist, psychiatrist, social worker, counselor, or any number of other helping professionals. Each of these mental health professionals is qualified to provide psychotherapeutic services. They all practice from any one or combination of the therapeutic orientations discussed in this chapter. They may also see people on an individual, one to one basis, or in small groups, as in group therapy. The critical question is, of course, how does someone go about selecting a therapist to help them? This is not as easy a question as it may appear at first glance. We may face many of the same problems when we try to find a 'good' medical doctor, accountant, or dentist; however, the way that most people go about finding these other professional services may not be the best way of selecting a therapist. Asking a friend for a good therapist ignores the fact that some approaches to therapy work better with some problems than others. Also, every therapeutic relationship is different, so one person's experience in therapy is not translatable to another person's. Below, we offer some general suggestions when looking for a therapist.

Identify the professional's credentials. Although all different types of mental health professionals may be competent, psychologists, psychiatrists, and social workers all differ in their approach to therapy based on differences in training: psychologists tend to be focused on the person's emotions and behaviors; psychiatrists are trained as medical doctors so their perspective is likely to involve physical aspects of psychological problems; and social workers will be inclined to take a person's entire family and social situation into account. Regardless of the exact profession, some minimal credentials should be considered important. All states have licensing regulations for professionals who provide public services. Thus, a therapist should be licensed or certified by a state in order to practice. In addition, in some cases it may be important for a professional to have some advanced, specialized training in a certain area. For example, if a person is seeking help with a specific problem, like drug abuse, alcohol abuse, or a sexual problem, the therapist should have some training in that area. You should ask about the professional's credentials either before or during a first visit.

When starting therapy, give it some time before making a judgment of how useful it is. Making changes is very difficult. Expecting too much too soon can result in premature dissatisfaction and disappointment. Because a large part of therapy involves the development of a relationship with the therapist, it may take several meetings to really know if things are going well. One suggestion is to give it between four and six weekly meetings. If it does not seem like things are going the way you would like, it is a good idea to discuss your progress with the therapist and ask what you should expect with regard to making progress. Setting specific goals with specific time expectations can be helpful. If your goals are not being met, you should consider a new therapist.

Be a thoughtful and careful consumer of mental health services. Just as is true for when you seek any services, the more informed you are about the services provided, the better decision you can make about whether or not they are the right services for you. Calling around and asking specific questions about approaches and specializations is one way to become informed about the services offered by therapists. Consider how important it may be that the therapist is of your same or opposite sex, whether it is important that they have experience with your specific difficulty, as well as other specific characteristics. You may also want to learn more about their theoretical orientation to therapy as described in this chapter. Another way to find out more about the therapist is to ask these kinds of questions during your first visit. Most professionals are quite comfortable talking about their background and training. Your confidence and trust in the professional is an important part of how well therapy will work for you.

These general guidelines should be used when first looking for a therapist. Remember that people should continually evaluate their own progress throughout therapy and when they feel dissatisfied with how it is going, they should discuss this with their therapist. Remember that therapy is like other services: When dissatisfied, you can always look for another therapist. Don't think that just because one therapist has not been helpful none will be. All therapists and therapeutic relationships are different. Finding the right therapist is one of the most important factors in therapy success (Kalichman, 1994).

Americans terminate psychotherapy after an initial session at a much higher rate than do White Americans (Sue, Allen, & Conaway, 1978). The social stigma of being a "mental patient," fear of hospitalization, conflict between their own belief system and the beliefs of modern mental health practitioners, and the availability of an alternate healer, are additional reasons ethnic minority individuals terminate therapy early.

Psychotherapy involves interpersonal interaction and communication. Verbal and nonverbal messages need to be accurately sent and received. Although, as we indicated earlier, very effective therapy can take place when the client and therapist are from different sociocultural backgrounds, barriers to communication can develop in such circumstances that can destroy and undermine the effectiveness of psychotherapy (Arrendondo, 1996; Parham, 1996).

Some Thoughts About Improvements in Therapy for Ethnic Minority Individuals

Some therapists recommend that, when working with Latinos, therapists reframe problems as being medical rather than psychological, to reduce resistance. The assumption is that Latinos will be more receptive to a medical orientation than to a psychological orientation. Some therapists recommend that, when working with African Americans, therapists use externally focused, action-oriented therapy rather than internally focused, intrapsychic therapy.

Such recommendations, however, raise some important questions. For example, isn't it impossible for therapists to effectively change their therapy orientation to work with ethnic minority groups? Thus, a psychoanalytic therapist might find it difficult to use the externally focused, action-oriented therapy recommended for African Americans. By using a specific approach, supposedly based on the client's cultural background, how does the therapist deal with diversity and individual differences in an ethnic or cultural group? Because of the problems raised by such questions, we cannot just say, "Know the cultural background of the client or use this approach with that particular ethnic or cultural group."

According to Stanley Sue (1991), what we can say is that when they see ethnic minority clients, therapists should emphasize two processes, at least in initial therapy sessions: (1) credibility, and (2) giving. **Credibility** *refers to a therapist's believability.* **Giving** *refers to clients' receiving some kind of benefit from treatment early in the therapy process.* Two factors are important in increasing credibility: ascribed status and achieved status. Ascribed status is one's position or role defined by others or cultural norms. In some cultures, the young are subordinate to the old, those who are naive abide by those in authority, and females have less power than males. Credibility must also be achieved. The therapist can achieve credibility by doing something that the client perceives as being helpful or competent. Lack of ascribed credibility may be the main reason ethnic minority individuals tend to steer clear of therapy; lack of achieved credibility may be the main reason ethnic minority individuals terminate therapy once it has begun as well as problems with rapport.

In terms of giving, clients may wonder how talking to a therapist will alleviate their problems. Therapists need to help ethnic minority clients see the relationship between therapy and why it will help a person get better (Caldwell, 1996). It is important for the therapist to make this association in the first session. Many ethnic minority clients do not understand Western psychotherapy. The first session should not be just an assessment session, but rather the therapist should find out about the client, give some recommendations for treatment, and say something concrete to the client so the client will leave the first session saying, "I got something out of it that I think will help me and I want to come back again."

In addition to culture and ethnicity, gender also plays a role in psychotherapy. As we see next, concern about gender bias in psychotherapy has increased dramatically in the last two decades.

Gender

One of the by-products of changing gender roles for women and men is a rethinking of approaches to psychotherapy. In some instances, the development of abnormal behavior and lack of effective psychotherapy may be due to traditional gender conditioning (Ballou, 1996; Mays, Caldwell, & Jackson, 1996; Worrell & Robinson, 1993). Our discussion of gender and therapy focuses on three areas: autonomy and relatedness in therapy, consciousness-raising groups, and feminist therapies, each of which we examine in turn.

Autonomy and Relatedness in Therapy

Autonomy and relatedness are central issues to an understanding of gender conditioning. For many years autonomy was championed as an important characteristic for maturity. As a result, autonomy was the unquestioned goal of many psychotherapies, relatedness was not. Thomas Szasz (1965), for example, claimed that the basic goal of psychotherapy is to foster autonomy, independence, and freedom. The humanistic therapies—Rogers, Maslow, and Perls—argued that to become psychologically healthy, an individual has to become self-actualized through self-determination and fulfillment of needs independent of social constraints or personal commitments.

But therapists are taking a new look at autonomy as the ideal goal of therapy for females. Should therapy with females focus more on the way most females have been socialized and place more emphasis on relationships? Can females, even with psychotherapy, achieve autonomy in a male-dominated society? Are conventional ways of thinking about autonomy and relatedness appropriate for capturing the complexity of human experience? Would psychotherapy for females, as well as for males, be improved if its goals were more

(a)

(b)

(c)

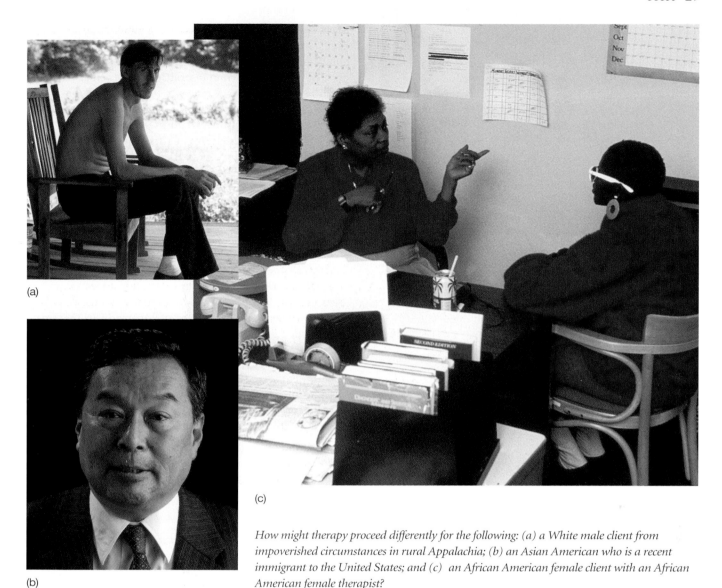

How might therapy proceed differently for the following: (a) a White male client from impoverished circumstances in rural Appalachia; (b) an Asian American who is a recent immigrant to the United States; and (c) an African American female client with an African American female therapist?

androgynous in nature, stressing better psychological functioning in *both* autonomy and relatedness?

Because traditional therapy often has not adequately addressed the specific concerns of women in a sexist society, several nontraditional approaches have arisen. These nontraditional therapies emphasize the importance of helping people break free from traditional gender roles and stereotypes. The nontraditional therapies avoid language that labels one sex as more socially desirable or valuable then the other. Let's now consider two such nontraditional therapies: consciousness-raising groups and feminist therapy.

Consciousness-Raising Groups

Consciousness-raising groups *are believed by some feminists to be important alternatives or adjuncts to traditional therapies; they often involve several people meeting in a member's home, are frequently leaderless (or members take turns facilitating discussion), and focus on the members' feelings and self-perceptions. Instead of seeking and accepting male-biased therapy, women may meet in consciousness-raising groups to define their own experiences with their own criteria.*

Some men followed suit and formed all-male consciousness-raising groups in which they discuss what it means to be male in our society. Several colleges and universities have rape-awareness programs, a form of consciousness-raising groups for men. Going even further, the University of Wisconsin group called Men Stopping Rape offers a version of their program to junior high and high school students (Paludi, 1995).

Feminist Therapies

Feminist therapies *are usually based on a critique of society wherein women are perceived to have less political and economic power than men have. Also, feminist therapies assume that the reasons for women's problems are social, not personal.* Many individuals assume that feminist therapies and nonsexist therapies are identical. However, some

Increased interest has focused on gender roles in psychotherapy. Might female psychotherapists be more likely to encourage autonomy and relatedness, rather than autonomy alone, as psychotherapy goals?

Rachel Hare-Mustin (left) and Jeanne Maracek (right) have made important contributions to understanding the role of gender in psychotherapy. They have been especially concerned about the inclusion of strategies in psychotherapy to help women break free from gender stereotypes and male bias.

feminists distinguish between the two. For example, **nonsexist therapy** *occurs when the therapist has become aware of and primarily overcome his or her own sexist attitudes and behavior.* Thus, a nonsexist therapist would not perceive a dependent man or an independent woman to be showing emotional problems just because they are acting in counterstereotypic ways. Nonsexist therapists do not view marriage as any better for women or men. And these therapists also encourage women and men to adopt androgynous gender roles rather than stereotypic masculine or feminine ones (Paludi, 1995).

Feminist therapists, both male and female, believe that traditional psychotherapy continues to carry considerable gender bias, and that women clients cannot realize their full potential without becoming aware of society's sexism. The goals of feminist therapists are no different than other therapists' goals. Feminist therapists make no effort to turn clients into feminists, but want the female client to be fully aware of how the nature of the female role in the American society can contribute to the development of a mental disorder. Feminist therapists believe women must become aware of the effects of social oppression on their own lives if they are to achieve their mental health goals.

In one feminist approach to therapy, women go through three phases enroute to mental health (Williams, 1987). First, in *harmful adaptation,* women accept dependency and the rules of a patriarchal society. In this phase, women harm themselves because they subordinate their own desires and needs to the values of the system. Second, in *corrective action,* when women realize what harmful adaptation has done to them, they begin to develop their own identity and to articulate personal goals. Third, in *health maintenance,* women develop pride in their new identity and form alliances with other women to work toward better conditions for all women. In this model of feminist therapy, women move from acceptance of a discriminating society to taking pride in a new, positive status and helping other women achieve the same.

So far we have discussed a variety of psychotherapies that can help individuals cope more effectively with stress and develop more adaptive, less harmful behavior. In recent years considerable progress has also been made in biomedical therapies, which we now discuss.

Biomedical Therapies

Biomedical therapies *are treatments to reduce or eliminate the symptoms of psychological disorders by altering the way an individual's body functions. Drug therapy is the most common form of biomedical therapy. Much less widely used biomedical therapies are electroconvulsive therapy and psychosurgery.* Psychologists and other mental health professionals may provide psychotherapy in conjunction with the biomedical therapy administered by psychiatrists and medical doctors.

Drug Therapy

Psychotherapeutic drugs are used to treat many different mental disorders—anxiety, depression, and schizophrenia, for example. In some instances, these drugs are effective when other forms of therapy are not (Smith & Darlington, 1996). Drug therapy has substantially reduced the amount of time schizophrenics must spend in hospitals, for example. Three main types of psychotherapeutic drugs are antianxiety drugs, antipsychotic drugs, and antidepressant drugs, each of which we discuss in turn.

Antianxiety Drugs

Antianxiety drugs *are commonly known as tranquilizers; these drugs reduce anxiety by making individuals less excitable* *and more tranquil.* Why are antianxiety drugs so widely used? Many individuals experience stress, anxiety, or an inability to sleep well; family physicians or psychiatrists prescribe these drugs to improve our abilities to cope with these situations more effectively. The most popular antianxiety drugs are Xanax and Valium.

The relaxed feelings brought on by antianxiety drugs is a welcome relief to individuals experiencing anxiety and stress in their lives. But these drugs often make individuals feel fatigued and drowsy; motor abilities can be impaired and work productivity reduced; and extended use can produce dependency. In some instances, the combination of antianxiety drugs and alcohol has caused death. When an individual feels anxious, it may be best to face the problems creating the anxiety rather than rely on antianxiety drugs to avoid the problems.

Antipsychotic Drugs

The **antipsychotic drugs** *are powerful drugs that diminish agitated behavior, reduce tension, decrease hallucinations and delusions, improve social behavior, and produce better sleep patterns in severely mentally disordered individuals, especially schizophrenics. Neuroleptics are the most widely used antipsychotic drugs.*

The most widely used explanation for the effectiveness of antipsychotic drugs is their ability to block the dopamine system's action in the brain (Rebec, 1996). Schizophrenics have too much of the neurochemical messenger dopamine. Numerous well-controlled investigations reveal that when used in sufficient doses, the neuroleptics reduce a variety of schizophrenic symptoms, at least in the short-term (Breier, 1996; Holcomb & others, 1996).

The most effective drug used to treat schizophrenia is clozapine (marketed as Clozaril). However, clozapine has a toxic effect on white blood cells in a small percentage of cases, which necessitates regular blood testing.

The neuroleptics do not cure schizophrenia, and they can have severe side effects. The neuroleptics treat the symptoms of schizophrenia, not its causes. If an individual stops taking the drug, the symptoms return. Neuroleptic drugs have substantially reduced the length of hospital stays for schizophrenics. Although schizophrenics are able to return to the community because drug therapy keeps their symptoms from reappearing, most have difficulty coping with the demands of society and most are chronically unemployed.

Tardive dyskinesia *is a major side effect of the neuroleptic drugs; it is a neurological disorder characterized by grotesque, involuntary movements of the facial muscles and mouth as well as extensive twitching of the neck, arms, and legs.* As many as 20 percent of schizophrenics taking neuroleptics develop this disorder. Elderly women are especially vulnerable. Long-term neuroleptic therapy also is associated with increased depression and anxiety. Schizophrenics who take neuroleptics for many years report that they feel miserable most of the time, for example. Nonetheless, for the majority of schizophrenics, the benefits of neuroleptic treatment outweigh its risk and discomforts.

Strategies to increase the effectiveness of the neuroleptics involve administering lower dosages over time rather than a large initial dose and combining drug therapy with psychotherapy. The small percentage of schizophrenics who are able to hold jobs suggests that drugs alone will not make them contributing members of society. Vocational, family, and social-skills training are needed in conjunction with drug therapy to facilitate improved psychological functioning and adaptation to society.

Antidepressant Drugs

Antidepressant drugs *regulate mood. The three main classes of antidepressant drugs are tricyclics, such as Elavil; SSRI drugs, such as Prozac; and MAO inhibitors, such as Nardil.* The *tricyclics,* so called because of their three-ringed molecular structure, probably work because they increase the level of certain neurotransmitters, especially norepinephrine and serotonin. The tricyclics reduce the symptoms of depression in approximately 60 to 70 percent of cases. The tricyclics are not effective in improving mood until 2 to 4 weeks after the individual begins taking them. And the tricyclics sometimes have adverse side effects—restlessness, faintness, and trembling, for example. The most prominent of the selective serotonin reuptake inhibiting (SSRI) type is Prozac. SSRI drugs work by interfering with the reabsorption of serotonin in the brain. Prozac is most frequently prescribed for dysthymia, a mild to moderate form of clinical depression, but it has also successfully treated anxiety, obsession, and shyness. Although many individuals report that they feel fully themselves when taking Prozac, the drug can be disinhibiting and dangerous for some individuals, who report an increase in suicidal feelings and aggressive impulses. The MAO inhibitors are not as widely used as the tricyclics because they are more toxic, require more dietary restrictions, and usually have less-potent therapeutic effects. Nonetheless, some severely depressed individuals who do not respond to the tricyclics do respond to the MAO inhibitors.

Lithium *is a drug that is widely used to treat bipolar disorder* (recall that this disorder involves wide mood swings of depression and mania). The amount of lithium that circulates in the bloodstream needs to be carefully monitored because its effective dosage is precariously close to toxic levels. Memory impairment is also associated with lithium use.

As with schizophrenia, the treatment of the affective disorders might also involve a combination of drug therapy and psychotherapy. One study showed that the combination of tricyclics and interpersonal psychotherapy produced a lower than normal relapse rate for depressed clients (10 percent versus 22 percent) (Frank & Kupfer, 1986). The interpersonal therapy focused on the client's ability to develop and maintain positive interpersonal relationships and included an educational workshop for clients and their families.

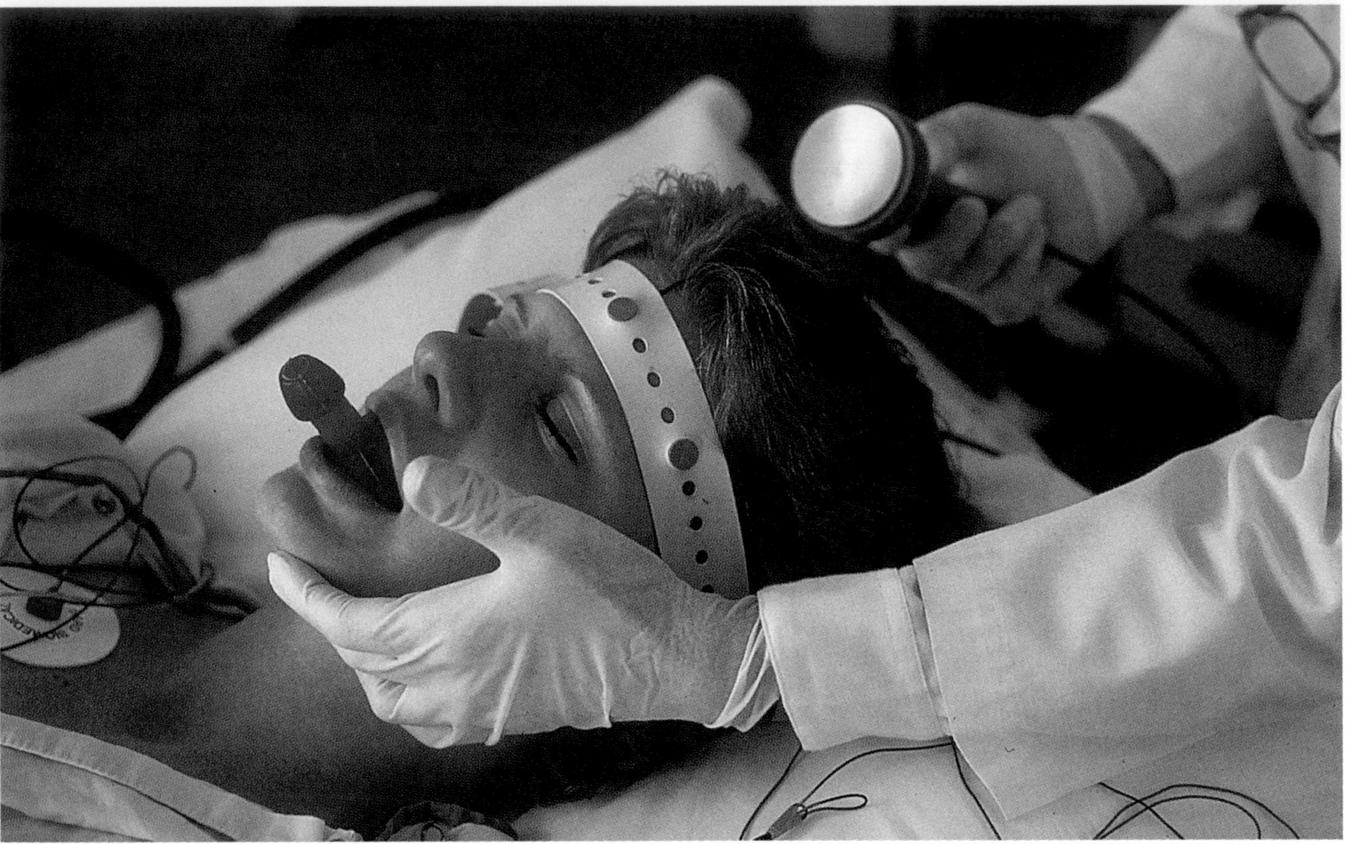

Electroconvulsive therapy (ECT), commonly called "shock therapy," causes a seizure in the brian. ECT still is given to as many as 60,000 people a year, mainly to treat major depression.

The use of psychotherapeutic drugs is the most widely practiced biomedical therapy. However, as we see next, in extreme circumstances, electroconvulsive therapy and even psychosurgery may be used.

Electroconvulsive Therapy

"Then something bent down and took hold of me and shook me like the end of the world. Wee-ee-ee-ee-ee, it shrilled, through an air crackling with blue light, and with each flash a great jot drubbed me until I thought my bones would break and the sap fly out of me like a split plant." Images such as this description from the late Sylvia Plath's (1971) autobiographic novel *The Bell Jar* have shaped the public's view of **electroconvulsive therapy (ECT),** *commonly called "shock treatment." ECT is sometimes used to treat severely depressed individuals. The goal of ECT is to cause a seizure in the brain much like what happens spontaneously in some forms of epilepsy.* A small electric current lasting for one second or less passes through two electrodes placed on the individual's head. The current excites neural tissue, stimulating a seizure that lasts for approximately 1 minute.

ECT has been used for more than 40 years. In earlier years it often was used indiscriminately, sometimes even as a punishment for patients. ECT is still used with as many as 60,000 individuals a year, mainly to treat major depression. Adverse side effects may include memory loss or other cognitive impairment. Today ECT is given mainly to individuals who have not responded to drug therapy or psychotherapy. ECT sounds as if it would entail intolerable pain, but the manner in which it is administered today involves little discomfort. The patient is given anesthesia and muscle relaxants before the current is applied; this allows the individual to sleep through the procedure, minimizes convulsions, and reduces the risk of physical injury. The individual awakens shortly afterward with no conscious memory of the treatment.

An example reveals how ECT, used as a last resort, was effective in reducing depression (Sackheim, 1985). Ann is a 36-year-old teacher and mother. She had been in psychotherapy for several years. Prior to entering the hospital, she took tricyclics with unsuccessful results. In the first 6 months of her hospital stay, doctors tried different drugs to reduce her depression; none of the drugs worked. She slept poorly, lost her appetite, and showed no interest in even reading newspaper headlines. Obsessed with the idea that she had ruined her children's lives, she repeatedly threatened suicide. With her consent, doctors began ECT; after five treatments, Ann returned to her family and job several days later. Not all cases of ECT turn out as positively. Even when ECT works, though, we do not know why it works.

Concept Table 3

The Effectiveness of Psychotherapy and Biomedical Therapies

Concept	Processes/Related Ideas	Characteristics/Description
The Effectiveness of Psychotherapy	Research on psychotherapy's effectiveness	Psychotherapy in general is effective, but no single treatment is more effective than others. Behavioral therapies are often most successful in treating specific behavioral problems, such as phobias; cognitive therapy is often successful in treating depression.
	Common themes and specificity	Common themes in successful therapies include expectations, sense of mastery, emotional arousal, and a confiding relationship. Further research is needed on which therapies work best with which individuals in what setting with which therapist.
	Culture and ethnicity	For too long the needs of people from poor and ethnic minority backgrounds were ignored by psychotherapists. Credibility and giving are two important therapy processes with ethnic minority individuals.
	Gender	Historically, the goal of therapy has been autonomy, but questions are raised about this as an ideal goal of therapy, especially for females. The goals of psychotherapy should include more attention to relatedness. Two nontraditional, gender-related forms of therapy are consciousness-raising groups and feminist therapy. Some feminist therapists distinguish between feminist therapy and nonsexist therapy.
Biomedical Therapies	Their nature	Treatment procedures are designed to reduce or eliminate the symptoms of psychological disorders by altering the way the body functions. Drug therapy is the most common biomedical therapy.
	Drug therapy	This may be effective when other therapies have failed, as in reducing the symptoms of schizophrenia. Three major classes of psychotherapeutic drugs are antianxiety, antipsychotic, and antidepressant.
	Electroconvulsive therapy	This is commonly called "shock therapy" and involves creation of a brain seizure; its most common use is as a last resort in treating severe depression.
	Psychosurgery	This refers to an irreversible procedure; brain tissue is destroyed in an attempt to improve psychological adjustment. Today's psychosurgery is more precise than the early prefrontal lobotomies. Psychosurgery is used only as a last resort.

Psychosurgery

One biomedical treatment is even more extreme than ECT. **Psychosurgery** *is a biomedical therapy that involves removal or destruction of brain tissue to improve the individual's psychological adjustment.* The effects of psychosurgery are irreversible. In the 1930s, Portuguese physician Egas Moniz developed a procedure known as a *prefrontal lobotomy.* In this procedure, a surgical instrument is inserted into the brain and rotated, severing fibers that connect the frontal lobe, important in higher thought processes, and the thalamus, important in emotion. Moniz theorized that by severing the connections between these brain structures the symptoms of severe mental disorders could be alleviated. Prefrontal lobotomies were conducted on thousands of patients from the 1930s through the 1950s. Moniz was even awarded the Nobel Prize for his work. However, while some patients may have benefited from the lobotomies, many were left in vegetable-like states because of the massive assaults on their brains.

These crude lobotomies are no longer performed. Since the 1960s, psychosurgery has become more precise. When psychosurgery is now performed, a small lesion is made in the amygdala or another part of the limbic system. Today only several hundred patients per year undergo psychosurgery. It is used as a last resort and with extreme caution.

At this point we have discussed a number of ideas about whether psychotherapy is effective and we reviewed the biomedical therapies. A summary of these ideas is presented in concept table 3.

Critical Thinking About Behavior

The Designer Brain and Enhanced Abilities

One pill makes you larger, And one pill makes you small.
Grace Slick

Lewis Carroll's *Alice in Wonderland* is often read as a whimsical metaphorical account of the adaptability that drugs can provide. When Alice was not tall enough to reach an opening, she drank a potion and magically grew to the required height. When she came upon another entrance that was too small for her giant frame, she drank another potion to shrink herself sufficiently.

Although science cannot produce the physical transformations described in Lewis Carroll's tale, many believe we are on the brink of a revolution in pharmacology that will produce mental health "designer drugs" not just to medicate the mentally disordered but to enhance the capacities of people with "normal" personalities. Once again, science may have made technological progress in areas where we have not fully considered the ethical and moral implications of implementing the technology.

Peter Kramer's depressed and anxious patients in *Listening to Prozac* are persuasive. They speak of feeling liberated from the edginess and depression that confused and confined them. They proclaim that they have discovered their true selves. They regret the span of their lives when they were without Prozac and wonder who they could have become if they had been able to be at their best throughout their lives.

However, the use of medication to enhance normal functioning is decidedly controversial. Many argue against the use of drugs to enhance normal function on religious grounds or because such interventions are "unnatural." Many believe philosophically that lives were meant to be lived fully, including feeling pain without the blunting caused by medication, in order to experience the full range of what life has to offer. Still others object on practical grounds. They express concern that we do not fully understand the long-term implications of using these drugs; they worry that there may be some serious bodily harms from long-term use that we simply have not had time to discover.

Those who advocate the development of mental health designer drugs view this technology as another step in helping humans adapt more effectively to their environments. For example, individuals who are born nearsighted use the technology of eyeglasses and contact lenses to compensate for their deficiencies and to adapt visually to their environments. People with chronic disease in our culture use any available technology to sustain life and promote a better quality of life. Advocates argue that designer drugs are a similar use of technology to adapt to ever worsening stress in contemporary life. They are optimistic that science will continue to produce cleaner and safer drugs for a variety of problems. They also suggest that society as a whole would benefit from citizens who are functioning closer to their maximum potential.

Where do you stand on the use of drugs to enhance normal functioning? If you had the opportunity legally to take a drug that would enhance your performance, would you? Or would you pass this opportunity by, regarding it as an example of human foolishness in trying to attain perfection using artificial methods? What personality characteristics or values undergird your position on designer drugs? Your position should reveal your ability to identify values that influence behavior.

Overview

We began this chapter by exploring the history of psychotherapy and then examined a number of therapy approaches. Our coverage of psychodynamic therapies focused on Freud's psychoanalysis and contemporary psychodynamic therapies, and our overview of humanistic therapies emphasized person-centered therapy and Gestalt therapy. We also studied the behavior therapies—classical conditioning approaches, operant conditioning approaches, cognitive behavior therapy, and the widespread use of behavior therapy. We learned about the cognitive therapies, including rational-emotive therapy and Beck's cognitive therapy. We evaluated group therapies and community psychology, and explored how effective psychotherapy is, including research on therapy effectiveness, common themes and specificity in therapy, culture and ethnicity, and gender. And we discussed the biomedical therapies—drug therapy, electroconvulsive therapy, and psychosurgery. Don't forget that you can obtain an overall summary of the chapter by again studying the three concept tables on pages 486, 499, and 507.

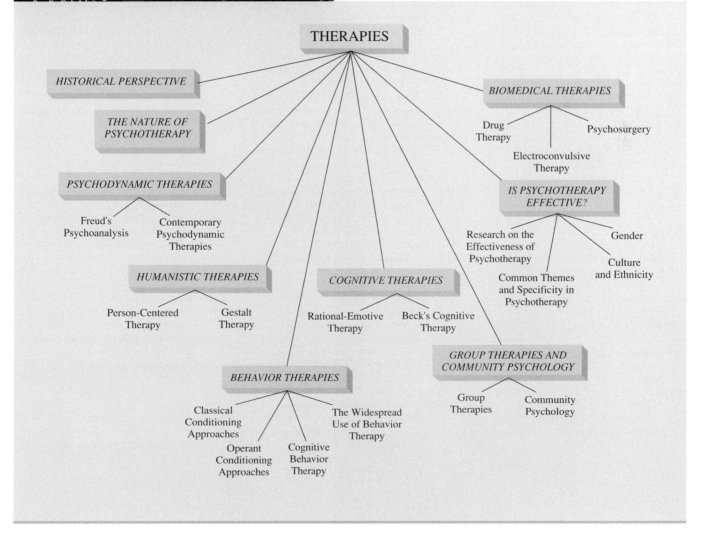

THERAPIES

- *HISTORICAL PERSPECTIVE*
- *THE NATURE OF PSYCHOTHERAPY*
- *PSYCHODYNAMIC THERAPIES*
  - Freud's Psychoanalysis
  - Contemporary Psychodynamic Therapies
- *HUMANISTIC THERAPIES*
  - Person-Centered Therapy
  - Gestalt Therapy
- *BEHAVIOR THERAPIES*
  - Classical Conditioning Approaches
  - Operant Conditioning Approaches
  - Cognitive Behavior Therapy
  - The Widespread Use of Behavior Therapy
- *COGNITIVE THERAPIES*
  - Rational-Emotive Therapy
  - Beck's Cognitive Therapy
- *GROUP THERAPIES AND COMMUNITY PSYCHOLOGY*
  - Group Therapies
  - Community Psychology
- *IS PSYCHOTHERAPY EFFECTIVE?*
  - Research on the Effectiveness of Psychotherapy
  - Common Themes and Specificity in Psychotherapy
  - Culture and Ethnicity
  - Gender
- *BIOMEDICAL THERAPIES*
  - Drug Therapy
  - Electroconvulsive Therapy
  - Psychosurgery

Key Terms

psychotherapy The process used by mental health professionals to help individuals recognize, define, and overcome their psychological and interpersonal difficulties and improve their adjustment. p. 479

insight therapy Therapy that encourages insight into and awareness of oneself. p. 479

managed health care A system in which external reviewers approve the type and length of treatment to justify insurance reimbursement. p. 480

psychodynamic therapies Therapies that stress the importance of the unconscious mind, extensive therapist interpretation, and the role of infant and early childhood experiences. p. 481

psychoanalysis Freud's therapeutic technique for analyzing an individual's unconscious thought. p. 481

free association The technique of encouraging individuals to say aloud whatever comes to mind, no matter how trivial or embarrassing. p. 482

catharsis The psychoanalytic term for clients' release of emotional tension when they relive an emotionally charged and conflicted experience. p. 482

dream analysis The psychotherapeutic technique psychoanalysts use to interpret a client's dreams. Psychoanalysts believe that dreams contain information about the individual's unconscious thoughts and conflicts. p. 482

manifest content The psychoanalytic term for the conscious, remembered aspects of a dream. p. 482

latent content The psychoanalytic term for the unconscious, unremembered, symbolic aspects of a dream. p. 482

transference The psychoanalytic term for a client's relating to an analyst in ways that reproduce or relive important relationships in the client's life. p. 483

resistance The psychoanalytic term for a client's unconscious defense strategies that prevent the analyst from understanding the client's problems. p. 483

humanistic psychotherapies Therapy in which clients are encouraged to understand themselves and to grow personally. In contrast to psychodynamic therapies, humanistic therapies emphasize conscious thoughts rather than unconscious thoughts, the present rather than the past, and growth and fulfillment rather than curing illness. p. 484

person-centered therapy A form of humanistic therapy developed by Carl Rogers, in which the therapist provides a warm, supportive atmosphere to improve the client's self-concept and encourage the client to gain insight about problems. p. 484

genuineness The Rogerian technique of being genuine and not hiding behind a facade. p. 485

accurate empathy Rogers' term for the therapist's identification with the client. p. 485

active listening Rogers' term for listening to another person with total attention to what the person says and means. p. 485

Gestalt therapy A humanistic therapy developed by Fritz Perls, in which the therapist questions and challenges clients to help them become more aware of their feelings and face their problems. p. 485

behavior therapies Therapies that use principles of learning to reduce or eliminate maladaptive behavior. p. 485

systematic desensitization A method of behavior therapy that treats anxiety by associating deep relaxation with successive visualizations of increasingly intense anxiety-producing situations; this technique is based on classical conditioning. p. 487

aversive conditioning An approach to behavior therapy that involves repeated pairings of an undesirable behavior with aversive stimuli to decrease the behavior's rewards so that the individual will stop doing it; this technique is based on classical conditioning. p. 487

behavior modification The application of operant conditioning principles to change human behavior; the main goal is to replace unacceptable responses with acceptable ones. p. 488

token economy A behavior modification system in which behaviors are reinforced with tokens (such as poker chips) that can be exchanged later for desired rewards (such as candy, money, or going to a movie). p. 488

cognitive behavior therapy An approach to behavior therapy that tries to help individuals behave more adaptively by modifying their thoughts. Cognitive behavior therapy stems from both cognitive psychology, with its emphasis on the effects of thoughts on behavior, and behaviorism, with its emphasis on behavior-change techniques. p. 489

self-efficacy The belief that one can master a situation and produce positive outcomes. p. 489

self-instructional methods Cognitive behavior techniques aimed at teaching individuals to modify their own behavior. p. 489

cognitive therapies Therapies that emphasize that the individual's cognitions or thoughts are the main source of abnormal behavior. Cognitive therapists attempt to change the individual's feelings and behaviors by changing cognitions. p. 490

rational-emotive therapy Therapy based on Albert Ellis' view that people become psychologically disordered because of their beliefs, especially those that are irrational and self-defeating. p. 490

family therapy Group therapy with family members. p. 493

couple therapy Group therapy with married or unmarried couples whose major problem is their relationship. p. 493

family systems therapy A form of therapy based on the assumption that psychological adjustment is related to patterns of interaction within the family unit. p. 493

personal growth groups Groups that have their roots in the humanistic therapies; they emphasize personal growth and increased openness and honesty in interpersonal relations. p. 494

encounter group A personal growth group designed to promote self-understanding through candid group interaction. p. 494

self-help groups Voluntary organizations of individuals who get together on a regular basis to discuss topics of common interest. The group leader and members give support to help individuals with their problems. Self-help groups are so-called because they are conducted without a professional therapist. p. 494

deinstitutionalization The movement to transfer the treatment of mental disorders from inpatient mental institutions to community-based facilities that stress outpatient care. p. 496

primary prevention A community psychology approach that attempts to reduce the number of new cases of mental disorders. p. 497

secondary prevention A community psychology approach that focuses on early detection of problems and early intervention. p. 498

tertiary prevention A community psychology approach that attempts to reduce the long-term consequences of mental health disorders that were not prevented or arrested earlier. p. 498

empowerment Helping individuals develop the skills they need to control their own lives. p. 498

meta-analysis A research strategy in which the results of many studies are statistically combined. p. 498

credibility A therapist's believability. p. 502

giving The therapist provides the client with some kind of benefit from treatment early in the therapy process. p. 502

consciousness-raising groups Groups that are believed by some feminists to be an important alternative or adjunct to traditional therapy; they often involve several people meeting in a member's home, frequently are leaderless, and focus on members' feelings and self-perceptions. Instead of seeking and accepting male-biased therapy, women might meet in consciousness-raising groups to define their own experiences with their own criteria. p. 503

feminist therapies Therapies usually based on a critique of society wherein women are perceived to have less political and economic power than men have. Also, feminist therapies assume that the reasons for women's problems are principally social, not personal. p. 503

nonsexist therapy Therapy that can occur when the therapist has become aware of and primarily overcome his or her sexist attitudes and behavior. p. 504

biomedical therapies Treatments to reduce or eliminate the symptoms of psychological disorders by altering the way an individual's body functions. Drug therapy is the most common form; less common are electroconvulsive therapy and psychosurgery. p. 504

antianxiety drugs Drugs that reduce anxiety by making individuals less excitable and more tranquil; commonly known as tranquilizers. p. 504

antipsychotic drugs Powerful drugs that diminish agitated behavior, reduce tension, decrease hallucinations and delusions, improve social behavior, and produce better sleep patterns in severely mentally disordered individuals; neuroleptics are the most common such drugs. p. 505

tardive dyskinesia A major side effect of the neuroleptic drugs; a neurological disorder characterized by grotesque, involuntary movements of the facial muscles and mouth, as well as extensive twitching of the neck, arms, and legs. p. 505

antidepressant drugs Drugs that regulate mood. The three main classes are tricyclics, such as Elavil; SSRI inhibitors, such as Prozac; and MAO inhibitors, such as Nardil. p. 505

lithium A drug that is widely used to treat bipolar disorder. p. 505

electroconvulsive therapy (ECT) "Shock treatment," sometimes used to treat severely depressed individuals. The goal is to cause a seizure in the brain, much like an epileptic seizure. p. 506

psychosurgery A biomedical therapy that involves removal or destruction of brain tissue to improve the individual's psychological adjustment. p. 507

Resources and Readings in Psychology

Behavior Therapy

This journal publishes a wide-ranging set of behavior therapy strategies and a number of fascinating case studies. Look through recent issues to learn how behavior therapy is conducted.

Case Approach to Counseling and Psychotherapy (1996, 4th ed.)

by Gerald Corey
Pacific Grove, CA: Brooks/Cole

A central client, Ruth, becomes the focus for the application of nine different therapies, including psychoanalytic, Adlerian, person-centered, Gestalt, cognitive-behavior, and family systems.

The Compleat Therapist (1991)

by Jeffrey Kottler
New York: Jossey-Bass

Kottler reveals the techniques all good therapists have in common and combines the most effective healing therapies into one framework. These characteristics include the therapist's personality, skillful thinking processes, communication skills, and intimate and trusting relationships. This book gives excellent insight into the characteristics of therapists that help clients improve regardless of the therapist's theoretical orientation.

The Consumer's Guide to Psychotherapy (1992)

by Jack Engler and Daniel Goleman
New York: Simon & Schuster

This is a comprehensive manual on psychotherapy for consumers. Among the questions the authors ask and evaluate are:

- How do I decide if I need therapy?
- Which therapy approach is best for me?
- How do I find the right therapist?
- What questions should I ask during the first session?
- How can I afford therapy?
- How can I tell if therapy is really working?
- How do I know when to end therapy?

The book is based on the clinical opinions of almost 1,000 therapists nationwide. Included are case studies and listings of mental health organizations, as well as therapist referral sources.

***Counseling American Minorities* (1993, 4th ed.)**
by Donald Atkinson, George Morten, and Derald Sue
Dubuque, IA: Brown & Benchmark

This book provides valuable information about counseling and psychotherapy with individuals from ethnic minority backgrounds. Entire sections are devoted to the American Indian client, the Asian American client, the African American client, and the Latino client. You might also want to read *Psychotherapy and Counseling with Minorities* (New York: Pergamon, 1991) by Manuel Ramirez.

***Current Psychotherapies* (1989, 2nd ed.)**
edited by Ray Corsini
Itasca, IL: Peacock

Therapists from various schools of psychotherapy describe their approaches.

***Five Therapists and One Client* (1991)**
by Raymond Corsini and contributors
Itasca, IL: Peacock

Therapists who have five distinctive approaches to helping clients describe their conceptual orientation, therapy techniques, and demonstrate how they would likely work with the same fictitious client. The imaginary client is a relatively normal individual with unusual and persistent problems—a common client for psychotherapists in private practice. Four clear-cut systems of psychotherapy were selected: Alfred Adler's individual therapy, Carl Rogers' person-centered therapy, Albert Ellis' rational-emotive therapy, and behavior therapy. Finally, a fifth therapy approach—eclectic therapy—was chosen. How therapists from these five different approaches would handle the same client serves as the core of the book, helping you to see distinctive ways therapists with different orientations conduct psychotherapy.

***Gestalt Therapy Verbatim* (1969)**
by Fritz Perls
Lafayette, CA: Real People Press

Fritz Perls, the founder of Gestalt therapy, lays out the main ideas of his approach in vivid detail.

***Great Cases in Psychotherapy* (1979)**
by D. Wedding and R. Corsini
Itasca, IL: Peacock

A complete description of a number of well-known cases in psychotherapy, including clients of Sigmund Freud, Fritz Perls, Alfred Adler, Carl Jung, and Carl Rogers.

***Heart and Mind* (1996)**
By Robert Allan and Stephan Scheidt (eds.)
Washington, DC : American Psychological Association

The intriguing link between cardiac health and human behavior is explored in this volume. State-of-the-art treatment solutions are given for coronary-prone-behavior.

Journal of Clinical and Consulting Psychology

This excellent journal publishes articles on many different topics in clinical psychology. Special sections feature a series of articles on a particular topic.

National Alliance of the Mentally Ill
2101 Wilson Road, Suite 302
Arlington, VA 22201
703–524–7600

This is an alliance of self-help/advocacy groups concerned with severe and chronically mentally disordered individuals. The objective is to provide emotional support and practical guidance to families. The Alliance has resource materials available and publishes a monthly newsletter, *NAMI Advocate.*

National Council of Community Mental Health Centers
12300 Twinbrook Parkway, No. 320
Rockville, MD 20852
301–984–6200

This organization's goal is to improve the quality of community mental health care; its divisions include consultation, education, and prevention. Publications and materials are available.

North American Society of Adlerian Psychology
202 S. State Street, Suite 1212
Chicago, IL 60604
312–939–0834

This organization involves mental health professionals and people interested in the therapy approach of Alfred Adler. It promotes the establishment of family education associations and parent study groups and publishes a monthly newsletter and a journal, *Individual Psychology.*

***Theory of Multicultural Counseling and Therapy* (1996)**
by Derald Wing Sue (ed.)
Pacific Grove, CA: Brooks/Cole

Experts in the field of multicultural counseling discuss many issues involving African American, Latino, Asian American, and Native American individuals.

CHAPTER

SCH

Stress, Coping, and Health

JOHN W. SANTROCK
In Torment

CHAPTER

SCH

Stress, Coping, and Health

Chapter Outline

Chapter Boxes

Life is not living, but living in health.

—Martial

If you can't fight and you can't flee, flow.

—**Robert Eliot**

Images of Psychology

Overwhelmed by Stress

Mort, age 52, has worked as an air traffic controller for the past 15 years. An excitable person, he compares the job to being in a cage. During peak air traffic, the tension is almost unbearable. In these frenzied moments, Mort's emotions are a mixture of rage, fear, and anxiety. Unfortunately, the tension also spills over into his family life. In his own words, "When I go home, my nerves are hopping. I take it out on the nearest person." Two years ago, Mort's wife, Sally, told him that if he could not calm his emotions and handle stress more effectively, she would leave him. She suggested that he change to a less upsetting job, but he ignored her advice. His intense emotional behavior continued, and she left him. Last week the roof fell in on Mort. That Sunday evening, the computer that monitors air traffic temporarily went down and Mort had a heart attack. Quadruple bypass surgery saved his life.

Yesterday his doctor talked with him about the stress in his life and what could be done to reduce it. Mort rarely gets enough sleep, weighs too much but frequently skips meals, never exercises, smokes two packs of cigarettes a day, and drinks two or three scotches every evening (more on weekends). He professes no religious interests. He rarely dates since his divorce and has no relatives living within 50 miles. He has only one friend and does not feel very close to him. Mort says that he never has enough time to do the things he wants to do and rarely has quiet time to himself during the day. He has fun only about once every 2 weeks.

The doctor gave Mort a test, shown in table 1, to reveal his vulnerability to stress. Mort scored 68 on the stress test, indicating he is seriously vulnerable to stress and close to the extremely vulnerable range. Stress is inevitable in our lives, so it is important to understand what factors are involved in managing stress and in maintaining a healthy lifestyle. How do *you* fare on the stress test?

Table 1
Stress Test

Rate yourself on each item, using a scale of 1–5:

1 = almost always
2 = often
3 = sometimes
4 = seldom
5 = never

1. I eat at least one hot, balanced meal a day.
2. I get 7 to 8 hours of sleep at least four nights a week.
3. I give and receive affection regularly.
4. I have at least one relative within 50 miles whom I can rely on.
5. I exercise to the point of perspiration at least twice a week.
6. I smoke less than half a pack of cigarettes a day.
7. I take fewer than five alcoholic drinks a week.
8. I am the appropriate weight for my height.
9. I have an income adequate to meet my basic expenses.
10. I get strength from my religious beliefs.
11. I regularly attend church.
12. I have a network of friends and acquaintances.
13. I have one or more friends to confide in about personal matters.
14. I am in good health (including eyesight, hearing, teeth).
15. I am able to speak openly about my feelings when angry or worried.
16. I have regular conversations with the people I live with about domestic problems (e.g., chores, money, and daily living issues).
17. I do something for fun at least once a week.
18. I am able to organize my time effectively.
19. I drink fewer than three cups of coffee (or tea or cola drinks) a day.
20. I take quiet time for myself during the day.

Total:

To get your total score, add up the figures and subtract 20. Any number over 30 indicates a vulnerability to stress. You are seriously vulnerable if your score is between 50 and 75 and extremely vulnerable if it is over 75.

Preview

There are too many Morts in the world who haven't figured out how to live a healthy lifestyle. This chapter is about the role psychology plays in understanding health, stress, and coping. We will examine how people like Mort can cope more effectively with stress and live more healthy lives. You will learn about effective and ineffective coping strategies. Before we tackle health, stress, and coping, we will examine the historical and contemporary approaches to understanding health concerns.

The Scope of Health Psychology

Around 2600 B.C. Asian physicians, and later around 500 B.C., Greek physicians recognized that good habits were essential for good health. They did not blame the gods for illness and think that magic would cure the illness. They realized that people have some control over their health. The physician's role was as a guide, assisting the patient in restoring a natural and emotional balance.

As we approach the twenty-first century, once again we recognize the power of lifestyles and psychological states in promoting health. We are returning to the ancient view that the ultimate responsibility for influencing health rests with the individuals themselves.

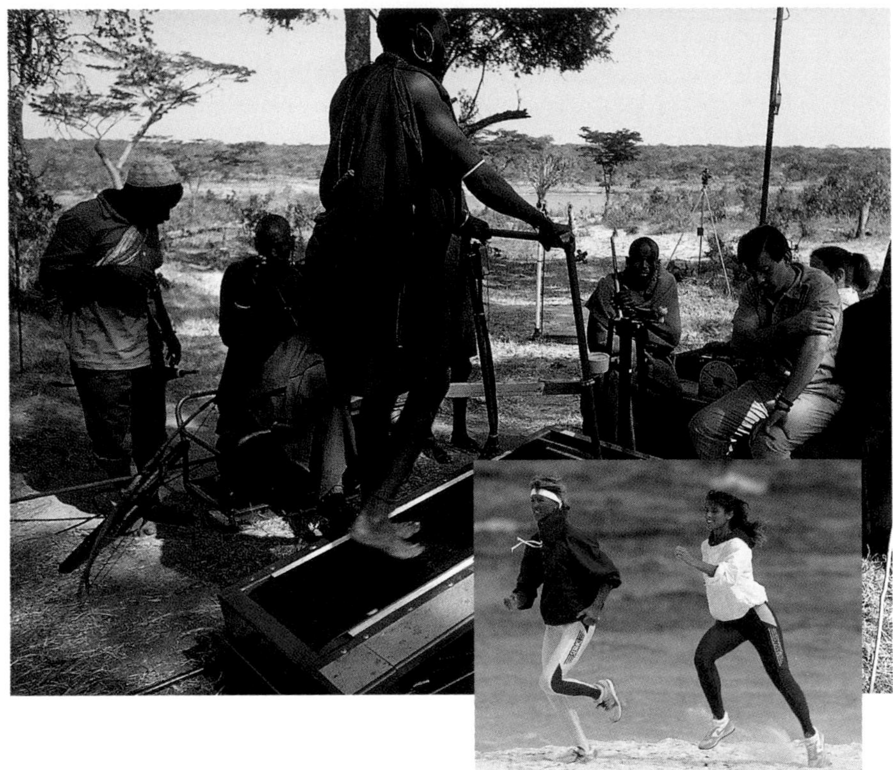

Members of the Masai tribe in Kenya, Africa, can stay on a treadmill for a long time because of their very active life. Heart disease is extremely low in the Masai tribe, which also can be attributed to their energetic lifestyle. (inset) Americans are increasingly recognizing the health benefits of exercise and an active lifestyle. The role of exercise in health is one of health psychology's many interests.

Health psychology *is a multidimensional approach to health that emphasizes psychological factors, lifestyle, and the nature of the health care delivery system.* To underscore the increasing interest in psychology's role in health, a new division of the American Psychological Association called "health psychology" was formed in 1978. **Behavioral medicine** *is a field closely related to health psychology; it attempts to combine medical and behavioral knowledge to reduce illness and to promote health.* The interests of health psychologists and behavioral medicine researchers are broad; they include examining why we do or do not comply with medical advice, how effective media campaigns are in reducing smoking, psychological factors involved in losing weight, and the role of exercise in reducing stress.

One of the main areas of research in health psychology and behavioral medicine is the link between stress and illness (Turpin & Slade, 1997). Both our psychological and physical well-being are related to stress and how we cope with it. Because stress is an inevitable part of each of our lives, we need to understand it better and learn how to handle it more effectively.

Stress

We live in a world that includes many stressful circumstances. According to the American Academy of Family Physicians, two-thirds of office visits to family doctors are for stress-related symptoms. And stress is believed to be a major contributor to coronary heart disease, cancer, lung problems, accidental injuries, cirrhosis of the liver, and suicide—six of the leading causes of death in the United States. In 1990, two of the five best-selling prescription drugs in the United States were an antianxiety drug (Xanax) and an ulcer medication (Zantac).

Stress is a sign of the times. Everywhere you look, people are jogging, going to health clubs, and following diets designed to reduce tension. Even corporations have developed elaborate stress management programs. No one really knows whether we experience more stress than our parents or grandparents, but it seems as if we do.

How can we define stress? Stress is one of those terms that is not easy to define. Initially, the word *stress* was loosely borrowed from physics. Humans, it was thought, are in some ways similar to physical objects such as metals that resist moderate outside forces but loose their resiliency at some point of greater pressure. But unlike metal, human beings can think and reason, and experience a myriad of social, environmental circumstances that make defining stress more complex in psychology than in physics (Hobfoll, 1989). In humans, is stress the threats and challenges our environment places on us, as when we say, "Sally's world is so stressful, it is overwhelming her"? Is stress our responses to such threats and challenges, as when we say, "Bob is not coping well with the problems in his life, he is experiencing a lot of stress, and his body is falling apart"? While psychologists debate whether stress is the threatening events in our world or whether it is our response to those demands, we will define stress broadly. **Stress** *is the response of individuals to the circumstances and events, called stressors, that threaten them and tax their coping abilities.* To understand stress, we need to know about the following factors: physical and biological, emotional, personality, cognitive, environmental, sociocultural, and coping skills (see figure 1).

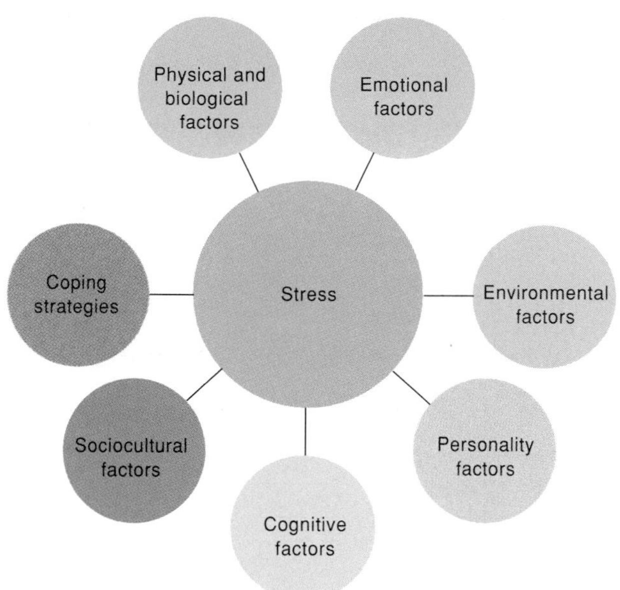

FIGURE 1

Factors Involved in Stress
Among the most important factors involved in understanding stress are physical and biological factors (such as our body's response to stress), emotional factors (such as happiness), environmental factors (such as the frustrating stressors we experience in our world), personality factors (such as how we handle anger and whether we trust others), cognitive factors (such as whether we perceive and appraise an event as threatening or challenging), sociocultural factors (such as negative contact with the mainstream society), and coping strategies (such as how we use our skills and abilities to manage stress).

Biological Factors in Stress

Among the important physical and biological factors in stress are the nervous system's role, the general adaptation syndrome and psychoneuroimmunology, each of which we discuss in turn.

The Nervous System

Many scientists now believe there are two main pathways in the nervous system that connect the brain and endocrine system in response to stress. The first pathway is through the autonomic nervous system (ANS). Your central nervous system perceives a stressor and then the sympathetic part of the ANS releases the stress hormones *epinephrine* (adrenaline) and *norepinephrine* (noradrenaline) from nerve endings in the inner portion of the adrenal glands. A surge of adrenaline not only elevates blood pressure, but has been linked to sudden death through heart disease. The autonomic nervous system changes in response to stress have also been linked to stomach problems, such as ulcers. The second pathway is used when the cerebral cortex perceives a stressor and the information is routed through the hypothalamus and pituitary gland to the outer part of the adrenal gland, where the hormone *cortisol* is released.

The General Adaptation Syndrome

According to the Austrian-born founder of stress research, the late Hans Selye (1974, 1983), stress simply is the wear and tear on the body due to the demands placed on it. Any number of environmental events or stimuli will produce the same stress response in the body. Selye observed patients with different problems: the death of someone close, loss of income, arrest for embezzlement. Regardless of which problem the patient had, similar symptoms appeared: loss of appetite, muscular weakness, and decreased interest in the world.

The **general adaptation syndrome (GAS)** *is Selye's term for the common effects on the body when demands are placed on it. The GAS consists of three stages: alarm, resistance, and exhaustion.* First, in the *alarm stage,* the body enters a temporary state of shock, a time when resistance to illness and stress fall below normal limits. In trying to cope with the initial effects of stress, the body quickly releases hormones, which, in a short time, adversely affect the immune system's functioning. It is during this time that the

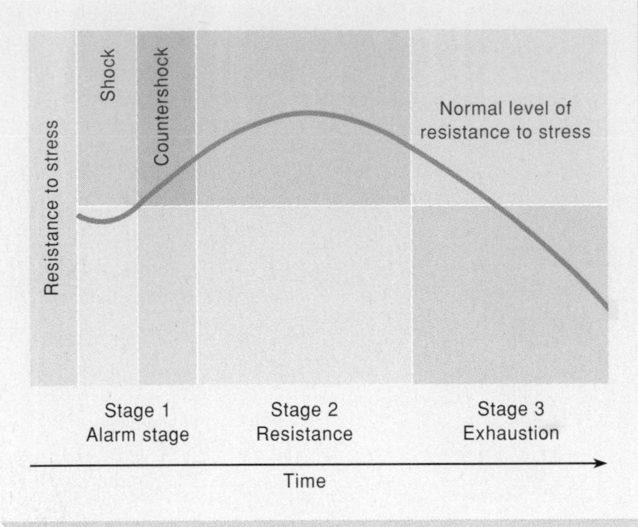

FIGURE 2

Selye's General Adaptation Syndrome
The general adaptation syndrome (GAS) describes an individual's general response to stress. In the first stage (alarm), the body enters a temporary state of shock, a time when resistance to stress is below normal. Then a rebound called "countershock" occurs, in which resistance to stress begins to pick up. Not much later, the individual moves into the second state (resistance), during which resistance to stress is intensified in an all-out effort to combat stress. If the effort fails and stress persists, the individual moves into the third and final state (exhaustion), when wear and tear on the body worsens, the person may collapse in a state of exhaustion, and vulnerability to disease increases.

individual is prone to infections from illness and injury. Fortunately, the alarm stage passes rather quickly as the body begins to build up its resistance. In the *resistance stage,* a number of glands throughout the body begin to manufacture different hormones that protect the individual in many ways. During this stage, the body's immune system can fight off infection with remarkable efficiency. Similarly, hormones that reduce inflammation normally associated with injury are present at high levels. If the all-out effort to combat stress fails and the stress persists, the individual moves into the *exhaustion stage.* Now the wear and tear on the body takes its toll—the person may collapse in a state of exhaustion and vulnerability to disease increases. Figure 2 provides an illustration of Selye's general adaptation syndrome.

Not all stress is bad, though. **Eustress** *is Selye's term for the positive features of stress.* Competing in an athletic event, writing an essay, or pursuing someone who is attractive requires the body to expend energy. Selye does not say we should avoid these fulfilling experiences in life, but he does emphasize that we should minimize the wear and tear on our bodies.

One of the main criticisms of Selye's view is that human beings do not always react to stress in the uniform way he proposed (Seffge-Krenke, 1995). There is much more to understanding stress in humans than knowing their physical reactions to it. We also need to know about their personality, their physical makeup, their perceptions, and the context in which the stressor occurred.

Illness and the Immune System

Psychoneuroimmunology *is the field that explores connections among psychological factors (such as attitudes and emotions), the nervous system, and the immune system.* The immune system keeps us healthy by recognizing foreign materials such as bacteria, viruses, and tumors, and then destroying them. Its machinery consists of billions of white blood cells located in the lymph system. The number of white blood cells and their effectiveness in killing foreign viruses or bacteria are related to stress levels. When in the alarm or exhaustion stage, for example, the immune system functions poorly. During these stages, viruses and bacteria are more likely to multiply and cause disease.

What are some of the biological pathways that might link stress and illness? What are some of the behavioral pathways? What interventions are effective in breaking down the connection between stress and illness?

Biological Pathways Stress can set in motion biological effects that involve the autonomic, endocrine, and immune systems (Anderson, Kiecolt-Glaser, & Glaser, 1994). The immune system may be one of the more important biological determinants in the control of certain malignant diseases. Are there stress-mediated immune responses and stress-mediated health effects?

There are three lines of support for stress-mediated immune response. First, acute stressors can produce immunological changes in healthy individuals. For example, in relatively healthy HIV-infected individuals, as well as individuals with cancer, the onset of acute stressors was associated with poorer immune system functioning (Roberts, Anderson, & Lubaroff, 1994).

Second, chronic stressors are associated with an increasing downturn in immune system responsiveness, rather than adaptation. This effect has been documented in a number of contexts, including living next to a damaged nuclear reactor, failures in close relationships (divorce, separation, and marital distress), and burdensome caregiving for a family member with progressive dementia (Kiecolt-Glaser & others, 1991).

Third, research with cancer patients links quality-of-life components with immunity. Social adjustment often predicts higher NK-cell levels (NK stands for natural killer), while negative-distress indicators often predict lower NK-cell levels (Levy & others, 1990). NK cells can attack tumor cells.

Two lines of research reveal the role of stress in health. First, acute stress is related to illness, especially infectious illness in young, healthy individuals. In one study, increased cold infection was associated with increased stress. Second, chronic stressors can affect health as well. In one study, "at risk" Alzheimer's caregivers had more and longer-lasting respiratory infections than did their non-at-risk counterparts (Kiecolt-Glaser & others, 1991).

Behavioral Pathways Behavioral pathways involving stress and illness focus on health behaviors and compliance. Individuals who experience psychological stress from an illness often develop other health-related problems. Distressed individuals often have appetite disturbances, resulting in eating less often or eating meals of lower nutritional value (Wellisch & others, 1989). Individuals who are depressed, anxious, or both are more likely to self-medicate with alcohol and other drugs (Grunberg & Baum, 1985). Thus, poor health behaviors can magnify the effects of stress on illness. Both poor nutrition and substance abuse can directly lower the immune system's functioning. On the positive side, there is increasing evidence that physical activity can improve immune system functioning. For example, in one study, exercise and fitness were linked with positive immune system functioning in HIV-infected men (LaPerriere & others, 1990).

Noncompliance is a general health problem that can influence the link between stress and illness (Anderson, in press). For instance, the psychological or behavioral effects of cancer treatments can be so disruptive that patients become discouraged and fail to complete, or even refuse, treatment.

Interventions Appropriately designed interventions can reduce stress and enhance the quality of life as well as improve behavioral responses, such as health behaviors and compliance (Anderson, Kiecolt-Glaser, & Glaser, 1994). Among the therapy components that have been effective in reducing stress in cancer patients are emotional support, coping strategies, and relaxation training (Gruber & others, 1993).

Recently researchers have found that certain interventions hold the possibility of not only reducing stress, but improving immune functioning and physical health as well. James Pennebaker and his colleagues (Pennebaker, Colder, & Sharp, 1990) revealed that beginning college students often find the first few months of college to be very stressful. Indeed, health problems during this time are significantly higher than in the later college years. One problem is that students frequently do not talk about their problems with others. In this research, individuals were asked to write for 20 minutes a day for 3 consecutive days about their deepest thoughts and feelings about coming to college. Other students wrote for the same amount of time about superficial topics, such as their plans for the day. Students who wrote about coming to college visited the student health center for illness at about half the rate as other students in the 4 months following the study.

Writing or talking about upsetting experiences does more than reduce physician visits. For example, individuals who wrote about traumatic experiences for 4 consecutive days had better immune system functioning than a control group of individuals who wrote about superficial topics (Pennebaker, Kiecolt-Glaser, & Glaser, 1988). Confronting painful topics, then, is often a good strategy in reducing stress. Consider, for instance, the intriguing research study conducted by David Spiegel and his colleagues (1989), in which eighty women with advanced breast cancer were randomly assigned to either a talk therapy group or a no-therapy control group. Women assigned to groups in which they could confide their thoughts and feelings about cancer lived an average of 1.5 years longer than women in the control group.

The scientific study of psychoneuroimmunology is relatively young. Much of what we know needs to be clarified, explained, and verified further. Researchers hope to clarify the precise links among psychological factors, the brain, and the immune system (Redd, 1995). Some preliminary hypotheses about the interaction that causes vulnerability to disease include the following: (1) Stressful experiences lower the efficiency of immune systems, making individuals more susceptible to disease; (2) stress directly promotes disease-producing processes; and (3) stressful experiences may cause the activation of dormant viruses that diminish the individual's ability to cope with disease. These hypotheses may lead to clues for more successful treatments for some of the most baffling diseases—cancer and AIDS among them. To increase your understanding of AIDS, turn to Explorations in Psychology 1.

Personality Factors in Stress

Do you have certain personality characteristics that help you cope more effectively with stress? Do other characteristics make you more vulnerable to stress? Two important candidates are the Type A behavior pattern and hardiness.

Type A Behavior Pattern

In the late 1950s a secretary for two California cardiologists, Meyer Friedman and Ray Rosenman, observed that the chairs in their waiting rooms were tattered and worn, but only on the front edges. The cardiologists had noticed the impatience of their cardiac patients, who often arrived exactly on time for an appointment and were in a great hurry to leave. Subsequently they conducted a study of 3,000 healthy men between the ages of 35 and 59 over a period of 8 years (Friedman & Rosenman, 1974). During the 8 years, one group of men had twice as many heart attacks or other forms of heart disease as anyone else. And autopsies of the men who died revealed that this same group had coronary arteries that were more obstructed than those of other men. Friedman and Rosenman described the coronary disease group as characterized by **Type A behavior pattern,** *a cluster of characteristics—being excessively competitive, hard-driven, impatient, and hostile—thought to be related to the incidence of heart disease.*

However, further research on the link between Type A behavior and coronary disease indicates that the association

Explorations in Psychology 1

Increasing Your Understanding of AIDS

Valerie and Tom had been dating for about 3 years. They mutually decided to think about a few things, including their level of sexual intimacy and where marriage fit in their plans. As they discussed these matters, Tom brought up the issue of birth control and wondered about the relative effectiveness of the different methods. Valerie and Tom knew little about this and wanted more information. Together, they visited the health department in their community and picked up brochures and pamphlets, including pamphlets about AIDS. After reading these, they realized that condoms are the only contraceptive method that protects against diseases. They also started to talk more about their past relationships, something they really never had done before. Sharing this information relieved them of many concerns and raised others. Together, though, they were able to work out many of the issues they were thinking about and were able to make several important informed decisions about their relationship that could have a dramatic impact on their health.

The most rapidly emerging threat to public health is infection from human immunodeficiency virus (HIV), which results in acquired immunodeficiency syndrome (AIDS). In fact, no disease has ever become such a major public health threat so soon after being recognized. As of early 1992, more than 200,000 persons had AIDS in the United States, with the last 100,000 cases occurring since 1989. HIV, the virus that causes AIDS, is transmitted from one person to another in

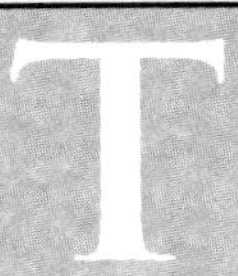

Table A

Knowledge of AIDS Risk Behavior

Instructions

This is a true/false test. Please do not skip any questions. Because this is a test, some of the statements are true and accurate, others are false and inaccurate.

Items

1. Most people who transmit the AIDS virus look unhealthy.
2. Anal intercourse is high-risk behavior for transmitting the AIDS virus.
3. Oral sex carries risk for AIDS virus transmission.
4. A person can be exposed to the AIDS virus in one sexual contact.
5. Keeping in good physical condition is the best way to prevent exposure to the AIDS virus.
6. It is unwise to touch a person with AIDS.
7. Condoms make intercourse completely safe.
8. Showering after sex greatly reduces the transmission of AIDS.
9. When people become sexually exclusive with one another, they no longer need to follow "safe sex" guidelines.
10. Oral sex is safe if the partners "don't swallow."
11. Most people who have been exposed to the AIDS virus quickly show symptoms of serious illness.
12. By reducing the number of different sexual partners, you are effectively protected from AIDS.
13. The AIDS virus does not penetrate unbroken skin.
14. Female-to-male transmission of the AIDS virus has not been documented.
15. Sharing toothbrushes and razors can transmit the AIDS virus.
16. Pre-ejaculatory fluids carry the AIDS virus.
17. Intravenous drug users are at risk for AIDS when they share needles.
18. A person must have many different sexual partners to be at risk from AIDS.
19. People carrying the AIDS virus generally feel quite ill.
20. Vaginal intercourse carries high risk for AIDS virus transmission.
21. Withdrawal immediately before orgasm makes intercourse safe.

Please turn to Table A.1 at the end of the chapter to score and interpret your responses.

only a few specific ways. A person can get infected with HIV from engaging in sexual intercourse with an infected partner or sharing syringes and other injection equipment when shooting up drugs. Some people have been infected after receiving blood transfusions; however, this is rare today because blood banks routinely test blood before using it in transfusions. The primary way that people are getting infected with HIV today is through sexual contact and injecting drugs. To evaluate your own knowledge of AIDS, turn to table A.

Recently in the United States, it was thought that gay men were the only people who needed to be concerned about HIV and AIDS. This could not be further from the truth. Although gay men were hit hardest early in the U.S. AIDS epidemic, today there are no boundaries to AIDS. People of all sexual orientations, ethnic backgrounds, incomes, and geographical locations can be at risk for HIV infection. It is the things a person *does,* not the person that they *are,* that puts people at risk. The public came to realize this most recently when basketball star Earvin "Magic" Johnson announced that he was infected with HIV. Magic Johnson's message was that anyone could get HIV if they engaged in behaviors that put them at risk, such as having sex without using a condom. Although condoms can break and are effective only when used properly, they do decrease the chances of HIV infections substantially. Condoms offer the best protection from the virus during sexual intercourse.

22. Persons who are exclusively heterosexual are not at risk from AIDS.
23. Healthy persons in AIDS risk groups should not donate blood.
24. Sharing kitchen utensils or a bathroom with a person with AIDS poses no risk.
25. Intravenous drug users become exposed to the AIDS virus because the virus is often contained in heroin, amphetamines, and the injected drugs.
26. A wholesome diet and plenty of sleep will keep a person from becoming exposed to the AIDS virus.
27. A cure for AIDS is expected within the next two years.
28. It is more important to take precautions against AIDS in large cities than in small cities.
29. A negative result on the AIDS virus antibody test can occur even for people who carry the virus.
30. A positive result on the AIDS virus antibody test can occur even for people who do not carry the virus.
31. Coughing does not spread AIDS.
32. Only receptive (passive) anal intercourse transmits AIDS.
33. Most present cases of AIDS are due to blood transfusions that took place before 1984.
34. Most persons exposed to the AIDS virus know they are exposed.
35. A great deal is now known about how the AIDS virus is transmitted.
36. Donating blood carries no AIDS risk for the donor.
37. No cases of AIDS have ever been linked to social (dry) kissing.
38. Mutual masturbation and body rubbing are low in risk unless the partners have cuts or scratches.
39. People who become exposed to the AIDS virus through needle-sharing can transmit the virus to others during sexual activities.
40. The AIDS virus can be transmitted by mosquitoes or cockroaches.

is not as strong as Friedman and Rosenman believed (Williams, 1995). Researchers have examined the components of Type A behavior, such as hostility, to determine a more precise link with coronary risk (Dolezal, Davison, & DeQuattro, 1996; Faber & Burns, 1996). People who are hostile or consistently turn anger inward, it turns out, are more likely to develop heart disease (Allan & Scheidt, 1996). Such people have been labeled "hot reactors," meaning they have intense physiological reactions to stress—their hearts race, their breathing quickens, and their muscles tense up—which could lead to heart disease. Redford Williams (1995), a leading researcher in charting the behavioral and psychological dimensions of heart disease, believes each of us has the ability to control our anger and develop more trust in others, which he believes will reduce the risk for heart disease.

Type C Behavior

Type C behavior *refers to the cancer-prone personality, which consists of being inhibited, uptight, lacking in emotional expressiveness, and being otherwise constrained. This type of individual is more likely to develop cancer than more expressive people* (Temoshok & Dreher, 1992). While still a very new concept, Type C behavior holds the promise of capturing as much attention as Type A behavior. The concept of Type C behavior fits with the findings of stress and health researchers, who have found that holding in one's problems and being inhibited about talking with others about problems can be an impairment to health.

Hardiness

Hardiness *is a personality style characterized by a sense of commitment (rather than alienation), control (rather than powerlessness), and a perception of problems as challenges (rather than threats).* In the Chicago Stress Project, male business managers 32 to 65 years of age were studied over a 5-year period. During the 5 years, most of the managers experienced stressful events, such as divorce, job transfers, the death of a close friend, inferior performance evaluations at work, and working at a job with an unpleasant boss. In one study, managers who developed an illness (ranging from the flu to a heart attack) were compared with those who did not (Kobasa, Maddi, & Kahn, 1982). The latter group was more likely to have a hardy personality. In another study, whether or not hardiness along with exercise and social support buffered stress and reduced illness in executives' lives was investigated (Kobasa & others, 1985). When all three factors were present in an executive's life the level of illness dropped dramatically. This suggests the power of multiple buffers of stress, rather than a single buffer, in maintaining health.

Cognitive Factors in Stress

Most of us think of stress as environmental events that place demands on our lives, such as losing one's notes from a class, being yelled at by a friend, failing a test, or being in a car wreck. While there are some common ways we all experience stress, not everyone perceives the same events as stressful. For example, one person may perceive an upcoming job interview as threatening, while another person may perceive it as challenging. One person may perceive a D grade on a paper as threatening, another person may perceive the same grade as challenging. To some degree, then, what is stressful depends on how people cognitively appraise and interpret events. This view has been most clearly presented by Richard Lazarus (1993). **Cognitive appraisal** *is Lazarus' term for individuals' interpretation of events in their lives as harmful, threatening, or challenging, and their determination of whether they have the resources to effectively cope with the events.*

In Lazarus' view, events are appraised in two steps: primary appraisal and secondary appraisal. In *primary appraisal,* individuals interpret whether an event involves *harm* or loss that has already occurred, a *threat* of some future danger, or a *challenge* to be overcome. *Harm* is the individual's appraisal of the damage the event has already inflicted. For example, if you overslept yesterday and missed an exam, the harm has already been done. *Threat* is the individual's appraisal of potential future damage an event may bring. For example, missing the exam may lower the instructor's opinion of you and increase the probability you will get a low grade in the course at the end of the semester. *Challenge* is the individual's appraisal of the potential to overcome the adverse circumstances of an event and ultimately to profit from it. For example, a student may use missing the exam as an opportunity to become acquainted with the instructor and actually benefit from what initially appeared to be a hopelessly bad circumstance.

After individuals cognitively appraise an event for its harm, threat, or challenge, Lazarus says that they subsequently engage in secondary appraisal. In *secondary appraisal,* individuals evaluate their resources and determine how effectively they can be used to cope with the event. This appraisal is called *secondary* because it comes after primary appraisal and depends on the degree to which the event has been appraised as harmful, threatening, or challenging. Coping involves a wide range of potential strategies, skills, and abilities for effectively managing stressful events. In the example of missing an exam, if you learn that a makeup will be given two days later, you may not experience much stress since you already have studied for the exam and have several additional days to study for it. But if the instructor says that you have to write a lengthy paper for missing the test, you may cognitively appraise your situation and determine that this additional requirement places considerable demands on your time and wonder whether you will be able to meet the requirement. In this case, your secondary appraisal indicates a more stressful situation than simply having to take a makeup test several days later (Sears, Paplau, & Taylor, 1997).

Lazarus believes an individual's experience of stress is a balance of primary and secondary appraisal. When harm and threat are high, and challenge and resources are low, stress is likely to be high; when harm and threat are low, and challenge and resources are high, stress is more likely to be low.

Environmental Factors in Stress

Many circumstances, large and small, can produce stress in our lives. In some instances, cataclysmic events such as war, an automobile accident, a fire, or the death of a loved one produce stress. In others, the everyday pounding of being overloaded with work, of being frustrated in an unhappy relationship, or of living in poverty produce stress. What makes some situations stressful and others less so?

Overload, Conflict, and Frustration

Sometimes stimuli become so intense that we can no longer cope with them. For example, persistent high levels of noise overload our adaptability. Overland can occur with work as well. How often have you said to yourself, "There are not enough hours in the day to do all I have to do." In today's computer age, we are especially faced with information overload. It is easy to develop the stressful feeling that we don't know as much about a topic as we should, even if we are a so-called "expert."

Today the buzzword for overload is **burnout,** *a hopeless, helpless feeling brought about by relentless work-related stress. Burnout leaves its sufferers in a state of physical and emotional exhaustion that includes chronic fatigue and low energy.* Burnout usually does not occur because of one or two traumatic events but because of a gradual accumulation of heavy, work-related stress. Burnout is most likely to occur among individuals who deal with others in highly emotional situations (such as nurses and social workers), but have only limited control over altering their clients'/patients' outcomes.

On a number of college campuses, burnout, reaching a rate of 25 percent at some schools, is the most frequent reason students leave school before earning their degrees. Dropping out of college for a semester or two used to be considered a sign of weakness. Now it is more accepted and is sometimes called "stopping out" because the student fully intends to return; counselors may actually encourage some students who feel overwhelmed with stress to take a break from college. Before recommending stopping out, though, most counselors first suggest that the student examine ways to reduce overload and possible coping strategies that would allow the student to remain in school. The simple strategy of taking a reduced or better-balanced class load sometimes works, for example. Most college counseling services have professionals who can effectively work with students to alleviate the sense of being overloaded and overwhelmed by life.

Stimuli not only overload us, but they also can be a source of conflict. Conflict occurs when we must decide between two or more incompatible stimuli. Three major types of conflict are approach/approach, avoidance/avoidance, and approach/avoidance. The **approach/approach conflict** *is a conflict in which the individual must choose between two attractive stimuli or circumstances.* Should you go out with the attractive blond or with the attractive brunette? Do you buy a Corvette or a Porsche? The approach/approach conflict is the least stressful of the three types of conflict because either choice leads to a positive result.

The **avoidance/avoidance conflict** *is a conflict in which the individual must choose between two unattractive stimuli or circumstances.* Will you go to the dentist to have a bad tooth pulled or endure the toothache? Do you go through the stress of giving an oral presentation in class or not show up and get a zero? You want to avoid both, but in each case, you must choose one. Obviously these conflicts are more stressful than having the luxury of having two enticing choices. In many instances, we delay our decision about the avoidance/avoidance conflict until the last possible moment.

The **approach/avoidance conflict** *is a conflict involving a single stimulus or circumstance that has both positive and negative characteristics.* Let's say you really like the person you are going with and are thinking about getting married. On the one hand you are attracted by the steady affection and love that marriage might bring, but on the other hand, marriage is a commitment you might not feel ready to make. You look at a menu and face a dilemma—the double chocolate delight would be sumptuous, but is it worth the extra pound of weight? Our world is full of approach/avoidance conflicts and they can be highly stressful. In these circumstances, we often vacillate before deciding (Miller, 1959).

Frustration is another circumstance that produces stress. **Frustration** *refers to any situation in which a person cannot reach a desired goal.* If we want something and cannot have it, we feel frustrated. Our world is full of frustrations that build up to make our life more stressful—not having enough money to buy the car we want, not getting promoted at work, not getting an A average, being delayed for an important appointment by traffic, and being rejected by a friend. Failures and losses are especially frustrating—not getting grades that are high enough to get into medical school or losing someone we are closely attached to through death, for example. Sometimes the frustrations we experience are major life events, as in the case of divorce and death. At other times, the accumulation of daily hassles may make us feel as though we're being nibbled to death by ducks.

Life Events and Daily Hassles

Think about your life. What events have created the most stress for you? A change in financial status, getting fired at work, a divorce, the death of someone you loved, a personal injury? And what about the everyday circumstances of your life? What hassles you the most? Not having enough time to study, arguing with your girlfriend or boyfriend, not getting enough credit for the work you do at your job?

Researchers have proposed that significant life events are a major source of stress and loosely have linked such life events with illnesses. The effects of individual life events, such as a tornado or volcanic eruption, can be evaluated, or the effects of *clusters* of events can be studied. Thomas Holmes and Richard Rahe (1967) devised a scale to measure clusters of life events and their possible impact on illness. Their widely used Social Readjustment Rating Scale includes events ranging from the death of a spouse (100 stress points) to minor violations of the law (11 stress points).

People who experience clusters of life events, such as divorce, being fired from a job, and sexual difficulties, are more likely to become ill (Maddi, 1989); however, the ability to predict illness from life events alone is modest. Total scores of life events scales such as the Social Readjustment Rating Scale are frequently ineffective at predicting future health problems. A life-events checklist tells us nothing about a person's physiological makeup, constitutional strengths and weaknesses, ability to cope with stressful circumstances, support systems, or the nature of the social relationships involved—all of which are important in understanding how stress is related to illness. A divorce, for example, might be less stressful than a marriage filled with day-to-day tension. In addition, the Holmes-Rahe scale includes positive events, such as marital reconciliation and gaining a new family member, which can also create stressors that must be faced. However, the changes that result from positive events are not as difficult to cope with as the changes that result from negative events.

Psychologists increasingly consider the nature of daily hassles and daily uplifts to gain better insight about the nature of stress (Kanner & Feldman, 1991; Pillow, Zautra, & Sandler, 1996). It might be our daily experiences, and not life's major events, that are the primary sources of stress. Enduring a boring but tense job or marriage and living in poverty do not show up on scales of major life events; yet the everyday tension involved in these living conditions adds up to a highly stressful life and in some cases psychological disorder or illness. In one study, people who experienced the most daily hassles had the most negative self-images (Tolan, Miller, & Thomas, 1988).

How about your own life? What are the biggest hassles? One study showed that the most frequent daily hassles of college students were wasting time, being lonely, and worrying about meeting high achievement standards (Kanner & others, 1981). In fact, the fear of failing in our success-oriented world often plays a role in college students' depression. College students also found that the small things in life—having fun, laughing, going to movies, getting along well with friends, and completing a task—were their main sources of feeling uplifted.

Critics of the daily hassles approach argue that some of the same problems with life events scales occur when assessing daily hassles (Dohrenwend & Shrout, 1985). For example, knowing about a person's daily hassles tell us nothing about the body's resilience to stress, coping ability or strategies, or how that person perceives stress. Further, the hassles scale has not been consistently related to objective measures of health and illness. Yet another criticism is that hassles can be conceived of as dependent measures rather than causes. People who complain about things, who report being anxious and unhappy, and who see the bad side of everything see more hassles in their daily lives. From this perspective, hassles don't predict bad moods; bad moods predict hassles. Supporters of the daily hassles concept contend that information about daily hassles can be used in concert with information about physiological reactions, coping, and how stress is perceived to provide a more complete picture of the causes and consequences of stress.

Sociocultural Factors in Stress

Sociocultural factors influence the stressors individuals are likely to encounter, whether events are perceived as stressful or not, and the expectations individuals have about how stressors should be confronted (Anderson, 1996; Chang, 1996; Liebkind, 1996). Among the sociocultural factors that influence stress are acculturation and socioeconomic status, each of which we discuss in turn.

Acculturation and Acculturative Stress

Cultural subgroups in the United States can find contacts with mainstream society stressful. **Acculturation** *refers to cultural change that results from continuous, firsthand contact between two distinctive cultural groups.* **Acculturative stress** *refers to the negative consequences of acculturation.*

Acculturation takes place over time in a series of phases (Berry & Kim, 1988). In the *precontact phase,* two cultural groups remain distinct, each with its own set of customs. The people within each culture represent a "normal" mix of people who range, by cultural definition, from mentally well-adjusted to maladjusted. In the *contact phase,* the groups meet, interact, and new stressors appear. The impetus toward contact may be the result of stressors (such as overpopulation, war, famine, and so on) in one of the cultures. In the contact phase, cultural and behavioral change begin to take place. The concept of acculturation allows for cultural exchange in both directions. In practice, the balance of flow is usually from the larger, more dominant culture to the smaller, less dominant group. As a result, more stress is placed on the smaller, more acculturating group. Common, but not inevitable, is a *conflict phase,* in which tension builds up and the smaller cultural group is pressured to change its way of life. Conflict can involve intergroup or psychological conflict. Intergroup conflict creates threats to person and property, while psychological (intrapsychic) conflict creates confusion and uncertainty. If conflict and tension do occur, a highly stressful *crisis phase* may evolve, in which the conflict comes to a head, and a resolution is required. The crisis phase is often associated with increased homicide, suicide, family abuse, and substance abuse in acculturating peoples. Finally, an *adaptation phase* may occur, in which the cultural relations are stabilized in some way. The kind of adaptation achieved has consequences for mental and physical health.

Canadian cross-cultural psychologist John Berry (1980) believes that a person facing acculturation can adapt to the pressures of change in four different ways—through assimilation, integration, separation, or marginalization. These four outcomes depend on how the individual answers two important questions: (1) Is my cultural identity of value and should I retain it? (2) Do I want to seek positive relations with the larger, dominant culture?

Assimilation *occurs when individuals relinquish their cultural identity and move into the larger society.* The nondominant group may be absorbed into an established "mainstream," or many groups may merge to form a new society (what is often called a "melting pot"). By contrast, **integration** *implies the maintenance of cultural integrity as well as the movement to become an integral part of the larger culture.* In this circumstance, a number of ethnic groups all cooperate within a large social system ("a mosaic"). **Separation** *refers to self-imposed withdrawal from the larger culture.* If imposed by the larger society, however, separation becomes *segregation.* People may maintain their traditional way of life because they desire an independent existence (as in the case of "separatist" movements) or the dominant culture may exercise its power to exclude the other culture (as in the circumstance of slavery and apartheid).

Finally, there also is an option that involves a considerable amount of confusion and anxiety because the essential features of one's culture are lost but do not become replaced by those of the larger society. **Marginalization** *refers to the process in which groups are put out of cultural and psychological contact with both their traditional society and the larger, dominant society.* Marginalization often involves feelings of alienation and a loss of identity. Marginilization does not mean that a group has no culture but indicates that this culture may be disorganized and unsupportive of the acculturating individual.

As you can see, separation and marginalization, especially, are the least adaptive responses to acculturation. While separation can have benefits under certain circumstances, it may be especially stressful for individuals who seek separation while most members of their group seek assimilation. Integration and assimilation are healthier adaptations to acculturative pressures. But assimilation means some cultural loss, so it may be more stressful than integration, where selective involvement in the two cultural systems may provide the supportive base for effective coping. More about the acculturative stress of ethnic minority individuals appears in Explorations in Psychology 2.

Socioeconomic Status

Poverty can cause considerable stress for individuals and families (Hoff-Ginsburg & Tardif, 1995; Huston, 1995). Chronic conditions such as inadequate housing, dangerous neighborhoods, burdensome responsibilities, and economic uncertainties are potent stressors in the lives of the poor (Chase-Lansdale & Brooks-Gunn, 1996). Ethnic minority families are disproportionately among the poor (Phillips, 1996). For example, Puerto Rican families headed by women are fifteen times more likely to live in poverty than are families headed by White men. Similarly, families headed by African American women are ten times more likely to live in poverty than are families headed by White men (National Advisory Council on Economic Opportunity, 1980). Many people who become poor during their lives remain so for only 1 or 2 years. However, African Americans and female heads of household are especially at risk for persistent poverty. The average poor African American child experiences poverty that will last almost 20 years (Wilson & Neckerman, 1986).

Poverty is also related to threatening and uncontrollable life events (Russo, 1990). For example, poor women are more likely to experience crime and violence than middle-class women are. And poverty undermines sources of social support that play a role in buffering the effects of stress. Poverty is related to marital unhappiness and with having spouses who are unlikely to serve as confidants (Brown, Bhrolchain, & Harris, 1975). Further, poverty means having to depend on many overburdened and unresponsive bureaucratic systems for financial, housing, and health assistance that may contribute to a poor person's perception of powerlessness.

At this point we have discussed many ideas about the nature of health psychology and stress. A summary of those ideas is presented in concept table 1. Next we turn our attention to an extremely important aspect of stress—how to cope with it more effectively.

Coping

What is the nature of coping? What roles do self-efficacy, positive thinking, and optimistic thinking play in coping? What is stress management and how can it help individuals cope more effectively?

The Nature of Coping

To explore the nature of coping we will examine what coping is; the importance of cognitive appraisal and problem-focused strategies in coping; the role of active-cognitive, active-behavioral, and avoidance strategies in coping; a number of other ways to effectively cope; and the importance of using multiple coping strategies.

Explorations in Psychology 2

The Acculturative Stress of Ethnic Minority Group Individuals

As upwardly mobile ethnic minority families have attempted to penetrate historically all-White neighborhoods, interracial tensions often mount (Huang & Gibbs, 1989). Although many Americans think of racial tensions and prejudice largely as Black/White issues, this no longer is the case. Racial tensions and hostility often emerge among the various ethnic minorities as each struggles for housing and employment opportunities, seeking a fair share of these limited markets. Clashes become inevitable as Latino family markets spring up in African American urban neighborhoods; as Vietnamese extended families displace Puerto Rican apartment dwellers; as the increasing enrollment of Asian students on college campuses is perceived as a threat to affirmative action policies by other ethnic minority students.

Although the dominant White society has on many occasions tried to enslave or dispossess entire populations, these ethnic minority groups have survived and flourished. In the face of severe stress and oppression, these groups have shown remarkable resilience and adaptation by developing their own communities and social structures—such as African American churches, Vietnamese American mutual assistance associations, Chinese American family associations, Japanese-language schools, American Indian "bands" and tribal associations, and Mexican American kin systems. In addition, they have learned to negotiate with the dominant White culture. They essentially have mastered two cultures and have developed impressive strategies for adapting to life in America. The resilience and adaptation of ethnic minority groups can teach us much about coping and survival in the face of overwhelming adversity.

To help buffer the stress in their lives, many ethnic minority groups have developed their own social structures, which include Mexican American kin systems, African American churches, Chinese American family associations, and Native American tribal associations. Shown above are members of a Chinese American family association.

What Is Coping?

Not everyone responds the same way to stress. Some individuals throw in the towel and give up even when the slightest thing goes wrong in their life. Others are motivated to work hard to seek solutions to personal problems and successfully adjust to even extremely taxing circumstances. Coping is an extremely important part of adjustment. Just what do we mean by coping? **Coping** *is the process of managing taxing circumstances, expending effort to solve personal and interpersonal problems, and seeking to master, minimize, reduce, or tolerate stress and conflict.* A stressful event can be rendered considerably less stressful when a person successfully copes with it.

Cognitive Appraisal, Problem-Focused Coping, and Emotion-Focused Coping

In our discussion of stress earlier in this chapter, we described Richard Lazarus' (1993) view that cognitive appraisal—interpreting events as harmful, threatening, or challenging, and determining whether one has the resources to effectively cope with the event—is critical to coping. Remember that Lazarus believes that events are appraised in two stages—primary appraisal (when individuals interpret whether an event involves harm or loss that has already occurred, a threat of some future danger, or a challenge to be overcome) and secondary appraisal (evaluation of one's resources and determining how effectively they can be used to cope with the stressful event).

Lazarus also believes that two general types of coping efforts can be distinguished. **Problem-focused coping** *is Lazarus' term for the cognitive strategy of squarely facing one's troubles and trying to solve them.* For example, if you are having trouble with a class, you might go to the study skills center at your college or university and enter a training program to learn how to study more effectively. You have faced your problem and attempted to do something about it. **Emotion-focused coping** *is Lazarus' term for responding to stress in an emotional manner, especially using defensive appraisal.* Emotion-focused coping involves using defense mechanisms. In emotion-focused coping, we might avoid something, rationalize what has happened to us, deny it is occurring, laugh it off, or call on our religious faith for support. If you use emotion-focused coping, you might avoid going to the class. You might say the class doesn't matter, deny that you are having a problem, laugh and joke about it with your friends, or pray that you will do better. In one study, depressed individuals used coping strategies to avoid facing their problems more than individuals who were not depressed (Ebata & Moos, 1989).

But there are times when emotion-focused coping is adaptive. For example, denial is one of the main protective psychological mechanisms that enables people to cope with the flood of feelings that occur when the reality of death or dying becomes too great. In other circumstances, emotion-focused coping is maladaptive. Denying that the person you were dating doesn't love you any more when that person has actually become engaged to someone else is not adaptive. Denial can be used to avoid the destructive impact of shock, however, by postponing the time when you have to deal with stress. Over the long term, though, we usually want to use problem-focused more than emotion-focused coping.

Many individuals use both problem-focused and emotion-focused coping when adjusting to a stressful circumstance. For example, in one study, individuals said they used both problem-focused and emotion-focused coping strategies in 98 percent of the stressful encounters they face (Folkman & Lazarus, 1980). But aren't there other ways to cope than just using a combination of problem-focused and emotion-focused strategies?

Active-Cognitive, Active-Behavioral, and Avoidance Coping Strategies

Coping strategies can also be categorized as active-cognitive, active-behavioral, and avoidance (Billings & Moos, 1981). **Active-cognitive strategies** *are coping responses in which individuals actively think about a situation in an effort to adjust more effectively.* For example, if you have had a problem that involved breaking up with a girlfriend or a boyfriend, you may have coped by logically reasoning through why you are better off in the long run without her or him. Or you might analyze why the relationship did not work and use this information to help you develop better dating experiences in the future.

Active-behavioral strategies *are coping responses in which individuals take some type of action to improve their problem situation.* For example, if we again consider the situation of having problems in dating, individuals may take the action of going to their college or university's counseling center where they might be "coached" to improve their dating skills.

Stress is so abundant in our society that many of us are confronted with more than one stressor at the same time. An extremely valuable active-behavioral strategy for coping with stress is to try to remove at least one of the stressors from our life. For example, a college student might be taking an extra course load, not have enough money to eat regularly, and have problems in a close relationship. Researchers have found that when several stressors are simultaneously experienced, the effects may be compounded (Rutter & Garmezy, 1983). For example, one study found that people who felt besieged by two chronic life stressors were four times more likely to eventually need psychological services than those who had to cope with only one chronic stressor (Rutter, 1979). The student facing the triple whammy of school, financial, and relationship difficulties probably would benefit from removing one of the stressors, such as dropping one class and taking a normal course load.

Concept Table 1

Health Psychology and Stress

Concept	Processes/Related Ideas	Characteristics/Description
Health Psychology	Its nature	Health psychology is a multidimensional approach to health that emphasizes psychological factors, lifestyle, and the nature of the health care delivery system. Closely aligned with health psychology is behavioral medicine, which combines medical and behavioral knowledge to create ways to reduce illness and promote health.
Defining Stress	Its nature	Stress is the way we respond to circumstances that threaten us and tax our coping abilities.
Physical and Biological Factors	The nervous system	Many scientists now believe there are two pathways through the nervous system that connect the brain and the endocrine system in response to stress—one route through the autonomic nervous system, the other through the hypothalamus and the pituitary.
	Selye's general adaptation syndrome	This refers to the common effects of stress on the body. Stress is the wear and tear on the body due to the demands placed on it. This involves three stages—alarm, resistance, and exhaustion. Not all stress is bad—Selye calls good stress "eustress." Critics argue that humans do not always respond as uniformly as Selye envisioned and that we also need to know about such factors as an individual's coping strategies.
	Illness and the immune system	Psychoneuroimmunology explores the connections among psychological factors, the nervous system, and the immune system. Biological pathways that connect stress and illness include stress-mediated immune responses and stress-mediated health effects. Behavioral pathways that link stress and illness include health behaviors and compliance. A number of interventions have been successful in improving the quality of life of individuals with illnesses, including cancer patients and individuals infected with AIDS.
Personality Factors	Type A behavior pattern	This involves a cluster of characteristics—being excessively competitive, hard-driven, impatient, and hostile—related to heart disease. The Type A pattern is controversial, with some researchers arguing that only specific components of the cluster, such as hostility, are associated with heart disease.
	Type C behavior	This refers to the cancer-prone personality, which consists of being inhibited, uptight, inexpressive, and otherwise constrained. This type of individual is more likely to develop cancer than more expressive people.

Avoidance strategies *are responses that individuals use to keep stressful circumstances out of awareness so they do not have to deal with them.* Everything we know about coping suggests that avoidance strategies are extremely harmful to individuals' adjustment. In the example of having problems in dating, an avoidance strategy is to simply do nothing about it, with the result of never thinking about better ways to cope with dating problems and never taking any actions either. Examples of active-cognitive, active-behavioral, and avoidance strategies are shown in figure 3.

So far we have described two ways to classify coping responses: (1) problem-focused and emotion-focused, and (2) active-cognitive, active-behavioral, and avoidance. In general, of these different ways to cope, problem-focused coping, active-cognitive coping, and active-behavioral coping are the best strategies.

More Ways to Cope

Aren't there even more varied ways to cope and adjust than we have discussed so far? In one study with married couples, there were (Folkman & others, 1986). The

Concept	Processes/Related Ideas	Characteristics/Description
Personality Factors (continued)	Hardiness	This is a personality style characterized by a sense of commitment, control, and a perception of problems as challenges rather than threats. Hardiness is a stress buffer and is related to reduced illness.
Cognitive Factors	Their nature	Lazarus believes that stress depends on how people cognitively appraise and interpret events. Cognitive appraisal is Lazarus' term that describes individuals' interpretations of events in their lives as harmful, threatening, or challenging (primary appraisal), and their determination of whether they have the resources to cope effectively with the event (secondary segregation, and marginalization. The resilience and adaptation of ethnic minority groups can teach us much about coping and survival in the face of overwhelming adversity appraisal).
Environmental Factors	Overload, conflict, and frustration	Stress is produced because stimuli become so intense and prolonged we cannot cope. Three types of conflict are approach/approach, avoidance/avoidance, and approach/avoidance. Frustration occurs when we cannot reach a goal.
	Life events and daily hassles	Stress may be produced by major life events or daily hassles. Life-events lists tell us nothing about how individuals cope with stress, their body strengths and weaknesses, and other important dimensions of stress. Daily hassles provide a more focused look, but their evaluation should include information about coping and body characteristics.
Sociocultural Factors	Acculturation and acculturative stress	Acculturation refers to cultural change that results from continuous, firsthand contact between two distinct cultural groups. Acculturative stress refers to the negative consequences of acculturation. Acculturation takes place over time in a series of phases: precontact, contact, conflict, crisis, and adaptation. Berry argues that a person can acculturate in four ways: assimilation, integration, segregation, or marginalization. The resilience and adaptation of ethnic minority groups can teach us much about coping and survival in the face of overwhelming adversity.
	Socioeconomic status	Poverty imposes considerable stress on individuals. Chronic conditions such as inadequate housing, dangerous neighborhoods, burdensome responsibilities, and economic uncertainties are potent stressors in the lives of the poor. The incidence of poverty is especially high in ethnic minority families.

couples were interviewed once a month for 6 months about the most stressful event that they had experienced in the previous week, and they were asked how they coped with the stressful event. Overall, the couples reported using eight different coping strategies in adjusting to the stressful event: confrontative coping, seeking social support, planful problem-solving, self-control, distancing, positive reappraisal, accepting responsibility, and escape/avoidance (see figure 4).

And there are even more ways to cope and effectively adjust to challenging and taxing circumstances. Experts on adjustment increasingly conclude that self-efficacy—the belief that one can master a situation and produce positive outcomes—is a powerful coping strategy. We will have more to say about self-efficacy's role in adjustment later in this chapter. Closely related to self-efficacy is the wise coping strategy of thinking positively and adopting an optimistic outlook, which we also will discuss later in this chapter.

Another very helpful coping strategy is to seek social support. Develop the orientation that you don't always have to solve each of your problems by yourself. In many instances, the emotional comfort that others can provide you in times of stress and difficult circumstances can benefit you enormously. You might seek emotional comforting through a spouse or partner, a friend, or possibly a mental health professional.

Developing stress management techniques—such as starting a relaxation program, developing a regular exercise routine, and adopting a better nutritional regimen—or participating in a stress management workshop or program benefit individuals in their effort to cope. We will study stress management techniques later in this chapter.

Multiple Coping Strategies

Yet another important idea to keep in mind when coping with stress is that multiple coping strategies are often better than a single strategy alone. As we have already seen, individuals who face stressful circumstances have many different strategies from which to choose, and often a good strategy is to choose more than one of them. For example, people who have experienced a stressful life event or a cluster of life events (such as the death of a parent, a divorce, and a significant reduction in income) might adopt the following plan of multiple coping strategies:

- Engage in problem-focused coping
- Engage in active-cognitive strategies
- Engage in active-behavioral strategies
- Use self-control
- Seek social support
- Exercise regularly
- Reduce drinking
- Practice relaxation

Active-cognitive strategies
Prepared for the worst
Tried to see the positive side of the situation
Considered several alternatives for handling the problem
Drew on my past experiences
Took things one day at a time
Tried to step back from the situation and be more objective
Went over the situation in my mind to try to understand it
Told myself things that helped me feel better
Made a promise to myself that things would be different next time
Accepted it; nothing could be done
Active-behavioral strategies
Tried to find out more about the situation
Talked with spouse or other relative about the problem
Talked with friend about the problem
Talked with professional person (e.g., doctor, lawyer, clergy)
Got busy with other things to keep my mind off the problem
Made a plan of action and followed it
Tried not to act too hastily or follow my first hunch
Got away from things for a while
Knew what had to be done and tried harder to make things work
Let my feelings out somehow
Sought help from persons or groups with similar experiences
Bargained or compromised to get something positive from the situation
Tried to reduce tension by exercising more
Avoidance strategies
Took it out on other people when I felt angry or depressed
Kept my feelings to myself
Avoided being with people in general
Refused to believe that it happened
Tried to reduce tension by drinking more
Tried to reduce tension by eating more
Tried to reduce tension by smoking more
Tried to reduce tension by taking more tranquilizing drugs

FIGURE 3

Active-Cognitive, Active-Behavioral, and Avoidance Coping Strategies

A summary of the coping strategies that frequently have positive outcomes in reducing stress and adjusting more effectively is presented in figure 5.

Developing Self-Efficacy

Self-efficacy—*the belief that one can master a situation and produce positive outcomes—can be an effective strategy in coping with stress and challenging circumstances.* Albert Bandura (1986, 1995) and others have shown that people's self-efficacy affects their behavior in a variety of circumstances, ranging from solving personal problems to going on diets. Self-efficacy influences whether people even try to develop healthy habits, how much effort they expend in coping with stress, how long they persist in the face of obstacles, and how much stress they experience.

Let's look at several examples of how self-efficacy might work in coping. Overweight individuals will likely have more success with their diets if they believe they have the self-control to restrict their eating. Smokers who believe they will not be able to break their habit probably won't try to quit smoking, even though they know that smoking is likely to cause poor health and shorten their life.

How can you increase your self-efficacy beliefs? The following steps can help (Watson & Tharp, 1989). First, select something you expect to be able to do, not something you expect to fail at accomplishing. As you

Way of coping	Definition	Example
Confrontative coping	Aggressive efforts to alter the situation	"I stood my ground and fought for what I wanted."
Distancing	Efforts to become detached	"I didn't let the problem get to me. I refused to think about it."
Self-control	Efforts to regulate one's own feelings and actions	"I kept others from knowing how bad things were. I tried not to act too hastily."
Seeking social support	Efforts to seek feedback and emotional support	"I talked with someone to find out more about the situation. I accepted sympathy and understanding from someone."
Accepting responsibility	Acknowledging one's own role in the problem	"I criticized or lectured myself. I realized I brought the problem on myself."
Escape/Avoidance	Describes wishful thinking and attempting to escape or avoid the problem	"I wished the situation would go away or somehow be over. I tried to make myself feel better by eating, drinking, or taking drugs."
Planful problem-solving	Describes deliberate problem-focused efforts to alter the situation coupled with an analytic approach to solving the problem	"I knew what had to be done, so doubled my efforts to make things work. I made a plan of action and followed it."
Positive reappraisal	Describes efforts to create positive meaning by focusing on personal growth	"I changed or grew as a person in a positive way."

FIGURE 4

Eight Strategies Married Couples Used to Cope with a Stressful Event

develop a stronger sense of self-efficacy, then you can tackle projects that you previously might not have thought possible. Second, distinguish between your past performance and your present project. You might have learned from past failures that you cannot do certain things. However, remind yourself that past failures are just that, in the past, and that you now have a new sense of confidence and accomplishment. Third, keep good records so you can be concretely aware of your successes. A person who sticks to a study schedule for four days and then fails to adhere to the schedule on the fifth day should not think, "I'm a failure. I can't do it." This statement ignores the student's 80 percent success rate of keeping to schedule on four of five days. Fourth, pay close attention to your successes. Some individuals have a tendency to remember their failures but not their successes. Fifth, make a list of the specific kinds of situations in which you expect to have the most difficulty and the least difficulty. Then, begin with the easier tasks and cope with the harder ones after you have experienced success and improved your coping skills.

In sum, the belief that you can cope does not by itself eliminate all problems you might face. But the self-confidence that self-efficacy brings to challenging situations goes a long way toward overcoming difficult problems and allows you to cope with stress less emotionally.

Thinking Positively and Optimistically

Thinking positively and avoiding negative thoughts is generally a good coping strategy when trying to handle stress more effectively. A positive mood improves our ability to process information more efficiently, makes us more altruistic, and gives us higher self-esteem. In most cases, an optimistic attitude is superior to a pessimistic one. It gives us a sense that we are controlling our environment, much like what Bandura talks about when he describes the importance of self-efficacy in coping. For example, sports psychologist Jim Loehr (1989) pieced together videotaped segments of 17-year-old Michael Chang's most outstanding tennis points in the past year. Chang periodically watched the videotape—he always saw himself winning, he never saw himself make mistakes, and he always saw himself in a positive mood. Several months later Chang became the youngest male to win the French Open tennis championship.

Cognitive Restructuring and Positive Self-Talk

Many cognitive therapists believe the process of **cognitive restructuring**—*modifying the thoughts, ideas, and beliefs that maintain an individual's problems*—can be used to get people to think more positively and optimistically. **Self-talk** (also called **self-statements**)—*the soundless, mental speech we use when we think about something, plan, or solve problems—is often very helpful in cognitive restructuring.* Positive self-talk can do a lot to give you the confidence that frees you to use your talents to the fullest. Since self-talk has a way of becoming a self-fulfilling prophecy, uncountered negative thinking can spell trouble. That's why it's so important to monitor your self-talk.

Several strategies can help you to monitor your self-talk. First, at random times during the day, ask yourself, "What am I saying to myself right now?" Then, if you can,

Strategy	Elaboration
Engage in cognitive appraisal — challenges	Work on interpreting events as challenges to overcome rather than as highly stressful forces that immobilize and emotionally blunt you.
Use cognitive appraisal—coping resources	Evaluate your resources and determine how effectively they can be used to cope with the stressful event.
Engage in problem-focused coping	Use the cognitive strategy of squarely facing your troubles and try to solve your personal and interpersonal problems.
Use emotion-focused coping	Use this strategy sparingly, although such emotion-focused strategies as calling on one's religious faith can be helpful.
Engage in active-cognitive strategies	Develop cognitive actions to cope with stress and adjust more effectively. Use such techniques as trying to see the positive side of situations, drawing on your past experiences, trying to step back from the situation to be more objective, and going over the situation in your mind and trying to understand it.
Engage in active behavioral strategies	Try to take some behavioral action to solve the problem and reduce stress. Use such strategies as: find out more about the situation, enact a plan, and seek professional help.
Reduce or eliminate avoidance strategies	Deal with stressful circumstances; don't avoid them. Don't keep your feelings to yourself, don't refuse to believe what happened, and don't try to reduce stress by drinking more, eating more, smoking more, or taking more drugs.
Develop self-efficacy	Develop a sense that your actions will produce favorable outcomes and expect to be able to master situations.
Engage in positive thinking and develop an optimistic outlook	Eliminate self-defeating, pessimistic thinking; develop a positive outlook that your world is going to be better and then make it better.
Engage in self-control	Work on controlling your negative emotions, such as anger and jealousy. Make an effort to keep yourself from getting into a frenzied state in which you can't think clearly about positive ways to cope. Develop patience and don't act too impulsively.
Seek social support	Obtain emotional comfort from others — either friends, your spouse or partner, or a mental health professional.
Follow a disinhibition strategy, engage in some enjoyable activities, and use humor	Open up and talk about your stressful experiences. Engage in at least some activities you enjoy doing instead of being immobilized and feeling sorry for yourself. Sometimes humor can help.
Use stress-management techniques or become involved in a stress management program	Develop a relaxation program, follow a better nutrition regimen, and engage in a more healthy lifestyle, or enroll in a workshop or program that teaches stress management.
Adopt multiple coping strategies	Use more than one coping strategy by examining all of the different coping strategies and analyzing which combination would likely serve you best.

FIGURE 5

A Summary of Positive Ways to Cope with Stress and Adjust More Effectively

write down your thoughts along with a few notes about the situation you are in and how you're feeling. Your goal is to fine-tune your self-talk to make it as accurate as possible. Before you begin, it is important to record your self-talk without any censorship.

You can also use uncomfortable emotions or moods—such as stress, depression, and anxiety—as cues for listening to your self-talk. When this happens, identify the feeling as accurately as possible. Then ask yourself, "What was I saying to myself right before I started feeling this way?" or "What have I been saying to myself since I've been feeling this way?"

Situations that you anticipate might be difficult for you also are excellent times to access your self-talk. Write down a description of the coming event. Then ask yourself, "What am I saying to myself about this event?" If your thoughts are negative, think how you can use your strengths to turn these disruptive feelings into more positive ones and help turn a potentially difficult experience into a success.

It is also useful to compare your self-talk predictions (what you thought would or should happen in a given situation) with what actually took place. If the reality conflicts with your predictions—as it often does when your self-talk is in error—pinpoint where your self-talk needs adjustment to fit reality.

You are likely to have a subjective view of your own thoughts. So it is helpful to enlist the assistance of a sympathetic but objective friend, partner, or therapist who is willing to listen, discuss your self-assessment with you, and help you to identify ways your self-talk is distorted and might be improved. And examples of how positive self-statements can be used to replace negative self-statements in coping with various stressful situations is presented in figure 6.

Positive Self-Illusion

For a number of years, mental health professionals believed that seeing reality as accurately as possible was the best path to health. Recently though, researchers have found increasing evidence that maintaining some positive illusions about oneself and the world is healthy. Happy people often have falsely high opinions of themselves, give self-serving explanations for events, and have exaggerated beliefs about their ability to control the world around them (Taylor & others, 1988; Taylor & Brown, 1994).

Situation	Negative self-statement	Positive self-statement
Having a long, difficult assignment due the next day	"I'll never get this work done by tomorrow."	"If I work real hard I may be able to get it all done for tomorrow." "This is going to be tough but it is still possible to do it." "Finishing this assignment for tomorrow will be a real challenge." "If I don't get it finished, I'll just have to ask the teacher for an extension."
Losing one's job	"I'll never get another job."	"I'll just have to look harder for another job." "There will be rough times ahead, but I've dealt with rough times before." "Hey, maybe my next job will be a better deal altogether." "There are agencies that can probably help me get some kind of job."
Moving away from friends and family	"My whole life is left behind."	"I'll miss everyone, but it doesn't mean we can't stay in touch." "Just think of all the new people I'm going to meet." "I guess it will be kind of exciting moving to a new home." "Now I'll have two places to call home."
Breaking up with a person you love	"I have nothing to live for. He/she was all I had."	"I really thought our relationship would work, but it's not the end of the world." "Maybe we can try again in the future." "I'll just have to try to keep myself busy and not let it bother me." "If I met him (her), there is no reason why I won't meet someone else someday."
Not getting into graduate school	"I guess I'm really dumb. I don't know what I'll do."	"I'll just have to reapply next year." "There are things I can do with my life other than going to grad school." "I guess a lot of good students get turned down. It's just so unbelievably competitive." "Perhaps there are a few other programs that I could apply to."
Having to participate in a class discussion	"Everyone else knows more than I do, so what's the use of saying anything."	"I have as much to say as anyone else in the class." "My ideas may be different, but they're still valid." "It's OK to be a bit nervous; I'll relax as I start talking." "I might as well say something; how bad could it sound?"

FIGURE 6

Examples of How Positive Self-Statements Can Be Used to Replace Negative Self-Statements in Coping with Stressful Situations

Illusions, whether positive or negative, are related to one's sense of self-esteem. Having too grandiose an idea of yourself or thinking too negatively about yourself both have negative consequences. Rather, the ideal overall orientation may be an optimal margin of illusion in which individuals see themselves as slightly above average (see figure 7).

A negative outlook can increase our chances of getting angry, feeling guilty, and magnifying our mistakes. And for some people, seeing things too accurately can lead to depression. Seeing one's suffering as meaningless and random does not help a person cope and move forward, even if the suffering *is* random and meaningless. An absence of illusions may also thwart individuals from undertaking the risky and ambitious projects that may yield the greatest rewards (Baumeister, 1993).

In some cases, though, a strategy of defensive pessimism may actually work best in handling stress. By imagining negative outcomes, people can prepare for stressful circumstances (Norem & Cantor, 1986). Think about the honors student who is worried that she will flunk the next test, or the nervous host who is afraid his lavish dinner party will fall apart. For these two people, thoughts of failure may not be paralyzing but instead may motivate them to do everything necessary to ensure that things go smoothly. By imagining potential problems, they may develop relevant strategies for dealing with or preventing negative outcomes. One study found that negative thinking spurred constructive thinking and feelings such as evaluating negative possibilities, wondering what the future held, psyching up for future experiences so they would be positive, feeling good about being prepared to cope with the worst, and forming positive expectations (Showers, 1986).

Developing an Optimistic Outlook

Although some individuals at times use a strategy of defensive pessimism to improve their ability to cope with stress, overall a positive feeling of optimism is the best strategy. Indeed, a number of books have recently promoted the power of optimism in effective coping. *Learned Optimism*

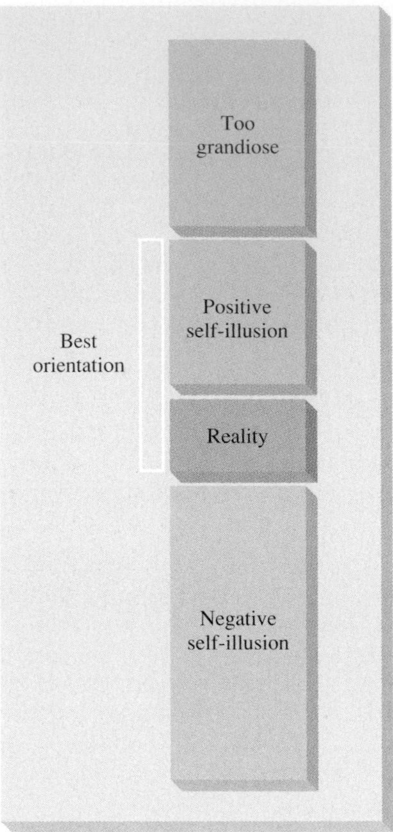

FIGURE 7

Reality and Self-Illusion
In Baumeister's model of self-illusion, the most healthy individuals often have self-illusions that are slightly above average. Having too grandiose an opinion of yourself or thinking negatively about yourself can have negative consequences. For some individuals, seeing things too accurately can be depressing. Overall, in most contexts, a reality orientation or a slightly above average self-illusion may be most effective.

by Martin Seligman (1991) and *Positive Illusions: Creative Self-Deception and the Healthy Mind* by Shelley Taylor (1989) both provide excellent recommendations for ways to develop a more optimistic outlook on life that will help you cope more effectively.

How can you develop a more optimistic outlook? Seligman (1991) believes that the best tools for overcoming chronic pessimism lie in cognitive therapy, an approach that emphasizes more positive thinking by challenging self-defeating attitudes. Some cognitive therapists believe that optimistic coping skills can be assembled in six to twelve sessions, although Seligman believes that some individuals can master the techniques on their own. One of cognitive therapy's recommendations is to not ruminate and wallow in self-pity when a bad event occurs. The tendency to repeatedly think and worry about negative circumstances and failures often prevents the development of positive coping strategies. Another recommendation of cognitive therapists is to dispute negative thoughts. Pessimists tend to use absolute, all-encompassing terms to describe defeats. They apply damaging labels to their behavior and pepper their langauge with words like *never* and *always*. Cognitive therapists advocate talking back to these negative thoughts in an optimistic style that limits self-blame and negative generalizations. According to Peterson, cognitive therapists are not telling people to be out of touch with reality, but rather to wear rose-colored glasses.

An optimistic outlook also may help individuals resist disease, as evidenced in a series of studies conducted by Christopher Peterson and his colleagues (Peterson & Seligman, 1984; Peterson, Seligman, & Vaillant, 1986; Peterson & Stunkard, 1986). For example, college students were given the Attributional Style Questionnaire that evaluates an individual's optimistic and pessimistic tendencies. Then, their health was monitored over the next year. The pessimists had twice as many infections and doctors' visits as the optimists.

Seeking Social Support

Our crowded, polluted, noisy, and achievement-oriented world can make us feel overwhelmed and isolated. Now more than ever, we may need support systems such as family members, friends, and co-workers to buffer stress. **Social support** *is information and feedback from others that one is loved and cared for, esteemed and valued, and included in a network of communication and mutual obligation.*

The benefits of social support can be grouped into three categories: tangible assistance, information, and emotional support (Taylor, 1995). Family and friends can provide *tangible assistance* by giving individuals actual goods and services in stressful circumstances. For example, gifts of food are often given after a death in the family occurs, meaning that bereaved family members won't have to cook for themselves and for visiting relatives in a time when their energy and motivation is low. Individuals who provide support can also give *information* by recommending specific actions and plans to help the person under stress cope more effectively. Friends may notice that a co-worker is overloaded with work and suggest ways for him or her to manage time more efficiently or delegate tasks more effectively. In stressful situations, individuals often suffer emotionally and may develop depression, anxiety, and loss of self-esteem. Friends and family can provide *emotional support* by reassuring the person under stress that he or she is a valuable individual who is loved by others. Knowing that others care allows a person to approach stress and cope with stress with greater assurance.

Researchers consistently have found that social support helps individuals cope with stress (Hobfoll, 1996). For example, in one study depressed persons had fewer and less supportive relationships with family members, friends, and co-workers than people who were not depressed (Billings, Cronkite, & Moos, 1983). In another study, the prognosticators of cancer, mental illness, and suicide included a lack of closeness to one's parents and a negative attitude toward one's family (Thomas, 1983). Widows die at a rate that is three to thirteen times higher than married women for every known cause of death. Close, positive attachments to others, both family and friends, consistently show up as important buffers of stress.

Consider Robert, who had been laid off by an automobile manufacturer when it was about to fold, then a decade later by a truck manufacturer, and more recently by yet another automobile manufacturer. By all accounts you would expect Robert to be down in the dumps or possibly feel that life had given him a bum deal. Yet he is one of the most well-adjusted individuals in the community. When asked his secret in the face of adversity and stress, he attributes his ability to cope to a wonderful family and some great friends. Far more important than Robert's trials and tribulations is the support he receives from others, which helps him to handle stress.

In thinking about ways to improve your coping, it is important for you to recognize the potential sources of social support in your own environment and learn how to effectively draw on these resources in times of stress (Taylor, 1995). Sometimes your coping can also be improved by joining community groups, interest groups, or informal social groups that meet regularly.

Meditation has been an important dimension of Asians' lives for centuries.

Stress Management

Because many people have difficulty in managing stress themselves, psychologists have developed a variety of stress management programs that can be taught to individuals. We will study the nature of these stress management programs and evaluate some of the techniques that are used in them, such as meditation, relaxation, and biofeedback.

Stress management programs *teach individuals how to appraise stressful events, how to develop skills for coping with stress, and how to put these skills into use in their everyday lives.* Stress management programs are often taught through workshops, which are increasingly offered in the workplace (Taylor, 1995). Aware of the high cost of lost productivity to stress-related disorders, many organizations have become increasingly motivated to help their workers identify and cope with stressful circumstances in their lives. Some stress management programs are broad in scope, teaching a variety of techniques to handle stress; others are more narrow, teaching a specific technique, such as relaxation or assertiveness training (Handelsman & Frielander, 1995). Some stress management programs are also taught to individuals who are experiencing similar kinds of problems—such as migraine headache sufferers or individuals with chronically high blood pressure. Colleges are increasingly developing stress management programs for students. If you are finding the experience of college extremely stressful and are having difficulty coping with taxing circumstances in your life, you might want to consider enrolling in a stress management program at your college or in your community. Let's now examine some of the techniques used in stress management programs.

Meditation and Relaxation

At one time, meditation was believed to have more in common with mysticism than science. While meditation has become popular in the United States only in recent years, it has been an important part of life in Asia for centuries.

Meditation *is the practice and system of thought that incorporates exercises to attain bodily or mental control and well-being, as well as enlightenment.* The strategies of meditation vary but usually take one of two forms: either cleansing the mind to have new experiences or increasing concentration. **Transcendental meditation (TM)** *is the most popular form of meditation in the United States; it is derived from an ancient Indian technique and involves a mantra, which is a resonant sound or phrase that is repeated mentally or aloud to focus attention.* One widely used TM mantra is the phrase *Om mani padme hum.* By concentrating on this phrase, the individual replaces other thoughts with the syllables *Om mani padme hum.* In transcendental meditation the individual learns to associate a mantra with a special meaning, such as beauty, peace, or tranquility.

As a physiological state, meditation shows qualities of both sleep and wakefulness, yet it is distinct from them. It resembles the hypnagogic state, which is the transition from wakefulness to sleep, but at the very least it is prolongation of that state.

In early research on meditation's effects on the body, oxygen consumption was lowered, heart rate slowed down, blood flow increased in the arms and forehead, and EEG patterns were predominantly of the alpha variety—regular and rhythmic (Wallace & Benson, 1972). Other researchers have found support for the positive physiological changes that result from meditation and believe that meditation is superior to relaxation in reducing body arousal and anxiety (Eppley, Abrams, & Shear, 1989). Yet other researchers acknowledge meditation's positive physiological effects but believe relaxation is just as effective (Holmes, 1987). To learn how to put more relaxation into your own life, try out the following exercise.

How relaxed are you right now? Would you like to feel more tranquil and peaceful? If so, you can probably reach that feeling state by following some simple instructions. First, you need to find a quiet place to sit. Get a comfortable chair and sit quietly and upright in it. Let your chin rest comfortably on your chest, your arms in your lap. Close your eyes. Then, pay attention to your breathing. Every time you inhale and every time you exhale, notice it and pay attention to the sensations of air flowing through your body, the feeling of your lungs filling and emptying. After you have done this for several breaths, begin to repeat silently to yourself a single word every time you breathe out. The word you choose does not have to mean anything. You can make the word up, you could use the word "one," or you could try a word that is associated with the emotion you want to produce, such as "trust," "love," "patience," or "happy." Try several different words to see which one works for you. At first, you will find that thoughts intrude and you are no longer attending to your breathing. Just return to your breathing and say the word each time you exhale. After you have practiced this exercise for 10 to 15 minutes, twice a day, every day for 2 weeks, you will be ready for a shortened version. If you notice stressful thoughts or circumstances appearing, simply engage in the relaxation response on the spot for several minutes. If you are in public, you don't have to close your eyes, just fix your gaze on some nearby object, attend to your breathing and say your word silently every time you exhale.

Audiotapes that induce the relaxation response are available in most bookstores. They usually include soothing background music along with instructions for how to do the relaxation response. These audiotapes can especially help induce a more relaxed state before you go to bed at night.

Biofeedback

For many years operant conditioning was believed to be the only effective means to deal with voluntary behaviors such as aggression, shyness, and achievement. Behavior modification helped people to reduce their aggression, to be more assertive and outgoing, and to get better grades, for example. Involuntary behaviors such as blood pressure, muscle tension, and pulse rate were thought to be outside the boundaries of operant conditioning and more appropriate for classical conditioning. Beginning in the 1960s, though, psychologist Neal Miller (1969) and others began to demonstrate that people can control internal behaviors. **Biofeedback** *is the process in which individuals' muscular or visceral activities are monitored by instruments and information from the instruments is given (fed back) to the individuals so they can learn to voluntarily control their physiological activities.*

How does biofeedback work? Let's consider the problem of reducing an individual's muscle tension. The individual's muscle tension is monitored and the level of tension is fed back to him. Often the feedback is in the form of an audible tone. As muscle tension rises, the tone becomes louder; as it drops, the tone becomes softer. The reinforcement in biofeedback is the raising and lowering of the tone (or in some cases, seeing a dot move up or down on a television screen) as the individual learns to control muscle tension.

When biofeedback was developed, some overzealous individuals exaggerated its success and potential for helping people with problems such as high blood pressure and migraine headaches. But as more carefully designed investigations were conducted, the wildly enthusiastic early claims were replaced with more realistic appraisal of biofeedback's effectiveness. For example, some success in lowering blood pressure has been achieved, although it is easier to raise blood pressure than to lower it through biofeedback. Relaxation training and more general stress management programs are often just as effective in reducing blood pressure (Achmon & others, 1989).

At this point we have discussed a number of ideas about coping. A summary of these ideas is presented in concept table 2. Next, we will examine another important aspect of coping—coping with illness.

Coping with Illness

Even if we manage stress effectively and practice good health habits, we cannot always prevent illness. How do we recognize, interpret, and seek treatment for the symptoms of an illness? What is a patient's role? How good are we at complying with medical advice and treatment?

Recognizing, Interpreting, and Seeking Treatment for Symptoms

How do you know if you are sick? Each of us diagnoses how we feel and interprets the meaning of symptoms to decide whether we have a cold, the flu, a sexually transmitted disease, an ulcer, heart disease, and so on. However, many of us are not very accurate at recognizing the symptoms of an illness. For example, most people believe that they can tell when their blood pressure is elevated. The facts say otherwise. The majority of heart attack victims have never sought medical attention for cardiac problems. Many of us do not go to the doctor when the early warning signs of cancer, such as a lump or cyst, appear. Also, we are better at recognizing the symptoms of illnesses we are more familiar with, such as a cold or the flu, than illnesses we are less familiar with, such as diabetes.

Whether or not we seek treatment for symptoms depends on our perception of their severity and the

Concept Table 2

Coping

Concept	Processes/Related Ideas	Characteristics/Description
The Nature of Coping	What is coping?	There is individual variation in how people cope, but for everyone, coping is an important dimension of adjustment. Coping is the process of managing taxing circumstances, expending effort to solve personal and interpersonal problems, and seeking to master, minimize, reduce, or tolerate stress. A stressful event can be rendered considerably less stressful when a person copes with it.
	Cognitive appraisal, problem-focused coping, and emotion-focused coping; active-cognitive, active-behavioral, avoidance strategies; and other ways to cope	According to Lazarus, cognitive appraisal and problem-focused coping are important aspects of effectively coping with stress. Active-cognitive and active-behavioral strategies are preferred coping strategies; avoidance is not. Other positive ways to cope include developing self-efficacy; engaging in positive thinking and developing an optimistic outlook; seeking social support; using stress management techniques or becoming involved in a stress management program; and adopting multiple coping strategies.
Developing Self-Efficacy, Thinking Positively and Optimistically, and Seeking Social Support	Developing self-efficacy, thinking positively, and having an optimistic outlook	Self-efficacy—the belief that one can master a situation and produce positive outcomes—can be an effective strategy in coping with stress. Self-efficacy provides individuals with self-confidence, influencing whether some people ever even get started in trying to develop better health habits. Judgments about self-efficacy also influence how much effort individuals expend in coping with stress, how long they persist in the face of obstacles, and how much stress they experience. Many cognitive therapists believe that cognitive restructuring can get people to think more positively and optimistically. Self-talk (also called self-statements) is often helpful in cognitive restructuring. Since self-talk has a way of becoming a self-fulfilling prophecy, uncountered negative thinking can spell trouble. That's why it is important to monitor your self-talk and replace negative self-statements with positive ones. Positive self-illusions can improve an individual's coping, but it is important to guard against unrealistic expectations. While some people use the strategy of defensive pessimism effectively, overall a feeling of optimism is the best strategy. An optimistic outlook can help individuals resist disease.
	Seeking social support	Social support is information and feedback from others that one is loved and cared for, esteemed and valued, and included in a network of communication and mutual obligation. Three important benefits of social support are: tangible assistance, information, and emotional support. Researchers have consistently found that social support helps individuals to cope more effectively with stress.
Stress Management, Meditation, Relaxation, and Biofeedback	The nature of stress management training	Stress management programs teach individuals how to appraise stressful events, how to develop skills for coping with stress, and how to put these skills into use in their everyday lives. Stress management programs are often taught through workshops. Among the techniques that are taught in stress management workshops are meditation, relaxation, and biofeedback.
	Meditation and relaxation	Meditation is a system of thought that incorporates exercises to attain bodily or mental control and well-being, as well as enlightenment. Transcendental meditation is the most popular form of meditation in the United States. Researchers have found that meditation reduces body arousal and anxiety, but whether more so than relaxation is debated. The "relaxation response" can be especially helpful in reducing arousal and calming a person.
	Biofeedback	Biofeedback has been successful in reducing muscle tension and blood pressure.

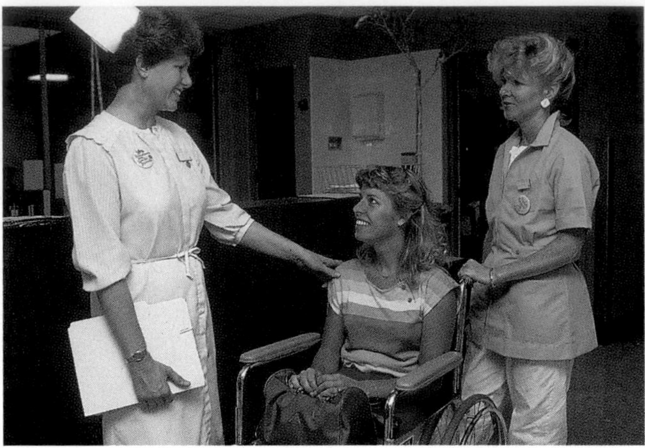

We are good at recognizing the symptoms of illnesses we are familiar with, such as a cold or the flu, but we are not very good when it comes to recognizing the symptoms of illnesses we are less familiar with, such as diabetes.

likelihood medical treatment will relieve or eliminate them. If a person's ankle is fractured so badly he cannot walk without assistance, he is more likely to seek treatment than if the fracture produces only a slight limp. Also, someone may not seek treatment for a viral infection if she perceives that no drug is available to combat it effectively. By contrast, a person is more likely to seek treatment if she believes that a fungus infection on her foot can be remedied by antibiotics.

When people direct their attention outward, they are less likely to notice symptoms than when they direct their attention inward. For example, a woman whose life is extremely busy and full of distracting activities is less likely to notice a lump on her breast than a woman who has a much less active life. People who have boring jobs, who are socially inactive, and who live alone are more likely to report symptoms than people who have interesting jobs, who have active social lives, and who live with others (Pennebaker, 1983). Perhaps people who lead more active lives have more distractions and focus their attention less on themselves than do people with quieter lives. Even for people who have active lives, situational factors influence whether they will be attentive to symptoms. In one experiment, joggers were more likely to experience fatigue and be aware of their running-related aches and pains when they ran on a boring course than on a more interesting and varied course (Pennebaker & Lightner, 1980). The boring course likely increased the joggers' tendency to turn their attention inward and, thus, recognize their fatigue and pain.

The Patient's Role

Shelley Taylor (1979) identified two general types of patient roles. According to her analysis, some hospitalized individuals take on a "good patient" role, others a "bad patient" role. In the **"good patient" role,** *a patient is passive and unquestioning and behaves "properly."* The positive consequences of this role include being well-liked by the hospital staff, who in turn respond quickly to the "good patient's" emergencies. Like many roles, however, the "good patient" is somewhat superficial, and Taylor believes that, behind the facade, the patient may feel helpless, powerless, anxious, and depressed. In the **"bad patient" role,** *a patient complains to the staff, demands attention, disobeys staff orders, and generally misbehaves.* The refusal to become helpless, and the accompanying anger, may actually have some positive consequences, because "bad patients" take an *active* role in their own health care. The negative side of "bad patient" behavior, however, may aggravate such conditions as hypertension and angina, and such behavior may stimulate staff members to ignore, overmedicate, or prematurely discharge the "bad patient."

How can the stress of hospitalization be relieved? Realistic expectations about the experience, predictable events, and social support reduce the stress of hospitalization (Spacapan, 1988). When doctors communicate clearly to their patients about the nature of the treatment procedures and what to expect when they are hospitalized, patients' confidence in the medical treatment also increases, and, as we learned in the earlier discussion of stress, the social network of individuals who deeply care about us goes a long way toward reducing stress. Visits, phone calls, cards, and flowers from family members and friends lift patients' spirits and improve their recovery from illness.

Compliance with Medical Advice and Treatment

An estimated one-third of patients fail to follow recommended treatments. Compliance depends on the disorder and the recommendation. Only about 15 percent of patients do not follow doctors' orders for tablets and ointments, but more than 90 percent of patients do not heed life-style advice, such as to stop smoking, to lose weight, or to stop drinking (DiNicola & DiMatteo, 1984).

Why do we pay money to doctors and then not follow their advice? We may not comply with a doctor's orders because we are not satisfied with the quality of the care we are receiving and because we have our own theories about our health and do not completely trust the doctor's advice. This mistrust is exacerbated when doctors use jargon and highly technical descriptions to inform patients about a treatment. Sometimes doctors do not give patients clear information or fully explain the risks of ignoring their orders. To be motivated to stop smoking, to eat more nutritionally, or to stop drinking, patients need a clear understanding of the dangers involved in noncompliance with the doctor's recommendations. Success or failure in treatment may depend on whether the doctor can convince patients that a valid, believable danger exists and offer an effective, concrete strategy for coping with the problem (Lau, 1988).

PROMOTING HEALTH

In our earlier discussion of stress, we described a number of coping strategies that individuals can adopt to deal with stress and that can also improve their health. Our nation's health profile can also be improved by reducing behaviors that impair health, such as smoking and overeating, and by engaging in healthier behaviors that include good nutrition and exercise.

Smoking

The year 1988 marked the seventy-fifth anniversary of the introduction of Camel cigarettes. Selected magazines surprised readers with elaborate pop-up advertisements for Camels. Camel's ad theme was "75 years and still smokin'." Coincidentally, 1988 was also the seventy-fifth anniversary of the American Cancer Society.

In 1989 the surgeon general and his advisory committee issued a report, *Reducing the Health Consequences of Smoking: 25 Years of Progress.* It was released 25 years after the original warnings that cigarettes are responsible for major health problems, especially lung cancer. New evidence was presented to show that smoking is even more harmful than previously thought. The report indicated that, in 1985, for example, cigarette smoking accounted for more than one-fifth of all deaths in the United States—20 percent higher than previously believed. Thirty percent of all cancer deaths are attributed to smoking, as are 21 percent of all coronary heart disease deaths and 82 percent of chronic pulmonary disease deaths.

Researchers are also increasingly finding that passive smoke (environmental smoke inhaled by nonsmokers who live or work around smokers) carries health risks (Sandler & others, 1989). Passive smoke is estimated to be the culprit in as many as 8,000 lung cancer deaths a year in the United States. Children of smokers are at special risk for respiratory and middle-ear diseases. For children under the age of 5, the risk of upper respiratory tract infection is doubled if their mothers smoke. And in one recent study, the greater the number of cigarettes the infant was passively exposed to after birth, the higher was the infant's risk of death from sudden infant death syndrome, a condition in which the infant stops breathing and suddenly dies (Klonoff-Cohen & others, 1995).

The surgeon general's report contains some good news, however. Fewer people smoke today and almost half of all living adults who ever smoked have quit. In particular, the prevalence of smoking among men fell from over 50 percent in 1965 to about 30 percent today. As a consequence, a half century's uninterrupted escalation in the rate of death due to lung cancer among males has ceased. And the incidence of lung cancer among White males has fallen. Although approximately 56 million Americans 15 to 84 years of age were smokers in 1985, the surgeon general's report estimates that 91 million would have been smoking had there been no changes in smoking and health knowledge, norms, and policy over the past quarter century.

Cigarette smoking accounted for 20 percent of all deaths in the United States in 1985.

However, the bad news is that over 50 million Americans *continue* to smoke, most having failed at attempts to quit. Why, in the face of the damaging figure that more than one-fifth of all deaths are due to smoking, do so many people still smoke?

Smoking Is Addictive and Reinforcing

Most adult smokers would like to quit, but their addiction to nicotine often turns their efforts into dismal failures. Nicotine, the active drug in cigarettes, is a stimulant that increases a smoker's energy and alertness, a pleasurable experience that is positively reinforcing (Payne & others, 1996). Nicotine also causes the release of acetylcholine and endorphin neurotransmitters, which have a calming and pain-reducing effect. However, smoking not only works as a positive reinforcer; it also works as a negative reinforcer by ending a smoker's painful craving for nicotine. A smoker gets relief from this painful aversive state simply by smoking another cigarette.

We are rational, cognitive beings. Can't we develop enough self-control to overcome these pleasurable, immediate, reinforcing circumstances by thinking about the delayed, long-term, damaging consequences of smoking? As indicated earlier, many adults have quit smoking because they recognize that it is "suicide in slow motion," but the immediate pleasurable effects of smoking are extremely difficult to overcome.

Preventing Smoking

Smoking usually begins during childhood and adolescence. Adolescent smoking reached its peak in the early 1980s when 29 percent of high school seniors smoked on a daily basis. The rate of adolescent smoking has dropped less than 2 percent since 1981 (Johnston, O'Malley, & Bachman, 1995). The smoking rate is at a level that will cut short the lives of many adolescents. Despite the growing awareness that it is important to keep children from starting to smoke in the first place, there are fewer restrictions on children's access to cigarettes today than there were in 1964, and the existing restrictions are rarely reinforced.

Traditional school health programs appear to have succeeded in educating adolescents about the long-term health consequences of smoking but have had little effect on adolescent smoking *behavior.* That is, teens who smoke know all the facts about the health risks such as lung cancer, emphysema, and "suicide in slow motion," but they go ahead and smoke just as much anyway (Miller & Slap, 1989). As a result of this gap between what teens "know" and what they "do" in regard to smoking, researchers are focusing on the factors that place teens at high risk for future smoking, especially social pressures from peers, family members, and the media. The tobacco industry preys on young people's desire to feel grown up by including "cool" people who smoke in their advertisements—successful young women smoking Virginia Slims cigarettes and rugged, handsome men smoking Marlboros, for example. The advertisements encourage adolescents to associate cigarette smoking with a successful and, ironically, athletic/active lifestyle. Legislators are trying to introduce more stringent laws to further regulate the tobacco industry.

In recent years, American health concerns have focused not only on smoking, but on eating as well. Next, we will discuss some of the eating habits that cause people problems.

Eating Disorders and Dieting

Even after a challenging workout, a tall, slender woman goes into the locker room of the fitness center, hurls her towel across the bench, looks squarely in the mirror, and says, "You fat pig. You are nothing but a fat pig." The alarm goes off and 35-year-old Robert jumps out of bed, throws on his jogging shorts, and begins his daily predawn 3-mile run. Returning to shower and dress, he too observes his body in the mirror, tugging at the flabby overhang and commenting, "Why did you eat that bowl of ice cream last night?"

We are a nation obsessed with food, spending an extraordinary amount of time thinking about, gobbling, and avoiding food. Here we will focus on the problem of our increasingly heavy population, dieting, and eating disorders.

Obesity

Understanding obesity is complex because body weight is affected by a number of factors—genetic inheritance, physiological mechanisms, cognitive factors, and environmental influences (Brownell, 1993; Friedman & Brownell, 1995).

Heredity Until recently, the genetic component in body weight had been underestimated by scientists. Some individuals do inherit a tendency to be overweight. Only 10 percent of children who do not have obese parents become obese themselves, whereas 40 percent of children who become obese have one obese parent and 70 percent of children who become obese have two obese parents. The actual extent to which this is due to genes rather than experience cannot be determined in research with humans, but research with animals documents that they can be inbred to develop a propensity for obesity (Blundell, 1984). Further, identical twins have similar weights, even when they are reared apart (Stunkard & others, 1990). Estimates of variance in body mass that can be explained by heredity range from 25 percent to 70 percent (Bouchard & others, 1990; Stunkard & others, 1990).

Set Point and BMR The amount of stored fat in your body is an important factor in your body weight **set point,** *the weight maintained when no effort is made to gain or lose weight.* Fat is stored in adipose cells. When these cells are filled, you do not get hungry. When people gain weight—because of genetic predisposition, early childhood eating patterns, or adult overeating—their number of fat cells increases, and they might not be able to get rid of them. A normal-weight individual has 30 to 40 billion fat cells. An obese individual has 80 to 120 billion fat cells. When individuals go on a diet, their fat cells may shrink, but they do not go away.

Another factor in weight is **basal metabolism rate (BMR),** *the minimal amount of energy an individual uses in a resting state.* As shown in figure 8, BMR varies with age and sex. Rates decline precipitously during adolescence and then more gradually during adulthood; they also are slightly higher for males than for females. Many individuals gradually increase their weight over a period of many years. Figure 8 suggests that to some degree the weight gain may be due to a declining basal metabolism rate. The declining BMR underscores the importance of reducing our food intake as we grow older if we want to maintain our weight.

Sociocultural Factors Balanced against the contribution of hereditary and biological factors is recognition that environmental factors are involved in weight and shape in important ways. The human gustatory system and taste preferences developed at a time when reliable sources of food were scarce. Our earliest ancestors probably developed a preference for sweets, since ripe fruit, which is a concentrated source of sugar (and thus, calories), was so accessible.

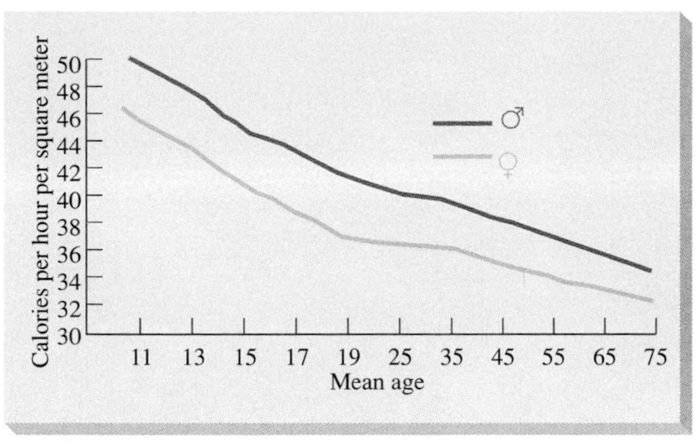

FIGURE 8

Basal Metabolic Rate in Females and Males
BMR varies with age and sex. Rates are usually higher for males and decline proportionately with age for both sexes.

Today many people still have a "sweet tooth," but unlike ancestors' ripe fruit, which contained sugar *plus* vitamins and minerals, the soft drinks and candy bars we snack on today too often fill us with just empty calories.

Strong evidence of the environment's influence is the doubling of obesity in the United States since 1900, likely due to greater availability of food (especially food high in fat content), energy-saving devices, and declining physical activity, unlikely due to heredity. Obesity is also six times more frequent among low-income women than among upper-income women, and more common among Americans than Europeans.

Obesity and Its Costs Estimates indicate that 31 percent of men and 24 percent of women in the United States are overweight, with 12 percent of both sexes severely overweight (National Academy of Sciences National Research Council, 1989). The economic costs of obesity are estimated at $39 billion per year, or more than 5 percent of all health care costs. The staggering costs stem from obesity's association with diabetes, hypertension, cardiovascular disease, and some cancers (Thompson, 1996).

Dieting

Many divergent interests are involved in the topic of dieting—the public, health professionals, policy makers, the media, and the powerful diet and food industries. On one side are societal norms that promote a very lean, aesthetic ideal, supported by an industry valued at more than $30 billion per year that provides diet books, programs, videos, foods, pills, and the like. On the other side are health professionals and a growing minority of the press and the public who, although recognizing the alarmingly high incidence of obesity, are frustrated by high relapse rates and are increasingly concerned that dieting may have negative effects on health and well-being (Brownell & Rodin, 1994).

Dieting is a pervasive concern of many individuals in the United States. Two large-scale national surveys revealed that approximately 40 percent of women and 24 percent of men are currently dieting (Horm & Anderson, 1993; Serdula & others, 1993). And in one of these surveys, 52 percent of women and 37 percent of men felt they were overweight (Horm & Anderson, 1993).

Following are some fundamental issues in the dieting debate and the current status of their empirical evaluation (Brownell & Rodin, 1994).

Does Weight Loss Reduce or Increase Health Risks? Few studies have explored the effects of weight loss on disease and death. The most common type of data comes from population studies in which some individuals lose weight and others do not and their mortality is compared. However, the subjects who lose weight are self-selected; possible mediating factors such as body fat distribution and dieting history are not considered. And subjects may be gaining or losing weight because of factors that are related to disease, such as starting and stopping smoking. The type of study required to address the connection between dieting and mortality—a longitudinal study with random assignment to weight-loss and no-weight-loss groups, with a sufficient sample size to evaluate mortality—has not been conducted and would be costly and difficult to undertake. Possibly because of such limitations, studies on weight loss and mortality are striking in the inconsistency of their results. In sum, the available data present a mixed picture of whether weight loss is related to mortality.

Do Diets Work? Some critics argue that all diets fail (Wooley & Garner, 1991). Although there are reports of poor long-term results (Wilson, 1994), some recent studies revealed that programs that combine very-low-calorie diets with intensive education and behavior modification produce good long-term results. In one such study, participants lost an average of 55 pounds and had kept off more than half of this weight 2½ years later (Nunn, Newton, & Faucher, 1992). Thus, it appears that some individuals do lose weight and maintain the loss. How often this occurs and whether some programs produce this outcome better than others are open questions (Brownell & Cohen, 1995).

Are Diets Harmful? One main concern about diets being harmful focuses on weight cycling (yo-yo dieting involving repeated cycles of dieting and weight gain) (Wadden & others, 1996). The empirical evidence does suggest a link between weight variability and chronic disease outcomes (Blair & Paffenbarger, 1993; Brownell & Rodin, in press). Another important concern about dieting is the possibility that it may lead to eating disorders. Dieting often does precede the development of eating disorders, but no causal link has been documented (Wilson, 1993). Also, overweight individuals who diet and maintain their weight

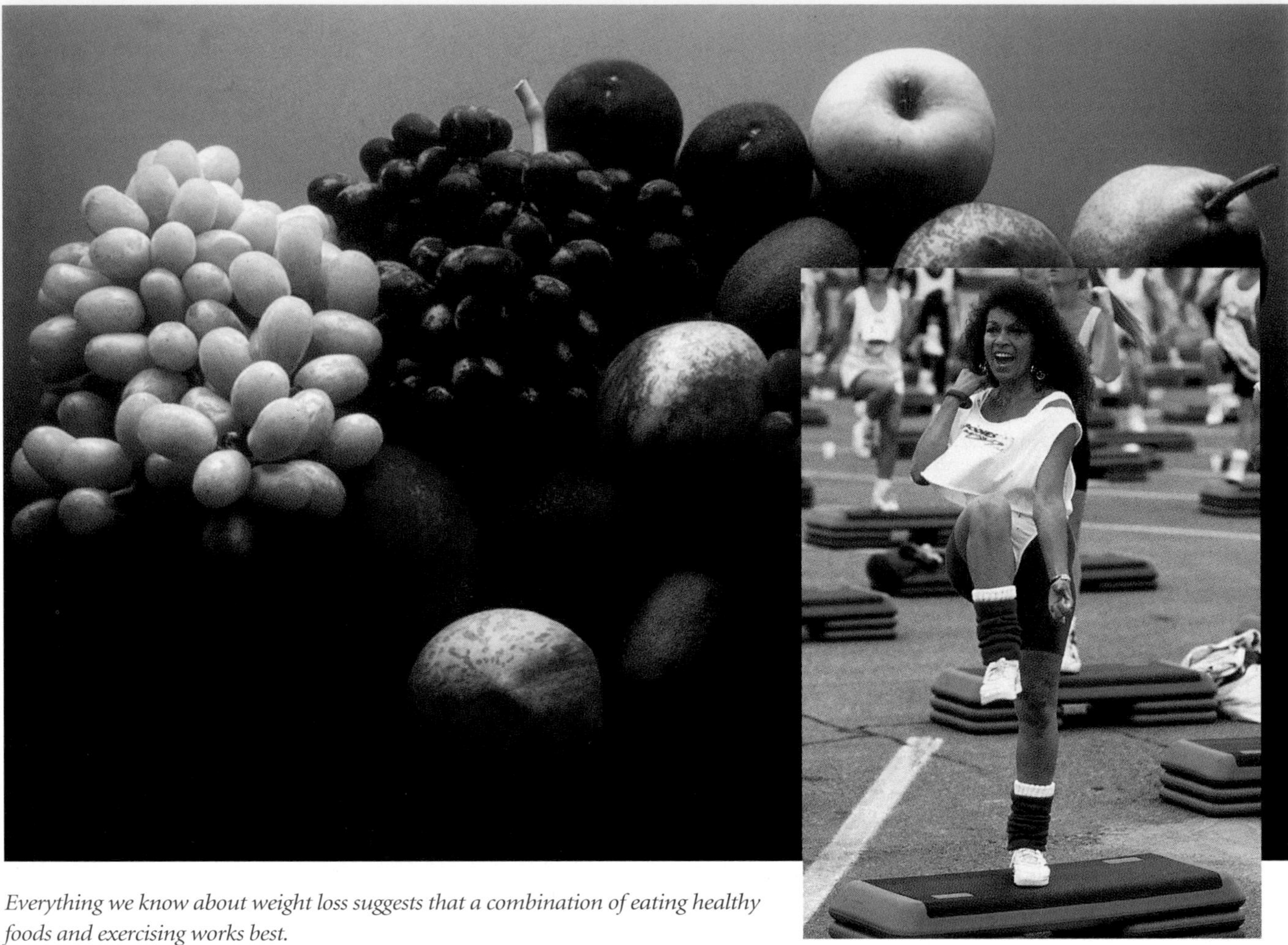

Everything we know about weight loss suggests that a combination of eating healthy foods and exercising works best.

do become less depressed and reduce their risk for a number of health-impairing disorders (Christensen, 1996).

Does Exercise Benefit Individuals Who Want to Lose Weight? Exercise not only burns up calories, but it continues to raise the metabolic rate for several hours *after* the exercise. Exercise actually lowers your body's set point for weight, making it much easier to maintain a lower weight (Bennett & Gurin, 1982). Nonetheless, it is difficult to convince obese individuals to exercise. One problem is that moderate exercise does not reduce calorie consumption, and many individuals who exercise take in more calories than their sedentary counterparts (Stern, 1984). Still, exercise combined with conscious self-control of eating habits can produce a viable weight-loss program (Stotland & Zuroff, 1991). When exercise is a component of weight-loss programs, individuals keep weight off longer than when calorie reduction alone is followed.

Who Should Diet? The population is not uniform, and clearly not everyone should go on a diet. A 10 percent reduction in body weight might produce striking benefits in an older, obese, hypertensive man but be unhealthy in an adolescent female who is not overweight. The pressure to be thin, and thus to diet, is greatest among young women, yet they are not the group in which the greatest risk of obesity exists or in which the benefits of dieting outweigh the risks.

Researchers have not adequately investigated the question of who should lose weight, and it will likely be best answered by consideration of the medical and psychosocial consequences of weight loss, which may be a highly individualized matter.

Anorexia Nervosa and Bulimia

Eighteen-year-old Jane gradually eliminated foods from her diet to the point she subsisted by eating *only* applesauce and eggnog. She spent hours observing her own body, wrapping her fingers around her waist to see if it was getting any thinner. She fantasized about becoming a beautiful fashion model and wearing designer bathing suits. However, even when she dropped to 85 pounds, Jane still felt fat. She continued to lose weight, eventually emaciating herself. She was hospitalized and treated for **anorexia nervosa,** *an eating disorder that involves the relentless pursuit of thinness through starvation.* Anorexia nervosa can eventually lead to death, as it did for popular singer Karen Carpenter.

Anorexia nervosa primarily afflicts females during adolescence and the early adulthood years (only about 5 percent of all anorexics are male). Most adolescents with this disorder are White and from well-educated, middle-and upper-income families. Although anorexics avoid eating, they have an intense interest in food. They cook for others, they talk about food, and they insist on watching others eat. Anorexics have a distorted body image, perceiving themselves as overweight even when they become skeletal. As self-starvation continues and the fat content of their body drops to a bare minimum, menstruation usually stops and their behavior often becomes hyperactive.

Numerous causes of anorexia nervosa have been proposed, including societal, psychological, and physiological factors (Lam, Goldner, & Grewal, 1996; Pomeroy, 1996; Striegel-Moore & others, 1993). The societal factor most often held responsible is the current fashion image of thinness, reflected in the saying "You can't be too rich or too thin." Psychological factors include motivation for attention, desire for individuality, denial of sexuality, and a need to cope with overcontrolling parents. Some anorexics have parents that place high demands for achievement on them. Unable to meet their parents' high standards, they feel unable to control their own lives. By limiting their food intake, anorexics gain some sense of self-control. Physiological causes involve the hypothalamus, which becomes abnormal in a number of ways when an adolescent becomes anorexic. Unfortunately, we are uncertain of the exact causes of anorexia at this time.

Bulimia *is an eating disorder in which the individual consistently follows a binge-and-purge eating pattern.* The bulimic goes on an eating binge and then purges by self-induced vomiting or using a laxative. Sometimes the binges alternate with fasting, at other times with normal eating. Like anorexia nervosa, bulimia is primarily a female disorder. Bulimia has become prevalent among traditional-age college women. Some estimates suggest that one in every two college women binges and purges at least some of the time. Recent estimates, however, suggest true bulimics—those who binge and purge on a regular basis—make up less than 2 percent of the college female population (Stunkard, 1987). Another survey of 1,500 high school and university students found that 4 percent of the high school students and 5 percent of the university students were bulimic (Howar & Saxton, 1988). Anorexics can control their eating, but bulimics cannot. Depression is a common characteristic of bulimics. Bulimia can produce gastric and chemical imbalance in the body. Many of the causes proposed for anorexia nervosa are also offered for bulimia (Fairburn, 1995).

Exercise

In 1961, President John F. Kennedy offered the following message: "We are underexercised as a nation. We look instead of play. We ride instead of walk. Our existence deprives us of the minimum of physical activity essential for healthy living." Without question, people are jogging, cycling, and aerobically exercising more today than in 1961, but far too many of us are still couch potatoes. **Aerobic exercise** *is sustained exercise—jogging, swimming, or cycling, for example—that stimulates heart and lung activity* (Cooper, 1970). The main focus of research on the effects of exercise on health has involved preventing heart disease. Most health experts recommend that you should try to raise your heart rate to 60 percent of your maximum heart rate. Your maximum heart rate is calculated as 220 minus your age divided by 0.6, so if you are 20, you should aim for an exercise heart rate of 120 ($220 - 20 = 200 \times 0.6 = 120$). If you are 45, you should aim for an exercise heart rate of 105 ($220 - 45 = 175 \times 0.6 = 105$).

People in some occupations get more vigorous exercise than those in others. For example, longshoremen have about half the risk of fatal heart attacks as co-workers like crane drivers and clerks who have physically less demanding jobs. Further, elaborate studies of 17,000 male alumni of Harvard University found that those who exercised strenuously on a regular basis had a lower risk of heart disease and were more likely to still be alive in their middle adulthood years than their more sedentary counterparts (Lee, Hsieh, & Paffenbarger, 1995; Paffenbarger & others, 1986). Based on such findings, some health experts conclude that, regardless of other risk factors (smoking, high blood pressure, overweight, heredity), if you exercise enough to burn more than 2,000 calories a week, you can cut your risk of heart attack by an impressive two-thirds (Sherwood, Light, & Blumenthal, 1989). Burning up 2,000 calories a week through exercise requires a lot of effort, far more than most of us are willing to expend. To burn 300 calories a day, through exercise, you would have to do one of the following: swim or run for about 25 minutes, walk for 45 minutes at about 4 miles an hour, or participate in aerobic dancing for 30 minutes.

The risk of heart attack can also be cut by as much as one-third over a 7-year period with such moderate exercise as rapid walking and gardening. The catch is that you have to spend an hour a day in these activities to get them to pay off. Health experts uniformly recommend that if you are unaccustomed to exercise, always start any exercise program slowly.

Robert Ornstein and David Sobel (1989) go against the grain of the "no pain, no gain" philosophy and believe that exercise should be pleasurable, not painful. They point out that 20 percent of joggers running 10 miles a week suffer significant injuries, such as torn knee cartilage and pulled hamstring muscles. Ornstein and Sobel argue that most people can stay healthy by participating in exercise that burns up only 500 calories a week. They believe it is overkill to run 8-minute miles, 3 miles at a time, 5 days a week, for example. Not only are fast walking and gardening on their recommended list of exercises, so are 20 minutes of sex (110 calories), 20 minutes of playing with children (106 calories), and 45 minutes of dancing (324 calories).

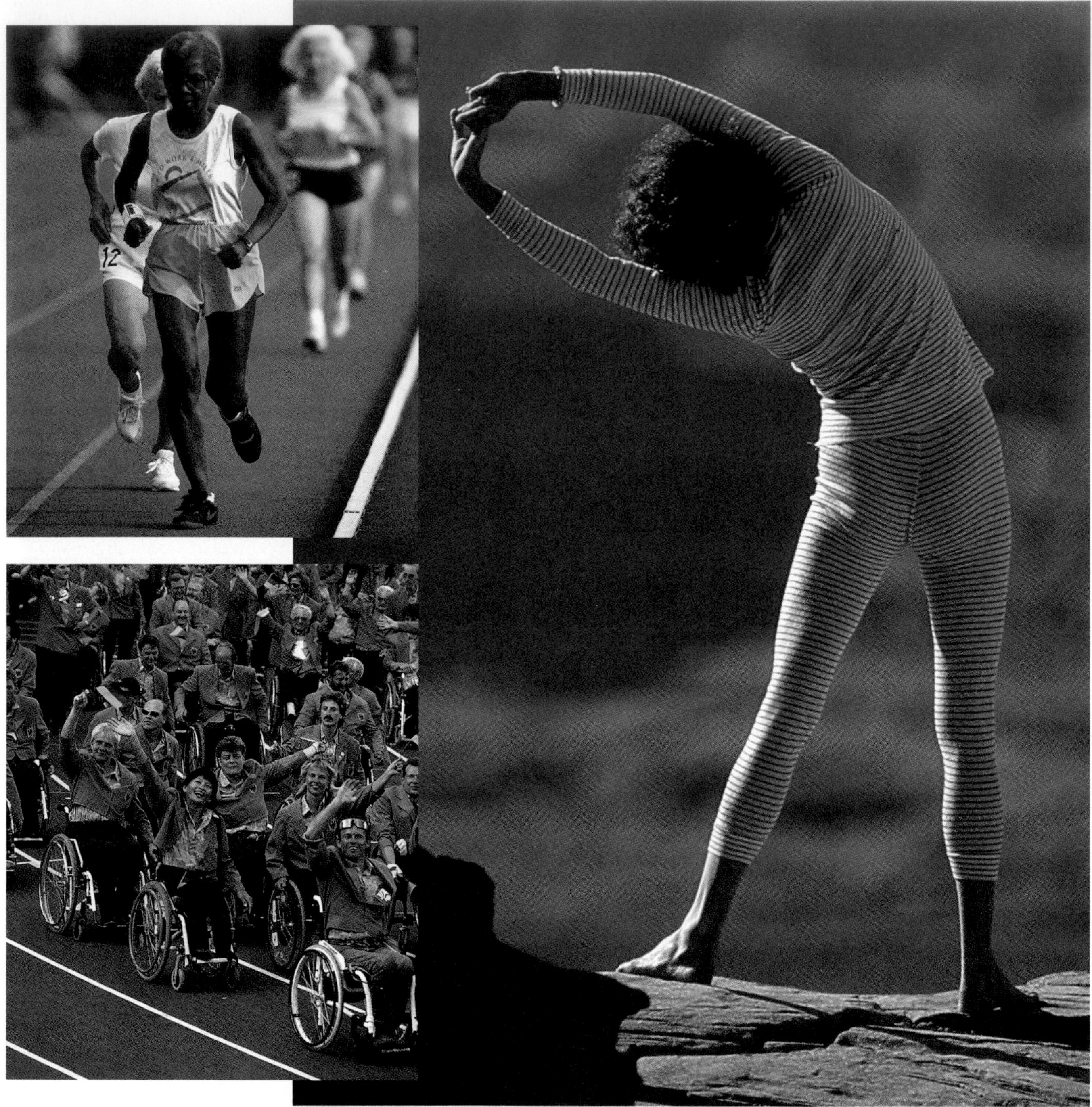

Researchers have found that exercise benefits not only physical health but mental health as well. And exercise can benefit individuals throughout their adult lives.

Researchers have found that exercise benefits not only physical health, but mental health as well. In particular, exercise improves self-concept and reduces anxiety and depression. In one study, 109 nonexercising volunteers were randomly assigned to one of four conditions: high-intensity aerobic training, moderate-intensity aerobic training, low-intensity nonaerobic training, and waiting list (Moses & others, 1989). In the high-intensity aerobic group, participants engaged in a continuous walk-jog program that elevated their heart rate to between 70 and 75 percent of maximum. In the moderate-intensity aerobic group, participants engaged in walking or jogging that elevated their heart rate to 60 percent of maximum. In the low-intensity nonaerobic group, participants engaged in strength, mobility, and flexibility exercises in a slow, discontinuous manner for approximately 30 minutes. Those who were assigned to exercise programs worked out three to five times a week. Those who were on the waiting list did not exercise. The programs lasted for 10 weeks. As expected, the group assigned to the high-intensity aerobic program showed the greatest aerobic fitness on a 12-minute walk-run. Fitness also improved for those assigned to moderate- and low-exercise programs. However, only the people assigned to the moderate-intensity aerobic training programs showed psychological benefits. These benefits appeared immediately in the form of reduced tension and anxiety, and after 3 months in the form of improved ability to cope with stress.

Why were the psychological benefits superior in the moderate-intensity aerobic condition? Perhaps the participants in the high-intensity program found the training too demanding, not so surprising since these individuals were nonexercisers prior to the study. The superiority of the moderate-intensity aerobic training program over the nonaerobic low-intensity exercise program suggests that a minimum level of aerobic conditioning may be required to obtain important psychological benefits.

Research on the benefits of exercise suggests that both moderate and intense activities produce important physical and psychological gains (Thayer & others, 1996). Some people enjoy rigorous, intense exercise. Others enjoy more moderate exercise routines. The enjoyment and pleasure we derive from exercise added to its aerobic benefits make exercise one of life's most important activities.

Increasingly, businesses are providing on-site exercise programs for their employees because they recognize the important role that health plays in productive work.

Toward Healthier Lives

In this chapter we have seen that being healthy involves far more than simply going to a doctor when you get sick and being treated for disease. We are becoming increasingly aware that our behavior determines whether we will develop a serious illness and when we will die (Minkler, 1989; Sarafine, 1994). Seven of the ten leading causes of death in the United States are associated with the *absence* of health behaviors. Diseases such as influenza, polio, and rubella no longer are major causes of death. More deaths now are caused by heart disease (36 percent), cancer (22 percent), and stroke (17 percent).

As we have seen repeatedly in this chapter, personal habits and lifestyle play key roles in these diseases. These findings lead health psychologists, behavioral medicine specialists, and public health professionals to predict that the next major step in improving the general health of the American population will be primarily behavioral, not medical.

The federal government and the Society for Public Health Education have set health objectives for the year 2000 (Schwartz & Erikson, 1989). Among them are these:

- The need to develop preventive services targeting diseases and problems such as cancer, heart disease, stroke, unintended pregnancy (especially among adolescents), and AIDS.
- The need for health promotion, including behavior modification and health education. Stronger programs are urged for dealing with smoking, alcohol and drug abuse, nutrition, physical fitness, and mental health.
- The need for cleaner air and water, and the need to improve workplace safety, including reducing exposure to toxic chemicals.
- Meeting the health needs of special populations, such as a better understanding of disease prevention in African American and Latino populations (Klonoff, 1991). Ethnic minority groups suffer disproportionately from cancer, heart disease, diabetes, and other major diseases.

According to a 1995 midcourse evaluation of year 2000 health goals, Americans are still eating too much, getting hurt on the job too frequently, and too often involved in violence. The good news is that more people are now eating lowfat foods and smoking less.

In Russia, though, health trends are worse than in the United States. In the first part of the 1990s in Russia, alcohol consumption increased more than 100 percent among men and smoking increased 25 percent among women. More than half of Russians over 30 are overweight—in the United States, 34 percent of individuals over 30 are overweight.

American's health costs have soared and are moving toward the $1 trillion mark annually. Health experts hope to make a dent in these costs by encouraging people to live healthier lives. Many corporations have begun to recognize that health promotion for their employees is cost effective. Businesses are increasingly examining their employees' health behavior and the workplace environment as they recognize the role health plays in productive work. Smoke-free work environments, on-site exercise programs, bonuses to quit smoking and lose weight, and company-sponsored athletic events are increasingly found in American businesses.

At this point we have discussed many ideas about coping with illness and promoting health. A summary of these ideas is presented in concept table 3.

Concept Table 3

Coping with Illness and Promoting Health

Concept	Processes/Related Ideas	Characteristics/Description
Coping with Illness	Recognizing, interpreting, and seeking treatment for symptoms	Many of us are not very accurate at diagnosing the symptoms of an illness. When our attention is directed outward, we are less likely to detect symptoms than when our attention is directed inward. Seeking treatment depends on our perception of the severity of the symptoms and the likelihood that medical treatment will reduce or eliminate the symptoms.
	The patient's role	In the "good patient" role, individuals are passive and unquestioning and behave properly. In the "bad patient" role, individuals complain to the staff, demand attention, disobey staff orders, and generally misbehave. Realistic prior expectations, predictable events, and social support reduce the stress of hospitalization.
	Compliance with medical advice and treatment	Approximately one-third of patients do not follow treatment recommendations. Compliance varies with the disorder and the treatment recommendation, whether we are satisfied with the quality of the care we are receiving, and our own theories about why we are sick and how we can get well. Clearer doctor-patient communication is needed for improved compliance.
Promoting Health	Smoking	In 1989 the surgeon general released an extensive document with new evidence that smoking is more harmful than previously believed, accounting for one-fifth of all deaths in the Untied States. Researchers are increasingly finding that passive smoke also carries health risks. Smoking is both addictive and reinforcing. Stronger educational and policy efforts regarding smoking are needed. Current prevention programs with youth focus on social pressures from family, peers, and the media.
	Eating disorders and dieting	Understanding obesity is complex because body weight involves a number of factors. Estimates of body mass that can be explained by heredity range from 25 to 78 percent. Set point and BMR are other biological processes involved in weight. Environmental factors also play a role in obesity—obesity has doubled in the United States since 1900. Obesity has high costs. Dieting is a pervasive concern of many individuals in the United States and raises many questions, such as whether weight loss reduces or increases health risks, whether diets work (some do, many don't), whether diets are harmful, whether exercise benefits individuals who want to lose weight, and who should diet. Two increasingly common eating disorders are anorexia nervosa and bulimia.
	Exercise	Both moderate and intense exercise produce important physical and psychological gains, such as lowered risk of heart disease and reduced anxiety. Experts increasingly recommend that the level of exercise you participate in should be pleasurable. Every indication suggests our nation's children are not getting enough exercise.
	Toward healthier lives	Seven of the ten leading causes of death—heart disease, cancer, and stroke, for example—are associated with the absence of health behaviors. The next major improvements in general health may be behavioral, not medical. A number of health goals for the year 2000 have been proposed, and businesses are increasingly interested in improving the health of their employees.

Critical Thinking About Behavior

All Stressed Up and Too Many Places to Go

We began this chapter with the story of Mort, whose life was seriously strained by a variety of stressors. Mort's score of 68 on the stress test diagnosed him as "seriously vulnerable" to stress. How high was your score? How vulnerable are you?

Well-constructed testing devices offer us an effective, systematic way to make accurate observations, descriptions, and inferences about behavior. For each test item, you indicated the degree to which the situation addressed by the item could contribute to your overall reactivity to stress; in effect, each item becomes a stress-related observation. The sum of your ratings produced your stress score.

Now what? If your test score suggests that you are vulnerable to stress, what kinds of predictions do you think you can make about your future physical and mental health? Have you already demonstrated particular patterns of "malfunctioning" that could be linked to the high degree of stress that you have reported?

After reading this chapter, you should have a new repertoire of ideas about how to address stress in more effective ways. In fact, scan the summary of positive coping strategies that you read about in figure 5. Pick three strategies that you think would be reasonable ways to improve your own coping style and reduce your vulnerability to stress. Think about the opportunities and challenges that would be involved in implementing these three strategies.

As a final reflection in this exercise, carefully examine the challenges that you identified in the implementation of your three strategies. Are these real challenges or convenient excuses? Just what would it take to encourage you to embark on a plan for a more healthful existence? Your implementation of a plan to improve your health would be a healthy example of applying psychological concepts to enhance personal adaptation.

OVERVIEW

We began this chapter by exploring the scope of health psychology and then turned our attention to stress, including biological, personality, cognitive, environmental, and sociocultural factors in stress. Our coverage of coping focused on the nature of coping, developing self-efficacy, thinking positively and optimistically, seeking social support, stress management, meditation and relaxation, and biofeedback. We also studied coping with illness—recognizing, interpreting, and seeking treatment for symptoms, the patient's role, and compliance with medical advice and treatment. We read about promoting health, including such topics as smoking, eating disorders and dieting, exercise, and moving toward healthier lives. Don't forget that you can obtain an overall summary of the chapter by again studying the three concept tables on pages 528, 537, and 546.

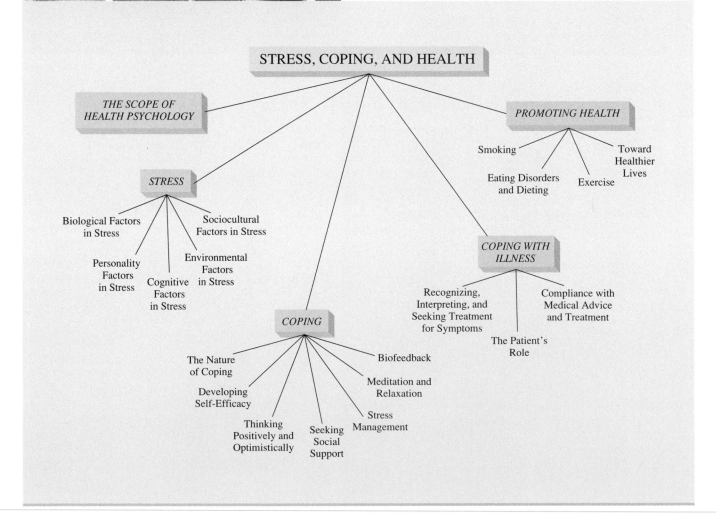

STRESS, COPING, AND HEALTH

- *THE SCOPE OF HEALTH PSYCHOLOGY*
- *STRESS*
  - Biological Factors in Stress
  - Personality Factors in Stress
  - Cognitive Factors in Stress
  - Environmental Factors in Stress
  - Sociocultural Factors in Stress
- *COPING*
  - The Nature of Coping
  - Developing Self-Efficacy
  - Thinking Positively and Optimistically
  - Seeking Social Support
  - Stress Management
  - Meditation and Relaxation
  - Biofeedback
- *COPING WITH ILLNESS*
  - Recognizing, Interpreting, and Seeking Treatment for Symptoms
  - The Patient's Role
  - Compliance with Medical Advice and Treatment
- *PROMOTING HEALTH*
  - Smoking
  - Eating Disorders and Dieting
  - Exercise
  - Toward Healthier Lives

Key Terms

health psychology A multidimensional approach to health that emphasizes psychological factors, lifestyle, and the nature of the health care delivery system. p. 516

behavioral medicine A field closely related to health psychology that attempts to combine medical and behavioral knowledge to reduce illness and promote health. p. 516

stress The response of individuals to the circumstances and events, called stressors, that threaten them and tax their coping abilities. p. 517

general adaptation syndrome (GAS) Selye's, term for common effects on the body when demands are placed on it. The GAS consists of three stages: alarm, resistance, and exhaustion. p. 517

eustress Selye's term for the positive features of stress. p. 518

psychoneuroimmunology The field that explores the connections among psychological factors (such as attitudes and emotions), the nervous system, and the immune system. p. 518

Type A behavior pattern A cluster of characteristics—being excessively competitive, hard-driven, impatient, and hostile—thought to be related to the incidence of heart disease. p. 519

Type C behavior The cancer-prone personality, which consists of being inhibited, uptight, lacking in emotional expression, and otherwise constrained. This type of person is more likely than more expressive persons to develop cancer. p. 522

hardiness A personality style characterized by a sense of commitment (rather than alienation), control (rather than powerlessness), and a perception of problems as challenges (rather than threats). p. 522

cognitive appraisal Lazarus' term for individuals' interpretation of events in their lives as harmful, threatening, or challenging, and their determination of whether they have the resources to effectively cope with the events. p. 522

burnout A hopeless, helpless feeling brought about by relentless work-related stress. Burnout leaves its sufferers in a state of physical and emotional exhaustion that includes chronic fatigue and low energy. p. 523

approach/approach conflict A conflict in which the individual must choose between two attractive stimuli or circumstances. p. S523

avoidance/avoidance conflict A conflict in which the individual must choose between two unattractive stimuli or circumstances. p. 523

approach/avoidance conflict A conflict involving a single stimulus or circumstance that has both positive and negative characteristics. p. 523

frustration Any situation in which a person cannot reach a desired goal. p. 523

acculturation Cultural change that results from continuous, firsthand contact between two distinctive cultural groups. p. 524

acculturative stress The negative consequences of acculturation. p. 524

assimilation Individuals' relinquishing their cultural identity and moving into the larger society. p. 525

integration Maintenance of cultural integrity as well as the movement to become an integral part of the larger culture. p. 525

separation Self-imposed withdrawal from the larger culture. p. 525

marginalization The process in which groups are put out of cultural and psychological contact with both their traditional society and the larger, dominant society. p. 525

coping The process of managing taxing circumstances, expending effort to solve personal and interpersonal problems, and seeking to master, minimize, reduce, or tolerate stress and conflict. p. 527

problem-focused coping Lazarus' term for the cognitive strategy of squarely facing one's own troubles and trying to solve them. p. 527

emotion-focused coping Lazarus' term for responding to stress in an emotional manner, especially using defensive appraisal. p. 527

active-cognitive strategies Coping responses in which individuals actively think about a situation in an effort to adjust more effectively. p. 527

active-behavioral strategies Coping responses in which individuals take some type of action to improve their problem situation. p. 527

avoidance strategies Responses that individuals use to keep stressful circumstances out of awareness so they do not have to deal with them. p. 528

self-efficacy The belief that one can master a situation and produce positive outcomes; an effective coping strategy. p. 530

cognitive restructuring Modifying the thoughts, ideas, and beliefs that maintain an individual's problems. p. 531

self-talk (self-statements) The soundless, mental speech people use when they think about something, plan, or solve problems; often helpful in cognitive restructuring. p. 531

social support Information and feedback from others that one is loved and cared for, esteemed and valued, and included in a network of communication and mutual obligation. p. 534

stress management programs Programs that teach individuals how to appraise stressful events, how to develop skills for coping with stress, and how to put these skills to use. p. 535

meditation The practice and system of thought that incorporates exercises to attain bodily or mental control and well-being, as well as enlightenment. p. 535

transcendental meditation (TM) The most popular form of meditation in the United States, TM is derived from an ancient Indian technique and involves a mantra, which is a resonant sound or phrase that is repeated mentally or aloud to focus attention. p. 535

biofeedback The process in which individuals' muscular or visceral activities are monitored by instruments and information is given (fed back) to the individuals so they can learn to voluntarily control their physiological activities. p. 536

"good patient" role As a hospitalized patient, being passive and unquestioning and behaving properly. p. 538

"bad patient" role As a hospitalized patient, complaining to the staff, demanding attention, disobeying staff orders, and generally misbehaving. p. 538

set point The weight maintained when no effort is made to gain or lose weight. p. 540

basal metabolism rate (BMR) The minimal amount of energy an individual uses in a resting state. p. 540

anorexia nervosa An eating disorder that involves the relentless pursuit of thinness through starvation. p. 542

bulimia An eating disorder in which the individual consistently follows a binge-and-purge eating pattern. p. 543

aerobic exercise Sustained exercise (such as jogging, swimming, or cycling) that stimulates heart and lung activity. p. 543

Resources and Readings in Psychology

American Anorexia/Bulimia Association
418 E. 76th Street
New York, NY 10021
212–734–1114

This association acts as an information and referral service related to anorexia nervosa and bulimia and publishes the *American Anorexia/Bulimia Association Newsletter.*

American Public Health Association
1815 15th Street
Washington, DC 20005
202–789–5600

This organization has available a number of books, manuals, and pamphlets on many areas of health. It also publishes a newsletter on the delivery and support of health services in developing countries.

Beyond the Relaxation Response (1984)
by Herbert Benson
New York: Times Books

Beyond the Relaxation Response is Herbert Benson's sequel to *The Relaxation Response.* A decade after he coined the term *the relaxation response,* Benson concluded that combining the relaxation response with another strategy is even more powerful in combating stress than the relaxation response alone. The other strategy is faith in a healing power either inside or outside of yourself.

Body Traps (1992)
by Judith Rodin
New York: William Morrow

Body Traps focuses on the relation of a person's body to self-image and the destructive effects of society's standards on women's perceptions of their bodies. Rodin recommends strategies for avoiding body traps and developing more positive ways of relating to ourselves as we are. This is a thoughtful, penetrating look at society's harmful preoccupation with women's appearance. *Body Traps* is informative, well written, and a helpful guide to women's bodies.

Exploring Sport & Exercise Psychology (1996)
by Judy Van Raalte and Britton Brewer (eds.)
Washington, DC: American Psychological Association

An up-to-date overview of the rapidly growing field of sports and exercise psychology is provided. Discussions include the psychological processes involved in peak performance, the use of exercise to reduce mental problems, imagery training, and goal-setting as well as strategies for developing a career in this area of specialization.

The LEARN Program for Weight Control (1988)
by Kelly Brownell
Dallas: American Health

This excellent book, written by a leading researcher, outlines an effective, healthy program for losing weight and maintaining the weight loss.

Learned Optimism (1990)
by Martin Seligman
New York: Pocket Books

Learned Optimism is one of the new breed of positive-thinking books, a breed that first began to appear in the late 1980s and has increased in number recently. Such books are based on psychological research and give specific strategies for optimistic thinking rather than earlier cheerleading books that were low on substance. Seligman's positive message is that since pessimism is learned, it can be unlearned. Included are self-tests to determine your levels of optimism, pessimism, and depression.

National Latina Health Organization
P.O. Box 7567
Oakland, CA 94601
510–534–1362

This organization seeks to improve the health of Puerto Rican, Chicana, Mexican, Cuban, and South and Central American women. It publishes a newsletter and is a source of information about health education, self-help methods, and bilingual access to health care.

The New Aerobics (1970)
by Kenneth Cooper
New York: Bantam

The New Aerobics lays out Cooper's age-adjusted recommendations for aerobic exercise. Cooper's book is research based and easy to read, and if you are in only average or poor physical shape, Cooper's recommended program will reap physical and psychological benefits for you. More than any other individual, Kenneth Cooper is responsible for getting a lot of people off their couches and out on the walking or jogging track. His positive influence is even international. In Brazil, when people go out to run, they call it "doing the Cooper." Another Cooper book we recommend is *The Aerobics Program for Well-Being.*

The New Aerobics for Women (1988)
by Kenneth Cooper and Mildred Cooper
New York: Bantam

This book tailors the concept of aerobic exercise to the capabilities and needs of women. It includes age-adjusted formulas for appropriate exercise that are tailored to a woman's lifestyle and current level of physical fitness.

The New Fit or Fat (1991, rev. ed.)
by Covert Bailey
Boston: Houghton Mifflin

The New Fit or Fat describes ways to become healthy by developing better diet and exercise routines. Bailey argues that the basic problem for overweight people is not losing weight, which fat people do periodically, but gaining weight, which fat people do more easily than those with a different body chemistry. This book offers solid, no-nonsense advice on how to lose weight and become more physically fit.

The Psychology of Women's Health (1995)
by Annette Stanton and Sherly Gallant (eds.)
Washington, DC: American Psychological Association

This book explores the roles of biological, psychological, and social factors that frame conceptions and assessments of women's health. Among the issues discussed are AIDS, smoking, exercise, eating disorders, heart disease, and alcohol use.

What to Say When You Talk to Yourself (1986)
by Shad Helmstetter
New York: Pocket Books

What to Say When You Talk to Yourself examines the success literature and concludes that in all of the many recommendations there are some missing ingredients, which include permanent solutions and a word-for-word set of directions for self-programming an individual's mind. Helmstetter describes several types of self-talk, such as silent self-talk, self-speak, self-conversation, self-write, tape-talk, and creating your own self-tapes. He covers many self-talk problem-solving strategies, how to change attitudes, how to change behaviors, and self-talk for different situations. You learn how to get started and how to create your own self-talk tape.

Women's Health
by Tracey Revenson, Nancy Adler, Hortensia Amaro, Ronald Kessler, Karen Matthews, Sally Schumaker, and Annette Stanton (eds.)

This relatively new scholarly journal focuses on psychological , social, cultural, and political factors that affect women's health. Among the journal's themes are how gender influences health-behavior relationships, illness, and health care.

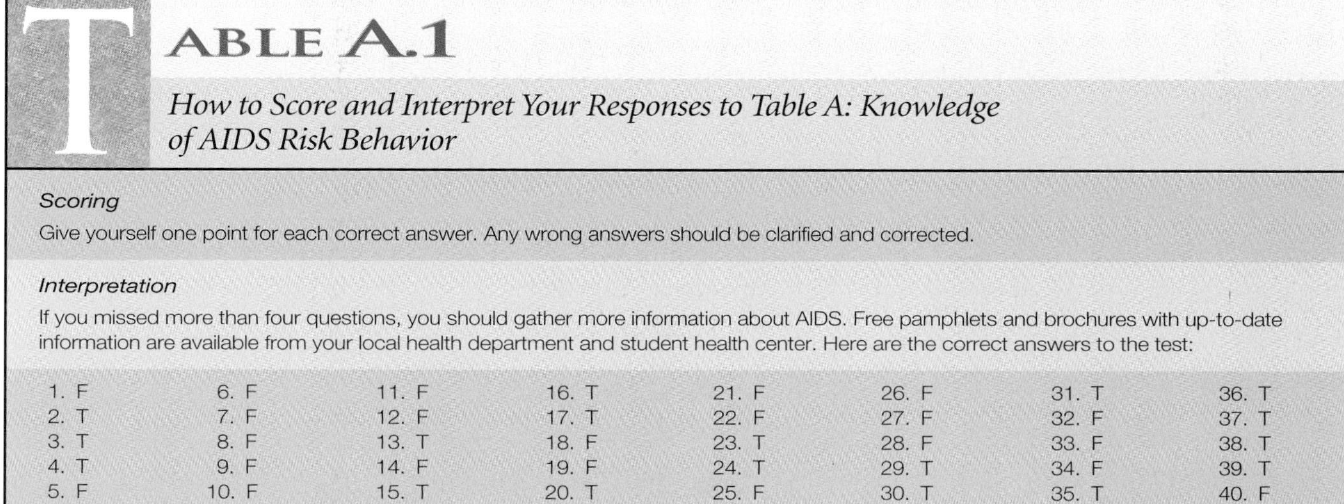

TABLE A.1

How to Score and Interpret Your Responses to Table A: Knowledge of AIDS Risk Behavior

Scoring

Give yourself one point for each correct answer. Any wrong answers should be clarified and corrected.

Interpretation

If you missed more than four questions, you should gather more information about AIDS. Free pamphlets and brochures with up-to-date information are available from your local health department and student health center. Here are the correct answers to the test:

1. F	6. F	11. F	16. T	21. F	26. F	31. T	36. T
2. T	7. F	12. F	17. T	22. F	27. F	32. F	37. T
3. T	8. F	13. T	18. F	23. T	28. F	33. F	38. T
4. T	9. F	14. F	19. F	24. T	29. T	34. F	39. T
5. F	10. F	15. T	20. T	25. F	30. T	35. T	40. F

Chapter

STI

Social Thinking and Influence

Georges Seurat
Sunday on the Isle Lagrande Jatte, detail

CHAPTER

STI

Social Thinking and Influence

Chapter Outline

Chapter Boxes

Man is by nature a social animal.

—**Aristotle**

In civilized society we all depend upon each other, and our happiness results from the good opinion of mankind.

—Samuel Johnson

Images of Psychology

The Reverend James Jones' Dark Side

With the noble intent of eliminating social injustice and improving interracial harmony, James W. Jones established a small church in Indiana in 1953. His congregation included a number of African Americans. He and his wife adopted seven children, including an African American, a Chinese, and a Korean. As a missionary for 2 years, Jones lived in Brazil, where he founded an orphanage and a mission. When he returned to the United States he changed the name of his church to the People's Temple Full Gospel.

Jones moved his church to northern California, where he increased his money-making efforts and community work. By the early 1970s, Jones had developed churches in the African American areas of San Francisco and Los Angeles. He was showered with accolades and his social programs were rated among the best in the country.

But Reverend Jones' dark side began to surface. As he stepped up fund-raising, he at first asked his congregation to make modest donations in the name of universal brotherhood and peace. Eventually he induced people to sell their homes and turn over all their money as a testament to their faith and loyalty. Rumors leaked that

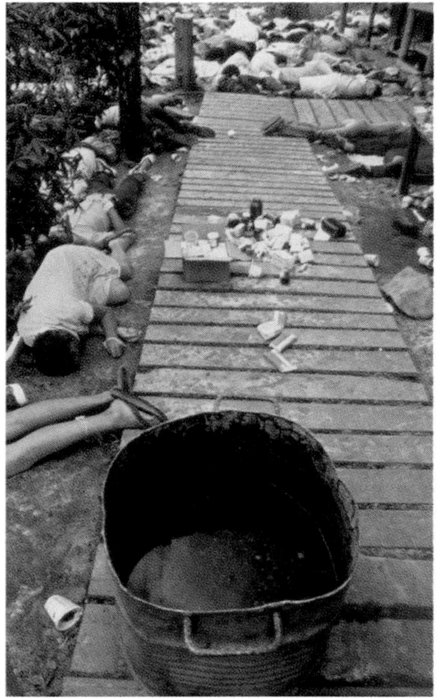

The Jonestown massacre, elaborately planned by People's Temple leader James Jones, reveals the macabre side of social thinking and influence.

physical abuse, death threats, and attempts to gain the guardianship of children were meted out to members who were disobedient or tried to leave Jones' church. Jones was able to deflect public investigations through his tight reign on information and his respectability in the community.

By the early 1970s, Jones increasingly saw parallels between himself and Christ. He portrayed himself as a messiah and required his congregation to call him "Father." Jones declared that everything he said was law. Jones was a charismatic leader and a master at getting members to conform to his wishes.

In 1977, shortly before an article exposing Jones' megalomania and repressive cruelty appeared in *New West* magazine, Jones' "flock" migrated en masse to Jonestown, Guyana. In Jonestown, the members of the People's Temple were isolated from their families and the world. They had been stripped of their possessions and individuality, and they were utterly obedient.

On November 17, 1978, United States Representative Leo Ryan and four of his aides, who were in Guyana to evaluate charges of abuse in the People's Temple, were gunned down by Jones' henchmen as they boarded a plane to leave the country. Jones convinced his congregation that hostile intruders were on their way to exterminate them in retaliation for the deaths at the airstrip.

The next day, Jones gathered before him more than 900 members of the People's Temple. It was time, he said, for them to die. Their death, the "martyr" Jones claimed, would be a revolutionary and positive act. Amidst few protests or acts of resistance, parents gave their children cyanide-laced Kool-Aid, drank it themselves, then lay down and waited to die.

PREVIEW

How could such a gruesome event as the Jonestown mass suicide happen? What forces could compel parents to poison their own children? The Jonestown massacre, as it is known, is a macabre example of social thinking and influence; it shows the power of obedience and conformity and how such power can be abused. The same processes help to determine the latest fashion fads, influence the outcome of political elections, and shape our everyday decisions. In this chapter we study these processes, beginning with an exploration of attitudes, attitude change, and persuasion. Then we will turn our attention to social perception and attribution. Finally, we will explore the many faces of conformity.

ATTITUDES AND PERSUASION

As Mark Twain once said, "It is a difference of opinion that makes horses race." **Attitudes** *are positive and negative dispositions to behave in certain ways toward some persons, groups, or objects.* We have attitudes about all sorts of things, and we live in a world in which we try to influence the attitudes of others.

Attitudes and Behavior

Think about your attitudes about religion, politics, and sex. Now think about your behavior in these areas. Consider sex, for example. How liberal or conservative are your sexual attitudes? Does your behavior match your attitudes? Researchers have found that we have more accepting attitudes toward sexual practices than our behavior actually shows. As we study the relation of attitudes to behavior, two questions arise: How strongly do attitudes influence behavior? and How strongly does behavior influence attitudes?

Predicting Behavior from Attitudes

More than 50 years ago Richard LaPiere (1934) toured the United States with a Chinese couple. LaPiere expected to encounter prejudice against Asians. He thought they would be banned from restaurants and hotels, for example. Surprisingly, in more than 10,000 miles of travel, the threesome was rejected only once. It appeared, LaPiere thought, that there were few negative attitudes toward Asians in the United States. To see if this actually was the case, LaPiere wrote a letter to all 251 places he and his Asian friends had visited, asking the proprietors if they would provide food or lodging to Asians. More than half responded; of these, a resounding 90 percent said they absolutely would not allow Asians in their restaurant or motel. LaPiere's study documented a powerful lesson in understanding mind and behavior: What we *say* and what we *do* may be different.

The connection between attitudes and behaviors may vary depending on the situation. In the study of attitudes toward Asians in the 1930s, the Chinese who accompanied LaPiere were well dressed and carried expensive luggage; they might have inspired different attitudes if they had appeared in cheaper attire. To consider further situational influences on attitude—behavior connections, imagine asking someone about his attitude toward people who drive pickup trucks. Let's say he responds, "Totally classless." A month later the guy stops for a cup of coffee in a small west Texas town. A burly man in the next booth is talking with his buddies about the merits of pickup trucks. He turns to our friend and asks, "How do you like that green pickup truck sitting outside?" Needless to say, his response was not "Totally classless." This example suggests that the demands of the situation can be powerful even when we hold strong beliefs.

Other guidelines help predict behavior from attitudes. When our attitudes are based on personal experiences, our behavior is more likely to reflect our attitudes. For example, Jane has a negative attitude about smoking yet smokes heavily; however, when a chain-smoking relative dies of lung cancer, Jane quits smoking, making her nonsmoking behavior match her negative attitude about smoking.

When we think about our attitudes at length, the connection between attitudes and behavior strengthens (Petty & Krosnick, 1995). For example, what is your attitude toward gun control, smoking in public places, or President Clinton? Chances are, you have thought about your attitudes toward gun control, smoking in public places, and Bill Clinton on a number of occasions. Because attitudes we have thought about at length quickly come to mind and are easily accessible, they influence our perceptions of events and, therefore, are more closely tied to our behavior. One study tested the idea that the more accessible the attitude, the more likely it will influence our behavior (Fazio & Williams, 1986). Attitudes toward Ronald Reagan and Walter Mondale and the accessibility of these attitudes as measured by how long subjects took to respond were assessed prior to the 1984 presidential election.

If individuals knew immediately that they liked Reagan, this attitude usually was reflected in their judgment of Reagan's performance during televised debates and in the way they voted in the election. The subjects' attitudes about the candidates that were quickly accessible were more strongly associated with their subsequent perceptions of the debates and their voting behavior.

Understanding of the attitude-behavior connection is furthered by the **model of reasoned action**, *which states that people act rationally and that it is intention that predicts behavior most directly* (Fishbein & Ajzen, 1974, 1975). Intentions are conscious efforts to carry out a specific act. For example, a woman who intends to take birth control pills to avoid getting pregnant is more likely to take them than is a woman who does not intend to. Likewise, if a man says that he intends to use condoms to avoid getting a female pregnant and/or to reduce the risk of sexually transmitted diseases, he is more likely to do so than is a man who does not intend to.

Intentions are the result of two main factors: (1) the person's attitudes toward the behavior (Does she think taking the pill is a good idea for her?) and (2) social norms, rules, and expectations about what members of a social group should do (in this case, the woman's perception of what others—such as her husband, her mother, her church—think she should do).

The model of reasoned action is appealing because it provides a positive view of human beings—describing them as rational and intentional. This model has been somewhat successful in predicting people's behavior (Chaiken & Stagnor, 1987; Cialdini, Petty, & Cacioppo, 1981).

No model, though, is perfect. What are some of the limitations of the model of reasoned action? One limitation is that what people have done in the past can influence their behavior beyond the boundaries of rational thinking. Possibly a male has so infrequently used condoms that this ingrained behavior outweighs his intention to use them. Another limitation involves emotions—sometimes people know what they should do but can't get themselves to do it for emotional reasons. Possibly a male becomes so passionately involved in a sexual encounter that he chooses to ignore reasoned action. Other limitations involve external constraints and opportunities, as well as perceived susceptibility and fear. In one study, college undergraduates were interviewed about their intentions to use condoms during sexual intercourse (Boyd & Wandersman, 1991). Three months after completing the initial questionnaire, they were recontacted by phone and interviewed about their frequency of condom use during the interim period. Although behavioral intention was a strong predictor of condom use, perceived susceptibility to and fear of AIDS predicted condom use as well. Access to condoms and willingness to use them probably also contributes to this behavior (Sears, Peplau, & Taylor, 1995).

Behavior's Influence on Attitudes

"The actions of men are the best interpreters of their thoughts," asserted the seventeenth-century English philosopher John Locke. Does doing change your believing? If you quit drinking, will you have a more negative attitude toward drinking? If you take up an exercise program, are you more likely to extol the benefits of cardiovascular fitness when someone asks your attitude about exercise?

Ample evidence exists that changes in behavior sometimes precede changes in attitudes (Bandura, 1989). Social psychologists offer two main explanations of why behavior influences attitudes. The first view is that we have a strong need for cognitive consistency; consequently, we change our attitudes to make them more consistent with our behavior (Carkenord & Bullington, 1995). The second view is that our attitudes are not completely clear, so we observe our behavior and make inferences about it to determine what our attitudes should be. Let's consider these two views in more detail.

Cognitive dissonance *is a concept developed by social psychologist Leon Festinger (1957); it refers to an individual's motivation toward consistency and away from inconsistency.* For example, we might feel uneasy about the discrepancy between our attitudes and behavior, which often leads us to justify our actions. Imagine the circumstance when you do something you do not feel good about—flunking a test or losing your temper, for example. We often justify our behavior in our mind, as George Bernard Shaw did with his father's alcoholism: "If you cannot get rid of the family skeleton, you may as well make it dance." Shaw's justification helped him reduce the tension between his attitude about his father's drinking problems and its actual occurrence. Cognitive dissonance is about making our skeletons dance, about trying to reduce tension by cognitively justifying things that are unpleasant (Aronson, 1988; Elliott & Devine, 1994).

A classic experiment in social psychology illustrates further how cognitive dissonance works. If you were paid $1 to tell a lie, would you end up believing the lie more than if you were paid $20 to tell the lie? A behavioral interpretation would predict that you would be more likely to believe the lie if you were paid $20; however, one experiment provided an elegant example of cognitive dissonance (Festinger & Carlsmith, 1959). Remember that cognitive dissonance theory states that we are rationalizing creatures who try to make our attitudes conform to our behavior. In the experiment, college students were asked to perform boring, repetitive tasks, such as packing spools in a tray or turning rows of screws one-quarter of a turn. The experimenter induced them to lie about the task; they were asked to tell a woman waiting to participate in the experiment (who was paid for her role) how interesting and enjoyable the experience was. When the experiment was over, an interviewer asked the "liars" how much they had enjoyed their work. The students who had been given

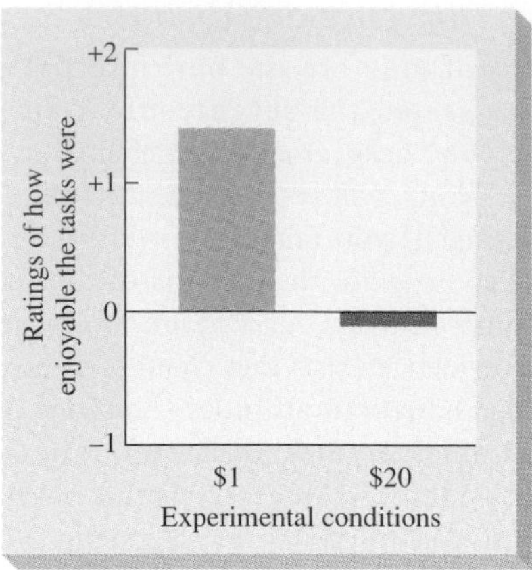

FIGURE 1

Festinger and Carlsmith's Classic Study on Cognitive Dissonance
Ratings were made on a scale of +5 to –5. The students who had been given $20 to lie rated the activity as dull; those who were paid only $1 said it was enjoyable.

$20 to lie to the woman rated the activity as dull; those who were paid only $1 said it was enjoyable (see figure 1). That is, students who were *externally justified* (paid $20) for lying told the lie but did not believe it. Those who experienced little external justification (paid only $1) told the lie and moved toward believing that what they said was true. These subjects needed an *internal justification* to tell the lie, since they lacked an external justification; therefore, they internally justified telling the lie by believing it.

We justify the negative things we do in life. We need to convince ourselves that we are decent, reasonable human beings. For example, when we have had a bad argument with someone, we often develop a negative attitude toward that person, which justifies the nasty things we said. We also have a strong need to justify the effort we put forth in life. We positively evaluate goals that require considerable effort. Whether we reach the goals or not, we engage in the process of *effort justification*. The reasoning goes like this: if we work hard to attain a goal but then evaluate that goal in a negative way, dissonance would occur. If we put forth considerable effort, yet still do not reach the goal, how could we reduce the dissonance? We could convince ourselves that we did not work as hard as we actually did, or we could say that the goal was not all that important in the first place.

Our most intense justifications of our actions take place when our self-esteem is involved. If you do something cruel, then it follows that you have to perform some mental gymnastics to keep yourself from thinking you are a cruel person. The clearest results in the hundreds of research studies on cognitive dissonance occur when self-esteem is involved, and it is when individuals with the highest self-esteem act in cruel ways that the most dissonance results. What about individuals with low self-esteem? They probably experience less dissonance because acting in a cruel way is consistent with their attitudes toward themselves—attitudes that might entail such labels as "loser," "jerk," "zero," or "bad guy." Put another way, individuals who think of themselves as bad may do bad things because it keeps dissonance at a minimum.

Not all of our thoughts and behaviors are aimed at reducing dissonance, however. Some of us learn from our mistakes. There are times when we need to catch ourselves, look in the mirror, and say, "You blew it. Now what can you do to prevent that from happening again?" Eliot Aronson (1988) offers three suggestions that can keep our lives from being a treadmill of dissonance reduction:

1. Know your defensive and dissonance-reducing tendencies. Be able to sense them before you get in over your head.
2. Realize that behaving in stupid and cruel ways does not necessarily mean that you are a stupid and cruel person.
3. Develop enough strengths and competencies to be able to tolerate your mistakes without having to spend a lifetime rationalizing them away.

Not all social psychologists, however, are satisfied with cognitive dissonance as an explanation for the influence of behavior on attitudes. Daryl Bem (1967), for example, believes that the cognitive dissonance view relies too heavily on internal factors, which are difficult to measure. Bem argues that we should move away from such fuzzy and nebulous concepts as "cognitions" and "psychological discomfort" and replace them with more behavioral terminology. **Self-perception theory** *is Bem's theory of the attitude–behavior connection; it stresses that individuals make inferences about their attitudes by perceiving their behavior.* For example, consider the remark, "I am spending all of my time thinking about the test I have next week. I must be anxious." Or, "This is the third time I have gone to the student union in two days. I must be lonely." Bem believes we look to our own behavior when our attitudes are not completely clear. This means that when we have clear ideas about something, we are less likely to look to our behavior for clues about our attitudes; but if we feel more ambivalent about something or someone, our behavior is a good place to look to determine our attitude. Figure 2 provides a comparison of cognitive dissonance and self-perception theories.

Which theory is right, the theory of cognitive dissonance or self-perception theory? Bem's self-perception theory has been more useful in understanding what happens to people's attitudes when they are offered an inducement to do something they would want to do anyway. The pattern of research on cognitive dissonance suggests that the heart of dissonance has to do with not wanting to feel cheap or stupid or guilty. Dissonance theory argues that individuals should avoid information inconsistent with

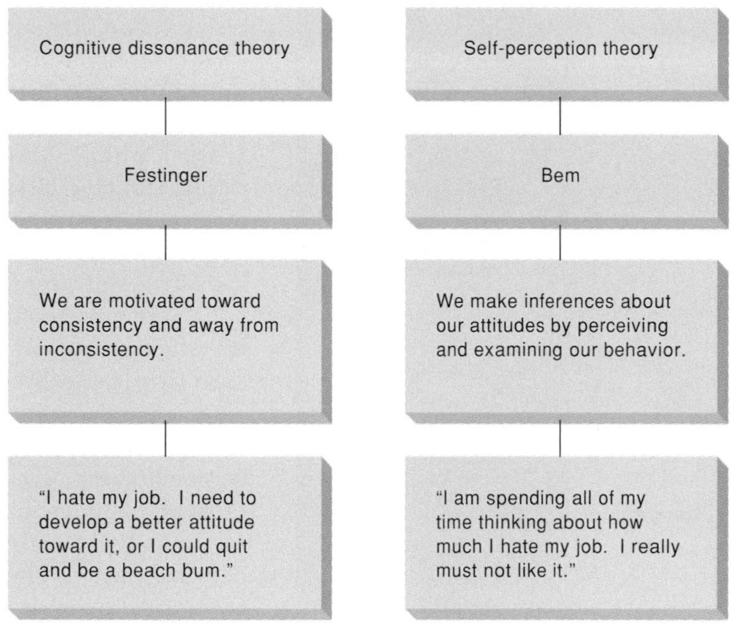

FIGURE 2

Two Views of Behavior's Influence on Attitudes

their views. Early attempts to document this selective exposure failed, although more recently researchers have found that people will avoid unpleasant information only if (1) they think they cannot refute the uncomfortable argument, and (2) they are irrevocably committed to their way of thinking or behaving. In sum, cognitive dissonance theory and self-perception theory both have merit in explaining different dimensions of the connection between attitudes and behavior (Sabini, 1995).

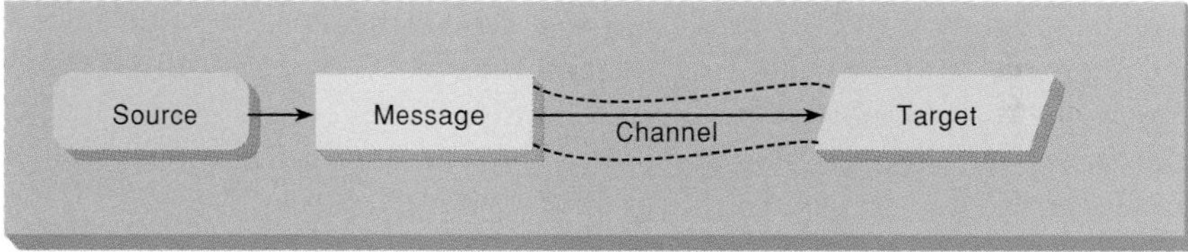

FIGURE 3

Factors in the Attitude Persuasion Process

Understanding the nature of attitudes not only involves the relation of attitudes to behavior, but also the nature of persuasion and attitude change. We form many attitudes as we go through our lives, attitudes that are often under pressure to be changed (Kimble, 1990; McGuire, 1989).

Persuasion and Attitude Change

We spend many hours of our lives trying to persuade people to do certain things. For example, the words from the song "Emotion in Motion" go like this, "I would do anything just to hold on to you. Just about anything that you want me to do." One person is trying to *persuade* another of the intensity of his or her love. Politicians, for example, have full arsenals of speech writers and image consultants to ensure that their words and behavior are as persuasive as possible.

Advertisers also go to great lengths to persuade people to buy their products. Consider trying to persuade someone to buy raisins. How would you make raisins appeal to consumers? An imaginative advertisement had a chorus line of animated raisins dancing to the tune of "I Heard It Through the Grapevine." What is it about this advertisement that persuades us to buy raisins? Social psychologists believe persuasion involves four key components: who conveys the message (the source), what the message is (the communication), what medium is used (the channel), and for whom the message is intended (the target) (see figure 3).

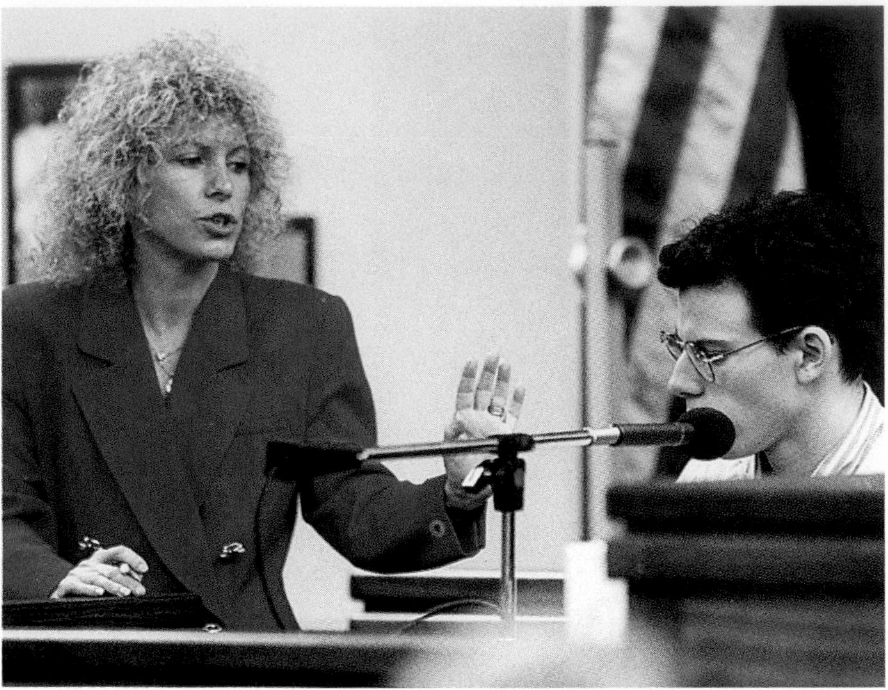

Leslie Abramson, the attorney for accused murderer Erik Menendez, presents her case to the judge and jury. In this context, Abramson is the source of the message, and the source plays an important role in the persuasion process.

The Communicator (Source)

Suppose you are running for president of the student body. You tell students you are going to make life at your college better. Would they believe you? That would depend on several different factors, which we will examine in turn.

One factor involved in whether or not we believe someone is the *expertise* and *credibility* of the communicator. Expertise depends on qualifications. If you had held other elective offices, students would be more likely to believe you have the expertise to be their president. We attribute competence to experts, believing they are knowledgeable about the topics they address.

In addition to expertise and credibility, trustworthiness is an important quality of an effective communicator. This factor depends on whether what you say and how you say it is perceived as honest or dishonest. It was in Abraham Lincoln's best interest, then, to be called "Honest Abe"; being perceived as honest increased the power of his communication.

Social psychologists believe that power, attractiveness, likableness, and similarity are four important characteristics that add to a communicator's ability to change people's attitudes. In running for student body president, you will probably have more clout with students if you have been on the university president's student issues committee. Power may be an important characteristic for a communicator because it is associated with the ability to impose sanctions or control rewards and punishments (Kelley & Thibaut, 1978).

In running for student body president, you are more likely to get votes if students perceive you as attractive and similar to themselves. That's why you often see presidential candidates putting on miners' helmets in West Virginia, speaking a Spanish phrase in San Antonio, or riding a tractor in Iowa. The candidates are striving to show that they share common interests and an identity with their audience.

Similarity is also widely used in advertising. In commercials we might see a homemaker scrubbing the floor while advertising a new cleaner or a laborer laughing with his buddies at a bar while drinking beer. The creators of these commercials hope you will relate to these people because you perceive them as similar to yourself. Of course, many products are promoted by appealing to our personal ideals. To do this, attractive or famous individuals are used in advertisements. Cher tries to persuade us to buy cologne and Michael Jordan tries to persuade us to buy athletic shoes, for example.

Another factor that influences attitudes is the sex of the communicator. To learn more about how gender might be a factor in attitudes about political candidates, turn to Explorations in Psychology 1. As we see next, the content of the message itself also is an important factor in influencing attitudes.

The Message

What should the content of a message be like to make it more persuasive? Should appeals be more positive than negative? Should a rational or emotional strategy be used?

How often have we seen politicians vow to run a clean campaign but as soon as the bell sounds come out swinging below the belt? In the 1988 presidential campaign, negative advertising became a big issue and proved to be effective. George Bush succeeded in branding Michael Dukakis with the "L" word (*liberal*) in the campaign. Negative appeals play on our emotions, while positive appeals are directed at our rational, logical thinking. The less informed we are, the more likely we will respond to an emotional appeal. For example, if we do not know anything about nuclear waste, an emotional appeal to keep a hazardous waste dump from being built near our home may influence our attitude about the project more than an appeal based on reasoning. For people who did not know much about Dukakis' political background, Bush's criticism of Dukakis was probably a wise strategy.

Explorations in Psychology 1

Gender and Politics—from Ferraro to County Clerk

It is the summer of 1984. The November presidential election is only months away; the Democrats are far behind in the polls. The economy is looking better and Republican incumbent Ronald Reagan's lead seems insurmountable. What could the Democratic party do to persuade the American population to switch their allegiance? It would have to be something bold, something never tried before in the history of American politics.

One of the areas in which Reagan seemed vulnerable was women's rights; the National Organization for Women (NOW) called Reagan insensitive to women, for example. For the first time in history, a woman—Geraldine Ferraro—was selected to fill the vice-presidential slot on the Democratic ticket. Although the Democrats did not win the 1984 presidential election, Ferraro's selection was an important step for women in their effort to achieve equality.

As more women have sought political office, the issue of gender has assumed a more important role in attitude change. Surveys reveal that, in today's political climate, we are more likely to vote for qualified female candidates, especially if they are running for lower political offices (Gallup, 1984). Discrimination still exists, though, especially in gubernatorial campaigns (Yankelovich, Skelly, & White, 1984).

The challenge is to determine for whom and under what circumstances gender makes the most difference. Social psychologist Carol Sigelman and her colleagues (1986) wanted to find out to what extent voters were influenced by the candidate's gender, physical attractiveness, prestige, and the responsibility of the office sought. The researchers gave college students information about six challengers to an incumbent in either a mayoral or county clerk's race. The challengers were men and women of high, moderate, or low physical attractiveness. The researchers found that male, but not female, voters discriminated against female candidates. In addition, they found that men saw women as less qualified, voted for them less, and placed them lower in the overall ratings of challengers. The antifemale bias of men was not offset by a preference for women by female voters. Female voters tended to vote evenly between the male and female candidates. Attractiveness was less consistently an asset for female candidates than it was for males.

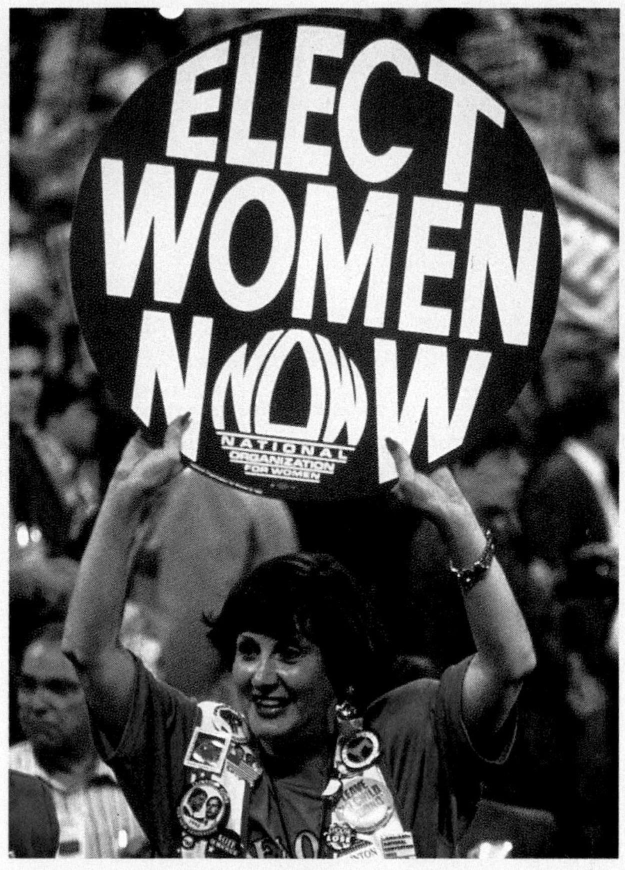

Women have made important gains in the political arena in recent years, but equality has not yet been reached.

Although it appears that less discrimination against female candidates occurs today than in past years, this research suggests that equality has not yet been reached.

All other things being equal, the more frightened we are, the more we will change our attitude. The day after the telecast of the vivid nuclear war film *The Day After,* more negative attitudes about the United States' massive nuclear arsenal surfaced (Schofield & Pavelchak, 1985, 1989). Advertisers also sometimes take advantage of our fears to stimulate attitude change. For example, you may have seen the Michelin tire ad that shows a baby playing near tires or the life insurance company ad that shows a widow and her young children moving out of their home which they lost because they did not have enough insurance.

Not all emotional appeals are negative, though. Music is widely used to make us feel good about messages. Think about how few television commercials you

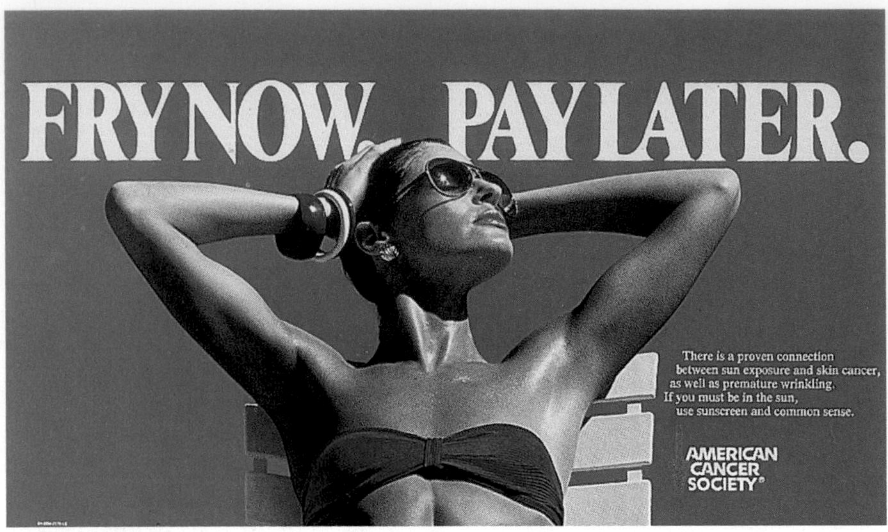

FRY NOW. PAY LATER.
There is a proven connection between sun exposure and skin cancer, as well as premature wrinkling. If you must be in the sun, use sunscreen and common sense.
AMERICAN CANCER SOCIETY®

All other things being equal, the more frightened we are, the more we will change our attitudes. Advertisers use this strategy at times, as reflected in this fear-oriented advertisement of the American Cancer Society designed to convince people to limit their sun exposure.

have seen without some form of music either in the background or as a prominent part of the message. When we watch such commercials, we may associate the pleasant feelings of the music with the product, even though the music itself does not provide any information about the product.

How extensively should messages differ from the audience's point of view? This depends on the credibility of the source. The more credible the communicator, the more she can advocate an extreme position and persuade the audience. By contrast, if a communicator's credibility is dubious, an opinion change is likely only when a moderate discrepancy is present between the audience's view and the communicator's view. For example, if a 60-year-old man who has completed the Boston marathon every year for the past 20 years and has a body that looks half his age tells an audience of sedentary office workers to exercise vigorously an hour a day to improve their health, they probably would believe him. However, they would probably be less influenced by the same message from someone who has just taken up running in the past several months.

Should the opposing side's arguments be acknowledged? This depends on the audience. If you perceive that the audience members may never hear the opposing side's argument, it makes no sense to tell them about it; however, when issues are highly controversial and the audience members are intelligent and well informed, reference to the opposing argument should be made.

Should you wait until the end of your presentation to make your strongest points or put your best foot forward at the beginning? In the **foot-in-the-door strategy,** *an individual presents a weaker point or makes a small request with which the listeners will probably comply in the beginning, saving the strongest point until the end.* In the words of social psychologist Robert Cialdini (1993), "Start small and build." For example, a sales pitch for a health spa might offer you 4 weeks' use of the facility for $10 and hope that, after the 4 weeks, you will pay $200 for a 1-year membership. In contrast, in the **door-in-the-face strategy,** *a communicator makes the strongest point or demand in the beginning, which the listeners probably will reject, then presents a weaker point or moderate "concessionary" demand toward the end.* For example, the salesperson for the health spa might initially offer you the 1-year membership for $200, which you turn down, then offer you a "bargain" 4-weeks-for-$10 package.

The Medium

While there are many factors to consider in regard to the message itself, the communicator also needs to be concerned about which medium to use to get the message across (Brehm & Kassin, 1996). Consider the difference between watching a presidential debate on television and reading about it in the newspaper. Television lets us see how the candidates deliver the message, what their appearance and mannerisms are like, and so on. Because it presents live images, television is considered the most powerful medium for changing attitudes. In one study, the winners of various political primaries were predicted by the amount of media exposure they had (Grush, 1980).

Television's power of persuasion is staggering. By the time the average American adolescent graduates from high school, he or she has watched 20,000 hours of television, far more than the number of hours spent in the classroom. Social scientists have studied television's influence on matters such as the impact of commercials on purchases, of mass media political campaigning on voting, of public service announcements on health, of broad-based ideological campaigns on lifestyles, and of television violence on aggression.

How strong is television's influence on an individual's attitudes and behavior? Some reviews of research conclude that there are few effects (Ziegler & Harmon, 1989). Other reviews conclude that television has a rather formidable effect (Clifford, Bunter, & McAleer, 1995).

How does television compare to other media in the effective delivery of a message? The superior attention-getting ability of the electronic media may be important for simple material, but the print medium provides more comprehensive coverage of difficult material.

Television's vividness also gives it an advantage when a communicator is highly credible, although print may be more persuasive when a communicator's credibility is suspect.

The Target (Audience)

What are some characteristics of the audience that determine whether a message will be effective? Age, gender, and self-esteem are three such factors. Younger people are more likely to change their attitudes than older ones, females are more susceptible to persuasion than males, and self-esteem is believed to be important but does not have a predictable pattern. Another factor is the strength of the audience's attitude. If the audience is not strongly committed to a particular attitude, change is more likely; if it is strong, the communicator will have more difficulty. Also, if uninvolved audience members hear others be enthusiastic, they are more likely to change attitudes than if they are highly involved in the issue addressed by the speaker (Axsom, Yates, & Chaiken, 1987). Another factor in message effectiveness is the audience's perception of who is responsible for an attitude change. If a communicator can convince an individual that it is she, rather than the communicator, who is responsible for changing her attitude, the message probably will be more influential.

Elaboration Likelihood Model

The **elaboration likelihood model** *states that there are two ways to persuade—by a central route and by a peripheral route* (Petty & Cacioppo, 1986). The central route to persuasion works by engaging someone thoughtfully. The peripheral route involves nonmessage factors, such as the source's credibility and attractiveness, or conditioned emotional responses. In the peripheral route to persuasion, people won't be persuaded by the logic of the arguments because they are not paying close attention to what the communicator is saying. Television commercials often involve the peripheral route to persuasion.

What determines whether people will take the central or the peripheral route to persuasion? That is, when will people be swayed by the logic of arguments, and when will they be influenced by something other than the message itself? A key factor is whether people have the ability, and are motivated, to pay attention to the facts. If people are truly interested in the topic and motivated to pay close attention to the arguments, they are more likely to take the central persuasion route. People are also likely to take the central route if they have the ability to pay attention—for example, if nothing is distracting them or keeping them from paying attention.

At this point, we have discussed the nature of attitudes and behavior and persuasion and attitude change. A summary of ideas about these topics is presented in concept table 1. In the past two decades, social psychologists have increasingly studied the cognitive aspects of interpersonal relationships. The next two topics—social perception and attribution—highlight this cognitive interest.

Social Perception and Attribution

As we interact with our world, we are both actors and spectators, doing and perceiving, acting and thinking. Social psychologists are interested in how we perceive our social world and how we try to make sense of it.

Social Perception

Social perception *is our judgment about the qualities of individuals, which involves how we form impressions of others, how we gain self-knowledge from our perception of others, and how we present ourselves to others to influence their perceptions of us.*

Developing Impressions of Others

Our evaluations of people often fall into broad categories—good or bad, happy or sad, introvert or extravert, for example. If someone asked for your impression of your psychology professor, you might respond, "She is great." Then you might go on to describe your perception of her characteristics, for example, "She is charming, intelligent, witty, and sociable." From this description we can infer that you have a positive impression of her.

As we form impressions of others, we cognitively organize the information in two important ways. First, our impressions are *unified*, and second, our impressions are *integrated.* Traits, actions, appearance, and all of the other information we obtain about a person are closely connected in memory even though the information may have been obtained in an interrupted or random fashion. We might obtain some information today, more next week, some more in 2 months. During those 2 months, we interacted with many other people and developed impressions of them as well. Nonetheless, we usually perceive the information about a particular person as unified, as a continuous block of information (Brown, 1986).

Impressions are integrated, in the sense that we reach beyond the information we have, adding, manipulating, and modifying the information to form a whole impression (Asch, 1946). When we do not have much information about an individual, we stretch it to form a complete impression of that person. In Solomon Asch's original work (1946), subjects were asked to think of a short list of traits for an individual. Asch then asked the subjects to write character sketches based on a brief list of traits. The sketches included many different combinations of the traits and went far beyond the original list. **Implicit personality theory** *is the term given to the public's or a layperson's conception of how personality traits go together in an individual* (Bruner & Tagiuri, 1954).

Concept Table 1

Attitudes and Persuasion

Concept	Processes/Related Ideas	Characteristics/Description
Attitudes and Behavior	Predicting behavior from attitudes	Attitudes are positive and negative dispositions to behave in certain ways toward some persons, groups, or objects. Social psychologists are interested in how strongly attitudes predict behavior. Today it is believed that, when situational influences are weak, when attitudes are based on personal experience, when we have thought about our attitudes, and when we have ready access to them, the attitude-behavior connection is strengthened. Understanding of the attitude-behavior connection is furthered by the model of reasoned action, which states that people act rationally and that it is intention that predicts behavior most directly. Intentions result from the person's attitude toward behavior and social norms. Limitations of the model of reasoned action have been documented.
	Behavior's influence on attitudes	Cognitive dissonance theory, developed by Festinger, argues that we have a strong need for cognitive consistency; we change our attitudes to make them more consistent with our behavior so that dissonance is reduced. In many cases, this involves justification of our actions. Justification is most intense when our self-esteem is an issue. Not all of our thoughts are dissonance reducing. Bem developed a more behavioral approach called self-perception theory; it stresses the importance of making inferences about our own behavior, especially when our attitudes are not clear.
Persuasion and Attitude Change	The communicator (source)	The source is most influential when he or she has expertise and credibility, trustworthiness, and power; attractiveness and similarity are also important.
	The message	The less informed we are, the more emotional appeals work; the more frightened we are, the more we will be influenced. Positive emotional appeals can also be persuasive, especially through the use of music. The more credible the communicator, the more extreme he or she can be; the less credible, the more moderation is needed. If audience members will not hear about an opposing argument, it makes no sense to tell them about it. If they are intelligent and well informed, reference to the opposition should be made. The foot-in-the-door and door-in-the-face strategies represent opposite tactics in persuasion.
	The medium	Because it delivers live images, television may be the most powerful medium; its persuasive capabilities are staggering, given the frequency of viewing. Experts debate television's influence. Television is superior for simple material but print is better for comprehensive coverage.
	The target (audience)	Younger individuals are more likely to change their attitudes than older individuals and females are more readily persuaded than males. Self-esteem is thought to be important, but a predictable effect for it has not been found. If audience members' attitudes are weak and they believe they are responsible for their attitude change, a communicator will be more effective.
	Elaboration likelihood model	This model states that there are two ways to persuade—by a central route or by a peripheral route.

When we integrate information about people, we follow certain rules. We use some evaluative dimensions more than others. Norman Anderson (1959, 1974, 1989) thinks we use three dimensions more than any others to categorize people. The most common dimension is good/bad. Think for a moment about the people you know. Chances are you categorize each of them as either good or bad. Our tendency to categorize people as good or bad is so strong that

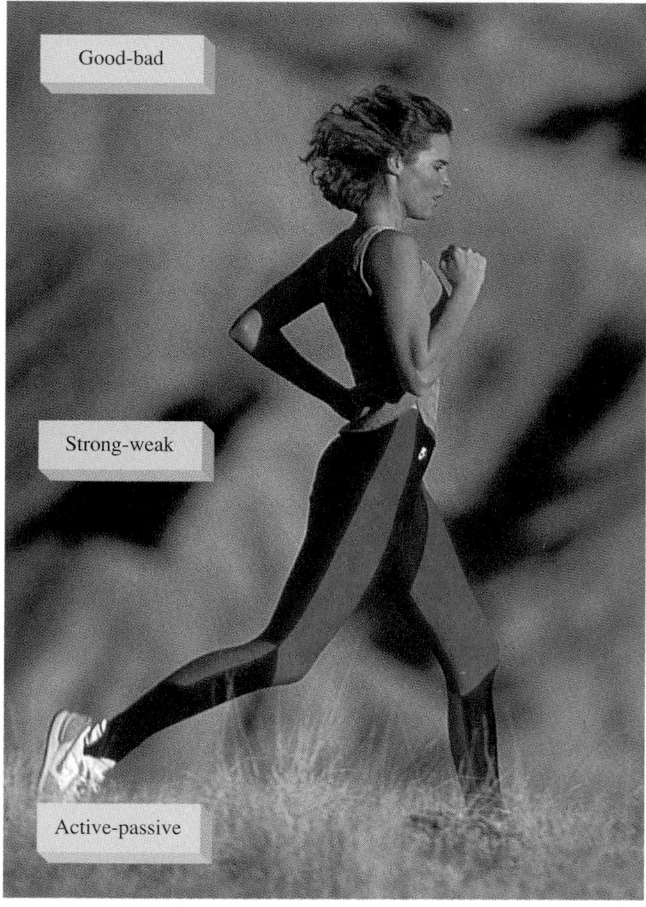

FIGURE 4

Developing Impressions of Others: Three Dimensions Used to Categorize People
Look at the individual running. What is your impression of her? You probably will categorize her as good or bad, possibly as strong or weak, or as active or passive.

Anderson calls this *the* evaluation dimension. Potency (strong/weak) and activity (active/passive) are two other dimensions we often use to categorize people (see figure 4).

When we integrate information about people, we fit the information into a schema. A schema is a category we use to organize information. When we read a book, we do not remember every paragraph word for word; rather, we get the gist of what the author says and fit the information into existing categories in our mind. We "read" people in a similar way. We don't remember everything about what they are like and what they do, but we get the gist of their personality and behavior, and we fit the information about them into existing categories of memory. One set of categories has been given special attention: **prototypes** *are abstract categorizations of traits that describe a particular personality type. Prototypes act as standards against which we match the individuals we evaluate.* For example, a prototype for extraversion is outgoing, talkative, and assertive.

We tend to simplify the task of understanding people by classifying them as members of groups or categories with which we are familiar. It takes more mental effort to consider a person's individual characteristics than it does to label her as a member of a particular group or category. Thus, when we categorize an individual, the categorization is often based on stereotypes.

What is the prototype for a business executive? How well does this man fit the prototype?

We do not always respond to others on the basis of categories, however. Imagine that you meet a salesman. Based on the category-classification system, you would develop an impression of him based on the "salesman" category. Without seeking any additional information, you might perceive that person as pushy, self-serving, and materialistic; however, as you interact with him, you discover that he is actually interesting, modest, bright, and altruistic. You would then have to revise your impression and perceive him differently. When impressions are formed in this manner, a more individualized, or *individuated*, orientation in impression formation occurs.

The information available largely determines whether a category-based or an individuated-based impression formation will occur. When we discover information that is inconsistent with a category or when we simply become more personally involved with someone, we are more likely to take an individuated approach.

Our first encounter with someone also contributes to the impression we form. First impressions are often enduring. **Primacy effect** *is the term used to describe the enduring quality of initial impressions.* One reason for the primacy effect is that we pay less attention to subsequent information about the individual (Anderson, 1965). Next time you want to impress someone, a wise strategy is to make sure that you put your best foot forward in your first encounter.

Gaining Self-Knowledge from Our Perceptions of Others: Social Comparison

How many times have you asked yourself questions such as "Am I as smart as Jill?" "Is Bob better looking than I am?" or "Is my taste as good as Carmen's?" We gain self-knowledge from our own behavior; we also gain it from others through **social comparison**, *the process in which individuals evaluate their thoughts, feelings, behaviors, and abilities in relation to other people.* Social comparison helps individuals to evaluate themselves, tells them what their distinctive characteristics are, and aids them in building an identity.

Some years ago Leon Festinger (1954) proposed a theory of social comparison. He stressed that when no objective means is available to evaluate our opinions and abilities, we compare ourselves with others. Festinger believed that we are more likely to compare ourselves with others who are similar to us than dissimilar to us. He reasoned that if we compare ourselves with someone who is very different from us, we will not be able to obtain an accurate appraisal of our own behavior and thoughts. This means that we will develop more accurate self-perceptions if we compare ourselves with people in communities similar to where we grew up and live, with people who have similar family backgrounds, and with people of the same sex, for example. Social comparison theory has been extended and modified over the years and continues to provide an important rationale for why we affiliate with others and how we come to know ourselves (Gibbons, Benbow, & Gerrard, 1994; Kulik, Mahler, & Earnst, 1994).

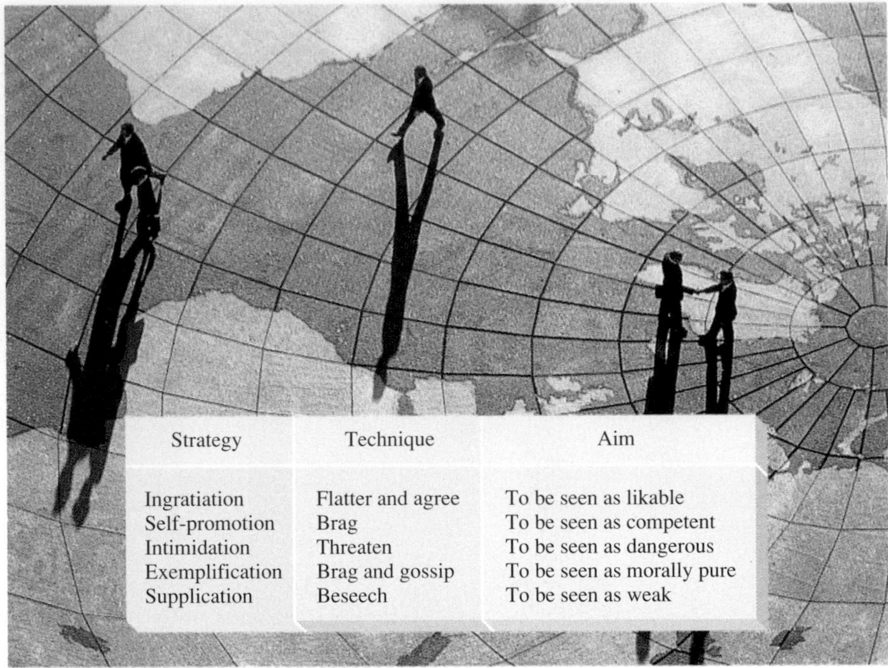

Strategy	Technique	Aim
Ingratiation	Flatter and agree	To be seen as likable
Self-promotion	Brag	To be seen as competent
Intimidation	Threaten	To be seen as dangerous
Exemplification	Brag and gossip	To be seen as morally pure
Supplication	Beseech	To be seen as weak

FIGURE 5

Five Impression Management Strategies

In contrast to Festinger's emphasis on the role of social comparison in evaluating one's abilities, recently researchers have focused more on the self-enhancing properties of downward comparisons (Banaji & Prentice, 1994; Wood, 1989). Individuals under threat (from negative feedback, low self-esteem, depression, and illness, for example) try to improve their well-being by comparing themselves with someone less fortunate (Gibbons & McCoy, 1991).

Presenting Ourselves to Others to Influence Their Social Perceptions

How do you present yourself to others? Do you try to act naturally and be yourself, or do you deliberately change your behavior to get other people to have a more favorable impression of you? Let's explore two dimensions of presenting ourselves to others to influence their social perceptions: impression management and self-monitoring.

Impression Management **Impression management (also called self-presentation)** *involves acting in a way to present an image of oneself as a certain sort of person, which might or might not be who one really is.* In most instances, we try to present ourselves to look better than we really are. We spend billions of dollars rearranging our faces, bodies, minds, and social skills, usually to make a favorable impression on others. We especially use self-presentational motives with people we are not familiar with and with people toward whom we have a sexual interest (Leary & others, 1994).

There are five strategies people can use to influence the impressions they make on others (Jones & Pittman, 1982) (see figure 5). First, **ingratiation** *is a self-presentation technique that involves illicitly making yourself likable in another person's eyes.* How might you go about doing this? One way is to simply agree with what others think. Another is to praise the other person's accomplishments, personality, and so on. Yet another way is to do favors for the person you want to impress. However, to succeed, the strategies have to be used subtly; if pushed too far, they will often be detected. Knowing how to effectively ingratiate involves knowing how much is too much.

A second impression management strategy is **self-promotion**, *a self-presentation technique in which individuals try to present themselves as competent.* In general, ingratiation is a strategy that involves trying to get other people to like us, while self-promotion strives to get other people to respect us.

A third impression management strategy is **intimidation**, *a self-presentation technique in which individuals present themselves as dangerous in an effort to coerce others into*

Explorations in Psychology 2

Impression Management and Job Interviewing

Most of us want to make a good impression the first time we meet someone. We especially want to make a good impression if the other person is interviewing us for a job. What nonverbal cues might we use to improve the likelihood that an interviewer will develop a favorable impression of us? People who are successful at impression management recognize that certain facial expressions, patterns of eye contact, and body postures or movements are part of the reason we are liked or disliked. For example, to improve the likelihood that an interviewer will have a favorable impression of you, you might smile often, lean forward, maintain a high degree of eye contact, and frequently nod your head in agreement with what the interviewer says.

Some people smile frequently, maintain good eye contact, and show a strong interest in what someone else is saying more naturally than others. Even if you don't normally behave this way when you are interacting with someone, you can make a conscious effort to control your nonverbal behavior. In general, researchers have found that individuals who use these impression management techniques receive more favorable ratings than individuals who do not (Riggio, 1986). These nonverbal cues, along with other impression management strategies such as behavioral matching, conforming to situational norms, and showing appreciation of others, apply to a number of social encounters in addition to interviews, including first dates and salesperson-customer situations. In one investigation, it was observed that individuals who were selected for engineering apprenticeships had smiled more, had maintained greater eye contact with the interviewer, and had nodded their heads affirmatively more during their interviews than had rejected applicants (Forbes & Jackson, 1980).

Is there a point, though, at which there can be too much of a good thing and we can overuse impression management? You *can* overdo it, using so many positive nonverbal cues that the other individual perceives you negatively and labels you as insincere. In one research investigation, the frequent use of positive nonverbal cues had favorable outcomes in a job interview situation only when the applicants also had competent qualification (Rasmussen, 1984).

In sum, using positive nonverbal cues can improve the way other people perceive you, but don't overdo it (Reece & Brandt, 1990).

---

treating them in a desired way. Intimidators try to convince others that they can and will cause trouble for others if they don't do what they want.

A fourth impression management strategy is **exemplification**, *a self-presentation technique in which individuals present themselves as having integrity and being morally worthy.* While self-promoters strive to project that they are competent, exemplifiers strive to project that they are morally pure. Exemplifiers risk being found out and called a hypocrite.

A fifth impression management strategy is **supplication**, *a self-presentation technique in which individuals try to make themselves appear weak and dependent.* Supplication might work because there are extensive norms in our society that suggest that we should feel sorry for people who are needy and handicapped.

Nonverbal cues can often be used in successful impression management. To read about how nonverbal cues can get other people to perceive you positively, especially in a job interview, turn to Explorations in Psychology 2.

Keep in mind, though, that impression management techniques that work in one cultural setting may not work in another. In particular, appreciation and flattery are often culture bound. For example, in some Eastern European countries, if one person expresses great admiration for another's watch, courtesy dictates that the watch should be given to the admirer! In the Native American culture of the Sioux, it's considered courteous to open a conversation with a compliment. Nonverbal cues also vary considerably from culture to culture. For example, the "thumbs up" sign, which means everything is OK or the desire to hitch a ride in most cultures, means something very different in Greece—an insult similar to a raised third finger in the United States.

Self-Monitoring Some people are more concerned about and aware of the impressions they make than others are. **Self-monitoring** *is individuals' attention to the impressions they make on others and the degree to which they fine-tune their performance accordingly.* Lawyers and actors are among the best self-monitors; salespeople, con artists, and politicians are not far behind. A former mayor of New York City, Fiorello LaGuardia, was so good at self-monitoring that, by watching silent films of his campaign speeches, it was possible to tell which ethnic group he was courting for votes.

Individuals who are very skilled at self-monitoring seek information about appropriate ways to present themselves and invest considerable time in trying to "read" and

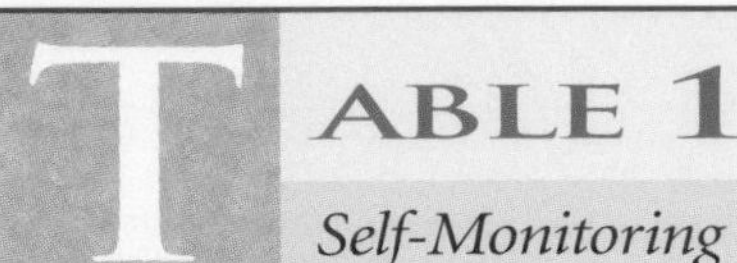

TABLE 1
Self-Monitoring

Instructions

These statements concern personal reactions to a number of situations. No two statements are exactly alike, so consider each statement carefully before answering. If a statement is true or mostly true as applied to you, circle the T. If a statement is false or not usually true as applied to you, circle the F.

1. I find it hard to imitate the behavior of other people. T F
2. I guess I put on a show to impress or entertain people. T F
3. I would probably make a good actor. T F
4. I sometimes appear to others to be experiencing deeper emotions than I actually am. T F
5. In a group of people, I am rarely the center of attention. T F
6. In different situations and with different people, I often act like very different persons. T F
7. I can only argue for ideas I already believe. T F
8. In order to get along and be liked, I tend to be what people expect me to be. T F
9. I may deceive people by being friendly when I really dislike them. T F
10. I'm not always the person I appear to be. T F

Scoring: Give yourself one point for each of questions 1, 5, and 7 that you answered F. Give yourself one point for each of the remaining questions that you answered T. Add up your points. If you are a good judge of yourself and scored 7 or above, you are probably a high-self-monitoring individual; 3 or below, you are probably a low-self-monitoring individual.

From Mark Snyder, *Journal of Personality and Social Psychology*, 30:526–537.

understand others (Simpson, 1995). Social psychologist Mark Snyder (1979) developed a scale to measure the extent to which an individual is a high or low self-monitor. To see how you fare as a self-monitor, refer to table 1, where items from Snyder's scale are presented.

The principle of self-monitoring stresses that individuals vary in how much they are tuned in to what is happening in the external world. A theory of psychology that has become prominent in recent years stresses that we seek to explain behavior in terms of internal or external causes; it is called attribution theory.

Attribution

Attribution theorists argue that we want to know why people do the things they do because the knowledge will enable us to cope more effectively with the situations that confront us (White & Lilly, 1995). **Attribution theory** *states that individuals are motivated to discover the underlying causes of behavior as part of their interest in making sense out of the behavior.* In a way, attribution theorists say people are much like intuitive scientists, seeking the reason something happens.

We can classify the reasons individuals behave the way they do in a number of ways, but one basic distinction stands out above all the others—the distinction between internal causes, such as the actor's personality traits or motives, and external causes, which are environmental, situation factors (Heider, 1958). If you don't do well on a test, do you attribute it to the fact that the professor plotted against you and made the test too difficult (external cause) or to the fact that you did not study hard enough (internal cause)? The answer to such a question influences how we feel about ourselves. If we believe our poor performance is the professor's fault (he gives unfair tests, for example), we don't feel as bad as when we do not spend enough time studying. To further your understanding of attribution, turn to Explorations in Psychology 3, where you will read about events involving a rock group and its fans.

Our attributions are not always accurate. In a given situation the person who acts, or the actor, produces the behavior to be explained. Then the onlooker, or the observer, offers a causal explanation of the actor's behavior or experience. Actors often explain their own behavior with external causes, while observers often explain the actor's behavior with internal causes. The **fundamental attribution error** *states that observers overestimate the importance of traits and underestimate the importance of situations when they seek explanations of an actor's behavior* (Ross, 1977) (see figure 6).

Since actors and observers often have different ideas about what causes behavior, many attributions are biased. Behavior is determined by a number of factors, so it is not surprising that our lives are full of squabbling and arguing about the causes of behavior. Attribution theory provides us with a more informed perspective on disagreements in marriages, the courts, the Senate, and many other social arenas (Harvey, 1995).

Our social world not only involves making attributions, it also involves our tendency to conform or not to conform to the attitudes and behavior of others. As we see next, conformity can occur in a variety of circumstances.

CONFORMITY

"Each of you, individually, walketh with the tread of a fox, but collectively, ye are geese," reflected the ancient Greek philosopher Solon on the importance of conformity in our lives.

Conformity in a Variety of Circumstances

Conformity comes in many forms and affects many areas in our lives. Do you take up jogging because everyone else is doing it? Does fashion dictate whether you let your hair grow long this year and cut it short the next? Would you take cocaine if pressured by others or would you resist? **Conformity** *occurs when individuals adopt the attitudes or behavior of others because of real or imagined pressure from others.*

Explorations in Psychology 3

The Who, Crowd Crush, and Attribution

It is December 3, 1979, in Cincinnati. A crowd of 8,000 Who fans presses forward toward the stage. Eleven of them are knocked down and suffocated. What happened?

Within 24 hours of the crowd crush in Cincinnati, it became apparent that there was disagreement about the causes of the eleven deaths. Drugs, alcohol, the weather, crowd size, the manner in which seats were sold, and a disposition for violence on the part of Who fans were all offered as explanations.

How did the Who fans, Roger Daltry of the Who, the mayors, and the city managers use attribution to explain the deaths of fans in Cincinnati?

The causes could be divided into those that were internal and those that were external to the actors, the individuals whose actions needed explanation. The actors in this situation were the Who fans. The internal causes included alcohol, drugs, and a disposition for violence. External causes included everything in the situation: the cold weather, a 5-hour wait, the allocation of seating, the number of police present, the manner of admission to the arena, and so on.

The mayor of Providence, Rhode Island, quickly canceled the December 17 Who concert in that city. When this date was offered to Portland, Maine, the city manager said no—it would be too risky. The cancellation and refusal reflected internal attributions, since the Cincinnati "situation" would not have recurred in Providence and Portland, but there would have been Who fans in those cities. If the fault was with the fans, then a recurrence would probably have taken place.

The cancellation had all the force of an accusation—The Who are bad news and so are the fans. In the December 12, 1979, edition of the *Cincinnati Post*, an editorial read, "Unfortunately there are thousands of impatient dopeheads who are more concerned about a good seat than a human life." Roger Daltry, one of the Who, said, "I don't think the crowd had anything to do with it." Neither did the mayor of Cincinnati, who stressed that causes external to the Who fans triggered the crowd crush. Fifty percent of the seats were reserved and 50 percent were on a nonreserved, first-come, first-served basis. Holders of the reserved seats already were in the arena when the crowd of 8,000 nonreserved ticket fans began their push forward. Of the fifty doors to the arena, only a few had been opened, apparently because there were only a few ticket takers working.

Officials in cities other than Providence where Who concerts were scheduled must have believed the external cause argument. In each instance, extensive evaluation, and caution was exercised: security forces were doubled, all doors were opened in advance, all seats were reserved, and fans were told not to come if they did not have a ticket. The next concert was in Buffalo, New York, on December 5. There was no trouble and the fans hoisted a banner that said, "These kids are all right" (which is the title of a famous Who song).

We use attribution in our everyday lives, just as the Who fans, Roger Daltry, the mayors, and the city managers did. We seek external and internal explanations of why events or behavior occur (Brown, 1986, pp.133–136).

Conformity to rules and regulations results in people's engaging in a number of behaviors that make society run more smoothly. For example, consider what would happen if most people did not conform to rules such as these: stopping at red lights, driving on the correct side of the road, not punching others in the face, and going to school regularly. However, in the following experiments, researchers reveal how conformity pressures can sometimes make us act against our better judgment and have dramatic, unfortunate consequences.

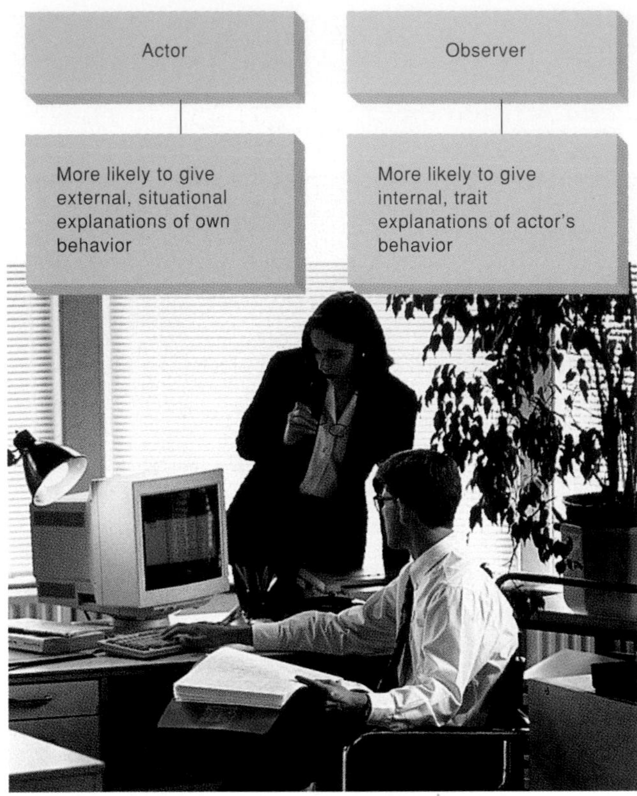

FIGURE 6

Actor-Observer Context and the Accuracy of Attributions
In this situation, the female supervisor is the observer and the male employee is the actor. If the employee has made an error in his work, how are the employee and his supervisor likely to differ in their explanations of his behavior, given what you have learned about actor/observer differences and the fundamental attribution error?

Put yourself in this situation. You are taken into a room where you see six other people seated around a table. A person in a white lab coat enters the room and announces that you are about to participate in an experiment on perceptual accuracy. The group is shown two cards, the first having only a single vertical line on it, the second card three vertical lines of varying length. You are told that the task is to determine which of the three lines on the second card is the same length as the line of the first card. You look at the cards and think, "What a snap. It's so obvious which is longest" (see figure 7).

The other people in the room are actually in league with the experimenter; they've been hired to perform in ways the experimenter dictates (of course, you are not aware of this). On the first several trials everyone agrees about which line matches the standard. Then on the fourth trial each of the others picks an incorrect line; you have a puzzled look on your face. As the last person to make a choice, you're in the dilemma of responding as your eyes tell you or conforming to what the others before you said. How do you think you would answer?

Solomon Asch conducted this classic experiment on conformity in 1951. He believed there would be little yielding to group pressure. To find out if this was so, Asch instructed the hired accomplices to give incorrect responses on 12 of the 18 trials. To his surprise, Asch found that the volunteer participants conformed to the incorrect answers 35 percent of the time. (Figure 7 shows the actual participants in Asch's experiment on conformity.) The pressure to conform is strong. Even in a clear-cut situation, such as the Asch experiment, we often conform to what others say and do. We don't want to be laughed at or have others be angry with us.

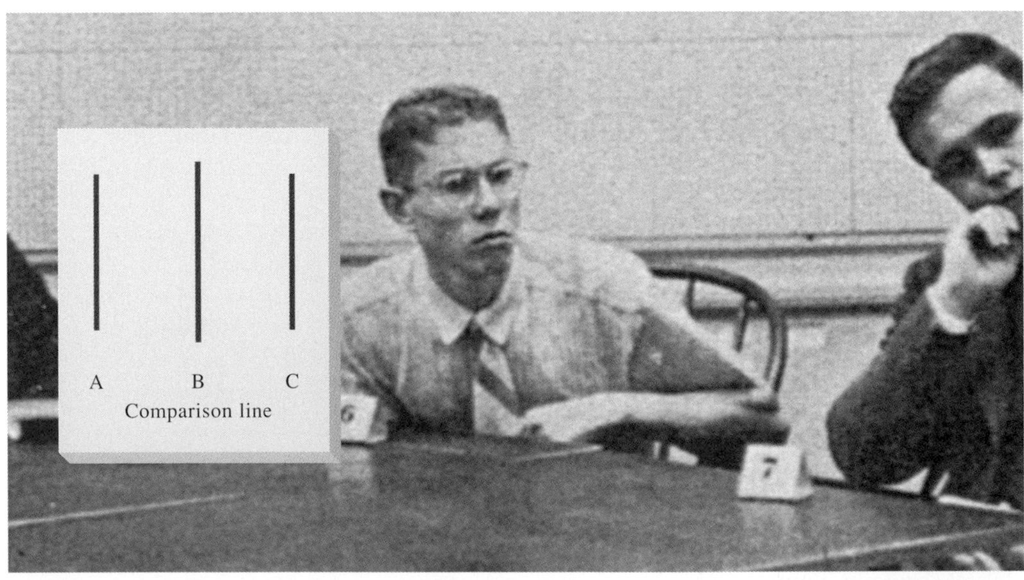

FIGURE 7

Asch's Conformity Experiment
The figures on the left show the stimulus materials for the Asch conformity experiment on group influence. The photograph shows the dilemma for one subject after five confederates of the experimenter chose the incorrect line.

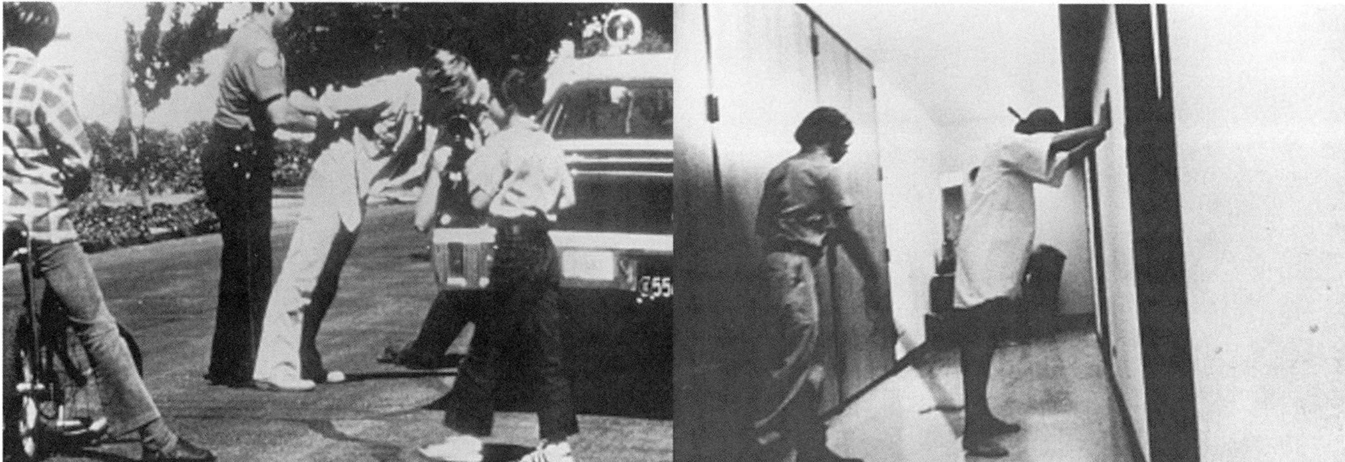

FIGURE 8

Zimbardo's Prisoner Experiment
At left, a volunteer for a psychology experiment is being picked up on campus—he had lost a coin flip and was designated a prisoner. At right, conformity to the hostile and abusive role of prison guard is shown.

In a more recent test of group pressure and conformity, college students watched the third Bush-Clinton presidential debate and then rated the candidates' performances (Fein & others, 1993). Students were randomly assigned to one of three groups: (1) a 30-student group that included 10 confederates of the experimenter who openly supported Bush and criticized Clinton, (2) a 30-student group that included 10 confederates who cheered Clinton and put down Bush, and (3) a 30-student group with no confederates of the experimenter. The effects of the group pressure exerted by the confederates were powerful; even Bush supporters rated Clinton's performance more favorably when their group included pro-Clinton confederates of the experimenter.

Put yourself in another situation. You have volunteered to participate in a psychology experiment. By the flip of a coin, half of the volunteers have been designated as prisoners and half as guards in a mock prison; you are one of the fortunate ones because you will be a guard. How much would you and your fellow volunteers conform to the social roles of "guard" and "prisoner"?

You are instructed to maintain law and order—to do a guard's job. You will make a fine guard, you think, because you are kind and respect the rights and dignity of others. But in just a few hours you find that your behavior, and that of the other "guards" and "prisoners," changes; each of you begins to conform to what you think are the expected social roles for guards and prisoners. Over the course of six days you and the other guards begin to make the prisoners obey petty, meaningless rules and force them to perform tedious, useless work. What's more, you find yourself insulting the prisoners and keeping them "in line" with night sticks. Many of the prisoners begin acting like dehumanized robots. They develop an intense hatred for you and the other guards and constantly think about ways to escape.

You may be thinking that the scenario we just described stretches credibility. No one you know, and certainly not you, would behave in such an abusive way. But psychologist Philip Zimbardo and his colleagues conducted just such an experiment with a group of normal, mature, stable, intelligent young men at Stanford University (Zimbardo & others, 1972). In fact, the prison study was scheduled to last two weeks but the behavior of the "guards" and "prisoners" changed so drastically that the experiment had to be stopped after six days. Although many of the prisoners resisted the guards and asked questions initially, after awhile they gave up and virtually stopped reacting. Five of the prisoners had to be released, four because of severe depression or anxiety and the fifth because he broke out in a rash all over his body. Several of the guards had become brutal with the prisoners. Figure 8 shows some of the actual circumstances in the prison study.

Factors That Contribute to Conformity

Many factors influence whether an individual will conform or not. In Asch's study with lines on cards, the group opinion was unanimous. When such unanimity is broken, the group's power is lessened and individuals feel less pressure to conform. Also, if you do not have a prior commitment to an idea or action, you are more likely to be influenced by others. If you publicly commit to a course of action, conformity to another point of view is less likely.

Three other factors that contribute to conformity involve an individual's characteristics, the characteristics of the group members, and the culture in which people live. People with low self-esteem and doubts about their abilities are more likely to conform (Campbell, Tesser, & Fairey, 1986), and you are more likely to conform if the group members are experts, attractive to you, or similar to you in

The Branch Davidian compound in Waco, Texas, going up in flames and David Koresh (inset). Koresh's charisma and power induced obedience on the part of his congregation, an offshoot of the Seventh-Day Adventist Church, the Branch Davidians. Koresh imposed all sorts of sacrifices on his followers that he decreed did not apply to him. Members donated their assets and paychecks to cover the compound's expenses. Members were fed with strict rations of vegetables. In contrast, Koresh had access to many things forbidden to members, such as meat, beer, and television. Men were required to be celibate; women were to be available to Koresh as "wives." Those who left the cult described Koresh as a zealous, imaginative preacher who paddled and humiliated rule breakers. When paddlings did not produce compliance, Koresh ordered the rule breakers to lie down in raw sewage and refused to let them bathe afterward. The Bureau of Alcohol, Tobacco, and Firearms believed that Koresh was holding cult members hostage and stockpiling ammunition, including machine guns, hand grenades, and radio-controlled aircrafts to carry explosives. They assaulted Koresh's compound on two separate occasions. On the second occasion, a raging fire developed; 25 children and 60 adults died in the fire, including Koresh himself. In the end, no one knew for certain what caused the fire, whether it was part of a mass suicide plan on the part of Koresh and his followers, whether the ATF started the fire, or whether it began by accident. The horrifying story of David Koresh reveals the macabre side of obedience.

any way. In experiments conducted in fourteen countries, conformity rates were lower in individualistic cultures (like that of the United States) and higher in collectivistic cultures (like that of China) (Bond & Smith, 1994).

Obedience

Obedience *is behavior that complies with the explicit demands of the individual in authority.* In Zimbardo's prison experiment, the prisoners and the guards were obedient. Obedient behavior sometimes can be destructive; it was rapidly becoming so with the prison guards. The mass suicides at Jonestown described at the beginning of the chapter, the massacre of Vietnamese civilians at My Lai, and the Nazi crimes against Jews in World War II are other examples of destructive obedience. Karl Adolf Eichmann, for example, has been described as an ambitious functionary who believed that it was his duty to obey Hitler's orders. An average middle-class man with no identifiable criminal tendencies, Eichmann ordered the killing of 6 million Jews. The following experiment by Stanley Milgram provides insight into such obedience.

As part of an experiment in psychology, you are asked to deliver a series of painful electric shocks to another person. You are told that the purpose of the study is to determine the effects of punishment on memory. Your role is to be the "teacher" and punish the mistakes

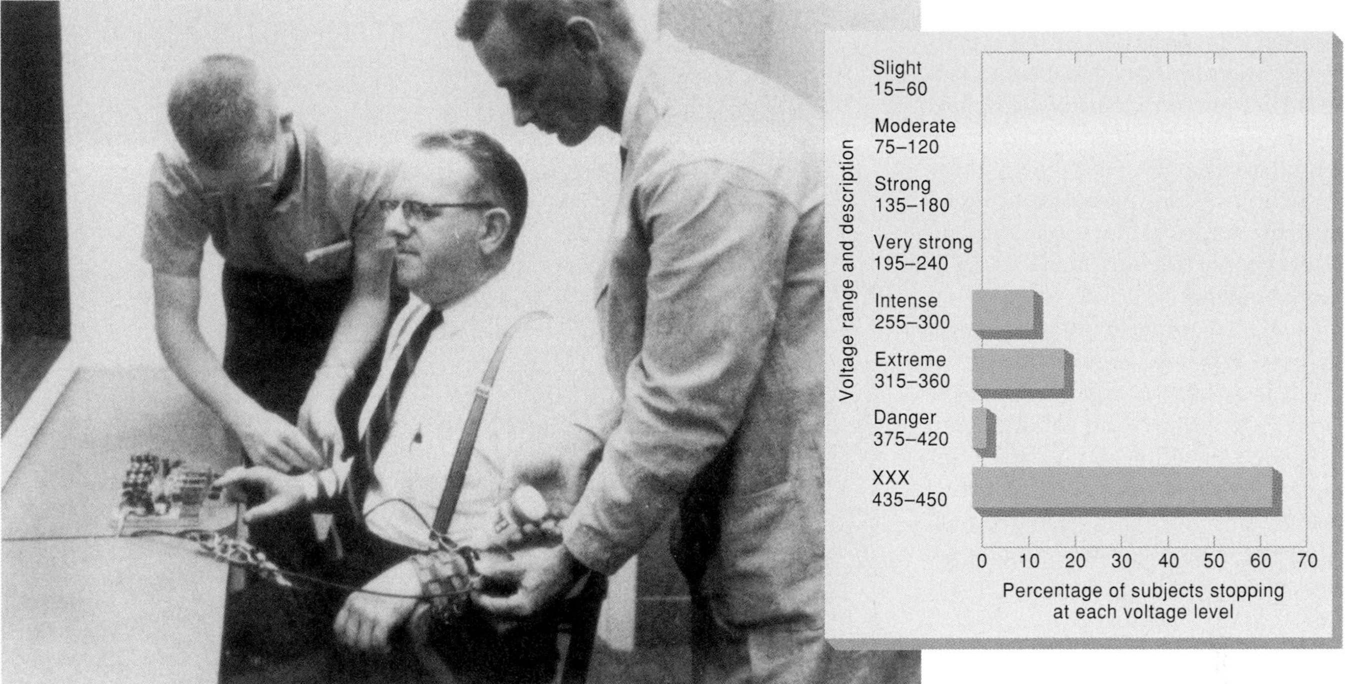

FIGURE 9

Miligram Obedience Study
A 50-year-old man ("learner") is strapped into a chair. The experimenter makes it look as if a shock generator is being connected to his body through several electrodes. The chart at the right shows the percentage of subjects ("teachers") who stopped shocking the experimenter at each voltage level.

made by the "learner." Each time the learner makes a mistake your job is to increase the intensity of the shock by a certain amount.

You are introduced to the "learner," a nice 50-year-old man who mumbles something about having a heart condition. He is strapped to a chair in the next room; he communicates with you through an intercom. As the trials proceed, the "learner" quickly runs into trouble and is unable to give the correct answers. Should you shock him? The apparatus in front of you has thirty switches, ranging from 15 volts (light) to 450 volts (marked as dangerous, "severe shock XXX"). Before this part of the experiment began, you had been given a 75-volt shock to see how it feels. As you raise the intensity of the shock, the "learner" says he's in pain. At 150 volts, he demands to have the experiment stopped. At 180 volts, he cries out that he can't stand it anymore. At 300 volts, he yells about his heart condition and pleads to be released. But if you hesitate in shocking the learner, the experimenter tells you that you have no choice, the experiment must continue.

The experiment just described is a classic one devised by Stanley Milgram (1963, 1965, 1974) to study obedience. As you might imagine, the "teachers" were uneasy about shocking the "learner." At 240 volts, one "teacher" responded, "240 volts delivered; Aw, no. You mean I've got to keep going with that scale? No sir, I'm not going to kill that man—I'm not going to give him 450 volts!" (Milgram, 1965). At the very high voltage, the "learner" quit responding. When the "teacher" asked the experimenter what to do, he simply instructed the "teacher" to continue the experiment and told him that it was his obligation to complete the job. Figure 9 shows the results of the study and what the situation in the Milgram experiment was like. By the way, the 50-year-old man was in league with the experimenter. He was not being shocked at all. Of course, the "teachers" were completely unaware of this.

Forty psychiatrists were asked how they thought individuals would respond to this situation. The psychiatrists predicted that most would go no further than 150 volts, that less than 1 in 25 would go as far as 300 volts, and that only 1 in 1,000 would deliver the full 450 volts. The psychiatrists, it turns out, were way off the mark. The majority of the individuals obeyed the experimenter. In fact, almost two of every three delivered the full 450 volts.

In subsequent studies, Milgram set up a storefront in Bridgeport, Connecticut, and recruited volunteers through newspaper ads. Milgram wanted to create a more natural environment for the experiment and to use a wider cross section of volunteers. In these additional studies, close to two-thirds of the individuals still selected the highest level of shock for the "learner." In variations of the experiment, Milgram discovered some factors that encouraged disobedience: When an opportunity was given to see others disobey, when the authority figure was not perceived to be legitimate and was not close by, and when the victim was made to seem more human.

In 1989, Chinese students led a massive demonstration against the Chinese government in Beijing. The students resisted the government's social influence by putting together resources to challenge the Chinese authorities; however, the government eventually eliminated the protests, massacring hundreds.

We're going to sidetrack for a moment and raise an important point about the Milgram experiments: How *ethical* were they? The volunteers in Milgram's experiment clearly felt anguish and some were very disturbed about "harming" another individual. After the experiment was completed, they were told that the "learner" was not actually shocked. Even though they were debriefed and told that they really had not shocked or harmed anyone, was the anguish imposed on them ethical?

Milgram argues that we have learned a great deal about human nature from the experiments. He claims that they tell us how far individuals will go in their obedience, even if it means being cruel to someone. The volunteers were interviewed later and more than four of every five said that they were glad they had participated in the study; none said they were sorry they participated. When Milgram conducted his studies on obedience, the ethical guidelines for research were not as stringent as they are today. The current ethical guidelines of the American Psychological Association stress that researchers should obtain informed consent from their volunteers. Deception should be used only for very important purposes. Individuals are supposed to feel as good about themselves when the experiment is over as they did when it began. Under today's guidelines, it is unlikely that the Milgram experiment would be conducted.

Resisting Social Influence

"If a man does not keep pace with his companions, perhaps it is because he hears a different drummer. Let him step to the music which he hears, however measured or far away." Thoreau's words suggest that some of us resist social influence. Most of us would prefer to think of ourselves as stepping to our own music, maybe even setting the rhythms for others, rather than trying to keep apace with our companions. However, a certain degree of conformity is required if society is to function at all. As we go through our lives we are both conformists and nonconformists. Sometimes we are overwhelmed by the persuasion and influence of others, in other circumstances we resist and gain personal control over our lives. It is important to remember that our relation to the social world is reciprocal. Individuals may be trying to control us, but we can exert personal control over our actions and influence others in turn (Bandura, 1986).

If you believe someone in a position of authority is making an unjust request or asking you to do something wrong, what choice of action do you have?

- You can comply.
- You also can give the appearance of complying but secretly do otherwise.
- You can publicly dissent by showing doubts and disenchantment but still follow directives.
- You can openly disregard the orders and refuse to comply.
- You can challenge or confront the authority.
- You might get higher authorities to intervene or organize a group of people who agree with you to show the strength of your view.

At this point we have discussed a number of ideas about social perception, attribution, and conformity. A summary of these ideas is presented in concept table 2.

Concept Table 2

Social Perception and Attribution

Concept	Processes/Related Ideas	Characteristics/Description
Social Perception	Developing impressions of others	Our impressions are unified and integrated. An individual's notion of how traits go together is called implicit personality theory. We have social schemas, or prototypes, that we use to evaluate others. We simplify our impressions by categorizing others; in some instances, though, we develop a more individuated approach to impression. First impressions are important and influence impressions at a later point.
	Gaining self-knowledge from our perceptions of others—social comparison	We evaluate ourselves by comparison with others. Festinger stresses that social comparison provides an important source of self-knowledge, especially when no other objective means is available; we are more likely to compare ourselves with similar others.
	Presenting ourselves to others to influence their social perceptions	Two dimensions of presenting ourselves to others to influence their social perceptions are impression management (self-presentation) and self-monitoring. Impression management involves acting in a way to present an image of oneself as a certain sort of person, which might or might not be who one is. Five impression management strategies are ingratiation, self-promotion, intimidation, exemplification, and supplication. Self-monitoring involves individuals' awareness of the impressions they make on others and the degree to which they fine-tune their performance accordingly.
Attribution	The nature of attribution theory	This theory focuses on the motivation to infer causes of behavior in order to make sense of the world. One of the most frequent and important ways we classify the causes of behavior is in terms of internal and external causes.
	The fundamental attribution error and actor-observer differences	Our attributions are not always accurate; the human mind has a built-in bias in making causal judgments. The fundamental attribution error involves overestimating the importance of traits and internal causes while underestimating the importance of situations and external causes. Actors are more likely to choose external causes, observers internal causes.
Conformity	Its nature	Conformity is change in an individual's behavior because of real or imagined pressure. Two experiments demonstrated conformity's power in our lives: Asch's study on judgments of line length and Zimbardo's study on social roles in a mock prison. Many factors influence whether or not we conform.
	Obedience	Obedience is behavior that complies with the explicit demands of an individual in authority. Milgram's classic experiment demonstrated obedience's power. Subjects followed the experimenter's direction, even though they perceived they were hurting someone. Milgram's experiments raise the question of ethics in psychological experimentation.
	Resisting social influence	As we go through our lives, we are both conformists and nonconformists. Sometimes we are overwhelmed by the power of persuasion; at other times, we exert personal control and resist such influence.

Critical Thinking About Behavior

The Media, Music, and Youth

Earlier in the chapter in our discussion of persuasion and attitude change, we indicated that one component of persuasion is the medium used to convey the message. We also suggested that the power of television as a medium can be staggering and commented that music can play a special role in influencing attitudes. Let's explore the roles of media and music in the lives of youth.

Anyone who has been around young people very long knows that many of them spend huge amounts of time listening to music on the radio, playing CDs or tapes, or watching music videos on television. Approximately two-thirds of all records and tapes are purchased by the 10- to 24-year-old age group. And one-third of the nation's 8,200 radio stations aim their broadcast music at this age group.

Are there links between preference for certain types of music and reckless/antisocial behavior? Researchers have found that heavy metal music is more popular among antisocial youth than among the general population (Wass, Miller, & Redditt, 1991). In one study, male fans of heavy metal music were more likely to engage in reckless driving, casual sex, and drug use than male non-fans of heavy metal music (Arnett, 1991). In this same study, female heavy metal fans were more likely to engage in sex without contraception, marijuana use, shoplifting, and vandalism than female non-heavy metal fans. In yet another study, heavy metal music was more popular among youth who used drugs than those who did not (King, 1988).

Can we conclude that heavy metal music causes reckless/antisocial behavior in youth? Think about the nature of the studies. Are they *correlational* in nature? Can we make a cause-and-effect statement based on a correlational study? No we cannot, so we cannot conclude from these studies that the music causes the problem behaviors, only that the music is related to them. That is, young people with particular views may be attracted to particular types of music, such as punk.

One of the frightening claims of heavy metal music's detractors is that the music causes some youth to attempt suicide. In highly publicized cases parents charged that songs by Judas Priest and Ozzy Osborne were responsible for the suicides of their adolescents. However, there are no research data that link depression or suicide to heavy metal or rap music (Ballard & Coates, in press).

Let's turn our attention to television and violence. In one study, the amount of violence watched on television at age 8 was significantly related to the seriousness of criminal acts performed as an adult (Huesmann, 1986). In another study, long-term exposure to television violence was significantly related to the likelihood of aggression in 1,565 12–17-year-old boys (Belson, 1978). Boys who watched the most aggression on television were the most likely to commit a violent crime, swear, be aggressive in sports, threaten violence toward another boy, write slogans on walls, and break windows.

Can we conclude from these studies that television violence causes aggression? No, we cannot because they too are *correlational* in nature. What type of study would it take to conclude that watching television violence causes aggression? We would have to conduct an *experimental* study like the following (Steur, Applefield, & Smith, 1971). Children were randomly assigned to one of two groups: One group watched shows taken directly from violent Saturday morning cartoon offerings on 11 different days; the second group watched cartoon shows with the violence removed. The children then were observed at play. The children who saw the television cartoon violence kicked, choked, and pushed their playmates more than the children who watched the nonviolent television cartoon shows did. Because the children were *randomly assigned* to the two conditions (violent and nonviolent versions of television cartoons), we can conclude that exposure to television violence *caused* the children's violence in this study.

In a review of more than three decades of research on television violence, several conclusions were reached (Comstock & Paik, 1991). First, television violence can affect behavior by influencing people's cognitive scripts. For example, frequent viewing of police violence can shape viewer conceptions of how to respond when first approached by a real police officer. Second, susceptibility to a given message varies considerably, depending on the viewer's interests, needs, and concerns. Third, various message characteristics affect individual interpretations of the televised violence, such as whether the violence is rewarded or punished, whether the violence is presented within the range of social norms, and whether the violence is familiar or useful to the viewer.

Through evaluating the roles of music and television in the lives of youth, you are learning to think critically by examining the evidence necessary to make cause-and-effect statements and examining the validity of conclusions about behavior.

OVERVIEW

We began this chapter by exploring the nature of attitudes and persuasion, attitudes and behavior, and persuasion and attitude change. Then we evaluated social perception and attribution. Our coverage of conformity focused on conformity in a variety of circumstances, factors that contribute to conformity, obedience, and resisting social influence. Remember that you can obtain an overall summary of the chapter by again studying the concept tables on pages 564 and 575.

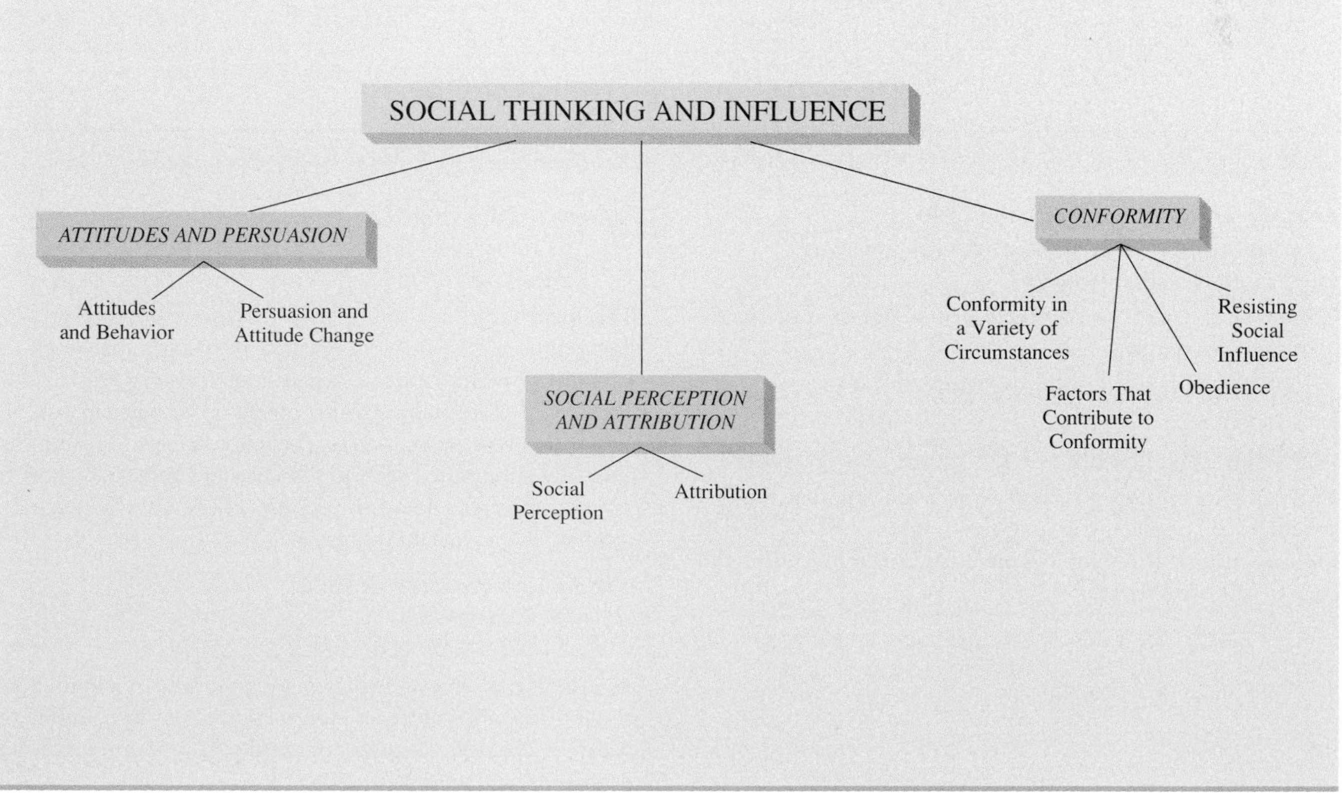

Key Terms

attitudes Positive and negative dispositions to behave in certain ways toward some persons, groups, or objects. p. 556

model of reasoned action A model according to which people act rationally and behavior can be most directly predicted based on intentions. p. 557

cognitive dissonance A concept developed by social psychologist Leon Festinger that refers to an individual's motivation toward consistency and away from inconsistency. p. 557

self-perception theory Bem's theory of attitude-behavior connection; it stresses that individuals make inferences about their attitudes by perceiving their behavior. p. 558

foot-in-the-door strategy A strategy in which an individual presents a weaker point or makes a small request with which listeners will probably comply in the beginning, saving the strongest point until the end. p. 562

door-in-the-face strategy The technique in which a communicator makes the strongest point or demand in the beginning, which listeners will probably reject, then presents a weaker point or moderate, "concessionary" demand toward the end. p. 562

elaboration likelihood model A model according to which there are two ways to persuade—by a central route and by a peripheral route. p. 563

social perception Judgment about the qualities of individuals, which involves how we form impressions of others, how we gain self-knowledge from perception of others, and how we present ourselves to others to influence their perceptions of us. p. 563

implicit personality theory The public's conception of how personality traits go together in an individual. p. 563

prototypes Abstract categorizations of traits that describe a particular personality type. Prototypes act as standards against which we match the individuals we evaluate. p. 565

primacy effect The enduring quality of initial impressions. p. 565

social comparison The process in which individuals evaluate their thoughts, feelings, behaviors, and abilities in relation to other people. p. 566

impression management (self-presentation) Presenting an image of oneself as a certain sort of person, which might or might not be who one really is. p. 566

ingratiation A self-presentation technique that involves illicitly making yourself likable to another person's eyes. p. 566

self-promotion A self-presentation technique in which individuals try to present themselves as competent. p. 566

intimidation A self-presentation technique in which individuals present themselves as dangerous in an effort to coerce others into treating them in a desired way. p. 566

exemplification A self-presentation technique in which individuals try to portray themselves as having integrity and being morally worthy. p. 567

supplication A self-presentation technique in which individuals try to make themselves appear weak and dependent. p. 567

self-monitoring Individuals' attention to the impressions they make on others and the degree to which they fine-tune their performance accordingly. p. 567

attribution theory The theory that individuals are motivated to discover the underlying causes of behavior as part of their interest in making sense out of the behavior. p. 568

fundamental attribution error Observers' tendency to overestimate the importance of traits and underestimate the importance of situations when they seek explanations of an actor's behavior. p. 568

conformity Adopting the attitudes or behavior of others because of real or imagined pressure from others. p. 568

obedience Behavior that complies with the explicit demands of an individual in authority. p. 572

Resources and Readings in Psychology

Attitude Structure and Function (1989)
edited by A. R. Pratkanis and A. G. Greenwald
Hillsdale, NJ: Erlbaum.

A number of experts present their ideas about the importance of attitudes in our lives.

Contact: The First Four Minutes (1972)
by L. Zunin and N. Zunin
New York: Ballantine

This book focuses on first impressions, arguing that the first 4 minutes are crucial to our long-term impressions of others. It includes information about nonverbal communication and how to cope with rejection.

Influence (1993, rev. ed.)
by Robert Cialdini
New York: Quill

This highly acclaimed book by a well-known social psychologist explores how influence works in today's marketplace. Cialdini provides valuable suggestions for persuading other people and understanding how others try to persuade us. He also covers how power works, the role of reciprocity in influence, the importance of commitment and consistency, how to say no, scarcity, relationships with others, advertising, sales techniques, and instant influence.

The Social Animal (1995, 7th ed.)
by E. Aronson
New York: W. H. Freeman

This book is an enjoyable presentation of research and thinking about many different topics in social psychology by a leading researcher. Aronson discusses conformity, mass communication, persuasion, and self-justification.

CHAPTER

SOR

Social Relations, Group Behavior, and Sociocultural Diversity

PAUL GAUGUIN
The Market, detail

C H A P T E R

SOR

Social Relations, Group Behavior, and Sociocultural Diversity

Chapter Outline

Chapter Boxes

Man is a knot, a web, a mesh into which relationships are tied.

—Saint Exupéry

Love is a canvas furnished by nature and embroidered by imagination.

—Voltaire

Images of Psychology

Looking for Love

Phil is a lovesick man. On two consecutive days he put expensive ads in New York City newspapers, urging, begging, pleading a woman named Edith to forgive him and continue their relationship. The first ad read as follows:

> **Edith**
> I was torn two ways.
> Too full of child
> to relinquish the lesser.
> Older now,
> a balance struck,
> that a child forever behind me.
> Please forgive me,
> reconsider.
> Help make a new us;
> better now than before.
> **Phil**

This ad was placed in the *New York Post* at a cost of $3,600. Another full-page ad appeared in the *New York Times* at a cost of $3,408. Phil's ads stirred up quite a bit of interest. Forty-two Ediths responded; Phil said he thought the whole process would be more private. As Phil would attest, relationships are very important to us. Some of us will go to almost any length and spend large sums of money to restore lost relationships (Worschel & Cooper, 1979).

Sherry is not searching for a particular man. She is at the point where she is, well, looking for Mr. Anybody. Sherry is actually more particular than she says, although she is frustrated by what she calls the great man shortage in this country. According to the 1980 United States Census, for every 100 men over 15 years of age who have never been married or are widowed or divorced, there are 123 women; for African Americans the ratio is 100 men for every 133 women.

William Novak (1983), author of *The Great Man Shortage,* believes it is the quality of the gap that bothers most women. He says the quality problem stems from the fact that in the last two decades, the combination of the feminist movement and women's tendency to seek therapy when their personal relationships do not work out has made women outgrow men emotionally. He points out that many women are saying to men, "You don't have to earn all the money anymore, and I don't want to have to do all the emotional work." Novak observes that the whole issue depresses many women because society has conditioned them to assume that their lack of a marriage partner is their fault. One 37-year-old woman told Novak, "I'm no longer waiting for a man on a white horse. Now I'd settle for the horse."

Preview

Our close relationships bring us warm and cherished moments. They also can bring us moments we would rather forget, moments that are stressful. Our relationships involve attraction and love. Some of our relationships also occur in groups. For example, we have relationships with other ethnic groups and nations. These relationships require an understanding of how conflict comes about, how it can be reduced, and sociocultural diversity. These are the themes of this chapter, themes that involve social relations, group behavior, and sociocultural diversity.

Attraction

What attracts us to others and motivates us to spend more time with them? Does just being around someone increase the likelihood a relationship will develop? Do birds of a feather flock together; that is, are we likely to associate with those who are similar to us? How important are the attractiveness and personality characteristics of another person?

Proximity and Similarity

Physical proximity does not guarantee that we will develop a positive relationship with another person. Familiarity can breed contempt, but familiarity is a condition that is necessary for a close relationship to develop. For the most part, friends and lovers have been around each other for a long time; they may have grown up together, gone to high school or college together, worked together, or gone to the same social events. Once we have been exposed to someone for a period of time, what is it that makes the relationship breed friendship and even love?

Birds of a feather do indeed flock together. One of the most powerful lessons generated by the study of close relationships is that we like to associate with people who are similar to us. Our friends, as well as our lovers, are much more like us than unlike us. We have similar attitudes, behavior, and characteristics, as well as clothes, intelligence, personality, other friends, values, lifestyle, physical attractiveness, and so on. In some limited cases and on some isolated characteristics, opposites may attract. An introvert may wish to be with an extravert, or someone with little money may wish to associate with someone who has a lot of money, for example. But overall we are attracted to individuals with similar rather than opposite characteristics. In one study, for example, the old adage "Misery loves company" was supported as depressed college students preferred to meet unhappy others while nondepressed college students preferred to meet happy others (Wenzlaff & Prohaska, 1989). The fact that individuals are attracted to each other on the basis of similar characteristics and attitudes is reflected in the questions that computer dating services ask their clients (see table 1).

Consensual validation *provides an explanation of why people are attracted to others who are similar to them. Our own attitudes and behavior are supported when someone else's attitudes and behavior are similar to ours—their attitudes and behavior validate ours.* People tend to shy away from the unknown. We may tend, instead, to prefer people whose attitudes and behavior we can predict. And similarity

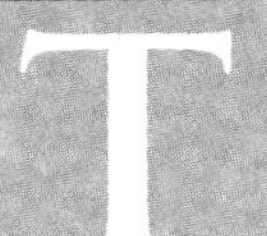

ABLE 1

Computer Dating Questionnaire

Computer dating is based almost entirely on the idea that people with similar interests and attitudes are compatible. In applying for a date, the person completes a questionnaire, such as the one below, and is then matched with a person of the opposite sex who has similar interests and attitudes.

Key A—Yes definitely! B—Yes C—Maybe D—No E—No definitely!

1. Do you sometimes look down at others?	A	B	C	D	E
2. Do you enjoy being the center of attention in group activities?	A	B	C	D	E
3. Do you think it proper for unmarried couples to go on a trip by themselves?	A	B	C	D	E
4. Do you think you would be content married to an unaffectionate mate?	A	B	C	D	E
5. Do you believe that our schools should teach evolution?	A	B	C	D	E
6. Do you find yourself getting angry easily or often?	A	B	C	D	E
7. Do you usually prefer being with groups of people to being alone?	A	B	C	D	E
8. Do you think that a theft is ever justifiable?	A	B	C	D	E
9. Do you think that sex is over-exploited in advertising?	A	B	C	D	E
10. Do you believe some religious instruction is necessary for all children?	A	B	C	D	E
11. Do you feel that your life as a child was enjoyable?	A	B	C	D	E
12. Do you ever go out of your way to avoid someone?	A	B	C	D	E
13. Do you think it proper for a schoolteacher to smoke or drink in public?	A	B	C	D	E
14. Do you think college campuses are too sexually liberated?	A	B	C	D	E
15. Do you believe you could permit your child to choose a different religion?	A	B	C	D	E

These are sample items from a dating questionnaire developed by a computer dating firm that matches up people who are interested in meeting someone they think they would like to date. The computer dating firm would take your responses to the items and try to match you with someone with similar characteristics and interests.

implies that we will enjoy doing things with the other person, which often requires a partner who likes the same things and has similar attitudes. In one recent study, self-verifying evaluations were especially important in marriage (Swann, De La Ronde, & Hixon, 1994).

One outcome of a desire for self-knowledge is that people tend to choose interaction partners who see them as they see themselves. In a series of studies, people used two general strategies to verify their views of themselves: (1) They created environments that confirmed their views of themselves, primarily by choosing appropriate interaction partners, and (2) they interpreted and remembered their interactions as confirming their views of themselves (Swann, 1987; Swan, Stein-Seroussi, & Giesler, 1992). The inclination to choose interaction partners who confirm one's view of oneself is likely rooted in a desire to predict and control interactions with others.

Physical Attraction

From the long list of characteristics on which partners in close relationships can be similar, one deserves special mention: physical attractiveness. How important is physical attractiveness in determining whether we like or love someone? In one experiment, college students assumed that a computer had determined their date on the basis of similar interests, but actually the dates were randomly assigned (Walster & others, 1966). The college students' social skills, physical appearance, intelligence, and personality were measured. Then a dance was set up for the matched partners. At intermission, the partners were asked in private to indicate the most positive aspects of their date that contributed to his or her attractiveness. The overwhelming reason was looks, not other factors such as personality or intelligence. Other research has documented the importance of physical attraction in close relationships; it has been associated with the number of dates female college students have in a year, how popular someone is with peers, attention given to an infant, positive encounters with teachers, and selection of a marital partner (Simpson, Campbell, & Berscheid, 1986).

Why do we want to be associated with attractive individuals? Again, as with similarity, it is rewarding to be around physically attractive people. It provides us with consensual validation that we too are attractive. As part of the rewarding experience, our self-image is enhanced. It also is aesthetically pleasing to look at physically attractive individuals. We assume that if individuals are physically attractive they will have other desirable traits that will interest us.

But we all can't have Cindy Crawford or Tom Cruise as our friend or lover. How do we deal with this in our relationships? While beautiful women and handsome men seem to have an advantage, in the end we usually seek out someone at our own level of attractiveness. Most of us come away with a reasonably good chance of finding a "good match." Research indicates that this **matching hypothesis**—*that while we may prefer a more attractive person in the abstract, in the real world we end up choosing someone who is close to our own level of attractiveness*—holds up (Kalick & Hamilton, 1986).

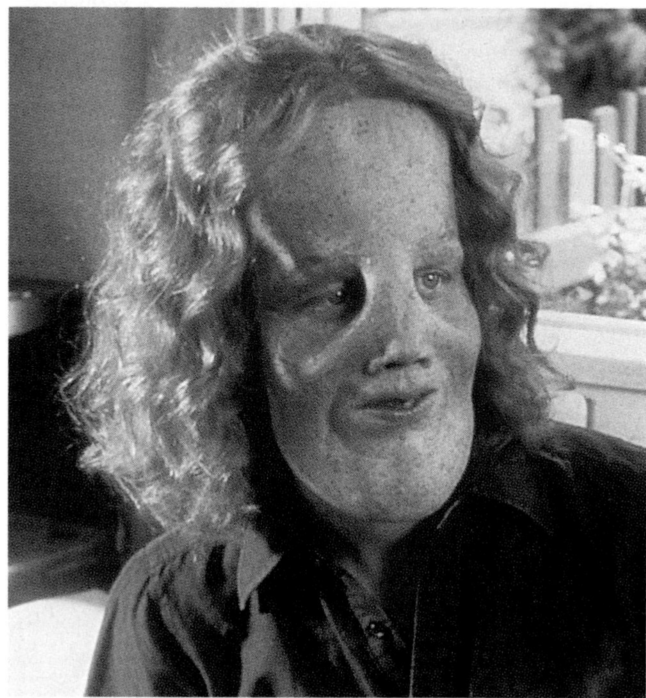

Eric Stoltz's portrayal of Rocky Dennis in the movie Mask. *Rocky was unloved and unwanted as a young child because of his grotesque features. As his mother and peers got to know him, they became much more attracted to him.*

Heterosexual men and women differ on the importance they place on good looks when they seek an intimate partner. Women tend to rate traits such as considerateness, honesty, dependability, kindness, and understanding as most important; men list good looks, cooking skills, and frugality first (Buss & Barnes, 1986).

Several additional points help to clarify the role of physical beauty and attraction in our close relationships. Much of the research has focused on initial or short-term encounters; attraction over the course of months and years often is not evaluated. As relationships endure, physical attraction probably assumes less importance. Rocky Dennis, as portrayed in the movie *Mask,* is a case in point. His peers and even his mother initially wanted to avoid Rocky, whose face was severely distorted. But over the course of his childhood and adolescent years, the avoidance turned into attraction and love as people got to know him.

Our criteria for beauty may vary from one culture to another and from one point in history to another, so, although attempts are being made to quantify beauty and to arrive at the ultimate criteria for such things as a beautiful female face, beauty is relative (Lamb & others, 1993). In the 1940s and 1950s in the United States, a Marilyn Monroe body build (a well-rounded, shapely appearance) and face was the cultural ideal for women. In the 1970s, some women aspired to look like Twiggy and other virtually anorexic females. In the 1990s, the desire for thinness has not ended, but what is culturally beautiful is no longer pleasingly plump or anorexic but, rather, a tall stature with moderate curves. The current image of attractiveness also includes the toning of one's body through physical exercise and healthy eating habits.

Exotic definitions of beauty not withstanding, some psychologists believe that certain aspects of attractiveness are consistent across cultures (Cunningham & others, 1995). One classic, early study found that health, feminine plumpness, and cleanliness were the criteria for attractiveness across a wide range of cultures (Ford & Beach, 1951). Evolutionary psychologists are not surprised by such findings—they argue that men are attracted to healthy women because their genes are more likely to lead to successful reproduction (Buss, 1995). In another investigation, men were most attracted to women with waists that were approximately one-third smaller than their hips, which, say evolutionary psychologists, suggests youthful fertility (Singh, 1993). Indeed, the more youthful the woman's appearance, the more attractive she was rated in 37 different cultures (Buss, 1989). By contrast, women rate men as more attractive if they are mature and dominant, which, according to evolutionary psychologists, signals an ability to support and protect (Buss, 1995). In a recent national study of gender differences in mate preference in the United States, men were attracted to women on the basis of physical attractiveness and youthfulness, while women were attracted to men on the basis of their earning potential (Sprecher, Sullivan, & Hatfield, 1994).

Personality Characteristics

When you think of what attracts you to someone else, certain personality characteristics probably come to mind. Wouldn't you rather be around someone who is sincere, honest, understanding, loyal, truthful, trustworthy, intelligent, and dependable than someone who is phony, mean, obnoxious, insulting, greedy, conceited, rude, and thoughtless? In one investigation, these and other personality traits were among those we like and do not like, respectively (Anderson, 1968) (see table 2).

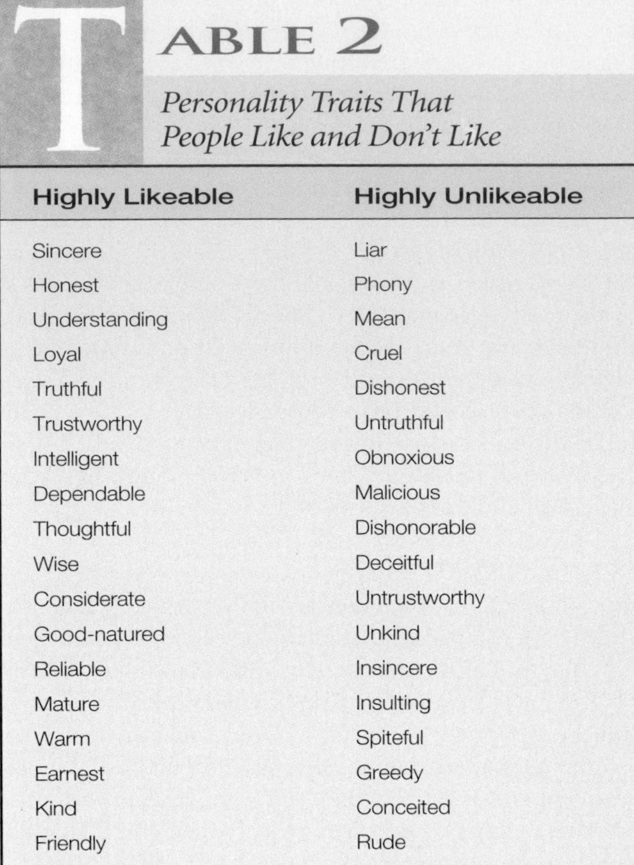

TABLE 2

Personality Traits That People Like and Don't Like

Highly Likeable	Highly Unlikeable
Sincere	Liar
Honest	Phony
Understanding	Mean
Loyal	Cruel
Truthful	Dishonest
Trustworthy	Untruthful
Intelligent	Obnoxious
Dependable	Malicious
Thoughtful	Dishonorable
Wise	Deceitful
Considerate	Untrustworthy
Good-natured	Unkind
Reliable	Insincere
Mature	Insulting
Warm	Spiteful
Earnest	Greedy
Kind	Conceited
Friendly	Rude
Kind-hearted	Thoughtless
Happy	Insolent

From N. H. Anderson, "Likeableness Ratings of 55 Personality Trait Words" in *Journal of Personality and Social Psychology,* 9:272–279. Copyright ©1968 by the American Psychological Association. Reprinted with permission.

The Faces of Love

A question that has intrigued philosophers, poets, and songwriters for centuries is, What is love? Is it lustful and passionate, or should we be more cautious in our pursuit of love, as a Czech proverb advises, "Do not choose your wife at a dance, but in the fields among the harvesters." Love refers to a vast and complex territory of human behavior. How can we classify and study such a phenomenon? A common classification is to describe four forms of love: altruism, friendship, romantic (or passionate) love, and affectionate (or companionate) love (Berscheid, 1988).

Altruism

Altruism *is an unselfish interest in helping someone else.* We often hear or read about acts of generosity and courage, such as rock concerts and fund raisers to help AIDS victims, the taxi driver who risks his life to save a woman in a dark alley, and volunteers who pull a baby from an abandoned well. You may have placed some of your hard-earned cash in the palm of a homeless person or perhaps cared for a wounded cat. How do psychologists account for such acts of human altruism?

The Biological Basis of Altruism

Evolutionary psychologists emphasize that some types of altruism help to perpetuate our genes (Buss, 1995). An act in the biological realm is altruistic if it increases another's prospects for survival and having the opportunity to reproduce.

Evolutionary psychologists believe that tremendous benefits can accrue to individuals who form cooperative reciprocal relationships (Trivers, 1971). By being good to someone now, individuals increase the likelihood that they

Examples of altruism: (a) Shown here is an example of animal altruism—a baboon plucking bugs from another baboon. Most acts of animal altruism involve kin. (b) A young woman assists a handicapped child.

will receive a benefit from the other person in the future. Through this reciprocal process, both gain something beyond what they could have by acting alone.

Evolutionary psychologists also stress that those who carry our genes—our children—have a special place in the domain of altruism. Natural selection favors parents who care for their children and improve their probability of surviving. A parent feeding its young is performing a biological altruistic act because the young's chance of survival is increased. So is a mother bird who performs a distraction ritual to lure predators away from the eggs in her nest. She is willing to sacrifice herself so that three or four of her young offspring will have the chance to survive, thus preserving her genes. Individuals also often show more empathy toward other relatives in relation to their genetic closeness. In the case of a natural disaster, people's uppermost concern is their family (Cunningham, 1986). In one recent study involving a hypothetical decision to help in life-or-death situations, college students chose to aid close kin over distant kin, the young over the old, the healthy over the sick, the wealthy over the poor, and the premenopausal woman over the postmenopausal woman (Burnstein, Crandall, & Kitayama, 1994). In this same study, when an everyday favor rather than a life-or-death situation was involved, the college students gave less weight to kinship and chose to help either the very young or the very old over those of intermediate age, the sick over the healthy, and the poor over the wealthy.

"All I'm saying is, giving a little something to the arts might help our image."

Psychological and Environmental Influences

Examples of human altruism are plentiful—a hardworking laborer who places a $5 bill in a Salvation Army kettle, rock concerts and fund-raisers to help AIDS victims, a taxi driver who risks his life to save a woman from being molested in a dark alley, a child who takes in a wounded cat and cares for it, volunteers who pull a baby from an abandoned well. How do psychologists account for such acts of human altruism?

Reciprocity and exchange are important aspects of altruism. Reciprocity, which encourages us to do unto others as we would have them do unto us, is present in every widely practiced religion in the world—Judaism, Christianity, Buddhism, and Islam, for example. Certain human sentiments are involved in reciprocity: Trust is probably the most important principle over the long run, guilt occurs if we do not reciprocate, and anger results if someone else does not reciprocate. Many examples of altruism that are reciprocal involve social exchanges. **Social exchange theory** *states that individuals should benefit those who benefit them, or that for a benefit received, an equivalent benefit should be returned at a certain point.* We exchange gifts, cards, and tips for competent service, for example. It sounds cold and calculating to describe altruism in terms of costs and benefits, but that is exactly what social exchange theory does.

Not all altruism is motivated by reciprocity and social exchange, but this view alerts us to the importance of considering interactions between oneself and others to understand altruism. And not all seemingly altruistic behavior is unselfish. Some psychologists even argue that true altruism has never been demonstrated, while others argue that a distinction between altruism and egoism is possible (Cialdini & others, 1987). **Egoism** *involves giving to another person to ensure reciprocity; to gain self-esteem; to present oneself as powerful, competent, or caring; or to avoid social and self-censure for failing to live up to normative expectations.* By contrast, altruism occurs when someone gives to another person with the ultimate goal of benefiting that other person. Any benefits that come to the giver are unintended.

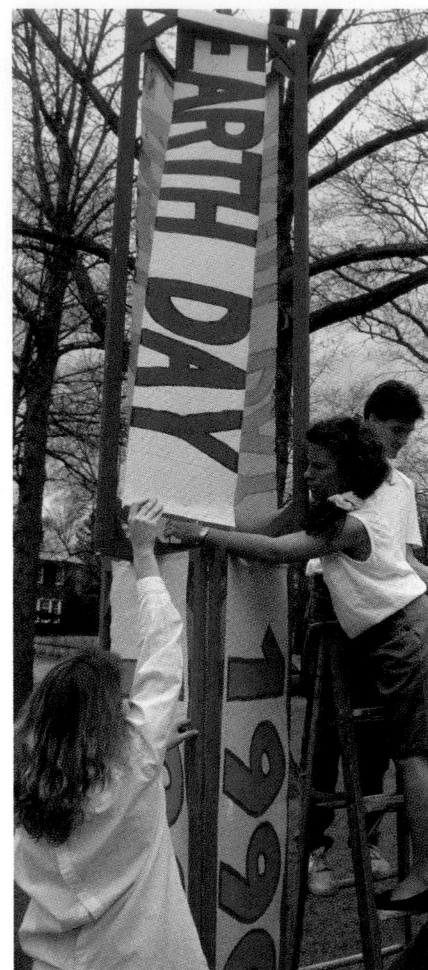

How strongly are today's college students interested in self-fulfillment versus helping others?

Describing individuals as having altruistic or egoistic motives implies that person variables are important in understanding altruistic behavior. Altruistic behavior is determined by both person and situational variables. A person's ability to empathize with the needy or to feel a sense of responsibility for another's welfare affects altruistic motivations. The stronger these personality dispositions, the less we would expect situational variables to influence whether giving, kindness, or helping occur.

But as with any human behavior, characteristics of the situation influence the strength of altruistic motivation. Some of these characteristics include the degree of need shown by the other individual, the needy person's responsibility for his plight, the cost of assisting the needy person, and the extent to which reciprocity is expected.

One of the most widely studied aspects of altruism is bystander intervention. Why does one person help a stranger in distress while another won't lift a finger? It often depends on the circumstances. More than 20 years ago a young woman named Kitty Genovese cried out repeatedly as she was brutally murdered. She was attacked at about 3 A.M. in a respectable area of New York City. The murderer left and returned three times; he finally put an end to Kitty's life as she crawled to her apartment door and screamed for help. It took the slayer about 30 minutes to kill Kitty. Thirty-eight neighbors watched the gory scene and heard Kitty Genovese's screams. No one helped or even called the police.

The **bystander effect** *is that individuals who observe an emergency help less when someone else is present than when they are alone.* The bystander effect helps to explain the apparent cold-blooded indifference to Kitty Genovese's murder. Social psychologists John Darley and Bibb Latané (1968) documented the bystander effect in a number of criminal and medical emergencies. Most of the bystander intervention studies show that when alone, a person will help 75 percent of the time, but when another bystander is present, the figure drops to 50 percent. Apparently the difference is due to the diffusion of responsibility among witnesses and our tendency to look to the behavior of others for clues about what to do. People may think that someone else will call the police or that since no one is helping, possibly the person does not need help.

Many other aspects of the situation influence whether the individual will intervene and come to the aid of the person in distress. Bystander intervention is less likely to occur in the following situations (Shotland, 1985): a situation is not clear; the individuals struggling or fighting are married or related; a victim is perceived to be intoxicated; the person is thought to be from a different ethnic group; the intervention might lead to personal harm, or retaliation by the criminal. Also, helping requires considerable time, such as days in court testifying. When bystanders have no prior history of victimization themselves, have seen few crimes and intervention efforts, or have not had training in first aid, rescue, or police tactics, intervention is less likely to occur.

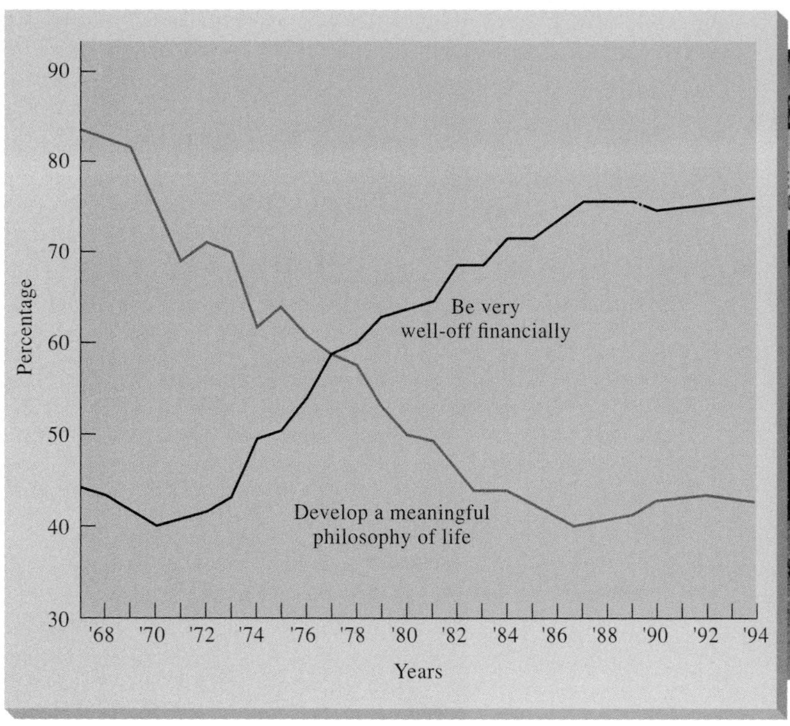

FIGURE 1

Changing Freshman Life Goals, 1968–1994
The percentages indicated are in response to the question of identifying a life goal as "essential" or "very important." There has been a significant reversal in freshman life goals in the last two decades, with a far greater percentage of today's college freshmen stating that a "very important" life goal is to be well-off financially, and far fewer stating that developing a meaningful philosophy of life is a "very important" life goal.

How altruistic are college students? Are they less altruistic than several decades ago? Over the past two decades, college students have shown an increased concern for personal well-being and a decreased concern for the well-being of others, especially the disadvantaged (Astin, Korn, & Berz, 1995). As shown in figure 1, today's college freshmen are more strongly motivated to be well-off financially and less motivated to develop a meaningful philosophy of life than were their counterparts of 20 years ago.

However, there are some signs that today's college students are shifting toward a stronger interest in the welfare of our society. For example, between 1986 and 1995, there was a small increase in the percentage of college freshman who said they were strongly interested in participating in community action programs (28 percent in 1994 compared to 18 percent in 1986) and helping promote racial understanding (40 percent in 1994 compared to 27 percent in 1986) (Astin, Korn, & Berz, 1995). Whether these small increments in concern for community and society will continue to increase in the remainder of the 1990s is difficult to predict. For successful adjustment in adult life, it is important to seek self-fulfillment *and* have a strong commitment to others.

Helping others improves our ability to get along with others in the world. As we see next, liking others and they us in the close relationship of friendship is an important aspect of our adjustment.

Friendship

True friendship is hard to come by. As the American historian Henry Adams succinctly put it, "One friend in life is much, two are many, and three hardly possible." **Friendship** *is a form of close relationship that involves enjoyment (we like to spend time with our friends), acceptance (we take our friends as they are without trying to change them), trust (we assume our friends will act in our best interest), respect (we think our friends make good judgments), mutual assistance (we help and support our friends and they us), openness (we share experiences and deeply personal matters with a friend), understanding (we feel that a friend knows us well and understands what we like), and spontaneity (we feel free to be ourselves around a friend).* In one study of more than 40,000 individuals, many of these characteristics were considered qualities of a best friend (Parlee, 1979).

How is friendship different from love? The difference can be seen by looking at the scales of liking and

Love scale
1. I feel that I can confide in ________ about virtually everything.
2. If I could never be with ________, I would feel miserable.
3. One of my primary concerns is ________'s welfare.

Liking scale
1. I would highly recommend ________ for a responsible job.
2. Most people would react favorably to ________ after a brief acquaintance.
3. ________ is the sort of person whom I myself would like to be.

Note: Subjects are asked to fill out the questionnaire in terms of their feelings for their boyfriend or girlfriend, and in terms of their feelings for a platonic friend of the opposite sex.

FIGURE 2

Sample Items from Rubin's Loving and Liking Scales

loving developed by Zick Rubin (1970) (see figure 2). Rubin says that liking involves our sense that someone else is similar to us; it includes a positive evaluation of the individual. Loving, he believes, involves being close to someone; it includes dependency, a more selfless orientation toward the individual, and qualities of absorption and exclusiveness.

Friends and lovers are also similar in some ways. Keith Davis (1985) has found that friends and romantic partners share the characteristics of acceptance, trust, respect, confiding, understanding, spontaneity, mutual assistance, and happiness. However, he found that relationships with spouses or lovers are also more likely to involve fascination and exclusiveness. Relationships with friends were perceived as more stable, especially more than those among unmarried lovers.

Are the friendships of women and men different? Females in general disclose significantly more intimate information about themselves to same-sex friends than males do (Sherrod, 1989). And when a close friendship lacks intimate self-disclosure, women are more disappointed about the low level than men are. However, several personality and situational variations need to be considered in the intimate self-disclosure of males and females. Androgynous males report that they disclose as much to their best male friend as traditional or androgynous women disclose to a best friend, and much more than traditional men do (Lavine & Lombardo, 1984). Also, in a laboratory situation, males revealed more intimate information about themselves to a female stranger than females disclosed to a male stranger, although first encounters between two men were less disclosing overall than those between two women (Derlega & others, 1985). Despite such personality and situational exceptions, we can conclude that in general females self-disclose intimate information in friendship relations more than males do (Berndt, 1996). Also, although it has been proposed that males treat friendships in terms of respect, and females in terms of affection (Tannen, 1990), tests of this difference have not always held up (Gaines, 1994).

Romantic or Passionate Love

Romantic love *is also called passionate love or eros; it has strong components of sexuality and infatuation, and it often predominates in the early part of a love relationship.* Poets, playwrights, and musicians through the ages have lauded the fiery passion of romantic love—and lamented the searing pain when it fails. Think for a moment about songs and books that hit the top of the charts. Chances are they're about love. Well-known love researcher Ellen Berscheid (1988) says that it is romantic love we mean when we say that we are "in love" with someone. It is romantic love she believes we need to understand if we are to learn what love is all about. To assess your experience with romantic or passionate love, turn to table 3.

Romantic love is the main reason we get married. In 1967, a well-known study showed that men maintained that they would not get married if they were not "in love." Women either were undecided or said that they would get married even if they did not love their prospective husband (Kephart, 1967). In the 1980s, women and men tended to agree that they would not get married unless they were "in love." And more than half of today's men and women said that not being "in love" is sufficient reason to dissolve a marriage (Berscheid, Snyder, & Omoto, 1989).

Romantic love is especially important among college students. One study of unattached college men and women found that more than half identified a romantic partner as their closest relationship rather than naming a parent, sibling, or friend (Berscheid, Snyder, & Omoto, 1989). We are referring to romantic love when we say, "I am *in love*," not just "I *love*."

Romantic love includes a complex intermingling of different emotions—fear, anger, sexual desire, joy, and jealousy, for example. Obviously, some of these emotions are a source of anguish. In one study, romantic loves were more likely to be the cause of depression than friends were (Berscheid & Fei, 1977).

Although Berscheid admits this is an inadequate answer, she concluded that romantic love is about 90 percent sexual desire. Berscheid (1988) believes sexual desire is vastly neglected in the study of romantic love. As she puts it, "To discuss romantic love without also prominently mentioning the role sexual arousal and desire plays in it is very much like printing a recipe for tiger soup that leaves out the main ingredient."

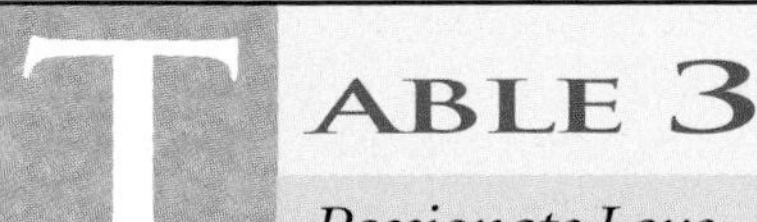

TABLE 3

Passionate Love

The items below ask you what it's like when you are passionately in love. Please think of the person you love most passionately *right now.* If you are not in love right now, please think of the person you loved passionately. If you have never been in love, think of the person you came closest to caring for in that way. Keep this person in mind as you complete the items. (The person you choose should be of the opposite sex if you are heterosexual or of the same sex if you are homosexual.) Try to tell how you felt at the time your feelings were the most intense. Select a number from 1–9 that best reflects your feelings for each item (1 = not true at all; 5 = moderately true; and 9 = definitely true).

1. I would feel deep despair if ___________ left me.
2. Sometimes I feel I can't control my thoughts; they are obsessively on ___________.
3. I feel happy when I am doing something to make ___________ happy.
4. I would rather be with ___________ than anyone else.
5. I'd get jealous if I thought ___________ was falling in love with someone else.
6. I yearn to know all about ___________ .
7. I want ___________—physically, emotionally, mentally.
8. I have an endless appetite for affection from ___________ .
9. For me, ___________ is the perfect romantic partner.
10. I sense my body responding when ___________ touches me.
11. ___________ always seems to be on my mind.
12. I want ___________ to know me—my thoughts, my fears, my hopes.
13. I eagerly look for signs indicating ___________'s desire for me.
14. I possess a powerful attraction for ___________ .
15. I get extremely depressed when things don't go right in my relationship with ___________ .

Total your responses for the 15 items on the passionate love scale. If your score is 15–45, your passionate love experience has not been a very passionate one; if your score is 60–90, it has been a moderately passionate one; and if your score is 105–135, your passionate love experience has been a very intense one.

Affectionate or Companionate Love

Love is more than just passion. **Affectionate love** *also called companionate love, is the type of love that occurs when individuals desire to have each other near and have a deep, caring affection for each other.*

There is a growing belief that the early stages of love have more romantic ingredients, but as love matures, passion tends to give way to affection. Phillip Shaver (1986, 1993) describes the initial phase of romantic love as a time that is fueled by a mixture of sexual attraction and gratification, a reduced sense of loneliness, uncertainty about the security of developing another attachment, and excitement from exploring the novelty of another human being. With time, he says, sexual attraction wanes, attachment anxieties either lessen or produce conflict and withdrawal, novelty is replaced with familiarity, and lovers either find themselves securely attached in a deeply caring relationship or distressed—feeling bored, disappointed, lonely, or hostile, for example. In the latter case, one or both partners may eventually seek another close relationship.

When two lovers go beyond their preoccupation with novelty, unpredictability, and the urgency of sexual attraction, they are more likely to detect deficiencies in each other's caring (Vannoy-Hiller & Philliber, 1989). This may be the point in a relationship when women, who often are better caregivers than men, sense that the relationship has problems. Wives are almost twice as likely as husbands to initiate a divorce, for example (National Center for Health Statitics, 1989).

So far we have discussed two forms of love: romantic (or passionate) and affectionate (or companionate). Robert J. Sternberg (1988, 1993) believes that affectionate love actually consists of two components: intimacy and commitment. The **triangular theory of love** *is Sternberg's theory that love has three main forms: passion, intimacy, and commitment.* Passion, as described earlier, is physical and sexual attraction to a lover. Intimacy is the emotional feelings of warmth, closeness, and sharing in a relationship. Commitment is our cognitive appraisal of the relationship and our intent to mantain the relationship even in the face of problems. If passion is the only ingredient

Explorations in Psychology 1

Ten Rules of Love

Sternberg (1988) spells out ten rules that people who seek a satisfying love relationship should find helpful:

1. *Successful partners do not take their relationship for granted.* The seeds of a relationship's destruction are planted when partners take one another for granted. When we are dating, we often make a special effort to impress each other by paying attention to the way we look, act, and set priorities. In dating, we are usually aware of the possibility of losing each other, so we put forth an extra effort to keep the relationship stimulating. Dating is like an agreement written in paper and pencil, whereas marriage is like an agreement etched in stone, says Sternberg, but stone is not indestructible and, under certain conditions, crumbles.
2. *Successful partners make their relationship a priority.* In dating, we often put the relationship first because we want something—the love and possibly the marital commitment of the other individual. As time passes, the press of careers, family, and other matters tempt us to give less attention to the relationship. The relationship can share first place with other priorities, but, once it drops below them, its life is jeopardized.
3. *Successful partners actively seek to meet each other's needs.* Active, self-initiated meeting of your partner's needs shows you care and understand your partner. Don't wait for your partner to request something; anticipate his or her wants and desires. Do whatever it is that satisfies your partner's needs before you are asked, and the value of what you do will be much greater.
4. *Successful partners know when, and when not, to change in response to the other.* Successful partners in a love relationship are flexible and adaptive, willing to change to satisfy a partner's needs. Only by being flexible can partners meet the challenge to grow that each change in the nature of the relationship demands. Successful partners not only know when to give in as the situation demands, but also when not to give in. They are aware of what they can be and what they cannot be; they do not strive to meet requests they know are impossible or compromise in being true to themselves.
5. *Successful partners value themselves.* Abraham Maslow distinguished between deficiency love and being love. In deficiency love, you seek out another individual to attain something you lack in yourself; in being love, you seek out another individual to enhance an already competent self. Most loves are probably a combination of deficiency and being loves, a blend that varies over time. If you seek self-worth in another individual that you cannot find in yourself, you probably will be disappointed.
6. *Successful partners love each other, not their idealization of each other.* It is much easier to fall in love with an ideal person than a real person. An ideal person is flawless, does not make unreasonable demands, has all

(with intimacy and commitment low or absent), *infatuation* occurs. This might happen in an affair or a fling in which there is little intimacy and even less commitment. A relationship marked by intimacy and commitment but low or lacking in passion is called *affectionate love,* a pattern often found among couples who have been married for many years. If passion and commitment are present but intimacy is not, Sternberg calls the relationship *fatuous love,* as when one person worships another from a distance. Couples must share all three components—passion, intimacy, and commitment—to experience the strongest, fullest type of love. Sternberg calls this *consummate love* (see figure 3). Based on his observations of love, Sternberg (1988) described a number of rules for a successful loving relationship. To read about these rules, turn to Explorations in Psychology 1.

Relationship Cognition

Researchers are increasingly interested in the role that cognition plays in understanding close relationships (Berscheid, 1994; Fletcher & Fitness, 1995). One area that has been fruitful in improving our knowledge of close relationships is attribution—our motivation to seek the causes of behavior (Finchum & Bradbury, 1992). A number of investigators have found that the attributions spouses make for marital events are related to their marital satisfaction (Karney & others, 1994). Specifically, distressed spouses are more likely than nondistressed spouses to attribute marital problems and negative partner behaviors to stable and global characteristics of the partner and to view the partner as behaving intentionally, in a blameworthy manner, and with selfish motivations. For example, a happily married, nondistressed spouse might attribute a sharp-tongued remark to a temporary circumstance ("Maybe he had a bad day at work"), whereas an unhappily married, distressed spouse might attribute the same caustic remark to a global trait of the partner ("Why did I marry such a loser").

Relationship memories are another aspect of relationship cognition that is currently being studied (Jussim, 1991). The accuracy of relationship memories may depend on who is doing the remembering. In one investigation, the characteristics we want in a true love, does not talk back. The problem with an ideal love is that such a person exists only in one's mind. You can be in love with an idealized person rather than a real person, and the relationship can go on for some time; you tend to see only what you want to see and ignore or make excuses about your lover's flaws. Sooner or later, though, the bubble bursts as you eventually get to know your partner. You become disappointed because your partner is not the ideal love you initially thought. In a successful relationship, partners love each other for who they are, not for what they want each other to be.

7. *Successful partners tolerate what they cannot change.* We can change some things in our partner; other things we cannot change. A key ingredient of a successful love relationship is the wisdom to recognize which is which. If your partner is short and you want someone tall, you are not going to be able to change that characteristic. You must either accept your partner's short stature or give up the relationship. If your partner is moody and has been that way for a long time, he or she will probably continue to be moody. If you want to make the relationship work, you may have to cope with your partner's moody tendencies.
8. *Successful partners are open with each other.* We all have faults, but most of us are not very willing to admit them. Sometimes the easy way out is to lie or hold back the truth instead of divulging errors and shortcomings. The problem is that omissions, distortions, and flat-out lies can be damaging to a relationship. Once they start, they tend to spread and can ultimately destroy the relationship. Once you see you can get by with a small lie, you may tell a bigger one next time. Eventually the relationship becomes only a shell. When the partners talk, they say empty things because the relationship has lost its depth and trust.
9. *Successful partners make good times together and grow through the bad ones.* They participate in joint activities that are enjoyable and provide companionship. Instead of waiting for good times to happen, they create them. At the same time, they recognize that life is not always perfect. Successful partners, though, use the bad times as opportunities to grow. You can be truly honest with each other and still not prevent problems from developing in a relationship; however, by using problems as an opportunity to cope and grow mutually, you can come out stronger.
10. *Successful partners do unto the other as they would have the other do unto them.* It is easy to want to give less than we get. If you really want a relationship to work, see things from your partner's point of view and treat your partner the way you want to be treated. This helps you develop the empathy and understanding that are important in a successful love relationship.

women were likely to recall relationship events (such as their first date) more vividly and in greater detail than their male partners were (Ross & Holmberg, 1990). This gender difference may stem from the greater importance of relationships to women and the tendency for women to reminisce about relationships. In another study that supports this viewpoint, when talking about a relationship, women showed more relationship awareness (such as awareness of the couple's interaction patterns) than men did (Acitelli & Holmberg, 1993). Women might also have more highly developed relationship schemas (a schema is a mental framework that organizes and guides perceptions) because they spend more time in social interaction than men do (Wong & Csikszentmihalyi, 1991).

Attachment security, which can be viewed as a relationship schema, is receiving increased attention in the study of close relationships (Shaver & Clark, 1996; Shaver, Collins, & Clark, 1995). Closely related to attachment security is relationship trust. Highly trusting partners often assimilate negative information about their partner without impairing their trust in the partner (Murray & Holmes, 1993).

Not all of us experience the passion, intimacy, and commitment of love. And often it is said that it is better to have loved and lost than to never have loved at all; however, as we see next, loneliness is a dark cloud that hangs over many lives, something few people want to feel.

Loneliness

Some of us are lonely. We may feel that no one knows us very well. We may feel isolated and sense that we do not have anyone we can turn to in times of need or stress. Our society's emphasis on self-fulfillment and achievement, the importance we attach to commitment in relationships, and the decline in stable close relationships are among the reasons loneliness is common today (de Jong-Gierveld, 1987).

Loneliness is associated with a person's gender, attachment history, self-esteem, and social skills. Both men and women who lack female companions have a greater risk of being lonely. Lonely people often have a history of poor relationships with their parents. Early experiences of rejection and loss (as when a parent dies) can cause a lasting

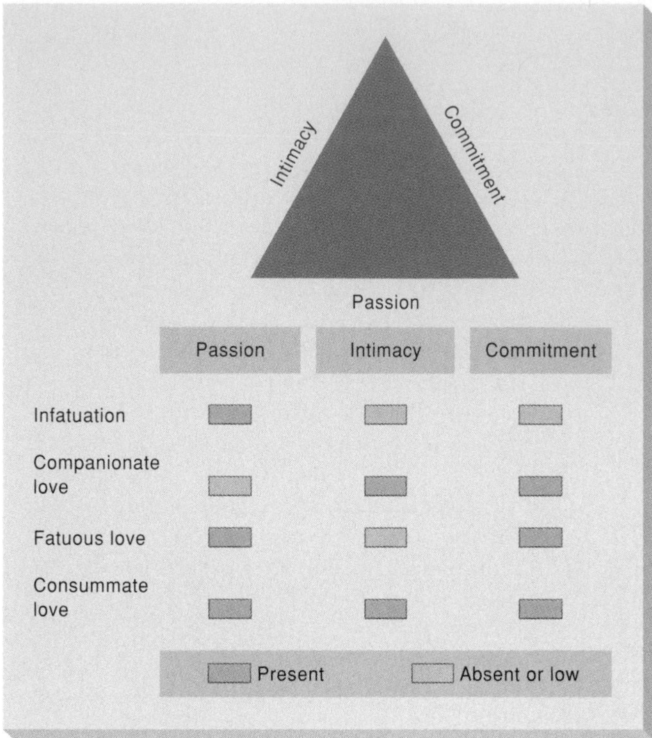

FIGURE 3
Sternberg's Triangle of Love

It is important to distinguish being alone from being lonely. Most of us cherish the moments we can be left alone for a while. Aloneness can heal, but loneliness can hurt.

effect of feeling alone. Lonely people often have low self-esteem and tend to blame themselves more than they deserve for their inadequacies. And lonely people usually have poor social skills (Jones, Hobbs, & Hockenbury, 1982). For example, they show inappropriate self-disclosure, self-attention at the expense of attention to a partner, or an inability to develop comfortable intimacy.

When students leave the familiar world of their hometown and family to enter college, they may feel especially lonely. Many college freshman feel anxious about meeting new people and developing a new social life. As one student commented:

> My first year here at the university has been pretty lonely. I wasn't lonely at all in high school. I lived in a fairly small town—I knew everybody and everyone knew me. I was a member of several clubs and played on the basketball team. It's not that way at the university. It is a big place and I've felt like a stranger on so many occasions. I'm starting to get used to my life here and the last few months I've been making myself meet people and get to know them, but it has not been easy.

As this comment illustrates, freshmen rarely bring their popularity and social standing from high school into the college environment. There may be a dozen high school basketball stars, National Merit scholars, and former student council presidents in a single dormitory wing. Especially if students attend college away from home, they face the task of forming completely new social relationships.

One study found that 2 weeks after the school year began, 75 percent of 354 college freshmen felt lonely at least part of the time since arriving on campus (Cutrona, 1982). More than 40 percent said their loneliness was moderate to severe in intensity. Students who were the most optimistic and had the highest self-esteem were more likely to overcome their loneliness by the end of their freshman year. Loneliness is not reserved only for college freshmen, though. Upperclassmen are often lonely as well.

Lonely males and females attribute their loneliness to different sources, with men more likely to blame themselves, women more likely to blame external factors. Men are socialized to initiate relationships, whereas women are traditionally socialized to wait, then respond. Perhaps men blame themselves because they feel they should do something about their loneliness, while women wonder why no one calls.

How do you determine if you are lonely? Scales of loneliness ask you to respond to items like "I don't feel in tune with the people around me" and "I can find companionship when I want it." If you consistently respond that you never or rarely feel in tune with people around you and

Concept Table 1

Attraction, the Faces of Love, and Loneliness

Concept	Processes/Related Ideas	Characteristics/Description
Attraction	Its nature	Familiarity precedes a close relationship. We like to associate with people who are similar to us. The principles of consensual validation and matching provide explanations of why we are attracted to people who are similar to us. Physical attraction is usually more important in the early part of a relationship, and it varies across cultures and historical time. Personality factors also influence attraction.
The Faces of Love	Altruism	Altruism is an unselfish interest in helping someone. Evolutionary psychologists stress that altruism involves increasing the prospects for survival as well as reproduction. Examples involve kin, as when a parent cares for its young. Examples of human altruism are plentiful. Reciprocity and social exchange often are involved, although not always. Motivation can be altruistic or egoistic. Psychologists have studied both the person and situation variables involved in altruism. Extensive research has been conducted on bystander intervention.
	Friendship	Friends and lovers have similar and dissimilar characteristics. Despite some personality and situational variations, females generally engage in more intimate self-disclosure than males do.
	Romantic or passionate love	Romantic love is involved when we say we are "in love"; it includes passion, sexuality, and a mixture of emotions, not all of which are positive.
	Affectionate or companionate love	Also called companionate love, this type of love is more important as relationships mature. Shaver proposed a developmental model of love and Sternberg a triangular model. Sternberg believes that affectionate love is made up of intimacy and commitment, which along with romantic love, comprise the three facets of his model of love.
	Relationship cognition	Researchers are increasingly interested in the role that cognition plays in close relationships. Areas of relationship cognition that are being studied include attribution, memory, attachment security and trust as relationship schemas.
Loneliness	Its nature	Loneliness is associated with a poor attachment history with parents and low self-esteem. It is important to remember the distinction between being alone and being lonely.

rarely or never can find companionship when you want it, you are likely to fall into the category of people who are described as moderately or intensely lonely (Russell, 1996).

How can people who are lonely reduce their loneliness? Two recommendations are to (1) change your actual social relations, or (2) change your social need and desires (Peplau & Perlman, 1982). Probably the most direct and satisfying way to become less lonely is to improve your social relations. You can do this by forming new relationships, by using your existing social network more competently, or by creating "surrogate" relationships with pets, television personalities, and the like. A second way to reduce loneliness is to reduce your desire for social contact. Over the short run, you might do this by choosing activities you can enjoy alone rather than activities that require someone's company. Over the long run, though, you should make an effort to form new relationships. A third, unfortunate coping strategy some people adopt is to distract themselves from their painful feelings by drinking to "drown their sorrows" or by becoming a workaholic. Some of the negative health consequences of loneliness may be the product of such maladaptive coping strategies. If you think of yourself as a lonely person, you might consider contacting the counseling center at your college for advice on ways to reduce your loneliness and improve your social skills.

At this point we have discussed a number of ideas about attraction, the faces of love, and loneliness. A summary of these ideas is presented in concept table 1. Next, we turn our attention to another important aspect of social relations—group behavior.

Group Relations

A student joining a fraternity, a jury making a decision about a criminal case, a president of a company delegating authority, a prejudiced remark against a minority group, conflict among nations, and attempts to reach peace—all of these circumstances reflect our lives as members of groups. Each of us belongs to many different groups. Some we choose, others we do not. We choose to belong to a club, but we are born into a particular ethnic group, for example. Some of the important questions about group relations are these: Why do we join groups? What is the structure of groups? How do we perform and make decisions in groups? Why are some people leaders and others followers? How do groups deal with each other, especially ethnic groups?

Motivation for Group Behavior and the Structure of Groups

Why does one student join a study group? A church? An athletic team? A company? Groups satisfy our personal needs, reward us, provide information, raise our self-esteem, and give us an identity. We might join a group because we think it will be enjoyable and exciting and satisfy our need for affiliation and companionship. We might join a group because we will receive rewards, either material or psychological. By taking a job with a company we get paid to work for a group, but we also reap prestige and recognition. Groups are an important source of information. For example, as we listen to other members talk in a Weight Watchers group we learn about their strategies for losing weight. As we sit in the audience at a real estate seminar we learn how to buy property with no money down. The groups in which you are a member—your family, college, a club, a team—make you feel good, raise your self-esteem, and provide you with an identity.

Any group to which you belong has certain things in common with all other groups. **Norms** *are rules that apply to all members of a group.* A sorority may require each of its members to maintain a 3.00 grade point average. This is a norm. The city government requires each of its workers to wear socks. Mensa requires individuals to have a high IQ. The Polar Bear club says its members must complete a 15-minute swim in below-freezing temperatures. These, too, are norms.

Roles *are rules and expectations that govern certain positions in the group. Roles define how people should behave in a particular position in the group.* In a family, parents have certain roles, siblings have other roles, and a grandparent has yet another role. On a football team, many different roles must be fulfilled: center, guard, tackle, end, quarterback, running back, and wide receiver, for example, and that only covers the offense. Roles and norms, then, tell us what is expected of a particular group.

Group Performance

Do we perform better in a group or when alone? The very first experiment in social psychology examined this question. Norman Triplett (1898) found that bicyclists performed better when they raced against each other than when they raced alone against the clock. Triplett also built a "competition machine" made out of fishing reels. The machine allowed two individuals to turn the reels side by side. Observing 40 children, he discovered that those who reeled next to another child worked faster than those who reeled alone.

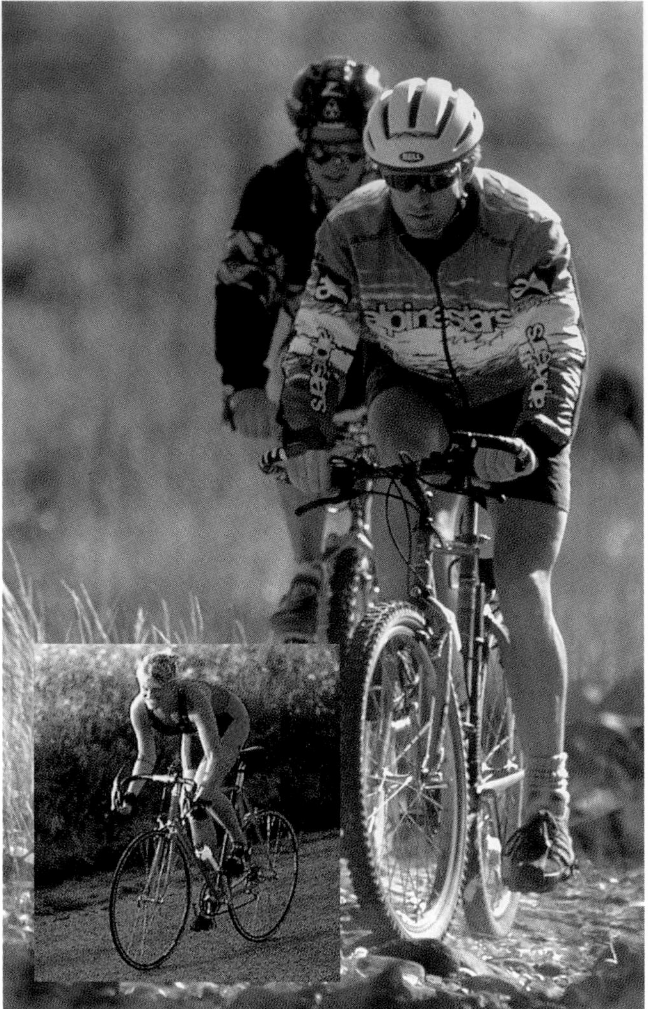

Do you perform better as a member of a group or as an individual?

Since Triplett's work almost a century ago, many investigations of group versus individual performance have been conducted. Some studies reveal that we do better in groups, others that we are more productive when we work alone (Paulus, 1989). Is there any way we can make sense out of these contradictory findings?

Social facilitation *is the phenomenon that occurs when an individual's performance improves because of the presence of others; social facilitation occurs with well-learned tasks but not with new or difficult tasks.* Robert Zajonc (1965) argued that the presence of other individuals arouses us. The arousal produces energy and facilitates our performance in groups. If our arousal is too high, however, we won't be able to learn new or difficult tasks efficiently. Social facilitation,

Our behavior in groups can become deindividuated. An example of a situation in which people can lose their individual identity is a Ku Klux Klan rally.

then, improves our performance on well-learned tasks. For new or difficult tasks, we might be best advised to work things out on our own before trying them in a group. If you are good at basketball, you might perform better when others are watching, but, if you are just learning to play golf, you probably will fare better if you step up to the first tee when no one else is around. In one investigation, expert and poor pool players were observed in the student union at Virginia Polytechnic Institute (Michaels & others, 1982). When they were observed unobtrusively, the experts hit 71 percent of their shots, the poor players 36 percent; when four individuals walked up to observe their play, however, the experts improved, making 80 percent of their shots, whereas the poor players got worse, making only 25 percent of their shots.

Another factor in group performance is how closely our behavior is monitored. **Social loafing** *is each person's tendency to exert less effort in a group because of reduced monitoring. The effect of social loafing is lowered group performance* (Latané, 1981). The larger the group, the more likely a person can loaf without being detected. One way to decrease social loafing is for people to develop a sense of personal responsibility (Brickner, Harkins, & Ostrom, 1986). Another way is to provide a standard that allows the group to evaluate its performance.

Our behavior in groups can also become deindividuated (Dodd, 1995). **Deindividuation** *is a state of reduced awareness, weakened self-restraints against impulsive actions, and apathy about negative social evaluation.* As early as 1895, Gustave LeBon observed that a group can foster uninhibited behavior, ranging from wild celebrations to mob activity. Ku Klux Klan violence, Mardi Gras wild times, and a mob rolling a car on spring break in Fort Lauderdale might be due to deindividuated behavior. One explanation of deindividuation is that groups give us anonymity. We may act in a disinhibited way because we believe that authority figures and victims are less likely to discover that we are the culprits.

Group Interaction and Decision Making

Many of the decisions we make take place in a group—juries, teams, families, clubs, school boards, the Senate, a class vote, for example (Davis, 1996; Laughlin, 1996). What happens when people put their minds to the task of making a group decision? How do they decide whether a criminal is guilty, a country should attack another, a family should stay home or go on vacation, or sex education should be part of a school curriculum? Three aspects of group decision making bear special mention: the risky shift and group polarization, groupthink, and majority-minority influence.

The Risky Shift and Group Polarization

When we make decisions in a group, do we take risks and stick our necks out or do we compromise our opinions and move toward the center? The **risky shift** *is the tendency for a group decision to be riskier than the average decision made by individual group members.* In one investigation, fictitious dilemmas were presented, and subjects were asked how much risk the characters in the dilemmas were willing to take (Stoner, 1961). When the individuals discussed the dilemmas as a group, they were more willing to say the characters would make risky decisions than when they were queried alone. Many studies have been conducted on this topic with similar results (Goethals & Demorest, 1995).

(a) (b)

Certain individuals in the minority have played important roles in history. (a) Martin Luther King, Jr., helped African Americans gain important rights. (b) Corazon Aquino, who became president of the Philippines after defeating Ferdinand Marcos, toppled a corrupt political regime and reduced the suffering of many Philippine citizens.

We do not always make riskier decisions in a group than when alone (Minsz, 1995); however, hundreds of research studies show that being in a group does move us even more strongly in the direction of the position we initially held (Moscovici, 1985). The **group polarization effect** *is the solidification and further strengthening of a position as a consequence of group discussion.* A "hawk" in the Senate may listen to endless hours of committee discussion about nuclear disarmament; a Senate "dove" hears the same words. After 2 years on the committee, each is even more strongly committed to her position than before the deliberation began. Initially held views often become even more polarized because of group discussion.

Why does group polarization occur? It may take place because people hear more persuasive arguments as group members than they knew about previously; such arguments strengthen their position. It might also occur because of social comparison. We may find that our position is not as extreme as others, which may motivate us to take a stand at least as strong as the most extreme advocate of the position.

Groupthink

Sometimes groups make rational decisions and come up with the best solution to a problem. But not always. Group members, especially leaders, often want to develop or maintain unanimity among group members. **Groupthink** *is the motivation of group members to maintain harmony and unanimity in decision making, suffocating differences of opinion in the process* (Janis, 1972). Groupthink evolves because members often boost each other's ego and increase each other's self-esteem by seeking conformity, especially in stressful circumstances. This motivation for harmony and unanimity may result in disastrous decisions and policy recommendations. Examples of groupthink include the United States invasion of Cuba (the Bay of Pigs), escalation of the Vietnam War, failure to prepare for the invasion of Pearl Harbor, the Watergate cover-up, and Irangate.

Leaders often have favored a solution and promoted it within the group. Members of the group also tend to be cohesive and isolate themselves from qualified outsiders who could influence their decisions. Leaders can avoid groupthink by encouraging dissident opinions, by not presenting a favored plan at the outset, and by having several independent groups work on the same problem.

Majority and Minority Influence

Think about the groups in which you have been a member. Who had the most influence, the majority or the minority? In most groups—whether a jury, family, or corporate meeting—the majority holds sway over the minority. The majority exerts both normative and informational pressure on the group. Its adherents set the group's norm; those who do not go along may be rejected or even given the boot. The majority also has a greater opportunity to provide information that will influence decision making.

In most cases the majority wins, but there are occasions when the minority has its day (Latané, 1996). How can the minority swing the majority? The minority cannot win through normative influence because it is outnumbered. It must do its work through *informational pressure.* If the minority presents its views consistently and confidently, then the majority is more likely to listen to the minority's views.

In group situations, some individuals are able to command the attention of others and thus have a better opportunity to shape and direct subsequent social outcomes. To achieve such a high social impact, they have to distinguish themselves in various ways from the rest of the group. They have to make themselves noticed by others—by the opinions they express, the jokes they tell, or their nonverbal style. They might be the first ones to raise a new idea, to disagree with a prevailing point of view, or to propose a creative alternative solution to a problem. People who have a strong social impact often are willing to be different. In one recent study, people high in individuation (those who are differentiated from other parts of the physical and social environment) had a stronger social impact on the group than their low-individuation counterparts did (Whitney, Sagrestano, & Maslach, 1994).

Certain individuals in a minority may play a crucial role. Individuals with a history of taking minority stands may trigger others to dissent, showing them that disagreement is possible and that it may be the best course. Such is the ground of some of history's greatest moments—when Lincoln spoke out against slavery, racism dominated and tore at the country; when Corazon Aquino became a candidate for president of the Philippines, few people thought Ferdinand Marcos could be beaten.

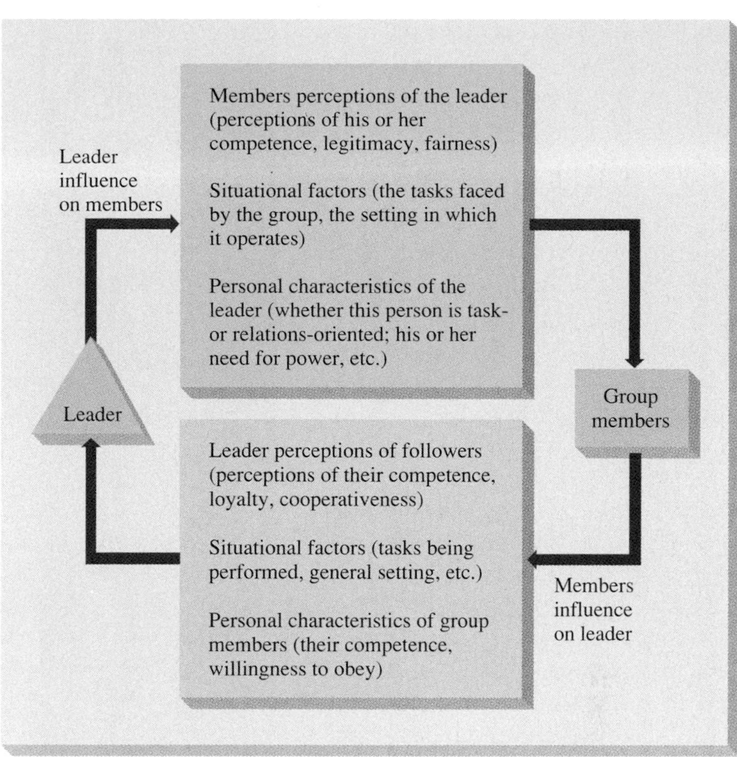

FIGURE 4

Contingency Model of Leadership
In the contingency model of leadership, leadership is viewed as a complex undertaking in which leaders influence their followers and followers influence their leaders.

Leadership

"I am certainly not one of those who needs to be prodded. In fact, if anything, I am the prod," the British Prime Minister Winston Churchill once said of himself. What made Churchill a great leader? Was it a set of personality traits, the situation into which he was thrust, or some combination of the two?

The **great-person theory** *says that some individuals have certain traits that are best suited for leadership positions.* Leaders are commonly thought to be assertive, cooperative, decisive, dominant, energetic, self-confident, tolerant of stress, willing to assume responsibility, diplomatic and tactful, and persuasive. While we can list traits and skills possessed by leaders, a large number of research studies conclude that we cannot predict who will become a leader solely from the individual's personality characteristics.

Is it the situation, then, that produces leaders? The situational view of leadership argues that the needs of a group change from time to time. The individual who emerges as the leader in one particular circumstance will not necessarily be the individual who becomes the leader in another circumstance.

The **contingency model of leadership** *states that both personality characteristics and situational influences determine who will become a leader; leadership is viewed as a complex undertaking in which leaders influence their followers and followers influence their leaders* (Fielder, 1978) (see figure 4). In the contingency model, leaders follow one of two styles: They direct leadership either toward getting a task completed or toward members' relationships (helping members get along). Is one of these two styles superior? The contingency model emphasizes that the appropriate style of leadership depends on the situation. If a group is working under very favorable or very unfavorable conditions, a task-oriented leader is better, but if group conditions are more moderate, a relationship-oriented leader is better. Full tests of these ideas have not been made, but the concept that leadership is a function of both personality characteristics and situational influences is an important one.

At this point our discussion of group relations has focused on why we join groups, the structure of groups, how we perform and make decisions in groups, and why some individuals are leaders and others are followers. Next we will discuss how groups deal with each other, especially ethnic groups and nations.

INTERGROUP RELATIONS

In 1966, in refusing to serve in Vietnam, Muhammad Ali said, "No Viet Cong ever called me a nigger." In response to the power of the United States in 1956, Nikita Khrushchev said, "Whether you like it or not, history is on our side. We will bury you." And in seeking to reduce conflict in 1963, John Kennedy said, "Peace is a daily, a weekly, a monthly process, gradually changing opinions, slowly eroding old barriers, quietly building new structures." In this chapter we will first discuss culture, then turn to prejudice, ethnocentrism, and racism. Finally, we will evaluate ways to reduce conflict and find peace.

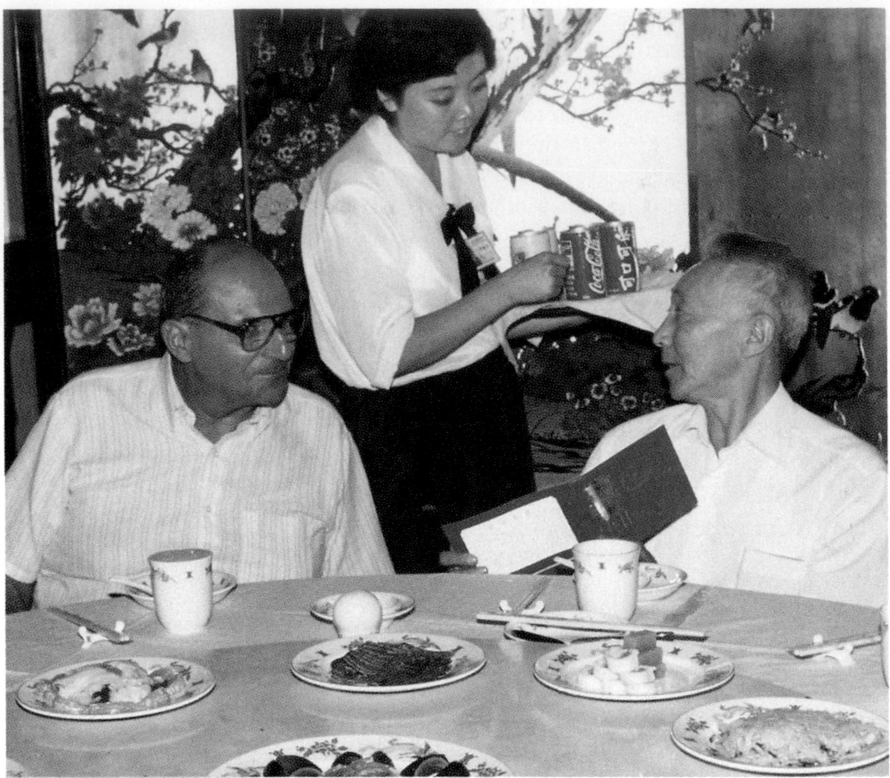

Harry Triandis (above left) has been a pioneer in the field of cross-cultural psychology. He is past president of the International Association of Cross-Cultural Psychology and has conducted insightful analyses of the individualistic and collectivistic dimensions of cultures.

Culture

Culture *consists of the behavior patterns, beliefs, and all other products of a particular group of people that are passed on from generation to generation.* The products result from the interaction between groups of people and their environments over many years. A cultural group can be as large as the United States or as small as an African hunter-gatherer group. Whatever its size, the group's culture influences the behavior of its members (Brislin, 1993; Lonner & Malpass, 1994; Matsumoto, 1994). For example, the United States is an achievement-oriented culture with a strong work ethic, but recent comparisons of American and Japanese children revealed that the Japanese were better at math, spent more time working on math in school, and did more math homework than the Americans (Stevenson, 1995). **Cross-cultural studies**—*comparisons of a culture with one or more other cultures—provide information about the degree to which people have characteristics that are similar, or universal, across cultures, or to what degree their behavior, thoughts, and feelings are culture-specific.*

Cross-cultural expert Richard Brislin (1993) recently described a number of features of culture. They include the following:

- Culture is made up of ideals, values, and assumptions about life that guide people's behavior.
- Culture refers to those aspects of the culture that people make.
- Culture is transmitted from generation to generation, with the responsibility for the transmission resting on the shoulders of parents, teachers, and community leaders.
- Culture's influence often becomes noticed the most in well-meaning clashes between people from very different cultural backgrounds.
- Despite compromises, cultural values still remain.
- When people's cultural values are violated or when cultural expectations are ignored, people react emotionally.
- It is not unusual for people to accept a cultural value at one point in their life and reject it at another point. For example, rebellious adolescents and young adults may accept a culture's values and expectations only after having children of their own.

In cross-cultural research, the search for basic traits has extended to characteristics common to a whole nation. In recent years, the most elaborate search for traits has focused on the dichotomy of individualism/collectivism (Hofstede, 1980; Triandis, 1994). **Individualism** *involves giving priority to personal goals rather than to group goals; it emphasizes values that serve the self, such as feeling good, personal distinction, and independence.* ***Collectivism*** *emphasizes values that serve the group by subordinating personal goals to preserve group integrity, interdependence of the members, and harmonious relationships.* Many Western cultures, such as the United States, Canada, Great Britain, and the Netherlands, are described as individualistic; many Eastern cultures, such as China, Japan, India, and Thailand, are described as collectivistic.

© Sidney Harris. Reprinted by permission.

Many of psychology's basic tenets developed in individualistic cultures such as the United States. Consider the flurry of *self-* terms in psychology that have an individualistic focus: *self-actualization, self-awareness, self-efficacy, self-reinforcement, self-criticism, self-serving, selfishness,* and *self-doubt* (Lonner, 1988; Rumpel, 1988).

Critics of the Western notion of psychology point out that human beings have always lived in groups, whether large or small, and have always needed one another for survival. They argue that the Western emphasis on individualism may undermine our species' basic need for relatedness (Kagitcibasi, 1988). Some social scientists believe that many of the problems in Western cultures are intensified by their emphasis on individualism. Individualistic cultures have been found to have higher rates of the following problems than collectivistic cultures: suicide, drug abuse, crime, teenage pregnancy, divorce, child abuse, and mental disorders (Triandis, 1994). The pendulum may have swung too far toward individualism in Western cultures. People, regardless of their cultural background, need a positive sense of *self* and *connectedness to others* to develop fully as human beings.

Some psychologists criticize the individualism/collectivism dichotomy. They argue that describing an entire nation of people as having a basic personality obscures the diversity and individual variation that characterizes any nation's people. Also, individual and collective interests share certain values, such as wisdom, mature love, and tolerance (Schwartz, 1990). Thus, individuals can possess *both* individualistic and collectivistic qualities (Gaines & Reed, 1994).

Prejudice, Stereotyping, and Ethnocentrism

Understanding the antagonism that develops between groups requires knowledge about prejudice, stereotyping, and ethnocentrism. These factors are involved in discrimination against groups.

Prejudice

Prejudice's dark nature has appeared on many occasions in human history. The population of North American Indians dropped from an estimated 3 million in the seventeenth century to about 600,000 today because of brutal slayings. More than 6 million Jews were murdered by the Nazis in the 1940s under the justification of "purifying" the European racial stock. Only a fraction of the world's Jews remain in Europe today.

Whites' racial prejudice against African Americans has characterized much of America's history. When Africans were imported into America as slaves, they were described as property and treated in subhuman ways. In the first half of the twentieth century, most African Americans still lived in the South and were still largely segregated by law—restaurants, movie theaters, and buses had separate areas for Whites and African Americans. Even with the downfall of segregation, much higher portions of African Americans than Whites live below the poverty line today.

African Americans and Native Americans are not the only ethnic minority groups that have been subjected to prejudice in the United States. Many Latinos also live below the poverty line and have low educational achievement and low-paying jobs. Historically, lesbians and gays have been subjected to considerable prejudice from the heterosexual majority. This prejudice has been so intense that most homosexuals stayed "in the closet" until recently, not revealing their sexual preferences for fear of prejudice and discrimination. In fact, virtually every social group has been the victim of prejudice at one time or another.

You probably are reasonably sure that you know what prejudice means. And, like most people, you probably don't think of yourself as prejudiced. In fact, each of us has prejudices and stereotypes. **Prejudice** *is an unjustified negative attitude toward an individual based on the individual's membership in a group.* The group against which the individual is prejudiced can be made up of people of a particular race, sex, age, religion, nation, or can have some other detectable difference (Aboud, 1988; Devine & Zuwerink, 1994).

Stereotyping

A **stereotype** *is a generalization about a group's characteristics that does not consider any variation from one individual to the next.* Think about your image of a dedicated accountant. Most of us would probably describe such a person as quiet, boring, unsociable, and so on. Rarely would we come up with a mental image of this person as extraverted, the life of the party, or artistic. Characterizing all accountants as boring is a clear example of a stereotype. Another stereotype is to describe all Italians as excitable. Researchers have found that we are less likely to detect variations among individuals who belong to "other" groups than those who belong to "our" group. For example, Whites are more likely to stereotype African Americans than other Whites during eye-witness identification (Brigham, 1986).

Stereotypes are often described as cognitive categories that people use when thinking about groups and individuals from those groups (Steele, 1996). Much of the last 25 years of research on stereotypes has emphasized and documented the role of cognitive mechanisms in the biased judgments of individuals (Jussim & others, 1995). In the *cognitive* perspective, the perceiver's *beliefs* about social groups are involved in stereotyping. Biased beliefs are often interpreted as reflecting any of several cognitive mechanisms, such as schemas, expectations, and prototypes. Some individuals also might engage in stereotyping without being aware of it (Greenwald & Benaji, 1995).

However, some researchers argue that *affective* factors are more responsible for stereotyping than cognitive factors are. For example, in the classic book *The Roots of Prejudice,* Gordon Allport (1954) argued that the emotional dimensions of prejudice, such as anger, produce irrational and biased judgments that lead to stereotyping. In the affective view, how much people *like* or *dislike* different groups (in contrast to the cognitive view's emphasis on a person's beliefs) generates stereotyping (see figure 5). In one recent study, affect, as reflected in liking or disliking, produced judgmental bias and stereotyping (Jussim & others, 1995). In sum, both cognitive and affective factors are likely involved in stereotyping.

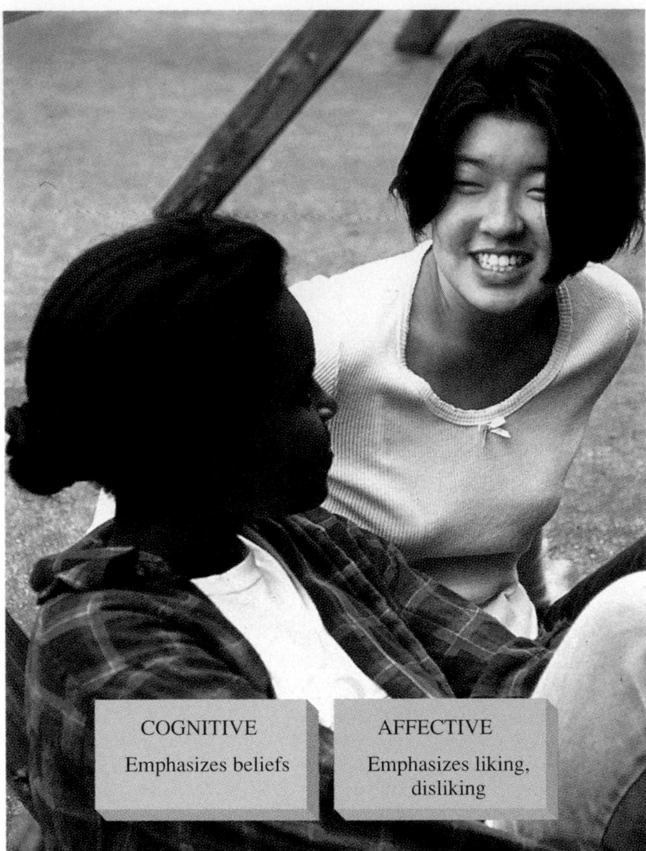

FIGURE 5

Cognitive and Affective Views of Stereotyping
How do stereotypes come into existence? For example, consider the African American and Asian American females shown here. How might a White American acquire stereotypes of them?

Ethnocentrism

Ethnocentrism *is the tendency to favor one's own group over other groups.* Ethnocentrism's positive side is that it fosters a sense of pride in our group that fulfills the human urge to attain and maintain a positive self-image. As we approach the end of the twentieth century, group pride has mushroomed. There's Black Pride and Gay Pride. The Scots grow more Scottish, the Irish more Irish.

There is something paradoxical, though, about such pride. Most members of a group will attest that the group does not discriminate against others. As the American radical Stokeley Carmichael said in 1966, "I'm for the Negro. I'm not against anything." Too often members of groups stress differences with others rather than solely emphasizing pride in their own group.

However, in-group pride does not always reflect ethnocentrism. What might be occurring in some in-group/out-group considerations is in-group/out-group bias, the tendency to view members of one's own group as having heterogeneous and desirable qualities *and* to view the members of other groups as having homogeneous and undesirable qualities. Members of socioeconomical and/or sociopolitical minority groups (such as women, African Americans, Latinos, and gays and lesbians) often assert in-group pride as a necessary counter to the many overt and covert messages transmitted by society that denigrate them simply by virtue of their group membership (Gaines & Reed, 1994, 1995).

Henry Tajfel (1978) proposed **social identity theory,** *which states that when individuals are assigned to a group,*

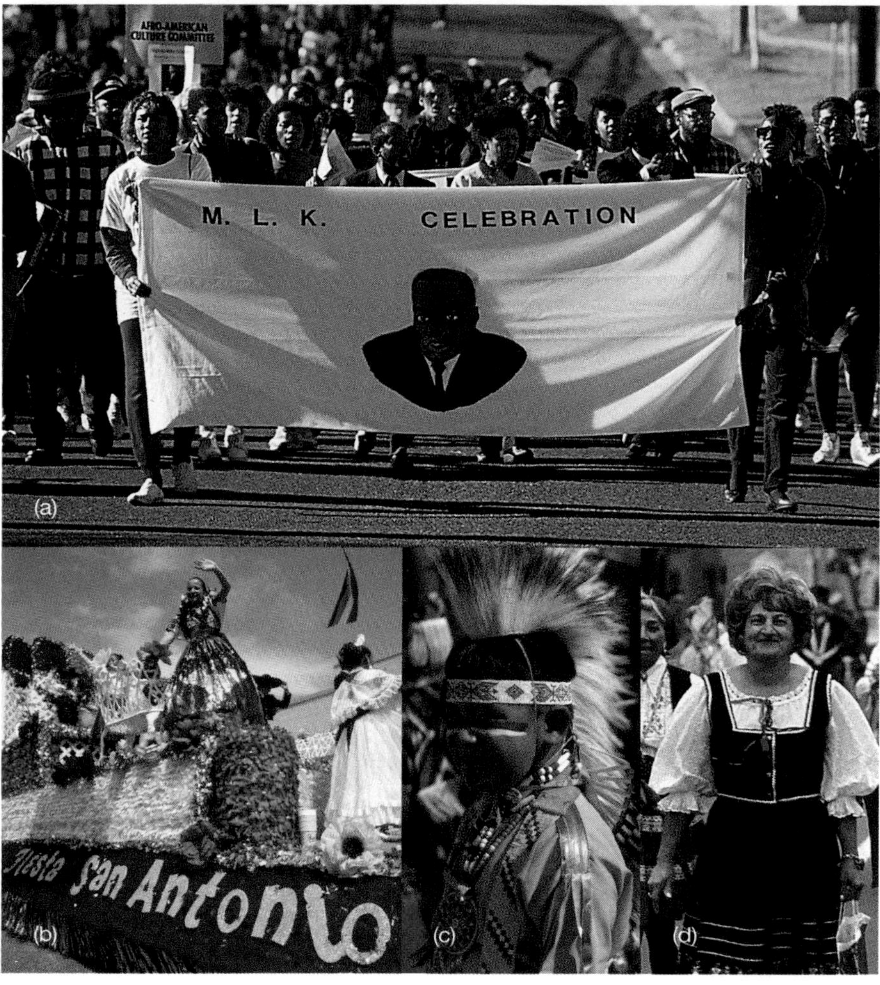

Group members often show considerable pride in their group identity, as reflected in (a) African Americans' celebration of Martin Luther King Day, (b) Mexican Americans' celebration of Cinco de Mayo, (c) Native Americans' celebration of their heritage, and (d) Polish Americans' celebration of their cultural background.

they invariably think of the group as an in-group for them. This occurs because individuals want to have a positive self-image. Social identity theory helps explain prejudice and conflict between groups. Tajfel is one of an increasingly small group of European Jews who survived World War II. His goal was to explain the extreme violence and prejudice his group experienced.

Self-image consists of both a personal identity and many different social identities. Tajfel argues that individuals can improve their self-image by enhancing either their personal or their social identity. Tajfel believes our social identity is especially important. When we compare the social identity of our group with the social identity of another group, we often maximize the distinctiveness of the two groups. Think about your social identity with your home town. Or imagine two fans of professional basketball teams, one of whom lives in Houston and is a Houston Rockets fan, the other of whom lives in Phoenix and is a Phoenix Suns fan. When the Rockets won the 1994 and 1995 NBA championships, the Rockets fans' self-image was enhanced.

As these two fans talk with each other, they argue about the virtues of their teams, reinforcing the distinctiveness of their social identities with two different groups. As they strive to promote their social identities, it is not long before they intersperse proud, self-congratulatory remarks with nasty comments about the opposing team. In a capsule, the theme of the conversation has become, "My team is good and I am good. Your team is bad and you are bad." And so it goes with the sexes, ethnic groups, nations, social classes, religions, sororities, fraternities, and countless other groups. These comparisons often lead to competition and even to "legitimizing" discrimination against other groups.

Tajfel showed that for us to think in terms of "we" and "they," it doesn't take much. For example, he assigned one person to a particular group because she overestimated the number of dots on a screen. He assigned another person to a different group because he underestimated the number. Once assigned to the two groups, the members were asked to award money to other participants. Those eligible to receive the money were distinguished only by their membership in one of the two groups just described. Invariably, an individual acted favorably (awarded money) toward a member of his or her own group. It is no wonder, then, that if we favor our own group based on such trivial criteria that we will show intense in-group favoritism when differences are not so trivial (Hogg, 1996; Rappaport, Bornstein, & Erev, 1989).

Racism

We live in a society that has discriminated against virtually every ethnic minority group—Asians, Latinos, eastern and southern Europeans—as they arrived on our shores. However, slavery and the system of segregation that followed it are unique to African Americans. Some psychologists argue that, as a result, African Americans have had more difficulty achieving equality than any other ethnic minority group (Sears, Peplau, & Taylor, 1997).

The treatment of African Americans by White police officers has been a source of racial conflict for many years in the United States. This is a frame of videotape showing Los Angeles policemen beating Rodney King. This beating was perceived by many African Americans as one more example of the long-standing police brutality toward African Americans. By contrast, many police officers explained the beating as a consequence of the high crime rate among urban African American males.

Intense Racism

For some people, virtually every member of an out-group is inferior. **Racism** *involves believing that the members of another race or ethnic group are inferior.* In many cases, racists believe that members of another race or ethnic group are inferior on a host of characteristics from morals to intelligence because they were born into the particular out-group.

Today it is unfashionable to express intense racism openly in many parts of the world, although in some countries, intense racism openly rears its ugly head (Brislin, 1993). The most recent occurrences have been in Germany where 1990s neo-Nazis seek an "ethnic cleansing" of Germany in an effort to deport non-German born individuals and restrict certain foreigners from entering the country and becoming citizens. In the United States, intense racism heated up when African American Rodney King was beaten by White American police in Los Angeles.

Some Contemporary Forms of Racism

Today, most Whites show more accepting attitudes toward African Americans than even a decade or two ago (Sears, Peplau, & Taylor 1997; Sears & Funk, 1991). The vast majority of Whites support African Americans' rights to public office, access to public accommodations, fair housing, and so on. Violence by Whites toward African Americans has diminished considerably. However, occasional incidents—such as the Rodney King beating—still spark conflict and hatred between African Americans and Whites. And often there still is resistance to programs that would help African Americans reach full equality—such as affirmative action and school desegregation.

Some social scientists engage in lively debate about whether White society will continue to move toward liberal racial attitudes or resist further change (Bowser & Hunt, 1996). While most Whites ostensibly support integration, it may just be *lip service.* That is, on the surface many Whites make socially correct comments about African Americans, but underneath they harbor racist feelings. Whites' support for general principles of equality may be *superficial.* It is easy to support equality in the abstract, but supporting its actual implementation has real and costly implications. White Americans also may have a genuine *ambivalence* about African Americans. In this view, Whites sympathize with the problems African Americans have faced and continue to face, but also perceive that African Americans have contributed to their plight by their lack of ambition and failure to take advantage of opportunities (Katz, Wackenhut, & Hass, 1986).

Another possibility is that old-fashioned racism has been replaced by a new form called *aversive racism,* which describes the conflict Whites experience between their genuinely egalitarian values and their own negative feelings toward African Americans (Dovidio & Gaertner, 1986). In this perspective, Whites are ashamed of their negative feelings and do not want them to be exposed, so they simply avoid African Americans. In old-fashioned racism, Whites felt hostility and hatred toward African Americans; in aversive racism, they feel discomfort, uneasiness, and fear. Yet another possiblity is that old-fashioned racism has been replaced by another version called *symbolic racism,* which consists of a combination of anti–African American feelings and traditional values such as those involved in the Protestant ethic (Sears & McConahay, 1973). Symbolic racism is the attitude that African Americans are pushing too hard, too fast, for equality, making unfair demands and getting undeserved special attention, such as favoritism in job hiring and college admissions (Nosworthy, Lea, & Lindsay, 1995; Sears, 1987). In sum, although old-fashioned intense racism has diminished, other forms of racism seem to have replaced it (Swim & others, 1995).

Improving Interethnic Relations

Martin Luther King once said, "I have a dream that my four little children will one day live in a nation where they will not be judged by the color of their skin but by the content of their character." How might we possibly reach the world Martin Luther King envisioned—a world without prejudice and racism? Beginning with Gordon Allport's classic study of prejudice in 1954, researchers have consistently found that contact itself does not improve relations with people from other ethnic backgrounds. What does improve interethnic relations?

Superordinate Goals

Years ago social psychologist Muzafer Sherif and his colleagues (1961) fueled "we/they" competition between two groups of 11-year-old boys at a summer camp called Robbers Cave in Oklahoma. In the first week one group hardly knew the other group existed. One group became known as

Eliot Aronson developed the concept of the jigsaw classroom to reduce ethnic conflict. How does the jigsaw classroom work?

the Rattlers (a tough and cussing group whose shirts were emblazoned with a snake insignia) and the other was known as the Eagles.

Near the end of the first week each group learned of the other's existence. It took little time for "we/they" talk to surface ("They had better not be on our ball field." "Did you see the way one of them was sneaking around?"). Sherif, who disguised himself as a janitor so he could unobtrusively observe the Rattlers and Eagles, arranged for the two groups to compete in baseball, touch football, and tug-of-war. Counselors manipulated and judged events so the teams were close. Each team perceived the other to be unfair. Raids, burning the other group's flag, and fights resulted. The Rattlers and Eagles further derided one another as they held their noses in the air as they passed each other. Rattlers described all Rattlers as brave, tough, and friendly, and called all Eagles sneaky and smart alecks. The Eagles reciprocated by labeling the Rattlers crybabies.

After we/they competition transformed the Rattlers and Eagles into opposing "armies," Sherif devised ways to reduce hatred between the groups. He tried noncompetitive contact but that didn't work. Only when both groups were required to work cooperatively to solve a problem did the Rattlers and Eagles develop a positive relationship. Sherif created superordinate tasks that required the efforts of both groups: working together to repair the only water supply to the camp, pooling their money to rent a movie, and cooperating to pull the camp truck out of a ditch.

Might Sherif's idea—that of creating cooperation between groups rather than competition—be applied to ethnic groups? When the schools of Austin, Texas, were desegregated through extensive busing, increased racial tension among African Americans, Mexican Americans, and Whites resulted in violence in the schools. The superintendent consulted Eliot Aronson, a prominent social psychologist, who was at the University of Texas in Austin at the time. Aronson (1986) thought it was more important to prevent ethnic hostility than to control it. He observed a number of elementary school classrooms in Austin and saw how fierce the competition was between children of unequal status.

Aronson stressed that the reward structure of the classrooms needed to be changed from a setting of unequal competition to one of cooperation among equals, without making any curriculum changes. To accomplish this, he put together the *jigsaw classroom.* The jigsaw classroom works by creating a situation where all of the students have to pull together to get the "big picture." Let's say we have a class of thirty students, some White, some African American, and some Latino. The academic goal is to learn about the life of Joseph Pulitzer. The class might be broken up into five study groups of six students each, with the groups being as equal as possible in terms of ethnic composition and academic achievement level. Learning about Pulitzer's life becomes a class project divided into six parts, with one part given to each member of the six-person group. The components might be paragraphs from Pulitzer's biography, such as how the Pulitzer family came to the United States, Pulitzer's childhood, his early work, and so on. The parts are like the pieces of a jigsaw puzzle. They have to be together to form the complete puzzle.

Each student has an allotted time to study her or his part. Then the group meets and each member tries to teach her or his part to the group. After an hour or so each student is tested on the life of Pulitzer. Each student must learn the entire lesson; learning depends on the cooperation

Intimate personal contact that involves sharing doubts, hopes, problems, ambitions, and much more is one way to improve interethnic relations.

and effort of other members. Aronson believes that this type of learning increases students' interdependence through cooperatively reaching a common goal.

The strategy of emphasizing cooperation rather than competition and the jigsaw approach have been widely used in classrooms in the United States. A number of studies reveal that this type of cooperative learning is associated with increased self-esteem, better academic performance, friendships among classmates, and improved interethnic perceptions (Slavin, 1989).

It is not easy to get groups who do not like each other to cooperate. The air of distrust and hostility is hard to overcome. Creating superordinate goals that require cooperation of both groups is one viable strategy, as evidenced in Sherif's and Aronson's work. Other strategies involve disseminating positive information about the "other" and reducing the potential threat of each group (Worschel, 1986).

Intimate Contact

We indicated earlier that contact by itself does not improve interethnic relations. However, one form of contact—intimate contact—can (Amir, 1994; Brislin, 1993). Intimate contact in this context does not mean sexual relations, rather it involves sharing one's personal worries, troubles, successes, failures, personal ambitions, and coping strategies. When people reveal personal information about themselves, they are more likely to be perceived as an individual rather than as a member of a category. And, the sharing of personal information often produces the discovery that others previously considered as "them" or the out-group have many of the same feelings, hopes, and concerns, which can help to breakdown in-group/out-group, we/they barriers.

In one of the initial investigations of extensive interethnic contact, African American and White residents in an integrated housing project were studied (Deutsch & Collins, 1951). The residents lived in small apartments, and the housing project included shared facilities, such as laundry rooms and playgrounds for children, which allowed for interethnic contact. Whites found it more enjoyable to talk with African Americans than to stare at the walls while their laundry was washing, and African American and White parents began to converse with each other as they watched their children play. The young African American and White children played with each other regardless of skin color. Initially the conversations focused on such nonintimate matters as the quality of the washing machines and the weather, but eventually they moved on to more personal matters. The Whites and African Americans discovered that they shared a number of similar concerns, such as jobs and work, the quality of their children's schools, and taxes. Their revelations that they shared many of the same concerns and problems helped to diminish in-group/out-group thoughts and feelings. Sharing intimate information and becoming friendly with someone from another ethnic group helps people become more tolerant and less prejudiced toward the other ethnic group.

Sociocultural Diversity and Issues

As the future brings extensive contact between people from quite different cultural backgrounds, schools and neighborhoods can no longer be the fortresses of one privileged group whose agenda is to exclude those whose skin color or customs are different. Increasingly, immigrants, refugees, and ethnic minority individuals are refusing to become part of a homogeneous melting pot, and instead are requesting that the nation's schools, employers, and governments honor many of their cultural customs. But our institutions cannot accommodate every aspect of every culture, and consequently children learn attitudes in school that may challenge traditional authority patterns in the home (Brislin, 1990, 1991, 1993). These are just a few of the sociocultural issues that must be addressed if we are to make psychology meaningful to culturally diverse people. Let's examine some others.

Understanding Diversity Within an Ethnic, Cultural, or Gender Group

An especially important fact is that there is diversity within every ethnic, cultural, and gender group. In Explorations in Psychology 2, we describe how no cultural characteristic is common to all (or even nearly all) members of a particular ethnic group; one exception might be, for African Americans, the experience of being Black and the beliefs that develop from that experience. Diversity also characterizes the members of any cultural group, such as Russians, Italians, and Indonesians. And diversity characterizes females and males. For example, some females excel at math; others do not; likewise, some males excel at math, others do not. Some females have highly connected friendships, others are lonely; and the same is true for males. Diversity and individual differences exist in every ethnic, cultural, and gender group. Failure to recognize this strong diversity and individual variation results in stereotyping and ineffective social interaction with individuals from other ethnic, cultural, and gender groups (Triandis, 1991).

Recognizing and Respecting Legitimate Differences in Ethnic, Cultural, and Gender Groups

Ours is a diverse, multicultural world teeming with different languages, family structures, and customs. A cascade of historical, economic, and social experiences have produced these differences between ethnic, cultural, and gender groups (Triandis, 1994). We need to recognize and respect these differences to facilitate communication and cooperation in our increasingly interdependent world. While someone's behavior may be different from ours, we can develop empathy and better understand them by taking their perspective and thinking about what life would be like if we were in their shoes. We can then begin to celebrate the richness that comes with diversity and appreciate the common ground we share with people whose ethnicity, cultural heritage, or gender differs from ours.

While this sounds reasonable to many of us now, for too long the dominant White culture disparaged ethnic minority differences. Virtually any difference—from the way people looked to the kind of music they listened to—was thought of as a deficit. Too often, these differences have been seized upon by segments of society seeking to justify their own biases, to exploit, or humiliate people from ethnic minority backgrounds (Jones, 1993). Historically, being female has also meant exposure to the world of restrictions, barriers, and unfair treatment. Many psychologists now seek to discover the psychological assets of females and the strengths of ethnic groups. This new trend is long overdue.

Searching for Similarities in Ethnic, Cultural, and Gender Groups When Differences Have Incorrectly Been Assumed

Almost every aspect of American society bears the imprint of a White, middle-class, male bias. Psychology is no exception. As a result, females and members of ethnic minorities have had inadequate opportunities to contribute their ideas and values to society and psychology. In addition, incorrect assumptions about the differences between White Americans and ethnic minority Americans, as well as between women and men, proliferate and take on a power all their own (for example, Asian men are effeminate, Jews are ambitious, and African Americans are naturally athletic). As members of ethnic minorities and women begin to have a stronger voice in society, similarities will emerge. Recognizing legitimate similarities between people, regardless of ethnicity or gender, will help break down the stereotypes that lead to prejudice.

Reducing Discrimination and Prejudice

In a recent Gallup poll, Americans said they believe the United States is tolerant of ethnic differences and that overt racism is basically unacceptable ("Poll Finds Racial Tension Decreasing," 1990). However, many ethnic minority members experience persistent forms of discrimination and prejudice in many domains of life—in the media, interpersonal interactions, and daily conversations (Sue, 1990). As we discussed earlier in this chapter, prejudice and racism today are often expressed in more subtle and indirect ways than they once were (Sears, Peplau & Taylor, 1997)).

In today's world, most people agree that children from different ethnic groups should attend the same school. However, despite more-accepting attitudes about many dimensions of ethnicity, a substantial portion of individuals say that they don't feel comfortable with people from other ethnic groups. For example, in a recent survey of students at 390 colleges and universities, more than half of the

Explorations in Psychology 2

The Changing Tapestry of American Culture

In 1989 one-fifth of all children and adolescents under the age of 17 were from ethnic minority groups—African Americans, Latinos, Native Americans (American Indians), and Asians. By the year 2000, one-third of all school-age children will fall into this category. This changing demographic tapestry promises national diversity, but it also carries the challenge of extending the American dream to people of all ethnic and minority groups. Historically, ethnic minorities have found themselves at the bottom of the economic and social order. They have been disproportionately among the poor and the inadequately educated. Today for instance, half of all African American children and one-third of all Latino children live in poverty, and the school dropout rate for minority youth is as high as 60 percent in some urban areas. Our social institutions can play an enormous part to help correct these discrepancies. By becoming more sensitive to ethnic issues and providing improved services to people of ethnic minority and low-income backgrounds, schools, colleges, social services, health and mental health agencies, and the courts can help bring minorities into the mainstream of American life.

An especially important fact for social planners to keep in mind is the tremendous diversity within each ethnic group. We're accustomed to thinking of American society as a melting pot of cultures—Whites, African Americans, Latinos, Native Americans, Asian Americans, Italian Americans, Polish Americans, and so on. But there is no cultural characteristic common to all African Americans and all Latinos.

African Americans make up the largest and most visible ethnic minority group in the United States. African Americans are distributed throughout the social class structure, although a disproportionate number are poor. In spite of social and economic disadvantage, the majority of African American youth stay in school, do not take drugs, do not get married prematurely, and grow up to lead productive lives. Latinos also are a diverse group of individuals. Not all Latinos are Catholic. Many are, but some are not. Not all Latinos have a Mexican heritage. Many do, but others have cultural ties with South American countries, with Puerto Rico or other Caribbean countries, or with Spain (Padilla, 1994).

Native Americans, with 511 identifiable tribal units, also are an extremely diverse and complicated ethnic group (Trimble & Fleming, 1989). So are Asian Americans, with more than 30 distinct groups listed under this designation (Wong, 1982). And within each of these 511 identifiable Native American tribes and 30 distinct Asian American groups, there is considerable diversity and individual variation.

America has embraced many cultures, and in the process the cultures have often mixed their beliefs and identities. Some of the culture of origin is retained, some of it lost, and some of it mixed with the American culture. As the population of ethnic minority groups continues to expand rapidly, one of psychology's most important agendas in the next decade is to better understand the role that culture and ethnicity play in the way we think and act.

The tapestry of American culture has changed dramatically in recent years. Nowhere is the change more noticeable than in the increasing ethnic diversity of America's citizens. Ethnic minority groups—African American, Latino, Native American (American Indian), and Asian American, for example—will make up approximately one-third of all individuals under the age of 17 in the United States by the year 2000. One of psychology's challenges is to become more sensitive to race and ethnic origin, and to provide improved services to ethnic minority individuals.

African Americans and almost one-fourth of the Asian Americans, but only 6 percent of the Whites, said that they felt excluded from school activities (Hurtado, Dey, & Trevino, 1994). We still have a long way to go in reducing discrimination and prejudice.

Value Conflicts: Underlying Factors in Ethnic Minority Issues

Most ethnic minorities want to participate fully in society, but they don't necessarily agree on how to accomplish that goal. People are often caught between conflicting values of assimilation and cultural pluralism (Sue, 1990).

Assimilation *refers to the absorption of an ethnic minority group into the dominant group, which often means the loss of some or all of the behavior and values of the ethnic minority group.* Those who advocate assimilation usually exhort ethnic minority groups to become more American. By contrast, **pluralism** *refers to the coexistence of distinct ethnic and cultural groups in the same society.* Those who advocate pluralism usually promote cultural differences, urging that those differences be maintained and appreciated. Because the mainstream way of life was considered superior for so many years, assimilation was thought to be the best course for American society. Although assimilation still has many supporters, many people now believe that pluralism is the best approach.

Value conflicts have been a source of considerable controversy (Amirkhan & others, 1995). According to Sue, without properly identifying the assumptions and effects of the conflicting values, it is difficult to resolve ethnic minority issues.

James Jones has been an important influence in improving our understanding of ethnic issues and discrimination. Jones believes that until we accept the fact that color does make a difference in our social relationships, we will never fully understand intergroup relations.

Globalizing Psychology and Understanding American Psychology's Ethnocentrism

For the most part, American psychology has been ethnocentric, emphasizing mainstream American values, especially those of middle-class White males. Of course, it is not just individuals in the United States who are ethnocentric; people in all societies are. One example of American psychology's ethnocentrism is American individualism. Yet many of the world's cultures—Japan, China, India, and Mexico, for example—are group oriented.

While people from different cultures may vary in how strongly they identify with their group, some attitudes appear to be constant from culture to culture. For example, American social psychologist Donald Campbell and his colleagues (Brewer & Campbell, 1976; Campbell & LeVine, 1968) found that people in all cultures have a tendency to:

- believe that what happens in their culture is "natural" and "correct" and what happens in other cultures is "unnatural" and "incorrect."
- perceive their cultural customs as universally valid; that is, what is good for us is good for everyone.
- behave in ways that favor their cultural group.
- feel proud of their cultural group.
- feel hostile toward other cultural groups.

In fact, many cultures define the word *human* in terms of their own characteristics. The ancient Greeks distinguished between those who spoke Greek and those whose languages sounded like "barber," a repetitive chatter; they called those who did not speak Greek *barbarians.* Similarly, the ancient Chinese labeled themselves "the central kingdom." In many languages, the word *human* is the same as the name of the tribe, suggesting that people from foreign cultures are not perceived as fully human (Triandis, 1990).

Global interdependence is no longer a matter of preference or choice. It is an inescapable reality. We are not just citizens of the United States or Canada. We are citizens of the world, a world that through modern communication and transport has become increasingly intertwined. By improving our understanding of the behavior and values of cultures around the world, we hope that we can interact more effectively with each other and make this a more hospitable, peaceful planet (Sloan, 1990).

Recognizing That the Behavior of Every Individual from Every Ethnic, Cultural, and Gender Group Is Multiply Determined

When we think about what causes a person's behavior and adjustment, we tend to think in terms of a single cause. But human behavior and adjustment is not that

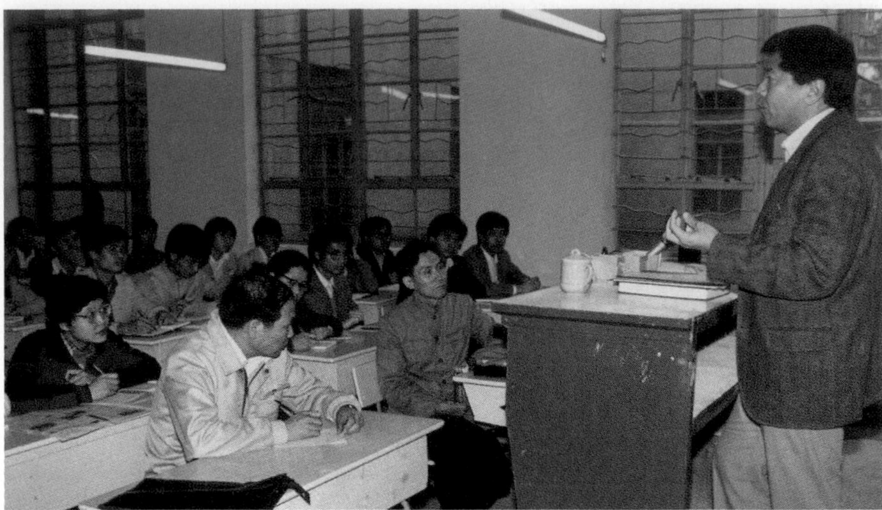

Stanley Sue, shown lecturing to Asian Americans, has been an important advocate of increased research on ethnic minority issues on psychology. Sue has conducted extensive research on the role of ethnicity in abnormal behavior and psychotherapy. He also has provided considerable insight into ethnic minority issues.

simple. For example, consider 19-year-old Tom, a Native American high school dropout. It's possible he quit school because his family did not adequately appreciate the importance of education; but even if that were true, it is likely that other factors were involved. For example, it is also possible that Tom comes from a low-income family that he helps to support. The school Tom attended may have had a poor history of helping Native Americans adapt to school; perhaps it has no multicultural programs and no Native Americans in the school administration. It may also turn out that the town in which Tom lives devotes few resources to youth programs. And there undoubtedly are more factors that contributed to Tom's dropping out of school. Because it is the result of many factors, behavior is said to be multiply determined.

Considering Different Sides of Sensitive Ethnic, Cultural, and Gender Issues

Seeing things from multiple points of view is as crucial to understanding ethnic, cultural, and gender issues as it is to understanding one person's behavior. If we do not seek out alternative explanations and interpretations of problems and issues, our conclusions may be based on our expectations, prejudices, and stereotypes.

Stanley Sue (1990) described the importance of considering different sides of the sociocultural issue involving equal opportunity and equality of outcomes. For example, in discussing his stance on ethnic issues, a university administrator commented that he believes in equality and does not discriminate against any group. He commented that in hiring teachers his university is ethnic and color blind, focusing only on the applicants' qualifications. By contrast, an administrator at a small college said that his college follows an affirmative action course and recruits faculty from different ethnic groups. He further commented that his college will not be happy until the ethnic composition of the college reflects that of the community. The administrators' statements illustrate a clash of values over the appropriate course of action to follow in addressing ethnic minority concerns. The position of the university administrator ensures that all members of society will have the same opportunity. That is, all individuals should be treated the same with regard to education, employment, and housing. By contrast, the position of the small college administrator advocates achieving equality of outcomes. That is, through affirmative action procedures, equality of outcomes may be attained. Such procedures might involve increasing the ethnic pool of applicants, practicing selection procedures that consider ethnicity, and using different criteria for selecting different groups.

According to Sue, proponents of equal opportunity want to eliminate discrimination. Their goal is to abolish racial or ethnic bias, intentional patterns of segregation, and discriminatory admissions or selection criteria. However, even if discrimination is eliminated, there is no guarantee that equal outcomes will be achieved. Realizing this, advocates of equal outcomes believe it is important to have special programs and affirmative action to narrow the gap between ethnic minority groups and Whites. In their view, color-blind policies that are applied to ethnic groups already showing negative disparities with Whites only serve to maintain differential achievements. In Sue's view, the dilemma here is apparent—advocates of equal opportunity run the risk of perpetuating unequal outcomes. The controversy has unfortunately been turned into one of discrimination. That is, if it is unfair to discriminate against ethnic minority groups, should we now discriminate in reverse against the majority group? A more meaningful question is, What kind of society do we want? According to Sue, the goal of our society should be to maximize the potential of every individual, irrespective of color, ethnic group, or sex.

Affirmative action initiatives have assumed a central role in the politics of the United States (Halonen & Santrock, 1997). Many White men feel the strain of being personally punished by cultural practices to try to promote stronger diversity in the workplace when it places them individually at a disadvantage. For example, a White male applicant who aspired to be a baggage handler for a major airline complained to his career counselor that the only applicants who seemed to be getting hired were women and minorities. He concluded that he was unlikely to be hired since he had the "wrong pigment and wrong plumbing" (Galen & Palmer, 1994).

White men still dominate in positions of power in corporate America. According to the Bureau of Labor Statistics, in 1993 nearly 92 percent of corporate officers were

We are not just citizens of the United States or Canada. We are citizens of the world. By increasing our understanding of the behavior and values of cultures around the world, we hope that we can interact with people from other cultures more effectively and make this planet a more hospitable, peaceful place in which to live.

CONCEPT TABLE 2

Group Relations, Intergroup Relations, and Sociocultural Diversity/Issues

Concept	Processes/Related Ideas	Characteristics/Description
Group Relations	Motivation for group behavior and the structure of groups	Groups satisfy our personal needs, reward us, provide us with information, raise our self-esteem, and enhance our identity. Every group has norms and roles.
	Group performance	Our performance in groups may be enhanced through social facilitation and lowered because of social loafing. Our behavior in the group may also take the form of deindividuation.
	Group interaction and decision making	The risky shift is the tendency for a group decision to be riskier than the average decision made by individual group members. Group polarization and groupthink are other concepts that help clarify our understanding of group performance. The majority usually has the most influence, but at times the minority has its day.
	Leadership	Theories of group leadership include the great-person theory; the situational approach; and the person/situation view, known as the contingency model of leadership.
Intergroup Relations	Culture	Culture refers to the behavior patterns, beliefs, and all other products of a particular group of people that are passed on from generation to generation. Cross-cultural studies involve the comparison of one culture with one or more other cultures. They provide information about the degree to which people are similar, or universal, across cultures, or to what degree their behavior, thoughts, and feelings are culture-specific. Some cross-cultural psychologists ascribe characteristics to entire cultures or nations. One such characteristic is the dichotomy of individualism/collectivism. Individualism involves giving priority to personal goals rather than to group goals; it emphasizes values that serve the self. Collectivism emphasizes values that serve the group by subordinating personal goals to preserve group integrity, interdependence of members, and harmonious relationships. Many Western cultures are described as individualistic, many Eastern cultures as collectivistic. Criticisms of the individualistic/collectivistic dichotomy have been made.

White males. Director positions showed an equivalent proportion at 88 percent. Despite this predominance, it is the men who are seeking entry level positions that increasingly report having to cope with diminished opportunities and expectations to step aside in order to create a more level playing field. In periods of corporate difficulties, White men who have established themselves in careers fear being laid off first as another corporate strategy for enhancing diversity.

Many advocates for dumping affirmative action argue that such practices promote "reverse racism" (Fish, 1993). They criticize such initiatives as undemocratic, penalizing individuals solely on the basis of gender and ethnicity—in this instance male and White. They also believe affirmative action undercuts the role of merit in employment decisions. They suggest that affirmative action may damage affirmative action candidates destined to fail because of underpreparation when other more qualified individuals have been bypassed or rejected in order to promote diversity (Sowell, 1994).

Many personnel departments report growing White male backlash from growing resentment about losing opportunity and being blamed for all the prejudices influencing employment practices in the past. One insidious effect of White male backlash is the attribution of recognition and promotion as solely a function of female gender or non-White ethnicity. One experiment demonstrated that attaching an affirmative action label to a list of employee characteristics prompted more negative attributions and competence concerns than for White candidates who did not have an affirmative action label (Heilman, Block, & Lucas, 1992). Their findings support

Concept	Processes/Related Ideas	Characteristics/Description
	Prejudice, stereotyping, and ethnocentrism	Prejudice is an unjustified negative attitude toward an individual based on the individual's membership in a group. A stereotype is a generalization about a group's characteristics that does not consider any variation from one individual to the next. Both cognitive and affective explanations of stereotyping have been offered. Ethnocentrism is the tendency to favor one's own group over other groups. One theory devised to explain prejudice and conflict is Tajfel's social identity theory, which states that when individuals are assigned to a group they invariably think of the group as an in-group for them. This occurs because they want to have a positive image.
	Racism	Racism occurs when the members of one race or ethnic group believe the members of another race or ethnic group are inferior. Intense racism is less prevalent today than in the past, but it still rears its ugly head from time to time. Some contemporary forms of racism that are less intense than old-fashioned racism include: superficial support for principles of equality, Whites' genuine ambivalence about Blacks, aversive racism, and symbolic racism.
	Improving interethnic relations	Contact, by itself, between ethnic groups does not decrease conflict and improve relations. One effective strategy is to develop a superordinate goal requiring the cooperation of both groups. Sherif initially studied the superordinate goal strategy in his work on in-group/out-group relations at a summer camp for boys, and Aronson showed its effectiveness in the jigsaw classroom designed to reduce ethnic tension. Another effective way to improve interethnic relations is the sharing of intimate information with someone from another ethnic group.
Sociocultural Diversity and Issues	Their nature	Increasing sociocultural diversity raises some important issues—among them: diversity itself; differences and similarities in ethnic, cultural, and gender groups; reducing discrimination and prejudice; understanding the importance of value conflicts; globalizing psychology and reducing ethnocentrism; multiple determination of behavior; and considering both sides of sensitive issues.

some concern that affirmative action programs may intensify ill feelings based on gender and ethnicity rather than improve the climate of the workplace.

Unfortunately many strategies used in the corporate world may make matters worse. Some ill-designed diversity training programs simply heap more responsibility for the employment misfortunes of ethnic and female candidates on White men, which fuels anger and resentment. Especially problematic is that a blaming atmosphere obscures the contribution many White males have made toward creating a diverse workplace (Galen & Palmer, 1994). Ironically, destructive diversity initiatives sometimes rely on brief, intense interventions that may stir up ill feelings without ongoing support to work such feelings through. Critical to the success of diversity initiatives is a broad-ranging diversity definition. For example, age, religious traditions, and family structure can also be aspects of diversity in the workplace. Senior managers need to make a substantial, concrete effort on an ongoing basis to stress that enriched diversity can be a corporate asset in global competition (Baker, 1996; Crowfoot & Chesler, 1996).

Our understanding of sociocultural diversity and issues is improving but there still are many gaps in our knowledge. The 1990s represent an outstanding opportunity for psychologists to make important contributions to our understanding of sociocultural diversity and issues.

At this point we have discussed a number of ideas about group relations, intergroup relations, and sociocultural diversity and issues. A summary of these ideas is presented in concept table 2.

CRITICAL THINKING ABOUT BEHAVIOR

Foundations for a Different Future

No one need wait a moment.
We can start now.
We can start changing the world.

Anne Frank

It is often quite daunting to maintain an optimistic outlook about what the future holds for ethnic and cultural relations in this country and across the globe. Headlines reinforce how little tolerance we have for people whose traditions are different from our own. Such unrest shows up in everything from petty insults and ethnic jokes to severe displays of hostility or bloodshed. Rarely is the world completely at peace, largely due to our human inability to cope with the attitudes, values, and behaviors of those who are unlike us.

This final critical-thinking exercise is a simple one. Identify someone whose cultural or ethnic traditions (or other sociocultural characteristics, such as economic status or sexual orientation) are different from your own. This individual can be from your class, your neighborhood, a civic organization, or interest group. Ask that individual to agree to sit down with you for a simple conversation of 15 minutes in order to help you complete an assignment for psychology. Your objective? Try to establish how similar you are in as many ways as you can.

What kinds of conclusions will you come to? You might identify that you both are "morning people." Perhaps you both rely on public transportation to get around. Maybe you both have a sister-in-law you can't abide. Perhaps you both like Beethoven or Boys II Men. Maybe you both have O-positive blood. The number of similarities you discover will be limited only by your imagination and your energy.

What does it mean? This exercise is designed to facilitate relationships that achieve intimacy. When you recognize how many similarities can be discovered between you and your partner, you may find it more difficult to think in ethnocentric or self-serving terms in relation to the group your partner represents. In addition, your curiosity may have been aroused by some of the differences you discovered.

This may be a small start, but it is through such intimate exchange that stronger bonds can be forged between people of different traditions and values. Stronger bonds offer promise for greater interethnic and intercultural understanding. By completing this exercise, you demonstrate your ability to appreciate individual differences. Your recognition of similarity encourages you to use psychological knowledge to promote human welfare through research and prevention. By achieving intimacy with "the other," you set the stage for a different kind of future.

Overview

We began this chapter by evaluating the nature of attraction, including proximity and similarity, physical attraction, and personality characteristics. Our coverage of the faces of love focused on altruism, friendship, romantic or passionate love, affectionate or companionate love, and relationship cognition. We also studied loneliness. We discussed group relations—the motivation for group behavior and the structure of groups, group performance, group interaction and decision making, and leadership. We learned about intergroup relations, evaluating culture, prejudice, ethnocentrism, and racism, as well as reducing conflict and seeking peace. And we examined sociocultural diversity and issues. Remember that you can obtain an overall summary of the chapter by again studying the concept tables on pages 593 and 610.

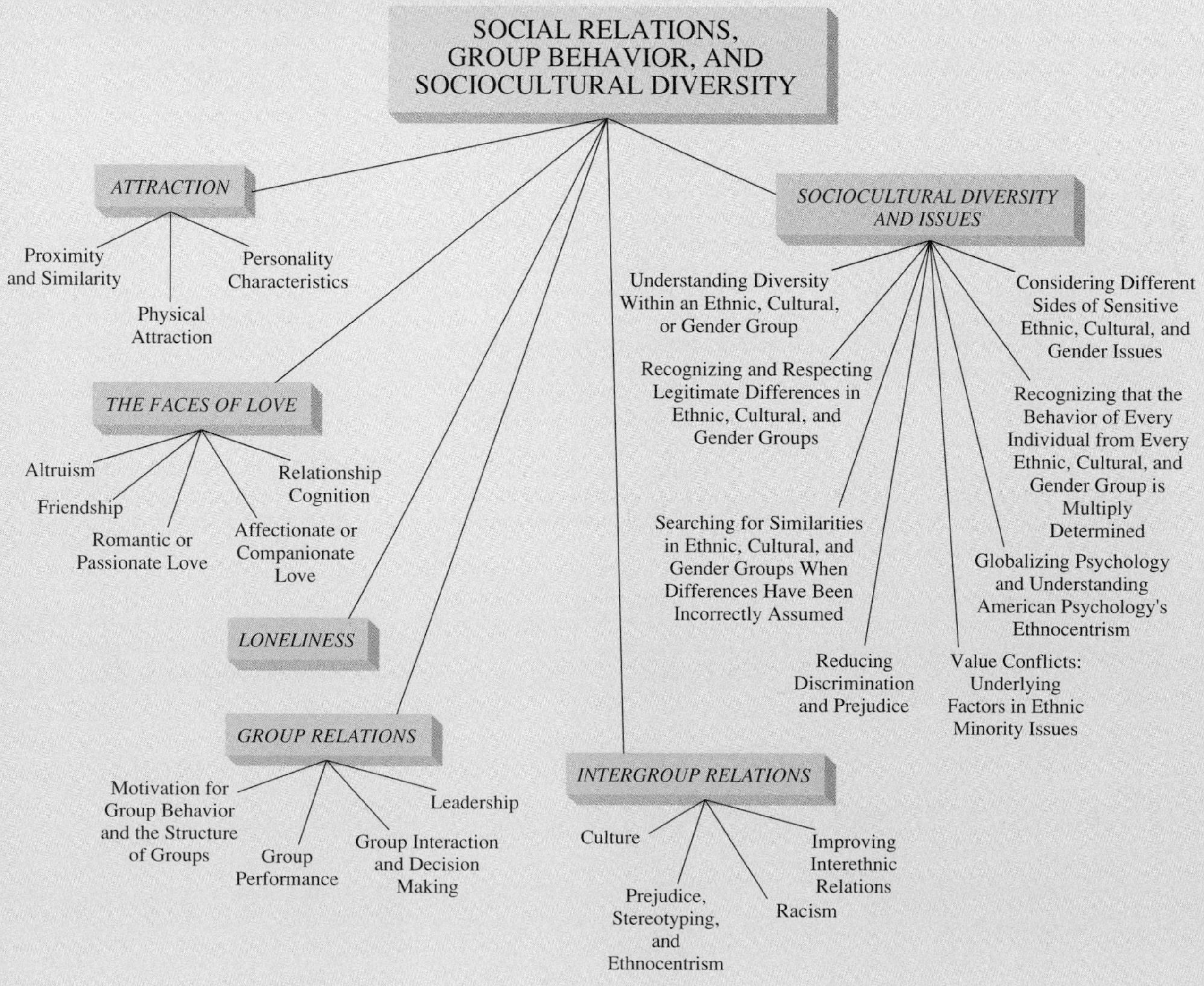

SOCIAL RELATIONS, GROUP BEHAVIOR, AND SOCIOCULTURAL DIVERSITY

- *ATTRACTION*
  - Proximity and Similarity
  - Physical Attraction
  - Personality Characteristics
- *THE FACES OF LOVE*
  - Altruism
  - Friendship
  - Romantic or Passionate Love
  - Affectionate or Companionate Love
  - Relationship Cognition
- *LONELINESS*
- *GROUP RELATIONS*
  - Motivation for Group Behavior and the Structure of Groups
  - Group Performance
  - Group Interaction and Decision Making
  - Leadership
- *INTERGROUP RELATIONS*
  - Culture
  - Prejudice, Stereotyping, and Ethnocentrism
  - Racism
  - Improving Interethnic Relations
- *SOCIOCULTURAL DIVERSITY AND ISSUES*
  - Understanding Diversity Within an Ethnic, Cultural, or Gender Group
  - Recognizing and Respecting Legitimate Differences in Ethnic, Cultural, and Gender Groups
  - Searching for Similarities in Ethnic, Cultural, and Gender Groups When Differences Have Been Incorrectly Assumed
  - Reducing Discrimination and Prejudice
  - Value Conflicts: Underlying Factors in Ethnic Minority Issues
  - Globalizing Psychology and Understanding American Psychology's Ethnocentrism
  - Recognizing that the Behavior of Every Individual from Every Ethnic, Cultural, and Gender Group is Multiply Determined
  - Considering Different Sides of Sensitive Ethnic, Cultural, and Gender Issues

Key Terms

consensual validation An explanation of why people are attracted to others who are similar to them: Our own attitudes and behavior are supported when someone else's attitudes and behavior are similar to ours—their attitudes and behaviors validate ours. p. 582

matching hypothesis The hypothesis that while we may prefer a more attractive person in the abstract, in the real world we end up choosing someone who is close to our own level of attractiveness. p. 583

altruism An unselfish interest in helping someone else. p. 584

social exchange theory The theory that individuals should benefit those who benefit them, or that for a benefit received, an equivalent benefit should be returned at some point. p. 586

egoism Giving to another to ensure reciprocity; to gain self-esteem; to appear powerful, competent, or caring; or to avoid social and self-censure for failing to live up to normative expectations. p. 586

bystander effect Individuals who observe an emergency help less when someone else is present than when they are alone. p. 586

friendship A form of close relationship that involves enjoyment, acceptance, trust, intimacy, respect, mutual assistance, understanding, and spontaneity. p. 587

romantic love Also called passionate love or eros, this type of love has strong components of sexuality and infatuation; it often predominates in the early part of a love relationship. p. 588

affectionate love Also called companionate love, this type of love occurs when individuals desire to have each other near and have a deep, caring affection for each other. p. 589

triangular theory of love Sternberg's view that love comes in three main forms: passion, intimacy, and commitment. p. 589

norms Rules that apply to the members of a group. p. 594

roles Rules and expectations that govern certain positions in a group. Roles define how people should behave in a particular position in the group. p. 594

social facilitation The phenomenon that occurs when an individual's performance improves because of the presence of others; occurs with well-learned tasks but not with new or difficult tasks. p. 594

social loafing Each person's tendency to exert less effort in a group because of reduced monitoring. The result is lowered group performance. p. 595

deindividuation A state of reduced self-awareness, weakened self-restraints against impulsive actions, and apathy about negative social evaluation. p. 595

risky shift The tendency for a group decision to be riskier, on the average, than decisions made by individual group members. p. 596

group polarization effect The solidification and further strengthening of a position as a consequence of group discussion. p. 596

groupthink The motivation of group members to maintain harmony and unanimity in decision making, suffocating differences of opinion in the process. p. 596

great-person theory The theory that some individuals have certain traits that are best suited for leadership positions. p. 597

contingency model of leadership The view that both personality characteristics and situational influences determine who will become a leader; leadership is viewed as a complex undertaking in which leaders influence their followers and followers influence their leaders. p. 597

culture The behavior patterns, beliefs, and all other products of a particular group of people that are passed on from generation to generation. p. 598

cross-cultural studies Studies that compare a culture with one or more other cultures and provide information about the degree to which people have characteristics that are similar, or universal, across cultures, and to what degree their behavior, thoughts, and feelings are culture-specific. p. 598

individualism Giving priority to personal goals rather than to group goals; an outlook that emphasizes values that serve the self, such as feeling good, personal distinction, and independence. p. 598

collectivism Giving priority to values that serve the group by subordinating personal goals to preserve group integrity, interdependence of group members, and harmonious relationships. p. 598

prejudice An unjustified negative attitude toward an individual based on the individual's membership in a group. p. 600

stereotype A generalization about a group's characteristics that does not consider any variation from one individual to another. p. 600

ethnocentrism The tendency to favor one's own group over other groups. p. 600

social identity theory The theory that when individuals are assigned to a group, they invariably think of the group as an in-group for them. This occurs because individuals want to have a positive self-image. Social identity theory helps to explain prejudice and conflict between groups. p. 600

racism The belief that members of another race or ethnic group are inferior. p. 602

assimilation The absorption of an ethnic minority group into the dominant group, which often means the loss of some or all of the behavior and values of the ethnic minority group. p. 607

pluralism The coexistence of distinct ethnic and cultural groups in the same society. p. 607

Resources and Readings in Psychology

***Culture and Psychology* (1996)**
by David Matsumoto
Pacific Grove, CA: Brooks/Cole

Matsumoto discusses the skills and knowledge necessary to interact in a pluralistic world. Among the topics covered are culture and social behavior, culture and health, culture and communication, and culture and gender.

***Culture and Social Behavior* (1994)**
by Harry Triandis
New York: McGraw-Hill

This insightful book by one of cross-cultural psychology's leading figures, Harry Triandis, aims to unveil how culture influences people's social behavior. Among the topics given considerable coverage are how to study cultures, how to analyze subjective culture, culture and communication, cultural influences on aggression, helping, dominance, and conformity, dealing with diversity in intercultural relations, and intercultural training.

***Getting the Love You Want* (1988)**
by Harvill Hendrix
New York: Henry Holt

Getting the Love You Want is a guide for couples to help them improve their relationship. The book is based on Hendrix's couples workshop techniques, which are designed to help couples construct a conscious marriage, a relationship based on awareness of unresolved childhood needs and conflicts that cause individuals to select a particular spouse.

International Association of Cross-Cultural Psychologists
c/o Jeff Lewis
Pitzer College
1050 N. Mills Avenue
Claremont, CA 91711

This organization of professionals and students interested in cross-cultural psychology publishes the *Journal of Cross-Cultural Psychology* and the *Cross-Cultural Psychology Bulletin.*

***Intimate Connections* (1985)**
by David Burns
New York: William Morrow

This book describes how to overcome loneliness. Burns believes lonely individuals need to change their patterns of perception. He tells you how to make social connections and develop closer relationships with others. Checklists, daily mood logs, and self-assessments are found throughout the book.

***Knowledge Structures in Close Relationships* (1995)**
Garth Fletcher and Julie Fitness (eds.)
Hillsdale, NJ: Erlbaum

A number of leading experts discuss issues related to the increasing interest cognition and close relationships. Topics discussed include attachment and working models of the self, construction of relationship realities, script analysis of anger, and lay persons' theories of close relationships.

***A Lifetime of Relationships* (1996)**
by Nelly Vanzetti and Steve Duck
Pacific Grove, CA: Brooks/Cole

The authors address relationships across the lifespan. Among the topics covered are social support, parent-infant relationships, courtship and marriage, the transition to parenthood, and midlife friendship patterns.

National Urban League
The Equal Opportunity Building
500 E. 62nd Street
New York, NY 10021
212–310–9000

The National Urban League is an influential social service and civil rights organization with more than 30,000 volunteers working to obtain equal opportunities for African Americans and other ethnic minority groups. If you are interested in helping, contact the affiliate where you live or contact the National Urban League at the address listed above.

***Psychology and Culture* (1994)**
edited by Walter Lonner and Roy Malpass
Boston: Allyn & Bacon

This recent book includes a large number of articles about ethnicity and culture written by a number of leading experts.

***Shyness* (1987)**
by Philip Zimbardo
Reading, MA: Addison-Wesley

According to Zimbardo, shyness is a widespread social problem that affects as many as four out of every five people at one time or another in their lives. He explores how and why people become shy and examines the roles that parents, teachers, spouses, and culture play in creating shy individuals.

***Understanding Group Behavior* (1996, Vols. I and II)**
by Erich Witte and James Davis
Hillsdale, NJ: Erlbaum

These books provide up-to-date coverage of current research on many different facets of group behavior. Topics discussed include issues involving task-oriented small groups, interpersonal relations in groups, jury decision making, minority opinions, social identity, and effective teamwork.

APPENDIX

DAT

Analyzing the Data: Statistics in Psychology and Everyday Life

JOHN W. SANTROCK
Spring Color, detail

APPENDIX

Analyzing the Data: Statistics in Psychology and Everyday Life

with Don H. Hockenbury

Appendix Outline

The true spirit of delight is to be found in mathematics as surely as in poetry.

—Bertrand Russell

> *What would life be without math?*
>
> —**Sydney Smith, 1835**

IMAGES OF PSYCHOLOGY

Everyday Exposure to Statistics

Whether or not you realize it, you are exposed to statistics every day. For example, the federal government releases reports showing the number of homeless people per 1,000 by regions of the country, the dramatic increase in the number of women in prisons, and so on. Advertisers use statistics to try to persuade you to buy their products by showing you how consumers prefer their products over the competition by five to one. High schools, colleges, and universities use statistics to track student demographics such as the number of students attending, the number of students in particular programs, and student grade point averages. Statistics are also widely used in sports such as football, baseball, and basketball. Statistics also are used in psychology and the other sciences to analyze data that have been collected. In short, statistics are so much a part of our lives that an understanding of basic statistics is essential if you want to be an informed member of society (Hastings, 1995). Thus, the purpose of this appendix is to help you make sense out of some basic statistical concepts that are used in everyday life as well as in scientific research.

PREVIEW

In this appendix, we will explore the nature of statistics, which psychologists use to analyze data. The main sections of this appendix focus on the nature of statistics, descriptive statistics, and inferential statistics.

THE NATURE OF STATISTICS

Statistics *are mathematical methods used to describe, summarize, and draw conclusions about data.* There are two basic categories of statistics: (1) descriptive and (2) inferential.

DESCRIPTIVE STATISTICS

Descriptive statistics *are mathematical procedures used to describe and summarize samples of data in a meaningful fashion.* More specifically, descriptive statistics can be used to describe the characteristics of either a single variable or an interaction between two variables. This is important in most psychological studies because, if we simply reported all the individual scores, it would be virtually impossible to summarize the results. Descriptive statistics allow us to avoid this situation by providing numerous measures that reveal the overall characteristics of the data. Let's look at some of those measures.

Descriptive Statistics for One Variable

The descriptive statistics for one variable include frequency distributions, histograms, and frequency polygons; measures of central tendency; measures of variability; and normal distribution.

Frequency Distributions, Histograms, and Frequency Polygons

Recently some researchers found a connection between how many siblings a student has and her academic performance. Let's assume your introductory psychology class is dubious about this finding, but your classmates want to see if a connection between number of siblings and academic

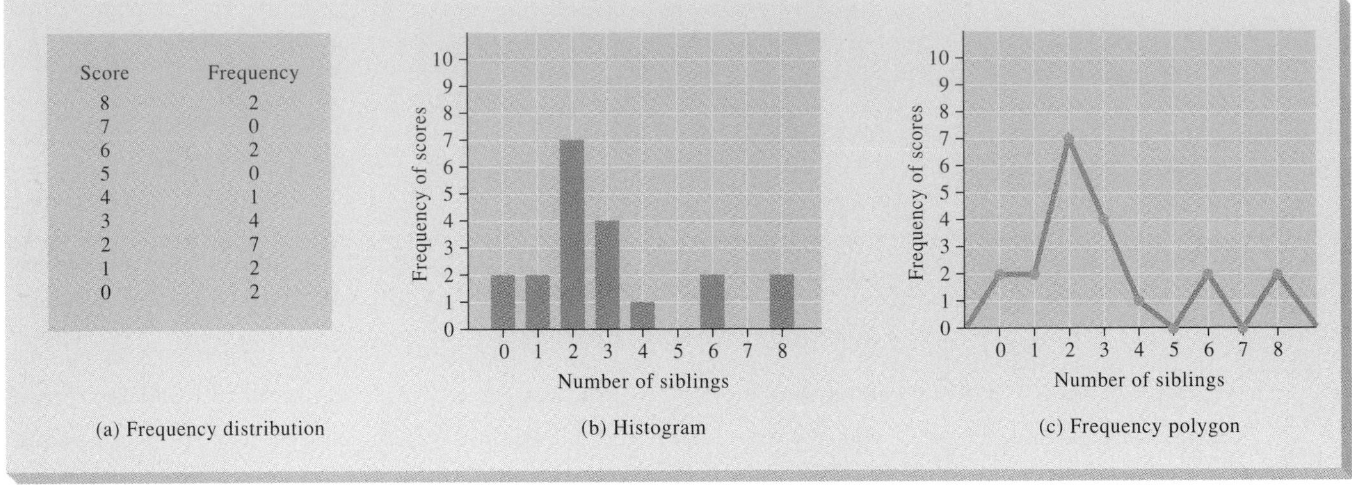

FIGURE 1

Frequency Distribution, Histogram, and Frequency Polygon

These data are from a hypothetical survey on number of siblings reported by 20 students in your psychology class. (*a*) A frequency distribution lists the scores from lowest to highest, with the number of times each score appears. (*b*) A histogram depicts the frequency distribution in graphic form, with vertical bars representing the frequency of scores. (*c*) A frequency polygon is basically the same as a histogram except that the data are represented with lines rather than bars. *Which of these formats do you find easiest to interpret?*

performance applies to them. All 20 students in your psychology class answer a short questionnaire, indicating the number of brothers and sisters they have, if any, and their cumulative high school grade point average. For now let's focus on the variable of number of siblings. Following are the number of siblings each member of your class indicated:

6	4	3	8
6	2	0	2
1	2	3	0
2	3	2	1
3	2	2	8

It is difficult to draw any general conclusions about the overall tendencies of the group just by looking at the raw data (that is, the number of brothers and sisters each person reported). It would be even more difficult if our sample size were 500 or 1,000 students instead of just 20. In any case, the first thing we need to do is to organize the data in a more meaningful way, such as in a frequency distribution. A **frequency distribution** *is simply a listing of scores from lowest to highest with the number of times each score appears in a sample.* Figure 1*a* shows the frequency distribution for our data on number of siblings. The column on the left lists the possible responses (number of siblings) and the column on the right shows how often that response was given.

Another way to present the data is visually through the use of either a histogram or a frequency polygon. A **histogram** *is a frequency distribution in graphic form, in which vertical bars represent the frequency of scores per category or class.* Figure 1*b* shows a histogram for our data on the category of number of siblings. A histogram is often called a *bar graph* or, occasionally, a *block diagram.*

A **frequency polygon** *is basically the same as a histogram except that the data are represented with lines rather than bars.* Figure 1*c* shows a frequency polygon for the data on number of siblings. Notice that, in both the histogram and the frequency polygon, the horizontal axis (the *y*-axis) indicates the possible scores and the vertical axis (the *x*-axis) indicates how often each score occurs in the set of data points.

Although frequency distributions, histograms, and frequency polygons can help *graphically* represent a group of scores, you may want to represent a group of scores *numerically* by providing a measure of central tendency, a measure of variability, or both. Let's look at these two measures.

Measures of Central Tendency

If you want to describe an "average" value for a set of scores, you would use one of the measures of central tendency. In essence, a **measure of central tendency** *is a single number that tells you the overall characteristics of a set of data.* There are three measures of central tendency: the mean, the median, and the mode.

The **mean** *is the numerical average for a group of scores or values.* The mean is calculated by adding all the scores and then dividing by the number of scores. To compute the mean for the data collected on number of siblings, we add all the scores, equalling 60, then divide by the total number of scores, 20. This gives us a mean of 3 siblings. This procedure is shown on the left side of figure 2.

In general the mean is a good indicator of the central tendency for a group of scores; it is the measure of central tendency that is used most often. One exception to this general rule is when a group of scores contains a few extreme scores. For example, consider the annual earnings for the

Mean	Median: Ranking	Median: Scores in order	Mode: Score	Mode: Frequency
6	1	0	8	2
6	2	0	7	0
1	3	1	6	2
2	4	1	5	0
3	5	2	4	1
4	6	2	3	4
2	7	2	2	7 ← Most frequent score
2	8	2	1	2
3	9	2	0	2
2	10	2 (Middle of rankings)		
3	11	2		
0	12	3		
3	13	3		
2	14	3		
2	15	3		
8	16	4		
2	17	6		
0	18	6		
1	19	8		
8	20	8		
60/20=3				

Mode = 2

0 1 2 3 4 5 6 7 8

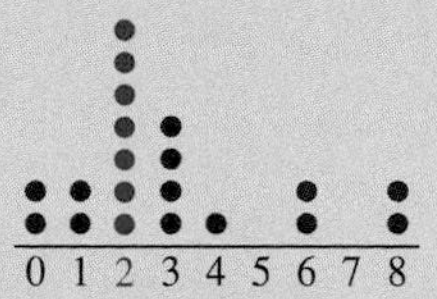

Because there is an even set of scores, median equals middle two scores added together, then divided by 2. Thus, $\frac{2+2}{2} = 2$

FIGURE 2

Mean, Median, and Mode

These data are from a hypothetical survey on number of siblings reported by 20 students in your psychology class. The mean is the numerical average for a group of scores; it is calculated by adding all the scores and then dividing by the number of scores. The median is the score that falls exactly in the middle of a distribution of scores after they have been ranked from highest to lowest. When there is an even number of scores, as there is here, you add the middle two scores and divide by 2 to calculate the median. The mode is the score that appears most often.

two groups of five people in the table that follows. Group 1 lists the earnings of five relatively average people. Group 2 is composed of the earnings of four average people plus the approximate earnings of movie director Steven Spielberg. The vast difference between the mean earnings for the two groups is due to the one extreme score. In such a situation, one of the other two measures of central tendency would more accurately describe the data's overall characteristics.

	Group 1		Group 2
	$17,000		$17,000
	21,000		21,000
	23,000		23,000
	24,000		24,000
	25,000		45,000,000
Mean =	$22,000	*Mean* =	$9,017,000
Median =	$23,000	*Median* =	$23,000
Mode =	N/A	*Mode* =	N/A

The **median** *is the score that falls exactly in the middle of a distribution of scores after they have been arranged (or ranked) from highest to lowest.* When you have an odd number of scores (say, 5 or 7 scores), the median is the score with the same number of scores above it as below it after they have been ranked. Thus, in our example comparing earnings, each group had a median income of $23,000. When you have an even number of scores (8, 10, or 20 scores, for example), you simply add the middle 2 scores and divide by 2 to arrive at the median. In our example using number of siblings, we have an even number of scores (20), so the median is the 10th and 11th scores added together and divided by 2, or (2 + 2)/2. Thus, the median number of siblings for our set of 20 responses is 2, as shown in the middle panel of figure 2.

Notice that, unlike the mean, the median is unaffected by one or a few extreme scores. Look again at the earnings of the two groups. The medians are the same for both groups ($23,000), but their means are extremely different ($22,000 versus $9,017,000).

The **mode** *is the score that occurs most often.* The mode can be determined very easily by looking at a frequency distribution, histogram, or frequency polygon. In our present example, the mode is 2, which is the number of siblings indicated most often by the members of your psychology class. Although the mode is the least used measure of central tendency, it has descriptive value because, unlike the mean and the median, there can be two or more modes. Consider the following 15 scores on a 10-point surprise quiz: 9, 3, 8, 5, 9, 3, 6, 9, 4, 10, 2, 3, 3, 9, 7. The quiz scores 9 and 3 each appear four times. No other score in this example appears as often or more often. Thus, this set of scores has two modes, or a *bimodal distribution.* It is, in fact, possible to have several modes, or a *multimodal distribution.* It also is possible to have no mode at all, which was the case when we compared the earnings of the two groups of five people. Depending on the research question being investigated, the mode may actually provide more meaningful information than either the mean or the median. For example, developers of a program to help people stop smoking would benefit more from knowing that the "modal" age of the greatest number of people who smoke is either 22 *or* 58 than from knowing that the mean age of smokers is 37. By knowing that smoking behavior is distributed bimodally in the population, they can more appropriately target their program to young adults and older adults rather than to middle-aged adults.

Selecting the right measure of central tendency can be challenging. In general, the mean is a good indicator of the central tendency for a group of scores; it is the measure of central tendency that researchers use most often. One exception to this rule is when a group of scores contains extreme scores.

Annual earnings represent a single variable that will illustrate the importance of selecting the right measure of central tendency to communicate about the data. Suppose we have collected annual earnings data on group 1, consisting of seven people. The frequency distribution is as follows:

Group 1	
$17,000	1
$21,000	2
$23,000	1
$24,000	1
$25,000	1
$28,000	1

Test yourself on the differences in concepts. What is the mode? What would be the median score? Calculate the mean by adding up the raw scores and dividing by the number of scores.

The mode is easy to determine from the frequency distribution. The value $21,000 occurs twice and stands out in the distribution as the only repeated value. We determine the median score by identifying the score that occupies the middle (or 4th) position in this frequency distribution: $24,000. In calculating the mean, the sum of all the earnings adds up to $159,000. When you divide that by 7, you discover that the mean is about $22,700. In this example the median, mode, and mean are all relatively close.

Suppose we examine another group in which all of the scores are identical except for the last one. In this case, we are including as the 7th score Steven Spielberg's approximate annual earnings as a highly successful movie director. The data for group 2 are as follows:

Group 2	
$17,000	1
$21,000	2
$23,000	1
$24,000	1
$25,000	1
$45,000,000	1

Which measures of central tendency would change? Which ones would *not* be influenced by the inclusion of an extreme score? As you have probably guessed, the median would stay the same. The fourth score in the distribution is still $24,000. The mode remains the same. The value of $21,000 still occurs twice. The mean is the measure that is dramatically influenced. In this case, the average salary is now over $6 million. This example illustrates how important it is to find out what kind of "average" figure is being presented to communicate the characteristics of any group of data. These insights may also help you develop appropriate skepticism when evaluating statistical claims. For example, radio humorist Garrison Keillor asserts that in his fictionalized hometown of Lake Woebegone, "all the women are strong, all the men are good-looking, and all the children are *above average.*"

Measures of Variability

Consider the following example. You are the owner of three clothing stores that all have the same mean annual earnings of $1,000,000. These three stores fluctuate widely in their monthly earnings, however. Store 1 consistently produces a monthly income of about $100,000. Store 2 generates no income some months but produces $250,000 of income other months. Store 3 loses money the first 9 months of every year but makes enormous profits during October, November, and December. It would be to your advantage to be able to represent the individual fluctuations of your three stores. Measures of variability can be very useful in this regard.

Along with obtaining the overall or central characteristics for a sample, *we can also ask how much the scores in a sample vary from one another. These measures are called* **measures of variability** *or* **measures of dispersion.** The two measures of variability are called the range and the standard deviation.

The **range** *is the distance between the highest and the lowest scores.* The range for our data on number of siblings would be 8 (high score) minus 0 (low score), for a range of 8. Generally speaking, the range is a rather simplistic estimate of variability, or dispersion, for a group of scores. More importantly, because the range involves only two scores, it can produce a misleading index of variability; thus, the range is rarely used as a measure of variability. The most commonly used measure of variability is the standard deviation.

The **standard deviation** *is a measure of how much the scores vary on the average around the mean of a sample.* Put another way, it indicates how closely scores are clustered around the mean. The smaller the standard deviation, the less variability from the mean and vice versa. A simple example will illustrate how this measure of variability works. Consider the following four race scores for each of three joggers:

	Jogger 1	Jogger 2	Jogger 3
Race 1	44 minutes	40 minutes	32 minutes
Race 2	36 minutes	40 minutes	48 minutes
Race 3	44 minutes	40 minutes	32 minutes
Race 4	36 minutes	40 minutes	48 minutes
Mean time	40 minutes	40 minutes	40 minutes
Standard deviation	4 minutes	0 minutes	8 minutes

Notice that all three joggers had the same mean race time of 40 minutes, but jogger 1 and jogger 3 each had race times that varied from race to race, whereas jogger 2 had exactly the same time for each of the four races. This variability from race to race, or the lack of it, is expressed by the three different standard deviations. Because jogger 2 had no variability from race to race, that person's standard deviation is 0. Jogger 1's race time varied 4 minutes on the average from his mean of 40 minutes. In other words, jogger 1 had a standard deviation of 4 minutes for his race times. Jogger 3's race times varied 8 minutes on the average from her mean time of 40 minutes. Thus, jogger 3 had a standard deviation of 8 minutes for her race times. The different standard deviations tell you that jogger 2 had no variability among his race scores, jogger 1 had some variability among his race scores, and jogger 3 had even more variability among her race scores.

Calculating a standard deviation is really not very difficult if you use a calculator capable of doing square roots. To compute a standard deviation, follow these four steps:

1. Calculate the mean of the scores.
2. From each score, subtract the mean and then square that difference. (Squaring the scores will eliminate any negative signs that result from subtracting the mean.)
3. Add the squares and then divide by the number of scores.
4. Calculate the square root of the value obtained in Step 3. This is the standard deviation.

The formula for these four steps is

$$\textbf{Standard deviation} = \sqrt{\frac{\Sigma x^2}{N}}$$

where x = the individual score minus the mean, N = the number of scores, and Σ = the sum of. The application of these four steps to our example of number of siblings is illustrated in figure 3. As you can see, when all the calculations are completed, the standard deviation equals 2.26.

Scores	Score minus mean (x)	Difference squared (x^2)
0	−3	9
0	−3	9
1	−2	4
1	−2	4
2	−1	1
2	−1	1
2	−1	1
2	−1	1
2	−1	1
2	−1	1
2	−1	1
3	0	0
3	0	0
3	0	0
3	0	0
4	1	1
6	3	9
6	3	9
8	5	25
8	5	25
Mean = 60/20 = 3		$\Sigma x^2 = 102$

$$\text{Standard deviation} = \sqrt{\frac{\Sigma x^2}{N}} = \sqrt{\frac{102}{20}} = \sqrt{5.1} = 2.26$$

FIGURE 3

Computing the Standard Deviation

The standard deviation is a measure of how much the scores vary on the average around the mean of a sample. In this figure, you can see how the standard deviation was calculated for the data gathered from a hypothetical survey on number of siblings reported by 20 students in your psychology class.

The Normal Distribution

As we saw earlier, the scores for any distribution can be plotted on a frequency polygon, and can take a variety of shapes. One shape in particular has been of considerable interest to psychologists—the **normal distribution,** or **bell-shaped curve.** *In this type of frequency polygon, most of the scores cluster around the mean. The farther above or below the mean a score appears, the less frequently it occurs.* Many naturally occurring phenomena, such as human intelligence, height, weight, and athletic abilities, follow or closely approximate a normal distribution. For example, the normal distribution of IQ scores as measured by the Wechsler Adult Intelligence Scale is shown in figure 4. Notice that the mean IQ is 100 and the standard deviation is 15 IQ points. We will come back to these numbers in a moment.

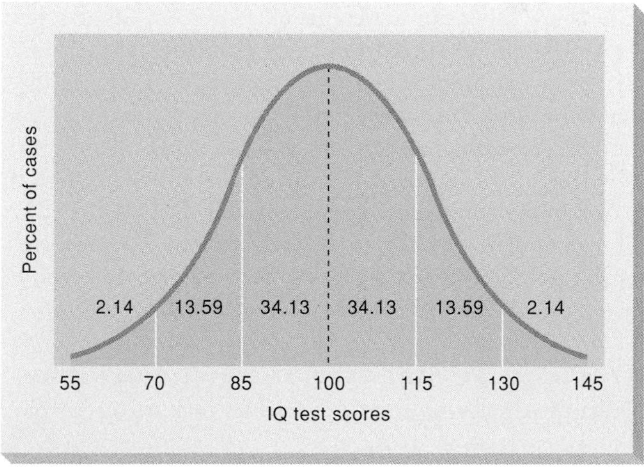

FIGURE 4

Normal Distribution, or Bell-Shaped Curve

This graph shows the normal distribution of IQ scores as measured by the Wechsler Adult Intelligence Scale. The normal distribution is a type of frequency polygon in which most of the scores are clustered around the mean. The scores become less frequent the farther they appear above or below the mean.

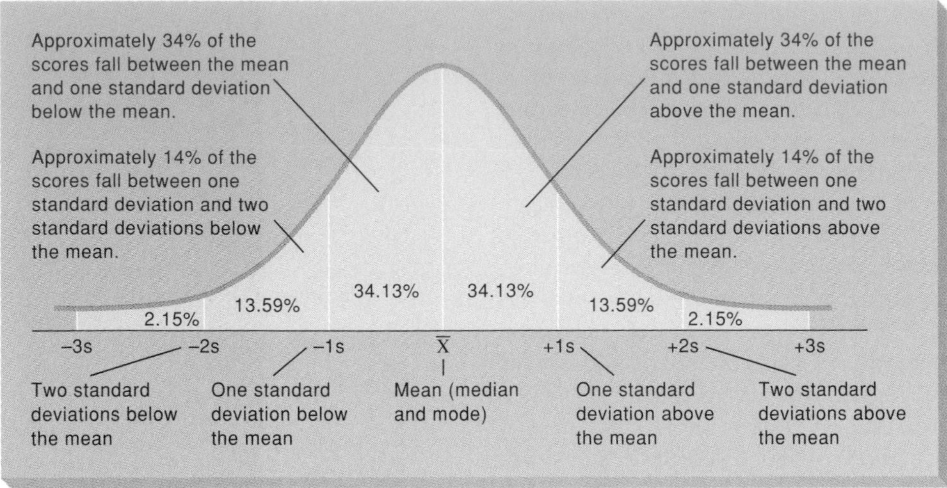

FIGURE 5

The Normal Distribution

Figure 5 illustrates several important characteristics of the normal distribution. First, it is perfectly symmetrical. There is the same number of scores above the mean as below it. Because of this perfect symmetry, the mean, median, and mode are identical in a normal distribution. Second, its bell shape illustrates that the most common scores are near the middle. The scores become less frequent and more extreme the farther away from the middle they appear. Third, the normal distribution incorporates information about both the mean and the standard deviation, as shown in figure 5. The area on the normal curve that is one standard deviation above the mean and one standard deviation below the mean represents 68.26 percent of the scores. At two standard deviations above and below the mean, 95.42 percent of the scores are represented. Finally, at three standard deviations above and below the mean, 99.74 percent of the scores are contained. If we apply this information to figure 4, which shows the normal distribution of IQ scores in the population, you can readily see that 68 percent of the population has an IQ between 85 and 115, 95 percent of the population has an IQ between 70 and 130, and 99 percent of the population has an IQ between 55 and 145.

Descriptive Statistics for Two Variables

Descriptive statistics for two variables include scatter plots and the correlation coefficient.

Scatter Plots

Up to this point, we've focused on descriptive statistics used to describe only one variable. Often the goal of research is to describe the relationship between two variables. In our example, we collected information from the 20 members of your psychology class on their number of siblings and their high school grade point average. The raw data we collected are shown on the left side of figure 6. Also shown is a scatter plot of those scores. A **scatter plot** *is a graph on which pairs of scores are represented.* In this case, we are looking at the possible relationship between number of siblings and academic performance. The possible scores for one variable—number of siblings—are indicated on the *x*-axis, and the scores for the second variable—grade point average—are indicated on the *y*-axis. Each dot on the scatter plot represents one pair of scores as reported by each member of your class. As you can see, there seems to be a distinct pattern to our scatter plot—that is, as the number of siblings increases, high school GPA decreases. Tentatively, at least, there appears to be an association between these two variables. Just how related are these two factors? It's difficult to go beyond a broad generalization from simply viewing a scatter plot.

The Correlation Coefficient

Just as we found measures of central tendency and measures of variability to be more precise than frequency distributions or histograms in describing one variable, it would be helpful if we had a type of measurement that is more precise than a scatter plot to describe the relationship between two variables. In such cases, we could compute a correlation coefficient (Toothaker & Miller, 1996).

A **correlation coefficient** *is a numerical value that expresses the degree of relationship between two variables.* For example, let's assume that we have calculated the correlation coefficient for the relationship between how long your instructor lectures (the *X* variable) and the number of times students yawn (the *Y* variable). For the sake of this example, let's assume these data produce a correlation coefficient (represented by the letter *r*) of +.70. Remember this number, as we will use it to illustrate what a correlation coefficient tells you.

The numeric value of a correlation coefficient falls within the range from +1.00 to −1.00. This is simply an arbitrary range that does *not* parallel an integer number line (for example, . . . −3, −2, −1, 0, 1, 2, 3, . . .). In other

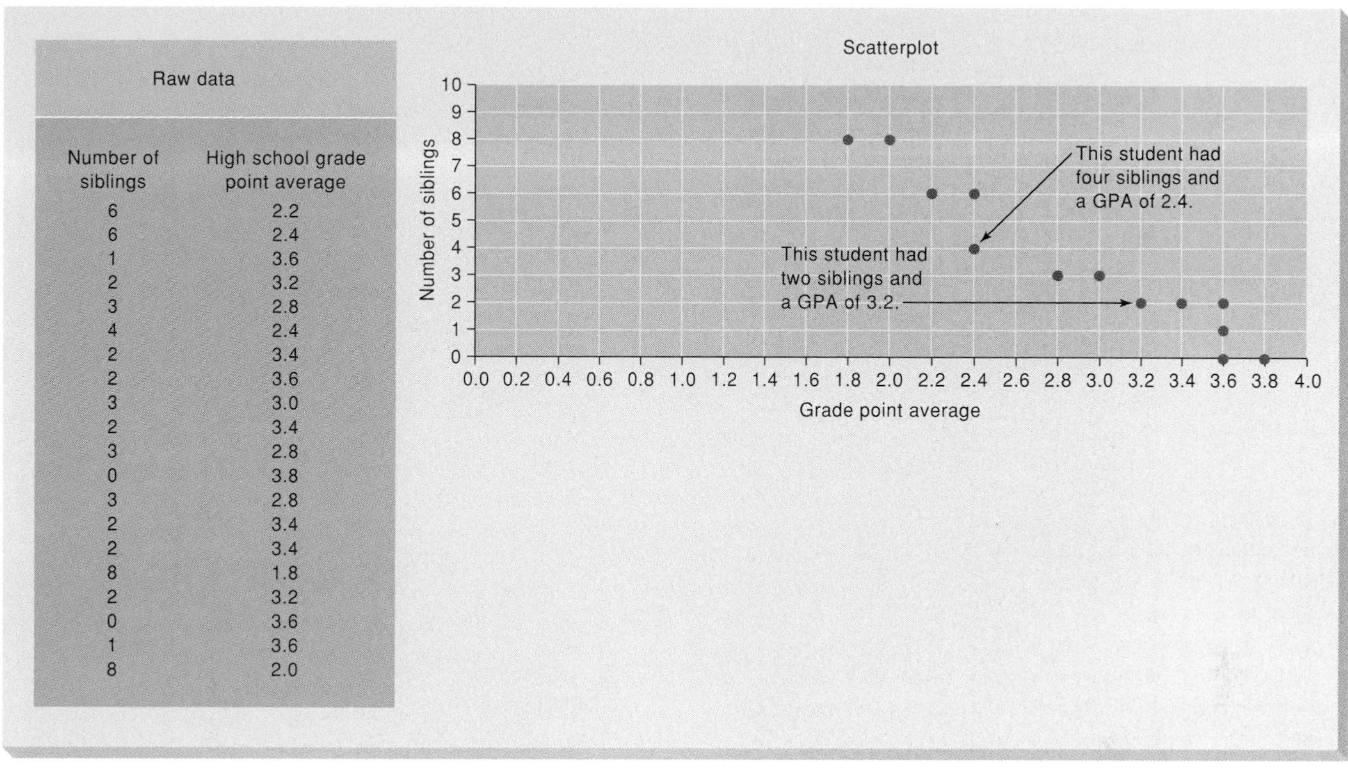

Raw data

Number of siblings	High school grade point average
6	2.2
6	2.4
1	3.6
2	3.2
3	2.8
4	2.4
2	3.4
2	3.6
3	3.0
2	3.4
3	2.8
0	3.8
3	2.8
2	3.4
2	3.4
8	1.8
2	3.2
0	3.6
1	3.6
8	2.0

FIGURE 6

Descriptive Measures for Two Variables
This scatter plot depicts the possible relationship between number of siblings and grade point average. Each dot on the scatter plot represents one pair of scores as reported by each member of your class in a hypothetical survey. The raw data from that survey are shown on the left.

words, negative numbers are *not* less than positive numbers. A correlation of +.65 is just as strong as a correlation of –.65. The plus or minus sign has a different meaning when applied to correlation coefficients, which we will discuss in a moment. Also, avoid the temptation to attach value judgments to correlational signs. A positive correlation is not "good" or "desirable" and a negative correlation is not "bad" or "undesirable."

There are two parts to a correlation coefficient: the number and the sign. The number tells you the strength of the relationship between the two factors. The rule is simple: regardless of the sign, the closer the number is to 1.00, the stronger the correlation; conversely, the closer the number is to .00, the weaker the correlation. Remember that the plus or minus sign tells you nothing about the strength of the correlation; thus, a correlation of –.87 is stronger than a correlation of +.45. Table 1 offers guidelines for interpreting correlational numbers.

TABLE 1

Guidelines for Interpreting Correlational Numbers

1.00	Perfect relationship; the two factors always occur together
.76–.99	Very strong relationship; the two factors occur together very often
.51–.75	Strong relationship; the two factors occur together frequently
.26–.50	Moderate relationship; the two factors occur together occasionally
.01–.25	Weak relationship; the two factors seldom occur together
.00	No relationship; the two factors never occur together

The plus or minus sign tells you the direction of the relationship between the two variables. A **positive correlation** *is a relationship in which the two factors vary in the same direction.* Both factors tend to go up together *or* both factors tend to go down together. Either relationship represents a positive correlation. A **negative correlation** *is a relationship in which the two factors vary in opposite directions.* As one factor increases, the other factor decreases. Thus, a correlation of +.15 would indicate a weak positive correlation, and a –.74 would indicate a strong negative correlation. Examples of scatter plots showing positive and negative correlations appear in figure 7.

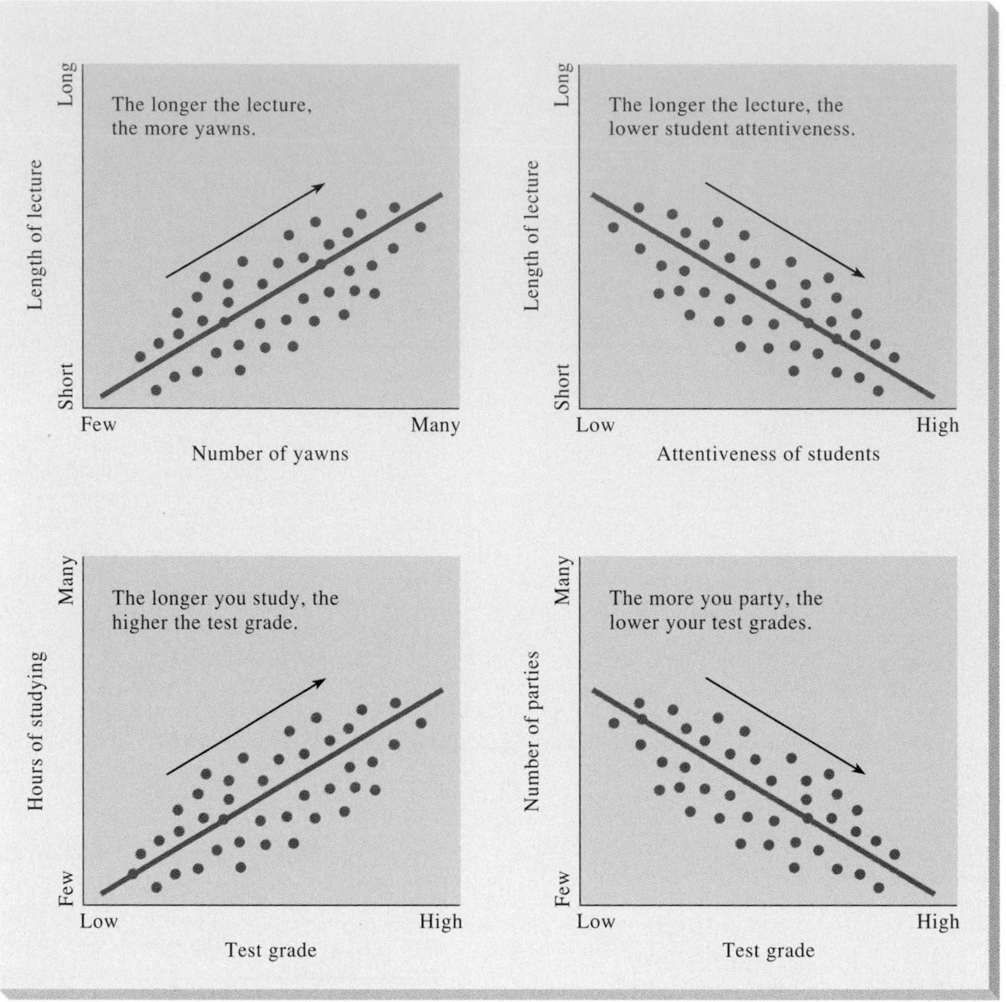

FIGURE 7

Scatter Plots Showing Positive and Negative Correlations
A positive correlation is a relationship in which two factors vary in the same direction, as shown in the two scatter plots on the left. A negative correlation is a relationship in which two factors vary in opposite directions, as shown in the two scatter plots on the right.

Let's return to our example about how long your professor lectures and the number of times students yawn. Those two variables produced a correlation coefficient of +.70. The number .70 tells us that these two factors happen together frequently. We also know from the preceding discussion that the positive sign indicates the two factors vary in the same direction. As the amount of time your professor lectures increases, the number of yawns increases. An example of a negative correlation in this situation might be the relationship between how long your instructor lectures and the level of student attentiveness. As the length of time your instructor lectures increases, the level of student attentiveness decreases—these two factors vary in opposite directions.

The following formula is used to calculate a correlation coefficient:

$$r = \frac{\sum xy}{\sqrt{\sum x^2 \Xi \sum y^2}}$$

where x is the difference between each X variable minus the mean; y is the difference between each Y variable minus the mean; $\sum xy$ is the sum of the cross products (each x score multiplied by its corresponding y score); $\sum x^2$ is the sum of the squares of the x scores; and $\sum y^2$ is the sum of the squares of the y scores.

Let's return to our original example examining the relationship between number of siblings and high school grade point average. Figure 8 contains the calculation of the correlation coefficient of –.95. From our previous discussion, we know that this is a very strong association indicating that, as number of siblings increases, grade point average decreases. What exactly does this mean? How are we supposed to interpret this hypothetical finding? Does this mean that, if you are an only child, you will have a 4.0 GPA? Does this mean that, if you grew up in a large family, you are destined to make poor grades?

Although correlation coefficients are frequently used by researchers to analyze the relationship between two

Student number	Number of siblings (*X* variable)	Score minus mean (3.0)	Difference squared	High school GPA (*Y* variable)	Score minus mean (3.0)	Difference squared	*x* multiplied by *y*
N	*X*	*x*	x^2	*Y*	*y*	y^2	*xy*
1	6	3	9	2.2	−.8	.64	−2.4
2	6	3	9	2.4	−.6	.36	−1.8
3	1	−2	4	3.6	.6	.36	−1.2
4	2	−1	1	3.2	.2	.04	−0.2
5	3	0	0	2.8	−.2	.04	0.0
6	4	1	1	2.4	−.6	.36	−0.6
7	2	−1	1	3.4	.4	.16	−0.4
8	2	−1	1	3.6	.6	.36	−0.6
9	3	0	0	3.0	0.0	.00	0.0
10	2	−1	1	3.4	.4	.16	−0.4
11	3	0	0	2.8	−.2	.04	0.0
12	0	−3	9	3.8	.8	.64	−2.4
13	3	0	0	2.8	−.2	.04	0.0
14	2	−1	1	3.4	.4	.16	−0.4
15	2	−1	1	3.4	.4	.16	−0.4
16	8	5	25	1.8	−1.2	1.44	−6.0
17	2	−1	1	3.2	.2	.04	−0.2
18	0	−3	9	3.6	.6	.36	−1.8
19	1	−2	4	3.6	.6	.36	−1.2
20	8	5	25	2.0	−1.0	1.00	−5.0
	N = 20	Mean = 3.0	$\Sigma x^2 = 102$	Mean = 3.0		$\Sigma y^2 = 6.72$	$\Sigma xy = -25.00$

$$r = \frac{\Sigma xy}{\sqrt{\Sigma x^2 \times \Sigma y^2}} = \frac{-25.00}{\sqrt{(102)\,(6.72)}} = \frac{-25.00}{\sqrt{685.44}} = \frac{-25.00}{26.18} = -.95$$

FIGURE 8

Computation of a Correlation Coefficient

These data are from a hypothetical survey on number of siblings and high school GPA reported by 20 students in your psychology class. The correlation coefficient of −.95 indicates a very strong negative relationship between number of siblings and high school GPA.

variables, they are almost as frequently misinterpreted by the general public. The problem is that *correlation does not necessarily indicate causality.* Causality means that one factor makes, produces, or creates change in a second factor. Correlation means that two factors *seem* to be related, associated, or connected such that, as one factor changes, the other factor seems to change. Correlation implies potential causality that may or may not actually be there. Even though two factors are strongly or even perfectly correlated, in reality a third factor may be responsible for the changes observed. Thus, in our hypothetical example showing a very strong negative correlation between number of siblings and GPA, the changes observed in these two variables could be due to a third factor. For example, perhaps children who grow up in larger families have a greater tendency to hold part-time jobs after school, thereby limiting the amount of time they can study, or children who grow up in small families may be more likely to have their own room, with a desk, thereby allowing them more uninterrupted study time. In any case, the point remains the same: correlation only potentially indicates a causal relationship.

Look at the terms in bold type in the following headlines:

Researchers **Link** Coffee Consumption to Cancer of Pancreas
Scientists Find **Connection** Between Ear Hair and Heart Attacks
Psychologists Discover **Relationship** Between Marital Status and Health
Researchers Identify **Association** Between Loneliness and Social Skills
Parental Discipline **Tied** to Personality Disorders in Children

All of the words in bold type are synonymous with correlation, not causality. The general public, however, tends to equate such terms as *connection* or *association* with causality. As you read about the findings of psychological studies, or findings in other sciences, guard against making the same interpretation. Remember, correlation means only that two factors seem to occur together (Cohen, 1996).

How, then, can a researcher provide compelling evidence of a causal relationship between two variables? In the experimental method, researchers try to hold all variables constant, then systematically manipulate the factor that they think produces change (the independent variable); finally, they measure the variable believed to be affected by these manipulations (the dependent variable). If the researchers have held all factors constant except for their manipulation of the independent variable, then any changes observed in the dependent variable can be attributed to the independent variable; changes in the independent variable *caused* changes to occur in the dependent variable. This is the most compelling evidence of causality that science can provide, assuming that the experiment was carefully designed and controlled to avoid such experimental pitfalls as experimenter bias, subject bias, situational bias, or invalid scores. Furthermore, experimental evidence of causality is even more compelling if the research can be *replicated,* or repeated by other researchers using different subjects.

Why do researchers even bother doing correlational studies if they only potentially indicate causality? Why don't researchers simply conduct experiments all the time, since experiments provide the most compelling evidence of causality? There are several reasons. One, it is not always ethically possible to conduct an experiment on the research question at hand. It may be unethical to conduct an experiment because it poses either physical or psychological danger to the subjects. For instance, it would be unethical to carry out an experiment in which expectant mothers are directed to smoke varying numbers of cigarettes (the independent variable) to see how cigarette smoke affects birth weight and fetal activity level (the dependent variable). Two, the issue under investigation may be post hoc (after the fact) or historical, such as studying the childhood backgrounds of people who are abusive parents. Three, sometimes the factors simply cannot be manipulated experimentally, such as the effects of the October 17, 1989, earthquake on the residents of San Francisco. Fourth, experiments can be incredibly costly to conduct. Correlational studies, on the other hand, are often less expensive. These are some of the limitations associated with the experimental method.

What do researchers do in the situations in which formal experiments are inappropriate or impossible? They use the correlational method and collect data based on *systematic observation* of subjects rather than *systematic manipulation* of the subjects. Systematic observation techniques include case studies, naturalistic observation, interviews, questionnaires, and standardized tests.

Thus, the correlation coefficient is a very useful and important statistical tool for psychological as well as for other kinds of research. By understanding how to interpret the number and sign of a correlation coefficient, you can judge how closely two factors are related and in what direction they vary. By understanding the difference between "correlation" and "causation," you are more likely to interpret correctly the research findings described in newspapers, magazines, and journals. Every time the words *association, link, tie, connection,* and *relationship* are used to explain research findings, a correlational study is being described, because all of those words imply correlation, not causation.

Although descriptive statistics can help us summarize and characterize a sample of data, they have limitations. For instance, descriptive statistics cannot tell us whether data are meaningful or significant. A different category of statistics is necessary to accomplish this—inferential statistics (Evans, 1996).

Inferential Statistics

Assume you have conducted a naturalistic observation investigating whether boys play more aggressively than girls. Assume further that you have followed all the procedures for a good research design to eliminate or minimize any bias or other factors that might distort the data you have collected. When you calculate the descriptive statistics comparing the aggressive behavior of boys with that of girls, it appears that there are large differences between the two groups. How large do those differences have to be before you are willing to conclude confidently that the differences are significant? Inferential statistics can help answer that question.

Inferential statistics *are complex mathematical methods used to draw conclusions about data that have been collected.* More specifically, inferential statistics are used to indicate whether or not data sufficiently support or confirm a research hypothesis. To accomplish this, inferential statistics rely on statements of probability and statistical significance, two important concepts that we will examine briefly.

There are many kinds of inferential statistics. Depending on the characteristics of the data and the number of groups being compared, different tests are applied. Some examples of inferential statistical measures include the *t*-test, the chi-square, analysis of variance, and the Mann-Whitney *U* Test. Although it's beyond the scope of this Appendix to look at these different measures of inferential statistics in detail, the logic behind inferential statistics is relatively simple. Measures of inferential statistics yield a statement of probability about the differences observed between two or more groups; this probability statement tells what the odds are that the observed differences were due simply to chance. If an inferential statistical measure tells

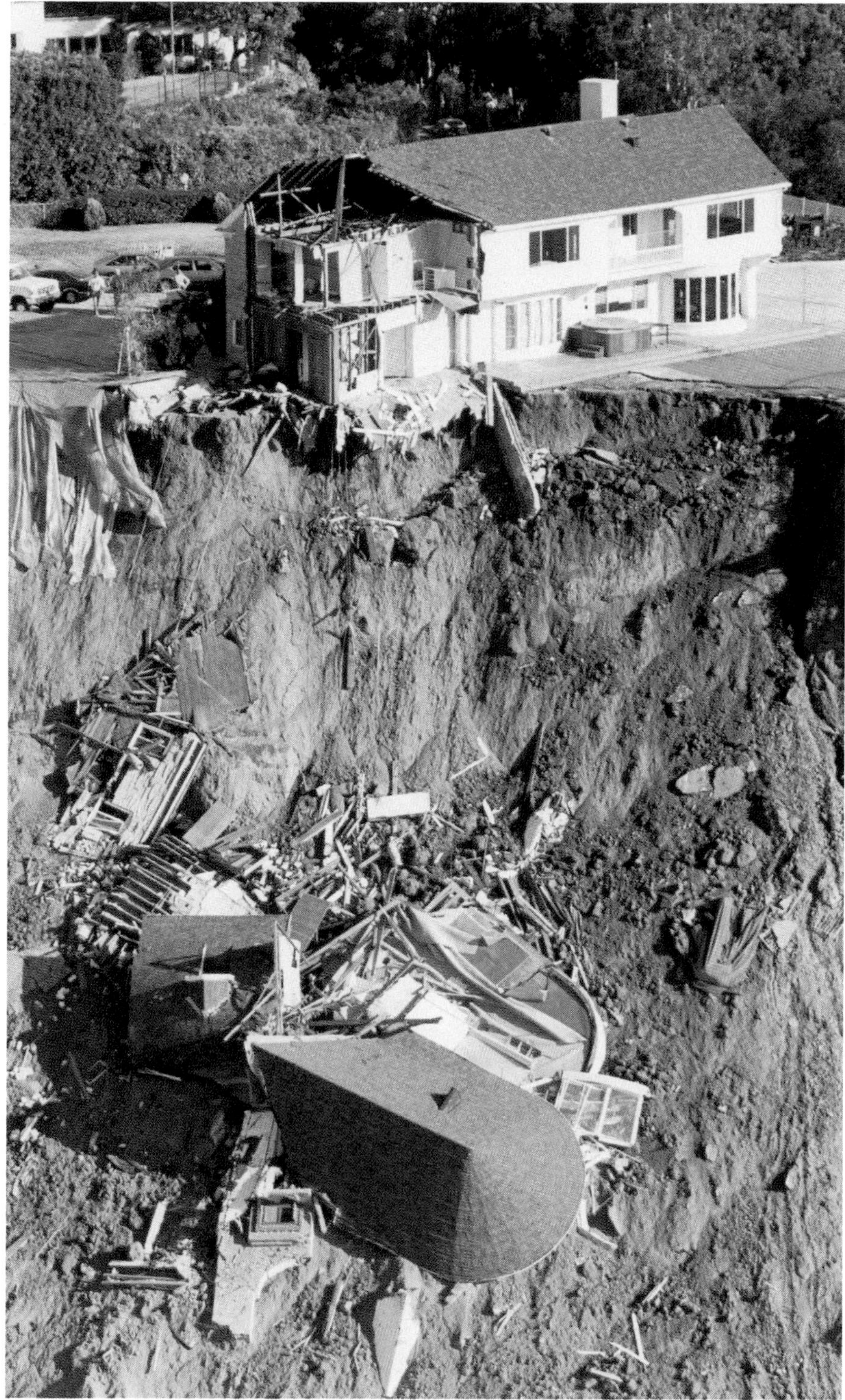

Correlation methods permit research in situations that cannot be experimentally manipulated, such as natural disasters like the 1993 earthquake in Los Angeles.

you that the odds are less than 5 out of 100 (or .05) that the differences are due to chance, the results are considered statistically significant. In statistical jargon, this is referred to as the *.05 level of statistical significance*, or the *.05 confidence level.* Put another way, **statistical significance** *means that the differences observed between two groups are so large that it is highly unlikely those differences are due merely to chance.*

The .05 level of statistical significance is considered the minimum level of probability that scientists will accept for concluding that the differences observed are real, thereby supporting a hypothesis. Some researchers prefer to use more rigorous levels of statistical significance, such as the .01 level of statistical significance (1 out of 100) or the .001 level of statistical significance (1 out of 1,000). Regardless of which level of statistical significance is used, by knowing that a research result is statistically significant, you can be reasonably confident that the finding is not due simply to chance. Of course, replication of the study, with similar significant results, can increase your confidence in the finding even further.

However, a statistically significant difference does not always translate into a difference that has meaning in everyday life. Before assuming that a finding is significant both statistically and in everyday terms, it's wise to look at the actual differences involved. Sometimes the differences are so small as to be inconsequential. For example, in comparisons of average scores for males and females on the math section of the Scholastic Aptitude Test, the difference is statistically significant, with males performing better than females (Benbow & Stanley, 1983). In reality, however, the average difference is only a few points. Caution, therefore, should be exercised in the practical interpretation of statistically significant findings.

At this point we have studied a number of ideas about the nature of statistics, descriptive statistics, and inferential statistics. A summary of these ideas is presented in concept table 1.

Concept Table 1

The Nature of Statistics, Descriptive Statistics, and Inferential Statistics

Concept	Processes/Related Ideas	Characteristics/Description
Nature of Statistics	Basic ideas	Statistics are a part of our everyday life. Therefore, an understanding of statistics helps us to be informed participants in today's society. Statistics are mathematical methods that are used to describe, summarize, and infer conclusions about data. The two basic categories of statistics are (1) descriptive and (2) inferential.
Descriptive Statistics	Descriptive statistics for one variable	Descriptive statistics used to describe the characteristics of one variable include frequency distributions, histograms, frequency polygons, measures of central tendency, and measures of variability. The most commonly used descriptive statistics are measures of central tendency and measures of variability. Measures of central tendency describe the overall or average characteristics of a group of scores. Measures of central tendency include the mean, median, and mode. Measures of variability describe how much scores differ from one another. The standard deviation is the most commonly used measure of variability. The normal distribution, or bell-shaped curve, is a frequency polygon of special interest to psychologists. A perfect normal distribution is completely symmetrical; thus, the mean, median, and mode are identical. By knowing the mean and the standard deviation for a normally distributed variable, you can determine what percentage of the population has a particular score.
	Descriptive statistics for two variables	Descriptive statistics examining the relationship between two variables include the scatter plot and the correlation coefficient. Whereas a scatter plot provides a graphic illustration of the relationship between two variables, correlation coefficients provide a numeric summary of the association between two variables. Although correlational research is widely used, many people confuse correlation and causality. Correlation simply means that two variables seem to occur together in a systematic fashion. Correlation, however, does not necessarily indicate causality. Causality means that one factor makes, produces, or creates change in a second factor. The most compelling evidence to demonstrate that one variable causes change to occur in a second variable comes from experiments. Formal experiments, however, cannot always be conducted for a variety of reasons; thus, scientists frequently rely on correlational research to demonstrate a potential relationship between two variables.
Inferential Statistics	Their nature	Inferential statistics are complex mathematical methods used to draw conclusions based on data. Inferential statistical measures yield a statement of probability about the differences observed between two or more groups. This probability statement tells you what the odds are that the observed differences were due simply to chance. If an inferential statistical measure tells you that the odds are less than 5 out of 100 (or .05) that the observed differences are due to chance, the results are considered statistically significant. Although research results may be statistically significant, they may actually have little or no implication in everyday terms. Thus, caution should be exercised in the practical interpretation of statistically significant findings.

Overview

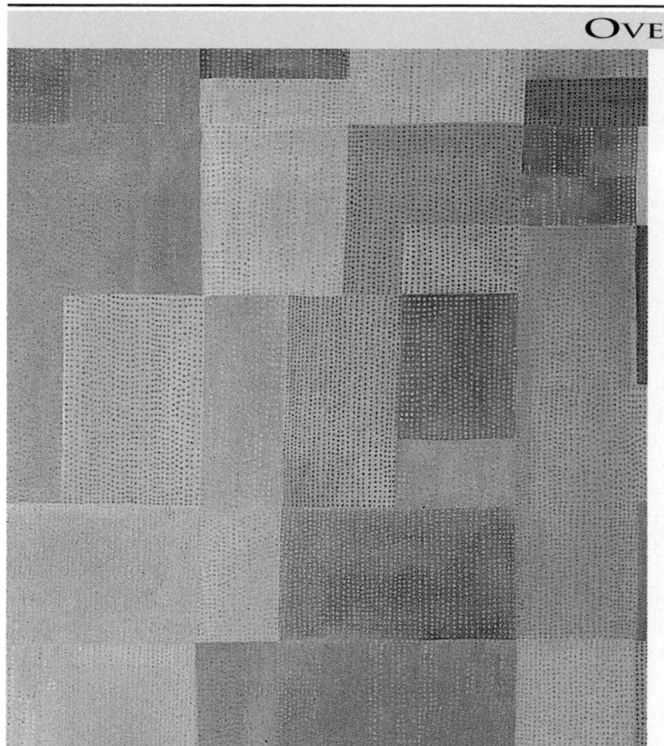

In this appendix we explored the basic nature of statistics, descriptive statistics, and inferential statistics. Don't forget that you can obtain an overall summary of the appendix by studying the concept table on page 630.

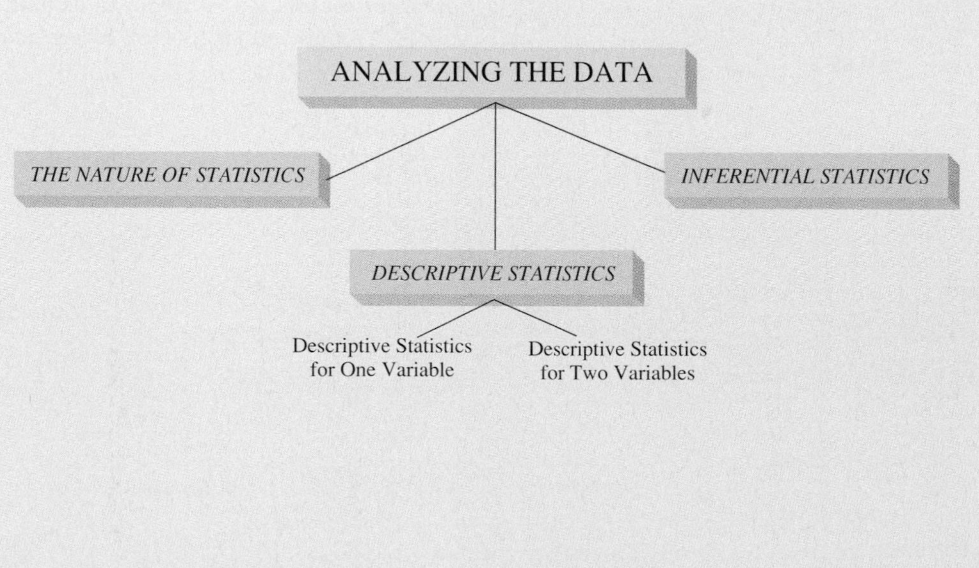

Key Terms

statistics Mathematical methods used to describe, summarize, and draw conclusions about data. p. 619

descriptive statistics Mathematical procedures used to describe and summarize samples of data in a meaningful fashion. p. 619

frequency distribution A listing of scores from lowest to highest with the number of times each score appears in a sample. p. 620

histogram Frequency distribution in a graphic form, in which vertical bars represent the frequency of scores per category or class. p. 620

frequency polygon Basically the same as a histogram except that the data are represented with lines rather than bars. p. 620

measure of central tendency A single number that tells you the overall characteristics of a set of data. p. 620

mean The numerical average for a group of scores or values. p. 620

median The score that falls exactly in the middle of a distribution of scores after they have been arranged (or ranked) from highest to lowest. p. 621

mode The score that occurs most often. p. 621

measures of variability (measures of dispersion) A measure of how much the scores in a sample vary from one another. p. 622

range The distance between the highest and lowest scores. p. 622

standard deviation A measure of how much the scores vary on the average around the mean of a sample. p. 622

normal distribution (bell-shaped curve) In this type of frequency polygon, most of the scores cluster around the mean. The farther above or below the mean a score appears, the less frequently it occurs. p. 623

scatter plot A graph on which pairs of scores are represented. p. 624

correlation coefficient A numerical value that expresses the degree of relationship between two variables. p. 624

positive correlation A relationship in which the two factors vary in the same direction. p. 625

negative correlation A relationship in which the two factors vary in opposite directions. p. 625

inferential statistics Complex mathematical methods used to draw conclusions about data that have been collected. p. 628

statistical significance The idea that the differences observed between two groups are so large that it is highly unlikely that those differences are due merely to chance. p. 629

Resources and Readings in Psychology

Elementary Statistics (1989, 2nd ed.)
by A. Comrey, P. Bott, and H. Lee
Dubuque, IA: Wm. C. Brown

This excellent introductory statistics text uses a step-by-step problem-solving approach to understanding statistics.

How to Lie with Statistics (1954)
by D. Huff
New York: W. W. Norton

This delightful book is the classic primer on how statistics are frequently used to mislead or deceive people. Originally published in 1954, the examples are not only humorous and effective, but they also provide a wonderful glimpse of everyday life in America over four decades ago. Currently in its thirty-seventh printing, this book is must reading for every college student.

GLOSSARY

A

abnormal behavior—behavior that is maladaptive and harmful.

absolute threshold—the minimum amount of energy that we can detect.

accommodation—the eye lens' changes in curvature; an individual's adjustment to new information.

acculturation—cultural change that results from continuous, firsthand contact between two distinctive cultural groups.

acculturative stress—the negative consequences of acculturation.

accurate empathy—Rogers' term for the therapist's identification with the client.

acetylcholine (ACh)—a neurotransmitter that produces contractions of skeletal muscles by acting on motor nerves.

achievement motivation (need for achievement)—the desire to accomplish something, to reach a standard of excellence, and to expend effort to excel.

achievement test—a test that measures what has been learned or what skills have been mastered.

action potential—the brief wave of electrical charge that sweeps down the axon.

activation-synthesis view—the view that dreams have no inherent meaning but, rather, reflect the brain's efforts to make sense out of or find meaning in the neural activity that takes place during REM sleep. In this view, the brain has considerable random activity during REM sleep, and dreams are an attempt to synthesize the chaos.

active-behavioral strategies—coping responses in which individuals take some type of action to improve their problem situation.

active-cognitive strategies—coping responses in which individuals actively think about a situation in an effort to adjust more effectively.

active listening—Rogers' term for listening to another person with total attention to what the person says and means.

active (niche-picking) genotype-environment interactions—the interactions that occur when children seek out environments they find compatible and stimulating. *Niche-picking* means finding a niche or setting that is especially suited to the child's abilities.

activity theory—the theory that the more active and involved older people are, the more satisfied they will be with their lives and the more likely they will stay healthy.

acupuncture—a technique in which thin needles are inserted at specific points in the body to produce various effects, such as local anesthesia.

adaptation—modifications in an organism's structure, function, and behavior that increase the likelihood of its continued existence or that of its relatives.

adaptive behavior—a concept that has been prevalent in biology; adaptive behavior is behavior that promotes the organism's survival in the natural habitat.

additive mixture—the mixing of beams of light from different parts of the color spectrum.

adolescence—the developmental period of transition from childhood to adulthood, which involves physical, cognitive, and socioemotional changes. In most cultures adolescence begins at about 10 to 13 years of age and ends at about 18 to 21 years of age.

adolescent egocentrism—the adolescent's belief that others are as preoccupied with the adolescent as she is herself, that she is unique, and that she is indestructible.

adoption study—a study in which investigators seek to discover whether, in behavior and psychological characteristics, adopted children are more like their adoptive parents, who provided a home environment, or their biological parents, who contributed their heredity. Another form of adoption study compares adoptive and biological siblings.

adrenal glands—glands that play an important role in our moods, energy level, and ability to cope with stress; each adrenal gland secretes epinephrine (also called adrenaline) and norepinephrine (also called noradrenaline).

aerobic exercise—sustained exercise (such as jogging, swimming, or cycling) that stimulates heart and lung activity.

affectionate love—a type of love in which individuals desire to have the other person near and have a deep, caring affection for the other person. Also called companionate love.

afferent nerves—sensory nerves that carry information to the brain.

afterimages—sensations that remain after a stimulus is removed.

ageism—prejudice against people based on their age; in particular, prejudice against older people.

agoraphobia—the fear of entering unfamiliar situations, especially open or public spaces; the most common phobic disorder.

AIDS—a sexually transmitted disease that is caused by the human immunodeficiency virus (HIV), which destroys the body's immune system.

alcoholism—a disorder that involves long-term, repeated, uncontrolled, compulsive, and excessive use of alcoholic beverages, impairing the drinker's health and interpersonal relationships.

algorithms—procedures that guarantee an answer to a problem.

all-or-none-principle—the principle that once the electrical impulse reaches a certain level of intensity, it fires and moves all the way down the axon, remaining at the same strength throughout its course.

alpha waves—brain waves that make up the EEG pattern of a person who is awake but relaxed.

altered states of consciousness—mental states that noticeably differ from normal awareness. Drugs, meditation, fatigue, hypnosis, and sensory deprivation can produce altered states of consciousness.

altruism—an unselfish interest in helping someone else.

Alzheimer's disease—a degenerative irreversible brain disorder that impairs memory and social behavior.

American Board of Professional Psychology (ABPP)—an organization that assesses clinical psychologists' competency and awards special diplomas to qualified clinicians.

amnesia—the loss of memory.

amplitude—a feature of waves that is measured in decibels (dB), the amount of pressure produced by a wave relative to a standard.

amygdala—a limbic system structure located within the base of the temporal lobe and involved in the discrimination of objects that are important for an organism's survival, such as appropriate food, mates, and social rivals.

analogy—a type of formal reasoning that is always made up of four parts, and the relationship between the first two parts is the same as the relationship between the last two.

anal stage—Freud's second stage of development, occurring between 1½ and 3 years of age, in which the child's greatest pleasure involves the anus or the eliminative functions associated with it.

androgens—the main class of male sex hormones.

androgyny—the presence of desirable masculine and feminine characteristics in an individual.

anorexia nervosa—an eating disorder that involves the relentless pursuit of thinness through starvation.

anterograde amnesia—a memory disorder that prevents the retention of new information or events; what was learned before the onset of the condition is not affected.

antianxiety drugs—drugs that reduce anxiety by making individuals less excitable and more tranquil; commonly known as tranquilizers.

antidepressant drugs—drugs that regulate mood. The three main classes are tricyclics, such as Elavil; SSRI inhibitors, such as Prozac; and MAO inhibitors, such as Nardil.

antipsychotic drugs—powerful drugs that diminish agitated behavior, reduce tension, decrease hallucinations and delusions, improve social behavior, and produce better sleep patterns in severely mentally disordered individuals; neuroleptics are the most common such drugs.

antisocial personality disorder—a disorder in the dramatic/emotional/erratic cluster; the most problematic personality disorder for society. Individuals with this disorder often resort to crime, violence, and delinquency.

anxiety disorders—psychological disorders that include the following main features: motor tension (jumpiness, trembling, inability to relax), hyperactivity (dizziness, racing heart, or perspiration), and apprehensive expectations and thoughts.

APA approval—the stamp of approval by the American Psychological Association that a graduate and internship program meets the standards established by the APA's education and training board.

aphasia—specific language loss resulting from brain damage.

apparent movement—our perception of a stationary object as being in motion.

applied behavior analysis (behavior modification)—the application of operant conditioning principles to change human behavior.

applied psychology—the use of psychological principles to improve the lives of human beings and solve human problems.

approach/approach conflict—a conflict in which the individual must choose between two attractive stimuli or circumstances.

approach/avoidance conflict—a conflict involving a single stimulus or circumstance that has both positive and negative characteristics.

aptitude test—a test that predicts an individual's ability to learn a skill or what the individual can accomplish with training.

archetype—the primordial influences in every individual's collective unconscious; Jung's psychoanalytic theory is often referred to as "depth psychology" because archetypes rest deep within the unconscious mind, far deeper than the Freudian personal unconscious.

arousal regulation theory of behavior—the theory that each individual seeks an optimal level of arousal. Physiologically, arousal is the activity of the brain's reticular formation. Subjectively, arousal is the degree to which an individual feels comfortably alert, awake, and aware.

artificial intelligence (AI)—the science of creating machines capable of performing activities that require intelligence when they are done by people.

assessment—the overall process of gathering information, a central activity of clinical psychologists.

assimilation—an individual's incorporation of new information into her or his existing knowledge. The absorption of an ethnic minority group into the dominant group, which often means the loss of some or all of the behavior and values of the ethnic minority group. Individuals' relinquishing their cultural identity and moving into the larger society.

association cortex (association areas)—the region of the neocortex involved in the highest intellectual functions, such as problem solving and thinking.

astrology—the pseudopsychology that uses the position of the stars and planets at the time of a person's birth to describe, explain, and predict that person's behavior. Scientific researchers have repeatedly demonstrated that astrology has no scientific merit.

attachment—a close emotional bond between the infant and its caregiver.

attitudes—positive and negative dispositions to behave in certain ways toward some persons, groups, or objects.

attribution theory—the theory that individuals are motivated to discover the underlying causes of behavior as part of their interest in making sense out of the behavior.

auditory nerve—the nerve that carries neural impulses to the brain's auditory areas.

authoritarian parenting—a restrictive punitive parenting style in which the parent exhorts the child to follow the parent's directions and to respect work and effort. The authoritarian parent places firm limits and controls on the child and allows little verbal exchange. Authoritarian parenting is associated with children's social incompetence.

authoritative parenting—a parenting style in which parents encourage children to be independent but still places limits and controls on their actions. Extensive verbal give-and-take is allowed, and parents are warm and nurturant toward the child. Authoritative parenting is associated with children's social competence.

automaticity—the ability to process information with little or no effort.

automatic processes—forms of consciousness that require minimal attention and do not interfere with other ongoing activities.

automatic processing—processing that does not require capacity, resources, or effort to encode information into memory.

autonomic nervous system—the system of nerves that takes messages to and from the body's internal organs, monitoring such processes as breathing, heart rate, and digestion.

autonomy versus shame and doubt—Erikson's second psychosocial stage, occurring from about 1 to 3 years of age. After developing trust, infants begin to discover that their behavior is their own. They start to assert their sense of independence, or autonomy; they realize their will.

availability heuristic—the strategy of judging the probability of an event by the ease with which prior occurrences come to mind.

aversive conditioning—an approach to behavior therapy that involves repeated pairings of an undesirable behavior with aversive stimuli to decrease the behavior's rewards so that the individual will stop doing it; this technique is based on classical conditioning.

avoidance/avoidance conflict—a conflict in which the individual must choose between two unattractive stimuli or circumstances.

avoidance strategies—responses that individuals use to keep stressful circumstances out of awareness so they do not have to deal with them.

avoiding the other's concerns—an ineffective communication technique that involves diversion and logical argument, which effectively derail conversations.

axon—the part of the neuron that carries information away from the cell body to other cells.

B

"bad patient" role—as a hospitalized patient, complaining to the staff, demanding attention, disobeying staff orders, and generally misbehaving.

barbiturates—depressant drugs, such as Nembutal and Seconal, that induce sleep or reduce anxiety.

Barnum effect—If you make your descriptions broad enough, any person can fit them.

basal ganglia—forebrain structures essential to starting and stopping voluntary movements.

basal metabolism rate (BMR)—the minimal amount of energy an individual uses in a resting state.

basilar membrane—a membrane housed inside the cochlea that runs its entire length.

behavior—everything we do that can be directly observed.

behavioral approach—an approach that emphasizes the scientific study of observable behavior responses and their environmental determinants.

behavioral ecology—the study of animals and their interaction with the living and nonliving environment.

behavioral medicine—an interdisciplinary approach to dealing with medical disorders from a psychological perspective; a field closely related to and sometimes overlapping with health psychology that attempts to combine medical and behavioral knowledge to reduce illness and promote health.

behavioral model of religion—a model that emphasizes the importance of analyzing a person's learning history to determine the extent to which, for that person, religious behavior has been and is being rewarded, punished, and imitated.

behavior genetics—the branch of genetics that is concerned with the degree and nature of heredity's influence on behavior.

behavior modification—the application of operant conditioning principles to change human behavior; the main goal is to replace unacceptable responses with acceptable ones.

behavior therapies—therapies that use principles of learning to reduce or eliminate maladaptive behavior.

between-person comparison—an aspect of performance appraisal in which one worker's performance is compared with that of other workers in the same unit.

binocular cues—depth cues that are based on both eyes working together.

biofeedback—the process in which individuals' muscular or visceral activities are monitored by instruments and information is given (fed back) to the individuals so they can learn to voluntarily control their physiological activities.

biological clocks—internal timing mechanisms that involve both a self-sustaining physiological pacemaker and an environmental cyclic sensitizer.

biological communication—a signal from one animal (sender) that influences the behavior of another animal (recipient).

biological processes—patterned changes in the individual's body.

biological rhythms—animal behavior patterns that can be directly related to distinct environmental features that occur with regular frequencies.

biomedical therapies—treatments to reduce or eliminate the symptoms of psychological disorders by altering the way an individual's body functions. Drug therapy is the most common form; less common are electroconvulsive therapy and psychosurgery.

bipolar disorder—a mood disorder characterized by extreme mood swings; an individual with this disorder might be depressed, manic, or both.

bisexual—being sexually attracted to people of both sexes.

blind spot—the area of the retina where the optic nerve leaves the eye on its way to the brain.

borderline personality disorder—a disorder in the dramatic/emotional/erratic cluster; behavior reflects these characteristics.

brain graft—the transplantation of healthy tissue into a damaged brain.

brain imaging—a technique for observing the activity of the brain as it performs perceptual, motor, and even cognitive tasks.

brightness—a characteristic of color based on its intensity.

brightness constancy—recognition that an object retains the same degree of brightness even when different amounts of light fall on it.

Broca's area—an area of the left frontal lobe of the brain that is involved in speech motor output.

bulimia—an eating disorder in which the individual consistently follows a binge-and-purge eating pattern.

burnout—a hopeless, helpless feeling brought about by relentless work-related stress. Burnout leaves its sufferers in a state of physical and emotional exhaustion that includes chronic fatigue and low energy.

bystander effect—individuals who observe an emergency help less when other bystanders are present than when they are alone.

C

canalization—the narrow path or developmental course that certain characteristics take. Apparently, preservative forces help to protect or buffer a person from environmental extremes.

Cannon-Bard theory—the theory that emotions and physiological states occur simultaneously.

care perspective—Carol Gilligan's theory of moral development, which sees people in terms of their connectedness with others and focuses on interpersonal communication, relationships with others, and concern for others.

carpentered-world hypothesis—the hypothesis that people who live in cultures in which straight lines, right angles, and rectangles predominate (for instance, in which most rooms and buildings are rectangular and many things, such as city streets, have right-angled corners) should be more susceptible to illusions involving straight lines, right angles, and rectangles (such as the Müller-Lyer illusion) than are people who live in noncarpentered cultures.

case study—an in-depth look at one individual. Clinical psychologists use case studies when, for either practical or ethical reasons, they cannot duplicate the unique aspects of an individual's life for study.

catatonic schizophrenia—a schizophrenic disorder characterized by bizarre motor behavior, which sometimes takes the form of an immobile stupor.

catharsis—the psychoanalytic term for clients' release of emotional tension when they relive an emotionally charged and conflicted experience. The release of anger or aggressive energy by directly or vicariously engaging in anger or aggression. The catharsis hypothesis states that behaving angrily or watching others behave angrily reduces subsequent anger.

cell body—the part of the neuron that contains the nucleus, which directs the manufacture of the substances the neuron uses for its growth and maintenance.

central nervous system (CNS)—the brain and spinal cord.

cerebellum—the part of the brain that extends from the rear of the hindbrain, above the medulla. It consists of two rounded structures thought to play important roles in motor control.

chaining—an operant conditioning technique used to teach a complex sequence, or chain, of behaviors. The procedure begins by shaping the final response in the sequence, then working backward until a chain of behaviors is learned.

chlamydia—the most common of all sexually transmitted diseases.

chromosomes—threadlike structures that come in 23 pairs, one member of each pair coming from each parent; chromosomes contain DNA.

chunking—the grouping or "packing" of information into higher-order units that can be remembered as single units. Chunking expands working memory by making large amounts of information more manageable.

circadian rhythm—a daily behavioral or physiological cycle, an example being the 24-hour sleep/wake cycle.

clairvoyance—the ability to perceive remote events that are not visible.

classical conditioning—a form of learning in which a neutral stimulus becomes associated with a meaningful stimulus and acquires the ability to produce a response originally produced by another stimulus.

clinical and counseling psychology—the most widely practiced specialization in psychology; clinical and counseling psychologists diagnose and treat people with psychological problems.

clinical psychology—the subdivision of psychology concerned with applying the theories and findings of the science of psychology and related fields to people experiencing clinical problems.

clinical referral—a situation in which the consumer has been sent to a psychologist by another service provider in order to find the answer to a question or obtain further services.

cochlea—a long tubular fluid-filled structure in the inner ear that is curled up like a snail.

cognition—mental processes—perception, memory, thought, and language—that together produce knowledge. The study of cognition deals with how information enters the mind, how it is transformed and stored in memory, and how it is retrieved to perform some mental activity such as forming a new concept, reasoning through an argument, or solving a difficult problem.

cognitive appraisal—Lazarus' term for individuals' interpretation of events in their lives as harmful, threatening, or challenging, and their determination of whether they have the resources to effectively cope with the events.

cognitive approach—an approach that emphasizes the mental processes involved in knowing: how we direct our attention, how we perceive, how we remember, and how we think and solve problems.

cognitive behavior therapy—an approach to behavior therapy that tries to help individuals behave more adaptively by modifying their thoughts. Cognitive behavior therapy stems from both cognitive psychology, with its emphasis on the effects of thoughts on behavior, and behaviorism, with its emphasis on behavior-change techniques.

cognitive developmental theory of gender—the theory that children's gender typing occurs after they have developed a concept of gender. Once they begin to consistently conceive themselves as male or female, children often organize their world on the basis of gender.

cognitive dissonance—a concept developed by social psychologist Leon Festinger that refers to an individual's motivation toward consistency and away from inconsistency.

cognitive map—an organism's mental representation of the structure of physical space; a mental representation of the spatial layout of a place.

cognitive mechanics—the hardware of the mind, reflecting the neurophysiological architecture of the brain as developed through evolution. At the operational level, cognitive mechanics involve speed and accuracy of the processes involving sensory input, visual and motor memory, discrimination, comparison, and categorization.

cognitive pragmatics—the culture-based "software" of the mind. At the operational level, cognitive pragmatics include reading and writing skills, language comprehension, educational qualifications, professional skills, and also the type of knowledge about the self and life skills that help us master or cope with life.

cognitive processes—processes involving the individual's thought, intelligence, and language.

cognitive restructuring—modifying the thoughts, ideas, and beliefs that maintain an individual's problems.

cognitive therapies—therapies that emphasize that the individual's cognitions or thoughts are the main source of abnormal behavior. Cognitive therapists attempt to change the individual's feelings and behaviors by changing cognitions.

cohorts—groups of individuals born in the same year or time period.

collateral sprouting—a form of regeneration in which the axons of some healthy neurons adjacent to damaged cells will grow new branches.

collective unconscious—according to Jung, the impersonal, deepest layer of the unconscious mind, which is shared by all human beings because of their ancestral past.

collectivism—giving priority to and emphasizing values that serve the group by subordinating personal goals to preserve group integrity, interdependence of group members, and harmonious relationships.

commons dilemma—a choice between harvesting heavily for a large reward but threatening the extinction of the resource, and harvesting lightly but reaping a small reward while others may receive large rewards.

community psychology—a branch of psychology that focuses on providing accessible care for people with psychological problems. Community-based mental health centers are one means of providing such services as outreach programs to people in need, especially those who traditionally have been underserved by mental health professions. An approach that emphasizes the role of ecological and sociocultural factors in the creation and treatment of psychological problems.

comparative psychology—an approach to the study of animal behavior that involves the comparison of two or more species to explore the ecology and evolution of behavior, as well as to draw analogies among the behavior patterns of diverse types of animals, including humans.

compensation—Adler's term for the individual's attempt to overcome imagined or real inferiorities or weaknesses by developing one's abilities.

competence motivation—our motivation to deal effectively with the environment, to be adept at what we attempt, to process information efficiently, and to make the world a better place.

complex sounds—sounds in which numerous frequencies of sound blend together.

comprehensive community mental health center—clusters of mental health services in a particular geographic area that provide comprehensive mental health care for that community.

computer-assisted axial tomography (CAT scan)—three-dimensional imaging obtained from X rays of the head that are assembled into a composite image by computer.

concept—a category used to group objects, events, and characteristics based on common properties.

conception—the penetration of a female's gamete (ovum) by a male's gamete (sperm); also called fertilization.

concrete operational thought—the term Piaget gave to the 7- to 11-year-old child's understanding of the world. At this stage of thought children can use operations. Logical reasoning replaces intuitive thought as long as the principles are applied to concrete examples.

concurrent validity—a form of criterion validity that assesses the relation of a test's scores to a criterion that is presently available (concurrent).

conditional positive regard—Rogers' term for love and praise being withheld if the individual does not conform to parental or social standards.

conditioned response (CR)—the learned response to the conditioned stimulus that occurs after CS-US association.

conditioned stimulus (CS)—a previously neutral stimulus that eventually elicits the conditioned response after being paired with the unconditioned stimulus.

cones—receptors in the retina for color perception.

conformity—adopting the attitudes or behavior of others because of real or imagined pressure from others to do so.

confounding factors—other uncontrolled factors that covary coincidentally with the causal factor.

connectionism (or parallel distributed processing [PDP])—the idea that memory is stored in a distributed fashion over a wide range of connections between neurons. Memory occurs or does not occur because of the extent, inhibitory or excitatory nature, and strength of neuron connections.

connotation—the subjective, emotional, or personal meaning of a word or message.

consciousness—awareness of both external and internal stimuli or events.

consciousness-raising groups—groups that are believed by some feminists to be an important alternative or adjunct to traditional therapy; they often involve several people meeting in a member's home, frequently are leaderless, and focus on members' feelings and self-perceptions. Instead of seeking and accepting male-biased therapy, women might meet in consciousness-raising groups to define their own experiences with their own criteria.

consensual validation—an explanation of why people are attracted to others who are similar to them: Our own attitudes and behavior are supported when someone else's attitudes and behavior are similar to ours—their attitudes and behaviors validate ours.

conservation—a belief in the permanence of certain attributes of objects or situations in spite of superficial changes.

conservative responders—people who set their decision criterion at very high intensity levels of the sensory continuum and thus respond only when they are very sure that the sensory activation level they are experiencing is due to the presence of a stimulus.

content validity—a test's ability to test a broad range of the content that is to be measured.

contingency model of leadership—the view that both personality characteristics and situational influences determine who will become a leader; leadership is viewed as a complex undertaking in which leaders influence their followers and followers influence their leaders.

continuity of development—the view that development involves gradual, cumulative change from conception to death.

contour—a location on a surface at which a sudden change of brightness occurs.

control group—a comparison group treated in every way like the experimental group except for the manipulated factor. The control group serves as a baseline against which the effects found in the manipulated condition can be compared.

controlled processes—the most alert states of consciousness, in which individuals actively focus their efforts toward a goal.

conventional level—Kohlberg's second level of moral thinking, in which an individual shows an intermediate level of internalization. The individual abides by certain standards (internal), but they are the standards of others (external), such as parents' standards (stage 3) or society's laws (stage 4).

convergent thinking—thinking that produces one correct answer and is characteristic of the kind of thinking required on standardized intelligence tests.

conversion disorder—a somatoform disorder in which an individual experiences genuine physical symptoms, even though no physiological problems can be found. Conversion disorder received its name from psychoanalytic theory, which stresses that anxiety is "converted" into a physical symptom.

coping—the process of managing taxing circumstances, expending effort to solve personal and interpersonal problems, and seeking to master, minimize, reduce, or tolerate stress and conflict.

cornea—a clear membrane in front of the eye. Its function is to bend the light falling on the surface of the eye just enough to focus it at the back of the eye.

corpus callosum—a large bundle of axons that connects the brain's two hemispheres.

correlation coefficient—a numerical value that expresses the degree of relationship between two variables.

correlational strategy—a strategy in which the goal is to describe the strength of the relation between two or more events or characteristics.

cortical columns—the basic units of cortical organization; each column contains only a few hundred nerve cells.

counterconditioning—a classical conditioning procedure for weakening a conditioned response of fear by associating the fear-provoking stimulus with a new response that is incompatible with the fear.

couple therapy—group therapy with married or unmarried couples whose major problem is their relationship.

covary—the value of one factor varies with the other factor.

crack—an intensified form of cocaine; chips of pure cocaine that are usually smoked.

creativity—the ability to think about something in a novel and unusual way and to come up with unique solutions to problems.

credibility—a therapist's believability.

criterion validity—a test's ability to predict an individual's performance when measured by other measures, or criteria, of an attribute.

critical period—a period in which there is learning readiness; beyond this period learning is difficult or impossible.

critical thinking—thinking that involves grasping the deeper meaning of problems, keeping an open mind about different approaches and perspectives, and deciding for oneself what to believe or do.

cross-cultural psychology—a branch of psychology that examines the role of culture in understanding behavior, thought, and emotion.

cross-cultural studies—studies that compare a culture with one or more other cultures and provide information about the degree to which people have characteristics that are similar, or universal, across cultures, and to what degree their behavior, thoughts, and feelings are culture-specific.

cross-sectional study—a study in which individuals of different ages are tested at the same time.

crowding—the psychological experience that others are too close to us.

cue-dependent forgetting—a form of forgetting information because of failure to use effective retrieval cues.

cultural evolution—adaptive change in a culture in response to recurring pressures over time.

cultural-familial retardation—mental retardation in which there is no evidence of organic brain damage; individuals' IQs range from 50 to 70.

culture—the behavior patterns, beliefs, and other products of a particular group of people, such as the values, work patterns, music, dress, diet, and ceremonies, that are passed on from generation to generation.

culture-fair tests—intelligence tests that are intended to not be culturally biased.

cupula—a small bit of tissue that is attached to the wall of each semicircular canal in the ear by hairlike cells and gets pulled to and fro with the fluid flow, functioning in the vestibular sense.

current concern—a state the person occupies between becoming committed to pursuing a goal and either attaining it or abandoning it.

D

date or acquaintance rape—coercive sexual activity directed at someone with whom the perpetrator is at least casually acquainted.

daydreaming—a form of consciousness that involves a low level of conscious effort.

debriefing—informing subjects of the purpose and methods used in a psychological study when the study is completed.

decay theory—the theory that when something new is learned, a neurochemical "memory trace" is formed, but over time this trace tends to disintegrate.

decision criterion—a criterion that each individual sets to divide the sensory continuum into two parts. When the sensory activation level is less than the decision criterion, we do not respond; when the level of sensory activation is greater than the criterion, we do respond.

declarative memory—the conscious recollection of information, such as specific facts or events, and at least in humans, information that can be verbally communicated. Because of its conscious and verbalizable nature, declarative memory has been called "explicit memory."

decline stage—Super's label for the period of 65 years and older when individuals' career activity declines and retirement takes place.

decoding—the act of understanding messages.

deductive reasoning—reasoning from the general to the specific; this often involves working with more abstract information or statements, usually called "premises," and deriving conclusions.

defense mechanisms—according to psychoanalytic theory, unconscious methods of dealing with conflict; the ego distorts reality, thereby protecting itself from anxiety.

deindividuation—a state of reduced self-awareness, weakened self-restraints against impulsive actions, and apathy about negative social evaluation.

deinstitutionalization—the movement to transfer the treatment of mental disorders from inpatient mental institutions to community-based facilities that stress outpatient care.

delta waves—large, slow brain waves associated with deep sleep.

dendrite—the receiving part of the neuron, serving the important function of collecting information and orienting it toward the cell body.

denotation—the objective meaning of a word or message.

density—the number of people per unit area.

deoxyribonucleic acid (DNA)—a complex molecule that contains genetic information.

dependent variable—the factor that is measured in an experiment; it may change when the independent variable is manipulated.

depth perception—the ability to perceive objects three-dimensionally.

descriptive statistics—mathematical procedures used to describe and summarize samples of data in a meaningful fashion.

development—the pattern of movement or change that begins at conception and continues through the life span.

developmental level of analysis—the level of analysis that involves the manner in which the organism's heredity interacts with the environment to produce the organism's traits and characteristics.

developmental psychology—a branch of psychology concerned with how we become who we are, from conception to death.

diathesis-stress view—the view that schizophrenia is caused by a combination of environmental stress and biogenetic disposition.

dichromats—people with only two kinds of visual cones.

difference threshold—the smallest difference in stimulation required to discriminate one stimulus from another 50 percent of the time. Also called the just noticeable difference (jnd).

discontinuity of development—the view that development involves distinct stages in the life span.

discrimination—in classical conditioning, the process of learning to respond to certain stimuli and not to respond to others. In operant conditioning, the tendency to respond only to those stimuli that are correlated with reinforcement.

discriminative stimuli—stimuli that signal that a response will be reinforced.

disease model of addiction—the view that addictions are biologically based, lifelong diseases that involve a loss of control over behavior and require medical and/or spiritual treatment for recovery.

disorganized schizophrenia—a schizophrenic disorder in which an individual has delusions and hallucinations that have little or no recognizable meaning—hence the label *disorganized.*

disparity—the difference between the images from the left and right eye that the brain uses as a binocular cue to determine the depth or distance of an object.

displacement—the use of language to communicate information about another place and time. The psychoanalytic defense mechanism that occurs when an individual shifts unacceptable feelings from one object to another, more acceptable object.

display rules—sociocultural standards that determine when, where, and how emotions should be expressed.

dissociative disorders—psychological disorders that involve a sudden loss of memory or change in identity. Under extreme stress or shock, an individual's conscious awareness becomes dissociated (separated or split) from previous memories and thoughts.

divergent thinking—thinking that produces many answers to a question and is characteristic of creativity.

dominance hierarchy—a relationship in which higher-ranking animals have access to some resources before lower-ranking animals do.

dominant-recessive genes principle—the principle that if one gene of a pair is dominant and the other is recessive, the dominant gene exerts its effect, overriding the potential influence of the recessive gene. A recessive gene exerts its influence only if both genes in the pair are recessive.

door-in-the-face strategy—the technique in which a communicator makes the strongest point or demand in the beginning, which listeners will probably reject, then presents a weaker point or moderate, "concessionary" demand toward the end.

dopamine—an inhibitory neurotransmitter related to movement, attention, learning, and mental health; too much dopamine in the brain's synapses is associated with the severe mental disorder schizophrenia.

double standard—the belief that many sexual activities are acceptable for males but not for females.

Down syndrome—a genetically transmitted form of mental retardation that is caused by the presence of an extra (47th) chromosome.

dream analysis—the psychotherapeutic technique psychoanalysts use to interpret a client's dreams. Psychoanalysts believe that dreams contain information about the individual's unconscious thoughts and conflicts.

drive—an aroused tension state that occurs because of a physiological need and motivated the organism to reduce the need.

DSM-IV—the *Diagnostic and Statistical Manual of Mental Disorders,* fourth edition. The DSM-IV is the most recent major classification of mental disorders and contains eighteen major classifications and more than 200 specific disorders.

dualism—the view that mind and body are separate, the mind being nonphysical, the brain being physical.

duty to warn—a clinical psychologist's ethical and legal responsibility to warn a possible victim of a client's harmful intent.

E

eardrum—a membrane in the middle ear that vibrates in response to sound. The sound is then transmitted by the hammer, anvil, and stirrup to the inner ear.

early adulthood—the developmental period that begins in the late teens or early twenties and lasts into the late thirties to early forties. It is a time when individuals establish personal and economic independence, intensely pursue a career, and seek intimacy with one or more individuals.

early childhood—the developmental period extending from the end of infancy to about 5 or 6 years of age; sometimes called preschool years.

early-later experience issue—the issue of whether early experiences (especially in infancy) or later experiences are the key determinants of development.

echoic memory—the auditory sensory memory in which information is retained for up to several seconds.

echoing—repeating something a child has said, especially if it is an incomplete phrase or sentence.

echolocation—a system, used by animals like bats, in which the animal emits loud sounds (too high in frequency for humans to hear) that travel through the environment, hitting objects and echoing back to the animal's ears or other auditory receptors.

eclectic psychotherapy (integrative psychotherapy)—therapy that involves a mixture of techniques—for instance, drawing from both psychodynamic and behavioral therapies.

ecological approach—a view of perception that stresses an active perceiver exploring and moving about the environment.

ecological level of analysis—the level of analysis that involves the interaction of animals with the living and nonliving environment (populations, ecological communities, and exosystems).

ecological theory—the relatively recent view that sleep is evolutionary based. This theory argues that the main purpose of sleep is to prevent animals from wasting their energy and harming themselves during the parts of the day or night to which they have not adapted.

ectomorph—Sheldon's term for a tall, thin, fragile person who is fearful, introverted, and restrained.

efferent nerves—motor nerves that carry the brain's output.

effortful processing—processing that requires capacity or resources to encode information into memory.

ego—the Freudian structure of personality that deals with the demands of reality; the ego is called the executive branch of personality because it makes decisions based on rationality.

egocentrism—a salient feature of preoperational thought; the inability to distinguish between one's own perspective and someone else's perspective.

egoism—giving to another to ensure reciprocity; to gain self-esteem; to appear powerful, competent, or caring; or to avoid social and self-censure for failing to live up to normative expectations.

elaboration—the extensiveness of processing at any given depth in memory.

elaboration likelihood model—a model according to which there are two ways to persuade—by a central route and by a peripheral route.

electroconvulsive therapy (ECT)—"shock treatment," sometimes used to treat severely depressed individuals. The goal is to cause a seizure in the brain, much like an epileptic seizure.

electroencephalograph (EEG)—a machine that records the electrical activity of the brain. Electrodes placed on an individual's scalp record brain-wave activity, which is reproduced on a chart known as an electroencephalogram.

embryonic period—the period of prenatal development that occurs from 3 to 8 weeks after conception. During the embryonic period, the rate of cell differentiation intensifies, support systems for the cells form, and the beginnings of organs appear.

emic approach—the goal is to describe behavior in one culture or ethnic group in terms that are meaningful and important to the people in that culture or group, without regard to other cultures or ethnic groups.

emotion—feeling, or affect, that involves a mixture of arousal (a fast heartbeat, for example), conscious experience (such as thinking about being in love with someone), and overt behavior (such as smiling or grimacing).

emotion-focused coping—Lazarus' term for responding to stress in an emotional manner, especially using defensive appraisal.

empirically keyed test—a test that relies on its items to predict a particular criterion; unlike tests based on face validity, empirically keyed tests make no assumptions about the nature of the items.

empiricism—the view that the mind at birth is devoid of ideas; rather, experience is the source of all ideas.

empowerment—helping individuals develop the skills they need to control their own lives.

encoding—the transformation and/or transfer of information into a memory system; the act of producing messages.

encoding specificity principle—states that remembering depends on your processing of a retrieval cue, as well as the contents of the record or "trace" that you previously stored in memory. The key factor is the similarity or match between your processing of the cue and the memory trace. If the match is good, retrieval probably will succeed, but if the match is poor, retrieval will probably fail.

encounter group—a personal growth group designed to promote self-understanding through candid group interaction.

endocrine glands—glands that release their chemical products, called hormones, directly into the bloodstream.

endomorph—Sheldon's term for a soft, round, large-stomached person who is relaxed, gregarious, and food loving.

endorphins—natural opiates that are neurotransmitters; endorphins are involved in pleasure and the control of pain.

engram—a physical trace that stores memory information.

environment—all of the surrounding conditions and influences that affect the development of living things.

environmental appraisals—an individual's use of environmental information to form a personal impression of a physical setting.

environmental assessments—the combining of individuals' environmental appraisals into broader-based impressions.

environmental psychology—the study of transactions between individuals, small groups, and the physical environment.

environmental shock—a worsening of mood and health in the days following a tourist's arrival day.

epigenetic principle—Erikson's term for the process that guides development through the life span. The epigenetic principle states that human beings unfold according to a blueprint, with each stage of development coming at a predictable time. Ultimately, all stages contribute to a complete identity.

episodic memory—the retention of information about the where and when of life's happenings—what it was like when your younger sister or brother was born, what happened to you on your first date, what you were doing when you heard Desert Storm had begun in the Persian Gulf, and what you had for breakfast this morning.

erogenous zones—according to Freud, parts of the body that have especially strong pleasure-giving qualities at particular stages of development.

establishment stage—Super's term for the period from 25-44 years of age when individuals pursue a permanent career and attain a pattern of stable work in a particular career.

estradiol—a hormone associated in girls with breast, uterine, and skeletal development.

estrogen—the main class of female sex hormones.

ethnic gloss—the use of an ethnic label, such as *Black, Hispanic, Asian,* or *Native American,* in a superficial way that makes an ethnic group seem more homogeneous than it actually is.

ethnicity—a dimension based on cultural heritage, nationality, race, religion, and language.

ethnocentrism—the tendency to favor one's own group over other groups.

ethogram—an inventory of the behavior of a species. Ethograms have been the starting point for many ethological studies.

ethology—the systematic study of the function and evolution of behavior (in natural habitats).

etic approach—the goal is to describe behavior in terms that allow cross-cultural generalizations to be made.

Euclidean bias—our tendency to see paths as straight when they have slight curves or to believe that paths turn at right angles when they do not.

eustress—Selye's term for the positive features of stress.

evocative genotype-environment interactions—the interactions that occur when a child's genotype elicits certain types of physical and social environments.

evolutionary level of analysis—the level of analysis that involves behavior patterns that develop over time in a particular species through natural selection.

evolutionary psychology—a contemporary approach that emphasizes that behavior is a function of mechanisms, requires input for activation, and is ultimately related to successful survival and reproduction.

exemplification—a self-presentation technique in which individuals try to portray themselves as having integrity and being morally worthy.

exhibitionism—a psychosexual disorder in which individuals obtain sexual gratification from exposing their sexual anatomy to others.

expanding—restating, in linguistically sophisticated form, what a child has said.

experiment—a carefully regulated procedure where one or more of the factors believed to influence the behavior being studied is manipulated and all the others are held constant. If the behavior under study changes when a factor is manipulated, we say that the manipulated factor causes the behavior to change.

experimental and physiological psychology—areas of psychology that involve pure research. Although psychologists in other areas conduct experiments, virtually all experimental and physiological psychologists follow precise, careful experimental strategies.

experimental group—the group, in an experiment, whose experience is manipulated.

experimental strategy—a strategy that allows us to precisely determine behavior's causes.

expert systems—computer-based systems for assessing knowledge and making decisions in advanced skill areas.

exploration stage—Super's term for late adolescence and beginning early adulthood years when individuals examine and evaluate the work world in a general way.

external validity—the capacity of an experiment's results to be generalized to the population of interest; a good experiment has external validity.

extinction—in classical conditioning, the weakening of the conditioned response in the absence of the unconditioned stimulus. In operant conditioning, a decrease in the tendency to perform a behavior that no longer receives either positive or negative reinforcement.

extrasensory perception (ESP)—perception that occurs without the use of any known sensory process.

extrinsic motivation—motivation produced by external rewards and punishments.

extrinsic religious orientation—religious motives that lie outside the person.

F

face validity—an assumption that the content of test items is a good indicator of an individual's personality.

false memory syndrome (FMS)—a syndrome presumed to occur when the client remembers events that never occurred. In some cases the memories conform to the therapist's suggestion of what happened in the client's past.

family systems therapy—a form of therapy based on the assumption that psychological adjustment is related to patterns of interaction within the family unit.

family therapy—group therapy with family members.

feminist therapies—therapies usually based on a critique of society wherein women are perceived to have less political and economic power than men have. Also, feminist therapies assume that the reasons for women's problems are principally social, not personal.

fetal alcohol syndrome (FAS)—a cluster of abnormalities that appear in the offspring of mothers who drink alcohol heavily during pregnancy. These abnormalities include a small head (microencephaly); defective limbs, face and heart; and, usually, below-average intelligence.

fetal period—the prenatal period of development that begins 2 months after conception and lasts for 7 months, on the average.

fetishism—psychosexual disorders in which an individual relies on inanimate objects or a specific body part for sexual gratification.

figure-ground relationship—the principle by which we organize the perceptual field into stimuli that stand out (figure) and those that are left over (ground).

fixation—the psychoanalytic defense mechanism that occurs when the individual remains locked in an earlier developmental stage because needs are under- or overgratified.

fixed action pattern—an unlearned behavior that is universal in a species, elicited by a specific environmental stimulus, and usually more complex than a reflex.

fixed-interval schedule—reinforcement of the first appropriate response after a fixed amount of time has elapsed.

fixed-ratio schedule—reinforcement of a behavior after a set number of responses.

flow—optimal experiences in life that are most likely to occur when people develop a sense of mastery. Flow involves a state of concentration in which an individual becomes absorbed while engaging in an activity.

foot-in-the-door strategy—a strategy in which an individual presents a weaker point or makes a small request with which listeners will probably comply in the beginning, saving the strongest point until the end.

forebrain—the highest region of the human brain. Its most important structures include the limbic system, amygdala, hippocampus, thalamus, basal ganglia, hypothalamus, and neocortex.

forensic clinical psychology—the branch of clinical psychology that deals with legal issues and interactions between the legal system and clinical psychologists.

formal groups—groups established by management to do the organization's work.

formal operational thought—Piaget's fourth stage of cognitive development, which appears between 11 and 15 years of age. Formal operational thought is abstract, idealistic, and logical.

fovea—a tiny area in the center of the retina where vision is at its best.

fraternal twins—twins that develop from separate eggs and separate sperm, making them no more genetically alike than nontwin siblings.

free association—the technique of encouraging individuals to say aloud whatever comes to mind, no matter how trivial or embarrassing.

frequency—the number of cycles of a wave (or full wavelengths) that pass through a point in a given time.

frequency distribution—a listing of scores from lowest to highest with the number of times each score appears in a sample.

frequency polygon—basically the same as a histogram except that the data are represented with lines rather than bars.

frequency theory—the theory that the perception of a sound's frequency is due to how often the auditory nerve fires.

friendship—a form of close relationship that involves enjoyment, acceptance, trust, intimacy, respect, mutual assistance, understanding, and spontaneity.

frontal lobe—the portion of the cerebral cortex located behind the forehead and involved in the control of voluntary muscles and in intelligence.

frustration—any situation in which a person cannot reach a desired goal.

frustration-aggression hypothesis—the hypothesis that frustration always leads to aggression.

fugue—a dissociative disorder in which the individual not only develops amnesia but also unexpectedly travels away from home and establishes a new identity; *fugue* means "flight."

function—in psychology, (1) how mental processes and behavior occur, (2) what mental processes and behavior accomplish, and (3) why mental processes and behavior occur.

functional fixedness—the inability to solve a problem because it is viewed only in terms of usual functions.

functionalism—an approach in psychology that emphasizes the functions of mental processes and behavior in adapting to the environment—William James' theory.

fundamental attribution error—the theory that observers overestimate the importance of traits and underestimate the importance of situations when they seek explanations of an actor's behavior.

fundamentalism—for research purposes, defined as a dogmatic and closed-minded way of holding religious beliefs.

G

GABA—gamma aminobutyric acid, a neurotransmitter that inhibits the firing of motor neurons.

gamblers' fallacy—the tendency to underestimate the probability of long runs of similar events.

gametes—human reproductive cells created in the ovaries of the female and the testes of the male.

gate-control theory—the theory that the spinal column contains a neural gate that can be opened (allowing the perception of pain) or closed (blocking the perception of pain).

gender—the sociocultural dimension of being female or male, especially how we learn to think and behave as females and males.

gender identity—the sense of being male or female, which most children begin to acquire by the time they are 3 years old.

gender role—a set of expectations that prescribes how females or males should think, act, or feel.

gender-role stereotypes—broad categories that reflect our impressions and beliefs about females and males.

gender-role transcendence—the belief that when an individual's competence is at issue, it should be conceptualized not on the basis of femininity, masculinity, or androgyny, but rather on a person basis.

gender schema—a cognitive structure that organizes the world in terms of female and male.

gender schema theory—the theory that children's attention and behavior are guided by an internal motivation to conform to gender-based sociocultural standards and stereotypes.

general adaptation syndrome (GAS)—Selye's term for common effects on the body when demands are placed on it. The GAS consists of three stages: alarm, resistance, and exhaustion.

generalization—in classical conditioning, the tendency of a new stimulus that is similar to the original conditioned stimulus to elicit a response that is similar to the conditioned response. In operant conditioning, giving the same response to similar stimuli.

generalized anxiety disorder—an anxiety disorder that consists of persistent anxiety for at least 1 month; an individual with this disorder is unable to specify the reasons for the anxiety.

generativity versus stagnation—Erikson's seventh stage of development, occurring mainly in middle adulthood. Middle-aged adults need to assist the younger generation in leading useful lives.

genes—short segments of chromosomes that are the units of hereditary information and are composed of DNA.

genital herpes—a sexually transmitted disease in which the symptoms are small, painful bumps or blisters on the genitals; caused by a large family of viruses.

genital stage—the fifth Freudian stage of development, occurring from puberty on; the genital stage is the time of sexual reawakening, and the source of sexual pleasure now becomes someone outside of the family.

genetic drift—a variety of chance events that may lead to changes in a gene pool.

genome—a complete set of genes.

genotype—a person's genetic inheritance; the actual genetic material.

genuineness—the Rogerian technique of being genuine and not hiding behind a facade.

germinal period—the period of prenatal development that takes place in the first 2 weeks after conception. It includes the creation of the zygote, continued cell division, and the attachment of the zygote to the uterine wall.

Gestalt psychology—an approach that states that people naturally organize their perceptions according to certain patterns. *Gestalt* is a German word that means "configuration" or "form." One of Gestalt psychology's main principles is that the whole is not equal to the sum of its parts.

Gestalt therapy—a humanistic therapy developed by Fritz Perls, in which the therapist questions and challenges clients to help them become more aware of their feelings and face their problems.

gesture—a motion of the limbs or body made to convey a message to someone else.

giftedness—having above-average intelligence (an IQ of 120 or higher) or a superior talent for something, or both.

giving—the therapist's providing the client with some kind of benefit from treatment early in the therapy process.

glass ceiling—a concept popularized in the 1980s to describe a subtle barrier that is virtually transparent, yet so strong that it prevents women and ethnic minorities from moving up the management hierarchy.

glial cells—non-neuron cells with supportive and nutritive functions.

gonorrhea—a sexually transmitted disease, commonly called "the drip" or "the clap," that is caused by a bacterium from the gonococcus family, which thrives in the moist mucous membranes lining the mouth, throat, vagina, cervix, urethra, and anal tract.

"good patient" role—as a hospitalized patient, being passive and unquestioning and behaving properly.

gradual conversion—a religious change that takes place over a period of time, ranging from several weeks or months to even years.

grand paradox—the paradox that individuals who attend church tend to be more prejudiced in ethnic matters than nonchurchgoers.

graphology—the use of handwriting analysis to determine an individual's personality.

great-person theory—the theory that some individuals have certain traits that are best suited for leadership positions.

group polarization effect—the solidification and further strengthening of a position as a consequence of group discussion.

groupthink—the motivation of group members to maintain harmony and unanimity in decision making, suffocating differences of opinion in the process.

growth stage—Super's label for the period of physical and cognitive development that takes place from birth through adolescence. In this stage, children move from no interest in vocations (0–3 years), to extensive fantasies about careers (4–10 years), to career interests based on likes and dislikes (10–12 years), to beginning to consider ability in their career choices (13–14 years).

H

habituation—reduced responding when an animal is repeatedly presented with the same stimulus.

hallucinogens—psychoactive drugs that modify a person's perceptual experiences and produce hallucinatory visual images; hallucinogens are called psychedelic ("mind altering") drugs.

hardiness—a personality style characterized by a sense of commitment (rather than alienation), control (rather than powerlessness), and a perception of problems as challenges (rather than threats).

hardware—in most digital computers, a central processing unit (CPU) or controller and a large number of memory storage locations.

health psychology—a multidimensional approach to health that emphasizes psychological factors, lifestyle, and the nature of the health care delivery system; a relatively new field that focuses on applying psychological principles to the promotion and maintenance of health, as well as the prevention and treatment of physical illness.

hearing—a physiological sensory process in which auditory sensations are received by the ears and transmitted to the brain.

hedonism—maximizing pleasure and minimizing pain. Early explanations of behavior, proposed by philosophers, emphasized that human beings were basically hedonistic.

helpless orientation—an orientation in which one seems trapped by the experience of difficulty and attributes one's difficulty to a lack of ability.

heritability—a statistical measure of the extent to which traits such as intelligence and personality are due to heredity. Heritability is the percentage of phenotypic (observed) variance that is due to genotypic variance.

herpes genitalis—a sexually transmitted disease in which the symptoms are small, painful bumps or blisters on the genitals; caused by a large family of viruses.

heuristics—strategies or rules of thumb that can suggest a solution to a problem but do not ensure that the solution will work.

hidden observer—Hilgard's term for the part of a hypnotized person's mind that is aware of what is happening. This part remains a passive, or hidden, observer until called upon to comment.

hierarchy of motives—according to Maslow, the main kinds of needs that each individual must satisfy, in this sequence: physiological needs, safety needs, the need for love and belongingness, the need for esteem, cognitive needs, aesthetic needs, and the need for self-actualization.

hindbrain—the lowest portion of the brain, located at the skull's rear. It consists of the spinal cord, lower brain stem (pons and medulla), and cerebellum.

hippocampus—a limbic system structure that has a special role in the storage of memories.

histogram—frequency distribution in a graphic form, in which vertical bars represent the frequency of scores per category or class.

holophrase hypothesis—the concept that a single word can be used to imply a complete sentence; an infant's first words characteristically are holophrastic.

homeostasis—the body's tendency to maintain an equilibrium, or steady state.

hue—a characteristic of color based on its wavelength content.

human factors psychology (engineering psychology)—the subdivision of I/O psychology that focuses on the design of machines that workers use to perform their jobs, and the environment in which humans function to make it safer and more efficient.

humanistic approach—an approach that emphasizes a person's capacity for personal growth, freedom to choose one's own destiny, and positive qualities.

humanistic model of religion—a model that emphasizes that a person's most important needs include needs for growth, purpose, and self-actualization. Humans have innate tendencies to fulfill their potential and express their values. Religion serves as an important vehicle for fulfilling potential and expressing values.

humanistic perspective—the most widely adopted phenomenological approach to personality; it stresses personal growth, choosing one's own destiny, and positive qualities.

humanistic psychotherapies—therapy in which clients are encouraged to understand themselves and to grow personally. In contrast to psychodynamic therapies, humanistic therapies emphasize conscious thoughts rather than unconscious thoughts, the present rather than the past, and growth and fulfillment rather than curing illness.

human sexual response pattern—the four phases of human sexual response—excitement, plateau, orgasm, and resolution—identified by Masters and Johnson.

hypnosis—a psychological state of altered attention and awareness in which the individual is unusually receptive to suggestions.

hypochondriasis—a somatoform disorder in which the individual has a pervasive fear of illness and disease.

hypothalamus—a forebrain structure located just below the thalamus that monitors three enjoyable activities—eating, drinking, and sex. The hypothalamus also helps to direct the endocrine system, through the pituitary gland, and it is involved in emotion, stress, and reward.

hypotheses—assumptions that can be tested to determine their accuracy.

hypothesis testing—the process of using our theories and intuitions to make predictions and then evaluating those predictions with further observations.

hypothetical-deductive reasoning—Piaget's name for adolescents' cognitive ability to develop hypotheses, or best guesses, about how to solve problems, such as algebraic equations. They then systematically deduce, or conclude, which is the best path to follow to solve the problem.

I

iconic memory—the visual sensory memory in which information is retained for about 1/4 second.

id—the Freudian structure of personality that consists of instincts, which are the person's reservoir of psychic energy.

identical twins—twins that develop from a single fertilized egg that splits into two genetically identical replicas, each of which becomes a person; also called "monozygotic" twins.

identification theory—a theory that stems from Freud's view that preschool children develop a sexual attraction to the opposite-sex parent, then, at 5 to 6 years of age, renounce the attraction because of anxious feelings, subsequently identifying with the same-sex parent and unconsciously adopting the same-sex parent's characteristics.

identity versus identity confusion—the fifth of Erikson's stages of human development, occurring primarily during the adolescent years. The development of identity involves finding out who we are, what we are all about, and where we are going in life.

idiographic needs—needs that are important for the individual, not for the group.

ill-defined problems—problems whose initial states, goal states, and/or permissible operations are only vaguely specified or not specified at all.

imitation—an animal's copying another animal's behavior.

implicit personality theory—the public's conception of how personality traits go together in an individual.

impression management (self-presentation)—presenting an image of oneself as a certain sort of person, which might or might not be who one really is.

imprinting—the ethological concept of rapid, innate learning within a limited critical period of time, that involves attachment to the first moving object seen or heard.

incentives—positive or negative external stimuli or events that motivate an individual's behavior.

incest—sex between close relatives, which is virtually universally taboo.

independent variable—the manipulated, influential, experimental factor in an experiment.

individual differences—the stable, consistent ways in which people are different from one another.

individualism—giving priority to personal goals rather than to group goals; an outlook that emphasizes values that serve the self, such as feeling good, personal achievement and distinction, and independence.

individual psychology—the name Adler gave to his theory of psychology to emphasize the uniqueness of every individual.

inductive reasoning—reasoning from the specific to the general—for instance, drawing conclusions about all members of a category based on observing only some of the members; the process of deriving abstract principles, concepts, or hypotheses from specific observations.

indulgent parenting—a parenting style in which the parents are highly involved with their children but place few demands or controls on them. Indulgent parenting is associated with children's social incompetence, especially a lack of self-control.

industrial/organizational (I/O) psychology—a branch of psychology that deals with the workplace, focusing on both the workers and the organizations that employ them.

industrial psychology—the subdivision of I/O psychology that focuses on personnel and human resource management. This branch consists of the various personnel activities that organizations engage in such as recruitment, selection, performance appraisal, training, and career development. A basic underlying theme of all of these activities is individual differences.

industry versus inferiority—Erikson's fourth stage of development, occurring during the elementary school years. In this stage, children's initiative brings them into contact with a wealth of new experiences. As they move into middle and late childhood, they direct their energy toward mastering knowledge and intellectual skills. With their expansive imaginations, children at this stage are eager to learn.

infancy—the developmental period extending from birth to 18 or 24 months of age.

inferential statistics—complex mathematical methods used to draw conclusions about data that have been collected.

inferiority complex—Adler's name for exaggerated feelings of inadequacy.

inferring—the process of taking information that is given in a problem and considering what this information implies beyond what is explicitly stated; it involves going beyond the information given.

infinite generativity—an individual's ability to generate an infinite number of meaningful sentences using a finite set of words and rules, which makes language a highly creative enterprise.

informal groups—clusters of workers formed by the group's members.

information-processing approach—the most widely adopted cognitive approach. Information-processing psychologists study how individuals process information—how they attend to information, how they perceive it, how they store it, how they think about it, and how they retrieve it for further use. It is the view that perception is the process of internally representing information from the world, subjecting it to a series of internal manipulations.

information theory—the contemporary explanation of how classical conditioning works: The key to understanding classical conditioning is the information the organism obtains from the situation.

informed consent—the process whereby individuals are made aware of what they are being asked to do or what treatment is being prescribed.

ingratiation—a self-presentation technique that involves illicitly making yourself likable in another person's eyes.

initiative versus guilt—Erikson's third stage of development, occurring during the preschool years. As preschool children encounter a widening social world, they are challenged more than they were as infants. Active, purposeful behavior is needed to cope with these challenges. Children in this stage are asked to assume responsibility for their bodies, their behavior, their toys, and their pets.

inner ear—the oval window, cochlea, and organ of Corti.

insanity—a legal term, not a psychological term. Individuals who are labeled "insane" are deemed mentally disordered and incapable of being responsible for their actions.

insanity defense—a plea of "innocent by reason of insanity," used as a legal defense in criminal trials.

insight learning—a form of learning in which an organism develops a sudden insight into or understanding of a problem's solution.

insight therapy—therapy that encourages insight into and awareness of oneself.

insomnia—a common sleep problem; the inability to sleep.

instinct—an innate, biological determinant of behavior.

instinctive drift—the tendency of animals to revert to instinctive behavior that interferes with learning.

integration—maintenance of cultural integrity as well as the movement to become an integral part of the larger culture.

integrity versus despair—Erikson's eighth and final stage of human development, which occurs mainly in late adulthood. It is a time of looking back at what we have done with our lives.

intelligence—verbal ability, problem-solving skills, and the ability to learn from and adapt to the experiences of everyday life.

intelligence quotient (IQ)—devised in 1912 by William Stern, IQ consists of mental age divided by chronological age, multiplied by 100.

interference theory—the theory that we forget, not because memories are actually lost from storage, but because other information gets in the way of what we want to remember.

internalization—the developmental change from behavior that is externally controlled to behavior that is controlled by internal, self-generated standards and principles.

internal validity—in experimental psychology, an experiment's capacity to generate causal inferences; a good experiment has internal validity.

interneurons—central nervous system neurons that go between sensory input and motor output. Interneurons make up most of the brain.

interpersonal communication—a transactional process that is ongoing over time. This process involves at least two individuals who each act as both sender and receiver, encoding and decoding messages, sometimes simultaneously. These messages are sent through verbal and nonverbal channels. Noise can interfere with accurate transmission or reception of the message. Communication always takes place in a context.

interpersonal distance—the distance component of interpersonal relations.

intimacy versus isolation—Erikson's sixth stage of development, occurring mainly in early adulthood. Intimacy is the ability to develop close, loving relationships.

intimidation—a self-presentation technique in which individuals present themselves as dangerous in an effort to coerce others into treating them in a desired way.

intrinsic motivation—the desire to be competent and to do something for its own sake.

intrinsic religious orientation—religious motives that lie within the person.

introspection—a technique whereby specially trained people carefully observe and analyze their own mental experiences.

ions—electrically charged particles. The neuron creates electrical signals by moving these charged ions back and forth through its membrane; the waves of electricity that are created sweep along the membrane.

iris—the colored part of the eye, which can range from light blue to dark brown.

J

James-Lange theory—the theory that emotion results from physiological states triggered by stimuli in the environment.

job analysis—the cornerstone of virtually all personnel activities. Depending on the type of job analysis conducted, it can provide information about either the task requirements of the job or the worker requirements necessary for successfully performing the job.

Johari Window—a model of self-disclosure that helps us understand the proportion of information about ourselves that we and others are aware of. This model categorizes self-disclosure in terms of four areas or quadrants: the open self, the blind self, the hidden self, and the unknown self.

judging—a barrier to effective communication that includes criticizing, name calling, labeling, and praising evaluatively.

justice perspective—a theory of moral development that focuses on the rights of the individual; individuals stand alone and independently make moral decisions. Kohlberg's theory is a justice perspective.

K

kinesthetic sense—the sense that provides information about balance and movement, posture, and orientation.

Klinefelter syndrome—a genetic disorder in which males have an extra X chromosome, making them XXY instead of XY.

knowledge-lean problems—problems that can be solved with little or no background knowledge.

knowledge-rich problems—problems whose solutions depend on considerable knowledge in a particular domain.

L

labeling—identifying the names of objects.

laboratory—a controlled setting with many of the complex factors of the "real world" removed.

language—a system of symbols used to communicate with others that involves infinite generativity, displacement, signal simultaneity and overlap, and rule systems.

late adulthood—the developmental period that begins around 60 to 70 years of age and lasts until an individual dies. It is a time of adjustment to decreased strength and health, retirement, reduced income, new social roles, and learning how to age successfully.

latency stage—the fourth Freudian stage of development, occurring approximately between 6 years of age and puberty; the child represses all interest in sexuality and develops social and intellectual skills.

latent content—the psychoanalytic term for the unconscious, unremembered, symbolic aspects of a dream.

law of effect—Robert Thorndike's law that behaviors followed by positive outcomes are strengthened, whereas behaviors followed by negative outcomes are weakened.

learned helplessness—a product of exposure to aversive stimulation, such as prolonged stress or pain, over which one has no control. The inability to avoid such aversive stimulation produces an apathetic state of helplessness.

learning—a relatively permanent change in behavior that occurs through experience.

learning set—the tendency to try to solve all problems with the same strategy.

lens model—the view that environmental perception begins with some actual quality of the environmental display. This model distinguishes between distal cues (objective features) and proximal cues (personal impressions).

lens of the eye—a transparent and somewhat flexible ball-like entity at the front of the eye, filled with a gelatinous material; its function is to bend the light falling on the surface of the eye just enough to focus it at the back of the eye.

levels of processing—Craik and Lockhart's theory that memory is on a continuum from shallow to deep; in this theory, deeper processing produces better memory.

liberal responders—people who set their decision criterion at very high low levels of the sensory continuum and thus will respond to any sensory activation level that might indicate the presence of a stimulus.

life-process model of addiction—the view that addiction is not a disease but rather a habitual response and a source of gratification and security that can be understood only in the context of social relationships and experiences.

life tasks—problems individuals are currently working on. These usually involve normal life transitions, such as going to college, getting married, and entering an occupation.

light—a form of electromagnetic energy that can be described in terms of wavelengths.

limbic system—a loosely connected network of structures under the cerebral cortex that plays an important role in both memory and emotion.

linguistic relativity hypothesis—Whorf's hypothesis that language determines the structure of thinking and shapes our basic ideas.

listening—the psychological process of interpreting and understanding the significance of what someone says.

lithium—a drug that is widely used to treat bipolar disorder.

longitudinal study—a research strategy in which the same individuals are retested after a period of years.

long-term memory—a relatively permanent type of memory that holds huge amounts of information for a long period of time.

loudness—the perception of a sound wave's amplitude.

lucid dreaming—dreaming while knowing that one is dreaming.

M

macroevolution—slow-paced evolution as Darwin described it.

magnetic resonance imaging (MRI)—a brain-imaging technology that measures blood flow and volume using the magnetic properties of hydrogen atoms in the blood after exposure to, and release from, an external magnetic field.

maintenance rehearsal—the conscious repetition of information that increases the length of time it stays in working memory.

maintenance stage—Super's label given to the period from about 45-64 years of age in which individuals continue in their career and maintain their career status.

major depression—a mood disorder in which the individual is deeply unhappy, demoralized, self-derogatory, and bored, showing changes in appetite and sleep patterns, decreased energy, feelings of worthlessness, concentration problems, and guilt feelings that may prompt thoughts of suicide.

managed health care—a system in which external reviewers approve the type and length of treatment to justify insurance reimbursement.

manifest content—the psychoanalytic term for the conscious, remembered aspects of a dream.

marginalization—the process in which groups are put out of cultural and psychological contact with both their traditional society and the larger, dominant society.

masochism—a psychosexual disorder in which individuals obtain sexual gratification from being subjected to pain, inflicted by others or themselves.

mastery orientation—an orientation in which one is task oriented and instead of focusing on one's ability, is concerned with learning strategies and the process of achievement rather than outcomes.

matching hypothesis—the hypothesis that while we may prefer a more attractive person in the abstract, in the real world we end up choosing someone who is close to our own level of attractiveness.

maturation—the orderly sequence of changes dictated by each person's genetic blueprint.

Maximally Discriminative Facial Movement Coding System (MAX)—Izard's system of coding infants' facial expressions related to emotion.

mean—the numerical average for a group of scores or values.

mean length of utterance (MLU)—an index of language development based on the number of morphemes per sentence a child produces in a sample of about 50 to 100 sentences.

means-end strategy—finding the biggest difference between where you are now in your work on a problem and where you want to be, and then trying to find an operation that can reduce this difference.

measure of central tendency—a single number that tells you the overall characteristics of a set of data.

measures of variability (measures of dispersion)—a measure of how much the scores in a sample vary from one another.

mechanoreceptors—the receptors for touch; they are embedded under the skin and are responsible for our ability to detect pressure applied to the skin. They deform to pressure, just as the surface skin does, and convert the mechanical pressure to nerve impulses that can be processed in the brain. The cortical destination of these nerve impulses is the parietal lobes of the brain.

median—the score that falls exactly in the middle of a distribution of scores after they have been arranged (or ranked) from highest to lowest.

medical model—the model that states that abnormal behavior is a disease or illness precipitated by internal physical causes; also called the disease model; the forerunner of the biological approach.

meditation—the practice and system of thought that incorporates exercise to attain bodily or mental control and well-being, as well as enlightenment.

medulla—the part of the brain located where the spinal cord enters the skull. It helps control breathing and regulates some of the reflexes that allow us to maintain an upright posture.

meiosis—the process of cell doubling and division, in which each pair of chromosomes in the cell separates, with one member of each pair going into each gamete, or daughter cell, produced by the cell division.

memory—the retention of information over time. Psychologists study how information is initially placed, or encoded into memory, how it is retained, or stored, after being encoded, and how it is found, or retrieved, for a certain purpose later.

memory processes—the encoding of new information into memory and the retrieval of what was previously stored.

memory span—the number of digits an individual can report back in order following a single presentation of them.

menopause—the time in middle age, usually in the late forties or early fifties, when a woman's menstrual periods cease completely.

mental age (MA)—an individual's level of mental development relative to others.

mental processes—the thoughts, feelings, and motives that each of us experiences privately but that cannot be observed directly.

mental retardation—a condition of limited mental ability in which individuals have a low IQ, usually below 70 on a traditional test of intelligence, and have difficulty adapting to everyday life.

mesomorph—Sheldon's term for a strong, athletic, and muscular person who is energetic, assertive, and courageous.

message—information being delivered from a sender to a receiver.

meta-analysis—a research strategy in which the results of many studies are statistically combined.

microevolution—small-scale evolution in which it is possible to observe not only the results, but also the actual process, of evolution through natural selection.

midbrain—an area of the brain located between the hindbrain and forebrain, where many nerve-fiber systems ascend and descend to connect lower and higher portions of the brain; in particular, the midbrain relays information between the brain and the eyes and ears.

middle adulthood—the developmental period that begins around 35 to 45 years of age and extends into the sixties. It is a time of expanding personal and social involvement, increased responsibility, adjustment to physical decline, and attainment and maintenance of career satisfaction.

middle and late childhood—the developmental period extending from about 6 to about 11 years of age; sometimes called elementary school years.

middle ear—the section of the ear that receives sounds from the auditory canal and has four main parts: eardrum, hammer, anvil, and stirrup.

migration—the movement of individuals into or out of populations.

Minnesota Multiphasic Personality Inventory (MMPI)—the self-report personality test most widely used in clinical and research settings.

mnemonics—techniques designed to make memory more efficient.

mode—the score that occurs most often.

model of reasoned action—a model according to which people act rationally and behavior can be most directly predicted based on intentions.

modern synthetic theory—theory that explains variation in terms of both Darwin's concept of natural selection and genetic influences.

monism—the view that a single substance underlies body and mind—that body and mind are inseparable.

monocular cues—depth cues based on each eye working independently.

monogamy—a mating system in which one male and one female bond exclusively with each other for one or more breeding seasons.

monothetic research—research that takes place at the level of the group.

mood disorders—psychological disorders characterized by wide emotional swings, ranging from deep depression to extreme euphoria and agitation. Depression can occur alone, as in major depression, or it can alternate with mania, as in bipolar disorder.

morphology—the study of the rules for combining morphemes, meaningful units of sound that contain no smaller meaningful parts.

motherese—the kind of speech often used by mothers and others to talk to babies—in higher pitch than normal and with simple words and sentences.

motivation—reasons why people behave, think, and feel the way they do. Motivated behavior is energized and directed.

movement aftereffects—an illusion of movement that occurs when people watch continuous movement and then look at another surface, which then appears to move in the opposite direction.

multiaxial system—a feature of DSM-IV in which individuals are classified on the basis of five dimensions or "axes" that include the individual's history and highest level of functioning in the last year. This system ensures that the individual will not be merely assigned to a mental disorder category, but instead will be characterized by a number of clinical factors.

multiple-factor theory—Thurstone's theory that intelligence consists of seven primary abilities: verbal comprehension, number ability, word fluency, spatial visualization, associative memory, reasoning, and perceptual speed.

multiple personality—the most dramatic but least common dissociative disorder; individuals with this disorder have two or more distinct personalities.

mutation—changes in genetic material.

myelin sheath—a layer of fat cells that encases most axons. It insulates the axon and helps the nerve impulse travel faster.

N

narcolepsy—the overpowering urge to fall asleep.

National Register of Health Service Providers in Psychology—a listing of clinical psychologists who have met the criteria of training and experience designated by a board of distinguished psychologists.

nativism—the view that we are born with some predetermined ways of organizing perceptual information.

naturalistic observation—the observation of individuals in real-world settings outside of the clinical setting, such as at school or in the home, with no attempt to manipulate or control the situation.

natural selection—the evolutionary process that favors individuals of a species that are best adapted to reproduce and survive in a given environment.

nature—an organism's biological inheritance.

nature/nurture controversy—the debate about whether development is primarily influenced by maturation or by experiences. *Nature* refers to an organism's biological inheritance, *nurture* to environmental experiences. "Nature" proponents claim biological inheritance is the most important influence on development; "nurture" proponents claim that environmental experiences are the most important.

need—a deprivation that energizes the drive to eliminate or reduce the deprivation.

need for affiliation—the motive to be with other people, which involves establishing, maintaining, and restoring warm, close, personal relationships.

need for power—the motivation to be in control, to have prestige and status, and to get others to conform to our wishes.

negative affectivity (NA)—emotions that are negatively toned, such as anxiety, anger, guilt, and sadness.

negative correlation—a relationship in which the two factors vary in opposite directions.

negative reinforcement—reinforcement in which the frequency of a response increases because the response either removes a stimulus or involves avoiding the stimulus.

neglected children—these children receive little attention from their peers but they are not necessarily disliked by their peers.

neglectful parenting—a parenting style in which the parents are very uninvolved in the child's life. Neglectful parenting is associated with children's social incompetence, especially a lack of self-control.

neocortex—the most recently evolved part of the brain; covering the lower portions of the brain almost like a cap, it is the largest part of the brain and makes up 80 percent of its volume.

neo-Piagetians—developmentalists who have elaborated on Piaget's theory, believing that children's cognitive development is more specific in many respects than Piaget thought.

neural network models—computational models that make use of simple interconnected computational elements (that is, simulated simplified neurons) acting in parallel to solve a problem.

neurobiological approach—an approach that assumes that the brain and nervous system is central to understanding behavior, thought, and emotion.

neurons—nerve cells, the basic units of the nervous system.

neurotic—a term for relatively mild mental disorders in which the individual has not lost contact with reality.

neurotransmitters—chemical substances that carry information across the synaptic gap to the next neuron.

New Age movement—a broad-based pseudopsychology that expresses a distrust of science and seeks to develop new levels of spiritual awareness. New Age proponents maintain that there are hidden "spiritual dimensions" to reality that cannot be discovered by science's experimental strategies.

nightmare—a frightening dream that awakens the sleeper from REM sleep.

night terror—sudden arousal from sleep, with intense fear, usually accompanied by a number of physiological reactions.

nociceptors—the pain system's receptors that respond to stimulation that produces injury to the body.

noise—irrelevant and competing stimuli; environmental, physiological, and psychological factors that decrease the likelihood that a message will be accurately expressed or understood.

nomothetic research—research that takes place at the level of the group.

nondeclarative memory—refers to a variety of phenomena of memory in which behavior is affected by prior experience, without that experience being consciously recollected. Because nondeclarative memory cannot be verbalized or consciously recollected, at least not in the form of specific events or facts, it also is called "implicit memory."

nondirective interviews—interviews that involve a skillful interviewer's following the information given by the interviewee to explore the questions posed.

nonsexist therapy—therapy that can occur when the therapist has become aware of and primarily overcome his or her sexist attitudes and behavior.

nonstate view—the view that hypnotic behavior is similar to other forms of social behavior and can be explained without resorting to special processes. Hypnotic behavior is purposeful, goal-directed action that is best understood by the way subjects interpret their situation and how they try to present themselves.

nonverbal communication—messages that are transmitted from one person to another by other than linguistic means, including bodily communication (gestures, facial expressions, eye communication, and touch), spatial communication, silence, vocalization, and paralanguage (such as tone of voice).

nonverbal leakage—the communication of true emotions through nonverbal channels even when the person tries to verbally conceal the truth.

norepinephrine—a neurotransmitter that usually inhibits the firing of neurons in the brain and spinal cord but excites the heart muscles, intestines, and urogenital tract.

normal distribution—a symmetrical configuration of scores, with most cases falling in the middle of the possible range of scores and few scores appearing toward the extremes of the range. **(bell-shaped curve)** In this type of frequency polygon, most of the scores cluster around the mean. The farther above or below the mean a score appears, the less frequently it occurs.

norms—established standards of performance for a test. Norms are established by giving the test to a large group of individuals representative of the population for whom the test is intended, which allows the test constructor to determine the distribution of test scores. Norms inform us which scores are considered high, low, or average. Rules that apply to the members of a group.

nurture—an organism's environmental experiences.

obedience—behavior that complies with the explicit demands of an individual in authority.

object permanence—the Piagetian term for one of an infant's most important accomplishments: understanding that objects and events continue to exist even when they cannot directly be seen, heard, or touched.

observational learning—learning that occurs when a person observes and imitates someone else's behavior; also called imitation or modeling.

observer-based environmental assessments (OBEAs)—assessments that use humans to measure key qualities of physical settings.

obsessive-compulsive disorder (OCD)—an anxiety disorder in which the individual has anxiety-provoking thoughts that will not go away (obsession) and/or urges to perform repetitive, ritualistic behaviors to prevent or produce a future situation.

obsessive-compulsive personality disorder—a disorder in the anxious/fearful cluster of personality disorders; anxious adjustment is the primary feature. Individuals with this disorder tend to be exacting, precise, and orderly.

occipital lobe—the portion of the cerebral cortex at the back of the head involved in vision.

Oedipus complex—Freud's idea that the young child develops an intense desire to replace the parent of the same sex and to enjoy the affections of the opposite-sex parent.

olfactory epithelium—tissue located at the top of the nasal cavity that contains a sheet of receptor cells for smell.

open-plan offices—large spaces with no walls in which employee work stations are separated by partitions and plants.

operant conditioning (instrumental conditioning)—a form of learning in which the consequences of behavior produce changes in the probability of the behavior's occurrence.

operational definition—a statement of what a construct is in terms of the procedures or methods used to assess it.

operations—internalized sets of actions that allow the child to do mentally what was done physically before; Piaget's term for mental representations that are reversible.

opiates—opium and its derivatives; these depress the central nervous system's activity.

opponent-process theory—the theory that cells in the visual system respond to red-green and blue-yellow colors; a given cell might be excited by red and inhibited by green, while another cell might be excited by yellow and inhibited by blue. Solomon's theory that pleasant or unpleasant stimuli can cause both a primary and a secondary process to occur in the brain. The secondary process is the central nervous system's reaction to the primary process of the autonomic nervous system. The secondary process reduces the intensity of feeling and increases equilibrium; it strengthens with repeated stimulation.

optic array—the constantly changing pattern of light that specifies the environment.

oral stage—the term Freud used to describe development during the first 18 month of life, in which the infant's pleasure centers on the mouth.

organic retardation—mental retardation caused by a genetic disorder or brain damage; *organic* refers to the tissue or organs of the body, so there is some physical damage in organic retardation.

organizational psychology—the subdivision of I/O psychology that examines the social and group influences within an organization, in contrast with the emphasis of industrial psychologists on individual differences.

organ of Corti—a part of the ear that runs the length of the cochlea and sits on the basilar membrane. It contains the ear's sensory receptors, which change the energy of sound waves into nerve impulses that can be processed by the brain.

outer ear—the pinna and the external auditory canal.

overcompensation—Adler's term for the individual's attempt to deny rather than acknowledge a real situation or the individual's exaggerated effort to conceal a weakness.

overextension—using a name too broadly; characteristic of young children's language use.

overload theory—Milgram's theory that the avalanche of incoming stimulation forces people in the city to carefully select from the vast array of information they experience. This requires them to avert their attention from cues that are less important. Higher density means more cues, and more cues mean individuals cannot pay attention to all of them.

P

pain—the sensation that warns us that damage is occurring to our bodies.

panic disorder—an anxiety disorder that is marked by the recurrent sudden onset of apprehension or terror.

papillae—bumps on the surface of the tongue that contain taste buds, the receptors for taste.

paralanguage—nonlinguistic aspects of verbal expression, such as the rapidity of speech, the volume of speech (loudness, softness), and the pitch of speech (based on a sound wave's frequency—a soprano voice is high-pitched, a bass voice low-pitched).

parallel machine—the brain's architecture; neurons are organized in such a way that many neurons can work on a problem at the same time.

paranoid schizophrenia—a schizophrenic disorder characterized by delusions of reference, grandeur, and persecution.

paraphilias—psychosexual disorders in which the source of an individual's sexual satisfaction is an unusual object, ritual, or situation.

paraphrasing—a concise response to a speaker that states the essence of the speaker's content in the listener's own words.

parasympathetic nervous system—the division of the autonomic nervous system that calms the body and promotes relaxation and healing.

parental investment—any behavior toward an offspring that increases the chances of the offspring's survival at the cost of the parent's ability to rear other offspring.

parietal lobe—the portion of the cerebral cortex at the top of the head, and toward the rear; it is involved in processing bodily sensations.

partial reinforcement—intermittent reinforcement; responses are not reinforced every time they occur.

passive genotype-environment interactions—the interactions that occur when parents who are genetically related to a child provide a rearing environment for the child.

pedophilia—a psychosexual disorder in which the sex object is a child and the intimacy usually involves manipulation of the child's genitals.

peers—children of about the same age or maturity level.

perception—the brain's process of organizing and interpreting sensory information to give it meaning.

perceptual representation system (PRS)—important in the perceptual identification of words, objects, faces, and other important types of stimuli in our world.

performance appraisal—the systematic description of an employee's strengths and weaknesses, including between-person and within-person comparison.

performance orientation—an orientation in which one focuses on achievement outcomes, winning is what matters most, and happiness is thought to result from winning.

peripheral nervous system—a network of nerves that connects the brain and spinal cord to other parts of the body. The peripheral nervous system takes information to and from the brain and spinal cord and carries out the commands of the CNS to execute various muscular and glandular activities.

personal growth groups—groups that have their roots in the humanistic therapies; they emphasize personal growth and increased openness and honesty in interpersonal relations.

personality—the enduring, distinctive thoughts, emotions, and behaviors that characterize the way an individual adapts to the world.

personality disorders—psychological disorders that develop when personality traits become inflexible, and thus, maladaptive.

personality psychology—a branch of psychology that focuses on relatively enduring traits and characteristics of individuals.

personality-type theory—vocational theorist John Holland's view that it is important to develop a match or fit between individual's personality type and the selection of a particular career.

personal projects—sequences of personally relevant action, similar to current concerns, but focusing more on behavioral enactment than thought.

personal strivings—relatively enduring, individualistic coherent patterns of goals. These strivings represent what an individual is typically trying to do.

person-centered therapy—a form of humanistic therapy developed by Carl Rogers, in which the therapist provides a warm, supportive atmosphere to improve the client's self-concept and encourage the client to gain insight about problems.

phallic stage—Freud's third stage of development, which occurs between the ages of 3 and 6. Its name comes from the Latin word *phallus,* which means "penis." During the phallic stage, pleasure focuses on the genitals as the child discovers that self-stimulation is enjoyable.

phenomenological perspective—the perspective that stresses the importance of our perceptions of ourselves and our world in understanding personality; it emphasizes that for each individual, the world is what that individual perceives.

phenotype—the way an individual's genotype is expressed in observed and measurable characteristics.

phenylketonuria (PKU)—a genetic disorder in which the individual cannot properly metabolize phenylalanine, an amino acid. Phenylketonuria is now easily detected, but if left untreated it can result in mental retardation and hyperactivity.

pheromones—odorous substances released by animals that are powerful attractants and a form of communication; chemical signals that are passed between members of the same species.

phobias—irrational fears.

phobic disorder—an anxiety disorder in which the individual has an irrational, overwhelming, persistent fear of a particular object or situation; commonly called a phobia.

phonology—the study of the sound systems of language.

phrenology—an approach developed by a German physician named Franz Joseph Gall, who argued that the bumps on the skull were associated with personality and intelligence.

physical dependence—the physical need for a drug that is accompanied by unpleasant withdrawal symptoms when the drug is discontinued.

physiological level of analysis—the level of analysis that involves biochemistry and the functions of cells, tissues, and organs that affect behavior. Internal physiological factors include heredity, the nervous system, the hormonal system, and biological clocks.

pitch—the perceptual interpretation of a sound's frequency.

pituitary gland—an important endocrine gland that sits at the base of the skull and is about the size of a pea; it controls growth and regulates other glands.

place theory—the theory of hearing that states that each frequency produces vibrations at a particular spot on the basilar membrane.

plasticity—the brain's capacity to modify and reorganize itself following damage.

play—pleasurable activity that is engaged in for its own sake.

pleasure principle—the Freudian concept that the id always seeks pleasure and avoids pain.

pluralism—the coexistence of distinct ethnic and cultural groups in the same society.

polygamy—a mating system in which an individual has more than one mate.

polygenic inheritance—a genetic principle that many genes can work together to produce a particular characteristic.

polygraph—a machine that is used to try to determine if someone is lying by monitoring changes in the body—heart rate, breathing, and electrodermal response (an index that detects skin resistance to passage of a weak electric current)—thought to be influenced by emotional states.

pons—a bridge in the hindbrain that contains several clusters of fibers involved in sleep and arousal.

population—a group of organisms of the same species in a particular place.

positive affectivity (PA)—the range of positive emotion, from high energy, enthusiasm, and excitement, to calm, quiet, and withdrawn. Joy and happiness involve positive affectivity.

positive correlation—a relationship in which the two factors vary in the same direction.

positive reinforcement—reinforcement in which the frequency of a response increases because the response is followed by a stimulus.

positron-emission tomography (PET scan)—a blood-imaging technology that measures blood flow, blood volume, and the metabolism of glucose and oxygen, elements vital to neural activity, in the brain of an awake human or animal.

postconventional level—Kohlberg's highest level of moral thinking, in which moral development is completely internalized and not based on others' standards. The individual recognizes alternative moral courses, explores the options, and then develops a personal moral code. The code is among the principles generally accepted by the community (stage 5) or it is more individualized (stage 6).

post-occupancy evaluation—determining how well a new building meets the design goals in actual use.

post-traumatic stress disorder (PTSD)—a mental disorder that develops through exposure to any of several traumatic events, such as war; severely oppressive situations, such as the holocaust; severe abuse, as in rape; natural disasters, such as floods and tornados; and accidental disasters, such as plane crashes. The disorder is characterized by anxiety symptoms that may be apparent immediately after the trauma, or their onset might be delayed by months or even years; an anxiety disorder that occurs after an individual has experienced a catastrophic event.

pragmatics—the use of appropriate conversation and knowledge of the rules underlying the use of language in context.

precognition—"knowing" events before they occur.

preconventional level—Kohlberg's lowest level of moral thinking, in which an individual shows no internalization of moral values—moral thinking is based on punishments (stage 1) or rewards (stage 2) that come from the external world.

predictive validity—a form of criterion validity that assesses the relation of a test's scores to an individual's performance at a point in the future.

prejudice—an unjustified negative attitude toward an individual based on the individual's membership in a group.

prenatal period—the time from conception to birth.

preoperational thought—the term Piaget gave to the 2- to 7-year-old's understanding of the world. Children at this stage of reasoning cannot understand such logical operations as the reversibility of mental representations.

preparedness—the species-specific biological predisposition to learn in certain ways but not in others.

prescriptive therapy—therapy that matches specific treatments with specific disorders.

preterm infant—an infant born prior to 38 weeks after conception (also called a premature infant).

primacy effect—superior recall for items at the beginning of a list. The enduring quality of initial impressions.

primary prevention—prevention that attempts to stop people from taking drugs by helping them to not start. A community psychology approach that attempts to reduce the number of new cases of mental disorders.

primary reinforcement—the use of reinforcers that are innately satisfying (that is, they do not require any learning on the organism's part to make them pleasurable).

priming—the facilitation in responding to a stimulus that immediately follows a related stimulus.

principle of closure—the principle that when people see a disconnected figure, they fill in the spaces and see it as a complete figure.

principle of proximity—the principle that when individuals see objects close to each other, they tend to group them together.

principle of similarity—the principle that when individuals see objects that are similar to each other, they tend to group them together.

privacy—selective control of access to oneself or to one's group.

proactive interference—disruption of recall of material that was learned earlier.

problem—something you experience when you have a goal but do not know immediately what you must do to reach it.

problem-focused coping—Lazarus' term for the cognitive strategy of squarely facing one's own troubles and trying to solve them.

problem solving—an attempt to find an appropriate way of attaining a goal when the goal is not readily available.

problem space—a representation of the possible states of work on a problem and the sequence of operations that will lead to those states.

procedural memory—knowledge in the form of skills and cognitive operations involved in how to do something. Procedural memory cannot be consciously recollected, at least not in the form of specific events or facts; this makes procedural memory difficult, if not impossible, to communicate verbally. Procedural memory has been called "knowing hows" and, more recently, "implicit memory."

process model—a research framework that examines the four main elements in the perception of environments: the perceiver, the display, the response format, and validational criteria.

projection—the psychoanalytic defense mechanism that occurs when we attribute our own shortcomings, problems, and faults to others.

projective test—a test that presents individuals with an ambiguous stimulus and then asks them to describe it or tell a story about it. Projective tests are based on the assumption that the ambiguity of the stimulus allows individuals to project into it their feelings, desires, needs, and attitudes.

proposing solutions—an ineffective communication pattern that can be transmitted caringly as advice, indirectly by questioning, authoritatively as an order, aggressively as a threat, or with a halo around it as moralizing.

protocol analysis—the procedure of having subjects talk out loud while solving a problem and recording and analyzing everything they say.

prototypes—abstract categorizations of traits that describe a particular personality type. Prototypes act as standards against which we match the individuals we evaluate.

proxemics—the study of the communicative function of space, especially how people unconsciously structure their space.

proximate causation—immediate causes of behavior, the ways behavior is directly produced and controlled; this type of analysis asks how behavior occurs.

pseudopsychology—a nonscientific system that resembles psychology. Pseudopsychologies, like astrology, lack a scientific basis. Their descriptions, explanations, and predictions either cannot be directly tested or, when tested, turn out to be unfounded.

psychiatrist—a physician (M.D.) who has completed a residency in the diagnosis and treatment of mental disorders.

psychiatry—a branch of medicine practiced by physicians with a doctor of medicine (M.D.) degree who subsequently specialize in abnormal behavior and psychotherapy.

psychoactive drugs—drugs that act on the nervous system to alter states of consciousness, modify perceptions, and change moods.

psychoanalysis—Freud's therapeutic technique for analyzing an individual's unconscious thought.

psychoanalyst—a specialist in the application of the theory of psychoanalysis first put forth by Freud and then elaborated and revised by numerous followers.

psychoanalytic approach—an approach that emphasizes the unconscious aspects of the mind, conflict between biological instincts and society's demands, and early childhood experiences.

psychoanalytic (psychodynamic) model of religion—a model that emphasizes that the key to understanding religiousness resides deep within the unconscious mind. Individuals are believed to have instinctual needs they are not aware of, such as needs for safety and security, which can be met by relating to a higher power.

psychodynamic therapies—therapies that stress the importance of the unconscious mind, extensive therapist interpretation, and the role of infant and early childhood experiences.

psychogenic amnesia—a dissociative disorder involving memory loss caused by extensive psychological stress.

psychokinesis—the mind-over-matter phenomenon of being able to move objects without touching them, closely associated with ESP.

psychological addiction—the subjective feeling of craving and perceived need for a drug.

psychology—the scientific study of behavior and mental processes.

psychology of women—a branch of psychology that emphasizes the importance of promoting the research and study of women, integrating this information about women with current psychological knowledge and beliefs, and applying the information to society and its institutions.

psychometrics—the field that involves assessment of individual differences.

psychoneuroimmunology—the field that explores the connections among psychological factors (such as attitudes and emotions,), the nervous system, and the immune system.

psychosexual disorders—sexual problems caused mainly by psychological factors.

psychosexual dysfunctions—disorders that involve impairments in the sexual response cycle, either in the desire for gratification or in the ability to achieve it.

psychosurgery—a biomedical therapy that involves removal or destruction of brain tissue to improve the individual's psychological adjustment.

psychotherapy—the process used by mental health professionals of working with individuals to reduce their emotional problems—to help individuals recognize, define, and overcome their psychological and interpersonal difficulties and improve their adjustment.

psychotic—a term for severe mental disorders in which the individual has lost contact with reality.

puberty—a period of rapid skeletal and sexual maturation that occurs in early adolescence.

punishment—a consequence that decreases the probability that a behavior will occur.

pupil—the opening in the center of the iris; it appears black. The iris contains muscles that control the size of the pupil and, hence, the amount of light that enters the eye.

quest—searching and exploring religious issues while being satisfied in not finding answers and being aware of one's limitations in their face of existential questions.

questionnaire—a method similar to a highly structured interview, except that respondents read the questions and mark their answers on a sheet of paper rather than respond directly to the interviewer.

R

racism—the belief that members of another race or ethnic group are inferior.

random assignment—the assignment of subjects to experimental and control conditions by chance. This practice reduces the probability that the results of the experiment will be due to preexisting differences in the two groups.

random sample—a sample for which every member of a population or group has an equal chance of being selected.

range—the distance between the highest and lowest scores.

rape—forcible sexual intercourse with a person who does not give consent.

rational-emotive therapy—therapy based on Albert Ellis' view that people become psychologically disordered because of their beliefs, especially those that are irrational and self-defeating.

rationalization—according to psychoanalytic theory, the defense mechanism that occurs when the real motive for an individual's behavior is not accepted by the ego and is replaced by a sort of cover motive.

reaction formation—the psychoanalytic defense mechanism that occurs when we express an unacceptable impulse by transforming it into its opposite.

reaction range—the range of possible phenotypes for each genotype, suggesting the importance of an environment's restrictiveness or enrichment.

reality principle—the Freudian principle that the ego tries to bring the individual pleasure within the norms of society.

reasoning—the mental activity of transforming information to reach conclusions.

recall—a memory measure in which the individual must retrieve previously learned information, as on an essay test.

recasting—rephrasing something said, perhaps turning it into a question.

recency effect—recall is superior for items at the end of a list.

reciprocal socialization—bidirectional socialization, in which children socialize their parents just as parents socialize their children.

recognition—a memory measure in which the individual only has to identify ("recognize") learned items, as on a multiple-choice test.

reflective listening—an effective communication strategy in which the listener restates the feelings and/or content of what the speaker has communicated and does so in a way that reveals understanding and acceptance.

reflexes—automatic stimulus-response connections that are "hardwired" into the brain.

regression—the psychoanalytic defense mechanism that occurs when we behave in a way that is characteristic of a previous developmental level.

reinforcement (reward)—a consequence that increases the probability that a behavior will occur.

rejected children—these children are more likely to be disruptive and aggressive than neglected children and are often disliked by their peers.

reliability—the extent to which a test yields a consistent, reproducible measure of performance; a good experiment has high reliability.

religious belief—the ideological dimension and doctrine of religious commitment—the content of what someone believes.

religious content—the ritualistic dimension of religious commitment—the behaviors someone is supposed to perform as part of a particular religion.

religious conversion—the change from having no religious belief to accepting a religious belief system as one's own, or the process of changing from one religious belief system to another.

religious effects—the consequential dimension of religious commitment, which includes the behaviors a person engages in during everyday life that are related to religion.

religious feeling—the experiential dimension of religious commitment, which consists of the emotions, states of consciousness, or sense of well-being, dread, freedom, or guilt that are part of a person's religiousness.

religious knowledge—the intellectual dimension of religious commitment—what a person knows and believes.

religious socialization—a lifelong process in which individuals cannot remember not having a religious faith.

REM sleep—a periodic, active stage of sleep during which dreaming occurs.

repair theory—the theory that sleep restores, replenishes, and rebuilds our brains and bodies, which are somehow worn out by the day's waking activities.

representativeness heuristic—the strategy of judging the probability of an event based on how well it matches a prototype (the most common or representative example).

repression—the most powerful and pervasive defense mechanism, according to Freud; it works to push unacceptable id impulses out of awareness and back into the unconscious mind.

reproduction—the process of creating offspring, which in humans begins with the fertilization of a female's gamete (ovum) by a male's gamete (sperm).

resistance—the psychoanalytic term for a client's unconscious defense strategies that prevent the analyst from understanding the client's problems.

resting potential—the stable, negative charge of an inactive neuron.

restrained eaters—individuals who chronically restrict their food intake to control their weight. Restrained eaters are often on diets, are very conscious of what they eat, and tend to feel guilty after splurging on sweets.

reticular formation—a diffuse collection of neurons involved in stereotyped patterns of behavior such as walking, sleeping, or turning to attend to a sudden noise.

retina—the light-sensitive surface at the back of the eye that houses light receptors called rods and cones.

retroactive interference—disruption of recall of material learned earlier by material that was learned later.

retrograde amnesia—memory loss for a segment of the past but not for new events.

right-wing authoritarianism—a profile involving being overly submissive, overly obedient to authority, and overly aggressive to individuals who violate the rules of authority.

risky shift—the tendency for a group decision to be riskier, on the average, than decisions made by individual group members.

rite of passage—a ceremony or ritual that marks an individual's transition from one status to another.

rods—the receptors in the retina that are exquisitely sensitive to light but are not very useful for color perception.

roles—rules and expectations that govern certain positions in a group. Roles define how people should behave in a particular position in the group.

romantic love—a type of love that has strong components of sexuality and infatuation; it often predominates in the early part of a love relationship. Also called passionate love or eros.

romantic script—a sexual script in which sex is synonymous with love. In this script, if people develop a relationship and fall in love, it is acceptable for them to have sex, whether married or not.

Rorschach inkblot test—the most well known projective test, developed in 1921 by Swiss psychiatrist Hermann Rorschach. It uses individuals' perceptions of inkblots to determine their personality.

S

sadism—a psychosexual disorder in which individuals obtain sexual gratification from inflicting pain on others.

saturation—a characteristic of color based on its purity.

scatter plot—a graph on which pairs of scores are represented.

schedules of reinforcement—timetables that determine when a response will be reinforced.

schema—information—concepts, events, and knowledge—that already exists in a person's mind. A cognitive structure, or network that organizes and guides an individual's perception.

schizophrenic disorders—severe psychological disorders characterized by distorted thoughts and perceptions, odd communication, inappropriate emotion, abnormal motor behavior, and social withdrawal. The term *schizophrenia* comes from the Latin words *schizo,* meaning "split," and *phrenia,* meaning "mind." The individual's mind is split from reality, and personality loses its unity.

schizotypal personality disorder—a personality disorder in the odd/eccentric cluster. Individuals with this disorder appear to be in contact with reality, but many aspects of their behavior are distasteful, which leads others to retreat or withdraw from them.

school and educational psychology—a branch of psychology concerned with children's learning and adjustment in school.

science—in psychology, the use of systematic methods to observe, describe, explain, and predict behavior.

scientific method—an approach used to discover accurate information; it includes the following steps: identify and analyze the problem, collect data, draw conclusions, and revise theories.

scientist-practitioner model—a philosophy in clinical psychology that emphasizes an integration of research and clinical practice in the training of graduate students.

sclera—the white outer part of the eye that helps maintain the shape of the eye and protect it from injury.

script—a schema for an event.

secondary prevention—prevention that attempts to minimize the harm caused by drug use with a high-risk population or with a group that is involved in experimental or occasional use. A community psychology approach that focuses on early detection of problems and early intervention; prevention concerned with the early recognition of and intervention of human problems to alleviate them before they become too hard to resolve.

secondary reinforcement—reinforcement that acquires its positive value through experience; secondary reinforcers are learned, or conditioned, reinforcers.

secure attachment—securely attached infants use the caregiver, usually the mother, as a secure base from which to explore the environment. Ainsworth believes that secure attachment in the first year of life provides an important foundation for psychological development later in life.

selective attention—the focusing of attention on a narrow band of information.

selective breeding—a genetic method in which animals are chosen for reproduction based on how much of a particular trait they display.

self-actualization—according to Maslow, the highest and most elusive human need; the motivation to develop to one's full potential as a human being.

self-concept—a central theme in the views of Rogers and other humanists; individuals' overall perceptions of their abilities, behavior, and personality.

self-disclosure—the communication of intimate details about ourselves to someone else.

self-efficacy—the belief that one has mastery over a situation and the ability to produce positive outcomes.

self-esteem—the evaluative and affective dimensions of self-concept, also referred to as self-worth or self-image.

self-help groups—voluntary organizations of individuals who get together on a regular basis to discuss topics of common interest. The group leader and members give support to help individuals with their problems. Self-help groups are so-called because they are conducted without a professional therapist.

self-instructional methods—cognitive behavior techniques aimed at teaching individuals to modify their own behavior.

self-monitoring—individuals' attention to the impressions they make on others and the degree to which they fine-tune their performance accordingly.

self-perception theory—Bem's theory of the connection between attitude and behavior. It stresses that individuals make inferences about their attitudes by perceiving their behavior.

self-promotion—a self-presentation technique in which individuals try to present themselves as competent.

self-report tests—tests that assess personality traits by asking what they are; these tests are not designed to reveal unconscious personality characteristics.

self-talk (self-statements)—the soundless, mental speech people use when they think about something, plan, or solve problems; often helpful in cognitive restructuring.

semantic memory—a person's knowledge about the world. It includes a person's field of expertise (knowledge of chess for a skilled chess player, for example); general academic knowledge of the sort learned in school (knowledge of geometry, for example); and "everyday" knowledge about meanings of words, famous individuals, important places, and common things (who Nelson Mandela and Mahatman Gandhi are, for example). A critical characteristic of semantic memory knowledge is that it appears to be independent of the individual's personal identity with the past.

semantics—the study of the meanings (for instance, of words, phrases, and sentences).

semicircular canals—canals in the inner ear that contain the sensory receptors that detect head motion caused by tilting the head or other bodily motion.

sensation—the process of detecting and encoding stimulus energy in the world.

sensorimotor thought—the first Piagetian stage, lasting from birth to about 2 years of age. In this stage, infants construct an understanding of the world by coordinating sensory experiences (such as seeing and hearing) with physical (motor) actions—hence the term *sensorimotor.*

sensory adaptation—a change in the responsiveness of the sensory system based on the average level of surrounding stimulation.

sensory memory—this form of memory holds information from the world in its original sensory form for only an instant, not much longer than it is exposed to the visual, auditory, and other senses.

sensory noise—the ever-present activity of the sensory system, which varies in intensity from moment to moment.

sensory registers—the initial part of the memory system, in which information is retained in its original sensory form for only an instant, not much longer than the time for which it is exposed to the visual, auditory, and other senses.

separation—self-imposed withdrawal from the larger culture.

serial position effect—superior recall for items at the beginning and end of a list.

serotonin—an inhibitory neurotransmitter involved in the regulation of sleep and depression.

set point—the body weight maintained when no effort is made to gain or lose weight.

sex—the biological dimension of being female or male.

sexism—prejudice and discrimination against an individual because of her or his sex.

sexually transmitted diseases (STDs)—diseases that are contracted primarily through sex—intercourse as well as oral-genital and anal-genital sex.

sexual script—a stereotyped pattern of role prescriptions for how individuals should behave sexually.

shape constancy—recognition that an object remains the same shape even though its orientation to us changes.

shaping—the process of rewarding approximations of desired behavior.

short-term memory—a limited-capacity memory system in which information is retained for as long as 30 seconds, unless the information is rehearsed, in which case it can be retained longer.

sickle-cell anemia—a genetic disorder affecting the red blood cells that is found most often in Africans and people of African descent.

signal detection theory—the theory that sensitivity to sensory stimuli depends on a variety of factors besides the physical intensity of the stimulus and the sensory abilities of the observer.

sign stimulus—in ethological theory, any stimulus or well-defined environmental event that produces a fixed action pattern.

simulation heuristic—the strategy of judging the probability of an event by the ease of imagining or constructing scenarios that would cause it to occur.

situationism—Mischel's view that personality often varies from one context to another.

size constancy—recognition that an object remains the same size even though the retinal image of the object changes.

sleep apnea—a sleep disorder in which the sleeper stops breathing because the windpipe fails to open or brain processes involved in respiration fail to work properly.

sleep spindles—brief bursts of higher-frequency waves that periodically occur during stage 2 sleep.

social comparison—the process in which individuals evaluate their thoughts, feelings, behaviors, and abilities in relation to other people.

social design—design that involves people in the planning and management of the spaces around them.

social desirability—a factor that can motivate individuals to say what they think the interviewer wants to hear or what they think will make them look better.

social exchange theory—the theory that individuals should benefit those who benefit them, or that for a benefit received, an equivalent benefit should be returned at some point.

social facilitation—the phenomenon that occurs when an individual's performance improves because of the presence of others; occurs with well-learned tasks but not with new or difficult tasks.

social identity theory—the theory that when individuals are assigned to a group, they invariably think of the group as an in-group for them. This occurs because individuals want to have a positive self-image. Social identity theory helps to explain prejudice and conflict between groups.

social learning theorists—theorists who believe that behavior is determined by its controlling environmental conditions, but also by how thought processes modify the impact of the environment on behavior.

social learning theory of gender—the theory that children's gender development occurs through observation and imitation of gender-related behavior, as well as through the rewards and punishments children experience for gender-appropriate and gender-inappropriate behaviors.

social level of analysis—the level of analysis that involves how animals interact and communicate.

social loafing—each person's tendency to exert less effort in a group because of reduced monitoring. The result is lowered group performance.

social motives—needs and desires that are learned through experience with the social world.

social perception—our judgment about the qualities of individuals, which involves how we form impressions of others, how we gain self-knowledge from perception of others, and how we present ourselves to others to influence their perceptions of us.

social policy—a national government's course of action designed to influence the welfare of its citizens.

social psychology—a branch of psychology that deals with people's social interactions, relationships, perceptions, and attitudes.

social support—information and feedback from others that one is loved and cared for, esteemed and valued, and included in a network of communication and mutual obligation.

society—a group of individuals of the same species that is organized in a cooperative manner that goes beyond sexual and parental behavior.

sociobiology—a research approach that relies on the principles of evolution to explain the social behavior.

sociocultural approach—an approach that emphasizes that culture, ethnicity, and gender are central to understanding behavior, thought, and emotion.

sociocultural model of religion—a model that emphasizes that individuals adopt a particular religious stance because of the experiences they have had in the culture in which they live.

socioemotional processes—processes that involve changes in the individual's relationships with other people, changes in emotions, and changes in personality.

software—a series of logical step-by-step instructions for combining the information stored in the memory locations of a computer in various ways.

somatic nervous system—the system of sensory nerves, which convey information from the skin and muscle to the CNS about such matters as pain and temperature, and the motor nerves, which tell muscles when to act.

somatoform disorders—mental disorders in which psychological symptoms take a physical, or somatic, form even though no physical causes can be found.

somatotype theory—Sheldon's theory that precise charts reveal distinct body types, which in turn are associated with certain personality characteristics.

somnambulism—the formal term for sleepwalking; somnambulism occurs during the deepest stages of sleep.

S-O-R model—a model of learning that gives some importance to cognitive factors. *S* stands for stimulus, *O* for organism, and *R* for response.

sounds—vibrations of air that are processed by the auditory (hearing) system; also called sound waves.

spatial cognition—the way we acquire, organize, store, and recall information about locations, distances, and arrangements of paths and places.

speaking—expressing thoughts and feelings in words and behavior with accuracy and clarity so that what you mean is understood by others.

special process theory—a view that hypnotic behavior is different from nonhypnotic behavior, and that hypnotic responses are elicited by suggestion rather than being voluntary reactions.

split-half reliability—a method in which test items are divided into two halves, such as odd-numbered items and even-numbered items. The items are different, and the two scores are compared to determine how consistently an individual performed.

spontaneous recovery—the process in classical conditioning by which a conditioned response can reappear after a time delay without further conditioning.

standard deviation—a measure of how much the scores vary on the average around the mean of a sample.

standardization—the development of uniform procedures for administering and scoring a test. It also involves the development of norms for the test.

standardized tests—tests that require people to answer a series of written or oral questions and have two distinct features: First, an individual's score usually is totaled to yield a single score, or set of scores, that reflects something about the individual. Second, the individual's score is compared to the scores of a large group of similar people to determine how the individual responded relative to others.

statistical significance—the idea that the differences observed between two groups are so large that it is highly unlikely that those differences are due merely to chance.

statistics—mathematical methods used to describe, summarize, and draw conclusions about data.

stereotype—a generalization about a group's characteristics that does not take into account any variation among group members.

stimulants—psychoactive drugs that increase the central nervous system's activity.

stimulus substitution—Pavlov's theory of how classical conditioning works: The nervous system is structured in such a way that the CS and US bond together and eventually the CS substitutes for the US.

storm-and-stress view—G. Stanley Hall's view that adolescence is a turbulent time charged with conflict and mood swings.

stream of consciousness—a continuous flow of changing sensations, images, thoughts, and feelings.

stress—the response of individuals to the circumstances and events, called stressors, that threaten them and tax their coping abilities.

stress management programs—programs that teach individuals how to appraise stressful events, how to develop skills for coping with stress, and how to put these skills to use.

striving for superiority—according to Jung, the human motivation to adapt, improve, and master the environment.

stroboscopic motion—the illusion of movement created when the image of an object is flashed on and off rapidly in succession at slightly different places on the retina.

structuralism—the early theory of psychology developed by Wundt and Titchener that emphasized the importance of conscious thought and classification of the mind's structures.

structured interview—an interview in which the questions to be asked are known in advance and are asked in a predetermined order.

structured observation—observation in which the setting is under the control of the observer and specific events are arranged to help assess how the observed person reacts.

subgoal strategy—finding an intermediate goal that will put you in a better position to reach the final goal.

sublimation—the psychoanalytic defense mechanism that occurs when a socially approved course of action replaces an unacceptable impulse.

substance-use disorder—a disorder characterized by one or more of the following features: (1) a pattern of pathological use that involves frequent intoxication, a need for daily use, and an inability to control use—in a sense, psychological dependence; (2) a significant impairment of social or occupational functioning attributed to drug use; and (3) physical dependence that involves serious withdrawal problems.

substitution of function—a form of brain repair in which the function of the damaged region is taken over by another area of the brain.

subtractive mixture—the mixing of pigments of different colors rather than beams of light.

sudden conversion—a religious change that occurs all at once with no prior warning.

superconducting quantum interference device (SQUID)—a brain-scanning device that senses tiny changes in the magnetic fields.

superego—the Freudian structure of personality that is the moral branch of personality. The superego takes into account whether something is right or wrong.

superiority complex—Adler's concept of exaggerated self-importance designed to mask feelings of inferiority.

supplication—a self-presentation technique in which individuals try to make themselves appear weak and dependent.

syllogism—a deductive reasoning task that consists of a major premise, a minor premise, and a conclusion.

sympathetic nervous system—the division of the autonomic nervous system that is involved in the arousal of the body, being responsible for quick reactions to a stressor—sometimes referred to as the fight-or-flight response.

synapses—tiny gaps between neurons. Most synapses are between the axon of one neuron and the dendrites or cell body of another neuron.

synchrony—the carefully coordinated interaction between the parent and child in which, often unknowingly, they are attuned to each other's behavior.

syntax—the ways words are combined to form acceptable phrases and sentences in a language.

syphilis—a sexually transmitted disease caused by the bacterium *Treponema pallidum,* a member of the spirochete family.

systematic desensitization—a method of behavior therapy that treats anxiety by associating deep relaxation with successive visualizations of increasingly intense anxiety-producing situations; this technique is based on classical conditioning.

T

Tarasoff case—a California legal case that established the responsibility of therapists to warn the appropriate parties when a client threatens harm.

tardive dyskinesia—a major side effect of the neuroleptic drugs; a neurological disorder characterized by grotesque, involuntary movements of the facial muscles and mouth, as well as extensive twitching of the neck, arms, and legs.

technical environmental assessments (TEAs)—assessments that use machines to measure aspects of the physical setting.

telegraphic speech—the use of short and precise words to communicate; characteristic of young children's two- or three-word combinations.

telepathy—the extrasensory transfer of thought from one person to another.

temporal lobe—the portion of the cerebral cortex located just above the ears, involved in hearing.

teratogen—(the word comes from the Greek word *tera,* meaning "monster.") Any agent that causes a birth defect. The field of study that investigates the causes of birth defects is called teratology.

territoriality—a pattern of behavior and attitudes that is related to the perceived or actual control of a physical space; a possessive or ownership-like reaction to an area of space or particular objects.

tertiary prevention—treatment for people who abuse drugs. A community psychology approach that attempts to reduce the long-term consequences of mental health disorders that were not prevented or arrested earlier; prevention that seeks to minimize the effects and duration of a mental health problem after it has occurred.

testosterone—a hormone associated in boys with development of the genitals, an increase in height, and a change of voice.

test-retest reliability—the extent to which a test yields the same measure of performance when an individual is given the same test on two different occasions.

thalamus—a forebrain structure that sits at the top of the brain stem in the central core of the brain. It serves as an important relay station, functioning much like a telephone switchboard between the diverse areas of the cortex and the reticular formation.

Thematic Apperception Test (TAT)—a projective test designed to elicit stories that reveal something about an individual's personality; developed by Henry Murray and Christina Morgan in the 1930s.

theory—a coherent set of ideas that helps to explain data and to make predictions. A theory has hypotheses, which are assumptions that can be tested to determine their accuracy.

thermoreceptors—receptors located under the skin that respond to changes in temperature.

timbre—the tone color or perceptual quality of a sound.

time precedence—the appearance of the causal factor before the caused factor.

tip-of-the-tongue phenomenon (TOT state)—a type of effortful retrieval that occurs when people are confident they know something but just can't quite seem to pull it out of memory.

token economy—a behavior modification system in which behaviors are reinforced with tokens (such as poker chips) that can be exchanged later for desired rewards (such as candy, money, or going to a movie).

tokenism—being treated as a representative of a group rather than as an individual.

tolerance—the need for a greater amount of a drug to produce the same effect.

traditional information-processing model—the model in which memory involves a sequence of three stages—sensory registers, short-term memory, and long-term memory.

traditional religious script—a sexual script in which sex is acceptable only within marriage; both premarital and extramarital sex are taboo, especially for women. In this script, sex is for reproduction and sometimes for affection.

trait theories—theories that propose that people have broad dispositions (traits) that are reflected in the basic ways they behave, such as whether they are outgoing and friendly or whether they are dominant and assertive.

tranquilizers—depressant drugs, such as Valium and Xanax, that reduce anxiety and induce relaxation.

transactional communication—communication that is an ongoing process between sender and receiver that unfolds over time; frequently information is communicated simultaneously between the participants.

transcendental meditation (TM)—the most popular form of meditation in the United States, TM is derived from an ancient Indian technique and involves a mantra, which is a resonant sound or phrase that is repeated mentally or aloud to focus attention.

transference—the psychoanalytic term for a client's relating to an analyst in ways that reproduce or relive important relationships in the client's life.

transsexualism—a psychosexual disorder in which an individual has an overwhelming desire to become a member of the opposite sex.

transvestism—psychosexual disorders in which an individual obtains sexual gratification by dressing up as a member of the opposite sex.

triangular theory of love—Sternberg's theory that love comes in three main forms: passion, intimacy, and commitment.

triarchic theory—Sternberg's theory that intelligence consists of componential intelligence, experiential intelligence, and contextual intelligence.

trichromatic theory—the theory that color perception is based on the existence of three types of receptors, which are maximally sensitive to different, but overlapping, ranges of wavelengths.

trichromats—people with normal color vision—they have three kinds of cone receptors.

trust versus mistrust—Erikson's first psychosocial stage, experienced in the first year of life. Trust is built when an infant's basic needs—such as needs for comfort, food, and warmth—are met.

Turner syndrome—a genetic disorder in which females are missing an X chromosome, making them XO instead of XX.

twin study—a study in which the behavior of identical twins is compared with the behavior of fraternal twins.

two-factor theory—Spearman's theory that individuals have both general intelligence, called *g,* and a number of specific types of intelligence, called *s.*

Type A behavior pattern—a cluster of characteristics—being excessively competitive, hard-driven, impatient, and hostile—thought to be related to the incidence of heart disease.

Type C behavior—the cancer-prone personality, which consists of being inhibited, uptight, lacking in emotional expression, and otherwise constrained. This type of person is more likely than more expressive persons to develop cancer.

ultimate causation—explanations of behavior at the evolutionary level. This type of explanation involves "why" questions that can be answered in terms of evolutionary function.

unconditional positive regard—Rogers' term for accepting, valuing, and being positive toward another person regardless of the other person's behavior.

unconditioned response (UR)—an unlearned response that is automatically elicited by the unconditional stimulus.

unconditioned stimulus (US)—a stimulus that produces a response without prior learning.

unconscious thought—according to Freud, a reservoir of unacceptable wishes, feelings, and thoughts that we are not consciously aware of.

underextension—using a name too narrowly; characteristic of young children's language use.

undifferentiated schizophrenia—a schizophrenic disorder characterized by disorganized behavior, hallucinations, delusions, and incoherence.

validity—the extent to which a test measures what it is intended to measure.

variable-interval schedule—reinforcement of a response after a variable amount of time has elapsed.

variable-ratio schedule—a timetable in which responses are rewarded an average number of times, but on an unpredictable basis.

ventromedial hypothalamus (VMH)—a region of the hypothalamus that plays an important role in controlling hunger.

vestibular sense—the sense that provides information about balance and movement.

visual illusion—an illusion that occurs when two objects produce exactly the same retinal image but are perceived as different images.

volley theory—the theory that high frequencies can be signaled by teams of neurons that fire at different offset times to create an overall firing rate that could signal a very high frequency.

voyeurism—a psychosexual disorder in which individuals obtain sexual gratification from observing the sex organs or sex acts of others, often from a secret vantage point.

wavelength—the distance from the peak of one wave to the peak of the next.

Weber's law—the law that states that the difference threshold is a constant percentage of the magnitude of the comparison stimulus rather than a constant amount. Weber's law generally holds true.

well-defined problems—problems whose initial states, goal states, and permissible operations are clearly specified.

Wernicke's area—a region of the brain's left hemisphere involved in language comprehension.

wisdom—according to Balters, expert knowledge about the practical aspects of life.

within-person comparison—an aspect of performance in which the individual worker's strength and weaknesses in different performance areas are assessed.

working memory—the concept currently used to describe short-term memory as a place for mental work. Working memory is a kind of mental "workbench" that allows us to manipulate and assemble information when making decisions, solving problems, and comprehending written and spoken language.

working memory model—the model in which long-term memory precedes working memory, and working memory uses long-term memory in a variety of flexible ways (such as rehearsal and imagery).

XYY syndrome—a genetic disorder in which the male has an extra Y chromosome.

Yerkes-Dodson law—the law that performance is best under conditions of moderate rather than low or high arousal.

zone of proximal development (ZPD)—Vygotsky's term for tasks that are too difficult for children to master alone, but that can be mastered with the guidance and assistance of adults or more skilled children.

zygote—a single cell formed through fertilization.

REFERENCES

Aamodt, M. G. (1996). *Applied industrial/organizational psychology (2nd ed.).* Pacific Grove, CA: Brooks/Cole.

Abbey, A., Ross, L. T., & McDuffie, D. (1993). Alcohol's role in sexual assault. In R. R. Watson (Eds.), *Drug and alcohol abuse reviews. Vol. 5: Addictive behaviors in women.* Totowa, NJ: Humana Press.

Abelson, J. L., & Curtis, G. C. (1996). Hypothalamic-pituitary-adrenal axis activity in panic disorder. *The American Journal of Psychiatry, 153,* 69–73.

Aboud, F. (1988). *Children and prejudice.* New York: Basil Blackwell.

Abraham, J. D., & Hansson, R. O. (1995). Successful aging at work: An applied study of selection, optimization, and compensation through impression management. *Journal of Gerontology, 50B,* P94–P103.

Achmon, J., Granek, M., Golomb, M., & Hart, J. (1989). Behavioral treatment of essential hypertension: A comparison between cognitive therapy and biofeedback of heart rate. *Psychosomatic Medicine, 51,* 152–164.

Acitelli, L. K., & Holmberg, D. (1993). Reflecting on relationships: The role of thoughts and memories. In D. Perlman & W. H. Jones (Eds.), *Advances in personal relationships* (Vol. 4). London: Kingsley.

Ackerman, P. L., & Kanfer, R. (in press). Integrating laboratory and field study of improving selection: Development of a battery for predicting air traffic controller success. *Journal of Applied Psychology.*

Adams, H. E., & Cassidy, J. F. (1993). The classification of abnormal behavior: An overview. In P. B. Sutker & H. E. Adams (Eds.), *Comprehensive textbook of psychopathology* (2nd ed.). New York: Plenum Press.

Adams, J. (1979). *Conceptual blockbusting* (2nd ed.). New York: W. W. Norton.

Adams, P. R., & Adams, G. R. (1984). Mount Saint Helens's ashfall: Evidence for a disaster stress reaction. *American Psychologist, 39,* 252–260.

Adler, A. (1927). *The theory and practice of individual psychology.* New York: Harcourt, Brace, & World.

Adler, T. (1991, January). Seeing double? Controversial twins study is widely reported, debated. *APA Monitor, 22,* 1, 8.

Adorno, T. W., Frenkel-Brunswik, E., Levinson, D. J., & Sanford, R. N. (1950). *The authoritarian personality.* New York: Harper.

Aiello, J. R., Thompson, D. E., & Brodzinsky, D. M. (1983). How funny is crowding anyway? Effects of room size, group size and the introduction of humor. *Basic and Applied Social Psychology, 4,* 193–207.

Aiken, L. R. (1996). *Assessment of intellectual functioning (2nd ed.).* New York: Plenum.

Ainsworth, M. D. S. (1967). Infancy in Uganda: Infant care and the growth of love. In B. M. Caldwell & H. N. Riccuiti (Eds.), *Review of child development research* (Vol. 3). Chicago: University of Chicago Press.

Ainsworth, M. D. S. (1979). Infant-mother attachment. *American Psychologist, 34,* 932–937.

Al-Issa, I. (1982). Does culture make a difference in psychopathology? In I. Al-Issa (Ed.), *Culture and psychopathology.* Baltimore: University Park Press.

Albee, G. (1986). Toward a just society: Lessons from observation on the primary prevention of psychopathology. *American Psychologist, 41,* 891–898.

Alcamo, I. E. (1996). *DNA technology.* Dubuque, IA: Wm. C. Brown.

Alcock, J. E. (1989). *Science and supernature: A critical appraisal of parapsychology.* Buffalo, NY: Prometheus Books.

Alderfer, C. P., Alderfer, C. J., Bell, E. L., & Jones, J. (in press). The race relations competence workshop. *Human Relations.*

Alderfer, C. P., & Tucker, R. C. (1996). A field experiment for studying race relations embedded in organizations. *Journal of Organizational Behavior, 17,* 43–58.

Alexander, R. D. (1974). The evolution of social behavior. *Annual Review of Ecology and Systematics, 5,* 324–383.

Allan, R., & Scheidt, S. (Eds.) (1996). *Heart and mind.* Washington, DC: American Psychological Association.

Allen, J. P., & Bell, K. L. (1995, March). *Attachment and communication with parents and peers in adolescence.* Paper presented at the meeting of the Society for Research in Child Development, Indianapolis.

Allen, L., & Mitchell, C. M. (in press). *Poverty and adolescent health.* Paper prepared for the U.S. Congress, Office of Technology Assessment.

Alliger, G. M., Lilienfeld, S. O., & Mitchell, K. E. (1996). The susceptibility of overt and covert integrity tests to coaching and faking. *Psychological Science, 7,* 32–39.

Allison, J. A., & Wrightsman, L. S. (1993). *Rape: The misunderstood crime.* Newbury Park, CA: Sage.

Allport, G. (1954). *The roots of prejudice.* Cambridge, MA: Addison-Wesley.

Allport, G. W. (1937). *Personality: A psychological interpretation.* New York: Holt.

Allport, G. W. (1966). The religious context of prejudice. *Journal for the Scientific Study of Religion, 5,* 447–457.

Allport, G. W., & Ross, J. M. (1967). Personal religious orientation and prejudice. *Journal of Personality and Social Psychology, 5,* 432–443.

Als, H. (1996). The effectiveness of early intervention for children in neonatal intensive care units. In M. J. Guralnick (Ed.), *The effectiveness of early intervention.* Baltimore, Md: Paul Brookes.

Altemeyer, B. (1988). *Enemies of freedom: Understanding right-wing authoritarianism.* San Francisco: Jossey-Bass.

Altemeyer, B., & Hunsberger, B. (1992). Authoritarianism, religious fundamentalism, quest, and prejudice. *International Journal for the Psychology of Religion, 2* (2), 113–133.

Altman, I. (1975). *The environment and social behavior: Privacy, personal space, territoriality and crowding.* Monterey, CA: Brooks/Cole.

Altman, I., & Chemers, M. (1980). *Culture and environment.* Monterey, CA: Brooks/Cole.

Alvarez, R., & Lopez, M. (1996). Effects of elements or compound preexposure on conditioned taste aversion as a function of retention interval. *Animal Learning & Behavior, 23,* 391–399.

Amabile, T. M. (1990, August). *Mechanisms of creativity: Motivation, affect, and cognition.* Paper presented at the meeting of the American Psychological Association, Boston.

Amabile, T. M., Phillips, E. D., & Collins, M. A. (1993, August). *Creativity by contract: Social influences on the creativity of professional artists.* Paper presented at the meeting of the American Psychological Association, Toronto.

American College Health Association. (1989, May). *Survey of AIDS on American college and university campuses.* Washington, DC: Author.

American Psychiatric Association. (1994). *Diagnostic and statistical manual of mental disorders* (4th ed. rev.). Washington, DC: Author.

American Psychological Association. (1954). *Technical recommendations for psychological tests and diagnostic techniques.* Washington, DC: Author.

American Psychological Association. (1978). APA guidelines for therapists working with women clients. *American Psychologist, 33,* 1122–1123.

American Psychological Association. (1987a). Model act for state licensure of psychologists. *American Psychologist, 42,* 696–703.

American Psychological Association. (1987b). *Casebook on ethical principles of psychologists* (rev. ed.). Washington, DC: Author.

American Psychological Association. (1992, May). APA continues to refine its ethics code. *APA Monitor,* pp. 38–42.

Ames, C., & Ames, R. (Eds.). (1989). *Research on motivation in education* (Vol. 3). San Diego: Academic Press.

Amirkhan, J., Betancourt, H., Graham, S., Loopez, S. R., & Weiner, B. (1995). Reflections on affirmative action goals in psychology admissions. *Psychological Science, 6,* 133–139.

Anastasi, A. (1988). *Psychological testing* (6th ed.). New York: Macmillan.

Andersen, B. L. (in press). Surviving cancer. *Cancer.*

Anderson, B. L. (1983). Primary orgasmic dysfunction: Diagnostic considerations and a review of treatment. *Psychological Bulletin, 93,* 105–136.

Anderson, B. L., Kiecolt, J. K., & Glaser, R. (1994). A biobehavioral model of cancer stress and disease course. *American Psychologist, 49,* 389–404.

Anderson, C. A. (1989). Temperature and aggression: Ubiquitous effects of heat on occurrence of human violence. *Journal of Personality and Social Psychology, 106,* 74–96.

Anderson, E. N., Jr. (1972). Some Chinese methods in dealing with crowding. *Urban Anthropology, 1,* 141–150.

Anderson, M. P. (1996). Frequently asked questions about NAEYC's linguistic and cultural diversity position paper. *Young Children, 51,* 13–16.

Anderson, N. (1996, June). *Socio-economic status and health.* Paper presented at the meeting of the American Psychological Society, San Francisco.

Anderson, N. H. (1959). Test of a model of opinion change. *Journal of Abnormal and Social Psychology, 59,* 371–381.

Anderson, N. H. (1965). Primacy effects in personality impression formation using a generalized order effect paradigm. *Journal of Personality and Social Psychology, 2,* 1–9.

Anderson, N. H. (1968). Likableness ratings of 55 personality trait words. *Journal of Personality and Social Psychology, 9,* 272–279.

Anderson, N. H. (1974). Cognitive algebra: Integration theory applied to social attribution. In L. Berkowitz (Ed.), *Advances in experimental social psychology* (Vol. 7). New York: Academic Press.

Anderson, N. H. (1989). Functional memory and on-line attribution. In J. N. Bassili (Ed.), *On-line cognition in person perception.* Hillsdale, NJ: Erlbaum.

Andreassi, J. L. (1989). *Psychophysiology* (2nd ed.). Hillsdale, NJ: Erlbaum.

Andronico, M. P. (Ed.) (1996). *Men in groups.* Washington, DC: American Psychological Association.

Aneshensel, C. S., Pearlin, L. I., Mullan, J. T., Zarit, S. H., & Whitlatch, C. (1996). *Profiles in caregiving.* San Diego, CA: Academic Press.

Aponte, H. (1979). Family therapy and the community. In M. S. Gibbs, J. R. Lachenmeyer, & J. Sigel (Eds.), *Community psychology: Theoretical and empirical approaches.* New York: Gardner Press, 1979.

Appelbaum, S. A. (1970). Science and persuasion in the psychological test report. *Journal of Consulting and Clinical Psychology, 35,* 349–355.

Aragones, J. I., & Arredondo, J. M. (1985). Structure of urban cognitive maps. *Journal of Environmental Psychology, 5,* 197–212.

Archea, J. (1990). Two earthquakes: Three human conditions. In Y. Yoshitake, R. B. Bechtel, T. Takahaski, & M. Asai (Eds.), *Current issues in environment-behavior research.* Tokyo: University of Tokyo.

Archer, D., & Gartner, R. (1976). Violent acts and violent times: A comparative approach in postwar homicide. *American Sociological Review, 41,* 937–963.

Arden, I. A., & Mellott, R. N. (1995, August). *Introducing feminist perspectives to counseling students: An assessment to change.* Paper presented at the meeting of the American Psychological Association, New York City.

Arkes, H. R. (1981). Impediments to accurate clinical judgment and possible ways to minimize their impact. *Journal of Consulting and Clinical Psychology, 49,* 323–330.

Armsden, G. G., & Greenberg, M. T. (1984). *The inventory of parent and peer attachment: Individual differences and their relationship to psychological well-being in adolescence.* Unpublished manuscript, University of Washington.

Arnett, J. (1991). Heavy metal music and reckless behavior among adolescents. *Journal of Youth and Adolescence, 20,* 573–592.

Arnhoff, F. N. (1968). Realities and mental health manpower. *Mental Hygiene, 52,* 181–189.

Aronson, E. (1986, August). *Teaching students things they think they already know all about: The case of prejudice and desegregation.* Paper presented at the meeting of the American Psychological Association, Washington, DC.

Aronson, E. (1988). *The social animal* (5th ed.). New York: W. H. Freeman.

Arrendondo, P. (1996). Multicultural counseling theory and Latino-Hispanic-American populations. In D. W. Sue (Ed.), *Theory of multicultural counseling and therapy.* Pacific Grove, CA: Brooks/Cole.

Asch, S. E. (1946). Forming impressions of personality. *Journal of Abnormal and Social Psychology, 41,* 258–290.

Asch, S. E. (1951). Effects of group pressure on the modification and distortion of judgments. In H. S. Guetzkow (Ed.), *Groups leadership and men.* Pittsburgh: Carnegie University Press.

Ashcraft, M. H. (1994). *Human memory and cognition* (2nd ed.). New York: HarperCollins.

Asnis, G. M., & van Praag, H. M. (1995). *Panic disorder.* New York: Wiley.

Astin, A. W., Korn, W. S., & Berz, E. R. (1989). *The American freshman: National norms for fall, 1989.* Los Angeles: Higher Education Research Institute, University of California, Los Angeles.

Atkinson, J. W., & Raynor, I. O. (1974). *Motivation and achievement.* Washington, DC: Winston.

Atkinson, R. C., & Shiffrin, R. M. (1968). Human Memory: A proposed system and its control processes. In K. W. Spence & J. T. Spence (Eds.), *The psychology of learning and motivation* (Vol. 2). San Diego: Academic Press.

Aune, K. S., & Aune, R. K. (1996). Cultural differences in self-reported experience and expression of emotion in relationships. *Journal of Cross-Cultural Psychology, 27,* 67–81.

Averill, J. R. (1983). Studies on anger and aggression: Implications for theories of emotion. *American Psychologist, 38,* 1145–1160.

Ax, A. F. (1953). The physiological differentiation of fear and anger in humans. *Psychosomatic Medicine, 15,* 433–442.

Axelrod, R. (1984). *The evolution of cooperation.* New York: Basic.

Axsom, D., Yates, S., & Chaiken, S. (1987). Audience response as a heuristic cue in persuasion. *Journal of Personality and Social Psychology, 53,* 30–40.

Azar, B. (1994, December). Research improves lives of animals. *APA Monitor,* p. 19.

Azar, B. (1996, January). Damaged area of brain can reorganize itself. *APA Monitor, 27,* 18–19.

Baars, B. J. (1989). *A cognitive theory of consciousness.* New York: Cambridge University Press.

Baars, B. J., & McGovern, K. (1994). Consciousness. In *Encyclopedia of Human Behavior* (Vol. 1). New York: Academic Press.

Bachman, J., O'Malley, P., & Johnston, L. (1978). *Youth in transition: Vol. 6. Adolescence to adulthood—Change and stability of the lives of young men.* Ann Arbor: Institute of Social Research, University of Michigan.

Bachman, J. G., Johnston, L. D., O'Malley, P. M., & Schulenberg, J. (1996). Transitions in drug use during late adolescence and early adulthood. In J. A. Graber, J. Brooks-Gunn, & A. C. Petersen (Eds.)., *Transitions through adolescence.* Hillsdale, NJ: Erlbaum.

Baddeley, A. (1990). *Human memory: Theory and practice.* Boston: Allyn & Bacon.

Baddeley, A. (1993). Working memory and conscious awareness. In A. F. Collins, S. E. Gathercole, M. A. Conway, & P. E. Morris (Eds.), *Theories of memory.* Hillsdale, NJ: Erlbaum.

Baddeley, A. (1995). Applying the psychology of memory to clinical problems. In D. Hermann, C. McEvoy, C. Hertzog, P. Hertel, & M. Johnson (Eds.), *Basic and applied memory research (Vol. 1).* Hillsdale, NJ: Erlbaum.

Baddeley, A. D., Bressi, S., Della Sala, S., Logie, R., & Spinnler, H. (in press). Working memory. *Brain.*

Baddeley, A. D. (1992). Working memory. *Science, 255,* 556–560.

Bagley, C. (1984). The social aetiology of schizophrenia in immigrant groups. In J. E. Mezzich & C. E. Berganza (Eds.), *Culture and psychopathology.* New York: Columbia University Press.

Bahill, A. T., & Karnavas, W. J. (1993). The perceptual illusion of baseball's rising fastball and breaking curveball. *Journal of Experimental Psychology: Human Perception and Performance, 19,* 3–14.

Bahrick, H. P., Bahrick, P. O., & Wittlinger, R. P. (1975). Fifty years of memory for names and faces: A cross-sectional approach. *Journal of Experimental Psychology: General, 104,* 54–75.

Bailey, J. M., & Pillard, R. C. (1991). A genetic study of male sexual orientation. *Archives of General Psychiatry, 48,* 1089–1096.

Baird, B. (1996). *The internship, practicum, and field placement book.* Upper Saddle River, NJ: Prentice Hall.

Baird, K. A., & Rupert, P. A. (1987). Clinical management of confidentiality: A survey of psychologists in seven states. *Professional Psychology: Research and Practice, 18,* 347–352.

Baker, O. (1996). Managing diversity: Implications for White managers. In B. P. Bowser & R. G. Hunt (Eds.), *Impacts of racism on White Americans.* Newbury Park, CA: Sage.

Balda, R. P., & Kamil, A. C. (1989). A comparative study of cache recovery by three corvid species. *Animal Behaviour, 38,* 486–495.

Ball, W., & Tronick, E. (1971). Infant responses to impending collision: Optical and real. *Science, 171,* 818–820.

Ballard, M. E., & Coates, S. (in press). The immediate effects of homicidal, suicidal, and non-violent heavy metal rap songs on the moods of college students. *Journal of Youth and Adolescence.*

Ballentine, S. F., & Inclan, J. B. (Eds.) (1995). *Diverse voices of women.* Mountain View, CA: Mayfield.

Ballou, M. (1996). Multicultural counseling theory and women. In D. W. Sue (Ed.), *Theory of multicultural counseling and therapy.* Pacific Grove, CA: Brooks/Cole.

Ballou, M., & Gabalac, N. W. (1985). *A feminist position on mental health.* Springfield, IL: Charles C. Thomas.

Baltes, P. B. (1987). Theoretical propositions life-span developmental psychology: On the dynamics between growth and decline. *Developmental Psychology, 23,* 611–626.

Baltes, P. B. (1993). The aging mind: Potentials and limits. *Gerontologist, 33,* 580–594.

Baltes, P. B., & Baltes, M. M. (Eds.). (1990). *Successful Aging.* New York: Cambridge University Press.

Baltes, P. B., & Baltes, M. M. (1990). Psychological perspectives on successful aging: The model of selective optimization with compensation. In P. B. Baltes & M. M. Baltes (Eds.), *Successful aging: Perspectives from the behavioral sciences.* New York: Cambridge University Press.

Baltes, P. B., & Staudinger, U. M. (1993). The search for a psychology of wisdom. *Current Directions in Psychological Science, 2,* 75–80.

Banaji, M., & Prentice, D. A. (1994). The self in social contexts. *Annual Review of Psychology, 45,* 297–332.

Bancroft, J. (1990). The impact of sociocultural influences on adolescent sexual development: Further considerations. In J. Bancroft & J. M. Reinisch (Eds.), *Adolescence and puberty.* New York: Oxford University Press.

Bandarage, A. (1986). Women of color: Toward a celebration of power. *Women of Power, 4,* 8–14.

Bandura, A. (1965). Influence of models' reinforcement contingencies on the acquisition of imitative responses. *Journal of Personality and Social Psychology, 1,* 589–596.

Bandura, A. (1969). *Principles of behavior modification.* New York: Holt, Rinehart & Winston.

Bandura, A. (1971). *Social learning theory.* New York: General Learning Press.

Bandura, A. (1971). Psychotherapy based upon modeling principles. In A. E. Bergin & S. L. Garfield (Eds.). *Handbook of psychotherapy and behavior change: An empirical analysis.* New York: Wiley.

Bandura, A. (1977). *Social learning theory.* Englewood Cliffs, NJ: Prentice Hall.

Bandura, A. (1986). *Social foundations of thought and action.* Englewood Cliffs, NJ: Prentice Hall.

Bandura, A. (1989). Social cognitive theory. In R. Vasta (Ed.), *Six theories of child development: Revised formulations and current issues.* Greenwich, CT: JAI Press.

Bandura, A. (1994). Social cognitive theory of mass communication. In J. Bryant & D. Zillman (Eds.), *Media effects.* Hillsdale, NJ: Erlbaum.

Bandura, A., Blanchard, E. B., & Ritter, B. (1969). Relative efficacy of desensitization and modeling approaches for inducing behavioral, affective, and attitudinal changes. *Journal of Personality and Social Psychology, 13,* 173–199.

Bandura, A., & Jourden, F. J. (1991). Self-regulatory mechanisms governing the impact of social comparison on complex decision making. *Journal of Personality and Social Psychology, 60,* 941–951.

Barak, A., & Fisher, W. A. (1989). Counselor and therapist gender bias? More questions than answers. *Professional Psychology: Research and Practice, 20,* 377–383.

Barash, D. P. (1977). *Sociobiology and behavior.* New York: Elsevier.

Barber, A. E., Hollenbeck, J. R., Tower, S. L., & Phillips, J. M. (1994). The effects of interview focus on recruitment effectiveness: A field experiment. *Journal of Applied Psychology, 79,* 886–896.

Bard, P. (1934). Emotion. In C. Murchison (Ed.), *Handbook of general experimental psychology.* Worcester, MA: Clark University Press.

Barker, L., Edwards, R., Gaines, C., Gladney, K., & Holley, F. (1981). An investigation of proportional time spent in various communication activities by college students. *Journal of Applied Communication Research, 8,* 101–109.

Barker, P. (1986). *Basic family therapy* (2nd ed.). New York: Oxford University Press.

Barkow, J., Cosmides, L., & Tooby, J. (Eds.). (1992). *The adapted mind.* New York: Oxford University Press.

Barlow, D. H., Blanchard, E. B., Vermilyea, J. A., Vermilyea, B. B., & Dimardo, P. A. (1986). Generalized anxiety and generalized anxiety disorder: Description and reconceptualization. *American Journal of Psychiatry, 143,* 40–44.

Barnlund, D. C. (1975). Communicative styles in two cultures: Japan and the United States. In A. Kendon, R. M. Harris, & M. R. Key (Eds.), *Organization of behavior in face-to-face interaction.* The Hague: Mouton.

Barrett, K. C. (1995, March). *Functionalism, contextualism, and emotional development.* Paper presented at the meeting of the Society for Research in Child Development, Indianapolis, IN.

Barrett, K. C., & Campos, J. J. (1987). A functionalist approach to emotions. In J. D. Osofsky (Ed.), *Handbook of infant development.* New York: Wiley.

Barrick, M. R., & Mount, M. K. (1991). The big five personality dimensions and job performance: A meta analysis. *Personnel Psychology, 44,* 1–26.

Barrom, C. P., Shadish, W. R., Jr., & Montgomery, L. M. (1988). PhDs, PsyDs, and real world constraints on scholarly activity: Another look at the Boulder model. *Professional Psychology: Research and Practice, 19,* 93–101.

Barron, F. (1989, April). The birth of a notion: Exercises to tap your creative potential. *Omni,* pp. 112–119.

Barry, H., Child, I. L., & Bacon, M. K. (1959). Relation of child training to subsistence economy. *American Anthropologist, 61,* 51–63.

Bartell, P. A., & Rubin, L. J. (1990). Dangerous liaisons: Sexual intimacies in supervision. *Professional Research and Practice, 21,* 442–450.

Bartlett, F. C. (1932). *Remembering.* Cambridge, England: Cambridge University Press.

Bartoshuk, L. M., & Beauchamp, G. K. (1994). Chemical senses. *Annual Review of Psychology, 45,* 419–449.

Baruth, L. G., & Manning, M. L. (1991). *Multicultural counseling and psychotherapy: A lifespan perspective.* New York: Macmillan.

Bass, D. M., Bowman, K., & Noelker, L. S. (1991). The influence of caregiving and bereavement support on adjusting to an older relative's death. *Gerontologist, 31,* 32–41.

Bateman, T., & Snell, S. (1996). *Management (3rd ed.).* Burr Ridge, IL: Irwin.

Bates, J. A. (1995). Teaching hypothesis testing by debunking a demonstration of telepathy. In M. E. Ware & D. E. Johnson (Eds.), *Handbook of demonstrations and activities in the teaching of psychology (Vol. 1).* Hillsdale, NJ: Erlbaum.

Batson, C. D., Bolen, M. H., Cross, J. A., & Jeuringer-Benefiel, H. E. (1986). Where is the altruism in the altruistic personality? *Journal of Personality and Social Psychology, 50,* 212–220.

Batson, C. D., Schoenrade, P., & Ventis, W. L. (1993). *Religion and the individual.* New York: Oxford University Press.

Baum, A., & Singer, J. E. (Eds.). (1987). *Handbook of psychology and health: Vol. 5. Stress.* Hillsdale, NJ: Erlbaum.

Baumeister, R. F. (1993). *Self-esteem: The puzzle of low self-regard.* New York: Plenum.

Baumgartner, M. P. (1993). Violent networks: The origins and management of domestic conflict. In R. B. Felson & J. T. Tedeschi (Eds.), *Aggression and violence.* Washington, DC: American Psychological Association.

Baumrind, D. (1971). Current patterns of parental authority. *Developmental Psychology Monographs, 4* (1, Pt. 2).

Baumrind, D. (1991). Parenting styles and adolescent development. In J. Brooks-Gunn, R. Lerner, & A. C. Petersen (Eds.), *The encyclopedia of adolescence.* New York: Garland.

Baumrind, D. (1993). The average expectable environment is not good enough. *Child Development, 64,* 1299–1317.

Beal, C. R. (1994). *Boys and girls: The development of gender roles.* New York: McGraw-Hill.

Beatty, J. (1995). *Principles of neuroscience.* Madison, WI: Brown & Benchmark.

Beck, A. (1976). *Cognitive therapies and the emotional disorders.* New York: International Universities Press.

Beck, A. T. (1967). *Depression.* New York: Harper & Row.

Beck, A. T. (1993). Cognitive therapy: Past, present, and future. **Journal of Consulting and Clinical Psychology, 61,** 194–198.

Beck, J. G. (1996). The crescendo of fear. *Contemporary Psychology, 41,* 262–263.

Becker, F. D. (1974). *Design for living: The residents' view of multi-family housing.* Ithaca, NY: Center for Urban Development Research.

Beckham, F. E., & Leber, W. R. (Eds.). (1995). *Handbook of depression* (2nd ed.). New York: Guilford Press.

Begley, S., Wright, W., Church, V., & Hager, M. (1992, April 20). Mapping the brain. *Newsweek,* pp. 66–70.

Beit-Hallahmi, B. (1989). *Prologomena to the psychological study of religion.* Lewisburg, PA: Bucknell University Press.

Bell, A. P., & Weinberg, M. S. (1978). *Homosexualities.* New York: Simon & Schuster.

Bell, A. P., Weinberg, M. S., & Mammersmith, S. K. (1981). *Sexual preference: Its development in men and women.* New York: Simon & Schuster.

Bell, K. L. (1995, March). *Attachment and flexibility at self-presentation during the transition to adulthood.* Paper presented at the meeting of the Society for Research in Child Development, Indianapolis.

Bell, P. A., & Greene, T. C. (1982). Thermal stress: Physiological, comfort, performance and social effects of hot and cold environments. In G. W. Evans (Ed.), *Environmental stress.* New York: Cambridge University Press.

Bellack, A. S., & Hersen, M. (Eds.). (1988). *Behavioral assessment: A practical handbook* (3rd ed.). New York: Pergamon.

Belsky, J. (1987, April). *Science, social policy, and day care: A personal odyssey.* Paper presented at the biennial meeting of the Society for Research in Child Development, Baltimore.

Belson, W. (1978). *Television violence and the adolescent boy.* London: Saxon House.

Bem, D. J. (1967). Self-perception. An alternative interpretation of cognitive dissonance phenomena. *Psychological Review,* 200.

Bem, S. L. (1977). On the utility of alternative procedures for assessing psychological androgyny. *Journal of Consulting and Clinical Psychology, 45,* 196–205.

Ben-Shakhar, G., Bar-Hillel, M., Yoram, B., Ben-Abba, E., & Flug, A. (1986). Can graphology predict occupational success? Two empirical studies and some methodological ruminations. *Journal of Applied Psychology, 71,* 645–653.

Benbow, C. P., & Stanley, J. C. (1983). Sex differences in mathematical reasoning ability: More facts. *Science, 222,* 1029–1031.

Benet, S. (1976). *How to live to be 100.* New York: Dial Press.

Bengston, V. L. (Ed.) (1996). *Adulthood and aging.* New York: Springer.

Benjamin, L. T. (1996). Lightner Witmer's legacy to American psychology. *American Psychologist, 51,* 235–236.

Bennett, S. K. (1994). The American Indian: A psychological overview. In W. J. Lonner & R. Malpass (Eds.), *Psychology and culture.* Needham Heights, MA: Allyn & Bacon.

Bennett, W. I., & Gurin, J. (1982). *The dieter's dilemma: Eating less and weighing more.* New York: Basic Books.

Benson, H., & Proctor, W. (1984). *Beyond the relaxation response.* New York: Times Books.

Benton, C., Hernandez, A., Schmidt, A., Schmitz, M., Stone, A., & Weiner, B. (1983). Is hostility linked with affiliation among males and with achievement among females? A critique of Pollak and Gilligan. *Journal of Personality and Social Psychology, 45,* 1167–1171.

Bereczkei, T. (1993). Selected reproductive strategies among Hungarian gypsies: A preliminary analysis. *Ethology and Sociobiology, 14,* 71–88.

Bergin, A. E., & Garfield, S. L. (1994). *Handbook of psychotherapy and behavior change.* New York: John Wiley.

Berk, S. F. (1985). *The gender factory: The apportionment of work in American households.* New York: Plenum.

Berkowitz, L. (1989). Frustration-aggression hypothesis: Examination and reformulation. *Psychological Bulletin, 106,* 59–73.

Berkowitz, L. (1990). On the formation and regulation of anger and aggression. A cognitive-neoassociationistic analysis. *American Psychologist, 45,* 494–503.

Berkowitz, M. W., Mueller, C. W., Schnell, S. V., & Padberg, M. T. (1986). Moral reasoning and judgments of aggression. *Journal of Personality and Social Psychology, 51,* 885–891.

Berndt, T. J. (1996). Transitions in friendships and friends' influence. In J. A. Graber, J. Brooks-Gunn, & A. C. Petersen (Eds.), *Transitions through adolescence.* Hillsdale, NJ: Erlbaum.

Berndt, T. J., & Perry, T. B. (1990). Distinctive features and effects of early adolescent friendships. In R. Montemayor (Ed.), *Advances in adolescent research.* Greenwich, CT: JAI.

Berninger, V. W. (1993, March). *Independent contributions of orthographic, phonological, and working memory skills to component reading skills.* Paper presented at the biennial meeting of the Society for Research in Child Development, New Orleans.

Bernstein, R., & Bernstein, S. (1996). *Biology.* Dubuque, IA: Wm. C. Brown.

Berry, G. L., & Asamen, J. K. (1993). *Children and television.* Newbury Park, CA: Sage.

Berry, J. W. (1969). On cross-cultural comparability. *International Journal of Psychology, 4,* 119–128.

Berry, J. W. (1971). Ecological and cultural factors in spatial perceptual development. *Canadian Journal of Behavioral Science, 3,* 324–336.

Berry, J. W. (1980). Acculturation as varieties of adaptation. In A. Padilla (Ed.), *Acculturation: Theory, model, and some new findings.* Washington, DC: American Association for the Advancement of Science.

Berry, J. W. (1983). Textured contexts: Systems and situations in cross-cultural psychology. In S. H. Irvine & J. W. Berry (Eds.), *Human assessment and cultural factors.* New York: Plenum.

Berry, J. W., & Kim, U. (1988). Acculturation and mental health. In P. R. Dasen, J. W. Berry, & N. Sartorius (Eds.), *Health and cross-cultural psychology: Toward applications.* Newbury Park, CA: Sage.

Berry, J. W., Poortinga, Y. H., Segall, M. H., & Dasen, P. R. (1992). *Cross-cultural psychology: Theory, method, and applications.* Cambridge, England: Cambridge University Press.

Berscheid, E. (1988). Some comments on love's anatomy. Or, whatever happened to an old-fashioned lust? In R. J. Sternberg & M. L. Barnes (Eds.), *Anatomy of love.* New Haven, CT: Yale University Press.

Berscheid, E. (1994). Interpersonal relationships. *Annual Review of Psychology, 45,* 79–129.

Berscheid, E., & Fei, J. (1977). Sexual jealousy and romantic love. In G. Clinton & G. Smith (Eds.), *Sexual jealousy.* Englewood Cliffs, NJ: Prentice-Hall.

Berscheid, E., Snyder, M., & Omoto, A. M. (1989). Issues in studying close relationships: Conceptualizing and measuring closeness. In C. Hendrick (Ed.), *Close relationships.* Newbury Park, CA: Sage.

Bersoff, D. N. (1996). The virtue of principle ethics. *The Counseling Psychologist, 24,* 86–91.

Bertelson, A. (1979). A Danish twin study of manic-depressive disorders. In M. Schous & E. Stromgren (Eds.), *Origin, prevention, and treatment of affective disorders.* Orlando, FL: Academic Press.

Bertenthal, B. (1993, March). *Emerging themes in perceptual development.* Paper presented at the biennial meeting of the Society for Research in Child Development, New Orleans.

Berzon, B. (1988). *Permanent partners.* New York: Plume.

Bexton, W. H., Heron, W., & Scott, T. H. (1954). Effects of decreased variation in the sensory environment. *Canadian Journal of Psychology, 8,* 70–76.

Bickman, L., & Ellis, H. C. (Eds.). (1990). *Preparing psychologists for the 21st century: Proceedings of the National Conference on Graduate Education in Psychology.* Hillsdale, NJ: Erlbaum.

Bijur, P. E., Wallston, K. A., Smith, C. A., Lifrak, S., & Friedman, S. B. (1993, August). *Gender differences in turning to religion for coping.* Paper presented at the meeting of the American Psychological Association, Toronto.

Biller, H. B. (1993). *Fathers and families: Paternal factors in child development.* Westport, CT: Auburn House.

Billings, A., & Moos, R. (1982). Social support and functioning among community and clinical groups: A panel model. *Journal of Behavioral Medicine, 5,* 295–311.

Billings, A. G., Cronkite, R. C., & Moos, R. H. (1983). Social-environment factors in unipolar depression. *Journal of Abnormal Psychology, 92,* 119–133.

Billings, A. G., & Moos, R. H. (1981). The role of coping responses and social resources in attenuating the stress of life events. *Journal of Behavioral Medicine, 4,* 157–189.

Billy, J. O. G., Tanfer, K., Grady, W. R., & Klepinger, D. H. (1993). The sexual behavior of men in the United States. *Family Planning Perspectives, 25,* 52–60.

Birren, J. E. (Ed.) (1996). *Encyclopedia of gerontology.* San Diego, CA: Academic Press.

Birren, J. E., & Salthouse, T. A. (in press). *The psychology of aging.* Cambridge, MA: Blackwell.

Birren, J. E., & Schaie, K. W. (Eds.) (1996). *Handbook of the psychology of aging (4th ed.).* Orlando, FL: Academic Press.

Birren, J. E., Schaie, K. W., Abeles, R. P., & Salthouse, T. J. (Eds.) (1996). *Handbook of the psychology of aging (4th ed.).* San Diego, CA: Academic Press.

Bitterman, M. E. (1965). Phyletic differences in learning. *American Psychologist, 20,* 396–410.

Bitterman, M. E. (1975). The comparative analysis of learning. *Science, 188,* 699–709.

Bjerklie, D., Dorfman, A., Gorman, C., & Nash, J. M. (1994, January 17). The genetic revolution. *Time,* pp. 46–53.

Blackmore, S. (1987). A report of a visit to Carl Sargent's laboratory. *Journal of the Society for Psychical Research, 54,* 186–198.

Blades, M. (1977). *Individual differences in intelligence.* In P. Scott & C. Spencer (Eds.), *Psychology.* Cambridge, MA: Blackwell.

Blair, C., & Ramey, C. (1996). Early intervention with low-birth weight infants: The path to second generation research. In M. J. Guralnick (Ed.), *The effectiveness of early intervention.* Baltimore, MD: Paul Brookes.

Blair, S. N. (1989, February). Personal communication, The Aerobics Institute, Dallas.

Blair, S. N. (1990, January). Personal communication. Aerobics Institute, Dallas.

Blair, S. N., & Kohl, H. W. (1988). Physical activity: Which is more important for health? *Medicine and Science and Sports and Exercise, 20,* (2, Suppl.), 5–7.

Blair, S. N., & Paffenbarger, R. S., Jr. (1993, March). *The influence of body weight and shape variation on the incidence of cardiovascular disease, diabetes, lung disease and cancer.* Paper presented at the annual meeting of the American Epidemiologic Society, Pittsburgh.

Blake, R. (1994). Gibson's inspired but latent prelude to visual motion perception. *Psychological Review, 101,* 324–328.

Blanck, P. D., Buck, R., & Rosenthal, R. (Eds.). (1986). *Nonverbal communication in the clinical context.* University Park: Pennsylvania State University Press.

Bland, S. H., O'Leary, E. S., Farinaro, E., Jossa, F., & Trevison, M. (1996). Long-term psychological effects of natural disasters. *Psychosomatic Medicine, 58,* 18–24.

Bloom, B. (1975). *Changing patterns of psychiatric care.* New York: Human Science Press.

Bloom, B. (1992). Computer-assisted intervention: A review and commentary. *Clinical Psychology Review, 128,* 169–198.

Bloom, B. L. (1985). *Community mental health: A general introduction* (2nd ed.). Monterey, CA: Brooks/Cole.

Bloom, B. S. (Ed.). (1985). *Developing talent in young people.* New York: Ballantine.

Bloom, F. E., Lazerson, A., & Hofstadter, L. (1985). *Brain, mind, and behavior.* New York: W. H. Freeman.

Bloor, C., & White, F. (1983). Unpublished manuscript, University of California at San Diego.

Blos, P. (1989). The inner world of the adolescent. In A. H. Esman (Ed.), *International annals of adolescent psychiatry.* Chicago: University of Chicago Press.

Blumstein, P. W., & Schwartz, P. (1983). *American couples: Money, work, sex.* New York: William Morrow.

Blundell, J. E. (1984). Systems and interactions: An approach to the pharmacology of feeding. In A. J. Stunkard & E. Stellar (Eds.), *Eating and its disorders.* New York: Raven Press.

Bly, R. (1990). *Iron John.* New York: Vintage Books.

Boden, M. A. (Ed.) (1996). *Computational psychology and artificial intelligence.* Orlando, FL: Academic Press.

Boggiano, A. K., & Pittman, T. S. (1993). *Achievement and motivation.* New York: Cambridge University Press.

Bohannon, J. N., III. (1988). Flashbulb memories for the space shuttle disaster: A tale of two theories. *Cognition, 29,* 179–186.

Bolles, R. (1993). *What color is your parachute?* Berkeley, CA: Ten Speed Press.

Bolt, M. (1975). Purpose in life and religious orientation. *Journal of Psychology and Theology, 3,* 116–118.

Bolton, R. (1979). *People skills.* New York: Touchstone.

Bond, R., & Smith, P. B. (1994). Culture and conformity: A meta-analysis of studies using the Asch-type perceptual judgment task. *British Psychological Society 1994 Proceedings,* p. 41.

Boray, P. F., Gifford, R., & Rosenblood, L. (1989). Effects of warm white, cool white, and full-spectrum lighting on simple cognitive performance, mood and ratings of others. *Journal of Environmental Psychology, 9,* 297–308.

Bordens, K. S., & Abbott, B. B. (1996). *Research design and methods (3rd ed.).* Mountain View, CA: Mayfield.

Boring, E. G. (1950). *A history of experimental psychology* (2nd ed.). New York: Appleton-Century-Crofts.

Bornstein, M. H. (1993, March). *Cross-cultural perspectives on parenting.* Paper presented at the biennial meeting of the Society for Research in Child Development, New Orleans.

Bouchard, C., Trembley, A., Despres, J. P., Nadeau, A., Lupien, P., Theriault, G., Dussault, J., Moorjani, S., Pinault, S., & Fournier, G. (1990). The response to long-term overfeeding in identical twins. *New England Journal of Medicine, 322,* 1477–1482.

Bouchard, T. J., Heston, L., Eckert, E., Keyes, M., & Resnick, S. (1981). The Minnesota Study of Twins Reared Apart: Project description and sample results in the developmental domain. *Twin Research, 3,* 227–233.

Bouchard, T. J., Lykken, D. T., McGue, M., Segal, N. L., & Tellegen, A. (1990). Source of human psychological differences: The Minnesota Study of Twins Reared Apart. *Science, 250,* 223–228.

Bouchard, T. J., Lykken, D. T., Tellegen, A., & McGue, M. (1996). Genes, drives, environment, and experience. In D. Lubinski & C. Benbow (Eds.), *Psychometrics and social issues concerning intellectual talent.* Baltimore, MD: Johns Hopkins University Press.

Boudewyns, P. A. (1996). Post-traumatic stress disorder. In M. Hersen & P. M. Miller (Eds.), *Progress in behavior modification (Vol. 30).* Pacific Grove, CA: Brooks/Cole.

Bower, G. H., Clark, M., Winzenz, D., & Lesgold, A. (1969). Hierarchical retrieval schemes in recall of categorized word lists. *Journal of Verbal Learning and Verbal Behavior, 3,* 323–343.

Bower, G. H., & Gilligan, S. G. (1979). Remembering information related to one's self. *Journal of Research in Personality, 13,* 404–419.

Bowers, J., & Schacter, D. L. (1993). Priming of novel information in amnesic patients: Issues and data. In P. Graf & M. E. J. Masson (Eds.), *Implicit memory.* Hillsdale, NJ: Erlbaum.

Bowers, T. G., & Clum, G. A. (1988). Relative contribution of specific and nonspecific treatment effects: Meta-analysis of placebo-controlled behavior therapy research. *Psychological Bulletin, 103,* 315–323.

Bowlby, J. (1969). *Attachment and loss* (Vol. 1). London: Hogarth Press.

Bowlby, J. (1980). Attachment and loss. In *Loss, sadness, and depression* (Vol. 3). New York: Basic Books.

Bowlby, J. (1989). *Secure and insecure attachment.* New York: Basic Books.

Bowlby, J. (1989). *Secure attachment.* New York: Basic Books.

Bowman, G. D., & Stern, M. (1995). Adjustment to occupational stress: The relationship of perceived control to effectiveness of coping strategies. *Journal of Counseling Psychology, 42,* 294–303.

Bowser, B. P., & Hunt, R. G. (Eds.) (1996). *Impacts of racism on White Americans.* Newbury Park, CA: Sage.

Boyd, B., & Wandersman, A. (1991). Predicting undergraduate condom use with the Fishbein and Ajzen and the Triandis attitude-behavior models: Implications for public health interventions. *Journal of Applied Social Psychology, 21,* 1810–1830.

Boyd-Franklin, N. (1989). *Black families in therapy.* New York: Guilford.

Bradley, M. M. (1996). Gonna change my way of thinking. *Contemporary Psychology, 41,* 258–259.

Brandtstädter, J., & Renner, G. (1990). Tenacious goal pursuit and flexible goal adjustment: Explication and age-related analysis of assimilative and accommodative strategies of coping. *Psychology and Aging, 5,* 58–67.

Bransford, J. D., Franks, J. J., Vye, N. J., & Sherwood, R. D. (1989). Multiple analogies for complex concepts. In S. Vosniadou & A. Ortony (Eds.), *Similarity and analogical reasoning.* New York: Cambridge University Press.

Bransford, J. D., & Stein, B. S. (1984). *The IDEAL problem solver.* New York: W. H. Freeman.

Bransford, J. D., & Stein, B. S. (1993). *The IDEAL problem solver* (2nd ed.). New York: W. H. Freeman.

Brean, H. (1958, March 31). What hidden sell is all about. *Life,* pp. 104–114.

Brehm, S. S., & Kassin, S. M. (1996). *Social psychology (3rd ed.).* Boston: Houghton Mifflin.

Breier, A. (Ed.). (1996). *The new pharmacotherapy of schizophrenia.* Washington, DC: American Psychiatric Association.

Breier, A., Charney, D. S., & Heninger, G. R. (1986). Agoraphobia with panic attacks. *Archives of General Psychiatry, 43,* 1029–1036.

Breland, K., & Breland, M. (1961). The misbehavior of organisms. *American Psychologist, 16,* 681–684.

Brennan, P., Mednick, S., & Kandel, E. (1991). Congenital determinants of violent and property offencing. In D. Pepler & K. Rubin (Eds.), *The development and treatment of childhood aggression.* Hillsdale, NJ: Erlbaum.

Bretherton, I. (1996). Attachment theory and research in historical and personal context. *Contemporary Psychology, 41,* 236–237.

Brewer, M. B., & Campbell, D. T. (1976). *Ethnocentrism and intergroup attitudes.* New York: Wiley.

Brewer, M. B., & Caporael, L. R. (1990). Selfish genes versus selfish people: Sociobiology as origin myth. *Motivation and Emotion, 14,* 237–243.

Brewer, W. F. (1996). Children's eyewitness memory research. In N. L. Stein, C. Brainerd, P. A. Ornstein, & B. Tversky (Eds.), *Memory for everyday and emotional events.* Hillsdale, NJ: Erlbaum.

Brickman, P., Coates, D., & Janoff-Bulman, R. J. (1978). Lottery winners and accident victims: Is happiness relative? *Journal of Personality and Social Psychology, 36,* 917–927.

Brickner, M. A., Harkins, S. G., & Ostrom, T. M. (1986). Effects of personal involvement: Thought-provoking implications for social loafing. *Journal of Personality and Social Psychology, 51,* 763–769.

Bridgwater, C. A. (1984, February). The work ethic lives. *Psychology Today,* p. 17.

Briggs, J. L. (1970). *Never in anger.* Cambridge, MA: Harvard University Press.

Brigham, J. C. (1986). Race and eyewitness identifications. In S. Worschel & W. G. Austin (Eds.), *Psychology of intergroup relations.* Chicago: Nelson-Hall.

Brigham, J. C., Maas, A., Snyder, L. D., & Spaulding, K. (1982). Accuracy of eyewitness identification in a field setting. *Journal of Personality and Social Psychology, 41,* 683–691.

Brim, G. (1992, December 7). Commentary, *Newsweek,* p. 52.

Brislin, R. (1993). *Understanding culture's influence on behavior.* Fort Worth, TX: Harcourt Brace.

Brislin, R. W. (1990). Applied cross-sultural psychology: An introduction. In R. W. Brislin (Ed.), *Applied cross-cultural psychology.* Newbury Park, CA: Sage.

Broadbent, D. E. (1979). Human performance and noise. In C. M. Harris (Ed.), *Handbook of noise control,* New York: McGraw-Hill.

Brobeck, J. R., Tepperman, T., & Long, C. N. (1943). Experimental hypothalamic hyperphagia in the albino rat. *Yale Journal of Biological Medicine, 15,* 831–853.

Brodie, J. D. (1996). Imaging for the clinical psychiatrist. *The American Journal of Psychiatry, 153,* 145–149.

Broman, C. L. (1996). Coping with personal problems. In H. W. Neighbors & J. S. Jackson (Eds.), *Mental health in Black America.* Newbury Park, CA: Sage.

Brone, R. J., & Fisher, C. B. (1988). Determinants of adolescent obesity: A comparison with anorexia nervosa. *Adolescence, 23,* 155–169.

Bronstein, P. A., & Paludi, M. (1988). The introductory course from a broader perspective. In P. A. Bronstein & M. Paludi (Eds.), *Teaching a psychology of people.* Washington, DC: American Psychological Association.

Bronstein, P. A., & Quina, K. (1988). Perspectives on gender balance and cultural diversity in the teaching of psychology. In P. A. Bronstein & K. Quina (Eds.), *Teaching a psychology of people: Resources for gender and sociocultural awareness.* Washington, DC: American Psychological Association.

Brook, J. S., Brook, D. W., Gordon, A. S., Whiteman, M., & Cohen, P. (1990). The psychological etiology of adolescent drug use: A family interactional approach. *Genetic Psychology Monographs, 116,* no. 2.

Brooks-Gunn, J. (1996, March). *The uniqueness of the early adolescent transition.* Paper presented at the meeting of the Society for Research on Adolescence, Boston.

Broverman, I., Broverman, D., Clarkson, F., Rosenkrantz, P., & Vogel, S. (1970). Sex-role stereotypes and clinical judgments of mental health. *Journal of Consulting and Clinical Psychology, 34,* 1–7.

Broverman, I., Vogel, S., Broverman, D., Clarkson, F., & Rosenkranz, P. (1972). Sex-role stereotypes: A current appraisal. *Journal of Social Issues, 28,* 59–78.

Brower, A. V. Z. (1996). Parallel race formation and the evolution of mimicry in *Heliconius* butterflies: A phylogenetic hypothesis from mitochondrial DNA sequences. *Evolution, 50,* 195–221.

Brower, I. O. (1989). Counseling Vietnamese. In D. R. Atkinson, G. Morten, & D. W. Sue (Eds.), *Counseling American minorities.* Dubuque, IA: Wm. C. Brown.

Brown, A. S., & Nix, L. A. (1996). Age-related changes in the tip-of the-tongue experiences. *American Journal of Psychology, 109,* 79–92.

Brown, B. B., & Lohr, M. J. (1987). Peer-group affiliation and adolescent self-esteem: An integration of ego-identity and symbolic-interaction theories. *Journal of Personality and Social Psychology, 52,* 47–55.

Brown, D. R., & Gary, L. E. (1985). Social support network differentials among married and nonmarried black females. *Psychology of Women Quarterly, 9,* 229–241.

Brown, E., Deffenbacher, K., & Sturgill, W. (1977). Memory for faces and the circumstances of encounter. *Journal of Applied Psychology, 6,* 311–318.

Brown, E. D., & Moye, J. A. (1995, August). *Toward consensus of geropsychology training.* Paper presented at the meeting of the American Psychological Association, New York City.

Brown, G., Bhrolchain, M., & Harris, T. (1975). Social class and psychiatric disturbance among women in an urban population. *Sociology, 9,* 225–254.

Brown, G. D. (1995). *Human evolution.* Dubuque, IA: Wm. C. Brown.

Brown, J. K. (1985). Introduction. In J. K. Brown & V. Kerns (Eds.), *In her prime: A new view of middle-aged women.* South Hadley, MA: Bergin & Garvey.

Brown, L., & Brodsky, A. (1992). The future of feminist therapy. *Psychotherapy, 29,* 39–43.

Brown, R. (1973). *A first language: The early stages.* Cambridge, MA: Harvard University Press.

Brown, R. (1986). *Social psychology* (2nd ed.). New York: Free Press.

Brown, R. T. (1995). Exercise demonstrating genetic-environment interaction. in M. E. Ware & D. E. Johnson (Eds.), *Demonstrations and activities in teaching of psychology (Vol. 2).* Hillsdale, NJ: Erlbaum.

Brown, W. S., & Caetano, C. (1992). Conversion, cognition, and neuropsychology. In H. Newton Malony & S. Southard (Eds.), *Handbook of religious conversion.* Birmingham, AL: Religious Education Press.

Browne, A., & Williams, K. R. (1993). Gender, intimacy, and lethal violence: Trends from 1976 through 1987. *Gender and Society, 7,* 78–98.

Browne, M. W. (1994, October 16). What is intelligence, and who has it? *New York Times Book Review,* pp. 2–3, 41–42.

Brownell, K. D. (1993). Whether obesity should be treated. *Health Psychology, 10,* 303–310.

Brownell, K. D., & Cohen, L. R. (1995). Adherence to dietary regimens. *Behavioral Medicine, 20,* 226–242.

Brownell, K. D., & Rodin, J. (1994). The dieting maelstrom: Is it possible and advisable to lose weight? *American Psychologist, 9,* 781–791.

Brownell, K. D., & Rodin, J. (in press). Medical, metabolic, and psychological effects of weight cycling and weight variability. *Archives of Internal Medicine.*

Bruce, C., Desimone, R., & Gross, C. G. (1981). Visual properties of neurons in a polysensory area in the superior temporal sulcus of the macaque. *Journal of Neurophysiology, 46,* 369–384.

Bruess, C. J., & Pearson, J. C. (1996). Gendered patterns in family communication. In J. T. Wood (Ed.), *Gendered relationships.* Mountain View, CA: Mayfield.

Bruner, J. S. (1964). The course of cognitive growth. *American Psychologist, 19,* 1–15.

Bruner, J. S., & Tagiuri, R. (1954). The perception of people. In G. Lindzey (Ed.), *Handbook of social psychology* (Vol. 2). Reading, MA: Addison-Wesley.

Brunswick, A. F., & Banaszak-Holl, J. (1996). HIV risk behavior and the health belief model. *Journal of Community Psychology, 24,* 44–65.

Brunswick, E. (1956). *Perception and the representative design of psychological experiments.* Berkeley: University of California Press.

Bryne, R. (1997). Evolution and sociobiology. In P. Scott & C. Spencer (Eds.), *Psychology.* Cambridge, MA: Blackwell.

Burgess, K. (1968). The behavior and training of a killer whale (*Orcinus orca*) at San Diego Sea World. *International Zoo Yearbook, 8,* 202–205.

Burmeister, S., Couvillon, P. A., & Bitterman, M. E. (1995). Performance of honeybees in analogues of the rodent radial maze. *Animal Learning and Behavior, 23,* 369–375.

Burnstein, E., Crandall, C., & Kitayama, S. (1994). Some neo-Darwinian decision rules for altruism: Weighing cues for inclusive fitness as a function of the biological importance of the decision. *Journal of Personality and Social Psychology, 67,* 773–789.

Bushman, B. J. (1993). Human aggression while under the influence of alcohol and other drugs: An integrative research review. *Current Directions in Psychological Science, 2,* 148–152.

Buss, D. M. (1986). Can social science be anchored in evolutionary biology? *Revue Europeane des Sciences Sociales, 234,* 41–50.

Buss, D. M. (1989). Sex differences in human mate preferences: Evolutionary hypotheses tested in 37 cultures. *Behavioral and Brain Sciences, 12,* 1–49.

Buss, D. M. (1991). Evolutionary personality psychology. *Annual Review of Psychology, 45,* 459–491.

Buss, D. M. (1994). *The evolution of desire.* New York: Basic Books.

Buss, D. M. (1995). Evolutionary psychology: A new paradigm for psychological science. *Psychological Inquiry, 6,* 1–30.

Buss, D. M. (1995). Psychological sex differences: Origins through sexual selection. *American Psychologist, 50,* 164–168.

Buss, D. M., & Barnes, M. (1986). Preferences in human mate selection. *Journal of Personality and Social Psychology, 50,* 559–570.

Buss, D. M., & Malamuth, N. (Eds.) (1996). *Sex, power, and conflict.* New York: Oxford University.

Buss, D. M., & others. (1990). International preferences in selecting mates: A study of 37 cultures. *Journal of Cross-Cultural Psychology, 21,* 5–47.

Buss, D. M., & Schmitt, D. P. (1993). Sexual strategies theory: An evolutionary perspective on human mating. *Psychological Review, 100,* 204–232.

Bustamente, A. (1992, April). *Beyond the DSM-III: The role of the therapist in affirming the development of a positive gay identity in lesbian and gay clients.* Symposium presented at the Annual Convention of the Society for the Exploration of Psychotherapy Integration, San Diego.

Butcher, J. N., Dahlstrom, W. G., Graham, J. R., Tellegen, A., & Kaemmer, B. (1989). *Manual for the restandardized Minnesota Multiphasic Personality Inventory (MMPI-2): An administrative and interpretive guide.* Minneapolis: University of Minnesota Press.

Butler, G., Fennell, M., Robson, P., & Gelder, M. (1991). Comparison of behavior therapy and cognitive behavior therapy in the treatment of generalized anxiety disorder. *Journal of Consulting and Clinical Psychology, 59,* 167–175.

Butler, R. A. (1953). Discrimination learning by rhesus monkeys to visual-exploration motivation. *Journal of Comparative and Physiological Psychology, 46,* 95–98.

Butters, N., Delis, D., & Lucas, J. (1995). Clinical assessment of memory disorders in amnesia and dementia. *Annual Review of Psychology, 46.* Palo Alto, CA: Annual Reviews.

Butters, N., Heindel, W. C., & Salmon, D. P. (1990). Dissociation of implicit memory in dementia: Neurological implications. *Bulletin of the Psychonomic Society, 28,* 359–366.

Butz, M. R. (1995). Psychopharmacology: Psychology's *Jurassic Park? Psychotherapy, 13,* 692–699.

Buunk, B. P., Collins, R. L., Taylor, S. E., Van Yperen, N. W., & Dakof, G. A. (1990). The affective consequences of social comparison: Either direction has its ups and downs. *Journal of Personality and Social Psychology, 59,* 1238–1249.

Byar, C. O., & Shainberg, L. W. (1997). *Dimensions of human sexuality (5th ed.).* Madison, WI: Brown & Benchmark.

Byrnes, J. P. (1988). Formal operations: A systematic reformulation. *Developmental Review, 8,* 66–87.

Cabeza de Vaca, S., Brown, B. L., & Hemmes, N. S. (1994). Internal clock and memory processes in animal timing. *Journal of Experimental Psychology: Animal Behavior Processes, 20,* 184–198.

Cahill, L., Prins, B., Weber, M. & McGaugh, J. L. (1995). /gb/-Adrenergic activation and memory for emotional events. *Nature, 376,* 702–704.

Cain, D. J. (1996). A person-centered therapist's perspective on Ruth. In G. Corey (Ed.), *Case approach to counseling and psychotherapy (4th ed.).* Pacific Grove, CA: Brooks/Cole.

Cairns, R. B. (1991). Multiple metaphors for a singular idea. *Developmental Psychology, 27,* 23–236.

Caldwell, B. (1964). The effects of infant care. In M. Hoffman & L. Hoffman (Eds.), *Review of child development research* (Vol. 1). New York: Russell Sage.

Caldwell, C. H. (1996). Predisposing, enabling, and need factors related to help-seeking in Black women. In H. W. Neighbors & J. S. Jackson (Eds.), *Mental health in Black America.* Newbury Park, CA: Sage.

Calhoun, J. B. (1971). Space and the strategy of life. In A. H. Esser (Eds.), *Behavior and environment: The use of space by animals and men.* New York: Plenum Press.

Cameron, N. (1963). *Personality development and psychopathology.* Boston: Houghton Mifflin.

Campbell, D. T., & LeVine, R. A. (1968). Ethnocentrism and intergroup relations. In R. Abelson & others (Eds.), *Theories of cognitive consistency: A sourcebook.* Chicago: Rand McNally.

Campbell, F. A., & Ramey, C. T. (1993, March). *Mid-adolescent outcomes for high risk students: An examination of the continuing effects of early intervention.* Paper presented at the biennial meeting of the Society for Research in Child Development, New Orleans.

Campbell, J. D., Tesser, A., & Fairey, P. J. (1986). Conformity and attention to the stimulus: Some temporal and contextual dynamics. *Journal of Personality and Social Psychology, 51,* 315–324.

Campos, J. (1994, Spring). The new functionalism in emotions. *SRCD Newsletter,* pp. 1, 7, 9–11, 14.

Campos, J. J., Kermoian, R., & Witherington, D. (1995). An epigenetic perspective on emotional development. In R. D. Kavanaugh, B. Zimmerberg, & S. Fein (Eds.), *Emotion.* Hillsdale, NJ: Erlbaum.

Candland, D. K. (1993). *Feral children and clever animals: Reflections on human nature.* New York: Oxford University Press.

Canfield, R. L., & Haith, M. M. (1991). Young infants' visual expectations for symmetric and asymmetric stimulus sequences. *Developmental Psychology, 27,* 198–208.

Cannon, W. B. (1927). The James-Lange theory of emotions: A critical examination and an alternative theory. *American Journal of Psychology, 39,* 106–124.

Cannon, W. B., & Washburn, A. L. (1912). An explanation of hunger. *American Journal of Physiology, 29,* 444–454.

Canter, M. B., Bennett, B. E., Jones, S. E., & Nagy, T. F. (1994). *Ethics for psychologists.* Washington, DC: American Psychological Association.

Cantor, N., & Langston, C. A. (1989). Ups and downs of life tasks in a life transition. In L. A. Pervin (Ed.), *Goal concepts in personality and social psychology* (pp. 127–167). Hillsdale, NJ: Erlbaum.

Capaldi, E. (Ed.) (1996). *Why we eat what we eat.* Washington, DC: American Psychological Association.

Caplan, G. (1964). *Principles of preventive psychiatry.* New York: Basic Books.

Caporael, L. R., & Brewer, M. B. (1995). Hierarchical evolutionary theory: There is an alternative and it's not creationism. *Psychological Inquiry, 6,* 31–34.

Carkenord, D. M., & Bullington, J. (1995). Bringing cognitive dissonance to the classroom. In M. E. Ware & D. E. Johnson (Eds.), *Demonstrations and activities in teaching of psychology (Vol. 3).* Hillsdale, NJ: Erlbaum.

Carp, F. M., & Carp, A. (1982). Perceived environmental quality of neighborhoods: Development of assessment scales and their relation to age and gender. *Journal of Environmental Psychology, 2,* 295–312.

Carpenter, P. A., & Just, M. A. (1981). Cognitive processes in reading: Models based on readers' eyes' fixations. In A. M. Lesgold & C. A. Perfetti (Eds.), *Interactive processes in reading.* Hillsdale, NJ: Erlbaum.

Carrera, M. (1981). *Sex: The facts, the acts, and your feelings.* New York: Crown.

Carstensen, L. L., Hanson, K. A., & Freund, A. M. (1995). Selection and compensation in adulthood. In R. A. Dixon & L. Backman (Eds.), *Compensating for psychological deficits and declines.* Hillsdale, NJ: Erlbaum.

Carter, D. B., & Levy, G. D. (1988). Cognitive aspects of children's early sex-role development: The influence of gender schemas on preschoolers' memories and preference for sex-typed toys and activities. *Child Development, 59,* 782–793.

Carter, D. B., & Taylor, R. D. (in press). The development of children's awareness and understanding of flexibility in sex-role stereotypes: Implications for preferences, attitude, and behavior. *Sex Roles.*

Cartwright, R. D. (1978, December). Happy endings for our dreams. *Psychology Today,* pp. 66–74.

Cascio, W. F. (1991). *Applied psychology in personnel management* (4th ed.). Englewood Cliffs, NJ: Prentice Hall.

Cascio, W. F., Oouttz, J., Zedeck, S., & Goldstin, I. L. (1991). Statistical implications of six methods of test score use in personnel selection. *Human Performance, 4,* 233–264.

Case, R. (1985). *Intellectual development: Birth to adulthood.* New York: Academic Press.

Case, R. (Ed.). (1992). *The mind's staircase: Exploring the conceptual underpinnings of children's thought and knowledge.* Hillsdale, NJ: Erlbaum.

Cass, R. C., & Hershberger, R. G. (1973). *Further toward a set of semantic scales to measure the meaning of designed environments.* Paper presented at the annual meeting of the Environmental Design Research Association, Blacksburg, VA.

Cassell, C. (1984). *Swept away: Why women fear their own sexuality.* New York: Simon & Schuster.

Cauce, A. M. (1996, June). *Culture and ethnicity: Between or within—which is it?* Informal talk at the Family Research Summer Consortium, San Diego.

Cavanagh, P., & Leclerc, Y. G. (1989). Shape from shadows. *Journal of Experimental Psychology, 15,* 3–27.

Cavett, D. (1974). *Cavett.* San Diego: Harcourt Brace Jovanovich.

Ceci, S. (1996). Review of *Child Development (8th ed.)* by John W. Santrock. Madison, WI: Brown & Benchmark.

Centers for Disease Control and Prevention. (1995, March). *Statistical report: AIDS in women.* Atlanta: Author.

Cervantes, R. C. (1987). Hispanics in psychology. In P. J. Woods & C. S. Wilkinson (Eds.), *Is psychology the major for you?* Washington, DC: American Psychological Association.

Chaffin, R., & Hermann, D. J. (1995). A classroom demonstration of depth of processing. In M. E. Ware & D. E. Johnson (Eds.), *Demonstrations and activities in teaching of psychology (Vol. 2).* Hillsdale, NJ: Erlbaum.

Chaiken, S., & Pliner, P. (1987). Women, but not men, are what they eat: The effect of meal size and gender on perceived femininity and masculinity. *Personality and Social Psychology Bulletin, 13,* 166–176.

Chaiken, S., & Stagnor, C. (1987). Attitudes and attitude change. *Annual Review of Psychology, 38,* 575–630.

Chan, W. S. (1963). *A source book in Chinese philosophy.* Princeton, NJ: Princeton University Press.

Chance, J. E., & Goldstein, A. G. (1995). The other-race effect and eyewitness identification. In S. L. Sporer, R. S. Malpass, & G. Koehnken (Eds.), *Psychological issues in eyewitness identification.* Hillsdale, NJ: Erlbaum.

Chance, P. (1979). *Learning and behavior.* Belmont, CA: Wadsworth.

Chandra, R. K., & Newberne, P. M. (1977). *Nutrition, immunity, and infection: Mechanisms of interactions.* New York: Plenum.

Chang, E. C. (1996). Cultural differences in optimism, pessimism, and coping. *Journal of Counseling Psychology, 43,* 113–123.

Changeux, J., & Chavillion, J. (1995). *Origins of the human brain.* New York: Oxford University Press.

Charles A. Dana Foundation Report. (1988, Spring). *Dana award winner's innovations in educating minority students in math and science attract nationwide attention.* New York: Charles A. Dana Foundation, pp. 1–5.

Charlesworth, W. R. (1995). An evolutionary approach to cognition and learning. In C. A. Nelson (Ed.), *Basic and applied perspectives on learning, cognition, and development.* Hillsdale, NJ: Erlbaum.

Charry, J. M.. & Hawkenshire, F. B. W. (1981). Effects of atmospheric electricity on some substrates of disordered social behavior. *Journal of Personal and Social Psychology, 41,* 185–197.

Chase, W. G., & Simon, H. A. (1973). Perception in chess. *Cognitive Psychology, 4,* 55–81.

Chase-Lansdale, P. L. (1996, June). *Effects of divorce on mental health through the life span.* Informal talk at the Family Research Summer Consortium, San Diego.

Chase-Lansdale, P. L., & Brooks-Gunn, J. (Eds.) (1996). *Escape from poverty.* New York: Cambridge University Press.

Chase-Lansdale, P. L., & Hetherington, E. M. (1992). The impact of divorce on life-span development: Short- and long-term effects. In P. B. Baltes, D. L. Featherman, & R. M. Lerner (Eds.), *Life-span development and behavior.* Hillsdale, NJ: Erlbaum.

Cheng, P. W., Holyoak, K. J., Nisbett, R. E., & Oliver, L. M. (1986). Pragmatic versus syntactic approaches to training deductive reasoning. *Cognitive Psychology, 18,* 293–328.

Chmiel, N. (1997). Psychology in the workplace. In P. Scott & C. Spencer (Eds.), *Psychology.* Cambridge, MA: Blackwell.

Chodorow, N. (1978). *The reproduction of mothering.* Berkeley: University of California Press.

Chodorow, N. (1989). *Feminism and psychoanalytic theory.* New Haven, CT: Yale University Press.

Chomsky, N. (1957). *Syntactic structure.* The Hague: Mouton.

Chomsky, N. (1975). *Reflections on language.* New York: Pantheon.

Chow, E. N., Wilkinson, D., & Baca Zinn, M. (1996). *Common bonds, different voices.* Newbury Park, CA: Sage.

Christensen, L. (1996). *Diet-behavior relationships.* Washington, DC: American Psychological Association.

Cialdini, R. B. (1993). *Influence: Science and practice* (3rd ed.). New York: HarperCollins.

Cialdini, R. B., Petty, R. E., & Cacioppo, J. T. (1981). Attitudes and attitude change. *Annual Review of Psychology, 32,* 357–404.

Cialdini, R. B., Schaller, M., Houlihan, D., Arps, K., Fultz, J., & Beaman, A. L. (1987). Empathy-based helping: Is it selflessly or selfishly motivated? *Journal of Personality and Social Psychology, 52,* 749–758.

Clark, D. A., & Beck, A. T. (1989). Cognitive theory and therapy of anxiety and depression. In P. C. Kendall & D. Watson (Eds.), *Anxiety and depression.* San Diego: Academic Press.

Clark, E. V. (1983). Meanings and concepts. In P. H. Mussen (Ed.), *Handbook of child psychology* (4th ed., Vol. 4). New York: Wiley.

Clark, K. B. (1971). The pathos of power: A psychological perspective. *American Psychologist, 26,* 1047–1057.

Clark, L. A., Watson, D., & Reynolds, S. (1995). Diagnosis and classification in psychopathology. *Annual Review of Psychology, 46.* Palo Alto, CA: Annual Reviews.

Clark, R. D., & Hatfield, E. (1989). Gender differences in receptivity to sexual offers. *Journal of Psychology and Human Sexuality, 2,* 39–55.

Clarke-Stewart, K. A. (1989). Infant day care: Maligned or malignant? *American Psychologist, 44,* 266–273.

Clarke-Stewart, K. A., Alhusen, V. D., & Clements, D. C. (1995). Nonparental caregiving. In M. H. Bornstein (Ed.), *Handbook of parenting* (Vol. 3). Hillsdale, NJ: Erlbaum.

Clausen, J. A. (1993). *American lives.* New York: Free Press.

Clifford, B. R., Bunter, B., & McAleer, I. L. (1995). *Television and children.* Hillsdale, NJ: Erlbaum.

Cloninger, C. R. (1988). Alcohol-related symptoms in heterogeneous families of hospitalized alcoholics. *Alcoholism: Clinical and Experimental Research, 12,* 670–678.

Cloninger, S. C. (1996). *Theories of personality (2nd ed.).* Upper Saddle River, NJ: Prentice Hall.

Cochran, S. D., de Leeuw, J., & Mays, V. M. (1995). Optimal scaling of HIV-related sexual risk behaviors in ethnically diverse homosexually active men. *Journal of Consulting and Clinical Psychology, 63,* 270–279.

Cochran, S. D., & Mays, V. M. (1990). Sex, lies, and HIV. *New England Journal of Medicine, 322, (11),* 774–775.

Coffman, S., Levitt, M. J., & Guacci-Franco, N. (1996). Infant-mother attachment: Relationships to maternal responsiveness and infant temperament. *Journal of Pediatric Nursing, 10,* 9–18.

Cohen, B. H. (1996). *Explaining psychological statistics.* Pacific Grove, CA: Brooks/Cole.

Cohen, J. D., & Scholer, J. W. (Eds.) (1996). *Scientific approaches to consciousness.* Hillsdale, NJ: Erlbaum.

Cohen, R. J., Swerdlik, M. E., & Phillips, S. M. (1996). *Psychological testing and assessment (3rd ed.).* Mountain View, CA: Mayfield.

Cohen, R. L., & Borsoi, D. (1996). The role of gestures in description-communication: A cross-sectional study of aging. *Journal of Nonverbal Behavior, 20,* 45–64.

Cohen, S., & Beckwith, L. (1996, March). *Mental health and attachment relationships.*

Coie, J. D. (1993, March). *The adolescence of peer relations research: Will we survive it?* Paper presented at the biennial meeting of the Society for Research in Child Development, New Orleans.

Colby, A., Kohlberg, L., Gibbs, J., & Lieberman, M. (1983). A longitudinal study of moral judgment. *Monographs of the Society for Research in Child Development.* (Serial No. 201).

Cole, M., & Cole, S. R. (1996). *The development of children* (3rd ed.). New York: W. H. Freeman.

Coleman, L. (1996, March). *What does it mean to be a Black man or a Black woman?* Paper presented at the meeting of the Society for Research on Adolescence, Boston.

Coles, R. (1986). *The political life of children.* Boston: Little, Brown.

Comas-Diaz, L. (1992). The future of psychotherapy with ethnic minorities. *Psychotherapy, 29,* 88–94.

Comstock, G., & Paik, H. (1991). *Television and the American Child.* San Diego, CA: Academic Press.

Condry, J. C. (1989). *The psychology of television.* Hillsdale, NJ: Erlbaum.

Conway, M. (1995). Failures of autobiographical memory. In D. Hermann, C. McEvoy, C. Hertzog, P. Hertel, & M. Johnson (Eds.), *Basic and applied memory research (Vol. 1).* Hillsdale, NJ: Erlbaum.

Conway, M., & Rubin, D. (1993). The structure of autobiographical memory. In A. F. Collins, S. E. Gathercole, M. A. Conway, & P. E. Morris (Eds.), *Theories of memory.* Hillsdale, NJ: Erlbaum.

Conway, M. A., Collins, A. F., Gathercole, S. E., & Anderson, S. J. (1996). Recollections of true and false autobiographical memories. *Journal of Experimental Psychology: General, 125,* 69–95.

Cooper, C., & Azmitia, M. (1996, March). *Bridging multiple worlds: Challenges and resources of immigrant youth and their families.* Paper presented at the meeting of the Society for Research on Adolescence, Boston.

Cooper, C. R., Grotevant, H. D., Moore, M. S., & Condon, S. M. (1982, August). *Family support and conflict: Both foster adolescent identity and role taking.* Paper presented at the meeting of the American Psychological Association, Washington, DC.

Cooper, C. R., & Ayers-Lopez, S. (1985). Family and peer systems in early adolescence: New models of the role of relationships in development. *Journal of Early Adolescence, 5,* 9–22.

Cooper, K. (1970). *The new aerobics.* New York: Bantam.

Cooper, R. M., & Zubek, J. P. (1958). Effects of enriched and restricted early environments on the learning ability of bright and dull rats. *Canadian Journal of Psychology, 12,* 159–164.

Cordes, C. (1983, May). Human factors and nuclear safety: Grudging respect for a growing field. *APA Monitor,* p. 1, 13–14.

Coren, S., & Girus, J. S. (1972). Illusion decrement in intersecting line figures. *Psychonomic Science, 26,* 108–110.

Coren, S., & Ward, I. M. (1989). *Sensation and perception.* San Diego: Harcourt Brace Jovanovich.

Coren, S., Ward, L. W., & Enns, J. T. (1994). *Sensation and perception.* Fort Worth, TX: Harcourt Brace.

Corless, I. B., & Pittman-Lindemann, M. (1989). *AIDS: Principles, practices, and politics.* New York: Hemisphere.

Cormier, W. H., & Cormier, L. S. (1979). *Interviewing strategies for helpers: A guide to assessment, treatment and evaluation.* Pacific Grove, CA: Brooks/Cole.

Cornelius, R. R. (1996). *The science of emotion.* Upper Saddle River, NJ: Prentice Hall.

Cornoldi, C., & De Beni, R. (1996). Mnemonics and metacognition. In D. Hermann, C. McEvoy, C. Hertzog, P. Hertel, & M. Johnson (Eds.), *Basic and applied memory research (Vol. 2).* Hillsdale, NJ: Erlbaum.

Cortes, J. B., & Gatti, F. M. (1970, April). Physique and propensity. *Psychology Today,* pp. 42–44.

Cosmides, L., & Tooby, J. (1989). Evolutionary psychology and the generation of culture (Part III). Case Study: A computational theory of social exchange. *Ethology and Sociobiology, 10,* 51–98.

Cosmides, L., & Tooby, J. (1992). Cognitive adaptations for social exchange. In J. Barkow, L. Cosmides, & J. Tooby (Eds.), *The adapted mind.* New York: Oxford University Press.

Costa, P. T. (1988, August). *Personality, continuity and the changes of adult life.* Paper presented at the American Psychological Association, Atlanta.

Costa, P. T., & McCrae, R. R. (1989). Personality continuity and the changes of adult life. In M. Storandt & G. R. VandenBos (Eds.), *The adult years: Continuity and change.* Washington, DC: American Psychological Association.

Costa, P. T., & McCrae, R. R. (1992). *Revised NEO personality inventory.* Odessa, FL: Psychological Assessment Resources.

Costa, P. T., & McCrae, R. R. (1995). Solid ground in the wetlands of personality: A reply to Block. *Psychological Bulletin, 117,* 216–220.

Costanzo, M. (1992). Training students to decode verbal and nonverbal cues: Effects on confidence and performance. *Journal of Educational Psychology, 84,* 308–313.

Costanzo, M., & Archer, D. (1995). A method for teaching about verbal and nonverbal communication. In M. E. Ware & D. E. Johnson (Eds.), *Demonstrations and activities in teaching of psychology (Vol. 3).* Hillsdale, NJ: Erlbaum.

Courneya, K. S., & Carron, A. V. (1992). The home advantage in sport competition: A literature review. *Journal of Sport and Exercise Psychology, 14,* 13–27.

Cowan, E. (1980). The wooing of primary prevention. *American Journal of Community Psychology, 8,* 258–284.

Cowan, P. A. (1988). Becoming a father. A time of change, an opportunity for development. In P. Bronstein & C. P. Cowan (Eds.), *Fatherhood today.* New York: Wiley.

Cowley, G. (1988, May 23). The wisdom of animals. *Newsweek,* pp. 52–58.

Cox, H., & Hammonds, A. (1988). Religiosity, aging, and life satisfaction. *Journal of Religion and Aging, 5,* 1–21.

Cozby, F. (1991). *Juggling.* New York: Macmillan.

Cozby, F. J. (1991). *Juggling: The unexpected advantages of balancing career and home for women and their families.* New York: Free Press.

Crabbe, J. C., Kosubud, A., Young, E. R., Tam, B. R., & McSwigan, J. D. (1985). Bidirectional selection for susceptibility to ethanol withdrawal seizures in *Mus musculus. Behavior Genetics, 15,* 521–536.

Craik, F. I. M. (1989). On the making of episodes. In H. L. Roediger & F. I. M. Craik (Eds.), *Varieties of memory and consciousness.* Hillsdale, NJ: Erlbaum.

Craik, F. I. M., & Lockhart, R. S. (1972). Levels of processing: A framework for memory research. *Journal of Verbal Learning and Verbal Behavior, 11,* 671–684.

Craik, F. I. M., & Tulving, E. (1975). Depth of processing and retention of words in episodic memory. *Journal of Experimental Psychology: General, 104,* 268–294.

Craik, K. H. (1968). The comprehension of the everyday physical environment. *Journal of the American Institute of Planners, 34,* 29–37.

Crasilneck, H. B. (1995). The use of the Crasilneck bombardment technique in problems of intractable organic pain. *American Journal of Clinical Hypnosis, 37,* 255–266.

Crawford, C. (1987). Sociobiology: Of what value to psychology? In C. Crawford, M. Smith, & D. Krebs (Eds.), *Sociobiology and psychology.* Hillsdale, NJ: Erlbaum.

Crick, M. (1977). *Explorations in language and meaning: Toward a scientific anthropology.* New York: Halsted Press.

Crooks, R., & Bauer, K. (1996). *Our sexuality (6th ed.).* Pacific Grove, CA: Brooks/Cole.

Crowfoot, J. E., & Chesler, M. A. (1996). White men's roles in multicultural coalitions. In B. P. Bowser & R. G. Hunt (Eds.), *Impacts of racism on White Americans.* Newbury Park, CA: Sage.

Csikszentmihalyi, M. (1990). *Flow: The psychology of optimal experience.* New York: Harper.

Culbertson, F. M. (1991, August). *Mental health of women: An international journey.* Paper presented at the meeting of the American Psychological Association, San Francisco.

Cunningham, M. R. (1986). Measuring the physical in physical attractiveness: Quasi-experiments on the sociobiology of female facial beauty. *Journal of Personality and Social Psychology, 50,* 925–935.

Cunningham, M. R., Roberts, A. R., Barbee, A. P., Druen, P. B., & Wu, C. (1995). "Their ideas of beauty are, on the whole, the same as ours": Consistency and variability in the cross-cultural perception of female physical attractiveness. *Journal of Personality and Social Psychology, 68,* 261–279.

Cunningham, W. P., & Saigo, B. W. (1995). *Environmental science (3rd ed.).* Dubuque, IA: Wm. C. Brown.

Curtis, H., & Barnes, N. S. (1989). *Biology* (5th ed.). New York: Worth.

Curtiss, S. (1977). *Genie.* New York: Academic Press.

Cushner, K., & Brislin, R. W. (1995). *Intercultural interactions* (2nd ed.). Newbury Park, CA: Sage.

d'Ansia, G. I. D. (1989). Familial analysis of panic disorder and agoraphobia. *Journal of Affective Disorders, 17,* 1–8.

Dabbs, J. M., Jr. (1992). Testosterone measurements in social and clinical psychology. *Journal of Social and Clinical Psychology, 11,* 302–321.

Dabbs, J. M., Jr., Frady, R. L., Carr, T. S., & Besch, N. F. (1987). Saliva, testosterone, and criminal violence in young adult prison inmates. *Psychosomatic Medicine, 49,* 174–182.

Dabbs, J. M., Jr., & Morris, R. (1990). Testosterone, social class, and antisocial behavior in a sample of 4,462 men. *Psychological Science, 1,* 209–211.

Daly, M., & Wilson, M. (1995). Evolutionary psychology: Adaptationist, selectionist, and comparative. *Psychological Inquiry, 6,* 34–38.

Dana, R. (1993). *Multicultural assessment perspectives for professional psychology.* Boston: Allyn & Bacon.

Daniel, T. C. (1990). Measuring the quality of the natural environment: A psychophysical approach. *American Psychologist, 45,* 633–637.

Darley, J. M., & Latané, B. (1968). Bystander intervention in emergencies: Diffusion of responsibility. *Journal of Personality and Social Psychology, 8,* 337–383.

Darling, C. A., Kallon, D. J., & Van Duesen, J. E. (1984). Sex in transition, 1900–1984. *Journal of Youth and Adolescence, 13,* 385–399.

Darwin, C. (1859). *On the origin of species.* London: John Murray.

Darwin, C. (1872/1965). *The expression of the emotions in man and animals.* Chicago: University of Chicago Press.

Davidson, R. J., Ekman, P., Saron, C. D., Senulis, J. A., & Friesen, W. V. (1990). Approach-withdrawal and cerebral asymmetry: Emotional expression and brain physiology. *Journal of Personality and Social Psychology, 58,* 330–341.

Davis, J. H. (1996). Group decision making and quantitative judgments: A consensus model. In E. H. Witte & J. H. Davis (Eds.), *Understanding group behavior (Vol. 1).* Hillsdale, NJ: Erlbaum.

Davis, K. (1996). *Families.* Pacific Grove, CA: Brooks/Cole.

Davis, K. E. (1985, February). Near and dear: Friendship and love compared. *Psychology Today,* pp. 22–29.

DeAngelis, T. (1996, March). Women's contributions large; recognition isn't. *APA Monitor, 27,* 12–13.

Deci, E. L. (1975). *Intrinsic motivation.* New York: Plenum.

DeCola, J. P., & Fanselow, M. S. (1995). Differential inflation with short and long CS-US intervals: Evidence of a nonassociative process in long delay taste avoidance. *Animal Learning & Behavior, 23,* 154–163.

DeCorte, W. (1993). Estimating sex-related bias in job evaluation. *Journal of Occupational and Organizational Psychology, 66,* 83–96.

DeFour, D. C., & Paludi, M. (1991, August). *Ethnicity, sex, and sexual harassment.* Paper presented at the meeting of the American Psychological Association, San Francisco.

DeFour, D. C., & Paludi, M. A. (in press). Integrating scholarship on ethnicity into the psychology of women course. *Teaching of Psychology.*

deGroot, A. D. (1965). *Thought and choice in chess.* The Hague: Mouton.

de Jong-Gierveld, J. (1987). Developing and testing a model of loneliness. *Journal of Personality and Social Psychology, 53,* 119–128.

Dement, W. C. (1978). *Some must watch while some must sleep.* New York: Norton.

DeNelsky, G. Y. (1996). The case against prescription privileges for psychologists. *American Psychologist, 51,* 207–212.

Denmark, F. L., & Paludi, M. A. (Eds.). (in press). *Handbook on the psychology of women.* Westport, CT: Greenwood.

Denmark, F. L., Russo, N. F., Frieze, I. H., & Eschzur, J. (1988). Guidelines for avoiding sexism in psychological research: A report of the ad hoc committee on nonsexist research. *American Psychologist, 43,* 582–585.

DePaulo, B. M. (1994). Spotting lies: Can humans learn to do better? *Current Directions in Psychological Science, 3,* 83–86.

Derlega, V. J. (1984). Self-disclosure and intimate relationships. In V. J. Derlega (Ed.), *Communication, intimacy, and close relationships.* New York: Academic Press.

Derlega, V. J., Metts, S., Petronio, S., & Marguilis, S. T. (1994). *Self-disclosure.* Newbury Park, CA: Sage.

Derlega, V. J., Winstead, B. A., Wong, P. T. P., & Hunter, S. (1985). Gender effects in an initial encounter: A case where men exceed women in self-disclosure. *Journal of Social and Personal Relationships, 2,* 25–44.

Derry, P. S. (1996). Buss and sexual selection: The issue of culture. *American Psychologist, 51,* 159–160.

DeSpelder, L. A., & Strickland, A. L. (1996). *The last dance (4th ed.). Mountain View, CA: Mayfield.*

Deutsch, F. M. (1991). Women's lives: The story not told by theories of development. *Contemporary Psychology, 36,* 237–238.

Deutsch, J. A., & Gonzales, M. F. (1980). Gastric nutrient content signals satiety. *Behavioral and Neural Biology, 30,* 113–116.

Deutsch, M., & Collins, M. (1951). *Interracial housing: A psychological evaluation of a social experiment.* Minneapolis: University of Minnesota Press.

de Villiers, J. (1996). Toward a rational empiricism: Why interactionism isn't behaviorism any more than biology is genetics. In M. E. Rice (Ed.), *Towards a genetics of language.* Hillsdale, NJ: Erlbaum.

DeVito, J. A. (1992). *The interpersonal communication book* (6th ed.). New York: HarperCollins.

Devlin, K. (1990). An examination of architectural interpretation: Architects versus non-architects. *Journal of Architectural and Planning Research, 7,* 235–244.

de Waal, F. B. M. (1992). *Peacemaking among primates.* Cambridge, MA: Harvard University Press.

Dewey, J. (1933). *How we think: A restatement of the relation of reflective thinking to the educative process.* Lexington, MA: D. C. Heath.

Dewsbury, D. A. (1984). *Comparative psychology in the twentieth century.* Stroudsburg, PA: Hutchinson Ross.

Dewsbury, D. A. (1992). Comparative psychology and ethology: A reassessment. *American Psychologist, 47,* 208–215.

Dewsbury, D. A. (1994). A classic in comparative psychology. *Contemporary Psychology, 39,* 797–799.

Diamond, E. E. (1988). Women's occupational plans and decisions: An introduction. *Applied Psychology: An International Review, 37,* 97–102.

Dickerscheid, J. D., Schwarz, P. M., Noir, S., & El-Taliawy, T. (1988). Gender concept development of preschool-aged children in the United States and Egypt. *Sex Roles, 18,* 669–677.

Dickinson, T. L. (1993). Attitudes about performance appraisal. In H. Schuler, J. L. Farr, & M. Smith (Eds.), *Personnel selection and assessment.* Hillsdale, NJ: Erlbaum.

Diener, E. (1984). Subjective well-being. *Psychological Bulletin, 95,* 542–575.

Diener, E. (1984). Subjective well-being. *Psychological Bulletin, 109,* 125–129.

Dietz, W. (1986, March). *Comments at the workshop on childhood obesity.* Washington, DC: National Institutes of Health.

DiNicola, D. D., & DiMatteo, M. R. (1984). Practitioners, patients, and compliance with medical regimens: A social psychological perspective. In A. Baum, S. E. Taylor, & J. E. Singer (Eds.), *Handbook of psychology and health* (Vol. 4). Hillsdale, NJ: Erlbaum.

DiPardo, A. (1996). Review of Writers in the Zone of Proximal Development by Petrick-Steward. *Contemporary Psychology, 41,* 51–52.

Dipboye, R. L. (1993). Bridging the gap between leadership theory and practice. *Contemporary Psychology, 38,* 597–599.

Dittman-Kohli, F. (1992). *The personal system of sense of life: A comparison between early and late adulthood.* Unpublished manuscript, Free University, Berlin, Germany.

Dixon, R. A., & Backman, L. (1995). Concept of compensation. In R. A. Dixon & L. Backman (Eds.), *Compensating for psychological deficits and declines.* Hillsdale, NJ: Erlbaum.

Dodd, D. K. (1995). Robbers in the classroom: A deindividuation exercise. In M. E. Ware & D. E. Johnson (Eds.), *Demonstrations and activities in teaching of psychology (Vol. 3).* Hillsdale, NJ: Erlbaum.

Dohrenwend, B. S., & Shrout, P. E. (1985). "Hassles" in the conceptualization and measurement of life stress variables. *American Psychologist, 40,* 780–785.

Dolezal, S. L., Davison, G. C., & DeQuattro, V. (1996, March). *Hostile behavior, Type A, cardiac damage and neuroendocrine response in hostility-provoking social interactions.* Paper presented at the meeting of the American Psychosomatic Society, Williamsburg, VA.

Dollard, J., Doob, L. W., Miller, N. E., Mowrer, O. H., & Sears, R. R. (1939). *Frustration and aggression.* New Haven, CT: Yale University Press.

Dolnick, E. (1988, December). The right (left) stuff. *Omni,* p. 45.

Domjan, M. P. (1996). *Essentials of conditioning and learning.* Pacific Grove, CA: Brooks/Cole.

Donnerstein, E. (1980). Aggressive erotica and violence against women. *Journal of Personality and Social Psychology, 39,* 269–277.

Donnerstein, E. (1987, May). *Pornography, sex, and violence.* Invited presentation, University of Texas at Dallas.

Dorn, L. D., & Chrousos, G. P. (1996, March). *Behavioral predictors of stress hormones.* Paper presented at the meeting of the Society for Research on Adolescence, Boston.

Doty, R. L., & Muller, Schwarze, D. (1992). *Chemical signals in vertebrates* (Vol. 6). New York: Plenum.

Dougherty, D. M., Cherek, D. R., & Bennett, R. H. (1996). The effects of alcohol on the aggressive responding of women. *Journal of Studies on Alcohol, 57,* 178–186.

Dovidio, J. F., & Gaertner, S. L. (Eds.). (1986). *Prejudice, discrimination, and racism.* New York: Academic Press.

Dow-Edwards, D. L. (1995). Developmental toxicity of cocaine: Mechanisms of action. In M. Lewis & M. Bendersky (Eds.), *Mothers, babies, and cocaine.* Hillsdale, NJ: Erlbaum.

Doweiko, H. E. (1996). *Concepts of chemical dependency (2nd ed.).* Pacific Grove, CA: Brooks/Cole.

Doyle, J. A., & Paludi, M. A. (1991). *Sex and gender: The human experience* (2nd ed.). Dubuque, IA: Wm. C. Brown.

Draguns, J. G. (1990). Applications of cross-cultural psychology in the field of mental health. In R. W. Brislin (Ed.), *Applied cross-cultural psychology.* Newbury Park, CA: Sage.

Dresher, E., & van der Hulst, H. (1994). Global determinacy and learnability in phonology. In J. Archibald (Ed.), *Phonological acquisition and phonological theory.* Hillsdale, NJ: Erlbaum.

Drickamer, L. C., & Vessey, S. H. (1996). *Animal behavior* (3rd ed). Dubuque, IA: Wm. C. Brown.

Drickamer, L. C., Vessey, S. H., & Miekle, D. (1996). *Animal behavior (4th ed.).* Dubuque, IA: Wm. C. Brown.

Druckman, D., & Bjork, R. A. (Eds.). (1994). *Learning, remembering, and believing.* Washington, DC: National Academy Press.

Drummond, R. J., & Ryan, C. W. (1995). *Career counseling.* Upper Saddle River, NJ: Prentice Hall.

Dryfoos, J. G. (1990). *Adolescents at risk: Prevalence and prevention.* New York: Oxford University Press.

Dryfoos, J. G. (1992, March). *Integrating services for adolescents: The community schools.* Paper presented at the meeting of the Society for Research on Adolescence, Washington, DC.

Dunn, J., & Kendrick, C. (1982). *Siblings.* Cambridge, MA: Harvard University Press.

Dunnett, S. B. (1989). Neural transplantation: Normal brain function and repair after damage. *Psychologist, 1,* 4–8.

Durup, M. J., & Leiter, M. P. (1995, August). *Role of environmental resources in managing family and work.* Paper presented at the meeting of the American Psychological Association, New York City.

Dutton, D., & Aron, A. (1974). Some evidence for heightened sexual attraction under conditions of high anxiety. *Journal of Personality and Social Psychology, 30,* 510–517.

Eagly, A. H. (1995). The science and politics of comparing men and women. *American Psychologist, 50,* 145–158.

Eagly, A. H. (1996). Differences between women and men. *American Psychologist, 51,* 158–159.

Eagly, A. H., & Crowley, M. (1986). Gender and helping behavior: A meta-analytic review of the social psychological literature. *Psychological Bulletin, 100,* 283–308.

East, P., & Felice, M. E. (1996). *Adolescent pregnancy and parenting.* Hillsdale, NJ: Erlbaum.

Ebata, A. T., & Moos, R. H. (1989, April). *Coping and adjustment in four groups of adolescents.* Paper presented at the biennial meeting of the Society for Research in Child Development, Kansas City.

Ebbinghaus, H. (1885/1964). *Memory: A contribution to experimental psychology* (H. A. Ruger & E. R. Bussemius, Trans.). New York: Dover. (Original work published 1885).

Eckert, E. D., Heston, L. L., & Bouchard, T. J. (1981). MZ twins reared apart. Preliminary findings of psychiatric disturbances and trait. In L. Gedda, P. Paris, & W. D. Nance (Eds.), *Twin research* (Vol. 1). New York: Alan Liss.

Edelman, M. W. (1995). *The state of America's children.* Washington, DC: Children's Defense Fund.

Edney, J. J. (1976). The psychological role of property rights in human behavior. *Environment and Planning, A, 8,* 811–822.

Educational Testing Service. (1992, February). *Cross-national comparisons of 9–13-year-olds' science and math achievement.* Princeton, NJ: Educational Testing Service.

Educational Testing Service. (1992). [Cross-national comparison of children's learning and achievement.] Unpublished data, Educational Testing Service, Princeton, NJ.

Edwards, B. (1979). *Drawing on the right side of the brain.* Los Angeles: Tarcher.

Efron, R. (in press). *The decline and fall of hemispheric specialization.* Hillsdale, NJ: Erlbaum.

Ehrhardt, A. A. (1987). A transactional perspective on the development of gender differences. In J. M. Reinisch, L. A. Rosenblum, & S. A. Sanders (Eds.), *Masculinity/femininity: Basic perspectives.* New York: Oxford University Press.

Eibl-Eibesfeldt, I. (1977). Evolution of destructive aggression. *Aggressive Behavior, 3,* 127–144.

Eich, E. (1990, June). *Searching for mood dependent memory.* Paper presented at the meeting of the American Psychological Society, Dallas.

Eich, E. (1995). Searching for mood dependent memory. *Psychological Science, 6,* 67–75.

Eichorn, D. H., Clausen, J. A., Haan, N., Honzik, M. P., & Mussen, P. H. (Eds.). (1981). *Present and past in middle life.* New York: Academic Press.

Eisenberg, N. (1989). The development of prosocial values. In N. Eisenberg & J. Reykowski (Eds.), *Social and moral values.* Hillsdale, NJ: Erlbaum.

Ekman, P. (1980). *The face of man.* New York: Garland STPM.

Ekman, P. (1994). Strong evidence for universals in facial expressions: A reply to Russel's mistaken critique. *Psychological Bulletin, 115,* 268–287.

Ekman, P. (1996). Lying and deception. In N. L. Stein, C. Brainerd, P. A. Ornstein, & B. Tversky (Eds.), *Memory for everyday and emotional events.* Hillsdale, NJ: Erlbaum.

Ekman, P., & Friesen, W. V. (1968). The repertoire of nonverbal behavior—Categories, origins, usage and coding. *Semiotica, 1,* 49–98.

Ekman, P., & Friesen, W. V. (1971). Constants across cultures in the face and emotion. *Journal of Personality and Social Psychology, 17,* 124–129.

Ekman, P., & Friesen, W. (1974). Detecting deception from the body or face. *Journal of Personality and Social Psychology, 29,* 288–298.

Ekman, P., Levenson, R. W., & Friesen, W. V. (1983). Autonomic nervous system activity distinguishes among emotions. *Science, 221,* 1208–1210.

Ekman, P., & O'Sullivan, M. (1991). Who can catch a liar? *American Psychologist, 46,* 913–920.

Eldridge, N. S. (1995, August). *Competence in working with lesbian and gay couples and families.* Paper presented at the meeting of the American Psychological Association, New York City.

Elkind, D. (1978). Understanding the young adolescent. *Adolescence, 13,* 127–134.

Elkind, D. (1981). *The hurried child.* Reading, MA: Addison-Wesley.

Elliott, A. J., & Devine, P. G. (1994). On the motivational nature of cognitive dissonance: Dissonance as psychological discomfort. *Journal of Personality Psychology, 67,* 382–394.

Ellis, A. (1962). *Reason and emotion in psychotherapy.* New York: Lyle Stuart.

Ellis, A. (1993). Reflections on rational-emotive therapy. *Journal of Consulting and Clinical Psychology, 61,* 199–201.

Ellis, A. (1996). A rational emotive behavior therapist's perspective on Ruth. In G. Corey (Ed.), *Case approach to counseling and psychotherapy.* Pacific Grove, CA: Brooks/Cole.

Ellis, H. C. (1987). Recent developments in human memory. In V. P. Makosky (Ed.), *The G. Stanley Hall Lecture Series.* Washington, DC: American Psychological Association.

Ellis, H. C., Thomas, R. L., & Rodriguez, I. A. (1984). Emotional mood states and memory: Elaborative encoding, semantic processing, and cognitive effort. *Journal of Experimental Psychology: Learning, Memory, and Cognition, 10,* 470–482.

Ellis, L., & Ames, M. A. (1987). Neurohormonal functioning and sexual orientation: A theory of homosexuality-heterosexuality. *Psychological Bulletin, 101,* 233–258.

Ellison, C. W., & Smith, J. (1991). Toward an integrative measure of health and well-being. *Journal of Psychology and Theology, 19* (1), 35–48.

Elner, R. W., & Hughes, R. N. (1978). Energy maximization in the diet of the shore crab. *Journal of Animal Ecology, 47,* 103–116.

Emlen, S. T. (1984). Cooperative breeding in birds and mammals. In J. R. Krebs & N. B. Davies (Eds.), *Behavioral ecology: An evolutionary approach* (2nd ed.). Oxford: Blackwell Scientific.

Emmons, R. A. (1989). The personal striving approach to personality. In L. A. Pervin (Ed.), *Goal concepts in personality and social psychology* (pp. 87–126). Hillsdale, NJ: Erlbaum.

Emmons, R. A., & Kaiser, H. A. (1995). Goal orientation and emotional well-being: Linking goals and affect through the self. In L. L. Martin & A. Tesser (Eds.), *Striving and feeling.* Hillsdale, NJ: Erlbaum.

Enger, E. D. (1995). *Environmental science (5th ed.).* Dubuque, IA: Wm. C. Brown.

Enger, E. D., Kormelink, R., Ross, F. C., & Otto, R. (1996). *Diversity of life.* Dubuque, IA: Wm. C. Brown.

Engler, B. (1995). *Personality theories (4th ed.).* Boston: Houghton Mifflin.

Eppley, K. R., Abrams, A. I., & Shear, J. (1989). Differential effects of relaxation effects on trait anxiety: A meta-analysis. *Journal of Clinical Psychology, 45,* 957–974.

Epstein, C. F. (1987). Multiple demands and multiple roles. The conditions of successful management. In F. J. Crosby (Ed.), *Spouse, parent, worker: On gender and multiple roles.* New Haven, CT: Yale University Press.

Ericsson, K. A., & Kintsch, W. (1995). Long-term working memory. *Psychological Review, 102,* 211–245.

Erikson, E. H. (1950). *Childhood and society.* New York: W. W. Norton.

Erikson, E. H. (1968). *Identity: Youth and crisis.* New York: W. W. Norton.

Eron, L. D., & Slaby, R. G. (1994). Introduction. In L. D. Eron, J. H. Gentry, & P. Schlegl (Eds.), *Reason to hope: A psychological perspective on youth and violence.* Washington, DC: American Psychological Association.

Erwin, E. J. (Ed.) (1996). *Putting children first.* Baltimore, MD: Paul Brookes.

Espinet, A., Iraola, J. A., Bennett, C. H., & Mackintosh, N. J. (1995). Inhibitory associations between neutral stimuli in flavor-aversion conditioning. *Animal Learning & Behavior, 23,* 361–368.

Evans, B. J., & Whitfield, J. R. (Eds.). (1988). *Black males in the United States: An annotated bibliography from 1967 to 1987.* Washington, DC: American Psychological Association.

Evans, G. W., & Jacobs, S. V. (1982). Air pollution and human behavior. In G. W. Evans (Ed.), *Environmental stress.* New York: Cambridge University Press.

Evans, G. W., Jacobs, S. V., & Frager, N. B. (1982). Adaptation to air pollution. *Journal of Environmental Psychology, 2,* 99–108.

Evans, J. D. (1996). *Straightforward statistics for the behavioral sciences.* Pacific Grove, CA: Brooks/Cole.

Evans, M. E. (1992, March). *Achievement and achievement-related beliefs in Asian and Western contexts: Cultural and gender differences.* Paper presented at the meeting of the Society for Research on Adolescence, Washington, DC.

Evans, P. (1989). *Motivation and emotion.* New York: Routledge.

Everett, F., Proctor, N., & Cartmela, B. (1989). Providing psychological services to American Indian children and families. In D. R. Atkinson, G. Morten, & D. W. Sue (Eds.), *Counseling American minorities.* Dubuque, IA: Wm. C. Brown.

Ewing, C. (1978). *Crisis intervention as psychotherapy.* New York: Oxford University Press.

Eysenck, H. J. (1952). The effects of psychotherapy: An evaluation. *Journal of Consulting Psychology, 16,* 319–324.

Eysenck, H. J. (1967). *The biological basis of personality.* Springfield, IL: Charles C Thomas.

Eysenck, H. J. (1973). *Eysenck on extraversion.* New York: Wiley.

Faber, S. D., & Burns, J. W. (1996). Anger management style, degree of expressed anger, and gender influence cardiovascular recovery from interpersonal harassment. *Journal of Behavioral Medicine, 19,* 55–72.

Fairburn, C. G. (1995). *Overcoming binge eating.* New York: Guilford.

Fancher, R. (1990). *Pioneers of psychology* (2nd ed.). New York: W. W. Norton.

Fanselow, M. S., DeCola, J. P., & Young, S. L. (1993). Mechanisms responsible for reduced contextual conditioning with massed unsignaled unconditioned stimuli. *Journal of Experimental Psychology: Animal Processes, 19,* 121–137.

Fasick, F. A. (1988). Patterns of formal education in high school as rites of passage. *Adolescence, 23,* 457–468.

Fassinger, R., & Gilbert, M. (1995, August). *Training issues: Preparing psychologists to provide competent services.* Paper presented at the meeting of the American Psychological Association, New York City.

Fazio, R. H., & Williams, C. J. (1986). Attributed accessibility as a moderator of the attitude-perception and attitude-behavior relations: An investigation of the 1984 presidential election. *Journal of Personality and Social Psychology, 51,* 505–514.

Fein, S., Goethals, G. R., Kassin, S. M., & Cross, J. (1993, August). *Social influence and presidential debates.* Paper presented at the meeting of the American Psychological Association, Toronto.

Feinman, S. (1981). Why is cross-sex-role behavior more approved for girls than for boys? A status characteristic approach. *Sex Roles, 7,* 289–299.

Feldman, D. H. (1989). Creativity: Proof that development occurs. In W. Damon (Ed.), *Child development today and tomorrow.* San Francisco: Jossey-Bass.

Feldman, D. H., & Piirto, J. (1995). Parenting talented children. In M. H. Borstein (Ed.), *Handbook of parenting.* Hillsdale, NJ: Erlbaum.

Feldman, M. A. (1996). The effectiveness of early intervention for children of parents with mental retardation. In M. J. Guralnick (Ed.), *The effectiveness of early intervention.* Baltimore, MD: Paul Brookes.

Feldman, S. S., & Elliott, G. R. (1990). Progress and promise of research on normal adolescent development. In S. S. Feldman & G. Elliott (Eds.), *At the threshold: The development adolescent.* Cambridge, MA: Harvard University Press.

Felton, K. A., Allard, C. B., Hovdestad, W., & Kristiansen, C. M. (1995, August). *Ottawa study of women sexually abused as children.* Paper presented at the meeting of the American Psychological Association, New York City.

Ferguson, D. M., Harwood, L. J., & Shannon, F. T. (1987). Breast-feeding and subsequent social adjustment in six- to eight-year-old children. *Journal of Child Psychology and Psychiatry, 28,* 378–386.

Ferrell, O. C., & Hirt, G. (1996). *Business: A changing world (2nd ed.).* Burr Ridge, IL: Irwin.

Ferrett, S. K. (1996). *Strategies: Getting and keeping the job you want.* Burr Ridge, IL: Irwin.

Feshbach, S., & Weiner, B. (1996). *Personality* (4th ed.). Lexington, MA: Heath.

Festinger, L. (1954). A theory of social comparison processes. *Human Relations, 7,* 117–140.

Festinger, L. (1957). *A theory of cognitive dissonance.* Evanston, IL: Row Peterson.

Festinger, L., & Carlsmith, J. (1959). Cognitive consequences of forced compliance. *Journal of Abnormal and Social Psychology, 58,* 203–210.

Field, T., Scafidi, F., & Schanberg, S. (1987). Massage of preterm newborns to improve growth and development. *Pediatric Nursing, 13,* 386–388.

Field, T M. (1992, September). Stroking babies helps growth, reduces stress. *Brown University Child and Adolescent Behavior Letter,* pp. 1, 6.

Field, T. M. (Ed.). (1995). *Touch in early development.* Hillsdale, NJ: Erlbaum.

Fielder, F. E. (1978). Contingency model and the leadership process. In L. Berkowitz (Ed.), *Advances in experimental social psychology* (Vol. 11). New York: Academic Press.

Fiez, J. A., Raife, E. A., Balota, D. A., Schwarz, J. P., Raichle, M. E., & Petersen, S. E. (1996). A positron emission tomography study of the short-term maintenance of verbal information. *The Journal of Neuroscience, 16,* 808–822.

Finchum, F. D., & Bradbury, T. N. (1992). Attributions and behavior in marital interaction. *Journal of Personality and Social Psychology, 63,* 613–628.

Fine, T. H., & Turner, J. W. (1985). REST-assisted relaxation and chronic pain. In J. J. Sanchez-Sosa (Ed.), *Health and clinical psychology.* American: Elsevier.

Fine, T. H., & Turner, J. W. (1987). *Proceedings of the Second International Conference on REST.* Toledo, OH: IRIS.

Fingerhut, L. A., & Kleinman, J. C. (1990). International and interstate comparisons of homicide among young males. *Journal of the American Medical Association, 263,* 3292–3295.

First, M. B., Frances, A., & Pincus, H. A. (1995). *DSM-IV handbook for differential diagnosis.* Washington, DC: American Psychiatric Press.

Fischer, J., & Gochros, H. L. (1975). *Planned behavior change.* New York: Free Press.

Fish, S. (1993). Reverse racism, or how the pot got to call the kettle black. *Atlantic Monthly, 272,* 128–136.

Fish, T. A., & Rye, B. J. (1991). Attitudes toward a homosexual or heterosexual person with AIDS. *Journal of Applied Psychology, 21,* 651–667.

Fishbein, M., & Ajzen, I. (1974). Attitudes toward objects as predictors of single and multiple behavioral criteria. *Psychological Review, 81,* 59–74.

Fishbein, M., & Ajzen, I. (1975). *Belief, attitude, intention, behavior: An introduction to theory and research.* Reading, MA: Addison-Wesley.

Fiske, S. T., Bersoff, D. N., Borgida, E., Deaux, K., & Heilman, M. E. (1991). Social science research on trial: Use of sex stereotyping research in *Price Waterhouse v. Hopkins. American Psychologist, 23,* 399–427.

Fitzgerald, L. F., & Osipow, S. H. (1986). An occupational analysis of counseling psychology: How special is the specialty? *American Psychologist, 41,* 535–544.

Fivush, R. (1995, March). *The development of narrative remembering: Implications for the recovered memory debate.* Paper presented at the meeting of the Society for Research in Child Development, Indianapolis.

Flavell, J. H. (1992). Cognitive development: Past, present, and future. *Developmental Psychology, 28,* 998–1005.

Fletcher, G., & Fitness, J. (Eds.) (1995). *Knowledge structures in close relationships.* Hillsdale, NJ: Erlbaum.

Foa, E. B., Steketze, G., & Young, M. C. (1984). Agoraphobia. *Clinical Psychology Review, 4,* 431–457.

Foley, V. (1975). Family therapy with black disadvantaged families: Some observations on roles, communications, and techniques. *Journal of Marriage and Family Counseling, 1,* 29–38.

Folkman, S., & Lazarus, R. S. (1980). An analysis of coping in a middle-aged community sample. *Journal of Health and Social Behavior, 21,* 219–239.

Folkman, S., Lazarus, R. S., Dunkel-Schetter, C., DeLongis, A., & Gruen, R. (1986). The dynamics of a stressful encounter: Cognitive appraisal, coping, and encounter outcomes. *Journal of Personality and Social Psychology, 50,* 992–1003.

Follette, W. C. (1996). Behavior therapy in the era of diagnostic categories. *Contemporary Psychology, 41,* 246–247.

Foner N. (1984). *Ages in conflict.* New York: Columbia University Press.

Fong, G. T., Krantz, D. H., & Nisbett, R. E. (1986). The effects of statistical training on thinking about everyday problems. *Cognitive Psychology, 18,* 253–292.

Forbes, R. J., & Jackson, P. R. (1980). Non-verbal behavior and the outcome of selection interviews. *Journal of Occupational Psychology, 53,* 65–72.

Ford, C., & Beach, F. (1951). *Patterns of sexual behavior.* New York: Harper.

Forgays, D. (1983). Primary prevention of psychopathology. In M. Hersen, A. Kazdin, & A. Bellack (Eds.), *The clinical psychology handbook.* New York: Pergamon.

Forsyth, B. W. C., Leventhal, J. M., & McCarthy, P. L. (1985). Mothers' perceptions of feeding and crying behaviors. *American Journal of Diseases of Children, 139,* 269–272.

Fowler, C. A., Wolford, G., Slade, R., & Tassinary, L. (1981). Lexical access with and without awareness. *Journal of Experimental Psychology: General, 110,* 341–362.

Fowler, J. W. (1981). *States of faith: The psychology of human development and the quest for faith.* New York: HarperCollins.

Fowler, J. W. (1986). Faith and the structuring of meaning. In C. Dykstra & S. Parks (Eds.), *Faith development and Fowler.* Birmingham, AL: Religious Education Press.

Fowler, J. W. (1991). The vocation of faith developmental theory. In J. W. Fowler, K. E. Nipkow, & F. Schweitzer (Eds.), *Stages of faith and religious development.* New York: Crossroad.

Fox, J. L. (1984). The brain's dynamic way of keeping in touch. *Science, 225,* 820–821.

Fox, N. (Ed.). (in press). The development of emotion regulation: Biological and behavioral considerations. *Monographs of the Society for Research in Development.*

Fox, S. I. (1996). *Human physiology (5th ed.).* Dubuque, IA: Wm. C. Brown.

France, K. (1982). *Crisis intervention: A handbook of immediate person-to-person help.* Springfield, IL: C. C. Thomas.

Frances, A., First, M. B., & Pincus, H. A. (1995). *DSM-IV guidebook.* Washington, DC: American Psychiatric Press.

Frances, A., & Ross, R. (1996). *DSM-IV case studies.* Washington, DC: American Psychiatric Association.

Frances, A. J., Pincus, H. A., & Widiger, T. A. (in press). DSM-IV and international communication in psychiatric diagnosis. In Y. Honda, M. Kastrup, & J. E. Mezzich (Eds.), *Psychiatric diagnosis: A world perspective.* New York: Springer.

Franck, K. A. (1980). Friends and strangers: The social experience of living in urban and non-urban settings. *Journal of Social Issues, 36,* 52–71.

Frank, E. & Kupfer, D. J. (1986). Psychotherapeutic approaches to treatment of recurrent unipolar depression. Work in progress. *Psychopharmacology Bulletin, 22,* 558–565.

Frank, J. D. (1982). Therapeutic components shared by all psychotherapies. In J. H. Harvey & M. M. Parks (Eds.), *Psychotherapy research and behavior change.* Washington, DC: American Psychological Association.

Franken, L. E. (1994). *Human motivation* (3rd ed.). Pacific Grove, CA: Brooks/Cole.

Franz, C. E., & McClelland, D. C. (1994). Lives of women and men active in the social protests of the 1960s: A longitudinal study. *Journal of Personality and Social Psychology, 66,* 196–205.

Fraser, S. (Ed.) (1995). *The bell curve wars: Race, intelligence, and the future of America.* New York: Basic Books.

Freedman, J. L. (1979). Current status of work on crowding and suggestions for housing design. In J. R. Aiello & A. Baum (Eds.), *Residential crowding and design.* New York: Plenum Press.

Freedman, J. L. (1984). Effects of television violence on aggressiveness. *Psychological Bulletin, 96,* 227–246.

Freeman, D. (1983). *Margaret Mead and Samoa.* Cambridge, MA: Harvard University Press.

Freeman, J. (Ed.) (1995). *Women: A feminist perspective (5th ed.).* Mountain View, CA: Mayfield.

Freud, S. (1900/1953). The interpretation of dreams. In J. Strachey (Ed.), *The standard edition of the complete psychological works of Sigmund Freud.* London: Hogarth Press.

Freud, S. (1908). Creative writers and day-dreaming. In *Collected works* (Vol. 9). London: Hogarth Press.

Freud, S. (1917). *A general introduction to psychoanalysis.* New York: Washington Square Press.

Freyd, J. J. (1993, August). *Human perceptual adaptations for entraining, tracking, and predicting animals' motion.* Paper presented at the meeting of the Human Behavior and Evolution Society, Binghamton, NY.

Friedman, H. S., Tucker, J. S., Schwartz, J. E., Tomlinson-Keasey, C., Martin, L. R., Wingard, D. L., & Criqui, M. H. (1995). Psychosocial and behavioral predictors of longevity: The aging and death of the "Termites." *American Psychologist, 50,* 69–78.

Friedman, M., & Rosenman, R. (1974). *Type A behavior and your heart.* New York: Knopf.

Friedman, M. A., & Brownell, K. D. (1995). Psychological correlates of obesity: Moving to the next generation of research. *Psychological Bulletin, 117,* 3–20.

Frischoltz, E. Z. (1995, August). *Discriminating hypnotic and nonhypnotic influences on human memory.* Paper presented at the meeting of the American Psychological Association, New York City.

Fromm, E. (1947). *Man for himself.* New York: Holt Rinehart.

Fuhrman, A., & Burlingame, G. M. (1995). *Handbook of group psychotherapy.* New York: Wiley.

Furnham, A. (1988). Write and wrong: The validity of graphological analysis. *Skeptical Inquirer, 13,* 64–69.

Furth, H. G. (1971). Linguistic deficiency and thinking: Research with deaf subjects. 1964–1969. *Psychological Bulletin, 75,* 52–58.

Furth, H. G., & Wachs, H. (1975). *Thinking goes to school.* New York: Oxford University Press.

Furumoto, L. (1989). The new history of psychology. In I. S. Cohen (Ed.), *The G. Stanley Hall Lecture Series* (Vol. 9). Washington, DC: American Psychological Association.

Furumoto, L., & Scarborough, E. (1986). Placing women in the history of psychology. *American Psychologist, 41,* 35–42.

Gadpaille, W. J. (1996). *Adolescent suicide.* Washington, DC: American Psychiatric Association.

Gage, F. H., & Bjorklund, A. (1986). Cholinergic septal grafts into the hippocampal formation improve spatial learning and memory in aged rats by an atropine-sensitive mechanism. *Journal of Neuroscience, 6,* 2837–2847.

Gagnon, J. H., & Simon, W. (1973). *Sexual conduct.* Chicago: Aldine.

Gaines, S. O., & Reed, E. S. (1995). Prejudice: From Allport to Dubois. *American Psychologist, 50,* 96–103.

Gaines, S. O., Jr. (1994). Reciprocity of respect-denying behavior in male-female friendships. *Journal of Social and Personal Relationships, 11,* 5–24.

Galen, M., & Palmer, A. T. (January 31, 1994). White, male, and worried. *Business Week,* 50–55.

Gallup, G. (1984, August–September). *Gallup Report,* Nos. 228 and 229, 2–9.

Gallup, G. (1985). *The Gallup poll.* New York: Random House.

Gallup, G. (1988). *The Gallup poll.* New York: Random House.

Gallup, G. H., Jr., & Bezilla, R. (1992). *The religious life of young Americans.* Princeton, NJ: Gallup Institute.

Gallup, G. H., Jr., & Jones, S. (1989). *100 questions and answers: Religion in America.* Princeton, NJ: Princeton Religion Research Center.

Gallup Report. (1987). Legalized gay relations. *Gallup Report,* No. 254, p. 25.

Galotti, K. M. (1989). Approaches to studying formal and everyday reasoning. *Psychological Bulletin, 105,* 331–351.

Gangestad, S. W. (1995). The new evolutionary psychology: Prospects and challenges. *Psychological Inquiry, 6,* 38–41.

Garcia, J. (1989). Food for Tolman: Cognition and cathexis in concert. In T. Archer & L. Nilsson (Eds.), *Aversion, avoidance, and anxiety.* Hillsdale, NJ: Erlbaum.

Garcia, J., Ervin, F. E., & Koelling, R. A. (1966). Learning with prolonged delay of reinforcement. *Psychonomic Science, 5,* 121–122.

Garden, R. A. (1987). The second IEA mathematics study. *Comparative Education Review, 31,* 47–68.

Gardner, B. T., & Gardner, R. A. (1971). Two-way communication with an infant chimpanzee. In A. Schrier & F. Stollnitz (Eds.), *Behavior of nonhuman primates* (Vol. 4). New York: Academic Press.

Gardner, H. (1983). *Frames of mind.* New York: Basic Books.

Gardner, H. (1985). *The mind's new science.* New York: Basic Books.

Gardner, H. (1989). Beyond a modular view of mind. In W. Damon (Ed.), *Child development today and tomorrow.* San Francisco: Jossey-Bass.

Gardner, J. M. (1995). The myth of the mental illness game. Sick is just a four letter word. In M. E. Ware & D. E. Johnson (Eds.), *Demonstrations and activities in psychology (Vol. 3).* Hillsdale, NJ: Erlbaum.

Gardner, R. A., & Gardner, B. T. (1978). Comparative psychology and language acquisition. *Annals of the New York Academy of Sciences, 309,* 37–76.

Garraghty, P. E. (1996, June). *Neuroplasticity: From mechanisms to behavior.* Paper presented at the meeting of the American Psychological Association, San Francisco.

Gash, D. M., Collier, T. J., & Sladek, J. R. (1985). Neural transplantation: A review of recent developments and potential applications to the aged brain. *Neurobiology of Aging, 6,* 131–150.

Gathercole, S., & Baddeley, A. D. (1989). Development of vocabulary in children and short-term phonological memory. *Journal of Memory and Language, 28,* 200–213.

Gazzaniga, M. S. (1983). Right hemisphere language following brain bisection: A 20-year perspective. *American Psychologist, 38,* 525–537.

Geary, D. C., & Brown, S. C. (1991). Cognitive addition: Strategy choice and speed-of-processing differences in gifted, normal, and mathematically disabled children. *Developmental Psychology, 27,* 398–406.

Gelman, R., & Au, T. K. (Eds.) (1996). *Perceptual and cognitive development (2nd ed.).* San Diego, CA: Academic Press.

Gerson, K. (1986). *Hard choices: How women decide about work, career, and motherhood.* Berkeley: University of California Press.

Getzels, J. W., & Csikszentmihalyi, M. (1975). From problem solving to problem finding. In I. A. Taylor & J. W. Getzels (Eds.), *Perspectives in creativity.* Chicago: Aldine.

Gibbons, F. X., & McCoy, S. B. (1991). Self-esteem, similarity, and reactions to active versus passive downward comparison. *Journal of Personality and Social Psychology, 60,* 414–424.

Gibbons, F. X., Benbow, C. P., & Gerrard, M. (1994). From top dog to bottom half: Social comparison strategies in response to poor performance. *Journal of Personality and Social Psychology, 67,* 638–652.

Gibbs, J. T. (1989). Black American adolescents. In J. T. Gibbs & L. N. Huang (Eds.), *Children of color.* San Francisco: Jossey-Bass.

Gibbs, N. (1990, fall). The dreams of youth. *Time* [Special Issue], pp. 10–14.

Gibson, E. J. (1989). Exploratory behavior in the development of perceiving, acting, and the acquiring of knowledge. *Annual Review of Psychology, 39.* Palo Alto, CA: Annual Reviews.

Gibson, E. J., & Walk, R. D. (1960). The visual cliff. *Scientific American, 202,* 64–71.

Gibson, J. J. (1966). *The senses considered as perceptual systems.* Boston: Houghton Mifflin.

Gifford, R. (1987). *Environmental psychology: Principles and practice.* Boston: Allyn & Bacon.

Gifford, R. (1994). Scientific evidence for claims about full-spectrum lamps: Past and future. In J. A. Veitch (Ed.), *Full-spectrum lighting effects on performance, mood, and health.* NRCC Internal Report 659. Ottawa: National Research Council Canada.

Gifford, R. (1995). Natural psychology. *Journal of Environmental Psychology, 15,* 167–168.

Gifford, R., Hine, D. W., & Veitch, J. A. (in press). Meta-analysis for environment-behavior research, illuminated with a study of lighting level effects on office task performance. In G. T. Moore & R. W. Marans (Eds.), *Advances in environment, behavior, and design* (Vol. 4). New York: Plenum Press.

Gifford, R., & Peacock, J. (1979). Crowding: More fearsome than crime-provoking? Comparison of an Asian city and a North American city. *Psychologia, 22,* 79–83.

Gilligan, C. (1982). *In a different voice.* Cambridge, MA: Harvard University Press.

Gilligan, C. (1990). Teaching Shakespeare's sister. In C. Gilligan, N. Lyons, and T. Hanmer (Eds.), *Making connections: The relational worlds of adolescent girls at Emma Willard School.* Cambridge: Harvard University Press.

Gilligan, C. (1992, May). *Joining the resistance: Girls' development in adolescence.* Paper presented at the symposium on development and vulnerability in close relationships, Montreal.

Gilligan, C. (1996). The centrality of relationships in psychological development: A puzzle, some evidence, and a theory. In G. G. Noam & K. W. Fischer (Eds.), *Development and vulnerability in close relationships.* Hillsdale, NJ: Erlbaum.

Gjerde, P. (1985, April). *Adolescent depression and parental socialization patterns: A prospective study.* Paper presented at the biennial meeting of the Society for Research in Child Development, Toronto.

Gladding, S. T. (1995). *Group work (2nd ed.).* Upper Saddle River, NJ: Prentice Hall.

Gladue, B. A. (1994, August). *Psychobiology of aggression in humans: Current status and future directions.* Paper presented at the meeting of the American Psychological Association, Los Angeles.

Gladue, B. A. (1994). The biopsychology of sexual orientation. *Current Directions in Psychological Science, 3,* 150–154.

Glaser, R., Rice, J., Sheridan, J., Fertel, R., Stout, J. C., Speicher, C. E., Pinsky, D., Kotur, M., Post, A., Beck, M., & Kiecolt-Glaser, J. K. (1987). Stress-related immune suppression: Health implications. *Brain, Behavior, and Immunity, 1,* 7–20.

Glassman, M. J. (1995, March). *Vygotsky's times: Their times, his times, our times.* Paper presented at the meeting of the Society for Research in Child Development, Indianapolis, IN.

Glick, J. (1975). Cognitive development in cross-cultural perspective. In F. Horowitz (Ed.), *Review of child development research* (Vol. 4). Chicago: University of Chicago Press.

Glisky, E. L., & Schacter, D. L. (1987). Acquisition of domain-specific knowledge in organic amnesia: Training for computer-related work. *Neuropsychologica, 25,* 893–906.

Glock, C. Y. (1962, July–August). On the study of religious commitment: Review of recent research bearing on religious character formation. *Religious Education, 42* (Suppl.), 98–110.

Glock, C. Y. (1964). The role of deprivation in the origin and evolution of religious groups. In R. Lee & M. E. Marty (Eds.), *Religion and social conflict.* New York: Oxford University Press.

Glock, C. Y., & Stark, R. (1965). *Religion and society in tension.* Chicago: Rand McNally.

Gluck, M. (1996, June). *What does the hippocampus do?* Paper presented at the meeting of the American Psychological Society, San Francisco.

Gluck, M. A., & Granger, R. (1993). Computational models of the neural bases of learning and memory. *Annual Review of Neuroscience, 16.* Palo Alto: CA: Annual Reviews.

Glueckauf, R. L., Frank, R. G., Bond, G. R., & McGrew, J. H. (Eds.) (1996). *Psychological practice in a changing health care system.* New York: Springer.

Godden, D. R., & Baddeley, A. D. (1975). Context-dependent memory in two natural environments: On land and under water. *British Journal of Psychology, 66,* 325–331.

Goethals, G. R., & Demorest, A. P. (1995). The risky shift is a sure bet. In M. E. Ware & D. E. Johnson (Eds.), *Demonstrations and activities in teaching of psychology (Vol. 3).* Hillsdale, NJ: Erlbaum.

Gold, M. (1987). Social ecology: In H. C. Quay (Ed.), *Handbook of juvenile delinquency.* New York: Wiley.

Goldberg, T. E., Berman, K. F., & Weinberger, D. R. (1995). Neuropsychology and neurophysiology of schizophrenia. *Current Opinion in Psychiatry, 8,* 34–40.

Goldernberg, I. (1996). *Family therapy (4th ed.).* Pacific Grove, CA: Brooks/Cole.

Goldin-Meadow, S., McNeill, D., & Singleton, J. (1996). Silence is liberating: Removing the handcuffs on grammatical expression in the manual modality. *Psychological Review, 103,* 34–55.

Goldman, R. (1964). *Religious thinking from childhood to adolescence.* London: Routledge & Kegan Paul.

Goldsmith, H. H. (1994, Winter). The behavior-genetic approach to development and experience: Contexts and constraints. *SRCD Newsletter, 1,* 6, 10–11.

Goldstein, E. B. (1996). *Sensation and perception (4th ed.).* Pacific Grove, CA: Brooks/Cole.

Goldstein, M. J. (1986, August). *Psychosocial factors in the course and onset of schizophrenia.* Paper presented at the meeting of the American Psychological Association, Washington, DC.

Goldstein, M. J., & Palmer, J. O. (1975). *The experience of anxiety.* New York: Oxford University Press.

Goldstein, W. N. (1995). The borderline patient. *American Journal of Psychotherapy, 49,* 317–337.

Goldston, S. (1986). Primary prevention: Historical perspectives and a blueprint for action. *American Psychologist, 41,* 453–460.

Goodchilds, J. D., & Zellman, G. L. (1984). Sexual signaling and sexual aggression in adolescent relationships. In N. M. Malamuth & E. D. Donnerstein (Eds.), *Pornography and sexual aggression.* New York: Academic Press.

Goodman, G. (1988). Silences. In G. Goodman & G. Esterly (Eds.), *The talk book.* New York: Ballantine.

Goodman, G., & Esterly, G. (1988). *The talk book.* New York: Ballantine.

Goodstein, L. D., & Calhoun, J. F. (1982). *Understanding abnormal behavior.* Reading, MA: Addison-Wesley.

Gordon, D. M. (1996). Soldier production under threat. *Behavioural Ecology, 379,* 583–585.

Gordon, S., & Gilgun, J. F. (1987). Adolescent sexuality. In V. B. Van Hasselt & M. Hersen (Eds.), *Handbook of adolescent psychology.* New York: Pergamon.

Gottesman, I. I. (1989). Vital statistics, demography, and schizophrenia. *Schizophrenia Bulletin, 15,* 5–8.

Gottesman, I. I., & Shields, J. (1982). *The schizophrenic puzzle.* New York: Cambridge University Press.

Gottfredson, G. D., & Holland, J. L. (1989). *Dictionary of Holland occupational titles* (2nd ed.). Odessa, FL: Psychological Assessment Resources.

Gottfredson, L. (1980). Construct validity of Holland's occupational typology in terms of prestige, census, Department of Labor, and other classification systems. *Journal of Applied Psychology, 651,* 697–714.

Gottlieb, G. (1991). Epigenetic systems view of human development. *Developmental Psychology, 27,* 33–34.

Gould, M., Wunsch-Hitzig, R., & Dohrenwend, B. S. (1981). Estimating the prevalence of childhood psychopathology. *Journal of American Academy of Child Psychiatry, 20,* 462–476.

Gould, S. J. (1981). *The mismeasure of man.* New York: W. W. Norton.

Gounin-Decarie, T. (1996). Revisiting Piaget, or the vulnerability of Piaget's infancy theory in the nineties. In G. G. Noam and K. W. Fischer (Eds.), *Development and vulnerability in close relationships.* Hillsdale, NJ: Erlbaum.

Graber, J. A., Petersen, A. C., & Brooks-Gunn, J. (1996). Pubertal processes: Methods, measures, and models. In J. A. Graber, J. Brooks-Gunn, & A. C. Petersen (Eds.), *Transitions through adolescence.* Hillsdale, NJ: Erlbaum.

Graham, S. (1986, August). *Can attribution theory tell us something about motivation in Blacks?* Paper presented at the meeting of the American Psychological Association, Washington, DC.

Graham, S. (1987, August). *Developing relations between attributions, affect, and intended social behavior.* Paper presented at the meeting of the American Psychological Association, New York.

Graham, S. (1990). Motivation in Afro-Americans. In G. L. Berry & J. K. Asamen (Eds.), *Black students: Psychosocial issues and academic achievement.* Newbury Park, CA: Sage.

Graham, S. (1994). Classroom motivation from an attributional perspective. In H. F. O'Neil & M. Drillings (Eds.), *Motivation: Theory and research.* Hillsdale, NJ: Erlbaum.

Gray, C. R., & Gummerman, K. (1975). The enigmatic eidetic image: A critical examination of methods, data, and theories. *Psychological Bulletin, 82,* 383–407.

Graziano, W. J. (1995). Evolutionary psychology: Old music, but now on CDs? *Psychological Inquiry, 6,* 41–44.

Greely, A. M. (1974). *Ecstasy: A way of knowing.* Englewood Cliffs, NJ: Prentice Hall.

Green, M. (1996). In quest of outcomes: The Larimer project. *Community Mental Health Journal, 32,* 11–22.

Green, P. (1995, March). *Sesame Street: More than a television show.* Paper presented at the meeting of the Society for Research in Child Development, Indianapolis, IN.

Greenberg, J. (1996). *Managing behavior in organizations.* Upper Saddle River, NJ: Prentice Hall.

Greene, B. (1993). Human diversity in clinical psychology: Lesbian and gay sexual orientations. *Clinical Psychologist, 46,* 74–82.

Greeno, J. G. (1994). Gibson's affordances. *Psychological Review, 101,* 336–342.

Greenwald, A. G., & Banaji, M. R. (1995). Implicit social cognition: Attitudes, self-esteem, and stereotypes. *Psychological Review, 102,* 4–27.

Greer, C. R. (1995). *Strategy and human resources.* Upper Saddle River, NJ: Prentice Hall.

Gregory, R. L. (1978). *Eye and brain: The psychology of seeing* (3rd ed.). New York: McGraw-Hill.

Grevious, C. (1985). The role of the family therapist with low-income black families. *Family Therapy, 12,* 115–122.

Griffin, D. R. (1958). *Listening in the dark.* New Haven: Yale University Press.

Griffin, D. R., & Galambos, R. (1941). The sensory basis of obstacle avoidance by flying bats. *Journal of Experimental Zoology, 86,* 481–506.

Griggs, R. A., & Cox, J. R. (1982). The elusive thematic materials effect in Wason's selection task. *British Journal of Psychology, 73,* 407–420.

Grill, C. P., & Juliano, S. A. (1996). Predicting species interactions based on behavior: Predation and competition in container-dwelling mosquitos. *Journal of Animal Ecology, 65,* 63–76.

Gruber, B. L., Hersh, S. P., Hall, N. R., Waletzky, L. R., Kunz, J. E., Carpenter, J. K., Kverno, K. S., & Weiss, S. M. (1993). Immunological responses of breast cancer patients to behavioral interventions. *Biofeedback and Self-Regulation, 18,* 1–22.

Grunberg, N. E., & Baum, A. (1985). Biological commonalities of stress and substance abuse. In S. Shiffman & T. A. Wills (Eds.), *Coping and substance use.* San Diego: Academic Press.

Grunwald, L., Goldberg, J., Berstein, S., & Hollister, A. (1993, July). The amazing mind of babies. *Life,* p. 52.

Grush, J. E. (1980). Impact of candidate expenditures, regionality, and prior outcomes on the 1976 Democratic presidential primaries. *Journal of Personality and Social Psychology, 38,* 337–347.

Guilford, J. P. (1967). *The structure of intellect.* New York: McGraw-Hill.

Gur, R. C., Mozley, L. H., Mozley, P. D., Resnick, S. M., Karp, J. S., Alavi, A., Arnold, S. E., & Gur, R. E. (1995). Sex differences in regional cerebral glucose metabolism during a resting state. *Science, 267,* 528–531.

Gutek, B. A. (1993). Responses to sexual harassment. In S. Oskamp & M. Costanzo (Eds.), *Gender issues in contemporary society.* Newbury Park, CA: Sage.

Guthrie, R. (1976). *Even the rat was white: A historical view of psychology.* New York: Harper & Row.

Guttman, N., & Kalish, H. I. (1956). Discriminability and stimulus generalization. *Journal of Experimental Psychology, 51,* 79–88.

Hackett, G., & Watkins, C. E. (1995). Research in career assessment. In W. B. Walsh & S. H. Osipow (Eds.), *Handbook of vocational psychology (2nd ed.).* Hillsdale, NJ: Erlbaum.

Hadani, I., & Julesz, B. (1994). Computational aspects of motion perception during self-motion. *Behavioral and Brain Sciences, 17,* 293–355.

Haier, R. J., Siegel, B., Tang, C., Abel, L., & Buchsbaum, M. S. (1992). Intelligence and changes in regional cerebral glucose metabolic rate following learning. *Intelligence, 16,* 415–426.

Hakuta, K., & Garcia, E. E. (1989). Bilingualism and education. *American Psychologist, 44,* 374–379.

Haley, J. (1976). *Problem-solving therapy.* San Francisco: Jossey-Bass.

Halford, G. S. (1993, March). *Experience and processing capacity in cognitive development: A PDP approach.* Paper presented at the biennial meeting of the Society for Research in Child Development, New Orleans.

Hall, C. C. I., Evans, B. J., & Selice, S. (Eds.). (1989). Black females in the United States: A bibliography from 1967 to 1987. Washington, DC: American Psychological Association.

Hall, E. (1969). *The hidden dimension.* Garden City, NY: Anchor Books.

Hall, G. S. (1904). *Adolescence* (Vols. I and II). Englewood Cliffs, NJ: Prentice Hall.

Halonen, J. (1995). Demystifying critical thinking. *Teaching of Psychology, 22,* 75–81.

Halonen, J. S., & Santrock, J. W. (1997). *Psychology: The contexts of behavior* (2nd ed.). Madison, WI: Brown & Benchmark.

Halonen, J. S., & Santrock, J. W. (1997). *Human adjustment* (2nd ed.). Madison, WI: Brown & Benchmark.

Halpern, D. F. (1995). *Thinking critically about critical thinking.* Hillsdale, NJ: Erlbaum.

Hammond, W. R. (1993, August). Participant in open forum with the APA Commission on Youth and Violence, meeting of the American Psychological Association, Washington, DC.

Hammond, W. R., & Yung, B. R. (1994). African Americans. In L. D. Eron, J. H. Gentry, & P. Schlegl (Eds.), *Reason to hope: A psychological perspective on youth and violence.* Washington, DC: American Psychological Association.

Handelsman, M. M., & Frielander, B. L. (1995). The use of an experiential exercise to teach about assertiveness. In M. E. Ware & D. E. Johnson (Eds.), *Demonstrations and activities in teaching of psychology (Vol. 3).* Hillsdale, NJ: Erlbaum.

Haney, W. V. (1986). *Communication and interpersonal relations: Text and cases.* Homewood, IL: Irwin.

Hanna, S. L. (1995). *Person to person (2nd ed.).* Upper Saddle River, NJ: Prentice Hall.

Hansen, J. P. (1995). An experimental investigation of configural, digital, and temporal information on process displays. *Human Factors, 37,* 539–552.

Hare-Muston, R., & Marecek, J. (1988). The meaning of difference: Gender theory, postmodernism, and psychology. *American Psychologist, 43,* 455–464.

Harlow, H. F. (1959, June). Love in infant monkeys. *Scientific American,* pp. 68–74.

Harlow, H. F., & Zimmerman, R. R. (1959). Affectional responses in the infant monkey. *Science, 130,* 421–432.

Harris, A. S. (1996). *Living with paradox: An introduction to Jungian psychology.* Pacific Grove, CA: Brooks/Cole.

Harris, L., & others. (1978). *The Steelcase national study of office environments: Do they work?* Grand Rapids, MI: Steelcase.

Harris, R. F., Wolf, N. M., & Baer, D. M. (1964). Effects of adult social reinforcement on child behavior. *Young Children, 20,* 8–17.

Harrison, C. A. (1991). Older women in our society: America's silent, invisible majority. *Educational Gerontology, 17,* 111–122.

Harter, S. (1988). Developmental and dynamic changes in the nature of the self-concept. In S. R. Shirk (Ed.), *Cognitive development and child psychotherapy.* New York: Plenum.

Harter, S. (1990). Self and identity development. In S. S. Feldman & G. R. Elliott (Eds.), *At the threshold: The developing adolescent.* Cambridge, MA: Harvard University Press.

Harter, S., & Marold, D. B. (1992). Psychological risk factors contributing to adolescent suicide ideation. In G. Noam & S. Borst (Eds.), *Child and adolescent suicide.* San Francisco: Jossey-Bass.

Hartig, T., Mang, M., & Evans, G. W. (1991). Restorative effects of natural environment experiences. *Environment and Behavior, 23,* 3–26.

Hartshorne, H., & May, M. S. (1928–1930). *Moral studies in the nature of character: Vol. 1. Studies in deceit. Vol. 2. Studies in self-control. Vol. 3. Studies in the organization of character.* New York: Macmillan.

Harvard Medical School Newsletter. (1981). Cambridge, MA: Harvard Medical School, Dept. of Continuing Education.

Harvey, J. H. (1995). *Odyssey of the heart.* New York: W. H. Freeman.

Hasher, L., & Zacks, R. T. (1979). Automatic and effortful processes in memory. *Journal of Experimental Psychology: General, 108,* 356–388.

Hassebrock, F. (1996). Tracing the cognitive revolution through a literature search. In M. E. Ware & D. E. Johnson (Eds.), *Demonstrations and activities in teaching of psychology (Vol. 3).* Hillsdale, NJ: Erlbaum.

Hassler, A. D. (1966). *Underwater guideposts: Homing of salmon.* Madison: University of Wisconsin Press.

Hastings, M. W. (1995). Statistics: Challenge for the students and the professor. In M. E. Ware & D. E. Johnson (Eds.), *Demonstrations and activities in teaching of psychology (Vol. 1).* Hillsdale, NJ: Erlbaum.

Hatcher, R., & others. (1988). *Contraceptive technology, 1988–1989* (14th ed.). New York: Irvington.

Hattie, J., Sharpley, C., & Rogers, H. (1984). Comparative effectiveness of professionals and paraprofessional helpers. *Psychological Bulletin, 95,* 534–541.

Hatvany, N., & Pucik, V. (1981). An integrated management system: Lessons from the Japanese experience. *Academy of Management Review, 6,* 469–480.

Hawkins, D. (1970). The effects of subliminal stimulation on drive level and brand preference. *Journal of Marketing Research, 7,* 322–326.

Hawkins, J., Pea, R. D., Glick, J., & Scribner, S. (1984). "Merds that laugh don't like mushrooms": Evidence for deductive reasoning by preschoolers. *Developmental Psychology, 20,* 584–594.

Hawkins, L. H. (1981). The influence of air ions, temperature, and humidity on subjective well-being and comfort. *Journal of Environmental Psychology, 1,* 279–292.

Hawkins, L. H., & Barker, T. (1978). Air ions and human performance. *Ergonomics, 21,* 273–278.

Hawkins, R. D., Kandel, E. R., & Siegelbaum, S. A. (1993). Learning to modulate neurotransmitter release: Themes and variations in synaptic plasticity. *Annual Review of Neuroscience, 16.* Palo Alto, CA: Annual Review.

Hayes, S. C., & Heiby, E. (1996). Psychology's drug problem. *American Psychologist, 51,* 198–206.

Hayflick, L. (1975, September). Why grow old? *Stanford Magazine,* pp. 36–43.

Hayflick, L. (1977). The cellular basis for biological aging. In C. E. Finch & L. Hayflick (Eds.), *Handbook of the biology of aging.* New York: Van Nostrand.

Haynes, S. N. (1990). Behavioral assessment of adults. In G. Goldstein & M. Hersen (Eds.), *Handbook of psychological assessment* (pp. 369–401). New York: Pergamon.

Heath, S. B. (1983). *Ways with words: Language, life, and work in communities and classrooms.* Cambridge, MA: Cambridge University Press.

Heatherton, T. F., & Baumeister, R. F. (1991). Binge-eating as an escape from self-awareness. *Psychological Bulletin, 110,* 86–108.

Heatherton, T. F., Herman, C. P., & Polivy, J. (1991). Effects of physical threat and ego threat on eating behavior. *Journal of Personality and Social Psychology, 60,* 138–143.

Heatherton, T. F., Herman, C. P., & Polivy, J. (1992). Effects of distress on eating: The importance of ego-involvement. *Journal of Personality and Social Psychology, 62,* 801–803.

Hebb, D. O. (1949). *The organization of behavior.* New York: Wiley.

Heckhausen, J., & Schulz, R. (1993). Optimization by selection and compensation: Balancing primary and secondary control in life-span development. *International Journal of Behavioral Development, 16,* 287–303.

Heider, F. (1946). Attitudes and cognitive organization. *Journal of Psychology, 21,* 107–112.

Heider, F. (1958). *The psychology of interpersonal relations.* New York: Wiley.

Heilman, M. E., Block, C. J., & Lucas, J. A. (1992). Presumed incompetent? Stigmatization and affirmative action efforts. *Journal of Applied Psychology, 77,* 536–544.

Heiman, G. W. (1995). *Research methods.* Boston: Houghton Mifflin.

Helgeson, V. S., & Sharpsteen, D. J. (1987). Perceptions of danger in achievement and affiliation situations: An extension of the Pollack and Gilligan versus Benton et al. debate. *Journal of Personality and Social Psychology, 53,* 727**733.**

Heller, J. F., Groff, B. D., & Solomon, S. A. (1977). Toward an understanding of crowding: The role of physical interaction. *Journal of Personality and Social Psychology, 35,* 183–190.

Hellige, J. B. (1990). Hemispheric asymmetry. *Annual Review of Psychology, 41.* Palo Alto, CA: Annual Reviews.

Helmreich, R. L. (1995). Culture shocks social psychology: Two views. *Contemporary Psychology, 40,* 108–109.

Helson, R., Mitchell, V., & Moane, G. (1984). Personality change in women from college to midlife. *Journal of Personality and Social Psychology, 53,* 176–186.

Helson, R., & Moane, G. (1987). Personality change in women from college to midlife. *Journal of Personality and Social Psychology, 53,* 176–186.

Helson, R., & Roberts, B. W. (1994). Ego development and personality change in adulthood. *Journal of Personality and Social Psychology, 5,* 911–920.

Helson, R., & Wink, P. (1992). Personality change in women from the early 40s to early 50s. *Psychology and Aging, 7,* 46–55.

Henderson, V. L., & Dweck, C. S. (1990). Motivation and achievement. In S. S. Feldman & G. R. Elliott (Eds.), *At the threshold: The developing adolescent.* Cambridge, MA: Harvard University Press.

Henrink, R. (Ed.) (1980). *The psychotherapy handbook: The A to Z guide to more than 250 different therapies in use today.* New York: New American Library.

Heppner, M. J., O'Brien, K. M., Hinkelman, J. M., & Flores, L. Y. (1996). Training counseling psychologists in career development. *The counseling psychologist, 24,* 105–125.

Herbert, J. (1988). The physiology of aggression. In J. Groebel & R. A. Hinde (Eds.), *Aggression and war: The biological and social bases.* New York: Cambridge University Press.

Hernandez, D. J. (1988). Demographic trends and the living arrangements of children. In E. M. Hetherington & J. D. Arasteh (Eds.), *Impact of divorce, single-parenting, and stepparenting on children.* Hillsdale, NJ: Erlbaum.

Hernstein, R. J., & Murray, C. (1994). *The bell curve: Intelligence and class structure in modern life.* New York: Free Press.

Hersch, L. (1995). Adapting to health care reform and managed care: Three strategies for survival and growth. *Professional Psychology, 26,* 16–26.

Hersen, M., & Miller, P. M. (Eds.) (1996). *Progress in behavior modification (Vol. 30).* Pacific Grove, CA: Brooks/Cole.

Hertel, P. (1995). Practical aspects of emotions and memory. In D. Hermann, C. McEvoy, C. Hertzog, P. Hertel, & M. Johnson (Eds.), *Basic and applied memory research (Vol. 1).* Hillsdale, NJ: Erlbaum.

Herzog, H. A. (1995). Naturalistic observation of behavior. In M. E. Ware & D. E. Johnson (Eds.), *Demonstrations and activities in teaching of psychology (Vol. 1).* Hillsdale, NJ: Erlbaum.

Herzog, H. A. (1995). Discussing animal rights and animal research in the classroom. In M. E. Ware & D. E. Johnson (Eds.), *Demonstrations and activities in teaching of psychology (Vol. 1).* Hillsdale, NJ: Erlbaum.

Hetherington, E. M. (1993, March). *An overview of the Virginia longitudinal study of divorce and remarriage with a focus on early adolescence.* Paper presented at the biennial meeting of the Society for Research in Child Development, New Orleans.

Hetherington, E. M., & Blechman, E. A. (Eds.) (1996). *Stress, coping, and resiliency in children and families.* Hillsdale, NJ: Erlbaum.

Hetherington, E. M., Hagan, M. S., & Anderson, E. R. (1989). Marital transitions: A child's perspective. *American Psychologist, 44,* 303–312.

Heyns, B. (1982). The influence of parents' work on children's school achievement. In S. B. Kamerman & C. D. Hayes (Eds.), *Families that work: Children in a changing world.* Washington, DC: National Academy Press.

Hickman, C. P, & Roberts, L. S. (1995). *Animal diversity.* Dubuque, IA: Wm. C. Brown.

Hilgard, E. R. (1965). *Hypnotic suggestibility.* New York: Harcourt Brace.

Hilgard, E. R. (1977). *Divided consciousness: Multiple controls in human thought and action.* New York: Wiley.

Hill, J. P., & Holmbeck, G. (1986). Attachment and autonomy in adolescence: In G. Whitehurst (Ed.), *Annals of child development.* Greenwich: JAI Press.

Hill, P. C. (1995). Affective theory and religious experience. In R. Hood, Jr., (Ed.), *Handbook of religious experience.* Birmingham, AL: Religious Education Press.

Himes, C. L., Hogan, D. P., & Eggebeen, D. J. (1996). Living arrangements of minority elders. *Journal of Gerontology, 51A,* S42–S48.

Hine, D. W. (1990). *The commons dilemma: A quantitative review.* Unpublished master's thesis, University of Victoria, Canada.

Hines, M. (1982). Prenatal gonadal hormones and sex differences in human behavior. *Psychological Bulletin, 92,* 56–80.

Hines, M. (1990). Gonadal hormones and human cognitive development. In J. Balthazart (Ed.), *Hormones, brain, and behavior in vertebrates.* Basel: Karger.

Hines, T. (1988). *Pseudoscience and the paranormal.* Buffalo, NY: Prometheus Books.

Hinsz, V. B. (1995). Group and individual decision making for task performance goals: Processes in the establishment of goals in groups. *Journal of Applied Social Psychology, 25,* 353–370.

Hirtle, S. C., & Jonides, J. (1985). Evidence of hierarchies in cognitive maps. *Memory and Cognition, 13,* 208–217.

Hoagwood, K., Jensen, P., & Fischer, C. (Eds.) (1996). *Ethical issues in mental health research with children and adolescents.* Hillsdale, NJ: Erlbaum.

Hobfoll, S. E. (1989). Conversation of resources: A new attempt at conceptualizing stress. *American Psychologist, 44,* 513–524.

Hobfoll, S. E. (1996). Social support. In N. Vanzetti & S. Duck (Eds.) (1996), *A lifetime of relationships.* Pacific Grove, CA: Brooks/Cole.

Hobson, J. A., & McCarley, R. W. (1977). The brain as a dream state generator: An activation-synthesis hypothesis of the dream process. *American Journal of Psychiatry, 134,* 1335–1348.

Hoff-Ginsburg, E., & Tardif, T. (1995). Socioeconomic status and parenting. In M. H. Bornstein (Ed.), *Handbook of parenting* (Vol. 1). Hillsdale, NJ: Erlbaum.

Hofferth, S. L. (1990). Trends in adolescent sexual activity, contraception, and pregnancy in the United States. In J. Bancroft & J. M. Reinisch (Eds.), *Adolescence and puberty.* New York: Oxford University Press.

Hoffman, L. W. (1989). Effects of maternal employment in the two-parent family. *American Psychologist, 44,* 283–292.

Hofstede, G. (1980). *Culture's consequences: International differences in work-related values.* Newbury Park, CA: Sage.

Hogan, R. T. (1987, August). *Conceptions of personality and the prediction of job performance.* Paper presented at the meeting of the American Psychological Association, New York.

Hogg, M. A. (1996). Social identity, self-categorization, and the small group. In E. H. Witte & J. H. Davis (Eds.), *Understanding group behavior (Vol. 2).* Hillsdale, NJ: Erlbaum.

Holcomb, H. H., Cascella, N. G., Thaker, G. K., Medoff, D. R., Dannals, R. F., & Tamminga, C. A. (1996). Functional sites of neuroleptic drug action in the human brain. *The American Journal of Psychiatry, 153,* 41–49.

Holden, G. W. (1996). *Parents and the dynamics of child rearing.* Boulder, CO: Westview Press.

Holland, J. L. (1973). *Making vocational choices: A theory of careers.* Englewood Cliffs, NJ: Prentice Hall.

Holland, J. L. (1987). Current status of Holland's theory of careers: Another perspective. *Career Development Quarterly, 36,* 24–30.

Holland, P. C. (1996). The effects of intertrial and feature-target intervals on operant serial feature-positive discrimination learning. *Animal Learning & Behavior, 23,* 411–428.

Hollender, M., & Mercer, A. (1976). Wish to be held and wish to hold in men and women. *Archives of General Psychiatry, 33,* 49–51.

Hollingshead, A. B., & Redlich, F. C. (1958). *Social class and mental illness.* New York: Wiley.

Holmbeck, G. N. (1996). A model of family relational transformations during the transition to adolescence: Parent-adolescent conflict and adaptation. In J. A. Graber, J. Brooks-Gunn, & A. C. Petersen (Eds.), *Transitions through adolescence.* Hillsdale, NJ: Erlbaum.

Holmbeck, G. N., Paikoff, R. L., Brooks-Gunn, J. (1995). Parenting adolescents. In M. H. Bornstein (Ed.), *Children and parenting* (Vol. 1). Hillsdale, NJ: Erlbaum.

Holmes, T. H., & Rahe, R. H. (1967). The social readjustment rating scale. *Journal of Psychosomatic Research, 11,* 213–218.

Holt, R. D. (1996). Demographic constraints in evolution: Towards unifying the evolutionary theories of senescence and niche conservation. *Evolutionary Ecology, 10,* 1–12.

Holtzmann, W. (1982). Cross-cultural comparisons of personality development in Mexico and the United States. In D. Wagner & H. W. Stevenson (Eds.), *Cultural perspectives on child development.* San Francisco: W. H. Freeman.

Holyoak, K. J., & Spellman, B. A. (1993). Thinking. *Annual Review of Psychology, 44,* 265–315.

Honts, C. R. (1994). Psychophysiological deception. *Current Directions in Psychological Science, 3,* 77–82.

Hood, R. W., Jr. (1970). Religious orientation and the report of religious experience. *Journal for the Scientific Study of Religion, 9,* 285–291.

Hood, R. W., Jr. (1995). *Handbook of religious experience.* Birmingham, AL: Religious Education Press.

Hood, R. W., Jr., & Morris, R. J. (1981). Sensory isolation and the differential elicitation of religious imagery in intrinsic and extrinsic persons. *Journal for the Scientific Study of Religion, 20,* 261–273.

Hood, R. W., Jr., Spilka, B., Hunsberger, B., & Gorsuch, R. (1996). *Psychology of religion: An empirical approach* (2nd ed.). New York: Guilford Press.

Hopkins, C. D. (1974). Electric communication in fish. *American Scientist, 62,* 426–437.

Hoptman, M. J., & Davidson, R. J. (1994). How and why do the two cerebral hemispheres interact? *Psychological Bulletin, 116,* 195–219.

Horm, J., & Anderson, K. (1993). Who in America is trying to lose weight? *Annals of Internal Medicine, 119,* 672–676.

Horn, J. L., & Donaldson, G. (1980). Cognitive development II: Adulthood development of human abilities. In O. G. Brim & J. Kagan (Eds.), *Constancy and change in human development.* Cambridge, MA: Harvard University Press.

Horney, K. (1945). *Our inner conflicts.* New York: Norton.

Horowitz, F. D., & O'Brien, M. (1989). In the interest of our nation. *American Psychologist, 44,* 441–445.

Horowitz, M. J. (1989). *Introduction to psychoanalysis.* New York: Basic Books.

Horwitz, L., Gabbard, G. O., Allen, J. G., Frieswyk, S. H., Colson, D. B., Newsom, G. E., & Coyne, L. (1996). *Borderline personality disorder.* Washington, DC: American Psychiatric Press.

Hothersall, D. (1996). *History of psychology* (3rd ed.). New York: McGraw-Hill.

Houston, M., & Wood, J. T. (1996). Difficult dialogues—communicating across race and class. In J. T. Wood (Ed.), *Gendered Relationships.* Mountain View, CA: Mayfield.

Howat, P. M., & Saxton, A. M. (1988). The incidence of bulimic behavior in a secondary and university school population. *Journal of Youth and Adolescence, 17,* 221–231.

Howe, M. L. (1995, March). *Early memory development and the emergence of autobiographical memory.* Paper presented at the meeting of the Society for Research in Child Development, Indianapolis.

Howell, W. C. (1993). Engineering psychology in a changing world. *Annual Review of Psychology,* 231–263.

Howes, C. (1988, April). *Can the age of entry and the quality of infant child care predict behaviors in kindergarten?* Paper presented at the International Conference on Infant Studies, Washington, DC.

Hoyenga, K. B., & Hoyenga, K. T. (1984). *Motivational explanations of behavior: Evolutionary, physiological, and cognitive ideas.* Monterey, CA: Brooks/Cole.

Huang, L. N., & Gibbs, J. T. (1989). Future directions: Implications for research, training, and practice. In J. T. Gibbs & L. N. Huang (Eds.), *Children of color.* San Francisco: Jossey-Bass.

Hubel, D. H., & Wiesel, T. N. (1962). Receptive fields, binocular interaction and functional architecture in the cat's visual cortex. *Journal of Physiology, 160,* 106–154.

Hubel, D. H., & Wiesel, T. N. (1965). Receptive fields and functional architecture in two nonstriate visual areas (18 and 19) of the cat. *Journal of Neurophysiology, 28,* 229–289.

Hudson Institute. (1987). *Workforce 2000: Work and workers for the twenty-first century.* Indianapolis: Author.

Huesmann, L. (1986). Psychological processes promoting the relation between exposure to media violence and aggressive behavior by the viewer. *Journal of Social Issues, 42,* 125–139.

Huesmann, L. R., Eron, L. D., Klein, R., Brice, P., & Fischer, P. (1983). Mitigating the imitation of aggressive behaviors by changing children's attitudes about media violence. *Journal of Personality and Social Psychology, 44,* 899–910.

Hull, C. L. (1943). *Principles of behavior.* New York: Appleton-Century-Crofts.

Hultsch, D. F., & Plemons, J. K. (1979). Life events and life-span development. In P. B. Baltes & O. G. Brim (Eds.), *Life-span development and behavior.* New York: Academic Press.

Humphreys, K. (1996). Clinical psychologists as psychotherapists. *American Psychologist, 51,* 190–197.

Hundert, E. M. (1989). *Philosophy, psychiatry, and neuroscience: Three approaches to mind.* New York: Oxford University Press.

Hunt, M. (1974). *Sexual behavior in the 1970s.* Chicago: Playboy.

Hunt, R. R., & Kelly, R. E. S. (1996). Accessing the particular from the general: The power of distinctiveness in the context of organization. *Memory & Cognition, 24,* 217–225.

Hurtado, S., Dey, E. L., & Trevino, J. G. (1994). *Exclusion or self-segregation? Interaction across racial/ethnic groups on college campuses.* Paper presented at the American Educational Research Association annual meeting.

Hurvich, L. M., & Jameson, D. (1969). Human color perception. *American Scientist, 57,* 143–166.

Huston, A. (1995, August). *Children in poverty.* Paper presented at the meeting of the American Psychological Association, New York City.

Huston, A. C., Watkins, B. A., & Kunkel, D. (1989). Public policy and children's television. *American Psychologist, 44,* 424–433.

Hy, L., & Loevinger, J. (1996). *Measuring ego development.* Hillsdale, NJ: Erlbaum.

Hyde, J. S. (1981). How large are cognitive gender differences? A meta-analysis using w^2 and *d. American Psychologist, 36,* 892–901.

Hyde, J. S. (1984). Children's understanding of sexist language. *Developmental Psychology, 20,* 697–706.

Hyde, J. S. (1990). Meta-analysis and the psychology of gender differences. *Signs: Journal of Women in Culture and Society, 16,* 55–69.

Hyde, J. S. (1991, August). *Gender and sex: So what has meta-analysis done for me?* Paper presented at the meeting of the American Psychological Association, San Francisco.

Hyde, J. S. (1993). Meta-analysis and the psychology of women. In F. L. Denmark & M. A. Paludi (Eds.), *Handbook on the psychology of women.* Westport, CT: Greenwood.

Hyde, J. S. (in press). Meta-analysis and the psychology of women. In F. L. Denmark & M. A. Paludi (Eds.), *Handbook of the psychology of women.* Dubuque, IA: Wm. C. Brown.

Hyde, J. S., & Plant, E. A. (1995). Magnitude of psychological gender differences: Another side of the story. *American Psychologist, 50,* 159–161.

Hyde, K. E. (1990). *Religion in childhood and adolescence: A comprehensive review of the research.* Birmingham, AL: Religious Education Press.

Hyde, T. S., & Jenkins, J. J. (1969). Differential effects of incidental tasks on the organization of recall of lists of highly associated words. *Journal of Experimental Psychology, 82,* 472–481.

Ikels, C. (1989). Becoming a human being in theory and practice: Chinese views of human development. In D. I. Kertzer & K. W. Schaie (Eds.), *Age structuring in comparative perspective.* Hillsdale, NJ: Erlbaum.

Intons-Peterson, M. J. (1993). External memory aids and their relation to memory. In C. Izawa (Ed.), *Cognitive Psychology Applied.* Hillsdale, NJ: Erlbaum.

Intons-Peterson, M. (1996). Memory aids. In D. Hermann, C. McEvoy, C. Hertzog, P. Hertel, & M. Johnson (Eds.), *Basic and applied memory research (Vol. 2).* Hillsdale, NJ: Erlbaum.

Irvine, M. J., Johnson, D. W., Jenner, D. A., & Marie, G. V. (1986). Relaxation and stress management in the treatment of essential hypertension. *Journal of Psychosomatic Research, 30,* 437–450.

Irvine, S. H., & Berry, J. W. (Eds.). (1988). *Human abilities in cultural context.* New York: Cambridge University Press.

Izard, C. (1991). Studies of the development of emotion-cognition relations. In C. E. Izard (Ed.), *The development of emotion-cognition relations.* Hillsdale, NJ: Erlbaum.

Izard, C. E. (1982). *Measuring emotions in infants and young children.* New York: Cambridge University Press.

Izard, C. E. (1994). Innate and universal facial expressions: Evidence from developmental and cross-cultural research. *Psychological Bulletin, 115,* 288–299.

Jackson, E. L. (1981). Response to earthquake hazard: The west coast of North America. *Environment and Behavior, 13,* 387–416.

Jackson, J. F. (1993). Human behavioral genetics, Scarr's theory, and her views on interventions: A critical review and commentary on their implications for African American children. *Child Development, 64,* 1318–1332.

Jackson, W. (1995). *Social research methods.* Upper Saddle River, NJ: Prentice Hall.

Jacobson, N. S. (1995, August). *Psychotherapy is dead! Long live psychotherapy!* Paper presented at the meeting of the American Psychological Association, New York City.

Jacquette, D. (1996). Lloyd on intrinsic natural representation in simple mechanical minds. *Minds and Machines, 6,* 47–60.

Jahoda, G. (1980). Theoretical and systematic approaches in cross-cultural psychology. In H. C. Triandis & J. G. Draguns (Eds.), *Handbook of cross-cultural psychology* (Vol. 1). Boston: Allyn & Bacon.

James, W. (1890/1950). *The principles of psychology.* New York: Dover.

James, W. (1902). *Varieties of religious experience.* New York: Longmans.

Jameson, D., & Hurvich, L. (1989). Essay concerning color constancy. *Annual Review of Psychology, 40.* Palo Alto, CA: Annual Reviews.

Janis, I. (1972). *Victims of groupthink: A psychological study of foreign-policy decisions and fiascos.* Boston: Houghton Mifflin.

Janos, P. M., & Robinson, N. M. (1985). Psychosocial development in intellectually gifted children. In F. D. Horowitz & M. O'Brien (Eds.), *The gifted and talented.* Washington, DC: American Psychological Association.

Janz, N. K., Zimmeran, M. A., Wren, P. A., Israel, B. A., Freudenberg, N., & Carter, R. J. (1996). Evaluation of 37 AIDS prevention projects: Successful approaches and barriers to program effectiveness. *Health Education Quarterly, 23,* 80–97.

Jenkins, J. J. (1969). Language and thought. In J. F. Voss (Ed.), *Approaches to thought.* Columbus, OH: Merrill.

Jensen, A. R. (1969). How much can we boost IQ and scholastic achievement? *Harvard Educational Review, 39,* 1–123.

Jensen, L. A. (1995, March). *The moral reasoning of orthodox and progressivist Indians and Americans.* Paper presented at the meeting of the Society for Research in Child Development, Indianapolis.

Johnson, C. (1990, May). The new woman's ethics report. *New Woman,* p. 6.

Johnson, M., Mullins, P., & Burnham, J. (1993, August). *Spirituality: Conceptualization and measurement.* Paper presented at the meeting of the American Psychological Association, Toronto.

Johnson, P. E. (1979, November). *Expert problem solving.* Paper presented at the meeting of the American Educational Research Association, San Francisco.

Johnson-Laird, P. N. (1989). *The computer and the mind.* Cambridge, MA: Harvard University Press.

Johnson-Laird, P. N., & Byrne, R. M. J. (1993). Precis of deduction. *Brain and Behavioral Sciences, 16,* 323–333.

Johnston, L., O'Malley, P., & Bachman, G. (1993, March). *Drug use among the nation's eight-grade students.* Ann Arbor: University of Michigan, Institute of Social Research.

Johnston, L., O'Malley, G., & Bachman, J. (1994, December). *Drug use continues to decline among American teenagers.* Unpublished manuscript, University of Michigan, Institute of Social Research.

Johnston, L. D., Bachman, J. G., & O'Malley, P. M. (1994). *Teen drug use.* Ann Arbor: University of Michigan, Institute of Social Research.

Johnston, L. D., O'Malley, P. M., & Bachman, J. G. (1995). National survey results on drug use from the *Monitoring the Future Study, Vol. 1: Secondary school students.* Ann Arbor, MI: Institute of Social Research.

Jones, A., & Seagull, A. (1977). Dimensions of the relationship between the Black client and the White therapist. *American Psychologist, 32,* 850–856.

Jones, J. M. (1987). Blacks in psychology. In P. J. Woods & C. S. Wilkinson (Eds.). *Is psychology the major for you?* Washington, DC: American Psychological Association.

Jones, J. M. (1993, August). *Racism and civil rights: Right problem, wrong solution.* Paper presented at the meeting of the American Psychological Association, Toronto.

Jones, J. M. (1994). *Racism and civil rights: Right problem, wrong solution.* Paper presented at the meeting of the American Psychological Association.

Jones, J. M. (1994). The African American: A duality dilemma? In W. J. Lonner & R. Malpass (Eds.), *Psychology and culture.* Needham Heights, MA: Allyn & Bacon.

Jones, L. (1996). *HIV/AIDS: What to do about it.* Pacific Grove, CA: Brooks/Cole.

Jones, M. C. (1924). A laboratory study of fear: The case of Peter. *Journal of Genetic Psychology, 31,* 308–315.

Jones, M. C. (1965). Psychological correlates of somatic development. *Child Development, 36,* 899–911.

Jones, S. L. (1994). A constructive relationship for religion with the science and profession of psychology. *American Psychologist, 49,* 184–199.

Jones, W. H., Hobbs, S. A., & Hockenbury, D. (1982). Loneliness and social skills deficits. *Journal of Personality and Social Psychology, 42,* 682–689.

Jordan, E., & Collins, F. S. (1996). Human Genome Project: A march of genetic maps. *Nature, 380,* 111–112.

Jou, J., Shanteau, J., & Harris, R. J. (1996). An information processing view of framing effects: The role of causal schemas in decision making. *Memory & Cognition, 24,* 1–15.

Jourard, S. M. (1971). *The transparent self.* New York: Van Nostrand Reinhold.

Julesz, B. (1985). *Dialogues on perception.* Cambridge, MA: MIT Press.

Jung, C. G. (1917). *Analytic psychology.* New York: Moffat, Yard.

Jussim, L. (1991). Social perception and social reality: A reflection-construction model. *Psychological Review, 98,* 54–73.

Jussim, L., Manis, M., Nelson, T. E., & Sofin, S. (1995). Prejudice, stereotypes, and labeling effects: Sources of bias in person perception. *Journal of Personality and Social Psychology, 68,* 228–246.

Kagan, J. (1984). *The nature of the child.* New York: Basic Books.

Kagan, J., Kearsley, R. B., & Zelazo, P. R. (1978). *Infancy.* Cambridge, MA: Harvard University Press.

Kagan, J., & Snidman, N. (1991). Temperamental factors in human development. *American Psychologist, 46,* 856–862.

Kagan, S., & Madsen, M. C. (1972). Experimental analysis of cooperation and competition of Anglo-American and Mexican children. *Developmental Psychology, 6,* 49–59.

Kagitcibasi, C. (1995). Is psychology relevant to global human development issues? Experience from Turkey. *American Psychologist, 50,* 293–300.

Kagitcibasi, C., & Berry, J. W. (1989). Cross-cultural psychology: Current research and trends. *Annual Review of Psychology, 40.* Palo Alto, CA: Annual Reviews.

Kahneman, D., & Tversky, A. (1982). The simulation heuristic. In D. Kahneman, D. Slovic, & A. Tversky (Eds.), *Judgment under uncertainty: Heuristics and biases* (pp. 201–208). Cambridge: Cambridge University Press.

Kail, R. (1993, March). *The nature of global developmental change in processing time.* Paper presented at the biennial meeting of the Society for Research in Child Development, New Orleans.

Kail, R., & Pellegrino, J. W. (1985). *Human intelligence.* New York: W. H. Freeman.

Kales, A. (1970). Sleep patterns following 205 hours of sleep deprivation. *Psychosomatic Medicine, 32,* 189–200.

Kalichman, S. C. (1996). *Answering your questions about AIDS.* Washington, DC: American Psychological Association.

Kamin, L. J. (1968). Attention-like processes in classical conditioning. In M. R. Jones (Ed.), *Miami Symposium on the prediction of behavior: Aversive stimuli.* Coral Gables, FL: University of Miami Press.

Kammann, R., Thomson, R., & Irwin, R. (1979). Unhelpful behavior in the street: City size or immediate pedestrian density? *Environment and Behavior, 11,* 245–250.

Kamo, Y. (1988). Determinants of the household division of labor: Resources, power, and ideology. *Journal of Family Issues, 9,* 177–200.

Kandel, E. R., & Schwartz, J. H. (1982). Molecular biology of learning: Modulation of transmitter release. *Science, 218,* 433–443.

Kane, J. M., & Barnes, T. R. E. (1995). Schizophrenia research: Challenges and opportunities. *Current Opinion in Psychiatry, 8,* 19–20.

Kanner, A. D., Coyne, J. C., Schaefer, C., & Lazarus, R. S. (1981). Comparisons of two modes of stress measurement. Daily hassles and uplifts versus major life events. *Journal of Behavioral Medicine, 4,* 1–39.

Kanner, A. D., & Feldman, S. S. (1991). Control over uplifts and hassles and its relationship to adaptational outcomes. *Journal of Behavioral Medicine, 14,* 187–198.

Kaplan, H. S. (1974). *The new sex therapy.* New York: Times Books.

Kaplan, S. (1992). Environmental preference in a knowledge-seeking, knowledge-using organism. In J. Barkow, L. Cosmides, & J. Tooby (Eds.), *The adapted mind.* New York: Oxford University Press.

Kaplan, S. (1995). The restorative benefits of nature: Toward an integrative framework. *Journal of Environmental Psychology, 15,* 169–182.

Kapur, S. (1994). Some applications of formal learning theory results to natural language acquisition. In B. Lust, G. Hermon, & J. Kornfilt (Eds.), *Syntactic theory and first language acquisition* (Vol. 2). Hillsdale, NJ: Erlbaum.

Kapur, S., Craik, F. I. M., Tulving, E., Wilson, A. A., Houle, S., & Brown, G. M. (1994). Neuroanatomical correlates of encoding in episodic memory: levels of processing effect. *Proceedings of the National Academy of Science of the United States of America, 91,* 2008–2111.

Karacek, R. (1979). Job demands, job decision latitude, and mental strain: Implications for job redesign. *Administrative Science Quarterly, 24,* 285–307.

Karacek, R. (1981). Job socialization and job strain: The implication of two related psychosocial mechanisms for job design. In B. Gardell & G. Johansson (Eds.), *Working life* (pp. 75–94). New York: Wiley.

Karasu, T. B. (1986). The psychotherapies: Benefits and limitations. *American Journal of Psychotherapy, 15,* 324–342.

Karney, B. R., Bradbury, T. N., Fincham, F. D., & Sullivan, K. T. (1994). The role of negative affectivity in the association between attributions and marital satisfaction. *Journal of Personality and Social Psychology, 66,* 413–424.

Karni, A., Tanne, D., Rubenstein, B. S., Askenasy, J. J. M., & Sagi, D. (1994). Overnight improvement in a perceptual skill. *Science, 265,* 679–681.

Karon, B. P. (1995). Provision of psychotherapy under managed health care: A growing crisis and national nightmare. *Professional Psychology, 26,* 5–9.

Katicibasi, C. (1995). Is psychology relevant to global human development issues? Experiences from Turkey. *American Psychologist, 50,* 293–300.

Katicibasi, C. (1996). *Family and human development across cultures.* Hillsdale, NJ: Erlbaum.

Katigbak, M. S., Church, A. T., & Akamine, T. X. (1996). Cross-cultural generalizability of personality dimensions: Relating indigenous and imported dimensions in two cultures. *Journal of Personality and Social Psychology, 70,* 99–114.

Katz, A. N. (1995). Inexpensive animal learning exercises for huge introductory psychology classes. In M. E. Ware & D. E. Johnson (Eds.), *Handbook of demonstrations and activities in psychology (Vol. 1).* Hillsdale, NJ: Erlbaum.

Katz, I., Wackenhut, J., & Hass, R. G. (1986). Racial ambivalence, value duality, and behavior. In J. F. Dovidio & S. L. Gaertner (Eds.), *Prejudice, discrimination, and racism.* New York: Academic Press.

Katz, L., & Chard, S. (1989). *Engaging the minds of young children: The project approach.* Norwood, NJ: Ablex.

Katz, R., & Rolde, E. (1981). Community alternatives to psychotherapy. *Psychotherapy: Theory, Research, and Practice, 18,* 365–374.

Keating, D. P. (1991). Cognition, adolescent. In R. M. Lerner, A. C. Petersen, & J. Brooks-Gunn (Eds.), *Encyclopedia of adolescence* (Vol. 1). New York: Garland.

Keil, F. C. (1989). *Concepts, kinds, and cognitive development.* Cambridge, MA: MIT Press.

Keith-Spiegel, P. (1991). *The complete guide to graduate school admission: Psychology and related fields.* Hillsdale, NJ: Erlbaum.

Kelley, H. H., & Thibaut, J. (1978). *Interpersonal relations: A theory of interdependence.* New York: Wiley.

Kelly, J. A., & Murphy, D. A. (1992). Psychological intervention with AIDS and HIV: Prevention and treatment. *Journal of Consulting and Clinical Psychology, 60,* 576–585.

Kennedy, P. G. E., & Fok-Seang, J. F. (1986). Studies on the development, antigenic phenotype and function of human glial cells in tissue culture. *Brain, 109,* 1261–1277.

Kenrick, D. T. (1987). Gender, genes, and the social environment. In P. C. Shaver & C. Hendrick (Eds.), *Review of Personality and Social Psychology, 8,* 14–43.

Kephart, W. M. (1967). Some correlates of romantic love. *Journal of Marriage and the Family, 29,* 470–474.

Kiecolt-Glaser, J. K., Dura, J. R., Speicher, C. E., Trask, O. J., & Glaser, R. (1991). Spousal caregivers of dementia victims: Longitudinal changes in immunity and health. *Psychosomatic Medicine, 53,* 345–362.

Kiecolt-Glaser, J. K., & Glaser, R. (1988). Behavioral influences on immune function. In T. Field, P. McCabe, & N. Schneiderman (Eds.), *Stress and coping across development.* Hillsdale, NJ: Erlbaum.

Kilbourne, B., & Richardson, J. T. (1984). Psychotherapy and new religions in a pluralistic society. *American Psychologist, 39* (3), 237–251.

Kimble, C. E. (1990). *Social psychology: Studying human interaction.* Dubuque, IA: Wm. C. Brown.

Kimble, G. A. (1961). *Hilgard and Marquis's conditioning and learning.* New York: Appleton-Century-Crofts.

Kimble, G. A. (1989). Psychology from the standpoint of a generalist. *American Psychologist, 44,* 491–499.

Kimble, G. A., Boneau, C. A., & Wertheimer, M. (1996). *Portraits of pioneers in psychology (Vol. II).* Washington, DC: American Psychological Association.

Kimble, M., McFadden, S. H., Ellor, J. W., & Seeber, J. J. (Eds.). (1995). *Handbook on religion, spirituality, and aging.* Minneapolis: Fortress Press.

Kimmel, A. (1996). *Ethical issues in behavioral research.* Cambridge, MA: Blackwell.

Kimmel, E. B., & Garco, M. G. (1991, August). *The experience of feminism by women of color.* Paper presented at the meeting of the American Psychological Association, San Francisco.

Kimmel, H. D. (1989). The importance of classical conditioning. *Behavioral and Brain Sciences, 12,* 147.

Kimura, D. (1989, November). How sex hormones boost—or cut—intellectual ability. *Psychology Today,* pp. 62–66.

King, B. M. (1996). *Human sexuality today (2nd ed.).* Upper Saddle River, NJ: Prentice Hall.

King, H. E. (1961). Psychological effects of excitation of the limbic system. In D. E. Sheer (Ed.), *Electrical stimulation of the brain.* Austin: University of Texas Press.

King, L. (1991). *Investigations in the relations, predictive validity and implications of implicit and explicit motives.* Unpublished dissertation, University of California, Davis.

King, L. A., & Pennebaker, J. W. (1995). Thinking about goals, glue, and the meaning of life. In R. S. Wyer (Ed.), *Ruminative thoughts.* Hillsdale, NJ: Erlbaum.

King, P. (1988). Heavy metal music and drug use in adolescents. *Postgraduate Medicine, 83,* 295–304.

Kinnaird, M. F. (1996). Indonesia's hornbill haven. *Natural History, 86,* 40–46.

Kinsey, A. C., Pomeroy, W. B., & Martin, E. E. (1948). *Sexual behavior in the human male.* Philadelphia: W. B. Saunders.

Kitayama, S., & Markus, H. R. (Eds.). (1994). *Emotion and culture.* Washington, DC: American Psychological Association.

Kitayama, S., & Markus, H. R. (in press). A cultural perspective on self-conscious emotions. In J. P. Tangney & K. W. Fisher (Eds.), *Shame, guilt, embarrassment, and pride.* New York: Guilford Press.

Kitchin, R. M. (1994). Cognitive maps: What are they and why study them? *Journal of Environmental Psychology, 14,* 1–20.

Klahr, D. (1989). Information-processing approaches. In R. Vasta (Ed.), *Six theories of child development: Revised formulations and current issues.* Greenwich, CT: JAI Press.

Klatsky, R. L. (1984). *Memory and awareness.* New York: W. H. Freeman.

Klein, R. G. (1996). Comments on expanding the clinical role of psychologists. *American Psychologist, 51,* 216–218.

Kleinke, C. L. (1994). *Common principles of psychotherapy.* Pacific Grove, CA: Brooks/Cole.

Kleinman, A. (1988). *Rethinking psychiatry.* New York: Macmillan.

Kline, N. (1962). Drugs are the greatest practical advance in the history of psychiatry. *New Medical Material, 4,* 49.

Kling, J. W. (1995). Demonstration experiments in learned taste aversion. In M. E. Ware & D. E. Johnson (Eds.), *Demonstrations and activities in teaching of psychology (Vol. 2).* Hillsdale, NJ: Erlbaum.

Klinger, E. (1987). The interview questionnaire technique: Reliability and validity of a mixed idiographic-nomothetic measure of motivation. In J. N. Butcher & C. D. Spielberger (Eds.), *Advances in personality assessment* (Vol. 6, pp. 32–48). Hillsdale, NJ: Erlbaum.

Klivington, K. (1989). *The science of mind.* Cambridge, MA: MIT Press.

Klonoff, E. A. (1991, August). *Ethnicity and women's health: The neglected women.* Paper presented at the meeting of the American Psychological Association, San Francisco.

Klonoff-Cohen, H. S., Edelstein, S. L., Lefkowitz, E. S., Srinivasan, I. P., Kaegi, D., Chang, J. C., & Wiley, K. J. (1995). The effect of passive smoke and tobacco exposure through breast milk on sudden infant death syndrome. *Journal of the American Medical Association, 293,* 795–798.

Kluft, R. P. (1995, August). *Evaluating hypnotically and nonhypnotically influenced memories in clinical and forensic contexts.* Paper presented at the meeting of the American Psychological Association, New York City.

Knesper, D. J., Pagnucco, D. J., & Wheeler, J. R. C. (1985). Similarities and differences across mental health services providers and practice settings in the United States. *American Psychologist, 40,* 1352–1369.

Knight, B. G., Teri, L., Wohlford, P., & Santos, J. (Eds.) (1996). *Mental health services for older adults.* Washington, DC: American Psychological Association.

Knight, R. A., Rosenberg, R., & Schneider, B. (1985). Classification of sexual offenders: Perspectives, methods, and validation. In A. W. Burgess (Ed.), *Rape and sexual assault.* New York: Garland.

Kobak, R., & Cole, C. (1993). Attachment and meta-monitoring: Implications for adolescent autonomy and psychopathology. In D. Cicchetti (Ed.), *Rochester Symposium on Development and Psychopathology. Vol. 5: Disorders of the Self.* Rochester, NY: University of Rochester Press.

Kobasa, N., Maddi, S., & Kahn, S. (1982). Hardiness and health. A prospective study. *Journal of Personality and Social Psychology, 42,* 168–177.

Kobasa, S. C., Maddi, S. R., Puccetti, M. C., & Zola, M. (1985). Relative effectiveness of hardiness, exercise, and social support as resources against illness. *Journal of Psychosomatic Research, 29,* 525–533.

Koenig, H. G., Kvale, J. N., & Ferrel, C. (1988). Religion and well-being in later life. *Gerontologist, 28* (1), 18–28.

Koenig, H. G., Smiley, M., & Gonzales, J. A. P. (1988). *Religion, health, and aging: A review and theoretical integration.* New York: Greenwood Press.

Koenig, W. D., Mumme, R. L., & Pitelka, F. A. (1984). The breeding system of the acorn woodpecker in central coastal California, *Z. Tierpsychol., 65,* 289–308.

Kogan, N., & Black, K. (in press). *Gender and aging.* Cambridge, MA: Blackwell.

Kohlberg, L. (1966). A cognitive-developmental analysis of children's sex-role concepts and attitudes. In E. E. Maccoby (Ed.), *The development of sex differences.* Palo Alto, CA: Stanford University Press.

Kohlberg, L. (1969). Stage and sequence: The cognitive-developmental approach to socialization. In D. A. Goslin (Ed.), *Handbook of socialization theory and research* (p. 379). Chicago: Rand McNally.

Kohlberg, L. (1976). Moral stages and moralization: The cognitive-developmental approach. In T. Lickona (Ed.), *Moral development and behavior.* New York: Holt, Rinehart & Winston.

Kohlberg, L. (1986). A current statement on some theoretical issues. In S. Modgil & C. Modgil (Eds.), *Lawrence Kohlberg.* Philadelphia: Falmer Press.

Kohlenberg, R. J., Tsai, M., & Kohlenberg, B. S. (1996). Functional analysis in behavior therapy. In M. Hersen & P. M. Miller (Eds.), *Progress in behavior modification (Vol. 30).* Pacific Grove, CA: Brooks/Cole.

Kohler, W. (1925). *The mentality of apes.* New York: Harcourt Brace Jovanovich.

Kohn, A, & Kalat, J. W. (1995). Preparing for an important event: Demonstrating the modern view of classical conditioning. In M. E. Ware & D. E. Johnson (Eds.), *Demonstrations and activities in teaching of psychology (Vol. 2).* Hillsdale, NJ: Erlbaum.

Kohout, J., Wicherski, M., & Pion, G. (1991). *Characteristics of graduate departments of psychology: 1988–89.* Washington, DC: American Psychological Association Education Directorate.

Kohut, H. (1977). *Restoration of the self.* New York: International Universities Press.

Kolb, B. (1989). Brain development, plasticity, and behavior. *American Psychologist, 44,* 1203–1212.

Kolb, L. (1973). *Modern clinical psychiatry* (8th ed.). Philadelphia: W. B. Saunders.

Koocher, G. P., & Keith-Spiegel, P. (1996). *Ethics in psychology.* New York: Oxford University Press.

Kopp, C. B. (1994). *Baby steps.* New York: W. H. Freeman.

Kopp, C. B., & Kaler, S. R. (1989). Risk in infancy: Origins and implications. *American Psychologist, 44,* 224–230.

Korchin, S. J. (1976). *Modern clinical psychology: Principles of intervention in the clinic and community.* New York: Basic Books.

Korman, M. (1974). National conference on levels and patterns of professional training in psychology: The major themes. *American Psychologist, 29,* 441–449.

Kornetsky, C. (1986, August). *Effects of opiates and stimulants on brain stimulation: Implications for abuse.* Paper presented at the meeting of the American Psychological Association, Washington, DC.

Koss, M. P. (1990). The women's mental health research agenda: Violence against women. *American Psychologist, 45,* 374–381.

Koss, M. P. (1993, August). *Sex gone wrong: Current perspectives on rape and sexual harassment.* Paper presented at the meeting of the American Psychological Association, Toronto.

Kosslyn, S. M. (1995). *Image and brain.* Cambridge, MA: MIT Press.

Kosslyn, S. M., Chabris, C. F., & Baker, D. P. (1995). Neural network models as evidence for different types of visual representation. *Cognitive Science, 19,* 575–580.

Krause, N., Jay, G., & Liang, J. (1991). Financial strain and psychological well-being among the American and Japanese elderly. *Psychology and Aging, 6,* 171–181.

Kristiansen, C. M., Hovdestad, W., Gareau, C., Mittleholt, J., & DeCourville, N. E. (1995, August). *Survivors' memory process.* Paper presented at the meeting of the American Psychological Association, New York City.

Kristof, A. L. (1996). Person-organization fit: An integration review of its conceptualization, measurement, and implications. *Personnel Psychology, 49,* 1–51.

Kübler-Ross, E. (1974). *Questions and answers on death and dying.* New York: Macmillan.

Kubovy, M. (1988). *The psychology of perspective and Renaissance art.* New York: Cambridge University Press.

Kulik, J. A., Bangert-Drowns, R. L., & Kulik, C. C. (1984). The effectiveness of coaching for aptitude tests. *Psychological Bulletin, 95,* 179–188.

Kulik, J. A., Kulik, C. C., & Bangert-Drowns, R. L. (1985). Effectiveness of computer-based education in elementary schools. *Computers in Human Behavior, 1,* 59–74.

Kulik, J. A., Mahler, H. I. M., & Earnest, A. (1994). Social comparison and affiliation under threat: Going beyond the affiliate-choice paradigm. *Journal of Personality and Social Psychology, 66,* 301–309.

Kupersmidt, J. B., & Patterson, C. (1993, March). *Developmental patterns of peer relations and aggression in the prediction of externalizing behavior problems.* Paper presented at the biennial meeting of the Society for Research in Child Development, New Orleans.

Kutchinsky, B. (1992). The child sexual abuse panic. *Nordisk Sexoligi, 10,* 30–42.

Kuyken, W., & Brewin, C. R. (1995). Autobiographical memory functioning in depression and reports of early abuse. *Journal of Abnormal Psychology, 104,* 585–591.

LaBerge, S. P. (1985). *Lucid dreaming.* Los Angeles: Tarcher.

Labouvie-Vief, G. (1986, August). *Modes of knowing and life-span cognition.* Paper presented at the meeting of the American Psychological Association, Washington, DC.

Ladany, N., Hill, C. E., Corbett, M. M., & Nutt, E. A. (1996). Nature, extent, and importance of what psychology trainees do not disclose to their supervisors. *Journal of Counseling Psychology, 43,* 10–24.

Ladd, G. W., & Le Sieur, K. D. (1995). Parents and children's peer relationships. In M. H. Bornstein (Ed.), *Children and parenting* (Vol. 4). Hillsdale, NJ: Erlbaum.

Lai, J., & Linden, W. (1993). The smile of Asia: Acculturation effects on symptom reporting. *Canadian Journal of Behavioural Research, 25,* 303–315.

LaJoie, S. P., & Derry, S. J. (1993). *Computers as cognitive tools.* Hillsdale, NJ: Erlbaum.

Lam, R. W., Goldner, E. M., & Grewal, A. (1996). Seasonality of symptoms in anorexia and bulimia nervosa. *Eating Disorders, 19,* 35–44.

Lamb, C. S., Jackson, L. A., Cassiday, P. B., & Priest, D. J. (1993). Body figure preferences of men and women: A comparison of two generations. *Sex Roles, 28,* 345–358.

Lamb, M. E., Frodi, A. M., Hwang, C. P., Frodi, M., & Steinberg, J. (1982). Mother- and father-infant interaction involving play and holding in traditional and nontraditional Swedish families. *Developmental Psychology, 18,* 215–221.

Lamberton, L., & Minor, L. (1995). *Human relations.* Burr Ridge, IL: Irwin.

Landrine, H. (Ed.). (1995). *Bringing cultural diversity to feminist psychology.* Washington, DC: American Psychological Association.

Lane, H. (1976). *The wild boy of Aveyron.* Cambridge, MA: Harvard University Press.

Lange, C. G. (1922). *The emotions.* Baltimore: Williams & Wilkins.

Langs, R. (1978). *Technique in transition.* New York: Jason Aronson.

La Pera, G., & Nicastro, A. (1996). A new treatment for premature ejaculation: The rehabilitation of the pelvic floor. *Journal of Sex & Marital Therapy, 22,* 22–26.

LaPerriere, A. R., Antoni, M. H., Schneiderman, N., Ironson, G., Klimas, N., Caralis, P., & Fletcher, M. A. (1990). Exercise intervention attenuates emotional distress and natural killer cell decrements following notification of positive serologic status for HIV-A. *Biofeedback and Self-Regulation, 15,* 229–242.

LaPiere, R. (1934). Attitudes versus actions. *Social Forces, 13,* 230–237.

Larson, J. H. (1988). The Marriage Quiz: College students' beliefs in selected myths about marriage. *Family Relations, 37,* 3–11.

Lashley, K. (1929). *Brain mechanisms and intelligence.* Chicago: University of Chicago Press.

Lashley, K. S. (1950). In search of the engram. In *Symposium of the Society for Experimental Biology* (Vol. 4). New York: Cambridge University Press.

Latané, B. (1981). The psychology of social impact. *American Psychologist, 36,* 343–356.

Latané, B. (1996). Strength from weakness: The fate of opinion minorities in spatially distributed groups. In E. H. Witte & J. H. Davis (Eds.), *Understanding group behavior (Vol. 1).* Hillsdale, NJ: Erlbaum.

Lau, R. R. (1988). Beliefs about control and health behavior. In D. S. Gochman (Ed.), *Health behavior: Emerging perspectives.* New York: Plenum.

Laughlin, P. L. (1996). Group decision making and quantitative judgments. In E. H. Witte & J. H. Davis (Eds.), *Understanding group behavior (Vol. 1).* Hillsdale, NJ: Erlbaum.

Lavine, L. O., & Lombardo, J. P. (1984). Self-disclosure: Intimate and non-intimate disclosures to parents and best friends as a function of Bem sex-role category. *Sex Roles, 11,* 735–744.

Lazarus, A. A. (1996). A multimodal behavior therapist's perspective on truth. In G. Corey (Ed.), *Case approach to counseling and psychotherapy (4th ed.).* Pacific Grove, CA: Brooks/Cole.

Lazarus, R. S. (1984). On the primacy of cognition. *American Psychologist, 39,* 124–129.

Lazarus, R. S. (1993). Coping theory and research: Past, present, and future. *Psychosomatic Medicine, 55,* 234–247.

Lazarus, R. S. (1993). From psychological stress to the emotions: A history of a changing outlook. *Annual Review of Psychology, 44,* 1–21.

Leach, P. (1990). *Your baby and child: From birth to age five.* New York: Knopf.

Leahey, T. H., & Harris, R. J. (1989). *Human learning* (2nd ed.). Englewood Cliffs, NJ: Prentice Hall.

Leary, M. R., Nezlek, J. B., Downs, D., Radford-Davenport, J., Martin, J., & McMullen, A. (1994). Self-presentation in everyday interactions: Effects of target familiarity and gender composition. *Journal of Personality and Social Psychology, 67,* 664–673.

LeBoeuf, B. J., & Peterson, R. S. (1969). Social status and mating activity in elephant seals. *Science, 163,* 91–93.

Lebow, J. L., & Gurman, A. S. (1995). Research assessing couple and family therapy. *Annual Review of Psychology, 46,* Palo Alto, CA: Annual Reviews.

Lecci, L., Okun, M. A., & Karoly, P. (1994). Life regrets and current goals as predictors of psychological adjustment. *Journal of Personality and Social Psychology, 66,* 731–741.

Lee, D. J., & Hall, C. C. I. (1994). Being Asian in North America. In W. J. Lonner & R. Malpass (Eds.), *Psychology and culture.* Needham Heights, MA: Allyn & Bacon.

Lee, I., Hsieh, C., & Paffenbarger, O. (1995). Exercise intensity and longevity in men. *Journal of the American Medical Association, 273,* 1179–1184.

LeFromboise, T., & Trimble, J. (1996). Multicultural counseling theory and American-Indian populations. In D. W. Sue (Ed.), *Theory of multicultural counseling and therapy.* Pacific Grove, CA: Brooks/Cole.

Leinster, C. (1988, January 18). Black executives: How they're doing. *Fortune* pp. 109–120.

Lenneberg, E. (1967).*The biological foundations of language.* New York: Wiley.

Lenneberg, E. H., Rebelsky, F. G., & Nichols, I. A. (1965). The vocalization of infants born to deaf and hearing parents. *Human Development, 8,* 23–27.

Leong, F. (1996). Multicultural counseling theory and Asian-American populations. In D. W. Sue (Ed.), *Theory of multicultural counseling and therapy.* Pacific Grove, CA: Brooks/Cole.

Lepper, M., Greene, D., & Nisbett, R. E. (1973). Undermining children's intrinsic interest with extrinsic rewards. *Journal of Personality and Social Psychology, 28,* 129–137.

Lerman, H., & Porter, N. (Eds.). (1990). *Feminist ethics in psychotherapy.* New York: Springer.

Lerner, H. G. (1989). *The dance of intimacy.* New York: Harper & Row.

Lerner, P., & Lerner, H. (1989). Rorschach measures of psychoanalytic theories of defense. In J. N. Butcher & C. D. Spielberger (Eds.), *Advances in Personality Assessment* (Vol. 8). Hillsdale, NJ: Erlbaum.

Lerner, R. M., Petersen, A. C., & Brooks-Gunn, J. (Eds.). (1991). *Encyclopedia of Adolescence.* New York: Garland.

Lester, B. M., Freier, K., & LcGasse, K. (1995). Prenatal cocaine exposure and child outcome: How much do we really know? In M. Lewis & M. Bendersky (Eds.), *Mothers, babies, and cocaine.* Hillsdale, NJ: Erlbaum.

Levant, R. (1996). The male code and parenting: A psychoeducational approach. In M. P. Andronico (Ed.), *Men in groups.* Washington, DC: American Psychological Association.

LeVay, S. (1991). A difference in hypothalamic structure between heterosexual and homosexual men. *Science, 253,* 1034–1037.

Leventhal, H., & Tomarken, A. J. (1986). Emotion: Today's problems. *Annual Review of Psychology, 37,* 565–610.

Levin, I., & Louviere, J. (1981). Psychological contributions to travel demand modeling. In I. Altman, J. F. Wohlwill, & P. B. Everett (Eds.), *Transportation and behavior.* New York: Plenum Press.

Levin, J. S. (Ed.). (1994). *Religion in aging and health.* Thousand Oaks, CA: Sage.

Levin, J. S., Taylor, R. J., & Chatters, L. M. (1994). Race and gender differences in religiosity among older adults: Findings from four national surveys. *Journal of Gerontology, 49,* S137–S145.

Levine, R. V., Martinez, T. S., Brase, G., & Sorenson, K. (1994). Helping in 36 U.S. cities. *Journal of Personality and Social Psychology, 67,* 69–82.

LeVine, S. (1979). *Mothers and wives: Gusii women of East Africa.* Chicago: University of Chicago Press.

Levinson, D. (1978). *The seasons of a man's life.* New York: Knopf.

Levinson, D. J. (1987, August). *The seasons of a woman's life.* Paper presented at the meeting of the American Psychological Association, New York.

Levy, L. (1979). Handwriting and hiring. *Dun's Review, 113,* 72–79.

Levy, L. H. (1984). The metamorphosis of clinical psychology: Toward a new charter as Human Services Psychology. *American Psychologist, 39,* 486–494.

Levy, S. M., Herberman, R. B., Lee, J., Whiteside, T., Kirkwood, J., & McFeeley, S. (1990). Estrogen receptor concentration and social factors as predictors of natural killer cell activity in early-stage breast cancer patients. *Natural Immunity and Cell Growth Regulation, 9,* 313–324.

Lewin, R. (1988). Brain graft puzzles. *Science, 240,* 879.

Lewinsohn, P. M. (1987). The Coping with Depression course. In R. F. Mu/at/noz (Ed.), *Depression prevention.* New York: Hemisphere.

Lewinsohn, P. M., Antonuccio, D. O., Steinmetz, J., & Teri, L. (1984). *The coping with depression course: A psychoeducational intervention for unipolar depression.* Eugene, OR: Castalia.

Lewis, M., Feiring, C., McGuffog, C., & Jaskir, J. (1984). Predicting psychopathology in six-year-olds from early social relations. *Child Development, 55,* 123–136.

Lieberman, M. A., Yalom, I. D., & Miles, M. B. (1973). *Encounter groups: First facts.* New York: Basic Books.

Liebert, R. M., & Sprafkin, J. (1988). *The early window* (3rd ed.). New York: Pergamon.

Liebkind, K. (1996). Acculturation and stress: Vietnamese refugees in Finland. *Journal of Cross-Cultural Psychology, 27,* 161–180.

Light, L. L., & Carter-Sobell, L. (1970). Effects of changed semantic context on recognition memory. *Journal of Verbal Learning and Verbal Behavior, 9,*1–11.

Limber, S. P., & Flekkoy, M. G. (1995, Winter). The U.N. Convention on the rights of the child: Its relevance for social scientists. *Social Poplicy Report, Society for Research in Child Development, Vol. 9.* No. 2, 1–15.

Linn, M. C., & Hyde, J. S. (1991). Cognitive and psychosocial gender differences, trends in. In R. M. Lerner, A. C. Petersen, & J. Brooks-Gunn (Eds.), *Encyclopedia of adolescence* (Vol. 1). New York: Garland.

Lipsey, M. W., & Wilson, D. B. (1993). The efficacy of psychological, educational, and behavioral treatment: Confirmation from meta-analyses. *American Psychologist, 48,* 1181–1209.

Little, B. (1995, August). *Influence of intermediaries and groups on the quality of person-environment transactions.* Paper presented at the meeting of the American Psychological Association, New York City.

Little, B. R. (1989). Personal projects analysis: Trivial pursuits, magnificent obsessions, and the search for coherence. In D. M. Buss & N. Cantor (Eds.), *Personality psychology: Recent trends and emerging directions* (pp. 15–31). New York: Springer-Verlag.

Livesley, W. J. (Ed.). (1995). *The DSM-IV personality disorders.* New York: Guilford.

Locke, E. A., & Latham, G. P. (1990). *A theory of goal setting and task performance.* Englewood Cliffs, NJ: Prentice Hall.

Loehlin, J. (1995, August). *Genes and environment in The Bell Curve.* Paper presented at the meeting of the American Psychological Association, New York City.

Loehlin, J. C. (1992). *Genes and environment in personality development.* Newbury Park, CA: Sage.

Loehr, J. (1989, May). [Personal communication.] United States Tennis Association Training Camp, Saddlebrook, FL.

Lofland, J., & Stark, R. (1965). Becoming a world-saver: A theory of conversion to a deviant perspective. *American Sociological Review, 30,* 862–875.

Loftus, E. F. (1975). Spreading activation within semantic categories: Comments on Rosch's "Cognitive representations of semantic categories." *Journal of Experimental Psychology, 104,* 234–240.

Loftus, E. F. (1979). *Eyewitness testimony.* Cambridge, MA: Harvard University Press.

Loftus, E. F. (1980). *Memory.* Reading, MA: Addison-Wesley.

Loftus, E. F. (1993). Psychologists in the eyewitness world. *American Psychologist, 48,* 550–552.

Loftus, E. F. (1993). The reality of repressed memories. *American Psychologist, 48,* 518–537.

Logue, A. W. (1995). *Self-control.* Upper Saddle River, NJ: Prentice Hall.

Lollis, C. M., Johnson, E. H., Antoni, M. H., & Hinkle, Y. (1996). Characteristics of African Americans with multiple risk factors associated with HIV/AIDS. *Journal of Behavioral Medicine, 19,* 55–72.

Long, B. (1986). The prevention of mental-emotional disabilities: A report from a National Mental Health Association Commission. *American Psychologist, 41,* 825–829.

Long, D., Elkind, D., & Spilka, B. (1967). The child's conception of prayer. *Journal for the Scientific Study of Religion, 6,* 101–109.

Long, T., & Long, L. (1984). *The handbook for latchkey children and their parents.* New York: Berkeley.

Lonner, W. J. (1988). *The introductory psychology text and cross-cultural psychology: A survey of cross-cultural psychologists.* Bellingham, WA: Western Washington University, Center for Cross-Cultural Research.

Lonner, W. J. (1990). An overview of cross-cultural testing and assessment. In R. W. Brislin (Ed.), *Applies cross-cultural psychology.* Newbury Park, CA: Sage.

Lonner, W. J., & Malpass, R. (1994). *Psychology and culture.* Needham Heights, MA: Allyn & Bacon.

Lopez, S., Grover, K. P., Holland, D., Johnson, M. J., Kain, C. D., Kanel, K., Mellins, C. A., Rhyne, M. C. (1989). Development of culturally sensitive psychotherapists. *Professional Psychology: Research and Practice, 6,* 369–376.

Lore, R. K., & Schultz, L. A. (1993). Control of human aggression: A comparative perspective. *American Psychologist, 48,* 16–25.

Lorenz, K. Z. (1965). *Evolution and modification of behavior.* Chicago: University of Chicago Press.

Lorenz, K. Z. (1966). *On aggression.* San Diego: Harcourt Brace Jovanovich.

Lorian, R. P. (1996). Applying our medicine to the psychopharmacology debate. *American Psychologist, 51,* 219–224.

Lorian, R. P., Iscoe, I., DeLeon, P. H., & VandenBos, G. R. (1996). *Psychology and public policy.* Washington, DC: American Psychological Association.

Lourenco, O., & Machado, A. (1996). In defense of Piaget's theory: A reply to 10 common criticisms. *Psychological Review, 103,* 143–164.

Lowman, R. L. (1991). *The clinical practice of career assessment.* Washington, DC: American Psychological Association.

Ludolph, P. (1982, August). *A reanalysis of the literature on multiple personality.* Paper presented at the American Psychological Association, Washington, DC.

Luria, A., & Herzog, E. (1985, April). *Gender segregation across and within settings.* Paper presented at the biennial meeting of the Society for Research in Child Development, Toronto.

Lussier, R. (1996). *Human relations in organizations (3rd ed.).* Burr Ridge, IL: Irwin.

Lykken, D. T. (1985). The probity of the polygraph. In S. M. Kassin & L. S. Wrightsman (Eds.), *The psychology of evidence and trial procedure.* Beverly Hills, CA: Sage.

Lykken, D. T. (1987, Spring). The validity of tests: Caveat emptor. *Jurimetrics Journal,* pp. 263–270.

Lykken, D. T. (1987). The probity of the polygraph. In S. M. Kassin & L. S. Wrightsman (Eds.), *The psychology of evidence and trial procedure.* Beverly Hills, CA: Sage.

Lyman, S. M., & Scott, M. B. (1967). Territoriality: A neglected sociological dimension. *Social Problems, 15,* 235–249.

Lynch, G. (1990, June). *The many shapes of memory and the several forms of synaptic plasticity.* Paper presented at the meeting of the American Psychological Society, Dallas.

Lynch, K. (1960). *The image of the city.* Cambridge, MA: MIT Press.

Lynn, S. J., Rhue, J. W., & Spanos, N. P. (1994). Hypnosis. In *The Encyclopedia of Human Behavior.* New York: Academic Press.

Maarse, G., & Lyons, C. (1992, April). *Growing up gay and lesbian: Implications for psychotherapy integration.* Discussion Group at the Annual Convention of the Society for the Exploration of Psychotherapy Integration, San Diego.

Maccoby, E. E. (1980). *Social development.* San Diego: Harcourt Brace Jovanovich.

Maccoby, E. E. (1987, November). Interview with Elizabeth Hall: All in the family. *Psychology Today,* pp. 54–60.

Maccoby, E. E. (1990, June). *Gender and relationships: A developmental account.* Paper presented at the meeting of the American Psychological Society, Dallas.

Maccoby, E. E. (1992). Trends in the study of socialization: Is there a Lewinian heritage? *Journal of Social Issues, 48,* 171–185.

Maccoby, E. E. (1993, March). *Trends and issues in the study of gender role development.* Paper presented at the biennial meeting of the Society for Research in Child Development, New Orleans.

Maccoby, E. E. (1995). The two sexes and their social systems. In P. Moen, G. H. Elder, & K. Luscher (Eds.), *Examining lives in context.* Washington, DC: American Psychological Association.

Maccoby, E. E., & Jacklin, C. N. (1974). *The psychology of sex differences.* Palo Alto, CA: Stanford University Press.

Maccoby, E. E., & Jacklin, C. N. (in press). Gender segregation in childhood. In H. Reese (Ed.), *Advances in child development and behavior* (Vol. 20). New York: Academic Press.

Maccoby, E. E., & Martin, J. A. (1983). Socialization in the context of the family: Parent-child interaction. In P. H. Mussen (Ed.), *Handbook of child psychology* (4th ed., Vol. 4). New York: Wiley.

Macdonald, J. E. (1994). *The restorative effects of a vacation from work: The role of novelty, positive affect, and nature.* Unpublished doctoral dissertation, University of Victoria.

Mace, W. M. (1974). Ecologically stimulating cognitive psychology: Gibsonian perspective. In W. B. Weimer & D. S. Palermo (Eds.), *Cognition and the symbolic processes.* Hillsdale, NJ: Erlbaum.

MacPhee, D., Fritz, J. J., & Miller-Heyl, J. (1993, March). *Ethnic variations in social support networks and child rearing.* Paper presented at the biennial meeting of the Society for Research in Child Development, New Orleans.

MacWhinney, B., & Chang, F. (1995). Connectionism and language learning. In C. A. Nelson (Ed.), *Basic and applied perspectives on learning, cognition, and development.* Hillsdale, NJ: Erlbaum.

Maddi, S. (1989). *Theories of personality* (5th ed.). Homewood, IL: Dorsey.

Maddi, S. (1996). *Personality theories (6th ed.).* Pacific Grove, CA: Brooks/Cole.

Mader, S. (1996). *Biology* (5th ed.). Dubuque, IA: Wm. C. Brown Publishers.

Magee, W. J. (1996). Agoraphobia, simple phobia, and social phobia in the national comorbidity survey. *Archives of General Psychiatry, 68,* 87–99.

Mager, R. F. (1972). *Goal analysis.* Belmont, CA: Fearon.

Mahoney, G. J. (1995, March). *The maternal behavior rating scale.* Paper presented at the meeting of the Society for Research in Child Development, Indianapolis.

Mahoney, M. J. (1989). Sport psychology. In *The G. Stanley Hall Lecture Series* (Vol. 9). Washington, DC: American Psychological Association.

Mahoney, M. J. (1991). *Human change processes: The scientific foundations of psychotherapy.* New York: Basic Books.

Mahoney, M. J. (1993). Introduction to special section: Theoretical developments in the cognitive psychotherapies. *Journal of Consulting and Clinical Psychology, 61,* 187–193.

Mahoney, M. J., Gabriel, T. J., & Perkins, T. S. (1987). Psychological skills and exceptional athletic performance. *The Sport Psychologist, 1,* 181–199.

Maier, N. R. F. (1931). Reasoning in humans. *Journal of Comparative Psychology, 12,* 181–194.

Malamuth, N. M., & Donnerstein, E. (Eds.). (1983). *Pornography and sexual aggression.* New York: Academic Press.

Malatesta, C. (1990, May 28). Commentary. *Newsweek,* p. 61.

Malinowski, B. (1927). *Sex and repression in savage society.* New York: Humanities Press.

Mandler, G. (1980). Recognizing: The judgment of previous occurrence. *Psychological Review, 87,* 252–271.

Mandler, G. (1984). *Mind and body.* New York: Norton.

Mandler, G. (1996). The situation of psychology: Landmarks and choicepoints. *American Journal of Psychology, 109,* 1–35.

Mandler, J. M. (1990). A new perspective on cognitive development. *American Scientist, 78,* 236–243.

Mandler, J. M. (in press-a). How to build a baby. II: Conceptual primitives. *Psychological Review.*

Mandler, J. M. (in press-b). The foundations of conceptual thought in infancy. *Cognitive Development.*

Mann, J. J., Malone, K. M., Diehl, D. J., Perel, J., Cooper, T. B., & Mintun, M. A. (1996). Demonstration of in vivo reduced serotonin responsivity in the brain of untreated depressed patients. *The American Journal of Psychiatry, 153,* 174–182.

Manning, A. (1989). The genetic bases of aggression. In J. Groebel & R. A. Hinde (Eds.), *Aggression and war: Their biological and social bases.* New York: Cambridge University Press.

Maracek, J. (1995). Gender, politics, and psychology's ways of knowing. *American Psychologist, 50,* 162–163.

Marecek, J., & Hare-Mustin, R. (1991). A short history of the future: Feminism and clinical psychology. *Psychology of Women Quarterly, 15,* 521–536.

Marin, G. (1993). Defining culturally appropriate community interventions: Hispanics as a case study. *Journal of Community Psychology,* 149–161.

Marin, G. (1994). The experience of being a Hispanic in the United States. In W. J. Lonner & R. Malpass (Eds.), *Psychology and culture.* Needham Heights, MA: Allyn & Bacon.

Marklein, M. B., & DeRosa, R. (1991, November 19). Magic's HIV affects health educators' game plans. *USA Today,* p. 8D.

Marks, I. M. (1987). *Fears, phobias, and rituals.* New York: Oxford University Press.

Marks, M. A., & Nelson, E. S. (1993). Sexual harassment on campus: Effects of professor gender on perception of sexually harassing behaviors. *Sex Roles, 28,* 207–218.

Markus, H. R., & Kitayama, S. (1991). Culture and the self: Implications for cognition, emotion, and motivation. *Psychological Review, 98,* 224–253.

Marler, P. (1995). Rating the Thorndike inheritance: By worth or by weight? *Contemporary Psychology, 40,* 11–14.

Marler, P., & Mundinger, P. (1971). Vocal learning in birds. In H. Moltz (Ed.), *Ontogeny of vertebrate behavior* (pp. 389–449). New York: Academic Press.

Marr, D. (1982). *Vision.* New York: W. H. Freeman.

Marsella, A. J., Friedman, M. J., Gerrity, E. T., & Scurfield, R. M. (Eds.) (1996). *Ethnocultural aspects of posttraumatic stress disorder.* Washington, DC: American Psychological Association.

Marsh, H. W. (1994). Relations between global and specific domains of self: The importance of individual importance, certainty, and ideals. *Journal of Personality and Social Psychology, 65,* 975–992.

Marshall, G. N., Wortman, C. B., Vickers, R. R., Kusulas, J. W., & Hervig, L. K. (1994). The five-factor model of personality as a framework for personality-health research. *Journal of Personality and Social Psychology, 67,* 278–286.

Marsiske, M., Lang, F. R., Baltes, P. B., & Baltes, M. M. (1995). Selective optimization with compensation. In R. A. Dixon & L. Backman (Eds.), *Compensating for psychological deficits and declines.* Hillsdale, NJ: Erlbaum.

Martin, C. L. (1993, March). *The influence of children's theories about groups on gender-based inferences.* Paper presented at the biennial meeting of the Society for Research in Child Development, New Orleans.

Martin, D. W. (1996). *Doing psychology experiments (4th ed.).* Pacific Grove, CA: Brooks/Cole.

Martin, G. L., & Pear, J. (1996). *Behavior modification (5th ed.).* Upper Saddle River, NJ: Prentice Hall.

Maslow, A. H. (1954). *Motivation and personality.* New York: Harper & Row.

Maslow, A. H. (1971). *The farther reaches of human nature.* New York: Viking.

Masters, W. H. (1993, August). *Sex therapy: Past, present, and future.* Paper presented at the meeting of the American Psychological Association, Toronto.

Masters, W. H., & Johnson, V. E. (1966). *Human sexual response.* Boston: Little, Brown.

Matas, L., Arend, R. A., & Sroufe, L. A. (1978). Continuity in adaptation: Quality of attachment and later competence. *Child Development, 49,* 547–556.

Matlin, M. (1989). *Cognition* (2nd ed.). New York: Holt, Rinehart & Winston.

Matlin, M. W. (1988). *Perception.* Needham Heights, MA: Allyn & Bacon.

Matlin, M. W. (1993). *The psychology of women* (2nd ed.). Fort Worth, TX: Harcourt Brace.

Maton, K. I., & Salem, D. A. (1995). Organizational characteristics of empowering community settings. *American Journal of Community Psychology, 23,* 631–636.

Matsumoto, D. (1989). Cultural influences on the perception of emotion. *Journal of Cross-Cultural Psychology, 20,* 92–105.

Matsumoto, D. (1994). *People: Psychology from a cultural perspective.* Pacific Grove, CA: Brooks/Cole.

Matsumoto, D. (1996). *Culture and psychology.* Pacific Grove, CA: Brooks/Cole.

Maupin, R. J. (1993). How can women's lack of upward mobility in accounting organizations be explained? Male and female accountants respond. *Group and Organization Management, 18,* 132**152.**

Mayer, F. S., & Sutton, K. (1996). *Theories of personality (2nd ed.).* Upper Saddle River, NJ: Prentice Hall.

Mayo, E. (1933). *The human problems of an industrial organization.* New York: Macmillan.

Mays, V., Caldwell, C. H., & Jackson, J. S. (1996). Mental health symptoms and service utilization patterns of help-seeking among Black women. In H. W. Neighbors & J. S. Jackson (Eds.), *Mental health in Black America.* Newbury Park, CA: Sage.

McAleer, N. (1989, April). On creativity. *Omni.* pp. 42–44, 98–102.

McAuley, E., & Duncan, T. E. (1991). The causal attribution process in sport and physical activity. In S. Graham & V. S. Folkes (Eds.), *Attribution theory: Applications to achievement, mental health, and interpersonal conflict.* Hillsdale, NJ: Erlbaum.

McBurney, D. H. (1996). *How to think like a psychologist.* Upper Saddle River, NJ: Prentice Hall.

McCallister, B. J. (1995). Cognitive theory and religious experience. In R. Hood, Jr., (Ed.), *Handbook of religious experience.* Birmingham, AL: Religious Education Press.

McClearn, G. C. (1976). Experimental behavior genetics. In D. Bartrop (Ed.), *Aspects of genetics in pediatrics.* London: Fellowship of Postdoctorate Medicine.

McClelland, D. C. (1955). Some social consequences of achievement motivation. In M. R. Jones (Ed.), *Nebraska Symposium on Motivation.* Lincoln: University of Nebraska Press.

McClelland, D. C. (1978). Managing motivation to expand human freedom. *American Psychologist, 33,* 201–210.

McClelland, D. C. (1985). *Human motivation.* Glenview, IL: Scott, Foresman.

McClelland, D. C., Atkinson, J. W., Clark, R., & Lowell, E. L. (1953). *The achievement motive.* New York: Appleton-Century-Crofts.

McClelland, J. L., & Rumelhart, D. E. (1986). *Parallel distributed processing: Explorations in the micro-structure of cognition* (Vol. 2). Cambridge, MA: MIT Press.

McClintock, C. G., & Allison, S. T. (1989). Social value orientation and helping behavior. *Journal of Applied Social Psychology, 19,* 353–362.

McClintock, M. K. (1971). Menstrual synchrony and suppression. *Nature, 229, 244–245.*

McConaghy, N. (1993). *Sexual behavior: Problems and management.* New York: Plenum.

McCormick, E. J. (1976). *Human factors in engineering and design.* New York: McGraw-Hill.

McDaniel, M., Waddill, P., & Shakesby, P. (1995). Study strategies, interest, and learning from text. In D. Hermann, C. McEvoy, C. Hertzog, P. Hertel, & M. Johnson (Eds.), *Basic and applied memory research (Vol. 1).* Hillsdale, NJ: Erlbaum.

McDaniel, M. A., & Pressley, M. (1987). *Imagery and related mnemonic processes.* New York: Springer-Verlag.

McDaniel, M. A., Whetzel, D. L., Schmidt, F. L., & Maurer, S. D. (1994). The validity of employment interviews: A comprehensive review and meta-analysis. *Journal of Applied Psychology, 79,* 599–616.

McDougall, W. (1908). *Social psychology.* New York: G. Putnam & Sons.

McDowell, C., & Acklin, M. W. (1996). Standardizing procedures for calculating Rorschach interrater reliability. *Journal of Personality Assessment, 66,* 308–320.

McGaugh, J. L., Bermudez-Rattoni, F., & Prado-Alcala, R. A. (Eds.) (1995). *Plasticity in the central nervous system.* Hillsdale, NJ: Erlbaum.

McGill, T. (1996). Commentary. In L. C. Drickamer & S. H. Vessey (Eds.), *Animal behavior* (4th ed.). Dubuque, IA: Wm. C. Brown.

McGrath, E., Keita, G. P., Strickland, B., & Russo, N. F. (1990). *Women and depression: Risk factors and treatment issues.* Washington, DC: American Psychological Association.

McGrath, J. E., Kelly, J. R., & Rhodes, J. E. (1993). A feminist perspective on research methodology. In S. Oskamp & M. Costanzo (Eds.), *Gender issues in contemporary society.* Newbury Park, CA: Sage.

McGue, M., & Carmichael, C. M. (1995). Life-span developmental psychology: A behavior-genetic perspective. In L. F. Dilla and S. M. C. Dollinger (Eds.), *Assessment of biological mechanisms across the life span.* Hillsdale, NJ: Erlbaum.

McGuffin, P. (1996). A hospital-based twin registry study of the heritability of DMS-IV unipolar depression. *Archives of General Psychiatry, 68,* 55–64.

McGuire, W. J. (1989). The structure of individual attitudes and of attitude systems. In A. R. Pratkanis, S. J. Breckler, & A. G. Greenwald (Eds.), *Attitude structure and function.* Hillsdale, NJ: Erlbaum.

McIver, T. (1988). Backward masking and other backward thoughts about music. *Skeptical Inquirer, 13,* 50–63.

McKinlay, S. M., & McKinlay, J. B. (1984). *Health status and health care utilization by menopausal women.* Unpublished manuscript, Cambridge Research Center, American Institutes for Research, Cambridge, MA.

McKnight, C. C., Crosswhite, F. J., Dossey, J. A., Kifer, E., Swafford, J. O., Travers, K. J., & Cooney, T. J. (1987). *The underachieving curriculum: Assessing U.S. school mathematics from an international perspective.* Champaign, IL: Stipes.

McLaughlin, B. (1987). *Theories of second language learning.* London: Edward Arnold.

McLoyd, V. C., & Ceballo, R. (1995, March). *Conceptualizing economic context.* Paper presented at the meeting of the Society for Research in Child Development, Indianapolis.

McMillan, B., Florin, P., Stevenson, J., Kenman, B., & Mitchell, R. E. (1995). Empowerment praxis in community coalitions. *American Journal of Community Psychology, 23,* 699–728.

McNeil, E. B. (1967). *The quiet furies.* Englewood Cliffs, NJ: Prentice Hall.

McReynolds, P. (1996). Lightner Witmer: A centennial tribute. *American Psychologist, 51,* 237–240.

Mead, M. (1928). *Coming of age in Samoa.* New York: Morrow.

Meara, N. M., Schmidt, L. D., & Day, J. D. (1996). A foundation for ethical decisions, policies, and character. *The Counseling Psychologist, 24,* 4–77.

Medvedev, A. A. (1974). The nucleic acids in the development of aging. In B. L. Strehler (Ed.), *Advances in gerontological research* (Vol. 1). San Diego: Academic Press.

Meehl, P. E. (1962). Schizotoma, schizotypy, schizophrenia. *American Psychologist, 17,* 827–838.

Meehl, P. E. (1986). Diagnostic taxa as open concepts. In T. Millon & G. I. Klerman (Eds.), *Contemporary directions in psychopathology.* New York: Guilford Press.

Mehrabian, A., & Wiener, M. (1967). Decoding of inconsistent communications. *Journal of Personality and Social Psychology, 6,* 109–114.

Mehrabian, A., & Russell, J. A. (1974). *An approach to environmental psychology.* Cambridge, MA: MIT Press.

Meichenbaum, D. (1977). *Cognitive-behavior modification: An integrative approach.* New York: Plenum Press.

Meichenbaum, D. (1986). Cognitive behavior modification. In F. H. Kanfer & A. P. Goldstein (Eds.), *Helping people change: A textbook of methods.* New York: Pergamon.

Meichenbaum, D. (1993). Changing conceptions of cognitive behavior modification: Retrospect and prospect. *Journal of Consulting and Clinical Psychology, 61,* 202–204.

Meichenbaum, D., Turk, D., & Burstein, S. (1975). The nature of coping with stress. In I. Sarason & C. Spielberger (Eds.), *Stress and anxiety.* Washington, DC: Hemisphere.

Meltzoff, A., & Kuhl, P. (1989). Infants' perceptions of faces and speech sounds: Challenges to developmental theory. In P. R. Zelazo & R. Barr (Eds.), *Challenges to developmental paradigms.* Hillsdale, NJ: Erlbaum.

Melzack, R. (1973). *The puzzle of pain.* New York: Basic Books.

Melzack, R., & Wall, P. D. (1965). Pain mechanisms: A new theory. *Science, 150,* 971–979.

Melzack, R., & Wall, P. D. (1983). *The challenge of pain.* New York: Basic Books.

Mercer, J. R., & Lewis, J. F. (1978). *System of multicultural pluralistic assessment.* New York: Psychological Corporation.

Merritt, A. C., & Helmreich, R. L. (1996). Human factors on the flight deck: The influence of national culture. *Journal of Cross-Cultural Psychology, 27,* 5–24.

Mervis, J. (1986, July). NIMH data point way to effective treatment. *APA Monitor, 17,* 1, 13.

Messinger, J. C. (1971). Sex and repression in an Irish folk community. In D. S. Marshall & R. C. Suggs (Eds.), *Human sexual behavior: Variations in the ethnic spectrum.* New York: Basic Books.

Metalsky, G. I., Joiner, T. E., Hardin, T. S., & Abramson, L. Y. (1993). Depressive reactions to failure in a naturalistic setting. *Journal of Abnormal Psychology, 102,* 101–109.

Meyer, K. A., Borgealt, D. A., Zurazesei, R. M., & Forshaun, S. (1996, March). *Attributions concerning adolescent suicide: The impact of gender, method, and outcome.* Paper presented at the meeting of the Society for Research on Adolescence, Boston.

Meyer, R. G., & Osborne, Y. V. H. (1982). *Case studies in abnormal behavior.* Boston: Allyn & Bacon.

Meyers, J. (1985). *Hemingway* (p. 559). New York: Harper & Row.

Mezzich, J. E., Fabegra, H., & Kleinman, A. (in press). On enhancing the cultural sensitivity of DSM-IV. *Journal of Nervous and Mental Disease.*

Michael, R. T., Gagnon, J. H., Laumann, E. O., & Kolata, G. (1994). *Sex in America.* Boston: Little, Brown.

Michaels, J. W., Bloomel, J. M., Brocato, R. M., Linkous, R. A., & Rowe, J. S. (1982). Social facilitation and inhibition in a natural setting. *Replications in Social Psychology, 2,* 21–24.

Michelozzi, B. N. (1996). *Coming alive from nine to five: The career search handbook.* Mountain View, CA: Mayfield.

Michelson, W. (1977). *Environmental choice, human behavior and residential satisfaction.* New York: Oxford University Press.

Milgram, S. (1963). Behavioral study of obedience. *Journal of Abnormal and Social Psychology, 67,* 171–178.

Milgram, S. (1965). Some conditions of obedience and disobedience to authority. *Human Relations, 18,* 56–76.

Milgram, S. (1970). The experience of living in cities. *Science, 167,* 1461–1468.

Milgram, S. (1974). *Obedience to authority.* New York: Harper & Row.

Milgram, S., Liberty, H. J., Toledo, R., & Wackenhut, J. (1986). Response to intrusion in waiting lines. *Journal of Personality and Social Psychology, 51,* 683–689.

Miller, A. S., & Hoffman, J. P. (1995). Risk and religion: An explanation of gender differences in religiosity. *Journal for the Scientific Study of Religion, 34,* 63–75.

Miller, D. B. (1995). The nature-nurture issue: Lessons from the Pillsbury doughboy. In M. E. Ware & D. E. Johnson (Eds.), *Demonstrations and activities in teaching of psychology.* Hillsdale, NJ: Erlbaum.

Miller, G. A. (1956). The magical number seven, plus or minus two: Some limits on our capacity for information processing. *Psychological Review, 48,* 337–442.

Miller, G. A. (1981). *Language and speech.* New York: W. H. Freeman.

Miller, H. L. (1996). Clinical and biochemical effects of catecholamine depletion on antidepressant-induced remission of depression. *Archives of General Psychiatry, 68,* 38–54.

Miller, J. B. (1976). *Toward a new psychology of women.* Boston: Beacon Press.

Miller, J. B. (1986). *Toward a new psychology of women* (2nd ed.). Boston: Beacon Press.

Miller, J. G. (1995, March). *Culture, context, and personal agency: The cultural grounding of self and morality.* Paper presented at the meeting of the Society for Research in Child Development, Indianapolis.

Miller, N. E. (1941). The frustration-aggression hypothesis. *Psychological Review, 48,* 337–442.

Miller, N. E. (1959). Liberalization of basic S-R concepts: Extension to conflict behavior, motivation, and social learning. In S. Koch (Ed.), *Psychology: A study of science.* New York: McGraw-Hill.

Miller, N. E. (1969). Learning of visceral glandular responses. *Science, 163,* 434–445.

Miller, N. E. (1985). The value of behavioral research on animals. *American Psychologist, 40,* 432–440.

Miller, S. A., & Harley, J. P. (1996). *Zoology (3rd ed.).* Dubuque, IA: Wm. C. Brown.

Miller, S. K., & Slap, G. B. (1989). Adolescent smoking: A review of prevalence and prevention. *Journal of Adolescent Health Care, 10,* 129–135.

Miller, W. R., & Jackson, K. A. (1995). *Practical psychology for pastors (2nd ed.).* Upper Saddle River, NJ: Prentice Hall.

Miller-Jones, D. (1989). Culture and testing. *American Psychologist, 44,* 360–366.

Milligan, S. E. (1990). Understanding diversity of the urban black aged: Historical perspectives. In Z. Harel, E. A. McKinney, & M. Williams (Eds.), *Black aged.* Newbury Park, CA: Sage.

Milner, P. M. (1996). Neural representations: Some old problems revisited. *Journal of Cognitive Neuroscience, 8,* 78–82.

Minkler, M. (1989). Health education, health promotion and the open society: An historical perspective. *Health Education Quarterly, 16,* 17–30.

Mintz, N., & Schwartz, D. (1964). Urban ecology and psychosis: Community factors in the incidence of schizophrenia and manic-depression among Italians in Greater Boston. *International Journal of Social Psychiatry, 10,* 101–118.

Minuchin, P. (1985). Families and individual development: Provocations from the field of family therapy. *Child Development, 56,* 289–302.

Mischel, W. (1968). *Personality and assessment.* New York: Wiley.

Mischel, W. (1970). Sex-typing and socialization. In P. H. Mussen (Ed.), *Manual of child psychology* (3rd ed., Vol. 2). New York: Wiley.

Mischel, W. (1973). Toward a cognitive social learning reconceptualization of personality. *Psychological Review, 80,* 252–283.

Mischel, W. (1994, August). *From good intentions to willpower.* Paper presented at the meeting of the American Psychological Association, Los Angeles.

Mischel, W. (1995, August). *Cognitive-affective theory of person-environment psychology.* Paper presented at the meeting of the American Psychological Association, New York City.

Mischel, W., & Baker, N. (1975). Cognitive transformations of reward objects through instructions. *Journal of Personality and Social Psychology, 31,* 254–261.

Mischel, W., Ebbesen, E. B., & Zeiss, A. R. (1972). Cognitive and attentional mechanisms in delay of gratification. *Journal of Personality and Social Psychology, 21,* 204–218.

Mischel, W., Peake, P. K., & Zeiss, A. R. (1984). *Longitudinal studies of delay behavior.* Unpublished manuscript, Stanford University.

Mischel, W., & Shoda, Y. (in press). A cognitive-affective system theory of personality: Reconceptualizing the invariances in personality and the role of situations. *Psychological Review.*

Mishkin, M., & Appenzellar, T. (1987). The anatomy of memory. *Scientific American, 256,* 80–89.

Moates, D. R., & Schumacher, G. M. (1980). *An introduction to cognitive psychology.* Belmont, CA: Wadsworth.

Monagle, K. (1990, October). Women around the world. *New Woman,* pp. 195–197.

Money, J. (1986). *Lovemaps: Clinical concepts of sexual/erotic health and pathology, paraphilia, and gender transposition in childhood, adolescence, and maturity.* New York: Irvington.

Montano, D., & Adamopoulos, J. (1984). The perception of crowding in interpersonal situations: Affective and behavioral responses. *Environment and Behavior, 16,* 643–666.

Montemayor, R., & Flannery, D. J. (1991). Parent-adolescent relations in middle and late adolescence. In R. M. Lerner, A. C. Petersen, & J. Brooks-Gunn (Eds.), *Encyclopedia of adolescence* (Vol. 2). New York: Garland.

Moore, E. O. (1982). A prison environment's effect on health care service demands. *Journal of Environmental Systems, 11,* 17–34.

Moore-Ede, M. C., Sulzman, F. M., & Fuller, C. A. (1982). *The clocks that time us.* Cambridge, MA: Harvard University Press.

Moos, R., & Moos, B. (1984). The process of recovery from alcoholism: III. Comparing functioning in families of alcoholics and matched control families. *Journal of Studies on Alcohol, 45,* 111–118.

Moos, R. H. (1986). Work as a human context. In M. S. Pallack & R. Perloff (Eds.), *Psychology and work: Productivity, change, and employment.* Washington, DC: American Psychological Association.

Moos, R. H., & Lemke, S. (1984). *Multiphasic environmental assessment procedure.* Unpublished manuscript, Stanford University, Social Ecology Laboratory, Palo Alto, CA.

Mori, D., Chaiken, S., & Pliner, P. (1987). "Eating lightly" and the self-presentation of femininity. *Journal of Personality and Social Psychology, 53,* 693–702.

Morris, D. (1977). *Manwatching.* New York: Abrams.

Morris, D., Collett, P., Marsh, P., & O'Shaugnessy, M. (1979). *Gestures.* New York: Stein & Day.

Morrow, L. (1988, August 6). Through the eyes of children. *Time,* pp. 32–33.

Moscovici, S. (1985). Social influence and conformity. In G. Lindzey & E. Aronson (Eds.), *Handbook of social psychology* (3rd ed., Vol. 2). New York: Random House.

Moses, J., Steptoe, A., Mathews, A., & Edwards, S. (1989). The effects of exercise training on mental well-being in the normal population: A controlled trial. **Journal of Psychosomatic Research, 33,** 47–61.

Moskowitz, D. S., Suh, E. J., & Desaulniers, J. (1994). Situational influences on gender differences in agency and communion. *Journal of Personality and Social Psychology, 66,* 753–761.

Moulton, D. G. (1977). Minimum odorant concentrations detectable by the dog and their implications for olfactory receptor sensitivity. In D. Miller-Schwarze & M. M. Mozell (Eds.), *Chemical signals in vertebrates* (pp. 455–464). New York: Plenum.

Mountcastle, V. B. (1986, August). *The parietal visual system and optic flow.* Paper presented at the annual meeting of the American Psychological Association, Washington, DC.

Mowday, R. T., & Sutton, R. I. (1993). Organizational behavior: Linking individuals and groups to organizational contexts. *Annual Review of Psychology, 44,* 195–229.

Moyer, D. M. (1995). An opposing view on prescription privileges for psychologists. *Professional Psychology, 26,* 586–590.

Munroe, R. H., Himmin, H. S., & Munroe, R. L. (1984). Gender understanding and sex role preference in four cultures. *Developmental Psychology, 20,* 673–682.

Munroe, R. L., & Munroe, R. H. (1975). *Cross-cultural human development.* Monterey, CA: Brooks/Cole.

Murphy, H. B. (1978). Cultural factors in the genesis of schizophrenia. In D. Rosenthal & S. S. Kety (Eds.), *The transmission of schizophrenia.* Elmsford, NY: Pergamon Press.

Murphy, K. R. (1993). *Honesty in the workplace.* Pacific Grove, CA: Brooks/Cole.

Murphy, S. T., & Zajonc, R. B. (1993). Affect, cognition, and awareness: Affective priming with optimal and suboptimal stimulus exposures. *Journal of Personality and Social Psychology, 64,* 723–739.

Murray, H. A. (1938). *Explorations in personality.* New York: Oxford University Press.

Murray, H. A., & Morgan, C. (1935). *The thematic apperception test.* Cambridge, MA: Harvard University Press.

Murray, S. L., & Holmes, J. G. (1992). Seeing virtues in faults: Negativity and the transformation of interpersonal narratives in close relationships. *Journal of Personality and Social Psychology, 65,* 707–722.

Murray, V. M. (1996, March). *Sexual and motherhood statuses: Subsequent life experiences of African-American high school graduates.* Paper presented at the meeting of the Society for Research on Adolescence, Boston.

Murstein, B. I., & Mathes, S. (1996). Projection on projective techniques = pathology: The problem that is not being addressed. *Journal of Personality Assessment, 66,* 337–351.

Mussen, P. H., Honzik, M., & Eichorn, D. (1982). Early adult antecedents of life satisfaction at age 70. *Journal of Gerontology, 37,* 316–322.

Muuss, R. E. (1989). *Theories of adolescence* (15th ed.). New York: Random House.

Myers, D. G. (1993). *The pursuit of happiness.* New York: William Morrow.

Myers, D. G., & Diener, E. (1995). Who is happy? *Psychological Science, 6,* 10–19.

Myers, N. A., Clifton, R. K., & Clarkson, M. G. (1987). When they were very young: Almost-threes remember two years ago. *Infant Behavior and Development, 10,* 123–132.

NAEYC (1996). NAEYC position statement: Responding to linguistic and cultural diversity—recommendations for effective early childhood education. *Young Children, 51,* 4–12.

Nagata, D. K. (1989). Japanese American children and adolescents. In J. T. Gibbs & L. N. Huang (Eds.), *Children of color.* San Francisco: Jossey-Bass.

Naisbitt, J., & Aburdene, P. (1990). *Megatrends 2000.* New York: William Morrow.

Nakayama, K. (1994). James J. Gibson—An appreciation. *Psychological Review, 101,* 329–335.

Nash, B. C. (1981). The effects of classroom spatial organization on four- and five-year-old children's learning. *British Journal of Educational Psychology, 51,* 144–155.

Natalie, E. J. (1996). Gendered issues in the workplace. In J. T. Wood (Ed.), *Gendered relationships.* Mountain View, CA: Mayfield.

Nathan, P. E. (1994). DSM-IV: Empirical, accessible, not yet ideal. *Journal of Clinical Psychology, 50,* 103–109.

National Academy of Sciences, National Research Council. (1989). *Diet and health: Implications for reducing chronic disease risk.* Washington, DC: National Academy Press.

National Advisory Council on Economic Opportunity. (1980). *Critical choices for the 80s.* Washington, DC: U.S. Government Printing Office.

National Center for Health Statistics. (1989, June). *Statistics on marriage and divorce.* Washington, DC: U.S. Government Printing Office.

Neighbors, H. W., & Jackson, J. S. (Eds.) (1996). *Mental health in Black America.* Newbury Park, CA: Sage.

Neill, S. (1982). Experimental alterations in playroom layout and their effect on staff and child behavior. *Educational Psychology, 2,* 103–119.

Neisser, U. (1982). Snapshots or benchmarks? In U. Neisser (Ed.), *Memory observed: Remembering in natural contexts* (pp. 43–48). San Francisco: W. H. Freeman.

Neisser, U., Boodoo, G., Bouchard, T. J., Boykin, A. W., Brody, N., Ceci, S. J., Halpern, D. F., Loehlin, J. C., Perloff, R., Sternberg, R. J., & Urbina S. (1996). Intelligence: Knowns & unknowns. *American Psychologist, 51,* 77–101.

Neisser, U., Winograd, E., & Weldon, M. S. (1991, November). *Remembering the earthquake: "What I experienced" versus "How I heard the news."* Paper presented at the 32nd annual meeting of the Psychonomic Society, San Francisco.

Nelson, T. O. (1996). Consciousness and metacognition. *American Psychologist, 51,* 102–116.

Neugarten, B. L. (1964). *Personality in middle and late life.* New York: Atherton Press.

Neugarten, B. L. (1980). Must everything be a mid-life crisis? Annual editions, *Human Development 80/81.* Guilford, CT: Dushkin.

Neugarten, B. L. (1986). The aging society. In A. Pifer & L. Bronte (Eds.), *Our aging society: Paradox and promise.* New York: W. W. Norton.

Neugarten, B. L. (1988, August). *Policy issues for an aging society.* Paper presented at the meeting of the American Psychological Association, Atlanta.

Nevo, B. (1986). *Scientific aspects of graphology.* Springfield, IL: Charles C Thomas.

Newell, A., & Simon, H. A. (1972). *Human problem solving.* Englewood Cliffs, NJ: Prentice Hall.

Newell, P. B. (1995). Perspectives on privacy. *Journal of Environmental Psychology, 15,* 87–104.

Newman, E. (1974). *Strictly speaking.* Indianapolis: Bobbs-Merrill.

Newman, J. (1995). How breast milk protects newborns. *Scientific American, 273,* 76–79.

Nickels, W. G., McHugh, J. M., & McHugh, S. M. (1996). *Understanding business (4th ed.).* Burr Ridge, IL: Irwin.

Ninio, A., & Snow, C. E. (1996). *Pragmatic development.* Boulder, CO: Westview Press.

Nisbett, R. E., Fong, G. T., Lehman, D. R., & Cheng, P. W. (1987). Teaching reasoning. *Science, 238,* 625–631.

Nisbett, Richard E. (1972, November). Hunger, obesity, and the ventromedial hypothalamus. *Psychological Review, 79,* 433–453.

Nolen-Hoeksema, S. (1990). *Sex differences in depression.* Stanford, CA: Stanford University Press.

Noonan, K. M. (1987). Evolution: A primer for psychologists. In C. Crawford, M. Smith, & D. Krebs (Eds.), *Sociobiology and psychology.* Hillsdale, NJ: Erlbaum.

Norem, J. K., & Cantor, N. (1986). Anticipatory and post-hoc cushioning strategies: Optimism and defensive pessimism in "risky" situation. *Cognitive Therapy Research, 10,* 347–362.

Norton, R., & Brenders, D. (1995). *Communication and consequences.* Hillsdale, NJ: Erlbaum.

Nosworthy, G. J., Lea, J. A., & Lindsay, C. L. (1995). Opposition to affirmative action: Racial affect and traditional value predictors across four programs. *Journal of Applied Social Psychology, 25,* 314–337.

Notarius, C. I. (1996). Marriage: Will I be happy or sad? In N. Vanzetti & S. Duck (Eds.), *A lifetime of relationships.* Pacific Grove, CA: Brooks/Cole.

Nottelman, E. D., Susman, E. J., Blue, J. H., Inoff-Germain, G., Doran, L. D., Loriaux, D. L., Cutler, G. B., & Chrousos, G. P. (1987). Gonadal and adrenal hormone correlates of adjustment in early adolescence. In R. M. Lerner & T. T. Foch (Eds.), *Biological-psychological interactions in early adolescence.* Hillsdale, NJ: Erlbaum.

Novak, C. A. (1977). Does youthfulness equal attractiveness? In L. E. Troll, J. Israel, & K. Israel (Eds.), *Looking ahead: A woman's guide to the problems and joys of growing older.* Englewood Cliffs, NJ: Prentice Hall.

Novak, W. (1983). *The great man shortage.* New York: Rawson.

Novlin, D., Robinson, B. A., Culbreth, L. A., & Tordoff, M. G. (1983). Is there a role for the liver in the control of food intake? *American Journal of Clinical Nutrition, 9,* 233–246.

O'Brien, E. J., & Myers, J. L. (1985). When comprehension difficulty improves memory for text. *Journal of Experimental Psychology: Learning, Memory, and Cognition, 11,* 12–21.

O'Brien, T. G., & Charlton, S. G. (1995). *Handbook of human factors testing and evaluation.* Hillsdale, NJ: Erlbaum.

O'Connor, B. P., Davidson, H., & Gifford, R. (1991). Window view, social exposure and nursing home adaptation. *Canadian Journal of Aging, 10,* 216–223.

O'Connor, S. C., & Rosenblood, L. K. (1996). Affiliation motivation in everyday experience: A theoretical comparison. *Journal of Personality and Social Psychology, 70,* 513–522.

O'Donahue, W., & Krasner, L. (Eds.). (1995). *Theories of behavior therapy.* Washington, DC: American Psychological Association.

O'Hara, J. M., Stubler, W. F., & Higgins, J. C. (1995). Human factors evaluation of advanced nuclear power plants. In T. G. O'Brien & S. G. Charlton (Eds.), *Handbook of human factors testing and evaluation.* Hillsdale, NJ: Erlbaum.

O'Neil, J. M. (1996). The gender role journey workshop. In M. P. Andronico (Ed.), *Men in groups.* Washington, DC: American Psychological Association.

Oatley, K., & Jenkins, J. M. (1996). *Understanding emotions.* Cambridge, MA: Blackwell.

Obler, L. K. (1993). Language beyond childhood. In J. B. Gleason (Ed.), *The development of language* (3rd ed.). New York: Macmillan.

Offer, D., Ostrov, E., Howard, K. I., & Atkinson, R. (1988). *The teenage world: Adolescents' self-image in ten countries.* New York: Plenum.

Offer, D., & Church, R. B. (1991). Turmoil, adolescent. In R. M. Lerner, A. C. Petersen, & J. Brooks-Gunn (Eds.), *Encyclopedia of adolescence* (Vol. 2). New York: Garland.

Ogbu, J. U. (1989, April). *Academic socialization of Black children: An inoculation against future failure?* Paper presented at the meeting of the Society for Research in Child Development, Kansas City.

Okabe, A., Aoki, K., & Hamamoto, W. (1986). Distance and direction judgment in a large-scale natural environment: Effects of a slope and winding trail. *Environment and Behavior, 18,* 755–772.

Oldman, J. M., Hollander, E., & Skodal, A. E. (Eds.) (1996). *Impulsivity and compulsivity.* Washington, DC: American Psychiatric Association.

Olds, J. M. (1958). Self-stimulation experiments and differentiated reward systems. In H. H. Jasper, L. D. Proctor, R. S. Knighton, W. C. Noshay, R. T. Costello (Eds.), *Reticular formation of the brain.* Boston: Little, Brown.

Olds, J. M., & Milner, P. M. (1954). Positive reinforcement produced by electrical stimulation of the septal area and other areas of the rat brain. *Journal of Comparative and Physiological Psychology, 47,* 419–427.

Oller, D. K. (1995, February). *Early speech and word learning in bilingual and monolingual children: Advantages of early bilingualism.* Paper presented at the meeting of the American Association for the Advancement of Science, Atlanta.

Olson, H. C., & Burgess, D. M. (1996). Early intervention with children prenatally exposed to alcohol and other drugs. In M. J. Guralnick (Ed.), *The effectiveness of early intervention.* Baltimore, MD: Paul Brookes.

Olson, J. M., & Zanna, M. P. (1993). Attitudes and attitude change. *Annual Review of Psychology, 44,* 117–154.

Omata, K. (1995). Territoriality in the house and its relationship to the use of rooms and the psychological well-being of Japanese married women. *Journal of Environmental Psychology, 15,* 147–154.

Ones, D., Viswesvaran, C., & Schmidt, F. (1993). Meta-analysis of integrity test validities: Findings and implications for personnel selection and theories of job performance. *Journal of Applied Psychology, 78,* 679–703.

Ones, D. S., Mount, M. K., Barrick, M. R., & Hunter, J. E. (1994). Personality and job performance: A critique of the Tett, Jackson, and Rothstein (1991) meta-analysis. *Personnel Psychology, 47,* 147–156.

Oostveen, T., Knibbe, R., & de Vries, H. (1996). Social influences on young adults' alcohol consumption: Norms, modeling, pressure, socializing, and conformity. *Addictive Behaviors, 21,* 187–198.

Orne, M. T. (1959). The nature of hypnosis: Artifact and essence. *Journal of Abnormal and Social Science, 58,* 277–299.

Ornstein, P. A. (1995, March). *Remembering the distant past.* Paper presented at the meeting of the Society for Research in Child Development, Indianapolis.

Ornstein, R., & Sobel, D. (1989). *Healthy pleasures.* Reading, MA: Addison-Wesley.

Orwell, G. (1949). *Nineteen Eighty-Four.* New York: Harcourt, Brace.

Oser, F., & Gmunder, P. (1991). *Religious judgment: A developmental perspective.* Birmingham, AL: Religious Education Press.

Osgood, C. E. (1962). *An alternative to war or surrender.* Urbana, IL: University of Illinois Press.

Oskamp, S. (1988). Nontraditional employment opportunities for applied psychologists. *American Psychologist, 43,* 484–485.

Ozer, D. J., & Reise, S. P. (1994). Personality assessment. *Annual Review of Psychology, 45,* 357–388.

Padilla, A. (Ed.). (1994). *Hispanic psychology.* Newbury Park, CA: Sage.

Padilla, A. M. (1980). The role of cultural awareness and ethnic loyalty in acculturation. In A. M. Padilla (Ed.), *Acculturation.* Boulder, CO: Westview.

Padilla, A. M. (Ed.). (1995). *Hispanic psychology.* Newbury Park, CA: Sage.

Paffenbarger, R. S., Hyde, R. T., Wing, A. L., & Hsieh, C. (1986). Physical activity, all-cause mortality, and longevity of college alumni. *New England Journal of Medicine, 314,* 605–612.

Pahnke, W. N. (1970). Drugs and mysticism. In B. Aaronson & H. Osmond (Eds.), *Psychedelics: The uses and implications of hallucinogenic drugs* (pp. 145–165). New York: Doubleday.

Paivio, A. (1971). *Imagery and verbal processes.* New York: Holt, Rinehart & Winston.

Paivio, A. (1986). *Mental representations: A dual coding approach.* New York: Oxford University Press.

Palmer, S., Schreiber, C., & Fox, C. (1991, November). *Remembering the earthquake: "Flashbulb" memory for experienced versus reported events.* Paper presented at the 32nd annual meeting of the Psychonomic Society, San Francisco.

Paloutzian, R. (1996). *Invitation to the psychology of religion* (2nd ed.). Needham Heights, MA: Allyn & Bacon.

Paloutzian, R. F. (1996). *Invitation to the psychology of religion* (2nd ed.). Needham Heights, MA: Allyn & Bacon.

Paloutzian, R. F., & Ellison, C. W. (1982). Loneliness, spiritual well-being, and the quality of life. In L. A. Peplau & D. Perlman (Eds.), *Loneliness: A sourcebook of current theory, research, and therapy* (pp. 224–237). New York: Wiley-Interscience.

Paludi, M. A. (1992). *The psychology of women.* Dubuque, IA: Wm. C. Brown.

Paludi, M. A. (1995). *The psychology of women* (2nd ed.). Madison, WI: Brown & Benchmark.

Paludi, M. A. (in press). *Ivory power: Sexual harassment on campus.* Albany, NY: SUNY Press.

Parducci, A. (1996). *Happiness, pleasure, and judgment.* Hillsdale, NJ: Erlbaum.

Pargament, K. E., & Park, C. L. (1995). Merely a defense? Examining psychologists' stereotype of religion. *Journal of Social Issues.*

Pargament, K. I. (1992). Of means and ends: Religion and the search for significance. *International Journal for the Psychology of Religion, 2* (4), 201–229.

Parham, T. (1996). Multicultural counseling theory and African-American populations. In D. W. Sue (Ed.), *Theory of multicultural counseling and therapy.* Pacific Grove, CA: Brooks/Cole.

Parham, T. A., & McDavis, R. J. (1993). Black men, an endangered species: Who's really pulling the trigger. In D. R. Atkinson, G. Morten, & D. W. Sue (Eds.), *Counseling American minorities.* Dubuque, IA: Wm. C. Brown.

Paris, S. G., & Lindauer, B. K. (1982). The development of cognitive skills during childhood. In B. B. Wolman (Ed.), *Handbook of developmental psychology.* Englewood Cliffs, NJ: Prentice Hall.

Park, D. C. (1992). Applied cognitive aging research. In F. I. M. Craik & T. A. Salthouse (Eds.), *The handbook of aging and cognition.* Hillsdale, NJ: Erlbaum.

Park, D. C. (in press). *The cognitive psychology of aging.* Cambridge, MA: Blackwell.

Parke, R. D. (1993, March). *Family research in the 1990s.* Paper presented at the biennial meeting of the Society for Research in Child Development, New Orleans.

Parke, R. D. (1996, June). *Tracking families across contexts.* Paper presented at the Family Research Summer Consortium, San Diego.

Parker, J. G., & Gottman, J. M. (1989). Social and emotional development in a relational context: Friendship interaction from early childhood to adolescence. In T. J. Berndt & G. W. Ladd (Eds.), *Peer relations in child development.* New York: Wiley.

Parkin, A. J. (1984). Levels of processing, context, and facilitation of pronunciation. *Acta Psychologica, 55,* 19–29.

Parkin, A. J. (1996). *Explorations in cognitive neuropsychology.* Cambridge, MA: Blackwell.

Parlee, M. B. (1979, April). The friendship bond: PT's survey report on friendship in America. *Psychology Today,* pp. 43–54, 113.

Passuth, P. M., Maines, D. R., & Neugarten, B. L. (1984). *Age norms and age constraints twenty years later.* Paper presented at the meeting of the Midwest Sociological Society, Chicago.

Patel, V. L., & Green, G. J. (1986). Knowledge based solution strategies in medical reasoning. *Cognitive Science, 10,* 91–116.

Patterson, C. J. (1995). Lesbian and gay parenthood. In M. H. Bornstein (Ed.), *Handbook of parenting* (Vol. 3). Hillsdale, NJ: Erlbaum.

Patterson, C. J. (1996, August). *Children of lesbian and gay parents: Research, law, and policy.* Paper presented at the meeting of the American Psychological Association, Toronto.

Patterson, G. R., Debaryshe, B. D., & Ramsey, E. (1989). A developmental perspective on antisocial behavior. *American Psychologist, 44,* 329–335.

Patterson, K., Vargha-Khadem, F., & Polkey, C. E. (1989). Reading with one hemisphere. *Brain, 112,* 39–63.

Paul, G. L. (1967). Strategy of outcome research in psychotherapy. *Journal of Consulting Psychology, 31,* 109–119.

Paulesu, E., Frith, C. D., & Frackowiak, S. J. (1993). The neural correlates of the verbal component of working memory. *Nature, 362,* 342–345.

Paulus, P. B. (1989). An overview and evaluation of group influence. In P. B. Paulus (Ed.), *Psychology of group influence.* Hillsdale, NJ: Erlbaum.

Paunonen, S., Jackson, D., Trzebinski, J., & Forserling, F. (1992). Personality structures across cultures: A multimethod evaluation. *Journal of Personality and Social Psychology, 62,* 447–456.

Pavlov, I. P. (1906). The scientific investigation of psychical faculties or processes in the higher animals. *Science, 24,* 613–619.

Pavlov, I. P. (1917). *Conditioned reflexes* (G. V. Anrep, Trans.). London: Oxford University Press.

Pavlov, I. P. (1927). *Conditioned reflexes* (F. V. Anrep, Trans. and Ed.). New York: Dover.

Pavlov, I. P. (1927). *Conditioned reflexes* (G. V. Anrep, Trans.). London: Oxford University Press.

Payne, D. G., Lang, V. A., & Blackwell, J. M. (1995). Mixed versus pure display format in integration and nonintegration visual display. *Human factors, 37,* 507–527.

Payne, L. R., Bergin, A. E., & Loftus, P. E. (1992). A review of attempts to integrate spiritual and standard psychotherapy techniques. *Journal of Psychotherapy Integration, 2,* 171–192.

Payne, T. J., Smith, P. O., Sturges, L. V., & Holleran, S. A. (1996). Reactivity to smoking cues: Mediating roles of nicotine and duration of deprivation. *Addictive Behaviors, 21,* 139–154.

Pearce, P. L. (1981). Environment shock: A study of tourists' reactions to two tropical islands. *Journal of Applied Social Psychology, 11,* 268–280.

Peele, S., & Brodsky, A. (1991). *The truth about addiction and recovery.* New York: Simon & Schuster.

Pelham, B. W., & Swann, W. B. (1989). From self-conceptions to self-worth: On the sources and structure of global self-esteem. *Journal of Personality and Social Psychology, 57,* 672–680.

Pellegrini, A. D. (1996). *Observing children in their natural worlds.* Hillsdale, NJ: Erlbaum.

Penfield, W. (1947). Some observations in the cerebral cortex of man. *Proceedings of the Royal Society, 134,* 349.

Pennebaker, J. W. (1990). *Opening up: The healing power of confiding in others.* New York: Avon Books.

Pennebaker, J. W., & Lightner, J. M. (1980). Competition of internal and external information in an exercise setting. *Journal of Personality and Social Psychology, 39,* 165–174.

Pennebaker, J. W. (1983). Accuracy of symptom perception. In A. Baum, S. E. Taylor, & J. Singer (Eds.), *Handbook of psychology and health* (Vol. 4). Hillsdale, NJ: Erlbaum.

Pennebaker, J. W., Colder, M., & Sharp, L. K. (1990). Accelerating the coping process. *Journal of Personality and Social Psychology, 58,* 528–537.

Pennebaker, J. W., Kiecolt-Glaser, J. K., & Glaser, R. (1988). Disclosure of traumas and immune function: Health implications for psychotherapy. *Journal of Consulting and Clinical Psychology, 56,* 239–245.

Pentz, M. A. (1993). Comparative effects of community-based drug abuse prevention. In J. S. Baer, G. A. Marlatt, & R. J. McMahon (Eds.), *Addictive behaviors across the life span.* Newbury Park, CA: Sage.

Peplau, L. A., & Perlman, D. (Eds.). (1982). *Loneliness: A sourcebook of current theory, research and therapy.* New York: Wiley.

Perkins, D. D., & Zimmerman, M. A. (1995). Empowerment theory, research, and application. *American Journal of Community Psychology, 23,* 569–580.

Perkins, D. N. (1984, September). Creativity by design. *Educational Leadership,* 18–25.

Perlin, M. L. (1996). The insanity defense. In B. D. Sales & D. W. Shuman (Eds.), *Law, mental health, and mental disorder.* Pacific Grove, CA: Brooks/Cole.

Perlmutter-Bowen, S., & Michal-Johnson, P. (1996). Being sexual in the shadow of AIDS. In J. T. Wood (Ed.), *Gendered relationships.* Mountain View, CA: Mayfield.

Perls, F. (1969). *Gestalt therapy verbatim.* Lafayette, CA: Real People Press.

Perris, E. E., Myers, N. A., & Clifton, R. K. (1990). Long-term memory for a single experience. *Child Development, 61,* 1796–1807.

Persinger, M. A., & Krippner, S. (in press). Experimental dream telepathy-clairvoyance and geomagnetic activity. *Journal of the American Society for Psychical Research.*

Pert, A. B., & Snyder, S. H. (1973). Opiate receptor: Demonstration in a nervous tissue. *Science, 179,* 1011.

Pert, C. (1986). Commentary. In J. Hooper & D. Teresi, *The three-pound universe.* New York: Macmillan.

Pervin, L. A. (1993). *Personality* (6th ed.). New York: John Wiley.

Peskin, H. (1967). Pubertal onset and ego functioning. *Journal of Abnormal Psychology, 72,* 1–15.

Peters, R. D., & McMahon, R. J. (Eds.) (1996). *Preventing childhood disorders, substance abuse, and delinquency.* Newbury Park, CA: Sage.

Petersen, A. C. (1979, January). Can puberty come any faster? *Psychology Today,* pp. 45–56.

Petersen, S. E., Fox, P. T., Snyder, A. Z., & Raichle, M. E. (1990). Activation of extrastriate and frontal cortical areas by visual words and work-like stimuli. *Science, 249,* 1041–1044.

Peterson, C. (1988). *Personality.* San Diego: Harcourt Brace Jovanovich.

Peterson, C., & Seligman, M. E. P. (1984). Causal explanations as a risk factor for depression: Theory and evidence. *Psychological Review, 91,* 347–374.

Peterson, C., Seligman, M. E. P., & Vaillant, G. E. (1986). *Explanatory style is a risk factor for physical illness.* Unpublished manuscript, Department of Psychology, University of Michigan, Ann Arbor.

Peterson, C., & Stunkard, A. J. (1986). *Personal control and health promotion.* Unpublished manuscript, Department of Psychology, University of Michigan, Ann Arbor.

Peterson, D. R. (1971). Status of the Doctor of Psychology program. *Professional Psychology, 2,* 271–275.

Petri, H. L. (1996). *Motivation.* Pacific Grove, CA: Brooks/Cole.

Petronovich, L. (1996). *Living and dying well.* New York: Plenum.

Pettito, L., & Marentette, P. F. (1991). Babbling in the manual mode: Evidence for the ontogeny of language. *Science, 251,* 1397–1536.

Petty, R. E., & Cacioppo, J. T. (1986). The elaboration likelihood of persuasion. In L. Berkowitz (Ed.), *Advances in experimental social psychology* (Vol. 19). New York: Academic Press.

Petty, R. E., & Krosnick, J. A. (Eds.) (1995). *Attitude strength.* Hillsdale, NJ: Erlbaum.

Phares, E. J. (1984). *Personality.* Columbus, OH: Merrill.

Philips, H. C., & Rachman, S. (1996). *The psychological management of chronic pain (2nd ed).* New York: Springer.

Piaget, J. (1952). *The origins of intelligence in children.* New York: W. W. Norton.

Piaget, J. (1952). *The origins of intelligence in children* (M. Cook, Trans.). New York: International Universities Press.

Piaget, J. (1952). *The origins of intelligence in children.* New York: Oxford University Press.

Piaget, J. (1960). *The child's conception of the world.* Totowa, NJ: Littlefield.

Pierce, W. D., & Epling, W. F. (1995). *Behavior analysis and learning.* Upper Saddle River, NJ: Prentice Hall.

Pillow, D. R., Zautra, A. J., & Sandler, I. (1996). Major life events and minor stressors: Identifying mediational links in the stress process. *Journal of Personality and Social Psychology, 70,* 381–394.

Pinel, J. P. J. (1993). *Biopsychology* (2nd ed.). Needham Heights, MA: Allyn & Bacon.

Pines, A., & Aronson, E. (1988). *Career burnout: Causes and cures.* New York: Free Press.

Pinker, S., & Bloom, P. (1990). Natural language and natural selection. *Behavioral and Brain Sciences, 13,* 707–784.

Piotrkowski, C. (1979). *Work and the family system: A naturalistic study of working class and lower middle class families.* New York: Free Press.

Pipes, P. (1988). Nutrition during infancy. In S. R. Williams and B. S. Worthington-Roberts (Eds.), *Nutrition through the life cycle.* St. Louis: Times Mirror/Mosby.

Pirsig, R. (1974). *Zen and the art of motorcycle maintenance.* New York: Morrow.

Plath, S. (1971). *The bell jar.* New York: Harper & Row.

Pleck, J. H. (1979). Men's family work: Three perspectives and some new data. *Family Coordinator, 28,* 481–488.

Pleck, J. H. (1983). The theory of male sex role identity: Its rise and fall, 1936–present. In M. Lewin (Ed.), *In the shadow of the past: Psychology portrays the sexes.* New York: Columbia University Press.

Pleck, J. H. (1995). The gender role strain paradigm: An update. In R. F. Levant & W. S. Pollack (Eds.), *A new psychology of men.* New York: Basic.

Pleck, J. H., Sonnenstein, F. L., & Ku, L. C. (1994). Problem behaviors and masculine ideology in adolescent males. In R. Ketterlinus & M. E. Lamb (Eds.), *Adolescent problem behaviors.* Hillsdale, NJ: Erlbaum.

Plomin, R. (1991, April). *The nature of nurture: Genetic influence on "environmental" measures.* Paper presented at the meeting of the Society for Research in Child Development, Seattle.

Plomin, R. (1996, August). *Nature and nurture together.* Paper presented at the meeting of the American Psychological Association, Toronto.

Plomin, R., DeFries, J. C., & McClearn, G. F. (1990). *Behavioral genetics: A primer.* New York: W. H. Freeman.

Plutchik, R. (1980). *Emotion: A psychoevolutionary synthesis.* New York: Harper & Row.

Polivy, J., Heatherton, T. F., & Herman, C. P. (1988). Self-esteem, restraints and eating behavior. *Journal of Abnormal Psychology, 97,* 354–356.

Poll finds racial tension decreasing. (1990, June 29). *Asian Week,* p. 4.

Pollack, S., & Gilligan, C. (1985). Killing the manager. *Journal of Personality and Social Psychology, 48,* 374–375.

Pomeroy, C. (1996). Anorexia nervosa, bulimia nervosa, and binge eating disorder. In J. K. Thompson (Ed.), *Body image, eating disorders, and obesity.* Washington, DC: American Psychological Association.

Ponterotto, J. G. (1996). Multicultural counseling in the 21st century. *The Counseling Psychologist, 24,* 259–268.

Ponterotto, J. G., Casas, J. M., Suzuki, L. A., & Alexander, C. M. (Eds.). (1995). *Handbook of multicultural counseling.* Newbury Park, CA: Sage.

Popper, K. R., & Eccles, J. C. (1977). *The self and its brain.* Berlin: Springer-Verlag.

Porcino, J. (1983). *Growing older, getting better: A handbook for women in the second half of life.* Reading, MA: Addison-Wesley.

Posner, M., & Rothbart, M. (1989, August). *Attention: Normal and pathological development.* Paper presented at the meeting of the American Psychological Association, New Orleans.

Poyatos, F. (Ed.). (1988). *Cross-cultural perspectives in nonverbal communication.* Toronto: C. J. Hogrefe.

Premack, D. (1986). *Gavagi! The future history of the ape language controversy.* Cambridge, MA: MIT Press.

Prentice, D. A., & Miller, D. T. (1993). Pluralistic ignorance and alcohol use on campus: Some consequences of misperceiving the social norm. *Journal of Personality and Social Psychology, 64,* 243–256.

Pressley, M. (1996). Personal reflections on the study of practical memory in the mid-1990s. In D. Hermann, C. McEvoy, C. Hertzog, P. Hertel, & M. Johnson (Eds.), *Basic and applied memory research (Vol. 2).* Hillsdale, NJ: Erlbaum.

Pribram, K. (in press). *Brain and perception.* Hillsdale, NJ: Erlbaum.

Pribram, K. H. (1994, August). *Varieties of conscious experience.* Paper presented at the meeting of the American Psychological Association, New York City.

Pritchard, D. J. (1996). Genetic analysis of schizophrenia as an example of a putative multifactorial trait. *Annals of Human Genetics, 60,* 105–123.

Prochaska, J., & Norcross, J. (1993). *Systems of psychotherapy.* Pacific Grove, CA: Brooks/Cole.

Purcell, T. V. (1980). Policies on minority employment. *Professional Psychology, 11,* 352–359.

Pylyshyn, Z. W. (1973). What the mind's eye tells the mind's brain: A critique of mental imagery. *Psychological Bulletin, 80,* 1–24.

Quarantelli, E. L. (1976). *Human response in stress situations.* Baltimore, MD: Johns Hopkins University Press.

Rabkin, J. (1979). Ethnic density and psychiatric hospitalization: Hazards of minority status. *American Journal of Psychiatry, 136,* 1562–1566.

Raimy, V. C. (Ed.). (1950). *Training in clinical psychology.* Englewood Cliffs, NJ: Prentice Hall.

Ramachandran, V. S. (1988). Perceiving shape from shading. *Scientific American, 259,* 76–83.

Rambo, L. R. (1993). *Understanding religious conversion.* New Haven, CT: Yale University Press.

Ramey, C. (1989, April). *Parent-child intellectual similarities in natural and altered ecologies.* Paper presented at the biennial meeting of the Society for Research in Child Development, Kansas City.

Ramirez, O. (1989). Mexican American children and adolescents. In J. T. Gibbs & L. N. Huang (Eds.), *Children of color.* San Francisco: Jossey-Bass.

Randi, J. (1980). *Flim-flam!* New York: Lippincott.

Rappaport, A., Bornstein, G., & Erev, I. (1989). Intergroup competition for public goods: Effects of unequal resources and relative group size. *Journal of Personality and Social Psychology, 5,* 748–756.

Rapaport, D. (1967). On the psychoanalytic theory of thinking. In M. M. Gill (Ed.), *The collected papers of David Rapaport.* New York: Basic Books.

Rasmussen, K. G. (1984). Nonverbal behavior, verbal behavior, résumé credentials, and selection interview outcomes. *Journal of Applied Psychology, 69,* 551–556.

Raven, P. H., & Johnson, G. B. (1996). *Biology (4th ed.).* Dubuque, IA: Wm. C. Brown.

Ravnikar, V. (1992, May 25). Commentary, *Newsweek,* p. 82.

Rebec, G. V. (1996, June). *Neurochemical and behavioral insights into the mechanisms of action of stimulant drugs.* Paper presented at the meeting of the American Psychological Society, San Francisco.

Redd, W. H. (1995). Behavioral research in cancer as a model for health psychology. *Health Psychology, 14,* 99–100.

Ree, M. J., Earles, J. A., & Teachout, M. S. (1994). Predicting job performance: Not much more than *g. Journal of Applied Psychology, 79,* 518–524.

Reece, B. L., & Brandt, R. (1990). *Effective human relations in organizations* (4th ed.). Boston: Houghton Mifflin.

Reed, E. S., Turiel, E., & Brown, T. (1995). *Values and knowledge.* Hillsdale, NJ: Erlbaum.

Reed, S. K. (1996). *Cognition (4th ed.).* Pacific Grove, CA: Brooks/Cole.

Regier, D. A., Hirschfeld, R. M. A., Goodwin, F. K., Burke, J. D., Lazar, J. B., & Judd, L. L. (1988). The NIMH Depression Awareness, Recognition, and Treatment Program: Structure, aims, and scientific basis. *American Journal of Psychiatry, 145,* 1351–1357.

Reid, P. T., & Bing, V. (1996). Women and the psychotherapeutic "color line." *Contemporary Psychology, 41,* 19–20.

Reilly, R. R., & Manese, W. R. (1983). The validation of a mini-course for telephone company switching technicians. *Personnel Psychology, 32,* 83–90.

Reinisch, J. (1992, December 7). Commentary, *Newsweek,* p. 54.

Reinisch, J. M. (1990). *The Kinsey Institute new report on sex: What you must know to be sexually literate.* New York: St. Martin's Press.

Reinitz, M. T., & Alexander, R. (1996). Mechanisms of facilitation in primed perceptual identification. *Memory & Cognition, 24,* 129–135.

Reiser, B. J., Black, J. B., & Abelson, R. P. (1985). Knowledge structures in the organization and retrieval of autobiographical memories. *Cognitive Psychology, 17,* 89–137.

Reisman, J. M. (1976). *A history of clinical psychology.* New York: Irvington.

Religion in America. (1993). Princeton, NJ: Princeton Religious Research Center.

Rescorla, R. A. (1988). Pavlovian conditioning: It's not what you think it is. *American Psychologist, 43,* 151–160.

Rescorla, R. A. (1996). Spontaneous recovery after training with multiple outcomes. *Animal Learning & Behavior, 24,* 11–18.

Reser, J. P. (1980). Automobile addiction: Real or imagined? *Man-Environment Systems, 10,* 279–287.

Resnick, J. H. (1991). Finally, a definition of clinical psychology: A message from the president, division 12. *Clinical Psychologist, 40,* 3–11.

Restak, R. M. (1988). *The mind.* New York: Bantam.

Revitch, E., & Schlesinger, L. B. (1978). Murder: Evaluation, classification, and prediction. In I. L. Kutash, S. B. Kutash, & L. B. Schlesinger (Eds.), *Violence.* San Francisco: Jossey-Bass.

Rhodes, S. R. (1983). Age-related differences in work attitudes and behavior: A review and conceptual analysis. *Psychological Bulletin, 93,* 328–367.

Rice, F. P. (1996). *Intimate relationships, marriages, and families (3rd ed.).* Mountain View, CA: Mayfield.

Rice, M. L. (1989). Children's language acquisition. *American Psychologist, 44,* 149–156.

Rice, M. L. (Ed.) (1996). *Toward a genetics of language.* Hillsdale, NJ: Erlbaum.

Richardson, J. T. (1985). The active vs. passive convert: Paradigm, conflict in conversion/recruitment research. *Journal for the Scientific Study of Religion, 24* (2), 119–236.

Richardson, J. T. (1989). The psychology of induction: A review and interpretation. In M. Galanter (Ed.), *Cults and new religious movements: A report of the American Psychiatric Association* (pp. 211–238). Washington, DC: American Psychiatric Association.

Richardson, J. T. E. (1996). Real science, *Contemporary Psychology, 41,* 213–215.

Richter, C. P. (1957). On the phenomenon of sudden death in animals and man. *Psychosomatic Medicine, 19,* 191–198.

Richwald, G. A., Schneider-Muńoz, M., & Valdez, R. B. (1989). Are condom instructions in Spanish readable? Implications for AIDS preventions. *Hispanic Journal of Behavioral Sciences, 11,* 70–82.

Riger, S., & Galligan, P. (1980). An exploration of competing paradigms. *American Psychologist, 35,* 902–910.

Riggio, R. E. (1986). Assessment of basic social skills. *Journal of Personality and Social Psychology, 51,* 649–660.

Robbins, M. M. (1995). A demographic analysis of male life history and social structure of mountain gorillas. *Behaviour, 132,* 21–47.

Robbins, S. P. (1995). *Organizational behavior (7th ed.).* Upper Saddle River, NJ: Prentice Hall.

Robbins, T. L, & DeNisi, S. (1994). A closer look at interpersonal affect as a distinct influence on cognitive processing in performance evaluations. *Journal of Applied Psychology, 79,* 341–353.

Roberts, D., Anderson, B. L., & Lubaroff, A. (1994). *Stress and immunity at cancer diagnosis.* Unpublished manuscript, Department of Psychology, Ohio State University, Columbus.

Robins, L., & Regier, D. A. (Eds.). (1990). *Psychiatric disorders in America.* New York: Macmillan.

Robins, L. N., Helzer, J. F., Weissman, M. M., Orvashcel, H., Gruenberg, F., Burke, J. D., & Regier, D. A. (1984). Lifetime prevalence of specific psychiatric disorders in three sites. *Archives of General Psychiatry, 41,* 949–958.

Robinson, F. P. (1961). *Effective study.* New York: Harper & Row.

Robinson, I., Ziss, K., Ganza, B., Katz, S., & Robinson, E. (1991). Twenty years of the sexual revolution, 1965–1985: An update. *Journal of Marriage and the Family, 53,* 216–220.

Robinson, J. P., & Shaver, P. R. (Eds.). (1973). *Measures of social psychological attitudes.* Ann Arbor: University of Michigan, Institute for Social Research.

Rodin, J. (1984, December). Interview: A sense of control. *Psychology Today,* pp. 38–45.

Roeder, K. D. (1962). The behavior of free flying moths in the presence of artificial ultrasonic pulses. *Animal Behavior, 10,* 300–304.

Roethlisberger, F. J., & Dickson, W. J. (1939). *Management and the worker.* Cambridge, MA: Harvard University Press.

Rogers, C. R. (1961). *On becoming a person.* Boston: Houghton Mifflin.

Rogers, C. R. (1974). In retrospect: Forty-six years. *American Psychologist, 29,* 115–123.

Rogers, C. R. (1980). *A way of being.* Boston: Houghton Mifflin.

Rogers, R. W. (1989). Deindividuation and the self-regulation of behavior. In P. B. Paulus (Ed.), *Psychology of group influence.* Hillsdale, NJ: Erlbaum.

Rohner, R. P., & Rohner, E. C. (1981). Parental acceptance-rejection and parental control: Cross-cultural codes. *Ethnology, 20,* 245–260.

Rollins, J. H. (1996). *Women's minds/women's bodies.* Upper Saddle River, NJ: Prentice Hall.

Rolls, E. T. (1990). Functions of the primate hippocampus in spatial processing and memory. In R. P. Kesner & D. S. Olton (Eds.), *Neurobiology and comparative cognition.* Hillsdale, NJ: Erlbaum.

Rosch, E. H. (1973). On the internal structure of perceptual and semantic categories. In T. E. Moore (Ed.), *Cognition and the acquisition of language.* New York: Academic Press.

Rose, H. A., & Martin, C. L. (1993, March). *Children's gender-based inferences about others' activities, emotions, and occupations.* Paper presented at the biennial meeting of the Society for Research in Child Development, New Orleans.

Rose, R. J., Koskenvuo, M., Kaprio, J., Sarna, S., & Langinvainio, H. (1988). Shared genes, shared experiences, and similarity of personality: Data from 14,228 adult Finnish co-twins. *Journal of Personality and Social Psychology, 54,* 161–171.

Rosen, J. C., Orosan, P., & Reiter, J. (1995). Cognitive behavior therapy for negative body image in obese women. *Behavior Therapy, 26,* 25–42.

Rosen, K. H., & Stith, S. M. (1995). Women terminating abusive dating relationships: A qualitative study. *Journal of Personal and Social Relationships, 12,* 155–160.

Rosen, R. C., & Leiblum, S. R. (1995). Treatment of sexual disorders in the 1990s: An integrated approach. *Journal of Consulting and Clinical Psychology, 63,* 877–890.

Rosenfeld, A. H. (1985, June). Depression: Dispelling despair. *Psychology Today,* pp. 28–34.

Rosenhan, D. L. (1973). On being sane in insane places. *Science, 179,* 250–258.

Rosenthal, D. (1963). *The Germain quadruplets.* New York: Basic Books.

Rosenthal, L. (1996). Phenomena of resistance in modern group analysis. *American Journal of Psychotherapy, 50,* 75–89.

Rosenthal, R., & Jacobsen, L. (1968). *Pygmalian in the classroom.* New York: Holt, Rinehart & Winston.

Rosnow, R. L. (1995). Teaching research ethnics through role-play and discussion. In M. E. Ware & D. E. Johnson (Eds.), *Demonstrations and activities in teaching of psychology (Vol. 1).* Hillsdale, NJ: Erlbaum.

Rosnow, R. L., & Rosenthal, R. (1996). *Beginning behavioral research (2nd ed.).* Upper Saddle River, NJ: Prentice Hall.

Ross, H. E. (1974). *Behavior and perception in strange environments.* London: Allen & Unwin.

Ross, L. (1977). The intuitive psychologist and his shortcomings: Distortions in the attribution process. In L. Berkowitz (Ed.), *Advances in experimental psychology* (Vol. 10). New York: Academic Press.

Ross, M., & Holmberg, D. (1990). Recounting the past: Gender differences in the recall of events in the history of a close relationship. In J. M. Olson & M. P. Zanna (Eds.), *Self-inference processes: The Ontario symposium.* Hillsdale, NJ: Erlbaum.

Rossi, A. (1989). A life course approach to gender, aging, and intergenerational relations. In K. W. Schaie & C. Schooler (Eds.), *Social structures and aging.* Hillsdale, NJ: Erlbaum.

Rotton, J., & Frey, J. (1985). Air pollution, weather, and violent crimes: Concomitant time-series analysis of archival data. *Journal of Personality and Social Psychology, 49,* 1207–1220.

Rovee-Collier, C. (1987). Learning and memory in children. In J. D. Osofsky (Ed.), *Handbook of infant development* (2nd ed.). New York: Wiley.

Rowe, J., & Kahn, R. (1987). Human aging: Usual and successful. *Science, 237,* 143–149.

Rubin, D. C., & Kozin, M. (1984). Vivid memories. *Cognition, 16* 81–95.

Rubin, L. B. (1984). *Intimate strangers: Men and women working together.* New York: Harper & Row.

Rubin, L. J., & Hampton, B. R. (1994, August). *Sexual harassment in academic psychology: Psychologists as educators.* Paper presented at the meeting of the American Psychological Association, New York City.

Rubin, Z. (1970). Measurement of romantic love. *Journal of Personality and Social Psychology, 16,* 265–273.

Rubin, Z. (1981, May). Does personality really change after 20? *Psychology Today.*

Rubin, Z., & Mitchell, C. (1976). Couples research as couples counseling. *American Psychologist, 31,* 17–25.

Ruderman, A. J. (1986). Dietary restraint: A theoretical and empirical review. *Psychological Bulletin, 99,* 247–262.

Rue, L., & Byars, L. (1996). *Supervision: Key link to productivity (5th ed.).* Burr Ridge, IL: Irwin.

Rumbaugh, D. M., Hopkins, W. D., Washburn, D. A., & Savage-Rumbaugh, E. S. (1991). Comparative perspectives on brain, cognition, and language. In N. A. Krasnegor, D. M. Rumbaugh, M. Studdert-Kennedy, & R. L. Schiefelbusch (Eds.), *Biological and behavioral determinants of language development.* Hillsdale, NJ: Erlbaum.

Rumbaugh, D. M., & Rumbaugh, E. S. (1990, June). *Chimpanzees: Language, speech, counting, and video tasks.* Paper presented at the meeting of the American Psychological Society, Dallas.

Rushton, J. P., Fulker, D. W., Neale, M. C., Nias, D. K. B., & Eysenck, H. J. (1986). Altruism and aggression: The heritability of individual differences. *Journal of Personality and Social Psychology, 50,* 1192–1198.

Russell, D. W. (1996). UCLA Loneliness Scale (Version 3): Reliability, validity, and factor structure. *Journal of Personality Assessment, 66,* 20–43.

Russell, M. J. (1976). Human olfactory communication. *Nature, 260,* 520–522.

Russell, M. J., Switz, G. M., & Thompson, K. (1980). Olfactory influences in the human menstrual cycle. *Pharmacology, Biochemistry, and Behavior, 13,* 737–738.

Russo, N. F. (1984). *Women in the American Psychological Association.* Washington, DC: American Psychological Association, Women's Program Office.

Russo, N. F. (1985). *A women's mental health agenda.* Washington, DC: American Psychological Association.

Russo, N. F. (1990). Overview: Forging research priorities for women's mental health. *American Psychologist, 45,* 368–373.

Ruth, S. (Ed.) (1995). *Issues in feminism.* Mountain View, CA: Mayfield.

Rutter, M. (1979). Protective factors in children's response to stress and disadvantage. In M. W. Kent & J. E. Rolf (Eds.), *Primary prevention in psychopathology* (Vol. 3). Hanover, NH: University Press of New England.

Rutter, M., & Garmezy, N. (1983). Developmental psychopathology. In P. H. Mussen (Ed.), *Handbook of child psychology* (4th ed., Vol. 4). New York: Wiley.

Rybash, J. M. (1996). A taxonomy of priming: Implications for aging. In D. Hermann, C. McEvoy, C. Hertzog, P. Hertel, & M. Johnson (Eds.), *Basic and applied memory research (Vol. 2).* Hillsdale, NJ: Erlbaum.

Rybash, J. M., Roodin, P. A., & Hoyer, W. J. (1995). *Adult development and aging* (3rd ed.). Madison, WI: Brown & Benchmark.

Rymer, R. (1992). *Genie.* New York: HarperCollins.

Saal, F. E., & Knight, P. A. (1995). *Industrial/organizational psychology (2nd ed.).* Pacific Grove, CA: Brooks/Cole.

Saarni, C. (1988). Children's understanding of the interpersonal consequences of dissemblance of nonverbal emotional-expressive behavior. *Journal of Nonverbal Behavior, 12,* 275–294.

Sabini, J. (1995). *Social psychology* (2nd ed.). New York: Norton.

Sackett, P. R. (1994). Integrity testing for personnel selection. *Current Directions in Psychological Science, 3,* 73–76.

Sackheim, H. A. (1985, June). The case for ECT. *Psychology Today,* pp. 37–40.

Sacks, O. (1985). *The man who mistook his wife for a hat.* New York: Summit Books.

Sadalla, E. K., & Magel, S. G. (1980). The perception of traversed distance. *Environment and Behavior, 12,* 65–79.

Sadalla, E. K., Burroughs, W. J., & Staplin, L. J. (1980). Reference points in spatial cognition. *Journal of Experimental Psychology: Human Learning and Memory, 5,* 516–528.

Sadalla, E. K., & Staplin, L. J. (1980). The perception of traversed distance: Intersections. *Environment and Behavior, 12,* 167–182.

Sadalla, E. K., & Oxley, D. (1984). The perception of room size: The rectangularity illusion. *Environment and Behavior, 16,* 394–405.

Sade, D. S. (1965). Some aspects of parent-offspring and sibling relations in a group of rhesus monkeys, with a discussion of grooming. *American Journal of Anthropology, 23,* 1–17.

Sadik, N. (1991, March–April). Success in development depends on women. *Popline.* New York: World Population News Service.

Sagan, C. (1980). *Cosmos.* New York: Random House.

Sagan, C., & Druyan, A. (1992). *Shadows of forgotten ancestors.* New York: W. W. Norton.

Saklofske, D. H., & Zeidner, M. (Eds.). (1995). *International handbook of personality and intelligence.* New York: Plenum.

Salling, M., & Harvey, M. E. (1981). Poverty, personality and sensitivity to residential stressors. *Environment and Behavior, 13,* 131–163.

Salthouse, T. A. (1996). General and specific speed mediation of adult age differences in memory. *Journal of Gerontology, 51A,* P30–P42.

Samovar, L. A., & Mills, J. (1992). *Oral communication: Message and response.* Dubuque, IA: Wm. C. Brown.

Sanderson, W. C. (1995, March). Which therapies are proven effective? *APA Monitor,* p. 4.

Sandler, D. P., Comstock, G. W., Helsing, K. J., & Shore, D. L. (1989). Deaths from all causes in non-smokers who lived with smokers. *American Journal of Public Health, 79,* 163–167.

Sangree, W. H. (1989). Age and power: Life-course trajectories and age structuring of power relations in East and West Africa. In D. I. Kertzer & K. W. Schaie (Eds.), *Age structuring in comparative perspective.* Hillsdale, NJ: Erlbaum.

Santrock, J. W. (1996). *Adolescence* (6th ed.). Madison, WI: Brown & Benchmark.

Santrock, J. W. (1996). *Child Development* (7th ed.). Madison, WI: Brown & Benchmark.

Santrock, J. W. (1997). *Life-Span Development* (6th ed.). Madison, WI: Brown & Benchmark.

Santrock, J. W., & Warshak, R. A. (1986). Development, relationships, and legal/clinical considerations in father custody families. In M. E. Lamb (Ed.), *The father's role: Applied perspectives.* New York: Wiley.

Sarafino, E. P. (1994). *Health psychology* (2nd ed.). New York: John Wiley.

Sarason, I. G., & Sarason, B. R. (1987). *Abnormal psychology* (5th ed.). Englewood Cliffs, NJ: Prentice Hall.

Sarason, I. G., & Sarason, B. R. (1996). *Abnormal psychology (8th ed.).* Upper Saddle River, NJ: Prentice Hall.

Saravi, R. D. (1993). The right hemisphere: An esoteric closet? *Skeptical Inquirer, 17,* 380–387.

Sargent, C. (1987). Skeptical fairytales from Bristol. *Journal of the Society for Psychical Research, 54.*

Sargent, P. B. (1993). The diversity of neuronal nicotinic acetylcholine receptors. *Annual Review of Neuroscience, 16.* Palo Alto, CA: Annual Reviews.

Sarrel, P., & Masters, W. (1982). Sexual molestation of men by women. *Archives of Human Sexuality, 11,* 117–131.

Sarter, M., Bernstson, G. G., & Cacioppo, J. T. (1996). Brain imaging and cognitive neuroscience: Toward strong inference in attributing function to structure. *American Psychologist, 51,* 13–21.

Sasaki, T., & Kennedy, J. L. (1995). Genetics of psychosis. *Current Opinion in Psychiatry, 8,* 25–28.

Saslow, C. (1982). *Basic research methods.* Reading, MA: Addison-Wesley.

Satir, V. (1964). *Conjoint family therapy.* Palo Alto, CA: Science and Behavior Books.

Savage-Rumbaugh, E. S., Murphy, J., Sevick, R. A., Brakke, K. E., Williams, S. L., & Rumbaugh, D. (1993). Language comprehension in ape and child. *Monographs of the Society for Research in Child Development, 58,* (3–4, Serial No. 233).

Sax, G. (1989). *Principles of educational and psychology measurement* (3rd ed.). Belmont, CA: Wadsworth.

Saxe, L., Dougherty, D., & Cross, T. (1985). The validity of polygraph testing: Scientific analysis and public controversy. *American Psychologist, 40,* 355–366.

Saxe, L. (1994). Detection of deception: Polygraph and integrity tests. *Current Directions in Psychological Science, 3,* 69–73.

Sayette, M., Mayne, T., & Norcross, J. (1992). *Insider's guide to graduate programs in clinical psychology.* New York: Guilford.

Scarr, S. (1984, May). Interview. *Psychology Today,* pp. 59–63.

Scarr, S. (1984). *Mother care/other care.* New York: Basic Books.

Scarr, S. (1991, April). *Developmental theories for the 1990s.* Presidential address, biennial meeting of the Society for Research in Child Development, Seattle.

Scarr, S. (1992). Developmental theories for the 1990s: Development and individual differences. *Child Development, 63,* 1–19.

Scarr, S. (1996). Best of human genetics. *Contemporary Psychology, 41,* 149–150.

Scarr, S., Lande, J., & McCartney, K. (1989). Child care and the family: Complements and interactions. In J. Lande, S. Scarr, and N. Gunzenhauser (Eds.), *Caring for children: Challenge to America.* Hillsdale, NJ: Erlbaum.

Scarr, S., & McCartney, K. (1983). How people make their own environments: A theory of genotype environment effects. *Child Development, 54,* 424–435.

Scarr, S., & McCartney, K. (1992). How people make their own environments: A theory of genotype environment effects. *Child Development, 54,* 424–435.

Scarr, S., & Ricciuti, A. (in press). What effects do parents have on their children? In L. Okagaki & R. J. Sternberg (Eds.), *Directors of development: Influences on the development of children's thinking.* Hillsdale, NJ: Erlbaum.

Scarr, S., & Weinberg, R. A. (1980). Calling all camps! The war is over. *American Sociological Review, 45,* 859–865.

Scarr, S., & Weinberg, R. A. (1983). The Minnesota adoption studies: Genetic differences and malleability. *Child Development, 54,* 253–259.

Schacter, D. L. (1995). Memory wars. *Scientific American, 172,* 135–139.

Schacter, D. L., & McGlynn, S. M. (1989). Implicit memory: Effects of elaboration depend on unitization. *American Journal of Psychology, 102,* 151–181.

Schacter, D. L., Reiman, E., Vecker, A., Polster, M. R., Yun, L. S., & Cooper, L. A. (1995). Brain regions associated with retrieval of structurally coherent visual information. *Nature, 376,* 587–590.

Schacter, D. L., & Tulving, E. (1994). What are the memory systems of 1994? In D. L. Schacter & E. Tulving (Eds.), *Memory systems 1994.* Cambridge, Mass.: Bradford/MIT press (pp. 1–38).

Schlachter, S. (1971). Some extraordinary facts about obese humans and rats. *American Psychologist, 26,* 129–144.

Schachter, S., & Singer, J. E. (1962). Cognitive, social, and physiological determinants of emotional state. *Psychological Review, 69,* 379–399.

Schaffer, H. R., & Emerson, P. E. (1964). The development of social attachments in infancy. *Monographs of the Society for Research in Child Development, 29* (3, Serial No. 94).

Schaie, K. W. (1984). The Seattle Longitudinal Study: A 21-year exploration of psychometric intelligence in adulthood. In K. W. Schaie (Ed.), *Longitudinal studies of adult psychological development.* New York: Guilford Press.

Schank, R., & Abelson, R. (1977). *Scripts, plans, goals, and understanding.* Hillsdale, NJ: Erlbaum.

Scheff, T. J. (1966). *Being mentally ill: A sociological theory.* Chicago: Aldine.

Schein, V. E., Mueller, R., Lituchy, T., & Liu, J. (1996). Think manager—think male? A global phenomenon? *Journal of Organizational Behavior, 17,* 33–42.

Schneider, E. L., Rowe, J. W., Johnson, T., Holbrook, N., & Morrison, J. (Eds.) (1996). *Handbook of the biology of aging (4th ed.).* Orlando, FL: Academic Press.

Schofield, J. W., & Pavelchak, M. A. (1985). The day after: The impact of a media event. *American Psychologist, 40,* 542–548.

Schofield, J. W., & Pavelchak, M. A. (1989). Fallout from *The Day After:* Impact of a TV film on attitudes related to nuclear war. *Journal of Applied Social Psychology, 19,* 433–448.

Schuetz-Mueller, D., Tiefer, L., & Melman, A. (1996). Follow-up of vacuum and nonvacuum constriction devices as treatment of erectile dysfunction. *Journal of Sex & Marital Therapy, 21,* 229–238.

Schultz, D. P., & Schultz, S. E. (1986). *Psychology and industry today* (4th ed.). New York: Macmillan.

Schulz, R., & Curnow, C. (1988). Peak performance and age among super athletes. Track and field, swimming, baseball, tennis, and golf. *Journal of Gerontology, 43,* 113–120.

Schumacher, R. M., Hardzinski, M. L., & Schwartz, A. L. (1995). Increasing the usability of interactive voice response systems. *Human Factors, 37,* 251–264.

Schumaker, J. F. (Ed.). (1992). *Religion and mental health.* New York: Oxford University Press.

Schunk, D. H. (1983). Developing children's self-efficacy and skills: The roles of social comparative information and goal-setting. *Contemporary Educational Psychology, 8,* 76–86.

Schutte, N. S., & Malouff, J. M. (1995). *Sourcebook of adult assessment strategies.* New York: Plenum.

Schwartz, R., & Erikson, M. (1989). Statement of the Society for Public Health Education on the national health promotion disease prevention objectives for the year 2000. *Health Education Quarterly, 16,* 3–7.

Schwartz, S. H. (1990). Individualism-collectivism. *Journal of Cross-Cultural Psychology, 21,* 139–157.

Schwartz, S. H., & Sagiv, L. (1995). Identifying culture-specifics in the content and structure of values. *Journal of Cross-Cultural Psychology, 26,* 92–116.

Scitovsky, A. A. (1988). Medical care in the last twelve months of life: Relation between age, functional status, and medical care expenditures. *Milbank Quarterly, 66,* 640–660.

Scott, P. (1997). Language. In P. Scott & C. Spencer (Eds.), *Psychology.* Cambridge, MA: Blackwell.

Scribner, S. (1977). Modes of thinking and ways of speaking: Culture and logic reconsidered. In P. N. Johnson-Laird & P. C. Watson (Eds.), *Thinking: Readings in cognitive science.* New York: Cambridge University Press.

Seager, J., & Olson, A. (Eds.). (1986). *Women of the world: An international atlas.* New York: Simon & Schuster.

Searle, J. R. (1984). *Minds, brains, and science.* Cambridge, MA: Harvard University Press.

Sears, D. O. (1987). Symbolic racism. In P. Katz & D. Taylor (Eds.), *Towards the elimination of racism: Profile in controversy.* New York: Plenum.

Sears, D. O., & Funk, C. (1991). The role of self-interest in social and political attitudes. In M. Zann (Ed.), *Advances in experimental social psychology* (Vol. 24). San Diego: Academic Press.

Sears, D. O., & McConahay, J. B. (1973). *The politics of violence: The new urban Blacks and the Watts riot.* Boston: Houghton Mifflin.

Sears, D. O., Peplau, L. A., Freedman, J. L., & Taylor, S. E. (1988). *Social psychology* (6th ed.). Englewood Cliffs, NJ: Prentice Hall.

Sears, D. O., Peplau, L. A., & Taylor, S. E. (1997). *Social psychology (9th ed.).* Englewood Cliffs, NJ: Prentice Hall.

Seffge-Krenke, I. (1995). *Stress, coping, and relationships in adolescence.* Hillsdale, NJ: Erlbaum.

Segall, M. H., Campbell, D. T., & Herskovits, M. J. (1963). Cultural differences in the perception of geometric illusions. *Science, 193,* 769–771.

Segall, M. H., Dasen, P. R., Berry, J. W., & Poortinga, Y. H. (1990). *Human behavior in global perspective.* New York: Pergamon.

Sehulster, J. R. (1996). Individual differences in memory style and autobiographical memory. In D. Hermann, C. McEvoy, C. Hertzog, P. Hertel, & M. Johnson (Eds.), *Basic and applied memory research (Vol. 2).* Hillsdale, NJ: Erlbaum.

Seidemann, E., Meilijson, I., Abeles, M., Bergman, H., & Vaadia, E. (1996). Simultaneously recorded single units in the frontal cortex go through sequences of discrete and stable states in monkeys performing a delayed localization task. *The Journal of Neuroscience, 16,* 752–768.

Seligman, C., Olson, J. M., & Zanna, M. P. (Eds.) (1996). *The psychology of values.* Hillsdale, NJ: Erlbaum.

Seligman, M. E. P. (1970). On the generality of the laws of learning. *Psychological Review, 77,* 406–418.

Seligman, M. E. P. (1975). *Helplessness: On depression, development and death.* San Francisco: W. H. Freeman.

Seligman, M. E. P. (1989). Why is there so much depression today? The waxing of the individual and the waning of the common. In *The G. Stanley Hall Lecture Series.* Washington, DC: American Psychological Association.

Seligman, M. E. P. (1991). *Learned optimism.* New York: Knopf.

Seligman, M. E. P. (1996, August). *Predicting and preventing depression.* Paper presented at the meeting of the American Psychological Association, Toronto.

Selye, H. (1974). *Stress without distress.* Philadelphia: W. B. Saunders.

Selye, H. (1983). The stress concept. Past, present, and future. In C. I. Cooper (Ed.), *Stress research.* New York: Wiley.

Semaj, L. T. (1985). Afrikanity, cognition, and extended self-identity. In M. B. Spencer, G. K. Brookins, & W. R. Allen (Eds.), *Beginnings: The social and affective development of Black children.* Hillsdale, NJ: Erlbaum.

Serbin, L. A., & Sprafkin, C. (1986). The salience of gender: The process of sex-typing in three- to seven-year-old children. *Child Development, 57,* 1188–1209.

Serdula, M. K., Collins, M. E., Williamson, D. F., Anda, R. F., Pamuk, E. R., & Byers, T. E. (1993). Weight control practices of U.S. adolescents and adults. *Annals of Internal Medicine, 119,* 667–671.

Seto, M. C., & Barbaree, H. E. (1995). The role of alcohol in sexual aggression. *Clinical Psychology Review, 15,* 545–566.

Shakow, D. (1949). *Report of the Commission on Clinical Training.* Washington, DC: American Psychological Association.

Shalev, A. Y., Peri, T., Canetti, L., & Schreiber, S. (1996). Predictors of PTSD in injured trauma survivors. *The American Journal of Psychiatry, 153,* 219–225.

Shanks, D. R. (1991). Categorization by a connectionist network. *Journal of Experimental Psychology: Learning, Memory, and Cognition, 17,* 433–443.

Shaver, P. (1986, August). *Being lonely, falling in love: Perspectives from attachment theory.* Paper presented at the meeting of the American Psychological Association, Washington, DC.

Shaver, P., Collins, N., & Clark, C. (1995). Attachment styles and internal working models of self and relationship partners. In G. Fletcher & J. Fitness (Eds.), *Knowledge structures in close relationships.* Hillsdale, NJ: Erlbaum.

Shaver, P., Schwartz, J., Kirson, D., & O'Connor, C. (1987). Emotion knowledge: Further exploration of a prototype approach. *Journal of Personality and Social Psychology, 52,* 1061–1086.

Shaver, P. R. (1993, March). *Where do adult romantic attachment patterns come from?* Paper presented at the biennial meeting of the Society for Research in Child Development, New Orleans.

Shaver, P. R., & Clark, C. L. (1996). Forms of adult romantic attachment and their cognitive and emotional underpinnings. In G. G. Noam & K. W. Fischer (Eds.), *Development and vulnerability in close relationships.* Hillsdale, NJ: Erlbaum.

Shaw, S. M. (1988). Gender differences in the definition and perception of household labor. *Family Relations, 37,* 333–337.

Sheehy, G. (1991). *The silent passage.* New York: Random House.

Sheldon, W. H. (1954). *Atlas of men.* New York: Harper.

Shepard, R. N. (1967). Recognition memory for words, sentences, and pictures. *Journal of Verbal Learning and Behavior, 6,* 156–163.

Shepard, R. N. (1992). The perceptual organization of colors: An adaptation to regulation of the terrestrial world? In J. Barkow, L. Cosmides, & J. Tooby (Eds.), *The adapted mind.* New York: Oxford University Press.

Shepard, R. N. (1996, August). *The eye's mind and the mind's eye.* Paper presented at the meeting of the American Psychological Association, Toronto.

Sheridan, E. P., Matarazzo, J. D., & Nelson, P. D. (1995). Accreditation of psychology's graduate professional education and training programs: An historical perspective. *Professional Psychology, 26,* 386–392.

Sherif, M., Harvey, O. J., White, B. J., Hood, W. R., & Sherif, C. W. (1961). *Intergroup cooperation and competition: The Robbers Cave experiment.* Norman, OK: University of Oklahoma Press.

Sherrod, D. (1989). The influence of same-sex friendships. In C. Hendrick (Ed.), *Close relationships.* Newbury Park, CA: Sage.

Sherwood, A., Light, K. C., & Blumenthal, J. A. (1989). Effects of aerobic exercise training on hemodynamic responses during psychosocial stress in normotensive and borderline hypertensive Type A men. A preliminary report. *Psychosomatic Medicine, 51,* 123–136.

Shettleworth, S. (1995). Review of animal behavior in J. W. Santrock, *Psychology* (5th ed.). Madison, WI: Brown & Benchmark.

Shettleworth, S. J. (1993). Varieties of learning and memory in animals. *Journal of Experimental Psychology: Animal Behavior Processes, 19,* 5–14.

Shields, S. A. (1991). Gender in the psychology of emotion: A selective research review. In K. T. Strongman (Ed.), *International Review of Studies on Emotion* (Vol. I). New York: John Wiley.

Shier, D., Butler, J., & Lewis, R. (1996). *Hole's human anatomy and physiology (7th ed.).* Dubuque, IA: Wm. C. Brown.

Shneidman, E. S. (1971). Suicide among the gifted. *Suicide and Life-Threatening Behavior, 1,* 23–45.

Shostrum, E. L. (1967). *Man, the manipulator.* New York: Bantam.

Shotland, R. L. (1985, June). When bystanders just stand by. *Psychology Today,* pp. 50–55.

Showers, C. (1986, August). *The motivational consequences of negative thinking: Those who imagine the worst try harder.* Paper presented at the meeting of the American Psychological Association, Washington, DC.

Showers, C. (1992). Compartmentalization of positive and negative self-knowledge: Keeping bad apples out of the bunch. *Journal of Personality and Social Psychology, 62,* 1036–1049.

Shrout, P. E., & Fiske, S. T. (Eds.) (1995). *Personality research, methods, and theories.* Hillsdale, NJ: Erlbaum.

Siegel, R. K. (1990). *Intoxication.* New York: Pocket Books.

Siegler, R. S. (1995, March). *Nothing is; everything becomes.* Paper presented at the meeting of the Society for Research in Child Development, Indianapolis, IN.

Siegried, T. (1994, August 1). Ability to learn while asleep not just in scientist's dreams. *Dallas Morning News,* p. 7D.

Siffre, M. (1975). Six months alone in a cave. *National Geographic, 147,* 426–435.

Sigelman, C. K., Thomas, D. B., Sigelman, L., & Ribich, F. D. (1986). Gender, physical attractiveness, and electability: An experimental investigation of vote biases. *Journal of Applied Social Psychology, 16,* 229–248.

Silverman, I., & Eals, M. (1992). Sex differences in spatial abilities: Evolutionary theory and data. In J. Barkow, L. Cosmides, & J. Tooby (Eds.), *The adapted mind.* New York: Oxford University Press.

Silverman, N. N., & Corsini, R. J. (1984). Is it true what they say about Adler's individual psychology? *Teaching of Psychology, 11,* 188–189.

Silverstein, L. B. (1996). Evolutionary psychology and the search for sex differences. *American Psychologist, 51,* 161–162.

Silverstone, B. (1996). Older people of tomorrow: A psychosocial profile. *The Gerontologist, 36,* 27–32.

Simmons, R. G., & Blyth, D. A. (1987). *Moving into adolescence.* Hawthorne, NY: Aldine.

Simon, H. A. (1969). *The sciences of the artificial.* Cambridge, MA: MIT Press.

Simon, H. A. (1996). Putting the story together. *Contemporary Psychology, 41,* 12–14.

Simpson, J. A. (1995). Self-monitoring and commitment to dating relationships: A classroom demonstration. In M. E. Ware & D. E. Johnson (Eds.), *Demonstrations and activities in teaching of psychology.* Hillsdale, NJ: Erlbaum.

Simpson, J. A., Campbell, B., & Berscheid, E. (1986). The association between love and marriage: Kephart (1967) twice revisited. *Personality and Social Psychology Bulletin, 12,* 363–372.

Singer, J. L. (1984). *The human personality.* San Diego: Harcourt Brace Jovanovich.

Singh, D. (1993). Adaptive significance of female physical attractiveness: Role of waist-to-hip ratio. *Journal of Personality and Social Psychology, 65,* 293–307.

Skinner, B. F. (1938). *The behavior of organisms: An experimental analysis.* New York: Appleton-Century-Crofts.

Skinner, B. F. (1948). *Walden two.* New York: Macmillan.

Skinner, B. F. (1961). Teaching machines. *Scientific American, 205,* 90–102.

Skinner, B. F. (1987, August). *Dialogue with B. F. Skinner.* Paper presented at the meeting of the American Psychological Association, New York City.

Skinner, B. F. (1989). The origins of cognitive thought. *American Psychologist, 44,* 13–18.

Slaby, R. G., Wilson-Brewer, R., & Dash, K. (1994). *Aggressors, victims, and bystanders: Thinking and acting to prevent violence.* Newton, MA: Education Development Center.

Slavin, R. (1989). Cooperative learning and student achievement. In R. Slavin (Ed.), *School and classroom organization.* Hillsdale, NJ: Erlbaum.

Sloan, P., Arsenault, L., Hilsenroth, M., Handler, L., & Harvill, L. (1996). Rorschach measures of posttraumatic stress in Persian Gulf War veterans: a three-year follow-up study. *Journal of Personality Assessment, 66,* 54–64.

Sloan, T. S. (1990). Psychology for the third world? *Journal of Social Issues, 46,* 1–20.

Slobin, D. (1972, July). Children and language: They learn the same all around the world. *Psychology Today,* pp. 71–76.

Slobogin, C. (1996). A jurisprudence of dangerousness as a criterion in the criminal process. In B. D. Sales & D. W. Shuman (Eds.), *Law, mental health, and mental disorder.* Pacific Grove, CA: Brooks/Cole.

Slovenko, R. (1995). *Psychiatry and criminal culpability.* New York: Wiley.

Slovic, P. (1978). The psychology of protective behavior. *Journal of Safety Research, 10,* 58–68.

Slum surgery in St. Louis. (1951). *Architectural Forum, 94* (4), 128–136.

Smith, C. A. B., & Stephens, D. A. (1996). Estimating linkage heterogeneity. *Annals of Human Genetics, 60,* 161–169.

Smith, J., & Baltes, P. B. (1991). A life-span perspective on thinking and problem solving. In M. Schwebel, C. A. Maher, & N. S. Fagley (Eds.), *Promoting cognitive growth over the life span.* Hillsdale, NJ: Erlbaum.

Smith, K. H., & Rogers, M. (1994). Effectiveness of subliminal messages in television commercials. *Journal of Applied Psychology, 79,* 866–874.

Smith, M. L., Glass, G. N., & Miller, R. L. (1980). *The benefit of psychotherapy.* Baltimore: Johns Hopkins University Press.

Smith, P. F., & Darlington, C. L. (1996). *Clinical psychopharmacology.* Hillsdale, NJ: Erlbaum.

Smither, J. W., Reilley, R. R., Millsap, R. E., Perlman, K., & Stoffey, R. W. (1993). Applicant reactions to selection procedures. *Personnel Psychology, 46,* 49–76.

Snarey, J. (1987, June). A question of morality. *Psychology Today,* pp. 6–8.

Snow, C. E. (1989). Understanding social interaction in language interaction: Sentences are not enough. In M. H. Bornstein & J. S. Bruner (Eds.), *Interaction in human development.* Hillsdale, NJ: Erlbaum.

Snow, C. E. (1996). Interactionist account of language acquisition. In M. E. Rice (Ed.), *Toward a genetics of language.* Hillsdale, NJ: Erlbaum.

Snowden, C. T. (1996, August). *Tamrin family values: Mechanisms maintaining monogamy and cooperative childcare.* Paper presented at the meeting of the American Psychological Association, Toronto.

Snowden, D. A. (1995). *An epidemiological study of aging in a select population and its relationship to Alzheimer's disease.* Unpublished manuscript, Sanders Brown Center on Aging, Lexington, KY.

Snowden, L. R., & Cheung, F. K. (1990). Use of inpatient mental health services by members of ethnic minority groups. *American Psychologist, 45,* 347–355.

Snowdon, C. T. (1990). Mechanisms maintaining monogamy in monkeys. In D. A. Dewsbury (Ed.), *Contemporary issues in comparative psychology.* Sunderland, MA: Sinauer.

Solano, C. H. (1982). Loneliness and patterns of self-disclosure. *Journal of Personality and Social Psychology, 43,* 524–531.

Solomon, R. L. (1980). The opponent-process theory of acquired motivation: The costs of pleasure and the benefits of pain. *American Psychologist, 35,* 691–712.

Solomon, Z. (1993). *Combat stress reaction.* New York: Plenum.

Sommer, R. (1983). *Social design.* Englewood Cliffs, NJ: Prentice Hall.

Sowell, T. (1994). *Race and culture: A world view.* New York: Basic Books.

Spacapan, S. (1988). Social psychology and health. In S. Spacapan & S. Oskamp (Eds.), *The social psychology of health.* Newbury Park, CA: Sage.

Spade, J. Z., & Reese, C. A. (1991). We've come a long way, maybe: College students' plans for work and family. *Sex Roles, 24,* 309–322.

Spanos, N. P. (1988). Misconceptions about influenceability research and sociocognitive approaches to hypnosis. *Behavioral and Brain Sciences, 11,* 714–716.

Spearman, C. E. (1927). *The abilities of man.* New York: Macmillan.

Spelke, E. S. (1988). The origins of physical knowledge. In L. Weiskrantz (Ed.), *Thought without language.* New York: Oxford University Press.

Spence, J. T., & Heimreich, R. (1978). *Masculinity and femininity: Their psychological dimensions.* Austin: University of Texas Press.

Spence, M., & DeCasper, A. J. (1982). *Human fetuses perceive human speech.* Paper presented at the International Conference on Infant Studies, Austin, TX.

Sperling, G. (1960). The information available in brief visual presentations. *Psychological Monographs, 74* (Whole No. 11).

Sperling, G. (1989, August). *Toward a computational theory of attention.* Paper presented at the meeting of the American Psychological Association, New Orleans.

Sperry, R. W. (1964). The great cerebral commissure. *Scientific American, 210,* 42–52.

Sperry, R. W. (1968). Hemisphere deconnection and unity in conscious awareness. *American Psychologist, 23,* 723–733.

Sperry, R. W. (1974). Lateral specialization in surgically separated hemispheres. In F. O. Schmitt & F. G. Worden (Eds.), *The neurosciences: Third study program.* Cambridge, MA: MIT Press.

Sperry, R. W. (1976). Mental phenomena as causal determinants in brain function. In G. G. Globus, G. Maxwell, & I. Savodnick (Eds.), *Consciousness and the brain.* New York: Plenum.

Sperry, R. W., & Gazzaniga, M. S. (1967). Language following surgical disconnection of the hemispheres. In C. H. Milikan & F. L. Darley (Eds.), *Brain mechanisms underlying speech and language.* New York: Grune & Stratton.

Spiegel, D., Bloom, Y. R., Kraemer, H. C., & Gottheil, E. (1989). Effects of psychosocial treatment of patients with metastatic breast cancer. *Lancet, 2,* 888–891.

Spilka, B. (1993, August). *Spirituality: Problems and directions in operationalizing a fuzzy concept.* Paper presented at the meeting of the American Psychological Association, Toronto.

Spilka, B., & McIntosh, D. N. (1995). Attribution theory and religious experience. In R. Hood, Jr., (Ed.), *Handbook of religious experience.* Birmingham, AL: Religious Education Press.

Spilka, B., Shaver, P., & Kirkpatrick, L. A. (1985). A general attribution theory for the psychology of religion. *Journal for the Scientific Study of Religion, 24*(1), 1–20.

Spiritual America. (1994, April 4). *U.S. News and World Report,* pp. 48–59.

Sporer, S. L., Malpass, R. S., & Koehnken, G. (Eds.) (1995). *Psychological issues in eyewitness identification.* Hillsdale, NJ: Erlbaum.

Sprecher, S., & McKinney, K. (1993). *Sexuality.* Newbury Park, CA: Sage.

Sprecher, S., Sullivan, Q., & Hatfield, E. (1994). Mate selection preferences: Gender differences examined in a national sample. *Journal of Personality and Social Psychology, 66,* 1074–1080.

Sprei, J. E., & Courtois, C. A. (1988). The treatment of women's sexual dysfunctions arising from sexual assault. In R. A. Brown & J. R. Fields (Eds.), *Treatment of sexual problems in individual and couples therapy.* Great Neck, NY: PMA.

Squire, C. (1993). *Women and AIDS.* Newbury Park, CA: Sage.

Squire, L. (1987). *Memory and brain.* New York: Oxford University Press.

Squire, L. (1990, June). *Memory and brain systems.* Paper presented at the meeting of the American Psychological Society, Dallas.

Squire, L. R. (1994). Declarative and nondeclarative memory: Multiple brain systems supporting learning and memory. In D. L. Schacter & E. Tulving (Eds.), *Memory systems 1994.* Cambridge, Mass.: Bradford/MIT press (pp. 203–232).

Squire, L. R., Knowlton, B., & Musen, G. (1993). The structure and organization of memory. *Annual Review of Psychology, 44,* 453–495.

Sroufe, L. A. (1985). Attachment classification from the perspective of infant-caregiver relationships and infant temperament. *Child Development, 56,* 1–14.

Sroufe, L. A. (1996). *Emotional development.* New York: Cambridge.

Staats, A. W. (1996). *Psychological behaviorism and personality.* New York: Springer.

Stanley, B., & Stanley, M. (1989). Biochemical studies in suicide victims: Current findings and future implications. *Suicide and Life-Threatening Behavior, 19,* 30–42.

Stanley, M. A., & Turner S. M. (1995). Current status of pharmacological and behavioral treatment of obsessive-compulsive disorder. *Behavior Therapy, 26,* 163–177.

Staples, S. L. (1996). Human response to environmental noise. *American Psychologist, 51,* 143–150.

Stark, R., & Bainbridge, W. S. (1985). *The future of religion: Secularization, revival, and cult formation.* Berkeley: University of California Press.

Staub, E. (1996). Cultural-societal roots of violence. *American Psychologist, 51,* 117–132.

St. Clair, M. (1996). *Object relations and self psychology.* Pacific Grove, CA: Brooks/Cole.

Steadman, H. J., Callahan, L. A., Robbins, P. C., & Morrissey, J. P. (1989). Maintenance of an insanity defense under Montana's "abolition" of the insanity defense. *American Journal of Psychiatry, 146,* 357–360.

Steele, C. M. (1996). *A burden of suspicion: The role of stereotypes in shaping intellectual identity.* Paper presented at the meeting of the American Psychological Association, Toronto.

Steele, F. I. (1973). *Physical settings and organizational behavior.* Don Mills, Ontario: Addison-Wesley.

Steers, R. M. (1988). *Introduction to organizational behavior* (2nd ed.). Glenview, IL: Scott, Foresman.

Stein, M. B. (Ed.) (1995). *Social phobia.* Washington, DC: American Psychiatric Association.

Steinberg, L. (1986). Latchkey children and susceptibility to peer pressure: An ecological analysis. *Developmental Psychology, 22,* 433–439.

Steinberg, L. (1991). Parent-adolescent relations. In R. M. Lerner, A. C. Petersen, & J. Brooks-Gunn (Eds.). *Encyclopedia of adolescence* (Vol. 2). New York: Garland.

Steinberg, L. D. (1988). Simple solutions to a complex problem: A response to Rodman, Pratto, & Nelson (1988). *Developmental Psychology, 24,* 295–296.

Stemberger, R. T., Turner, S. M., Beidel, D. C., & Calhoun, K. S. (1995). Social phobia: An analysis of possible developmental factors. *Journal of Abnormal Psychology, 104,* 526–531.

Stenhouse, G. (1996). *Practical parenting.* New York: Oxford.

Stern, J. S. (1984). Is obesity a disease of inactivity? In A. J. Stunkard & E. Stellar (Eds.), *Eating and its disorders.* New York: Raven.

Sternberg, R. J. (1985, November). Teaching critical thinking. Part 1: Are we making critical mistakes? *Phi Delta Kappan,* 194–198.

Sternberg, R. J. (1986). *Intelligence applied.* San Diego: Harcourt Brace Jovanovich.

Sternberg, R. J. (1988). *The triangle of love.* New York: Basic Books.

Sternberg, R. J. (1989). Introduction. In R. J. Sternberg (Ed.), *Advances in the psychology of human intelligence (Vol. 5).* Hillsdale, NJ: Erlbaum.

Sternberg, R. J. (1993, August). Recent advances in the psychology of love. Paper presented at the meeting of the American Psychological Association, Toronto.

Sternberg, R. J. (1993). Procedures for identifying intellectual potential in the gifted. In K. A. Heller, F. J. Monks, & A. H. Passow (Eds.), *International Handbook of Research and Development of Giftedness and Talent.* New York: Pergamon.

Sternberg, R. J., Conway, B. E., Ketron, J. L., & Berstein, M. (1981). People's conceptions of intelligence. *Journal of Personality and Social Psychology, 41,* 37–55.

Steur, F. B., Applefield, J. M., & Smith, R. (1971). Televised aggression and the interpersonal aggression of preschool children. *Journal of Experimental Child Psychology, 11,* 442–447.

Stevens, R. (1997). Neuroscience. In P. Scott & C. Spencer (Eds.), *Psychology.* Cambridge, MA: Blackwell.

Stevenson, H. W., Lee, S., Chen, C., Stigler, J., Hsu, C., & Kitamura, G. (1990). Contexts of achievement. *Monograph of the Society for Research in Child Development* (Serial No. 221, Vol. 55, Nos. 1–2).

Stevenson, H. W., Chen, C., & Lee, S. Y. (1993). Mathematics achievement of Chinese, Japanese, and American children: Ten years later. *Science, 259,* 53–58.

Stevenson, H. W. (1995, March). *Missing date: On the forgotten substance of race, ethnicity, and socioeconomic classification.* Paper presented at the meeting of the Society for Research in Child Development, Indianapolis.

Stevenson, H. W. (1995). Mathematics achievement of American students: First in the world by the year 2000? In C. A. Nelson (Ed.), *Basic and applied perspectives on learning, cognition, and development.* Minneapolis: University of Minnesota Press.

Stevenson, M. R., & Black, K. N. (1996). *How divorce affects offspring.* Boulder: Co: Westview Press.

Stewart, E. S. (1995, August). *Ethical decisions in social relationships with clients: Reasons for behavior.* Paper presented at the meeting of the American Psychological Association, New York City.

Stokols, D., & Novaco, R. W. (1981). Transportation and well-being: An ecological perspective. In I. Altman, J. F. Wohlwill, & P. B. Everett (Eds.), *Transportation and behavior.* New York: Plenum Press.

Stokols, D., Shumaker, S. A., & Martinez, J. (1983). Residential mobility and personal well-being. *Journal of Environmental Psychology, 3,* 5–19.

Stoner, J. (1961). *A comparison of individual and group decisions, including risk.* Unpublished master's thesis, School of Industrial Management, MIT.

Stoppard, J. M., & Gruchy, C. D. G. (1993). Gender, context, and expression of positive emotion. *Personality and Social Psychology Bulletin, 19,* 143–150.

Stotland, S., & Zuroff, D. C. (1991). Relations between multiple measures of dieting, self-efficacy, and weight change in a behavioral weight control program. *Behavior Therapy, 22,* 47–59.

Strean, H. S. (1996). Resistance viewed from different perspectives. *American Journal of Psychotherapy, 50,* 29–31.

Streissguth, A. P., Martin, D. C., Sandman, B. M., Kirchner, G. L., & Darby, B. L. (1984). Intrauterine alcohol and nicotine exposure: Attention and reaction time in four-year-old children. *Developmental Psychology, 20,* 533–541.

Strier, K. B. (1992). *Faces in the forest: The endangered muriqui monkeys of Brazil.* New York: Oxford University Press.

Strupp, H. H. (1989). Psychotherapy. *American Psychologist, 44,* 717–724.

Strupp, H. H. (1995). The psychotherapist's skills revised. *Clinical Psychology: Science and Practice, 2,* 70–74.

Studer, M., & Thornton, A. (1987). Adolescent religiosity and contraceptive usage. *Journal of Marriage and the Family, 49,* 117–128.

Studer, M., & Thornton, A. (1989). The multifaceted impact of religiosity on adolescent sexual experience and contraceptive usage: A reply to Shornack and Ahmed. *Journal of Marriage and the Family, 51,* 1085–1089.

Stunkard, A. J. (1989). Perspectives on human obesity. In A. J. Stunkard & A. Baum (Eds.), *Perspectives on behavioral medicine: Eating, sleeping, and sex.* Hillsdale, NJ: Erlbaum.

Stunkard, A. J., Harris, J. R., Pedersen, N. L., & McClearn, G. E. (1990). A separated twin study of the body mass index. *New England Journal of Medicine, 322,* 1483–1487.

Subich, L. M., & Billingsley, K. D. (1995). Integrating career assessment into counseling. In W. B. Walsh & S. H. Osipow (Eds.), *Handbook of vocational psychology (2nd ed.).* Hillsdale, NJ: Erlbaum.

Sue, D. W. (1996). Multicultural counseling: Models, methods, and actions. *The Counseling Psychologist, 24,* 279–284.

Sue, D. W. (Ed.) (1996). *Theory of multicultural counseling and therapy.* Pacific Grove, CA: Brooks/Cole.

Sue, D. W., Ivey, A. E., & Petersen, P. (1996). Research, practice, and training implications of multicultural counseling theory. In D. W. Sue (Ed.), *Theory of multicultural counseling and therapy.* Pacific Grove, CA: Brooks/Cole.

Sue, S. (1990, August). *Ethnicity and culture in psychological research and practice.* Paper presented at the meeting of the American Psychological Association, Boston.

Sue, S. (1991, August). *Ethnicity and culture in psychological research and practice.* Paper presented at the meeting of the American Psychological Association, Boston.

Sue, S., Allen, D., & Conaway, L. (1978). The responsiveness and equality of mental health care to Chicanos and Native Americans. *American Journal of Community Psychology, 6,* 137–146.

Suedfeld, P., & Coren, S. (1989). Perceptual isolation, sensory deprivation, and rest: Moving introductory psychology texts out of the 1950s. *Canadian Psychology, 30,* 17–29.

Suedfeld, P., Metcalfe, J., & Bluck, S. (1987). Enhancement of scientific creativity by flotation REST (Restricted Environmental Stimulation Technique). *Journal of Environmental Psychology, 7,* 219–231.

Suinn, R. M. (1984). *Fundamentals of abnormal psychology.* Chicago: Nelson-Hall.

Suinn, R. M. (1987). Asian Americans in psychology. In P. J. Woods & C. S. Wilkinson (Eds.), *Is psychology the major for you?* Washington, DC: American Psychological Association.

Sullivan, H. S. (1953). *The interpersonal theory of psychiatry.* New York: W. W. Norton.

Sullivan, L. (1991, May 25). US secretary urges TV to restrict "irresponsible sex and reckless violence." *Boston Globe,* p. A1.

Sulloway, E. J. (1994). *Born to rebel: Radical thinking in science and social thought.* Unpublished manuscript, Massachusetts Institute of Technology, Program in Science, Technology, and Society, Cambridge.

Suls, J. (1989). Self-awareness and self-identity. In J. Worrell & F. Danner (Eds.), *The adolescent as decision maker.* New York: Academic Press.

Suomi, S. J. (1996). *Behavioral physiological and physical changes associated with adolescence in Rhesus monkeys.* Paper presented at the meeting of the Society for Research on Adolescence, Boston.

Super, C. M. (1980). Cross-cultural research on infancy. In H. C. Triandis & A. Heron (Eds.), *Handbook of cross-cultural psychology, developmental psychology* (Vol. 4). Boston: Allyn & Bacon.

Super, C. M., & Harkness, S. (1982). The development of affect in infancy and early childhood. In D. A. Wagner & H. W. Stevenson (Eds.), *Cultural perspectives on child development.* San Francisco: W. H. Freeman.

Super, D. E. (1967). *The psychology of careers.* New York: Harper & Row.

Super, D. E. (1976). *Career education and the meanings of work.* Washington, DC: U.S. Office of Education.

Super, D. E. (1988). Vocational adjustment: Implementing a self-concept. *Vocational Guidance Quarterly, 36,* 351–357.

Susman, E. J., Murowchick, E., Worrall, B. K., & Murray, D. A. (1995, March). *Emotionality, adrenal hormones, and context interactions during puberty and pregnancy.* Paper presented at the meeting of the Society for Research in Child Development, Indianapolis.

Susman, E. J., Worrall, B. K., Murowchiick, E., Frobose, C. A., & Schwab, J. E. (1996). Experience and neuroendocrine parameters of development: Aggressive behavior and competencies. In D. M. Stoff & R. B. Cairns (Eds.), *Aggression and violence.* Hillsdale, NJ: Erlbaum.

Sutton, R. G., & Kessler, M. (1986). National study of the effects of clients' socioeconomic status on clinical psychologists' professional judgments. *Journal of Consulting and Clinical Psychology, 54,* 275–276.

Suzman, R. M., Harris, T., Hadley, E. C., Kovar, M. G., & Weindruch, R. (1992). The robust oldest old: Optimistic perspectives for increasing healthy life expectancy. In R. M. Suzman, D. P. Willis, & K. G. Manton (Eds.), *The oldest old.* New York: Oxford University Press.

Swann, W. B. (1987). Identity negotiation: Where two roads meet. *Journal of Personality and Social Psychology, 53,* 1038–1051.

Swann, W. B., De La Ronde, C., & Hixon, J. G. (1994). Authenticity and positive strivings in marriage and courtship. *Journal of Personality and Social Psychology, 66,* 857–869.

Swann, W. B., Stein-Seroussi, A., Giesler, R. B. (1992). Why people self-verify. *Journal of Personality and Social Psychology, 62,* 392–401.

Swets, J. A. (1964). *Signal detection and recognition by human observers.* New York: Wiley.

Swim, J. K., Aikin, K. J., Hall, W. S., & Hunter, B. A. (1995). Sexism and racism: Old-fashioned and modern prejudices. *Journal of Personality and Social Psychology, 68,* 199–214.

Symons, D. (1979). *The evolution of human sexuality.* New York: Oxford University Press.

Synder, M. (1979). Self-monitoring processes. In L. Berkowitz (Ed.), *Advances in experimental social psychology* (Vol. 12). New York: Academic Press.

Szasz, I. (1977). *Psychiatric slavers: When confinement and coercion masquerade as cure.* New York: Free Press.

Szasz, T. (1965). *The ethics of psychoanalysis.* New York: Basic Books.

Taber, T. D., & Alliger, G. M. (1995). A task-level assessment of job satisfaction. *Journal of Organizational Behavior, 16,* 101–111.

Tafoya, T. (1993, August). *Who's parenting the parents? Shattered scripts, missing models, and AIDS.* Paper presented at the meeting of the American Psychological Association, Toronto.

Tager-Flusberg, H. (Ed.). (1994). *Constraints on language acquisition.* Hillsdale, NJ: Erlbaum.

Tajfel, H. (1978). The achievement of group differentiation. In H. Tajfel (Ed.), *Differentiation between social groups: Studies in the social psychology of intergroup relations.* London: Academic Press.

Takanishi, R., & DeLeon, P. H. (1994). A Head Start for the 21st century. *American Psychologist, 49,* 120–122.

Talbert, F. S., & Pipes, R. B. (1988). Informed consent for psychotherapy: Content analysis of selected forms. *Professional Psychology, 19,* 131–132.

Tamarin, R. (1996). *Principles of genetics (5th ed.).* Dubuque, IA: Wm. C. Brown.

Tamir, L. M. (1982). *Men in their forties.* New York: Springer.

Tamminen, K. (1991). *Religious development in childhood and youth: An empirical study.* Helsinki: Suomen Tiedeakatemia. (Available from the Finnish Academy of Science and Letters, Tiedekirja, Kirkkokatu 14, 00170, Helsinki, Finland.

Tannen, D. (1990). *You just don't understand: Women and men in conversation.* New York: Ballantine.

Tauber, R. T. (1995). Overcoming misunderstandings about the concept of negative reinforcement. In M. E. Ware & D. E. Johnson (Eds.), *Demonstrations and activities in teaching of psychology (Vol. 2).* Hillsdale, NJ: Erlbaum.

Tavris, C. (1982, November). Anger diffused. *Psychology Today,* pp. 25–35.

Tavris, C. (1989). *Anger: The misunderstood emotion* (2nd ed.). New York: Touchstone.

Tavris, C., & Wade, C. (1984). *The longest war: Sex differences in perspective* (2nd ed.). San Diego: Harcourt Brace Jovanovich.

Taylor, S. E. (1979). Hospital patient behavior: Reactance, helplessness, or control? *Journal of Social Issues, 35,* 156–184.

Taylor, S. E. (1995). *Health psychology* (3rd ed.). New York: McGraw-Hill.

Taylor, S. E., & Brown, J. D. (1994). Positive illusions and well-being revisited: Separating fact from fiction. *Psychological Bulletin, 116,* 21–27.

Taylor, S. E., Collins, R., Skokan, L., & Aspinwall, L. (1988, August). *Illusion, reality, and adjustment in coping with victimizing events.* Paper presented at the meeting of the American Psychological Association, Atlanta.

Taylor, S. E., Kemeny, M. E., Schneider, S. G., & Aspinwall, L. G. (1993). Coping with the threat of AIDS. In J. B. Pryor & G. D. Reeder (Eds.), *The social psychology of HIV infection.* Hillsdale, NJ: Erlbaum.

Taylor, S. E., Peplau, L. A., & Sears, D. O. (1994). *Social psychology* (8th ed.). Englewood Cliffs, NJ: Prentice Hall.

Taylor, S. E., Peplau, L. A., & Sears, D. O. (1997). *Social psychology (8th ed.).* Upper Saddle River, NJ: Prentice Hall.

Teachman, J. D., & Polonko, K. A. (1990). Cohabitation and marital stability in the United States. *Social Forces, 69,* 207–220.

Teasdale, J. D., Taylor, M. J., Cooper, Z., Hayhurst, H., & Paykel, E. S. (1996). Depressive thinking: Shifts in construct accessibility or in schematic mental models? *Journal of Abnormal Psychology, 104,* 500–507.

Tedeschi, J. T., & Felson, R. B. (1994). *Violence, aggression, and coercive actions.* Washington, DC: American Psychological Association.

Temoshok, L., & Dreher, H. (1992). *The Type C syndrome.* New York: Random House.

Tenopyr, M. L. (1996, June). *The future of personnel research in America.* Paper presented at the meeting of the American Psychological Society, San Francisco.

Terman, L. H., & Oden, M. H. (1959). *Genetic studies of genius: Vol. 5. The gifted group at mid-life.* Stanford, CA: Stanford University Press.

Terrace, H. (1979). *Nim.* New York: Knopf.

Teti, D. M., & Teti, L. O. (1996). Infant-parent relationships. In N. Vanzetti & S. Duck (Eds.), *A lifetime of relationships.* Pacific Grove, CA: Brooks/Cole.

Tetrick, L. E., & Barling, J. (Eds.) (1995). *Changing employment relations.* Washington, DC: American Psychological Association.

Tett, R. P., Jackson, D. N., & Rothstein, M. (1991). Personality measures as predictors of job performance: A meta-analytic review. *Personnel Psychology, 44,* 703–742.

Thayer, J. F., Rossy, L., Sollers, J., Friedman, B. H., & Allen, M. T. (1996, March). *Relationships among heart period variability and cardiodynamic measures vary as a function of fitness.* Paper presented at the meeting of the American Psychosomatic Society, Williamsburg, VA.

Thieman, T. J. (1995). A classroom demonstration of encoding specificity. In M. E. Ware & D. E. Johnson (Eds.), *Demonstrations and activities in teaching of psychology.* Hillsdale, NJ: Erlbaum.

Thigpen, C. H., & Cleckley, H. M. (1957). *Three Faces of Eve.* New York: McGraw-Hill.

Thomas, C. B. (1983). Unpublished manuscript, Johns Hopkins University, Baltimore.

Thomas, D. A., & Alderfer, C. P. (1989). The influence of race on career dynamics: Theory and research on minority career experiences. In M. Arthur, D. Hall, & B. Lawrence (Eds.), *Handbook of career theory.* Cambridge, England: Cambridge University Press.

Thompson, C. P., Skowronski, J. J., Larsen, S. F., & Betz, A. (1996). *Autobiographical memory.* Hillsdale, NJ: Erlbaum.

Thompson, J. K. (Ed.) (1996). *Body image, eating disorders, and obesity.* Washington, DC: American Psychological Association.

Thompson, R. (1996, June). *Memory , mind, and behavior.* Commentary at the presidential symposium of the American Psychological Society, San Francisco.

Thompson, R. A. (1991). Construction and reconstruction of early attachments: Taking perspective on attachment theory and research. In D. P. Keating & H. G. Rosen (Eds.), *Constructivist perspectives on atypical development.* Hillsdale, NJ: Erlbaum.

Thompson, R. A., & Cimbolic, P. (1978). Black students' counselor preference and attitudes toward counseling center use. *Journal of Counseling Psychology, 25,* 570–575.

Thompson, R. F. (1989). A model system approach to memory. In P. R. Solomon, G. R. Goethals, C. M. Kelley, & B. R. Stephens (Eds.), *Memory: Interdisciplinary approaches.* New York: Springer-Verlag.

Thornburg, H. D. (1981). Sources of sex education among early adolescents. *Journal of Early Adolescence, 1,* 171–184.

Thorndike, E. L. (1898). Some experiments on animal intelligence. *Science, 7,* 818–824.

Thorndike, E. (1906). *Principles of teaching.* New York: Seiler.

Thorndike, E. L. (1911). *Animal intelligence.* New York: Macmillan.

Thornton, A., & Camburn, D. (1989). Religious participation and sexual behavior and attitudes. *Journal of Marriage and the Family, 51,* 641–653.

Thurstone, L. L. (1938). *Primary mental abilities.* Chicago: University of Chicago Press.

Tinbergen, N. (1963). On aims and methods of ethology. *Zeitschrift für Tierpsychologie, 20,* 410–429.

Tinbergen, N. (1969). *The study of instinct.* New York: Oxford University Press. (Originally published 1951)

Tobin, J. J. (1987). The American idealization of old age in Japan. *Gerontologist, 27,* 53–58.

Tolan, P., Miller, L., & Thomas, P. (1988). Perception and experience of types of social stress and self-image among adolescents. *Journal of Youth and Adolescence, 17,* 147–163.

Tolman, E. C. (1932). *Purposive behavior in animals and man.* New York: Appleton-Century-Crofts.

Tolman, E. C. (1948). Cognitive maps in rats and men. *Psychological Review, 55,* 189–208.

Tomlinson-Keasey, C. (1990). The working lives of Terman's gifted women. In H. W. Grossman & N. L. Chester (Eds.), *The experience and meaning of work in women's lives.* Hillsdale, NJ: Erlbaum.

Tomlinson-Keasey, C. (1993, August). *Tracing the lives of gifted women.* Paper presented at the meeting of the American Psychological Association, Toronto.

Tomlinson-Keasey, C., Warren, L. W., & Elliott, J. F. (1986). Suicide among gifted women. A prospective study. *Journal of Abnormal Psychology, 95,* 123–130.

Tompkins, S. S. (1962). *Affect, imagery, and consciousness* (Vol. 1). New York: Springer.

Tompkins, S. S. (1981). The quest for primary motives: Biography and autobiography of an idea. *Journal of Personality and Social Psychology, 41,* 306–329.

Toothaker, L. E., & Miller, L. (1996). *Introductory statistics for the behavioral sciences (2nd ed.).* Pacific Grove, CA: Brooks/Cole.

Torney-Purta, J. (1993, August). *Cross-cultural examination of measures of faith development.* Paper presented at the meeting of the American Psychological Association, Toronto.

Torrey, E. F., & others. (1984). Endemic psychosis in western Ireland. *American Journal of Psychiatry, 141,* 966–970.

Trankina, F. (1983). Clinical issues and techniques in working with Hispanic children and their families. In G. J. Powell, J. Yamamoto, A. Romero, & A. Morales (Eds.), *The psychosocial development of minority group children.* New York: Brunner/Mazel.

Treboux D. A., & Busch-Rossnagel, N. A. (1991). Sexual behavior, sexual attitudes, and contraceptive use, age differences in adolescent. In R. M. Lerner, A. C. Petersen, & J. Brooks-Gunn (Eds.), *Encyclopedia of adolescence* (Vol. 2). New York: Garland.

Tremblay, R. E., & Schaal, B. (1995, March). *Testosterone levels of physically active boys.* Paper presented at the meeting of the Society for Research in Child Development, Indianapolis.

Triandis, H. C. (1991, August). *Training for diversity.* Paper presented at the meeting of the American Psychological Association, San Francisco.

Triandis, H. C. (1994). Culture and social behavior. In W. J. Lonner & R. Malpass (Eds.), *Psychology and culture.* Needham Heights, MA: Allyn & Bacon.

Trimble, J. E. (1989). *The enculturation of contemporary psychology.* Paper presented at the meeting of the American Psychological Association, New Orleans.

Trimble, J. E., & Fleming, C. (1989). Client, counselor, and community characteristics. In P. Pedersen, J. Draguns, W. Lonner, & J. Trimble (Eds.), *Counseling across cultures* (3rd ed.). Honolulu: University of Hawaii Press.

Triplett, N. (1898). The dynamogenic factors in peacemaking and competition. *American Journal of Psychology, 9,* 507–533.

Trivers, R. (1971). The evolution of reciprocal altruism. *Quarterly Review of Biology, 46,* 35–57.

Tryon, R. C. (1940). Genetic differences in maze-learning ability in rats. In the *39th Yearbook, National Society for the Study of Education.* Chicago: University of Chicago Press.

Tulving, E. (1972). Episodic and semantic memory. In E. Tulving & W. Donaldson (Eds.), *Origins of memory.* San Diego: Academic Press.

Tulving, E. (1983). *Elements of episodic memory.* New York: Oxford University Press.

Tulving, E. (1989). Remembering and knowing the past. *American Scientist, 77,* 361–367.

Tulving, E., & Schacter, D. L. (1990). Priming and human memory systems. *Science, 247,* 301–306.

Tulving, E., Schacter, D. L., & Stark, H. A. (1982). Priming effects in word-fragment completion are independent of recognition memory. *Journal of Experimental Psychology: Learning, Memory, and Cognition, 8,* 336–342.

Tunnell, G. B. (1995, August). *Treatment model for couples therapy with HIV-positive gay men.* Paper presented at the meeting of the American Psychological Association, New York City.

Turnbull, C. (1961). Some observations regarding the experiences and behavior of the Bambuti Pygmies. *American Journal of Psychology, 74,* 304–308.

Turnbull, C. (1972). *The mountain people.* New York: Simon & Schuster.

Turpin, G., & Slade, P. (1997). Psychology and health. In P. Scott & C. Spencer (Eds.), *Psychology.* Cambridge, MA: Blackwell.

Tversky, A., & Kahneman, D. (1973). Availability: A heuristic for judging frequency and probability. *Cognitive Psychology, 5,* 207–232.

Tyler, C. (1983). Sensory processing of binocular disparity. In C. M. Schor & K. J. Ciuffreda (Eds.), *Vergence eye movements.* Boston: Butterworths.

U.S. Bureau of the Census. (1990). *Statistical abstracts of the United States, 1900.* Washington, DC: U.S. Department of Commerce.

U.S. Department of Justice, Bureau of Justice Statistics. (1983, October). *Report to the nation on crime and violence* (Report No. NJC-87068). Washington, DC: U.S. Government Printing Office.

Ulbrich, P. M. (1988). The determinants of depression in two-income marriages. *Journal of Marriage and the Family, 50,* 121–131.

Ulrich, R. S. (1984). View through a window may influence recovery from surgery. *Science, 224,* 420–421.

Ulrich, R. S., Simons, R. F., Losito, B. D., Fiorito, E., Miles, M. A., & Zelson, M. (1991). Stress recovery during exposure to natural and urban environments. *Journal of Environmental Psychology, 11,* 201–230.

Unger, R. (1992). Time and time again. *Psychology of Women Newsletter, 19,* 1–2.

Unger, R., & Crawford, M. (1992). *Women and gender* (2nd ed.). New York: McGraw-Hill.

Unger, R., & Crawford, M. (1996). *Women and gender: A feminist psychology* (2nd ed.). New York: McGraw-Hill.

United Nations. (1992). *1991 demographic yearbook.* New York: United Nations.

Usui, C. (1989). Can Japanese society promote individualism? In D. I. Kertzer & K. W. Schaie (Eds.), *Age structuring in comparative perspective.* Hillsdale, NJ: Erlbaum.

Vaillant, G. E. (1977). *Adaptation to life.* Boston: Little, Brown.

Van Deventer, W. (1983, November). Graphoanalysis as a management tool. *United States Banker,* pp. 74–76.

Vandell, D. L., & Corasaniti, M. A. (1988). Variations in early child care: Do they predict subsequent social, emotional, and cognitive differences? *Child Development, 59,* 176–186.

Vannoy-Hiller, D., & Philliber, W. W. (1989). *Equal partners: Successful women in marriage.* Newbury Park, CA: Sage.

Veitch, J. A., Gifford, R., & Hine, D. W. (1993). End-users' knowledge, beliefs, and preferences for lighting. *Journal of Interior Design, 19* (2), 15–26.

Veitch, R., & Arkkelin, D. (1995). *Environmental psychology.* Upper Saddle River, NJ: Prentice Hall.

Ventis, W. L. (1995). The relationships between religion and mental health. *Journal of Social Issues.*

Veraa, R. P., & Grafstein, B. (1981). Cellular mechanisms for recovery from nervous system injury: A conference report. *Experimental Neurology, 71,* 6–75.

Vernoy, M. W. (1995). Demonstrating classical conditioning in introductory psychology: Needles do not always make balloons pop! In M. E. Ware & D. E. Johnson (Eds.), *Demonstrations and activities in teaching of psychology (Vol. 2).* Hillsdale, NJ: Erlbaum.

Visconti, R. (1991). Introduction. In J. M. Hummerow (Ed.), *New directions in career planning and the workplace.* Palo Alto, CA: Consulting Psychologists Press.

Vokey, J. R., & Read, J. D. (1985). Subliminal messages: Between the devil and the media. *American Psychologist, 40,* 1231–1239.

Von Békésy, G. (1960). Vibratory patterns of the basilar membrane. In E. G. Wever (Ed.), *Experiments in hearing.* New York: McGraw-Hill.

von Frisch, K. (1974). Decoding the language of a bee. *Science, 185,* 663–668.

von Helmholtz, H. (1866/1962). *Treatise on physiological optics* (3 Vol.). New York: Dover.

Vosniadou, S., & Ortony, A. (Eds.). (1989). *Similarity and analogical reasoning.* New York: Cambridge University Press.

Voss, J. F., & Post, T. A. (1988). On the solving of ill-structured problems. In M. Chi, R. Glaser, & M. J. Farr (Eds.), *The nature of expertise* (pp. 261–285). Hillsdale, NJ: Erlbaum.

Vygotsky, L. S. (1962). *Thought and language.* Cambridge: MIT Press.

Wadden, T. A., Foster, G. D., Stunkard, A. J., & Conill, A. M. (1996). Effects of weight cycling on the resting energy expenditure and body composition of obese women, *Eating Disorders, 19,* 5–12.

Waddington, C. H. (1957). *The strategy of the genes.* London: Allen & Son.

Wagner, R. K. (1987). Tacit knowledge in everyday intelligent behavior. *Journal of Personality and Social Psychology, 52,* 1236–1247.

Wahlstrom, B. J. (1992). *Perspectives on human communication.* Dubuque, IA: Wm. C. Brown.

Walborn, F. S. (1996). *Process variables.* Pacific Grove, CA: Brooks/Cole.

Wald, G., & Brown, P. K. (1964). Human color vision and color blindness. *Cold Spring Harbor Symposia on Quantitative Biology, 30,* 345–359.

Wallace, R. K., & Benson, H. (1972). The physiology of meditation. *Scientific American, 226,* 85–90.

Waller, N. G., Kosetin, B. A., Bouchard, T. J., Jr., Lykken, D. T., & Tellegen, A. (1990). Genetic and environmental influences on religious interests, attitudes, and values: A study of twins reared apart and together. *Psychological Science, 1* (2), 138–142.

Wallerstein, J. S. (1989). *Second chances.* New York: Ticknor & Fields.

Wallerstein, R. S. (1989). The psychotherapy research project of the Menninger Foundation: An overview. *Journal of Consulting and Clinical Psychology, 57,* 195–205.

Wallis, C. (1985, December 9). Children having children. *Time,* pp. 78–88.

Walsh, W. B. (1995, August). *Personal-environment psychology: Contemporary models and perspectives.* Paper presented at the meeting of the American Psychological Association, New York City.

Walsh, W. B., & Betz, N. E. (1995). *Tests and assessment (3rd ed.).* Upper Saddle River, NJ: Prentice Hall.

Walster, E., Aronson, E., Abrahams, D., & Rottman, L. (1966). Importance of physical attractiveness in dating behavior. *Journal of Personality and Social Psychology, 4,* 508–516.

Wang, Z. X., & Novak, M. A. (1992). Influence of the social environment on parental behavior and pup development of meadow voles (*Mictrotus pennsylvanicus*) and prairie voles (*Microtus ochrogaster*). *Journal of Comparative Psychology, 106,* 163–171.

Ward, R. A., & Grashail, A. F. (1996). Using astrology to teach research methods to introductory psychology students. In M. E. Ware & D. E. Johnson (Eds.), *Demonstrations and activities in teaching of psychology (Vol. 1).* Hillsdale, NJ: Erlbaum.

Wass, H., Miller, M. D., & Readitt, C. A. (1991). Adolescents and destructive themes in rock music: A follow-up. *Omega, 23,* 199–206.

Wasserman, G. S. (1978). *Color vision: An historical introduction.* New York: Wiley.

Waterman, A. S., & Archer, S. I. (in press). A life-span perspective on identity formation. In P. B. Baltes, D. L. Featherman, & R. M. Lerner (Eds.), *Life-span development and behavior* (Vol. 10). Hillsdale, NJ: Erlbaum.

Waterman, J. A. (1991). Career and life planning: A personal gyroscope in times of change. In J. M. Hummerow (Ed.), *New directions in career planning and the workplace.* Palo Alto, CA: Consulting Psychologists Press.

Waters, E. (1991). Individual differences in infant-mother attachment. In J. Columbo & J. W. Fagen (Eds.), *Individual differences in infancy.* Hillsdale, NJ: Erlbaum.

Waters, E., Merrick, S. K., Albersheim, L. J., & Treboux, E. (1995, March). *Attachment security from infancy to early adulthood: A 20-year longitudinal study.* Paper presented at the meeting of the Society for Research in Child Development, Indianapolis.

Waters, H. S. (1989, April). *Problem solving at two: A year-long naturalistic study of two children.* Paper presented at the Society for Research in Child Development conference, Kansas City.

Watkins, C. E., Campbell, V. L., Nieberding, R., & Hallmark, R. (1995). Contemporary practice of psychological assessment by clinical psychologists. *Professional Psychology, 26,* 54–60.

Watkins, C. W., Lopez, F. G., Campbell, V. L., & Himmell, C. D. (1986). Counseling psychology and clinical psychology: Some preliminary comparative data. *American Psychologist, 41,* 581–582.

Watson, D. L., & Tharp, R. G. (1989). *Self-directed behavior* (5th ed.). Pacific Grove, CA: Brooks/Cole.

Watson, J. B. (1913). Psychology as the behaviorist views it. *Psychological Review, 20,* 158–177.

Watson, J. B. (1928). *Psychological care of the infant and child.* New York: Norton.

Watson, J. B., & Raynor, R. (1920). Emotional reactions. *Journal of Experimental Psychology, 3,* 1–14.

Watson, R. I. (1963). *The great psychologists.* Philadelphia: Lippincott.

Watt, N. F. (1984). *Children at risk for schizophrenia: A longitudinal perspective.* New York: Cambridge University Press.

Weary, G., Stanley, M. A., & Harvey, J. H. (1989). *Attribution.* New York: Springer-Verlag.

Weaver, C. A. (1993). Do you need a "flash" to form a flashbulb memory? *Journal of Experimental Psychology: General, 122,* 39–46.

Weaver, R. F., & Hedrick, P. W. (1996). *Genetics (2nd ed.).* Dubuque, IA: Wm. C. Brown.

Webb, W. B. (1978). Sleep and dreams. *Annual Review of Psychology.* Palo Alto, CA: Annual Reviews.

Wechsler, D. (1949). *Wechsler Intelligence Scale for Children.* New York: Psychological Corporation.

Wechsler, D. (1955). *Wechsler Adult Intelligence Scale manual.* New York: Psychological Corporation.

Wechsler, D. (1967). *Wechsler Preschool and Primary Scale of Intelligence.* New York: Psychological Corporation.

Wechsler, D. (1972). "Hold" and "Don't Hold" test. In S. M. Chown (Ed.), *Human aging.* New York: Penguin.

Wechsler, D. (1974). *Wechsler Intelligence Scale for Children—Revised.* New York: Psychological Corporation.

Wechsler, D. (1981). *Wechsler Adult Intelligence Scale—Revised.* New York: Psychological Corporation.

Weinberg, R. A. (1989). Intelligence and IQ: Landmark issues and great debates. *American Psychologist, 44,* 98–104.

Weinberger, D. R., Berman, K. F., & Zec, R. F. (1986). Physiological dysfunction of the dorsolateral prefrontal cortex in schizophrenia. *Archives of General Psychiatry, 43,* 114–124.

Weisberg, R. W., & Alba, J. W. (1981). An examination of the alleged role of "fixation" in the solution of several "insight" problems. *Journal of Experimental Psychology: General, 110,* 169–192.

Weissman, M. M., & Boyd, J. H. (1985). Affective disorders: Epidemiology. In H. I. Kaplan & B. J. Sadock (Eds.), *Comprehensive textbook of psychiatry/IV.* Baltimore: Williams & Wilkins.

Wellisch, D. K., Wolcott, D. L., Pasnau, R. O., Fawzy, F. I., & Landsverk, J. (1989). An evaluation of the psychosocial problems of the homebound cancer patient: Relationship of patient adjustment to family problems. *Journal of Psychosocial Research, 7,* 55–76.

Wells, G. L. (1993). What do we know about eyewitness identification? *American Psychologist, 48,* 553–571.

Wender, P. H., Kety, S. S., Rosenthal, D., Schulsinger, F., Ortmann, J., & Lunde, I. (1986). Psychiatric disorders in the biological and adoptive families of adopted individuals with affective disorders. *Archives of General Psychiatry, 43,* 923–929.

Wenger, M. J., & Payne, D. G. (1996). Comprehension and retention of nonlinear text: Considerations of working memory and material-appropriate processing. *American Journal of Psychology, 109,* 93–130.

Wenzlaff, R. M., & Prohaska, M. L. (1989). When misery loves company: Depression, attributions, and responses to others' moods. *Journal of Experimental Social Psychology, 25,* 220–223.

Wertheimer, M. (1945). *Productive thinking.* New York: Harper.

West, M. J. (1985). *Landscape views and stress response in the prison environment.* Unpublished master's thesis, Department of Landscape Architecture, University of Washington, Seattle.

Westin, A. F. (1967). *Privacy and freedom.* New York: Atheneum.

Westman, M., & Etzion, D. (1995). Crossover of stress, strain, and resources from one spouse to another. *Journal of Organizational Behavior, 16,* 169–182.

Whaley, L. F., & Wong, D. L. (1988). *Essentials of pediatric nursing* (3rd ed.). St. Louis: C. V. Mosby.

Whiston, S. C., & Sexton, T. L. (1993). An overview of psychotherapy outcome research: Implications for practice. *Professional Psychology, 24,* 43–51.

Whitam, F. L., Diamond, M., & Martin, J. (1993). Homosexual orientation in twins: A report of 61 pairs and three triplet sets. *Archives of Sexual Behavior, 22,* 187–198.

Whitbourne, S. K. (1996). *The aging individual.* New York: Springer.

White, B. L. (1988). *Educating the infant and toddler.* Lexington, MA: Lexington Books.

White, H. R., Brick, J., & Hansell, S. (1993). A longitudinal investigation of alcohol use and aggression in adolescence. *Journal of Studies on Alcohol,* Supplement No. 11, 62–77.

White, M. J., & Lilly, D. L. (1995). Teaching attribution theory with a videotaped illustration. In M. E. Ware & D. E. Johnson (Eds.), *Demonstrations and activities in teaching of psychology (Vol. 3).* Hillsdale, NJ: Erlbaum.

White, R. W. (1959). Motivation reconsidered: The concept of competence. *Psychological Review, 66,* 297–333.

Whiting, B. B. (1989, April). *Culture and interpersonal behavior.* Paper presented at the biennial meeting of the Society for Research in Child Development, Kansas City.

Whiting, B. B., & Whiting, J. W. M. (1975). *Children of six cultures.* Cambridge, MA: Harvard University Press.

Whitley, B. E. (1996). *Principles of research in behavioral science.* Mountain View, CA: Mayfield.

Whitman, F. L., Diamond, M., & Martin, J. (1993). Homosexual orientation in twins: A report of 61 pairs of three triplet sets. *Archives of Sexual Behavior, 22,* 187–198.

Whitney, K., Sagrestano, L. M., & Maslach, C. (1994). Establishing the social impact of individuation. *Journal of Personality and Social Psychology, 66,* 1140–1153.

Whorf, B. L. (1956). *Language, thought, and creativity.* New York: Wiley.

Wickelgren, W. A. (1974). *How to solve problems.* New York: W. H. Freeman.

Wilcox, K. J., & Bouchard, T. J. (1996). Behavior genetics. *Encyclopedia of Science and Technology.* New York: McGraw-Hill.

Wilder, D. (1991, March 28). To save the Black family, the young must abstain. *Wall Street Journal,* p. A14.

Wilding, J., & Valentine, E. (1996). Memory and expertise. In D. Hermann, C. McEvoy, C. Hertzog, P. Hertel, & M. Johnson (Eds.), *Basic and applied memory research. (Vol. 1).* Hillsdale, NJ: Erlbaum.

Wiles, J., & Humphreys, M. S. (1993). Using artificial neural nets to model implicit and explicit memory test performance. In Graf, P., & Masson, M. E. J. (Eds.). *Implicit memory.* Hillsdale: NJ: Erlbaum.

Wilkinson, S., & Kitzinger, C. (1993). *Heterosexuality.* Newbury Park, CA: Sage.

William T. Grant Foundation Commission. (1988). *The forgotten half: Non-college bound youth in America.* New York: William T. Grant Foundation.

Williams, G. C. (1966). *Adaptation and natural selection: A critique of some current evolutionary thought.* Princeton, NJ: Princeton University Press.

Williams, J. (1987). *Psychology of women: Behavior in a biosocial context* (3rd ed.). New York: W. W. Norton.

Williams, J. E., & Best, D. L. (1982). *Measuring sex stereotypes: A thirty nation study.* Newbury Park, CA: Sage.

Williams, J. E., & Best, D. L. (1989). *Sex and psyche: Self-concept viewed cross-culturally.* Newbury Park, CA: Sage.

Williams, R. B. (1989). Biological mechanisms mediating the relationship between behavior and coronary prone behavior. In A. W. Siegman & T. Dembrowski (Eds.), *In search of coronary-prone behavior: Beyond Type A.* Hillsdale, NJ: Erlbaum.

Williams, R. B. (1995). Coronary prone behaviors, hostility, and cardiovascular health: Implications for behavioral and pharmacological interventions. In K. Orth-Gomer & N. Schneiderman (Eds.), *Behavioral medicine approaches to cardiovascular disease prevention.* Hillsdale, NJ: Erlbaum.

Williamson, S. J., & Kaufman, L. (1989). Advances in neuromagnetic instrumentation and studies of spontaneous brain activity. *Brain Topography, 2,* 129–139.

Wilson, E. O. (1975). *Sociobiology: The new synthesis.* Cambridge, MA: Harvard University Press.

Wilson, E. O. (1992). *The diversity of life.* New York: W. W. Norton.

Wilson, E. O. (1995, February). *Unity in biodiversity.* Paper presented at the meeting of the American Association for the Advancement of Science, Atlanta.

Wilson, G. T. (1993). Relationship of dieting and voluntary weight loss to psychological functioning and binge eating. *Annals of Internal Medicine, 119,* 727–730.

Wilson, G. T. (1994). Behavioral treatment of obesity: Thirty years and counting. *Advances in Behaviour Research and Therapy, 16,* 31–75.

Wilson, M. (1993). DSM-III and the transformation of American psychiatry. *American Journal of Psychiatry, 150,* 399–410.

Wilson, M. A., & McNaughton, B. L. (1994). Reactivation of hippocampal ensemble memories during sleep. *Science, 265,* 676–678.

Wilson, W. J., & Neckerman, K. M. (1986). Poverty and family structure: The widening gap between evidence and public policy issues. In S. Danziger & D. Weinberg (Eds.), *Fighting poverty.* Cambridge, MA: Harvard University Press.

Wineman, J. D. (1982). The office environment as a source of stress. In G. W. Evans (Ed.), *Environmental stress.* New York: Cambridge University Press.

Winner, E. (1986, August). Where pelicans kiss seals. *Psychology Today,* pp. 24–35.

Winter, D. G. (1973). *The power motive.* New York: Free Press.

Wippich, W. (1995). Priming on verbal perceptual tests: Roles of lexical, surface, and conceptual processes. *Psychological Research, 57,* 250–259.

Wise, R. A. (1980). Action of drugs of abuse on brain reward systems. *Pharmacology and Biochemical Behavior, 13,* 213–223.

Wise, R. A. (1988). Neurobiology of craving: Implications for the understanding and treatment of addiction. *Journal of Abnormal Psychology, 8,* 118–132.

Wise, R. A., & Rompre, P. P. (1989). Brain dopamine and reward. *Annual Review of Psychology, 40.* Palo Alto, CA: Annual Reviews.

Witkin, H. A., Mednick, S. A. Schulsinger, R., Bakkestrom, E., Christiansen, K. O., Goodenbough, D. R., Hirchhorn, K., Lunsteen, C., Owen, D. R., Philip, J., Ruben, D. B., & Stocking, M. (1976). Criminality in XYY and XXY men. *Science, 193,* 547–555.

Wober, M. (1966). Sensotypes. *Journal of Social Psychology, 70,* 181–189.

Wolpe, J. (1963). Behavior therapy in complex neurotic states. *British Journal of Psychiatry, 110,* 28–34.

Wong, H. Z. (1982). Asian and Pacific Americans. In L. Snowden (Ed.), *Reaching the undeserved: Mental health needs of neglected populations.* Beverly Hills, CA: Sage.

Wong, M. M., & Csikszentmihalyi, M. (1991). Affiliation motivation and daily experience: Some issues on gender differences. *Journal of Personality and Social Psychology, 609,* 154–164.

Wood, J. M., Nezworski, M. T., & Stejskal, W. J. (1996). The comprehensive system for the Rorschach: A critical examination. *Psychological Science, 7,* 3–10.

Wood, J. T. (1996). Gender, relationships, and communication. In J. T. Wood (Ed.), *Gendered relationships.* Mountain View, CA: Mayfield.

Wood, J. V. (1989). Theory and research concerning social comparisons of personal attributes. *Psychological Bulletin, 106,* 231–248.

Woods, P. J., & Wilkinson, C. S. (1987). *Is psychology the major for you?* Washington, DC: American Psychological Association.

Wooley, S. C., & Garner, D. M. (1991). Obesity treatment: The high cost of false hope. *Journal of the American Dietetic Association, 91,* 1248–1251.

Woolfenden, G. E. (1975). Florida scrub jay helpers at the nest. *Auk, 92,* 1–15.

Work in America. *Report of a special task force to the Secretary of Health, Education, and Welfare.* (1973). Cambridge: MIT Press.

Worrell, J., & Robinson, D. (1993). Feminist counseling therapy for the 21st century. *The Counseling Psychologist, 21,* 92–96.

Worschel, S. (1986). The role of cooperation in reducing intergroup conflict. In S. Worschel & W. G. Austin (Eds.), *Psychology of intergroup relations.* Chicago: Nelson-Hall.

Worschel, S., & Cooper, J. (1979). *Understanding social psychology.* Homewood, IL: Dorsey.

Wright, J. C. (1995, March). *Effects of viewing Sesame Street: The longitudinal study of media and time use.* Paper presented at the meeting of the Society for Research in Child Development, Indianapolis.

Wulff, D. M. (1991). *Psychology of religion: Classic and contemporary views.* New York: Wiley.

Yalom, I. D. (1975). *The therapy and practice of group psychotherapy.* New York: Basic Books.

Yalom, I. D. (Ed.). (1995). *The theory and practice of group psychotherapy* (4th ed.). New York: Basic Books.

Yang, K., & Bond, M. (1990). Exploring implicit personality constructs with indigenous or imported constructs: the Chinese case. *Journal of Personality and Social Psychology, 58,* 1085–1087.

Yankelovich, D., Skelly, F., & White, A. (1984). *Sex stereotypes and candidacy for high level political office.* New York: Yankelovich, Skelly, & White.

Yarmey, A. D. (1973). I recognize your face but I can't remember your name: Further evidence on the tip of the tongue phenomenon. *Memory and Cognition, 1,* 287–290.

Yeni-Komshian, G. H. (1995, February). *What happens to our first language when we learn a second language?* Paper presented at the meeting of the American Association for the Advancement of Science, Atlanta.

Yerkes, R. M. (1907). *The dancing mouse: A study of animal behavior.* New York: Macmillan.

Yinger, J. M. (1967). Pluralism, religion, and secularism. *Journal for the Scientific Study of Religion, 6,* 17–28.

Yoder, J. (1995). Teaching students to do interviewing. In M. E. Ware & D. E. Johnson (Eds.), *Demonstrations and activities in teaching of psychology (Vol. 1).* Hillsdale, NJ: Erlbaum.

Young, K. T. (1990). American conceptions of infant development from 1955 to 1984: What the experts are telling parents. *Child Development, 61,* 17–28.

Young, S. K., & Shahinfar, A. (1995, March). *The contributions of maternal sensitivity and child temperament to attachment status at 14 months.* Paper presented at the meeting of the Society for Research in Child Development, Indianapolis.

Yuill, N., Oakhill, J., & Parkin, A. (1989). Working memory, comprehension ability and the resolution of text anomaly. *British Journal of Psychology, 80,* 351–361.

Yutrzenka, B. A. (1995). Making a case for ethnic and cultural diversity in increasing treatment efficacy. *Journal of Consulting and Clinical Psychology, 63,* 197–206.

Zabin, L. S. (1986, May/June). Evaluation of a pregnancy prevention program for urban teenagers. *Family Planning Perspectives,* p. 119.

Zahn-Waxler, C. (1990, May 28). Commentary. *Newsweek,* p. 61.

Zajonc, R. B. (1965). Social facilitation. *Science, 149,* 269–274.

Zajonc, R. B. (1984). On the primacy of affect. *American Psychologist, 39,* 117–123.

Zatorre, R. J., Halpern, A. R., Perry, D. W., Meyer, E., & Evans, A. C. (1996). Hearing in the mind's ear: A PET investigation of musical imagery and perception. *Journal of Cognitive Neuroscience, 8,* 29–46.

Zeigler, L. H., & Harmon, W. (1989). More bad news about the news. *Public Opinion, 12,* 50–52.

Zelnik, M., & Kantner, J. F. (1977). Sexual and contraceptive experiences of young unmarried women in the United States, 1976 and 1971. *Family Planning Perspectives, 9,* 55–71.

Zeren, A. S., & Makosky, V. P. (1995). Teaching observational methods. In M. E. Ware & D. E. Johnson (Eds.), *Demonstrations and activities in teaching of psychology (Vol. 1).* Hillsdale, NJ: Erlbaum.

Ziegert, K. A. (1983). The Wedesih prohibition of corporal punishment: A preliminary report. *Journal of Marriage and the Family, 45,* 917–926.

Zigler, E. (1991, October). *Day care in America: What is needed.* Paper presented at the symposium on day care for children, Arlington, VA.

Zigler, E., & Frank, M. (Eds.). (1988). *The parental leave crisis: Toward a national policy.* New Haven, CT: Yale University Press.

Zigler, E., & Styfco, S. J. (1994). Head Start: Criticisms in a constructive context. *American Psychologist, 49,* 127–132.

Zilbergeld, B. (1992). *The new male sexuality.* New York: Bantam Books.

Zimbardo, P., Haney, C., Banks, W., & Jaffe, D. (1972). *The psychology of imprisonment: Privation, power, and pathology.* Unpublished manuscript, Stanford University, Stanford, CA.

Zola, S. (1996, June). *The medial temporal lobe memory system: Findings from human and non-human primates.* Paper presented at the meeting of the American Psychological Society, San Francisco.

Zorumski, C. F., & Isenberg, K. E. (1991). Insights into the structure and function of GABA-benzodiazepine receptors: Ion channels and psychiatry. *American Journal of Psychiatry, 148,* 162–171.

Zube, E. H., Pitt, D. G., & Anderson, T. W. (1975). Perception and prediction of scenic resource values of the Northeast. In E. H. Zube, R. O. Brush, & J. G. Fabos (Eds.), *Landscape assessment: Values, perceptions, and resources.* Stroudsburg, PA: Dowden, Hutchinson & Ross.

Zuckerman, M. (1978). Sensation seeking. In H. London and J. E. Exner (Eds.), *Dimensions of personality* (pp. 487–560). New York: Wiley.

Zuckerman, M. (1979). *Sensation seeking: Beyond the optimal level of arousal.* Hillsdale, NJ: Erlbaum.

Credits

Photographs

Chapter WIP

Opener: © Superstock; WIP.1 A&B: The Bettmann Archive; p. 6: © The Bettmann Archive; p. 8: © Brett Froomer/The Image Bank-Chicago; p. 9: © Tom McHugh/Photo Researchers; p. 10: © Jay Dickman; p. 12: © Mark Richards/PhotoEdit; WIP.2 A&B: The Bettmann Archive; WIP.2 C: Courtesy of Ruth Howard; WIP.2 D: The Bettmann Archive; WIP.2 E: Courtesy of Keith and Mamie Clark; WIP.2 F: The Bettmann Archive; WIP.2 G: Center for the Study of the Person; WIP.2 H: Courtesy of Albert Bandura; WIP.2 I: Courtesy of Eleanor Macoby; WIP.2 J: Courtesy of John Berry; photo credit Monica Hart; WIP.2 K: Courtesy of Sandra Bem; WIP.2 L: Courtesy of Judith Rodin; WIP.2 M: Courtesy of Roger Sperry; WIP.2 N,O&P: The Bettmann Archive; WIP.2 Q: Jane Reed; WIP.2 R: The Bettmann Archive; WIP.2 S: Courtesy of Archives of the History of American Psychology, University of Akron; WIP.2 T,U&V: The Bettmann Archive; WIP.2 W&X: Courtesy of Archives of the History of American Psychology, University of Akron; p. 14: The Bettmann Archive

Chapter MET

Opener: © Superstock; MET.1 A: © Rob Atkins/ The Image Bank-Chicago; p. 28: © Sharon Beals/Insight; p. 29: © Ken Regan Pictures; p. 31: © John Madere/Psychology Today, 1/85; p. 32: © Ed Tronick/Anthro Photo; MET.2 A: © 1996 The Museum of Modern Art, New York Guggenheim; MET.3 A: © Marc Romanelli/ The Image Bank-Chicago; MET.4 A: © Richard Hutchings/PhotoEdit; p. 41: Courtesy of Dr. Florence L. Denmark/Photo by Robert Wesner

Chapter BFB

Opener: © 1995 Artists Rights Society (ARS), New York/ADAGP, Paris; p. 51: © Enrico Ferorelli; BFB.1: © Regents of University of California; BFB.2 B: © Superstock; BFB.2 C: © Elyse Lewin/The Image Bank-Texas; BFB.3 A: © Michael P. Gadomski/Photo Researchers, Inc.; BFB.3 B: © John P. Kelly/The Image Bank-Chicago; BFB.4 A&B: Dept. of Health and Human Services; BFB.4 C: © Ed Kashi; BFB.5: National Library of Medicine; p. 58: © Dr. Francis Schiller; BFB.8 C: © Lennart Nilsson, Bonnier Alba AB, "Behold Man," Little, Brown & Company; BFB.12&13 A: © Lennart Nilsson, Bonnier Alba AB, "Behold Man," Little, Brown & Company; BFB.14 A: © Hank Morgan/Photo Researchers; BFB.17 B: John Wiley, California Institute of Technology, estate of James Olds; BFB.18: © A. Glauberman/Photo Researchers; BFB.20: © Wilder Penfield Papers/Montreal Neurological Institute; p. 73: © Rex USA, Ltd.; p. 75 (left): Courtesy of Jerre Levy; p. 75 (top left): The Bettmann Archive; p. 75 (top right): © Picture Group; p. 75(bottom left): NASA; p. 75 (bottom right): The Bettmann Archive; BFB.B 2: © James Balog/Tony Stone Images; BFB.24: © Charles Gupton/Picturesque; BFB.25: © Steven Peterson; BFB.26 A&B: © Hank Morgan/Rainbow; BFB.26 C: © Dan McCoy/ Rainbow; BFB.28 A: AP/Wide World Photos; BFB.28 B: © Personality Photos

Chapter S&P

Opener: Courtesy of John W. Santrock; S&P.1 A: © Bob Coyle; p. 93: © Shooting Star/Werb; S&P.2 B: © Helmut Gritscher/Peter Arnold, Inc.; S&P.2 C: © Douglas B. Nelson/Peter Arnold, Inc.; S&P.5: © Morris Karol; S&P.6 B: © Burton McNeely/The Image Bank-Texas; S&P.8: Courtesy of Mac Beth, Division of Koll Morgen; S&P.9 A&B: © Fritz Goro/Life Magazine, 1944, Time Inc.; S&P.14 B: © Chuck Kuhn/ The Image Bank-Chicago; S&P.14 C: © Chuck Mason/ The Image Bank-Chicago; S&P.17 A: © J.P. Laffont/ Sygma; S&P.17 B: Peabody Museum of Salem, Photograph by Mark Sexton; S&P.18 B: © Lennart Nilsson, Bonnier Alba AB, "Behold Man," Little, Brown & Company; S&P.19 A: © Lennart Nilsson, Bonnier Alba AB, "Behold Man," Little, Brown & Company; S&P.19 B: © Lou Jones/The Image Bank-Chicago; S&P.20 B: © Dr. Paul A. Zahl/Photo Researchers; S&P.22: © 1995 M.C. Escher/Cordon Art-Baarn-Holland; S&P.23: © Asahi Shimbun; S&P.25: © 1994 Jun Oi; S&P.26: Reproduction by courtesy of the Trustees, The National Gallery, London; S&P.A: 1996 Museum of Modern Art, New York; S&P.B: © Scala/Art Resource, New York; S&P.C: © Erich Lessing/ Art Resource, New York; S&P.D: © National Gallery of Art; S&P.29: © 1992 Lawrence Migdale; S&P.34 A: © Herman Eisenbeiss/Photo Researchers; S&P.34 B: © Emillo Mercado/ Jeroboam; S&P.36: © Dr. Peter Thompson; S&P.37: © Enrico Ferorelli; S&P.39: © R. Joedecke/The Image Bank-Chicago; S&P.40: © Psychology Today/Sussex Publishers; p. S&P.42: © Dana Fineman/Sygma

Chapter SOC

Opener: Courtesy of John W. Santrock; SOC.1 B: © Art Wolfe/Tony Stone Images; SOC.2 B: © Steve Dunwell/The Image Bank-Texas; SOC.2 C: © David Young-Wolff/PhotoEdit; SOC.2 D: © David Frazier Photolibrary; SOC.2 E: © Randy Duchaine/The Stock Market; SOC.2 F: © Luis Castaneda/The Image Bank-Chicago; SOC.2 G: © Caesar Paredes/The Stock Market; SOC.2 H: © Barry Christensen/Stock Boston; p. 140 A: © Joel Gordon; p. 140 B: © Dean Press Images/The Image Works; SOC.4: © J. Allan Hobson & Hoffman LaRoche/Massachusetts Mental Health Center; p. 144: © Michel Siffre; SOC.6 A: Scala/Art Resource, New York; SOC.6 B: Detroit Institute of Art; p. 149: © James Wilson/Woodfin Camp; p. 151 (top): © James Wilson/Woodfin Camp; p. 151 (bottom): © Ed Kashi/Psychology Today; p. 153: © Billy E. Barnes/PhotoEdit; p. 154: © John T. Barr/ Gamma-Liaison; SOC.7: none; SOC.8 B: © Derik Murray/The Image Bank-Chicago; SOC.8 C,D,E,F&G: Courtesy of Drug Enforcement Administration

Chapter LRN

Opener: © Superstock; p. 169: © 1992 Children's Television Workshop. Used by permission of Television Workshop; p. 170: © Whitney Lane/The Image Bank-Texas; LRN.1C: The Bettmann Archive; LRN.4 A: Courtesy of Dr. Ben Harris; LRN.5 B: © Marc Romanelli/The Image Bank-Chicago; LRN.7 B: © G&M David de Lossey/The Image Bank-Chicago; LRN.8 B: © David Frazier Photolibrary; LRN.10: © Richard Wood/The Picture Cube; p. 183: © Leo de Wys/Bob Krist; p. 187 (top): © Richard Hutchings/Photo Researchers; p. 187 (bottom): © Alan Becker/The Image Bank-Chicago; LRN.14 A&B: Courtesy of Albert Bandura; LRN.16 B: © John P. Kelly/The Image Bank-Chicago; LRN.20: Courtesy of Animal Behavior Enterprises, Inc.

Chapter MEM

Opener: Courtesy of John W. Santrock; MEM.2 B: © R. Kawakami/The Image Bank-Texas; p. 206: © Photo Researchers; MEM.8: Gary Matthiesen/Light Images; p. 212: © Max Winter/Stock Boston; MEM.10 A: © Derek Berwin/The Image Bank-Texas; p. 219 (top): © Spencer Grant/Stock Boston; p. 219 (bottom): The Bettmann Archive; p. 221: AP/ Wide World Photos; p. 224: © James L. Shaffer

Chapter T&L

Opener: © Scala/Art Resource, NY; p. 237 (top left): © Peter Menzel/Stock Boston; p. 237 (top right): © Makoto Iwafuji/Stock Market; p. 237 (bottom left): © Bob Gomel/Stock Market; p. 237 (bottom right): © Seth Resnick/Stock Boston; T&L.5 A: © P. & G. Bowater/The Image Bank-Chicago; T&L.6 A: © HMS Images/The Image Bank; p. 248: © Shooting Star; p. 251 (left): © V. J. Lorero/S.I. Picture Collection; p. 251 (right): © Jeff Greenberg/PhotoEdit; p. 253: © Superstock; T&L.18: New Yorker Magazine, Apr. 13, 1992, p. 41; p. 261: © Anthony Bannister/Animal Animals; T&L.19 A: Courtesy of Roger Brown; p. 263 (bottom): © Superstock; p. 263 (top): © Holton/Superstock; T&L.20: © Enrico Ferorelli; T&L.A: © Ed Kashi

Chapter INT

Opener: © Tate Gallery/Art Resource, NY; p. 277: © Stephen Collins/Photo Researchers; INT.1 A: © Monkmeyer Press/Merrim; INT.2 A: © David Hamilton/The Image Bank-Chicago; INT.2 B: © Steve Dunwell/The Image Bank-Texas; INT.2 C: © Meike Maas/The Image Bank-Texas; INT.5 B: © Historical Pictures/Stock Montage; INT.5 C: © Dictionary of American Portraits, Dover Publications; INT.5 D: © Culver Pictures; INT.5 E: Courtesy of Archives of the History of American Psychology, University of Akron; INT.5 F&G: © Historical Pictures/Stock Montage; INT.6 A: © David Young-Wolff/Tony Stone Images; INT.6 B: © Charles Place/The Image Bank-Chicago; INT.6 C: © Bill Varies/The Image Bank-Chicago; INT.6 D: © John P. Kelly/The Image Bank-Chicago; INT.6 E: © Steve Niedorf/The Image Bank-Chicago; INT.6 F: © Jan Halaska, 1993/Photo Researchers; INT.6 G: © Myrleen Ferguson/PhotoEdit; INT.7 A: © G&J Anders/The Image Bank-Texas; INT.7 B: © Meike Maas/The Image Bank-Texas; INT.7 C: © Bob Daemmrich/The Image Works; INT.8 A: © David Austin/Stock Boston; INT.8 B: © Ben Simmons/The Stock Market; p. 293: © Will & Deni McIntyre/Photo Researchers; INT.11: © Jill Cannefax/EKM Nepenthe; p. 295 (all): The Bettmann Archive

Chapter HMD

Opener: The National Gallery; HMD.2 B: © Elyse Lewin/Image Bank-Chicago; HMD.2 C: © Rhoda Sidney/Leo de Wys; HMD.2 D: © Dan Esgro/Image Bank-Chicago; HMD.2 E: © James L. Shaffer; HMD.2 F: © Michael Salas/Image Bank-Chicago; HMD.2 G: © Joe Sohm/Image Works; HMD.2 H: Courtesy of John W. Santrock; HMD.2 I: Courtesy of Dr. Landrum B. Shettles; HMD.4 A, B&C: © Lennart Nilsson, "Behold Man," Little, Brown & Co. 1974; HMD.3 A: © Jerry Alexander/Tony Stone Images; HMD.3 B: © James Rowan/Tony Stone Images; HMD.3 C: © Jacques Jangoux/Tony Stone Images; p. 309: © Chas Cancellare/Picture Group; p. 310: Courtesy of Dr. Tiffany Fields; p. 313: © Yves DeBraine/Black Star; HMD.6 A&B: © D. Goodman/Monkmeyer Press; HMD.7 A: © Denise Marcotte/The Picture Cube; HMD.A A, B&C: Courtesy of Rovee-Collier; HMD.9 C: © Paul Fusco/Magnum Photos, Inc.; HMD.10 A: © Owen Franken/Stock Boston; HMD.12 A: © Richard Hutchings/Photo Researchers; HMD.13 B: © William Hopkins; HMD.13 C&D: © Suzanne Szasz/Photo Researchers; HMD.13 E: © Mel Digiacomo/The Image Bank-Chicago; HMD.14: © Martin Rogers/Stock Boston; HMD.15: Photo by Nina Leen/Time Life Magazine, © Time Inc.; p. 324: © Tim Bieber/The Image Bank-Chicago; p. 325 (top): © Pieter Breughel/Kunsthistorisches Museum; p. 325 (bottom): © Bob Daemmrich/The Image Works; p. 333: © Lanpher Productions; HMD.19 B: © Paul S. Conklin; HMD.20 A: © Michael Melford/The Image Bank-Texas; p. 337: © Keith Carter Photography; HMD.21 B: © John P. Kelly/The Image Bank-Chicago; HMD.21 C: © G&M David de Lossey/The Image Bank-Chicago; HMD.21 D: © Kaz Mori/The Image Bank-Texas; p. 342 A: © Owen Franken/Stock Boston; p. 342 B: The Bettmann Archive; p. 343 (left): © John Goodman; HMD.22: Courtesy of University of California; HMD.23 A: © Nilo Lima/Photo Researchers; p. HMD.45 A: © Linda Creighton/ U.S. News and World Report; p. 344 (bottom): © Elizabeth Crews; p.345 B: © John Lannois/ Black Star; p.346: © Elyse Lewin/The Image Bank-Texas; p. 347: © Harold Sund/The Image Bank-Chicago; HMD.25 A: © Jackson Hill/ Southern Lights Photography; HMD.25 B: © Spencer Swanger/Tom Stack & Associates

Chapter M&E

Opener: © Bill Rane; p. 359: ASSOCIATED PRESS 1991 L.A. TIMES; M&E.1 B: © Paul Trummer/The Image Bank-Chicago; M&E.1 C: © Photo Libr. Int'l/Leo de Wys, Inc.; M&E.1 D: © Rick Rusing/Leo de Wys, Inc.; M&E.1 E: © Ted Kawaleski/The Image Bank-Texas; M&E.1 F: © James L. Shaffer; M&E.1 G: © James L. Shaffer; M&E.1 H: © 1992 Lawrence Migdale; M&E.3 B: Courtesy Dr. Philip Teitelbaum, Published in the Proceedings of the American Philosophical Society, 1964, Vol. 108; p. 368 (top left): © Bob Coyle; p. 368 (top right): © Anthony Mercieca/Photo Researchers; p. 368 (bottom left): © Sven-Olof Lindblad/Photo Researchers; p. 368 (bottom right): © Jill Cannefax/EKM Nepenthe; p. 371 (right): © Randy Taylor/Sygma; p. 371 (left): © R. Maiman/Sygma; M&E.6: © University of Wisconsin Primate Laboratory; p. 374 (large): © Brian Drake/Sportslight, 1994; p. 374 (inset): AP/Wide World Photos; M&E.8 A: © Nick Pavloff/The Image Bank-Texas; p. 376: Courtesy of Sandra Graham; p. 377: © Robert A. Isaacs/Photo Researchers; p. 382: Self Help Book Inc; p. 383: © Leo Sporting Pictures/Leo de Wys, Inc.; M&E.10: © Bernard Gottfryd/Woodfin Camp; M&E.12: © Frank Whitney/The Image Bank-Texas; M&E.13 A&B: © Donald Dutton; M&E.14 B: © Michel Tcherevkoff/The Image Bank-Chicago; M&E.15: © Enrico Ferorelli; M&E.16: © Joe McNally/ SYGMA; M&E.17 A&B: © John Urban; M&E.17 C&D: © Paul Eckman; p. 391 (bottom): © Robert Harding Library

Chapter PER

Opener: © 1996 The Museum of Modern Art, New York; p. 401: UPI Bettmann; p. 403: The Bettmann Archive; PER.A: Planet Art; PER.B: © 1996 The Museum of Modern Art, New York; PER.2 A: © Robert Eckert/EKM Nepenthe; PER.2 B: © James Marshall; PER.2 C: © Burton McNeely/The Image Bank-Texas; PER.2 D: © Antman/The Image Works; PER.2 E: © Richard Hutchings/Photo Researchers; p. 407: © Superstock; p. 409 (left): The Bettmann Archives; p. 409 (right): Courtesy of Nancy Chodorow, photo by Jean Margolis; PER.3: © Jonathan Wright/Bruce Coleman; p. 410 (right): The Bettmann Archive; p. 413 (left): Courtesy of Albert Bandura; p. 413 (right): Courtesy of Dr. Walter Mischel; p. 415: Center for the Study of the Person; p. 417 : © David Frazier Photolibrary; PER.4 A: Alinari/Art Resource, New York; PER.4 B: Scala/Art Resource, New York; PER.4 C: © 1988 The Metropolitan Museum of Art, Gift of Thelma Chrysler Foy, 1952; p. 422: © Robert Brenner/PhotoEdit; p. 425 (top left): © Owen Franken/Stock Boston; p. 425 (bottom left): The Bettmann Archive; p. 425 (right): © The Bettmann Archive; p. 426 (bottom): © Kamuski/Woodfin Camp Associates; p. 426 (top): © Mark Lewis/ Tony Stone Images; PER.9: Reprinted by permission of the Publishers from Henry A. Murray; "Thematic Apperception Test," Cambridge, MA: Harvard University Press, Copyright © 1943 by the President and Fellows of Harvard College, © 1971 by Henry A. Murray; PER.10 B: © Spencer Grant/Marilyn Gartman Agency; PER.11 A&D: The Bettmann Archive; PER.11 B: © Joe McNally/Sygma; PER.11 C: Center for the Study of the Person

Chapter ABN

Opener: The Metropolitan Museum of Art, The Berggruen Klee Collection, 1984. (1984.531) (160); p. 446: © Adam Tanner/Comstock, Inc.; p. 446: © Stephen Marks/The Image Bank-Chicago; p. 451: © Alvis Upitis/The Image Bank; ABN.1 B: © Scala/Art Resource, New York; ABN.3: © Gerald Martineau/The Washington Post. Reprinted with permission; p. 456: Courtesy of Nancy Felipe Russo; ABN.5: Courtesy of University of Heidelberg; ABN.6: © Grunnitus/Monkmeyer Press; ABN.A: © Monte S. Buschbaum; ABN.B A&B: © Nora Buschbaum; p. 467 (left): AP/Wide World Photos; p. 467 (right): The Bettmann Archive

Chapter THR

Opener: Courtesy of John W. Santrock; THR.1: © Nation Museum of Denmark; THR.2: © Scala/Art Resource, New York; THR.3: © Historical Pictures/Stock Montage; p. 482: © Historical Pictures/ Stock Montage; THR.4 A: © Scala/Art Resource, New York; p. 485: Courtesy of Deke Simen; THR.5 A: © Superstock; THR.6: Courtesy of Albert Bandura; p. 493: © Michael Newman/PhotoEdit; p. 494: © Bob Daemmrich/The Image Bank; p. 495: © Alex Webb/Magnum Photos; p. 497: © Jay Lurie Photography; p. 503: © J.Y. Rabeuf/The Image Works; p. 503: © Peter Menzel/Stock Boston; p. 503: © Robert Houser/Comstock, Inc.; p. 504 (top): © Russ Kinne/Comstock, Inc.; p. 504 (bottom): Courtesy of Rachel Hare-Mustin & Jeanne Maracek; p. 506: © W & D McIntyre/Photo Researchers

Chapter SCH

Opener: Courtesy of John W. Santrock; p. 516 (large): © George V. Mann, Sc.D., M.D.; p. 516 (inset): © David Stoecklein/The Stock Market; p. 526: © Catherine Gehm; p. 535: © Cary Wolkinsky/Stock Boston; p. 538: © Vladimir Lange/The Image Bank-Chicago; p. 539: © Suki

Hill; p. 542 (left): © Jamie Villasseca/The Image Bank-Chicago; p. 542 (right): © David Young-Wolff/PhotoEdit; p. 544 (right): © John p. Kelly/ The Image Bank-Texas; p. 544 (bottom): © Bob Daemmrich/Tony Stone Images; p. 544(top): © Bob Daemmrich/Tony Stone Images; p. 545: © David Young-Wolff/PhotoEdit

Chapter STI

Opener: © 1995 The Art Institute of Chicago, All Rights Reserved; p. 555: AP/Wide World Photos; STI.2 A: © Stephen Wilkes/The Image Bank-Chicago; p. 560: The Bettmann Archive; p. 561: Courtesy of American Cancer Society; p. 562: © Paul Conklin/PhotoEdit; STI.4 A: © John P. Kelly/The Image Bank-Chicago; p. 565 (right): © Steve Hanson/Stock Boston; STI.5 A: © Greg Pease/Tony Stone Images; STI.6 B: © Romilly Lockyear/The Image Bank-Chicago; p. 569 (top): © Ken Kaminsky/Pangraphics; STI.7 A: Courtesy of William Vandivert; STI.8 A&B: Courtesy of Philip Zimbardo; p. 572 (large): The Bettmann Archive; p. 572 (inset): © A Current Affair/Sygma; STI.9 A: Courtesy of Alexandra Milgram; p. 574: AP/Wide World Photos

Chapter SOR

Opener: © Jon Riley/Tony Stone Images; p. 583: Courtesy of Academy of Motion Picture Arts and Sciences; p. 585 (left): © David Young-Wolff/PhotoEdit; p. 585 (right): © Kent Reno/ Jeroboam; SOR.1 A: © D.W. Productions/ The Image Bank-Texas; p. 586: © Randall Hyman/ Stock Boston; p. 592: © Brett Froomer/The Image Bank-Chicago; p. 594 (inset): John P. Kelly/The Image Bank-Texas; p. 594 (large): © David Frazier Photolibrary; p. 595: Michael Edrington/The Image Works; p. 596 A: AP/Wide World Photos; p. 596 B: © Alberto Garcia/Gamma Liaison; p. 598: Courtesy of Harry Triandis; SOR.5 A: © Mary Kate Denny/PhotoEdit; p. 601 A: © Larry Kolvoord/ The Image Works; p. 601 B: © Bob Daemmrich/ The Image Works; p. 601 C: © Bill Gillette/Stock Boston; p. 601 D: © Ellis Herwig/ The Picture Cube; p. 602: © Rob Crandall/Stock Boston; p. 603: © Cleo; p. 604: © Ellis Herwig/Stock Boston; p. 606 (right): © Bob Daemmrich/The Image Works; p. 606 (left): © Diane Carter; p. 607: Courtesy of James Jones; p. 608: Courtesy of Stanley Sue; p. 609 (top left): © Connie Coleman, Allstock/Tony Stone Images; p. 609 (top right): © Carlos Navajas/The Image Bank; p. 609 (middle right): © David Frazier Photolibrary; p. 609 (bottom right): © Phil Borges/Tony Stone Images; p. 609 (bottom left): © Marvin E. Newman/ The Image Bank-Chicago

Appendix DAT

Opener: Courtesy of John W. Santrock; p. 629: The Bettmann Archive

---

Line Art and Text

Chapter MET

Page 42: From Florence Denmark, et al., "Guidelines for Avoiding Sexism in Psychological Research" in *American Psychologist,* 43:582–585. Copyright © 1988 by the American Psychological Association. Reprinted with permission.

Chapter BFB

Figure BFB 7: Source: Floyd E. Bloom, et al., *Brain, Mind, and Behavior,* W. H. Freeman and Company, 1985; Figure BFB 18: From *Functional Neuroscience* by Michael Gazzaniga, Diana Steen and Bruce T. Volpe. Copyright © 1979 by Harper & Row, Publishers, Inc. Reprinted by permission of HarperCollins Publishers, Inc.; Figure BFB 24: From *The Neurosciences: A Third Study Program,* Schmitt and Worden (eds.). Copyright © The MIT Press. Reprinted by permission; Figure BFB 28: From Schmitt, *The Neurosciences: A Third Study Program.* Copyright © 1974 The MIT Press. Reprinted by permission.

Chapter S&P

Figure S&P 7: From H. R. Schiffman, *Sensations and Perception,* 2d ed. Copyright © 1982 John Wiley & Sons, Inc. Reprinted by permission of John Wiley & Sons, Inc.; Figure S&P 11: Figure from *Introduction to Psychology,* Seventh Edition by Ernest R. Hilgard, Rita L. Atkinson and Richard C. Atkinson, copyright © 1979 by Harcourt Brace & Company, reproduced by permission of the publisher; Figure S&P 18: From John W. Hole, Jr., *Human Anatomy and Physiology,* 5th ed. Copyright © 1990 Times Mirror Higher Education Group, Inc., Dubuque, Iowa. All Rights Reserved. Reprinted by permission; Figure S&P 28: From Wathen-Dunn, *Models for the Perception of Visual Form.* Copyright © The MIT Press. Reprinted by permission; Figure S&P 30: James J. Gibson, *The Perception of the Visual World.* Copyright © 1951 by Houghton Mifflin Company. Used with permission; Figure S&P 38: From R. L. Gregory and J. C. Wallace, "Recovery from Early Blindness" in *Experimental Psychological Society Monograph,* No. 2. Copyright © 1963 Cambridge University Press. Reprinted with the permission of Cambridge University Press.

Chapter LRN

Figure LRN 1a: From *Learning and Behavior* by Paul Chance. Copyright © 1994, 1987, 1979 Wadsworth Publishing Company. By permission of Brooks/Cole Publishing Company, Pacific Grove, CA 93950, a division of International Thomson Publishing Inc.; Figure LRN 1b: From Benjamin B. Lahey, *Psychology: An Introduction,* 3d ed. Copyright © 1989 Times Mirror Higher Education Group, Inc., Dubuque, Iowa. All Rights Reserved. Reprinted by permission; Figure LRN 7: Source: E. L. Thorndike, "Animal Intelligence: An Experimental Study of the Associative Process in Animals" in *Psychological Review Monographs Supplement,* 2(4, whole no. 8), American Psychological Association, 1898; Figure LRN 10: Source: B. F. Skinner, "Pigeons In a Pelican" in *American Psychologist,* 5:28–37, American Psychological Association, 1960; Figure LRN 12: From *Learning and Behavior,* by Paul Chance. Copyright © 1979 by Wadsworth, Inc. Used with the permission of Brooks/Cole Publishing Company, Pacific Grove, CA 93950; Figure LRN 14: Source: N. Guttman and H. I. Kalish, "Discriminability and Stimulus Generalization" in *Journal of Experimental Psychology,* 51:81, American Psychological Association, 1956; Figure LRN 15: Source: Data from Paul Chance, *Learning and Behavior,* Wadsworth Publishing, 1979; Figure LRN 17: From A. Bandura, "Influence of Model's Reinforcement Contingencies on the Acquisition of Imitative Responses" in *Journal of Personality and Social Psychology,* 1:589–595. Copyright © 1965 by the American Psychological Association. Reprinted by permission; Figure LRN 20: Source: E. C. Tolman, et al., "Studies in Spatial Learning I: Orientation and Short-Cut" in *Journal of Experimental Psychology,* 36:13–24, American Psychological Association, 1946.

Chapter MEM

Figure MEM 5: From L. R. Squire, "Declarative and Nondeclarative Memory: Multiple Brain Systems Supporting Learning and Memory" in *Memory Systems 1994,* D. L. Schacter and E. Tulving (eds.). Copyright © 1994 The MIT Press. Reprinted by permission; Figure MEM 11: From B. Murdock, Jr., *Human Memory: Theory and Data.* Copyright © 1974 Lawrence Erlbaum Associates, Inc. Reprinted by permission of the author.

Chapter T&L

Figure T&L 2: From *Human Memory and Cognition,* 2nd Edition by Mark H. Ashcraft. Copyright © 1994 by HarperCollins College Publishers. Reprinted by permission; Figure T&L 3: Reprinted with the permission of Simon & Schuster from *The Universe Within* by Morton Hunt. Copyright © 1982 by Morton Hunt; Figure T&L 13: Source: Data from M. Matlin, *Cognition,* Harcourt Brace, 1989; Figure T&L 16: From Danny R. Moates and Gary M. Schumacher, *An Introduction to Cognitive Psychology.* Copyright © 1980 Wadsworth Publishing Company. Reprinted by permission of Brooks/Cole Publishing Company; Figure T&L 19: From Roger Brown, et al., *Minnesota Symposium on Child Psychology,* Vol. 2. Copyright © 1969 University of Minnesota Press. Reprinted by permission.

Chapter INT

Figure INT 10: Courtesy of Dr. John Berry.

Chapter HMD

Page 303: Reprinted by permission from *The Family of Man,* copyright The Museum of Modern Art; Figure HMD 5: From W. K. Frankenburg and J. B. Dodds, "The Denver Development Screening Test" in *Journal of Pediatrics,* 71:181–191. Copyright © 1967 Mosby-Year Book, Inc. Reprinted by permission; Figure HMD 9a: Joshua Nove/Dennie Palmer Wolf. Reprinted by permission; Figure HMD 9b: Reprinted with permission of Ellen Winner; Figure HMD 22: From *The Seasons of a Man's Life* by Daniel J. Levinson, et al. Copyright © 1978 by Daniel J. Levinson. Reprinted by permission of Alfred A. Knopf, Inc.; Figure HMD 24: Source: U.S. Census data; Social Security Administration, *The Statistical History of the United States, 1976.*

Chapter M&E

Figure M&E 2: Reprinted from W. B. Cannon, "Hunger and Thirst" in C. Murchison (ed.), *The Foundations of Experimental Psychology,* 1928, with permission from Clark University Press; Figure M&E 3: Reprinted from the *1961 Nebraska Symposium on Motivation,* by permission of the University of Nebraska Press. Copyright © 1961 by the University of Nebraska Press. Copyright © renewed 1989 by the University of Nebraska Press; Figure M&E 4: From W. H. Masters and V. E. Johnson, *Human Sexual Response,* 1966, Little, Brown and Company. Reprinted by permission; Figure M&E 5: From Alfred C. Kinsey, et al., *Sexual Behavior in the Human Male.* Copyright © 1948 The Kinsey Institute. Reprinted by permission of The Kinsey Institute for Research in Sex, Gender, and Reproduction, Inc.; Figure M&E 8: From M. R. Lepper, et al., "Undermining Children's Intrinsic Interest with Extrinsic Rewards" in *Journal of Personality and Social Psychology,* 28. Copyright © 1973 by the American Psychological Association. Reprinted by permission; Page 382: From *Flow* by Mihaly Csikszentmihalyi. Cover copyright HarperCollins Publishers, Inc. Reprinted by permission.

Chapter PER

Figure PER 1: From *Psychology: A Scientific Study of Human Behavior,* by L. S. Wrightsman, C. K. Sigelman, and F. H. Sanford. Copyright © 1979, 1975, 1970, 1965, 1961 Brooks/Cole Publishing Company, a division of International Thomson Publishing Inc. By permission of the publisher; Figure PER C: From W. Mischel, et al., "Cognitive and Attentional Mechanisms in Delay of Gratification" in *Journal of Personality and Social Psychology,* 21:204–218. Copyright © 1972 by the American Psychological Association. Reprinted by permission; Figure PER D: From *Man, the Manipulator* by Everett L. Shostrum. Copyright © 1967 by Abingdon Press. Used by permission; Figure PER 5: Courtesy of Dr. Hans J. Eysenck; Figure PER 7: From C. Showers, "Compartmentalization of Positive and Negative Self-Knowledge: Keeping Bad Apples Out of the Bunch" in *Journal of Personality and Social Psychology,* 62:1038. Copyright © 1992 by the American Psychological Association. Reprinted with permission; Figure PER 10: From N. S. Jacobson, et al., "Toward a Behavioral Profile of Marital Distress" in *Journal of Consulting and Clinical Psychology,* 48:696–703. Copyright © 1980 by the American Psychological Association. All Rights Reserved.

Chapter ABN

Figure ABN 1: From A. Breier, et al., "Agoraphobia with Panic Attacks" in *Archives of General Psychiatry,* 43:1029–1036. Copyright © 1986 American Medical Association. Reprinted by permission; Figure ABN 2: From R. Bootzin, et al., *Abnormal Psychology.* Copyright © 1972 McGraw Hill, Inc. Reprinted by permission; Figure ABN 4: Reprinted with permission from Moshen Mirabi, *DSM-III Training Guide,* L. J. Webb, et al (eds.). Copyright © 1981 Brunner/Mazel, Inc.; Figure ABN 7: From I. I. Gottesman and J. Shields, *Schizophrenia: The Epigenetic Puzzle.* Copyright © 1992 Cambridge University Press. Reprinted with the permission of Cambridge University Press.

Chapter THR

Page 480: Source: National Library of Medicine.

Chapter SCH

Figure SCH 2: From Hans Selye, *The Stress of Life,* Copyright © 1976 McGraw-Hill, Inc. Reprinted by permission; Figure SCH 3: From C. J. Holahan and R. H. Moose, "Personal and Contextual Determinants of Coping Strategies" in *Journal of Personality and Social Psychology,* 52. Copyright © 1987 by the American Psychological Association. Reprinted with permission; Figure SCH 4: Modified and reproduced by special permission of the Publisher, Consulting Psychologists Press, Inc., Palo Alto, CA 94303 from *Manual of the Ways of Coping* by Susan Folkman, Ph.D. and Richard S. Lazarus, Ph.D. Copyright 1988 by Consulting Psychologists Press, Inc. All rights reserved. Further reproduction is prohibited without the Publisher's written consent; Figure SCH 6: From *Contemporary Behavior Therapy,* by M. D. Spiegler and D. C. Guevremont. Copyright © 1993 Brooks/Cole Publishing Company, Pacific Grove, CA 93950, a division of International Thomson Publishing Inc. By permission of the publisher; Figure SCH 8: From L. L. Langley, *Physiology of Man.* Copyright © 1971 Van Nostrand Reinhold Company. Reprinted by permission of the author.

Chapter STI

Figure STI 1: Source: L. Festinger and J. Carlsmith, "Cognitive Consequences of Forced Compliance" in *Journal of Abnormal and Social Psychology,* 58:203–210, American Psychological Association, 1959; Figure STI 5: Source: Data from E. E. Jones and T. S. Pittman, "Toward a General Theory of Strategic Self-Presentation" in *Psychological Perspectives on the Self,* 1982; Figure STI 7: Source: S. E. Asch, "Studies of Independence and Conformity: A Minority of One Against a Unanimous Majority" in *Psychological Monographs,* 90 (whole no. 416), American Psychological Association, 1956; Figure STI 9: Source: Data from Stanley Milgram, "Behavioral Study of Obedience" in *Journal of Abnormal and Social Psychology,* 67:371–378, 1963.

Chapter SOR

Figure SOR 1: From E. L. Dey, et al., *The American Freshman: Twenty-Five-Year Trends,* 1991; A. W. Astin, et al., *The American Freshman: National Norms for Fall 1991,* 1991; E. L. Dey, et al., *The American Freshman: National Norms for Fall 1992,* 1992; A. W. Astin, et al., *The American Freshman: National Norms for Fall 1993,* 1993, and A. W. Astin, et al., *The American Freshman: National Norms for Fall 1994,* 1994. All works © Higher Education Research Institute, UCLA; Figure SOR 2: Courtesy of Zick Rubin, 1970; Page 590: "Sternberg's 10 Rules of Love" from *The Triangle of Love* by Robert J. Sternberg. Copyright © 1988 by Basic Books, Inc. Reprinted by permission of Basic Books, a division of HarperCollins Publishers, Inc.; Figure SOR 3: Source: Data from R. J. Sternberg, *The Triangle of Love,* Basic Books, Inc., 1988; Figure SOR 4: From Robert A. Baron and Donn Byrne, *Social Psychology: Understanding Human Interaction.* Copyright © 1984 by Allyn and Bacon. Reprinted by permission.

Appendix

Figure DAT 1: From *Psychology Applied to Modern Life: Adjustment in the 90s* by W. Weiten, M. A. Lloyd, and R. Lashley. Copyright © 1991, 1986, 1983 Brooks/Cole Publishing Company, Pacific Grove, CA 93950, a division of International Thomson Publishing Inc. By permission of the publisher.

Name Index

G

H

I

J

K

L

M

N

P

Q

R

S

T

U

V

W

Y

Z

Subject Index

A

B

C

F

G

H

I

N

O

P

Q

R

S